Reading Between the Lines and Policy Watch

Reading Between the Lines news articles build critical thinking skills and demonstrate how economic principles can be used to interpret daily news events. The icon ✛ identifies Policy Watch news articles with "You're the Voter" questions. You can communicate your policy ideas and economic reasoning with your congressional representative through a direct link from the Parkin Home Page to the Congressional E-mail Directory at:
http://www.congress.org

CONGRATULATIONS!

As a student purchasing Parkin's *Economics* 6e, you are entitled to a prepaid subscription to premium services on The Economics Place Web site at www.economicsplace.com. You will have unlimited online access to the *eText, eStudy Guide, Economics in Action* software tutorial, *Office Hours* feature, and many other Web resources.

The duration of your subscription is 12 months.

To activate your prepaid subscription:

1. Launch your Web browser and go to the Companion Web site at www.economicsplace.com.

2. Select the *Economics* book. Click on *Register*.

3. Follow the instructions on the screen to register yourself as a new user. Your pre-assigned Access Code is located below:

Access Code:

WSPES-JEDDA-GAPPY-ZONED-COLZA-THRAW

4. During registration, you will choose a personal Login Name and Password for use in logging into the Companion Web site.

5. Once your personal Login Name and Password are confirmed, you can begin using the Companion Web site.

This Access code can be used only once to establish a subscription. This subscription is not transferable.

IS SOMETHING MISSING?

If the tear-out card is missing from this book, then you're missing out on an important part of your learning package. Choose to buy a new textbook, or visit the Companion Web site at www.economicsplace.com for information on purchasing a subscription.

Tear Here ------------►

If you did not purchase a new textbook, this Access Code may not be valid!

ECONOMICS

Sixth Edition

PARKIN

The cover depicts an everyday dawn scene—a field of dew-laden grass—viewed through the lens of the Parkin icon. You can look at this cover in many different ways. Here is what I see. ◆ First, I see a metaphor for what my text, Web site, and other supplements and the extraordinary publishing effort that has created them seek to be—a window that gives students a sharply focused view of the world based on a clear and compelling account of timeless principles. ◆ Second, I see a symbol of what economics (and all scientific endeavor) is about. The Parkin icon is like an economic model. We use models to understand reality. The model is abstract, like the diamond and its hole or aperture. The model distorts our view of the world by omitting some details. But it permits us to see the focus of our interest in the brightest and clearest possible light.

ECONOMICS

MICHAEL PARKIN

University of Western Ontario

SIXTH EDITION

Boston San Francisco New York
London Toronto Sydney Tokyo Singapore Madrid
Mexico City Munich Paris Cape Town Hong Kong Montreal

Editor-in-Chief:	Denise J. Clinton
Senior Editor:	Victoria Warneck
Senior Project Manager:	Mary Clare McEwing
Supplements Editor:	Andrea Basso
Associate Editor:	Roxanne Hoch
Senior Administrative Assistant:	Dottie Dennis
Managing Editor:	James Rigney
Senior Production Supervisor:	Nancy Fenton
Senior Design Supervisor:	Gina Kolenda
Cover Designer:	Leslie Haimes
Cover photo:	Digital Vision
Interior Design:	Gina Kolenda
Technical Illustrator:	Richard Parkin
Electronic Production Manager:	Scott Silva
Senior Electronic Production Specialist:	Sally Simpson
Senior Media Producer:	Melissa Honig
Copyeditor:	Barbara Willette
Proofreader:	Kathy Smith
Indexer:	Robin Bade
Senior Manufacturing Buyer:	Hugh Crawford
Media Buyer:	Ginny Michaud
Marketing Manager:	Adrienne D'Ambrosio
Marketing Specialist:	Jennifer Berkley

0-321-13103-7

TO
ROBIN

ABOUT MICHAEL PARKIN

MICHAEL PARKIN received his training as an economist at the Universities of Leicester and Essex in England. Currently in the Department of Economics at the University of Western Ontario, Canada, Professor Parkin has held faculty appointments at Brown University, the University of Manchester, the University of Essex, and Bond University. He is a past president of the Canadian Economics Association and has served on the editorial boards of the *American Economic Review* and the *Journal of Monetary Economics* and as managing editor of the *Canadian Journal of Economics*. Professor Parkin's research on macroeconomics, monetary economics, and international economics has resulted in over 160 publications in journals and edited volumes, including the *American Economic Review*, the *Journal of Political Economy*, the *Review of Economic Studies*, the *Journal of Monetary Economics*, and the *Journal of Money, Credit and Banking*. He became most visible to the public with his work on inflation that discredited the use of wage and price controls. Michael Parkin also spearheaded the movement toward European monetary union. Professor Parkin is an experienced and dedicated teacher of introductory economics.

PREFACE

This book presents economics as a serious, lively, and evolving science. Its goal is to open students' eyes to the "economic way of thinking" and to help them gain insights into how the economy works and how it might be made to work better. ◆ I provide a thorough and complete coverage of the subject, using a straightforward, precise, and clear writing style. ◆ I am conscious that many students find economics hard, so I place the student at center stage and write for the student. I use language that doesn't intimidate and that allows the student to concentrate on the substance. ◆ I open each chapter with a clear statement of learning objectives, a real-world student-friendly vignette to grab attention, and a brief preview. I illustrate principles with examples that are selected to hold the student's interest and to make the subject lively. And I put principles to work by using them to illuminate current real-world problems and issues. ◆ I present some new ideas, such as dynamic comparative advantage, game theory, the modern theory of the firm, public choice theory, rational expectations, new growth theory, and real business cycle theory. But I explain these topics with familiar core ideas and tools. ◆ Today's course springs from today's issues—the information revolution, energy deregulation, the 2001 recession, the stock market bubble, and the expansion of global trade and investment. But the principles that we use to understand these issues remain the core principles of our science. ◆ Governments and international agencies place continued emphasis on long-term fundamentals as they seek to promote economic growth. This book reflects this emphasis. ◆ To help promote a rich, active learning experience, I have developed a comprehensive online learning environment featuring a dynamic e-book, interactive tutorials and quizzes, daily news updates, and more.

The Sixth Edition Revision

Economics, Sixth Edition, retains all of the improvements achieved in its predecessor with its thorough and detailed presentation of modern economics, emphasis on real-world examples and critical thinking skills, diagrams renowned for pedagogy and precision, and path-breaking technology.

New to this edition are

- Rewritten introductory chapter
- All-new chapter on stock markets
- Revised and updated microeconomics content
- Revised and updated macroeconomics content
- Web-based current policy topics
- Expanded Web-based *Economics in Action*

Rewritten Introductory Chapter

Chapter 1 has been completely rewritten to emphasize the central role of tradeoffs in economics, setting the tone for the rest of the book.

All-New Chapter 34 on Global Stock Markets

This exciting addition provides a valuable framework for addressing your students' questions about how the stock market works. *What is a stock? What determines stock prices? Why are stock prices volatile? Why is it rational to diversify? How does the stock market influence the economy, and vice-versa?*

Revised and Updated Microeconomics Content

The five major revisions in the microeconomics chapters are

1. The Economic Problem (Chapter 2): A revised and more carefully paced explanation of the gains from specialization and exchange.

2. Monopolistic Competition and Oligopoly (Chapter 13): An expanded explanation of repeated games and sequential games. These traditionally advanced topics are explained with examples and illustrations that bring the ideas within the grasp of beginning students.

3. Economic Inequality (Chapter 15): Two chapters from the Fifth Edition have been combined, streamlined, and given a new focus to explain the sources of the trend in the distribution of income—the widening gap between the highest- and lowest-income households.

4. Regulation and Antitrust Law (Chapter 17): Now explains the effects of price caps in monopoly markets and contrasts their effects with price ceilings in competitive markets.

5. Externalities (Chapter 18): Reorganized to explain the full range of positive and negative production and consumption externalities.

Revised and Updated Macroeconomics Content

The five major revisions in the macroeconomics chapters are

1. Measuring GDP and Economic Growth (Chapter 19): Reorganized and more focused explanation of GDP and its measurement, along with a new and simplified explanation of the chain-weighted method of calculating real GDP.

2. Monitoring Cycles, Jobs, and the Price Level (Chapter 20): A much reorganized chapter that describes how the NBER defines recession, how the BLS measures the labor market, and how the Census Bureau measures the CPI. The chapter also explains the significance and interpretation of data on the labor market and price level.

3. Economic Growth (Chapter 24): A simplified and mainstreamed explanation and illustration of the classical, neoclassical, and new theories of economic growth.

4. Macroeconomic Policy Challenges (Chapter 31): Explanation of the Taylor rule and comparison of Fed interest rate decisions with such a rule.

5. Thorough and extensive updating to reflect the U.S. economy and the global economy of 2001 and 2002, including events such as the 2001 recession and the response to the September 11 attacks.

Web-Based Current Policy Topics

To achieve the most up-to-date coverage possible on current policy issues, *The Economics Place* Web site features:

1. Markets in Action (Chapter 6): New coverage of the Farm Bill and farm subsidies.

2. Regulation and Antitrust Law (Chapter 17): Application of price caps in the California power industry

3. Fiscal Policy (Chapter 26): The 2002 Tax Act (stimulus package).

Other topics will be added as new developments occur.

Expanded Web-Based *Economics in Action*

Parkin's market-leading interactive tutorial software program may now be accessed on the Web. This Java-based learning tool has been expanded to cover each and every chapter in the textbook.

Economics in Action is a powerful and wide-ranging program. Each *Fast Track* summary gives students a quick review of the topic at hand, while the *Demo* feature provides a more detailed lesson on graph movements. In *Action*, students may manipulate figures from the textbook by changing the conditions that lie behind them and observing how the economy responds to events. Quizzes that use five question types (fill-in-the-blank, true-or-false, multiple-choice, numeric, and complete-the-graph) can be worked with or without detailed feedback.

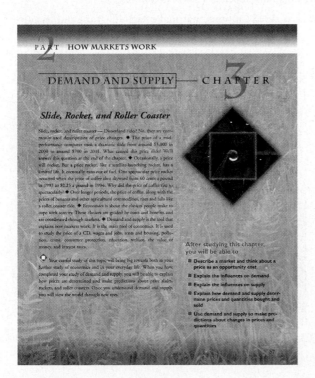

Features to Enhance Teaching and Learning

HERE I DESCRIBE THE CHAPTER FEATURES THAT ARE designed to enhance the learning process. Each chapter contains the following learning aids.

Chapter Opener

Each chapter opens with a one-page student-friendly, attention-grabbing vignette. The vignette raises questions that both motivate the student and focus the chapter. The Sixth Edition now carries this story into the main body of the chapter, and relates it to the chapter-ending *Reading Between the Lines* feature.

Chapter Objectives

A list of learning objectives enables students to see exactly where the chapter is going and to set their goals before they begin the chapter. I link these goals directly to the chapter's major headings.

After studying this chapter, you will be able to

- Describe a market and think about a price as an opportunity cost
- Explain the influences on demand
- Explain the influences on supply
- Explain how demand and supply determine prices and quantities bought and sold
- Use demand and supply to make predictions about changes in prices and quantities

In-Text Review Quizzes

A review quiz at end of most major sections enables students to determine whether a topic needs further study before moving on.

REVIEW QUIZ

1 What is scarcity?
2 Give some examples of scarcity in today's world.
3 Define economics.
4 Use the headlines in today's news to illustrate the distinction between microeconomics and macroeconomics.

Key Terms

Highlighted terms within the text simplify the student's task of learning the vocabulary of economics. Each highlighted term appears in an end-of-chapter list with page numbers, in an end-of-book glossary, boldfaced in the index, in the *Economics in Action* software, and on the Parkin Web site.

Diagrams That Show the Action

This book has set new standards of clarity in its diagrams. My goal has always been to show "where the economic action is." The diagrams in this book continue to generate an enormously positive response, which confirms my view that graphical analysis is the most powerful tool available for teaching and learning economics. But many students find graphs hard to work with. For this reason, I have developed the entire art program with the study and review needs of the student in mind. The diagrams feature:

■ Shifted curves, equilibrium points, and other important features highlighted in red

■ Color-blended arrows to suggest movement

■ Graphs paired with data tables

■ Diagrams labeled with boxed notes

■ Extended captions that make each diagram and its caption a self-contained object for study and review.

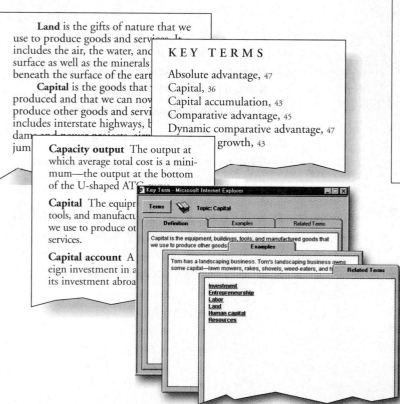

Reading Between the Lines

Each chapter ends with an economic analysis of a significant news article from the popular press together with a thorough economic analysis of the issues raised in the article. The Sixth Edition features all new *Reading Between the Lines* articles. I have chosen each article so that it sheds additional light on the questions first raised in the Chapter Opener.

Special "You're the Voter" sections in selected chapters invite students to analyze typical campaign topics and to probe their own stances on key public policy issues. Critical Thinking Questions about the article appear with the end-of-chapter questions and problems.

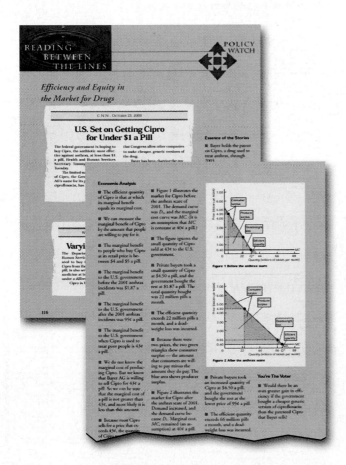

End-of-Chapter Study Material

Each chapter closes with a concise summary organized by major topics, lists of key terms (all with page references), problems, and critical thinking questions. In the Sixth Edition, I have added a new set of Web Exercises to the end of each chapter. In addition, I have replaced most of the even-numbered problems throughout the entire text.

The end-of-chapter problems are organized in pairs. The solution to the odd-numbered problem in each pair may be found at the end of the text; the parallel even-numbered problem is left for students to solve on their own. This arrangement offers help to students and flexibility to instructors who want to assign problems for credit.

For the Instructor

THIS BOOK ENABLES YOU TO ACHIEVE THREE objectives in your principles course:

- Focus on the economic way of thinking.
- Explain the issues and problems of our time.
- Choose your own course structure.

Focus on the Economic Way of Thinking

You know how hard it is to encourage a student to think like an economist. But that is your goal. Consistent with this goal, the text focuses on and repeatedly uses the central ideas: choice; tradeoff; opportunity cost; the margin; incentives; the gains from voluntary exchange; the forces of demand, supply, and equilibrium; the pursuit of economic rent; and the effects of government actions on the economy.

Explain the Issues and Problems of Our Time

Students must use the central ideas and tools if they are to begin to understand them. There is no better way to motivate students than by using the tools of economics to explain the issues that confront them in today's world. These issues include the 2001 recession and what lies beyond, environment, immigration, widening income gaps, energy deregulation, budget deficits or surpluses, restraining inflation, understanding the stock market, avoiding protectionism, and the long-term growth of output and incomes.

Choose Your Own Course Structure

You want to teach your own course. I have organized this book to enable you to do so. I demonstrate the book's flexibility in the flexibility chart and alternative sequences table that appear on pp. xxii–xxv. You can use this book to teach a traditional course that blends theory and policy or a current policy issues course. Your micro course can emphasize theory or policy. You can structure your macro course to emphasize long-term growth and supply-side fundamentals. Or you can follow a traditional macro sequence and emphasize short-term fluctuations. The choices are yours.

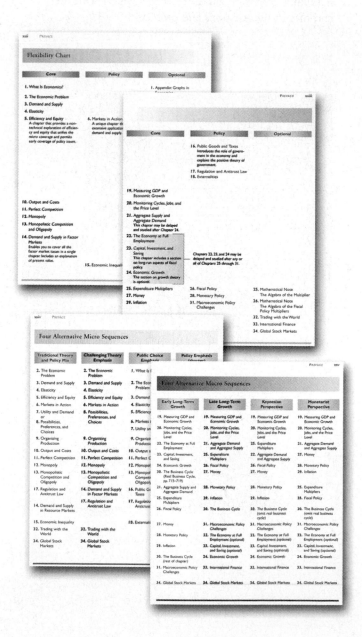

Instructor's Manual

The Instructor's Manual, written by me, Michael Stroup of Stephen F. Austin State University, and James Cobbe of Florida State University, integrates the teaching and learning package and is a guide to all the supplements. Each chapter contains a chapter outline, what's new in the Sixth Edition, teaching suggestions, a look at where we have been and where we are going, lists of available overhead transparencies, descriptions of the electronic supplements, additional discussion questions, answers to the Review Quizzes, solutions to end-of-chapter problems, additional problems, and solutions to the additional problems. The chapter outline and teaching suggestions sections are keyed to the PowerPoint lecture notes.

Three Test Banks

Three separate Test Banks, with nearly 13,000 questions, provide multiple-choice, true-false, numerical, fill-in-the-blank, short-answer, and essay questions. Mark Rush of the University of Florida reviewed and edited all existing questions to ensure their clarity and consistency with the Sixth Edition and incorporated over 2,000 new questions written by Della Lee Sue of Marist College, Carol Dole of the State University of West Georgia, Ed Price of Oklahoma State University, John Graham of Rutgers University, and Sang Lee of Southeastern Louisiana University.

PowerPoint Resources

Robin Bade and I have developed a full-color Microsoft PowerPoint Lecture Presentation for each chapter that includes all the figures from the text, animated graphs, and speaking notes. The slide outlines are based on the chapter outlines in the Instructor's Manual, and the speaking notes are based on the Instructor's Manual teaching suggestions. The presentations can be used electronically in the classroom or can be printed to create hard-copy transparency masters. This item is available for Macintosh and Windows.

Overhead Transparencies

Full-color transparencies of over 200 figures from the text will improve the clarity of your lectures. They are available to qualified adopters of the text (contact your Addison-Wesley sales representative).

Instructor's CD-ROM with Computerized Test Banks

This CD-ROM contains Computerized Test Bank files, Test Bank and Instructor's Manual files in Microsoft Word, and PowerPoint files. All three test banks are available in Test Generator Software (TestGen-EQ with QuizMaster-EQ). Fully networkable, it is available for Windows and Macintosh. TestGen-EQ's new graphical interface enables instructors to view, edit, and add questions; transfer questions to tests; and print different forms of tests. Tests can be formatted with varying fonts and styles, margins, and headers and footers, as in any word-processing document. Search and sort features let the instructor quickly locate questions and arrange them in a preferred order. QuizMaster-EQ, working with your school's computer network, automatically grades the exams, stores the results on disk, and allows the instructor to view or print a variety of reports.

CourseCompass

A dynamic, interactive online learning environment tool powered by Blackboard, CourseCompass provides flexible tools and rich content resources that enable instructors to easily and effectively customize online course materials to suit their needs. Now instructors can track and analyze student performance on an array of Internet activities. Please contact your Addison-Wesley representative for more details.

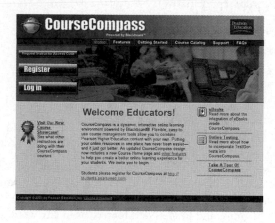

Economics in Action Software

Instructors can use *Economics in Action* interactive software in the classroom. Its many analytical graphs can be used as "electronic transparencies" for live graph manipulation in lectures. Its real-world data sets and graphing utility bring animated time-series graphs and scatter diagrams to the classroom.

The Parkin Web Site

The Sixth Edition of the textbook continues the tradition of path-breaking technology with *The Economics Place* at www.economicsplace.com. The instructor side of *The Economics Place* includes all of the same resources as the student side, but with the addition of PowerPoint lecture notes, easy access to Instructor's Manual files, and an online "Consult the Author" feature: Ask your questions and make your suggestions via e-mail, and I will answer you within 24 hours.

For the Student

Study Guide

The Sixth Edition Study Guide by Mark Rush of the University of Florida is carefully coordinated with the main text and the Test Banks. For the first time, each copy of the textbook comes bundled with a CD-ROM containing a color, electronic version of the Study Guide. Print copies are also available as an option.

Each chapter of the Study Guide contains:

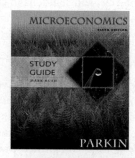

- Key concepts
- Helpful hints
- True/false/uncertain questions that ask students to explain their answers
- Multiple-choice questions
- Short-answer questions
- Common questions or misconceptions that the student explains as if he or she were the teacher

Each part allows students to test their cumulative understanding with sample midterm tests.

Economics in Action Interactive Software

With *Economics in Action* Release 6.0, which is now available on the Web, students will have fun working the tutorials, answering questions that give instant explanations, and testing themselves ahead of their midterm tests. One of my students told me that using EIA is like having a private professor in your dorm room! New modules now cover each and every chapter in the text.

The Parkin Web Site

The Economics Place is the market-leading Web site for Parkin. On the Web site, students will find:

- The textbook—the *entire textbook in Adobe Acrobat and PDF* with hyperlinks and animated figures with step-by-step audio explanations.

- *Economics in Action*—tutorials, quizzes, and graph tools that with a click of the mouse make curves shift and graphs come to life

- The Study Guide—the entire Study Guide, free, online

- Economics in the News updated daily during the school year

- Online "Office Hours": Ask your question via e-mail, and I will answer within 24 hours!

- Economic links—links to sites that keep you up-to-date with what's going on in the economy and that enable you to work end-of-chapter Web-based exercises

The power of *The Economics Place* lies not just in the

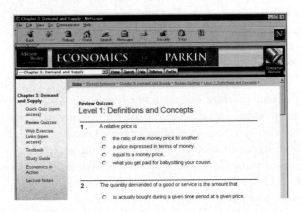

breadth and depth of learning tools available, but also in the way that we have linked the tools together. For example, suppose that a student logs onto *The Economics Place* to take a multiple-choice quiz. When the quiz is submitted for a grade, the student receives a scorecard with an explanation of why answers are correct or incorrect *and a hyperlink to the part of the e-book that the student should read to better understand the concept.* The student is thus able to navigate easily through the site and to maximize the payoff from her or his study efforts.

Economist.com Edition

The premier online source of economic news analysis, Economist.com provides your students with insight and opinion on current economic events. Through an agreement between Addison-Wesley and *The Economist*, your students can receive a low-cost subscription to this premium Web site for 12 weeks, including the complete text of the current issue of *The Economist* and access to *The Economist*'s searchable archives. Other features include Web-only weekly articles, news feeds with current world and business news, and stock market and currency data. Professors who adopt this special edition will receive a complimentary one-year subscription to Economist.com.

The Wall Street Journal Edition

Addison-Wesley is also pleased to provide your students with access to *The Wall Street Journal*, the most respected and trusted daily source for information on business and economics. For a small additional charge, Addison-Wesley offers your students a 10-week subscription to *The Wall Street Journal* and WSJ.com. Adopting professors will receive a complimentary one-year subscription to *The Wall Street Journal* as well as access to WSJ.com.

Financial Times Edition

Featuring international news and analysis from FT journalists in more than 50 countries, the *Financial Times* will provide your students with insights and perspectives on economic developments around the world. The *Financial Times Edition* provides your students with a 15-week subscription to one of the world's leading business publications. Adopting professors will receive a complimentary one-year subscription to the *Financial Times* as well as access to FT.com.

The Econ Tutor Center

Staffed by qualified, experienced college economics instructors, the Econ Tutor Center is open five days a week, seven hours a day. Tutors can be reached by phone, fax, e-mail or White Board technology. The Econ Tutor Center hours are designed to meet your students' study schedules, with evening hours Sunday through Thursday. Students receive one-on-one tutoring on examples, related exercises, and problems. Please contact your Addison-Wesley representative for information on how to make this service available to your students.

Acknowledgments

I THANK MY CURRENT AND FORMER COLLEAGUES and friends at the University of Western Ontario who have taught me so much. They are Jim Davies, Jeremy Greenwood, Ig Horstmann, Peter Howitt, Greg Huffman, David Laidler, Phil Reny, Chris Robinson, John Whalley, and Ron Wonnacott. I also thank Doug McTaggart and Christopher Findlay, co-authors of the Australian edition, and Melanie Powell and Kent Matthews, co-authors of the European edition. Suggestions arising from their adaptations of earlier editions have been helpful to me in preparing this edition.

I thank the several thousand students whom I have been privileged to teach. The instant response that comes from the look of puzzlement or enlightenment has taught me how to teach economics.

It is an especial joy to thank the many outstanding editors and others at Addison-Wesley who contributed to the concerted publishing effort that brought this edition to completion. Denise Clinton, Editor-in-Chief for Economics and Finance, is a constant source of inspiration and encouragement and provided overall direction. Victoria Richardson Warneck, Senior Editor for Economics and my sponsoring editor, played a major role in shaping this revision and the many outstanding supplements that accompany it. Victoria is an author's dream editor. Her knowledge of economics, economists, and the mood of the evolving marketplace is remarkable. Mary Clare McEwing, Senior Project Manager, brought her huge experience and dedicated professionalism to the development effort. Dottie Dennis, Senior Administrative Assistant, worked tirelessly to bring reviews in on time and consolidate and summarize them. Andrea Basso, Supplements Editor, working with the most able team of authors, managed the creation of a large and complex supplements package. Roxanne Hoch, Associate Editor, cheerfully performed many helpful tasks at a moment's notice. Melissa Honig, Senior Media Producer, developed the new version of *The Economics Place*, directed the development of the tools that enabled us to create and run *Economics in Action*, and is an appreciated and admired source of guidance on all matters relating to the electronic supplements. Adrienne D'Ambrosio, Marketing Manager, provided inspired marketing direction. Her brochures and, more important, her timely questions and prodding for material had a significant impact on the shape of the text. Regina Hagen Kolenda, Senior Designer, designed the cover, text, and package and surpassed the challenge of ensuring that we meet the highest design standards. Managing Editor James Rigney, Senior Production Supervisor Nancy Fenton, and Senior Electronic Production Specialist, Sally Simpson, worked miracles on a tight production schedule and coped calmly with late-changing content. Senior Manufacturing Buyer, Hugh Crawford, and Ginny Michaud, Media Buyer, ensured the highest standards of print and CD production. Barbara Willette copyedited the text manuscript and Sheryl Nelson the Instructor's Manual. I thank all of these wonderful people. It has been inspiring to work with them and to share in creating what I believe is a truly outstanding educational tool.

I thank our talented sixth-edition supplements authors — Michael Stroup of Stephen F. Austin State University, James Cobbe of Florida State University, Della Lee Sue of Marist College, Carol Dole of the State University of West Georgia, Ed Price of Oklahoma State University, John Graham of Rutgers University, and Sang Lee of Southeastern Louisiana University. I especially thank Mark Rush, who yet again played a crucial role in creating another edition of this text and package. Mark has been a constant source of good advice and good humor. And I particularly thank John Graham for his extraordinarily careful accuracy review of near-final pages.

I thank the people who work directly with me. Jeannie Gillmore provided outstanding research assistance on many topics, including all the *Reading Between the Lines* news articles. Jane McAndrew provided excellent library help. Richard Parkin created the electronic art files and offered many ideas that improved the figures in this book. And Laurel Davies managed an ever-growing and ever more complex *Economics in Action* database.

As with the previous editions, this one owes an enormous debt to Robin Bade. I dedicate this book to her and again thank her for her work. I could not have written this book without the unselfish help she has given me. My thanks to her are unbounded.

Classroom experience will test the value of this book. I would appreciate hearing from instructors and students about how I can continue to improve it in future editions.

Michael Parkin
London, Ontario, Canada
michael.parkin@uwo.ca

Reviewers

Eric Abrams, Hawaii Pacific University
Christopher Adams, University of Vermont
Tajudeen Adenekan, Bronx Community College
Syed Ahmed, Cameron University
Milton Alderfer, Miami-Dade Community College
William Aldridge, Shelton State Community College
Donald L. Alexander, Western Michigan University
Terence Alexander, Iowa State University
Stuart Allen, University of North Carolina, Greensboro
Sam Allgood, University of Nebraska, Lincoln
Neil Alper, Northeastern University
Alan Anderson, Fordham University
Lisa R. Anderson, College of William and Mary
Jeff Ankrom, Wittenberg University
Fatma Antar, Manchester Community Technical College
Kofi Apraku, University of North Carolina, Asheville
Moshen Bahmani-Oskooee, University of Wisconsin, Milwaukee
Donald Balch, University of South Carolina
Mehmet Balcilar, Wayne State University
Paul Ballantyne, University of Colorado
Sue Bartlett, University of South Florida
Jose Juan Bautista, Xavier University of Louisiana
Valerie R. Bencivenga, University of Texas, Austin
Ben Bernanke, Princeton University
Margot Biery, Tarrant County Community College South
John Bittorowitz, Ball State University
William T. Bogart, Case Western Reserve University
Giacomo Bonanno, University of California, Davis
Sunne Brandmeyer, University of South Florida
Audie Brewton, Northeastern Illinois University
Baird Brock, Central Missouri State University
Byron Brown, Michigan State University
Jeffrey Buser, Columbus State Community College
Alison Butler, Florida International University
Tania Carbiener, Southern Methodist University
Kevin Carey, American University
Kathleen A. Carroll, University of Maryland, Baltimore County
Michael Carter, University of Massachusetts, Lowell
Edward Castronova, California State University, Fullerton
Subir Chakrabarti, Indiana University-Purdue University
Joni Charles, Southwest Texas University
Adhip Chaudhuri, Georgetown University
Gopal Chengalath, Texas Tech University
Daniel Christiansen, Albion College
John J. Clark, Community College of Allegheny County, Allegheny Campus
Meredith Clement, Dartmouth College
Michael B. Cohn, U. S. Merchant Marine Academy
Robert Collinge, University of Texas, San Antonio
Carol Condon, Kean University

Doug Conway, Mesa Community College
Larry Cook, University of Toledo
Bobby Corcoran, Middle Tennessee State University
Kevin Cotter, Wayne State University
James Peery Cover, University of Alabama, Tuscaloosa
Erik Craft, University of Richmond
Eleanor D. Craig, University of Delaware
Jim Craven, Clark College
Elizabeth Crowell, University of Michigan, Dearborn
Stephen Cullenberg, University of California, Riverside
David Culp, Slippery Rock University
Norman V. Cure, Macomb Community College
Dan Dabney, University of Texas, Austin
Andrew Dane, Angelo State University
Joseph Daniels, Marquette University
Gregory DeFreitas, Hofstra University
David Denslow, University of Florida
Mark Dickie, University of Georgia
James Dietz, California State University, Fullerton
Carol Dole, State University of West Georgia
Ronald Dorf, Inver Hills Community College
John Dorsey, University of Maryland, College Park
Amrik Singh Dua, Mt. San Antonio College
Thomas Duchesneau, University of Maine, Orono
Lucia Dunn, Ohio State University
Donald Dutkowsky, Syracuse University
John Edgren, Eastern Michigan University
David J. Eger, Alpena Community College
Harry Ellis, Jr., University of North Texas
Ibrahim Elsaify, State University of New York, Albany
Kenneth G. Elzinga, University of Virginia
Antonina Espiritu, Hawaii Pacific University
Gwen Eudey, University of Pennsylvania
M. Fazeli, Hofstra University
Philip Fincher, Louisiana Tech University
F. Firoozi, University of Texas, San Antonio
Steven Francis, Holy Cross College
David Franck, University of North Carolina, Charlotte
Roger Frantz, San Diego State University
Alwyn Fraser, Atlantic Union College
Richard Fristensky, Bentley College
James Gale, Michigan Technological University
Susan Gale, New York University
Roy Gardner, Indiana University
Eugene Gentzel, Pensacola Junior College
Andrew Gill, California State University, Fullerton
Robert Giller, Virginia Polytechnic Institute and State University
Robert Gillette, University of Kentucky
James N. Giordano, Villanova University
Maria Giuili, Diablo College
Susan Glanz, St. John's University
Robert Gordon, San Diego State University
Richard Gosselin, Houston Community College
John Graham, Rutgers University

John Griffen, Worcester Polytechnic Institute
Wayne Grove, Syracuse University
Robert Guell, Indiana State University
Jamie Haag, University of Oregon
Gail Heyne Hafer, Lindenwood University
Rik W. Hafer, Southern Illinois University, Edwardsville
Daniel Hagen, Western Washington University
David R. Hakes, University of Northern Iowa
Craig Hakkio, Federal Reserve Bank, Kansas City
Ann Hansen, Westminster College
Seid Hassan, Murray State University
Jonathan Haughton, Northeastern University
Randall Haydon, Wichita State University
Denise Hazlett, Whitman College
Jolien A. Helsel, Kent State University
James Henderson, Baylor University
Jill Boylston Herndon, University of Florida
Gus Herring, Brookhaven College
John Herrmann, Rutgers University
John M. Hill, Delgado Community College
Lewis Hill, Texas Tech University
Steve Hoagland, University of Akron
Tom Hoerger, Vanderbilt University
Calvin Hoerneman, Delta College
George Hoffer, Virginia Commonwealth University
Dennis L. Hoffman, Arizona State University
Paul Hohenberg, Rensselaer Polytechnic Institute
Jim H. Holcomb, University of Texas, El Paso
Harry Holzer, Michigan State University
Linda Hooks, Washington and Lee University
Jim Horner, Cameron University
Djehane Hosni, University of Central Florida
Harold Hotelling, Jr., Lawrence Technical University
Calvin Hoy, County College of Morris
Julie Hunsaker, Wayne State University
Beth Ingram, University of Iowa
Michael Jacobs, Lehman College
S. Hussain Ali Jafri, Tarleton State University
Dennis Jansen, Texas A&M University
Frederick Jungman, Northwestern Oklahoma State University
Paul Junk, University of Minnesota, Duluth
Leo Kahane, California State University, Hayward
Veronica Kalich, Baldwin-Wallace College
John Kane, State University of New York, Oswego
Eungmin Kang, St. Cloud State University
Arthur Kartman, San Diego State University
Louise Keely, University of Wisconsin at Madison
Manfred W. Keil, Claremont McKenna College
Elizabeth Kelly, University of Wisconsin at Madison
Rose Kilburn, Modesto Junior College
Robert Kirk, Indiana University—Purdue University, Indianapolis
Norman Kleinberg, City University of New York, Baruch College
Robert Kleinhenz, California State University, Fullerton
Joseph Kreitzer, University of St. Thomas

David Lages, Southwest Missouri State University
W. J. Lane, University of New Orleans
Leonard Lardaro, University of Rhode Island
Kathryn Larson, Elon College
Luther D. Lawson, University of North Carolina, Wilmington
Elroy M. Leach, Chicago State University
Jim Lee, Fort Hays State University
Sang Lee, Southeastern Louisiana University
Robert Lemke, Florida International University
Mary Lesser, Iona College
Jay Levin, Wayne State University
Arik Levinson, University of Wisconsin, Madison
Tony Lima, California State University, Hayward
William Lord, University of Maryland, Baltimore County
Nancy Lutz, Virginia Polytechnic Institute and State University
Murugappa Madhavan, San Diego State University
K. T. Magnusson, Salt Lake Community College
Mark Maier, Glendale Community College
Beth Maloan, University of Tennessee, Martin
Jean Mangan, California State University, Sacramento
Michael Marlow, California Polytechnic State University
Akbar Marvasti, University of Houston
Wolfgang Mayer, University of Cincinnati
John McArthur, Wofford College
Amy McCormick, College of William and Mary
Russel McCullough, Iowa State University
Gerald McDougall, Wichita State University
Stephen McGary, Ricks College
Richard D. McGrath, College of William and Mary
Richard McIntyre, University of Rhode Island
John McLeod, Georgia Institute of Technology
Kimberly Merritt, Cameron University
Charles Meyer, Iowa State University
Peter Mieszkowski, Rice University
John Mijares, University of North Carolina, Asheville
Richard A. Miller, Wesleyan University
Judith W. Mills, Southern Connecticut State University
Glen Mitchell, Nassau Community College
Jeannette C. Mitchell, Rochester Institute of Technology
Khan Mohabbat, Northern Illinois University
Bagher Modjtahedi, University of California, Davis
W. Douglas Morgan, University of California, Santa Barbara
William Morgan, University of Wyoming
Joanne Moss, San Francisco State University
Edward Murphy, Southwest Texas State University
Kevin J. Murphy, Oakland University
Kathryn Nantz, Fairfield University
William S. Neilson, Texas A&M University
Bart C. Nemmers, University of Nebraska, Lincoln
Melinda Nish, Salt Lake Community College
Anthony O'Brien, Lehigh University
Mary Olson, Washington University
Terry Olson, Truman State University
James B. O'Neill, University of Delaware

Farley Ordovensky, University of the Pacific

Z. Edward O'Relley, North Dakota State University

Donald Oswald, California State University, Bakersfield

Jan Palmer, Ohio University

Michael Palumbo, University of Houston

Chris Papageorgiou, Louisiana State University

G. Hossein Parandvash, Western Oregon State College

Randall Parker, East Carolina University

Robert Parks, Washington University

David Pate, St. John Fisher College

Donald Pearson, Eastern Michigan University

Mary Anne Pettit, Southern Illinois University, Edwardsville

Kathy Phares, University of Missouri, St. Louis

William A. Phillips, University of Southern Maine

Dennis Placone, Clemson University

Charles Plot, California Institute of Technology, Pasadena

Mannie Poen, Houston Community College

Kathleen Possai, Wayne State University

Ulrika Praski-Stahlgren, University College in Gavle-Sandviken, Sweden

Edward Price, Oklahoma State University

Rula Qalyoubi, Colorado State University

K. A. Quartey, Talladega College

Herman Quirmbach, Iowa State University

Jeffrey R. Racine, University of South Florida

Peter Rangazas, Indiana University-Purdue University, Indianapolis

Vaman Rao, Western Illinois University

Laura Razzolini, University of Mississippi

Rob Rebelein, University of Cincinnati

J. David Reed, Bowling Green State University

Robert H. Renshaw, Northern Illinois University

W. Gregory Rhodus, Bentley College

Jennifer Rice, Indiana University, Bloomington

John Robertson, Paducah Community College

Malcolm Robinson, University of North Carolina, Greensboro

Richard Roehl, University of Michigan, Dearborn

Thomas Romans, State University of New York, Buffalo

David R. Ross, Bryn Mawr College

Thomas Ross, St. Louis University

Robert J. Rossana, Wayne State University

Jeffrey Rous, University of North Texas

Rochelle Ruffer, Youngstown State University

Mark Rush, University of Florida

Gary Santoni, Ball State University

John Saussy, Harrisburg Area Community College

Don Schlagenhauf, Florida State University

David Schlow, Pennsylvania State University

Paul Schmitt, St. Clair County Community College

Jeremy Schwartz, Indiana University, Bloomington

Martin Sefton, Indianapolis University

Esther-Mirjam Sent, University of Notre Dame

Rod Shadbegian, University of Massachusetts, Dartmouth

Gerald Shilling, Eastfield College

Dorothy R. Siden, Salem State College

Scott Simkins, North Carolina Agricultural and Technical State University

Chuck Skoro, Boise State University

Phil Smith, DeKalb College

William Doyle Smith, University of Texas, El Paso

Sarah Stafford, College of William and Mary

Frank Steindl, Oklahoma State University

Jeffrey Stewart, New York University

Allan Stone, Southwest Missouri State University

Courtenay Stone, Ball State University

Paul Storer, Western Washington University

Mark Strazicich, Ohio State University, Newark

Michael Stroup, Stephen F. Austin State University

Robert Stuart, Rutgers University

Della Lee Sue, Marist College

Gilbert Suzawa, University of Rhode Island

David Swaine, Andrews University

Jason Taylor, University of Virginia

Janet Thomas, Bentley College

Kay Unger, University of Montana

Anthony Uremovic, Joliet Junior College

David Vaughn, City University, Washington

Don Waldman, Colgate University

Francis Wambalaba, Portland State University

Rob Wassmer, Wayne State University

Paul A. Weinstein, University of Maryland, College Park

Lee Weissert, St. Vincent College

Robert Whaples, Wake Forest University

Mark Wheeler, Western Michigan University

Charles H. Whiteman, University of Iowa

Brenda Wilson, Brookhaven College

Larry Wimmer, Brigham Young University

Mark Witte, Northwestern University

Willard E. Witte, Indiana University

Mark Wohar, University of Nebraska, Omaha

Cheonsik Woo, Clemson University

Douglas Wooley, Radford University

Arthur G. Woolf, University of Vermont

Ann Al Yasiri, University of Wisconsin, Platteville

John T. Young, Riverside Community College

Michael Youngblood, Rock Valley College

Peter Zaleski, Villanova University

Jason Zimmerman, South Dakota State University

Supplements Authors

James Cobbe, Florida State University

Carol Dole, State University of West Georgia

John Graham, Rutgers University

Jill Herndon, University of Florida

Sang Lee, Southeastern Louisiana University

Edward Price, Oklahoma State University

Mark Rush, University of Florida

Della Lee Sue, Marist College

Michael Stroup, Stephen F. Austin State University

Flexibility Chart

Core	Policy	Optional

Core

1. What Is Economics?

2. The Economic Problem

3. Demand and Supply

4. Elasticity

5. Efficiency and Equity
A chapter that provides a non-technical explanation of efficiency and equity that unifies the micro coverage and permits early coverage of policy issues.

10. Output and Costs

11. Perfect Competition

12. Monopoly

13. Monopolistic Competition and Oligopoly

14. Demand and Supply in Factor Markets
Enables you to cover all the factor market issues in a single chapter. Includes an explanation of present value.

Policy

6. Markets in Action
A unique chapter that gives extensive applications of demand and supply.

15. Economic Inequality

Optional

1. Appendix: Graphs in Economics
A good appendix to assign to the student with a fear of graphs.

3. Mathematical Note
Demand, Supply, and Equilibrium

7. Utility and Demand
Although this chapter is optional, it may be covered if desired *before* demand in Chapter 3.

8. Possibilities, Preferences, and Choices
A full chapter on this strictly optional topic to ensure that it is covered clearly with intuitive explanations and illustrations. The standard short appendix treatment of this topic makes it indigestible.

9. Organizing Production
This chapter may be skipped or assigned as a reading.

14. Appendix: Labor Unions

Core	**Policy**	**Optional**

Four Alternative Micro Sequences

Traditional Theory and Policy Mix	Challenging Theory Emphasis	Public Choice Emphasis	Policy Emphasis (shorter)
2. The Economic Problem	2. The Economic Problem	1. What Is Economics?	1. What Is Economics?
3. Demand and Supply	3. Demand and Supply	2. The Economic Problem	2. The Economic Problem
4. Elasticity	4. Elasticity	3. Demand and Supply	3. Demand and Supply
5. Efficiency and Equity	5. Efficiency and Equity	4. Elasticity	4. Elasticity
6. Markets in Action	6. Markets in Action	5. Efficiency and Equity	5. Efficiency and Equity
7. Utility and Demand or	8. Possibilities, Preferences, and Choices	6. Markets in Action	6. Markets in Action
8. Possibilities, Preferences, and Choices		7. Utility and Demand	
9. Organizing Production	9. Organizing Production	9. Organizing Production	14. Demand and Supply in Factor Markets
10. Output and Costs	10. Output and Costs	10. Output and Costs	15. Economic Inequality
11. Perfect Competition	11. Perfect Competition	11. Perfect Competition	16. Public Goods and Taxes
12. Monopoly	12. Monopoly	12. Monopoly	18. Externalities
13. Monopolistic Competition and Oligopoly	13. Monopolistic Competition and Oligopoly	13. Monopolistic Competition and Oligopoly	32. Trading with the World
17. Regulation and Antitrust Law	14. Demand and Supply in Factor Markets	16. Public Goods and Taxes	
14. Demand and Supply in Factor Markets	17. Regulation and Antitrust Law	17. Regulation and Antitrust Law	
15. Economic Inequality		18. Externalities	
32. Trading with the World	32. Trading with the World		
34. Global Stock Markets	34. Global Stock Markets		

Four Alternative Macro Sequences

Early Long-Term Growth	Late Long-Term Growth	Keynesian Perspective	Monetarist Perspective
19. Measuring GDP and Economic Growth	19. Measuring GDP and Economic Growth	19. Measuring GDP and Economic Growth	19. Measuring GDP and Economic Growth
20. Monitoring Cycles, Jobs, and the Price Level	20. Monitoring Cycles, Jobs, and the Price Level	20. Monitoring Cycles, Jobs, and the Price Level	20. Monitoring Cycles, Jobs, and the Price Level
22. The Economy at Full Employment	21. Aggregate Demand and Aggregate Supply	25. Expenditure Multipliers	21. Aggregate Demand and Aggregate Supply
23. Capital, Investment, and Saving	25. Expenditure Multipliers	22. Aggregate Demand and Aggregate Supply	27. Money
24. Economic Growth	26. Fiscal Policy	26. Fiscal Policy	28. Monetary Policy
30. The Business Cycle (Real Business Cycle, pp. 715–719)	27. Money	27. Money	29. Inflation
21. Aggregate Supply and Aggregate Demand	28. Monetary Policy	28. Monetary Policy	25. Expenditure Multipliers
25. Expenditure Multipliers	29. Inflation	29. Inflation	26. Fiscal Policy
26. Fiscal Policy	30. The Business Cycle	30. The Business Cycle (omit real business cycle)	30. The Business Cycle (omit real business cycle)
27. Money	31. Macroeconomic Policy Challenges	31. Macroeconomic Policy Challenges	31. Macroeconomic Policy Challenges
28. Monetary Policy	22. The Economy at Full Employment (optional)	22. The Economy at Full Employment (optional)	22. The Economy at Full Employment (optional)
29. Inflation	23. Capital, Investment, and Saving (optional)	23. Capital, Investment, and Saving (optional)	23. Capital, Investment, and Saving (optional)
30. The Business Cycle (rest of chapter)	24. Economic Growth	24. Economic Growth	24. Economic Growth
31. Macroeconomic Policy Challenges	33. International Finance	33. International Finance	33. International Finance
34. Global Stock Markets	34. Global Stock Markets	34. Global Stock Markets	34. Global Stock Markets

CREDITS

BRIEF CONTENTS

CONTENTS

Summary (Key Points, Key Figures and Tables, and Key Terms), Problems, Critical Thinking, and Web Exercises appear at the end of each chapter.

PART 8   AGGREGATE SUPPLY AND ECONOMIC GROWTH

ECONOMICS

1

WHAT IS ECONOMICS? — CHAPTER

1

Choice, Change, Challenge, and Opportunity

You are studying economics, the science of choice, at a time of enormous change, challenge, and opportunity. Economics studies the choices that we make as we cope with the hard fact of life: We can't have everything we want. The engine of change is information technology, which has created the Internet and transformed our lives at both work and play. This transformation will continue but in 2001 it was challenged by the onset of recession in March and the terrorist attacks of September 11. The events of September 11 have brought long-lasting changes to the political and security landscape. They also changed the economic landscape. Suddenly, people faced choices they had not previously imagined. Some people avoided air travel, a choice that sent shock waves through travel agencies, airports, airlines, airplane builders, hotels and restaurants, casinos, and theme parks. Airports installed more closed-circuit television and security equipment, and the U.S. government ordered more missiles and warplanes, choices that increased the output of electronics and weapons producers. ◆ The effects of recession, unlike those of terrorism, are temporary. But a recession can be deep and it was not clear as 2002 began, just how deep the recession would be. But all recessions are followed by new waves of expansion and prosperity. So as 2002 began the question was not whether the economy would again expand, but when would the expansion begin?

◆ You've just glimpsed some of the economic issues in today's world. Your course in economics will help you to understand the powerful forces that are shaping this world. This chapter takes the first step. It describes the questions that economists try to answer, the way they think about choices, and the methods they use. An appendix provides a guide to the graphical methods that are widely used in economics.

After studying this chapter, you will be able to

- **Define economics and distinguish between microeconomics and macroeconomics**

- **Explain the three big questions of microeconomics**

- **Explain the three big questions of macroeconomics**

- **Explain the ideas that define the economic way of thinking**

- **Explain how economists go about their work as social scientists**

Definition of Economics

ALL ECONOMIC QUESTIONS ARISE BECAUSE WE want more than we can get. We want a peaceful and secure world. We want clean air, lakes, and rivers. We want long and healthy lives. We want good schools, colleges, and universities. We want spacious and comfortable homes. We want an enormous range of sports and recreational gear from running shoes to jet skis. We want the time to enjoy sports, games, novels, movies, music, travel, and hanging out with our friends.

Scarcity

What each one of us can get is limited by time, by the incomes we earn, and by the prices we must pay. Everyone ends up with some unsatisfied wants. What as a society we can get is limited by our productive resources. These resources include the gifts of nature, human labor and ingenuity, and tools and equipment that we have produced.

Our inability to satisfy all our wants is called **scarcity**. The poor and the rich alike face scarcity. A child wants a $1.00 can of soda and two 50¢ packs of gum but has only $1.00 in his pocket. He faces scarcity. A millionaire wants to spend the weekend playing golf *and* spend the same weekend at the office attending a business strategy meeting. She faces scarcity. A society wants to provide improved health care, install a computer in every classroom, explore space, clean polluted lakes and rivers, and so on. Even parrots face scarcity!

Faced with scarcity, we must make choices. We must *choose* among the available alternatives. The child must *choose* the soda *or* the gum. The millionaire must *choose* the golf game *or* the meeting. As a society, we must *choose* among health care, national defense, the environment, and so on.

Economics is the social science that studies the choices that individuals, businesses, governments, and entire societies make as they cope with scarcity. The subject divides into two main parts:

- Microeconomics
- Macroeconomics

Microeconomics

Microeconomics is the study of the choices that individuals and businesses make, the way these choices interact, and the influence that governments exert on them. Some examples of microeconomic questions are: Why are more people buying SUVs and fewer people buying minivans? How will a decline in air travel affect the producers of airplanes? How would a tax on e-commerce affect the growth of the Internet? Who benefits from minimum wage laws?

Macroeconomics

Macroeconomics is the study of the effects on the national economy and the global economy of the choices that individuals, businesses, and governments make. Some examples of macroeconomic questions are: Why did production and jobs shrink in 2001? Why has Japan been in a long period of economic stagnation? Can the government bring prosperity by cutting interest rates? Will a tax cut increase the number of jobs and total production?

Not only do I want a cracker — we all want a cracker!

REVIEW QUIZ

1 What is scarcity?
2 Give some examples of scarcity in today's world.
3 Define economics.
4 Use the headlines in today's news to illustrate the distinction between microeconomics and macroeconomics.

Three Big Microeconomic Questions

LOOK AT THE WORLD AROUND YOU. YOU SEE AN enormous range of things that you might buy and jobs that you might do. You also see a huge range of incomes and wealth. Microeconomics explains much of what you see by addressing three big questions:

- What goods and services are produced?
- How are goods and services produced?
- For whom are goods and services produced?

What Goods and Services Are Produced?

The objects that people value and produce to satisfy wants are called **goods and services**. Goods are

physical objects such as golf balls. Services are tasks performed for people such as haircuts.

What *are* the goods and services that we produce in the United States today? Figure 1.1 shows the surprising answer. We are a service economy. The largest item produced is real estate services (realtors). Retail and wholesale trades come next, and health services and education complete the largest five. The largest categories of goods — construction, electronic equipment such as computers, food, industrial equipment, and chemicals — each account for less than 4 percent of the value of total production.

Figure 1.2 shows the trends in what we produce. Sixty years ago, 25 percent of Americans worked on farms, 30 percent in mining, construction, and manufacturing, and 45 percent produced services. By 2000, almost 80 percent of working Americans had jobs producing services. Mining, construction, and manufacturing jobs had shrunk to 20 percent, and farm jobs had almost disappeared.

You've reviewed some of the facts about *what* we produce in the United States. These facts raise the deeper question: What determines the quantities of realtor services, new homes, DVD players, and corn that we produce? Microeconomics provides some answers to these questions.

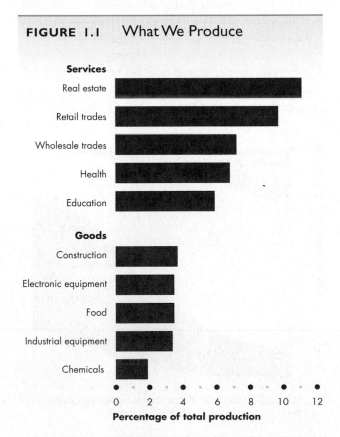

FIGURE 1.1   What We Produce

The production of real estate services and retail trades greatly exceeds the production of goods such as electronic equipment.

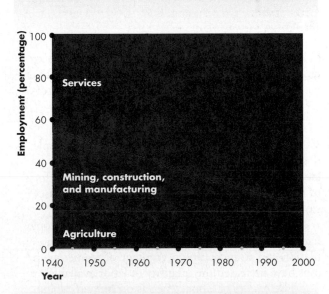

FIGURE 1.2   Trends in What We Produce

Services have expanded, and agriculture, mining, construction, and manufacturing have shrunk.

How Are Goods and Services Produced?

The range of jobs that you might do keeps changing. When Henry Ford built the world's first auto assembly line, he destroyed the jobs of the skilled craft workers who built cars using hand tools and created jobs for a new type of auto assembly worker. Every year, as businesses adopt new production technologies, similar changes occur. Today, it is information technology businesses that are producing new products, creating new jobs, and destroying old ones.

We call the resources that businesses use to produce goods and services **factors of production**. Factors of production are grouped into four categories:

- Land
- Labor
- Capital
- Entrepreneurship

Land The "gifts of nature" that we use to produce goods and services are called **land**. In economics, land is what in everyday language we call natural resources. It includes land in the everyday sense, minerals, and water.

The United States covers 2 billion acres and we live on about 5 percent of this land. The other 95 percent is equally divided between farmland and other use such as lakes and rivers, national parks, and forests. Urban land is expanding and rural land is shrinking, but slowly.

Our land surface and water resources are renewable, and some of our mineral resources can be recycled. But many mineral resources, and all those that we use to create energy, are nonrenewable resources — they can be used only once.

Labor The work time and work effort that people devote to producing goods and services is called **labor**. Labor includes the physical and mental efforts of all the people who work on farms and construction sites and in factories, shops, and offices.

In the United States in 2001, 141 million people had jobs or were available for work. An increasing population and an increasing percentage of women with jobs have increased the quantity of labor available.

The *quality* of labor depends on **human capital**, which is the knowledge and skill that people obtain from education, on-the-job training, and work experience. You are building your own human capital right now as you work on your economics course, and your human capital will continue to grow as you become better at your job. Today, more than 80 percent of the U.S. population has completed high school and 25 percent has a college or university degree. Figure 1.3 shows a measure of the growth of human capital in the United States over the past century.

Capital The tools, instruments, machines, buildings, and other constructions that businesses now use to produce goods and services are called **capital**. The quantity of capital grows steadily over time.

Entrepreneurship The human resource that organizes labor, land, and capital is called **entrepreneurship**. Entrepreneurs come up with new ideas about what and how to produce, make business decisions, and bear the risks that arise from these decisions.

You've reviewed some of the facts about *how* we produce in the United States. These facts raise deeper questions such as: What determines the quantities of labor and capital that get used? Microeconomics provides some answers to these questions.

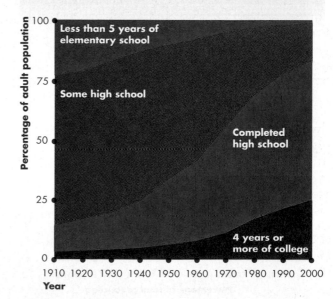

FIGURE 1.3   A Measure of Human Capital

In 2000, 25 percent of the population had 4 years or more of college, up from 3 percent in 1910. A further 58 percent had completed high school, up from 11 percent in 1910.

For Whom Are Goods and Services Produced?

Who gets the goods and services that are produced depends on the incomes that people earn. The movie star who earns a few million dollars a year buys a large quantity of goods and services. A homeless unemployed person has few options and a small quantity of goods and services.

To earn an income, people sell the services of the factors of production they own:

- Land earns **rent**.
- Labor earns **wages**.
- Capital earns **interest**.
- Entrepreneurship earns **profit**.

Which factor of production earns the most income? The answer is labor. Total wages (including fringe benefits) were 71 percent of total income in 2000. Land, capital, and entrepreneurship share the remaining 29 percent. And over time, these percentages have been remarkably constant.

Knowing how income is shared among the factors of production doesn't tell us how it is shared among individuals. You know of lots of people who earn very large incomes. The average baseball player's salary in 2002 was $5 million, and one star, the Texas Rangers' Alex Rodriguez, earned $22 million. You know of even more people who earn very small incomes. Servers at McDonald's average around $6.35 an hour; checkout clerks, gas station attendants, and textile and leather workers earn less than $10 an hour.

You probably know about other persistent differences in incomes. Men, on the average, earn more than women. Whites, on the average, earn more than minorities. College graduates, on the average, earn more than high-school graduates. Americans, on the average, earn more than Europeans, who in turn earn more, on the average, than Asians and Africans.

Figure 1.4 shows the incomes for five groups, each of which represents 20 percent of the population. If incomes were equal, each 20 percent group would earn 20 percent of total income. You know that incomes are unequal, and the figure provides a measure of just how unequal they are.

The 20 percent of individuals with the lowest incomes earn only 4 percent of total income. The second lowest 20 percent earn about 9 percent of total income. The next 20 percent — the middle 20 percent — earn 15 percent of total income. The

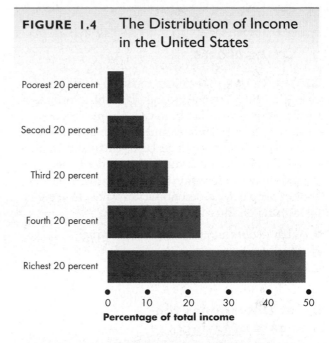

FIGURE 1.4   The Distribution of Income in the United States

Percentage of total income

In 1999, the richest 20 percent of the population earned 49 percent of total income. The poorest 20 percent earned only 4 percent of total income.

second highest 20 percent earn 23 percent of total income. And the richest 20 percent of individuals earn 49 percent of total income.

You've reviewed some of the facts about *for whom* we produce in the United States. These facts raise deeper questions such as: Why do women and minorities earn less than white males?

The three big microeconomic questions give you a sense of the *scope of microeconomics.* Next, we'll look at the big questions of macroeconomics.

REVIEW QUIZ

1 Does the United States produce more goods than services? What item accounts for the largest percent of the value of what we produce?
2 What are the trends in what we produce?
3 What are the factors of production and what are some of the changes in the way we produce goods and services?
4 Describe the distribution of income that shows for whom goods and services are produced.

Three Big Macroeconomic Questions

YOU'VE LIVED THROUGH A PERIOD OF DRAMATIC change in the way we work and play. The information age has created what has been called a "new economy" with rising living standards and new job opportunities. At the same time, prices have been remarkably stable. But you've also seen that our economy does not always expand. In 2001, recession brought job losses for millions of people. Macroeconomics explains these events by focusing on three big questions:

- What determines the standard of living?
- What determines the cost of living?
- Why does our economy fluctuate?

What Determines the Standard of Living?

What is the standard of living? How do we measure it? How do we compare the standard of living in Africa with that in the United States?

The **standard of living** is the level of consumption that people enjoy, on the average, and is measured by average income per person. The greater is income per person, the higher is the standard of living, other things remaining the same.

Figure 1.5 shows the number of dollars per day earned on the average in different places. You can see that in the United States, the average is $95 a day. This number tells you that an average person in the United States can buy goods and services that cost $95 — about five times the world average. Living standards fall off as we move down the figure, with average incomes in India and Africa of only $5 a day.

Most people live in the countries that have incomes below the world average. You can see this fact by looking at the population numbers shown in the figure. The poorest five countries or regions — China, Central Asia, Other Asia, India, and Africa — have a total population of 4 billion, which is two thirds of the world's population.

What makes the standard of living rise? What can Indians and Africans do to increase their standard of living? Your study of macroeconomics will help you to understand some answers to questions like these.

FIGURE 1.5   Living Standards Around the World

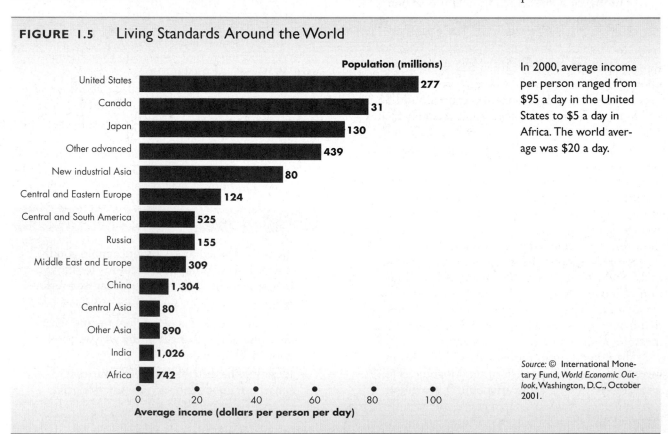

In 2000, average income per person ranged from $95 a day in the United States to $5 a day in Africa. The world average was $20 a day.

Source: © International Monetary Fund, *World Economic Outlook,* Washington, D.C., October 2001.

What Determines the Cost of Living?

In your great-grandparents' youth, when the electric light bulb was the latest big thing, the average American earned a $1 a day. But your great-grandparents' dime would buy what you need a dollar to buy. The dollar of 2002 is worth only one tenth of the dollar of 1902. The value of the dollar is shrinking and the cost of living is rising.

The **cost of living** is the amount of money it takes to buy the goods and services that a typical family consumes. In the United States, we measure money in dollars. So the cost of living in the United States is the number of dollars it takes to buy the goods and services that typical family buys. In the United Kingdom, it is the number of pounds; in Japan, the number of yen; and in Russia, the number of rubles.

Prices in Different Currencies   To make this idea concrete think about what a Big Mac costs. Table 1.1 shows some prices in 10 countries. The average price of a Big Mac in the United States is $2.50. In the United Kingdom, it costs £1.90, and in Japan, it costs ¥294. So in the United Kingdom, it costs a smaller number of money units to buy a Big Mac than it does in the United States, and in Japan, it costs a larger number of money units. But the cost of a Big Mac is similar in the three countries. The reason is that a

pound is worth more than a dollar and £1.90 is a price similar to $2.50. And a yen is worth a bit less than a cent, so a price of ¥294 is also similar to $2.50.

The number of money units that something costs is not very important. But the rate at which the number is changing is very important. A rising cost of living is called **inflation** and a falling cost of living is called **deflation**. Inflation brings a shrinking value of the dollar and deflation brings a rising value of the dollar.

Inflation and Deflation   Have we experienced inflation and a rising cost of living or deflation and a falling cost of living? If we look back over the past 100 years, we see that the cost of living has increased and the value of the dollar has shrunk.

In the United States, on the average during the 1980s and 1990s, the cost of living increased by 3.4 percent a year. To put this number in perspective, it means that a Big Mac that cost $1.30 in 1982 cost $1.80 in 1992 and $2.50 in 2002. Inflation at this rate is not generally regarded as a big problem. But it does mean that if the same trend continues, the dollar of 2052 will be worth about one third of the value of the dollar of 2002.

Most of the advanced economies have similarly low inflation. But the developing economies have higher inflation rates, some of them spectacularly so. In Central and South America, the average inflation rate during the 1980s and 1990s was 107 percent. A 100 percent change means a doubling. At this inflation rate, a Big Mac that cost 1.2 pesos in Santiago in 1992 costs 1,260 pesos in 2002. Inflation this rapid poses huge problems as people struggle to cope with an ever-falling value of money.

During the past few years, the cost of living has increased slowly. Can we count on it rising slowly in the future? What will the dollar buy next year? What will it buy in 10 years when you are paying off your student loan? And what will it buy in 50 years when you are spending your life's savings in retirement?

You've seen that over the years, our standard of living has increased. Why doesn't a rising *cost* of living mean that people must constantly cut back on their spending and endure a falling *standard* of living? Although the cost of living has increased steadily, incomes have increased more quickly. And because incomes have increased faster than the cost of living, the standard of living has increased.

What causes inflation? What can we do to avoid it? Your study of macroeconomics will help you to understand some answers to these questions.

TABLE 1.1	The Price of a Big Mac in 10 Countries	
Country	**Name of Currency**	**Price of a Big Mac**
United Kingdom	Pound	1.90
United States	Dollar	2.50
Brazil	Real	2.95
South Africa	Rand	9.00
China	Yuan	9.90
France	Franc	18.50
Russia	Ruble	39.50
Japan	Yen	294
Chile	Peso	1,260
Italy	Lira	4,500

Source: Economist.com

Why Does Our Economy Fluctuate?

Over long periods, both the standard of living and the cost of living increase. But these increases are not smooth and continuous. During 2001, more than two million American jobs disappeared as the expansion of the 1990s and 2000 turned into recession. We call the periodic but irregular up-and-down movement in production and jobs the **business cycle**.

When production and jobs are increasing more rapidly than normal, the economy is in a business cycle expansion. When production and jobs are shrinking, the economy is in a recession.

Figure 1.6 illustrates the phases and turning points of a business cycle. A *recession* runs from year 2 to year 4, followed by an *expansion* from year 4 through year 8. Another recession runs from year 8 through year 10. A recession ends at a *trough*, and an expansion ends at a *peak*.

The most recent expansion in the United States began in 1991 and ended in 2001. The deepest recession of the 1990s was in Russia, where production fell by almost 30 percent between 1990 and 1994. The most persistent recession of recent years has been in Japan. The worst recession ever experienced occurred during the 1930s in an episode called the Great Depression. During this period, production shrank by more than 20 percent.

When a recession occurs, unemployment increases. During the Great Depression, a quarter of the labor force was unable to find jobs. During the recession of the early 1980s, the unemployment rate climbed to 10 percent of the labor force.

What causes the business cycle? What can we do to smooth out the business cycle? Economists remain unsure about the answers to these questions. But in your study of macroeconomics, you will learn what economists have discovered about economic fluctuations.

REVIEW QUIZ

1 What are the three big issues that macroeconomics addresses?
2 What do we mean by the standard of living and what is its range from the richest to the poorest countries?
3 What do we mean by the cost of living? If the cost of living keeps rising, does the standard of living keep falling?
4 What are the phases of the business cycle?

FIGURE 1.6   Business Cycle Phases and Turning Points

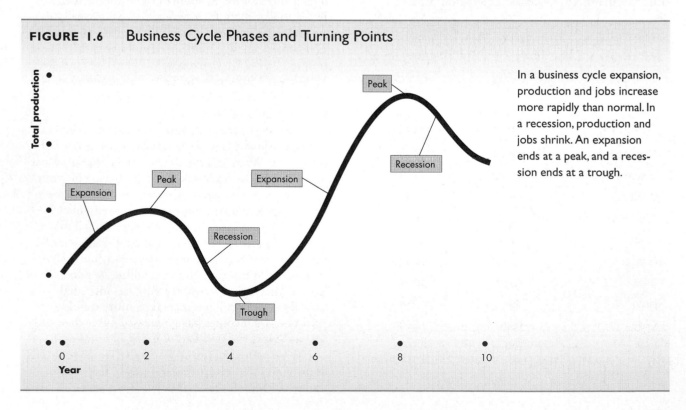

In a business cycle expansion, production and jobs increase more rapidly than normal. In a recession, production and jobs shrink. An expansion ends at a peak, and a recession ends at a trough.

The Economic Way of Thinking

THE DEFINITION OF ECONOMICS AND THE questions of microeconomics and macroeconomics tell you about the *scope of economics.* But they don't tell you how economists *think* about these questions and go about seeking answers to them.

You're now going to begin to see how economists approach economic questions. First, in this section, we'll look at the ideas that define the *economic way of thinking.* This way of thinking needs practice, but it is a powerful way of thinking and as you become more familiar with it, you'll begin to see the world around you with a new and sharp focus.

Choices and Tradeoffs

Because we face scarcity, we must make choices. And when we make a choice, we select from the available alternatives. For example, you can spend the weekend studying for your next economics test and having fun with your friends, but you can't do both of these activities at the same time. You must choose how much time to devote to each. Whatever choice you make, you could have chosen something else instead.

You can think about your choice as a tradeoff. A **tradeoff** is an exchange — giving up one thing to get something else. When you choose how to spend your weekend, you trade off between studying and hanging out with your friends.

Guns Versus Butter The classic tradeoff is guns versus butter. "Guns" and "butter" stand for any pair of goods. They might actually be guns and butter. Or they might be broader categories such as national defense and food. Or they might be any pair of specific goods or services such as cola and bottled water, baseball bats and tennis rackets, colleges and hospitals, realtor services and career counseling.

Regardless of the specific objects that guns and butter represent, the guns-versus-butter tradeoff captures a hard fact of life: If we want more of one thing, we must trade something else in exchange for it.

The idea of a tradeoff is central to the whole of economics. We can pose all the questions of microeconomics and macroeconomics in terms of tradeoffs. Let's return to these questions and view them in terms of tradeoffs.

Microeconomic Tradeoffs

The questions what, how, and for whom goods and services are produced all involve tradeoffs that are similar to that of guns versus butter.

"What" Tradeoffs What goods and services get produced depends on choices made by each one of us, by our government, and by the businesses that produce the things we buy. Each of these choices involves a tradeoff.

Each one of us faces a tradeoff when we choose how to spend our income. You go to the movies this week, but you forgo a few cups of coffee to buy the ticket — you trade off coffee for a movie.

The federal government faces a tradeoff when it chooses how to spend our tax dollars. Congress votes for more national defense but cuts back on educational programs — Congress trades off education for national defense.

Businesses face a tradeoff when they decide what to produce. Nike hires Tiger Woods and allocates resources to designing and marketing a new golf ball but cuts back on its development of a new running shoe. Nike trades off running shoes for golf balls.

"How" Tradeoffs How goods and services get produced depends on choices made by the businesses that produce the things we buy. These choices involve a tradeoff. For example, Krispy Kreme opens a new doughnut store with an automated production line and closes an older store with a traditional kitchen. Krispy Kreme trades off labor for capital.

"For Whom" Tradeoffs For whom goods and services are produced depends on the distribution of buying power. Buying power can be redistributed — transferred from one person to another — in three ways: by voluntary payments, by theft, or through taxes and benefits organized by government. Redistribution brings tradeoffs.

Each of us faces a "for whom" tradeoff when we choose how much to contribute to the United Nations famine relief fund. You donate $50 and cut your spending. You trade off your own spending for a small increase in economic equality.

We make choices that influence redistribution by theft when we vote to make theft illegal and to devote resources to law enforcement. We trade off goods and services for an increase in the security of our property.

We also vote for taxes and social programs that redistribute buying power from the rich to the poor. Government redistribution confronts society with what has been called the **big tradeoff** — the tradeoff between equality and efficiency. Taxing the rich and making transfers to the poor bring greater economic equality. But taxing productive activities such as running a business, working hard, and saving and investing in capital discourages these activities. So taxing productive activities means producing less — it creates inefficiency.

You can think of the big tradeoff as being the problem of how to share a pie that everyone contributes to baking. If each person receives a share of the pie that reflects the size of her or his effort, everyone will work hard and the pie will be as large as possible. But if the pie is shared equally, regardless of contribution, some talented bakers will slacken off and the pie will shrink. The big tradeoff is one between the size of the pie and how equally it is shared. We trade off some efficiency for increased equality.

We've reviewed some microeconomic tradeoffs. Let's now look at some macroeconomic tradeoffs.

Macroeconomic Tradeoffs

The three macroeconomic questions about the standard of living, the cost of living, and the business cycle involve tradeoffs that are similar to that of guns versus butter.

Standard of Living Tradeoffs The standard of living is higher in the United States than in Africa. And the standard of living improves over time, so today it is higher than it was a generation ago. Our standard of living and its rate of improvement depend on the many choices made by each one of us, by governments, and by businesses. And these choices involve tradeoffs.

One choice is that of how much of our income to consume and how much to save. Our saving can be channeled through the financial system to finance businesses and to pay for new capital that increases productivity. The more we save and invest, the faster our productivity and our standard of living increase. When you decide to save an extra $1,000 and forgo a vacation, you trade off the vacation for a higher future income. If everyone saves an extra $1,000 and businesses invest in more equipment that increases productivity, the average income per person rises and the standard of living improves. As a society, we trade off current consumption for economic growth and a higher future standard of living.

A second choice is how much effort to devote to education and training. By becoming better educated and more highly skilled, we become more productive and our standard of living rises. When you decide to remain in school for another two years to complete a professional degree and forgo a huge chunk of leisure time, you trade off leisure for a higher future income. If everyone becomes better educated, productivity increases, income per person rises, and the standard of living improves. As a society, we trade off current consumption and leisure time for economic growth and a higher future standard of living.

A third choice, usually made by businesses, is how much effort to devote to research and the development of new products and production methods. Ford Motor Company can hire engineers to do research on a new robot assembly line or to operate the existing plant and produce cars. More research brings greater productivity in the future but means smaller current production — a tradeoff of current production for greater future production.

Output-Inflation Tradeoff When policy actions lower the interest rate and speed the pace at which money is created, spending, output, and employment increase. Higher spending brings rising inflation — the cost of living rises more rapidly. Eventually, output returns to its previous level. But the higher inflation rate has been accompanied by a temporary increase in output.

Similarly, when policy actions raise the interest rate and slow the pace at which money is created, spending, output, and employment all decrease. Lower spending brings falling inflation — the cost of living rises more slowly. Again, output eventually returns to its previous level and the lower inflation rate has been accompanied by a temporary decrease in output.

When the inflation rate is too high, policy makers would like to lower inflation without lowering output. But they face an **output-inflation tradeoff** because the policy action that lowers inflation also lowers output and a policy action that boosts output increases inflation.

Seeing choices as tradeoffs emphasizes the idea that to get something, we must give up something. What we give up is the *cost* of what we get. Economists call this cost the *opportunity cost*.

Opportunity Cost

The highest-valued alternative that we give up to get something is the **opportunity cost** of the activity chosen. "There's no such thing as a free lunch" is not just a clever throwaway line. It expresses the central idea of economics: that every choice involves a cost.

You can quit school right now, or you can remain in school. If you quit school and take a job at McDonald's, you might earn enough to buy some CDs, go to the movies, and spend lots of free time with your friends. If you remain in school, you can't afford these things. You will be able to buy these things later, and that is one of the payoffs from being in school. But for now, when you've bought your books, you might have nothing left for CDs and movies. And doing assignments means that you've got less time for hanging around with your friends. The opportunity cost of being in school is the highest-valued alternative that you would have done if you had quit school.

All of the tradeoffs that we've just considered involve opportunity cost. The opportunity cost of some guns is the butter forgone; the opportunity cost of a movie ticket is the number of cups of coffee forgone; the opportunity cost of lower inflation is the output temporarily forgone.

Margins and Incentives

You can allocate the next hour between studying and e-mailing your friends. But the choice is not all or nothing. You must decide how many minutes to allocate to each activity. To make this decision, you compare the benefit of a little bit more study time with its cost — you make your choice at the **margin**.

The benefit that arises from an increase in an activity is called **marginal benefit**. For example, suppose that you're working four nights a week at your courses and your grade point average is 3.0. You decide that you want a higher grade and decide to study an extra night each week. Your grade now rises to 3.5. The marginal benefit from studying for one additional night a week is the 0.5 increase in your grade. It is *not* the 3.5 grade. The reason is that you already have the benefit from studying for four nights a week, so we don't count this benefit as resulting from the decision you are now making.

The cost of an increase in an activity is called **marginal cost**. For you, the marginal cost of increasing your study time by one night a week is the cost of the additional night not spent with your friends (if that is your best alternative use of the time). It does not include the cost of the four nights you are already studying.

To make your decision, you compare the marginal benefit from an extra night of study with its marginal cost. If the marginal benefit exceeds the marginal cost, you study the extra night. If the marginal cost exceeds the marginal benefit, you do not study the extra night.

By evaluating marginal benefits and marginal costs and choosing only those actions that bring greater benefit than cost, we use our scarce resources in the way that makes us as well off as possible.

Our choices respond to incentives. An **incentive** is an inducement to take a particular action. The inducement can be a benefit — a carrot — or a cost — a stick. A change in marginal cost and a change in marginal benefit change the incentives that we face and lead us to change our choices.

For example, suppose your economics instructor gives you some problem sets and tells you that all the problems will be on the next test. The marginal benefit from working these problems is large, so you diligently work them all. Suppose, in contrast, that your math instructor gives you some problem sets and tells you that none of the problems will be on the next test. The marginal benefit from working these problems is lower, so you skip most of them.

The central idea of economics is that we can predict the way choices will change by looking at changes in incentives. More of an activity is undertaken when its marginal cost falls or marginal benefit rises; less of an activity is undertaken when its marginal cost rises or marginal benefit falls.

REVIEW QUIZ

1 What is a tradeoff?
2 Provide three examples of microeconomic tradeoffs.
3 What is the big tradeoff and how does it arise?
4 Provide two examples of macroeconomic trade-offs.
5 What is the short-run tradeoff of macroeconomics?
6 What is opportunity cost?
7 How do economists predict changes in choices?

Economics: A Social Science

ECONOMICS IS A SOCIAL SCIENCE (ALONG WITH political science, psychology, and sociology). Economists try to discover how the economic world works, and in pursuit of this goal (like all scientists), they distinguish between two types of statements:

- What *is*
- What *ought to be*

Statements about what *is* are called *positive* statements and they might be right or wrong. We can test a positive statement by checking it against the facts. When a chemist does an experiment in her laboratory, she is attempting to check a positive statement against the facts.

Statements about what *ought to be* are called *normative* statements. These statements depend on values and cannot be tested. When Congress debates a motion, it is ultimately trying to decide what ought to be. It is making a normative statement.

To see the distinction between positive and normative statements, consider the controversy over global warming. Some scientists believe that centuries of the burning of coal and oil are increasing the carbon dioxide content of the earth's atmosphere and leading to higher temperatures that eventually will have devastating consequences for life on this planet. "Our planet is warming because of an increased carbon dioxide buildup in the atmosphere" is a positive statement. It can (in principle and with sufficient data) be tested. "We ought to cut back on our use of carbon-based fuels such as coal and oil" is a normative statement. You can agree with or disagree with this statement, but you can't test it. It is based on values. Health-care reform provides an economic example of the distinction. "Universal health care will cut the amount of work time lost to illness" is a positive statement. "Every American should have equal access to health care" is a normative statement.

The task of economic science is to discover positive statements that are consistent with what we observe and that help us to understand the economic world. This task can be broken into three steps:

- Observation and measurement
- Model building
- Testing models

Observation and Measurement

Economists observe and measure data on such things as natural and human resources, wages and work hours, the prices and quantities of the different goods and services produced, taxes and government spending, and the quantities of goods and services bought from and sold to other countries.

Model Building

The second step toward understanding how the economic world works is to build a model. An **economic model** is a description of some aspect of the economic world that includes only those features of the world that are needed for the purpose at hand. A model is simpler than the reality it describes. What a model includes and what it leaves out result from assumptions about what is essential and what are inessential details.

You can see how ignoring details is useful — even essential — to our understanding by thinking about a model that you see every day: the TV weather map. The weather map is a model that helps to predict the temperature, wind speed and direction, and precipitation over a future period. The weather map shows lines called isobars — lines of equal barometric pressure. It doesn't show the interstate highways. The reason is that our theory of the weather tells us that the pattern of air pressure, not the location of the highways, determines the weather.

An economic model is similar to a weather map. It tells us how a number of variables are determined by a number of other variables. For example, an economic model of the 2002 Salt Lake City Winter Olympic Games might tell us the effects of the games on the number of houses and apartments, rents and prices, jobs, and transportation facilities, and the outputs and profits of the businesses in the region.

Testing Models

The third step is testing the model. A model's predictions might correspond to the facts or be in conflict with them. By comparing the model's predictions with the facts, we can test a model and develop an economic theory. An **economic theory** is a generalization that summarizes what we think we understand about the economic choices that people make and the performance of industries and entire economies. It is a bridge between an economic model and the real economy.

The process of building and testing models creates theories. For example, meteorologists have a theory that if the isobars form a particular pattern at a particular time of the year (a model), then it will snow (reality). They have developed this theory by repeated observation and by carefully recording the weather that follows specific pressure patterns.

Economics is a young science. It was born in 1776 with the publication of Adam Smith's *Wealth of Nations* (see p. 52). Over the years since then, economists have discovered many useful theories. But in many areas, economists are still looking for answers. The gradual accumulation of economic knowledge gives most economists some faith that their methods will, eventually, provide usable answers to the big economic questions.

But progress in economics comes slowly. Let's look at some of the obstacles to progress in economics.

Obstacles and Pitfalls in Economics

We cannot easily do economic experiments. And most economic behavior has many simultaneous causes. For these two reasons, it is difficult in economics to unscramble cause and effect.

Unscrambling Cause and Effect By changing one factor at a time and holding all the other relevant factors constant, we isolate the factor of interest and are able to investigate its effects in the clearest possible way. This logical device, which all scientists use to identify cause and effect, is called *ceteris paribus*. **Ceteris paribus** is a Latin term that means "other things being equal" or "if all other relevant things remain the same." Ensuring that other things are equal is crucial in many activities, and all successful attempts to make scientific progress use this device.

Economic models (like the models in all other sciences) enable the influence of one factor at a time to be isolated in the imaginary world of the model. When we use a model, we are able to imagine what would happen if only one factor changed. But *ceteris paribus* can be a problem in economics when we try to test a model.

Laboratory scientists, such as chemists and physicists, perform experiments by actually holding all the relevant factors constant except for the one under investigation. In non-experimental sciences such as economics (and astronomy), we usually observe the outcomes of the simultaneous operation of many factors. Consequently, it is hard to sort out the effects of each individual factor and to compare them with what a model predicts. To cope with this problem, economists take three complementary approaches.

First, they look for pairs of events in which other things were equal (or similar). An example might be to study the effects of unemployment insurance on the unemployment rate by comparing the United States with Canada on the presumption that the people in the two economies are sufficiently similar. Second, economists use statistical tools — called econometrics. Third, when they can, they perform experiments. This relatively new approach puts real subjects (usually students) in a decision-making situation and varies their incentives in some way to discover how they respond to a change in one factor at a time.

Economists try to avoid fallacies — errors of reasoning that lead to a wrong conclusion. But two fallacies are common, and you need to be on your guard to avoid them. They are the

- Fallacy of composition
- *Post hoc* fallacy

Fallacy of Composition The fallacy of composition is the (false) statement that what is true of the parts is true of the whole or that what is true of the whole is true of the parts. Think of the true statement "Speed kills" and its implication: Going more slowly saves lives. If an entire freeway moves at a lower speed, everyone on the highway has a safer ride.

But suppose that only one driver slows down and all the other drivers try to maintain their original speed. In this situation, there will probably be more accidents because more cars will change lanes to overtake the slower vehicle. So in this example, what is true for the whole is not true for a part.

The fallacy of composition arises mainly in macroeconomics, and it stems from the fact that the parts interact with each other to produce an outcome for the whole that might differ from the intent of the parts. For example, a firm lays off some workers to cut costs and improve its profits. If all firms take similar actions, income falls and so does spending. The firm sells less, and its profits don't improve.

Post Hoc Fallacy Another Latin phrase — *post hoc, ergo propter hoc* — means "after this, therefore because of this." The *post hoc* fallacy is the error of reasoning that a first event *causes* a second event because the first occurred before the second. Suppose you are a visitor from a far-off world. You observe lots of people shopping in early December, and then you see them opening gifts and partying in the holiday season. "Does the shopping cause the holiday season?," you wonder. After a deeper study, you discover that the holiday season causes the shopping. A later event causes an earlier event.

Unraveling cause and effect is difficult in economics. And just looking at the timing of events often doesn't help. For example, the stock market booms, and some months later the economy expands — jobs and incomes grow. Did the stock market boom cause the economy to expand? Possibly, but perhaps businesses started to plan the expansion of production because a new technology that lowered costs had become available. As knowledge of the plans spread, the stock market reacted to *anticipate* the economic expansion. To disentangle cause and effect, economists use economic models and data and, to the extent that they can, perform experiments.

Economics is a challenging science. Does the difficulty of getting answers in economics mean that anything goes and that economists disagree on most questions? Perhaps you've heard the joke "If you laid all the economists in the world end to end, they still wouldn't reach agreement." Surprisingly, perhaps, the joke does not describe reality.

Agreement and Disagreement

Economists agree on a remarkably wide range of questions. And often the agreed-upon view of economists disagrees with the popular and sometimes politically correct view. When Federal Reserve Chairman Alan Greenspan testifies before the Senate Banking Committee, his words are rarely controversial among economists, even when they generate endless debate in the press and Congress.

Here are 12 propositions with which at least 7 out of every 10 economists broadly agree:

- Tariffs and import restrictions make most people worse off.
- A large budget deficit has an adverse effect on the economy.
- A minimum wage increases unemployment among young workers and low-skilled workers.

- Cash payments to welfare recipients make them better off than do transfers-in-kind of equal cash value.
- A tax cut can help to lower unemployment when the unemployment rate is high.
- The distribution of income in the United States should be more equal.
- Inflation is primarily caused by a rapid rate of money creation.
- The government should restructure welfare along the lines of a "negative income tax."
- Rent ceilings cut the availability of housing.
- Pollution taxes are more effective than pollution limits.
- The redistribution of income is a legitimate role for the U.S. government.
- The federal budget should be balanced on the average over the business cycle but not every year.

Which of these propositions are positive and which are normative? Notice that economists are willing to offer their opinions on normative issues as well as their professional views on positive questions. Be on the lookout for normative propositions dressed up as positive propositions.

REVIEW QUIZ

1 What is the distinction between a positive statement and a normative statement? Provide an example (different from those in the chapter) of each type of statement.

2 What is a model? Can you think of a model that you might use (probably without thinking of it as a model) in your everyday life?

3 What is a theory? Why is the statement "It might work in theory, but it doesn't work in practice" a silly statement?

4 What is the *ceteris paribus* assumption and how is it used?

5 Try to think of some everyday examples of the fallacy of composition and the *post hoc* fallacy.

SUMMARY

KEY POINTS

Definition of Economics (p. 2)

- All economic questions arise from scarcity — from the fact that wants exceed the resources available to satisfy them.
- Economics is the social science that studies the choices that people make as they cope with scarcity.
- The subject divides into microeconomics and macroeconomics.

Three Big Microeconomic Questions (pp. 3–5)

- Three big questions that summarize the scope of microeconomics are
  1. What goods and services are produced?
  2. How are goods and services produced?
  3. For whom are goods and services produced?

Three Big Macroeconomic Questions (pp. 6–8)

- Three big questions that summarize the scope of macroeconomics are
  1. What determines the standard of living?
  2. What determines the cost of living?
  3. Why does our economy fluctuate?

The Economic Way of Thinking (pp. 9–11)

- Every choice is a tradeoff — exchanging more of something for less of something else.
- The classic guns-versus-butter tradeoff represents all tradeoffs.
- All economic questions involve tradeoffs.
- The big social tradeoff is that between equality and efficiency.
- A macroeconomic tradeoff is the short-run tradeoff between output and inflation.
- The highest-valued alternative forgone is the opportunity cost of what is chosen.
- Choices are made at the margin and respond to incentives.

Economics: A Social Science (pp. 12–14)

- Economists distinguish between positive statements — what is — and normative statements — what ought to be.
- To explain the economic world, economists develop theories by building and testing economic models.
- Economists use the *ceteris paribus* assumption to try to disentangle cause and effect and are careful to avoid the fallacy of composition and the *post hoc* fallacy.
- Economists agree on a wide range of questions about how the economy works.

KEY TERMS

Big tradeoff, 10
Business cycle, 8
Capital, 4
Ceteris paribus, 13
Cost of living, 7
Deflation, 7
Economic model, 12
Economics, 2
Economic theory, 12
Entrepreneurship, 4
Factors of production, 4
Goods and services, 3
Human capital, 4
Incentive, 11
Inflation, 7
Interest, 5
Labor, 4
Land, 4
Macroeconomics, 2
Margin, 11
Marginal benefit, 11
Marginal cost, 11
Microeconomics, 2
Opportunity cost, 11
Output-inflation tradeoff, 10
Profit, 5
Rent, 5
Scarcity, 2
Standard of living, 6
Tradeoff, 9
Wages, 5

PROBLEMS

*1. Your friends go the movies one evening and you decide to stay home and do your economics assignment and practice test. You get 80 percent on your next economics exam compared with the 70 percent that you normally score. What is the opportunity cost of your extra points?

2. You go to the movies one evening instead of doing your economics assignment and practice test. You get 50 percent on your next economics exam compared with the 70 percent that you normally score. What is the opportunity cost of going to the movies?

*3. You plan to go to school this summer. If you do, you won't be able to take your usual job that pays $6,000 for the summer, and you won't be able to live at home for free. The cost of tuition is $2,000 and textbooks is $200, and living expenses are $1,400. What is the opportunity cost of going to summer school?

4. You plan to go skiing next weekend. If you do, you'll have to miss doing your usual weekend job that pays $100. You won't be able study for 8 hours and you won't be able to use your pre-paid college meal plan. The cost of your travel and accommodations will be $350, the cost of renting skis is $60, and your food will cost $40. What is the opportunity cost of the weekend ski trip?

*5. The local mall has free parking, but the mall is always very busy, and it usually takes 30 minutes to find a parking space. Today when you found a vacant spot, Harry also wanted it. Is parking really free at this mall? If not, what did it cost you to park today? When you parked your car today, did you impose any costs on Harry? Explain your answers.

6. The university has built a new movie house. Admission for students is free and there are always plenty of empty seats. But when the movie house screened *Lord of the Rings*, the lines were long. So the movie house decided to charge $4 per student. Cadbury Schweppes offered students a free soft drink. Compare the student's opportunity cost of seeing the movie *Lord of the Rings* with that of any other movie screened this year. Which is less costly and by how much?

CRITICAL THINKING

1. Use the three big questions of microeconomics, the three big questions of macroeconomics, and the economic way of thinking to organize a short essay about the economic life of a homeless man. Does he face scarcity? Does he make choices? Can you interpret his choices as being in his own best interest? Can either his own choices or the choices of others make him better off? If so, how?

WEB EXERCISES

1. Use the link on the Parkin Web site to visit *CNNfn*.
   a. What is the top economic news story today?
   b. With which of the big questions does it deal? (It must deal with at least one of them and might deal with more than one.)
   c. What tradeoffs does the news item discus?
   d. Write a brief summary of the news item in a few bulleted points using as much as possible of the economic vocabulary that you have learned in this chapter and that is in the key terms list on p. 15.

2. Use the link on the Parkin Web site to visit *Resources For Economists on the Internet*. This site is a good place from which to search for economic information on the Internet.
   a. Scroll down the page and click on General Interest.
   b. Visit the "general interest" sites and become familiar with the types of information they contain.

3. Use the link on the Parkin Web site to visit the Bureau of Labor Statistics.
   a. What is the number of people employed (nonfarm employment) in your area?
   b. Has employment increased or decreased?
   c. What is income per person (per capita income) in your area?

* You can obtain the solutions to odd-numbered problems on pp. 831–860.

APPENDIX

Graphs in Economics

After studying this appendix, you will be able to

- Make and interpret a time-series graph, a cross-section graph, and a scatter diagram

- Distinguish between linear and nonlinear relationships and between relationships that have a maximum and a minimum

- Define and calculate the slope of a line

- Graph relationships among more than two variables

Graphing Data

A GRAPH REPRESENTS A QUANTITY AS A DISTANCE on a line. Figure A1.1 shows two examples. Here, a distance on the horizontal line represents temperature, measured in degrees Fahrenheit. A movement from left to right shows an increase in temperature. The point marked 0 represents zero degrees Fahrenheit. To the right of 0, the temperature is positive. To the left of 0 (as indicated by the minus sign), the temperature is negative. A distance on the vertical line represents altitude or height, measured in thousands of feet above sea level. The point marked 0 represents sea level. Points above 0 represent feet above sea level. Points below 0 (indicated by a minus sign) represent feet below sea level.

By setting two scales perpendicular to each other, as in Fig. A1.1, we can visualize the relationship between two variables. The scale lines are called *axes*. The vertical line is the *y*-axis, and the horizontal line is the *x*-axis. Each axis has a zero point, which is shared by the two axes. This zero point, common to both axes, is called the *origin*.

To show something in a two-variable graph, we need two pieces of information: the value of the *x* variable and the value of the *y* variable. For example, off the coast of Alaska on a winter's day, the temperature is 32 degrees — the value of *x*. A fishing boat is located at 0 feet above sea level — the value of *y*. These two bits of information appear as point *A* in Fig. A1.1. A climber at the top of Mount McKinley on

FIGURE A1.1 Making a Graph

Graphs have axes that measure quantities as distances. Here, the horizontal axis (*x*-axis) measures temperature, and the vertical axis (*y*-axis) measures height. Point *A* represents a fishing boat at sea level (0 on the *y*-axis) on a day when the temperature is 32°F. Point *B* represents a climber at the top of Mt. McKinley 20,320 feet above sea level at a temperature of 0°F. Point *C* represents a climber at the top of Mt. McKinley, 20,320 feet above sea level at a temperature of 32°F.

a cold day is 20,320 feet above sea level in a zero-degree gale. These two pieces of information appear as point *B*. The position of the climber on a warmer day might be at the point marked *C*. This point represents the peak of Mt. McKinley at a temperature of 32 degrees.

We can draw two lines, called *coordinates*, from point *C*. One, called the *y*-coordinate, runs from *C* to the horizontal axis. Its length is the same as the value marked off on the *y*-axis. The other, called the *x*-coordinate, runs from *C* to the vertical axis. Its length is the same as the value marked off on the *x*-axis. We describe a point in a graph by the values of its *x*-coordinate and its *y*-coordinate.

Graphs like that in Fig. A1.1 can show any type of quantitative data on two variables. Economists use three types of graphs based on the principles in Fig. A1.1 to reveal and describe the relationships among variables. They are

- Time-series graphs
- Cross-section graphs
- Scatter diagrams

17

Time-Series Graphs

A **time-series graph** measures time (for example, months or years) on the *x*-axis and the variable or variables in which we are interested on the *y*-axis. Figures 1.2 and 1.3 on pp. 3 and 4 are examples of time-series graphs. So is Fig. A1.2, which provides some information about the price of coffee.

In Fig. A1.2, we measure time in years running from 1970 to 2000. We measure the price of coffee (the variable that we are interested in) on the *y*-axis.

The point of a time-series graph is to enable us to visualize how a variable has changed over time and how its value in one period relates to its value in another period.

A time-series graph conveys an enormous amount of information quickly and easily, as this example illustrates. It shows:

- The *level* of the price of coffee — when it is *high* and *low*. When the line is a long way from the *x*-axis, the price is high, as it was, for example, in 1977. When the line is close to the *x*-axis, the price is low, as it was, for example, in 1992.
- How the price *changes* — whether it *rises* or *falls*. When the line slopes upward, as in 1976, the price is rising. When the line slopes downward, as in 1978, the price is falling.
- The *speed* with which the price changes — whether it rises or falls *quickly* or *slowly*. If the line is very steep, then the price rises or falls quickly. If the line is not steep, the price rises or falls slowly. For example, the price rose quickly in 1976 and 1977 and slowly in 1993. The price fell quickly in 1978 and slowly during the early 1980s.

A time-series graph also reveals whether there is a trend. A **trend** is a general tendency for a variable to move in one direction. A trend might be upward or downward. In Fig. A1.2, you can see that the price of coffee had a general tendency to fall from the mid-1970s to the early 1990s. That is, although the price rose and fell, the general tendency was for it to fall — the price had a downward trend.

A time-series graph also helps us to detect cycles in variables. Figure 1.6 on page 8 illustrates the business cycle. We rarely see a cycle that is as clear as the one shown in that figure, but you can see some peaks and troughs in the price of coffee in Fig. A1.1.

Finally, a time-series graph also lets us compare the variable in different periods quickly. Figure A1.2 shows that the 1980s were different from the 1970s.

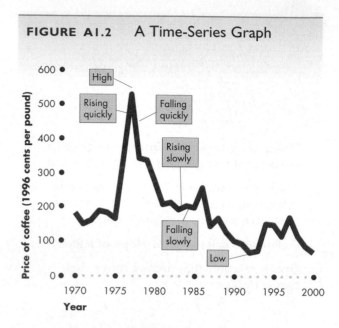

FIGURE A1.2   A Time-Series Graph

A time-series graph plots the level of a variable on the *y*-axis against time (day, week, month, or year) on the *x*-axis. This graph shows the price of coffee (in 1996 cents per pound) each year from 1970 to 2000. It shows us when the price of coffee was *high* and when it was *low*, when the price *increased* and when it *decreased*, and when it changed *quickly* and when it changed *slowly*.

The price of coffee fluctuated more violently in the 1970s than it did in the 1980s.

You can see that a time-series graph conveys a wealth of information. And it does so in much less space than we have used to describe only some of its features. But you do have to "read" the graph to obtain all this information.

Cross-Section Graphs

A **cross-section graph** shows the values of an economic variable for different groups in a population at a point in time. Figure 1.4 on p. 5, called a *bar chart*, is an example of a cross-section graph. Figure A1.3 shows another example.

The bar chart in Fig. A1.3 shows the population across the 10 largest metropolitan areas in the United States in 2000. The length of each bar indicates the population size. This figure enables you to compare the population in these 10 metropolitan areas. And you can do so much more quickly and clearly than by looking at a list of numbers.

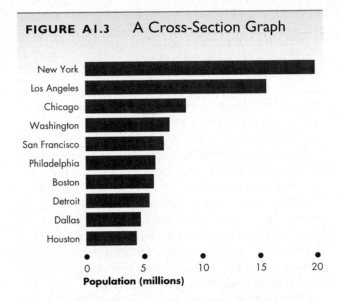

FIGURE A1.3   A Cross-Section Graph

A cross-section graph shows the level of a variable across the members of a population. This bar chart shows the population in each of the 10 largest metropolitan areas in the United States in 1999.

Scatter Diagrams

A **scatter diagram** plots the value of one variable against the value of another variable. Such a graph reveals whether a relationship exists between two variables and describes their relationship. Figure A1.4(a) shows the relationship between expenditure and income. Each point shows expenditure per person and income per person in a given year from 1990 to 2000. The points are "scattered" within the graph. The point labeled A tells us that in 1996, income per person was $20,613 and expenditure per person was $18,888. The dots in this graph form a pattern, which reveals that as income increases, expenditure increases.

Figure A1.4(b) shows the relationship between the number of international phone calls and the price of a call. This graph shows that as the price per minute falls, the number of calls increases.

Figure A1.4(c) shows a scatter diagram of inflation and unemployment in the United States. Here, the dots show no clear relationship between these two variables. The dots in this graph reveal that there is no simple relationship between these variables.

FIGURE A1.4   Scatter Diagrams

(a) Expenditure and income

(b) International phone calls and prices

(c) Unemployment and inflation

A scatter diagram reveals the relationship between two variables. Part (a) shows the relationship between expenditure and income. Each point shows the values of the two variables in a specific year. For example, point A shows that in 1996, average income was $20,613 and average expenditure was $18,888. The pattern formed by the points shows that as income increases, expenditure increases.

Part (b) shows the relationship between the price of an international phone call and the number of calls made. This graph shows that as the price of a phone call falls, the number of calls made increases. Part (c) shows a scatter diagram of the inflation rate and unemployment rate in the United States. This graph shows that inflation and unemployment are not closely related.

Breaks in the Axes Two of the graphs you've just looked at, Fig. A1.4(a) and Fig. A1.4(c), have breaks in their axes, as shown by the small gaps. The breaks indicate that there are jumps from the origin, 0, to the first values recorded.

In Fig. A1.4(a), the breaks are used because the lowest value of expenditure exceeds $14,000 and the lowest value of income exceeds $16,000. With no breaks in the axes of this graph, there would be a lot of empty space, all the points would be crowded into the top right corner, and we would not be able to see whether a relationship exists between these two variables. By breaking the axes, we are able to bring the relationship into view.

Putting a break in the axes is like using a zoom lens to bring the relationship into the center of the graph and magnify it so the relationship fills the graph.

Misleading Graphs Breaks can be used to highlight a relationship. But they can also be used to mislead — to make a graph that lies. The most common way of making a graph lie is to use axis breaks and either to stretch or compress a scale. For example, suppose that in Fig. A1.4(a), the y-axis that measures expenditure ran from zero to $45,000 while the x-axis was the same as the one shown. The graph would now create the impression that despite a huge increase in income, expenditure had barely changed.

To avoid being misled, it is a good idea to get into the habit of always looking closely at the values and the labels on the axes of a graph before you start to interpret it.

Correlation and Causation A scatter diagram that shows a clear relationship between two variables, such as Fig. A1.4(a) or Fig. A1.4(b), tells us that the two variables have a high correlation. When a high correlation is present, we can predict the value of one variable from the value of the other variable. But correlation does not imply causation.

Sometimes a high correlation is a coincidence, but sometimes it does arise from a causal relationship. It is likely, for example, that rising income causes rising expenditure (Fig. A1.4a) and that the falling price of a phone call causes more calls to be made (Fig. A1.4b).

You've now seen how we can use graphs in economics to show economic data and to reveal relationships between variables. Next, we'll learn how economists use graphs to construct and display economic models.

Graphs Used in Economic Models

THE GRAPHS USED IN ECONOMICS ARE NOT ALWAYS designed to show real-world data. Often they are used to show general relationships among the variables in an economic model.

An *economic model* is a stripped down, simplified description of an economy or of a component of an economy such as a business or a household. It consists of statements about economic behavior that can be expressed as equations or as curves in a graph. Economists use models to explore the effects of different policies or other influences on the economy in ways that are similar to the use of model airplanes in wind tunnels and models of the climate.

You will encounter many different kinds of graphs in economic models, but there are some repeating patterns. Once you've learned to recognize these patterns, you will instantly understand the meaning of a graph. Here, we'll look at the different types of curves that are used in economic models, and we'll see some everyday examples of each type of curve. The patterns to look for in graphs are the four cases in which

- Variables move in the same direction.
- Variables move in opposite directions.
- Variables have a maximum or a minimum.
- Variables are unrelated.

Let's look at these four cases.

Variables That Move in the Same Direction

Figure A1.5 shows graphs of the relationships between two variables that move up and down together. A relationship between two variables that move in the same direction is called a **positive relationship** or a **direct relationship**. A line that slopes upward shows such a relationship.

Figure A1.5 shows three types of relationships, one that has a straight line and two that have curved lines. But all the lines in these three graphs are called curves. Any line on a graph — no matter whether it is straight or curved — is called a *curve*.

A relationship shown by a straight line is called a **linear relationship**. Figure A1.5(a) shows a linear

FIGURE A1.5   Positive (Direct) Relationships

(a) Positive linear relationship   **(b) Positive, becoming steeper**   **(c) Positive, becoming less steep**

Each part of this figure shows a positive (direct) relationship between two variables. That is, as the value of the variable measured on the *x*-axis increases, so does the value of the variable measured on the *y*-axis. Part (a) shows a linear relationship — as the two variables increase together, we move along a straight line. Part (b) shows a positive relationship such that as the two variables increase together, we move along a curve that becomes steeper. Part (c) shows a positive relationship such that as the two variables increase together, we move along a curve that becomes flatter.

relationship between the number of miles traveled in 5 hours and speed. For example, point *A* shows that we will travel 200 miles in 5 hours if our speed is 40 miles an hour. If we double our speed to 80 miles an hour, we will travel 400 miles in 5 hours.

Figure A1.5(b) shows the relationship between distance sprinted and recovery time (the time it takes the heart rate to return to its normal resting rate). This relationship is an upward-sloping one that starts out quite flat but then becomes steeper as we move along the curve away from the origin. The reason this curve slopes upward and becomes steeper is because the additional recovery time needed from sprinting an additional 100 yards increases. It takes less than 5 minutes to recover from the first 100 yards but more than 10 minutes to recover from the third 100 yards.

Figure A1.5(c) shows the relationship between the number of problems worked by a student and the amount of study time. This relationship is an upward-sloping one that starts out quite steep and becomes flatter as we move away from the origin. Study time becomes less productive as you increase the hours worked and become more tired.

Variables That Move in Opposite Directions

Figure A1.6 shows relationships between things that move in opposite directions. A relationship between variables that move in opposite directions is called a **negative relationship** or an **inverse relationship**.

Figure A1.6(a) shows the relationship between the number of hours available for playing squash and the number of hours for playing tennis when the total is 5 hours. One extra hour spent playing tennis means one hour less playing squash and vice versa. This relationship is negative and linear.

Figure A1.6(b) shows the relationship between the cost per mile traveled and the length of a journey. The longer the journey, the lower is the cost per mile. But as the journey length increases, the cost per mile decreases, and the fall in the cost is smaller, the longer the journey. This feature of the relationship is shown by the fact that the curve slopes downward, starting out steep at a short journey length and then becoming flatter as the journey length increases. This relationship arises because some of the costs are fixed, such as auto insurance, and the fixed costs are spread over a longer journey.

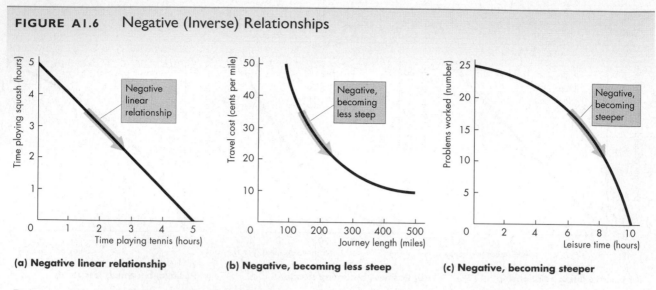

FIGURE A1.6   Negative (Inverse) Relationships

(a) Negative linear relationship

(b) Negative, becoming less steep

(c) Negative, becoming steeper

Each part of this figure shows a negative (inverse) relationship between two variables. That is, as the value of the variable measured on the x-axis increases, the value of the variable measured on the y-axis decreases. Part (a) shows a linear relationship. The total time spent playing tennis and squash is 5 hours. As the time spent playing tennis increases, the time spent playing squash decreases, and we move along a straight line. Part (b) shows a negative relationship such that as the journey length increases, the travel cost decreases as we move along a curve that becomes less steep. Part (c) shows a negative relationship such that as leisure time increases, the number of problems worked decreases as we move along a curve that becomes steeper.

Figure A1.6(c) shows the relationship between the amount of leisure time and the number of problems worked by a student. Increasing leisure time produces an increasingly large reduction in the number of problems worked. This relationship is a negative one that starts out with a gentle slope at a small number of leisure hours and becomes steeper as the number of leisure hours increases. This relationship is a different view of the idea shown in Fig. A1.5(c).

Variables That Have a Maximum or a Minimum

Many relationships in economic models have a maximum or a minimum. For example, firms try to make the maximum possible profit and to produce at the lowest possible cost. Figure A1.7 shows relationships that have a maximum or a minimum.

Figure A1.7(a) shows the relationship between rainfall and wheat yield. When there is no rainfall, wheat will not grow, so the yield is zero. As the rainfall increases up to 10 days a month, the wheat yield increases. With 10 rainy days each month, the wheat yield reaches its maximum at 40 bushels an acre (point *A*). Rain in excess of 10 days a month starts to lower the yield of wheat. If every day is rainy, the wheat suffers from a lack of sunshine and the yield decreases to zero. This relationship is one that starts out sloping upward, reaches a maximum, and then slopes downward.

Figure A1.7(b) shows the reverse case — a relationship that begins sloping downward, falls to a minimum, and then slopes upward. Most economic costs are like this relationship. An example is the relationship between the cost per mile and speed for a car trip. At low speeds, the car is creeping in a traffic snarl-up. The number of miles per gallon is low, so the cost per mile is high. At high speeds, the car is traveling faster than its efficient speed, using a large quantity of gasoline, and again the number of miles per gallon is low and the cost per mile is high. At a speed of 55 miles an hour, the cost per mile is at its minimum (point *B*). This relationship is one that starts out sloping downward, reaches a minimum, and then slopes upward.

FIGURE A1.7   Maximum and Minimum Points

Part (a) shows a relationship that has a maximum point, A. The curve slopes upward as it rises to its maximum point, is flat at its maximum, and then slopes downward.

Part (b) shows a relationship with a minimum point, B. The curve slopes downward as it falls to its minimum, is flat at its minimum, and then slopes upward.

(a) Relationship with a maximum

(b) Relationship with a minimum

Variables That Are Unrelated

There are many situations in which no matter what happens to the value of one variable, the other variable remains constant. Sometimes we want to show the independence between two variables in a graph, and Fig. A1.8 shows two ways of achieving this.

In describing the graphs in Fig. A1.5 through A1.7, we have talked about curves that slope upward or slope downward, and curves that become less steep or steeper. Let's spend a little time discussing exactly what we mean by slope and how we measure the slope of a curve.

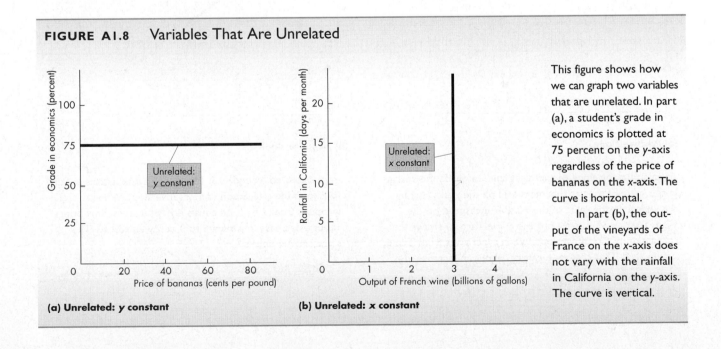

FIGURE A1.8   Variables That Are Unrelated

This figure shows how we can graph two variables that are unrelated. In part (a), a student's grade in economics is plotted at 75 percent on the y-axis regardless of the price of bananas on the x-axis. The curve is horizontal.

In part (b), the output of the vineyards of France on the x-axis does not vary with the rainfall in California on the y-axis. The curve is vertical.

(a) Unrelated: y constant

(b) Unrelated: x constant

The Slope of a Relationship

WE CAN MEASURE THE INFLUENCE OF ONE variable on another by the slope of the relationship. The **slope** of a relationship is the change in the value of the variable measured on the y-axis divided by the change in the value of the variable measured on the x-axis. We use the Greek letter Δ (*delta*) to represent "change in." Thus Δy means the change in the value of the variable measured on the y-axis, and Δx means the change in the value of the variable measured on the x-axis. Therefore the slope of the relationship is

$$\Delta y / \Delta x$$

If a large change in the variable measured on the y-axis (Δy) is associated with a small change in the variable measured on the x-axis (Δx), the slope is large and the curve is steep. If a small change in the variable measured on the y-axis (Δy) is associated with a large change in the variable measured on the x-axis (Δx), the slope is small and the curve is flat.

We can make the idea of slope sharper by doing some calculations.

The Slope of a Straight Line

The slope of a straight line is the same regardless of where on the line you calculate it. The slope of a straight line is constant. Let's calculate the slopes of the lines in Fig. A1.9. In part (a), when x increases from 2 to 6, y increases from 3 to 6. The change in

---

FIGURE A1.9   The Slope of a Straight Line

(a) Positive slope

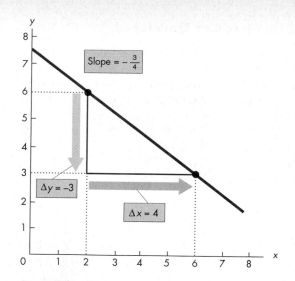

(b) Negative slope

To calculate the slope of a straight line, we divide the change in the value of the variable measured on the y-axis (Δy) by the change in the value of the variable measured on the x-axis (Δx), as we move along the curve. Part (a) shows the calculation of a positive slope. When x increases from 2 to 6, Δx equals 4. That change in x brings about an increase in y

from 3 to 6, so Δy equals 3. The slope ($\Delta y / \Delta x$) equals ¾. Part (b) shows the calculation of a negative slope. When x increases from 2 to 6, Δx equals 4. That increase in x brings about a decrease in y from 6 to 3, so Δy equals −3. The slope ($\Delta y / \Delta x$) equals −¾.

x is +4 — that is, Δx is 4. The change in y is +3 — that is, Δy is 3. The slope of that line is

$$\frac{\Delta y}{\Delta x} = \frac{3}{4}.$$

In part (b), when x increases from 2 to 6, y decreases from 6 to 3. The change in y is *minus* 3 — that is, Δy is –3. The change in x is *plus* 4 — that is, Δx is 4. The slope of the curve is

$$\frac{\Delta y}{\Delta x} = \frac{-3}{4}.$$

Notice that the two slopes have the same magnitude (¾) but the slope of the line in part (a) is positive (+3/+4 = ¾), while that in part (b) is negative (–3/+4 = –¾). The slope of a positive relationship is positive; the slope of a negative relationship is negative.

The Slope of a Curved Line

The slope of a curved line is trickier. The slope of a curved line is not constant. Its slope depends on where on the line we calculate it. There are two ways to calculate the slope of a curved line: You can calculate the slope at a point, or you can calculate the slope across an arc of the curve. Let's look at the two alternatives.

Slope at a Point To calculate the slope at a point on a curve, you need to construct a straight line that has the same slope as the curve at the point in question. Figure A1.10 shows how this is done. Suppose you want to calculate the slope of the curve at point A. Place a ruler on the graph so that it touches point A and no other point on the curve, then draw a straight line along the edge of the ruler. The straight red line is this line, and it is the tangent to the curve at point A. If the ruler touches the curve only at point A, then the slope of the curve at point A must be the same as the slope of the edge of the ruler. If the curve and the ruler do not have the same slope, the line along the edge of the ruler will cut the curve instead of just touching it.

Now that you have found a straight line with the same slope as the curve at point A, you can calculate the slope of the curve at point A by calculating the slope of the straight line. Along the straight line, as x

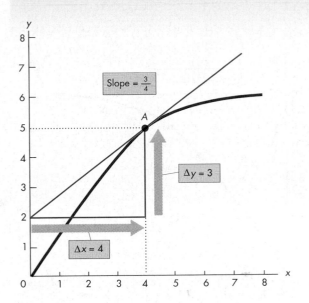

FIGURE A1.10   Slope at a Point

To calculate the slope of the curve at point A, draw the red line that just touches the curve at A — the tangent. The slope of this straight line is calculated by dividing the change in y by the change in x along the line. When x increases from 0 to 4, Δx equals 4. That change in x is associated with an increase in y from 2 to 5, so Δy equals 3. The slope of the red line is ¾. So the slope of the curve at point A is ¾.

increases from 0 to 4 ($\Delta x = 4$) y increases from 2 to 5 ($\Delta y = 3$). Therefore the slope of the line is

$$\frac{\Delta y}{\Delta x} = \frac{3}{4}.$$

Thus the slope of the curve at point A is ¾.

Slope Across an Arc An arc of a curve is a piece of a curve. In Fig. A1.11, you are looking at the same curve as in Fig. A1.10. But instead of calculating the slope at point A, we are going to calculate the slope across the arc from B to C. You can see that the slope at B is greater than at C. When we calculate the slope across an arc, we are calculating the average slope between two points. As we move along the arc from B to C, x increases from 3 to 5 and y increases from 4 to 5.5. The change in x is 2 ($\Delta x = 2$), and the change

FIGURE A1.11   Slope Across an Arc

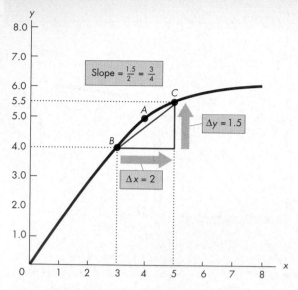

To calculate the average slope of the curve along the arc *BC*, draw a straight line from *B* to *C*. The slope of the line *BC* is calculated by dividing the change in *y* by the change in *x*. In moving from *B* to *C*, Δx equals 2 and Δy equals 1.5. The slope of the line *BC* is 1.5 divided by 2, or ¾. So the slope of the curve across the arc *BC* is ¾.

in *y* is 1.5 ($\Delta y = 1.5$). Therefore the slope of the line is

$$\frac{\Delta y}{\Delta x} = \frac{1.5}{2} = \frac{3}{4}.$$

Thus the slope of the curve across the arc *BC* is ¾.

This calculation gives us the slope of the curve between points *B* and *C*. The actual slope calculated is the slope of the straight line from *B* to *C*. This slope approximates the average slope of the curve along the arc *BC*. In this particular example, the slope across the arc *BC* is identical to the slope of the curve at point *A*. But the calculation of the slope of a curve does not always work out so neatly. You might have some fun constructing some more examples and some counterexamples.

You now know how to make and interpret a graph. But so far, we've limited our attention to graphs of two variables. We're now going to learn how to graph more than two variables.

Graphing Relationships Among More Than Two Variables

WE HAVE SEEN THAT WE CAN GRAPH THE relationship between two variables as a point formed by the *x*- and *y*-coordinates in a two-dimensional graph. You may be thinking that although a two-dimensional graph is informative, most of the things in which you are likely to be interested involve relationships among many variables, not just two. For example, the amount of ice cream consumed depends on the price of ice cream and the temperature. If ice cream is expensive and the temperature is low, people eat much less ice cream than when ice cream is inexpensive and the temperature is high. For any given price of ice cream, the quantity consumed varies with the temperature; and for any given temperature, the quantity of ice cream consumed varies with its price.

Figure A1.12 shows a relationship among three variables. The table shows the number of gallons of ice cream consumed each day at various temperatures and ice cream prices. How can we graph these numbers?

To graph a relationship that involves more than two variables, we use the *ceteris paribus* assumption.

Ceteris Paribus We noted in the chapter (see p. 13) that every laboratory experiment is an attempt to create *ceteris paribus* and isolate the relationship of interest. We use the same method to make a graph when more than two variables are involved.

Figure A1.12(a) shows an example. There, you can see what happens to the quantity of ice cream consumed when the price of ice cream varies and the temperature is held constant. The line labeled 70°F shows the relationship between ice cream consumption and the price of ice cream if the temperature remains at 70°F. The numbers used to plot that line are those in the third column of the table in Fig. A1.12. For example, if the temperature is 70°F, 10 gallons are consumed when the price is 60¢ a scoop, and 18 gallons are consumed when the price is 30¢ a scoop. The curve labeled 90°F shows consumption as the price varies if the temperature remains at 90°F.

We can also show the relationship between ice cream consumption and temperature when the price of ice cream remains constant, as shown in

FIGURE A1.12   Graphing a Relationship Among Three Variables

(a) Price and consumption at a given temperature

(b) Temperature and consumption at a given price

(c) Temperature and price at a given consumption

Price (cents per scoop)	Ice cream consumption (gallons per day)			
	30°F	50°F	70°F	90°F
15	12	18	25	50
30	10	12	18	37
45	7	10	13	27
60	5	7	10	20
75	3	5	7	14
90	2	3	5	10
105	1	2	3	6

The quantity of ice cream consumed depends on its price and the temperature. The table gives some hypothetical numbers that tell us how many gallons of ice cream are consumed each day at different prices and different temperatures. For example, if the price is 60¢ a scoop and the temperature is 70°F, 10 gallons of ice cream are consumed. This set of values is highlighted in the table and each part of the figure.

To graph a relationship among three variables, the value of one variable is held constant. Part (a) shows the relationship between price and consumption when temperature is held constant. One curve holds temperature at 90°F and the other at 70°F. Part (b) shows the relationship between temperature and consumption when price is held constant. One curve holds the price at 60¢ a scoop and the other at 15¢ a scoop. Part (c) shows the relationship between temperature and price when consumption is held constant. One curve holds consumption at 10 gallons and the other at 7 gallons.

Fig. A1.12(b). The curve labeled 60¢ shows how the consumption of ice cream varies with the temperature when ice cream costs 60¢ a scoop, and a second curve shows the relationship when ice cream costs 15¢ a scoop. For example, at 60¢ a scoop, 10 gallons are consumed when the temperature is 70°F and 20 gallons when the temperature is 90°F.

Figure A1.12(c) shows the combinations of temperature and price that result in a constant consumption of ice cream. One curve shows the combination that results in 10 gallons a day being consumed, and the other shows the combination that results in 7

gallons a day being consumed. A high price and a high temperature lead to the same consumption as a lower price and a lower temperature. For example, 10 gallons of ice cream are consumed at 70°F and 60¢ a scoop, at 90°F and 90¢ a scoop, and at 50°F and 45¢ a scoop.

◆With what you have learned about graphs, you can move forward with your study of economics. There are no graphs in this book that are more complicated than those that have been explained in this appendix.

SUMMARY

KEY POINTS

Graphing Data (pp. 17–20)

- A time-series graph shows the trend and fluctuations in a variable over time.
- A cross-section graph shows how variables change across the members of a population.
- A scatter diagram shows the relationship between two variables. It shows whether two variables are positively related, negatively related, or unrelated.

Graphs Used in Economic Models (pp. 20–23)

- Graphs are used to show relationships among variables in economic models.
- Relationships can be positive (an upward-sloping curve), negative (a downward-sloping curve), positive and then negative (have a maximum point), negative and then positive (have a minimum point), or unrelated (a horizontal or vertical curve).

The Slope of a Relationship (pp. 24–26)

- The slope of a relationship is calculated as the change in the value of the variable measured on the y-axis divided by the change in the value of the variable measured on the x-axis — that is, $\Delta y/\Delta x$.
- A straight line has a constant slope.
- A curved line has a varying slope. To calculate the slope of a curved line, we calculate the slope at a point or across an arc.

Graphing Relationships Among More Than Two Variables (pp. 26–27)

- To graph a relationship among more than two variables, we hold constant the values of all the variables except two.
- We then plot the value of one of the variables against the value of another.

KEY FIGURES

Figure A1.1   Making a Graph, 17
Figure A1.5   Positive (Direct) Relationships, 21
Figure A1.6   Negative (Inverse) Relationships, 22
Figure A1.7   Maximum and Minimum Points, 23
Figure A1.9   The Slope of a Straight Line, 24
Figure A1.10 Slope at a Point, 25
Figure A1.11 Slope Across an Arc, 26

KEY TERMS

Cross-section graph, 18
Direct relationship, 20
Inverse relationship, 21
Linear relationship, 20
Negative relationship, 21
Positive relationship, 20
Scatter diagram, 19
Slope, 24
Time-series graph, 18
Trend, 18

REVIEW QUIZ

1. What are the three types of graphs used to show economic data?
2. Give an example of a time-series graph.
3. List three things that a time-series graph shows quickly and easily.
4. Give three examples, different from those in the chapter, of scatter diagrams that show a positive relationship, a negative relationship, and no relationship.
5. Draw some graphs to show the relationships between two variables
   a. That move in the same direction.
   b. That move in opposite directions.
   c. That have a maximum.
   d. That have a minimum.
6. Which of the relationships in question 5 is a positive relationship and which a negative relationship?
7. What are the two ways of calculating the slope of a curved line?
8. How do we graph a relationship among more than two variables?

PROBLEMS

The spreadsheet provides data on the U.S. economy: Column A is the year, column B is the inflation rate, column C is the interest rate, column D is the growth rate, and column E is the unemployment rate. Use this spreadsheet to answers problems 1, 2, 3, and 4.

	A	B	C	D	E
1	1991	4.2	5.7	–0.5	6.7
2	1992	3.0	3.6	3.0	7.4
3	1993	3.0	3.1	2.7	6.8
4	1994	2.6	4.6	4.0	6.1
5	1995	2.8	5.8	2.7	5.6
6	1996	3.0	5.3	3.6	5.4
7	1997	2.3	5.5	4.4	4.9
8	1998	1.6	5.4	4.3	4.5
9	1999	2.2	5.2	4.1	4.2
10	2000	3.4	6.2	4.1	4.0
11	2001	2.8	3.6	1.1	4.8

*1. a. Draw a time-series graph of the inflation rate.
   b. In which year(s) (i) was inflation highest, (ii) was inflation lowest, (iii) did it increase, (iv) did it decrease, (v) did it increase most, and (vi) did it decrease most?
   c. What was the main trend in inflation?

2. a. Draw a time-series graph of the interest rate.
   b. In which year(s) was the interest rate highest, (ii) was the interest rate lowest, (iii) did it increase, (iv) did it decrease, (v) did it increase most, and (vi) did it decrease most.
   c. What was the main trend in the interest rate?

*3. Draw a scatter diagram to show the relationship between the inflation rate and the interest rate. Describe the relationship.

4. Draw a scatter diagram to show the relationship between the growth rate and the unemployment rate. Describe the relationship.

*5. Draw a graph to show the relationship between the two variables x and y:

x	0	1	2	3	4	5	6	7	8
y	0	1	4	9	16	25	36	49	64

   a. Is the relationship positive or negative?
   b. Does the slope of the relationship increase or decrease as the value of x increases?
   c. Think of some economic relationships that might be similar to this one.

6. Draw a graph that shows the relationship between the two variables x and y:

x	0	1	2	3	4	5
y	25	24	22	16	8	0

   a. Is the relationship positive or negative?
   b. Does the slope of the relationship increase or decrease as the value of x increases?
   c. Think of some economic relationships that might be similar to this one.

*7. In problem 5, calculate the slope of the relationship between x and y when x equals 4.

8. In problem 6, calculate the slope of the relationship between x and y when x equals 3.

*9. In problem 5, calculate the slope of the relationship across the arc when x increases from 3 to 4.

10. In problem 6, calculate the slope of the relationship across the arc when x increases from 4 to 5.

*11. Calculate the slope of the relationship shown at point A in the following figure.

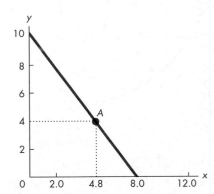

12. Calculate the slope of the relationship shown at point A in the following figure.

*13. Use the following figure to calculate the slope of the relationship:

a. At points *A* and *B*.
b. Across the arc *AB*.

14. Use the following figure to calculate the slope of the relationship:

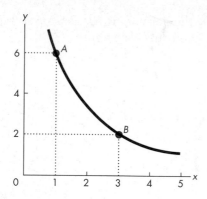

a. At points *A* and *B*.
b. Across the arc *AB*.

*15. The table gives the price of a balloon ride, the temperature, and the number of rides a day.

Price	Balloon rides (number per day)		
(dollars per ride)	50°F	70°F	90°F
5.00	32	40	50
10.00	27	32	40
15.00	18	27	32
20.00	10	18	27

Draw graphs to show the relationship between
a. The price and the number of rides, holding the temperature constant.
b. The number of rides and temperature, holding the price constant.

c. The temperature and price, holding the number of rides constant.

16. The table gives the price of an umbrella, the amount of rainfall, and the number of umbrellas purchased.

Price	Umbrellas (number per day)		
(dollars per umbrella)	0	1	2
	(inches of rainfall)		
10	7	8	12
20	4	7	8
30	2	4	7
40	1	2	4

Draw graphs to show the relationship between
a. The price and the number of umbrellas purchased, holding the amount of rainfall constant.
b. The number of umbrellas purchased and the amount of rainfall, holding the price constant.
c. The amount of rainfall and the price, holding the number of umbrellas purchased constant.

WEB EXERCISES

1. Use the link on the Parkin Web site and find Consumer Price Index (CPI) for the latest 12 months. Make a graph of the CPI. During the most recent month, was the CPI rising or falling? Was the rate of rise or fall increasing or decreasing?

2. Use the link on the Parkin Web site and find the unemployment rate for the latest 12 months. Graph the unemployment rate. During the most recent month, was it rising or falling? Was the rate of rise or fall increasing or decreasing?

3. Use the data that you obtained in problems 1 and 2. Make a graph to show whether the CPI and the unemployment rate are related to each other.

4. Use the data that you obtained in problems 1 and 2. Calculate the percentage change in the CPI each month. Make a graph to show whether the percentage change in the CPI and the unemployment rate are related to each other.

THE ECONOMIC PROBLEM

Good, Better, Best!

We live in a style that surprises our grandparents and would have astonished our great-grandparents. MP3s, video games, cell phones, gene splicing, and personal computers, which didn't exist even 25 years ago, have transformed our daily lives. For most of us, life is good, and getting better. But we still make choices and face costs. We still choose what we think is best for us. ◆ Perhaps the biggest choice that you will make is when to quit school and begin full-time work. When you've completed your current program, will you remain in school and work toward a postgraduate degree or a professional degree? What are the costs and consequences of this choice? We'll return to this question at the end of this chapter. ◆ We see an incredible amount of specialization and trade in the world. Each one of us specializes in a particular job — as a lawyer, a journalist, a home maker. Why? How do we benefit from specialization and trade? ◆ Over many centuries, social institutions have evolved that we take for granted. One of them is property rights and a political and legal system that protects them. Another is markets. Why have these institutions evolved?

◆ These are the questions that we study in this chapter. We begin with the core economic problem — scarcity and choice — and the concept of the production possibilities frontier. We then learn about the central idea of economics: efficiency. We also discover how we can expand production by accumulating capital and by specializing and trading with each other. What you will learn in this chapter is the foundation on which all economics is built.

After studying this chapter, you will be able to

■ Define the production possibilities frontier and calculate opportunity cost

■ Distinguish between production possibilities and preferences and describe an efficient allocation of resources

■ Explain how current production choices expand future production possibilities

■ Explain how specialization and trade expand our production possibilities

■ Explain why property rights and markets have evolved

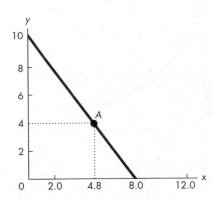

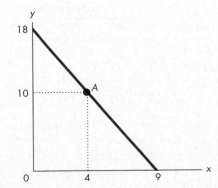

Production Possibilities and Opportunity Cost

EVERY WORKING DAY, IN MINES, FACTORIES, shops, and offices and on farms and construction sites across the United States, 135 million people produce a vast variety of goods and services valued at more than $30 billion. But the quantities of goods and services that we can produce are limited by our available resources and by technology. And if we want to increase our production of one good, we must decrease our production of something else — we face tradeoffs. You are going to learn about the production possibilities frontier, which describes the limit to what we can produce and provides a neat way of thinking about and illustrating the idea of a tradeoff.

The **production possibilities frontier** (*PPF*) is the boundary between those combinations of goods and services that can be produced and those that cannot. To illustrate the *PPF*, we focus on two goods at a time and hold the quantities produced of all the other goods and services constant. That is, we look at a *model* economy in which everything remains the same (*ceteris paribus*) except for the production of the two goods we are considering.

Let's look at the production possibilities frontier for the classic general example of "guns" and "butter," which stand for *any* pair of goods or services.

Production Possibilities Frontier

The *production possibilities frontier* for guns and butter shows the limits to the production of these two goods, given the total resources available to produce them. Figure 2.1 shows this production possibilities frontier. The table lists some combinations of the quantities of butter and guns that can be produced in a month given the resources available. The figure graphs these combinations. The *x*-axis shows the quantity of butter produced, and the *y*-axis shows the quantity of guns produced.

Because the *PPF* shows the *limits* to production, we cannot attain the points outside the frontier. They are points that describe wants that can't be satisfied. We can produce at all the points *inside* the *PPF* and *on* the *PPF*. They are attainable points. Suppose that in a typical month, we produce 4 tons of butter and 5 guns. Figure 2.1 shows this combination as point *E* and as possibility *E* in the table. The figure also shows

FIGURE 2.1   Production Possibilities Frontier

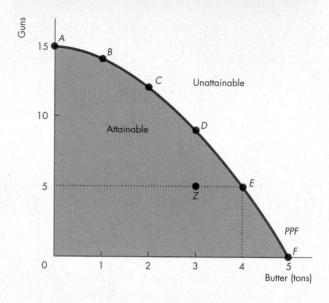

Possibility	Butter (tons)		Guns (units)
A	0	and	15
B	1	and	14
C	2	and	12
D	3	and	9
E	4	and	5
F	5	and	0

The table lists six points on the production possibilities frontier for guns and butter. Row A tells us that if we produce no butter, the maximum quantity of guns we can produce is 15. Points A, B, C, D, E, and F in the figure represent the rows of the table. The line passing through these points is the production possibilities frontier (*PPF*). It separates the attainable from the unattainable. Production is possible at any point inside the orange area or on the frontier. Points outside the frontier are unattainable. Points inside the frontier such as point Z are inefficient because resources are wasted or misallocated. At such points, it is possible to use the available resources to produce more of either or both goods.

other production possibilities. For example, we might stop producing butter and move all the people who produce it into producing guns. Point *A* in the figure and possibility *A* in the table show this case. The quantity of guns produced increases to 15, and butter production dries up. Alternatively, we might close the gun factories and switch all the resources into producing butter. In this situation, we produce 5 tons of butter. Point *F* in the figure and possibility *F* in the table show this case.

Production Efficiency

We achieve **production efficiency** if we cannot produce more of one good without producing less of some other good. When production is efficient, we are at a point *on* the *PPF*. If we are at a point *inside* the *PPF*, such as point *Z*, production is *inefficient* because we have some *unused* resources or we have some *misallocated* resources or both.

Resources are unused when they are idle but could be working. For example, we might leave some of the factories idle or some workers unemployed.

Resources are *misallocated* when they are assigned to tasks for which they are not the best match. For example, we might assign skilled butter-making machine operators to work in a gun factory and skilled gun makers to work in a dairy. We could get more butter *and* more guns from these same workers if we reassigned them to the tasks that more closely match their skills.

If we produce at a point inside the *PPF* such as *Z*, we can use our resources more efficiently to produce more butter, more guns, or more of *both* butter and guns. But if we produce at a point *on* the *PPF*, we are using our resources efficiently and we can produce more of one good only if we produce less of the other. That is, along the *PPF*, we face a *tradeoff*.

Tradeoff Along the *PPF*

Every choice *along* the *PPF* involves a *tradeoff*—we must give up something to get something else. On the *PPF* in Fig. 2.1, we must give up some guns to get more butter or give up some butter to get more guns.

Tradeoffs arise in every imaginable real-world situation, and you reviewed several of them in Chapter 1. At any given point in time, we have a fixed amount of labor, land, capital, and entrepreneurship. By using our available technologies, we can employ these resources to produce goods and services. But we are limited in what we can produce. This limit defines a boundary between what we can attain and what we cannot attain. This boundary is the real-world's production possibilities frontier, and it defines the tradeoffs that we must make. On our real-world *PPF*, we can produce more of any one good or service only if we produce less of some other goods or services.

When doctors say that we must spend more on AIDS and cancer research, they are suggesting a tradeoff: more medical research for less of some other things. When the President says that he wants to spend more on education and health care, he is suggesting a tradeoff: more education and health care for less national defense or less private spending (because of higher taxes). When an environmental group argues for less logging, it is suggesting a tradeoff: greater conservation of endangered wildlife for less paper. When your parents say that you should study more, they are suggesting a tradeoff: more study time for less leisure or sleep.

All tradeoffs involve a cost — an opportunity cost.

Opportunity Cost

The *opportunity cost* of an action is the highest-valued alternative forgone. The *PPF* helps us to make the concept of opportunity cost precise and enables us to calculate it. Along the *PPF*, there are only two goods, so there is only one alternative forgone: some quantity of the other good. Given our current resources and technology, we can produce more butter only if we produce fewer guns. The opportunity cost of producing an additional ton of butter is the number of guns we must forgo. Similarly, the opportunity cost of producing an additional gun is the quantity of butter we must forgo.

For example, at point *C* in Fig. 2.1, we produce less butter and more guns than at point *D*. If we choose point *D* over point *C*, the additional ton of butter *costs* 3 guns. One ton of butter costs 3 guns.

We can also work out the opportunity cost of choosing point *C* over point *D* in Fig. 2.1. If we move from point *D* to point *C*, the quantity of guns produced increases by 3 and the quantity of butter produced decreases by 1 ton. So if we choose point *C* over point *D*, the additional 3 guns *cost* 1 ton of butter. One gun costs 1/3 of a ton of butter.

Opportunity Cost Is a Ratio Opportunity cost is a ratio. It is the decrease in the quantity produced of one good divided by the increase in the quantity produced of another good as we move along the production possibilities frontier.

Because opportunity cost is a ratio, the opportunity cost of producing an additional gun is equal to the *inverse* of the opportunity cost of producing an additional ton of butter. Check this proposition by returning to the calculations we've just worked through. When we move along the *PPF* from *C* to *D*, the opportunity cost of a ton of butter is 3 guns. The inverse of 3 is 1/3, so if we decrease the production of butter and increase the production of guns by moving from *D* to *C*, the opportunity cost of a gun must be 1/3 of a ton of butter. You can check that this number is correct. If we move from *D* to *C*, we produce 3 more guns and 1 ton less of butter. Because 3 guns costs 1 ton of butter, the opportunity cost of 1 gun is 1/3 of a ton of butter.

Increasing Opportunity Cost   The opportunity cost of a ton of butter increases as the quantity of butter produced increases. Also, the opportunity cost of a gun increases as the quantity of guns produced increases. This phenomenon of increasing opportunity cost is reflected in the shape of the *PPF* — it is bowed outward.

When a large quantity of guns and a small quantity of butter are produced — between points *A* and *B* in Fig. 2.1 — the frontier has a gentle slope. A given increase in the quantity of butter *costs* a small decrease in the quantity of guns, so the opportunity cost of a ton of butter is a small quantity of guns.

When a large quantity of butter and a small quantity of guns are produced — between points *E* and *F* in Fig. 2.1 — the frontier is steep. A given increase in the quantity of butter *costs* a large decrease in the quantity of guns, so the opportunity cost of a ton of butter is a large quantity of guns.

The *PPF* is bowed outward because resources are not all equally productive in all activities. People with many years of experience working for Smith & Wesson are very good at producing guns but not very good at making butter. So if we move some of these people from Smith & Wesson to Land O'Lakes Dairies, we get a small increase in the quantity of butter but a large decrease in the quantity of guns.

Similarly, people who have spent years working at Land O'Lakes are good at producing butter but not so good at producing guns. So if we move some of these people from Land O'Lakes to Smith & Wesson, we get a small increase in the quantity of guns but a large decrease in the quantity of butter. The more we try to produce of either good, the less

productive are the additional resources we use to produce that good and the larger is the opportunity cost of a unit of that good.

Increasing Opportunity Costs Are Everywhere
Just about every activity that you can think of is one with an increasing opportunity cost. We allocate the most skillful farmers and the most fertile land to the production of food. And we allocate the best doctors and the least fertile land to the production of health-care services. If we shift fertile land and tractors away from farming to hospitals and ambulances and ask farmers to become hospital porters, the production of food drops drastically and the increase in the production of health-care services is small. The opportunity cost of a unit of health-care services rises. Similarly, if we shift our resources away from health care toward farming, we must use more doctors and nurses as farmers and more hospitals as hydroponic tomato factories. The decrease in the production of health-care services is large, but the increase in food production is small. The opportunity cost of a unit of food rises.

This example is extreme and unlikely, but these same considerations apply to any pair of goods that you can imagine.

REVIEW QUIZ

1 How does the production possibilities frontier illustrate scarcity?

2 How does the production possibilities frontier illustrate production efficiency?

3 How does the production possibilities frontier show that every choice involves a tradeoff?

4 How does the production possibilities frontier illustrate opportunity cost?

5 Why is opportunity cost a ratio?

6 Why does the *PPF* for most goods bow outward so that opportunity cost increases as the quantity produced of a good increases?

We've seen that what we can produce is limited by the production possibilities frontier. We've also seen that production on the *PPF* is efficient. But we can produce many different quantities on the *PPF*. How do we choose among them? How do we know which point on the *PPF* is the best one?

Using Resources Efficiently

YOU'VE SEEN THAT POINTS INSIDE THE *PPF* waste resources or leave them unused and are inefficient. You've also seen that points *on* the *PPF* are efficient — we can't produce more of one good unless we forgo some units of another good. But there are many such points on the *PPF*. Each point on the *PPF* achieves production efficiency. Which point is the best? How can we choose among them? What are the efficient quantities of butter and guns to produce?

These questions are examples of real-world questions of enormous consequence such as: How much should we spend on treating AIDS and how much on cancer research? Should we expand education and health-care programs or cut taxes? Should we spend more on the environment and the conservation of endangered wildlife?

To determine the efficient quantities to produce, we must compare costs and benefits.

The *PPF* and Marginal Cost

The limits to production, which are summarized by the *PPF*, determine the marginal cost of each good or service. **Marginal cost** is the opportunity cost of producing *one more unit*. We can calculate marginal cost in a way that is similar to the way we calculate opportunity cost. *Marginal cost* is the opportunity cost of *one* additional ton of butter — the quantity of guns that must be given up to get one more ton of butter — as we move along the *PPF*.

Figure 2.2 illustrates the marginal cost of butter. If butter production increases from zero to 1 ton — a move from *A* to *B* — the quantity of guns decreases from 15 to 14. So the opportunity cost of the first ton of butter is 1 gun.

If butter production increases from 1 ton to 2 tons — a move from *B* to *C* — the quantity of guns decreases by 2. So the second ton of butter costs 2 guns.

You can repeat this calculation for an increase in butter production from 2 to 3 tons, from 3 to 4 tons, and finally from 4 to 5 tons. Figure 2.2 shows the opportunity costs as a series of steps. Each additional ton of butter costs more guns than the preceding ton.

We've just calculated the opportunity cost of a ton of butter and generated the steps in Fig. 2.2(a). The opportunity cost of a ton of butter is also the *marginal cost* of producing a ton of butter. In Fig. 2.2(b), the line labeled *MC* shows the marginal cost.

FIGURE 2.2   The *PPF* and Marginal Cost

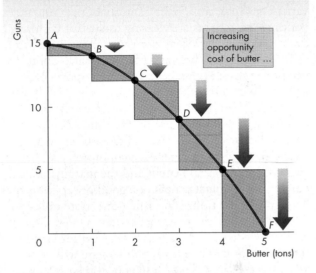

(a) *PPF* and opportunity cost

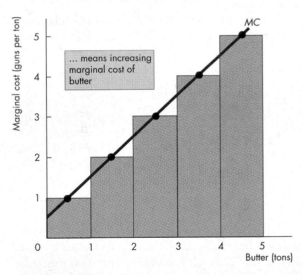

(b) Marginal cost

Opportunity cost is measured along the *PPF* in part (a). If the production of butter increases from zero to 1 ton, the opportunity cost of a ton of butter is 1 gun. If the production of butter increases from 1 to 2 tons, the opportunity cost of a ton of butter is 2 guns. The opportunity cost of butter increases as the production of butter increases. Part (b) shows the marginal cost of a ton of butter as the *MC* curve.

Preferences and Marginal Benefit

Look around your classroom and notice the wide variety of shirts, caps, pants, and shoes that you and your fellow students are wearing today. Why is there such a huge variety? Why don't you all wear the same styles and colors? The answer lies in what economists call preferences. **Preferences** are a description of a person's likes and dislikes.

You've seen that we have a concrete way of describing the limits to production: the *PPF*. We need a similarly concrete way of describing preferences. To describe preferences, economists use the concepts of marginal benefit and the marginal benefit curve. The **marginal benefit** of a good or service is the benefit received from consuming one more unit of it.

We measure the marginal benefit of a good or service by what a person is *willing to pay* for an additional unit of it. The idea is that you are willing to pay what the good is worth to you. It is worth its marginal benefit, and you're willing to pay an amount up to the marginal benefit. So willingness to pay measures marginal benefit.

The **marginal benefit curve** shows the relationship between the marginal benefit of a good and the quantity of that good consumed. It is a general principle that the more we have of any good or service, the smaller is its marginal benefit and the less we are willing to pay for an additional unit of it. This tendency is so widespread and strong that we call it a principle — the *principle of decreasing marginal benefit*.

The basic reason why marginal benefit decreases as we consume more of any one item is that we like variety. The more we consume of any one good or service, the more we can see of other things that we would like better.

Think about your willingness to pay for butter (or any other item). If butter is hard to come by and you can buy only a few ounces a year, you might be willing to pay a high price to get an additional ounce. But if butter is readily available and you have as much as you can use, you are willing to pay almost nothing for another pound.

In everyday life, we think of what we pay for goods and services as the money that we give up — dollars. But you've learned to think about cost as other goods or services forgone, not a dollar cost. You can think about willingness to pay in the same terms. The price you are willing to pay for something is the quantity of other goods and services that you are willing to forgo. Let's continue with the example of guns and butter and illustrate preferences this way.

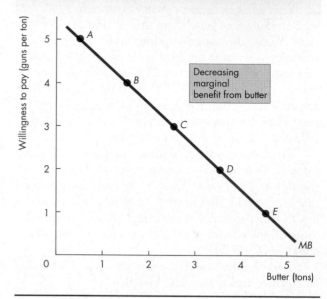

FIGURE 2.3   Preferences and the Marginal Benefit Curve

Possibility	Butter (tons)	Willingness to pay (guns per ton)
A	0.5	5
B	1.5	4
C	2.5	3
D	3.5	2
E	4.5	1

The smaller the quantity of butter produced, the more guns people are willing to give up for an additional ton of butter. If butter production is 0.5 tons, people are willing to pay 5 guns per ton. But if butter production is 4.5 tons, people are willing to pay only 1 gun per ton. Willingness to pay measures marginal benefit. And decreasing marginal benefit is a universal feature of people's preferences.

Figure 2.3 illustrates preferences as the willingness to pay for butter in terms of guns. In row A, butter production is 0.5 tons, and at that quantity, people are willing to pay 5 guns per ton. As the quantity of butter produced increases, the amount that people are willing to pay for it falls. When butter production is 4.5 tons, people are willing to pay only 1 gun per ton.

Let's now use the concepts of marginal cost and marginal benefit to describe the efficient quantity of butter to produce.

Efficient Use of Resources

When we cannot produce more of any one good without giving up some other good, we have achieved *production efficiency*, and we're producing at a point on the *PPF*. When we cannot produce more of any good without giving up some other good that we *value more highly*, we have achieved **allocative efficiency**, and we are producing at the point on the *PPF* that we prefer above all other points.

Suppose in Fig. 2.4, we produce 1.5 tons of butter. The marginal cost of butter is 2 guns per ton and the marginal benefit from butter is 4 guns per ton. Because someone values an additional ton of butter more highly than it costs to produce, we can get more value from our resources by moving some of them out of producing guns and into producing butter.

Now suppose we produce 3.5 tons of butter. The marginal cost of butter is now 4 guns per ton, but the marginal benefit from butter is only 2 guns per ton. Because the additional butter costs more to produce than anyone thinks it is worth, we can get more value from our resources by moving some of them away from producing butter and into producing guns.

But suppose we produce 2.5 tons of butter. Marginal cost and marginal benefit are now equal at 3 guns per ton. This allocation of resources between butter and guns is efficient. If more butter is produced, the forgone guns are worth more than the additional butter. If less butter is produced, the forgone butter is worth more than the additional guns.

REVIEW QUIZ

1 What is marginal cost? How is it measured?
2 What is marginal benefit? How is it measured?
3 How does the marginal benefit from a good change as the quantity produced of that good increases?
4 What is production efficiency and how does it relate to the production possibilities frontier?
5 What conditions must be satisfied if resources are used efficiently?

You now understand the limits to production and the conditions under which resources are used efficiently. Your next task is to study the expansion of production possibilities.

FIGURE 2.4   Efficient Use of Resources

(a) On the PPF

(b) Marginal benefit equals marginal cost

The greater the quantity of butter produced, the smaller is the marginal benefit (*MB*) from it — the fewer guns people are willing to give up to get an additional ton of butter. But the greater the quantity of butter produced, the greater is the marginal cost (*MC*) of butter — the more guns people must give up to get an additional ton of butter. When marginal benefit equals marginal cost, resources are being used efficiently.

Economic Growth

DURING THE PAST 30 YEARS, PRODUCTION PER person in the United States has doubled. Such an expansion of production is called **economic growth**. Economic growth increases our *standard of living*, but it doesn't overcome scarcity and avoid opportunity cost. To make our economy grow, we face a tradeoff — the *standard of living tradeoff* (p. 10) — and the faster we make production grow, the greater is the opportunity cost of economic growth.

The Cost of Economic Growth

Two key factors influence economic growth: technological change and capital accumulation. **Technological change** is the development of new goods and of better ways of producing goods and services. **Capital accumulation** is the growth of capital resources, which include *human capital*.

As a consequence of technological change and capital accumulation, we have an enormous quantity of cars that enable us to produce more transportation than was available when we had only horses and carriages; we have satellites that make global communications possible on a scale that is much larger than that produced by the earlier cable technology. But new technologies and new capital have an opportunity cost. To use resources in research and development and to produce new capital, we must decrease our production of consumption goods and services. Let's look at this opportunity cost.

Instead of studying the *PPF* of butter and guns, we'll hold the quantity of guns produced constant and examine the *PPF* for butter and butter-making machines. Figure 2.5 shows this *PPF* as the blue curve *ABC*. If we devote no resources to producing butter-making machines, we produce at point *A*. If we produce 3 tons of butter, we can produce 6 butter-making machines at point *B*. If we produce no butter, we can produce 10 machines at point *C*.

The amount by which our production possibilities expand depends on the resources we devote to technological change and capital accumulation. If we devote no resources to this activity (point *A*), our *PPF* remains at *ABC* — the blue curve in Fig. 2.5. If we cut the current production of butter and produce 6 machines (point *B*), then in the future, we'll have more capital and our *PPF* will rotate outward to the position shown by the red curve.

FIGURE 2.5 Economic Growth

PPF_0 shows the limits to the production of butter and butter-making machines, with the production of all other goods and services remaining the same. If we devote no resources to producing butter-making machines and produce 5 tons of butter, we remain at point *A*. But if we decrease butter production to 3 tons and produce 6 machines, at point *B*, our production possibilities expand. After one period, the *PPF* rotates outward to PPF_1 and we can produce at point *B'*, a point outside the original *PPF*. We can rotate the *PPF* outward, but we cannot avoid opportunity cost. The opportunity cost of producing more butter in the future is less butter today.

The fewer resources we devote to producing butter and the more resources we devote to producing machines, the greater is the expansion of our production possibilities.

Economic growth is not free. To make it happen, we devote resources to producing new machines and less to producing butter. In Fig. 2.5, we move from *A* to *B*. There is no free lunch. The opportunity cost of more butter in the future is less butter today. Also, economic growth is no magic formula for abolishing scarcity. On the new production possibilities frontier, we continue to face a tradeoff and opportunity cost.

The ideas about economic growth that we have explored in the setting of the dairy industry also apply to nations. Let's look at two examples.

Economic Growth in the United States and Hong Kong

If as a nation we devote all our resources to producing consumer goods and none to research and capital accumulation, our production possibilities in the future will be the same as they are today. To expand our production possibilities in the future, we must devote fewer resources to producing consumption goods and some resources to accumulating capital and developing technologies so that we can produce more consumption goods in the future. The decrease in today's consumption is the opportunity cost of an increase in future consumption.

The experiences of the United States and Hong Kong make a striking example of the effects of our choices on the rate of economic growth. In 1960, the production possibilities per person in the United States were more than four times those in Hong Kong (see Fig. 2.6). The United States devoted one fifth of its resources to accumulating capital and the other four fifths to consumption. In 1960, the United States was at point *A* on its *PPF*. Hong Kong devoted one third of its resources to accumulating capital and two thirds to consumption. In 1960, Hong Kong was at point *A* on its *PPF*.

Since 1960, both countries have experienced economic growth, but growth in Hong Kong has been more rapid than that in the United States. Because Hong Kong devoted a bigger fraction of its resources to accumulating capital, its production possibilities have expanded more quickly.

By 2000, the production possibilities per person in Hong Kong had reached 80 percent of those in the United States. If Hong Kong continues to devote more resources to accumulating capital than we do (at point *B* on its 2000 *PPF*), it will continue to grow more rapidly than the United States. But if Hong Kong increases consumption and decreases capital accumulation (moving to point *D* on its 2000 *PPF*), then its rate of economic growth will slow.

The United States is typical of the rich industrial countries, which include Western Europe and Japan. Hong Kong is typical of the fast-growing Asian economies, which include Taiwan, Thailand, South Korea, and China. Growth in these countries slowed during the Asia crisis of 1998 but quickly rebounded. Production possibilities expand in these countries by between 5 percent a year and almost 10 percent a year. If these high growth rates are maintained, these other Asian countries will eventually close the gap on the United States as Hong Kong has done.

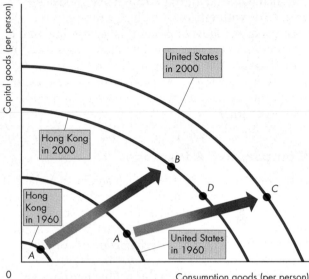

FIGURE 2.6 Economic Growth in the United States and Hong Kong

In 1960, the production possibilities per person in the United States were much larger than those in Hong Kong. But Hong Kong devoted more of its resources to accumulating capital than did the United States, so its production possibilities frontier has shifted outward more quickly than has that of the United States. In 2000, Hong Kong's production possibilities per person were 80 percent of those in the United States.

REVIEW QUIZ

1 What are the two key factors that generate economic growth?
2 How does economic growth influence the production possibilities frontier?
3 What is the opportunity cost of economic growth?
4 Why has Hong Kong experienced faster economic growth than the United States has?

Next, we're going to study another way in which we expand our production possibilities — the amazing fact that *both* buyers and sellers gain from specialization and trade.

Gains from Trade

PEOPLE CAN PRODUCE FOR THEMSELVES ALL THE goods that they consume, or they can concentrate on producing one good (or perhaps a few goods) and then trade with others — exchange some of their own goods for those of others. Concentrating on the production of only one good or a few goods is called *specialization.* We are going to discover how people gain by specializing in the production of the good in which they have a *comparative advantage* and trading with each other.

Comparative Advantage

A person has a **comparative advantage** in an activity if that person can perform the activity at a lower opportunity cost than anyone else. Differences in opportunity costs arise from differences in individual abilities and from differences in the characteristics of other resources.

No one excels at everything. One person is an outstanding pitcher but a poor catcher; another person is a brilliant lawyer but a poor teacher. In almost all human endeavors, what one person does easily, someone else finds difficult. The same applies to land and capital. One plot of land is fertile but has no mineral deposits; another plot of land has outstanding views but is infertile. One machine has great precision but is difficult to operate; another is fast but often breaks down.

Although no one excels at everything, some people excel and can outperform others in many activities. But such a person does not have a *comparative* advantage in each of those activities. For example, John Grisham is a better lawyer than most people. But he is an even better writer of fast-paced thrillers. So his *comparative* advantage is in writing.

Because people's abilities and the quality of their resources differ, they have different opportunity costs of producing various goods. Such differences give rise to comparative advantage. Let's explore the idea of comparative advantage by looking at two CD factories: one operated by Tom and the other operated by Nancy.

Tom's Factory To simplify the story quite a lot, suppose that CDs have just two components: a disc and a plastic case. Tom has two production lines: one for discs and one for cases. Figure 2.7 shows Tom's production possibilities frontier for discs and cases.

FIGURE 2.7 Production Possibilities in Tom's Factory

Tom's opportunity costs:
1 disc costs 1/3 case,
and 1 case costs 3 discs

Tom's *PPF*

Tom can produce discs and cases along the production possibilities frontier *PPF*. For Tom, the opportunity cost of 1 disc is ⅓ of a case and the opportunity cost of 1 case is 3 discs. If Tom produces at point A, he can produce 1,000 cases and 1,000 discs an hour.

It tells us that if Tom uses all his resources to make discs, he can produce 4,000 discs an hour. The *PPF* in Fig. 2.7 also tells us that if Tom uses all his resources to make cases, he can produce 1,333 cases an hour. But to produce cases, Tom must decrease his production of discs. For each case produced, he must decrease his production of discs by 3. So

Tom's opportunity cost of producing 1 case is 3 discs.

Similarly, if Tom wants to increase his production of discs, he must decrease his production of cases. And for each 1,000 discs produced, he must decrease his production of cases by 333. So

Tom's opportunity cost of producing 1 disc is 0.333 of a case.

Tom's *PPF* is linear because his workers have similar skills so if he reallocates them from one activity to another, he faces a constant opportunity cost.

Nancy's Factory The other factory, operated by Nancy, also produces cases and discs. But Nancy's factory has machines that are custom made for case production, so they are more suitable for producing cases than discs. Also, Nancy's work force is more skilled in making cases.

These differences between the two factories mean that Nancy's production possibilities frontier — shown along with Tom's *PPF* in Fig. 2.8 — is different from Tom's. If Nancy uses all her resources to make discs, she can produce 1,333 an hour. If she uses all her resources to make cases, she can produce 4,000 an hour. To produce discs, Nancy must decrease her production of cases. For each 1,000 additional discs produced, she must decrease her production of cases by 3,000. So

Nancy's opportunity cost of producing 1 disc is 3 cases.

Similarly, if Nancy wants to increase her production of cases, she must decrease her production of discs. For each 1,000 additional cases produced, she must decrease her production of discs by 333. So

Nancy's opportunity cost of producing 1 case is 0.333 of a disc.

Suppose that Tom and Nancy produce both discs and cases and that each produces 1,000 discs and 1,000 cases — 1,000 CDs — an hour. That is, each produces at point *A* on their production possibilities frontiers. Total production is 2,000 CDs an hour.

In which of the two goods does Nancy have a comparative advantage? Recall that comparative advantage is a situation in which one person's opportunity cost of producing a good is lower than another person's opportunity cost of producing that same good. Nancy has a comparative advantage in producing cases. Nancy's opportunity cost of producing a case is 0.333 of a disc, whereas Tom's is 3 discs.

You can see Nancy's comparative advantage by looking at the production possibilities frontiers for Nancy and Tom in Fig. 2.8. Nancy's production possibilities frontier is steeper than Tom's. To produce one more case, Nancy must give up fewer discs than Tom has to. Hence Nancy's opportunity cost of producing a case is less than Tom's. This means that Nancy has a comparative advantage in producing cases.

Tom's comparative advantage is in producing discs. His production possibilities frontier is less steep than Nancy's. This means that to produce one more

FIGURE 2.8   Comparative Advantage

Nancy's opportunity costs:
1 disc costs 3 cases, and
1 case costs 1/3 disc

Nancy's *PPF*

Tom's opportunity costs:
1 disc costs 1/3 case, and
1 case costs 3 discs

Tom's *PPF*

Along Tom's *PPF*, the opportunity cost of 1 disc is ⅓ of a case and the opportunity cost of 1 case is 3 discs. Along Nancy's *PPF*, the opportunity cost of 1 disc is 3 cases. Like Tom, Nancy produces at point *A*, where she produces 1,000 cases and 1,000 discs an hour. Nancy's opportunity cost of cases is less than Tom's, so Nancy has a comparative advantage in cases. Tom's opportunity cost of discs is less than Nancy's, so Tom has a comparative advantage in discs.

disc, Tom must give up fewer cases than Nancy has to. Tom's opportunity cost of producing a disc is 0.333 of a case, which is less than Nancy's 3 cases per disc. So Tom has a comparative advantage in producing discs.

Because Nancy has a comparative advantage in producing cases and Tom has a comparative advantage in producing discs, they can both gain from specialization and exchange.

Achieving the Gains from Trade

If Tom, who has a comparative advantage in producing discs, puts all his resources into that activity, he can produce 4,000 discs an hour — point *B* on his *PPF*. If Nancy, who has a comparative advantage in producing cases, puts all her resources into that activity, she can produce 4,000 cases an hour — point *B'* on her *PPF*. By specializing, Tom and Nancy together can produce 4,000 cases and 4,000 discs an hour, double the total production they can achieve without specialization.

By specialization and exchange, Tom and Nancy can get *outside* their individual production possibilities frontiers. To achieve the gains from specialization, Tom and Nancy must trade with each other.

Figure 2.9 shows how Tom and Nancy gain from trade. They make the following deal: Tom agrees to increase his production of discs from 1,000 an hour to 4,000 an hour — a move along his *PPF* from point *A* to point *B* in Fig. 2.9(a). Nancy agrees to increase her production of cases from 1,000 an hour to 4,000 an hour — a move along her *PPF* from point *A* to point *B'* in Fig. 2.9(b).

They also agree to exchange cases and discs at a "price" of one case for one disc. So Tom sells discs to Nancy for one case per disc, and Nancy sells cases to Tom for one disc per case.

With this deal in place, Tom and Nancy exchange along the red "Trade line." They exchange 2,000 cases and 2,000 discs, and each moves to point *C* (in both parts of the figure). At point *C*, each has 2,000 discs and 2,000 cases, or 2,000 CDs. So each now produces 2,000 CDs an hour — double the previous production rate. This increase in production of 2,000 CDs an hour is the gain from specialization and trade.

Both parties to the trade share the gains. Nancy, who can produce discs at an opportunity cost of 3 cases per disc, can buy discs from Tom at a cost of 1 case per disc. Tom, who can produce cases at an opportunity cost of 3 discs per case, can buy cases from Nancy at a cost of 1 disc per case.

For Nancy, the cost of a disc falls from 3 cases per disc to 1 case per disc. So she gets her discs more cheaply than she can produce them herself.

For Tom, the cost of a case falls from 3 discs per case to 1 disc per case. So he gets his cases more cheaply than he can produce them himself.

Because both Tom and Nancy obtain the items they buy from the other at a lower cost than that at which they can produce the items themselves, they both gain from specialization and trade.

The gains that we achieve from international trade are similar to those achieved by Tom and Nancy in this example. When Americans buy T-shirts from

---

FIGURE 2.9   The Gains from Trade

(a) Tom

(b) Nancy

Tom and Nancy initially produce at point *A* on their respective *PPFs*. Tom has a comparative advantage in discs, and Nancy has a comparative advantage in cases. If Tom specializes in discs, he produces at point *B* on his *PPF*. If Nancy specializes in cases, she produces at point *B'* on her *PPF*. They exchange cases for discs along the red "Trade line." Nancy

buys discs from Tom for less than her opportunity cost of producing them, and Tom buys cases from Nancy for less than his opportunity cost of producing them. Each goes to point *C* — a point outside his or her *PPF* — where each produces 2,000 CDs an hour. Tom and Nancy increase production with no change in resources.

China and when China buys Boeing 747 airplanes from the United States, both countries gain. We get our shirts at a lower cost than that at which we can produce them, and China gets its airplanes at a lower cost than that at which it can produce them.

Tom and Nancy are equally productive. Tom can produce the same quantities of discs as Nancy can produce cases. But this equal productivity is not the source of the gains from specialization and trade. The gains arise from comparative advantage and would be available even if one of the trading partners was much more productive than the other. To see that comparative advantage is the source of the gains, let's look at Tom and Nancy when Nancy is much more productive than Tom.

Absolute Advantage

A person has an **absolute advantage** if that person can produce more goods with a given amount of resources than another person can. Absolute advantage arises from differences in productivity. A person who has a better technology, more capital, or is more skilled than another person has an absolute advantage. (Absolute advantage also applies to nations.)

The gains from trade arise from *comparative* advantage, so people can gain from trade in the presence of *absolute* advantage. To see how, suppose that Nancy invents and patents a new production process that makes her *four* times as productive as she was before in the production of both cases and discs. With her new technology, Nancy can produce 16,000 cases an hour (4 times the original 4,000) if she puts all her resources into making cases. Alternatively, she can produce 5,332 discs (4 times the original 1,333) if she puts all her resources into making discs. Nancy now has an absolute advantage.

But Nancy's *opportunity cost* of 1 disc is still 3 cases. And this opportunity cost is higher than Tom's. So Nancy can still get discs at a lower cost by exchanging cases for discs with Tom.

In this example, Nancy will no longer produce only cases. With no trade, she would produce 4,000 discs and 4,000 cases. With trade, she will increase her production of cases to 7,000 and decrease her production of discs to 3,000. Tom will produce 4,000 discs and no cases. Tom will provide Nancy with 2,000 discs in exchange for 2,000 cases. So Tom's CD production will increase from 1,000 to 2,000 as before. Nancy's CD production will increase from 4,000 to 5,000.

Both Tom and Nancy have gained 1,000 CDs by taking advantage of comparative advantage, the same gains as before.

The key point to recognize is that even though someone (or some nation) has an absolute advantage, this fact does not destroy comparative advantage.

Dynamic Comparative Advantage

At any given point in time, the resources and technologies available determine the comparative advantages that individuals and nations have. But just by repeatedly producing a particular good or service, people become more productive in that activity, a phenomenon called **learning-by-doing**. Learning-by-doing is the basis of *dynamic* comparative advantage. **Dynamic comparative advantage** is a comparative advantage that a person (or country) possesses as a result of having specialized in a particular activity and, as a result of learning-by-doing, having become the producer with the lowest opportunity cost.

Hong Kong and Singapore are examples of countries that have pursued dynamic comparative advantage vigorously. They have developed industries in which initially they did not have a comparative advantage but, through learning-by-doing, became low opportunity cost producers in those industries. A specific example is the decision to develop a genetic engineering industry in Singapore. Singapore probably did not have a comparative advantage in genetic engineering initially. But it might develop one as its scientists and production workers become more skilled in this activity.

REVIEW QUIZ

1 What gives a person a comparative advantage?
2 Is production still efficient when people specialize?
3 Why do people specialize and trade?
4 What are the gains from specialization and trade?
5 What is the source of the gains from trade?
6 Distinguish between comparative advantage and absolute advantage.
7 How does dynamic comparative advantage arise?

The Market Economy

INDIVIDUALS AND COUNTRIES GAIN BY SPECIALIZ-ing in the production of those goods and services in which they have a comparative advantage and then trading with each other. Adam Smith identified this source of economic wealth in his *Wealth of Nations,* published in 1776 — see p. 52.

To enable billions of people who specialize in producing millions of different goods and services to reap these gains, trade must be organized. But trade need not be *planned* or *managed* by a central author-ity. In fact, when such an arrangement has been tried, as it was for 60 years in Russia, the result has been less than dazzling.

Trade is organized by using social institutions. Two key ones are

- Property rights
- Markets

Property Rights

Property rights are social arrangements that govern the ownership, use, and disposal of resources, goods, and services. *Real property* includes land and build-ings — the things we call property in ordinary speech — and durable goods such as factories and equip-ment. *Financial property* includes stocks and bonds and money in the bank. *Intellectual property* is the intangible product of creative effort. This type of property includes books, music, computer programs, and inventions of all kinds and is protected by copy-rights and patents.

If property rights are not enforced, the incentive to specialize and produce the goods in which each person has a comparative advantage is weakened, and some of the potential gains from specialization and trade are lost. If people can easily steal the production of others, then time, energy, and resources are devoted not to production but to protecting possessions.

Property rights evolved because they enable soci-eties to reap the gains from trade. If we had not developed property rights, we would still be hunting and gathering like our Stone Age ancestors.

Even in countries where property rights are well established, such as the United States, protecting intellectual property is proving to be a challenge in the face of modern technologies that make it rela-tively easy to copy audio and video material, com-puter programs, and books.

Markets

In ordinary speech, the word *market* means a place where people buy and sell goods such as fish, meat, fruits, and vegetables. In economics, a *market* has a more general meaning. A **market** is any arrangement that enables buyers and sellers to get information and to do business with each other. An example is the market in which oil is bought and sold — the world oil market. The world oil market is not a place. It is the network of oil producers, oil users, wholesalers, and brokers who buy and sell oil. In the world oil market, decision makers do not meet physically. They make deals throughout the world by telephone, fax, and direct computer link.

Nancy and Tom can get together and do a deal without markets. But for billions of individuals to specialize and trade millions of goods and services, markets are essential. Like property rights, markets have evolved because they facilitate trade. With-out organized markets, we would miss out on a substantial part of the potential gains from trade. Enterprising individuals, each pursuing their own goals, have profited from making markets, stand-ing ready to buy or sell the items in which they specialize.

Circular Flows in the Market Economy

Figure 2.10 identifies two types of markets: goods markets and factor markets. *Goods markets* are those in which goods and services are bought and sold. *Factor markets* are those in which factors of produc-tion are bought and sold.

Households decide how much of their labor, land, capital, and entrepreneurship to sell or rent in factor markets. Households receive incomes in the form of wages, rent, interest, and profit. Households also decide how to spend their incomes on goods and services produced by firms. Firms decide the quantities of factors of production to hire, how to use them to produce goods and services, what goods and services to produce, and in what quantities to produce them.

Figure 2.10 shows the flows that result from these decisions by households and firms. The red flows are the factors that go from households through factor markets to firms and the goods and services that go from firms through goods markets to house-holds. The green flows in the opposite direction are the payments made in exchange for these items.

How do markets coordinate all these decisions?

FIGURE 2.10   Circular Flows in the Market Economy

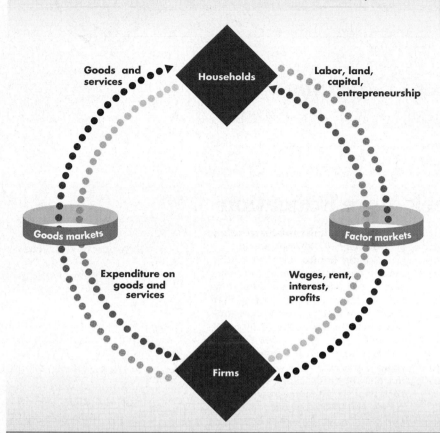

Households and firms make economic choices. Households choose the quantities of labor, land, capital, and entrepreneurship to sell or rent to firms in exchange for wages, rent, interest, and profit. Households also choose how to spend their incomes on the various types of goods and services available. Firms choose the quantities of factors of production to hire and the quantities of the various goods and services to produce. Goods markets and factor markets coordinate these choices of households and firms. Factors of production and goods flow clockwise (red), and money payments flow counterclockwise (green).

Coordinating Decisions

Markets coordinate individual decisions through price adjustments. To see how, think about your local market for hamburgers. Suppose that some people who want to buy hamburgers are not able to do so. To make the choices of buyers and sellers compatible, buyers must scale down their appetites or more hamburgers must be offered for sale (or both must happen). A rise in the price of hamburgers produces this outcome. A higher price encourages producers to offer more hamburgers for sale. It also encourages some people to change their lunch plans. Fewer people buy hamburgers, and more buy hot dogs. More hamburgers (and more hot dogs) are offered for sale.

Alternatively, suppose that more hamburgers are available than people want to buy. In this case, to make the choices of buyers and sellers compatible, more hamburgers must be bought or fewer hamburgers must be offered for sale (or both). A fall in the price of a hamburger achieves this outcome. A lower price encourages firms to produce a smaller quantity of hamburgers. It also encourages people to buy more hamburgers.

1 Why are social arrangements such as markets and property rights necessary?
2 What are the main functions of markets?

◆ You have now begun to see how economists approach economic questions. Scarcity, choice, and divergent opportunity costs explain why we specialize and trade and why property rights and markets have developed. You can see all around you the lessons you've learned in this chapter. *Reading Between the Lines* on pp. 46–47 gives an example. It explores the *PPF* of a student like you and the choices that students must make that influence their own economic growth — the growth of their incomes.

The Cost and Benefit of Education

NEWS & RECORD (GREENSBORO, NC), May 24, 2001

Graduates to Seek More Education

More than 840 graduating seniors at four Randolph County public high schools tonight will ... accept diplomas that conclude 13 years of education.

For some, those diplomas will be calling cards to signify their readiness to enter the working world.

For others, it's the first in possibly a string of diplomas.

If the 2001 class holds true to the history of previous classes, nearly 80 percent will go on to attend two- or four-year colleges. ...

Almost half of the people working in Randolph County are employed in the manufacturing industry at an average wage of $527.30 a week.

Bonnie Renfro, director of the county economic corporation, cautioned graduates who may think they will be able to start off earning that right out of high school. Most manufacturing jobs start off at $7.50 to $8 an hour.

But, she said, it is possible for today's graduates to make that and more, if they are "willing to improve their skills by attending a community college and the universities. The more you can improve yourself definitely enhances your earning potentials." ...

Essence of the Stories

■ High school graduates in Randolph County, North Carolina, can earn between $7.50 and $8 an hour in manufacturing jobs.

■ Students who increase their skills by attending community college and university can increase their earning potential.

■ The average starting salary in 2001 for graduates with a bachelor's degree in business administration from the Anderson Schools of Management at the University of New Mexico was $38,541.

■ The average starting salary in 2001 for graduates with an MBA from the Anderson Schools of Management at the University of New Mexico was $54,176.

THE ALBUQUERQUE TRIBUNE, August 6, 2001

UNM Business Graduates See Rise in Starting Salaries

The Anderson Schools of Management at the University of New Mexico have released the results of [the] graduate exit-salary survey. Despite reports of a sluggish economy, the survey showed that Anderson graduates far outpaced the state's average salaries as they entered the market.

For graduates with a bachelor's in business administration, the average starting salary was $38,541, ... For MBA graduates, the average starting salary was $54,176, ...

By May's commencement ceremony, 88 percent of bachelor's graduates and 90 percent of MBA graduates had jobs lined up and waiting for them. ...

Economic Analysis

■ Education increases human capital and expands production possibilities.

■ The opportunity cost of a college degree is forgone consumption. The payoff is an increase in lifetime production possibilities.

■ Figure 1 shows the choices facing a high school graduate who can consume education goods and services and consumption goods and services on the blue *PPF*.

■ Working full time, this person earns $8 an hour, or $16,000 a year, at point *A* on the blue *PPF* in Fig. 1, and the *PPF* remains the blue curve.

■ By attending college, the student moves from point *A* to point *B* along her *PPF*, forgoes current consumption (the opportunity cost of attending college), and increases the use of educational goods and services.

■ On graduating from college, a person can earn $38,000 a year, so production possibilities expand to the red *PPF* in Fig. 1.

■ Figure 2 shows a college graduate's choices. The blue curve is the same *PPF* as the red *PPF* in Fig. 1.

■ Working full time, this person earns $38,000 a year at point *C* on the blue *PPF* in Fig. 2, and the *PPF* remains the blue curve.

■ By pursuing an MBA, the student moves from point *C* to point *D* along her *PPF*, forgoes current consumption (the opportunity cost of an MBA), and increases the use of educational goods and services.

■ With an MBA, a person can earn $54,000 a year, so production possibilities expand to the red *PPF* in Fig. 2.

■ For people who have the required ability, the benefits of education exceed the costs.

You're The Voter

■ Political leaders of all parties say that they want every American to have access to a college education.

■ Why do you think political leaders need to be concerned about college education?

■ With the huge return from education, why don't more people remain in school for longer?

■ What is the opportunity cost of providing a college education to every American?

■ Would you vote for or against a tax increase to enable everyone to attend college? Why?

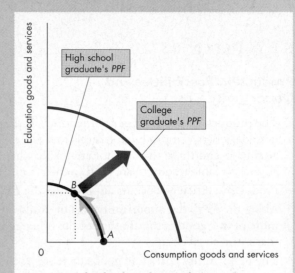

Figure 1 High school graduate's choices

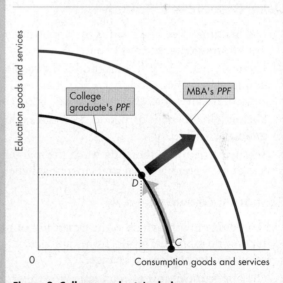

Figure 2 College graduate's choices

SUMMARY

KEY POINTS

Production Possibilities and Opportunity Cost (pp. 32–34)

- The production possibilities frontier, *PPF*, is the boundary between production levels that are attainable and those that are not attainable when all the available resources are used to their limit.
- Production efficiency occurs at points on the *PPF*.
- Along the *PPF*, the opportunity cost of producing more of one good is the amount of the other good that must be given up.
- The opportunity cost of all goods increases as the production of the good increases.

Using Resources Efficiently (pp. 35–37)

- The marginal cost of a good is the opportunity cost of producing one more unit.
- The marginal benefit from a good is the maximum amount of another good that a person is willing to forgo to obtain more of the first good.
- The marginal benefit of a good decreases as the amount available increases.
- Resources are used efficiently when the marginal cost of each good is equal to its marginal benefit.

Economic Growth (pp. 38–39)

- Economic growth, which is the expansion of production possibilities, results from capital accumulation and technological change.
- The opportunity cost of economic growth is forgone current consumption.

Gains from Trade (pp. 40–43)

- A person has a comparative advantage in producing a good if that person can produce the good at a lower opportunity cost than everyone else.
- People gain by specializing in the activity in which they have a comparative advantage and trading with others.
- Dynamic comparative advantage arises from learning-by-doing.

The Market Economy (pp. 44–45)

- Property rights and markets enable people to gain from specialization and trade.
- Markets coordinate decisions and help to allocate resources to *higher* valued uses.

KEY FIGURES

KEY TERMS

PROBLEMS

*1. Use the figure to calculate Wendell's opportunity cost of one hour of tennis when he increases the time he plays tennis from:
   a. 4 to 6 hours a week.
   b. 6 to 8 hours a week.

2. Use the figure to calculate Tina's opportunity cost of a day of skiing when she increases her time spent skiing from:
   a. 2 to 4 days a month.
   b. 4 to 6 days a month.

*3. In problem 1, describe the relationship between the time Wendell spends playing tennis and the opportunity cost of an hour of tennis.

4. In problem 2, describe the relationship between the time Tina spends skiing and the opportunity cost of a day of skiing.

*5. Wendell, in problem 1, has the following marginal benefit curve:

   a. If Wendell is efficient, what is his grade?
   b. Why would Wendell be worse off getting a higher grade?

6. Tina, in problem 2, has the following marginal benefit curve:

   a. If Tina is efficient, how much does she ski?
   b. Why would Tina be worse off spending more days a month skiing?

*7. Sunland's production possibilities are:

Food (pounds per month)		Sunscreen (gallons per month)
300	and	0
200	and	50
100	and	100
0	and	150

   a. Draw a graph of Sunland's production possibilities frontier.

b. What are Sunland's opportunity costs of producing food and sunscreen at each output?

8. Jane's Island's production possibilities are:

Corn (pounds per month)		Cloth (yards per month)
6	and	0
4	and	2
2	and	4
0	and	6

a. Draw a graph of the *PPF* on Jane's Island.
b. What are Jane's opportunity costs of producing corn and cloth at each output in the table?

*9. In problem 7, to get a gallon of sunscreen the people of Sunland are willing to give up 5 pounds of food if they have 25 gallons of sunscreen, 2 pounds of food if they have 75 gallons of sunscreen, and 1 pound of food if they have 125 gallons of sunscreen.
a. Draw a graph of Sunland's marginal benefit from sunscreen.
b. What is the efficient quantity of sunscreen?

10. In problem 8, to get a yard of cloth Jane is willing to give up 1.50 pounds of corn if she has 2 yards of cloth; 1.00 pounds of corn if she has 4 yards of cloth; and 0.50 pound of corn if she has 6 yards of cloth.
a. Draw a graph of Jane's marginal benefit from cloth.
b. What is Jane's efficient quantity of cloth?

*11. Busyland's production possibilities are:

Food (pounds per month)		Sunscreen (gallons per month)
150	and	0
100	and	100
50	and	200
0	and	300

Calculate Busyland's opportunity costs of food and sunscreen at each output in the table.

12. Joe's Island's production possibilities are:

Corn (pounds per month)		Cloth (yards per month)
12	and	0
8	and	1
4	and	2
0	and	3

What are Joe's opportunity costs of producing corn and cloth at each output in the table?

*13. In problems 7 and 11, Sunland and Busyland each produce and consume 100 pounds of food and 100 gallons of sunscreen per month, and they do not trade. Now the countries begin to trade with each other.
a. What good does Sunland sell to Busyland and what good does it buy from Busyland?
b. If Sunland and Busyland divide the total output of food and sunscreen equally, what are the gains from trade?

14. In problems 8 and 12, Jane's Island and Joe's Island each produce and consume 4 pounds of corn and 2 yards of cloth and they do not trade. Now the islands begin to trade.
a. What good does Jane sell to Joe and what good does Jane buy from Joe?
b. If Jane and Joe divide the total output of corn and cloth equally, what are the gains from trade?

CRITICAL THINKING

1. After you have studied *Reading Between the Lines* on pp. 46–47, answer the following questions:
a. At what point on the blue *PPF* in Figure 1 on p. 47 is the combination of education goods and services and consumption goods and services efficient? Explain your answer.
b. Students are facing rising tuition. How does higher tuition change the opportunity cost of education and how does it change the *PPF*s in Figures 1 and 2?
c. Who receives the benefits from education? Is the marginal cost of education equal to the marginal benefit of education? Is resource use in the market for education efficient?

WEB EXERCISES

1. Use the links on the Parkin Web site and obtain data on the tuition and other costs of enrolling in the MBA program of a school that interests you. If an MBA graduate can earn as much as the amounts reported in the news article in *Reading Between the Lines* on pp. 46–47, does the marginal benefit of an MBA exceed its marginal cost? Why doesn't everyone get an MBA?

UNDERSTANDING THE SCOPE OF ECONOMICS

PART 1

Your Economic Revolution

You are making progress in your study of economics. You've already encountered the big questions and big ideas of economics. And you've learned about the key insight of Adam Smith, the founder of economics: specialization and exchange create economic wealth. ◆ You are studying economics at a time that future historians will call the *Information Revolution*. We reserve the word 'Revolution' for big events that influence all future generations. ◆ During the *Agricultural Revolution*, which occurred 10,000 years ago, people learned to domesticate animals and plant crops. They stopped roaming in search of food and settled in villages and eventually towns and cities, where they developed markets in which to exchange their products. ◆ During the *Industrial Revolution*, which began 240 years ago, people used science to create new technologies. This revolution brought extraordinary wealth for some but created conditions in which others were left behind. It brought social and political tensions that we still face today. ◆ During today's *Information Revolution*, people who embraced the new technologies prospered on an unimagined scale. But the incomes and living standards of the less educated are falling behind, and social and political tensions are increasing. Today's revolution has a global dimension. Some of the winners live in previously poor countries in Asia, and some of the losers live here in the United States. ◆ So you are studying economics at an interesting time. Whatever *your* motivation is for studying economics, *my* objective is to help you do well in your course, to enjoy it, and to develop a deeper understanding of the economic world around you. ◆ There are three reasons why I hope that we both succeed: First, a decent understanding of economics will help you to become a full participant in the Information Revolution. Second, an understanding of economics will help you play a more effective role as a citizen and voter and enable you to add your voice to those who are looking for solutions to our social and political problems. Third, you will enjoy the sheer fun of *understanding* the forces at play and how they are shaping our world. ◆ If you are finding economics interesting, think seriously about majoring in the subject. A degree in economics gives the best training available in problem solving, offers lots of opportunities to develop conceptual skills, and opens doors to a wide range of graduate courses, including the MBA, and to a wide range of jobs. You can read more about the benefits of an economics degree in Robert Whaples's essay in your *Study Guide*. ◆ Economics was born during the Industrial Revolution. We'll look at its birth and meet its founder, Adam Smith. Then we'll talk about the progress that economists have made and some of the outstanding policy problems of today with one of today's most distinguished economists, Lawrence H. Summers, President of Harvard University.

The Sources of Economic Wealth

"It is not from the benevolence of the butcher, the brewer, or the baker that we expect our dinner, but from their regard to their own interest."

ADAM SMITH
The Wealth of Nations

ADAM SMITH *was a giant of a scholar who contributed to ethics and jurisprudence as well as economics. Born in 1723 in Kirkcaldy, a small fishing town near Edinburgh, Scotland, Smith was the only child of the town's customs officer (who died before Adam was born).*

His first academic appointment, at age 28, was as Professor of Logic at the University of Glasgow. He subsequently became tutor to a wealthy Scottish duke, whom he accompanied on a two-year grand European tour, following which he received a pension of £300 a year — ten times the average income at that time.

With the financial security of his pension, Smith devoted ten years to writing An Inquiry into the Nature and Causes of **The Wealth of Nations***, which was published in 1776. Many people had written on economic issues before Adam Smith, but he made economics a science. Smith's account was so broad and authoritative that no subsequent writer on economics could advance ideas without tracing their connections to those of Adam Smith.*

Why are some nations wealthy while others are poor? This question lies at the heart of economics. And it leads directly to a second question: What can poor nations do to become wealthy?

Adam Smith, who is regarded by many scholars as the founder of economics, attempted to answer these questions in his book *The Wealth of Nations*, published in 1776. Smith was pondering these questions at the height of the Industrial Revolution. During these years, new technologies were invented and applied to the manufacture of cotton and wool cloth, iron, transportation, and agriculture.

Smith wanted to understand the sources of economic wealth, and he brought his acute powers of observation and abstraction to bear on the question. His answer:

- The division of labor
- Free markets

The division of labor — breaking tasks down into simple tasks and becoming skilled in those tasks — is the source of "the greatest improvement in the productive powers of labor," said Smith. The division of labor became even more productive when it was applied to creating new technologies. Scientists and engineers, trained in extremely narrow fields, became specialists at inventing. Their powerful skills accelerated the advance of technology, so by the 1820s, machines could make consumer goods faster and more accurately than any craftsman could. And by the 1850s, machines could make other machines that labor alone could never have made.

But, said Smith, the fruits of the division of labor are limited by the extent of the market. To make the market as large as possible, there must be no impediments to free trade both within a country and among countries.

Smith argued that when each person makes the best possible economic choice, that choice leads as if by "an invisible hand" to the best outcome for society as a whole. The butcher, the brewer, and the baker each pursue their own interests but, in doing so, also serve the interests of everyone else.

THEN

Adam Smith speculated that one person, working hard, using the hand tools available in the 1770s, might possibly make 20 pins a day. Yet, he observed, by using those same hand tools but breaking the process into a number of individually small operations in which people specialize — by the **division of labor** — ten people could make a staggering 48,000 pins a day. One draws out the wire, another straightens it, a third cuts it, a fourth points it, a fifth grinds it. Three specialists make the head, and a fourth attaches it. Finally, the pin is polished and packaged. But a large market is needed to support the division of labor: One factory employing ten workers would need to sell more than 15 million pins a year to stay in business.

NOW

If Adam Smith were here today, the computer chip would fascinate him. He would see it as an extraordinary example of the productivity of the division of labor and of the use of machines to make machines that make other machines. From a design of a chip's intricate circuits, cameras transfer an image to glass plates that work like stencils. Workers prepare silicon wafers on which the circuits are printed. Some slice the wafers, others polish them, others bake them, and yet others coat them with a light-sensitive chemical. Machines transfer a copy of the circuit onto the wafer. Chemicals then etch the design onto the wafer. Further processes deposit atom-sized transistors and aluminum connectors. Finally, a laser separates the hundreds of chips on the wafer. Every stage in the process of creating a computer chip uses other computer chips. And like the pin of the 1770s, the computer chip of today benefits from a large market — a global market — to buy chips in the huge quantities in which they are produced efficiently.

Many economists have worked on the big themes that Adam Smith began. One of these is Lawrence H. Summers, President of Harvard University and a distinguished economist.

TALKING WITH

LAWRENCE H. SUMMERS

is President of Harvard University. Born in 1954 in New Haven, Connecticut, into a family of distinguished economists, he was an undergraduate at the Massachusetts Institute of Technology and a graduate student at Harvard University. While still in his 20s, he became one of the youngest tenured economics professors at Harvard University. In Washington, he has held a succession of public service jobs at the World Bank and in the U.S. government, culminating in 1999 with his appointment as Secretary of the Treasury— the chief financial officer of the United States and the president's highest-ranking adviser.

Dr. Summers's research has covered an enormous range of macroeconomic and public policy issues that include capital taxation, unemployment, global financial crises, the transition to a market economy in Eastern Europe, and the problem of speeding progress in the developing countries.

Michael Parkin talked with Lawrence Summers about his career and the progress that economists have made since the pioneering days of Adam Smith.

How does Adam Smith's assessment of the "nature and causes of the wealth of nations" look today in light of the lessons that economists have learned over the past two centuries?

Adam Smith is looking very good today. I think one of the most important insights of the social sciences of the last several centuries is Smith's idea that good things can come from the invisible hand—from decentralization rather than from central planning and direction. But Smith is also prescient in recognizing the various qualifications to the argument for the invisible hand, whether involving fairness, externalities, or monopoly.

What do we know today that Adam Smith didn't know?

We know today much more than Smith did about economic fluctuations and about the role of money—about what we today call macroeconomics. We know more today about economic situations that involve bargaining, whether between two individuals or between small numbers of firms in an industry, or between a buyer and a seller. We know much more today about markets without perfect information. I know how good my used car is when I sell it—you don't when you buy it. I know whether I'm sick when I buy medical insurance, but you the insurance company have to try to figure it out. The role of information in markets, which turns out to be quite profound, is something we understand much better today. And we also understand much better today the role of politics and governments in shaping the economy, which is far larger than it was in Smith's day.

Coincidentally, a few days before we're holding this conversation, a new nation was born—East Timor. What advice can economists offer a new and extremely poor nation as it takes its first steps?

Much of economic success involves strong rights to property. Has anyone ever washed a rented car or taken as good care of their hotel room as their home? When people own their farmlands, they're much more likely to farm them sustainably. When businesses own their machinery, they're much more likely to take care of it. When individuals own what they produce, they're much more likely to work hard.

Strong property rights and the framework of laws that support them are profoundly important to the market-based exchanges that are essential to economic success. So also is stable money that can be a basis for exchange. So also is an educated and capable population. But if there is a single lesson that is important for a starting economy, it is that strong property rights can motivate individuals.

One lesson that we've learned from your work at the World Bank is that the return to educating girls in developing countries is very high. What did you discover in that work?

Primary education, and especially for girls, may be the highest return investment available in the developing world. Those who read produce more and therefore earn more. Girls who are educated grow up to be better mothers who have smaller, happier, healthier families. Women who are educated are empowered with greater career options. They are less likely to fall into prostitution, and that reduces the spread of AIDS. Women who are educated are much more likely to take care of the environment. So it is in many respects that primary education, and especially that of girls, generates very large returns.

Are there any other activities that yield comparable returns for developing countries?

Maybe some investments in health care that generate very large returns—it's a difficult evaluation to make. The really crucial lesson is that a country's most

"The really crucial lesson is that a country's most precious assets are its people, and investments in people are likely to be the most important investments of all."

precious assets are its people, and investments in people are likely to be the most important investments of all.

Some of your earliest research was on taxing the income from capital. Why isn't the income from capital just like the income from labor?

Think about it this way: two individuals both earn a hundred dollars. One spends it all this year; the other saves half of it and earns 10 percent interest next year. Who should pay more total taxes? Plausibly, for fairness, both should pay the same tax. A tax on income will lead to the same taxes in the first year for the two individuals; and higher taxes in the second year for the individual who saved.

In effect, taxes on capital income are taxes on future consumption, and it is far from clear why a society should want to tax future consumption more highly than present consumption.

On the other hand, very large fortunes often show up as capital income, and so designing a workable and fair tax system that doesn't tax investment income is something that is very difficult to do.

Would you say that we have not yet managed to figure this one out?

We'll all be working on finding the best tax systems for a long time to come. And it may mean that the income tax is, as Churchill said of democracy, terrible but the best alternative.

The United States has a large and persistent current account deficit, a low personal saving rate, and a projected deficit in the Social Security and Medicare trust funds. Are you concerned about these problems?

Herb Stein, who was a leading American policy economist, once said that the unsustainable cannot be sustained and must surely end!

This is a concern, given that U.S. national debt to foreigners is rising faster than U.S. income. And it's a concern in terms of the financing of Social Security and Medicare as our population ages. In a way, the solution to both these problems is more American saving, because that will put us in a stronger position as our population ages, and will allow us to have

55

investment in the United States without incurring debts to foreigners.

Probably the most potent way of increasing a country's national savings is to improve the position of its budget. Whether to increase taxes or cut expenditures is a judgment for the congress to debate. My guess is that some combination would be appropriate. There are aspects of expenditures that are going to be hard to control. On the other hand, there are other aspects in terms of transfer payments and terms of various subsidies where economies probably are possible. And one virtue of a strong fiscal position is that it reduces interest expense down the road.

Did you always want to be an economist? How did you choose economics?

I thought I would be a mathematician or a physicist, but found myself very interested in questions of public policy. I was very involved in debate when I was in college. So I found myself wanting very much to combine an interest in public policy issues with an analytical approach, and economics gave me a way to do that. I also found that I had some aptitude, relative to my aptitude for pure mathematics or physics, so I gravitated to economics.

What led a brilliant academic economist to Washington? What did you want to achieve?

I hoped to put to use some of what I had learned in my studies in a direct way and to enhance my understanding of the way actual economies work by seeing how the policy process operated. I had a great time in Washington and feel that my economics training made a huge difference in everything I did. Whether it was thinking about how to respond to the Mexican and Asian financial crises or working on financial deregulation. Whether it was choosing optimal investments for the Customs Department in protecting our borders or designing tax incentives to promote saving. Whether it was supporting the protection of the Social Security trust fund or thinking about enforcement policies against corporate tax shelters. Principles of economics — in terms of maximizing benefits relative to costs, in terms of always thinking of the margin, in terms of always recognizing the opportunity cost of choices taken, in terms of always needing to see things add up — was quite valuable.

And what insights does economics bring to the task of running a major university?

I came to Harvard because I thought after my time in government the two most important resources that were going to shape the economies of the future were leaders and new ideas, and those are the two things that a university produces.

Successful leadership in a university is all about what economists think about all the time—incentives — whether it's for professors to do a good job teaching, attracting the best scholars in a particular area, or motivating concern and research about the most important problems.

Leadership and management for the university are very much about economics because they're very much about incentives. Some of them are pecuniary and involve money, but other incentives come from people's feelings of being appreciated; they come from the teams in which people have an opportunity to work; they come from the way in which the university is organized. If working at the treasury was heavily about applied macroeconomics, leadership in the university is heavily about applied microeconomics.

What is your advice to a student who is just setting out to become an economist? What other subjects work well with economics?

The best advice to students is, don't be a commodity that's available in a perfectly competitive market. Stand out by developing your own distinctive expertise in something you care deeply about. It matters much less what it is and much more that it be yours and it not be a hundred other people's.

I think there is enormous potential in almost every area of economics, but I think that the people who will contribute the most to economics over the next quarter century will be those who have some keen understanding of the context in which economics is playing out—the international context, the technological context, and the political context. So my hope would be that those interested in economics would understand that economics is very different from physics in that it is tracking a changing reality and that in order to do the best economics in a given period, you have to be able to track that changing reality, and that means understanding international, technological, and political contexts.

DEMAND AND SUPPLY —— CHAPTER 3

Slide, Rocket, and Roller Coaster

Slide, rocket, and roller coaster — Disneyland rides? No, they are commonly used descriptions of price changes. ◆ The price of a mid-performance computer took a dramatic slide from around $3,000 in 2000 to around $700 in 2001. What caused this price slide? We'll answer this question at the end of the chapter. ◆ Occasionally, a price will rocket. But a price rocket, like a satellite-launching rocket, has a limited life. It eventually runs out of fuel. One spectacular price rocket occurred when the price of coffee shot skyward from 60 cents a pound in 1993 to $2.25 a pound in 1994. Why did the price of coffee rise so spectacularly? ◆ Over longer periods, the price of coffee, along with the prices of bananas and other agricultural commodities, rises and falls like a roller coaster ride. ◆ Economics is about the choices people make to cope with scarcity. These choices are guided by costs and benefits and are coordinated through markets. ◆ Demand and supply is the tool that explains how markets work. It is the main tool of economics. It is used to study the price of a CD, wages and jobs, rents and housing, pollution, crime, consumer protection, education, welfare, the value of money, and interest rates.

◆ Your careful study of this topic will bring big rewards both in your further study of economics and in your everyday life. When you have completed your study of demand and supply, you will be able to explain how prices are determined and make predictions about price slides, rockets, and roller coasters. Once you understand demand and supply, you will view the world through new eyes.

After studying this chapter, you will be able to

- Describe a market and think about a price as an opportunity cost
- Explain the influences on demand
- Explain the influences on supply
- Explain how demand and supply determine prices and quantities bought and sold
- Use demand and supply to make predictions about changes in prices and quantities

Markets and Prices

WHEN YOU NEED A NEW PAIR OF RUNNING SHOES, want a bagel and a latte, plan to upgrade your stereo system, or need to fly home for Thanksgiving, you must find a place where people sell those items or offer those services. The place in which you find them is a *market*. You learned in Chapter 2 (p. 44) that a market is any arrangement that enables buyers and sellers to get information and to do business with each other.

A market has two sides: buyers and sellers. There are markets for *goods* such as apples and hiking boots, for *services* such as haircuts and tennis lessons, for *resources* such as computer programmers and earth-movers, and for other manufactured *inputs* such as memory chips and auto parts. There are also markets for money such as Japanese yen and for financial securities such as Yahoo! stock. Only our imagination limits what can be traded in markets.

Some markets are physical places where the buyers and sellers meet and where an auctioneer or a broker helps to determine the prices. Examples of this type of market are the New York Stock Exchange and the wholesale fish, meat, and produce markets.

Some markets are groups of people spread around the world who never meet and know little about each other but are connected through the Internet or by telephone and fax. Examples are the e-commerce markets and currency markets.

But most markets are unorganized collections of buyers and sellers. You do most of your trading in this type of market. An example is the market for basketball shoes. The buyers in this $3 billion-a-year market are the 45 million Americans who play basketball (or want to make a fashion statement). The sellers are the tens of thousands of retail sports equipment and footwear stores. Each buyer can visit several different stores, and each seller knows that the buyer has a choice of stores.

Markets vary in the intensity of competition that buyers and sellers face. In this chapter, we're going to study a **competitive market** — a market that has many buyers and many sellers, so no single buyer or seller can influence the price.

Producers offer items for sale only if the price is high enough to cover their opportunity cost. And consumers respond to changing opportunity cost by seeking cheaper alternatives to expensive items.

We are going to study the way people respond to *prices* and the forces that determine prices. But to pursue these tasks, we need to understand the relationship between a price and an opportunity cost.

In everyday life, the *price* of an object is the number of dollars that must be given up in exchange for it. Economists refer to this price as the *money price*.

The *opportunity cost* of an action is the highest-valued alternative forgone. If, when you buy a coffee, the highest-valued thing you forgo is some gum, then the opportunity cost of the coffee is the *quantity* of gum forgone. We can calculate the quantity of gum forgone from the money prices of coffee and gum.

If the money price of coffee is $1 a cup and the money price of gum is 50¢ a pack, then the opportunity cost of one cup of coffee is two packs of gum. To calculate this opportunity cost, we divide the price of a cup of coffee by the price of a pack of gum and find the *ratio* of one price to the other. The ratio of one price to another is called a **relative price**, and a *relative price is an opportunity cost*.

We can express the relative price of coffee in terms of gum or any other good. The normal way of expressing a relative price is in terms of a "basket" of all goods and services. To calculate this relative price, we divide the money price of a good by the money price of a "basket" of all goods (called a *price index*). The resulting relative price tells us the opportunity cost of an item in terms of how much of the "basket" we must give up to buy it.

The theory of demand and supply that we are about to study determines *relative prices,* and the word "price" means *relative* price. When we predict that a price will fall, we do not mean that its *money* price will fall — although it might. We mean that its *relative* price will fall. That is, its price will fall *relative* to the average price of other goods and services.

REVIEW QUIZ

1 What is the distinction between a money price and a relative price?

2 Explain why a relative price is an opportunity cost.

3 Can you think of an example of a good whose money price and relative price have risen?

4 Can you think of an example of a good whose money price and relative price have fallen?

Let's begin our study of demand and supply, starting with demand.

Demand

IF YOU DEMAND SOMETHING, THEN YOU

1. Want it,
2. Can afford it, and
3. Have made a definite plan to buy it.

Wants are the unlimited desires or wishes that people have for goods and services. How many times have you thought that you would like something "if only you could afford it" or "if it weren't so expensive"? Scarcity guarantees that many — perhaps most — of our wants will never be satisfied. Demand reflects a decision about which wants to satisfy.

The **quantity demanded** of a good or service is the amount that consumers plan to buy during a given time period at a particular price. The quantity demanded is not necessarily the same as the quantity actually bought. Sometimes the quantity demanded exceeds the amount of goods available, so the quantity bought is less than the quantity demanded.

The quantity demanded is measured as an amount per unit of time. For example, suppose that you buy one cup of coffee a day. The quantity of coffee that you demand can be expressed as 1 cup per day, 7 cups per week, or 365 cups per year. Without a time dimension, we cannot tell whether the quantity demanded is large or small.

What Determines Buying Plans?

The amount of any particular good or service that consumers plan to buy depends on many factors. The main ones are

1. The price of the good
2. The prices of related goods
3. Expected future prices
4. Income
5. Population
6. Preferences

We first look at the relationship between the quantity demanded and the price of a good. To study this relationship, we keep all other influences on consumers' planned purchases the same and ask: How does the quantity demanded of the good vary as its price varies, other things remaining the same?

The Law of Demand

The **law of demand** states

> Other things remaining the same, the higher the price of a good, the smaller is the quantity demanded.

Why does a higher price reduce the quantity demanded? For two reasons:

- Substitution effect
- Income effect

Substitution Effect When the price of a good rises, other things remaining the same, its *relative* price — its opportunity cost — rises. Although each good is unique, it has *substitutes* — other goods that can be used in its place. As the opportunity cost of a good rises, people buy less of that good and more of its substitutes.

Income Effect When a price rises and all other influences on buying plans remain unchanged, the price rises *relative* to people's incomes. So faced with a higher price and an unchanged income, people cannot afford to buy all the things they previously bought. They must decrease the quantities demanded of at least some goods and services, and normally, the good whose price has increased will be one of the goods that people buy less of.

To see the substitution effect and the income effect at work, think about the effects of a change in the price of a recordable compact disc — a CD-R. Several different goods are substitutes for a CD-R. For example, an audiotape and prerecorded CD provide services similar to those of a CD-R.

Suppose that a CD-R initially sells for $3 and then its price falls to $1.50. People now substitute CD-Rs for audiotapes and prerecorded CDs — the substitution effect. And with a budget that now has some slack from the lower price of a CD-R, people buy more CD-Rs — the income effect. The quantity of CD-Rs demanded increases for these two reasons.

Now suppose that a CD-R initially sells for $3 each and then the price doubles to $6. People now substitute prerecorded CDs and audiotapes for CD-Rs — the substitution effect. And faced with a tighter budget, people buy fewer CD-Rs — the income effect. The quantity of CD-Rs demanded decreases for these two reasons.

Demand Curve and Demand Schedule

You are now about to study one of the two most used curves in economics: the demand curve. And you are going to encounter one of the most critical distinctions: the distinction between *demand* and *quantity demanded*.

The term **demand** refers to the entire relationship between the price of the good and the quantity demanded of the good. Demand is illustrated by the demand curve and the demand schedule. The term *quantity demanded* refers to a point on a demand curve — the quantity demanded at a particular price.

Figure 3.1 shows the demand curve for CD-Rs. A **demand curve** shows the relationship between the quantity demanded of a good and its price when all other influences on consumers' planned purchases remain the same.

The table in Fig. 3.1 is the demand schedule for CD-Rs. A *demand schedule* lists the quantities demanded at each price when all the other influences on consumers' planned purchases — prices of related goods, expected future prices, income, population, and preferences — remain the same. For example, if the price of a CD-R is 50¢, the quantity demanded is 9 million a week. If the price is $2.50, the quantity demanded is 2 million a week. The other rows of the table show the quantities demanded at prices of $1.00, $1.50, and $2.00.

We graph the demand schedule as a demand curve with the quantity demanded of CD-Rs on the *x*-axis and the price of a CD-R on the *y*-axis. The points on the demand curve labeled *A* through *E* represent the rows of the demand schedule. For example, point *A* on the graph represents a quantity demanded of 9 million CD-Rs a week at a price of 50¢ a disc.

Willingness and Ability to Pay Another way of looking at the demand curve is as a willingness-and-ability-to-pay curve. And the willingness and ability to pay is a measure of *marginal benefit.*

If a small quantity is available, the highest price that someone is willing and able to pay for one more unit is high. But as the quantity available increases, the marginal benefit of each additional unit falls and the highest price that someone is willing and able to pay also falls along the demand curve.

In Fig. 3.1, if only 2 million CD-Rs are available each week, the highest price that someone is willing to pay for the 2 millionth CD-R is $2.50. But if 9 million CD-Rs are available each week, someone is willing to pay 50¢ for the last CD-R bought.

FIGURE 3.1   The Demand Curve

	Price (dollars per disc)	**Quantity** (millions of discs per week)
A	0.50	9
B	1.00	6
C	1.50	4
D	2.00	3
E	2.50	2

The table shows a demand schedule for CD-Rs. At a price of 50¢ a disc, 9 million a week are demanded; at a price of $1.50 a disc, 4 million a week are demanded. The demand curve shows the relationship between quantity demanded and price, everything else remaining the same. The demand curve slopes downward: As price decreases, the quantity demanded increases. The demand curve can be read in two ways. For a given price, the demand curve tells us the quantity that people plan to buy. For example, at a price of $1.50 a disc, the quantity demanded is 4 million discs a week. For a given quantity, the demand curve tells us the maximum price that consumers are willing and able to pay for the last discs available. For example, the maximum price that consumers will pay for the 6 millionth disc is $1.00.

A Change in Demand

When any factor that influences buying plans other than the price of the good changes, there is a **change in demand**. Figure 3.2 illustrates an increase in demand. When demand increases, the demand curve shifts rightward and the quantity demanded is greater at each and every price. For example, at a price of $2.50, on the original (blue) demand curve, the quantity demanded is 2 million discs a week. On the new (red) demand curve, the quantity demanded is 6 million discs a week. Look closely at the numbers in the table in Fig. 3.2 and check that the quantity demanded is greater at each price.

Let's look at the factors that bring a change in demand. There are five key factors to consider.

1. Prices of Related Goods The quantity of CD-Rs that consumers plan to buy depends in part on the prices of substitutes for CD-Rs. A **substitute** is a good that can be used in place of another good. For example, a bus ride is a substitute for a train ride; a hamburger is a substitute for a hot dog; and a prerecorded CD is a substitute for a CD-R. If the price of a substitute for a CD-R rises, people buy less of the substitute and more CD-Rs. For example, if the price of a prerecorded CD rises, people buy fewer CDs and more CD-Rs. The demand for CD-Rs increases.

The quantity of CD-Rs that people plan to buy also depends on the prices of complements with CD-Rs. A **complement** is a good that is used in conjunction with another good. Hamburgers and fries are complements. So are spaghetti and meat sauce, and so are CD-Rs and CD-R burners. If the price of a CD burner falls, people buy more CD burners *and more* CD-Rs. A fall in the price of a CD burner increases the demand for CD-Rs in Fig. 3.2.

2. Expected Future Prices If the price of a good is expected to rise in the future and if the good can be stored, the opportunity cost of obtaining the good for future use is lower today than it will be when the price has increased. So people retime their purchase — they substitute over time. They buy more of the good now before its price is expected to rise (and less after), so the current demand for the good increases.

For example, suppose that Florida is hit by a frost that damages the season's orange crop. You expect the price of orange juice to rise in the future. So you fill your freezer with enough frozen juice to get you through the next six months. Your current demand for frozen orange juice has increased and your future demand has decreased.

FIGURE 3.2   An Increase in Demand

Original demand schedule CD burner $300			New demand schedule CD burner $100		
	Price (dollars per disc)	Quantity (millions of discs per week)		Price (dollars per disc)	Quantity (millions of discs per week)
A	0.50	9	A'	0.50	13
B	1.00	6	B'	1.00	10
C	1.50	4	C'	1.50	8
D	2.00	3	D'	2.00	7
E	2.50	2	E'	2.50	6

A change in any influence on buyers' plans other than the price of the good itself results in a new demand schedule and a shift of the demand curve. A change in the price of a CD burner changes the demand for CD-Rs. At a price of $1.50 a disc, 4 million discs a week are demanded when a CD burner costs $300 (row C of the table) and 8 million CD-Rs a week are demanded when a CD burner costs $100. A *fall* in the price of a CD burner *increases* the demand for CD-Rs. The demand curve shifts *rightward*, as shown by the shift arrow and the resulting red curve.

Similarly, if the price of a good is expected to fall in the future, the opportunity cost of buying the good today is high relative to what it is expected to be in the future. So again, people retime their purchases. They buy less of the good now before its price falls, so the demand for the good decreases today and increases in the future.

Computer prices are constantly falling, and this fact poses a dilemma. Will you buy a new computer now, in time for the start of the school year, or will you wait until the price has fallen some more? Because people expect computer prices to keep falling, the current demand for computers is less (the future demand is greater) than it otherwise would be.

3. Income Consumers' income influences demand. When income increases, consumers buy more of most goods, and when income decreases, consumers buy less of most goods. Although an increase in income leads to an increase in the demand for *most* goods, it does not lead to an increase in the demand for *all* goods. A **normal good** is one for which demand increases as income increases. An **inferior good** is one for which demand decreases as income increases. Long-distance transportation has examples of both normal goods and inferior goods. As incomes increase, the demand for air travel (a normal good) increases and the demand for long-distance bus trips (an inferior good) decreases.

4. Population Demand also depends on the size and the age structure of the population. The larger the population, the greater is the demand for all goods and services; the smaller the population, the smaller is the demand for all goods and services.

For example, the demand for parking spaces or movies or CD-Rs or just about anything that you can imagine is much greater in New York City (population 7.5 million) than it is in Boise, Idaho (population 150,000).

Also, the larger the proportion of the population in a given age group, the greater is the demand for the goods and services used by that age group.

For example, between 1988 and 1998, the number of Americans aged 20 to 24 years decreased by 2 million. As a result, the demand for college places decreased during those years. During those same years, the number of Americans aged 85 years and over increased by more than 1 million. As a result, the demand for nursing home services increased.

TABLE 3.1   The Demand for CD-Rs

The Law of Demand

The quantity of CD-Rs demanded

Decreases if:	Increases if:
■ The price of a CD-R rises	■ The price of a CD-R falls

Changes in Demand

The demand for CD-Rs

Decreases if:	Increases if:
■ The price of a substitute falls	■ The price of a substitute rises
■ The price of a complement rises	■ The price of a complement falls
■ The price of a CD-R is expected to fall in the future	■ The price of a CD-R is expected to rise in the future
■ Income falls*	■ Income rises*
■ The population decreases	■ The population increases

*A CD-R is a normal good.

---

5. Preferences Demand depends on preferences. *Preferences* are an individual's attitudes toward goods and services. For example, a rock music fanatic has a much greater preference for CD-Rs than does a tone-deaf technophobic. As a consequence, even if they have the same incomes, their demands for CD-Rs will be very different.

Table 3.1 summarizes the influences on demand and the direction of those influences.

A Change in the Quantity Demanded Versus a Change in Demand

Changes in the factors that influence buyers' plans cause either a change in the quantity demanded or a change in demand. Equivalently, they cause either a movement along the demand curve or a shift of the demand curve. The distinction between a change in the quantity demanded and a change in demand is the same as that between a movement along the demand curve and a shift of the demand curve.

A point on the demand curve shows the quantity demanded at a given price. So a movement along the demand curve shows a **change in the quantity demanded**. The entire demand curve shows demand. So a shift of the demand curve shows a *change in demand*. Figure 3.3 illustrates and summarizes these distinctions.

Movement Along the Demand Curve If the price of a good changes but everything else remains the same, there is a movement along the demand curve. Because the demand curve slopes downward, a fall in the price of a good increases the quantity demanded of it and a rise in the price of the good decreases the quantity demanded of it — the law of demand.

In Fig. 3.3, if the price of a good falls when everything else remains the same, the quantity demanded of that good increases and there is a movement down the demand curve D_0. If the price rises when everything else remains the same, the quantity demanded of that good decreases and there is a movement up the demand curve D_0.

A Shift of the Demand Curve If the price of a good remains constant but some other influence on buyers' plans changes, there is a change in demand for that good. We illustrate a change in demand as a shift of the demand curve. For example, if the price of a CD burner falls, consumers buy more CD-Rs regardless of whether the price of a CD-R is high or low. That is what a rightward shift of the demand curve shows — more CD-Rs are bought at each and every price.

In Fig. 3.3, when any influence on buyers' planned purchases changes, other than the price of the good, there is a *change in demand* and the demand curve shifts. Demand *increases* and the demand curve *shifts rightward* (to the red demand curve D_1) if the price of a substitute rises, the price of a complement falls, the expected future price of the good rises, income increases (for a normal good), or the population increases. Demand *decreases* and the demand curve *shifts leftward* (to the red demand curve D_2) if the price of a substitute falls, the price of a complement rises, the expected future price of the good falls, income decreases (for a normal good), or the population decreases. (For an inferior good, the effects of changes in income are in the direction opposite to those described above.)

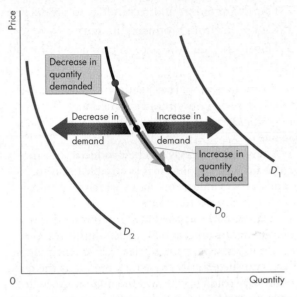

FIGURE 3.3 A Change in the Quantity Demanded Versus a Change in Demand

When the price of the good changes, there is a movement along the demand curve and *a change in the quantity demanded,* shown by the blue arrows on demand curve D_0. When any other influence on buyers' plans changes, there is a shift of the demand curve and a *change in demand*. An increase in demand shifts the demand curve rightward (from D_0 to D_1). A decrease in demand shifts the demand curve leftward (from D_0 to D_2).

REVIEW QUIZ

1 Define the quantity demanded of a good or service.
2 What is the law of demand and how do we illustrate it?
3 If a fixed amount of a good is available, what does the demand curve tell us about the price that consumers are willing to pay for that fixed quantity?
4 List all the influences on buying plans that change demand, and for each influence say whether it increases or decreases demand.
5 What happens to the quantity of Palm Pilots demanded and the demand for Palm Pilots if the price of a Palm Pilot falls and all other influences on buying plans remain the same?

Supply

IF A FIRM SUPPLIES A GOOD OR SERVICE, THE FIRM

1. Has the resources and technology to produce it,
2. Can profit from producing it, and
3. Has made a definite plan to produce it and sell it.

A supply is more that just having the *resources* and the *technology* to produce something. *Resources and technology* are the constraints that limit what is possible.

Many useful things can be produced, but they are not produced unless it is profitable to do so. Supply reflects a decision about which technologically feasible items to produce.

The **quantity supplied** of a good or service is the amount that producers plan to sell during a given time period at a particular price. The quantity supplied is not necessarily the same amount as the quantity actually sold. Sometimes the quantity supplied is greater than the quantity demanded, so the quantity bought is less than the quantity supplied.

Like the quantity demanded, the quantity supplied is measured as an amount per unit of time. For example, suppose that GM produces 1,000 cars a day. The quantity of cars supplied by GM can be expressed as 1,000 a day, 7,000 a week, or 365,000 a year. Without the time dimension, we cannot tell whether a particular number is large or small.

What Determines Selling Plans?

The amount of any particular good or service that producers plan to sell depends on many factors. The main ones are

1. The price of the good
2. The prices of resources used to produce the good
3. The prices of related goods produced
4. Expected future prices
5. The number of suppliers
6. Technology

Let's first look at the relationship between the price of a good and the quantity supplied. To study this relationship, we keep all other influences on the quantity supplied the same. We ask: How does the quantity supplied of a good vary as its price varies?

The Law of Supply

The **law of supply** states:

Other things remaining the same, the higher the price of a good, the greater is the quantity supplied.

Why does a higher price increase the quantity supplied? It is because *marginal cost increases*. As the quantity produced of any good increases, the marginal cost of producing the good increases. (You can refresh your memory of increasing marginal cost in Chapter 2, p. 35.)

It is never worth producing a good if the price received for it does not at least cover the marginal cost of producing it. So when the price of a good rises, other things remaining the same, producers are willing to incur the higher marginal cost and increase production. The higher price brings forth an increase in the quantity supplied.

Let's now illustrate the law of supply with a supply curve and a supply schedule.

Supply Curve and Supply Schedule

You are now going to study the second of the two most used curves in economics: the supply curve. And you're going to learn about the critical distinction between *supply* and *quantity supplied*.

The term **supply** refers to the entire relationship between the quantity supplied and the price of a good. Supply is illustrated by the supply curve and the supply schedule. The term *quantity supplied* refers to a point on a supply curve — the quantity supplied at a particular price.

Figure 3.4 shows the supply curve of CD-Rs. A **supply curve** shows the relationship between the quantity supplied of a good and its price when all other influences on producers' planned sales remain the same. The supply curve is a graph of a supply schedule.

The table in Fig. 3.4 sets out the supply schedule for CD-Rs. A *supply schedule* lists the quantities supplied at each price when all the other influences on producers' planned sales remain the same. For example, if the price of a CD-R is 50¢, the quantity supplied is zero — in row *A* of the table. If the price of a CD-R is $1.00, the quantity supplied is 3 million CD-Rs a week — in row *B*. The other rows of the table show the quantities supplied at prices of $1.50, $2.00, and $2.50.

FIGURE 3.4   The Supply Curve

The table shows the supply schedule of CD-Rs. For example, at a price of $1.00, 3 million discs a week are supplied; at a price of $2.50, 6 million discs a week are supplied. The supply curve shows the relationship between the quantity supplied and price, everything else remaining the same. The supply curve usually slopes upward: As the price of a good increases, so does the quantity supplied.

A supply curve can be read in two ways. For a given price, it tells us the quantity that producers plan to sell. And for a given quantity, it tells us the minimum price that producers are willing to accept for that quantity.

	Price (dollars per disc)	Quantity (millions of discs per week)
A	0.50	0
B	1.00	3
C	1.50	4
D	2.00	5
E	2.50	6

To make a supply curve, we graph the quantity supplied on the x-axis and the price on the y-axis, just as in the case of the demand curve. The points on the supply curve labeled A through E represent the rows of the supply schedule. For example, point A on the graph represents a quantity supplied of zero at a price of 50¢ a CD-R.

Minimum Supply Price   Just as the demand curve has two interpretations, so too does the supply curve. The demand curve can be interpreted as a willingness-and-ability-to-pay curve. The supply curve can be interpreted as a minimum-supply-price curve. It tells us the lowest price at which someone is willing to sell another unit.

If a small quantity is produced, the lowest price at which someone is willing to produce one more unit is low. But if a large quantity is produced, the lowest price at which someone is willing to sell one more unit is high.

In Fig. 3.4, if 6 million CD-Rs a week are produced, the lowest price that a producer is willing to accept for the 6 millionth disc is $2.50. But if only 4 million CD-Rs are produced each week, the lowest price that a producer is willing to accept for the 4 millionth disc is $1.50.

A Change in Supply

When any factor that influences selling plans other than the price of the good changes, there is a **change in supply**. Let's look at the five key factors that change supply.

1. Prices of Productive Resources   The prices of productive resources influence supply. The easiest way to see this influence is to think about the supply curve as a minimum-supply-price curve. If the price of a productive resource rises, the lowest price a producer is willing to accept rises, so supply decreases. For example, during 2001, the price of jet fuel increased and the supply of air transportation decreased. Similarly, a rise in the minimum wage decreases the supply of hamburgers. If the wages of disc producers rise, the supply of CD-Rs decreases.

2. Prices of Related Goods Produced   The prices of related goods and services that firms produce influence supply. For example, if the price of a prerecorded CD rises, the supply of CD-Rs decreases. CD-Rs and prerecorded CDs are *substitutes in production* — goods that can be produced by using the same resources. If the price of beef rises, the supply of cowhide increases. Beef and cowhide are *complements in production* — goods that must be produced together.

3. Expected Future Prices If the price of a good is expected to rise, the return from selling the good in the future is higher than it is today. So supply decreases today and increases in the future.

4. The Number of Suppliers The larger the number of firms that produce a good, the greater is the supply of the good. And as firms enter an industry, the supply in that industry increases. As firms leave an industry, the supply in that industry decreases. For example, over the past two years, there has been a huge increase in the number of firms that design and manage Web sites. As a result of this increase, the supply of Internet and World Wide Web services has increased enormously.

5. Technology New technologies create new products and lower the costs of producing existing products. As a result, they change supply. For example, the use of new technologies in the Taiwan factories that make CD-Rs for Imation Enterprises Corporation, a Minnesota based firm, have lowered the cost of producing a CD-R and increased its supply.

Figure 3.5 illustrates an increase in supply. When supply increases, the supply curve shifts rightward and the quantity supplied is larger at each and every price. For example, at a price of $1.00, on the original (blue) supply curve, the quantity supplied is 3 million discs a week. On the new (red) supply curve, the quantity supplied is 6 million discs a week. Look closely at the numbers in the table in Fig. 3.5 and check that the quantity supplied is larger at each price.

Table 3.2 summarizes the influences on supply and the directions of those influences.

A Change in the Quantity Supplied Versus a Change in Supply

Changes in the factors that influence producers' planned sales cause either a change in the quantity supplied or a change in supply. Equivalently, they cause either a movement along the supply curve or a shift of the supply curve.

A point on the supply curve shows the quantity supplied at a given price. A movement along the supply curve shows a **change in the quantity supplied**. The entire supply curve shows supply. A shift of the supply curve shows a *change in supply*.

FIGURE 3.5   An Increase in Supply

Original supply schedule Old technology			New supply schedule New technology		
	Price (dollars per disc)	**Quantity** (millions of discs per week)		**Price** (dollars per disc)	**Quantity** (millions of discs per week)
A	0.50	0	A'	0.50	3
B	1.00	3	B'	1.00	6
C	1.50	4	C'	1.50	8
D	2.00	5	D'	2.00	10
E	2.50	6	E'	2.50	12

A change in any influence on sellers' plans other than the price of the good itself results in a new supply schedule and a shift of the supply curve. For example, if Imation invents a new, cost-saving technology for producing CD-Rs, the supply of CD-Rs changes. At a price of $1.50 a disc, 4 million discs a week are supplied when producers use the old technology (row *C* of the table) and 8 million CD-Rs a week are supplied when producers use the new technology. An advance in technology *increases* the supply of CD-Rs. The supply curve shifts *rightward*, as shown by the shift arrow and the resulting red curve.

Figure 3.6 illustrates and summarizes these distinctions. If the price of a good falls and everything else remains the same, the quantity supplied of that good decreases and there is a movement down the supply curve S_0. If the price of a good rises and everything else remains the same, the quantity supplied increases and there is a movement up the supply curve S_0. When any other influence on selling plans changes, the supply curve shifts and there is a *change in supply*. If the supply curve is S_0 and if production costs fall, supply increases and the supply curve shifts to the red supply curve S_1. If, production costs rise, supply decreases and the supply curve shifts to the red supply curve S_2.

TABLE 3.2   The Supply of CD-Rs

The Law of Supply

The quantity of CD-Rs supplied

Decreases if:
- The price of a CD-R falls

Increases if:
- The price of a CD-R rises

Changes in Supply

The supply of CD-Rs

Decreases if:
- The price of a resource used to produce CD-Rs rises
- The price of a substitute in production rises
- The price of a complement in production falls
- The price of a CD-R is expected to rise in the future
- The number of CD-R producers decreases

Increases if:
- The price of a resource used to produce CD-Rs falls
- The price of a substitute in production falls
- The price of a complement in production rises
- The price of a CD-R is expected to fall in the future
- The number of CD-R producers increases
- More efficient technologies for producing CD-Rs are discovered

FIGURE 3.6   A Change in the Quantity Supplied Versus a Change in Supply

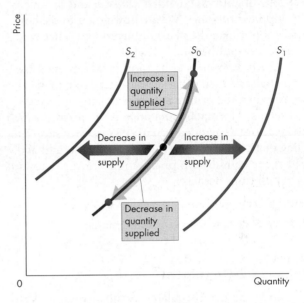

When the price of the good changes, there is a movement along the supply curve and *a change in the quantity supplied*, shown by the blue arrows on supply curve S_0. When any other influence on selling plans changes, there is a shift of the supply curve and a *change in supply*. An increase in supply shifts the supply curve rightward (from S_0 to S_1), and a decrease in supply shifts the supply curve leftward (from S_0 to S_2).

REVIEW QUIZ

1 Define the quantity supplied of a good or service.
2 What is the law of supply and how do we illustrate it?
3 What does the supply curve tell us about the price at which firms will supply a given quantity of a good?
4 List all the influences on selling plans, and for each influence say whether it changes supply.
5 What happens to the quantity of Palm Pilots supplied and the supply of Palm Pilots if the price of a Palm Pilot falls?

Your next task is to use what you've learned about demand and supply and learn how prices and quantities are determined.

Market Equilibrium

W̲E̲ ̲H̲A̲V̲E̲ ̲S̲E̲E̲N̲ ̲T̲H̲A̲T̲ ̲W̲H̲E̲N̲ ̲T̲H̲E̲ ̲P̲R̲I̲C̲E̲ ̲O̲F̲ ̲A̲ ̲G̲O̲O̲D̲ rises, the quantity demanded *decreases* and the quantity supplied *increases*. We are now going to see how prices coordinate the plans of buyers and sellers and achieve an equilibrium.

An *equilibrium* is a situation in which opposing forces balance each other. Equilibrium in a market occurs when the price balances the plans of buyers and sellers. The **equilibrium price** is the price at which the quantity demanded equals the quantity supplied. The **equilibrium quantity** is the quantity bought and sold at the equilibrium price. A market moves toward its equilibrium because

- Price regulates buying and selling plans.
- Price adjusts when plans don't match.

Price as a Regulator

The price of a good regulates the quantities demanded and supplied. If the price is too high, the quantity supplied exceeds the quantity demanded. If the price is too low, the quantity demanded exceeds the quantity supplied. There is one price at which the quantity demanded equals the quantity supplied. Let's work out what that price is.

Figure 3.7 shows the market for CD-Rs. The table shows the demand schedule (from Fig. 3.1) and the supply schedule (from Fig. 3.4). If the price of a disc is 50¢, the quantity demanded is 9 million discs a week, but no discs are supplied. There is a shortage of 9 million discs a week. This shortage is shown in the final column of the table. At a price of $1.00 a disc, there is still a shortage, but only of 3 million discs a week. If the price of a disc is $2.50, the quantity supplied is 6 million discs a week, but the quantity demanded is only 2 million. There is a surplus of 4 million discs a week. The one price at which there is neither a shortage nor a surplus is $1.50 a disc. At that price, the quantity demanded is equal to the quantity supplied: 4 million discs a week. The equilibrium price is $1.50 a disc, and the equilibrium quantity is 4 million discs a week.

Figure 3.7 shows that the demand curve and the supply curve intersect at the equilibrium price of $1.50 a disc. At each price *above* $1.50 a disc, there is a surplus of discs. For example, at $2.00 a disc, the surplus

FIGURE 3.7   Equilibrium

Price (dollars per disc)	Quantity demanded	Quantity supplied	Shortage (–) or surplus (+)
	(millions of discs per week)		
0.50	9	0	–9
1.00	6	3	–3
1.50	**4**	**4**	**0**
2.00	3	5	+2
2.50	2	6	+4

The table lists the quantities demanded and quantities supplied as well as the shortage or surplus of discs at each price. If the price is $1.00 a disc, 6 million discs a week are demanded and 3 million are supplied. There is a shortage of 3 million discs a week, and the price rises. If the price is $2.00 a disc, 3 million discs a week are demanded and 5 million are supplied. There is a surplus of 2 million discs a week, and the price falls. If the price is $1.50 a disc, 4 million discs a week are demanded and 4 million are supplied. There is neither a shortage nor a surplus. Neither buyers nor sellers have any incentive to change the price. The price at which the quantity demanded equals the quantity supplied is the equilibrium price.

is 2 million discs a week, as shown by the blue arrow. At each price *below* $1.50 a disc, there is a shortage of discs. For example, at $1.00 a disc, the shortage is 3 million discs a week, as shown by the red arrow.

Price Adjustments

You've seen that if the price is below equilibrium, there is a shortage and that if the price is above equilibrium, there is a surplus. But can we count on the price to change and eliminate a shortage or surplus? We can, because such price changes are beneficial to both buyers and sellers. Let's see why the price changes when there is a shortage or a surplus.

A Shortage Forces the Price Up   Suppose the price of a CD-R is $1. Consumers plan to buy 6 million discs a week, and producers plan to sell 3 million discs a week. Consumers can't force producers to sell more than they plan, so the quantity that is actually offered for sale is 3 million discs a week. In this situation, powerful forces operate to increase the price and move it toward the equilibrium price. Some producers, noticing lines of unsatisfied consumers, raise the price. Some producers increase their output. As producers push the price up, the price rises toward its equilibrium. The rising price reduces the shortage because it decreases the quantity demanded and increases the quantity supplied. When the price has increased to the point at which there is no longer a shortage, the forces moving the price stop operating and the price comes to rest at its equilibrium.

A Surplus Forces the Price Down   Suppose the price of a CD-R is $2. Producers plan to sell 5 million discs a week, and consumers plan to buy 3 million discs a week. Producers cannot force consumers to buy more than they plan, so the quantity that is actually bought is 3 million discs a week. In this situation, powerful forces operate to lower the price and move it toward the equilibrium price. Some producers, unable to sell the quantities of CD-Rs they planned to sell, cut their prices. In addition, some producers scale back production. As producers cut the price, the price falls toward its equilibrium. The falling price decreases the surplus because it increases the quantity demanded and decreases the quantity supplied. When the price has fallen to the point at which there is no longer a surplus, the forces moving the price stop operating and the price comes to rest at its equilibrium.

The Best Deal Available for Buyers and Sellers
When the price is below equilibrium, it is forced up toward the equilibrium. Why don't buyers resist the increase and refuse to buy at the higher price? Because they value the good more highly than the current price and they cannot satisfy all their demands at the current price. In some markets — an example is the market for rental accommodations in Salt Lake City during the 2002 Winter Olympic Games — the buyers might even be the ones who force the price up by offering to pay higher prices.

When the price is above equilibrium, it is bid down toward the equilibrium. Why don't sellers resist this decrease and refuse to sell at the lower price? Because their minimum supply price is below the current price and they cannot sell all they would like to at the current price. Normally, it is the sellers who force the price down by offering lower prices to gain market share from their competitors.

At the price at which the quantity demanded and the quantity supplied are equal, neither buyers nor sellers can do business at a better price. Buyers pay the highest price they are willing to pay for the last unit bought, and sellers receive the lowest price at which they are willing to supply the last unit sold.

When people freely make offers to buy and sell and when demanders try to buy at the lowest possible price and suppliers try to sell at the highest possible price, the price at which trade takes place is the equilibrium price — the price at which the quantity demanded equals the quantity supplied. The price coordinates the plans of buyers and sellers.

REVIEW QUIZ

1 What is the equilibrium price of a good or service?
2 Over what range of prices does a shortage arise?
3 Over what range of prices does a surplus arise?
4 What happens to the price when there is a shortage?
5 What happens to the price when there is a surplus?
6 Why is the price at which the quantity demanded equals the quantity supplied the equilibrium price?
7 Why is the equilibrium price the best deal available for both buyers and sellers?

Predicting Changes in Price and Quantity

THE DEMAND AND SUPPLY THEORY THAT WE HAVE just studied provides us with a powerful way of analyzing influences on prices and the quantities bought and sold. According to the theory, a change in price stems from a change in demand, a change in supply, or a change in both demand and supply. Let's look first at the effects of a change in demand.

A Change in Demand

What happens to the price and quantity of CD-Rs if the demand for CD-Rs increases? We can answer this question with a specific example. Between 1998 and 2001, the price of a CD burner fell from $300 to $100. Because the CD burner and CD-R discs are complements, the demand for discs increased, as is shown in the table in Fig. 3.8. The original demand schedule and the new one are set out in the first three columns of the table. The table also shows the supply schedule for CD-Rs.

The original equilibrium price is $1.50 a disc. At that price, 4 million discs a week are demanded and supplied. When demand increases, the price that makes the quantity demanded equal the quantity supplied is $2.50 a disc. At this price, 6 million discs are bought and sold each week. When demand increases, both the price and the quantity increase.

Figure 3.8 shows these changes. The figure shows the original demand for and supply of CD-Rs. The original equilibrium price is $1.50 a CD-R, and the quantity is 4 million CD-Rs a week. When demand increases, the demand curve shifts rightward. The equilibrium price rises to $2.50 a CD-R, and the quantity supplied 69increases to 6 million CD-Rs a week, as highlighted in the figure. There is an *increase in the quantity supplied* but *no change in supply* — a movement along, but no shift of, the supply curve.

We can reverse this change in demand. Start at a price of $2.50 a disc with 6 million CD-Rs a week being bought and sold, and then work out what happens if demand decreases to its original level. Such a decrease in demand might arise from a fall in the price of an MP3 player (a substitute for CD-R technology). The decrease in demand shifts the demand curve leftward. The equilibrium price falls to $1.50 a disc, and the equilibrium quantity decreases to 4 million discs a week.

FIGURE 3.8   The Effects of a Change in Demand

Price (dollars per disc)	Quantity demanded (millions of discs per week)		Quantity supplied (millions of discs per week)
	CD burner $300	CD burner $100	
0.50	9	13	0
1.00	6	10	3
1.50	**4**	8	**4**
2.00	3	7	5
2.50	2	**6**	**6**

With the price of a CD burner at $300, the demand for CD-Rs is the blue demand curve. The equilibrium price is $1.50 a disc, and the equilibrium quantity is 4 million discs a week. When the price of a CD burner falls from $300 to $100, the demand for CD-Rs increases and the demand curve shifts rightward to become the red curve.

At $1.50 a disc, there is now a shortage of 4 million discs a week. The price of a disc rises to a new equilibrium of $2.50. As the price rises to $2.50, the quantity supplied increases — shown by the blue arrow on the supply curve — to the new equilibrium quantity of 6 million discs a week. Following an increase in demand, the quantity supplied increases but supply does not change — the supply curve does not shift.

We can now make our first two predictions:

1. When demand increases, both the price and the quantity increase.
2. When demand decreases, both the price and the quantity decrease.

A Change in Supply

When Imation and other producers introduce new cost-saving technologies in their CD-R production plants, the supply of CD-Rs increases. The new supply schedule (the same one that was shown in Fig. 3.5) is presented in the table in Fig. 3.9. What are the new equilibrium price and quantity? The answer is highlighted in the table: The price falls to $1.00 a disc, and the quantity increases to 6 million a week. You can see why by looking at the quantities demanded and supplied at the old price of $1.50 a disc. The quantity supplied at that price is 8 million discs a week, and there is a surplus of discs. The price falls. Only when the price is $1.00 a disc does the quantity supplied equal the quantity demanded.

Figure 3.9 illustrates the effect of an increase in supply. It shows the demand curve for CD-Rs and the original and new supply curves. The initial equilibrium price is $1.50 a disc, and the quantity is 4 million discs a week. When the supply increases, the supply curve shifts rightward. The equilibrium price falls to $1.00 a disc, and the quantity demanded increases to 6 million discs a week, highlighted in the figure. There is an *increase in the quantity demanded* but *no change in demand* — a movement along, but no shift of, the demand curve.

We can reverse this change in supply. If we start out at a price of $1.00 a disc with 6 million discs a week being bought and sold, we can work out what happens if supply decreases to its original level. Such a decrease in supply might arise from an increase in the cost of labor or raw materials. The decrease in supply shifts the supply curve leftward. The equilibrium price rises to $1.50 a disc, and the equilibrium quantity decreases to 4 million discs a week.

We can now make two more predictions:

1. When supply increases, the quantity increases and the price falls.
2. When supply decreases, the quantity decreases and the price rises.

FIGURE 3.9   The Effects of a Change in Supply

Price (dollars per disc)	Quantity demanded (millions of discs per week)	Quantity supplied (millions of discs per week)	
		Old technology	New technology
0.50	9	0	3
1.00	**6**	3	**6**
1.50	**4**	4	8
2.00	3	5	10
2.50	2	6	12

With the old technology, the supply of CD-Rs is shown by the blue supply curve. The equilibrium price is $1.50 a disc, and the equilibrium quantity is 4 million discs a week. When the new technology is adopted, the supply of CD-Rs increases and the supply curve shifts rightward to become the red curve.

At $1.50 a disc, there is now a surplus of 4 million discs a week. The price of a CD-R falls to a new equilibrium of $1.00 a disc. As the price falls to $1.00, the quantity demanded increases — shown by the blue arrow on the demand curve — to the new equilibrium quantity of 6 million discs a week. Following an increase in supply, the quantity demanded increases but demand does not change — the demand curve does not shift.

A Change in Both Demand and Supply

You can now predict the effects of a change in either demand or supply on the price and the quantity. But what happens if *both* demand and supply change together? To answer this question, we look first at the case in which demand and supply move in the same direction — either both increase or both decrease. Then we look at the case in which they move in opposite directions — demand decreases and supply increases or demand increases and supply decreases.

Demand and Supply Change in the Same Direction We've seen that an increase in the demand for CD-Rs raises its price and increases the quantity bought and sold. And we've seen that an increase in the supply of CD-Rs lowers its price and increases the quantity bought and sold. Let's now examine what happens when both of these changes occur together.

The table in Fig. 3.10 brings together the numbers that describe the original quantities demanded and supplied and the new quantities demanded and supplied after the fall in the price of the CD burner and the improved CD-R production technology. These same numbers are illustrated in the graph. The original (blue) demand and supply curves intersect at a price of $1.50 a disc and a quantity of 4 million discs a week. The new (red) supply and demand curves also intersect at a price of $1.50 a disc but at a quantity of 8 million discs a week.

An increase in either demand or supply increases the quantity. So when both demand and supply increase, so does the quantity.

An increase in demand raises the price, and an increase in supply lowers the price, so we can't say whether the price will rise or fall when demand and supply increase together. In this example, the price does not change. But notice that if demand increases by slightly more than the amount shown in the figure, the price will rise. And if supply increases by slightly more than the amount shown in the figure, the price will fall.

We can now make two more predictions:

1. When *both* demand and supply increase, the quantity increases and the price might increase, decrease, or remain the same.
2. When *both* demand and supply decrease, the quantity decreases and the price might increase, decrease, or remain the same.

FIGURE 3.10   The Effects of an Increase in Both Demand and Supply

Price (dollars per disc)	Original quantities (millions of discs per week)		New quantities (millions of discs per week)	
	Quantity demanded CD burner $300	Quantity supplied old technology	Quantity demanded CD burner $100	Quantity supplied new technology
0.50	9	0	13	3
1.00	6	3	10	6
1.50	4	4	8	8
2.00	3	5	7	10
2.50	2	6	6	12

When a CD burner costs $300 and firms use the old technology to produce discs, the price of a disc is $1.50 and the quantity is 4 million discs a week. A fall in the price of the CD burner increases the demand for CD-Rs, and improved technology increases the supply of CD-Rs. The new supply curve intersects the new demand curve at $1.50 a disc, the same price as before, but the quantity increases to 8 million discs a week. These increases in demand and supply increase the quantity but leave the price unchanged.

Demand and Supply Change in Opposite Directions Let's now see what happens when demand and supply change together in *opposite* directions. A new production technology increases the supply of CD-Rs as before. But now the price of an MP3 download rises. An MP3 download is a *complement* of a CD-R. With more costly MP3 downloads, some people switch from buying CD-Rs to buying prerecorded CDs. The demand for CD-Rs decreases.

The table in Fig. 3.11 describes the original and new demand and supply schedules and the original (blue) and new (red) demand and supply curves. The original equilibrium price is $2.50 a disc, and the quantity is 6 million discs a week. The new supply and demand curves intersect at a price of $1.00 a disc and at the original quantity of 6 million discs a week.

A decrease in demand or an increase in supply lowers the price. So when a decrease in demand and an increase in supply occur together, the price falls.

A decrease in demand decreases the quantity, and an increase in supply increases the quantity, so we can't say for sure which way the quantity will change when demand decreases and supply increases at the same time. In this example, the quantity doesn't change. But notice that if demand had decreased by slightly more than is shown in the figure, the quantity would have decreased. And if supply had increased by slightly more than is shown in the figure, the quantity would have increased. So

1. When demand decreases and supply increases, the price falls and the quantity might increase, decrease, or remain the same.

2. When demand increases and supply decreases, the price rises and the quantity might increase, decrease, or remain the same.

REVIEW QUIZ

1 What is the effect on the price of a CD-R and the quantity of CD-Rs if (a) the price of a PC falls or (b) the price of an MP3 download rises or (c) more firms produce CD-Rs or (d) CD-R producers' wages rise or (e) any two of these events occur together? (Draw the diagrams!)

◆ To complete your study of demand and supply, take a look at *Reading Between the Lines* on pp. 74–75, which answers the question that we posed at the start of the chapter about falling PC prices.

FIGURE 3.11 The Effects of a Decrease in Demand and an Increase in Supply

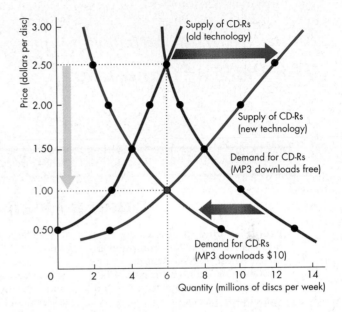

	Original quantities (millions of CD-Rs per week)		New quantities (millions of CD-Rs per week)	
Price (dollars per disc)	Quantity demanded MP3 download free	Quantity supplied old technology	Quantity demanded MP3 download $10	Quantity supplied new technology
0.50	13	0	9	3
1.00	10	3	6	6
1.50	8	4	4	8
2.00	7	5	3	10
2.50	6	6	2	12

When MP3 downloads are free and firms use the old technology to produce discs, the price of a CD-R is $2.50 and the quantity is 6 million discs a week. A rise in the price of an MP3 download decreases the demand for CD-Rs, and improved technology increases the supply of CD-Rs. The new equilibrium price is $1.00 a disc, a lower price, but in this case the quantity remains constant at 6 million discs a week. This decrease in demand and increase in supply lower the price but leave the quantity unchanged.

Demand and Supply:
The Price of Computers

THE BUFFALO NEWS, SEPTEMBER 1, 2001

Such a Deal!

People looking to buy a new computer are in luck: The computer industry's first-ever sales slump means retailers and manufacturers are taking drastic measures to offer consumers low prices.

How low?

These computers are so cheap, it megahertz.

Try a $900, $700 or even $400 personal computer package, depending on make and model. Laptops are selling for as little as $1,200. ...

Computer prices have been falling for years as manufacturers introduced mass production. Now they are finding that most people looking to buy a computer for their home already have one. ...

But there are consumers who always want the latest upgrade. "It's become about keeping up with the Joneses, ..." said Frank Bocchino, director of marketing at Beanstalk Networks, a Florida-based software service company.

Mike Budzich of Lancaster is one consumer who already has a second home computer.

"I bought a Dell this January," he said.

... Consumers like Budzich, who are already glutted at home, are why some predict prices will drop even lower to move merchandise.

Jennifer Read, 18, of Buffalo, is headed to college next week without a computer.

"I'm waiting to see if prices go down even more," she said.

Read said she wants to "see if I'll really need one," because of the proliferation of computing centers on campuses. ...

Computer prices are also being slashed to make way for new machines that are hitting stores next week. Top-of-the-line models will have Intel's new 2-gigahertz microprocessor, yet will be priced lower than what had been top-of-the-line a year ago. ...

"Every time new technology is introduced, other models instantly become older, and the price goes down," Bocchino said, referring to the new Intel technology. ...

The Buffalo News, 2001.

Essence of the Story

■ Mass production of computers leads to falling computer prices.

■ Most consumers looking for a computer already own one.

■ Top-of-the-line computers with the new Intel 2-gigahertz microprocessor are priced lower than the top-of-the line computers were a year ago.

■ Because buyers expect prices to keep falling, some people hold off buying.

■ When new technology is introduced, the price of older models falls.

Economic Analysis

■ Figure 1 shows how the market for personal computers evolved between 1982 and 1997.

■ In 1982, the demand curve was D_{82} and the supply curve was S_{82}. The equilibrium quantity was 14 million PCs, and the equilibrium price (an index number) was 100.

■ Between 1982 and 1997, advances in PC technology and in PC production technology increased the supply of PCs and the supply curve shifted rightward to S_{97}.

■ The demand for PCs also increased, and the demand curve shifted rightward to D_{97}.

■ In 1997, the equilibrium quantity of PCs was 300 million and the equilibrium price (index number) was 4.4, which means that the price of a PC in 1997 was 4.4 percent of the 1982 price.

■ The price of a PC fell because the supply of PCs increased by more than the demand for PCs increased.

■ Figure 2(a) shows the market for old technology PCs in 2001. The supply curve was S, and the demand curve at the beginning of 2001 was D_0. The price of a PC at the beginning of 2001 was $3,000.

■ Figure 2(b) shows the market for new technology (2-gigahertz) PCs in 2001. The demand curve

was D, and the supply curve at the beginning of 2001 was S_0. None of these PCs were available at the beginning of 2001.

■ During 2001, technology advanced and the supply curve of new technology PCs increased to S_1. The price of a new technology PC fell to $1,700.

■ During 2001, the fall in the price of the new technology PC decreased the demand for the old technology PC (a substitute). The demand curve for an old new technology PC shifted leftward to D_1 in Fig. 2(a), and the price fell to $700.

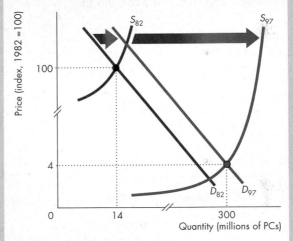

Figure 1 The PC market in 1982

(a) Old technology PC

Figure 2 The PC market in 2001

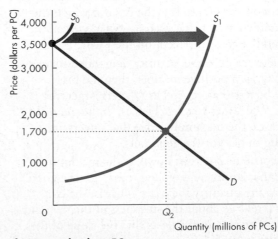

(b) New technology PC

75

Mathematical Note
Demand, Supply, and Equilibrium

Demand Curve

The law of demand says that as the price of a good or service falls, the quantity demanded of that good or service increases. We illustrate the law of demand by setting out a demand schedule, by drawing a graph of the demand curve, or by writing down an equation. When the demand curve is a straight line, the following linear equation describes it:

$$P = a - bQ_D,$$

where P is the price and Q_D is the quantity demanded. The a and b are positive constants.

This equation tells us three things:

1. The price at which no one is willing to buy the good (Q_D is zero). That is, if the price is a, then the quantity demanded is zero. You can see the price a on the graph. It is the price at which the demand curve hits the y-axis — what we call the demand curve's "intercept on the y-axis."

2. As the price falls, the quantity demanded increases. If Q_D is a positive number, then the price P must be less than a. And as Q_D gets larger, the price P becomes smaller. That is, as the quantity increases, the maximum price that buyers are willing to pay for the good falls.

3. The constant b tells us how fast the maximum price that someone is willing to pay for the good falls as the quantity increases. That is, the constant b tells us about the steepness of the demand curve. The equation tells us that the slope of the demand curve is $-b$.

Supply Curve

The law of supply says that as the price of a good or service rises, the quantity supplied of that good increases. We illustrate the law of supply by setting out a supply schedule, by drawing a graph of the supply curve, or by writing down an equation. When the supply curve is a straight line, the following linear equation describes it:

$$P = c + dQ_S,$$

where P is the price and Q_S is the quantity supplied. The c and d are positive constants.

This equation tells us three things:

1. The price at which sellers are not willing to supply the good (Q_S is zero). That is, if the price is c, then no one is willing to sell the good. You can see the price c on the graph. It is the price at which the supply curve hits the y-axis — what we call the supply curve's "intercept on the y-axis."

2. As the price rises, the quantity supplied increases. If Q_S is a positive number, then the price P must be greater than c. And as Q_S increases, the price P get larger. That is, as the quantity increases, the minimum price that sellers are willing to accept rises.

3. The constant d tells us how fast the minimum price at which someone is willing to sell the good rises as the quantity increases. That is, the constant d tells us about the steepness of the supply curve. The equation tells us that the slope of the supply curve is d.

Market Equilibrium

Demand and supply determine market equilibrium. The figure shows the equilibrium price (P^*) and equilibrium quantity (Q^*) at the intersection of the demand curve and the supply curve.

We can use the equations to find the equilibrium price and equilibrium quantity. The price of a good adjusts until the quantity demanded equals the quantity supplied. That is,

$$Q_D = Q_S.$$

So at the equilibrium price (P^*) and equilibrium quantity (Q^*),

$$Q_D = Q_S = Q^*.$$

To find the equilibrium price and equilibrium quantity, substitute Q^* for Q_D in the demand equation and Q^* for Q_S in the supply equation. Then the price is the equilibrium price (P^*), which gives

$$P^* = a - bQ^*$$
$$P^* = c + dQ^*.$$

Notice that

$$a - bQ^* = c + dQ^*.$$

Now solve for Q^*:

$$a - c = bQ^* + dQ^*$$
$$a - c = (b + d)Q^*$$
$$Q^* = \frac{a - c}{b + d}.$$

To find the equilibrium price, (P^*), substitute for Q^* in either the demand equation or the supply equation.

Using the demand equation, we have

$$P^* = a - b\left(\frac{a - c}{b + d}\right)$$

$$P^* = \frac{a(b + d) - b(a - c)}{b + d}$$

$$P^* = \frac{ad + bc}{b + d}.$$

Alternatively, using the supply equation, we have

$$P^* = c + d\left(\frac{a - c}{b + d}\right)$$

$$P^* = \frac{c(b + d) + d(a - c)}{b + d}$$

$$P^* = \frac{ad + bc}{b + d}.$$

An Example

The demand for ice-cream cones is

$$P = 800 - 2Q_D.$$

The supply of ice-cream cones is

$$P = 200 + 1Q_S.$$

The price of a cone is expressed in cents, and the quantities are expressed in cones per day.

To find the equilibrium price (P^*) and equilibrium quantity (Q^*), substitute Q^* for Q_D and Q_S and P^* for P. That is,

$$P^* = 800 - 2Q^*$$
$$P^* = 200 + 1Q^*.$$

Now solve for Q^*:

$$800 - 2Q^* = 200 + 1Q^*$$
$$600 = 3Q^*$$
$$Q^* = 200.$$

And

$$P^* = 800 - 2(200)$$
$$= 400.$$

The equilibrium price is $4 a cone, and the equilibrium quantity is 200 cones per day.

SUMMARY

KEY POINTS

Markets and Prices (p. 58)

- A competitive market is one that has so many buyers and sellers that no one can influence the price.
- Opportunity cost is a relative price.
- Demand and supply determine relative prices.

Demand (pp. 59–63)

- Demand is the relationship between the quantity demanded of a good and its price when all other influences on buying plans remain the same.
- The higher the price of a good, other things remaining the same, the smaller is the quantity demanded — the law of demand.
- Demand depends on the prices of substitutes and complements, expected future prices, income, population, and preferences.

Supply (pp. 64–67)

- Supply is the relationship between the quantity supplied of a good and its price when all other influences on selling plans remain the same.
- The higher the price of a good, other things remaining the same, the greater is the quantity supplied — the law of supply.
- Supply depends on the prices of resources used to produce a good, the prices of related goods produced, expected future prices, the number of suppliers, and technology.

Market Equilibrium (pp. 68–69)

- At the equilibrium price, the quantity demanded equals the quantity supplied.
- At prices above equilibrium, there is a surplus and the price falls.
- At prices below equilibrium, there is a shortage and the price rises.

Predicting Changes in Price and Quantity (pp. 70–73)

- An increase in demand brings a rise in price and an increase in the quantity supplied. (A decrease in demand brings a fall in price and a decrease in the quantity supplied.)

- An increase in supply brings a fall in price and an increase in the quantity demanded. (A decrease in supply brings a rise in price and a decrease in the quantity demanded.)
- An increase in demand and an increase in supply bring an increased quantity, but the price might rise, fall, or remain the same. An increase in demand and a decrease in supply bring a higher price, but the quantity might increase, decrease, or remain the same.

KEY FIGURES

KEY TERMS

PROBLEMS

*1. What is the effect on the price of an audiotape and the quantity of audiotapes sold if:
  a. The price of a CD rises?
  b. The price of a Walkman rises?
  c. The supply of CD players increases?
  d. Consumers' incomes increase?
  e. Workers who make audiotapes get a pay raise?
  f. The price of a Walkman rises at the same time as the workers who make audiotapes get a pay raise?

2. What is the effect on the price of a DVD player and the quantity of DVD players sold if:
  a. The price of a DVD rises?
  b. The price of a DVD falls?
  c. The supply of DVD players increases?
  d. Consumers' incomes decrease?
  e. The wage rate of workers who produce DVD players increases?
  f. The wage rate of workers who produce DVD players rises and at the same time the price of a DVD falls?

*3. Suppose that the following events occur one at a time:
  (i)   The price of crude oil rises.
  (ii) The price of a car rises.
  (iii) All speed limits on highways are abolished.
  (iv) Robot technology cuts car production costs.

  Which of these events will increase or decrease (state which):

  a. The demand for gasoline?
  b. The supply of gasoline?
  c. The quantity of gasoline demanded?
  d. The quantity of gasoline supplied?

4. Suppose that the following events occur one at a time:
  (i)   The price of airfares halve.
  (ii) The price of beef falls.
  (iii) A cheap new strong cloth, a close substitute for leather, is invented.
  (iv) A new high-speed technology for cutting leather is invented.

  Which of these events will increase or decrease (state which):

  a. The demand for leather bags?
  b. The supply of leather bags?
  c. The quantity of leather bags demanded?
  d. The quantity of leather bags supplied?

*5. The figure illustrates the market for pizza.
  a. Label the curves in the figure.
  b. What are the equilibrium price of a pizza and the equilibrium quantity of pizza?

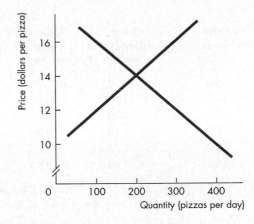

6. The figure illustrates the market for fish.
  a. Label the curves in the figure.
  b. What are the equilibrium price of a fish and the equilibrium quantity of fish?

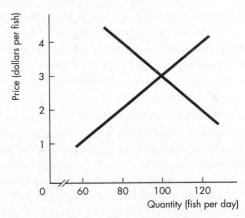

*7. The demand and supply schedules for gum are:

Price (cents per pack)	Quantity demanded	Quantity supplied
	(millions of packs a week)	
20	180	60
30	160	80
40	140	100
50	120	120
60	100	140
70	80	160
80	60	180

  a. Draw a graph of the gum market and mark in the equilibrium price and quantity.

b. Suppose that gum is 70 cents a pack. Describe the situation in the gum market and explain how the price of gum adjusts.

8. The demand and supply schedules for potato chips are

Price (cents per bag)	Quantity demanded	Quantity supplied
	(millions of bags per week)	
50	160	130
60	150	140
70	140	150
80	130	160
90	120	170
100	110	180

a. Draw a graph of the potato chip market and mark in the equilibrium price and quantity.

b. Suppose that chips are 60 cents a bag. Describe the situation in the market for chips and explain how the price adjusts.

*9. In problem 7, suppose that a fire destroys some gum-producing factories and the supply of gum decreases by 40 million packs a week.

a. Has there been a shift of or a movement along the supply curve of gum?

b. Has there been a shift of or a movement along the demand curve for gum?

c. What are the new equilibrium price and equilibrium quantity of gum?

10. In problem 8, suppose a new dip comes onto the market, which is very popular and the demand for potato chips increases by 30 million bags per week.

a. Has there been a shift of or a movement along the supply curve of potato chips?

b. Has there been a shift of or a movement along the demand curve for potato chips?

c. What are the new equilibrium price and equilibrium quantity of potato chips?

*11. In problem 9, suppose an increase in the teenage population increases the demand for gum by 40 million packs per week at the same time as the fire occurs. What are the new equilibrium price and quantity of gum?

12. In problem 10, suppose that a virus destroys several potato farms with the result that the supply of potato chips decreases by 40 million bags a week at the same time as the dip comes onto the market. What are the new equilibrium price and quantity of potato chips?

CRITICAL THINKING

1. After you have studied *Reading Between the Lines* on pp. 74–75, answer the following questions:

a. Why did the supply of PCs increase by more than the demand for PCs increased during the 1980s and 1990s?

b. Why did the introduction of the Intel 2-gigahertz processor decrease the demand for slower PCs?

c. How do you think the development of CD-R technology changed the demand for PCs? What was the effect on the equilibrium price of a PC?

WEB EXERCISES

1. Use the links on the Parkin Web site and obtain data on the prices and quantities of wheat.

a. Make a figure similar to Fig. 3.7 on p. 68 to illustrate the market for wheat in 1999 and 2000.

b. Show the changes in demand and supply and the changes in the quantity demanded and the quantity supplied that are consistent with the price and quantity data.

2. Use the link on the Parkin Web site and obtain data on the price of oil.

a. Describe how the price of oil has changed over the past five years.

b. Draw a demand-supply diagram to explain what happens to the price when there is an increase or a decrease in supply and no change in demand.

c. What do you predict would happen to the price of oil if a new drilling technology permitted deeper ocean sources to be used?

d. What do you predict would happen to the price of oil if a clean and safe nuclear technology were developed?

e. What do you predict would happen to the price of oil if automobiles were powered by batteries instead of by internal combustion engines?

ELASTICITY ——— CHAPTER 4

Predicting Prices

The Organization of Oil Exporting Countries (OPEC) is a big enough player in the global oil market to influence the price of oil. To raise the price, OPEC must cut production. If it does so, by how much will the price rise? Will non-OPEC producers also cut production? Or will they produce more to take advantage of the higher price achieved by OPEC's actions? To answer questions like these, we need to know the quantitative relationship between price and the quantities demanded and supplied. ◆ All firms are interested in the factors that influence prices and in predicting prices. A pizza producer wants to know if the arrival of a new competitor will lower the price of pizza, whether as people's incomes rise they will spend more or less on pizza. A labor union wants to know whether, if it goes for a large wage rise the number of people employed will fall by a lot or a little.

◆ In this chapter, you will learn about a tool that helps us to answer questions like the ones we've just considered. You will learn about the elasticity of demand and supply. At the end of the chapter, we'll return to the questions that the OPEC needs to answer and see how the concept of elasticity helps us to understand the effects of OPEC's actions on the price of crude oil, a price that has a big impact on the price that you end up paying for gasoline.

After studying this chapter, you will be able to

■ Define, calculate, and explain the factors that influence the price elasticity of demand

■ Define, calculate, and explain the factors that influence the cross elasticity of demand and the income elasticity of demand

■ Define, calculate, and explain the factors that influence the elasticity of supply

Price Elasticity of Demand

YOU KNOW THAT WHEN SUPPLY INCREASES, THE equilibrium price falls and the equilibrium quantity increases. But does the price fall by a large amount and the quantity increase by a little? Or does the price barely fall and the quantity increase by a large amount?

The answer depends on the responsiveness of the quantity demanded to a change in price. You can see why by studying Fig. 4.1, which shows two possible scenarios in a local pizza market. Figure 4.1(a) shows one scenario, and Fig. 4.1(b) shows the other.

In both cases, supply is initially S_0. In part (a), the demand for pizza is shown by the demand curve D_A. In part (b), the demand for pizza is shown by the demand curve D_B. Initially, in both cases, the price is $20 a pizza and the quantity of pizza produced and consumed is 10 pizzas an hour.

Now a large pizza franchise opens up, and the supply of pizza increases. The supply curve shifts rightward to S_1. In case (a), the price falls by an enormous $15 to $5 a pizza, and the quantity increases by only 3 to 13 pizzas an hour. In contrast, in case (b), the price falls by only $5 to $15 a pizza and the quantity increases by 7 to 17 pizzas an hour.

The different outcomes arise from differing degrees of responsiveness of the quantity demanded to a change in price. But what do we mean by responsiveness? One possible answer is slope. The slope of demand curve D_A is steeper than the slope of demand curve D_B.

In this example, we can compare the slopes of the two demand curves. But we can't always do so. The reason is that the slope of a demand curve depends on the units in which we measure the price and quantity. And we often must compare the demand curves for different goods and services that are measured in unrelated units. For example, a pizza producer might want to compare the demand for pizza with the demand for soft drinks. Which quantity demanded is more responsive to a price change? This question can't be answered by comparing the slopes of two demand curves. The units of measurement of pizza and soft drinks are unrelated. The question can be answered with a measure of responsiveness that is independent of units of measurement. Elasticity is such a measure.

The **price elasticity of demand** is a units-free measure of the responsiveness of the quantity demanded of a good to a change in its price when all other influences on buyers' plans remain the same.

FIGURE 4.1   How a Change in Supply Changes Price and Quantity

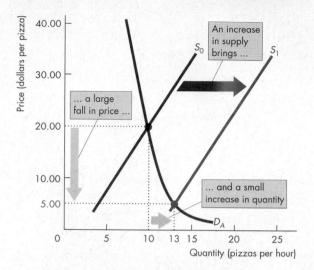

(a) Large price change and small quantity change

(b) Small price change and large quantity change

Initially the price is $20 a pizza and the quantity sold is 10 pizzas an hour. Then supply increases from S_0 to S_1. In part (a), the price falls by $15 to $5 a pizza, and the quantity increases by only 3 to 13 pizzas an hour. In part (b), the price falls by only $5 to $15 a pizza, and the quantity increases by 7 to 17 pizzas an hour. This price change is smaller and the quantity change is larger than in case (a). The quantity demanded is more responsive to price in case (b) than in case (a).

Calculating Elasticity

We calculate the *price elasticity of demand* by using the formula:

$$\text{Price elasticity of demand} = \frac{\text{Percentage change in quantity demanded}}{\text{Percentage change in price}}.$$

To use this formula, we need to know the quantities demanded at different prices when all other influences on buyers' plans remain the same. Suppose we have the data on prices and quantities demanded of pizza and we calculate the price elasticity of demand for pizza.

Figure 4.2 zooms in on the demand curve for pizza and shows how the quantity demanded responds to a small change in price. Initially, the price is $20.50 a pizza and 9 pizzas an hour are sold — the original point in the figure. The price then falls to $19.50 a pizza, and the quantity demanded increases to 11 pizzas an hour — the new point in the figure. When the price falls by $1 a pizza, the quantity demanded increases by 2 pizzas an hour.

To calculate the price elasticity of demand, we express the changes in price and quantity demanded as percentages of the *average price* and the *average quantity*. By using the average price and average quantity, we calculate the elasticity at a point on the demand curve midway between the original point and the new point. The original price is $20.50 and the new price is $19.50, so the average price is $20. The $1 price decrease is 5 percent of the average price. That is,

$$\Delta P/P_{ave} = (\$1/\$20) \times 100 = 5\%.$$

The original quantity demanded is 9 pizzas and the new quantity demanded is 11 pizzas, so the average quantity demanded is 10 pizzas. The 2 pizza increase in the quantity demanded is 20 percent of the average quantity. That is,

$$\Delta Q/Q_{ave} = (2/10) \times 100 = 20\%.$$

So the price elasticity of demand, which is the percentage change in the quantity demanded (20 percent) divided by the percentage change in price (5 percent) is 4. That is,

$$\text{Price elasticity of demand} = \frac{\%\Delta Q}{\%\Delta P}$$
$$= \frac{20\%}{5\%} = 4.$$

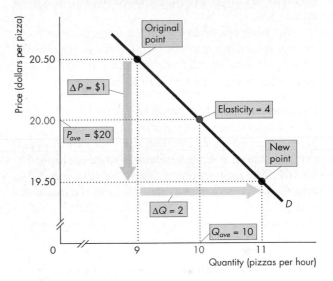

FIGURE 4.2   Calculating the Elasticity of Demand

The elasticity of demand is calculated by using the formula:*

$$\text{Price elasticity of demand} = \frac{\text{Percentage change in quantity demanded}}{\text{Percentage change in price}}$$
$$= \frac{\%\Delta Q}{\%\Delta P}$$
$$= \frac{\Delta Q/Q_{ave}}{\Delta P/P_{ave}}$$
$$= \frac{2/10}{1/20}$$
$$= 4.$$

This calculation measures the elasticity at an average price of $20 a pizza and an average quantity of 10 pizzas an hour.

* In the formula, the Greek letter delta (Δ) stands for "change in" and %Δ stands for "percentage change in."

Average Price and Quantity   Notice that we use the *average* price and *average* quantity. We do this because it gives the most precise measurement of elasticity — at the midpoint between the original price and the new price. If the price falls from $20.50 to $19.50, the $1 price change is 4.8 percent of $20.50. The 2 pizza change in quantity is 22.2 percent of 9, the original quantity. So if we use these numbers, the elasticity of demand is 22.2 divided by 4.8, which equals 4.5. If the price rises from $19.50 to $20.50, the $1 price change is 5.1 percent of $19.50. The 2 pizza change in quantity is 18.2 percent of 11, the original quantity. So if we use these numbers, the elasticity of demand is 18.2 divided by 5.1, which equals 3.6.

By using percentages of the *average* price and *average* quantity, we get the same value for the elasticity regardless of whether the price falls from $20.50 to $19.50 or rises from $19.50 to $20.50.

Percentages and Proportions Elasticity is the ratio of two percentage changes. So when we divide one percentage change by another, the 100s cancel. A percentage change is a *proportionate* change multiplied by 100. The proportionate change in price is $\Delta P/P_{ave}$, and the proportionate change in quantity demanded is $\Delta Q/Q_{ave}$. So if we divide $\Delta Q/Q_{ave}$ by $\Delta P/P_{ave}$ we get the same answer as we get by using percentage changes.

A Units-Free Measure Now that you've calculated a price elasticity of demand, you can see why it is a *units-free measure*. Elasticity is a units-free measure because the percentage change in each variable is independent of the units in which the variable is measured. And the ratio of the two percentages is a number without units.

Minus Sign and Elasticity When the price of a good *rises*, the quantity demanded *decreases* along the demand curve. Because a *positive* change in price brings a *negative* change in the quantity demanded, the price elasticity of demand is a negative number. But it is the magnitude, or *absolute value*, of the price elasticity of demand that tells us how responsive — how elastic — demand is. To compare elasticities, we use the magnitude of the price elasticity of demand and ignore the minus sign.

Inelastic and Elastic Demand

Figure 4.3 shows three demand curves that cover the entire range of possible elasticities of demand. In Fig. 4.3(a), the quantity demanded is constant regardless of the price. If the quantity demanded remains constant when the price changes, then the price elasticity of demand is zero and the good is said to have **perfectly inelastic demand**. One good that has a very low price elasticity of demand (perhaps zero over some price range) is insulin. Insulin is of such importance to some diabetics that if the price rises or falls, they do not change the quantity they buy.

If the percentage change in the quantity demanded equals the percentage change in price, then the price elasticity equals 1 and the good is said to have **unit elastic demand**. The demand in Fig. 4.3(b) is an example of unit elastic demand.

Between the cases shown in Fig. 4.3(a) and Fig. 4.3(b) is the general case in which the percentage change in the quantity demanded is less than the

FIGURE 4.3   Inelastic and Elastic Demand

(a) Perfectly inelastic demand

(b) Unit elastic demand

(c) Perfectly elastic demand

Each demand illustrated here has a constant elasticity. The demand curve in part (a) illustrates the demand for a good that has a zero elasticity of demand. The demand curve in part (b) illustrates the demand for a good with a unit elasticity of demand. And the demand curve in part (c) illustrates the demand for a good with an infinite elasticity of demand.

percentage change in price. In this case, the price elasticity of demand is between zero and 1 and the good is said to have **inelastic demand**. Food and housing are examples of goods with inelastic demand.

If the quantity demanded changes by an infinitely large percentage in response to a tiny price change, then the price elasticity of demand is infinity and the good is said to have **perfectly elastic demand**. Figure 4.3(c) shows perfectly elastic demand. An example of a good that has a very high elasticity of demand (almost infinite) is a soft drink from two campus machines located side by side. If the two machines offer the same soft drinks for the same price, some people buy from one machine and some from the other. But if one machine's price is higher than the other's, by even a small amount, no one will buy from the machine with the higher price. Soft drinks from the two machines are perfect substitutes.

Between the cases in Fig. 4.3(b) and Fig. 4.3(c) is the general case in which the percentage change in the quantity demanded exceeds the percentage change in price. In this case, the price elasticity is greater than 1 and the good is said to have **elastic demand**. Automobiles and furniture are examples of goods that have elastic demand.

Elasticity Along a Straight-Line Demand Curve

Along a straight-line demand curve, like the one shown in Fig. 4.4, the elasticity varies. At high prices and small quantities, the elasticity is large; and at low prices and large quantities, the elasticity is small. To convince yourself of this fact, calculate the elasticity at three different average prices.

First, suppose the price falls from $25 to $15 a pizza. The quantity demanded increases from zero to 20 pizzas an hour. The average price is $20, so the percentage change in price is $10 divided by $20 multiplied by 100, which equals 50. The average quantity is 10 pizzas, so the percentage change in quantity is 20 pizzas divided by 10 pizzas, multiplied by 100, which equals 200. So dividing the percentage change in the quantity demanded (200) by the percentage change in price (50), you see that the elasticity of demand at an average price of $20 is 4.

Next, suppose that the price falls from $15 to $10 a pizza. The quantity demanded increases from 20 to 30 pizzas an hour. The average price is now $12.50, so the percentage change in price is $5

divided by $12.50 multiplied by 100, which equals 40 percent. The average quantity is 25 pizzas an hour, so the percentage change in the quantity demanded is 10 pizzas divided by 25 pizzas multiplied by 100, which also equals 40 percent. So dividing the percentage change in the quantity demanded (40) by the percentage change in price (40), you see that the elasticity of demand at an average price of $12.50 is 1. The elasticity of demand is always equal to 1 at the midpoint of a straight-line demand curve.

Finally, suppose that the price falls from $10 to zero. The quantity demanded increases from 30 to 50 pizzas an hour. The average price is now $5, so the percentage change in price is $10 divided by $5 multiplied by 100, which equals 200 percent. The average quantity is 40 pizzas an hour, so the percentage change in the quantity demanded is 20 pizzas divided by 40 pizzas multiplied by 100, which also equals 50 percent. So dividing the percentage change in the quantity demanded (50) by the percentage change in price (200), you see that the elasticity of demand at an average price of $5 is ¼.

FIGURE 4.4   Elasticity Along a Straight-Line Demand Curve

On a straight-line demand curve, elasticity decreases as the price falls and the quantity demanded increases. Demand is unit elastic at the midpoint of the demand curve (elasticity is 1). Above the midpoint, demand is elastic; below the midpoint, demand is inelastic.

Total Revenue and Elasticity

The **total revenue** from the sale of a good equals the price of the good multiplied by the quantity sold. When a price changes, total revenue also changes. But a rise in price does not always increase total revenue. The change in total revenue depends on the elasticity of demand in the following way:

■ If demand is elastic, a 1 percent price cut increases the quantity sold by more than 1 percent and total revenue increases.

■ If demand is inelastic, a 1 percent price cut increases the quantity sold by less than 1 percent and total revenue decreases.

■ If demand is unit elastic, a 1 percent price cut increases the quantity sold by 1 percent and so total revenue does not change.

   Figure 4.5 shows how we can use this relationship between elasticity and total revenue to estimate elasticity using the total revenue test. The **total revenue test** is a method of estimating the price elasticity of demand by observing the change in total revenue that results from a change in the price, when all other influences on the quantity sold remain the same.

■ If a price cut increases total revenue, demand is elastic.

■ If a price cut decreases total revenue, demand is inelastic.

■ If a price cut leaves total revenue unchanged, demand is unit elastic.

   In Fig. 4.5(a), over the price range from $25 to $12.50, demand is elastic. Over the price range from $12.50 to zero, demand is inelastic. At a price of $12.50, demand is unit elastic.

   Figure 4.5(b) shows total revenue. At a price of $25, the quantity sold is zero, so total revenue is also zero. At a price of zero, the quantity demanded is 50 pizzas an hour but total revenue is again zero. A price cut in the elastic range brings an increase in total revenue — the percentage increase in the quantity demanded is greater than the percentage decrease in price. A price cut in the inelastic range brings a decrease in total revenue — the percentage increase in the quantity demanded is less than the percentage decrease in price. At unit elasticity, total revenue is at a maximum.

FIGURE 4.5 Elasticity and Total Revenue

(a) Demand

(b) Total revenue

When demand is elastic, in the price range from $25 to $12.50, a decrease in price (part a) brings an increase in total revenue (part b). When demand is inelastic, in the price range from $12.50 to zero, a decrease in price (part a) brings a decrease in total revenue (part b). When demand is unit elastic, at a price of $12.50 (part a), total revenue is at a maximum (part b).

Your Expenditure and Your Elasticity

When a price changes, the change in your expenditure on the good depends on *your* elasticity of demand.

- If your demand is elastic, a 1 percent price cut increases the quantity you buy by more than 1 percent and your expenditure on the item increases.
- If your demand is inelastic, a 1 percent price cut increases the quantity you buy by less than 1 percent and your expenditure on the item decreases.
- If your demand is unit elastic, a 1 percent price cut increases the quantity you buy by 1 percent and your expenditure on the item does not change.

So if when the price of an item falls, you spend more on it, your demand for that item is elastic; if you spend the same amount, your demand is unit elastic; and if you spend less, your demand is inelastic.

The Factors That Influence the Elasticity of Demand

Table 4.1 lists some estimates of actual elasticities in the real world. You can see that these real-world elasticities of demand range from 1.52 for metals, the item with the most elastic demand in the table, to 0.05 for oil, the item with the most inelastic demand in the table. What makes the demand for some goods elastic and the demand for others inelastic?

Elasticity depends on three main factors:

- The closeness of substitutes
- The proportion of income spent on the good
- The time elapsed since a price change

Closeness of Substitutes The closer the substitutes for a good or service, the more elastic is the demand for it. For example, oil from which we make gasoline has substitutes but none that are currently very close (imagine a steam-driven, coal-fueled car). So the demand for oil is inelastic. Plastics are close substitutes for metals, so the demand for metal is elastic.

The degree of substitutability between two goods also depends on how narrowly (or broadly) we define them. For example, the elasticity of demand for meat is low, but the elasticity of demand for beef or pork is high. The elasticity of demand for personal computers is low, but the elasticity of demand for a Compaq, Dell, or IBM is high.

In everyday language we call some goods, such as food and housing, *necessities* and other goods, such as exotic vacations, *luxuries*. A necessity is a good

TABLE 4.1	Some Real-World Price Elasticities of Demand
Good or Service	**Elasticity**
Elastic Demand	
Metals	1.52
Electrical engineering products	1.39
Mechanical engineering products	1.30
Furniture	1.26
Motor vehicles	1.14
Instrument engineering products	1.10
Professional services	1.09
Transportation services	1.03
Inelastic Demand	
Gas, electricity, and water	0.92
Chemicals	0.89
Drinks (all types)	0.78
Clothing	0.64
Tobacco	0.61
Banking and insurance services	0.56
Housing services	0.55
Agricultural and fish products	0.42
Books, magazines, and newspapers	0.34
Food	0.12
Oil	0.05

Sources: Ahsan Mansur and John Whalley, "Numerical Specification of Applied General Equilibrium Models: Estimation, Calibration, and Data," in *Applied General Equilibrium Analysis*, eds. Herbert E. Scarf and John B. Shoven (New York: Cambridge University Press, 1984), 109, and Henri Theil, Ching-Fan Chung, and James L. Seale, Jr., *Advances in Econometrics, Supplement 1, 1989, International Evidence on Consumption Patterns* (Greenwich, Conn.: JAI Press Inc., 1989), and Geoffrey Heal, Columbia University, Web site.

that has poor substitutes and that is crucial for our well-being. So generally, a necessity has an inelastic demand. In Table 4.1, food and oil might be classified as necessities that have inelastic demand.

A luxury is a good that usually has many substitutes, one of which is not buying it. So a luxury generally has an elastic demand. In Table 4.1, furniture and motor vehicles might be classified as luxuries that have elastic demand.

Proportion of Income Spent on the Good Other things remaining the same, the greater the proportion of income spent on a good, the more elastic is the demand for it.

Think about your own elasticity of demand for chewing gum and housing. If the price of chewing gum doubles, you consume almost as much gum as before. Your demand for gum is inelastic. If apartment rents double, you shriek and look for more students to share accommodation with you. Your demand for housing is more elastic than your demand for gum. Why the difference? Housing takes a large proportion of your budget, and gum takes only a tiny proportion. You don't like either price increase, but you hardly notice the higher price of gum, while the higher rent puts your budget under severe strain.

Figure 4.6 shows the proportion of income spent on food and the price elasticity of demand for food in 10 countries. This figure confirms the general tendency we have just described. The larger the proportion of income spent on food, the larger is the price elasticity of demand for food. For example, in Tanzania,

a nation where average incomes are 3.3 percent of incomes in the United States and where 62 percent of income is spent on food, the price elasticity of demand for food is 0.77. In contrast, in the United States, where 12 percent of income is spent on food, the price elasticity of demand for food is 0.12.

Time Elapsed Since Price Change The longer the time that has elapsed since a price change, the more elastic is demand. When the price of oil increased by 400 percent during the 1970s, people barely changed the quantity of oil and gasoline they consumed. But gradually, as more efficient auto and airplane engines were developed, the quantity consumed decreased. The demand for oil has become more elastic as more time has elapsed since the huge price hike. Similarly, when the price of a PC fell, the quantity of PCs demanded increased only slightly at first. But as more people have become better informed about the variety of ways of using a PC, the quantity of PCs bought has increased sharply. The demand for PCs has become more elastic.

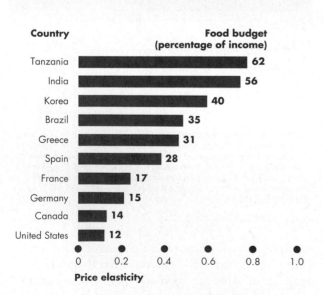

FIGURE 4.6   Price Elasticities in 10 Countries

As income increases and the proportion of income spent on food decreases, the demand for food becomes less elastic.

Source: Henri Theil, Ching-Fan Chung, and James L. Seale, Jr., *Advances in Econometrics, Supplement 1, 1989, International Evidence on Consumption Patterns* (Greenwich, Conn.: JAI Press, Inc., 1989).

REVIEW QUIZ

1 Why do we need a units-free measure of the responsiveness of the quantity demanded of a good or service to a change in its price?
2 Can you define and calculate the price elasticity of demand?
3 Why, when we calculate the price elasticity of demand, do we express the change in price as a percentage of the *average* price and the change in quantity as a percentage of the *average* quantity?
4 What is the total revenue test and why does it work?
5 What are the main influences on the elasticity of demand that make the demand for some goods elastic and the demand for other goods inelastic?
6 Why is the demand for a luxury generally more elastic than the demand for a necessity?

You've now completed your study of the *price* elasticity of demand. Two other elasticity concepts tell us about the effects of other influences on demand. Let's look at these other elasticities of demand.

More Elasticities of Demand

BACK AT THE PIZZERIA, YOU ARE TRYING TO WORK out how a price cut by the burger shop next door will affect the demand for your pizza. You know that pizzas and burgers are substitutes. And you know that when the price of a substitute for pizza falls, the demand for pizza decreases. But by how much?

You also know that pizza and soft drinks are complements. And you know that if the price of a complement of pizza falls, the demand for pizza increases. So you wonder whether you might keep your customers by cutting the price you charge for soft drinks. But again by how much?

To answer these questions, you need to calculate the cross elasticity of demand. Let's examine this elasticity measure.

Cross Elasticity of Demand

We measure the influence of a change in the price of a substitute or complement by using the concept of the cross elasticity of demand. The **cross elasticity of demand** is a measure of the responsiveness of the demand for a good to a change in the price of a substitute or complement, other things remaining the same. We calculate the *cross elasticity of demand* by using the formula:

$$\text{Cross elasticity of demand} = \frac{\text{Percentage change in quantity demanded}}{\text{Percentage change in price of a substitute or complement}}.$$

The cross elasticity of demand can be positive or negative. It is *positive* for a *substitute* and *negative* for a *complement*.

Substitutes Suppose that the price of pizza is constant and 9 pizzas an hour are sold. The price of a burger then rises from \$1.50 to \$2.50. No other influence on buying plans changes and the quantity of pizzas sold increases to 11 an hour.

The change in the quantity demanded is the new quantity, 11 pizzas, minus the original quantity, 9 pizzas, which is +2 pizzas. The average quantity is 10 pizzas. So the quantity of pizzas demanded increases by 20 percent (+20). That is,

$$\Delta Q/Q_{ave} = (+2/10) \times 100 = +20\%.$$

The change in the price of a burger, a substitute for pizza, is the new price, \$2.50, minus the original price, \$1.50, which is +\$1. The average price is \$2. So the price of a burger rises by 50 percent (+50). That is,

$$\Delta P/P_{ave} = (+1/2) \times 100 = +50\%.$$

So the cross elasticity of demand for pizza with respect to the price of a burger is

$$\frac{+20\%}{+50\%} = 0.4.$$

Figure 4.7 illustrates the cross elasticity of demand. Pizza and burgers are substitutes. Because they are substitutes, when the price of a burger rises, the demand for pizza increases. The demand curve for pizza shifts rightward from D_0 to D_1. Because a *rise* in the price of a burger brings a *increase* in the demand for pizza, the cross elasticity of demand for pizza with respect to the price of a burger is *positive*. Both the price and the quantity change in the same direction.

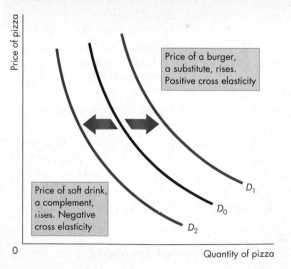

FIGURE 4.7   Cross Elasticity of Demand

Price of pizza

Price of a burger, a substitute, rises. Positive cross elasticity

Price of soft drink, a complement, rises. Negative cross elasticity

D_1

D_0

D_2

0   Quantity of pizza

A burger is a *substitute* for pizza. When the price of a burger rises, the demand for pizza increases and the demand curve for pizza shifts rightward from D_0 to D_1. The cross elasticity of the demand is *positive*.

Soft drinks are a *complement* of pizza. When the price of soft drinks rises, the demand for pizza decreases and the demand curve for pizza shifts leftward from D_0 to D_2. The cross elasticity of the demand is *negative*.

Complements Now suppose that the price of pizza is constant and 11 pizzas an hour are sold. The price of a soft drink rises from $1.50 to $2.50. No other influence on buying plans changes and the quantity of pizzas sold falls to 9 an hour.

The change in the quantity demanded is the opposite of what we've just calculated: The quantity of pizzas demanded decreases by 20 percent (−20).

The change in the price of a soft drink, a complement of pizza, is the same as the percentage change in the price of a burger that we've just calculated: The price rises by 50 percent (+50). So the cross elasticity of demand for pizza with respect to the price of a soft drink is

$$\frac{-20\%}{+50\%} = -0.4.$$

Because pizza and soft drinks are complements, when the price of a soft drink rises, the demand for pizza decreases. The demand curve for pizza shifts leftward from D_0 to D_2. Because a *rise* in the price of soft drinks brings a *decrease* in the demand for pizza, the cross elasticity of demand for pizza with respect to the price of soft drinks is *negative*. The price and quantity change in *opposite* directions.

The magnitude of the cross elasticity of demand determines how far the demand curve shifts. The larger the cross elasticity (absolute value), the greater is the change in demand and the larger is the shift in the demand curve.

If two items are very close substitutes, such as two brands of spring water, the cross elasticity is large. If two items are close complements, such as movies and popcorn, the cross elasticity is large.

If two items are somewhat unrelated to each other, such as newspapers and orange juice, the cross elasticity is small — perhaps even zero.

Income Elasticity of Demand

Suppose the economy is expanding and people are enjoying rising incomes. This prosperity is bringing an increase in the demand for most types of goods and services. But by how much will the demand for pizza increase? The answer depends on the **income elasticity of demand**, which is a measure of the responsiveness of the demand for a good or service to a change in income, other things remaining the same.

The income elasticity of demand is calculated by using the formula:

$$\text{Income elasticity of demand} = \frac{\text{Percentage change in quantity demanded}}{\text{Percentage change in income}}.$$

Income elasticities of demand can be positive or negative and fall into three interesting ranges:

- Greater than 1 (*normal* good, income elastic)
- Positive and less than 1 (*normal* good, income inelastic)
- Negative (*inferior* good)

Income Elastic Demand Suppose that the price of pizza is constant and 9 pizzas an hour are sold. Then incomes rise from $975 to $1,025 a week. No other influence on buying plans changes and the quantity of pizzas sold increases to 11 an hour.

The change in the quantity demanded is +2 pizzas. The average quantity is 10, so the quantity demanded increases by 20 percent. The change in income is +$50 and the average income is $1,000, so incomes increase by 5 percent. The income elasticity of demand for pizza is

$$\frac{20\%}{5\%} = 4.$$

As income increases, the quantity of pizza demanded increases faster than income. The demand for pizza is income-elastic. Other goods in this category include ocean cruises, international travel, jewelry, and works of art.

Income Inelastic Demand If the percentage increase in the quantity demanded is less than the percentage increase in income, the income elasticity of demand is positive and less than 1. In this case, the quantity demanded increases as income increases, but income increases faster than the quantity demanded. The demand for the good is income inelastic. Goods in this category include food, clothing, newspapers, and magazines.

Inferior Goods If when income increases the quantity demanded of a good decreases, the income elasticity of demand is negative. Goods in this category include small motorcycles, potatoes, and rice. Low-income consumers buy most of these goods.

Real-World Income Elasticities of Demand

Table 4.2 shows estimates of some real-world income elasticities of demand. The demand for a necessity such as food or gasoline is income inelastic, while the demand for a luxury such as transportation, which includes airline and foreign travel, is income elastic.

But what is a necessity and what is a luxury depends on the level of income. For people with a low income, food and clothing can be luxuries. So the *level* of income has a big effect on income elasticities of demand. Figure 4.8 shows this effect on the income elasticity of demand for food in 10 countries. In countries with low incomes, such as Tanzania and India, the income elasticity of demand for food is high. In countries with high incomes, such as the United States, the income elasticity of demand for food is low.

TABLE 4.2	Some Real-World Income Elasticities of Demand
Elastic Demand	
Airline travel	5.82
Movies	3.41
Foreign travel	3.08
Electricity	1.94
Restaurant meals	1.61
Local buses and trains	1.38
Haircuts	1.36
Automobiles	1.07
Inelastic Demand	
Tobacco	0.86
Alcoholic drinks	0.62
Furniture	0.53
Clothing	0.51
Newspapers and magazines	0.38
Telephone	0.32
Food	0.14

Sources: H.S. Houthakker and Lester D. Taylor, *Consumer Demand in the United States* (Cambridge, Mass.: Harvard University Press, 1970), and Henri Theil, Ching-Fan Chung, and James L. Seale, Jr., *Advances in Econometrics, Supplement 1, 1989, International Evidence on Consumption Patterns* (Greenwich, Conn.: JAI Press, Inc., 1989).

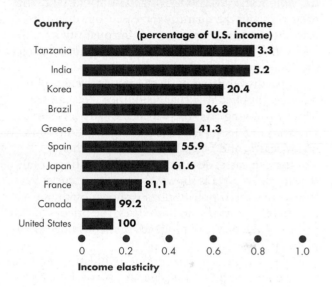

FIGURE 4.8   Income Elasticities in 10 Countries

Country	Income (percentage of U.S. income)
Tanzania	3.3
India	5.2
Korea	20.4
Brazil	36.8
Greece	41.3
Spain	55.9
Japan	61.6
France	81.1
Canada	99.2
United States	100

As income increases, the income elasticity of demand for food decreases. For low-income consumers, a larger percentage of any increase in income is spent on food than for high-income consumers.

Source: Henri Theil, Ching-Fan Chung, and James L. Seale, Jr., *Advances in Econometrics, Supplement 1, 1989, International Evidence on Consumption Patterns* (Greenwich, Conn.: JAI Press, Inc., 1989).

REVIEW QUIZ

1 What does the cross elasticity of demand measure?
2 What does the sign (positive versus negative) of the cross elasticity of demand tell us about the relationship between two goods?
3 What does the income elasticity of demand measure?
4 What does the sign (positive versus negative) of the income elasticity of demand tell us about a good?
5 Why does the level of income influence the magnitude of the income elasticity of demand?

You've now completed your study of the *cross elasticity* of demand and the *income elasticity* of demand. Let's look at the other side of a market and examine the elasticity of supply.

Elasticity of Supply

YOU KNOW THAT WHEN DEMAND INCREASES, THE price rises and the quantity increases. But does the price rise by a large amount and the quantity increase by a little? Or does the price barely rise and the quantity increase by a large amount?

The answer depends on the responsiveness of the quantity supplied to a change in price. You can see why by studying Fig. 4.9, which shows two possible scenarios in a local pizza market. Figure 4.9(a) shows one scenario, and Fig. 4.9(b) shows the other.

In both cases, demand is initially D_0. In part (a), the supply of pizza is shown by the supply curve S_A. In part (b), the supply of pizza is shown by the supply curve S_B. Initially, in both cases, the price is $20 a pizza and the quantity produced and consumed is 10 pizzas an hour.

Now increases in income and population increase the demand for pizza. The demand curve shifts rightward to D_1. In case (a), the price rises by $10 to $30 a pizza, and the quantity increases by only 3 to 13 an hour. In contrast, in case (b), the price rises by only $1 to $21 a pizza, and the quantity increases by 10 to 20 pizzas an hour.

The different outcomes arise from differing degrees of responsiveness of the quantity supplied to a change in price. We measure the degree of responsiveness by using the concept of the elasticity of supply.

Calculating the Elasticity of Supply

The **elasticity of supply** measures the responsiveness of the quantity supplied to a change in the price of a good when all other influences on selling plans remain the same. It is calculated by using the formula:

$$\text{Elasticity of supply} = \frac{\text{Percentage change in quantity supplied}}{\text{Percentage change in price}}.$$

We use the same method that you learned when you studied the elasticity of demand. (Refer back to page 83 to check this method.) Let's calculate the elasticity of supply for the supply curves in Fig. 4.9.

In Fig. 4.9(a), when the price rises from $20 to $30, the price rise is $10 and the average price is $25, so the price rises by 40 percent of the average price. The quantity increases from 10 to 13, so the increase

FIGURE 4.9   How a Change in Demand Changes Price and Quantity

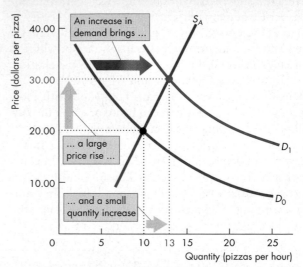

(a) Large price change and small quantity change

(b) Small price change and large quantity change

Initially, the price is $20 a pizza, and the quantity sold is 10 pizzas an hour. Then increases in incomes and population increase the demand for pizza. The demand curve shifts rightward to D_1. In part (a) the price rises by $10 to $30 a pizza, and the quantity increases by only 3 to 13 pizzas an hour. In part (b) the price rises by only $1 to $21 a pizza, and the quantity increases by 10 to 20 pizzas an hour. The price change is smaller and the quantity change is larger in case (b) than in case (a). The quantity supplied is more responsive to price in case (b) than in case (a).

is 3, the average quantity is 11.5, and the quantity increases by 26 percent. The elasticity of supply is equal to 26 percent divided by 40 percent, which equals 0.65.

In Fig. 4.9(b), when the price rises from $20 to $21, the price rise is $1 and the average price is $20.50, so the price rises by 4.8 percent of the average price. The quantity increases from 10 to 20, so the increase is 10, the average quantity is 15, and the quantity increases by 67 percent. The elasticity of supply is equal to 67 percent divided by 4.8 percent, which equals 13.67.

Figure 4.10 shows the range of supply elasticities. If the quantity supplied is fixed regardless of the price, the supply curve is vertical and the elasticity of supply is zero. Supply is perfectly inelastic. This case is shown in Fig. 4.10(a). A special intermediate case is when the percentage change in price equals the percentage change in quantity. Supply is then unit elastic. This case is shown in Fig. 4.10(b). No matter how steep the supply curve is, if it is linear and passes through the origin, supply is unit elastic. If there is a price at which sellers are willing to offer any quantity for sale, the supply curve is horizontal and the elasticity of supply is infinite. Supply is perfectly elastic. This case is shown in Fig. 4.10(c).

The Factors That Influence the Elasticity of Supply

The magnitude of the elasticity of supply depends on

- Resource substitution possibilities
- Time frame for the supply decision

Resource Substitution Possibilities Some goods and services can be produced only by using unique or rare productive resources. These items have a low, even perhaps a zero, elasticity of supply. Other goods and services can be produced by using commonly available resources that could be allocated to a wide variety of alternative tasks. Such items have a high elasticity of supply.

A Van Gogh painting is an example of a good with a vertical supply curve and a zero elasticity of supply. At the other extreme, wheat can be grown on land that is almost equally good for growing corn. So it is just as easy to grow wheat as corn, and the opportunity cost of wheat in terms of forgone corn is almost constant. As a result, the supply curve of wheat is almost horizontal and its elasticity of supply is very large. Similarly, when a good is produced in many different countries (for example, sugar and beef), the supply of the good is highly elastic.

FIGURE 4.10   Inelastic and Elastic Supply

(a) Perfectly inelastic supply **(b) Unit elastic supply** **(c) Perfectly elastic supply**

Each supply illustrated here has a constant elasticity. The supply curve in part (a) illustrates the supply of a good that has a zero elasticity of supply. The supply curve in part (b) illustrates the supply for a good with a unit elasticity of supply. All linear supply curves that pass through the origin illustrate supplies that are unit elastic. The supply curve in part (c) illustrates the supply for a good with an infinite elasticity of supply.

The supply of most goods and services lies between the two extremes. The quantity produced can be increased but only by incurring a higher cost. If a higher price is offered, the quantity supplied increases. Such goods and services have an elasticity of supply between zero and infinity.

Time Frame for Supply Decisions To study the influence of the length of time elapsed since a price change, we distinguish three time frames of supply:

1. Momentary supply
2. Long-run supply
3. Short-run supply

When the price of a good rises or falls, the *momentary supply curve* shows the response of the quantity supplied immediately following a price change.

Some goods, such as fruits and vegetables, have a perfectly inelastic momentary supply — a vertical supply curve. The quantities supplied depend on crop-planting decisions made earlier. In the case of oranges, for example, planting decisions have to be made many years in advance of the crop being available. The momentary supply curve is vertical because, on a given day, no matter what the price of oranges, producers cannot change their output. They have picked, packed, and shipped their crop to market, and the quantity available for that day is fixed.

In contrast, some goods have a perfectly elastic momentary supply. Long-distance phone calls are an example. When many people simultaneously make a call, there is a big surge in the demand for telephone cables, computer switching, and satellite time, and the quantity bought increases. But the price remains constant. Long-distance carriers monitor fluctuations in demand and reroute calls to ensure that the quantity supplied equals the quantity demanded without changing the price.

The *long-run supply curve* shows the response of the quantity supplied to a change in price after all the technologically possible ways of adjusting supply have been exploited. In the case of oranges, the long run is the time it takes new plantings to grow to full maturity — about 15 years. In some cases, the long-run adjustment occurs only after a completely new production plant has been built and workers have been trained to operate it — typically a process that might take several years.

The *short-run supply curve* shows how the quantity supplied responds to a price change when only *some* of the technologically possible adjustments to production have been made. The short-run response to a price change is a sequence of adjustments. The first adjustment that is usually made is in the amount of labor employed. To increase output in the short run, firms work their labor force overtime and perhaps hire additional workers. To decrease their output in the short run, firms either lay off workers or reduce their hours of work. With the passage of time, firms can make additional adjustments, perhaps training additional workers or buying additional tools and other equipment.

The short-run supply curve slopes upward because producers can take actions quite quickly to change the quantity supplied in response to a price change. For example, if the price of oranges falls, growers can stop picking and leave oranges to rot on the trees. Or if the price rises, they can use more fertilizer and improved irrigation to increase the yields of their existing trees. In the long run, they can plant more trees and increase the quantity supplied even more in response to a given price rise.

REVIEW QUIZ

1 Why do we need to measure the responsiveness of the quantity supplied of a good or service to a change in its price?
2 Can you define and calculate the elasticity of supply?
3 What are the main influences on the elasticity of supply that make the supply of some goods elastic and the supply of other goods inelastic?
4 Can you provide examples of goods or services whose elasticity of supply are (a) zero, (b) greater than zero but less than infinity, and (c), infinity?
5 How does the time frame over which a supply decision is made influence the elasticity of supply?

◆You have now studied the theory of demand and supply, and you have learned how to measure the elasticities of demand and supply. All the elasticities that you've met in this chapter are summarized in Table 4.3. In the next chapter, we are going to study the efficiency of competitive markets. But before doing that, take a look at *Reading Between the Lines* on pp. 96–97 to see elasticity in action.

TABLE 4.3   A Compact Glossary of Elasticities

Price Elasticities of Demand

A relationship is described as	When its magnitude is	Which means that
Perfectly elastic or infinitely elastic	Infinity	The smallest possible increase in price causes an infinitely large decrease in the quantity demanded*
Elastic	Less than infinity but greater than 1	The percentage decrease in the quantity demanded exceeds the percentage increase in price
Unit elastic	1	The percentage decrease in the quantity demanded equals the percentage increase in price
Inelastic	Greater than zero but less than 1	The percentage decrease in the quantity demanded is less than the percentage increase in price
Perfectly inelastic or completely inelastic	Zero	The quantity demanded is the same at all prices

Cross Elasticities of Demand

A relationship is described as	When its value is	Which means that
Perfect substitutes	Infinity	The smallest possible increase in the price of one good causes an infinitely large increase in the quantity demanded of the other good
Substitutes	Positive, less than infinity	If the price of one good increases, the quantity demanded of the other good also increases
Independent	Zero	If the price of one good increases, the quantity demanded of the other good remains the same
Complements	Less than zero	If the price of one good increases, the quantity demanded of the other good decreases

Income Elasticities of Demand

A relationship is described as	When its value is	Which means that
Income elastic (normal good)	Greater than 1	The percentage increase in the quantity demanded is greater than the percentage increase in income
Income inelastic (normal good)	Less than 1 but greater than zero	The percentage increase in the quantity demanded is less than the percentage increase in income
Negative income elastic (inferior good)	Less than zero	When income increases, quantity demanded decreases

Elasticities of Supply

A relationship is described as	When its magnitude is	Which means that
Perfectly elastic	Infinity	The smallest possible increase in price causes an infinitely large increase in the quantity supplied
Elastic	Less than infinity but greater than 1	The percentage increase in the quantity supplied exceeds the percentage increase in the price
Inelastic	Greater than zero but less than 1	The percentage increase in the quantity supplied is less than the percentage increase in the price
Perfectly inelastic	Zero	The quantity supplied is the same at all prices

*In each description, the directions of change may be reversed. For example, in this case, the smallest possible *decrease* in price causes an infinitely large *increase* in the quantity demanded.

Elasticities of Demand and Supply in the Global Oil Market

CNN MONEY, NOVEMBER 15, 2001

Oil Prices Slide Anew

Oil prices tumbled again Thursday afternoon, hitting two-year lows, as OPEC ministers warned that prices could fall toward $10 a barrel if non-OPEC producers don't follow suit and cut back on output. ...

The drop came a day after the Organization of Petroleum Exporting Countries said it would cut oil production by 1.5 million barrels a day, or 6 percent, but stressed it would only do so if non-OPEC members made deep cuts of their own.

Analysts said OPEC was taking a risk since it appears unlikely that other countries with economies less dependent on oil sales would pledge substantial cuts in output. ...

OPEC wants oil prices to rise. But the prime minister of Russia, the world's second biggest exporter after Saudi Arabia, said Thursday he saw little chance his country would make big cuts in output despite pressure from OPEC.

Essence of the Story

■ The Organization of Petroleum Exporting Countries (OPEC) said that it would cut oil production by 1.5 million barrels a day, or 6 percent, if non-OPEC members also made deep cuts to production.

■ On the same day, the price of oil fell and OPEC ministers predicted a price of $10 a barrel if non-OPEC producers didn't decrease output.

■ Analysts did not expect other producers to decrease output.

Economic Analysis

- Demand and supply in a global market determine the price of crude oil.

- OPEC is the largest supplier of oil (with a 36 percent market share), and it tries to limit production to raise the price.

- But the actions of individual OPEC members and of non-OPEC producers make it impossible for OPEC to control the price of crude oil.

- Figure 1 shows that the price of crude oil fluctuates (an example of a price roller coaster).

- During 2001, the price fell below $20 a barrel and OPEC worried that without a decrease in supply, the price might fall to $10 a barrel.

- Figure 2 shows demand and supply in the market for crude oil.

- The elasticity of demand is 0.05, and the elasticity of supply is 0.1. These elasticity values are suggested by Geoffrey Heal of Columbia University, a leading natural resource economist.

- In 2001, the supply curve was S_{2001} and the demand curve was D_{2001}. The quantity was 75 million barrels a day, and the price was $18 a barrel.

- OPEC predicted that demand would decrease in 2002 to D_{2002} so with no change in supply, the price would fall to $10 a barrel and the quantity would decrease to 71 million barrels a day.

- If OPEC cuts production by 1.5 million barrels a day, supply in 2002 would decrease to S_{2002}.

- We can work out the effect of OPEC's cut in production on price and quantity because we have estimates of the price elasticity of demand and the elasticity of supply.

- Figure 3 shows that the price would rise to $11.50 a barrel and the quantity would decrease to 70.5 million barrels a day.

- Because demand is inelastic, a small quantity decrease brings a large price rise.

- But because the price rises, non-OPEC producers *increase* production — an increase in the quantity supplied.

- The decrease in quantity of 0.5 million barrels a day equals OPEC's cut of 1.5 million barrels a day minus the 1 million barrels a day increase in production by the rest of the world.

Figure 1 The price of crude oil

Figure 2 The oil market with no production cuts

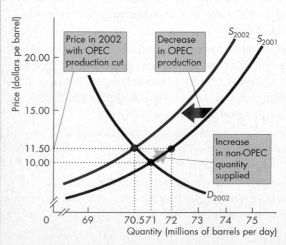

Figure 3 OPEC production cut

97

SUMMARY

KEY POINTS

Price Elasticity of Demand (pp. 82–88)

- Elasticity is a measure of the responsiveness of the quantity demanded of a good to a change in its price.
- Price elasticity of demand equals the percentage change in the quantity demanded divided by the percentage change in price.
- The larger the magnitude of the elasticity of demand, the greater is the responsiveness of the quantity demanded to a given change in price.
- Price elasticity of demand depends on how easily one good serves as a substitute for another, the proportion of income spent on the good, and the length of time elapsed since the price change.
- If demand is elastic, a decrease in price leads to an increase in total revenue. If demand is unit elastic, a decrease in price leaves total revenue unchanged. And if demand is inelastic, a decrease in price leads to a decrease in total revenue.

More Elasticities of Demand (pp. 89–91)

- Cross elasticity of demand measures the responsiveness of demand for one good to a change in the price of a substitute or a complement.
- The cross elasticity of demand with respect to the price of a substitute is positive. The cross elasticity of demand with respect to the price of a complement is negative.
- Income elasticity of demand measures the responsiveness of demand to a change in income. For a normal good, the income elasticity of demand is positive. For an inferior good, the income elasticity of demand is negative.
- When the income elasticity is greater than 1, as income increases, the percentage of income spent on the good increases.
- When the income elasticity is less than 1 but greater than zero, as income increases, the percentage of income spent on the good decreases.

Elasticity of Supply (pp. 92–94)

- Elasticity of supply measures the responsiveness of the quantity supplied of a good to a change in its price.
- The elasticity of supply is usually positive and ranges between zero (vertical supply curve) and infinity (horizontal supply curve).
- Supply decisions have three time frames: momentary, long run, and short run.
- Momentary supply refers to the response of sellers to a price change at the instant that the price changes.
- Long-run supply refers to the response of sellers to a price change when all the technologically feasible adjustments in production have been made.
- Short-run supply refers to the response of sellers to a price change after some of the technologically feasible adjustments in production have been made.

KEY FIGURES AND TABLE

KEY TERMS

PROBLEMS

*1. Rain spoils the strawberry crop. As a result, the price rises from $4 to $6 a box and the quantity demanded decreases from 1,000 to 600 boxes a week. Over this price range,
   a. What is the price elasticity of demand?
   b. Describe the demand for strawberries.

 2. Good weather brings a bumper tomato crop. The price falls from $7 to $5 a basket, and the quantity demanded increases from 300 to 500 baskets a day. Over this price range,
   a. What is the price elasticity of demand?
   b. Describe the demand for tomatoes.

*3. The figure shows the demand for videotape rentals.

   a. Calculate the elasticity of demand for a rise in rental price from $3 to $5.
   b. At what price is the elasticity of demand equal to 1?

 4. The figure shows the demand for pens.

   a. Calculate the elasticity of demand for a rise in price from $6 to $10.

   b. At what prices is the elasticity of demand equal to 1, greater than 1, and less than 1?

*5. If the quantity of dental services demanded increases by 10 percent when the price of dental services falls by 10 percent, is the demand for dental service inelastic, elastic, or unit elastic?

 6. If the quantity of haircuts demanded decreases by 10 percent when the price of a haircut rises by 5 percent, is the demand for haircuts elastic, inelastic, or unit elastic?

*7. The demand schedule for computer chips is

Price (dollars per chip)	Quantity demanded (millions of chips per year)
200	50
250	45
300	40
350	35
400	30

   a. What happens to total revenue if the price of a chip falls from $400 to $350?
   b. What happens to total revenue if the price of a chip falls from $350 to $300?
   c. At what price is total revenue at a maximum? Use the total revenue test to answer this question.
   d. At an average price of $350, is the demand for chips elastic or inelastic? Use the total revenue test to answer this question.

 8. The demand schedule for sugar is

Price (dollars per pound)	Quantity demanded (millions of pounds per year)
5	25
10	20
15	15
20	10
25	5

   a. What happens to total revenue if the price of sugar rises from $5 to $15 per pound?
   b. What happens to total revenue if the price rises from $15 to $25 per pound?
   c. At what price is total revenue at a maximum? Use the total revenue test to answer this question.
   d. At an average price of $20 a pound, is the demand for sugar elastic or inelastic? Use the total revenue test to answer this question.

*9. In problem 7, at $250 a chip, is the demand for chips elastic or inelastic? Use the total revenue test to answer this question.

10. In problem 8, at $10 a pound, is the demand for sugar elastic or inelastic? Use the total revenue test to answer this question.

*11. If a 12 percent rise in the price of orange juice decreases the quantity of orange juice demanded by 22 percent and increases the quantity of apple juice demanded by 14 percent, calculate the cross elasticity of demand between orange juice and apple juice.

12. If a 5 percent fall in the price of chicken decreases the quantity of beef demanded by 20 percent and increases the quantity of chicken demanded by 15 percent, calculate the cross elasticity of demand between chicken and beef.

*13. Alex's income has increased from $3,000 to $5,000. Alex increased his consumption of bagels from 4 to 8 a month and decreased his consumption of doughnuts from 12 to 6 a month. Calculate Alex's income elasticity of demand for (a) bagels and (b) doughnuts.

14. Judy's income has increased from $13,000 to $17,000. Judy increased her demand for concert tickets by 15 percent and decreased her demand for bus rides by 10 percent. Calculate Judy's income elasticity of demand for (a) concert tickets and (b) bus rides.

*15. The table gives the supply schedule for long-distance phone calls.

Price (cents per minute)	Quantity supplied (millions of minutes per day)
10	200
20	400
30	600
40	800

Calculate the elasticity of supply when

a. The price falls from 40 cents to 30 cents a minute.

b. The price is 20 cents a minute.

16. The table gives the supply schedule for jeans.

Price (dollars per pair)	Quantity supplied (millions of pairs per year)
120	2,400
125	2,800
130	3,200
135	3,600

Calculate the elasticity of supply when

a. The price rises from $125 to $135 a pair.

b. The price is $125 a pair.

CRITICAL THINKING

1. Study *Reading Between the Lines* (pp. 96–97) on the market for crude oil and then answer the following questions:
   a. Why did the price of oil fall during 2001?
   b. What is the elasticity that tells us the effect of a change in supply on the price and quantity of crude oil?
   c. What is the elasticity that tells us the effect of a change in demand on the price and quantity of crude oil?
   d. Why did OPEC want to cut production during 2002?
   e. Calculate the elasticity of supply in Figure 2 on page 97 when demand decreases and confirm that it is (approximately) 0.1.
   f. Calculate the elasticity of demand in Figure 3 on page 97 when supply decreases and confirm that it is (approximately) 0.05.
   g. By how much would OPEC have needed to cut production to raise the price to $15 a barrel (assuming demand D_{2002})?

WEB EXERCISES

1. Use the link on the Parkin Web site and
   a. Find the price of gasoline in the summer of 2002.
   b. Use the concepts of demand, supply, and elasticity to explain recent changes in the price of gasoline.
   c. Find the price of crude oil.
   d. Use the concepts of demand, supply, and elasticity to explain recent changes in the price of crude oil.

2. Use the link of the Parkin Web site and:
   a. Find the number of gallons in a barrel and the cost of crude oil in a gallon of gasoline.
   b. What are the other costs that make up the total cost of a gallon of gasoline?
   c. If the price of crude oil falls by 10 percent, by what percentage would you expect the price of gasoline to change, other things remaining the same?
   d. Which demand do you think is more elastic: that for crude oil or gasoline? Why?

3. Use the link of the Parkin Web site to review and write a brief report on *Geoffrey Heal's* lecture on the market for oil during the 1990s.

EFFICIENCY AND EQUITY

More for Less

People constantly strive to get more for less. Tommy Thompson, the Secretary of Health and Human Services, was pleased when he beat down the price the United States paid Bayer AG for Cipro (the drug used to treat anthrax) from the $4.50 a pill that you would pay to 95¢ a pill. Every time we buy something or decide *not* to buy something, we express our view about how scarce resources should be used. We try to spend our incomes in ways that get the most out of our scarce resources. ◆ Is the allocation of our resources between leisure and education, pizza and sandwiches, inline skates and squash balls, Cipro and AIDS treatments and all the other things we buy the right one? Can we get more out of our resources if we spend more on some goods and services and less on others? ◆ Some firms make huge profits year after year. Microsoft, for example, has generated enough profit over the past ten years to rocket Bill Gates, one of its founders, into the position of being one of the richest people in the world. Is that kind of business success a sign of efficiency? ◆ And is it fair that Bill Gates is so incredibly rich while others live in miserable poverty?

◆ These are the kinds of questions you'll explore in this chapter. You will discover that competitive markets can be efficient. But you will also discover some sources of inefficiency that can be addressed with government action. You will also discover that firms that make huge profits, while efficient in one sense, might be inefficient in a broader sense.

After studying this chapter, you will be able to

■ Define efficiency

■ Distinguish between value and price and define consumer surplus

■ Distinguish between cost and price and define producer surplus

■ Explain the conditions under which markets move resources to their highest-valued uses and the sources of inefficiency in our economy

■ Explain the main ideas about fairness and evaluate claims that markets result in unfair outcomes

Efficiency: A Refresher

IT IS HARD TO TALK ABOUT EFFICIENCY IN ORDI-nary conversation without generating disagreement. To an engineer, an entrepreneur, a politician, a working mother, or an economist, getting more for less seems like a sensible thing to aim for. But some people think that the pursuit of efficiency conflicts with other, worthier goals. Environmentalists worry about contamination from "efficient" nuclear power plants. And car producers worry about competition from "efficient" foreign producers.

Economists use the idea of efficiency in a special way that avoids these disagreements. An **efficient allocation** of resources occurs when we produce the goods and services that people value most highly (see Chapter 2, pp. 35–37). Equivalently, resource use is efficient when we cannot produce more of a good or service without giving up some other good or service that we value more highly.

If people value a nuclear-free environment more highly than they value cheap electric power, it is efficient to use higher-cost, nonnuclear technologies to produce electricity. Efficiency is not a cold, mechanical concept. It is a concept based on value, and value is based on people's feelings.

Think about the efficient quantity of pizza. To produce more pizza, we must give up some other goods and services. For example, we might give up some sandwiches. So to produce more pizzas, we forgo sandwiches. If we have fewer pizzas, we can have more sandwiches. What is the efficient quantity of pizza to produce? The answer depends on marginal benefit and marginal cost.

Marginal Benefit

If we consume one more pizza, we receive a marginal benefit. **Marginal benefit** is the benefit that a person receives from consuming one more unit of a good or service. The marginal benefit from a good or service is measured as the maximum amount that a person is willing to pay for one more unit of it. So the marginal benefit from a pizza is the maximum amount of other goods and services that people are willing to give up to get one more pizza. The marginal benefit from pizza decreases as the quantity of pizza consumed increases — the principle of *decreasing marginal benefit.*

We can express the marginal benefit from a pizza as the number of sandwiches that people are willing to forgo to get one more pizza. But we can also express marginal benefit as the dollar value of other goods and services that people are willing to forgo. Figure 5.1 shows the marginal benefit from pizza expressed in this way. As the quantity of pizza increases, the value of other items that people are willing to forgo to get yet one more pizza decreases.

Marginal Cost

If we produce one more pizza, we incur a marginal cost. **Marginal cost** is the opportunity cost of producing *one more unit* of a good or service. The marginal cost of a good or service is measured as the value of the best alternative forgone. So the marginal cost of a pizza is the value of the best alternative forgone to get one more pizza. The marginal cost of a pizza increases as the quantity of pizza produced increases — the principle of *increasing marginal cost.*

FIGURE 5.1   The Efficient Quantity of Pizza

The marginal benefit curve (*MB*) shows what people *are willing to* forgo to get one more pizza. The marginal cost curve (*MC*) shows what people *must* forgo to get one more pizza. If fewer than 10,000 pizzas a day are produced, marginal benefit exceeds marginal cost. Greater value can be obtained by producing more pizzas. If more than 10,000 pizzas a day are produced, marginal cost exceeds marginal benefit. Greater value can be obtained by producing fewer pizzas. If 10,000 pizzas a day are produced, marginal benefit equals marginal cost and the efficient quantity of pizza is available.

We can express marginal cost as the number of sandwiches we must forgo to produce one more pizza. But we can also express marginal cost as the dollar value of other goods and services we must forgo. Figure 5.1 shows the marginal cost of pizza expressed in this way. As the quantity of pizza produced increases, the value of other items we must forgo to produce yet one more pizza increases.

Efficiency and Inefficiency

To determine the efficient quantity of pizza, we compare the marginal cost of a pizza with the marginal benefit from a pizza. There are three possible cases:

- Marginal benefit exceeds marginal cost.
- Marginal cost exceeds marginal benefit.
- Marginal benefit equals marginal cost.

Marginal Benefit Exceeds Marginal Cost Suppose the quantity of pizza produced is 5,000 a day. Figure 5.1 shows that at this quantity, the marginal benefit of a pizza is $20. That is, when the quantity of pizza available is 5,000 a day, people are willing to pay $20 for the 5,000th pizza.

Figure 5.1 also shows that the marginal cost of the 5,000th pizza is $10. That is, to produce one more pizza, the value of other goods and services that we must forgo is $10. If pizza production increases from 4,999 to 5,000, the value of the additional pizza is $20 and its marginal cost is $10. If this pizza is produced, the value of the pizza produced exceeds the value of the goods and services we must forgo by $10. Resources will be used more efficiently — they will create more value — if we produce an extra pizza and fewer other goods and services. This same reasoning applies all the way up to the 9,999th pizza. Only when we get to the 10,000th pizza does marginal benefit not exceed marginal cost.

Marginal Cost Exceeds Marginal Benefit Suppose the quantity of pizza produced is 15,000 a day. Figure 5.1 shows that at this quantity, the marginal benefit of a pizza is $10. That is, when the quantity of pizza available is 15,000 a day, people are willing to pay $10 for the 15,000th pizza.

Figure 5.1 also shows that the marginal cost of the 15,000th pizza is $20. That is, to produce one more pizza, the value of the other goods and services that we must forgo is $20.

If pizza production decreases from 15,000 to 14,999, the value of the one pizza forgone is $10 and its marginal cost is $20. So if this pizza is not produced, the value of the other goods and services produced exceeds the value of the pizza forgone by $10. Resources will be used more efficiently — they will create more value — if we produce one fewer pizza and more other goods and services. This same reasoning applies all the way down to the 10,001st pizza. Only when we get to the 10,000th pizza does marginal cost not exceed marginal benefit.

Marginal Benefit Equals Marginal Cost Suppose the quantity of pizza produced is 10,000 a day. Figure 5.1 shows that at this quantity, the marginal benefit of a pizza is $15. That is, when the quantity of pizza available is 10,000 a day, people are willing to pay $15 for the 10,000th pizza.

Figure 5.1 also shows that the marginal cost of the 10,000th pizza is $15. That is, to produce one more pizza, the value of other goods and services that we must forgo is $15.

In this situation, we cannot increase the value of the goods and services produced by either increasing or decreasing the quantity of pizza. If we increase the quantity of pizza, the 10,001st pizza costs more to produce than it is worth. And if we decrease the quantity of pizza produced, the 9,999th pizza is worth more than it costs to produce. So when marginal benefit equals marginal cost, resource use is efficient.

REVIEW QUIZ

1 If the marginal benefit of pizza exceeds the marginal cost of pizza, are we producing too much pizza and too little of other goods, or are we producing too little pizza and too much of other goods?

2 If the marginal cost of pizza exceeds the marginal benefit of pizza, are we producing too much pizza and too little of other goods, or are we producing too little pizza and too much of other goods?

3 What is the relationship between the marginal benefit of pizza and the marginal cost of pizza when we are producing the efficient quantity of pizza?

Does a competitive market in pizza produce the efficient quantity of pizza? Let's answer this question.

Value, Price, and Consumer Surplus

TO INVESTIGATE WHETHER A COMPETITIVE market is efficient, we need to learn about the connection between demand and marginal benefit and the connection between supply and marginal cost.

Value, Willingness to Pay, and Demand

In everyday life, we talk about "getting value for money." When we use this expression, we are distinguishing between *value* and *price*. Value is what we get, and the price is what we pay.

The **value** of one more unit of a good or service is its *marginal benefit*. Marginal benefit can be expressed as the maximum price that people are willing to pay for another unit of the good or service. The willingness to pay for a good or service determines the demand for it.

In Fig. 5.2(a), the demand curve D shows the quantity demanded at each price. For example, when the price of a pizza is $15, the quantity demanded

is 10,000 pizzas a day. In Fig. 5.2(b), the demand curve D shows the maximum price that people are willing to pay when there is a given quantity. For example, when 10,000 pizzas a day are available, the most that people are willing to pay for the 10,000[th] pizza is $15. This second interpretation of the demand curve means that the marginal benefit from the 10,000th pizza is $15. The demand curve is also the marginal benefit curve *MB*.

When we draw a demand curve, we use a *relative price*, not a *money* price. We express the relative price in dollars, but the relative price measures the number of dollars' worth of other goods and services forgone to obtain one more unit of the good in question (see Chapter 3, p. 58). So a demand curve tells us the value of other goods and services that people are willing to forgo to get an additional unit of a good. But this is what a marginal benefit curve tells us too. So

A demand curve is a marginal benefit curve.

We don't always have to pay the maximum price that we are willing to pay. When we buy something, we often get a bargain. Let's see how.

FIGURE 5.2   Demand, Willingness to Pay, and Marginal Benefit

(a) Price determines quantity demanded

(b) Quantity determines willingness to pay

The demand curve for pizza, D, shows the quantity of pizza demanded at each price, other things remaining the same. It also shows the maximum price that consumers are willing to pay if a given quantity of pizza is available. At a price of $15 a

pizza, the quantity demanded is 10,000 pizzas a day (part a). If 10,000 pizzas a day are available, the maximum price that consumers are willing to pay for the 10,000th pizza is $15 (part b).

Consumer Surplus

When people buy something for less than it is worth to them, they receive a consumer surplus. A **consumer surplus** is the value of a good minus the price paid for it, summed over the quantity bought.

To understand consumer surplus, let's look at Lisa's demand for pizza in Fig. 5.3. Lisa likes pizza, but the marginal benefit she gets from it decreases quickly as her consumption increases.

To keep things simple, suppose Lisa can buy pizza by the slice and that there are 10 slices in a pizza. If a pizza costs $2.50 a slice (or $25 a pizza), Lisa spends her fast-food budget on items that she values more highly than pizza. At $2 a slice (or $20 a pizza), she buys 10 slices (1 pizza) a week. At $1.50 a slice, she buys 20 slices a week; at $1 a slice, she buys 30 slices a week; and at 50 cents a slice ($5 a pizza), she eats nothing but pizza and buys 40 slices a week.

Lisa's demand curve for pizza in Fig. 5.3 is also her *willingness-to-pay* or marginal benefit curve. It tells us that if Lisa can have only 10 slices (1 pizza) a week, she is willing to pay $2 a slice. Her marginal benefit from the 10th slice is $2. If she can have 20 slices (2 pizzas) a week, she is willing to pay $1.50 for the 20th slice. Her marginal benefit from the 20th slice is $1.50.

Figure 5.3 also shows Lisa's consumer surplus from pizza when the price is $1.50 a slice. At this price, she buys 20 slices a week. The most that Lisa is willing to pay for the 20th slice is $1.50 a slice, so its marginal benefit equals the price she pays for it.

But Lisa is willing to pay almost $2.50 for the first slice. So the marginal benefit from this slice is close to $1 more than she pays for it. So on her first slice of pizza, she receives a *consumer surplus* of almost $1. At a quantity of 10 slices of pizza a week, Lisa's marginal benefit is $2 a slice. So on the 10th slice, she receives a consumer surplus of 50 cents.

To calculate Lisa's consumer surplus, we find the consumer surplus on each slice she buys and add them together. This sum is the area of the green triangle — the area below the demand curve and above the market price line. This area is equal to the base of the triangle (20 slices a week) multiplied by the height of the triangle ($1) divided by 2, which is $10.

The area of the blue rectangle in Fig. 5.3 shows what Lisa pays for pizza, which is $30. This area is equal to 20 slices a week multiplied by $1.50 a slice.

All goods and services are like the pizza example you've just studied. Because of decreasing marginal benefit, people receive more benefit from their consumption than the amount they pay.

FIGURE 5.3   A Consumer's Demand and Consumer Surplus

Lisa's demand curve for pizza tells us that at $2.50 a slice, she does not buy pizza. At $2 a slice, she buys 10 slices a week; at $1.50 a slice, she buys 20 slices a week. Lisa's demand curve also tells us that she is willing to pay $2 for the 10th slice and $1.50 for the 20th. She actually pays $1.50 a slice — the market price — and buys 20 slices a week. Her consumer surplus from pizza is $10 — the area of the green triangle.

You've seen how we distinguish between value — marginal benefit — and price. And you've seen that buyers receive a consumer surplus because marginal benefit exceeds price. Next, we're going to study the connection between supply and marginal cost and learn about producer surplus.

Cost, Price, and Producer Surplus

WHAT YOU ARE NOW GOING TO LEARN ABOUT cost, price, and producer surplus parallels the related ideas about value, price, and consumer surplus that you've just studied.

Firms are in business to make a profit. To do so, they must sell their output for a price that exceeds the cost of production. Let's investigate the relationship between cost and price.

Cost, Minimum Supply-Price, and Supply

Earning a profit means receiving more (or at least receiving no less) for the sale of a good or service than the cost of producing it. Just as consumers distinguish between *value* and *price*, so producers distinguish between *cost* and *price*. Cost is what a producer gives up, and price is what a producer receives.

The cost of producing one more unit of a good or service is its *marginal cost*. And marginal cost is the minimum price that producers must receive to induce them to produce another unit of the good or service. This minimum acceptable price determines supply.

In Fig. 5.4(a), the supply curve S shows the quantity supplied at each price. For example, when the price of a pizza is $15, the quantity supplied is 10,000 pizzas a day. In Fig. 5.4(b), the supply curve shows the minimum price that producers must be offered to produce a given quantity of pizza. For example, the minimum price, which producers must be offered to get them to produce 10,000 pizzas a day is $15 a pizza. This second view of the supply curve means that the marginal cost of the 10,000th pizza is $15. The supply curve is also the marginal cost curve MC.

Because the price is a relative price, a supply curve tells us the quantity of other goods and services that *sellers must forgo* to produce one more unit of the good. But a marginal cost curve also tells us the quantity of other goods and services that we must

---

FIGURE 5.4 Supply, Minimum Supply-Price, and Marginal Cost

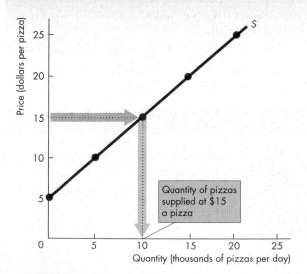

(a) Price determines quantity supplied

(b) Quantity determines minimum supply-price

The supply curve of pizza, S, shows the quantity of pizza supplied at each price, other things remaining the same. It also shows the minimum price that producers must be offered to get them to produce a given quantity of pizza. At a price of

$15 a pizza, the quantity supplied is 10,000 pizzas a day (part a). To get firms to produce 10,000 pizzas a day, the minimum price they must be offered for the 10,000th pizza is $15 (part b).

forgo to get one more unit of the good. So

A supply curve is a marginal cost curve.

If the price producers receive exceeds the cost they incur, they earn a producer surplus. This producer surplus is analogous to consumer surplus.

Producer Surplus

When price exceeds marginal cost, the firm obtains a producer surplus. A **producer surplus** is the price of a good minus the opportunity cost of producing it, summed over the quantity sold. To understand producer surplus, let's look at Max's supply of pizza in Fig. 5.5.

Max can produce pizza or bake bread that people like a lot. The more pizza he bakes, the less bread he can bake. His opportunity cost of pizza is the value of the bread he must forgo. This opportunity cost increases as Max increases his production of pizza. If a pizza sells for only $5, Max produces no pizza. He uses his kitchen to bake bread. Pizza just isn't worth producing. But at $10 a pizza, Max produces 50 pizzas a day, and at $15 a pizza, he produces 100 a day.

Max's supply curve is also his *minimum supply-price* curve. It tells us that if Max can sell only one pizza a day, the minimum that he must be paid for it is $5. If he can sell 50 pizzas a day, the minimum that he must be paid for the 50th pizza is $10, and so on.

Figure 5.5 also shows Max's producer surplus. If the price of a pizza is $15, Max plans to sell 100 pizzas a day. The minimum that he must be paid for the 100th pizza is $15. So its opportunity cost is exactly the price he receives for it. But his opportunity cost of the first pizza is only $5. So this first pizza costs $10 less to produce than he receives for it. Max receives a *producer surplus* from his first pizza of $10. He receives a slightly smaller producer surplus on the second pizza, less on the third, and so on until he receives no producer surplus on the 100th pizza.

Figure 5.5 shows Max's producer surplus as the blue triangle — the area above the supply curve and below the market price line. This area is equal to the base of the triangle (100 pizzas a week) multiplied by the height ($10 a slice) divided by 2, which equals $500 a week. Figure 5.5 also shows Max's opportunity costs of production as the red area below the supply curve.

FIGURE 5.5   A Producer's Supply and Producer Surplus

Max's supply curve of pizza tells us that at a price of $5, Max plans to sell no pizza. At a price of $10, he plans to sell 50 pizzas a day; and at a price of $15, he plans to sell 100 pizzas a day. Max's supply curve also tells us that the minimum he must be offered is $10 for the 50th pizza a day and $15 for the 100th pizza a day. If the market price is $15 a pizza, he sells 100 pizzas a day and receives $1,500. The red area shows Max's cost of producing pizza, which is $1,000 a day, and the blue area shows his producer surplus, which is $500 a day.

REVIEW QUIZ

1 What is the relationship between the marginal cost or opportunity cost of producing a good or service and the minimum supply-price — the minimum price that producers must be offered?
2 What is the relationship between marginal cost and the supply curve?
3 What is producer surplus? How do we measure it?

Consumer surplus and producer surplus can be used to measure the efficiency of a market. Let's see how we can use these concepts to study the efficiency of a competitive market.

Is the Competitive Market Efficient?

FIGURE 5.6 SHOWS THE MARKET FOR PIZZA. THE demand curve D shows the demand for pizza. The supply curve S shows the supply of pizza. The equilibrium price is $15 a pizza, and the equilibrium quantity is 10,000 pizzas a day.

The market forces that you studied in Chapter 3 (pp. 68–69) will pull the pizza market to this equilibrium. If the price is greater than $15 a pizza, a surplus will force the price down. If the price is less than $15 a pizza, a shortage will force the price up. Only if the price is $15 a pizza is there neither a surplus nor a shortage and no forces operate to change the price.

So the market price and quantity are pulled toward their equilibrium values. But is this competitive equilibrium efficient? Does a competitive market produce the efficient quantity of pizza?

Efficiency of Competitive Equilibrium

The equilibrium in Fig. 5.6 is efficient. Resources are being used to produce the quantity of pizza that people value most highly. It is not possible to produce more pizza without giving up some other good or service that is valued more highly. And if a smaller quantity of pizza is produced, resources are used to produce some other good that is not valued as highly as the pizza forgone.

To see why the equilibrium in Fig. 5.6 is efficient, think about the interpretation of the demand curve as the marginal benefit curve and the supply curve as the marginal cost curve. The demand curve tells us the marginal benefit from pizza. The supply curve tells us the marginal cost of pizza. So where the demand curve and the supply curve intersect, marginal benefit equals marginal cost.

But this condition — marginal benefit equals marginal cost — is the condition that delivers an efficient use of resources. A competitive market puts resources to work in the activities that create the greatest possible value. So a competitive equilibrium is efficient.

If production is less than 10,000 pizzas a day, the marginal pizza is valued more highly than its opportunity cost. If production exceeds 10,000 pizzas a day, the marginal pizza costs more to produce than the value that consumers place on it. Only when 10,000

FIGURE 5.6   An Efficient Market for Pizza

Resources are used efficiently when the sum of consumer surplus and producer surplus is maximized. Consumer surplus is the area below the demand curve and above the market price line — the green triangle. Producer surplus is the area below the price line and above the supply curve — the blue triangle. Here, consumer surplus is $50,000, producer surplus is $50,000, and the sum is $100,000. This sum of consumer surplus and producer surplus is maximized when the willingness to pay equals the opportunity cost. The efficient quantity of pizza is 10,000 pizzas per day.

pizzas a day are produced is the marginal pizza worth exactly what it costs. The competitive market pushes the quantity of pizza produced to its efficient level of 10,000 a day. If production is less than 10,000 a day, a shortage raises the price, which increases production. If production exceeds 10,000 a day, a surplus lowers the price, which decreases production.

In a competitive equilibrium, resources are used efficiently to produce the goods and services that people value most highly. And when the competitive market uses resources efficiently, the sum of consumer surplus and producer surplus is maximized.

Buyers and sellers each attempt to do the best they can for themselves, and no one plans for an efficient outcome for society as a whole. Buyers seek the lowest possible price, and sellers seek the highest possible price. And the market comes to an equilibrium in which resources are allocated efficiently.

The Invisible Hand

Writing in his *Wealth of Nations* in 1776, Adam Smith was the first to suggest that competitive markets send resources to the uses in which they have the highest value (see pp. 52–53). Smith believed that each participant in a competitive market is "led by an invisible hand to promote an end [the efficient use of resources] which was no part of his intention."

You can see the invisible hand at work in the cartoon. The cold drinks vendor has both cold drinks and shade. He has an opportunity cost of each and a minimum supply-price of each. The park-bench reader has a marginal benefit from a cold drink and from shade. You can see that the marginal benefit from shade exceeds the marginal cost, but the marginal cost of a cold drink exceeds its marginal benefit. The transaction that occurs creates producer surplus and consumer surplus. The vendor obtains a producer surplus from selling the shade for more than its opportunity cost, and the reader obtains a consumer surplus from buying the shade for less than its marginal benefit. In the third frame of the cartoon, both the consumer and the producer are better off than they were in the first frame. The umbrella has moved to its highest-valued use.

The Invisible Hand at Work Today

The market economy relentlessly performs the activity illustrated in the cartoon and in Fig. 5.6 to achieve an efficient allocation of resources. And rarely has the market been working as hard as it is today. Think about a few of the changes taking place in our economy that the market is guiding toward an efficient use of resources.

New technologies have cut the cost of producing computers. As these advances have occurred, supply has increased and the price has fallen. Lower prices have encouraged an increase in the quantity demanded of this now less costly tool. The marginal benefit from computers is brought to equality with their marginal cost.

A Florida frost cuts the supply of oranges. With fewer oranges available, the marginal benefit from oranges increases. A shortage of oranges raises their price, so the market allocates the smaller quantity available to the people who value them most highly.

Market forces persistently bring marginal cost and marginal benefit to equality and maximize the sum of consumer surplus and producer surplus.

© The New Yorker Collection 1985
Mike Twohy from cartoonbank.com. All Rights Reserved.

Obstacles to Efficiency

Although markets generally do a good job of sending resources to where they are most highly valued, markets do not always get the correct answer. Sometimes they overproduce a good or service, and sometimes they underproduce. The most significant obstacles to achieving an efficient allocation of resources in the market economy are

- Price ceilings and price floors
- Taxes, subsidies, and quotas
- Monopoly
- Public goods
- External costs and external benefits

Price Ceilings and Price Floors A *price ceiling* is a regulation that makes it illegal to charge a price higher than a specified level. An example is a price ceiling on apartment rents, which some cities impose. A *price floor* is a regulation that makes it illegal to pay a lower price than a specified level. An example is the minimum wage. (We study both of these restrictions on buyers and sellers in Chapter 6.)

The presence of a price ceiling or a price floor blocks the forces of demand and supply and might result in a quantity produced that differs from the quantity determined in an unregulated market.

Taxes, Subsidies, and Quotas *Taxes* increase the prices paid by buyers and lower the prices received by sellers. Taxes decrease the quantity produced (for reasons that are explained in Chapter 6, on pp. 129–132). All kinds of goods and services are taxed, but the highest taxes are on gasoline, alcohol, and tobacco.

Subsidies, which are payments by the government to producers, decrease the prices paid by buyers and increase the prices received by sellers. Subsidies increase the quantity produced.

Quotas, which are limits to the quantity that a firm is permitted to produce, restrict output below the quantity that a competitive market produces. Farms are sometimes subject to quotas.

Monopoly A *monopoly* is a firm that has sole control of a market. For example, Microsoft has a near monopoly on operating systems for personal computers. Although a monopoly can earn a large profit, it prevents the market from achieving an efficient use of resources. The goal of a monopoly is to maximize profit. To achieve this goal, it restricts production and raises price. (We study monopoly in Chapter 12.)

Public Goods A *public good* is a good or service that is consumed simultaneously by everyone, even if they don't pay for it. Examples are national defense and the enforcement of law and order. Competitive markets would produce too small a quantity of public goods because of a *free-rider problem*. It is not in each person's interest to buy her or his share of a public good. So a competitive market produces less than the efficient quantity. (We study public goods in Chapter 16.)

External Costs and External Benefits An *external cost* is a cost that is borne not by the producer but by other people. The cost of pollution is an example of an external cost. When an electric power utility burns coal to generate electricity, it puts sulfur dioxide into the atmosphere. This pollutant falls as acid rain and damages vegetation and crops. The utility does not consider the cost of pollution when it decides the quantity of electric power to supply. Its supply curve is based on its own costs, not on the costs that it inflicts on others. As a result, the utility produces more power than the efficient quantity.

An *external benefit* is a benefit that accrues to people other than the buyer of a good. An example is when someone in a neighborhood paints her home or landscapes her yard. The homeowner does not consider her neighbor's marginal benefit when she decides whether to do this type of work. So the demand curve for house painting and yard improvement does not include all the benefits that accrue. In this case, the quantity falls short of the efficient quantity. (We study externalities in Chapter 18.)

The impediments to efficiency that we've just reviewed and that you will study in greater detail in later chapters result in two possible outcomes:

■ Underproduction
■ Overproduction

Underproduction

Suppose that one firm owns all the pizza outlets in a city and that it produces only 5,000 pizzas a day. Figure 5.7(a) shows that at this quantity, consumers are willing to pay $20 for the marginal pizza — marginal benefit is $20. The marginal cost of a pizza is only $10. So there is a gap between what people are willing to pay and what producers must be offered — between marginal benefit and marginal cost.

The sum of consumer surplus and producer surplus is decreased by the amount of the gray triangle in Fig. 5.7(a). This triangle is called deadweight loss. **Deadweight loss** is the decrease in consumer surplus and producer surplus that results from an inefficient level of production.

The 5,000th pizza brings a benefit of $20 and costs only $10 to produce. If we don't produce this pizza, we are wasting $10. Similar reasoning applies all the way up to the 9,999th pizza. By producing more pizza and less of other goods and services, we get more value from our resources.

The deadweight loss is borne by the entire society. It is not a loss for the consumers and a gain for the producer. It is a *social* loss.

FIGURE 5.7 Underproduction and Overproduction

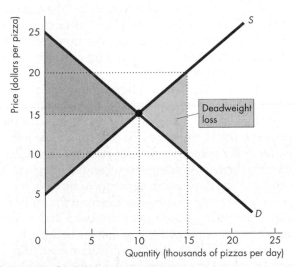

(a) Underproduction

(b) Overproduction

If pizza production is cut to only 5,000 a day, a deadweight loss (the gray triangle) arises (part a). Consumer surplus and producer surplus (the green and blue areas) are reduced. At 5,000 pizzas, the benefit of one more pizza exceeds its cost. The same is true for all levels of production up to 10,000 pizzas a day. If production increases to 15,000, a deadweight loss arises (part b). At 15,000 pizzas a day, the cost of the 15,000th pizza exceeds its benefit. The cost of each pizza above 10,000 exceeds its benefit. Consumer surplus plus producer surplus equals the sum of the green and blue areas minus the gray deadweight loss triangle.

Overproduction

Suppose the pizza lobby gets the government to pay the pizza producers a fat subsidy and that production increases to 15,000 a day. Figure 5.7(b) shows that at this quantity, consumers are willing to pay only $10 for that marginal pizza but the opportunity cost of that pizza is $20. It now costs more to produce the marginal pizza than consumers are willing to pay for it. The gap gets smaller as production approaches 10,000 pizzas a day, but it is present at all quantities greater than 10,000 a day.

Again, deadweight loss is shown by the gray triangle. The sum of consumer surplus and producer surplus is smaller than its maximum by the amount of deadweight loss. The 15,000th pizza brings a benefit of only $10 but costs $20 to produce. If we produce this pizza, we are wasting $10. Similar reasoning applies all the way down to the 10,001st pizza. By producing fewer pizzas and more of other goods and services, we get more value from our resources.

REVIEW QUIZ

1 Do competitive markets use resources efficiently? Explain why or why not.
2 Do markets with a price ceiling or price floor, taxes, subsidies, or quotas, monopoly power, public goods, or externalities result in the quantity produced being the efficient quantity?
3 What is deadweight loss and under what conditions does it occur?
4 Does a deadweight loss occur in a competitive market when the quantity produced equals the competitive equilibrium quantity and the resource allocation is efficient?

You now know the conditions under which the resource allocation is efficient. You've seen how a competitive market can be efficient, and you've seen some impediments to efficiency.

But is an efficient allocation of resources fair? Does the competitive market provide people with fair incomes for their work? And do people always pay a fair price for the things they buy? Don't we need the government to step into some competitive markets to prevent the price from rising too high or falling too low? Let's now study these questions.

Is the Competitive Market Fair?

WHEN A NATURAL DISASTER STRIKES, SUCH AS A severe winter storm or a hurricane, the prices of many essential items jump. The reason the prices jump is that some people have a greater demand and greater willingness to pay when the items are in limited supply. So the higher prices achieve an efficient allocation of scarce resources. News reports of these price hikes almost never talk about efficiency. Instead, they talk about equity or fairness. The claim often made is that it is unfair for profit-seeking dealers to cheat the victims of natural disaster.

Similarly, when low-skilled people work for a wage that is below what most would regard as a "living wage," the media and politicians talk of employers taking unfair advantage of their workers.

How do we decide whether something is fair or unfair? You know when *you* think something is unfair. But how do you know? What are the *principles* of fairness?

Philosophers have tried for centuries to answer this question. Economists have offered their answers too. But before we look at the proposed answers, you should know that there is no universally agreed answer.

Economists agree about efficiency. That is, they agree that it makes sense to make the economic pie as large as possible and to bake it at the lowest possible cost. But they do not agree about equity. That is, they do not agree about what are fair shares of the economic pie for all the people who make it. The reason is that ideas about fairness are not exclusively economic ideas. They touch on politics, ethics, and religion. Nevertheless, economists have thought about these issues and have a contribution to make. So let's examine the views of economists on this topic.

To think about fairness, think of economic life as a game — a serious game. All ideas about fairness can be divided into two broad groups. They are

- It's not fair if the *result* isn't fair.
- It's not fair if the *rules* aren't fair.

It's Not Fair If the *Result* Isn't Fair

The earliest efforts to establish a principle of fairness were based on the view that the result is what matters. And the general idea was that it is unfair if people's incomes are too unequal. It is unfair that

bank presidents earn millions of dollars a year while bank tellers earn only thousands of dollars a year. It is unfair that a store owner enjoys a larger profit and her customers pay higher prices in the aftermath of a winter storm.

There was a lot of excitement during the nineteenth century when economists thought they had made the incredible discovery that efficiency requires equality of incomes. To make the economic pie as large as possible, it must be cut into equal pieces, one for each person. This idea turns out to be wrong, but there is a lesson in the reason that it is wrong. So this nineteenth century idea is worth a closer look.

Utilitarianism The nineteenth century idea that only equality brings efficiency is called *utilitarianism*. **Utilitarianism** is a principle that states that we should strive to achieve "the greatest happiness for the greatest number." The people who developed this idea were known as utilitarians. They included the most eminent thinkers, such as Jeremy Bentham and John Stuart Mill.

Utilitarians argued that to achieve "the greatest happiness for the greatest number," income must be transferred from the rich to the poor up to the point of complete equality — to the point at which there are no rich and no poor.

They reasoned in the following way: First, everyone has the same basic wants and a similar capacity to enjoy life. Second, the greater a person's income, the smaller is the marginal benefit of a dollar. The millionth dollar spent by a rich person brings a smaller marginal benefit to that person than the marginal benefit of the thousandth dollar spent by a poorer person. So by transferring a dollar from the millionaire to the poorer person, more is gained than is lost and the two people added together are better off.

Figure 5.8 illustrates this utilitarian idea. Tom and Jerry have the same marginal benefit curve, *MB*. (Marginal benefit is measured on the same scale of 1 to 3 for both Tom and Jerry.) Tom is at point *A*. He earns $5,000 a year, and his marginal benefit of a dollar of income is 3. Jerry is at point *B*. He earns $45,000 a year, and his marginal benefit of a dollar of income is 1. If a dollar is transferred from Jerry to Tom, Jerry loses 1 unit of marginal benefit and Tom gains 3 units. So together, Tom and Jerry are better off. They are sharing the economic pie more efficiently. If a second dollar is transferred, the same thing happens: Tom gains more than Jerry loses. And the same is true for every dollar transferred until they both reach point *C*. At point *C*, Tom and Jerry have

FIGURE 5.8 Utilitarian Fairness

Tom earns $5,000 and has 3 units of marginal benefit at point A. Jerry earns $45,000 and has 1 unit of marginal benefit at point B. If income is transferred from Jerry to Tom, Jerry's loss is less than Tom's gain. Only when each of them has $25,000 and 2 units of marginal benefit (at point C) can the sum of their total benefit increase no further.

$25,000 each, and each has a marginal benefit of 2 units. Now they are sharing the economic pie in the most efficient way. It is bringing the greatest attainable happiness to Tom and Jerry.

The Big Tradeoff One big problem with the utilitarian ideal of complete equality is that it ignores the costs of making income transfers. Recognizing the cost of making income transfers leads to what is called the **big tradeoff**, which is a tradeoff between efficiency and fairness.

The big tradeoff is based on the following facts. Income can be transferred from people with high incomes to people with low incomes only by taxing incomes. Taxing people's income from employment makes them work less. It results in the quantity of labor being less than the efficient quantity. Taxing people's income from capital makes them save less. It results in the quantity of capital being less than the efficient quantity. With smaller quantities of both labor and capital, the quantity of goods and services produced is less than the efficient quantity. The economic pie shrinks.

The tradeoff is between the size of the economic pie and the degree of equality with which it is shared. The greater the amount of income redistribution through income taxes, the greater is the inefficiency — the smaller is the economic pie.

There is a second source of inefficiency. A dollar taken from a rich person does not end up as a dollar in the hands of a poorer person. Some of it is spent on administration of the tax and transfer system. The cost of tax-collecting agencies, such as the IRS, and welfare-administering agencies, such as the Health Care Financing Administration, which administers Medicaid and Medicare, must be paid with some of the taxes collected. Also, taxpayers hire accountants, auditors, and lawyers to help them ensure that they pay the correct amount of taxes. These activities use skilled labor and capital resources that could otherwise be used to produce goods and services that people value.

You can see that when all these costs are taken into account, transferring a dollar from a rich person does not give a dollar to a poor person. It is even possible that with high taxes, those with low incomes end up being worse off. Suppose, for example, that highly taxed entrepreneurs decide to work less hard and shut down some of their businesses. Low-income workers get fired and must seek other, perhaps even lower-paid work.

Because of the big tradeoff, those who say that fairness is equality propose a modified version of utilitarianism.

Make the Poorest as Well Off as Possible A Harvard philosopher, John Rawls, proposed a modified version of utilitarianism in a classic book entitled *A Theory of Justice*, published in 1971. Rawls says that, taking all the costs of income transfers into account, the fair distribution of the economic pie is the one that makes the poorest person as well off as possible. The incomes of rich people should be taxed, and after paying the costs of administering the tax and transfer system, what is left should be transferred to the poor. But the taxes must not be so high that they make the economic pie shrink to the point at which the poorest person ends up with a smaller piece. A bigger share of a smaller pie can be less than a smaller share of a bigger pie. The goal is to make the piece enjoyed by the poorest person as big as possible. Most likely, this piece will not be an equal share.

The "fair results" ideas require a change in the results after the game is over. Some economists say that these changes are themselves unfair and propose a different way of thinking about fairness.

It's Not Fair If the *Rules* Aren't Fair

The idea that it's not fair if the rules aren't fair is based on a fundamental principle that seems to be hardwired into the human brain: the symmetry principle. The **symmetry principle** is the requirement that people in similar situations be treated similarly. It is the moral principle that lies at the center of all the big religions and that says, in some form or other, "behave toward other people in the way you expect them to behave toward you."

In economic life, this principle translates into *equality of opportunity*. But equality of opportunity to do what? This question is answered by the late Harvard philosopher, Robert Nozick, in a book entitled *Anarchy, State, and Utopia*, published in 1974.

Nozick argues that the idea of fairness as an outcome or result cannot work and that fairness must be based on the fairness of the rules. He suggests that fairness obeys two rules:

1. The state must enforce laws that establish and protect private property.
2. Private property may be transferred from one person to another only by voluntary exchange.

The first rule says that everything that is valuable must be owned by individuals and that the state must ensure that theft is prevented. The second rule says that the only legitimate way a person can acquire property is to buy it in exchange for something else that the person owns. If these rules, which are the only fair rules, are followed, then the result is fair. It doesn't matter how unequally the economic pie is shared, provided that it is baked by people, each one of whom voluntarily provides services in exchange for the share of the pie offered in compensation.

These rules satisfy the symmetry principle. And if these rules are not followed, the symmetry principle is broken. You can see these facts by imagining a world in which the laws are not followed.

First, suppose that some resources or goods are not owned. They are common property. Then everyone is free to participate in a grab to use these resources or goods. The strongest will prevail. But when the strongest prevails, the strongest effectively *owns* the resources or goods in question and prevents others from enjoying them.

Second, suppose that we do not insist on voluntary exchange for transferring ownership of resources from one person to another. The alternative is *involuntary* transfer. In simple language, the alternative is theft.

Both of these situations violate the symmetry principle. Only the strong get to acquire what they want. The weak end up with only the resources and goods that the strong don't want.

In contrast, if the two rules of fairness are followed, everyone, strong and weak, is treated in a similar way. Everyone is free to use their resources and human skills to create things that are valued by themselves and others and to exchange the fruits of their efforts with each other. This is the only set of arrangements that obeys the symmetry principle.

Fairness and Efficiency   If private property rights are enforced and if voluntary exchange takes place in a competitive market, resources will be allocated efficiently if there are no

1. Price ceilings and price floors
2. Taxes, subsidies, and quotas
3. Monopolies
4. Public goods
5. External costs and external benefits

And according to the Nozick rules, the resulting distribution of income and wealth will be fair. Let's study a concrete example to examine the claim that if resources are allocated efficiently, they are also allocated fairly.

A Price Hike in a Natural Disaster   An earthquake has broken the pipes that deliver drinking water to a city. The price of bottled water jumps from $1 a bottle to $8 a bottle in the 30 or so shops that have water for sale.

First, let's agree that the water is being used *efficiently*. There is a fixed amount of bottled water in the city, and given the quantity available, some people are willing to pay $8 to get a bottle. The water goes to the people who value it most highly. Consumer surplus and producer surplus are maximized.

So the water resources are being used efficiently. But are they being used fairly? Shouldn't people who can't afford to pay $8 a bottle get some of the available water for a lower price that they can afford? Isn't the fair solution for the shops to sell water for a lower price that people can afford? Or perhaps it might be fairer if the government bought the water and then made it available to people through a government store at a "reasonable" price? Let's think about these alternative solutions to the water problem of this city. Should water somehow be made available at a more reasonable price?

Shop Offers Water for $5 Suppose that Kris, a shop owner, offers water at $5 a bottle. Who will buy it? There are two types of buyers. Chuck is an example of one type. He values water at $8—is willing to pay $8 a bottle. Recall that given the quantity of water available, the equilibrium price is $8 a bottle. If Chuck buys the water, he consumes it. Chuck ends up with a consumer surplus of $3 on the bottle, and Kris receives $3 less of producer surplus.

Mitch is an example of the second type of buyer. Mitch would not pay $8 for a bottle. In fact, he wouldn't even pay $5 to consume a bottle of water. But he buys a bottle for $5. Why? Because he plans to sell the water to someone who is willing to pay $8 to consume it. When Mitch buys the water, Kris again receives a producer surplus of $3 *less* than she would receive if she charged the going market price. Mitch now becomes a water dealer. He sells the water for the going price of $8 and earns a producer surplus of $3.

So by being public-spirited and offering water for less than the market price, Kris ends up $3 a bottle worse off and the buyers end up $3 a bottle better off. The same people consume the water in both situations. They are the people who value the water at $8 a bottle. But the distribution of consumer surplus and producer surplus is different in the two cases. When Kris offers the water for $5 a bottle, she ends up with a smaller producer surplus and Chuck and Mitch with a larger consumer surplus and producer surplus.

So which is the fair arrangement? The one that favors Kris or the one that favors Chuck and Mitch? The fair-rules view is that both arrangements are fair. Kris voluntarily sells the water for $5, so in effect, she is helping the community to cope with its water problem. It is fair that she should help, but the choice is hers. She owns the water. It is not fair that she should be compelled to help.

Government Buys Water Now suppose instead that the government buys all the water. The going price is $8 a bottle, so that's what the government pays. Now the government offers the water for sale for $1 a bottle, its "normal" price.

The quantity of water supplied is exactly the same as before. But now, at $1 a bottle, the quantity demanded is much larger than the quantity supplied. There is a shortage of water.

Because there is a large water shortage, the government decides to ration the amount that anyone may buy. Everyone is allocated one bottle. So everyone lines up to collect his or her bottle. Two of these people are Chuck and Mitch. Chuck, you'll recall, is

willing to pay $8 a bottle. Mitch is willing to pay less than $5. But they both get a bargain. Chuck drinks his $1 bottle and enjoys a $7 consumer surplus. What does Mitch do? Does he drink his bottle? He does not. He sells it to another person who values the water at $8. And he enjoys a $7 producer surplus from his temporary water-trading business.

So the people who value the water most highly consume it. But the consumer and producer surpluses are distributed in a different way from what the free market would have delivered. Again the question arises, which arrangement is fair?

The main difference between the government scheme and Kris's private charitable contributions lies in the fact that to buy the water for $8 and sell it for $1, the government must tax someone $7 for each bottle sold. So whether this arrangement is fair depends on whether the taxes are fair.

Taxes are an involuntary transfer of private property, so according to the fair-rules view, they are unfair. But most economists, and most people, think that there is such a thing as a fair tax. So it seems that the fair-rules view needs to be weakened a bit. Agreeing that there is such a thing as a fair tax is the easy part. Deciding what is a fair tax brings endless disagreement and debate.

REVIEW QUIZ

1 What are the two big approaches to thinking about fairness?
2 What is the utilitarian idea of fairness and what is wrong with it?
3 Explain the big tradeoff. What idea of fairness has been developed to deal with it?
4 What is the main idea of fairness based on fair rules?

◆ You've now studied the two biggest issues that run right through the whole of economics: efficiency and equity, or fairness. In the next chapter, we study some sources of inefficiency and unfairness. And at many points throughout this book — and in your life — you will return to and use the ideas about efficiency and fairness that you've learned in this chapter. *Reading Between the Lines* on pp. 116–117 looks at an example of an inefficiency and, some would argue, an unfairness in our economy today.

Efficiency and Equity in the Market for Drugs

CNN, October 23, 2001

U.S. Set on Getting Cipro for Under $1 a Pill

The federal government is hoping to buy Cipro, the antibiotic most effective against anthrax, at less than $1 a pill, Health and Human Services Secretary Tommy Thompson said Tuesday.

The limited supply and high cost of Cipro, the Germany-based Bayer AG's name for its patented version of ciprofloxacin, has led to suggestions that Congress allow other companies to make cheaper, generic versions of the drug.

Bayer has been charging the government $1.87 a pill. ...

Bayer, which holds the patent on Cipro through 2003, has promised to triple its production and ship 200 million tablets in the next three months.

THE WASHINGTON POST, October 26, 2001

Varying Costs for Cipro Criticized

The Department of Health and Human Services, which just negotiated to buy the anti-anthrax drug Cipro from Bayer Corp. at 95 cents a pill, is also arranging to get the same medicine at less than half that price under a different program.

Cipro is being sold by Bayer for about 43 cents a tablet under an HHS program, known as "340B," in which the agency negotiates low prices on pharmaceuticals for hospitals and clinics that treat poor people and underserved areas. ...

Cipro retails for between $4 and $5 a pill. ...

Essence of the Stories

■ Bayer holds the patent on Cipro, a drug used to treat anthrax, through 2003.

■ The U.S. government buys Cipro for several different prices: 43¢ a pill under a program to provide drugs to poor people, 95¢ a pill under the deal negotiated by Tommy Thompson, and $1.87 a pill before the latest negotiation.

■ The retail price of Cipro is between $4 and $5 a pill.

■ Some people have suggested that Congress should allow other companies to make cheaper, generic versions of ciprofloxacin.

■ Bayer has promised to triple output to 200 million tablets during the last three months of 2001.

Economic Analysis

■ The efficient quantity of Cipro is that at which its marginal benefit equals its marginal cost.

■ We can measure the marginal benefit of Cipro by the amount that people are willing to pay for it.

■ The marginal benefit to people who buy Cipro at its retail price is between $4 and $5 a pill.

■ The marginal benefit to the U.S. government before the 2001 anthrax incidents was $1.87 a pill.

■ The marginal benefit to the U.S. government after the 2001 anthrax incidents was 95¢ a pill.

■ The marginal benefit to the U.S. government when Cipro is used to treat poor people is 43¢ a pill.

■ We do not know the marginal cost of producing Cipro. But we know that Bayer AG is willing to sell Cipro for 43¢ a pill. So we can be sure that the marginal cost of a pill is not greater than 43¢, and most likely it is less than this amount.

■ Because most Cipro sells for a price that exceeds 43¢, the quantity of Cipro produced is less than the efficient quantity.

■ Figure 1 illustrates the market for Cipro before the anthrax scare of 2001. The demand curve was D_0, and the marginal cost curve was MC. (It is an assumption that MC is constant at 40¢ a pill.)

■ The figure ignores the small quantity of Cipro sold at 43¢ to the U.S. government.

■ Private buyers took a small quantity at $4.50 a pill, and the government bought the rest at $1.87 a pill. The total quantity bought was 22 million pills a month.

■ The efficient quantity exceeds 22 million pills a month, and a deadweight loss was incurred.

■ Because there were two prices, the two green triangles show consumer surplus. The blue area shows producer surplus.

■ Figure 2 illustrates the market for Cipro after the anthrax scare of 2001. Demand increased, and the demand curve became D_1. Marginal cost, MC, remained (an assumption) at 40¢ a pill.

■ Total production tripled from 22 to 66 million pills a month.

■ Private buyers took an increased quantity of

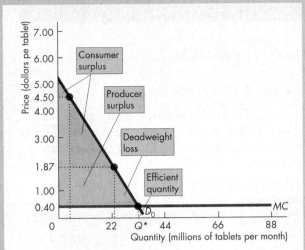

Figure 1 Before the anthrax scare

Figure 2 After the anthrax scare

Cipro at $4.50 a pill, and the government bought the rest at the lower price of 95¢ a pill.

■ The efficient quantity exceeds 66 million pills a month, and a deadweight loss was incurred.

■ Consumer surplus and producer surplus both increased.

You're The Voter

■ Would there be an even greater gain in efficiency if the government bought a cheaper generic version of ciprofloxacin than the patented Cipro that Bayer sells?

117

SUMMARY

KEY POINTS

Efficiency: A Refresher (pp. 102–103)

- The marginal benefit received from a good or service — the benefit of consuming one additional unit — is the *value* of the good or service to its consumers.
- The marginal cost of a good or service — the cost of producing one additional unit — is the *opportunity cost* of one more unit to its producers.
- Resource allocation is efficient when marginal benefit equals marginal cost.
- If marginal benefit exceeds marginal cost, an increase in production uses resources more efficiently.
- If marginal cost exceeds marginal benefit, a decrease in production uses resources more efficiently.

Value, Price, and Consumer Surplus (pp. 104–105)

- Marginal benefit is measured by the maximum price that consumers are willing to pay for a good or service.
- Marginal benefit determines demand, and a demand curve is a marginal benefit curve.
- Value is what people are *willing to* pay; price is what people *must* pay.
- Consumer surplus equals value minus price, summed over the quantity consumed.

Cost, Price, and Producer Surplus (pp. 106–107)

- Marginal cost is measured by the minimum price producers must be offered to increase production by one unit.
- Marginal cost determines supply, and a supply curve is a marginal cost curve.
- Opportunity cost is what producers pay; price is what producers receive.
- Producer surplus equals price minus opportunity cost, summed over the quantity produced.

Is the Competitive Market Efficient? (pp. 108–111)

- In a competitive equilibrium, marginal benefit equals marginal cost and resource allocation is efficient.
- Monopoly restricts production and creates deadweight loss.
- A competitive market provides too small a quantity of public goods because of the free-rider problem.
- A competitive market provides too large a quantity of goods and services that have external costs and too small a quantity of goods and services that have external benefits.

Is the Competitive Market Fair? (pp. 112–115)

- Ideas about fairness can be divided into two groups: fair *results* and fair *rules*.
- Fair-results ideas require income transfers from the rich to the poor.
- Fair-rules ideas require property rights and voluntary exchange.

KEY FIGURES

KEY TERMS

PROBLEMS

*1. The figure shows the market for floppy discs.

a. What are the equilibrium price and equilibrium quantity of floppy discs?
b. Calculate the amount consumers paid for floppy discs bought.
c. Calculate the consumer surplus.
d. Calculate the producer surplus.
e. Calculate the cost of producing the floppy discs sold.
f. What is the efficient quantity?

2. The figure illustrates the market for CDs.

a. What are the equilibrium price and equilibrium quantity of CDs?
b. Calculate the amount consumers paid for CDs.
c. Calculate the consumer surplus.
d. Calculate the producer surplus.
e. Calculate the cost of producing the CDs sold.
f. What is the efficient quantity of CDs?

*3. The table gives the demand and supply schedules for sandwiches.

Price (dollars per sandwich)	Quantity demanded (sandwiches per hour)	Quantity supplied
0	400	0
1	350	50
2	300	100
3	250	150
4	200	200
5	150	250
6	100	300
7	50	350
8	0	400

a. What is the maximum price that consumers are willing to pay for the 250th sandwich?
b. What is the minimum price that producers are willing to accept for the 250th sandwich?
c. Are 250 sandwiches a day less than or greater than the efficient quantity?
d. If the sandwich market is efficient, what is the consumer surplus? (Draw the graph.)
e. If the sandwich market is efficient, what is the producer surplus? (Draw the graph.)
f. If sandwich makers produce 250 a day, what is the deadweight loss? (Draw the graph.)

4. The table gives the demand and supply schedules for sunscreen.

Price (dollars per bottles)	Quantity demanded (bottles per day)	Quantity supplied
0	900	0
1	800	100
2	700	200
3	600	300
4	500	400
5	400	500
6	300	600
7	200	700
8	100	800
9	0	900

a. What is the maximum price that consumers are willing to pay for the 300th bottle?
b. What is the minimum price that producers are willing to accept for the 300th bottle?
c. Are 300 bottles a day less than or greater than the efficient quantity? (Draw the graphs.)
d. If the market for sunscreen is efficient, what is the consumer surplus? (Draw the graphs.)

e. If the market for sunscreen is efficient, what is the producer surplus?

f. If sunscreen bottlers produce 300 bottles a day, what is the deadweight loss?

*5. The table gives the demand schedules for train travel for Ben, Beth, and Bo.

Price	Quantity demanded (passenger miles)		
(cents per passenger mile)	Ben	Beth	Bo
10	500	300	60
20	450	250	50
30	400	200	40
40	350	150	30
50	300	100	20
60	250	50	10
70	200	0	0

a. If the price of train travel is 40 cents a passenger mile, what is the consumer surplus of each traveler?

b. Which traveler has the largest consumer surplus? Explain why.

c. If the price rises to 50 cents a passenger mile, what is the change in consumer surplus of each traveler?

6. The table gives the demand schedules for airline travel for Ann, Arthur, and Abby.

Price	Quantity demanded (passenger miles)		
(dollars per passenger mile)	Ann	Arthur	Abby
10.00	500	600	300
12.50	450	500	250
15.00	400	400	200
17.50	350	300	150
20.00	300	200	100
22.50	250	100	50
25.00	200	0	0

a. If the price is $20 a passenger mile, what is the consumer surplus of each traveler?

b. Which consumer has the largest consumer surplus? Explain why.

c. If the price falls to $15 a passenger mile, what is the change in consumer surplus of each traveler?

CRITICAL THINKING

1. Study *Reading Between the Lines* on pp. 116–117 about Cipro and then answer the following questions:

a. Is the quantity of Cipro produced greater than, less than, or equal to the efficient quantity? Explain your answer by using the concepts of marginal benefit, marginal cost, price, consumer surplus, and producer surplus.

b. What, if anything, do you think could be done to increase the quantity of Cipro and decrease its price?

c. Bayer sells some Cipro for 43¢ a pill to the U.S. government. Does this deal increase or decrease consumer surplus? Does it increase or decrease Bayer's producer surplus? Does it bring the quantity of Cipro closer to the efficient quantity? Explain your answer by using the concepts of marginal benefit, marginal cost, price, consumer surplus, and producer surplus.

d. Drug producers could make a generic ciprofloxacin and sell it at a much lower price than Bayer's price. Do generic drugs increase or decrease consumer surplus? Does a generic ciprofloxacin increase or decrease Bayer's producer surplus? Does it bring the quantity of antibiotics closer to the efficient quantity? Explain your answer by using the concepts of marginal benefit, marginal cost, price, consumer surplus, and producer surplus.

WEB EXERCISES

1. Use the links on the Parkin Web site and read the article by Augustine Faucher entitled "Cipro and the Free Riders." Then answer the following questions:

a. What does the author claim is the problem in the market for antibiotics that can treat anthrax?

b. What does the author claim is the solution to the problem in this market?

c. Explain why you agree or disagree with the author.

MARKETS IN ACTION ── CHAPTER 6

Turbulent Times

Apartment rents are skyrocketing in Washington, and people are screaming for help. Can the government limit rent increases to help renters live in affordable housing? ◆ Almost every day, a new machine is invented that saves labor and increases productivity. Take a look at the machines in McDonald's that have replaced some low-skilled workers. Can we protect low-skilled workers with minimum wage laws that enable people to earn a living wage? ◆ Almost everything we buy is taxed. Beer is one of the most heavily taxed items. How much of the beer tax gets paid by the buyer and how much by the seller? Do taxes help or hinder the market in its attempt to move resources to where they are valued most highly? ◆ Trade in items such as drugs, automatic firearms, and enriched uranium is illegal. What are the effects of laws that make trading in a good or service illegal on its price and the quantity bought and sold? ◆ In 1996, ideal conditions brought record yields and global grain production increased. But in 2000 and 2001, yields were low and global grain production decreased. How do farm prices and revenues react to such output fluctuations?

◆ In this chapter, we use the theory of demand and supply (Chapter 3) and the concepts of elasticity (Chapter 4) and efficiency (Chapter 5) to answer questions like those that we've just posed. In *Reading Between the Lines* at the end of the chapter, we explore who would benefit most from a proposed cut in the beer tax. And in a special feature on the Economics Place Web site, we examine the 2002 Farm Bill.

After studying this chapter, you will be able to

■ Explain how housing markets work and how price ceilings create housing shortages and inefficiency

■ Explain how labor markets work and how minimum wage laws create unemployment and inefficiency

■ Explain the effects of the sales tax

■ Explain how markets for illegal goods work

■ Explain why farm prices and revenues fluctuate and how speculation and price stabilization agencies influence farm prices and revenues

121

Housing Markets and Rent Ceilings

To SEE HOW A HOUSING MARKET WORKS, LET'S transport ourselves to San Francisco in April 1906, as the city is suffering from a massive earthquake and fire. You can sense the enormity of San Francisco's problems by reading a headline from the April 19, 1906, *New York Times* about the first days of the crisis:

> Over 500 Dead, $200,000,000 Lost in
> San Francisco Earthquake
> Nearly Half the City Is in Ruins and 50,000
> Are Homeless

The commander of federal troops in charge of the emergency described the magnitude of the problem:

> Not a hotel of note or importance was left standing. The great apartment houses had vanished . . . two hundred-and-twenty-five thousand people were . . . homeless.[1]

Almost overnight, more than half the people in a city of 400,000 had lost their homes. Temporary shelters and camps alleviated some of the problem, but it was also necessary to utilize the apartment buildings and houses left standing. As a consequence, they had to accommodate 40 percent more people than they had before the earthquake.

The *San Francisco Chronicle* was not published for more than a month after the earthquake. When the newspaper reappeared on May 24, 1906, the city's housing shortage — what would seem to be a major news item that would still be of grave importance — was not mentioned. Milton Friedman and George Stigler describe the situation:

> *There is not a single mention of a housing shortage!* The classified advertisements listed sixty-four offers of flats and houses for rent, and nineteen of houses for sale, against five advertisements of flats or houses wanted. Then and thereafter a considerable number of all types of accommodation except hotel rooms were offered for rent.[2]

How did San Francisco cope with such a devastating reduction in the supply of housing?

---

[1] Reported in Milton Friedman and George J. Stigler, "Roofs or Ceilings? The Current Housing Problem," in *Popular Essays on Current Problems*, vol. 1, no. 2 (New York: Foundation for Economic Education, 1946), pp. 3–159.
[2] *Ibid.*, p. 3.

The Market Response to a Decrease in Supply

Figure 6.1 shows the market for housing in San Francisco. The demand curve for housing is *D*. There is a short-run supply curve, labeled *SS*, and a long-run supply curve, labeled *LS*.

The short-run supply curve shows the change in the quantity of housing supplied as the rent changes while the number of houses and apartment buildings remains constant. The short-run supply response arises from changes in the intensity with which existing buildings are used. The quantity of housing supplied increases if families rent out rooms that they previously used themselves, and it decreases if families use rooms that they previously rented out to others.

The long-run supply curve shows how the quantity of housing supplied responds to a change in price after enough time has elapsed for new apartment buildings and houses to be erected or for existing ones to be destroyed. In Fig. 6.1, the long-run supply curve is *perfectly elastic*. We do not actually know that the long-run supply curve is perfectly elastic, but it is a reasonable assumption. It implies that the cost of building an apartment is pretty much the same regardless of whether there are 50,000 or 150,000 apartments in existence.

The equilibrium price (rent) and quantity are determined at the point of intersection of the *short-run* supply curve and the demand curve. Before the earthquake, the equilibrium rent is $16 a month and the quantity is 100,000 units of housing.

Figure 6.1(a) shows the situation immediately after the earthquake. The destruction of buildings decreases the supply of housing and shifts the short-run supply curve *SS* leftward to SS_A. If the rent remains at $16 a month, only 44,000 units of housing are available. But with only 44,000 units of housing available, the maximum rent that someone is willing to pay for the last available apartment is $24 a month. So rents rise. In Fig. 6.1(a), the rent rises to $20 a month.

As the rent rises, the quantity of housing demanded decreases and the quantity supplied increases to 72,000 units. These changes occur because people economize on their use of space and make spare rooms, attics, and basements available to others. The higher rent allocates the scarce housing to the people who value it most highly and are willing to pay the most for it.

But the higher rent has other, long-run effects. Let's look at these long-run effects.

FIGURE 6.1   The San Francisco Housing Market in 1906

(a) After earthquake

(b) Long-run adjustment

Part (a) shows that before the earthquake, 100,000 housing units were rented at $16 a month. After the earthquake, the short-run supply curve shifts from SS to SS$_A$. The rent rises to $20 a month, and the quantity of housing decreases to 72,000 units.

With rent at $20 a month, there is profit in building new apartments and houses. As the building proceeds, the short-run supply curve shifts rightward (part b). The rent gradually falls to $16 a month, and the quantity of housing increases to 100,000 units — as the arrowed line shows.

Long-Run Adjustments

With sufficient time for new apartments and houses to be constructed, supply increases. The long-run supply curve tells us that in the long run, housing is supplied at a rent of $16 a month. Because the rent of $20 a month exceeds the long-run supply price of $16 a month, there is a building boom. More apartments and houses are built, and the short-run supply curve shifts gradually rightward.

Figure 6.1(b) shows the long-run adjustment. As more housing is built, the short-run supply curve shifts gradually rightward and intersects the demand curve at lower rents and larger quantities. The market equilibrium follows the arrows down the demand curve. The building boom comes to an end when there is no further profit in building new apartments and houses. The process ends when the rent is back at $16 a month, and 100,000 units of housing are available.

We've just seen how a housing market responds to a decrease in supply. And we've seen that a key part of the adjustment process is a rise in the rent. Suppose the government passes a law to stop the rent from rising. What happens then?

A Regulated Housing Market

We're now going to study the effects of a price ceiling in the housing market. A **price ceiling** is a regulation that makes it illegal to charge a price higher than a specified level. When a price ceiling is applied to housing markets, it is called a **rent ceiling**. How does a rent ceiling affect the housing market?

The effect of a price (rent) ceiling depends on whether it is imposed at a level that is above or below the equilibrium price (rent). A price ceiling set above the equilibrium price has no effect. The reason is that the price ceiling does not constrain the market forces. The force of the law and the market forces are not in conflict. But a price ceiling below the equilibrium price has powerful effects on a market. The reason is that it attempts to prevent the price from regulating the quantities demanded and supplied. The force of the law and the market forces are in conflict, and one (or both) of these forces must yield to some degree. Let's study the effects of a price ceiling that is set below the equilibrium price by returning to San Francisco. What would have happened in San Francisco if a rent ceiling of $16 a month — the rent before the earthquake — had been imposed?

FIGURE 6.2   A Rent Ceiling

A rent above $16 a month is illegal (in the gray-shaded illegal region). At a rent of $16 a month, the quantity of housing supplied after the earthquake is 44,000 units. Someone is willing to pay $24 a month for the 44,000th unit. Frustrated renters spend time searching for housing and frustrated renters and landlords make deals in a black market.

Figure 6.2 enables us to answer this question. A rent that exceeds $16 a month is in the gray-shaded illegal region in the figure. At a rent of $16 a month, the quantity of housing supplied is 44,000 units and the quantity demanded is 100,000 units. So there is a shortage of 56,000 units of housing.

But the story does not end here. Somehow, the 44,000 units of available housing must be allocated among people who demand 100,000 units. How is this allocation achieved? When a rent ceiling creates a housing shortage, two developments occur. They are

■ Search activity
■ Black markets

Search Activity

The time spent looking for someone with whom to do business is called **search activity**. We spend some time in search activity almost every time we buy something. You want the latest hot CD, and you know four stores that stock it. But which store has the best deal? You need to spend a few minutes on the telephone finding out. In some markets, we spend a lot of time searching. An example is the used car market. People spend a lot of time checking out alternative dealers and cars.

But when a price is regulated and there is a shortage, search activity increases. In the case of a rent-controlled housing market, frustrated would-be renters scan the newspapers, not only for housing ads but also for death notices! Any information about newly available housing is useful. And they race to be first on the scene when news of a possible supplier breaks.

The *opportunity cost* of a good is equal not only to its price but also to the value of the search time spent finding the good. So the opportunity cost of housing is equal to the rent (a regulated price) plus the time and other resources spent searching for the restricted quantity available. Search activity is costly. It uses time and other resources, such as telephones, cars, and gasoline that could have been used in other productive ways. A rent ceiling controls the rent portion of the cost of housing, but it does not control the opportunity cost, which might even be *higher* than the rent would be if the market were unregulated.

Black Markets

A **black market** is an illegal market in which the price exceeds the legally imposed price ceiling. Black markets occur in rent-controlled housing, and scalpers run black markets in tickets for big sporting events and rock concerts.

When rent ceilings are in force, frustrated renters and landlords constantly seek ways of increasing rents. One common way is for a new tenant to pay a high price for worthless fittings, such as charging $2,000 for threadbare drapes. Another is for the tenant to pay an exorbitant price for new locks and keys — called "key money."

The level of a black market rent depends on how tightly the rent ceiling is enforced. With loose enforcement, the black market rent is close to the unregulated rent. But with strict enforcement, the black market rent is equal to the maximum price that renters are willing to pay.

With strict enforcement of the rent ceiling in the San Francisco example shown in Fig. 6.2, the quantity of housing available remains at 44,000 units. A small number of people offer housing for rent at $24 a month — the highest rent that someone is willing to pay — and the government detects and punishes some of these black market traders.

Inefficiency of Rent Ceilings

In an unregulated market, the market determines the rent at which the quantity demanded equals the quantity supplied. In this situation, scarce housing resources are allocated efficiently. *Marginal benefit* equals *marginal cost* (see Chapter 5, p. 108).

Figure 6.3 shows the inefficiency of a rent ceiling. If the rent is fixed at $16 per month, 44,000 units are supplied. Marginal benefit is $24 a month. The blue triangle above the supply curve and below the rent ceiling line shows producer surplus. Because the quantity of housing is less than the competitive quantity, there is a deadweight loss, shown by the gray triangle. This loss is borne by the consumers who can't find housing and by producers who can't supply housing at the new lower price. Consumers who do find housing at the controlled rent gain. If no one incurs search cost, consumer surplus is shown by the sum of the green triangle and the red rectangle. But search costs might eat up part of the consumer surplus, possibly as much as the entire amount that consumers are willing to pay for the available housing (the red rectangle).

Equity? So rent ceilings prevent scarce resources from flowing to their highest-valued use. But don't rent ceilings ensure that scarce housing goes to the people whose need is greatest and make the allocation of scarce housing fair?

The complex ideas about fairness are explored in Chapter 5 (pp. 112–115). Blocking rent adjustments that bring the quantity of housing demanded into equality with the quantity supplied doesn't end scarcity. So when the law prevents rents from adjusting and blocks the price mechanism from allocating scarce housing, some other allocation mechanism must be used. One of these factors might be discrimination on the basis of race, ethnicity, or sex. Are these mechanisms fair?

Paris, New York, and Santa Monica are three cities that have rent ceilings; the best example is New York. One consequence of New York's rent ceilings is that families that have lived in the city for a long time — including some rich and famous ones — enjoy low rents, while newcomers pay high rents for hard-to-find apartments. At the same time, landlords in rent-controlled Harlem abandon entire city blocks to rats and drug dealers. Swedish economist Assar Lindbeck has suggested that rent ceilings are the most effective means yet for destroying cities, even more effective than the hydrogen bomb.

FIGURE 6.3   The Inefficiency of a Rent Ceiling

A rent ceiling of $16 a month decreases the quantity of housing supplied to 44,000 units. Producer surplus shrinks, and a deadweight loss arises. If people use no resources in search activity, consumer surplus is the green triangle plus the red rectangle. But if people use resources in search activity equal to the amount they are willing to pay for available housing, the red rectangle, the consumer surplus shrinks to the green triangle.

REVIEW QUIZ

1 How does a decrease in the supply of housing change the equilibrium rent in the short run?
2 What are the effects of a rise in rent? And who gets to consume the scarce housing resources?
3 What are the long-run effects of higher rents following a decrease in the supply of housing?
4 What is a rent ceiling and what are its effects if it is set above the equilibrium rent?
5 What are the effects of a rent ceiling that is set below the equilibrium rent?
6 How do scarce housing resources get allocated when a rent ceiling is in place?

You now know how a price ceiling (rent ceiling) works. Next, we'll learn about the effects of a price floor by studying minimum wages in the labor market.

The Labor Market and the Minimum Wage

FOR EACH ONE OF US, THE LABOR MARKET IS THE market that influences the jobs we get and the wages we earn. Firms decide how much labor to demand, and the lower the wage rate, the greater is the quantity of labor demanded. Households decide how much labor to supply, and the higher the wage rate, the greater is the quantity of labor supplied. The wage rate adjusts to make the quantity of labor demanded equal to the quantity supplied.

But the labor market is constantly hit by shocks, and wages and employment prospects constantly change. The most pervasive source of these shocks is the advance of technology.

New labor-saving technologies become available every year. As a result, the demand for some types of labor, usually the least skilled types, decreases. During the 1980s and 1990s, for example, the demand for telephone operators and television repair technicians decreased. Throughout the past 200 years, the demand for low-skilled farm laborers has steadily decreased.

How does the labor market cope with this continuous decrease in the demand for low-skilled labor? Doesn't it mean that the wage rate of low-skilled workers is constantly falling?

To answer these questions, we must study the market for low-skilled labor. And just as we did when we studied the housing market, we must look at both the short run and the long run.

In the short run, there are a given number of people who have a given skill, training, and experience. Short-run supply of labor describes how the number of hours of labor supplied by this given number of workers changes as the wage rate changes. To get workers to work more hours, they must be offered a higher wage rate.

In the long run, people can acquire new skills and find new types of jobs. The number of people in the low-skilled labor market depends on the wage rate in this market compared with other opportunities. If the wage rate of low-skilled labor is high enough, people will enter this market. If the wage rate is too low, people will leave it. Some will seek training to enter higher-skilled labor markets, and others will stop working.

The long-run supply of labor is the relationship between the quantity of labor supplied and the wage rate after enough time has passed for people to enter or leave the low-skilled labor market. If people can freely enter and leave the low-skilled labor market, the long-run supply of labor is *perfectly elastic*.

Figure 6.4 shows the market for low-skilled labor. Other things remaining the same, the lower the wage rate, the greater is the quantity of labor demanded by firms. The demand curve for labor, D in part (a), shows this relationship between the wage rate and the quantity of labor demanded. Other things remaining the same, the higher the wage rate, the greater is the quantity of labor supplied by households. But the longer the period of adjustment, the greater is the *elasticity of supply* of labor. The short-run supply curve is SS, and the long-run supply curve is LS. In the figure, long-run supply is assumed to be perfectly elastic (the LS curve is horizontal). This market is in equilibrium at a wage rate of $5 an hour and 22 million hours of labor employed.

What happens if a labor-saving invention decreases the demand for low-skilled labor? Figure 6.4(a) shows the short-run effects of such a change. The demand curve before the new technology is introduced is the curve labeled D. After the introduction of the new technology, the demand curve shifts leftward to D_A. The wage rate falls to $4 an hour, and the quantity of labor employed decreases to 21 million hours. But this short-run effect on the wage rate and employment is not the end of the story.

People who are now earning only $4 an hour look around for other opportunities. They see many other jobs (in markets for other types of skills) that pay more than $4 an hour. One by one, workers decide to go back to school or take jobs that pay less but offer on-the-job training. As a result, the short-run supply curve begins to shift leftward.

Figure 6.4(b) shows the long-run adjustment. As the short-run supply curve shifts leftward, it intersects the demand curve D_A at higher wage rates and lower levels of employment. The process ends when workers have no incentive to leave the low-skilled labor market and the short-run supply curve has shifted to SS_A. At this point, the wage rate has returned to $5 an hour and employment has decreased to 20 million hours a year.

Sometimes, the adjustment process that we've just described is rapid. At other times, it is slow and the wage rate remains low for a long period. To boost the incomes of the lowest-paid workers, the government intervenes in the labor market and sets the minimum wage that employers are required to pay. Let's look at the effects of the minimum wage.

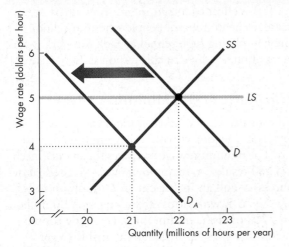

FIGURE 6.4   A Market for Low-Skilled Labor

(a) After invention

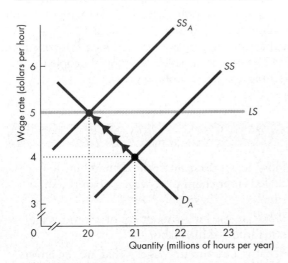

(b) Long-run adjustment

Part (a) shows the immediate effect of a labor-saving invention on the market for low-skilled labor. Initially, the wage rate is $5 an hour and 22 million hours are employed. A labor-saving invention shifts the demand curve from D to D_A. The wage rate falls to $4 an hour, and employment decreases to 21 million hours a year. With the lower wage rate, some workers leave this market, and the short-run supply curve starts to shift gradually leftward to SS_A (part b). The wage rate gradually increases, and the employment level decreases. In the long run, the wage rate returns to $5 an hour and employment decreases to 20 million hours a year.

The Minimum Wage

A **price floor** is a regulation that makes it illegal to trade at a price lower than a specified level. When a price floor is applied to labor markets, it is called a **minimum wage**. If the minimum wage is set *below* the equilibrium wage, the minimum wage has no effect. The minimum wage and market forces are not in conflict. If the minimum wage is set *above* the equilibrium wage, the minimum wage is in conflict with market forces and does have some effects on the labor market. Let's study these effects by returning to the market for low-skilled labor.

Suppose that with an equilibrium wage of $4 an hour (Fig. 6.4a), the government sets a minimum wage at $5 an hour. What are the effects of this minimum wage? Figure 6.5 answers this question. It shows the minimum wage as the horizontal red line labeled "Minimum wage." A wage below this level is in the gray-shaded illegal region. At the minimum wage rate, 20 million hours of labor are demanded (point *A*) and 22 million hours of labor are supplied (point *B*), so 2 million hours of available labor are unemployed.

With only 20 million hours demanded, some workers are willing to supply that 20 millionth hour

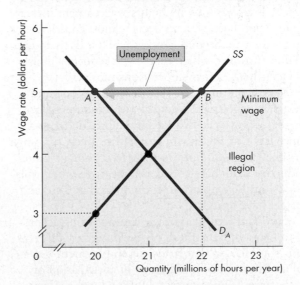

FIGURE 6.5   Minimum Wage and Unemployment

A wage below $5 an hour is illegal (in the gray-shaded illegal region). At the minimum wage of $5 an hour, 20 million hours are hired but 22 million hours are available. Unemployment — *AB* — of 2 million hours a year is created.

for $3. Frustrated unemployed workers spend time and other resources searching for hard-to-find jobs.

The Minimum Wage in Practice

The minimum wage in the United States is set by the federal government's Fair Labor Standards Act. In 2002, the federal minimum wage is $5.15 an hour. Some state governments have passed state minimum wage laws that exceed the federal minimum wage. The minimum wage has increased from time to time and has fluctuated between 35 percent and more than 50 percent of the average wage of production workers.

You saw in Fig. 6.5 that the minimum wage brings unemployment. But how much unemployment does it bring? Economists do not agree on the answer to this question. Until recently, most economists believed that the minimum wage was a big contributor to high unemployment among low-skilled young workers. But this view has recently been challenged and the challenge rebutted.

David Card of the University of California at Berkeley and Alan Krueger of Princeton University say that increases in the minimum wage have not decreased employment and created unemployment. From their study of minimum wages in California, New Jersey, and Texas, Card and Krueger say that the employment rate of low-income workers increased following an increase in the minimum wage. They suggest three reasons why higher wages might increase employment. First, workers become more conscientious and productive. Second, workers are less likely to quit, so labor turnover, which is costly, is reduced. Third, managers make a firm's operations more efficient.

Most economists are skeptical about Card and Krueger's suggestions. They ask two questions. First, if higher wages make workers more productive and reduce labor turnover, why don't firms freely pay wage rates above the equilibrium wage to encourage more productive work habits? Second, are there other explanations for the employment responses that Card and Krueger have found?

Card and Krueger got the timing wrong according to Daniel Hamermesh of the University of Texas at Austin. He says that firms cut employment *before* the minimum wage is increased in anticipation of the increase. If he is correct, looking for the effects of an increase *after* it has occurred misses its main effects. Finis Welch of Texas A&M University and Kevin Murphy of the University of Chicago say the employment effects that Card and Krueger found are caused by regional differences in economic growth, not by changes in the minimum wage.

One effect of the minimum wage, according to Fig. 6.5, is an increase in the quantity of labor supplied. If this effect occurs, it might show up as an increase in the number of people who quit school before completing high school to look for work. Some economists say that this response does occur.

Inefficiency of the Minimum Wage

An unregulated labor market allocates scarce labor resources to the jobs in which they are valued most highly. The minimum wage frustrates the market mechanism and results in unemployment — wasted labor resources — and an inefficient amount of job search.

In Fig. 6.5, with firms employing only 20 million hours of labor at the minimum wage, many people who are willing to supply labor are unable to get hired. You can see that the 20 millionth hour of labor is available for $3. That is, the lowest wage at which someone is willing to supply the 20 millionth hour — read off from the supply curve — is $3. Someone who manages to find a job earns $5 an hour — $2 an hour more than the lowest wage rate at which someone is willing to work. So it pays unemployed people to spend time and effort looking for work.

REVIEW QUIZ

1 How does a decrease in the demand for low-skilled labor change the wage rate in the short run?
2 What are the long-run effects of a lower wage rate for low-skilled labor?
3 What is a minimum wage? What are the effects of a minimum wage set below the equilibrium wage?
4 What is the effect of a minimum wage that is set above the equilibrium wage?

Next we're going to study a more widespread government action in markets: taxes, such as the sales taxes that many states impose. We'll see how taxes change prices and quantities and discover that usually a sales tax is not paid entirely by the buyer. And we'll see that a tax usually creates a deadweight loss.

Taxes

ALMOST EVERYTHING YOU BUY IS TAXED. But who really pays the tax? Because the sales tax is added to the price of a good or service when it is sold, isn't it obvious that the *buyer* pays the tax? Isn't the price higher than it otherwise would be by an amount equal to the tax? It can be, but usually it isn't. And it is even possible that the buyer actually pays none of the tax! Let's see how we can make sense of these apparently absurd statements.

Who Pays a Sales Tax?

Suppose the government puts a $10 sales tax on CD players. What are the effects of the sales tax on the price and quantity of CD players? To answer this question, we need to work out what happens to demand and supply in the market for CD players.

Figure 6.6 shows this market. The demand curve is *D*, and the supply curve is *S*. With no sales tax, the equilibrium price is $100 per CD player and 5,000 CD players are bought and sold each week.

When a good is taxed, it has two prices: a price that excludes the tax and a price that includes the tax. Buyers respond only to the price that includes the tax, because that is the price they pay. Sellers respond only to the price that excludes the tax, because that is the price they receive. The tax is like a wedge between these two prices.

Think of the price on the vertical axis of Fig. 6.6 as the price paid by buyers — the price that *includes* the tax. When a tax is imposed and the price changes, there is a change in the quantity demanded but no change in demand. That is, there is a movement along the demand curve and no shift of the demand curve.

But supply changes, and the supply curve shifts. The sales tax is like an increase in cost, so supply decreases and the supply curve shifts leftward to *S* + *tax*. To determine the position of this new supply curve, we add the tax to the minimum price that sellers are willing to accept for each quantity sold. For example, with no tax, sellers are willing to offer 5,000 CD players a week for $100 a player. So with a $10 tax, they will supply 5,000 CD players a week for $110 — a price that includes the tax. The curve *S* + *tax* describes the terms under which sellers are willing to offer CD players for sale now that there is a $10 tax.

Equilibrium occurs where the new supply curve intersects the demand curve — at a price of $105 and

FIGURE 6.6   A Sales Tax

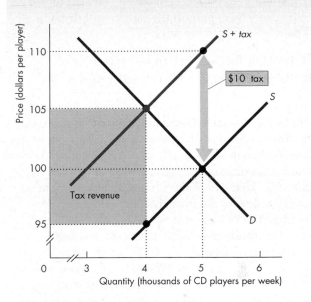

With no sales tax, 5,000 CD players a week are bought and sold at $100 each. A sales tax of $10 a CD player is imposed, and the supply curve shifts leftward to *S* + *tax*. In the new equilibrium, the price rises to $105 a CD player and the quantity decreases to 4,000 CD players a week. The sales tax raises the price by less than the tax, lowers the price received by the seller, and decreases the quantity. The sales tax brings in revenue to the government equal to the purple rectangle.

a quantity of 4,000 CD players a week. The $10 sales tax increases the price paid by the buyer by $5 a CD player and it decreases the price received by the seller by $5 a CD player. So the buyer and the seller pay the $10 tax equally.

The tax brings in tax revenue to the government equal to the tax per item multiplied by the number of items sold. The purple area in Fig. 6.6 illustrates the tax revenue. The $10 tax on CD players brings in tax revenue of $40,000 a week.

In this example, the buyer and the seller split the tax equally: The buyer pays $5 a CD player, and so does the seller. This equal sharing of the tax is a special case and does not usually occur. But some sharing of the tax between the buyer and seller is usual. And in other special cases, either the buyer or the seller pays the entire tax. The division of the tax between the buyer and the seller depends on the elasticities of demand and supply.

Tax Division and Elasticity of Demand

The division of the tax between the buyer and the seller depends in part on the elasticity of demand. There are two extreme cases:

- Perfectly inelastic demand — buyer pays.
- Perfectly elastic demand — seller pays.

Perfectly Inelastic Demand   Figure 6.7(a) shows the market for insulin, a vital daily medication of diabetics. Demand is perfectly inelastic at 100,000 doses a day, regardless of the price, as shown by the vertical curve *D*. That is, a diabetic would sacrifice all other goods and services rather than not consume the insulin dose that provides good health. The supply curve of insulin is *S*. With no tax, the price is $2 a dose and the quantity is 100,000 doses a day.

If insulin is taxed at 20¢ a dose, we must add the tax to the minimum price at which drug companies are willing to sell insulin. The result is the new supply curve *S* + *tax*. The price rises to $2.20 a dose, but the quantity does not change. The buyer pays the entire sales tax of 20¢ a dose.

Perfectly Elastic Demand   Figure 6.7(b) shows the market for pink marker pens. Demand is perfectly elastic at $1 a pen, as shown by the horizontal curve *D*. If pink pens are less expensive than the others, everyone uses pink. If pink pens are more expensive than the others, no one uses pink. The supply curve is *S*. With no tax, the price of a pink marker is $1, and the quantity is 4,000 pens a week.

If a sales tax of 10¢ a pen is imposed on pink marker pens but not on other colors, we add the tax to the minimum price at which sellers are willing to offer pink pens for sale, and the new supply curve is *S* + *tax*. The price remains at $1 a pen, and the quantity decreases to 1,000 a week. The 10¢ sales tax leaves the price paid by the buyer unchanged but lowers the amount received by the seller by the full amount of the sales tax. The seller pays the entire tax, and the quantity decreases.

We've seen that when demand is perfectly inelastic, the buyer pays the entire tax and when demand is perfectly elastic, the seller pays it. In the usual case, demand is neither perfectly inelastic nor perfectly elastic and the tax is split between the buyer and the seller. But the division depends on the elasticity of demand. The more inelastic the demand, the larger is the amount of the tax paid by the buyer.

FIGURE 6.7   Sales Tax and the Elasticity of Demand

(a) Perfectly inelastic demand

(b) Perfectly elastic demand

Part (a) shows the market for insulin, where demand is perfectly inelastic. With no tax, the price is $2 a dose and the quantity is 100,000 doses a day. A sales tax of 20¢ a dose shifts the supply curve to *S* + *tax*. The price rises to $2.20 a dose, but the quantity bought does not change. The buyer pays the entire tax.

Part (b) shows the market for pink pens, in which demand is perfectly elastic. With no tax, the price of a pen is $1 and the quantity is 4,000 pens a week. A sales tax of 10¢ a pink pen shifts the supply curve to *S* + *tax*. The price remains at $1 a pen, and the quantity of pink pens sold decreases to 1,000 a week. The seller pays the entire tax.

Tax Division and Elasticity of Supply

The division of the tax between the buyer and the seller also depends, in part, on the elasticity of supply. Again, there are two extreme cases:

- Perfectly inelastic supply — seller pays.
- Perfectly elastic supply — buyer pays.

Perfectly Inelastic Supply Figure 6.8(a) shows the market for water from a mineral spring that flows at a constant rate that can't be controlled. Supply is perfectly inelastic at 100,000 bottles a week, as shown by the supply curve *S*. The demand curve for the water from this spring is *D*. With no tax, the price is 50¢ a bottle and the 100,000 bottles that flow from the spring are bought.

Suppose this spring water is taxed at 5¢ a bottle. The supply curve does not change because the spring owners still produce 100,000 bottles a week even though the price they receive falls. But buyers are willing to buy the 100,000 bottles only if the price is 50¢ a bottle. So the price remains at 50¢ a bottle. The sales tax reduces the price received by sellers to 45¢ a bottle, and the seller pays the entire tax.

Perfectly Elastic Supply Figure 6.8(b) shows the market for sand from which computer-chip makers extract silicon. Supply of this sand is perfectly elastic at a price of 10¢ a pound, as shown by the supply curve *S*. The demand curve for sand is *D*. With no tax, the price is 10¢ a pound and 5,000 pounds a week are bought.

If this sand is taxed at 1¢ a pound, we must add the tax to the minimum supply price. Sellers are now willing to offer any quantity at 11¢ a pound along the curve *S + tax*. A new equilibrium is determined where the new supply curve intersects the demand curve: at a price of 11¢ a pound and a quantity of 3,000 pounds a week. The sales tax has increased the price paid by the buyer by the full amount of the tax — 1¢ a pound — and has decreased the quantity sold. The buyer pays the entire tax.

We've seen that when supply is perfectly inelastic, the seller pays the entire tax and when supply is perfectly elastic, the buyer pays it. In the usual case, supply is neither perfectly inelastic nor perfectly elastic and the tax is split between the buyer and the seller. But how the tax is split depends on the elasticity of supply. The more elastic the supply, the larger is the amount of the tax paid by the buyer.

FIGURE 6.8   Sales Tax and the Elasticity of Supply

(a) Perfectly inelastic supply

(b) Perfectly elastic supply

Part (a) shows the market for water from a mineral spring. Supply is perfectly inelastic. With no tax, the price is 50¢ a bottle. With a sales tax of 5¢ a bottle, the price remains at 50¢ a bottle. The number of bottles bought remains the same, but the price received by the seller decreases to 45¢ a bottle. The seller pays the entire tax.

Part (b) shows the market for sand. Supply is perfectly elastic. With no tax, the price is 10¢ a pound. The sales tax of 1¢ a pound increases the minimum supply-price to 11¢ a pound. The supply curve shifts to *S + tax*. The price increases to 11¢ a pound. The buyer pays the entire tax.

Sales Taxes in Practice

We've looked at the range of possible effects of a sales tax by studying the extreme cases. In practice, supply and demand are rarely perfectly elastic or perfectly inelastic. They lie somewhere in between. But some items tend toward one of the extremes. For example, a heavily taxed item such as alcohol, tobacco, or gasoline has a low elasticity of demand. Consequently, the buyer pays most of the tax. Also, because demand is inelastic, the quantity bought does not decrease much and the government collects a large tax revenue. It is unusual to tax an item heavily if its demand is elastic. Such a good or service has close substitutes. If a tax is levied on such a good or service, people will reduce their purchases of the taxed good and increase their purchases of an untaxed substitute. That is, the quantity of the taxed good bought decreases by a large amount and the government will not collect much tax revenue. This explains why the items that are taxed are those that have inelastic demands and why buyers pay most of the taxes.

Taxes and Efficiency

You've seen that a sales tax places a wedge between the price paid by buyers and the price received by sellers. The price paid by buyers is also the buyers' willingness to pay, which measures marginal benefit. And the price received by sellers is the sellers' minimum supply-price, which equals marginal cost.

So because a tax places a wedge between the buyers' price and the sellers' price, it also puts a wedge between marginal benefit and marginal cost and creates inefficiency. With a higher buying price and a lower selling price, the tax decreases the quantity produced and consumed and a deadweight loss arises. Figure 6.9 shows the inefficiency of a sales tax. With a sales tax, both consumer surplus and producer surplus shrink. Part of each surplus goes to the government in tax revenue — the purple area in the figure. And part of each surplus becomes a deadweight loss — the gray area.

In the extreme cases of perfectly inelastic demand and perfectly inelastic supply, the quantity does not change and there is no deadweight loss. The more inelastic is either demand or supply, the smaller is the decrease in quantity and the smaller is the deadweight loss. When demand or supply is perfectly inelastic, the quantity remains constant and there is no deadweight loss.

FIGURE 6.9   Taxes and Efficiency

With no sales tax, 5,000 CD players a week are bought and sold at $100 each. With a sales tax of $10 a CD player, the buyer's price rises to $105 a player, the seller's price falls to $95 a player, and the quantity decreases to 4,000 CD players a week. Consumer surplus shrinks to the green area, and the producer surplus shrinks to the blue area. Part of the loss of consumer surplus and producer surplus goes to the government as tax revenue, which is shown as the purple area. A deadweight loss arises, which is shown by the gray area.

REVIEW QUIZ

1 How does the elasticity of demand influence the effect of a sales tax on the price paid by the buyer, the price received by the seller, the quantity, the tax revenue, and the deadweight loss?
2 How does the elasticity of supply influence the effect of a sales tax on the price paid by the buyer, the price received by the seller, the quantity, the tax revenue, and the deadweight loss?
3 Why does a tax create a deadweight loss?

Governments make some types of goods, such as drugs, illegal. Let's see how the market works when trade in an illegal good takes place.

Markets for Illegal Goods

THE MARKETS FOR MANY GOODS AND SERVICES are regulated, and buying and selling some goods is illegal. The best-known examples of such goods are drugs, such as marijuana, cocaine, Ecstasy, and heroin.

Despite the fact that these drugs are illegal, trade in them is a multibillion-dollar business. This trade can be understood by using the same economic model and principles that explain trade in legal goods. To study the market for illegal goods, we're first going to examine the prices and quantities that would prevail if these goods were not illegal. Next, we'll see how prohibition works. Then we'll see how a tax might be used to limit the consumption of these goods.

A Free Market for Drugs

Figure 6.10 shows the market for drugs. The demand curve, *D*, shows that, other things remaining the same, the lower the price of drugs, the larger is the quantity of drugs demanded. The supply curve, *S*, shows that, other things remaining the same, the lower the price of drugs, the smaller is the quantity supplied. If drugs were not illegal, the quantity bought and sold would be Q_C and the price would be P_C.

A Market for Illegal Drugs

When a good is illegal, the cost of trading in the good increases. By how much the cost increases and on whom the cost falls depend on the penalties for violating the law and the effectiveness with which the law is enforced. The larger the penalties and the more effective the policing, the higher are the costs. Penalties might be imposed on sellers, buyers, or both.

Penalties on Sellers Drug dealers in the United States face large penalties if their activities are detected. For example, a marijuana dealer could pay a $200,000 fine and serve a 15-year prison term. A heroin dealer could pay a $500,000 fine and serve a 20-year prison term. These penalties are part of the cost of supplying illegal drugs, and they bring a decrease in supply — a leftward shift in the supply curve. To determine the new supply curve, we add the cost of breaking the law to the minimum price that drug dealers are willing to accept. In Fig. 6.10, the cost of breaking the law by selling drugs (*CBL*)

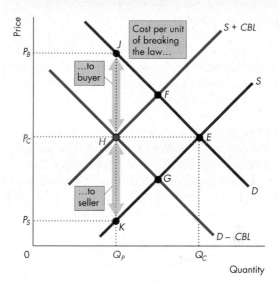

FIGURE 6.10   A Market for an Illegal Good

The demand curve for drugs is *D*, and the supply curve is *S*. If drugs are not illegal, the quantity bought and sold is Q_C at a price of P_C — point *E*. If selling drugs is illegal, the cost of breaking the law by selling drugs (*CBL*) is added to the minimum supply-price and supply decreases to *S + CBL*. The market moves to point *F*. If buying drugs is illegal, the cost of breaking the law is subtracted from the maximum price that buyers are willing to pay, and demand decreases to *D – CBL*. The market moves to point *G*. With both buying and selling illegal, the supply curve and the demand curve shift and the market moves to point *H*. The market price remains at P_C, but the market price plus the penalty for buying rises — point *J* — and the market price minus the penalty for selling falls — point *K*.

is added to the minimum price that dealers will accept and the supply curve shifts leftward to *S + CBL*. If penalties were imposed only on sellers, the market would move from point *E* to point *F*.

Penalties on Buyers In the United States, it is illegal to *possess* drugs such as marijuana, cocaine, Ecstasy, and heroin. For example, possession of marijuana can bring a prison term of 1 year, and possession of heroin can bring a prison term of 2 years. Penalties fall on buyers, and the cost of breaking the law must be subtracted from the value of the good to determine the maximum price buyers are willing to pay for the drugs. Demand decreases, and the demand curve shifts leftward. In Fig. 6.10, the demand curve shifts to $D - CBL$. If penalties were imposed only on buyers, the market would move from point E to point G.

Penalties on Both Sellers and Buyers If penalties are imposed on both sellers *and* buyers, both supply and demand decrease and both the supply curve and the demand curve shift. In Fig. 6.10 the costs of breaking the law are the same for both buyers and sellers, so both curves shift leftward by the same amount. The market moves to point H. The market price remains at the competitive market price P_C, but the quantity bought decreases to Q_P. The buyer pays P_C plus the cost of breaking the law, which is P_B. And the seller receives P_C minus the cost of breaking the law, which is P_S.

The larger the penalties and the greater the degree of law enforcement, the larger is the decrease in demand and/or supply. If the penalties are heavier on sellers, the supply curve shifts farther than the demand curve and the market price rises above P_C. If the penalties are heavier on buyers, the demand curve shifts farther than the supply curve and the market price falls below P_C. In the United States, the penalties on sellers are larger than those on buyers, so the quantity of drugs traded decreases and the market price increases compared with a free market.

With high enough penalties and effective law enforcement, it is possible to decrease demand and/or supply to the point at which the quantity bought is zero. But in reality, such an outcome is unusual. It does not happen in the United States in the case of illegal drugs. The key reason is the high cost of law enforcement and insufficient resources for the police to achieve effective enforcement. Because of this situation, some people suggest that drugs (and other illegal goods) should be legalized and sold openly but should also be taxed at a high rate in the same way that legal drugs such as alcohol are taxed. How would such an arrangement work?

Legalizing and Taxing Drugs

From your study of the effects of taxes, it is easy to see that the quantity of drugs bought could be decreased if drugs were legalized and taxed. A sufficiently high tax could be imposed to decrease supply, raise the price, and achieve the same decrease in the quantity bought as with a prohibition on drugs. The government would collect a large tax revenue.

Illegal Trading to Evade the Tax It is likely that an extremely high tax rate would be needed to cut the quantity of drugs bought to the level prevailing with a prohibition. It is also likely that many drug dealers and consumers would try to cover up their activities to evade the tax. If they did act in this way, they would face the cost of breaking the law — the tax law. If the penalty for tax law violation is as severe and as effectively policed as drug-dealing laws, the analysis we've already conducted applies also to this case. The quantity of drugs bought would depend on the penalties for law breaking and on the way in which the penalties are assigned to buyers and sellers.

Taxes Versus Prohibition: Some Pros and Cons Which is more effective: prohibition or taxes? In favor of taxes and against prohibition is the fact that the tax revenue can be used to make law enforcement more effective. It can also be used to run a more effective education campaign against illegal drug use. In favor of prohibition and against taxes is the fact that prohibition sends a signal that might influence preferences, decreasing the demand for illegal drugs. Also, some people intensely dislike the idea of the government profiting from trade in harmful substances.

REVIEW QUIZ

1 How does the imposition of a penalty for selling a drug influence demand, supply, price, and the quantity of the drug consumed?

2 How does the imposition of a penalty for possessing a drug influence demand, supply, price, and the quantity of the drug consumed?

3 How does the imposition of a penalty for selling *or* possessing a drug influence demand, supply, price, and the quantity of the drug consumed?

4 Is there any case for legalizing drugs?

You've seen how government action in markets in the form of price ceilings, minimum wages, and taxes limits the quantity and creates inefficient resource use. You've also seen how in a market for an illegal good, the quantity can be decreased by imposing penalties on either buyers or sellers or by legalizing and taxing the good. In the final section of this chapter, we look at agricultural markets and see how governments try to stabilize farm revenues.

Stabilizing Farm Revenues

EARLY FROST, DROUGHT, HEAVY RAIN, AND flooding all fill the lives of farmers with uncertainty. Fluctuations in the weather bring big fluctuations in farm output. How do changes in farm output affect farm prices and farm revenues? And how might farm revenues be stabilized? Let's begin to answer these questions by looking at an agricultural market.

An Agricultural Market

Figure 6.11 shows the market for wheat. In both parts, the demand curve for wheat is D. Once farmers have harvested their crop, they have no control over the quantity supplied, and supply is inelastic along a *momentary supply curve*. In normal climate conditions, the momentary supply curve is MS_0 (in both parts of the figure).

The price is determined at the point of intersection of the momentary supply curve and the demand curve. In normal conditions, the price is $4 a bushel. The quantity of wheat produced is 20 billion bushels, and farm revenue is $80 billion. Suppose the opportunity cost to farmers of producing wheat is also $80 billion. Then in normal conditions, farmers just cover their opportunity cost.

Poor Harvest Suppose there is a bad growing season, resulting in a poor harvest. What happens to the price of wheat and the revenue of farmers? These questions are answered in Fig. 6.11(a). The poor harvest decreases supply to 15 billion bushels and the momentary supply curve shifts leftward to MS_1. With a decrease in supply, the price rises to $6 a bushel.

What happens to total farm revenue? It *increases* to $90 billion. A decrease in supply has brought an increase in price and an increase in farm revenue. It does so because the demand for wheat is *inelastic*. The percentage decrease in the quantity demanded is less than the percentage increase in price. You can verify this fact by noticing in Fig. 6.11(a) that the increase in revenue from the higher price ($30 billion — the light blue area) exceeds the decrease in revenue from the smaller quantity ($20 billion — the red area). Farmers are now making revenue in excess of their opportunity cost.

Although total farm revenue increases when there is a poor harvest, some farmers, whose entire crop is wiped out, suffer a decrease in revenue. Others, whose crop is unaffected, make an enormous gain.

FIGURE 6.11   Harvests, Farm Prices, and Farm Revenue

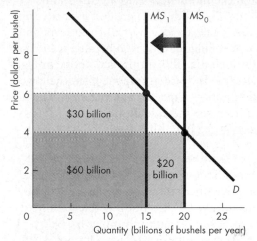

(a) Poor harvest: revenue increases

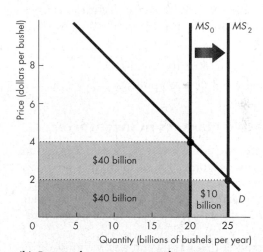

(b) Bumper harvest: revenue decreases

The demand curve for wheat is D. In normal times, the supply curve is MS_0 and 20 billion bushels are sold for $4 a bushel. In part (a), a poor harvest decreases supply to MS_1. The price rises to $6 a bushel, and farm revenue increases to $90 billion — the $30 billion increase from the higher price (light blue area) exceeds the $20 billion decrease from the smaller quantity (red area).

In part (b), a bumper harvest increases supply to MS_2. The price falls to $2 a bushel, and farm revenue decreases to $50 billion — the $40 billion decrease from the lower price (red area) exceeds the $10 billion increase from the increase in the quantity sold (light blue area).

Bumper Harvest Figure 6.11(b) shows what happens in the opposite situation, when there is a bumper harvest. Now supply increases to 25 billion bushels, and the momentary supply curve shifts rightward to MS_2. With the increased quantity supplied, the price falls to $2 a bushel. Farm revenue decreases to $50 billion. It does so because the demand for wheat is inelastic. To see this fact, notice in Fig. 6.11(b) that the decrease in revenue from the lower price ($40 billion — the red area) exceeds the increase in revenue from the increase in the quantity sold ($10 billion — the light blue area).

Elasticity of Demand In the example we've just worked through, demand is inelastic. If demand is elastic, the price fluctuations go in the same directions as those we've worked out but revenue fluctuates in the opposite direction. Bumper harvests increase revenue, and poor harvests decrease it. But the demand for most agricultural products is inelastic, and the case we've studied is the relevant one.

Because farm prices fluctuate, institutions have evolved to stabilize them. There are two types of institutions:

■ Speculative markets in inventories
■ Farm price stabilization policies

Speculative Markets in Inventories

Many goods, including a wide variety of agricultural products, can be stored. These inventories provide a cushion between production and consumption. If production decreases, goods can be sold from inventory; if production increases, goods can be put into inventory.

In a market that has inventories, we must distinguish production from supply. The quantity produced is not the same as the quantity supplied. The quantity supplied exceeds the quantity produced when goods are sold from inventory. And the quantity supplied is less than the quantity produced when goods are put into inventory. Supply therefore depends on the behavior of inventory holders.

The Behavior of Inventory Holders Inventory holders speculate. They hope to buy at a low price and sell at a high price. That is, they hope to buy goods and put them into inventory when the price is low and sell them from inventory when the price is high. They make a profit or incur a loss equal to their

selling price minus their buying price and minus the cost of storage.

But how do inventory holders know when to buy and when to sell? How do they know whether the price is high or low? To decide whether a price is high or low, inventory holders forecast the future price. If the current price is above the forecasted future price, inventory holders sell goods from inventory. If the current price is below the forecasted future price, inventory holders buy goods to put into inventory. This behavior by inventory holders makes the supply of the good perfectly elastic at the price forecasted by inventory holders.

Let's work out what happens to price and quantity in a market in which inventories are held when production fluctuates. Let's look again at the wheat market.

Fluctuations in Production In Fig. 6.12, the demand curve for wheat is D. Inventory holders expect the future price to be $4 a bushel. The supply curve is S — supply is perfectly elastic at the price expected by inventory holders. Production fluctuates between Q_1 and Q_2.

When production fluctuates and there are no inventories, the price and the quantity fluctuate. We saw this result in Fig. 6.11. But if there are inventories, the price does not fluctuate. When production decreases to Q_1, or 15 billion bushels, inventory holders sell 5 billion bushels from inventory and the quantity bought by consumers is 20 billion bushels. The price remains at $4 a bushel. When production increases to Q_2, or 25 billion bushels, inventory holders buy 5 billion bushels and consumers continue to buy 20 billion bushels. Again, the price remains at $4 a bushel. The actions of inventory holders reduce price fluctuations. In Fig. 6.12, the price fluctuations are entirely eliminated. When there are costs of carrying inventories and when inventories become almost depleted, some price fluctuations do occur, but these fluctuations are smaller than those occurring in a market without inventories.

Farm Revenue Even if inventory speculation succeeds in stabilizing the price, it does not stabilize farm revenue. With the price stabilized, farm revenue fluctuates as production fluctuates. But now bumper harvests always bring larger revenues than poor harvests do because the price remains constant and only the quantity fluctuates.

FIGURE 6.12   How Inventories Limit Price Changes

Inventory holders sell wheat from inventory if the price rises above $4 a bushel and buy wheat to hold in inventory if the price falls below $4 a bushel, making supply (S) perfectly elastic. When production decreases to Q_1, 5 billion bushels are sold from inventory; when production increases to Q_2, 5 billion bushels are added to inventory. The price remains at $4 a bushel.

Farm Price Stabilization Policy

Governments intervene in agricultural markets in four ways. They

- Provide subsidies.
- Set production limits.
- Set price floors.
- Hold inventories.

A *subsidy* is a payment to farmers, and it works like a negative tax. It lowers the market price and brings overproduction and deadweight loss. The 2002 Farm Bill increased subsidies to U.S. farms (see the Economics Place special feature on this topic.)

Production limits, which are called *quotas*, restrict the quantity produced and can result in the price exceeding the price in an unregulated market. Farmers

benefit from quotas because the price rises above the minimum supply-price. But consumers lose, and quotas create deadweight loss. Quotas exist because of the power of the farm lobby.

Price floors, which are set above the equilibrium price, create surpluses. Price floors work in a similar way to the minimum wage that we studied earlier. The minimum wage creates unemployment, and price floors in agricultural markets create surpluses of food products. To make a price floor work, the government's price stabilization agency must buy the surplus. If the price is persistently above the equilibrium price, the government agency buys more than it sells and ends up with a large inventory. Such has been the outcome in Europe, where they have "mountains" of butter and "lakes" of wine! The cost of buying and storing the inventory falls on the taxpayers, and the main gainers are large, low-cost farms.

If the government price stabilization agency operates like a private inventory holder, the agency's actions maintain the price close to the equilibrium price. The agency sells from inventory when price is above normal, and it buys to add to inventory when the price is below normal. But this type of intervention is not necessary because private trading can achieve the same outcome.

REVIEW QUIZ

1 How do poor harvests and bumper harvests influence farm prices and farm revenues?

2 Explain how inventories and speculation influence farm prices and farm revenues.

3 What are the main actions that price stabilization agencies take and how do these actions influence farm prices and farm revenues?

◆ You now know how to use the demand and supply model to predict prices, to study government actions in markets, and to study the sources and costs of inefficiency. Before you leave this topic, take a look at *Reading Between the Lines* on pp. 138–139 and see what would happen in the market for beer if a proposed cut in the federal beer tax were implemented.

Who Pays the Taxes on Beer?

THE SUNDAY GAZETTE MAIL, CHARLESTON, N.C., AUGUST 5, 2001

Drink Up: Lower Taxes on Beer May Be Ahead

... Legislation being proposed ... would significantly reduce the federal alcohol tax, cutting the rate on a case of beer by half.

While such a reduction would cost the federal government about $1.7 billion in revenue, it would ... create a more efficient tax... [and]... it would reduce the overall tax burden on the poorest Americans.

... The way the federal government taxes beer is inefficient. According to Standard and Poor's DRI, when additional state and federal sales tax revenues are included, brewers pay more than $25 billion a year in taxes. Significantly, federal taxes are levied on beer makers during production.

Thus, they become part of the cost of production passed along to distributors, wholesalers and retailers. This inevitably means consumers pay higher prices.

In fact — rather than hops, barley or labor — taxes are the single most expensive ingredient in beer, accounting for 44 percent of the total retail price of the average bottle. ...

The industry was hit hard by the 1991 tax hike, which doubled the federal tax on a barrel of beer from $9 to $18, causing a drop in sales by more than 4 million barrels. ...

... The beer tax is unfair because it disproportionately affects low-income Americans who consume beer — rather than other forms of alcohol — but who are least equipped to pay high prices. ...

Essence of the Story

■ The federal beer tax was doubled from $9 to $18 a barrel in 1991, and beer sales fell by more than 4 million barrels.

■ In 2001, a proposal was made for a cut in the federal beer tax from $18 back to $9 a barrel that would reduce the federal government's tax revenue by $1.7 billion.

■ Total taxes on beer account for 44 percent of the retail price of beer.

■ Taxes are passed along to distributors, wholesalers, and retailers, and the consumers pay higher prices.

■ The beer tax is unfair because it disproportionately affects low-income Americans.

Economic Analysis

■ The average price of beer is 80¢ a bottle. Total taxes on beer are 44 percent of the retail price, so the tax paid is 35¢ a bottle and the supplier receives 45¢ per bottle.

■ The news article says that the beer producer passes the tax along to distributors, wholesalers, and retailers and that consumers end up paying higher prices.

■ Who pays the beer tax depends on the elasticities of demand for and supply of beer.

■ The elasticity of demand for alcoholic beverages has been estimated to be 1.3. It is likely that the elasticity of demand for beer is greater than 1.3, but we'll use 1.3 as a lower limit for its likely value.

■ If we use our estimate of the elasticity of demand, there is enough information in the news article to figure out the elasticity of supply and to answer the question: Who pays the beer tax?

■ The news article tells us that when the federal beer tax increased from $9 to $18 a barrel in 1991, the quantity of beer sold decreased by more than 4 million barrels (about 1.6 billion bottles).

■ The quantity sold actually decreased from 75.3 to 73.7 billion bottles. This change in quantity is 2.14 percent of the average quantity.

■ With an elasticity of demand of 1.3, we can calculate the percentage change in the retail price, which increased by about 1 cent a bottle.

■ The tax increase of $9 a barrel translates to 2.3 cents per bottle, so the price received by the seller decreased by about 1.3 cents per bottle — a decrease of 5.5 percent.

■ Because a 5.5 percent fall in price brought a 2.14 percent decrease in the quantity supplied, the elasticity of supply is 2.14 ÷ 5.5, which is about 0.4.

■ Figure 1 shows the market for beer in the United States based on the above calculations and assumptions.

■ The demand curve, *D*, has a constant elasticity of demand of 1.3. The supply curve, *S*, has

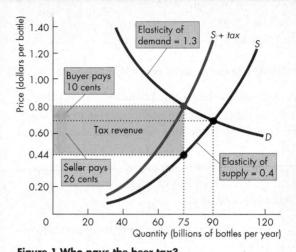

Figure 1 Who pays the beer tax?

a constant elasticity of supply of 0.4.

■ With the existing taxes of 44 percent of the retail price, the supply curve is *S + tax*.

■ The equilibrium quantity is 75 billion bottles a year, and the equilibrium price is 80¢ a bottle.

■ With no taxes, the equilibrium quantity is 90 billion bottles a year and the equilibrium price is 70¢ a bottle.

■ The beer tax increases the price paid by the consumer by 10¢ a bottle and decreases the price received by the supplier (the producer, distributor, wholesaler,

and retailer) by 26¢ a bottle.

■ The seller pays most of the tax because supply is inelastic and demand is elastic.

■ A cut in the federal beer tax of $9 a barrel will benefit the seller by more than twice as much as it will benefit the buyer.

You're The Voter

■ Why might it be efficient to have a high tax on beer?

■ Would you vote for a cut, an increase, or no change in the beer tax? Why?

SUMMARY

KEY POINTS

Housing Markets and Rent Ceilings (pp. 122–125)

- A decrease in the supply of housing raises rents.
- Higher rents stimulate building, and in the long run, the quantity of housing increases and rents fall.
- A rent ceiling that is set below the equilibrium rent creates a housing shortage, wasteful search, and a black market.

The Labor Market and the Minimum Wage (pp. 126–128)

- A decrease in the demand for low-skilled labor lowers the wage rate and reduces employment.
- The lower wage rate encourages people with low skill to acquire more skill, which decreases the supply of low-skilled labor and, in the long run, raises their wage rate.
- A minimum wage set above the equilibrium wage rate creates unemployment and increases the amount of time people spend searching for a job.
- A minimum wage hits low-skilled young people hardest.

Taxes (pp. 129–132)

- A sales tax raises price but usually by less than the tax.
- The shares of a tax paid by the buyer and by the seller depend on the elasticity of demand and the elasticity of supply.
- The less elastic the demand and the more elastic the supply, the greater is the price increase, the smaller is the quantity decrease, and the larger is the share of the tax paid by the buyer.
- If demand is perfectly elastic or supply is perfectly inelastic, the seller pays the entire tax. And if demand is perfectly inelastic or supply is perfectly elastic, the buyer pays the entire tax.

Markets for Illegal Goods (pp. 133–134)

- Penalties on sellers of an illegal good increase the cost of selling the good and decrease its supply. Penalties on buyers decrease their willingness to pay and decrease the demand for the good.
- The higher the penalties and the more effective the law enforcement, the smaller is the quantity bought.
- A tax that is set at a sufficiently high rate will decrease the quantity of drug consumed, but there will be a tendency for the tax to be evaded.

Stabilizing Farm Revenues (pp. 135–137)

- Farm revenues fluctuate because supply fluctuates.
- The demand for most farm products is inelastic, so a decrease in supply increases the price and increases farm revenue, while an increase in supply decreases price and decreases farm revenues.
- Inventory holders and government agencies act to stabilize farm prices and revenues.

KEY FIGURES

KEY TERMS

PROBLEMS

*1. The figure shows the demand for and supply of rental housing in the Village.

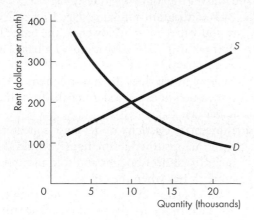

a. What are the equilibrium rent and equilibrium quantity of rental housing?

If a rent ceiling is set at $150 a month, what is

b. The quantity of housing rented?
c. The shortage of housing?
d. The maximum price that someone is willing to pay for the last unit of housing available?

2. The figure shows the demand for and supply of rental housing in Townsville.

a. What are the equilibrium rent and equilibrium quantity of rental housing?

If a rent ceiling is set at $300 a month, what is

b. The quantity of housing rented?
c. The shortage of housing?
d. The maximum price that someone is willing to pay for the last unit available?

*3. The table gives the demand for and supply of teenage labor.

Wage rate (dollars per hour)	Quantity demanded	Quantity supplied
	(hours per month)	
2	3,000	1,000
3	2,500	1,500
4	2,000	2,000
5	1,500	2,500
6	1,000	3,000

a. What are the equilibrium wage rate and level of employment?
b. What is the quantity of unemployment?
c. If a minimum wage of $3 an hour is set for teenagers, how many hours do they work?
d. If a minimum wage of $3 an hour is set for teenagers, how many hours of their labor is unemployed?
e. If a minimum wage is set at $5 an hour for teenagers, what are quantities of employment and unemployment?
f. If a minimum wage is set at $5 an hour and demand increases by 500 hours a month, what is the wage rate paid to teenagers and how many hours of their labor are unemployed?

4. The table gives the demand for and supply of labor of high school graduates.

Wage rate (dollars per hour)	Quantity demanded	Quantity supplied
	(hours per month)	
6	10,000	4,000
7	8,000	6,000
8	6,000	8,000
9	4,000	10,000
10	2,000	12,000

a. On a graph, mark in the equilibrium wage rate and level of employment.
b. What is the level of unemployment?
c. If a minimum wage is set at $7 an hour, how many hours do high school graduates work?
d. If a minimum wage is set at $7 an hour, how many hours of labor are unemployed?
e. If a minimum wage is set at $8 an hour, what are employment and unemployment?
f. If the minimum wage is $8 an hour and demand decreases by 2,000 hours a month, what is the wage rate paid to high school graduates and how many hours of their labor are unemployed?

*5. The table gives the demand and supply schedules for chocolate brownies:

Price (cents per brownie)	Quantity demanded	Quantity supplied
	(millions per day)	
50	5	3
60	4	4
70	3	5
80	2	6
90	1	7

a. If brownies are not taxed, what is the price of a brownie and how many are consumed?

b. If brownies are taxed at 20¢ each, what is the price and how many brownies are consumed? Who pays the tax?

6. The demand and supply schedules for roses are

Price (dollars per bunch)	Quantity demanded	Quantity supplied
	(bunches per week)	
10	100	40
12	90	60
14	80	80
16	70	100
18	60	120

a. If there is no tax on roses, what is the price and how many bunches are bought?

b. If a tax of $6 a bunch is introduced, what is the price and how many bunches are bought? Who pays the tax?

*7. The demand and supply schedules for rice are

Price (dollars per box)	Quantity demanded	Quantity supplied
	(boxes per week)	
1.20	3,000	500
1.30	2,750	1,500
1.40	2,500	2,500
1.50	2,250	3,500
1.60	2,000	4,500

A storm destroys part of the crop and decreases supply by 500 boxes a week.

a. What do inventory holders do?

b. What is the price and what is farm revenue?

8. In problem 7, instead of a storm, good weather increases supply by 250 boxes a week.

a. What do inventory holders do?

b. What is the price and what is farm revenue?

CRITICAL THINKING

1. Study *Reading Between the Lines* on the market for beer in the United States on pp. 138–139 and answer the following questions:

a. Draw a diagram similar to Fig. 1 on p. 139 to show the effects of lowering the federal beer tax from $18 a barrel to $9 a barrel and then to zero.

b. By how much does the buyer benefit and by how much does the seller benefit from the lower tax?

c. If the price elasticity of demand is greater than that assumed in the figure, would the quantity of beer bought and sold increase by more or less when the tax is cut?

d. If the elasticity of supply is greater than that assumed in the figure, would the quantity of beer bought and sold increase by more or less when the tax is cut?

e. Do you think the market would deliver the efficient quantity of beer if there were no taxes on it? Explain why or why not.

WEB EXERCISES

1. Use the links on the Parkin Web site to obtain information about cigarette tax rates, tax revenues, purchases, population, and income in the 50 states. Then answer the following questions about the relationship between the number of packs of cigarettes purchased and the price of a pack across the states.

a. How would you describe the relationship?

b. What does the relationship tell you about the demand for cigarettes?

c. What does the relationship tell you about the amount of cigarette smuggling?

2. Use the links on the Parkin Web site to obtain information about farm programs in the United States. What are the main programs and what are their effects on the quantities of farm products, their prices, and economic efficiency?

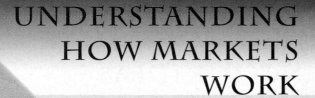

UNDERSTANDING HOW MARKETS WORK

The Amazing Market

The four chapters that you've just studied explain how markets work. The market is an amazing instrument. It enables people who have never met and who know nothing about each other to interact and do business. It also enables us to allocate our scarce resources to the uses that we value most highly. Markets can be very simple or highly organized. ◆ A simple market is one that the American historian Daniel J. Boorstin describes in The Discoverers (p. 161). In the late fourteenth century,

> *The Muslim caravans that went southward from Morocco across the Atlas Mountains arrived after twenty days at the shores of the Senegal River. There the Moroccan traders laid out separate piles of salt, of beads from Ceutan coral, and cheap manufactured goods. Then they retreated out of sight. The local tribesmen, who lived in the strip mines where they dug their gold, came to the shore and put a heap of gold beside each pile of Moroccan goods. Then they, in turn, went out of view, leaving the Moroccan traders either to take the gold offered for a particular pile or to reduce the pile of their merchandise to suit the offered price in gold. Once again the Moroccan traders withdrew, and the process went on. By this system of commercial etiquette, the Moroccans collected their gold.*

An organized market is the New York Stock Exchange, which trades many millions of stocks each day. Another is an auction at which the U.S. government sells rights to broadcasters and cellular telephone companies for the use of the airwaves. ◆ All of these markets determine the prices at which exchanges take place and enable both buyers and sellers to benefit. ◆ Everything and anything that can be exchanged is traded in markets. There are markets for goods and services; for resources such as labor, capital, and raw materials; for dollars, pounds, and yen; for goods to be delivered now and for goods to be delivered in the future. Only the imagination places limits on what can be traded in markets. ◆ You began your study of markets in Chapter 3 by learning about the laws of demand and supply. There, you discovered the forces that make prices adjust to coordinate buying plans and selling plans. In Chapter 4, you learned how to calculate and use the concept of elasticity to predict the responsiveness of prices and quantities to changes in supply and demand. In Chapter 5, you studied efficiency and discovered the conditions under which a competitive market sends resources to uses in which they are valued most highly. And finally, in Chapter 6, you studied markets in action. There, you learned how markets cope with change and discovered how they operate when governments intervene to fix prices, impose taxes, or make some goods illegal. ◆ The laws of demand and supply that you've learned and used in these four chapters were discovered during the nineteenth century by some remarkable economists. We conclude our study of demand and supply and markets by looking at the lives and times of some of these economists and by talking to one of today's most influential economists who studies and creates sophisticated auction markets. 143

Discovering the Laws of Demand and Supply

THE ECONOMIST

ALFRED MARSHALL *(1842–1924) grew up in an England that was being transformed by the railroad and by the expansion of manufacturing. Mary Paley was one of Marshall's students at Cambridge, and when Alfred and Mary married, in 1877, celibacy rules barred Alfred from continuing to teach at Cambridge. By 1884, with more liberal rules, the Marshalls returned to Cambridge, where Alfred became Professor of Political Economy.*

Many others had a hand in refining the theory of demand and supply, but the first thorough and complete statement of the theory as we know it today was set out by Alfred Marshall, with the acknowledged help of Mary Paley Marshall. Published in 1890, this monumental treatise, The Principles of Economics, *became the textbook on economics on both sides of the Atlantic for almost half a century. Marshall was an outstanding mathematician, but he kept mathematics and even diagrams in the background. His supply and demand diagram appears only in a footnote.*

THE ISSUES

The laws of demand and supply that you studied in Chapter 3 were discovered during the 1830s by Antoine-Augustin Cournot (1801–1877), a professor of mathematics at the University of Lyon, France. Although Cournot was the first to use demand and supply, it was the development and expansion of the railroads during the 1850s that gave the newly emerging theory its first practical applications. Railroads then were at the cutting edge of technology just as airlines are today. And as in the airline industry today, competition among the railroads was fierce.

Dionysius Lardner (1793–1859), an Irish professor of philosophy at the University of London, used demand and supply to show railroad companies how they could increase their profits by cutting rates on long-distance business on which competition was fiercest and by raising rates on short-haul business on which they had less to fear from other transportation suppliers. Today, economists use the principles that Lardner worked out during the 1850s to calculate the freight rates and passenger fares that will give airlines the largest possible profit. And the rates calculated have a lot in common with the railroad rates of the nineteenth century. On local routes on which there is little competition, fares per mile are highest, and on long-distance routes on which the airlines compete fiercely, fares per mile are lowest.

Known satirically among scientists of the day as "Dionysius Diddler," Lardner worked on an amazing range of problems from astronomy to railway engineering to economics. A colorful character, he would have been a regular guest of David Letterman if late-night talk shows had been around in the 1850s. Lardner visited the École des Ponts et Chaussées (School of Bridges and Roads) in

Paris and must have learned a great deal from Jules Dupuit.

In France, Jules Dupuit (1804–1866), a French engineer/ economist, used demand to calculate the benefits from building a bridge and, once the bridge was built, for calculating the toll to charge for its use. His work was the forerunner of what is today called *cost-benefit analysis*. Working with the principles invented by Dupuit, economists today calculate the costs and benefits of highways and airports, dams, and power stations.

THEN

Dupuit used the law of demand to determine whether a bridge or canal would be valued enough by its users to justify the cost of building it. Lardner first worked out the relationship between the cost of production and supply and used demand and supply theory to explain the costs, prices, and profits of railroad operations. He also used the theory to discover ways of increasing revenue by raising rates on short-haul business and lowering them on long-distance freight.

Now

Today, using the same principles that Dupuit devised, economists calculate whether the benefits of expanding airports and air-traffic control facilities are sufficient to cover their costs. Airline companies use the principles developed by Lardner to set their prices and to decide when to offer "seat sales." Like the railroads before them, the airlines charge a high price per mile on short flights, for which they face little competition, and a low price per mile on long flights, for which competition is fierce.

Markets do an amazing job. And the laws of demand and supply help us to understand how markets work. But in some situations, a market must be designed and institutions must be created to enable the market to operate. In recent years, economists have begun to use their tools to design and create markets. And one of the chief architects of new-style markets is John McMillan, whom you can meet on the following pages.

145

TALKING WITH

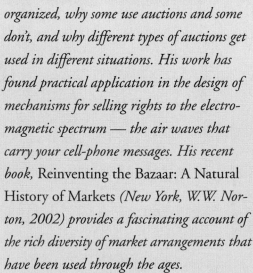

JOHN MCMILLAN *holds the Jonathan B. Lovelace Chair and teaches international management and economics in the Graduate School of Business at Stanford University. Born in Christchurch, New Zealand in 1951, he was an undergraduate at the University of Canterbury, where he studied first mathematics and then economics. For graduate school, he went to the University of New South Wales. John McMillan's research focuses on the way markets work. He wants to dig more deeply than demand and supply and explain how prices get determined, how markets are organized, why some use auctions and some don't, and why different types of auctions get used in different situations. His work has found practical application in the design of mechanisms for selling rights to the electromagnetic spectrum — the air waves that carry your cell-phone messages. His recent book,* Reinventing the Bazaar: A Natural History of Markets *(New York, W.W. Norton, 2002) provides a fascinating account of the rich diversity of market arrangements that have been used through the ages.*

John McMillan

Michael Parkin talked with John McMillan about his career and the progress that economists have made in understanding markets since the pioneering work of Alfred Marshall.

Professor McMillan, how does Alfred Marshall's assessment of how competitive markets work look today in the light of the progress that economists have made?

Supply and demand is still our basic tool of analysis, but modern microeconomics has dug deeper than Marshall was able to. The supply-demand diagram tells us what prices can do, but it sidesteps the question of where prices come from.

The main insight underlying much of modern microeconomics (and discussed in my book *Reinventing the Bazaar*) is that transaction costs can impede the smooth functioning of markets. Transaction costs include the time and money spent locating trading partners, assessing their reliability, negotiating an agreement, and monitoring performance.

Information is a major source of transaction costs. Often information is unevenly distributed: the seller knows more about the quality of the item for sale than the potential buyer; the buyer knows her willingness to pay but the seller doesn't. Informational asymmetries such as these can mean that transactions that would be mutually beneficial might fail to be realized.

The tools for analyzing the details of deal-making are game theory (as developed by John Nash, the hero of the motion picture "A Beautiful Mind"), and information economics (which was recognized by the Nobel committee in its 2001 economics award to George Akerlof, Michael Spence, and Joseph Stiglitz).

Marshall's economics is like physics without friction. For some questions, the assumption of a frictionless world is a useful short cut: for analyzing, say, the effects of rent controls or minimum-wage laws. For other questions, we need to examine the frictions explicitly. For example, to understand why financial markets are organized as they are we need to bring informational asymmetries and transaction costs into the picture.

> *"The main insight underlying much of modern microeconomics…is that transaction costs can impede the smooth functioning of markets."*

The focus on the costs of transacting has brought a recognition that markets can't operate in thin air. A market is a social construction. To operate well, with transaction costs minimized, any market needs rules and procedures. Some of these rules, perhaps most of them, arise from the bottom up: that is, they evolve through the everyday trial and error of the market participants. Others are set from the top down: government-set laws and regulations can help foster efficient transacting.

Are there any contemporary or recent examples that illustrate the way markets get created, and that perhaps hold some lessons about what works and what doesn't?

Yes. An experiment in the creation of markets is offered to us by the ex-communist countries. In the early 1990s, a common view among those advising Russia, for example, was that the overriding objective was to get the government out. Russia's approach to reform was to abolish all the mechanisms that had run the planned economy and to start with a clean slate. Once the prohibitions on market activity were abolished, the reformers believed, the private sector would quickly take over. Later, in light of Russia's grim performance in the 1990s, this simple view was supplanted by recognition that building a market economy is exceedingly hard. Success requires a complex package of microeconomic reform, macroeco-nomic stability, and institution-building. Markets don't operate well in an institutional vacuum.

China provides a telling contrast to Russia. China's reforms consisted of leaving the old institutions of the planned economy in place and letting markets grow up around the plan. China boomed during reform; its spectacular economic growth lifted millions out of dire poverty. This growth resulted from the emergence and expansion of the scope of markets and the gradual erosion of the formerly planned economy.

Markets developed in China, paradoxically, in the absence of any laws of contract and of any formal recognition of property rights. In place of the usual market-economy institutions, the pre-existing mechanisms of the planned economy served as a transitional substitute. Highly imperfect as these institutions were, they were enough to support the rapid development of markets. The lesson from the Russia-China comparison is that, for markets to work well, some institutions are better than none.

What is the most remarkable market that you've encountered?

In the Dutch village of Aalsmeer, just outside Amsterdam, operates a flower market of almost unbelievable size and complexity. Its warehouses, full of flowers, cover an area the size of 125 soccer fields. Each morning, 2,000 or so buyers bid around US$5 million for them. The flowers are flown in from far away, from places like Israel, Colombia, and Zimbabwe, and are later dispatched to buyers around the globe.

Sophisticated technology is needed to operate a global market in as perishable an item as cut flowers. The flower auctions are run via a giant clock at the front of the bidding hall, which winds down to successively lower prices. The bidders can stop the clock by pushing a button, meaning they have bought the flowers at the price shown on the clock. Computers then automatically organize the flowers' delivery to the buyer's address.

The auction that you've just described, appropriately called a Dutch auction, starts at a high price and goes down until someone accepts the price. It contrasts with a so-called English

147

auction, where the price starts low and rises until only one buyer is left. Which works best?

The Dutch auction is used at Aalsmeer because of its speed: a huge volume of flowers must be sold in a few hours. Both buyers and sellers value the speed of the Dutch auction. In other circumstances, the English auction works better from the seller's point of view, but not necessarily from the buyer's point of view.

Consider a situation where there is significant uncertainty about the value of the item for sale. The item has the same value whichever bidder ends up owning it, but at the time of bidding each of the bidders has a different estimate of the value. (This describes, for example, bidding for the right to drill for oil on a tract of land, and each of the bidders has an imperfect estimate of the amount of oil there.) In this situation, there is a risk of what is called the "winner's curse." The bidder who wins is the one with the highest value estimate, which might well be an overestimate. Winning thus conveys bad news: it tells the winner that everyone else believed the item was worth less than the winner believed.

Bidders who understand the winner's curse tend to bid cautiously. But they tend to bid less cautiously — that is, higher — in an English auction than in a Dutch auction. This is because they can see and react to each other's bids. The bids, as they ascend, convey some information about how highly the others value the item, mitigating the winner's curse and thereby usually inducing a higher price. The higher bids induced by the English auction than the other forms of auction are probably the reason that the English auction is the most commonly used auction form around the world.

What is special about selling airwaves that enables expensive economic consultants like you to show governments how to do it?

The spectrum auctions were unusually complex. Thousands of licenses were offered. The sale procedure had to recognize complementarities among the licenses: that is, the value to a bidder of a license covering, say, New Jersey, was probably higher if that bidder was going to end up owning a New York license as well (because the firm could spread its marketing costs across the wider region and in other ways offer more efficient service). None of the tried- and-true auction

forms allowed the bidding process to encompass such complementarities. As Vice President Al Gore said at the opening ceremony of one of the auctions, "They couldn't just go look it up in a book."

The auction form that we economists recommended and the government adopted was what came to be known as the "simultaneous ascending auction." Multiple licenses were offered for sale at the same time. The ascending bids allowed the bidders to avoid the winner's curse, and the simultaneous bidding on multiple licenses allowed the bidders to express their demands for packages of complementary licenses. The new auction form has raised many billions of dollars.

What does the Internet mean for markets today? Is it creating gains from trade that were previously unattainable?

It certainly has. By lowering transaction costs — especially the costs of search — to close to zero, it has created global markets in goods that before, because of their low value, previously had only a local sale. Before the internet, if you wanted some obscure object, you had to hunt in antique shops, flea markets, and so on. Now you simply use your Internet search engine. Buyers and sellers can quickly and easily contact each other where before it would have been prohibitively expensive. The result is better matches of buyer and seller — and larger gains from trade.

You began your university life studying math. Why did you switch to economics?

I was intrigued that mathematics could be used to help understand how the world works. Of course, as I was to learn, any good piece of economic analysis contains much more than just mathematics, but the mathematics lends the study rigor and precision.

What other subjects work well with economics?

Almost any subject. Mathematics is essential; you can't get to the frontiers of economics research without it. But that's not the only discipline of relevance. Economics uses ideas from fields like biology (for example, natural selection), history (the origins of institutions), sociology (networks and social capital), and philosophy (what is meant by fairness).

UTILITY AND DEMAND — CHAPTER **7**

Water, Water, Everywhere

We need water to live. We don't need diamonds for much besides decoration. If the benefits of water far outweigh the benefits of diamonds, why does water cost practically nothing while diamonds are expensive? ◆ When a winter storm cuts off the power supply, the prices of alternative sources of heat and light, such as firewood and candles, rise dramatically. But people buy as much firewood and as many candles as they can get their hands on. Our demand for goods that provide heat and light is price inelastic. Why? ◆ When the personal computer (PC) was introduced in 1980, it cost more than $5,000 and consumers didn't buy very many. Since then, the price has tumbled and people are buying PCs in enormous quantities. Our demand for PCs is price elastic. What makes the demand for some things price elastic while the demand for others is price inelastic? ◆ When a public transit authority has a free-rides day, the number of people taking trips increases, but there is a limit to the number who use the system. What limits the quantity bought when something is "free"?

◆ In the preceding four chapters, we saw that demand has an important effect on the price of a good. But we did not analyze what exactly shapes a person's demand. This chapter examines household behavior and its influence on demand. It explains why demand for some goods is elastic and the demand for other goods is inelastic. It also explains why the prices of some things, such as diamonds and water, are so out of proportion to their total benefits. And in *Reading Between the Lines* at the end of the chapter, we look at demand when the price falls to zero.

After studying this chapter, you will be able to

■ Describe preferences using the concept of utility and distinguish between total utility and marginal utility

■ Explain the marginal utility theory of consumer choice

■ Use marginal utility theory to predict the effects of changing prices and incomes

■ Explain the paradox of value

Household Consumption Choices

A HOUSEHOLD'S CONSUMPTION CHOICES ARE determined by many factors, but we can summarize all of these factors in terms of two concepts:

- Consumption possibilities
- Preferences

Consumption Possibilities

A household's consumption choices are constrained by the household's income and by the prices of the goods and services it buys. The household has a given amount of income to spend and cannot influence the prices of the goods and services it buys.

A household's *budget line* describes the limits to its consumption choices. Let's consider Lisa's household. Lisa has an income of $30 a month, and she plans to buy only two goods: movies and soda. The price of a movie is $6; the price of soda is $3 a six-pack. If Lisa spends all her income, she will reach the limits to her consumption of movies and soda.

Figure 7.1 illustrates Lisa's possible consumption of movies and soda. Rows *A* through *F* in the table show six possible ways of allocating $30 to these two goods. For example, Lisa can see 2 movies for $12 and buy 6 six-packs of soda for $18 (row *C*). Points *A* through *F* in the figure illustrate the possibilities presented in the table. The line passing through these points is Lisa's budget line.

Lisa's budget line is a constraint on her choices. It marks the boundary between what she can afford and what she cannot afford. She can afford all the points on the line and inside it. She cannot afford the points outside the line. Lisa's consumption possibilities depend on the price of a movie, the price of soda, and her income. Her consumption possibilities change when the price of a movie, the price of a six-pack of soda, or her income changes.

Preferences

How does Lisa divide her $30 between these two goods? The answer depends on her likes and dislikes — her *preferences*. Economists use the concept of utility to describe preferences. The benefit or satisfaction that a person gets from the consumption of a good or service is called **utility**. Let's now see how we can use the concept of utility to describe preferences.

FIGURE 7.1   Consumption Possibilities

Possibility	Movies		Soda	
	Quantity	Expenditure (dollars)	Six-packs	Expenditure (dollars)
A	0	0	10	30
B	1	6	8	24
C	2	12	6	18
D	3	18	4	12
E	4	24	2	6
F	5	30	0	0

Rows *A* through *F* in the table show six possible ways in which Lisa can allocate $30 to movies and soda. For example, Lisa can buy 2 movies and 6 six-packs of soda (row *C*). The combination in each row costs $30. These possibilities are points *A* through *F* in the figure. The line through those points is a boundary between what Lisa can afford and what she cannot afford. Her choices must lie along the line *AF* or inside the orange area.

Total Utility

Total utility is the total benefit that a person gets from the consumption of goods and services. Total utility depends on the level of consumption — more consumption generally gives more total utility. The units of utility are arbitrary. Suppose we tell Lisa that we want to measure her utility. We're going to call the utility from no consumption zero. And we are going

TABLE 7.1	Lisa's Total Utility from Movies and Soda		
Movies		**Soda**	
Quantity per month	Total utility	Six-packs per month	Total utility
0	0	0	0
1	50	1	75
2	88	2	117
3	121	3	153
4	150	4	181
5	175	5	206
6	196	6	225
7	214	7	243
8	229	8	260
9	241	9	276
10	250	10	291
11	256	11	305
12	259	12	318
13	261	13	330
14	262	14	341

to call the utility she gets from 1 movie a month 50 units. We then ask her to tell us, on the same scale, how much she would like 2, 3, and more movies up to 14 a month. We also ask her to tell us, on the same scale, how much she would like 1 six-pack of soda a month, 2 six-packs, and more up to 14 six-packs a month. Table 7.1 shows Lisa's answers.

Marginal Utility

Marginal utility is the change in total utility that results from a one-unit increase in the quantity of a good consumed. When the number of six-packs Lisa buys increases from 4 to 5 a month, her total utility from soda increases from 181 units to 206 units. Thus for Lisa, the marginal utility of consuming a fifth six-pack each month is 25 units. The table in Fig. 7.2 shows Lisa's marginal utility from soda. Notice that marginal utility appears midway between the quantities of soda. It does so because it is the change in consumption from 4 to 5 six-packs that produces the marginal utility of 25 units. The table displays calculations of marginal utility for each number of six-packs that Lisa buys from 1 to 5.

Figure 7.2(a) illustrates the total utility that Lisa gets from soda. The more soda Lisa drinks in a month, the more total utility she gets. Figure 7.2(b) illustrates her marginal utility. This graph tells us that as Lisa drinks more soda, the marginal utility that she gets from soda decreases. For example, her marginal utility decreases from 75 units for the first six-pack to 42 units from the second six-pack and to 36 units from the third. We call this decrease in marginal utility as the quantity of the good consumed increases the principle of **diminishing marginal utility**.

Marginal utility is positive but diminishes as consumption of a good increases. Why does marginal utility have these two features? In Lisa's case, she likes soda, and the more she drinks the better. That's why marginal utility is positive. The benefit that Lisa gets from the last six-pack consumed is its marginal utility. To see why marginal utility diminishes, think about the following two situations: In one, you've just been studying all through the day and evening and you've been too busy finishing an assignment to go shopping. A friend drops by with a six-pack of soda. The utility you get from that soda is the marginal utility from one six-pack. In the second situation, you've been on a soda binge. You've been working on an assignment all day but you've guzzled three six-packs while doing so. You are up to your eyeballs in soda. You are happy enough to have one more can. But the thrill that you get from it is not very large. It is the marginal utility of the nineteenth can in a day.

Temperature: An Analogy

Utility is similar to temperature. Both are abstract concepts, and both have units of measurement that are arbitrary. You know when you feel hot, and you know when you feel cold. But you can't *observe* temperature. You can observe water turning to steam if it is hot enough or turning to ice if it is cold enough. And you can construct an instrument — a thermometer — that can help you to predict when such changes will occur. We call the scale on the thermometer temperature and we call the units of temperature degrees. But these degree units are arbitrary. For example, we can accurately predict that when a Celsius thermometer shows a temperature of 0, water will turn to ice. This same event occurs when a Fahrenheit thermometer shows a temperature of 32. So the units of measurement of temperature don't matter.

The concept of utility helps us make predictions about consumption choices in much the same way

FIGURE 7.2   Total Utility and Marginal Utility

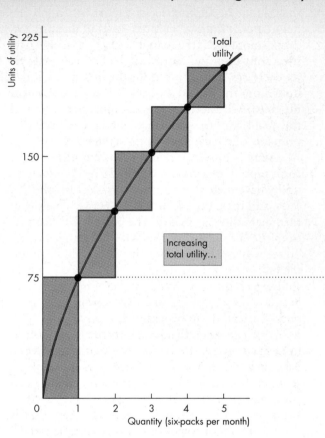

Quantity	Total utility	Marginal utility
0	0	
		 75
1	75	
		 42
2	117	
		 36
3	153	
		 28
4	181	
		 25
5	206	

(a) Total utility

(b) Marginal utility

The table shows that as Lisa consumes more soda, her total utility from soda increases. The table also shows her marginal utility — the change in total utility resulting from the last six-pack she consumes. Marginal utility declines as consumption increases. The figure graphs Lisa's total utility and marginal

utility from soda. Part (a) shows her total utility. It also shows as a bar the extra total utility she gains from each additional six-pack — her marginal utility. Part (b) shows how Lisa's marginal utility from soda diminishes by placing the bars shown in part (a) side by side as a series of declining steps.

that the concept of temperature helps us make predictions about physical phenomena.

Admittedly, marginal utility theory does not enable us to predict how buying plans change with the same precision that a thermometer enables us to predict when water will turn to ice or steam. But the theory provides important insights into buying plans and has some powerful implications, as you are about to discover. It helps us to understand why people buy more of a good or service when its price falls, why people buy more of most goods when their incomes increase, and it resolves the paradox of value.

REVIEW QUIZ

1 Explain how a consumer's income and the prices of goods limit consumption possibilities.
2 What is utility and how do we use the concept of utility to describe a consumer's preferences?
3 What is the distinction between total utility and marginal utility?
4 What is the key assumption about marginal utility?

Maximizing Utility

A HOUSEHOLD'S INCOME AND THE PRICES THAT it faces limit the household's consumption choices, and the household's preferences determine the utility that it can obtain from each consumption possibility. The key assumption of marginal utility theory is that the household chooses the consumption possibility that maximizes its total utility. This assumption of utility maximization is a way of expressing the fundamental economic problem: scarcity. People's wants exceed the resources available to satisfy those wants, so they must make hard choices. In making choices, they try to get the maximum attainable benefit — they try to maximize total utility.

Let's see how Lisa allocates $30 a month between movies and soda to maximize her total utility. We'll continue to assume that movies cost $6 each and soda costs $3 a six-pack.

The Utility-Maximizing Choice

The most direct way of calculating how Lisa spends her income to maximize her total utility is by making a table like Table 7.2. The rows of this table show the affordable combinations of movies and soda that lie along Lisa's budget line in Fig. 7.1. The table records three things: first, the number of movies seen and the total utility derived from them (the left side of the table); second, the number of six-packs consumed and the total utility derived from them (the right side of the table); and third, the total utility derived from both movies and soda (the center column).

The first row of Table 7.2 records the situation when Lisa watches no movies and buys 10 six-packs. In this case, Lisa gets no utility from movies and 291 units of total utility from soda. Her total utility from movies and soda (the center column) is 291 units. The rest of the table is constructed in the same way.

The consumption of movies and soda that maximizes Lisa's total utility is highlighted in the table. When Lisa sees 2 movies and buys 6 six-packs of soda, she gets 313 units of total utility. This is the best Lisa can do, given that she has only $30 to spend and given the prices of movies and six-packs. If she buys 8 six-packs of soda, she can see only 1 movie. She gets 310 units of total utility, 3 less than the maximum attainable. If she sees 3 movies, she can drink only 4 six-packs. She gets 302 units of total utility, 11 less than the maximum attainable.

TABLE 7.2   Lisa's Utility-Maximizing Combinations

	Movies		Total utility from movies and soda	Soda	
	Quantity per month	Total utility		Total utility	Six-packs per month
A	0	0	291	291	10
B	1	50	310	260	8
C	2	88	313	225	6
D	3	121	302	181	4
E	4	150	267	117	2
F	5	175	175	0	0

We've just described Lisa's consumer equilibrium. A **consumer equilibrium** is a situation in which a consumer has allocated all his or her available income in the way that, given the prices of goods and services, maximizes his or her total utility. Lisa's consumer equilibrium is 2 movies and 6 six-packs.

In finding Lisa's consumer equilibrium, we measured her *total* utility from movies and soda. But there is a better way of determining a consumer equilibrium, which uses the idea that you first met in Chapter 1 that choices are made at the margin. Let's look at this alternative.

Equalizing Marginal Utility per Dollar Spent

A consumer's total utility is maximized by following the rule:

Spend all the available income and equalize the marginal utility per dollar spent on all goods.

The **marginal utility per dollar spent** is the marginal utility from a good divided by its price. For example, Lisa's marginal utility from seeing 1 movie a month, MU_M, is 50 units of utility. The price of a movie, P_M, is $6, which means that the marginal utility per dollar spent on 1 movie a month, MU_M/P_M, is 50 units divided by $6, or 8.33 units of utility per dollar.

You can see why following this rule maximizes total utility by thinking about a situation in which Lisa has spent all her income but the marginal utilities per dollar spent are not equal. Suppose that Lisa's marginal utility per dollar spent on soda, MU_S/P_S, exceeds that on movies. By spending a dollar more on soda and a dollar less on movies, her total utility from soda rises and her total utility from movies falls. But her utility gain from soda exceeds her utility loss from movies, so her total utility increases. Because she's consuming more soda, her marginal utility from soda has fallen. And because she sees fewer movies, her marginal utility from movies has risen. Lisa keeps increasing her consumption of soda and decreasing her consumption of movies until the two marginal utilities per dollar spent are equal, or when

$$\frac{MU_M}{P_M} = \frac{MU_S}{P_S}.$$

Table 7.3 calculates Lisa's marginal utility per dollar spent on each good. Each row exhausts Lisa's income of $30. In row B, Lisa's marginal utility from movies is 50 units (use Table 7.1 to calculate the marginal utilities). Because the price of a movie is $6, Lisa's marginal utility per dollar spent on movies is 50 units divided by $6, which is 8.33. Marginal utility per dollar spent on each good, like marginal utility, decreases as more of the good is consumed.

Lisa maximizes her total utility when the marginal utility per dollar spent on movies is equal to the marginal utility per dollar spent on soda — possibility C. Lisa consumes 2 movies and 6 six-packs.

Figure 7.3 shows why the rule "equalize marginal utility per dollar spent on all goods" works. Suppose that instead of consuming 2 movies and 6 six-packs (possibility C), Lisa consumes 1 movie and 8 six-packs (possibility B). She then gets 8.33 units of utility per dollar spent on movies and 5.67 units per dollar spent on soda. Lisa can increase her total utility by buying less soda and seeing more movies. If she sees one additional movie and spends less on soda, her total utility from movies increases by 8.33 units per dollar and her total utility from soda decreases by 5.67 units per dollar. Her total utility increases by 2.66 units per dollar, as shown by the blue area.

FIGURE 7.3 Equalizing Marginal Utilities per Dollar Spent

If Lisa consumes 1 movie and 8 six-packs (possibility B), she gets 8.33 units of utility from the last dollar spent on movies and 5.67 units of utility from the last dollar spent on soda. She can get more total utility by seeing one more movie. If she consumes 4 six-packs and sees 3 movies (possibility D), she gets 5.50 units of utility from the last dollar spent on movies and 9.33 units of utility from the last dollar spent on soda. She can increase her total utility by seeing one fewer movie. When Lisa's marginal utility per dollar spent on both goods is equal, her total utility is maximized.

TABLE 7.3 Equalizing Marginal Utilities per Dollar Spent

	Movies ($6 each)			Soda ($3 per six-pack)		
	Quantity	Marginal utility	Marginal utility per dollar spent	Six-packs	Marginal utility	Marginal utility per dollar spent
A	0	0		10	15	5.00
B	1	50	8.33	8	17	5.67
C	2	38	6.33	6	19	6.33
D	3	33	5.50	4	28	9.33
E	4	29	4.83	2	42	14.00
F	5	25	4.17	0	0	

Or suppose that Lisa consumes 3 movies and 4 six-packs (possibility *D*). In this situation, her marginal utility per dollar spent on movies (5.50) is less than her marginal utility per dollar spent on soda (9.33). Lisa can now increase her total utility by seeing one less movie and spending more on soda, as the green area shows.

The Power of Marginal Analysis The method we've just used to find Lisa's utility-maximizing choice of movies and soda is an example of the power of marginal analysis. By comparing the marginal gain from having more of one good with the marginal loss from having less of another good, Lisa is able to ensure that she gets the maximum attainable utility.

The rule to follow is simple: If the marginal utility per dollar spent on movies exceeds the marginal utility per dollar spent on soda, see more movies and buy less soda; if the marginal utility per dollar spent on soda exceeds the marginal utility per dollar spent on movies, buy more soda and see fewer movies.

More generally, if the marginal gain from an action exceeds the marginal loss, take the action. You will meet this principle time and again in your study of economics. And you will find yourself using it when you make your own economic choices, especially when you must make a big decision.

Units of Utility In maximizing total utility by making the marginal utility per dollar spent equal for both goods, the units in which utility is measured do not matter. Any arbitrary units will work. It is in this respect that utility is like temperature. Predictions about the freezing point of water don't depend on the temperature scale; and predictions about a household's consumption choice don't depend on the units of utility.

REVIEW QUIZ

1 What is Lisa's goal when she chooses the quantities of movies and soda to consume?

2 What are the two conditions that are met if a consumer is maximizing utility?

3 Explain why equalizing the marginal utility of each good does *not* maximize utility.

4 Explain why equalizing the marginal utility per dollar spent on each good *does* maximize utility.

Predictions of Marginal Utility Theory

WE'RE NOW GOING TO USE MARGINAL UTILITY theory to make some predictions. In Chapter 3, we assumed that a fall in the price of a good, other things remaining the same, brings an increase in the quantity demanded of that good — the law of demand. We also assumed that a fall in the price of a substitute decreases demand and a rise in income increases demand for a normal good. We're now going to see that these assumptions are predictions of marginal utility theory.

A Fall in the Price of a Movie

A fall in the price of a movie, other things remaining the same, changes the quantity of movies demanded and brings a movement along the demand curve for movies. We've already found one point on Lisa's demand curve for movies. When the price of a movie is $6, Lisa sees 2 movies a month. Figure 7.4 shows this point on Lisa's demand curve for movies.

To find another point on her demand curve for movies, we need to work out what Lisa buys when the price of a movie changes. Suppose that the price of a movie falls from $6 to $3 and nothing else changes.

To work out the effect of this change in the price of a movie on Lisa's buying plans, we must first determine the combinations of movies and soda that she can afford at the new prices. Then we calculate the new marginal utilities per dollar spent. Finally, we determine the combination that makes the marginal utilities per dollar spent on movies and soda equal.

The rows of Table 7.4 show the combinations of movies and soda that exhaust Lisa's $30 of income when the price of a movie is $3 and the price of a six-pack is $3. Lisa's preferences do not change when prices change, so her marginal utility schedule remains the same as that in Table 7.3. Divide her marginal utility from movies by $3 to get the marginal utility per dollar spent on movies.

Lisa now sees 5 movies and drinks 5 six-packs. She *substitutes* movies for soda. Figure 7.4 shows both of these effects. In part (a), we've found another point on Lisa's demand curve for movies. And we've discovered that her demand curve obeys the law of demand. In part (b), we see that a fall in the price of a movie decreases the demand for soda. The demand curve for soda shifts leftward. For Lisa, soda and movies are substitutes.

TABLE 7.4	How a Change in Price of Movies Affects Lisa's Choices		
Movies ($3 each)		**Soda** ($3 per six-pack)	
Quantity	Marginal utility per dollar spent	Six-packs	Marginal utility per dollar spent
0		10	5.00
1	16.67	9	5.33
2	**12.67**	8	5.67
3	11.00	7	6.00
4	9.67	**6**	**6.33**
5	8.33	5	8.33
6	7.00	4	9.33
7	6.00	3	12.00
8	5.00	2	14.00
9	4.00	1	25.00
10	3.00	0	

FIGURE 7.4   A Fall in the Price of a Movie

(a) Demand for movies

(b) Demand for soda

When the price of a movie falls and the price of soda remains the same, the quantity of movies demanded by Lisa increases, and in part (a), Lisa moves along her demand curve for movies. Also, when the price of a movie falls, Lisa's demand for soda decreases, and in part (b), her demand curve for soda shifts leftward.

A Rise in the Price of Soda

In Fig. 7.4(b), we know only one point on Lisa's demand curve for soda when the price of a movie is $3. To find Lisa's demand curve for soda, we must see how she responds to a change in the price of soda. Suppose that the price of soda rises from $3 to $6 a six-pack. The rows of Table 7.5 show the combinations of movies and soda that exhaust Lisa's $30 of income when the price of a movie is $3 and the price of a six-pack is $6. Again, Lisa's preferences don't change when the price changes. Divide Lisa's marginal utility from soda by $6 to get her marginal utility per dollar spent on soda.

Lisa now drinks 2 six-packs a month and sees 6 movies a month. Lisa *substitutes* movies for soda. Figure 7.5 shows both of these effects. In part (a), we've found another point on Lisa's demand curve for soda. And we've confirmed that this demand curve obeys the law of demand. In part (b), we see that a rise in the price of soda increases the demand

for movies. The demand curve for movies shifts rightward. This change again tells us that for Lisa, soda and movies are substitutes.

TABLE 7.5   How a Change in Price of Soda Affects Lisa's Choices

Movies ($3 each)		Soda ($6 per six-pack)	
Quantity	Marginal utility per dollar spent	Six-packs	Marginal utility per dollar spent
0		5	4.17
2	12.67	4	4.67
4	9.67	3	6.00
6	7.00	2	7.00
8	5.00	1	12.50
10	3.00	0	

Marginal utility theory predicts these two results:

1. When the price of a good rises, the quantity demanded of that good decreases.
2. If the price of one good rises, the demand for another good that can serve as a substitute increases.

These predictions of marginal utility theory sound familiar because they correspond to the assumptions that we made about demand in Chapter 3. There, we assumed that the demand curve for a good slopes downward and that a rise in the price of a substitute increases demand.

We have now seen that marginal utility theory predicts how the quantities of goods and services that people demand respond to price changes. The theory enables us to derive the consumer's demand curve and predict how the demand curve for one good shifts when the price of another good changes.

Marginal utility theory also helps us to predict how demand changes when income changes. Let's study the effects of a change in income on demand.

FIGURE 7.5   A Rise in the Price of Soda

(a) Demand for soda

(b) Demand for movies

When the price of soda rises and the price of a movie remains the same, the quantity of soda demanded by Lisa decreases, and in part (a), Lisa moves along her demand curve for soda. Also, when the price of soda rises, Lisa's demand for movies increases, and in part (b), her demand curve for movies shifts rightward.

A Rise in Income

Let's suppose that Lisa's income increases to $42 a month and that the price of a movie is $3 and the price of a six-pack is $3. We saw in Table 7.4 that with these prices and with an income of $30 a month, Lisa sees 5 movies and drinks 5 six-packs a month. We want to compare this choice of movies and soda with Lisa's choice when her income is $42. Table 7.6 shows the calculations needed to make the comparison. With $42, Lisa can see 14 movies a month and buy no soda or buy 14 six-packs a month and see no movies or choose any combination of the two goods in the rows of the table. We calculate the marginal utility per dollar spent in exactly the same way as we did before and find the quantities at which the marginal utility per dollar spent on movies and

the marginal utility per dollar spent on soda are equal. When Lisa's income is $42, the marginal utility per dollar spent on each good is equal when she sees 7 movies and drinks 7 six-packs of soda a month.

By comparing this situation with that in Table 7.4, we see that with an additional $12 a month, Lisa buys 2 more six-packs and sees 2 more movies a month. Lisa's response arises from her preferences, as described by her marginal utilities. Different preferences would produce different quantitative responses. With a larger income, the consumer always buys more of a *normal* good and less of an *inferior* good. For Lisa, soda and movies are normal goods. When her income increases, Lisa buys more of both goods.

You have now completed your study of the marginal utility theory of a household's consumption choices. Table 7.7 summarizes the key assumptions, implications, and predictions of the theory.

| TABLE 7.6 | Lisa's Choices with an Income of $42 a Month | | |

Movies ($3 each)		Soda ($3 per six-pack)	
Quantity	Marginal utility per dollar spent	Six-packs	Marginal utility per dollar spent
0		14	3.67
1	16.67	13	4.00
2	12.67	12	4.33
3	11.00	11	4.67
4	9.67	10	5.00
5	**8.33**	9	5.33
6	7.00	8	5.67
7	**6.00**	**7**	**6.00**
8	5.00	6	6.33
9	4.00	**5**	**8.33**
10	3.00	4	9.33
11	2.00	3	12.00
12	1.00	2	14.00
13	0.67	1	25.00
14	0.33	0	

| TABLE 7.7 | Marginal Utility Theory |

Assumptions

- A consumer derives utility from the goods consumed.
- Each additional unit of consumption yields additional total utility — marginal utility is positive.
- As the quantity of a good consumed increases, marginal utility decreases.
- A consumer's aim is to maximize total utility.

Implication

Total utility is maximized when all the available income is spent and when the marginal utility per dollar spent is equal for all goods.

Predictions

- Other things remaining the same, the higher the price of a good, the smaller is the quantity bought (the law of demand).
- The higher the price of a good, the greater is the quantity bought of substitutes for that good.
- The larger the consumer's income, the greater is the quantity demanded of normal goods.

Individual Demand and Market Demand

Marginal utility theory explains how an individual household spends its income and enables us to derive an individual household's demand curve. In the earlier chapters, we've used *market* demand curves. We can derive a market demand curve from individual demand curves. Let's see how.

The relationship between the total quantity demanded of a good and its price is called **market demand**. The market demand curve is what you studied in Chapter 3. The relationship between the quantity demanded of a good by a single individual and its price is called *individual demand*.

Figure 7.6 illustrates the relationship between individual demand and market demand. In this example, Lisa and Chuck are the only people. The market demand is the total demand of Lisa and Chuck. At $3 a movie, Lisa demands 5 movies a month and Chuck demands 2, so the total quantity demanded by the market is 7 movies a month. Lisa's demand curve for movies in part (a) and Chuck's in part (b) sum *horizontally* to give the market demand curve in part (c).

The market demand curve is the horizontal sum of the individual demand curves and is formed by adding the quantities demanded by each individual at each price.

Because marginal utility theory predicts that individual demand curves slope downward, it also predicts that market demand curves slope downward.

FIGURE 7.6   Individual and Market Demand Curves

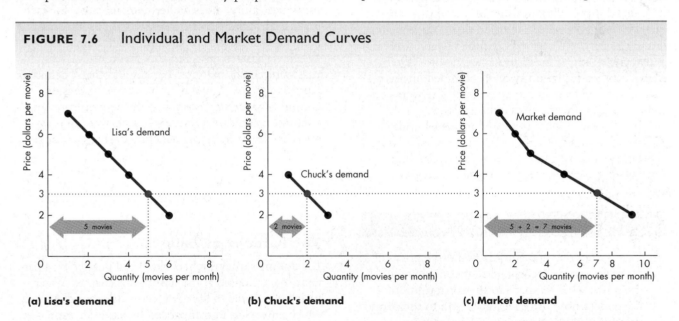

(a) Lisa's demand

(b) Chuck's demand

(c) Market demand

Price	Quantity of movies demanded		
(dollars per movie)	Lisa	Chuck	Market
7	1	0	1
6	2	0	2
5	3	0	3
4	4	1	5
3	5	2	7
2	6	3	9

The table and figure illustrate how the quantity of movies demanded varies as the price of a movie varies. In the table, the market demand is the sum of the individual demands. For example, at a price of $3, Lisa demands 5 movies and Chuck demands 2 movies, so the total quantity demanded in the market is 7 movies. In the figure, the market demand curve is the horizontal sum of the individual demand curves. Thus when the price is $3, the market demand curve shows that the quantity demanded is 7 movies, the sum of the quantities demanded by Lisa and Chuck.

Marginal Utility and Elasticity

At the beginning of this chapter, we asked why the demand for some things is price elastic while the demand for others is price inelastic. The main answer in Chapter 4 (p. 87) is that a good with close substitutes has an elastic demand and a good with poor substitutes has an inelastic demand. This answer is correct. But you can now provide a deeper answer based on marginal utility theory.

You know that for any pair of goods, X and Y, the consumer maximizes utility when

$$\frac{MU_X}{P_X} = \frac{MU_Y}{P_Y}.$$

If the price of X falls, the consumer will buy more of X to drive the marginal utility of X, MU_X, down. If the marginal utility of X diminishes only slightly as the quantity of X consumed increases, then a large increase in the quantity of X restores consumer equilibrium and demand is elastic. If the marginal utility of X diminishes steeply as the quantity of X consumed increases, then a small increase in the quantity of X restores consumer equilibrium and demand is inelastic.

If X has close substitutes, the marginal utility of X diminishes slightly as its quantity consumed increases. If X has poor substitutes, its marginal utility diminishes steeply as its quantity consumed increases.

REVIEW QUIZ

1 When the price of a good falls and the prices of other goods and a consumer's income remain the same, what happens to the consumption of the good whose price has fallen and to the consumption of other goods?
2 Elaborate on your answer to the previous question by using demand curves. For which good is there a change in demand and for which is there a change in the quantity demanded?
3 If a consumer's income increases and if all goods are normal goods, how does the quantity bought of each good change?

We're going to end this chapter by returning to a recurring theme throughout your study of economics: the concept of efficiency and the distinction between price and value.

Efficiency, Price, and Value

MARGINAL UTILITY THEORY HELPS US TO DEEPEN our understanding of the concept of efficiency and also helps us to see more clearly the distinction between value and price. Let's find out how.

Consumer Efficiency and Consumer Surplus

When Lisa allocates her limited budget to maximize utility, she is using her resources efficiently. Any other allocation of her budget wastes some resources.

But when Lisa has allocated her limited budget to maximize utility, she is *on* her demand curve for each good. A demand curve is a description of the quantity demanded at each price when utility is maximized. When we studied efficiency in Chapter 5, we learned that value equals marginal benefit and that a demand curve is also a willingness-to-pay curve. It tells us a consumer's *marginal benefit* — the benefit from consuming an additional unit of a good. You can now give the idea of marginal benefit a deeper meaning:

Marginal benefit is the maximum price a consumer is willing to pay for an extra unit of a good or service when utility is maximized.

The Paradox of Value

For centuries, philosophers have been puzzled by a paradox that we raised at the start of this chapter. Water, which is essential to life itself, costs little, but diamonds, which are useless in comparison to water, are expensive. Why? Adam Smith tried to solve this paradox. But not until the theory of marginal utility had been developed could anyone give a satisfactory answer.

You can solve this puzzle by distinguishing between *total* utility and *marginal* utility. The total utility that we get from water is enormous. But remember, the more we consume of something, the smaller is its marginal utility. We use so much water that its marginal utility — the benefit we get from one more glass of water — diminishes to a small value. Diamonds, on the other hand, have a small total utility relative to water, but because we buy few diamonds, they have a high marginal utility. When a household has maximized its total utility, it has allocated its budget in the way that makes the marginal

FIGURE 7.7 The Paradox of Value

(a) Water

(b) Diamonds

Part (a) shows the demand for water, D, and the supply of water, S. The supply is assumed to be perfectly elastic at the price P_W. At this price, the quantity of water consumed is Q_W and the consumer surplus from water is the large green triangle. Part (b) shows the demand for diamonds, D, and the supply of diamonds, S. The supply is assumed to be perfectly inelastic at the quantity Q_D. At this quantity, the price of diamonds is P_D and the consumer surplus from diamonds is the small green triangle. Water is valuable — has a large consumer surplus — but cheap. Diamonds are less valuable than water — have a smaller consumer surplus — but are expensive.

utility per dollar spent equal for all goods. That is, the marginal utility from a good divided by the price of the good is equal for all goods.

This equality of marginal utilities per dollar spent holds true for diamonds and water: Diamonds have a high price and a high marginal utility. Water has a low price and a low marginal utility. When the high marginal utility of diamonds is divided by the high price of diamonds, the result is a number that equals the low marginal utility of water divided by the low price of water. The marginal utility per dollar spent is the same for diamonds as for water.

Another way to think about the paradox of value uses *consumer surplus*. Figure 7.7 explains the paradox of value by using this idea. The supply of water (part a) is perfectly elastic at price P_W, so the quantity of water consumed is Q_W and the consumer surplus from water is the large green area. The supply of diamonds (part b) is perfectly inelastic at price Q_D, so the price of diamonds is P_D and the consumer surplus from diamonds is the small green area. Water is cheap but brings a large consumer surplus, while diamonds are expensive but bring a small consumer surplus.

REVIEW QUIZ

1 Can you explain why, along a demand curve, a consumer's choices are efficient?
2 Can you explain the paradox of value?
3 Does water or diamonds have the greater marginal utility? Does water or diamonds have the greater total utility? Does water or diamonds have the greater consumer surplus?

◆ You have now completed your study of the marginal utility theory. And you've seen how the theory can be used to explain our real-world consumption choices. You can see the theory in action once again in *Reading Between the Lines* on PP. 162–163, where it is used to interpret what happened when the Maryland Transit Authority ran a free-ride day on its system.

The next chapter presents an alternative theory of household behavior. To help you see the connection between the two theories of consumer behavior, we'll continue with the same example. We'll meet Lisa again and discover another way of understanding how she gets the most out of her $30 a month.

What's the Marginal Utility of a Free Bus Ride?

THE BALTIMORE SUN, September 13, 2001

Riders Enjoy Fare-Free Day

Yesterday was free ride day courtesy of the Mass Transit Administration, intended as a light-hearted campaign to encourage mass transit — and get people to leave their cars at home — by offering unlimited free passage on all MTA buses, Metro, light rail and MARC trains. ...

When [Darla Aye of Catonsville] learned the rides were free, she decided to add a trip to see her mother. In all, she estimated, she had saved $9 in fares. ...

Average daily ridership on all MTA vehicles is 355,000, most of them Baltimore city and county bus riders. While yesterday's ridership estimates were not immediately available, Jones said MTA officials were optimistic that it would reach or pass 400,000. ...

The point of the exercise was clear to Penny Hopkins, a former MTA employee, who took the light rail to and from a doctor's appointment in the city.

"It's good to observe how many people ride, what percentage of the public comes out," she said.

A Cherry Hill mother, Valerie Smothers, 28, said she knew of the program in advance and seized the chance to head downtown with her 7-year-old daughter, Alexus.

"I got my nails done and some children's clothes," she said. If free rides were instituted regularly, she said, "I'd be out more often."

Essence of the Story

■ To get people to leave their cars at home and try public transit, the Maryland Transit Administration (MTA) offered unlimited free travel for one day on all its vehicles.

■ One woman decided to take a trip to see her mother when she learned the rides were free, and she saved $9 in fares.

■ Another woman took the light rail to and from a doctor's appointment in the city.

■ Yet another woman took her daughter downtown and said that she would do so more often if free rides were instituted regularly.

■ On an average day, 355,000 people ride the MTA system, but MTA officials hoped the number would exceed 400,000 on the free day.

Economic Analysis

- The people who live in the region served by the MTA system choose the method of transportation and number of trips that maximize utility.

- When the MTA has a free day, consumption possibilities expand and there is no longer a trade-off between buying MTA tickets and buying other goods and services.

- Figure 1 shows this expansion of consumption possibilities. The consumer has a budget of $16 a day. One trip costs $2, and other goods and services cost $1 each.

- On a normal day, the consumer faces the trade-off shown by the downward-sloping budget line. She can buy 8 trips and no other goods and services or any combination that costs $16.

- On a free day, the consumer can spend the entire budget of $16 on other goods and services and take as many trips as she chooses.

- Choices depend on preferences and the budget line. Table 1 shows an example of a consumer's preferences described by her marginal utility schedules. Each row is an affordable combination of trips and other goods (and services).

- The consumer maximizes utility by choosing the combination at which the marginal utilities per dollar spent on the two goods are equal.

- This outcome occurs when the consumer takes 2 trips a day and buys 12 units of other goods.

- On a free day, the consumer takes trips until the marginal utility of a trip is zero, which in the example occurs when 8 trips per day are taken.

- Figure 2 shows this consumer's demand curve for trips based on the marginal utility numbers in the table.

- All three women mentioned in the news article behave in the way described by the hypothetical consumer in the table and Figure 2.

You're The Voter

- Who pays for MTA rides when they are "free"?

- Do you think it is a good idea to have free days on the urban public transit systems? Why or why not?

Figure 1 Consumption possibilities

Figure 2 Demand for MTA rides

MTA trips ($2 each)			Other goods ($1 each)		
Quantity	Marginal utility	Marginal utility per dollar spent	Quantity	Marginal utility	Marginal utility per dollar spent
0			16	1	1.00
1	10	5.00	14	2	2.00
2	8	4.00	12	4	4.00
3	6	3.00	10	6	6.00
4	4	2.00	8	8	8.00
5	3	1.50	6	10	10.00
6	2	1.00	4	12	12.00
7	1	0.50	2	14	14.00
8	0	0	0		

Table 1 MTA traveler's choices on a normal day

SUMMARY

KEY POINTS

Household Consumption Choices (pp. 150–152)

- A household's choices are determined by its consumption possibilities and preferences.
- A household's consumption possibilities are constrained by its income and by the prices of goods and services. Some combinations of goods and services are affordable, and some are not affordable.
- A household's preferences can be described by marginal utility.
- The key assumption of marginal utility theory is that the marginal utility of a good or service decreases as consumption of the good or service increases.
- Marginal utility theory assumes that people buy the affordable combination of goods and services that maximizes their total utility.

Maximizing Utility (pp. 153–155)

- Total utility is maximized when all the available income is spent and when the marginal utility per dollar spent on each good is equal.
- If the marginal utility per dollar spent on good *A* exceeds that on good *B*, total utility increases if the quantity purchased of good *A* increases and the quantity purchased of good *B* decreases.

Predictions of Marginal Utility Theory (pp. 155–160)

- Marginal utility theory predicts the law of demand. That is, other things remaining the same, the higher the price of a good, the smaller is the quantity demanded of that good.
- Marginal utility theory also predicts that other things remaining the same, the larger the consumer's income, the larger is the quantity demanded of a normal good.
- The market demand curve is found by summing horizontally all the individual demand curves.

Efficiency, Price, and Value (pp. 160–161)

- When a consumer maximizes utility, he or she is using resources efficiently.
- Marginal utility theory resolves the paradox of value.
- When we talk loosely about value, we are thinking of *total* utility or consumer surplus. But price is related to *marginal* utility.
- Water, which we consume in large amounts, has a high total utility and a large consumer surplus, but the price of water is low and the marginal utility from water is low.
- Diamonds, which we consume in small amounts, have a low total utility and a small consumer surplus, but the price of a diamond is high and the marginal utility from diamonds is high.

KEY FIGURES AND TABLE

KEY TERMS

PROBLEMS

*1. Jason enjoys rock CDs and spy novels and spends $60 a month on them. The table shows the utility he gets from each good:

Quantity per month	Utility from rock CDs	Utility from spy novels
1	60	20
2	110	38
3	150	53
4	180	64
5	200	70
6	206	75

a. Draw graphs showing Jason's utility from rock CDs and from spy novels.
b. Compare the two utility graphs. Can you say anything about Jason's preferences?
c. Draw graphs that show Jason's marginal utility from rock CDs and from spy novels.
d. What do the two marginal utility graphs tell you about Jason's preferences?
e. If the price of a rock CD is $10 and the price of a spy novel is $10, how does Jason spend the $60?

2. Martha enjoys classical CDs and travel books and spends $75 a month on them. The table shows the utility she gets from each good:

Quantity per month	Utility from classical CDs	Utility from travel books
1	90	120
2	110	136
3	126	148
4	138	152
5	146	154

a. Draw graphs showing Martha's utility from classical CDs and from travel books.
b. Compare the two utility graphs. Can you say anything about Martha's preferences?
c. Draw graphs that show Martha's marginal utility from classical CDs and from travel books.
d. What do the two marginal utility graphs tell you about Martha's preferences?
e. If the price of a classical CD is $15 and the price of a travel book is $15, how does Martha spend the $75 a month?

*3. Max enjoys windsurfing and snorkeling. The table shows the marginal utility he gets from each activity:

Hours per day	Marginal utility from windsurfing	Marginal utility from snorkeling
1	120	40
2	100	36
3	80	30
4	60	22
5	40	12
6	12	10
7	10	8

Max has $35 to spend, and he can spend as much time as he likes on his leisure pursuits. Windsurfing equipment rents for $10 an hour, and snorkeling equipment rents for $5 an hour.

How long does Max spend windsurfing and how long does he spend snorkeling?

4. Pete enjoys rock concerts and the opera. The table shows the marginal utility he gets from each activity:

Number per month	Marginal utility from rock concerts	Marginal utility from operas
1	120	200
2	100	160
3	80	120
4	60	80
5	40	40
6	20	0

Pete has $200 a month to spend on concerts. The price of a rock concert ticket is $20, and the price of an opera ticket is $40.

How many rock concerts and how many operas does Pete attend?

*5. In problem 3, Max's sister gives him $20 to spend on his leisure pursuits, so he now has $55.

a. Draw a graph that shows Max's consumption possibilities.
b. How many hours does Max choose to windsurf and how many hours does he choose to snorkel now that he has $55 to spend?

6. In problem 4, Pete's uncle gives him $60 to spend on concert tickets, so he now has $260.
   a. Draw a graph that shows Pete's consumption possibilities.
   b. How many rock concerts and how many operas does Pete now attend?

*7. In problem 5, if the rent on windsurfing equipment decreases to $5 an hour, how many hours does Max now windsurf and how many hours does he snorkel?

8. In problem 4, if the price of an opera ticket decreases to $20, how many rock concerts and operas will Pete attend?

*9. Max, in problem 3, takes a Club Med vacation, the cost of which includes unlimited sports activities. There is no extra charge for equipment. If Max windsurfs and snorkels for 6 hours a day, how many hours does he windsurf and how many hours does he snorkel?

10. Pete, in problem 4, wins a prize and has more than enough money to satisfy his desires for rock concerts and opera. He decides that he would like to buy a total of 7 tickets each month. How many rock concerts and how many operas does he now attend?

*11. Shirley's and Dan's demand schedules for popcorn are

Price	Quantity demanded by	
(cents per carton)	Shirley	Dan
	(cartons per week)	
10	12	6
30	9	5
50	6	4
70	3	3
90	1	2

If Shirley and Dan are the only two individuals, what is the market demand for popcorn?

12. Lee's and Lou's demand schedules for CDs are

Price	Quantity demanded by	
(dollars per CD)	Lee	Lou
	(CDs per year)	
6	12	10
8	9	8
10	6	6
12	3	4
14	0	2

If Lee and Lou are the only two individuals, what is the market demand for CDs?

CRITICAL THINKING

1. Study *Reading Between the Lines* on pp. 162–163 on the Maryland Transit Administration's free-ride day and then answer the following questions:
   a. If the price of a ride is zero, are the rides really free?
   b. List the components of the opportunity cost of a ride when its price is zero.
   c. Suppose the MTA made the price of a ride zero *every* day. Do you think the number of riders would be greater than, less than, or equal to the number of riders on a single free-ride day?
   d. What does marginal utility theory predict will happen to the demand for public transit as incomes rise?

2. Smoking is banned on most airline flights. Use marginal utility theory to explain
   a. The effect of the ban on the utility of smokers.
   b. How the ban influences the decisions of smokers.
   c. The effects of the ban on the utility of non-smokers.
   d. How the ban influences the decisions of nonsmokers.

WEB EXERCISES

1. Use the links on the Parkin Web site and read what Henry Schimberg, former CEO of Coca-Cola, said about the market for bottled water. Use marginal utility theory to explain and interpret his remarks.

2. Use the links on the Parkin Web site and obtain information about the prices on the Maryland Transit Administration system.
   a. Show the effects of the different ticket options on the consumer's budget line.
   b. How would a person decide whether to pay for each trip, to buy a day pass, or to buy a pass for a longer period? Use marginal utility theory to answer this question.
   c. How do you think the number of riders would change if the price of a single trip fell and the price of a day pass increased?

POSSIBILITIES, PREFERENCES, AND CHOICES

CHAPTER 8

Subterranean Movements

Like the continents floating on the earth's mantle, our spending patterns change steadily over time. On such subterranean movements, business empires rise and fall. One of these movements is occurring with the expansion of Internet access. We now can choose whether to download our music and audio books or buy them on discs and tapes. The price charged by recording companies for music is similar regardless of whether it is sold as a download or on a CD. But people are increasingly buying downloads. In contrast, the price of an audio book download is around half the price of an audiocassette. Yet almost no one downloads audio books. Why, when downloaded audio books are cheaper and music is not cheaper, are people downloading music but not audio books? ◆ Subterranean movements also govern the way we spend our time. The average workweek has fallen steadily from 70 hours a week in the nineteenth century to 35 hours a week today. While the average workweek is now much shorter than it once was, far more people now have jobs. Why has the average workweek declined?

◈ In this chapter, we're going to study a model of choice that predicts the effects of changes in prices and incomes on what people buy; that explains why we download music, even though we don't get it cheaper, and don't download books, even though we could get them cheaper that way; and that explains how much work people do.

After studying this chapter, you will be able to

■ Describe a household's budget line and show how it changes when prices or income changes

■ Make a map of preferences by using indifference curves and explain the principle of diminishing marginal rate of substitution

■ Predict the effects of changes in prices and income on consumption choices

■ Predict the effects of changes in wage rates on work-leisure choices

Consumption Possibilities

CONSUMPTION CHOICES ARE LIMITED BY INCOME and by prices. A household has a given amount of income to spend and cannot influence the prices of the goods and services it buys. A household's **budget line** describes the limits to its consumption choices.

Let's look at Lisa's budget line.[1] Lisa has an income of $30 a month to spend. She buys two goods: movies and soda. The price of a movie is $6, and the price of soda is $3 a six-pack. Figure 8.1 shows alternative affordable ways for Lisa to consume movies and soda. Row *A* says that she can buy 10 six-packs of soda and see no movies, a combination of movies and soda that exhausts her monthly income of $30. Row *F* says that Lisa can watch 5 movies and drink no soda — another combination that exhausts the $30 available. Each of the other rows in the table also exhausts Lisa's income. (Check that each of the other rows costs exactly $30.) The numbers in the table define Lisa's consumption possibilities. We can graph Lisa's consumption possibilities as points *A* through *F* in Fig. 8.1.

Divisible and Indivisible Goods Some goods — called divisible goods — can be bought in any quantity desired. Examples are gasoline and electricity. We can best understand household choice if we suppose that all goods and services are divisible. For example, Lisa can consume a half a movie a month on the average by seeing one movie every two months. When we think of goods as being divisible, the consumption possibilities are not just the points *A* through *F* shown in Fig. 8.1, but those points plus all the intermediate points that form the line running from *A* to *F*. Such a line is a budget line.

Lisa's budget line is a constraint on her choices. It marks the boundary between what is affordable and what is unaffordable. She can afford any point on the line and inside it. She cannot afford any point outside the line. The constraint on her consumption depends on prices and her income, and the constraint changes when the price of a good or her income changes. Let's see how by studying the budget equation.

---

[1] If you have studied Chapter 7 on marginal utility theory, you have already met Lisa. This tale of her thirst for soda and zeal for movies will sound familiar to you — up to a point. But in this chapter, we're going to use a different method for representing preferences — one that does not require us to resort to the idea of utility.

FIGURE 8.1 The Budget Line

Consumption possibility	Movies (per month)	Soda (six-packs per month)
A	0	10
B	1	8
C	2	6
D	3	4
E	4	2
F	5	0

Lisa's budget line shows the boundary between what she can and cannot afford. The rows of the table list Lisa's affordable combinations of movies and soda when her income is $30, the price of soda is $3 a six-pack, and the price of a movie is $6. For example, row *A* tells us that Lisa spends all of her $30 income when she buys 10 six-packs and sees no movies. The figure graphs Lisa's budget line. Points *A* through *F* on the graph represent the rows of the table. For divisible goods, the budget line is the continuous line *AF*. To calculate the equation for Lisa's budget line, start with expenditure equal to income:

$$\$3Q_S + \$6Q_M = \$30.$$

Divide by $3 to obtain

$$Q_S + 2Q_M = 10.$$

Subtract $2Q_M$ from both sides to obtain

$$Q_S = 10 - 2Q_M.$$

The Budget Equation

We can describe the budget line by using a *budget equation*. The budget equation starts with the fact that

$$\text{Expenditure} = \text{Income}.$$

Expenditure is equal to the sum of the price of each good multiplied by the quantity bought. For Lisa,

$$\text{Expenditure} = (\text{Price of soda} \times \text{Quantity of soda})$$
$$+ (\text{Price of movie} \times \text{Quantity of movies}).$$

Call the price of soda P_S, the quantity of soda Q_S, the price of a movie P_M, the quantity of movies Q_M, and income Y. We can now write Lisa's budget equation as

$$P_S Q_S + P_M Q_M = Y.$$

Or, using the prices Lisa faces, $3 for a six-pack and $6 for a movie, and Lisa's income, $30, we get

$$\$3 Q_S + \$6 Q_M = \$30.$$

Lisa can choose any quantities of soda (Q_S) and movies (Q_M) that satisfy this equation. To find the relationship between these quantities, divide both sides of the equation by the price of soda (P_S) to get

$$Q_S + \frac{P_M}{P_S} \times Q_M = \frac{Y}{P_S}.$$

Now subtract the term $P_M/P_S \times Q_M$ from both sides of this equation to get

$$Q_S = \frac{Y}{P_S} - \frac{P_M}{P_S} \times Q_M.$$

For Lisa, income (Y) is $30, the price of a movie (P_M) is $6, and the price of soda (P_S) is $3 a six-pack. So Lisa must choose the quantities of movies and soda to satisfy the equation

$$Q_S = \frac{\$30}{\$3} - \frac{\$6}{\$3} \times Q_M,$$

or

$$Q_S = 10 - 2Q_M.$$

To interpret the equation, look at the budget line in Fig. 8.1 and check that the equation delivers that budget line. First, set Q_M equal to zero. The budget equation tells us that Q_S, the quantity of soda, is Y/P_S, which is 10 six-packs. This combination of Q_M and Q_S is the one shown in row A of the table in Fig. 8.1. Next set Q_M equal to 5. Q_S now equals zero (row F of the table). Check that you can derive the other rows.

The budget equation contains two variables chosen by the household (Q_M and Q_S) and two variables (Y/P_S and P_M/P_S) that the household takes as given. Let's look more closely at these variables.

Real Income A household's **real income** is the household's income expressed as a quantity of goods the household can afford to buy. Expressed in terms of soda, Lisa's real income is Y/P_S. This quantity is the maximum number of six-packs that she can buy. It is equal to her money income divided by the price of soda. Lisa's income is $30 and the price of soda is $3 a six-pack, so her real income in terms of soda is 10 six-packs, which is shown in Fig. 8.1 as the point at which the budget line intersects the *y*-axis.

Relative Price A **relative price** is the price of one good divided by the price of another good. In Lisa's budget equation, the variable P_M/P_S is the relative price of a movie in terms of soda. For Lisa, P_M is $6 a movie and P_S is $3 a six-pack, so P_M/P_S is equal to 2 six-packs per movie. That is, to see one more movie, Lisa must give up 2 six-packs.

You've just calculated Lisa's opportunity cost of a movie. Recall that the opportunity cost of an action is the best alternative forgone. For Lisa to see 1 more movie a month, she must forgo 2 six-packs. You've also calculated Lisa's opportunity cost of soda. For Lisa to consume 2 more six-packs a month, she must forgo seeing 1 movie. So her opportunity cost of 2 six-packs is 1 movie.

The relative price of a movie in terms of soda is the magnitude of the slope of Lisa's budget line. To calculate the slope of the budget line, recall the formula for slope (see the Chapter 1 Appendix): Slope equals the change in the variable measured on the *y*-axis divided by the change in the variable measured on the *x*-axis as we move along the line. In Lisa's case (Fig. 8.1), the variable measured on the *y*-axis is the quantity of soda and the variable measured on the *x*-axis is the quantity of movies. Along Lisa's budget line, as soda decreases from 10 to 0 six-packs, movies increase from 0 to 5. So the magnitude of the slope of the budget line is 10 six-packs divided by 5 movies, or 2 six-packs per movie. The magnitude of this slope is exactly the same as the relative price we've just calculated. It is also the opportunity cost of a movie.

A Change in Prices When prices change, so does the budget line. The lower the price of the good measured on the horizontal axis, other things remaining the same, the flatter is the budget line. For example, if the price of a movie falls from $6 to $3, real

FIGURE 8.2   Changes in Prices and Income

(a) A change in price

(b) A change in income

In part (a), the price of a movie changes. A fall in the price from $6 to $3 rotates the budget line outward and makes it flatter. A rise in the price from $6 to $12 rotates the budget line inward and makes it steeper.

In part (b), income falls from $30 to $15 while the prices of movies and soda remain constant. The budget line shifts leftward, but its slope does not change.

income in terms of soda does not change but the relative price of a movie falls. The budget line rotates outward and becomes flatter, as Fig. 8.2(a) illustrates. The higher the price of the good measured on the horizontal axis, other things remaining the same, the steeper is the budget line. For example, if the price of a movie rises from $6 to $12, the relative price of a movie increases. The budget line rotates inward and becomes steeper, as Fig. 8.2(a) illustrates.

A Change in Income A change in money income changes real income but does not change the relative price. The budget line shifts, but its slope does not change. The bigger a household's money income, the bigger is real income and the farther to the right is the budget line. The smaller a household's money income, the smaller is real income and the farther to the left is the budget line. Figure 8.2(b) shows the effect of a change in money income on Lisa's budget line. The initial budget line when Lisa's income is $30 is the same one that we began with in Fig. 8.1. The new budget line shows how much Lisa can consume if her income falls to $15 a month. The two budget lines have the same slope because the relative price is the same. The new budget line is closer to the origin because Lisa's real income has decreased.

REVIEW QUIZ

1 What does a household's budget line show?
2 How does the relative price and a household's real income influence its budget line?
3 If a household has an income of $40 and buys only bus rides at $4 each and magazines at $2 each, what is the equation of the household's budget line?
4 If the price of one good changes, what happens to the relative price and to the slope of the household's budget line?
5 If a household's money income changes and prices do not change, what happens to the household's real income and budget line?

We've studied the limits to what a household can consume. Let's now learn how we can describe preferences and make a map that contains a lot of information about a household's preferences.

Preferences and Indifference Curves

YOU ARE GOING TO DISCOVER A VERY NEAT IDEA: that of drawing a map of a person's preferences. A preference map is based on the intuitively appealing idea that people can sort all the possible combinations of goods into three groups: preferred, not preferred, and indifferent. To make this idea more concrete, let's ask Lisa to tell us how she ranks various combinations of movies and soda.

Figure 8.3 shows part of Lisa's answer. She tells us that she currently consumes 2 movies and 6 six-packs a month at point *C*. She then lists all the combinations of movies and soda that she says are just as acceptable to her as her current consumption. When we plot these combinations of movies and soda, we get the green curve in Fig. 8.3(a). This curve is the key element in a map of preferences and is called an indifference curve.

An **indifference curve** is a line that shows combinations of goods among which a consumer is *indifferent*. The indifference curve in Fig. 8.3(a) tells us that Lisa is just as happy to consume 2 movies and 6 six-packs a month at point *C* as she is to consume the combination of movies and soda at point *G* or at any other point along the curve.

Lisa also says that she prefers all the combinations of movies and soda above the indifference curve in Fig. 8.3(a) — the yellow area — to those on the indifference curve. And she prefers any combination on the indifference curve to any combination in the gray area below the indifference curve.

The indifference curve in Fig. 8.3(a) is just one of a whole family of such curves. This indifference curve appears again in Fig. 8.3(b) labeled I_1. The curves labeled I_0 and I_2 are two other indifference curves. Lisa prefers any point on indifference curve I_2 to any point on indifference curve I_1, and she prefers any point on I_1 to any point on I_0. We refer to I_2 as being a higher indifference curve than I_1 and I_1 as being higher than I_0.

A preference map is a series of indifference curves that resemble the contour lines on a map. By looking at the shape of the contour lines on a map, we can draw conclusions about the terrain. Similarly, by looking at the shape of indifference curves, we can draw conclusions about a person's preferences.

Let's learn how to "read" a preference map.

FIGURE 8.3   A Preference Map

(a) An indifference curve

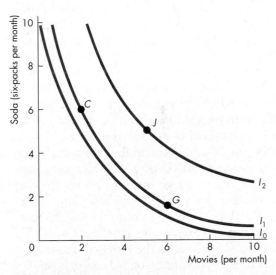

(b) Lisa's preference map

In part (a), Lisa consumes 6 six-packs of soda and 2 movies a month at point *C*. She is indifferent between all the points on the green indifference curve such as *C* and *G*. She prefers any point above the indifference curve (the yellow area) to any point on it, and she prefers any point on the indifference curve to any point below it (the gray area). A preference map is a number of indifference curves. Part (b) shows three indifference curves — I_0, I_1, and I_2 — that are part of Lisa's preference map. She prefers point *J* to point *C* or *G*, so she prefers any point on I_2 to any point on I_1.

Marginal Rate of Substitution

The **marginal rate of substitution** (*MRS*) is the rate at which a person will give up good *y* (the good measured on the *y*-axis) to get an additional unit of good *x* (the good measured on the *x*-axis) and at the same time remain indifferent (remain on the same indifference curve). The magnitude of the slope of an indifference curve measures the marginal rate of substitution.

- If the indifference curve is *steep*, the marginal rate of substitution is *high*. The person is willing to give up a large quantity of good *y* to get an additional unit of good *x* while remaining indifferent.

- If the indifference curve is *flat*, the marginal rate of substitution is *low*. The person is willing to give up a small amount of good *y* to get an additional unit of good *x* to remain indifferent.

Figure 8.4 shows you how to calculate the marginal rate of substitution. Suppose that Lisa drinks 6 six-packs and sees 2 movies at point *C* on indifference curve I_1. To calculate her marginal rate of substitution we measure the magnitude of the slope of the indifference curve at point *C*. To measure this magnitude, place a straight line against, or tangent to, the indifference curve at point *C*. Along that line, as the quantity of soda decreases by 10 six-packs, the number of movies increases by 5 — an average of 2 six-packs per movie. So at point *C*, Lisa is willing to give up soda for movies at the rate of 2 six-packs per movie — a marginal rate of substitution of 2.

Now suppose that Lisa drinks 1.5 six-packs and sees 6 movies at point *G* in Fig. 8.4. Her marginal rate of substitution is now measured by the slope of the indifference curve at point *G*. That slope is the same as the slope of the tangent to the indifference curve at point *G*. Here, as the quantity of soda decreases by 4.5 six-packs, the number of movies increases by 9 — an average of 1/2 six-pack per movie. So at point *G*, Lisa is willing to give up soda for movies at the rate of 1/2 six-pack per movie — a marginal rate of substitution of 1/2.

As Lisa sees more movies and drinks less soda, her marginal rate of substitution diminishes. Diminishing marginal rate of substitution is the key assumption of consumer theory. A **diminishing marginal rate of substitution** is a general tendency for a person to be willing to give up less of good *y* to get one more unit of good *x*, and at the same time remain indifferent, as the quantity of *x* increases. In Lisa's case, she is less willing to give up soda to see one more movie, the more movies she sees.

FIGURE 8.4   The Marginal Rate of Substitution

The magnitude of the slope of an indifference curve is called the marginal rate of substitution (*MRS*). The red line at point *C* tells us that Lisa is willing to give up 10 six-packs to see 5 movies. Her marginal rate of substitution at point *C* is 10 divided by 5, which equals 2. The red line at point *G* tells us that Lisa is willing to give up 4.5 six-packs to see 9 movies. Her marginal rate of substitution at point *G* is 4.5 divided by 9, which equals ½.

Your Own Diminishing Marginal Rate of Substitution Think about your own diminishing marginal rate of substitution. Imagine that in a week, you drink 10 six-packs of soda and see no movies. Most likely, you are willing to give up a lot of soda so that you can see just 1 movie. But now imagine that in a week, you drink 1 six-pack and see 6 movies. Most likely, you will now not be willing to give up much soda to see a seventh movie. As a general rule, the greater the number of movies you see, the smaller is the quantity of soda you are willing to give up to see one additional movie.

The shape of a person's indifference curves incorporates the principle of the diminishing marginal rate of substitution because the curves are bowed toward the origin. The tightness of the bend of an indifference curve tells us how willing a person is to substitute one good for another while remaining indifferent. Let's look at some examples that make this point clear.

Degree of Substitutability

Most of us would not regard movies and soda as being close substitutes. We probably have some fairly clear ideas about how many movies we want to see each month and how many cans of soda we want to drink. But to some degree, we are willing to substitute between these two goods. No matter how big a soda freak you are, there is surely some increase in the number of movies you can see that will compensate you for being deprived of a can of soda. Similarly, no matter how addicted you are to the movies, surely some number of cans of soda will compensate you for being deprived of seeing one movie. A person's indifference curves for movies and soda might look something like those shown in Fig. 8.5(a).

Close Substitutes Some goods substitute so easily for each other that most of us do not even notice which we are consuming. The different brands of personal computers are an example. As long as it has an "Intel inside" and runs Windows, most of us don't care whether our PC is a Dell, a Compaq, a Sony, or any of a dozen other brands. The same holds true for

marker pens. Most of us don't care whether we use a marker pen from the campus bookstore or one from the local supermarket. When two goods are perfect substitutes, their indifference curves are straight lines that slope downward, as Fig. 8.5(b) illustrates. The marginal rate of substitution is constant.

Complements Some goods cannot substitute for each other at all. Instead, they are complements. The complements in Fig. 8.5(c) are left and right running shoes. Indifference curves of perfect complements are L-shaped. One left running shoe and one right running shoe are as good as one left shoe and two right ones. Having two of each is preferred to having one of each, but having two of one and one of the other is no better than having one of each.

The extreme cases of perfect substitutes and perfect complements shown here don't often happen in reality. But they do illustrate that the shape of the indifference curve shows the degree of substitutability between two goods. The more perfectly substitutable the two goods, the more nearly are their indifference curves straight lines and the less quickly does the

FIGURE 8.5   The Degree of Substitutability

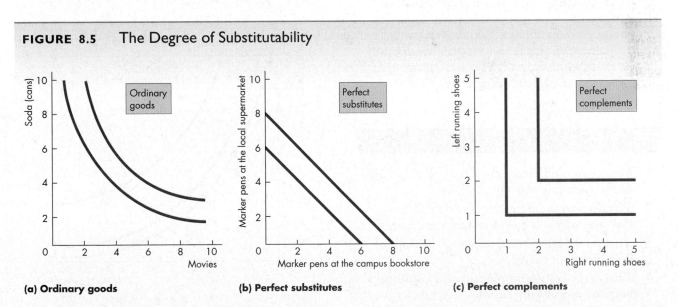

(a) Ordinary goods   **(b) Perfect substitutes**   **(c) Perfect complements**

The shape of the indifference curves reveals the degree of substitutability between two goods. Part (a) shows the indifference curves for two ordinary goods: movies and soda. To drink less soda and remain indifferent, one must see more movies. The number of movies that compensates for a reduction in soda increases as less soda is consumed. Part (b) shows the indifference curves for two perfect substitutes. For the

consumer to remain indifferent, one fewer marker pen from the local supermarket must be replaced by one extra marker pen from the campus bookstore. Part (c) shows two perfect complements — goods that cannot be substituted for each other at all. Having two left running shoes with one right running shoe is no better than having one of each. But having two of each is preferred to having one of each.

*"With the pork I'd recommend an Alsatian
white or a Coke."*

marginal rate of substitution diminish. Poor substitutes for each other have tightly curved indifference curves, approaching the shape of those shown in Fig. 8.5(c).

As you can see in the cartoon, according to the waiter's preferences, Coke and Alsatian white wine are perfect substitutes and each is a complement of pork. We hope the customers agree with him.

REVIEW QUIZ

1 What is an indifference curve and how does an indifference map show preferences?

2 Why does an indifference curve slope downward and why is it bowed toward the origin?

3 What do we call the magnitude of the slope of an indifference curve?

4 What is the key assumption about a consumer's marginal rate of substitution?

The two components of the model of household choice are now in place: the budget line and the preference map. We will now use these components to work out the household's choice and to predict how choices change when prices and income change.

Predicting Consumer Behavior

WE ARE NOW GOING TO PREDICT THE QUANTITIES of movies and soda that Lisa chooses to buy. Figure 8.6 shows Lisa's budget line from Fig. 8.1 and her indifference curves from Fig. 8.3(b). We assume that Lisa consumes at her best affordable point, which is 2 movies and 6 six-packs — at point *C*. Here, Lisa

- Is on her budget line.
- Is on her highest attainable indifference curve.
- Has a marginal rate of substitution between movies and soda equal to the relative price of movies and soda.

For every point inside the budget line, such as point *I*, there are points *on* the budget line that Lisa prefers. For example, she prefers all the points on the

FIGURE 8.6   The Best Affordable Point

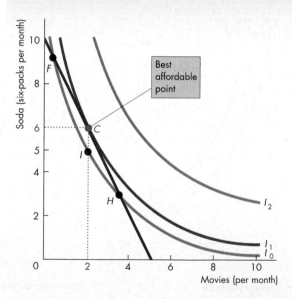

Lisa's best affordable point is *C*. At that point, she is on her budget line and also on the highest attainable indifference curve. At a point such as *H*, Lisa is willing to give up more movies in exchange for soda than she has to. She can move to point *I*, which is just as good as point *H*, and have some unspent income. She can spend that income and move to *C*, a point that she prefers to point *I*.

budget line between *F* and *H* to point *I*. So she chooses a point on the budget line.

Every point on the budget line lies on an indifference curve. For example, point *H* lies on the indifference curve I_0. At point *H*, Lisa's marginal rate of substitution is less than the relative price. Lisa is willing to give up more movies in exchange for soda than the budget line says she must. So she moves along her budget line from *H* toward *C*. As she does so, she passes through a number of indifference curves (not shown in the figure) located between indifference curves I_0 and I_1. All of these indifference curves are higher than I_0, and therefore Lisa prefers any point on them to point *H*. But when Lisa gets to point *C*, she is on the highest attainable indifference curve. If she keeps moving along the budget line, she starts to encounter indifference curves that are lower than I_1. So Lisa chooses point *C*.

At the chosen point, the marginal rate of substitution (the magnitude of the slope of the indifference curve) equals the relative price (the magnitude of the slope of the budget line).

Let's use this model of household choice to predict the effects on consumption of changes in prices and income. We'll begin by studying the effect of a change in price.

A Change in Price

The effect of a change in the price on the quantity of a good consumed is called the **price effect**. We will use Fig. 8.7(a) to work out the price effect of a fall in the price of a movie. We start with the price of a movie at $6, the price of soda at $3 a six-pack, and Lisa's income at $30 a month. In this situation, she drinks 6 six-packs and sees 2 movies a month at point *C*.

Now suppose that the price of a movie falls to $3. With a lower price of a movie, the budget line rotates outward and becomes flatter. (Check back to Fig. 8.2(a) for a refresher on how a price change affects the budget line.) The new budget line is the dark orange one in Fig. 8.7(a).

Lisa's best affordable point is now point *J*, where she sees 5 movies and drinks 5 six-packs of soda. Lisa drinks less soda and watches more movies now that movies are cheaper. She cuts her soda consumption from 6 to 5 six-packs and increases the number of movies she sees from 2 to 5 a month. Lisa substitutes movies for soda when the price of a movie falls and the price of soda and her income remain constant.

FIGURE 8.7   Price Effect and Demand Curve

(a) Price effect

(b) Demand curve

Initially, Lisa consumes at point *C* (part a). If the price of a movie falls from $6 to $3, Lisa consumes at point *J*. The move from *C* to *J* is the price effect.

At a price of $6 a movie, Lisa sees 2 movies a month, at point *A* in part (b). At a price of $3 a movie, she sees 5 movies a month, at point *B*. Lisa's demand curve traces out her best affordable quantity of movies as the price of a movie varies.

The Demand Curve In Chapter 3, we asserted that the demand curve slopes downward. We can now derive a demand curve from a consumer's budget line and indifference curves. By doing so, we can see that the law of demand and the downward-sloping demand curve are consequences of the consumer's choosing his or her best affordable combination of goods.

To derive Lisa's demand curve for movies, lower the price of a movie and find her best affordable point at different prices. We've just done this for two movie prices in Fig. 8.7(a). Figure 8.7 highlights these two prices and two points that lie on Lisa's demand curve for movies. When the price of a movie is $6, Lisa sees 2 movies a month at point A. When the price falls to $3, she increases the number of movies she sees to 5 a month at point B. The demand curve is made up of these two points plus all the other points that tell us Lisa's best affordable consumption of movies at each movie price, given the price of soda and Lisa's income. As you can see, Lisa's demand curve for movies slopes downward — the lower the price of a movie, the more movies she watches each month. This is the law of demand.

Next, let's see how Lisa changes her consumption of movies and soda when her income changes.

A Change in Income

The effect of a change in income on consumption is called the **income effect**. Let's work out the income effect by examining how consumption changes when income changes and prices remain constant. Figure 8.8 shows the income effect when Lisa's income falls. With an income of $30 and with the price of a movie at $3 and the price of soda at $3 a six-pack, she consumes at point J — 5 movies and 5 six-packs. If her income falls to $21, she consumes at point K — she sees 4 movies and drinks 3 six-packs. When Lisa's income falls, she consumes less of both goods. Movies and soda are normal goods.

The Demand Curve and the Income Effect A change in income leads to a shift in the demand curve, as shown in Fig. 8.8(b). With an income of $30, Lisa's demand curve is D_0, the same as in Fig. 8.7(b). But when her income falls to $21, she plans to see fewer movies at each price, so her demand curve shifts leftward to D_1.

FIGURE 8.8 Income Effect and Change in Demand

(a) Income effect

(b) Demand curve

A change in income shifts the budget line and changes the best affordable point and changes consumption. In part (a), when Lisa's income decreases from $30 to $21, she consumes less of both movies and soda. In part (b), Lisa's demand curve for movies when her income is $30 is D_0. When Lisa's income decreases to $21, her demand curve for movies shifts leftward to D_1. Lisa's demand for movies decreases because she now sees fewer movies at each price.

Substitution Effect and Income Effect

For a normal good, a fall in price *always* increases the quantity bought. We can prove this assertion by dividing the price effect into two parts:

- Substitution effect
- Income effect.

Figure 8.9 shows the price effect, and Fig. 8.9(b) divides the price effect into its two parts.

Substitution Effect The **substitution effect** is the effect of a change in price on the quantity bought when the consumer (hypothetically) remains indifferent between the original situation and the new one. To work out Lisa's substitution effect, when the price of a movie falls, we cut her income by enough to leave her on the same indifference curve as before.

When the price of a movie falls from $6 to $3, suppose (hypothetically) that we cut Lisa's income to $21. What's special about $21? It is the income that is just enough, at the new price of a movie, to keep Lisa's best affordable point on the same indifference curve as her original consumption point *C*. Lisa's budget line is now the light orange line in Fig. 8.9(b). With the lower price of a movie and a smaller income, Lisa's best affordable point is *K* on indifference curve I_1. The move from *C* to *K* is the substitution effect of the price change. The substitution effect of the fall in the price of a movie is an increase in the consumption of movies from 2 to 4. The direction of the substitution effect never varies: When the relative price of a good falls, the consumer substitutes more of that good for the other good.

Income Effect To calculate the substitution effect, we gave Lisa a $9 pay cut. To calculate the income effect, we give Lisa her $9 back. The $9 increase in income shifts Lisa's budget line outward, as shown in Fig. 8.9(b). The slope of the budget line does not change because both prices remain constant. This change in Lisa's budget line is similar to the one illustrated in Fig. 8.8. As Lisa's budget line shifts outward, her consumption possibilities expand and her best affordable point becomes *J* on indifference curve I_2. The move from *K* to *J* is the income effect of the price change. In this example, as Lisa's income increases, she increases her consumption of movies. For Lisa, a movie is a normal good. For a normal good, the income effect reinforces the substitution effect.

FIGURE 8.9   Substitution Effect and Income Effect

(a) Price effect

(b) Substitution effect and income effect

The price effect in part (a) can be separated into a substitution effect and an income effect in part (b). To isolate the substitution effect, we confront Lisa with the new price but keep her on her original indifference curve, I_1. The substitution effect is the move from *C* to *K*. To isolate the income effect, we confront Lisa with the new price of movies but increase her income so that she can move from the original indifference curve, I_1, to the new one, I_2. The income effect is the move from *K* to *J*.

Inferior Goods The example that we have just studied is that of a change in the price of a normal good. The effect of a change in the price of an inferior good is different. Recall that an inferior good is one whose consumption decreases as income increases. For an inferior good, the income effect is negative. Thus for an inferior good, a lower price does not always lead to an increase in the quantity demanded. The lower price has a substitution effect that increases the quantity demanded. But the lower price also has a negative income effect that reduces the demand for the inferior good. Thus the income effect offsets the substitution effect to some degree. If the negative income effect exceeded the positive substitution effect, the demand curve would slope upward. This case does not appear to occur in the real world.

Back to the Facts

We started this chapter by observing how consumer spending has changed over the years. The indifference curve model explains those changes. Spending patterns are determined by best affordable choices. Changes in prices and incomes change the best affordable choice and change consumption patterns.

REVIEW QUIZ

1 When a consumer chooses the combination of goods and services to buy, what is she or he trying to achieve?
2 Can you explain the conditions that are met when a consumer has found the best affordable combination of goods to buy? (Use the terms budget line, marginal rate of substitution, and relative price in your explanation.)
3 If the price of a normal good falls, what happens to the quantity demanded of that good?
4 Into what two effects can we divide the effect of a price change?
5 For a normal good, does the income effect reinforce the substitution effect or does it partly offset the substitution effect?

The model of household choice can explain many other household choices. Let's look at one of them.

Work-Leisure Choices

HOUSEHOLDS MAKE MANY CHOICES OTHER THAN those about how to spend their income on the various goods and services available. We can use the model of consumer choice to understand many other household choices. Some of these choices are discussed on pp. 186–190. Here we'll study a key choice: how much labor to supply.

Labor Supply

Every week, we allocate our 168 hours between working — called *labor* — and all other activities — called *leisure.* How do we decide how to allocate our time between labor and leisure? We can answer this question by using the theory of household choice.

The more hours we spend on *leisure,* the smaller is our income. The relationship between leisure and income is described by an *income-time budget line.* Figure 8.10(a) shows Lisa's income-time budget line. If Lisa devotes the entire week to leisure — 168 hours — she has no income and is at point Z. By supplying labor in exchange for a wage, she can convert hours into income along the income-time budget line. The slope of that line is determined by the hourly wage rate. If the wage rate is $5 an hour, Lisa faces the flattest budget line. If the wage rate is $10 an hour, she faces the middle budget line. And if the wage rate is $15 an hour, she faces the steepest budget line.

Lisa buys leisure by not supplying labor and by forgoing income. The opportunity cost of an hour of leisure is the hourly wage rate forgone.

Figure 8.10(a) also shows Lisa's indifference curves for income and leisure. Lisa chooses her best attainable point. This choice of income and time allocation is just like her choice of movies and soda. She gets onto the highest possible indifference curve by making her marginal rate of substitution between income and leisure equal to her wage rate. Lisa's choice depends on the wage rate she can earn. At a wage rate of $5 an hour, Lisa chooses point A and works 20 hours a week (168 minus 148) for an income of $100 a week. At a wage rate of $10 an hour, she chooses point B and works 35 hours a week (168 minus 133) for an income of $350 a week. And at a wage rate of $15 an hour, she chooses point C and works 30 hours a week (168 minus 138) for an income of $450 a week.

FIGURE 8.10   The Supply of Labor

(a) Time allocation decision

(b) Labor supply curve

In part (a), at a wage rate of $5 an hour, Lisa takes 148 hours of leisure and works 20 hours a week at point A. If the wage rate increases from $5 to $10, she decreases her leisure to 133 hours and increases her work to 35 hours a week at point B. But if the wage rate increases from $10 to $15, Lisa *increases* her leisure to 138 hours and *decreases* her work to 30 hours a week at point C. Part (b) shows Lisa's labor supply curve. Points A, B, and C on the supply curve correspond to Lisa's choices on her income-time budget line in part (a).

The Labor Supply Curve

Figure 8.10(b) shows Lisa's labor supply curve. This curve shows that as the wage rate increases from $5 an hour to $10 an hour, Lisa increases the quantity of labor supplied from 20 hours a week to 35 hours a week. But when the wage rate increases to $15 an hour, she decreases her quantity of labor supplied to 30 hours a week.

Lisa's supply of labor is similar to that described for the economy as a whole at the beginning of this chapter. As wage rates have increased, work hours have decreased. At first, this pattern seems puzzling. We've seen that the hourly wage rate is the opportunity cost of leisure. So a higher wage rate means a higher opportunity cost of leisure. This fact on its own leads to a decrease in leisure and an increase in work hours. But instead, we've cut our work hours. Why? Because our incomes have increased. As the wage rate increases, incomes increase, so people demand more of all normal goods. Leisure is a normal good, so as incomes increase, people demand more leisure.

The higher wage rate has both a *substitution effect* and an *income effect*. The higher wage rate increases the opportunity cost of leisure and so leads to a substitution effect away from leisure. And the higher wage rate increases income and so leads to an income effect toward more leisure. This outcome of rational household choice explains why the average workweek has fallen steadily as wage rates have increased. With higher wage rates, people have decided to use their higher incomes in part to consume more leisure.

REVIEW QUIZ

1 What is the opportunity cost of leisure?
2 Why might a rise in the wage rate lead to an increase in leisure and a decrease in work hours?

◆ *Reading Between the Lines* on pp. 180-181 shows you how the theory of household choice explains why, when downloaded audio books are cheaper and downloaded music is not cheaper, people are downloading music but not audio books.

In the chapters that follow, we study firms' choices. We'll see how, in the pursuit of profit, firms make choices that determine the supply of goods and services and the demand for productive resources.

The Marginal Rate of Substitution Between Discs and Downloads

THE HOLLYWOOD REPORTER, May 11, 2000

EMI Tunes Up for Future in Digital Download Era

EMI Recorded Music is turning up the volume on its digital music download initiative. The label group has announced plans to release more than 100 albums and 40 associated singles for sale through major online retailers starting July 1. ... "Our goal is to make digital just another format, just like you have cassette and you have CD," EMI Recorded Music senior VP new media Jay Samit said. ...

The pricing of the digital downloads will fall in the ballpark of the label's traditional off-line suggested retail price. ...

THE ATLANTA JOURNAL-CONSTITUTION, June 12, 2001

Audio Cyberbooks Make Dent in Market

Bob Muir is not your stereotypical MP3-player kind of guy. He's no rockin' Gen X-er fretting over the fate of Napster, the music-sharing Web site. For all he cares, Napster could be someone who sleeps a lot during the day.

When Muir plugs into his MP3, he listens to mysteries, histories and best sellers, audio books downloaded from the Web. And so, apparently, do a growing number of people in metro Atlanta and around the country.

Though audio books sold as digital downloads remain a tiny fraction of the $2.4 billion audio books industry ... .

... downloads of most single audio books cost $12.95, about half the price of books on tape. ...

... But MediaBay, which began offering digital downloads a year ago, is being cautious about expansion because of questions about formats and compatibility of listening devices. ...

Essence of the Stories

■ An increasing variety of recorded music is becoming available for purchase on the Internet.

■ The price of an album is about the same whether it is bought on a CD or downloaded.

■ Audio books are also becoming available for purchase on the Internet.

■ The price of an audio book download is about a half the price of a book on an audiocassette.

■ Audio book downloads are a tiny fraction of audio book sales.

Economic Analysis

■ For many people, music delivered on a CD and music delivered as a download are almost perfect substitutes.

■ When two goods are almost perfect substitutes, the indifference curves that describe preferences are almost linear and their slope is –1.

■ Figure 1 shows an example of these indifference curves for Andy. At point A on I_0, Andy buys 2 CDs and 2 downloads.

■ Andy would be equally happy with no CDs and 4 downloads and almost as happy with 4 CDs and no downloads.

■ If CDs and downloads have the same price, and if Andy can afford to buy 7 CDs or 7 downloads, his budget line is the orange line in Figure 1.

■ Andy's best affordable point is B on curve I_1. He buys 5 CDs and 2 downloads.

■ If downloads were slightly cheaper than CDs, Andy would buy only downloads; and if CDs were slightly cheaper than downloads, he would buy only downloads.

■ Andy's marginal rate of substitution between CDs and downloads is almost constant and is close to 1.

■ For most people, audio books delivered on a tape and audio books delivered as a download are poor substitutes. A book on tape is more convenient for most people.

■ When two goods are poor substitutes, the indifference curves that describe preferences are curved and almost horizontal.

■ Figure 2 shows an example of these indifference curves for Beth.

■ Beth really likes to get her audio books on tape, and almost no quantity of downloads would be as good as a tape.

■ If tapes and downloads have the same price, and if Beth can afford to buy 4 tapes or 4 downloads, her budget line is the pale orange line in Figure 2.

■ Beth's best affordable point is C on curve I_1. She buys 4 tapes and no downloads.

Figure 1 CDs and music downloads

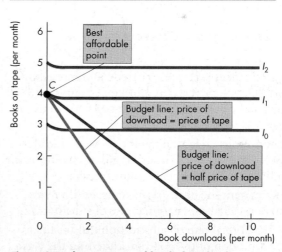

Figure 2 Books on tape and book downloads

■ Even with the price of a download at half the price of a tape (the dark orange budget line in Figure 2), Beth still buys only tapes.

■ Downloads would have to be almost free to induce Beth to switch from tapes to downloading her audio books.

SUMMARY

KEY POINTS

Consumption Possibilities (pp. 168–170)

- The budget line is the boundary between what the household can and cannot afford given its income and the prices of goods.
- The point at which the budget line intersects the y-axis is the household's real income in terms of the good measured on that axis.
- The magnitude of the slope of the budget line is the relative price of the good measured on the x-axis in terms of the good measured on the y-axis.
- A change in price changes the slope of the budget line. A change in income shifts the budget line but does not change its slope.

Preferences and Indifference Curves (pp. 171–174)

- A consumer's preferences can be represented by indifference curves. An indifference curve joins all the combinations of goods among which the consumer is indifferent.
- A consumer prefers any point above an indifference curve to any point on it and any point on an indifference curve to any point below it.
- The magnitude of the slope of an indifference curve is called the marginal rate of substitution.
- The marginal rate of substitution diminishes as consumption of the good measured on the y-axis decreases and consumption of the good measured on the x-axis increases.

Predicting Consumer Behavior (pp. 174–178)

- A household consumes at its best affordable point. This point is on the budget line and on the highest attainable indifference curve and has a marginal rate of substitution equal to relative price.
- The effect of a price change (the price effect) can be divided into a substitution effect and an income effect.
- The substitution effect is the effect of a change in price on the quantity bought when the consumer

(hypothetically) remains indifferent between the original and the new situation.

- The substitution effect always results in an increase in consumption of the good whose relative price has fallen.
- The income effect is the effect of a change in income on consumption.
- For a normal good, the income effect reinforces the substitution effect. For an inferior good, the income effect works in the opposite direction to the substitution effect.

Work-Leisure Choices (pp. 178–179)

- The indifference curve model of household choice enables us to understand how a household allocates its time between work and leisure.
- Work hours have decreased and leisure hours have increased because the income effect on the demand for leisure has been greater than the substitution effect.

KEY FIGURES

KEY TERMS

PROBLEMS

*1. Sara's income is $12 a week. The price of popcorn is $3 a bag, and the price of cola is $3 a can.
   a. What is Sara's real income in terms of cola?
   b. What is her real income in terms of popcorn?
   c. What is the relative price of cola in terms of popcorn?
   d. What is the opportunity cost of a can of cola?
   e. Calculate the equation for Sara's budget line (placing bags of popcorn on the left side of the equation).
   f. Draw a graph of Sara's budget line with cola on the *x*-axis.
   g. In (f), what is the slope of Sara's budget line? What determines its value?

2. Rashid's income is $100 per week. The price of a CD is $10, and the price of a book is $20.
   a. What is Rashid's real income in terms of CDs?
   b. What is his real income in terms of books?
   c. What is the relative price of a CD in terms of books?
   d. What is the opportunity cost of a book?
   e. Calculate the equation for Rashid's budget line (placing books on the left side of the equation).
   f. Draw a graph of Rashid's budget line with CDs on the *x*-axis.
   g. In (f), what is the slope of Rashid's budget line? What determines its value?

*3. Sara's income and the prices of popcorn and cola are the same as those in problem 1. The figure illustrates Sara's preferences.

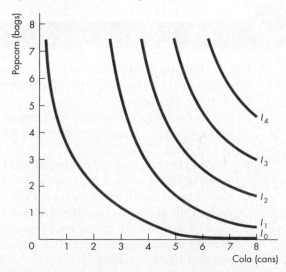

   a. What quantities of popcorn and cola does Sara buy?
   b. What is Sara's marginal rate of substitution at the point at which she consumes?

4. Rashid's income and the prices of CDs and books are the same as those in problem 2. The figure illustrates his preferences.

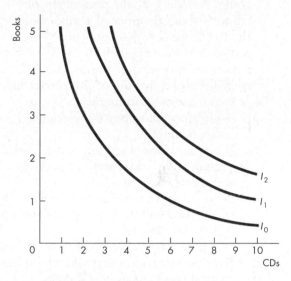

   a. What quantities of CDs and books does Rashid buy?
   b. What is Rashid's marginal rate of substitution at the point at which he consumes?

*5. Now suppose that in problem 3, the price of cola falls to $1.50 a can and the price of popcorn and Sara's income remain the same.
   a. What quantities of cola and popcorn does Sara now buy?
   b. Find two points on Sara's demand curve for cola.
   c. Find the substitution effect of the price change.
   d. Find the income effect of the price change.
   e. Is cola a normal good or an inferior good for Sara?

6. Now suppose that in problem 4, the price of a CD rises to $20 and the price of a book and Rashid's income remain the same.
   a. What quantities of CDs and books does Rashid now buy?
   b. Find two points on Rashid's demand curve for CDs.
   c. Find the substitution effect of the price change.

d. Find the income effect of the price change.

e. Is a CD a normal good or an inferior good for Rashid?

*7. Pam buys cookies and comic books. The price of a cookie is $1, and the price of a comic book is $2. Each month, Pam spends all of her income and buys 30 cookies and 5 comic books. Next month, the price of a cookie will fall to 50¢ and the price of a comic book will rise to $5. Assume that Pam's preference map is similar to that in Fig. 8.3(b). Use a graph to answer the following questions.

a. Will Pam be able to buy 30 cookies and 5 comic books next month?

b. Will Pam want to buy 30 cookies and 5 comic books?

c. Which situation does Pam prefer: cookies at $1 and comic books at $2 or cookies at 50¢ and comic books at $3?

d. If Pam changes the quantities that she buys, which good will she buy more of and which will she buy less of?

e. When the prices change next month, will there be an income effect and a substitution effect at work or just one of them?

8. Yangjie buys smoothies and sushi. The price of a smoothie is $5, and the price of sushi is $1 a piece. Each month, Yangjie spends all of her income and buys 10 smoothies and 20 pieces of sushi. Next month, the price of a smoothie will fall to $3 and the price of sushi will rise to $2 a piece. Assume that Yangjie's preference map is similar to that in Fig. 8.3(b). Use a graph to answer the following questions.

a. Will Yangjie be able to buy 10 smoothies and 20 pieces of sushi next month?

b. Will Yangjie want to buy 10 smoothies and 20 pieces of sushi? Explain why.

c. Which situation does Yangjie prefer: smoothies at $5 each and sushi at $1 a piece or smoothies at $3 each and sushi at $2 a piece?

d. If Yangjie changes the quantities that she buys, which good will she buy more of and which will she buy less of?

e. When the prices change next month, will there be an income effect and a substitution effect at work or just one of them? Explain.

CRITICAL THINKING

1. Study *Reading Between the Lines* about music and audio book downloads on pp. 180–181, and then answer the following questions.

a. How do you buy music?

b. Sketch your budget constraint for music and other items.

c. Sketch your indifference curves for music and other goods.

d. What do you predict would happen to the way that you buy music if the price of a CD increased and the price of a music download decreased, leaving you able to buy exactly the same quantity of music as you buy now?

2. The sales tax is a tax on goods. Some people say that a consumption tax, a tax that is paid on both goods and services, would be better. If we replaced the sales tax with a consumption tax:

a. What would happen to the relative price of CD-Rs and haircuts?

b. What would happen to the budget line showing the quantities of CD-Rs and haircuts you can afford to buy?

c. How would you change your purchases of CD-Rs and haircuts?

d. Which type of tax is better for the consumer and why?

Use a graph to illustrate your answers and to show the substitution effect and the income effect of the price change.

WEB EXERCISES

1. Use the links on your Parkin Web site to obtain information about the prices of cell phone service and first-class mail.

a. Sketch the budget constraint for a consumer who spent $50 a month on these two goods in 1999 and 2001.

b. Can you say whether the consumer was better off or worse off in 2001 than in 1999?

c. Sketch some indifference curves for cell phone calls and first-class letters mailed and show the income effect and the substitution effect of the changes in prices that occurred between 1999 and 2001.

UNDERSTANDING HOUSEHOLDS' CHOICES

Making the Most of Life

The powerful forces of demand and supply shape the fortunes of families, businesses, nations, and empires in the same unrelenting way that the tides and winds shape rocks and coastlines. You saw in Chapters 3 through 6 how these forces raise and lower prices, increase and decrease quantities bought and sold, cause revenues to fluctuate, and send resources to their most valuable uses. ◆ These powerful forces begin quietly and privately with the choices that each one of us makes. Chapters 7 and 8 probe these individual choices. Chapter 7 explores the marginal utility theory of human decisions. This theory explains people's consumption plans. It also explains people's consumption of leisure time and its flip side, the supply of work time. Marginal utility theory can even be used to explain "non-economic" choices, such as whether to marry and how many children to have. In a sense, there are no non-economic choices. If there is scarcity, there must be choice. And economics studies all such choices. Chapter 8 describes a tool that enables us to make a map of people's likes and dislikes, a tool called an *indifference curve*. Indifference curves are considered an advanced topic, so this chapter is *strictly optional*. But the presentation of indifference curves in Chapter 8 is the clearest and most straightforward available, so if you want to learn about this tool, this chapter is the place to do so. ◆ The earliest economists (Adam Smith and his contemporaries) did not have a very deep understanding of households' choices. It was not until the nineteenth century that progress was made in this area. On the following pages, you can spend some time with Jeremy Bentham, the person who pioneered the use of the concept of utility to the study of human choices, and with Gary Becker of the University of Chicago, who is one of today's most influential students of human behavior.

PROBING THE IDEAS
People as Rational Decision Makers

"... *It is the greatest happiness of the greatest number that is the measure of right and wrong.*"

JEREMY
BENTHAM
*Fragment on
Government*

THE ECONOMIST

JEREMY BENTHAM *(1748–1832),
who lived in London, was the son and
grandson of a lawyer and was himself trained
as a barrister. But he rejected the opportunity
to maintain the family tradition and, instead, spent his life as a writer, activist, and
Member of Parliament in the pursuit of rational laws that would bring the greatest
happiness to the greatest number of people.*

*Bentham, whose embalmed body is pre-
served to this day in a glass cabinet in the
University of London, was the first person to
use the concept of utility to explain human
choices. But in Bentham's day, the distinction
between explaining and prescribing was not
a sharp one, and Bentham was ready to use
his ideas to tell people how they ought to behave. He was one of the first to propose pen-
sions for the retired, guaranteed employment,
minimum wages, and social benefits such as
free education and free medical care.*

THE ISSUES

The economic analysis of human behavior in
the family, the workplace, the markets for
goods and services, the markets for labor
services, and financial markets is based on
the idea that our behavior can be understood
as a response to scarcity. Everything we do
can be understood as a choice that maximizes total benefit subject to the constraints
imposed by our limited resources and technology. If people's preferences are stable in
the face of changing constraints, then we
have a chance of predicting how they will
respond to an evolving environment.

The economic approach explains the
incredible change that has occurred during
the past 100 years in the way women allocate
their time as the consequence of changing
constraints, not of changing attitudes.
Technological advances have equipped the
nation's farms and factories with machines
that have increased the productivity of both
women and men, thereby raising the wages
they can earn. The increasingly technological
world has increased the return to education
for both women and men and has led to a
large increase in high school and college
graduates of both sexes. And equipped with
an ever-widening array of gadgets and appliances that cut the time taken to do household jobs, an increasing proportion of
women have joined the labor force.

The economic explanation might not be
correct, but it is a powerful one. And if it is
correct, the changing attitudes are a consequence, not a cause, of the economic advance-
ment of women.

By 2002, more than 60 percent of women were in the labor force, and although many had low-paying jobs, women were increasingly found in the professions and in executive positions. What brought about this dramatic change compared with 100 years earlier? Was it a change in preferences or a change in the constraints that women face?

THEN

Economists explain people's actions as the consequences of choices that maximize total utility subject to constraints. In the 1890s, fewer than 20 percent of women chose market employment, and most of those who did had low-paying and unattractive jobs. The other 80 percent of women chose nonmarket work in the home. What constraints led to these choices?

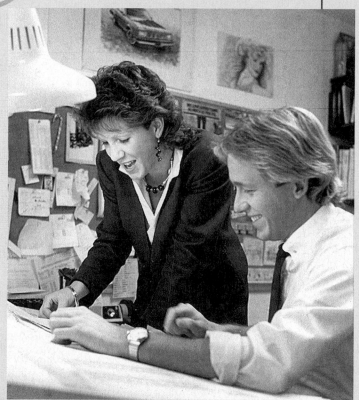

Today, one economist who stands out above all others and who stands on the shoulders of Jeremy Bentham is Gary Becker of the University of Chicago. Professor Becker has transformed the way we think about human choices. You can meet him on the following pages.

TALKING WITH

GARY S. BECKER *is Professor of Economics and Sociology at the University of Chicago. Born in 1930 in Pottsville, Pennsylvania, he was an undergraduate at Princeton University and a graduate student at the University of Chicago. His graduate supervisor was Milton Friedman, and his Ph.D. thesis became the book* The Economics of Discrimination, *a work that profoundly changed the way we think about discrimination and economic ways of reducing it.*

Professor Becker's other major book, Human Capital, *first published in 1964, has become a classic that influenced the thinking of the Clinton Administration on education issues. In 1992 he was awarded the Nobel Prize for Economic Science for his work on human capital.*

Professor Becker has revolutionized the way we think about human decisions in all aspects of life. Michael Parkin talked with Professor Becker about his work and how it uses and builds on the work of Jeremy Bentham.

Professor Becker, why are you an economist?

When I went to Princeton, I was interested in mathematics, but I wanted to do something for society. I took economics in my freshman year by accident, and it was a lucky accident. I found economics to be tremendously exciting intellectually because it could be used to understand the difference between capitalism and socialism, what determined wages, and how people are taxed. This was so exciting to me that I didn't even worry about job opportunities at the time.

Can we really hope to explain all human choices by using models that were invented initially to explain and predict choices about the allocation of income among alternative consumer goods and services?

I think we can hope to explain all human choices. All choices involve making comparisons and assessing how to allocate our time between work, leisure, and taking care of children. These are choices that are not in principle very different from the type of choices involved in allocating income. Whether economists succeed at the goal of explaining everything, of course, remains to be seen. We certainly haven't done that yet, but I think we've made considerable progress in expanding our horizons with the theory of choice.

You are a professor of both economics and sociology. Do you see these same techniques that we've developed in economics being used to address questions that are the traditional domain of the sociologist? Or is sociology just a totally different discipline?

Sociology is a discipline with many different approaches. There is a small but growing and vocal group of sociologists who believe in what they call *rational choice theory*, which is the theory economists have used to explain choices in markets. My late colleague, James Coleman, was the leader of that group. One of the issues they deal with is the influence of peers on behavior. For example, imagine that I am a teenager facing choices of getting involved with drugs or heavy drinking or smoking because of peer pressure. How would rational choice theorists incorporate this peer pressure into an analysis of these choices? The simple approach they take is that my utility, or pleasure, depends not only on what I'm consuming but also on what my peers are doing. If they're doing something very different from what I'm doing, that reduces my utility partly because I receive less respect from them and feel less part of the group.

Therefore when I am trying to get as much utility as possible, I take into account what my peers are doing. But since we're all doing that, this leads to some equilibrium in this peer market. Instead of us all behaving independently, we are all behaving interdependently. I think economists have given social structures such as peer pressure far too little attention. One of the things I learned during my association with Coleman and other sociologists is a better appreciation of the importance of social factors in individual behavior.

Can you identify the historical figures that have been most influential to your thinking and your career?

Economics is a cumulative field in which we build on the giants who went earlier, and we try to add a little bit. And then other people build on our generation's contributions. The view I take of the broad scope of

> *Very few people's work, certainly not mine, spring out of nowhere. They have continuity with the past. What we do is try to build on the work of past economists and do a little more and a little better than what they did.*

the economic approach has had a number of major practitioners, including Jeremy Bentham, who stated and applied a very general view of utility-maximizing behavior to many problems, such as the factors that reduce crime.

Other nineteenth century people like Wicksteed and Marshall highlighted the rational choice aspect of economics. In the eighteenth century, Adam Smith already applied economic reasoning to political behavior. My work on human capital was very much influenced by Irving Fisher, Alfred Marshall, Milton Friedman, and Ted Schultz. Very few people's work, certainly not mine, spring out of nowhere. They have continuity with the past. What we do is try to build on the work of past economists and do a little more and a little better than what they did.

How would you characterize the major achievements of the economics of human behavior? What questions, for example, would have convincing answers?

The area of law and economics has been very successful in analyzing criminal behavior. Work by many lawyers and economists, particularly Judge Richard Posner and William Landes of the University of Chicago Law School, has produced many successful applications. The question that economics of crime seeks to answer is: What determines the amount of crime that we have and how effective are various actions that governments can take in reducing the amount of crime? This analysis discusses apprehending and punishing criminals, giving better education to people who might commit crimes, reducing unemployment, and so on. They have basically said that fundamentally, the factors determining criminal behavior are not so different from the factors determining whether people become professors or not. People make choices, and these choices are conditional on their expected benefits and the cost. You can affect the number of people who decide to enter criminal activities by affecting the benefits and costs. To the extent that people make these calculations, they are more likely to enter crime when benefits are high relative to the cost.

One way to affect costs is to make it more likely that if somebody commits a crime they'll be captured, apprehended, convicted, and punished. That raises the cost and reduces crime. I think now that people accept this conclusion for most crimes.

But the economic approach is not simply a law and order approach. It also says that if you can increase the attractiveness to people of working at legal activities rather than illegal or criminal activities, you will also have less crime. One way to increase the attractiveness is to make it easier for people to find jobs and to earn more by improving their skills, their education, and their training and also by improving the functioning of labor markets.

You've made a significant contribution to demographic economics. Nearly 40 years ago, you introduced the idea of children being durable goods. Can you talk about the evolution of this idea?

Demographers initially were extremely hostile to my point of view. However, I recently received the Irene Taeuber Award from the Population Association of America, their most prestigious demographic award. It was given to me in recognition of the value of the economic way of looking at demographic questions, including birth and marriage rates. Over time, the cumulative work of many economists working on population problems around the world made an impact.

The main payoffs from this work have been in our understanding of fertility. The conclusions from the economic approach are that the number of children people have is very much a function of two variables: costs and choices. Costs depend not only on how much food and shelter you give children, but also on the time of parents. In most societies, most of that time is the mother's time, which has a value. As we have become richer, and as women have become better educated and are working outside the home more, the cost to them of spending time on children has risen.

> *There are about 15 countries of the world that now have birth rates well below replacement levels. If families continue with these rates, the populations will eventually decline — and decline rapidly.*

As these costs have risen, families are deterred from having as many children as they had in the past. So one of the factors explaining the big decline in birth rates is the increasing costs of children.

The second variable that economists recognize is that families are making choices about the quality of children's lives in terms of their education, training, and health. In modern economies, this quality component has become very important because the emphasis in modern economies is on knowledge, technology,

and skills. But there is a tradeoff. If you spend more on each child's skills, education, and training, you make children more costly and you are likely to have fewer children. Over the past 30 years, birth rates have been decreasing in most countries of the world, including India, China, parts of Asia, Latin America, some parts of Africa, Europe, and the United States.

How do you respond to people who feel that explaining choices such as how many children to raise is deeply personal and that it is therefore immoral to think of children in these terms?

I think morality is misplaced in this area. We are trying to understand very major changes in the world. There are about 15 countries of the world that now have birth rates well below replacement levels. If families continue with these rates, these populations will eventually decline — and decline rapidly. This includes Germany, Italy, Spain, Portugal, France, and Japan. It is important to understand why birth rates are going down. If this way of looking at it is a powerful tool for understanding why families have made these choices, then it would be immoral, I believe, to neglect this approach. If we are concerned about low birth rates, how can we go about raising them? Or if we want to understand what to expect in other countries that are experiencing significant economic development, we will miss out if we neglect an important set of considerations that help us to understand what's going on.

Is economics a subject that a young person can happily enter today? What are the major incentives for pursuing economics as an undergraduate?

I would certainly encourage a young person to enter economics for several reasons. There are many employment opportunities in economics, and it is also valuable if you decide to go into other areas such as the law, business, or even medicine. Economic issues, including the budget deficit, entitlement programs, minimum wages, and how to subsidize the elderly, are extremely important public policy issues.

I want also to stress that economics is a wonderful intellectual activity. To be able to take this very mysterious world we live in and to illuminate parts of it, important parts of it, through the use of economics is enormously intellectually satisfying and challenging for an undergraduate or for anybody else. So I would say it's both practical and satisfying. Who can ask for a better combination?

4

ORGANIZING PRODUCTION ── CHAPTER 9

Spinning a Web

In the fall of 1990, a British scientist named Tim Berners-Lee invented the World Wide Web. This remarkable idea paved the way for the creation and growth of thousands of profitable businesses. One of these businesses, Yahoo! Inc., is one of the largest Web portal providers. ◆ How do Yahoo! Inc. and the other 20 million firms that operate in the United States make their business decisions? How do they operate efficiently? ◆ Businesses range from multinational giants, such as Microsoft, to small family restaurants and local Internet service providers. Three quarters of all firms are operated by their owners. But corporations (such as Yahoo! and Microsoft) account for 86 percent of all business sales. What are the different forms a firm can take? Why do some firms remain small while others become giants? Why are most firms owner-operated? ◆ Many businesses operate in a highly competitive environment and struggle to make a profit. Others, like Microsoft, seem to have cornered the market for their products and make a large profit. What are the different types of market in which firms operate and why is it harder to make a profit in some markets than in others? ◆ Most of the components of a Dell personal computer are made by other firms. Microsoft created its Windows operating system, and Intel makes its processor chip. Other firms make the hard drive and modem, and yet others make the CD drive, sound card, and so on. Why doesn't Dell make all its own computer components? Why does it leave these activities to other firms and buy from them in markets? How do firms decide what to make themselves and what to buy in the marketplace from other firms?

◻ In this chapter, we are going to learn about firms and the choices they make to cope with scarcity. We begin by studying the economic problems and choices that all firms face.

After studying this chapter, you will be able to

- ■ Explain what a firm is and describe the economic problems that *all* firms face
- ■ Distinguish between technological efficiency and economic efficiency
- ■ Define and explain the principal-agent problem and describe how different types of business organizations cope with this problem
- ■ Describe and distinguish between different types of markets in which firms operate
- ■ Explain why markets coordinate some economic activities and firms coordinate others

The Firm and Its Economic Problem

THE 20 MILLION FIRMS IN THE UNITED STATES differ in size and in the scope of what they do. But they all perform the same basic economic functions. Each **firm** is an institution that hires factors of production and organizes those factors to produce and sell goods and services.

Our goal is to predict firms' behavior. To do so, we need to know a firm's goals and the constraints it faces. We begin with the goals.

The Firm's Goal

If you asked a group of entrepreneurs what they are trying to achieve, you would get many different answers. Some would talk about making a high-quality product, others about business growth, others about market share, and others about the job satisfaction of their work force. All of these goals might be pursued, but they are not the fundamental goal. They are means to a deeper goal.

A firm's goal is to maximize profit. A firm that does not seek to maximize profit is either eliminated or bought out by firms that do seek to maximize profit.

What exactly is the profit that a firm seeks to maximize? To answer this question, let's look at Sidney's Sweaters.

Measuring a Firm's Profit

Sidney runs a successful business that makes sweaters. Sidney's Sweaters receives $400,000 a year for the sweaters it sells. Its expenses are $80,000 a year for wool, $20,000 for utilities, $120,000 for wages, and $10,000 in interest on a bank loan. With receipts of $400,000 and expenses of $230,000, Sidney's Sweaters' annual surplus is $170,000.

Sidney's accountant lowers this number by $20,000, which he says is the depreciation (fall in value) of the firm's buildings and knitting machines during the year. (Accountants use Internal Revenue Service rules based on standards established by the Financial Accounting Standards Board to calculate the depreciation.) So the accountant reports that the profit of Sidney's Sweaters is $150,000 a year.

Sidney's accountant measures cost and profit to ensure that the firm pays the correct amount of income tax and to show the bank how its loan has

been used. But we want to predict the decisions that a firm makes. These decisions respond to *opportunity cost* and *economic profit*.

Opportunity Cost

The *opportunity cost* of any action is the highest-valued alternative forgone. The action that you choose not to take — the highest-valued alternative forgone — is the cost of the action that you choose to take. For a firm, the opportunity cost of production is the value of the firm's best alternative use of its resources.

Opportunity cost is a real alternative forgone. But so that we can compare the cost of one action with that of another action, we express opportunity cost in money units. A firm's opportunity cost includes both

- Explicit costs
- Implicit costs

Explicit Costs Explicit costs are paid in money. The amount paid for a resource could have been spent on something else, so it is the opportunity cost of using the resource. For Sidney, his expenditures on wool, utilities, wages, and bank interest are explicit costs.

Implicit Costs A firm incurs implicit costs when it forgoes an alternative action but does not make a payment. A firm incurs implicit costs when it

1. Uses its own capital.
2. Uses its owner's time or financial resources.

The cost of using its own capital is an implicit cost — and an opportunity cost — because the firm could rent the capital to another firm. The rental income forgone is the firm's opportunity cost of using its own capital. This opportunity cost is called the **implicit rental rate** of capital.

People rent houses, apartments, cars, and videotapes. And firms rent photocopiers, earth-moving equipment, satellite-launching services, and so on. If a firm rents capital, it incurs an explicit cost. If a firm buys the capital it uses, it incurs an implicit cost. The implicit rental rate of capital is made up of

1. Economic depreciation
2. Interest forgone

Economic depreciation is the change in the *market* value of capital over a given period. It is calculated as the market price of the capital at the beginning of the period minus its market price at the end of the period. For example, suppose that Sidney could have sold his buildings and knitting machines on December 31, 2001, for $400,000. If he can sell the same capital on December 31, 2002, for $375,000, his economic depreciation during 2002 is $25,000 — the fall in the market value of the machines. This $25,000 is an implicit cost of using the capital during 2002.

The funds used to buy capital could have been used for some other purpose. And in their next best use, they would have yielded a return — an interest income. This forgone interest is part of the opportunity cost of using the capital. For example, Sidney's Sweaters could have bought government bonds instead of a knitting factory. The interest forgone on the government bonds is an implicit cost of operating the knitting factory.

Cost of Owner's Resources A firm's owner often supplies entrepreneurial ability — the factor of production that organizes the business, makes business decisions, innovates, and bears the risk of running the business. The return to entrepreneurship is profit, and the return that an entrepreneur can expect to receive on the average is called **normal profit**. Normal profit is part of a firm's opportunity cost, because it is the cost of a forgone alternative — running another firm. If normal profit in the textile business is $50,000 a year, this amount must be added to Sidney's costs to determine his opportunity cost.

The owner of a firm also can supply labor (in addition to entrepreneurship). The return to labor is a wage. And the opportunity cost of the owner's time spent working for the firm is the wage income forgone by not working in the best alternative job. Suppose that Sidney could take another job that pays $40,000 a year. By working for his knitting business and forgoing this income, Sidney incurs an opportunity cost of $40,000 a year.

Economic Profit

What is the bottom line — the profit or loss of the firm? A firm's **economic profit** is equal to its total revenue minus its opportunity cost. The firm's opportunity cost is the sum of its explicit costs and implicit costs. And the implicit costs, remember, include *normal profit*. The return to entrepreneurial ability is greater than normal in a firm that makes a positive economic profit. And the return to entrepreneurial ability is less than normal in a firm that makes a negative economic profit — a firm that incurs an economic loss.

Economic Accounting: A Summary

Table 9.1 summarizes the economic accounting concepts that you've just studied. Sidney's Sweaters' total revenue is $400,000. Its opportunity cost (explicit costs plus implicit costs) is $365,000. And its economic profit is $35,000.

To achieve the objective of maximum profit — maximum economic profit — a firm must make five basic decisions:

1. What goods and services to produce and in what quantities
2. How to produce — the techniques of production to use
3. How to organize and compensate its managers and workers
4. How to market and price its products
5. What to produce itself and what to buy from other firms

In all these decisions, a firm's actions are limited by the constraints that it faces. Our next task is to learn about these constraints.

TABLE 9.1   Economic Accounting

Item		Amount
Total Revenue		**$400,000**
Opportunity Costs		
Wool	$80,000	
Utilities	20,000	
Wages paid	120,000	
Bank interest paid	10,000	
Total Explicit Costs		$230,000
Sidney's wages forgone	40,000	
Sidney's interest forgone	20,000	
Economic depreciation	$25,000	
Normal profit	$50,000	
Total Implicit Costs		$135,000
Total Cost		**$365,000**
Economic Profit		**$35,000**

The Firm's Constraints

Three features of its environment limit the maximum profit a firm can make. They are

- Technology
- Information
- Market

Technology Constraints Economists define technology broadly. A **technology** is any method of producing a good or service. Technology includes the detailed designs of machines. It also includes the layout of the workplace. And it includes the organization of the firm. For example, the shopping mall is a technology for producing retail services. It is a different technology from the catalog store, which in turn is different from the downtown store.

It might seem surprising that a firm's profits are limited by technology because it seems that technological advances are constantly increasing profit opportunities. Almost every day, we learn about some new technological advance that amazes us. With computers that speak and recognize our own speech and cars that can find the address we need in a city we've never visited before, we can accomplish ever more.

Technology advances over time. But at each point in time, to produce more output and gain more revenue, a firm must hire more resources and incur greater costs. The increase in profit that the firm can achieve is limited by the technology available. For example, by using its current plant and work force, Ford can produce some maximum number of cars per day. To produce more cars per day, Ford must hire more resources, which increases Ford's costs and limits the increase in profit that Ford can make by selling the additional cars.

Information Constraints We never possess all the information we would like to have to make decisions. We lack information about both the future and the present. For example, suppose you plan to buy a new computer. When should you buy it? The answer depends on how the price is going to change in the future. Where should you buy it? The answer depends on the prices at hundreds of different computer shops. To get the best deal, you must compare the quality and prices in every shop. But the opportunity cost of this comparison exceeds the cost of the computer! Similarly, a firm is constrained by limited information about the quality and effort of its work force,

the current and future buying plans of its customers, and the plans of its competitors. Workers might slacken off when the manager believes they are working hard. Customers might switch to competing suppliers. Firms must compete against competition from a new firm.

Firms try to create incentive systems for workers to ensure that they work hard even when no one is monitoring their efforts. And firms spend millions of dollars on market research. But none of these efforts and expenditures eliminate the problems of incomplete information and uncertainty. And the cost of coping with limited information itself limits profit.

Market Constraints What each firm can sell and the price it can obtain are constrained by its customers' willingness to pay and by the prices and marketing efforts of other firms. Similarly, the resources that a firm can buy and the prices it must pay for them are limited by the willingness of people to work for and invest in the firm. Firms spend billions of dollars a year marketing and selling their products. Some of the most creative minds strive to find the right message that will produce a knockout television advertisement. Market constraints and the expenditures firms make to overcome them limit the profit a firm can make.

REVIEW QUIZ

1 Why do firms seek to maximize profit? What happens to firms that don't pursue this goal?
2 Why do accountants and economists calculate a firm's cost and profit in different ways?
3 What are the items that make opportunity cost differ from the accountant's cost measure?
4 Why is normal profit an opportunity cost?
5 What are the constraints that a firm faces? How does each constraint limit the firm's profit?

In the rest of this chapter and in Chapters 10 through 13, we study the decisions that firms make. We're going to learn how we can predict a firm's behavior as the response to the constraints that it faces and to changes in those constraints. We begin by taking a closer look at the technology constraints that firms face.

Technological and Economic Efficiency

MICROSOFT EMPLOYS A LARGE WORK FORCE, AND most Microsoft workers possess a large amount of human capital. But the firm uses a small amount of physical capital. In contrast, a coal-mining company employs a huge amount of mining equipment (physical capital) and almost no labor. Why? The answer lies in the concept of efficiency. There are two concepts of production efficiency: technological efficiency and economic efficiency. **Technological efficiency** occurs when the firm produces a given output by using the least amount of inputs. **Economic efficiency** occurs when the firm produces a given output at the least cost. Let's explore the two concepts of efficiency by studying an example.

Suppose that there are four alternative techniques for making TV sets:

A. *Robot production.* One person monitors the entire computer-driven process.
B. *Production line.* Workers specialize in a small part of the job as the emerging TV set passes them on a production line.
C. *Bench production.* Workers specialize in a small part of the job but walk from bench to bench to perform their tasks.
D. *Hand-tool production.* A single worker uses a few hand tools to make a TV set.

Table 9.2 sets out the amounts of labor and capital required by each of these four methods to make 10 TV sets a day.

Which of these alternative methods are technologically efficient?

Technological Efficiency

Recall that technological efficiency occurs when the firm produces a given output by using the least inputs. Inspect the numbers in the table and notice that method A uses the most capital but the least labor. Method D uses the most labor but the least capital. Method B and method C lie between the two extremes. They use less capital but more labor than method A and less labor but more capital than method D. Compare methods B and C. Method C requires 100 workers and 10 units of capital to produce 10 TV sets. Those same 10 TV sets can be produced by method B with 10 workers and the same 10 units of capital. Because method C uses the same amount of capital and more labor than method B, method C is not technologically efficient.

Are any of the other methods not technologically efficient? The answer is no. Each of the other three methods is technologically efficient. Method A uses more capital but less labor than method B, and method D uses more labor but less capital than method B.

Which of the alternative methods are economically efficient?

Economic Efficiency

Recall that economic efficiency occurs when the firm produces a given output at the least cost. Suppose that labor costs $75 per person-day and that capital costs $250 per machine-day. Table 9.3(a) calculates the costs of using the different methods. By inspecting the table, you can see that method B has the lowest cost. Although method A uses less labor, it uses too much expensive capital. And although method D uses less capital, it uses too much expensive labor.

Method C, which is technologically inefficient, is also economically inefficient. It uses the same amount of capital as method B but 10 times as much labor. So it costs more. A technologically inefficient method is never economically efficient.

Although B is the economically efficient method in this example, method A or D could be economically efficient with different input prices.

Suppose that labor costs $150 a person-day and capital costs only $1 a machine-day. Table 9.3(b) now shows the costs of making a TV set. In this case, method A is economically efficient. Capital is now so

TABLE 9.2	Four Ways of Making 10 TV Sets a Day		
		Quantities of inputs	
	Method	**Labor**	**Capital**
A	Robot production	1	1,000
B	Production line	10	10
C	Bench production	100	10
D	Hand-tool production	1,000	1

TABLE 9.3   The Costs of Different Ways of Making 10 TV Sets a Day

(a) Four ways of making TVs

Method	Labor cost ($75 per day)		Capital cost ($250 per day)		Total cost	Cost per TV set
A	$75	+	$250,000	=	$250,075	$25,007.50
B	**750**	**+**	**2,500**	**=**	**3,250**	**325.00**
C	7,500	+	2,500	=	10,000	1,000.00
D	75,000	+	250	=	75,250	7,525.00

(b) Three ways of making TVs: High labor costs

Method	Labor cost ($150 per day)		Capital cost ($1 per day)		Total cost	Cost per TV set
A	**$150**	**+**	**$1,000**	**=**	**$1,150**	**$115.00**
B	1,500	+	10	=	1,510	151.00
D	150,000	+	1	=	150,001	15,000.10

(c) Three ways of making TVs: High capital costs

Method	Labor cost ($1 per day)		Capital cost ($1,000 per day)		Total cost	Cost per TV set
A	$1	+	$1,000,000	=	$1,000,001	$100,000.10
B	10	+	10,000	=	10,010	1,001.00
D	**1,000**	**+**	**1,000**	**=**	**2,000**	**200.00**

cheap relative to labor that the method that uses the most capital is the economically efficient method.

Next, suppose that labor costs only $1 a person-day while capital costs $1,000 a machine-day. Table 9.3(c) shows the costs in this case. Method *D*, which uses a lot of labor and little capital, is now the least-cost method and the economically efficient method.

From these examples, you can see that while technological efficiency depends only on what is feasible, economic efficiency depends on the relative costs of resources. The economically efficient method is the one that uses a smaller amount of a more expensive resource and a larger amount of a less expensive resource.

A firm that is not economically efficient does not maximize profit. Natural selection favors efficient firms and opposes inefficient firms. Inefficient firms go out of business or are taken over by firms with lower costs.

REVIEW QUIZ

1 Is a firm technologically efficient if it uses the latest technology? Why or why not?
2 Is a firm economically inefficient if it can cut costs by producing less? Why or why not?
3 Explain the key distinction between technological efficiency and economic efficiency.
4 Why do some firms use large amounts of capital and small amounts of labor while others use small amounts of capital and large amounts of labor?

Next we study information constraints that firms face and the diversity of organization structures they generate.

Information and Organization

EACH FIRM ORGANIZES THE PRODUCTION OF goods and services by combining and coordinating the productive resources it hires. But there is variety across firms in how they organize production. Firms use a mixture of two systems:

- Command systems
- Incentive systems

Command Systems

A **command system** is a method of organizing production that uses a managerial hierarchy. Commands pass downward through the hierarchy, and information passes upward. Managers spend most of their time collecting and processing information about the performance of the people under their control and making decisions about commands to issue and how best to get those commands implemented.

The military uses the purest form of command system. A commander-in-chief (in the United States, the President) makes the big decisions about strategic objectives. Beneath this highest level, generals organize their military resources. Beneath the generals, successively lower ranks organize smaller and smaller units but pay attention to ever-increasing degrees of detail. At the bottom of the managerial hierarchy are the people who operate weapons systems.

Command systems in firms are not as rigid as those in the military, but they share some similar features. A chief executive officer (CEO) sits at the top of a firm's command system. Senior executives who report to and receive commands from the CEO specialize in managing production, marketing, finance, personnel, and perhaps other aspects of the firm's operations. Beneath these senior managers might be several tiers of middle management ranks that stretch downward to the managers who supervise the day-to-day operations of the business. Beneath these managers are the people who operate the firm's machines and who make and sell the firm's goods and services.

Small firms have one or two layers of managers, while large firms have several layers. As production processes have become ever more complex, management ranks have swollen. Today, more people have management jobs than ever before. But the information revolution of the 1990s slowed the growth of management, and in some industries, it reduced the number of layers of managers and brought a shakeout of middle managers.

Managers make enormous efforts to be well informed. And they try hard to make good decisions and issue commands that end up using resources efficiently. But managers always have incomplete information about what is happening in the divisions of the firm for which they are responsible. It is for this reason that firms use incentive systems as well as command systems to organize production.

Incentive Systems

An **incentive system** is a method of organizing production that uses a market-like mechanism inside the firm. Instead of issuing commands, senior managers create compensation schemes that will induce workers to perform in ways that maximize the firm's profit.

Selling organizations use incentive systems most extensively. Sales representatives who spend most of their working time alone and unsupervised are induced to work hard by being paid a small salary and a large performance-related bonus.

But incentive systems operate at all levels in a firm. CEOs' compensation plans include a share in the firm's profit, and factory floor workers sometimes receive compensation based on the quantity they produce.

Mixing the Systems

Firms use a mixture of commands and incentives. And they choose the mixture that maximizes profit. They use commands when it is easy to monitor performance or when a small deviation from an ideal performance is very costly. They use incentives when monitoring performance is either not possible or too costly to be worth doing.

For example, it is easy to monitor the performance of workers on a production line. And if one person works too slowly, the entire line slows. So a production line is organized with a command system.

In contrast, it is costly to monitor a CEO. For example, what did Ken Lay (former CEO of Enron) contribute to the initial success and subsequent failure of Enron? This question can't be answered with certainty, yet Enron's stockholders had to put someone in charge of the business and provide that person with an incentive to maximize their returns. The performance of Enron illustrates the nature of this problem, known as the principal-agent problem.

The Principal-Agent Problem

The **principal-agent problem** is the problem of devising compensation rules that induce an *agent* to act in the best interest of a *principal*. For example, the stockholders of Enron are *principals,* and the firm's managers are *agents*. The stockholders (the principals) must induce the managers (agents) to act in the stockholders' best interest. Similarly, Bill Gates (a principal) must induce the programmers who are working on the next generation of Windows (agents) to work efficiently.

Agents, whether they are managers or workers, pursue their own goals and often impose costs on a principal. For example, the goal of stockholders of Citicorp (principals) is to maximize the firm's profit — its true profit, not some fictitious paper profit. But the firm's profit depends on the actions of its managers (agents), and they have their own goals. Perhaps a manager takes a customer to a ball game on the pretense that she is building customer loyalty, when in fact she is simply enjoying on-the-job leisure. This same manager is also a principal, and her tellers are agents. The manager wants the tellers to work hard and attract new customers so that she can meet her operating targets. But the workers enjoy conversations with each other and take on-the-job leisure. Nonetheless, the firm constantly strives to find ways of improving performance and increasing profits.

Coping with the Principal-Agent Problem

Issuing commands does not address the principal-agent problem. In most firms, the shareholders can't monitor the managers and often the managers can't monitor the workers. Each principal must create incentives that induce each agent to work in the interests of the principal. Three ways of attempting to cope with the principal-agent problem are

■ Ownership
■ Incentive pay
■ Long-term contracts

Ownership By assigning to a manager or worker ownership (or part-ownership) of a business, it is sometimes possible to induce a job performance that increases a firm's profits. Part-ownership schemes for senior managers are quite common, but they are less

common for workers. When United Airlines was running into problems a few years ago, it made most of its employees owners of the company.

Incentive Pay Incentive pay schemes — pay related to performance — are very common. They are based on a variety of performance criteria such as profits, production, or sales targets. Promoting an employee for good performance is another example of an incentive pay scheme.

Long-Term Contracts Long-term contracts tie the long-term fortunes of managers and workers (agents) to the success of the principal(s) — the owner(s) of the firm. For example, a multiyear employment contract for a CEO encourages that person to take a long-term view and devise strategies that achieve maximum profit over a sustained period.

These three ways of coping with the principal-agent problem give rise to different types of business organization. Each type of business organization is a different response to the principal-agent problem. Each type uses ownership, incentives, and long-term contracts in different ways. Let's look at the main types of business organization.

Types of Business Organization

The three main types of business organization are

■ Proprietorship
■ Partnership
■ Corporation

Proprietorship A *proprietorship* is a firm with a single owner — a proprietor — who has unlimited liability. *Unlimited liability* is the legal responsibility for all the debts of a firm up to an amount equal to the entire wealth of the owner. If a proprietorship cannot pay its debts, those to whom the firm owes money can claim the personal property of the owner. Some farmers, computer programmers, and artists are examples of proprietorships.

The proprietor makes management decisions, receives the firm's profits, and is responsible for its losses. Profits from a proprietorship are taxed at the same rate as other sources of the proprietor's personal income.

Partnership A *partnership* is a firm with two or more owners who have unlimited liability. Partners must agree on an appropriate management structure and on how to divide the firm's profits among themselves. The profits of a partnership are taxed as the personal income of the owners. But each partner is legally liable for all the debts of the partnership (limited only by the wealth of that individual partner). Liability for the full debts of the partnership is called *joint unlimited liability*. Most law firms are partnerships.

Corporation A *corporation* is a firm owned by one or more limited liability stockholders. *Limited liability* means that the owners have legal liability only for the value of their initial investment. This limitation of liability means that if the corporation becomes bankrupt, its owners are not required to use their personal wealth to pay the corporation's debts.

Corporations' profits are taxed independently of stockholders' incomes. Because stockholders pay taxes on the income they receive as dividends on stocks, corporate profits are taxed twice. The stockholders also pay a capital gains tax on the profit they earn when they sell a stock for a higher price than they paid for it. Corporate stocks generate capital gains when a corporation retains some of its profit and reinvests it in profitable activities. So even retained earnings are taxed twice because the capital gains they generate are taxed.

Pros and Cons of Different Types of Firms

The different types of business organization arise as different ways of trying to cope with the principal-agent problem. Each has advantages in particular situations. And because of its special advantages, each type continues to exist. Each type also has its disadvantages, which explains why it has not driven out the other two.

Table 9.4 summarizes these pros and cons of the different types of firms.

TABLE 9.4   The Pros and Cons of Different Types of Firms

Type of Firm	Pros	Cons
Proprietorship	■ Easy to set up ■ Simple decision making ■ Profits taxed only once as owner's income	■ Bad decisions not checked by need for consensus ■ Owner's entire wealth at risk ■ Firm dies with owner ■ Capital is expensive ■ Labor is expensive
Partnership	■ Easy to set up ■ Diversified decision making ■ Can survive withdrawal of partner ■ Profits taxed only once as owners' incomes	■ Achieving consensus may be slow and expensive ■ Owners' entire wealth at risk ■ Withdrawal of partner may create capital shortage ■ Capital is expensive
Corporation	■ Owners have limited liability ■ Large-scale, low-cost capital available ■ Professional management not restricted by ability of owners ■ Perpetual life ■ Long-term labor contracts cut labor costs	■ Complex management structure can make decisions slow and expensive ■ Profits taxed twice as company profit and as stockholders' income

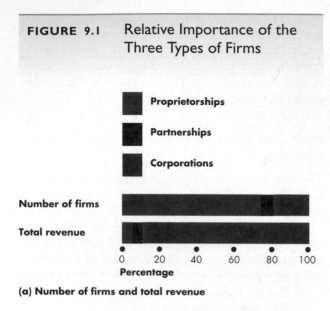

FIGURE 9.1   Relative Importance of the Three Types of Firms

(a) Number of firms and total revenue

(b) Total revenue in various industries

Three quarters of all firms are proprietorships, almost one fifth are corporations, and only a twentieth are partnerships. Corporations account for 86 percent of business revenue (part a). But proprietorships and partnerships account for a significant percentage of business revenue in some industries (part b).

Source: U.S. Bureau of the Census, *Statistical Abstract of the United States: 2001*

The Relative Importance of Different Types of Firms

Figure 9.1(a) shows the relative importance of the three main types of firms in the U.S. economy. The figure also shows that the revenue of corporations is much larger than that of the other types of firms. Although only 18 percent of all firms are corporations, they generate 86 percent of revenue.

Figure 9.1(b) shows the percentage of revenue generated by the different types of firms in various industries. Proprietorships in agriculture, forestry, and fishing generate about 40 percent of the total revenue in those sectors. Proprietorships in the service sector, construction, and retail trades also generate a large percentage of total revenue. Partnerships in agriculture, forestry, and fishing generate about 15 percent of total revenue. Partnerships are more prominent in services; mining; and finance, insurance, and real estate than in other sectors. Corporations are important in all sectors and have the manufacturing field almost to themselves.

Why do corporations dominate the business scene? Why do the other types of business survive? And why are proprietorships and partnerships more prominent in some sectors? The answers to these questions lie in the pros and cons of the different types of business organization that are summarized in Table 9.4. Corporations dominate where a large amount of capital is used. But proprietorships dominate where flexibility in decision making is critical.

REVIEW QUIZ

1 Explain the distinction between a command system and an incentive system.
2 What is the principal-agent problem? What are three ways in which firms try to cope with it?
3 What are the three types of firm? Explain the major advantages and disadvantages of each.
4 Why do all three types of firms survive and in which sectors is each type most prominent?

You've now seen how technology constraints and information constraints influence firms. We'll now look at market constraints and see how they influence the environment in which firms compete for business.

Markets and the Competitive Environment

THE MARKETS IN WHICH FIRMS OPERATE VARY A great deal. Some are highly competitive, and profits in these markets are hard to come by. Some appear to be almost free from competition, and firms in these markets earn large profits. Some markets are dominated by fierce advertising campaigns in which each firm seeks to persuade buyers that it has the best products. And some markets display a warlike character.

Economists identify four market types:

1. Perfect competition
2. Monopolistic competition
3. Oligopoly
4. Monopoly

Perfect competition arises when there are many firms, each selling an identical product, many buyers, and no restrictions on the entry of new firms into the industry. The many firms and buyers are all well informed about the prices of the products of each firm in the industry. The worldwide markets for corn, rice, and other grain crops are examples of perfect competition.

Monopolistic competition is a market structure in which a large number of firms compete by making similar but slightly different products. Making a product slightly different from the product of a competing firm is called **product differentiation**. Product differentiation gives the firm in monopolistic competition an element of market power. The firm is the sole producer of the particular version of the good in question. For example, in the market for running shoes, Nike, Reebok, Fila, New Balance, and Asics all make their own version of the perfect shoe. Each of these firms is the sole producer of a particular brand of shoe. Differentiated products are not necessarily different products. What matters is that consumers perceive them to be different. For example, different brands of aspirin are chemically identical (salicylic acid) and differ only in their packaging.

Oligopoly is a market structure in which a small number of firms compete. Computer software, airplane manufacture, and international air transportation are examples of oligopolistic industries. Oligopolies might produce almost identical products, such as the colas produced by Coke and Pepsi. Or they might produce differentiated products such as Chevrolet's Lumina and Ford's Taurus.

Monopoly arises when there is one firm, which produces a good or service that has no close substitutes and in which the firm is protected by a barrier preventing the entry of new firms. In some places, the phone, gas, electricity, and water suppliers are local monopolies — monopolies restricted to a given location. Microsoft Corporation, the software developer that created Windows, the operating system used by PCs, is an example of a global monopoly.

Perfect competition is the most extreme form of competition. Monopoly is the most extreme absence of competition. The other two market types fall between these extremes.

Many factors must be taken into account to determine which market structure describes a particular real-world market. One of these factors is the extent to which the market is dominated by a small number of firms. To measure this feature of markets, economists use indexes called measures of concentration. Let's look at these measures.

Measures of Concentration

Economists use two measures of concentration:

■ The four-firm concentration ratio
■ The Herfindahl-Hirschman Index

The Four-Firm Concentration Ratio The **four-firm concentration ratio** is the percentage of the value of sales accounted for by the four largest firms in an industry. The range of the concentration ratio is from almost zero for perfect competition to 100 percent for monopoly. This ratio is the main measure used to assess market structure.

Table 9.5 shows two calculations of the four-firm concentration ratio: one for tire makers and one for

printers. In this example, 14 firms produce tires. The largest four have 80 percent of the sales, so the four-firm concentration ratio is 80 percent. In the printing industry, with 1,004 firms, the largest four firms have only 0.5 percent of the sales, so the four-firm concentration ratio is 0.5 percent.

A low concentration ratio indicates a high degree of competition, and a high concentration ratio indicates an absence of competition. A monopoly has a concentration ratio of 100 percent — the largest (and only) firm has 100 percent of the sales. A four-firm concentration ratio that exceeds 60 percent is regarded as an indication of a market that is highly concentrated and dominated by a few firms in an oligopoly. A ratio of less than 40 percent is regarded as an indication of a competitive market.

The Herfindahl-Hirschman Index The **Herfindahl-Hirschman Index** — also called the HHI — is the square of the percentage market share of each firm summed over the largest 50 firms (or summed over all the firms if there are fewer than 50) in a market. For example, if there are four firms in a market and the market shares of the firms are 50 percent, 25 percent, 15 percent, and 10 percent, the Herfindahl-Hirschman Index is

$$HHI = 50^2 + 25^2 + 15^2 + 10^2 = 3,450.$$

TABLE 9.5   Concentration Ratio Calculations

Tiremakers		Printers	
Firm	**Sales** (millions of dollars)	**Firm**	**Sales** (millions of dollars)
Top, Inc.	200	Fran's	2.5
ABC, Inc.	250	Ned's	2.0
Big, Inc.	150	Tom's	1.8
XYZ, Inc.	100	Jill's	1.7
Largest 4 firms	700	Largest 4 firms	8.0
Other 10 firms	175	Other 1,000 firms	1,592.0
Industry	875	Industry	1,600.0

Four-firm concentration ratios:

Tiremakers: $\dfrac{700}{875} \times 100 = 80\%$ Printers: $\dfrac{8}{1,600} \times 100 = 0.5\%$

In perfect competition, the HHI is small. For example, if each of the largest 50 firms in an industry has a market share of 0.1 percent, then the HHI is $0.1^2 \times 50 = 0.5$. In a monopoly, the HHI is 10,000 — the firm has 100 percent of the market: $100^2 = 10,000$.

The HHI became a popular measure of the degree of competition during the 1980s, when the Justice Department used it to classify markets. A market in which the HHI is less than 1,000 is regarded as being competitive. A market in which the HHI lies between 1,000 and 1,800 is regarded as being moderately competitive. But a market in which the HHI exceeds 1,800 is regarded as being uncompetitive. The Justice Department scrutinizes any merger of firms in a market in which the HHI exceeds 1,000 and is likely to challenge a merger if the HHI exceeds 1,800.

Concentration Measures for the U.S. Economy

Figure 9.2 shows a selection of concentration ratios and HHIs for the United States calculated by the U.S. Department of Commerce.

Industries that produce chewing gum, household laundry equipment, light bulbs, breakfast cereal, and motor vehicles have a high degree of concentration and are oligopolies. The ice cream, milk, clothing, concrete block and brick, and commercial printing industries have low concentration measures and are highly competitive. The pet food and cookies and crackers industries are moderately concentrated. They are examples of monopolistic competition.

Concentration measures are a useful indicator of the degree of competition in a market. But they must be supplemented by other information to determine a market's structure. Table 9.6 summarizes the range of other information, along with the measures of concentration that determine which market structure describes a particular real-world market.

Limitations of Concentration Measures

The three main limitations of concentration measures alone as determinants of market structure are their failure to take proper account of

■ The geographical scope of the market

■ Barriers to entry and firm turnover

■ The correspondence between a market and an industry

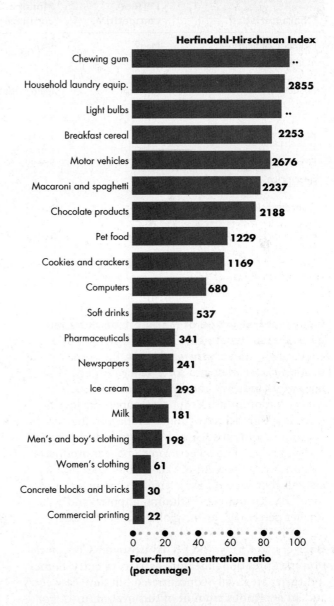

FIGURE 9.2   Concentration Measures in the United States

The industries that produce chewing gum, household laundry equipment, light bulbs, breakfast cereal, and motor vehicles are highly concentrated, while those that produce ice cream, milk, clothing, concrete blocks and bricks, and commercial printing are highly competitive. The industries that produce pet foods and cookies and crackers have an intermediate degree of concentration.

Source: Concentration Ratios in Manufacturing, (Washington, D.C.: U.S. Department of Commerce, 1996).

TABLE 9.6   Market Structure

Characteristics	Perfect competition	Monopolistic competition	Oligopoly	Monopoly
Number of firms in industry	Many	Many	Few	One
Product	Identical	Differentiated	Either identical or differentiated	No close substitutes
Barriers to entry	None	None	Moderate	High
Firm's control over price	None	Some	Considerable	Considerable or regulated
Concentration ratio	0	Low	High	100
HHI (approx. ranges)	Less than 100	101 to 999	More than 1,000	10,000
Examples	Wheat, corn	Food, clothing	Automobiles, cereals	Local water supply

Geographical Scope of Market   Concentration measures take a national view of the market. Many goods are sold in a *national* market, but some are sold in a *regional* market and some in a *global* one. The newspaper industry consists of local markets. The concentration measures for newspapers are low, but there is a high degree of concentration in the newspaper industry in most cities. The auto industry has a global market. The biggest three U.S. car producers account for 92 percent of cars sold by U.S. producers, but they account for a smaller percentage of the total U.S. car market (including imports) and a smaller percentage of the global market for cars.

Barriers to Entry and Firm Turnover   Concentration measures don't measure barriers to entry. Some industries are highly concentrated but have easy entry and an enormous amount of turnover of firms. For example, many small towns have few restaurants, but there are no restrictions on opening a restaurant and many firms attempt to do so.

Also, an industry might be competitive because of *potential entry* — because a few firms in a market face competition from many firms that can easily enter the market and will do so if economic profits are available.

Market and Industry Correspondence   To calculate concentration ratios, the Department of Commerce classifies each firm as being in a particular industry. But markets do not always correspond closely to industries for three reasons.

First, markets are often narrower than industries. For example, the pharmaceutical industry, which has a low concentration ratio, operates in many separate markets for individual products — for example, measles vaccine and AIDS-fighting drugs. These drugs do not compete with each other, so this industry, which looks competitive, includes firms that are monopolies (or near monopolies) in markets for individual drugs.

Second, most firms make several products. For example, Westinghouse makes electrical equipment and, among other things, gas-fired incinerators and plywood. So this one firm operates in at least three separate markets. But the Department of Commerce classifies Westinghouse as being in the electrical goods and equipment industry. The fact that Westinghouse competes with other producers of plywood does not show up in the concentration numbers for the plywood market.

Third, firms switch from one market to another depending on profit opportunities. For example,

Motorola, which today produces cellular telephones and other communications products, has diversified from being a TV and computer chip maker. Motorola produces no TVs today. Publishers of newspapers, magazines, and textbooks are today rapidly diversifying into Internet and multimedia products. These switches among industries show that there is much scope for entering and exiting an industry, and so measures of concentration have limited usefulness.

Despite their limitations, concentration measures do provide a basis for determining the degree of competition in an industry when they are combined with information about the geographical scope of the market, barriers to entry, and the extent to which large, multiproduct firms straddle a variety of markets.

Market Structures in the U.S. Economy

How competitive are the markets of the United States? Do most U.S. firms operate in competitive markets or in non-competitive markets?

Figure 9.3 provides part of the answer to these questions. It shows the market structure of the U.S. economy and the trends in market structure between 1939 and 1980. (Unfortunately, comparable data for the 1980s and 1990s are not available.)

In 1980, three quarters of the value of goods and services bought and sold in the United States was traded in markets that are essentially competitive — markets that have almost perfect competition or monopolistic competition. Monopoly and the dominance of a single firm accounted for about 5 percent of sales. Oligopoly, which is found mainly in manufacturing, accounted for about 18 percent of sales.

Over the period covered by the data in Fig. 9.3, the U.S. economy became increasingly competitive. You can see that the competitive markets have expanded most (the blue areas) and the oligopoly markets have shrunk most (the red areas).

But also during the past decades, the U.S. economy has become much more exposed to competition from the rest of the world. Figure 9.3 does not capture this international competition.

FIGURE 9.3   The Market Structure of the U.S. Economy

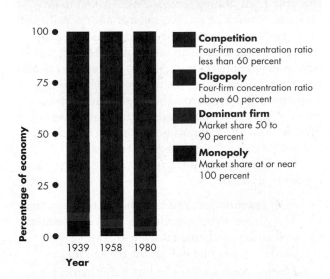

Three quarters of the U.S. economy is effectively competitive (perfect competition or monopolistic competition), one fifth is oligopoly, and the rest is monopoly. The economy became more competitive between 1939 and 1980. (Professor Shepherd, whose 1982 study remains the latest word on this topic, suspects that although some industries have become more concentrated, others have become less concentrated, so the net picture has probably not changed much since 1980.)

Source: William G. Shepherd, "Causes of Increased Competition in the U.S. Economy, 1939–1980," *Review of Economics and Statistics*, November 1982, pp. 613–626. © MIT Press Journals. Reprinted by permission.

REVIEW QUIZ

1 What are the four market types? Explain the distinguishing characteristics of each.
2 What are the two measures of concentration? Explain how each measure is calculated.
3 Under what conditions do the measures of concentration give a good indication of the degree of competition in a market?
4 Is our economy competitive? Is it becoming more competitive or less competitive?

You now know the variety of market types and the way we classify firms and industries into the different market types. Our final question in this chapter is: What determines the things that firms decide to buy from other firms rather than produce for themselves?

Markets and Firms

A FIRM IS AN INSTITUTION THAT HIRES FACTORS of production and organizes them to produce and sell goods and services. To organize production, firms coordinate the economic decisions and activities of many individuals. But firms are not the only coordinators of economic decisions. You learned in Chapter 3 that markets also coordinate decisions. They do so by adjusting prices and making the decisions of buyers and sellers consistent — making the quantity demanded equal to the quantity supplied for each good and service.

Market Coordination

Markets can coordinate production. For example, markets might coordinate the production of a rock concert. A promoter hires a stadium, some stage equipment, audio and video recording engineers and technicians, some rock groups, a superstar, a publicity agent, and a ticket agent — all market transactions — and sells tickets to thousands of rock fans, audio rights to a recording company, and video and broadcasting rights to a television network — another set of market transactions. Alternatively, if rock concerts were produced like cornflakes, the firm producing them would own all the capital used (stadiums, stage, sound and video equipment) and would employ all the labor needed (singers, engineers, and salespeople).

Outsourcing, buying parts or products from other firms, is another example of market coordination. Dell uses outsourcing for all the components of the computers it produces. The major automakers use outsourcing for windshields and windows, gearboxes, tires, and many other car parts.

What determines whether a firm or markets coordinate a particular set of activities? How do firms decide whether to buy from another firm or manufacture an item themselves? The answer is cost. Taking account of the opportunity cost of time as well as the costs of the other inputs, people use the method that costs least. In other words, they use the economically efficient method.

Firms coordinate economic activity when they can perform a task more efficiently than markets can. In such a situation, it is profitable to set up a firm. If markets can perform a task more efficiently than a firm can, people will use markets, and any attempt to set up a firm to replace such market coordination will be doomed to failure.

Why Firms?

Firms are often more efficient than markets as coordinators of economic activity because they can achieve

- Lower transactions costs
- Economies of scale
- Economies of scope
- Economies of team production

Transactions Costs The idea that firms exist because there are activities in which firms are more efficient than markets was first suggested by University of Chicago economist and Nobel Laureate Ronald Coase. Coase focused on the firm's ability to reduce or eliminate transactions costs. **Transactions costs** are the costs that arise from finding someone with whom to do business, of reaching an agreement about the price and other aspects of the exchange, and of ensuring that the terms of the agreement are fulfilled. Market transactions require buyers and sellers to get together and to negotiate the terms and conditions of their trading. Sometimes, lawyers have to be hired to draw up contracts. A broken contract leads to still more expenses. A firm can lower such transactions costs by reducing the number of individual transactions undertaken.

Consider, for example, two ways of getting your creaking car fixed.

Firm coordination: You take the car to the garage. The garage owner coordinates parts and tools as well as the mechanic's time, and your car gets fixed. You pay one bill for the entire job.

Market coordination: You hire a mechanic, who diagnoses the problems and makes a list of the parts and tools needed to fix them. You buy the parts from the local wrecker's yard and rent the tools from ABC Rentals. You hire the mechanic again to fix the problems. You return the tools and pay your bills — wages to the mechanic, rental to ABC, and the cost of the parts used to the wrecker.

What determines the method that you use? The answer is cost. Taking account of the opportunity cost of your own time as well as the costs of the other inputs that you would have to buy, you will use the method that costs least. In other words, you will use the economically efficient method.

The first method requires that you undertake only one transaction with one firm. It's true that the firm has to undertake several transactions — hiring the labor and buying the parts and tools required to do the job. But the firm doesn't have to undertake those transactions simply to fix your car. One set of such transactions enables the firm to fix hundreds of cars. Thus there is an enormous reduction in the number of individual transactions that take place if people get their cars fixed at the garage rather than going through an elaborate sequence of market transactions.

Economies of Scale When the cost of producing a unit of a good falls as its output rate increases, **economies of scale** exist. Automakers, for example, experience economies of scale because as the scale of production increases, the firm can use cost-saving equipment and highly specialized labor. An automaker that produces only a few cars a year must use hand-tool methods that are costly. Economies of scale arise from specialization and the division of labor that can be reaped more effectively by firm coordination rather than market coordination.

Economies of Scope A firm experiences **economies of scope** when it uses specialized (and often expensive) resources to produce a *range of goods and services*. For example, Microsoft hires specialist programmers, designers, and marketing experts and uses their skills across a range of software products. As a result, Microsoft coordinates the resources that produce software at a lower cost than an individual can who buys all these services in markets.

Economies of Team Production A production process in which the individuals in a group specialize in mutually supportive tasks is team production. Sport provides the best example of team activity. In baseball, some team members specialize in pitching and some in batting. In basketball, some team members specialize in defense and some in offense. The production of goods and services offers many examples of team activity. For example, production lines in automobile and TV manufacturing plants work most efficiently when individual activity is organized in teams, each specializing in a small task. You can also think of an entire firm as being a team. The team has buyers of raw material and other inputs, production workers, and salespeople. Each individual member of the team specializes, but the value of the output of the team and the profit that it earns depend on the coordinated activities of all the team's members. The

idea that firms arise as a consequence of the economies of team production was first suggested by Armen Alchian and Harold Demsetz of the University of California at Los Angeles.

Because firms can economize on transactions costs, reap economies of scale and economies of scope, and organize efficient team production, it is firms rather than markets that coordinate most of our economic activity. But there are limits to the economic efficiency of firms. If a firm becomes too big or too diversified in the things that it seeks to do, the cost of management and monitoring per unit of output begins to rise, and at some point, the market becomes more efficient at coordinating the use of resources. IBM is an example of a firm that became too big to be efficient. In an attempt to restore efficient operations, IBM split up its large organization into a number of "Baby Blues," each of which specializes in a segment of the computer market.

Sometimes firms enter into long-term relationships with each other that make it difficult to see where one firm ends and another begins. For example, GM has long-term relationships with suppliers of windows, tires, and other parts. Wal-Mart has long-term relationships with suppliers of the goods it sells. Such relationships make transactions costs lower than they would be if GM or Wal-Mart went shopping on the open market each time it wanted new supplies.

REVIEW QUIZ

1 What are the two ways in which economic activity can be coordinated?
2 What determines whether a firm or markets coordinate production?
3 What are the main reasons why firms can often coordinate production at a lower cost than markets can?

◆ *Reading Between the Lines* on pp. 208–209 explores the economic problem faced by Yahoo! Inc. We continue to study firms and their decisions in the next four chapters. In Chapter 10, we learn about the relationships between cost and output at different output levels. These cost-output relationships are common to all types of firms in all types of markets. We then turn to problems that are specific to firms in different types of markets.

Yahoo! Inc.'s Economic Problem

THE SUNNYVALE SUN, APRIL 25, 2001

Yahoo! Lays Off One-Eighth of Employees

Residents of the Silicon Valley know the economy is slowing down. Many have already been affected by the slowdown or know someone who has. ... [But]... it was a shock when Internet stalwart Yahoo! Inc. recently laid off one-eighth of its employees....

Last year Yahoo! decided to move its headquarters from Santa Clara to Sunnyvale. The construction began a little over a year ago and is already near completion. Though the company is currently operating out of the building, the move won't be completed until the end of the summer. ...

In regards to whether the slowing down or lowering the cost of construction could have enabled the retention of more employees, Diana Lee, director of public relations at Yahoo!, said, "Centralizing all of Yahoo!'s Silicon Valley locations to a facility in Sunnyvale will not only retain the speed, efficiency and effectiveness at which the organization operates, but we will also be reaping economic benefits as well, including lower costs, capital appreciation and less cost per square foot." ...

On March 7, [2001] ... Yahoo! Inc. ... said it expected its first quarter revenues to be in the range of $170 million to $180 million. These statistics didn't bode well for Yahoo! employees.

In January of 2001, ... Yahoo! ... expected revenues between $220 million and $240 million, which supposedly reflected an expectation of slower advertising expenditures, but was reliant on a continuation of the then current economic conditions. This estimate is a far cry from the expectation made only a few months later of approximately $180 million in March. It was expected that the company's success was not going to be as great as last year's, but there was still the expectation of significant revenue.

The Sunnyvale Sun.
© SVCN LLC.

Essence of the Story

■ Yahoo! Inc. laid off one eighth of its employees in April 2001.

■ In 2000, Yahoo! decided to move its headquarters from Santa Clara to Sunnyvale, a move that would be completed during 2001.

■ The move was expected to make Yahoo! more efficient, lower costs, and yield capital appreciation.

■ Not spending on a new headquarters would not have prevented the layoffs.

■ Yahoo! repeatedly lowered its forecast of revenue during early 2001.

Economic Analysis

■ Yahoo! Inc. is an Internet portal company that operates in 24 countries and normally gets 57 million visitors a month to its sites.

■ From its headquarters in Silicon Valley, Yahoo! Inc. hires labor, installs and operates servers, and produces Internet portal services.

■ Yahoo! Inc.'s goal is to maximize profit, and the news article illustrates three aspects of the economic problem that confronted the company during 2001: (1) a shrinking market for its product, (2) a change in its use of capital and labor, and (3) an attempt to lower the cost of its capital.

■ Yahoo! Inc.'s main competitors are AOL, MSN, and Lycos.

■ Internet portal companies generate revenue from advertisers, and when the economy slowed during 2001, advertising revenue began to shrink.

■ With a decrease in the demand for its services, Yahoo! Inc. decreased its work force — it employed less labor.

■ Yahoo! Inc. had made a decision *before* the economic slowdown to build a new headquarters.

■ The plan was to move to a lower-cost building and one that offered a better opportunity of capital appreciation.

■ Capital appreciation is the opposite of depreciation. If a firm can buy land that is likely to rise in value, it lowers the cost of its capital because the appreciation of the land value is set off against the depreciation of buildings and other equipment.

■ By lowering its labor costs and lowering the cost of its headquarters, Yahoo! Inc. attempted to decrease the impact on its economic profit of the loss of revenue that it experienced during 2001.

Yahoo! Inc.'s new headquarters

Yahoo! Inc.'s home page

SUMMARY

KEY POINTS

The Firm and Its Economic Problem (pp. 192–194)

- Firms hire and organize resources to produce and sell goods and services.
- Firms seek to maximize economic profit, which is total revenue minus opportunity cost.
- Technology, information, and markets limit a firm's profit.

Technological and Economic Efficiency (pp. 195–196)

- A method of production is technologically efficient when it is not possible to increase output without using more inputs.
- A method of production is economically efficient when the cost of producing a given output is as low as possible.

Information and Organization (pp. 197–200)

- Firms use a combination of command systems and incentive systems to organize production.
- Faced with incomplete information and uncertainty, firms induce managers and workers to perform in ways that are consistent with the firm's goals.
- Proprietorships, partnerships, and corporations use ownership, incentives, and long-term contracts to cope with the principal-agent problem.

Markets and the Competitive Environment (pp. 201–205)

- Perfect competition occurs when there are many buyers and sellers of an identical product and when new firms can easily enter a market.
- Monopolistic competition occurs when a large number of firms compete with each other by making slightly different products.
- Oligopoly occurs when a small number of producers compete with each other.

- Monopoly occurs when one firm produces a good or service for which there are no close substitutes and the firm is protected by a barrier that prevents the entry of competitors.

Markets and Firms (pp. 206–207)

- Firms coordinate economic activities when they can perform a task more efficiently — at lower cost — than markets can.
- Firms economize on transactions costs and achieve the benefits of economies of scale, economies of scope, and economies of team production.

KEY FIGURES AND TABLES

KEY TERMS

PROBLEMS

*1. One year ago, Jack and Jill set up a vinegar-bottling firm (called JJVB). Use the following information to calculate JJVB's explicit costs and implicit costs during its first year of operation:
   a. Jack and Jill put $50,000 of their own money into the firm.
   b. They bought equipment for $30,000.
   c. They hired one employee to help them for an annual wage of $20,000.
   d. Jack gave up his previous job, at which he earned $30,000, and spent all his time working for JJVB.
   e. Jill kept her old job, which paid $30 an hour, but gave up 10 hours of leisure each week (for 50 weeks) to work for JJVB.
   f. JJVB bought $10,000 of goods and services from other firms.
   g. The market value of the equipment at the end of the year was $28,000.

2. One year ago, Ms. Moffat and Mr. Spieder opened a cheese firm (called MSCF). Use the following information to calculate MSCF's explicit costs and implicit costs during its first year of operation:
   a. Moffat and Spieder put $70,000 of their own money into the firm.
   b. They bought equipment for $40,000.
   c. They hired one employee to help them for an annual wage of $18,000.
   d. Moffat gave up her previous job, at which she earned $22,000, and spent all her time working for MSCF.
   e. Spieder kept his old job, which paid $20 an hour, but gave up 20 hours of leisure each week (for 50 weeks) to work for MSCF.
   f. MSCF bought $5,000 of goods from other firms.
   g. The market value of the equipment at the end of the year was $37,000.

*3. Four methods for doing a tax return are with a personal computer, a pocket calculator, a pocket calculator with pencil and paper, and a pencil and paper. With a PC, the job takes an hour; with a pocket calculator, it takes 12 hours; with a pocket calculator and paper and pencil, it takes 12 hours; and with a pencil and paper, it takes 16 hours. The PC and its software cost $1,000, the pocket calculator costs $10, and the pencil and paper cost $1.

   a. Which, if any, of the methods is technologically efficient?
   b. Which method is economically efficient if the wage rate is
   (i) $5 an hour?
   (ii) $50 an hour?
   (iii) $500 an hour?

4. Shawn is a part-time student and he can do his engineering assignment by using a personal computer, a pocket calculator, a pocket calculator and a pencil and paper, or a pencil and paper. With a PC, Shawn completes the job in 1 hour; with a pocket calculator, it takes 15 hours; with a pocket calculator and paper and pencil, it takes 7 hours; and with a pencil and paper, it takes 30 hours. The PC and its software cost $1,000, the pocket calculator costs $20, and the pencil and paper cost $5.
   a. Which, if any, of the methods is technologically efficient?
   b. Which method is economically efficient if Shawn's wage rate is
   (i) $10 an hour?
   (ii) $20 an hour?
   (iii) $250 an hour?

*5. Alternative ways of laundering 100 shirts are:

Method	Labor (hours)	Capital (machines)
A	1	10
B	5	8
C	20	4
D	50	1

   a. Which methods are technologically efficient?
   b. Which method is economically efficient if the hourly wage rate and implicit rental rate of capital is
   (i)   Wage rate is $1, rental rate is $100?
   (ii) Wage rate is $5, rental rate is $50?
   (iii) Wage rate is $50, rental rate is $5?

6. Four ways of making 10 surfboards a day are:

Method	Labor (hours)	Capital (machines)
A	40	10
B	40	20
C	20	30
D	10	40

   a. Which methods are technologically efficient?
   b. Which method is economically efficient if the hourly wage rate and implicit rental rate

of capital are

(i) Wage rate is $1, rental rate $100?

(ii) Wage rate is $5, rental rate is $50?

(iii) Wage rate is $50, rental rate is $5?

*7. Sales of the firms in the tattoo industry are

Firm	Sales (dollars)
Bright Spots	450
Freckles	325
Love Galore	250
Native Birds	200
Other 15 firms	800

a. Calculate the four-firm concentration ratio.

b. What is the structure of the tattoo industry?

8. Sales of the firms in the dry cleaning industry are

Firm	Sales (thousands of dollars)
Squeaky Clean, Inc.	15
Village Cleaners, Inc.	25
Plaza Cleaners, Inc.	30
The Cleanery, Inc.	40
Other 20 firms	300

a. Calculate the four-firm concentration ratio.

b. What is the structure of the industry?

*9. Market shares of chocolate makers are

Firm	Market share (percent)
Mayfair, Inc.	15
Bond, Inc.	10
Magic, Inc.	20
All Natural, Inc.	15
Truffles, Inc.	25
Gold, Inc.	15

a. Calculate the Herfindahl-Hirschman Index.

b. What is the structure of the industry?

10. Market shares of OJ suppliers are

Firm	Market share (percent)
Natural Fresh, Inc.	75
Fresh Squeezed, Inc.	10
Juice-to-Go, Inc.	8
Juiced-Out, Inc.	7

a. Calculate the Herfindahl-Hirschman Index.

b. What is the structure of the industry?

CRITICAL THINKING

1. Study *Reading Between the Lines* about Yahoo! Inc.'s economic problem on pp. 208–209, and then answer the following questions.

   a. What are the three aspects of Yahoo! Inc.'s economic problem in the news article?

   b. What actions did Yahoo! take in response to its falling revenues in 2001?

   c. Why would not building the new headquarters not avoid the layoffs?

   d. If Yahoo! sees its revenues increasing during 2002 and 2003 to its 2000 level, do you expect the firm to increase its work force back to its 2000 level? Why or why not?

2. What is the principal-agent problem? Do you think Yahoo! has such a problem? Describe the problem and explain how Yahoo! might cope with it.

3. Do you think that Yahoo! buys any services from other firms? If so, what types of services do you predict that Yahoo! buys? Why do you think Yahoo! doesn't produce these services for itself?

WEB EXERCISES

1. Use the link on your Parkin Web site and read James D. Miller's views on providing airport security services.

   a. What does Mr. Miller argue concerning the best way to organize airport security?

   b. Explain Mr. Miller's views using the principal-agent analysis. Who is the principal and who is the agent?

   c. What exactly is the principal-agent problem in providing airport security services?

   d. Why might a private provider offer better security than a public provider?

   e. Do you think that a private provider would operate at a lower cost than a public provider? Why or why not?

OUTPUT AND COSTS

The ATM Is Everywhere!

Have you noticed how common the ATM is these days? More and more supermarkets, gas stations, and 7–11s have one. And have you noticed how much harder it is to find a drive-through bank? Every year, banks install more ATMs and close more conventional teller-operated banks. Why? ◆ Firms differ in lots of ways — from mom-and-pop convenience stores to multinational giants producing high-tech goods. But regardless of their size or what they produce, all firms must decide how much to produce and how to produce it. How do firms make these decisions? ◆ Most automakers in the United States could produce more cars than they can sell. Why do automakers have expensive equipment lying around that isn't fully used? Many electric utilities in the United States don't have enough production equipment on hand to meet demand on the coldest and hottest days and must buy power from other producers. Why don't these firms install more equipment so that they can supply the market themselves?

◆ We are going to answer these questions in this chapter. To do so, we are going to study the economic decisions of a small, imaginary firm: Cindy's Sweaters, Inc., a producer of knitted sweaters. The firm is owned and operated by Cindy. By studying the economic problems of Cindy's Sweaters and the way Cindy copes with them, we will be able to get a clear view of the problems that face all firms — small ones like Cindy's Sweaters and a mom-and-pop convenience store as well big firms such as banks, automakers, and electric utilities. We're going to begin by setting the scene and describing the time frames in which Cindy makes her business decisions.

After studying this chapter, you will be able to

- ■ Distinguish between the short run and the long run

- ■ Explain the relationship between a firm's output and labor employed in the short run

- ■ Explain the relationship between a firm's output and costs in the short run

- ■ Derive and explain a firm's short-run cost curves

- ■ Explain the relationship between a firm's output and costs in the long run

- ■ Derive and explain a firm's long-run average cost curve

213

Decision Time Frames

PEOPLE WHO OPERATE FIRMS MAKE MANY DECI-sions. And all of the decisions are aimed at one over-riding objective: maximum attainable profit. But the decisions are not all equally critical. Some of the decisions are big ones. Once made, they are costly (or impossible) to reverse. If such a decision turns out to be incorrect, it might lead to the failure of the firm. Some of the decisions are small ones. They are easily changed. If one of these decisions turns out to be incorrect, the firm can change its actions and survive.

The biggest decision that any firm makes is what industry to enter. For most entrepreneurs, their back-ground knowledge and interests drive this decision. But the decision also depends on profit prospects. No one sets up a firm without believing that it will be profitable — that total revenue will exceed opportu-nity cost (see Chapter 9, pp. 192–193).

The firm that we study has already chosen the industry in which to operate. It has also chosen its most effective method of organization. But it has not decided the quantity to produce, the quantities of resources to hire, or the price at which to sell its output.

Decisions about the quantity to produce and the price to charge depend on the type of market in which the firm operates. Perfect competition, monopolistic competition, oligopoly, and monopoly all confront the firm with their own special problems.

But decisions about how to produce a given out-put do not depend on the type of market in which the firm operates. These decisions are similar for *all* types of firms in *all* types of markets.

The actions that a firm can take to influence the relationship between output and cost depend on how soon the firm wants to act. A firm that plans to change its output rate tomorrow has fewer options than one that plans to change its output rate six months from now.

To study the relationship between a firm's output decision and its costs, we distinguish between two decision time frames:

- The short run
- The long run

The Short Run

The **short run** is a time frame in which the quantities of some resources are fixed. For most firms, the fixed resources are the firm's technology, buildings, and capital. The management organization is also fixed in the short run. We call the collection of fixed resources the firm's *plant*. So in the short run, a firm's plant is fixed.

For Cindy's Sweaters, the fixed plant is its factory building and its knitting machines. For an electric power utility, the fixed plant is its buildings, genera-tors, computers, and control systems. For an airport, the fixed plant is the runways, terminal buildings, and traffic control facilities.

To increase output in the short run, a firm must increase the quantity of variable inputs it uses. Labor is usually the variable input. So to produce more out-put, Cindy's Sweaters must hire more labor and oper-ate its knitting machines for more hours per day. Similarly, an electric power utility must hire more labor and operate its generators for more hours per day. And an airport must hire more labor and operate its runways, terminals, and traffic control facilities for more hours per day.

Short-run decisions are easily reversed. The firm can increase or decrease its output in the short run by increasing or decreasing the amount of labor it hires.

The Long Run

The **long run** is a time frame in which the quantities of *all* resources can be varied. That is, the long run is a period in which the firm can change its *plant*.

To increase output in the long run, a firm is able to choose whether to change its plant as well as whether to increase the quantity of labor it hires. Cindy's Sweaters can decide whether to install some additional knitting machines, use a new type of machine, reorganize its management, or hire more labor. An electric power utility can decide whether to install more generators. And an airport can decide whether to build more run-ways, terminals, and traffic control facilities.

Long-run decisions are *not* easily reversed. Once a plant decision is made, the firm usually must live with it for some time. To emphasize this fact, we call the past cost of buying a plant that has no resale value a **sunk cost**. A sunk cost is irrelevant to the firm's decisions. The only costs that influence its deci-sions are the short-run cost of changing its labor inputs and the long-run cost of changing its plant.

We're going to study costs in the short run and the long run. We begin with the short run and describe the technology constraint the firm faces.

Short-Run Technology Constraint

TO INCREASE OUTPUT IN THE SHORT RUN, A FIRM must increase the quantity of labor employed. We describe the relationship between output and the quantity of labor employed by using three related concepts:

1. Total product
2. Marginal product
3. Average product

These product concepts can be illustrated either by product schedules or by product curves. Let's look first at the product schedules.

TABLE 10.1 Total Product, Marginal Product, and Average Product

	Labor (workers per day)	Total product (sweaters per day)	Marginal product (sweaters per additional worker)	Average product (sweaters per worker)
A	0	0		
			4	
B	1	4		4.00
			6	
C	2	10		5.00
			3	
D	3	13		4.33
			2	
E	4	15		3.75
			1	
F	5	16		3.20

Total product is the total amount produced. Marginal product is the change in total product that results from a one-unit increase in labor. For example, when labor increases from 2 to 3 workers a day (row C to row D), total product increases from 10 to 13 sweaters. The marginal product of going from 2 to 3 workers is 3 sweaters. Average product is total product divided by the quantity of labor employed. For example, the average product of 3 workers is 4.33 sweaters per worker (13 sweaters a day divided by 3 workers).

Product Schedules

Table 10.1 shows some data that describe Cindy's Sweaters' total product, marginal product, and average product. The numbers tell us how Cindy's Sweaters' production increases as more workers are employed. They also tell us about the productivity of Cindy's Sweaters' labor force.

Focus first on the columns headed "Labor" and "Total product." **Total product** is the total output produced. You can see from the numbers in these columns that as Cindy employs more labor, total product increases. For example, when Cindy employs 1 worker, total product is 4 sweaters a day, and when Cindy employs 2 workers, total product is 10 sweaters a day. Each increase in employment brings an increase in total product.

The **marginal product** of labor is the increase in total product that results from a one-unit increase in the quantity of labor employed with all other inputs remaining the same. For example, in Table 10.1, when Cindy increases employment from 2 to 3 workers and keeps her capital the same, the marginal product of the third worker is 3 sweaters — total product goes from 10 to 13 sweaters.

Average product tells how productive workers are on the average. The **average product** of labor is equal to total product divided by the quantity of labor employed. For example, in Table 10.1, the average product of 3 workers is 4.33 sweaters per worker — 13 sweaters a day divided by 3 workers.

If you look closely at the numbers in Table 10.1, you can see some patterns. As employment increases, marginal product at first increases and then begins to decrease. For example, marginal product increases from 4 sweaters a day for the first worker to 6 sweaters a day for the second worker and then decreases to 3 sweaters a day for the third worker. Also average product at first increases and then decreases. You can see the relationships between employment and the three product concepts more clearly by looking at the product curves.

Product Curves

The product curves are graphs of the relationships between employment and the three product concepts you've just studied. They show how total product, marginal product, and average product change as employment changes. They also show the relationships among the three concepts. Let's look at the product curves.

Total Product Curve

Figure 10.1 shows Cindy's Sweaters' total product curve, *TP*. As employment increases, so does the number of sweaters knitted. Points *A* through *F* on the curve correspond to the same rows in Table 10.1.

The total product curve is similar to the *production possibilities frontier* (explained in Chapter 2). It separates the attainable output levels from those that are unattainable. All the points that lie above the curve are unattainable. Points that lie below the curve, in the orange area, are attainable. But they are inefficient — they use more labor than is necessary to produce a given output. Only the points *on* the total product curve are technologically efficient.

Notice especially the shape of the total product curve. As employment increases from zero to 1 worker per day, the curve becomes steeper. Then, as employment increases to 3, 4, and 5 workers a day, the curve becomes less steep. The steeper the slope of the total product curve, the greater is marginal product, as you are about to see.

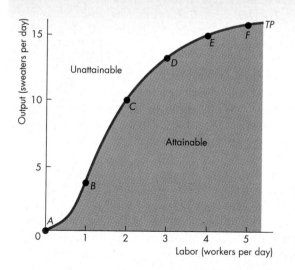

FIGURE 10.1   Total Product Curve

The total product curve, *TP*, is based on the data in Table 10.1. The total product curve shows how the quantity of sweaters changes as the quantity of labor employed changes. For example 2 workers can produce 10 sweaters a day (point *C*). Points *A* through *F* on the curve correspond to the rows of Table 10.1. The total product curve separates attainable outputs from unattainable outputs. Points below the *TP* curve are inefficient.

Marginal Product Curve

Figure 10.2 shows Cindy's Sweaters' marginal product of labor. Part (a) reproduces the total product curve from Fig. 10.1. Part (b) shows the marginal product curve, *MP*.

In part (a), the orange bars illustrate the marginal product of labor. The height of each bar measures marginal product. Marginal product is also measured by the slope of the total product curve. Recall that the slope of a curve is the change in the value of the variable measured on the *y*-axis — output — divided by the change in the variable measured on the *x*-axis — labor input — as we move along the curve. A one-unit increase in labor input, from 2 to 3 workers, increases output from 10 to 13 sweaters, so the slope from point *C* to point *D* is 3, the same as the marginal product that we've just calculated.

We've calculated the marginal product of labor for a series of unit increases in the quantity of labor. But labor is divisible into smaller units than one person. It is divisible into hours and even minutes. By varying the amount of labor in the smallest imaginable units, we can draw the marginal product curve shown in Fig. 10.2(b). The *height* of this curve measures the *slope* of the total product curve at a point. Part (a) shows that an increase in employment from 2 to 3 workers increases output from 10 to 13 sweaters (an increase of 3). The increase in output of 3 sweaters appears on the vertical axis of part (b) as the marginal product of going from 2 to 3 workers. We plot that marginal product at the midpoint between 2 and 3 workers. Notice that marginal product shown in Fig. 10.2(b) reaches a peak at 1.5 workers, and at that point, marginal product is 6. The peak occurs at 1.5 workers because the total product curve is steepest when employment increases from 1 worker to 2 workers.

The total product and marginal product curves are different for different firms and different types of goods. Ford Motor Company's product curves are different from those of Jim's Burger Stand, which in turn are different from those of Cindy's Sweaters. But the shapes of the product curves are similar because almost every production process has two features:

■ Increasing marginal returns initially
■ Diminishing marginal returns eventually

Increasing Marginal Returns Increasing marginal returns occur when the marginal product of an additional worker exceeds the marginal product of the

FIGURE 10.2   Marginal Product

(a) Total product

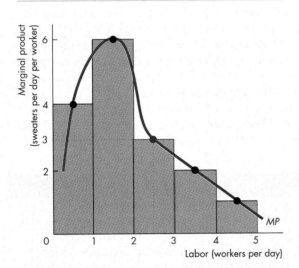

(b) Marginal product

Marginal product is illustrated by the orange bars. For example, when labor increases from 2 to 3, marginal product is the orange bar whose height is 3 sweaters. (Marginal product is shown midway between the labor inputs to emphasize that it is the result of *changing* inputs.) The steeper the slope of the total product curve (*TP*) in part (a), the larger is marginal product (*MP*) in part (b). Marginal product increases to a maximum (in this example when the second worker is employed) and then declines — diminishing marginal product.

previous worker. Increasing marginal returns arise from increased specialization and division of labor in the production process.

For example, if Cindy employs just one worker, that person must learn all the aspects of sweater production: running the knitting machines, fixing breakdowns, packaging and mailing sweaters, buying and checking the type and color of the wool. All these tasks must be performed by that one person.

If Cindy hires a second person, the two workers can specialize in different parts of the production process. As a result, two workers produce more than twice as much as one. The marginal product of the second worker is greater than the marginal product of the first worker. Marginal returns are increasing.

Diminishing Marginal Returns Most production processes experience increasing marginal returns initially. But all production processes eventually reach a point of *diminishing* marginal returns. **Diminishing marginal returns** occur when the marginal product of an additional worker is less than the marginal product of the previous worker.

Diminishing marginal returns arise from the fact that more and more workers are using the same capital and working in the same space. As more workers are added, there is less and less for the additional workers to do that is productive. For example, if Cindy hires a third worker, output increases but not by as much as it did when she hired the second worker. In this case, after two workers are hired, all the gains from specialization and the division of labor have been exhausted. By hiring a third worker, the factory produces more sweaters, but the equipment is being operated closer to its limits. There are even times when the third worker has nothing to do because the machines are running without the need for further attention. Hiring more and more workers continues to increase output but by successively smaller amounts. Marginal returns are diminishing. This phenomenon is such a pervasive one that it is called a "law" — the law of diminishing returns. The **law of diminishing returns** states that

As a firm uses more of a variable input, with a given quantity of fixed inputs, the marginal product of the variable input eventually diminishes.

You are going to return to the law of diminishing returns when we study a firm's costs. But before we do that, let's look at the average product of labor and the average product curve.

Average Product Curve

Figure 10.3 illustrates Cindy's Sweaters' average product of labor, *AP*. It also shows the relationship between average product and marginal product. Points *B* through *F* on the average product curve correspond to those same rows in Table 10.1. Average product increases from 1 to 2 workers (its maximum value at point *C*) but then decreases as yet more workers are employed. Notice also that average product is largest when average product and marginal product are equal. That is, the marginal product curve cuts the average product curve at the point of maximum average product. For the number of workers at which marginal product exceeds average product, average product is increasing. For the number of workers at which marginal product is less than average product, average product is decreasing.

The relationship between the average and marginal product curves is a general feature of the relationship between the average and marginal values of any variable. Let's look at a familiar example.

FIGURE 10.3 Average Product

The figure shows the average product of labor and the connection between the average product and marginal product. With 1 worker per day, marginal product exceeds average product, so average product is increasing. With 2 workers per day, marginal product equals average product, so average product is at its maximum. With more than 2 workers per day, marginal product is less than average product, so average product is decreasing.

Marginal Grade and Grade Point Average

To see the relationship between average product and marginal product, think about the similar relationship between Cindy's average grade and marginal grade over five semesters. (Suppose Cindy is a part-time student who takes just one course each semester.) In the first semester, Cindy takes calculus and her grade is a C(2). This grade is her marginal grade. It is also her average grade — her GPA. In the next semester, Cindy takes French and gets a B(3). French is Cindy's marginal course, and her marginal grade is 3. Her GPA rises to 2.5. Because her marginal grade exceeds her average grade, it pulls her average up. In the third semester, Cindy takes economics and gets an A(4) — her new marginal grade. Because her marginal grade exceeds her GPA, it again pulls her average up. Cindy's GPA is now 3, the average of 2, 3, and 4. The fourth semester, she takes history and gets a B(3). Because her marginal grade is equal to her average, her GPA does not change. In the fifth semester, Cindy takes English and gets a D(2). Because her marginal grade, a 2, is below her GPA of 3, her GPA falls.

Cindy's GPA increases when her marginal grade exceeds her GPA. Her GPA falls when her marginal grade is below her GPA. And her GPA is constant when her marginal grade equals her GPA. The relationship between Cindy's marginal and average grades is exactly the same as that between marginal product and average product.

REVIEW QUIZ

1 Explain how the marginal product of labor and the average product of labor change as the quantity of labor employed increases (a) initially and (b) eventually.
2 What is the law of diminishing returns? Why does marginal product eventually diminish?
3 Explain the relationship between marginal product and average product. How does average product change when marginal product exceeds average product? How does average product change when average product exceeds marginal product? Why?

Cindy's cares about its product curves because they influence its costs. Let's look at Cindy's costs.

Short-Run Cost

To produce more output in the short run, a firm must employ more labor, which means that it must increase its costs. We describe the relationship between output and cost by using three cost concepts:

- Total cost
- Marginal cost
- Average cost

Total Cost

A firm's **total cost** (TC) is the cost of the productive resources it uses. Total cost includes the cost of land, capital, and labor. It also includes the cost of entrepreneurship, which is *normal profit* (see Chapter 9, p. 193). We divide total cost into total fixed cost and total variable cost.

Total fixed cost (TFC) is the cost of the firm's fixed inputs. Because the quantity of a fixed input does not change as output changes, total fixed cost does not change as output changes.

Total variable cost (TVC) is the cost of the firm's variable inputs. Because to change its output, a firm must change the quantity of variable inputs, total variable cost changes as output changes.

Total cost is the sum of total fixed cost and total variable cost. That is,

$$TC = TFC + TVC.$$

The table in Fig. 10.4 shows Cindy's total costs. With one knitting machine that Cindy rents for $25 a day, TFC is $25. To produce sweaters, Cindy hires labor, which costs $25 a day. TVC is the number of workers multiplied by $25. For example, to produce 13 sweaters a day, Cindy hires 3 workers and TVC is $75. TC is the sum of TFC and TVC, so to produce 13 sweaters a day, Cindy's total cost, TC, is $100. Check the calculation in each row of the table.

Figure 10.4 shows Cindy's total cost curves, which graph total cost against total product. The green total fixed cost curve (TFC) is horizontal because total fixed cost does not change when output changes. It is a constant at $25. The purple total variable cost curve (TVC) and the blue total cost curve (TC) both slope upward because total variable cost increases as output increases. The arrows highlight total fixed cost as the vertical distance between the TVC and TC curves.

Let's now look at Cindy's marginal cost.

FIGURE 10.4   Total Cost Curves

$TC = TFC + TVC$

	Labor (workers per day)	Output (sweaters per day)	Total fixed cost (TFC)	Total variable cost (TVC)	Total cost (TC)
				(dollars per day)	
A	0	0	25	0	25
B	1	4	25	25	50
C	2	10	25	50	75
D	3	13	25	75	100
E	4	15	25	100	125
F	5	16	25	125	150

Cindy rents a knitting machine for $25 a day. This amount is Cindy's total fixed cost. Cindy hires workers at a wage rate of $25 a day, and this cost is Cindy's total variable cost. For example, if Cindy employs 3 workers, total variable cost is 3 × $25, which equals $75. Total cost is the sum of total fixed cost and total variable cost. For example, when Cindy employs 3 workers, total cost is $100 — total fixed cost of $25 plus total variable cost of $75. The graph shows Cindy's Sweaters' total cost curves. Total fixed cost (TFC) is constant — it graphs as a horizontal line — and total variable cost (TVC) increases as output increases. Total cost (TC) increases as output increases. The vertical distance between the total cost curve and the total variable cost curve is total fixed cost, as illustrated by the two arrows.

Marginal Cost

In Fig. 10.4, total variable cost and total cost increase at a decreasing rate at small levels of output and then begin to increase at an increasing rate as output increases. To understand these patterns in the changes in total cost, we need to use the concept of *marginal cost*.

A firm's **marginal cost** is the increase in total cost that results from a one-unit increase in output. We calculate marginal cost as the increase in total cost divided by the increase in output. The table in Fig. 10.5 shows this calculation. When, for example, output increases from 10 sweaters to 13 sweaters, total cost increases from $75 to $100. The change in output is 3 sweaters, and the change in total cost is $25. The marginal cost of one of those 3 sweaters is ($25 ÷ 3), which equals $8.33.

Figure 10.5 graphs the marginal cost data in the table as the red marginal cost curve, *MC*. This curve is U-shaped because when Cindy hires a second worker, marginal cost decreases, but when she hires a third, a fourth, and a fifth worker, marginal cost successively increases.

Marginal cost decreases at low outputs because of economies from greater specialization. It eventually increases because of *the law of diminishing returns.* The law of diminishing returns means that each additional worker produces a successively smaller addition to output. So to get an additional unit of output, ever more workers are required. Because more workers are required to produce one additional unit of output, the cost of the additional output — marginal cost — must eventually increase.

Marginal cost tells us how total cost changes as output changes. The final cost concept tells us what it costs, on the average, to produce a unit of output. Let's now look at Cindy's Sweaters' average costs.

Average Cost

There are three average costs:

1. Average fixed cost
2. Average variable cost
3. Average total cost

Average fixed cost (*AFC*) is total fixed cost per unit of output. **Average variable cost** (*AVC*) is total variable cost per unit of output. **Average total cost** (*ATC*) is total cost per unit of output. The average

cost concepts are calculated from the total cost concepts as follows:

$$TC = TFC + TVC.$$

Divide each total cost term by the quantity produced, *Q*, to get

$$\frac{TC}{Q} = \frac{TFC}{Q} + \frac{TVC}{Q},$$

or

$$ATC = AFC + AVC.$$

The table in Fig. 10.5 shows the calculation of average total cost. For example, in row *C* output is 10 sweaters. Average fixed cost is ($25 ÷ 10), which equals $2.50, average variable cost is ($50 ÷ 10), which equals $5.00, and average total cost is ($75 ÷ 10), which equals $7.50. Note that average total cost is equal to average fixed cost ($2.50) plus average variable cost ($5.00).

Figure 10.5 shows the average cost curves. The green average fixed cost curve (*AFC*) slopes downward. As output increases, the same constant total fixed cost is spread over a larger output. The blue average total cost curve (*ATC*) and the purple average variable cost curve (*AVC*) are U-shaped. The vertical distance between the average total cost and average variable cost curves is equal to average fixed cost — as indicated by the two arrows. That distance shrinks as output increases because average fixed cost declines with increasing output.

The marginal cost curve (*MC*) intersects the average variable cost curve and the average total cost curve at their minimum points. That is, when marginal cost is less than average cost, average cost is decreasing, and when marginal cost exceeds average cost, average cost is increasing. This relationship holds for both the *ATC* curve and the *AVC* curve and is another example of the relationship you saw in Fig. 10.3 for average product and marginal product and in Cindy's course grades.

Why the Average Total Cost Curve Is U-Shaped

Average total cost, *ATC*, is the sum of average fixed cost, *AFC*, and average variable cost, *AVC*. So the shape of the *ATC* curve combines the shapes of the *AFC* and *AVC* curves. The U shape of the average

FIGURE 10.5   Marginal Cost and Average Costs

$$ATC = AFC + AVC$$

Marginal cost is calculated as the change in total cost divided by the change in output. When output increases from 4 to 10, an increase of 6, total cost increases by $25 and marginal cost is $25 ÷ 6, which equals $4.17. Each average cost concept is calculated by dividing the related total cost by output. When 10 sweaters are produced, *AFC* is $2.50 ($25 ÷ 10), *AVC* is $5 ($50 ÷ 10), and *ATC* is $7.50 ($75 ÷ 10).

The graph shows that the marginal cost curve (*MC*) is U-shaped and intersects the average variable cost curve and the average total cost curve at their minimum points. Average fixed cost (*AFC*) decreases as output increases. The average total cost curve (*ATC*) and average variable cost curve (*AVC*) are U-shaped. The vertical distance between these two curves is equal to average fixed cost, as illustrated by the two arrows.

	Labor (workers per day)	Output (sweaters per day)	Total fixed cost (TFC)	Total variable cost (TVC)	Total cost (TC)	Marginal cost (MC) (dollars per additional sweater)	Average fixed cost (AFC)	Average variable cost (AVC)	Average total cost (ATC)
			(dollars per day)				(dollars per sweater)		
A	0	0	25	0	25		—	—	—
						.... 6.25			
B	1	4	25	25	50		6.25	6.25	12.50
						.... 4.17			
C	2	10	25	50	75		2.50	5.00	7.50
						.... 8.33			
D	3	13	25	75	100		1.92	5.77	7.69
						.... 12.50			
E	4	15	25	100	125		1.67	6.67	8.33
						.... 25.00			
F	5	16	25	125	150		1.56	7.81	9.38

total cost curve arises from the influence of two opposing forces:

1. Spreading total fixed cost over a larger output
2. Eventually diminishing returns

When output increases, the firm spreads its total fixed cost over a larger output and so its average fixed cost decreases — its average fixed cost curve slopes downward.

Diminishing returns means that as output increases, ever-larger amounts of labor are needed to produce an additional unit of output. So average variable cost eventually increases, and the *AVC* curve eventually slopes upward.

The shape of the average total cost curve combines these two effects. Initially, as output increases, both average fixed cost and average variable cost decrease, so average total cost decreases and the *ATC* curve slopes downward. But as output increases further and diminishing returns set in, average variable cost begins to increase. Eventually, average variable cost increases more quickly than average fixed cost decreases, so average total cost increases and the *ATC* curve slopes upward.

Cost Curves and Product Curves

The technology that a firm uses determines its costs. Figure 10.6 shows the links between the firm's technology constraint (its product curves) and its cost curves. The upper part of the figure shows the average product curve and the marginal product curve — like those in Fig. 10.3. The lower part of the figure shows the average variable cost curve and the marginal cost curve — like those in Fig. 10.5.

The figure highlights the links between technology and costs. As labor increases initially, marginal product and average product rise and marginal cost and average variable cost fall. Then, at the point of maximum marginal product, marginal cost is a minimum. As labor increases further, marginal product diminishes and marginal cost increases. But average product continues to rise, and average variable cost continues to fall. Then, at the point of maximum average product, average variable cost is a minimum. As labor increases further, average product diminishes and average variable cost increases.

Shifts in the Cost Curves

The position of a firm's short-run cost curves depend on two factors:

■ Technology
■ Prices of productive resources

Technology A technological change that increases productivity shifts the total product curve upward. It also shifts the marginal product curve and the average product curve upward. With a better technology, the same inputs can produce more output, so technological change lowers costs and shifts the cost curves downward.

For example, advances in robot production techniques have increased productivity in the automobile industry. As a result, the product curves of Chrysler, Ford, and GM have shifted upward, and their cost curves have shifted downward. But the relationships between their product curves and cost curves have not changed. The curves are still linked in the way shown in Fig. 10.6.

Often, a technological advance results in a firm using more capital, a fixed input, and less labor, a variable input. For example, today the telephone companies use computers to provide directory assistance

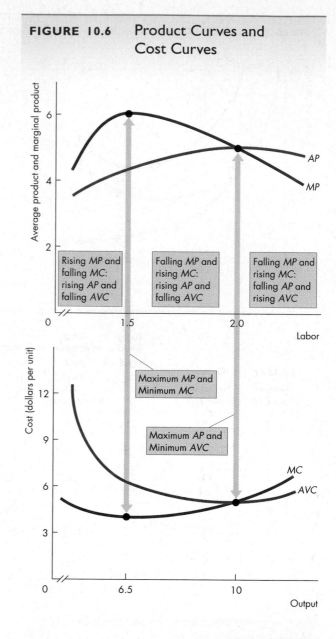

FIGURE 10.6   Product Curves and Cost Curves

A firm's marginal product curve is linked to its marginal cost curve. If marginal product rises, marginal cost falls. If marginal product is a maximum, marginal cost is a minimum. If marginal product diminishes, marginal cost rises. A firm's average product curve is linked to its average variable cost curve. If average product rises, average variable cost falls. If average product is a maximum, average variable cost is a minimum. If average product diminishes, average variable cost rises.

TABLE 10.2   A Compact Glossary of Costs

Term	Symbol	Definition	Equation
Fixed cost		Cost that is independent of the output level; cost of a fixed input	
Variable cost		Cost that varies with the output level; cost of a variable input	
Total fixed cost	TFC	Cost of the fixed inputs	
Total variable cost	TVC	Cost of the variable inputs	
Total cost	TC	Cost of all inputs	$TC = TFC + TVC$
Output (total product)	TP	Total quantity produced (output Q)	
Marginal cost	MC	Change in total cost resulting from a one-unit increase in total product	$MC = \Delta TC \div \Delta Q$
Average fixed cost	AFC	Total fixed cost per unit of output	$AFC = TFC \div Q$
Average variable cost	AVC	Total variable cost per unit of output	$AVC = TVC \div Q$
Average total cost	ATC	Total cost per unit of output	$ATC = AFC + AVC$

in place of the human operators they used in the 1980s. When such a technological change occurs, costs decrease, but fixed costs increase and variable costs decrease. This change in the mix of fixed cost and variable cost means that at low output levels, average total cost might increase, while at high output levels, average total cost decreases.

Prices of Resources An increase in the price of a productive resource increases costs and shifts the cost curves. But how the curves shift depends on which resource price changes. An increase in rent or some other component of *fixed* cost shifts the fixed cost curves (*TFC* and *AFC*) upward and shifts the total cost curve (*TC*) upward but leaves the variable cost curves (*AVC* and *TVC*) and the marginal cost curve (*MC*) unchanged. An increase in wages or some other component of *variable* cost shifts the variable cost curves (*TVC* and *AVC*) upward and shifts the marginal cost curve (*MC*) upward but leaves the fixed cost curves (*AFC* and *TFC*) unchanged. So, for example, if truck drivers' wages increase, the variable cost and marginal cost of transportation services

increase. If the interest expense paid by a trucking company increases, the fixed cost of transportation services increases.

You've now completed your study of short-run costs. All the concepts that you've met are summarized in a compact glossary in Table 10.2.

REVIEW QUIZ

1 What relationships do a firm's short-run cost curves show?
2 How does marginal cost change as output increases (a) initially and (b) eventually?
3 What does the law of diminishing returns imply for the shape of the marginal cost curve?
4 What is the shape of the average fixed cost curve and why?
5 What are the shapes of the average variable cost curve and the average total cost curve and why?

Long-Run Cost

IN THE SHORT RUN, A FIRM CAN VARY THE QUANtity of labor but the quantity of capital is fixed. So the firm has variable costs of labor and fixed costs of capital. In the long run, a firm can vary both the quantity of labor and the quantity of capital. So in the long run, all the firm's costs are variable. We are now going to study the firm's costs in the long run, when all costs are variable costs and when the quantities of labor and capital vary.

The behavior of long-run cost depends on the firm's *production function*, which is the relationship between the maximum output attainable and the quantities of both labor and capital.

The Production Function

Table 10.3 shows Cindy's Sweaters' production function. The table lists total product schedules for four different quantities of capital. We identify the quantity of capital by the plant size. The numbers for Plant 1 are for a factory with 1 knitting machine — the case we've just studied. The other three plants have 2, 3, and 4 machines. If Cindy's Sweaters doubles its capital to 2 knitting machines, the various amounts of labor can produce the outputs shown in the second column of the table. The other two columns show the outputs of yet larger quantities of capital. Each column of the table could be graphed as a total product curve for each plant.

Diminishing Returns Diminishing returns occur at all four quantities of capital as the quantity of labor increases. You can check that fact by calculating the marginal product of labor in plants with 2, 3, and 4 machines. At each plant size, as the quantity of labor increases, the marginal product of labor (eventually) diminishes.

Diminishing Marginal Product of Capital
Diminishing returns also occur as the quantity of capital increases. You can check that fact by calculating the marginal product of capital at a given quantity of labor. The *marginal product of capital* is the change in total product divided by the change in capital when the quantity of labor is constant — equivalently, the change in output resulting from a one-unit increase in the quantity of capital. For example, if

TABLE 10.3	The Production Function			
Labor (workers per day)	**Output** (sweaters per day)			
	Plant 1	**Plant 2**	**Plant 3**	**Plant 4**
1	4	10	13	15
2	10	15	18	20
3	13	18	22	24
4	15	20	24	26
5	16	21	25	27
Knitting machines (number)	1	2	3	4

The table shows the total product data for four quantities of capital. The greater the plant size, the larger is the total product for any given quantity of labor. But for a given plant size, the marginal product of labor diminishes. And for a given quantity of labor, the marginal product of capital diminishes.

Cindy's has 3 workers and increases its capital from 1 machine to 2 machines, output increases from 13 to 18 sweaters a day. The marginal product of capital is 5 sweaters per day. If Cindy increases the number of machines from 2 to 3, output increases from 18 to 22 sweaters per day. The marginal product of the third machine is 4 sweaters per day, down from 5 sweaters per day for the second machine.

Let's now see what the production function implies for long-run costs.

Short-Run Cost and Long-Run Cost

Continue to assume that Candy can hire workers for $25 per day and rent knitting machines for $25 per machine per day. Using these input prices and the data in Table 10.3, we can calculate and graph the average total cost curves for factories with 1, 2, 3, and 4 knitting machines. We've already studied the costs of a factory with 1 machine in Figs. 10.4 and 10.5. In Fig. 10.7, the average total cost curve for that case is ATC_1. Figure 10.7 also shows the average total cost curve for a factory with 2 machines, ATC_2, with 3 machines, ATC_3, and with 4 machines, ATC_4.

FIGURE 10.7   Short-Run Costs of Four Different Plants

The figure shows short-run average total cost curves for four different quantities of capital. Cindy's can produce 13 sweaters a day with 1 knitting machine on ATC_1 or with 3 knitting machines on ATC_3 for an average cost of $7.69 per sweater. Cindy's can produce the same number of sweaters by using 2 knitting machines on ATC_2 for $6.80 per sweater or by using 4 machines on ATC_4 for $9.50 per sweater. If Cindy's produces 13 sweaters a day, the least-cost method of production — the long-run method — is with 2 machines on ATC_2.

You can see, in Fig. 10.7, that plant size has a big effect on the firm's average total cost. Two things stand out:

1. Each short-run *ATC* curve is U-shaped.
2. For each short-run *ATC* curve, the larger the plant, the greater is the output at which average total cost is a minimum.

Each short-run average total cost curve is U-shaped because, as the quantity of labor increases, its marginal product at first increases and then diminishes. And these patterns in the marginal product of labor, which we examined in some detail for the plant with 1 knitting machine on pp. 216–217, occur at all plant sizes.

The minimum average total cost for a larger plant occurs at a greater output than it does for a smaller plant because the larger plant has a higher total fixed cost and therefore, for any given output level, a higher average fixed cost.

Which short-run average cost curve Cindy's operates on depends on its plant size. But in the long run, Cindy chooses the plant size. And which plant size she chooses depends on the output she plans to produce. The reason is that the average total cost of producing a given output depends on the plant size.

To see why, suppose that Cindy plans to produce 13 sweaters a day. With 1 machine, the average total cost curve is ATC_1 (in Fig. 10.7) and the average total cost of 13 sweaters a day is $7.69 per sweater. With 2 machines, on ATC_2, average total cost is $6.80 per sweater. With 3 machines, on ATC_3, average total cost is $7.69 per sweater, the same as with 1 machine. Finally, with 4 machines, on ATC_4, average total cost is $9.50 per sweater.

The economically efficient plant size for producing a given output is the one that has the lowest average total cost. For Cindy's, the economically efficient plant to use to produce 13 sweaters a day is the one with 2 machines.

In the long run, Cindy's chooses the plant size that minimizes average total cost. When a firm is producing a given output at the least possible cost, it is operating on its *long-run average cost curve*.

The **long-run average cost curve** is the relationship between the lowest attainable average total cost and output when both the plant size and labor are varied.

The long-run average cost curve is a planning curve. It tells the firm the plant size and the quantity of labor to use at each output to minimize cost. Once the plant size is chosen, the firm operates on the short-run cost curves that apply to that plant size.

The Long-Run Average Cost Curve

Figure 10.8 shows Cindy's Sweaters' long-run average cost curve, $LRAC$. This long-run average cost curve is derived from the short-run average total cost curves in Fig. 10.7. For output rates up to 10 sweaters a day, average total cost is the lowest on ATC_1. For output rates between 10 and 18 sweaters a day, average total cost is the lowest on ATC_2. For output rates between 18 and 24 sweaters a day, average total cost is the lowest on ATC_3. And for output rates in excess of 24 sweaters a day, average total cost is the lowest on ATC_4. The segment of each of the four average total cost curves for which that quantity of capital has the lowest average total cost is highlighted in dark blue in Fig. 10.8. The scallop-shaped curve made up of these four segments is the long-run average cost curve.

Economies and Diseconomies of Scale

Economies of scale are features of a firm's technology that lead to falling long-run average cost as output increases. When economies of scale are present, the $LRAC$ curve slopes downward. The $LRAC$ curve in Fig. 10.8 shows that Cindy's Sweaters experiences economies of scale for outputs up to 15 sweaters a day.

With given input prices, economies of scale occur if the percentage increase in output exceeds the percentage increase in all inputs. For example, if when a firm increases its labor and capital by 10 percent, output increases by more than 10 percent, its average total cost falls. Economies of scale are present.

The main source of economies of scale is greater specialization of both labor and capital. For example, if GM produces 100 cars a week, each worker must perform many different tasks and the capital must be general-purpose machines and tools. But if GM produces 10,000 cars a week, each worker specializes and becomes highly proficient in a small number of tasks. Also, the capital is specialized and productive.

Diseconomies of scale are features of a firm's technology that lead to rising long-run average cost as output increases. When diseconomies of scale are present, the $LRAC$ curve slopes upward. In Fig. 10.8, Cindy's Sweaters experiences diseconomies of scale at outputs greater than 15 sweaters a day.

With given input prices, diseconomies of scale occur if the percentage increase in output is less than the percentage increase in inputs. For example, if when a firm increases its labor and capital by 10 percent,

---

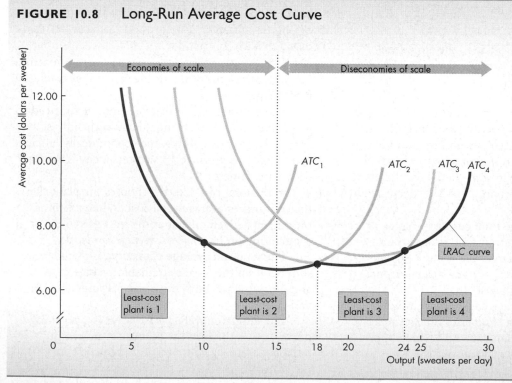

FIGURE 10.8   Long-Run Average Cost Curve

In the long run, Cindy's can vary both capital and labor inputs. The long-run average cost curve traces the lowest attainable average total cost of production. Cindy's produces on its long-run average cost curve if it uses 1 machine to produce up to 10 sweaters a day, 2 machines to produce between 10 and 18 sweaters a day, 3 machines to produce between 18 and 24 sweaters a day, and 4 machines to produce more than 24 sweaters a day. Within these ranges, Cindy's varies its output by varying its labor input.

output increases by less than 10 percent, its average total cost rises. Diseconomies of scale are present.

The main source of diseconomies of scale is the difficulty of managing a very large enterprise. The larger the firm, the greater is the challenge of organizing it and the greater is the cost of communicating both up and down the management hierarchy and among managers. Eventually, management complexity brings rising average cost.

Diseconomies of scale occur in all production processes but perhaps only at a very large output rate.

Constant returns to scale are features of a firm's technology that lead to constant long-run average cost as output increases. When constant returns to scale are present, the *LRAC* curve is horizontal.

Constant returns to scale occur if the percentage increase in output equals the percentage increase in inputs. For example, if when a firm increases its labor and capital by 10 percent, output increases by exactly 10 percent, then constant returns to scale are present.

For example, General Motors can double its production of Cavaliers by doubling its production facility for those cars. It can build an identical production line and hire an identical number of workers. With the two identical production lines, GM produces exactly twice as many cars.

Minimum Efficient Scale A firm experiences economies of scale up to some output level. Beyond that level, it moves into constant returns to scale or diseconomies of scale. A firm's **minimum efficient scale** is the smallest quantity of output at which long-run average cost reaches its lowest level.

The minimum efficient scale plays a role in determining market structure, as you will learn in the next three chapters. The minimum efficient scale also helps to answer some questions about real businesses.

Economies of Scale at Cindy's Sweaters The production technology that Cindy's Sweaters uses, shown in Table 10.3, illustrates economies of scale and diseconomies of scale. If Cindy's Sweaters increases its inputs from 1 machine and 1 worker to 2 of each, a 100 percent increase in all inputs, output increases by more than 100 percent from 4 sweaters to 15 sweaters a day. Cindy's Sweaters experiences economies of scale, and its long-run average cost decreases. But if Cindy's Sweaters increases its inputs to 3 machines and 3 workers, a 50 percent increase, output increases by less than 50 percent, from 15

sweaters to 22 sweaters a day. Now Cindy's Sweaters experiences diseconomies of scale, and its long-run average cost increases. Its minimum efficient scale is at 15 sweaters a day.

Producing Cars and Generating Electric Power
Why do automakers have expensive equipment lying around that isn't fully used? You can now answer this question. An automaker uses the plant that minimizes the average total cost of producing the output that it can sell. But it operates below the efficient minimum scale. Its short-run average total cost curve looks like ATC_1. If it could sell more cars, it would produce more cars and its average total cost would fall.

Why do many electric utilities have too little production equipment to meet demand on the coldest and hottest days and have to buy power from other producers? You can now see why this happens and why an electric utility doesn't build more generating capacity. A power producer uses the plant size that minimizes the average total cost of producing the output that it can sell on a normal day. But it produces above the minimum efficient scale and experiences diseconomies of scale. Its short-run average total cost curve looks like ATC_3. With a larger plant size, its average total costs of producing its normal output would be higher.

REVIEW QUIZ

1 What does a firm's production show and how is it related to a total product curve?
2 Does the law of diminishing returns apply to capital as well as labor? Explain why or why not.
3 What does a firm's long-run average cost curve show? How is it related to the firm's short-run average cost curves?
4 What are economies of scale and diseconomies of scale? How do they arise? What do they imply for the shape of the long-run average cost curve?
5 How is a firm's minimum efficient scale determined?

◆ *Reading Between the Lines* on pp. 228–229 applies what you've learned about a firm's short-run and long-run cost curves. It looks at the cost curves of a bank and compares the cost of using human tellers with the cost of operating ATMs.

ATMs Versus Human Tellers

THE PROVIDENCE JOURNAL-BULLETIN, March 17, 2001

This Window Closed — Fleet Touts Replacement ATMs as Always Open

At more and more FleetBoston bank branches, the drive-through teller's greeting "Have a nice day," has been replaced with the ATM keypad's boop-beep-boop.

The Boston-based bank is eliminating all drive-up windows at its Rhode Island branches as part of a company-wide initiative to replace the service with car-side ATMs. ...

"It makes more sense because of the automation and it's easier," said Matt Snowling, a banking analyst with Friedman, Billings, Ramsey. "It's open 24 hours and there's no staffing costs." ...

FleetBoston ... is spending about $100,000 per ATM site for equipment purchase and installation. That does not include maintenance and operations costs after the first year.

But industry experts say the machines save banks money in the long term because they cost less to operate than drive-throughs. A teller transaction costs from $1 to $2 to conduct, while an ATM transaction costs 15 cents to 50 cents, ...

Essence of the Story

■ FleetBoston bank branches are replacing teller-operated drive-through windows with ATMs.

■ Each ATM site costs about $100,000 for equipment and installation.

■ Machines save banks money in the long term because they cost less to operate than drive-through windows.

■ A teller transaction costs from $1 to $2, while an ATM transaction costs 15 cents to 50 cents.

Economic Analysis

■ Banks must choose between two main technologies in deciding how to conduct transactions: human tellers or ATMs.

■ ATM transactions use more capital and less labor than do teller transactions. The cost of the capital is a fixed cost, and the cost of the labor is a variable cost.

■ The average fixed cost of an ATM transaction exceeds the average fixed cost of a teller transaction.

■ The average variable cost of a teller transaction exceeds the average variable cost of an ATM transaction.

■ Average total cost (ATC) is the sum of average fixed cost and average variable cost. The figure shows the ATC curves for the two technologies.

■ ATC_T is the average total cost curve for a teller transaction, and ATC_A is the average total cost curve for an ATM transaction.

■ Small banks that make fewer than Q transactions a month minimize cost by using tellers.

■ Larger banks (like FleetBoston) that make more than Q transactions a month minimize cost by using ATMs.

■ The figure shows the long-run average cost curve, $LRAC$, for bank transactions.

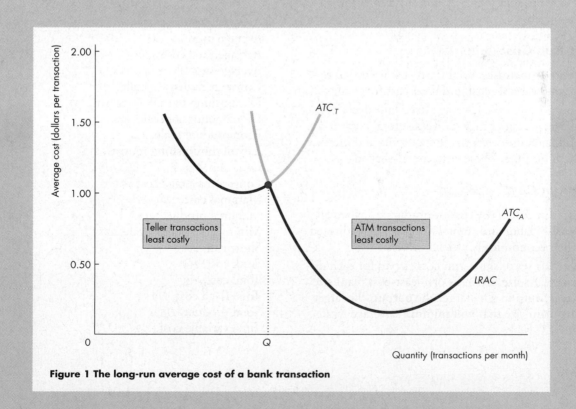

Figure 1 The long-run average cost of a bank transaction

SUMMARY

KEY POINTS

Decision Time Frames (p. 214)

- In the short run, the quantity of one resource is fixed and the quantities of the other resources can be varied.
- In the long run, the quantities of all resources can be varied.

Short-Run Technology Constraint (pp. 215–218)

- A total product curve shows the quantity a firm can produce with a given quantity of capital and different quantities of labor.
- Initially, the marginal product of labor increases as the quantity of labor increases, but eventually, marginal product diminishes — the law of diminishing returns.
- Average product increases initially and eventually diminishes.

Short-Run Cost (pp. 219–223)

- As output increases, total fixed cost is constant, and total variable cost and total cost increase.
- As output increases, average fixed cost decreases and average variable cost, average total cost, and marginal cost decrease at low outputs and increase at high outputs. These costs are U-shaped.

Long-Run Cost (pp. 224–227)

- Long-run cost is the cost of production when all inputs — labor and capital — have been adjusted to their economically efficient levels.
- There is a set of short-run cost curves for each different plant size. There is one least-cost plant size for each output. The larger the output, the larger is the plant size that will minimize average total cost.

- The long-run average cost curve traces out the lowest attainable average total cost at each output when both capital and labor inputs can be varied.
- With economies of scale, the long-run average cost curve slopes downward. With diseconomies of scale, the long-run average cost curve slopes upward.

KEY FIGURES AND TABLE

KEY TERMS

PROBLEMS

🖥 *1. Rubber Duckies' total product schedule is

Labor (workers per week)	Output (rubber boats per week)
1	1
2	3
3	6
4	10
5	15
6	21
7	26
8	30
9	33
10	35

a. Draw the total product curve.
b. Calculate the average product of labor and draw the average product curve.
c. Calculate the marginal product of labor and draw the marginal product curve.
d. What is the relationship between average product and marginal product when Rubber Duckies produces (i) fewer than 30 boats a week and (ii) more than 30 boats a week?

2. Sue's SurfBoards' total product schedule is

Labor (workers per week)	Output (surfboards per week)
0	0
1	40
2	100
3	140
4	170
5	190
6	200

a. Draw the total product curve.
b. Calculate the average product of labor and draw the average product curve.
c. Calculate the marginal product of labor and draw the marginal product curve.
d. What is the relationship between the average product and marginal product when Sue's SurfBoards produces (i) less than 100 surfboards a week and (ii) more than 100 surfboards a week?

🖥 *3. In problem 1, the price of labor is $400 a week and total fixed cost is $1,000 a week.
a. Calculate total cost, total variable cost, and total fixed cost for each output and draw the short-run total cost curves.
b. Calculate average total cost, average fixed cost, average variable cost, and marginal cost at each output and draw the short-run average and marginal cost curves.

4. In problem 2, the price of labor is $100 per week and total fixed costs are $200 per week.
a. Calculate total cost, total variable cost, and total fixed costs for each level of output and draw the short-run total cost curves.
b. Calculate average total cost, average fixed cost, average variable cost, and marginal cost at each level of output and draw the short-run average and marginal cost curves.

🖥 *5. In problem 3, suppose that Rubber Duckies' total fixed cost increases to $1,100 a week. Explain what changes occur in the short-run average and marginal cost curves.

6. In problem 4, suppose that the price of labor increases to $150 per week. Explain what changes occur in the short-run average and marginal cost curves.

*7. In problem 3, Rubber Duckies buys a second plant and the total product of each quantity of labor doubles. The total fixed cost of operating each plant is $1,000 a week. The wage rate is $400 a week.
a. Set out the average total cost schedule when Rubber Duckies operates two plants.
b. Draw the long-run average cost curve.
c. Over what output ranges is it efficient to operate one plant and two plants?

8. In problem 4, Sue's SurfBoards buys a second plant and the total product of each quantity of labor increases by 50 percent. The total fixed cost of operating each plant is $200 a week. The wage rate is $100 a week.
a. Set out the average total cost curve when Sue's SurfBoards operates two plants.
b. Draw the long-run average cost curve.
c. Over what output ranges is it efficient to operate one plant and two plants?

*9. The table shows the production function of Bonnie's Balloon Rides.

Labor (workers per day)	Output (rides per day)			
	Plant 1	Plant 2	Plant 3	Plant 4
1	4	10	13	15
2	10	15	18	21
3	13	18	22	24
4	15	20	24	26
5	16	21	25	27
Balloons (number)	1	2	3	4

Bonnie pays $500 a day for each balloon she rents and $250 a day for each balloon operator she hires.
a. Find and graph the average total cost curve for each plant size.
b. Draw Bonnie's long-run average cost curve.
c. What is Bonnie's minimum efficient scale?
d. Explain how Bonnie uses her long-run average cost curve to decide how many balloons to rent.

10. The table shows the production function of Cathy's Cakes.

Labor (workers per day)	Output (cakes per day)			
	Plant 1	Plant 2	Plant 3	Plant 4
1	20	40	55	65
2	40	60	75	85
3	65	75	90	100
4	65	85	100	110
Ovens (number)	1	2	3	4

Cathy pays $100 a day for each oven she rents and $50 a day for each kitchen worker she hires.
a. Find and graph the average total cost curve for each plant size.
b. Draw Cathy's long-run average cost curve.
c. Over what output range does Cathy experience economies of scale?
d. Explain how Cathy uses her long-run average cost curve to decide how many ovens to rent.

CRITICAL THINKING

1. Study *Reading Between the Lines* on pp. 228–229 and then answer the following questions:
   a. What is the main difference, from a cost point of view, between human tellers and ATM machines?
   b. Why do you think ATMs have become so popular?
   c. Would it ever make sense for a bank in the United States not to use ATMs?
   d. Do you think that ATMs are as common in China as they are in the United States? Explain why or why not.
   e. Suppose the government put a tax on banks for each ATM transaction but did not put on a similar tax for human teller transactions. How would the tax affect a bank's costs and cost curves? Would it change the number of ATMs and the number of tellers that banks hire? If so, how? Explain.

WEB EXERCISES

1. Use the link on your Parkin Web site to obtain information about the cost of producing pumpkins.
   a. List all the costs referred to on the Web page.
   b. For each item, say whether it is a fixed cost or a variable cost.
   c. Make some assumptions and sketch the average cost curves and the marginal cost curve for producing pumpkins.
2. Use the link on your Parkin Web site to obtain information about the cost of producing vegetables. For one of the vegetables (your choice):
   a. List all the costs referred to on the Web page.
   b. For each item, say whether it is a fixed cost or a variable cost.
   c. Sketch the average cost curves and the marginal cost curve for producing the vegetable you've chosen.

PERFECT COMPETITION

Sweet Competition

Maple syrup is sweet, but producing it and selling it is a tough competitive business. More than 2,000 farms that stretch from Wisconsin to Vermont and another nearly 10,000 farms in Canada produce 8 million gallons of syrup in a good year. New firms have entered, while others have been squeezed out of the business. How does competition affect prices and profits? What causes some firms to enter an industry and others to leave it? What are the effects on profits and prices of new firms entering and old firms leaving an industry? ◆ In October 2001, more than three million people were unemployed because they had been laid off by the firms that previously employed them. Why do firms lay off workers? Why do firms temporarily shut down? ◆ Over the past few years, there has been a dramatic fall in the prices of personal computers. For example, a slow computer cost almost $4,000 a few years ago, and a fast one costs only $1,000 today. What goes on in an industry when the price of its output falls sharply? What happens to the profits of the firms producing such goods? Ice cream, computers, and most other goods are produced by more than one firm, and these firms compete with each other for sales.

◆ To study competitive markets, we are going to build a model of a market in which competition is as fierce and extreme as possible — more extreme than in the examples we've just considered. We call this situation "perfect competition."

After studying this chapter, you will be able to

- Define perfect competition
- Explain how price and output are determined in perfect competition
- Explain why firms sometimes shut down temporarily and lay off workers
- Explain why firms enter and leave the industry
- Predict the effects of a change in demand and of a technological advance
- Explain why perfect competition is efficient

233

Competition

THE FIRMS THAT YOU STUDY IN THIS CHAPTER face the force of raw competition. We call this extreme form of competition perfect competition. **Perfect competition** is an industry in which

- Many firms sell identical products to many buyers.
- There are no restrictions on entry into the industry.
- Established firms have no advantage over new ones.
- Sellers and buyers are well informed about prices.

Farming, fishing, wood pulping and paper milling, the manufacture of paper cups and plastic shopping bags, grocery retailing, photo finishing, lawn service, plumbing, painting, dry cleaning, and the provision of laundry services are all examples of highly competitive industries.

How Perfect Competition Arises

Perfect competition arises if the minimum efficient scale of a single producer is small relative to the demand for the good or service. A firm's *minimum efficient scale* is the smallest quantity of output at which long-run average cost reaches its lowest level. (See Chapter 10, p. 227.) Where the minimum efficient scale of a firm is small relative to demand, there is room for many firms in an industry.

Second, perfect competition arises if each firm is perceived to produce a good or service that has no unique characteristics so that consumers don't care which firm they buy from.

Price Takers

Firms in perfect competition must make many decisions. But one thing they do *not* decide is the price at which to sell their output. Firms in perfect competition are said to be price takers. A **price taker** is a firm that cannot influence the price of a good or service.

The key reason why a perfectly competitive firm is a price taker is that it produces a tiny proportion of the total output of a particular good and buyers are well informed about the prices of other firms.

Imagine that you are a wheat farmer in Kansas. You have a thousand acres under cultivation — which sounds like a lot. But compared to the millions of acres in Colorado, Oklahoma, Texas, Nebraska, and the Dakotas, as well as the millions more in Canada,

Argentina, Australia, and Ukraine, your thousand acres is a drop in the ocean. Nothing makes your wheat any better than any other farmer's, and all the buyers of wheat know the price at which they can do business.

If everybody else sells their wheat for $4 a bushel and you want $4.10, why would people buy from you? They can go to the next farmer and the next and the one after that and buy all they need for $4 a bushel. This price is determined in the market for wheat, and you are a *price taker*.

A price taker faces a perfectly elastic demand curve. One farm's wheat is a *perfect substitute* for wheat from the farm next door or from any other farm. Note, though, that the *market* demand for wheat is not perfectly elastic. The market demand curve is downward-sloping, and its elasticity depends on the substitutability of wheat for other grains such as barley, rye, corn, and rice.

Economic Profit and Revenue

A firm's goal is to maximize *economic profit*, which is equal to total revenue minus total cost. Total cost is the *opportunity cost* of production, which includes *normal profit*, the return that the entrepreneur can expect to receive on the average in an alternative business. (See Chapter 9, p. 193.)

A firm's **total revenue** equals the price of its output multiplied by the number of units of output sold (price × quantity). **Marginal revenue** is the change in total revenue that results from a one-unit increase in the quantity sold. Marginal revenue is calculated by dividing the change in total revenue by the change in the quantity sold.

Figure 11.1 illustrates these revenue concepts. Cindy's Sweaters is one of a thousand such small firms. Demand and supply in the sweater market determine the price of a sweater. Cindy must take this price. Cindy's Sweaters cannot influence the price by its own actions, so the price remains constant when Cindy changes the quantity of sweaters produced.

The table shows three different quantities of sweaters produced. As the quantity varies, the price remains constant — in this example at $25 a sweater. Total revenue is equal to the price multiplied by the quantity sold. For example, if Cindy sells 8 sweaters, total revenue is 8 × $25, which equals $200.

Marginal revenue is the change in total revenue resulting from a one-unit change in quantity. For example, when the quantity sold increases from 8 to 9, total revenue increases from $200 to $225, so

FIGURE 11.1   Demand, Price, and Revenue in Perfect Competition

(a) Sweater market　　　　　**(b) Cindy's marginal revenue**　　　　　**(c) Cindy's total revenue**

Quantity sold (Q) (sweaters per day)	Price (P) (dollars per sweater)	Total revenue (TR = P × Q) (dollars)	Marginal revenue (MR = ΔTR/ΔQ) (dollars per additional sweater)
8	25	200	
			 25
9	25	225	
			 25
10	25	250	

Market demand and supply determine the market price. In part (a), the market price is $25 a sweater and 9,000 sweaters are bought and sold. Cindy's Sweaters faces a perfectly elastic demand at the market price of $25 a sweater. Part (b) shows Cindy's marginal revenue curve (MR). This curve is also the demand curve for Cindy's sweaters. The table calculates total revenue, average revenue, and marginal revenue. Part (c) shows Cindy's total revenue curve (TR). Point A corresponds to the second row of the table.

marginal revenue is $25 a sweater. (Notice that in the table, marginal revenue appears *between* the lines for the quantities sold to remind you that marginal revenue results from the *change* in the quantity sold.)

Because the price remains constant when the quantity sold changes, the change in total revenue resulting from a one-unit increase in the quantity sold equals price. Therefore in perfect competition, marginal revenue equals price.

Figure 11.1 shows Cindy's marginal revenue curve (MR). This curve tells us the change in total revenue that results from selling one more sweater. This same curve is also the firm's demand curve. The firm, being a price taker, can sell any quantity it chooses at this price. The firm faces a perfectly elastic demand for its output.

The total revenue curve (TR) in Fig. 11.1(c) shows the total revenue at each quantity sold. For example, if Cindy sells 9 sweaters, total revenue is

$225 (point A). Because each additional sweater sold brings in a constant amount — $25 — the total revenue curve is an upward-sloping straight line.

The Firm's Decisions in Perfect Competition

FIRMS IN A PERFECTLY COMPETITIVE INDUSTRY face a given market price and have the revenue curves that you've studied. These revenue curves summarize the market constraint faced by a perfectly competitive firm.

Firms also face a technology constraint, which is described by the product curves (total product, average product, and marginal product) that you studied in Chapter 10. The technology available to the firm determines its costs, which are described by the cost curves (total cost, average cost, and marginal cost) that you also studied in Chapter 10.

The task of the competitive firm is to make the maximum economic profit possible, given the constraints it faces. To achieve this objective, a firm must make four key decisions: two in the short run and two in the long run.

Short-Run Decisions   The short run is a time frame in which each firm has a given plant and the number of firms in the industry is fixed. But many things can change in the short run, and the firm must react to these changes. For example, the price for which the firm can sell its output might have a seasonal fluctuation, or it might fluctuate with general business conditions. The firm must react to such short-run price fluctuations and decide

1. Whether to produce or to shut down
2. If the decision is to produce, what quantity to produce

Long-Run Decisions   The long run is a time frame in which each firm can change the size of its plant and decide whether to leave the industry. Other firms can decide whether to enter the industry. So in the long run, both the plant size of each firm and the number of firms in the industry can change. Also in the long run, the constraints that firms face can change. For example, the demand for the good can permanently fall, or a technological advance can change the industry's costs. The firm must react to such long-run changes and decide

1. Whether to increase or decrease its plant size
2. Whether to stay in an industry or leave it

The Firm and the Industry in the Short Run and the Long Run   To study a competitive industry, we begin by looking at an individual firm's short-run decisions. We then see how the short-run decisions of all firms in a competitive industry combine to determine the industry price, output, and economic profit. We then turn to the long run and study the effects of long-run decisions on the industry price, output, and economic profit. All the decisions we study are driven by the pursuit of a single objective: maximization of economic profit.

Profit-Maximizing Output

A perfectly competitive firm maximizes economic profit by choosing its output level. One way of finding the profit-maximizing output is to study a firm's total revenue and total cost curves and find the output level at which total revenue exceeds total cost by the largest amount. Figure 11.2 shows how to do this for Cindy's Sweaters. The table lists Cindy's total revenue and total cost at different outputs, and part (a) of the figure shows Cindy's total revenue and total cost curves. These curves are graphs of the numbers shown in the first three columns of the table. The total revenue curve (TR) is the same as that in Fig. 11.1(c). The total cost curve (TC) is similar to the one that you met in Chapter 10: As output increases, so does total cost.

Economic profit equals total revenue minus total cost. The fourth column of the table in Fig. 11.2 shows Cindy's economic profit, and part (b) of the figure illustrates these numbers as Cindy's profit curve. This curve shows that Cindy makes an economic profit at outputs between 4 and 12 sweaters a day. At outputs less than 4 sweaters a day, Cindy incurs an economic loss. She also incurs an economic loss if output exceeds 12 sweaters a day. At outputs of 4 sweaters and 12 sweaters a day, total cost equals total revenue and Cindy's economic profit is zero. An output at which total cost equals total revenue is called a *break-even point*. The firm's economic profit is zero, but because normal profit is part of total cost, a firm makes normal profit at a break-even point. That is, at the break-even point, the entrepreneur makes an income equal to the best alternative return forgone.

Notice the relationship between the total revenue, total cost, and profit curves. Economic profit is measured by the vertical distance between the total

FIGURE 11.2   Total Revenue, Total Cost, and Economic Profit

(a) Revenue and cost

(b) Economic profit and loss

Quantity (Q) (sweaters per day)	Total revenue (TR) (dollars)	Total cost (TC) (dollars)	Economic profit (TR − TC) (dollars)
0	0	22	−22
1	25	45	−20
2	50	66	−16
3	75	85	−10
4	100	100	0
5	125	114	11
6	150	126	24
7	175	141	34
8	200	160	40
9	**225**	**183**	**42**
10	250	210	40
11	275	245	30
12	300	300	0
13	325	360	−35

The table lists Cindy's total revenue, total cost, and economic profit. Part (a) graphs the total revenue and total cost curves. Economic profit, in part (a), is the height of the blue area between the total cost and total revenue curves. Cindy's makes maximum economic profit, $42 a day ($225 − $183), when it produces 9 sweaters — the output at which the vertical distance between the total revenue and total cost curves is at its largest. At outputs of 4 sweaters a day and 12 sweaters a day, Cindy makes zero economic profit — these are break-even points. At outputs less than 4 and greater than 12 sweaters a day, Cindy incurs an economic loss. Part (b) of the figure shows Cindy's profit curve. The profit curve is at its highest when economic profit is at a maximum and cuts the horizontal axis at the break-even points.

revenue and total cost curves. When the total revenue curve in Fig. 11.2(a) is above the total cost curve, between 4 and 12 sweaters, the firm is making an economic profit and the profit curve in Fig. 11.2(b) is above the horizontal axis. At the break-even point, where the total cost and total revenue curves intersect, the profit curve intersects the horizontal axis. The profit curve is at its highest when the distance between *TR* and *TC* is greatest. In this example, profit maximization occurs at an output of 9 sweaters a day. At this output, Cindy's economic profit is $42 a day.

Marginal Analysis

Another way of finding the profit-maximizing output is to use *marginal analysis* and compare marginal revenue, *MR,* with marginal cost, *MC.* As output increases, marginal revenue remains constant but marginal cost changes. At low output levels, marginal cost decreases, but it eventually increases. So where the marginal cost curve intersects the marginal revenue curve, marginal cost is rising.

If marginal revenue exceeds marginal cost (if *MR > MC*), then the extra revenue from selling one more unit exceeds the extra cost incurred to produce it. The firm makes an economic profit on the marginal unit, so its economic profit increases if output *increases.*

If marginal revenue is less than marginal cost (if *MR < MC*), then the extra revenue from selling one more unit is less than the extra cost incurred to produce it. The firm incurs an economic loss on the marginal unit, so its economic profit decreases if output increases and its economic profit increases if output *decreases.*

If marginal revenue equals marginal cost (if *MR = MC*), economic profit is maximized. The rule *MR = MC* is an example of marginal analysis. Let's check that this rule works to find the profit-maximizing output by returning to Cindy's Sweaters.

Look at Fig. 11.3. The table records Cindy's marginal revenue and marginal cost. Marginal revenue is a constant $25 a sweater. Over the range of outputs shown in the table, marginal cost increases from $19 a sweater to $35 a sweater.

Focus on the highlighted rows of the table. If Cindy increases output from 8 sweaters to 9 sweaters, marginal revenue is $25 and marginal cost is $23. Because marginal revenue exceeds marginal cost, economic profit increases. The last column of the table shows that economic profit increases from $40 to $42, an increase of $2. This economic profit from the ninth sweater is shown as the blue area in the figure.

If Cindy increases output from 9 sweaters to 10 sweaters, marginal revenue is still $25 but marginal cost is $27. Because marginal revenue is less than marginal cost, economic profit decreases. The last column of the table shows that economic profit decreases from $42 to $40. This loss from the tenth sweater is shown as the red area in the figure.

Cindy maximizes economic profit by producing 9 sweaters a day, the quantity at which marginal revenue equals marginal cost.

FIGURE 11.3 Profit-Maximizing Output

Quantity (Q) (sweaters per day)	Total revenue (TR) (dollars)	Marginal revenue (MR) (dollars per additional sweater)	Total cost (TC) (dollars)	Marginal cost (MC) (dollars per additional sweater)	Economic profit (TR – TC) (dollars)
7	175		141		34
		25		19	
8	200		160		40
		25		23	
9	225		183		42
		25		27	
10	250		210		40
		25		35	
11	275		245		30

Another way of finding the profit-maximizing output is to determine the output at which marginal revenue equals marginal cost. The table shows that if output increases from 8 to 9 sweaters, marginal cost is $23, which is less than the marginal revenue of $25. If output increases from 9 to 10 sweaters, marginal cost is $27, which exceeds the marginal revenue of $25. The figure shows that marginal cost and marginal revenue are equal when Cindy produces 9 sweaters a day. If marginal revenue exceeds marginal cost, an increase in output increases economic profit. If marginal revenue is less than marginal cost, an increase in output decreases economic profit. If marginal revenue equals marginal cost, economic profit is maximized.

Profits and Losses in the Short Run

In short-run equilibrium, although the firm produces the profit-maximizing output, it does not necessarily end up making an economic profit. It might do so, but it might alternatively break even (earn a normal profit) or incur an economic loss. To determine which of these outcomes occurs, we compare the firm's total revenue and total cost or, equivalently, we compare price with average total cost. If price equals average total cost, a firm breaks even — makes normal profit. If price exceeds average total cost, a firm makes an economic profit. If price is less than average total cost, a firm incurs an economic loss. Figure 11.4 shows these three possible short-run profit outcomes.

Three Possible Profit Outcomes In Fig. 11.4(a), the price of a sweater is $20. Cindy produces 8 sweaters a day. Average total cost is $20 a sweater, so Cindy breaks even and makes normal profit (zero economic profit).

In Fig. 11.4(b), the price of a sweater is $25. Profit is maximized when output is 9 sweaters a day. Here, price exceeds average total cost (*ATC*), so

Cindy makes an economic profit. This economic profit is $42 a day. It is made up of $4.67 per sweater ($25.00 − $20.33) multiplied by the number of sweaters ($4.67 × 9 = $42). The blue rectangle shows this economic profit. The height of that rectangle is profit per sweater, $4.67, and the length is the quantity of sweaters produced, 9 a day, so the area of the rectangle is Cindy's economic profit of $42 a day.

In Fig. 11.4(c), the price of a sweater is $17. Here, price is less than average total cost and Cindy incurs an economic loss. Price and marginal revenue are $17 a sweater, and the profit-maximizing (in this case, loss-minimizing) output is 7 sweaters a day. Cindy's total revenue is $119 a day (7 × $17). Average total cost is $20.14 a sweater, so the economic loss is $3.14 per sweater ($20.14 − $17.00). This loss per sweater multiplied by the number of sweaters is $22 ($3.14 × 7 = $22). The red rectangle shows this economic loss. The height of that rectangle is economic loss per sweater, $3.14, and the length is the quantity of sweaters produced, 7 a day, so the area of the rectangle is Cindy's economic loss of $22 a day.

FIGURE 11.4   Three Possible Profit Outcomes in the Short Run

(a) Normal profit

(b) Economic profit

(c) Economic loss

In the short run, the firm might break even (making a normal profit), make an economic profit, or incur an economic loss. If the price equals minimum average total cost, the firm breaks even and makes a normal profit (part a). If the price exceeds the average total cost of producing the profit-maximizing output, the firm makes an economic profit (the blue rectangle in part b). If the price is below minimum average total cost, the firm incurs an economic loss (the red rectangle in part c).

The Firm's Short-Run Supply Curve

A perfectly competitive firm's short-run supply curve shows how the firm's profit-maximizing output varies as the market price varies, other things remaining the same. Figure 11.5 shows how to derive Cindy's supply curve. Part (a) shows Cindy's marginal cost and average variable cost curves, and part (b) shows its supply curve. There is a direct link between the marginal cost and average variable cost curves and the supply curve. Let's see what that link is.

Temporary Plant Shutdown In the short run, a firm cannot avoid incurring its fixed cost. But the firm can avoid variable costs by temporarily laying off its workers and shutting down. If a firm shuts down, it produces no output and it incurs a loss equal to total fixed cost. This loss is the largest that a firm need incur. A firm shuts down if price falls below the minimum of average variable cost. The **shutdown point** is the output and price at which the firm just covers its total variable cost — point *T* in Fig. 11.5(a). If the price is $17, the marginal revenue curve is MR_0 and the profit-maximizing output is 7 sweaters a day at point *T*. But both price and average variable cost equal $17, so Cindy's total revenue equals total variable cost. Cindy incurs an economic loss equal to total fixed cost. At a price below $17, no matter what quantity Cindy produces, average *variable* cost exceeds price and the firm's loss exceeds total fixed cost. At a price below $17, the firm shuts down temporarily.

The Short-Run Supply Curve If the price is above minimum average variable cost, Cindy maximizes profit by producing the output at which marginal cost equals price. We can determine the quantity produced at each price from the marginal cost curve. At a price of $25, the marginal revenue curve is MR_1 and Cindy maximizes profit by producing 9 sweaters. At a price of $31, the marginal revenue curve is MR_2 and Cindy produces 10 sweaters.

Cindy's short-run supply curve, shown in Fig. 11.5(b), has two separate parts: First, at prices that exceed minimum average variable cost, the supply curve is the same as the marginal cost curve above the shutdown point (*T*). Second, at prices below minimum average variable cost, Cindy shuts down and produces nothing. The supply curve runs along the vertical axis. At a price of $17, Cindy is indifferent between shutting down and producing 7 sweaters a day. Either way, Cindy incurs a loss of $22 a day.

FIGURE 11.5 A Firm's Supply Curve

(a) Marginal cost and average variable cost

(b) Cindy's short-run supply curve

Part (a) shows Cindy's profit-maximizing output at various market prices. At $25 a sweater, Cindy produces 9 sweaters. At $17 a sweater, Cindy produces 7 sweaters. At any price below $17 a sweater, Cindy produces nothing. Cindy's shutdown point is *T*. Part (b) shows Cindy's supply curve — the number of sweaters Cindy will produce at each price. It is made up of the marginal cost curve (part a) at all points above minimum average variable cost and the vertical axis at all prices below minimum average variable cost.

Short-Run Industry Supply Curve

The **short-run industry supply curve** shows the quantity supplied by the industry at each price when the plant size of each firm and the number of firms remain constant. The quantity supplied by the industry at a given price is the sum of the quantities supplied by all firms in the industry at that price.

Figure 11.6 shows the supply curve for the competitive sweater industry. In this example, the industry consists of 1,000 firms exactly like Cindy's Sweaters. At each price, the quantity supplied by the industry is 1,000 times the quantity supplied by a single firm.

The table in Fig. 11.6 shows the firm's and the industry's supply schedule and how the industry supply curve is constructed. At prices below $17, every firm in the industry shuts down; the quantity supplied by the industry is zero. At a price of $17, each firm is indifferent between shutting down and producing nothing or operating and producing 7 sweaters a day. Some firms will shut down, and others will supply 7 sweaters a day. The quantity supplied by each firm is *either* 0 or 7 sweaters, but the quantity supplied by the industry is *between* 0 (all firms shut down) and 7,000 (all firms produce 7 sweaters a day each).

To construct the industry supply curve, we sum the quantities supplied by the individual firms. Each of the 1,000 firms in the industry has a supply schedule like Cindy's. At prices below $17, the industry supply curve runs along the price axis. At a price of $17, the industry supply curve is horizontal — supply is perfectly elastic. As the price rises above $17, each firm increases its quantity supplied and the quantity supplied by the industry increases by 1,000 times that of each firm.

FIGURE 11.6   Industry Supply Curve

	Price (dollars per sweater)	Quantity supplied by Cindy's Sweaters (sweaters per day)	Quantity supplied by industry (sweaters per day)
A	17	0 or 7	0 to 7,000
B	20	8	8,000
C	25	9	9,000
D	31	10	10,000

The industry supply schedule is the sum of the supply schedules of all individual firms. An industry that consists of 1,000 identical firms has a supply schedule similar to that of the individual firm, but the quantity supplied by the industry is 1,000 times as large as that of the individual firm (see the table). The industry supply curve is S_I. Points A, B, C, and D correspond to the rows of the table. At the shutdown price of $17, each firm produces either 0 or 7 sweaters per day. The industry supply is perfectly elastic at the shutdown price.

So far, we have studied a single firm in isolation. We have seen that the firm's profit-maximizing actions depend on the market price, which the firm takes as given. But how is the market price determined? Let's find out.

Output, Price, and Profit in Perfect Competition

TO DETERMINE THE MARKET PRICE AND THE quantity bought and sold in a perfectly competitive market, we need to study how market demand and market supply interact. We begin this process by studying a perfectly competitive market in the short run when the number of firms is fixed and each firm has a given plant size.

Short-Run Equilibrium

Industry demand and industry supply determine the market price and industry output. Figure 11.7 shows a short-run equilibrium. The supply curve S is the same as S_I in Fig. 11.6. If demand is shown by the demand curve D_1, the equilibrium price is $20. Each firm takes this price as given and produces its profit-maximizing output, which is 8 sweaters a day. Because the industry has 1,000 firms, industry output is 8,000 sweaters a day.

A Change in Demand

Changes in demand bring changes to short-run industry equilibrium. Figure 11.7 shows these changes.

If demand increases, the demand curve shifts rightward to D_2. The price rises to $25. At this price, each firm maximizes profit by increasing output. The new output level is 9 sweaters a day for each firm and 9,000 sweaters a day for the industry.

If demand decreases, the demand curve shifts leftward to D_3. The price now falls to $17. At this price, each firm maximizes profit by decreasing its output. The new output level is 7 sweaters a day for each firm and 7,000 sweaters a day for the industry.

If the demand curve shifts farther leftward than D_3, the price remains constant at $17 because the industry supply curve is horizontal at that price. Some firms continue to produce 7 sweaters a day, and others temporarily shut down. Firms are indifferent between these two activities, and whichever they choose, they incur an economic loss equal to total fixed cost. The number of firms continuing to produce is just enough to satisfy the market demand at a price of $17.

FIGURE 11.7 Short-Run Equilibrium

(a) Equilibrium

(b) Change in equilibrium

In part (a), the industry supply curve is S. Demand is D_1, and the price is $20. At this price, each firm produces 8 sweaters a day and the industry produces 8,000 sweaters a day. In part (b), when demand increases to D_2, the price rises to $25 and

each firm increases its output to 9 sweaters a day. Industry output is 9,000 sweaters a day. When demand decreases to D_3, the price falls to $17 and each firm decreases its output to 7 sweaters a day. Industry output is 7,000 sweaters a day.

Long-Run Adjustments

In short-run equilibrium, a firm might make an economic profit, incur an economic loss, or break even (make normal profit). Although each of these three situations is a short-run equilibrium, only one of them is a long-run equilibrium. To see why, we need to examine the forces at work in a competitive industry in the long run.

In the long run, an industry adjusts in two ways:

■ Entry and exit
■ Changes in plant size

Let's look first at entry and exit.

Entry and Exit

In the long run, firms respond to economic profit and economic loss by either entering or exiting an industry. Firms enter an industry in which firms are making an economic profit, and firms exit an industry in which firms are incurring an economic loss. Temporary economic profit and temporary economic loss do not trigger entry and exit. But the prospect of persistent economic profit or loss does.

Entry and exit influence price, the quantity produced, and economic profit. The immediate effect of these decisions is to shift the industry supply curve. If more firms enter an industry, supply increases and the industry supply curve shifts rightward. If firms exit an industry, supply decreases and the industry supply curve shifts leftward.

Let's see what happens when new firms enter an industry.

The Effects of Entry Figure 11.8 shows the effects of entry. Suppose that all the firms in this industry have cost curves like those in Fig. 11.4. At any price greater than $20, firms make an economic profit. At any price less than $20, firms incur an economic loss. And at a price of $20, firms make zero economic profit. Also suppose that the demand curve for sweaters is D. If the industry supply curve is S_1, sweaters sell for $23, and 7,000 sweaters a day are produced. Firms in the industry make an economic profit. This economic profit is a signal for new firms to enter the industry. As these events unfold, supply increases and the industry supply curve shifts rightward to S_0. With the greater supply and unchanged demand, the market price falls from $23 to $20 a

sweater and the quantity produced by the industry increases from 7,000 to 8,000 sweaters a day.

Industry output increases, but Cindy's Sweaters, like each other firm in the industry, *decreases* output! Because the price falls, each firm moves down its supply curve and produces less. But because the number of firms in the industry increases, the industry as a whole produces more.

Because price falls, each firm's economic profit decreases. When the price falls to $20, economic profit disappears and each firm makes a normal profit.

You have just discovered a key proposition:

As new firms enter an industry, the price falls and the economic profit of each existing firm decreases.

An example of this process occurred during the 1980s in the personal computer industry. When IBM introduced its first PC, there was little competition

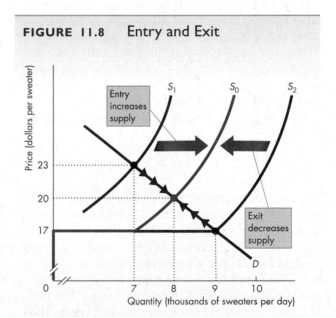

FIGURE 11.8   Entry and Exit

When new firms enter the sweater industry, the industry supply curve shifts rightward, from S_1 to S_0. The equilibrium price falls from $23 to $20, and the quantity produced increases from 7,000 to 8,000 sweaters.

When firms exit the sweater industry, the industry supply curve shifts leftward, from S_2 to S_0. The equilibrium price rises from $17 to $20, and the quantity produced decreases from 9,000 to 8,000 sweaters.

and the price of a PC gave IBM a big profit. But new firms such as Compaq, NEC, Dell, and a host of others entered the industry with machines that were technologically identical to IBM's. In fact, they were so similar that they came to be called "clones." The massive wave of entry into the personal computer industry shifted the supply curve rightward and lowered the price and the economic profit.

Let's now look at the effects of exit.

The Effects of Exit Figure 11.8 also shows the effects of exit. Suppose that firms' costs and the market demand are the same as before. But now suppose the supply curve is S_2. The market price is $17, and 9,000 sweaters a day are produced. Firms in the industry now incur an economic loss. This economic loss is a signal for some firms to exit the industry. As firms exit, the industry supply curve shifts leftward to S_0. With the decrease in supply, industry output decreases from 9,000 to 8,000 sweaters and the price rises from $17 to $20.

As the price rises, Cindy's Sweaters, like each other firm in the industry, moves up along its supply curve and increases output. That is, for each firm that remains in the industry, the profit-maximizing output increases. Because the price rises and each firm sells more, economic loss decreases. When the price rises to $20, each firm makes a normal profit.

You've now discovered a second key proposition:

As firms leave an industry, the price rises and the economic loss of each remaining firm decreases.

The same PC industry that saw a large amount of entry during the 1980s and 1990s is now beginning to see some exit. In 2001, IBM, the firm that first launched the PC, announced that it would no longer produce PCs. The intense competition from Compaq, NEC, Dell, and the host of others that entered the industry following IBM's lead has lowered the price and eliminated the economic profit on PCs. So IBM will now concentrate on servers and other parts of the computer market.

IBM exited the PC market because it was incurring economic losses on that line of business. Its exit decreased supply and made it possible for the remaining firms in the industry to earn normal profit.

You've now seen how economic profits induce entry, which in turn lowers profits. And you've seen how economic losses induce exit, which in turn eliminates losses. Let's now look at changes in plant size.

Changes in Plant Size

A firm changes its plant size if, by doing so, it can lower its costs and increase its economic profit. You can probably think of lots of examples of firms that have changed their plant size.

One example that has almost certainly happened near your campus in recent years is a change in the plant size of Kinko's or similar copy shops. Another is the number of FedEx vans that you see on the streets and highways. And another is the number of square feet of retail space devoted to selling computers and video games. These are examples of firms increasing their plant size to seek larger profits.

There are also many examples of firms that have decreased their plant size to avoid economic losses. One of these is Schwinn, the Chicago-based maker of bicycles. As competition from Asian bicycle makers became tougher, Schwinn cut back. Many firms have scaled back their operations — a process called *downsizing* — in recent years.

Figure 11.9 shows a situation in which Cindy's Sweaters can increase its profit by increasing its plant size. With its current plant, Cindy's marginal cost curve is MC_0, and its short-run average total cost curve is $SRAC_0$. The market price is $25 a sweater, so Cindy's marginal revenue curve is MR_0, and Cindy maximizes profit by producing 6 sweaters a day.

Cindy's Sweaters' long-run average cost curve is *LRAC*. By increasing its plant size — installing more knitting machines — Cindy's Sweaters can move along its long-run average cost curve. As Cindy's Sweaters increases its plant size, its short-run marginal cost curve shifts rightward.

Recall that a firm's short-run supply curve is linked to its marginal cost curve. As Cindy's marginal cost curve shifts rightward, so does its supply curve. If Cindy's Sweaters and the other firms in the industry increase their plants, the short-run industry supply curve shifts rightward and the market price falls. The fall in the market price limits the extent to which Cindy's can profit from increasing its plant size.

Figure 11.9 also shows Cindy's Sweaters in a long-run competitive equilibrium. This situation arises when the market price has fallen to $20 a sweater. Marginal revenue is MR_1, and Cindy maximizes profit by producing 8 sweaters a day. In this situation, Cindy cannot increase her profit by changing the plant size. Cindy's is producing at minimum long-run average cost (point *M* on *LRAC*).

Because Cindy's Sweaters is producing at minimum long-run average cost, it has no incentive to increases industry supply, shifts the industry supply curve rightward, lowers the price, and decreases economic profit.

Firms continue to enter the industry and profit decreases as long as firms in the industry are earning positive economic profits. When economic profit has been eliminated, firms stop entering the industry. And when firms are operating with the least-cost plant size, they stop expanding.

If the firms in a competitive industry are incurring an economic loss, some firms exit the industry. If firms can lower their costs by decreasing their plant size, they downsize. Each of these actions decreases industry supply, shifts the industry supply curve leftward, raises the price, and decreases economic loss.

Firms continue to exit and economic loss continues to decrease as long as firms in the industry are incurring economic losses. When economic loss has been eliminated, firms stop exiting the industry. And when firms are operating with the least-cost plant size, they stop downsizing.

So in long-run equilibrium in a competitive industry, firms neither enter nor exit the industry and old firms neither expand nor downsize. Each firm earns normal profit.

FIGURE 11.9 Plant Size and Long-Run Equilibrium

Initially, Cindy's plant has marginal cost curve MC_0 and short-run average total cost curve $SRAC_0$. The market price is $25 a sweater, and Cindy's marginal revenue is MR_0. The short-run profit-maximizing quantity is 6 sweaters a day. Cindy can increase profit by increasing the plant size. If all firms in the sweater industry increase their plant sizes, the short-run industry supply increases and the market price falls. In long-run equilibrium, a firm operates with the plant size that minimizes its average cost. Here, Cindy's Sweaters operates the plant with short-run marginal cost MC_1 and short-run average cost $SRAC_1$. Cindy's is also on its long-run average cost curve $LRAC$ and produces at point M. Its output is 8 sweaters a day, and its average total cost equals the price of a sweater: $20.

change its plant size. Either a bigger plant or a smaller plant has a higher long-run average cost. If Fig. 11.9 describes the situation of all firms in the sweater industry, the industry is in long-run equilibrium. No firm has an incentive to change its plant size. Also, because each firm is making zero economic profit (normal profit), no firm has an incentive to enter the industry or to leave it.

Long-Run Equilibrium

Long-run equilibrium occurs in a competitive industry when economic profit is zero (when firms earn normal profit). If the firms in a competitive industry are making an economic profit, new firms enter the industry. If firms can lower their costs by increasing their plant size, they expand. Each of these actions

REVIEW QUIZ

1 When a firm in perfect competition produces the quantity that maximizes profit, what is the relationship between the firm's marginal cost, marginal revenue, and price?
2 If the firms in a competitive industry earn an economic profit, what happens to supply, price, output, and economic profit in the long run?
3 If the firms in a competitive industry incur an economic loss, what happens to supply, price, output, and economic profit in the long run?

You've seen how a competitive industry adjusts toward its long-run equilibrium. But a competitive industry is rarely in a state of long-run equilibrium. A competitive industry is constantly and restlessly evolving toward such an equilibrium. But the constraints that firms in the industry face are constantly changing. The two most persistent sources of change are in tastes and technology. Let's see how a competitive industry reacts to such changes.

Changing Tastes and Advancing Technology

INCREASED AWARENESS OF THE HEALTH HAZARDS of smoking has caused a decrease in the demand for tobacco and cigarettes. The development of inexpensive car and air transportation has caused a huge decrease in the demand for long-distance trains and buses. Solid-state electronics have caused a large decrease in the demand for TV and radio repair. The development of good-quality inexpensive clothing has decreased the demand for sewing machines. What happens in a competitive industry when there is a permanent decrease in the demand for its products?

The development of the microwave oven has produced an enormous increase in demand for paper, glass, and plastic cooking utensils and for plastic wrap. The widespread use of the personal computer has brought a huge increase in the demand for CD-Rs. What happens in a competitive industry when the demand for its output increases?

Advances in technology are constantly lowering the costs of production. New biotechnologies have dramatically lowered the costs of producing many food and pharmaceutical products. New electronic technologies have lowered the cost of producing just about every good and service. What happens in a competitive industry when technological change lowers its production costs?

Let's use the theory of perfect competition to answer these questions.

A Permanent Change in Demand

Figure 11.10(a) shows a competitive industry that initially is in long-run equilibrium. The demand curve is D_0, the supply curve is S_0, the market price is P_0, and industry output is Q_0. Figure 11.10(b) shows a single firm in this initial long-run equilibrium. The firm produces q_0 and makes a normal profit and zero economic profit.

Now suppose that demand decreases and the demand curve shifts leftward to D_1, as shown in Fig. 11.10(a). The price falls to P_1, and the quantity supplied by the industry decreases from Q_0 to Q_1 as the industry slides down its short-run supply curve S_0. Figure 11.10(b) shows the situation facing a firm. Price is now below the firm's minimum average total

cost, so the firm incurs an economic loss. But to keep its loss to a minimum, the firm adjusts its output to keep marginal cost equal to price. At a price of P_1, each firm produces an output of q_1.

The industry is now in short-run equilibrium but not long-run equilibrium. It is in short-run equilibrium because each firm is maximizing profit. But it is not in long-run equilibrium because each firm is incurring an economic loss — its average total cost exceeds the price.

The economic loss is a signal for some firms to leave the industry. As they do so, short-run industry supply decreases and the supply curve gradually shifts leftward. As industry supply decreases, the price rises. At each higher price, a firm's profit-maximizing output is greater, so the firms remaining in the industry increase their output as the price rises. Each firm slides up its marginal cost or supply curve in Fig. 11.10(b). That is, as firms exit the industry, industry output decreases but the output of the firms that remain in the industry increases. Eventually, enough firms leave the industry for the industry supply curve to have shifted to S_1 in Fig. 11.10(a). At this time, the price has returned to its original level, P_0. At this price, the firms remaining in the industry produce q_0, the same quantity that they produced before the decrease in demand. Because firms are now making normal profit (zero economic profit), no firm wants to enter or exit the industry. The industry supply curve remains at S_1, and industry output is Q_2. The industry is again in long-run equilibrium.

The difference between the initial long-run equilibrium and the final long-run equilibrium is the number of firms in the industry. A permanent decrease in demand has decreased the number of firms. Each remaining firm produces the same output in the new long-run equilibrium as it did initially and earns a normal profit. In the process of moving from the initial equilibrium to the new one, firms incur economic losses.

We've just worked out how a competitive industry responds to a permanent *decrease* in demand. A permanent increase in demand triggers a similar response, except in the opposite direction. The increase in demand brings a higher price, economic profit, and entry. Entry increases industry supply and eventually lowers the price to its original level and economic profit to normal profit.

The demand for airline travel in the world economy increased permanently during the 1990s and

FIGURE 11.10   A Decrease in Demand

(a) Industry

(b) Firm

An industry starts out in long-run competitive equilibrium. Part (a) shows the industry demand curve D_0, the industry supply curve S_0, the equilibrium quantity Q_0, and the market price P_0. Each firm sells its output at price P_0, so its marginal revenue curve is MR_0 in part (b). Each firm produces q_0 and makes a normal profit.

Demand decreases permanently from D_0 to D_1 (part a). The equilibrium price falls to P_1, each firm decreases its output to q_1 (part b), and industry output decreases to Q_1 (part a).

In this new situation, firms incur economic losses and some firms leave the industry. As they do so, the industry supply curve gradually shifts leftward, from S_0 to S_1. This shift gradually raises the market price from P_1 back to P_0. While the price is below P_0, firms incur economic losses and some firms leave the industry. Once the price has returned to P_0, each firm makes a normal profit. Firms have no further incentive to leave the industry. Each firm produces q_0, and industry output is Q_2.

the deregulation of the airlines freed up firms to seek profit opportunities in this industry. The result was a massive rate of entry of new airlines. The process of competition and change in the airline industry is similar to what we have just studied (but with an increase in demand rather than a decrease in demand).

We've now studied the effects of a permanent change in demand for a good. To study these effects, we began and ended in a long-run equilibrium and examined the process that takes a market from one equilibrium to another. It is this process, not the equilibrium points, that describes the real world.

One feature of the predictions that we have just generated seems odd: In the long run, regardless of whether demand increases or decreases, the price returns to its original level. Is this outcome inevitable? In fact, it is not. It is possible for the long-run equilibrium price to remain the same, rise, or fall.

External Economies and Diseconomies

The change in the long-run equilibrium price depends on external economies and external diseconomies. **External economies** are factors beyond the control of an individual firm that lower the firm's costs as the *industry* output increases. **External diseconomies** are factors outside the control of a firm that raise the firm's costs as industry output increases. With no external economies or external diseconomies, a firm's costs remain constant as the industry output changes.

Figure 11.11 illustrates these three cases and introduces a new supply concept: the long-run industry supply curve.

A **long-run industry supply curve** shows how the quantity supplied by an industry varies as the market price varies after all the possible adjustments have been made, including changes in plant size and the number of firms in the industry.

Figure 11.11(a) shows the case we have just studied — no external economies or diseconomies. The long-run industry supply curve (LS_A) is perfectly elastic. In this case, a permanent increase in demand from D_0 to D_1 has no effect on the price in the long run. The increase in demand brings a temporary increase in price to P_S and a short-run quantity increase from Q_0 to Q_S. Entry increases short-run supply from S_0 to S_1, which lowers the price to its original level, P_0, and increases the quantity to Q_1.

Figure 11.11(b) shows the case of external diseconomies. The long-run supply industry curve (LS_B) slopes upward. A permanent increase in demand from D_0 to D_1 increases the price in both the short run and the long run. As in the previous case, the increase in demand brings a temporary increase in price to P_S and a short-run quantity increase from Q_0 to Q_S. Entry increases short-run supply from S_0 to S_2, which lowers the price to P_2 and increases the quantity to Q_2.

One source of external diseconomies is congestion. The airline industry provides a good example. With bigger airline industry output, there is more congestion of airports and airspace, which results in longer delays and extra waiting time for passengers and airplanes. These external diseconomies mean that as the output of air transportation services increases (in the absence of technological advances), average cost increases. As a result, the long-run supply curve is upward sloping. So a permanent increase in demand brings an increase in quantity and a rise in the price. (Industries with external diseconomies might nonetheless have a falling price because technological advances shift the long-run supply curve downward.)

Figure 11.11(c) shows the case of external economies. In this case, the long-run industry supply curve (LS_C) slopes downward. A permanent increase in demand from D_0 to D_1 increases the price in the short run and lowers it in the long run. Again, the increase in demand brings a temporary increase in price to P_S, and a short-run quantity increase from Q_0 to Q_S. Entry increases short-run supply from S_0 to S_3, which lowers the price to P_3 and increases the quantity to Q_3.

An example of external economies is the growth of specialist support services for an industry as it

---

FIGURE 11.11 Long-Run Changes in Price and Quantity

(a) Constant-cost industry

(b) Increasing-cost industry

(c) Decreasing-cost industry

Three possible changes in price and quantity occur in the long run. When demand increases from D_0 to D_1, entry occurs and the industry supply curve shifts rightward from S_0 to S_1. In part (a), the long-run supply curve, LS_A, is horizontal. The quantity increases from Q_0 to Q_1, and the price remains constant at P_0. In part (b), the long-run supply curve is LS_B; the price rises to P_2, and the quantity increases to Q_2. This case occurs in industries with external diseconomies. In part (c), the long-run supply curve is LS_C; the price falls to P_3, and the quantity increases to Q_3. This case occurs in an industry with external economies.

expands. As farm output increased in the nineteenth and early twentieth centuries, the services available to farmers expanded. New firms specialized in the development and marketing of farm machinery and fertilizers. As a result, average farm costs decreased. Farms enjoyed the benefits of external economies. As a consequence, as the demand for farm products increased, the output increased but the price fell.

Over the long term, the prices of many goods and services have fallen, not because of external economies but because of technological change. Let's now study this influence on a competitive market.

Technological Change

Industries are constantly discovering lower-cost techniques of production. Most cost-saving production techniques cannot be implemented, however, without investing in new plant and equipment. As a consequence, it takes time for a technological advance to spread through an industry. Some firms whose plants are on the verge of being replaced will be quick to adopt the new technology, while other firms whose plants have recently been replaced will continue to operate with an old technology until they can no longer cover their average variable cost. Once average variable cost cannot be covered, a firm will scrap even a relatively new plant (embodying an old technology) in favor of a plant with a new technology.

New technology allows firms to produce at a lower cost. As a result, as firms adopt a new technology, their cost curves shift downward. With lower costs, firms are willing to supply a given quantity at a lower price or, equivalently, they are willing to supply a larger quantity at a given price. In other words, industry supply increases, and the industry supply curve shifts rightward. With a given demand, the quantity produced increases and the price falls.

Two forces are at work in an industry undergoing technological change. Firms that adopt the new technology make an economic profit. So there is entry by new-technology firms. Firms that stick with the old technology incur economic losses. They either exit the industry or switch to the new technology.

As old-technology firms disappear and new-technology firms enter, the price falls and the quantity produced increases. Eventually, the industry arrives at a long-run equilibrium in which all the firms use the new technology and make a zero economic profit (a

normal profit). Because in the long run competition eliminates economic profit, technological change brings only temporary gains to producers. But the lower prices and better products that technological advances bring are permanent gains for consumers.

The process that we've just described is one in which some firms experience economic profits and others experience economic losses. It is a period of dynamic change for an industry. Some firms do well, and others do badly. Often, the process has a geographical dimension — the expanding new technology firms bring prosperity to what was once the boondocks, and traditional industrial regions decline. Sometimes, the new-technology firms are in a foreign country, while the old-technology firms are in the domestic economy. The information revolution of the 1990s produced many examples of changes like these. Commercial banking, which was traditionally concentrated in New York, San Francisco, and other large cities now flourishes in Charlotte, North Carolina, which has become the nation's number three commercial banking city. Television shows and movies, traditionally made in Los Angeles and New York, are now made in large numbers in Orlando.

Technological advances are not confined to the information and entertainment industries. Even milk production is undergoing a major technological change because of genetic engineering.

REVIEW QUIZ

1 Describe the course of events in a competitive industry following a permanent decrease in demand. What happens to output, price, and economic profit in the short run and in the long run?

2 Describe the course of events in a competitive industry following a permanent increase in demand. What happens to output, price, and economic profit in the short run and in the long run?

3 Describe the course of events in a competitive industry following the adoption of a new technology. What happens to output, price, and economic profit in the short run and in the long run?

Competition and Efficiency

A COMPETITIVE INDUSTRY CAN ACHIEVE AN EFFIcient use of resources. You studied efficiency in Chapter 5 using only the concepts of demand, supply, consumer surplus, and producer surplus. But now that you have learned what lies behind the demand and supply curves of a competitive market, you can gain a deeper understanding of how the competitive market achieves efficiency.

Efficient Use of Resources

Recall that resource use is efficient when we produce the goods and services that people value most highly (see Chapter 5, pp. 102–103). If someone can become better off without anyone else becoming worse off, resources are *not* being used efficiently. For example, suppose we produce a computer that no one wants and that no one will ever use. Suppose also that some people are clamoring for more video games. If we produce one less computer and reallocate the unused resources to produce more video games, some people will become better off and no one will be worse off. So the initial resource allocation was inefficient.

In the more technical language that you have learned, resource use is efficient when marginal benefit equals marginal cost. In the computer and video games example, the marginal benefit of video games exceeds the marginal cost. And the marginal cost of a computer exceeds its marginal benefit. So by producing fewer computers and more video games, we move resources toward a higher-valued use.

Choices, Equilibrium, and Efficiency

We can use what you have learned about the decisions made by consumers and competitive firms and market equilibrium to describe an efficient use of resources.

Choices Consumers allocate their budgets to get the most value possible out of them. And we derive a consumer's demand curve by finding how the best budget allocation changes as the price of a good changes. So consumers get the most value out of their resources at all points along their demand curves, which are also their marginal benefit curves.

Competitive firms produce the quantity that maximizes profit. And we derive the firm's supply curve by finding the profit-maximizing quantity at each price. So firms get the most value out of their resources at all points along their supply curves, which are also their marginal cost curves. (On their supply curves, firms are *technologically efficient* — they get the maximum possible output from given inputs — and *economically efficient* — they combine resources to minimize cost. See Chapter 9, pp. 195–196.)

Equilibrium In competitive equilibrium, the quantity demanded equals the quantity supplied. So the price equals the consumers' marginal benefit and the producers' marginal cost. In this situation, the gains from trade between consumers and producers are maximized. These gains from trade are the consumer surplus plus the producer surplus.

The gains from trade for consumers are measured by *consumer surplus*, which is the area below the demand curve and above the price paid. (See Chapter 5, p. 105.) The gains from trade for producers are measured by *producer surplus*, which is the area above the marginal cost curve and below the price received. (See Chapter 5, p. 107.) The total gains from trade are the sum of consumer surplus and producer surplus.

Efficiency If the people who consume and produce a good or service are the only ones affected by it and if the market for the good or service is in equilibrium, then resources are being used efficiently. They cannot be reallocated to increase their value.

In such a situation, there are no external benefits or external costs. **External benefits** are benefits that accrue to people other than the buyer of a good. For example, you might get a benefit from your neighbor's expenditure on her garden. Your neighbor buys the quantities of garden plants that make her as well off as possible, not her *and* you.

In the absence of external benefits, the market demand curve measures marginal *social* benefit — the value that *everyone* places on one more unit of a good or service.

External costs are costs that are borne not by the producer of a good or service but by someone else. For example, a firm might lower its costs by polluting. The cost of pollution is an external cost. Firms produce the output level that maximizes their own profit, and they do not count the cost of pollution as a charge against their profit.

In the absence of external costs, the market supply curve measures marginal *social* cost — the entire marginal cost that *anyone* bears to produce one more unit of a good or service.

An Efficient Allocation Figure 11.12 shows an efficient allocation. Consumers are efficient at all points on the demand curve, D (which is also the marginal benefit curve MB). Producers are efficient at all points on the supply curve, S (which is also the marginal cost curve MC). Resources are used efficiently at the quantity Q^* and price P^*. Marginal benefit equals marginal cost, and the sum of producer surplus (blue area) and consumer surplus (green area) is maximized.

If output is Q_0, marginal cost is C_0 and marginal benefit is B_0. Producers can supply more of the good for a cost lower than the price consumers are willing to pay, and everyone gains by increasing the quantity produced. If output is greater than Q^*, marginal cost exceeds marginal benefit. It costs producers more to supply the good than the price consumers are willing to pay, and everyone gains by decreasing the quantity produced.

Efficiency of Perfect Competition

Perfect competition achieves efficiency if there are no external benefits and external costs. In such a case, the benefits accrue to the buyers of the good and the costs are borne by its producer. In Fig. 11.12, the equilibrium quantity Q^* at the price P^* is efficient.

There are three main obstacles to efficiency:

- Monopoly
- Public goods
- External costs and external benefits

Monopoly Monopoly (Chapter 12) restricts output below its competitive level to raise price and increase profit. Government policies (Chapter 17) arise to limit such use of monopoly power.

Public Goods Goods such as national defense, the enforcement of law and order, the provision of clean drinking water, and the disposal of sewage and garbage are examples of public goods. Left to competitive markets, too small a quantity of them would be produced. Government institutions and policies (Chapter 16) help to overcome the problem of providing an efficient quantity of public goods.

External Costs and External Benefits The production of steel and chemicals can generate air and water pollution, and perfect competition might produce too large a quantity of these goods. Government policies (Chapter 18) attempt to cope with external costs and benefits.

◆ You've now completed your study of perfect competition. And *Reading Between the Lines* on pp. 252–253 gives you an opportunity to use what you have learned to understand recent events in the highly competitive maple syrup market.

Although many markets approximate the model of perfect competition, many do not. In Chapter 12, we study markets at the opposite extreme of market power: monopoly. Then, in Chapter 13, we'll study markets that lie between perfect competition and monopoly: monopolistic competition (competition with monopoly elements) and oligopoly (competition among a few producers). When you have completed this study, you'll have a tool kit that will enable you to understand the variety of real-world markets.

FIGURE 11.12   Efficiency of Competition

The efficient use of resources requires consumers to be efficient, which occurs when they are on their demand curves; firms to be efficient, which occurs when they are on their supply curves; and the market to be in equilibrium, with no external benefits or external costs. Resources are used efficiently at the quantity Q^* and the price P^*. With no external benefits or external costs, perfect competition achieves an efficient use of resources. If output is Q_0, the cost of producing one more unit, C_0, is less than its marginal benefit, B_0, and resources are not used efficiently.

Perfect Competition in Maple Syrup

THE HARTFORD COURANT, July 3, 2001

Connecticut's Syrup Output a Sweet Surprise to Producers

With all of New England reporting lower-than-normal maple syrup yields this year over the 2000 season, Connecticut producers were scratching their heads recently after the state's statistics for 2001 showed production had actually increased.

According to the crop report released last month by the New England Agricultural Statistics Service of Concord, N.H., Connecticut producers reported they boiled down about 369,000 gallons of maple sap to make about 9,000 gallons of maple syrup during a colder-than-normal season.

The yield was about 2,000 gallons more than the 7,000 gallons produced in Connecticut in 2000. ...

Across the United States, maple syrup production totaled 1.05 million gallons, down 15 percent from last year and 12 percent below 1999. Vermont led the country in production with 275,000 gallons, 40 percent less than last season. ...

With sugar makers producing less syrup, consumers may be worried about rising prices. But Lamothe doesn't see drastic increases for Connecticut syrup. Those who shop at farmer's markets or stands across the state can expect to pay an average of $5.50 for a pint and about $16.90 for a half-gallon.

"This is a high-end commodity with not a lot of profit margin," he said.

"It's very labor intensive and requires expensive equipment. But if we become too expensive, people will go to Mrs. Butterworth or Aunt Jemima."

Essence of the Story

■ New England reported lower-than-normal maple syrup yields in 2001.

■ But Connecticut producers increased their output by 2,000 gallons to 9,000 gallons.

■ For the United States, maple syrup production was down 15 percent from 2000 and 12 percent from 1999.

■ Vermont had the largest decrease in production, down 40 percent from 2000.

■ Despite the decrease in production, the price didn't change.

■ Maple syrup producers earn a small profit.

■ If maple syrup became too expensive, people would switch to synthetic syrup.

Economic Analysis

■ Maple syrup — the real kind, not the synthetic syrup such as Aunt Jemima — is produced in the United States and Canada by about 11,500 firms.

■ The market for maple syrup is close to perfectly competitive.

■ The demand for maple syrup is highly elastic — perhaps perfectly elastic — for two reasons.

■ First, Aunt Jemima and other synthetic varieties are close substitutes for the real product for many consumers.

■ Second, syrup can be stored. It does not have to be sold to its final consumer in the year in which it is produced.

■ During 1999, 2000, and 2001, the average (wholesale) price of maple syrup was roughly constant at $27 a gallon.

■ But the quantity produced fluctuated from 7 million gallons in 1999 to 8 million in 2000 and down to 5 million in 2001.

■ Production in Connecticut, the topic of the news article, is almost exactly one thousandth of world production.

■ Figure 1 shows the (global) market for maple syrup based on the information and assumptions that we've just provided.

■ Demand is highly elastic (perfectly elastic in the figure), shown by the demand curve D.

■ Fluctuations in the temperature and other climatic factors that influence yields bring fluctuations in supply. The supply curve shifted from S_{99} in 1999 to S_{00} in 2000 and to S_{01} in 2001.

■ Because demand is highly elastic (perfectly elastic in the figure), fluctuations in supply bring fluctuations in the quantity and no change in the price.

■ Figure 2 shows the situation facing a representative producer in Connecticut. Each firm is a price taker and maximizes profit by producing the quantity at which marginal cost (MC) equals marginal revenue (MR).

■ Figure 2 shows the situation in long-run equilibrium: The firm earns normal profit with price equal to average total cost (ATC).

Figure 1 The market for maple syrup

Figure 2 Connecticut maple syrup producers

SUMMARY

KEY POINTS

Competition (pp. 234–235)

- A perfectly competitive firm is a price taker.

The Firm's Decisions in Perfect Competition (pp. 236–241)

- The firm produces the output at which marginal revenue (price) equals marginal cost.
- In short-run equilibrium, a firm can make an economic profit, incur an economic loss, or break even.
- If price is less than minimum average variable cost, the firm temporarily shuts down.
- A firm's supply curve is the upward-sloping part of its marginal cost curve above minimum average variable cost.
- An industry supply curve shows the sum of the quantities supplied by each firm at each price.

Output, Price, and Profit in Perfect Competition (pp. 242–245)

- Market demand and market supply determine price.
- The firm produces the output at which price, which is marginal revenue, equals marginal cost.
- Economic profit induces entry. Economic loss induces exit.
- Entry and plant expansion increase supply and lower price and profit. Exit and downsizing decrease supply and raise price and profit.
- In long-run equilibrium, economic profit is zero (firms earn normal profit). There is no entry, exit, plant expansion, or downsizing.

Changing Tastes and Advancing Technology (pp. 246–249)

- A permanent decrease in demand leads to a smaller industry output and a smaller number of firms.
- A permanent increase in demand leads to a larger industry output and a larger number of firms.

- The long-run effect of a change in demand on price depends on whether there are external economies (the price falls) or external diseconomies (the price rises) or neither (the price remains constant).
- New technologies increase supply and in the long run lower the price and increase the quantity.

Competition and Efficiency (pp. 250–251)

- Resources are used efficiently when we produce goods and services in the quantities that people value most highly.
- When there are no external benefits and external costs, perfect competition achieves an efficient allocation. Marginal benefit equals marginal cost, and the sum of consumer surplus and producer surplus is maximized.
- The existence of monopoly, public goods, and external costs and external benefits presents obstacles to efficiency.

KEY FIGURES

KEY TERMS

PROBLEMS

*1. Quick Copy is one of the many copy shops near the campus. The figure shows Quick Copy's cost curves.

a. If the market price of copying one page is 10 cents, what is Quick Copy's profit-maximizing output?
b. Calculate Quick Copy's profit.
c. With no change in demand or technology, how will the price change in the long run?

2. Jerry's is one of many ice cream stands along the beach. The figure shows Jerry's cost curves.

a. If the market price of an ice cream cone is $3, what is Jerry's profit-maximizing output?
b. Calculate Jerry's profit.
c. With no change in demand or technology, how will the price change in the long run?

*3. Pat's Pizza Kitchen is a price taker. Its costs are

Output (pizzas per hour)	Total cost (dollars per hour)
0	10
1	21
2	30
3	41
4	54
5	69

a. What is Pat's profit-maximizing output and how much economic profit does Pat make if the market price is (i) $14, (ii) $12, and (iii) $10?
b. What is Pat's shutdown point?
c. Derive Pat's supply curve.
d. At what price will Pat exit the pizza industry?

4. Luigi's Lasagna is a price taker. Its costs are

Output (plates per day)	Total cost (dollars per day)
0	14
1	38
2	48
3	62
4	80
5	102
6	128

a. What is Luigi's profit-maximizing output and how much profit does Luigi make if the market price is (i) $24 a plate, (ii) $20 a plate, and (iii) $12 a plate?
b. What is Luigi's shutdown point?
c. What is Luigi's profit at the shutdown point?
d. At what prices will firms with costs the same as Luigi's enter the lasagna market?

*5. The market demand schedule for cassettes is:

Price (dollars per cassette)	Quantity demanded (thousands of cassettes per week)
3.65	500
5.20	450
6.80	400
8.40	350
10.00	300
11.60	250
13.20	200
14.80	150

The market is perfectly competitive, and each firm has the following cost structure:

Output (cassettes per week)	Marginal cost (dollars per additional cassette)	Average variable cost	Average total cost
		(dollars per cassette)	
150	6.00	8.80	15.47
200	6.40	7.80	12.80
250	7.00	7.00	11.00
300	7.65	7.10	10.43
350	8.40	7.20	10.06
400	10.00	7.50	10.00
450	12.40	8.00	10.22
500	20.70	9.00	11.00

There are 1,000 firms in the industry.
a. What is the market price?
b. What is the industry's output?
c. What is the output produced by each firm?
d. What is the economic profit made by each firm?
e. Do firms enter or exit the industry?
f. What is the number of firms in the long run?

6. The same demand conditions as those in problem 5 prevail and there are 1,000 firms in the industry, but fixed costs increase by $980. What now are your answers to the questions in problem 5?

 *7. In problem 5, the price of a CD decreases the demand for cassettes permanently and the demand schedule becomes

Price (dollars per cassette)	Quantity demanded (thousands of cassettes per week)
2.95	500
4.13	450
5.30	400
6.48	350
7.65	300
8.83	250
10.00	200
11.18	150

What now are your answers to the questions in problem 5?

8. In problem 6, the price of a CD decreases the demand for cassettes permanently and the demand schedule becomes that given in problem 7. What now are your answers to the questions in problem 6?

CRITICAL THINKING

1. After you have studied *Reading Between the Lines* on pp. 252–253, answer the following questions.
   a. What are the features of the market for maple syrup that make it an example of perfect competition?
   b. During the 1980s, the technology for extracting sap advanced. What effect do you predict that this development had on the price of syrup and the number of firms that produce it?
   c. Suppose that Aunt Jemima invents a syrup that no one can distinguish (in a blind test) from the real thing and can produce it for $10 a gallon. What effect would you expect this development to have on the market for real maple syrup?

2. Why have the prices of pocket calculators and VCRs fallen? What do you think has happened to the costs and economic profits of the firms that make these products?

3. What has been the effect of an increase in world population on the wheat market and the individual wheat farmer?

4. How has the diaper service industry been affected by the decrease in the U.S. birth rate and the development of disposable diapers?

WEB EXERCISES

1. Use the link on your Parkin Web site and study the *Web Reading Between the Lines*, "Dumping Steel." Then answer the following questions:
   a. What is the argument in the news article about limiting steel imports?
   b. Do you agree with the argument? Why or why not?
   c. Why does the United States claim that foreign steel is being dumped here? (Use the links in the *Web Reading Between the Lines* to answer this question.)

CHAPTER 12

MONOPOLY

The Profits of Generosity

When you buy a new PC, it comes already loaded with the Microsoft Windows operating system, whether you want it or not. And you don't have much choice about the operating system to use because the most commonly used applications (word processing and so on) run only in Windows. Microsoft is obviously not like firms in perfect competition. It doesn't face a market-determined price. It can choose its own price. How do Microsoft and firms like it behave? How do these firms choose the quantity to produce and the price at which to sell it? How does their behavior compare with that of firms in perfectly competitive industries? Do these firms charge prices that are too high and that damage the interests of consumers? Do they bring any benefits? ◆ As a student, you get lots of discounts: when you get your hair cut, go to a museum, or go to a movie. When you take a trip by air, you almost never pay the full fare. Instead, you buy a discounted ticket. Are the people who operate barber shops, museums, movie theaters, and airlines simply generous folks who don't maximize profit? Aren't they throwing profit away by offering discounts?

◆ In this chapter, we study markets in which the firm can influence the price. We also compare the performance of the firm in such a market with that of a competitive market and examine whether monopoly is as efficient as competition.

After studying this chapter, you will be able to

- Explain how monopoly arises and distinguish between single-price monopoly and price-discriminating monopoly

- Explain how a single-price monopoly determines its output and price

- Compare the performance and efficiency of single-price monopoly and competition

- Define rent seeking and explain why it arises

- Explain how price discrimination increases profit

- Explain how monopoly regulation influences output, price, economic profit, and efficiency

Market Power

MARKET POWER AND COMPETITION ARE THE TWO forces that operate in most markets. **Market power** is the ability to influence the market, and in particular the market price, by influencing the total quantity offered for sale.

The firms in perfect competition that you studied in Chapter 11 have no market power. They face the force of raw competition and are price takers. The firms that we study in this chapter operate at the opposite extreme. They face no competition and exercise raw market power. We call this extreme monopoly. A **monopoly** is an industry that produces a good or service for which no close substitute exists and in which there is one supplier that is protected from competition by a barrier preventing the entry of new firms.

Examples of monopoly include your local phone, gas, electricity, and water suppliers as well as De Beers, the South African diamond producer, and Microsoft Corporation, the software developer that created the Windows operating system.

How Monopoly Arises

Monopoly has two key features:

- No close substitutes
- Barriers to entry

No Close Substitutes If a good has a close substitute, even though only one firm produces it, that firm effectively faces competition from the producers of substitutes. Water supplied by a local public utility is an example of a good that does not have close substitutes. While it does have a close substitute for drinking — bottled spring water — it has no effective substitutes for showering or washing a car.

Monopolies are constantly under attack from new products and ideas that substitute for products produced by monopolies. For example, FedEx, UPS, the fax machine, and e-mail have weakened the monopoly of the U.S. Postal Service. Similarly, the satellite dish has weakened the monopoly of cable television companies.

But new products also are constantly creating monopolies. An example is Microsoft's monopoly in the DOS operating system during the 1980s and in the Windows operating system today.

Barriers to Entry Legal or natural constraints that protect a firm from potential competitors are called **barriers to entry**. A firm can sometimes create its own barrier to entry by acquiring a significant portion of a key resource. For example, De Beers controls more than 80 percent of the world's supply of natural diamonds. But most monopolies arise from two other types of barrier: legal barriers and natural barriers.

Legal Barriers to Entry Legal barriers to entry create legal monopoly. A **legal monopoly** is a market in which competition and entry are restricted by the granting of a public franchise, government license, patent, or copyright.

A *public franchise* is an exclusive right granted to a firm to supply a good or service. Examples are the U.S. Postal Service, which has the exclusive right to carry first-class mail. A *government license* controls entry into particular occupations, professions, and industries. Examples of this type of barrier to entry occur in medicine, law, dentistry, schoolteaching, architecture, and many other professional services. Licensing does not always create monopoly, but it does restrict competition.

A *patent* is an exclusive right granted to the inventor of a product or service. A *copyright* is an exclusive right granted to the author or composer of a literary, musical, dramatic, or artistic work. Patents and copyrights are valid for a limited time period that varies from country to country. In the United States, a patent is valid for 20 years. Patents encourage the *invention* of new products and production methods. They also stimulate *innovation* — the use of new inventions — by encouraging inventors to publicize their discoveries and offer them for use under license. Patents have stimulated innovations in areas as diverse as soybean seeds, pharmaceuticals, memory chips, and video games.

Natural Barriers to Entry Natural barriers to entry create **natural monopoly**, which is an industry in which one firm can supply the entire market at a lower price than two or more firms can.

Figure 12.1 shows a natural monopoly in the distribution of electric power. Here, the market demand curve for electric power is *D*, and the average total cost curve is *ATC*. Because average total cost decreases as output increases, economies of scale prevail over the entire length of the *ATC* curve. One firm can produce 4 million kilowatt-hours at 5 cents a kilowatt-hour. At this price, the quantity demanded is 4 million kilowatt-hours. So if the price was 5 cents, one firm could supply the entire market. If two firms shared the market, it would cost each of them 10 cents a kilowatt-hour to produce a total of 4 million kilowatt-hours. If four firms shared the market, it would cost each of them 15 cents a kilowatt-hour to produce a total of 4 million kilowatt-hours. So in conditions like those shown in Fig. 12.1, one firm can supply the entire market at a lower cost than two or more firms can. The distribution of electric power is an example of natural monopoly. So is the distribution of water and gas.

Most monopolies are regulated in some way by government agencies. We will study such regulation at the end of this chapter. But for two reasons, we'll first study unregulated monopoly. First, we can better understand why governments regulate monopolies and the effects of regulation if we also know how an unregulated monopoly behaves. Second, even in industries with more than one producer, firms often have a degree of monopoly power, and the theory of monopoly sheds light on the behavior of such firms and industries.

A major difference between monopoly and competition is that a monopoly sets its own price. But in doing so, it faces a market constraint. Let's see how the market limits a monopoly's pricing choices.

Monopoly Price-Setting Strategies

All monopolies face a tradeoff between price and the quantity sold. To sell a larger quantity, the monopolist must charge a lower price. But there are two broad monopoly situations that create different tradeoffs. They are

- Price discrimination
- Single price

Price Discrimination Many firms price discriminate and most are *not* monopolies. Airlines offer a dizzying array of different prices for the same trip. Pizza producers charge one price for a single pizza and almost give away a second pizza. These are examples of *price discrimination*. **Price discrimination** is the practice of selling different units of a good or service for different prices. Different customers might pay different prices (like airline passengers), or one customer might pay different prices for different quantities bought (like the bargain price for a second pizza).

When a firm price discriminates, it looks as though it is doing its customers a favor. In fact, it is charging the highest possible price for each unit sold and making the largest possible profit.

Not all monopolies can price discriminate. The main obstacle to price discrimination is resale by customers who buy for a low price. Because of resale possibilities, price discrimination is limited to monopolies that sell services that cannot be resold.

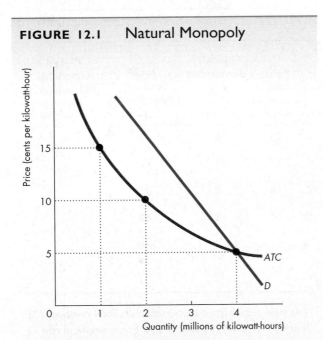

FIGURE 12.1   Natural Monopoly

The market demand curve for electric power is *D*, and the average total cost curve is *ATC*. Economies of scale exist over the entire *ATC* curve. One firm can distribute 4 million kilowatt-hours at a cost of 5 cents a kilowatt-hour. This same total output costs 10 cents a kilowatt-hour with two firms and 15 cents a kilowatt-hour with four firms. So one firm can meet the market demand at a lower cost than two or more firms can, and the market is a natural monopoly.

Single Price De Beers sells diamonds (of a given size and quality) for the same price to all its customers. If it tried to sell at a low price to some customers and at a higher price to others, only the low-price customers would buy from De Beers. Others would buy from De Beers' low-price customers.

De Beers is a *single-price* monopoly. A **single-price monopoly** is a firm that must sell each unit of its output for the same price to all its customers.

We'll look first at single-price monopoly.

A Single-Price Monopoly's Output and Price Decision

To UNDERSTAND HOW A SINGLE-PRICE MONOPOLY makes its output and price decision, we must first study the link between price and marginal revenue.

Price and Marginal Revenue

Because in a monopoly there is only one firm, the demand curve facing the firm is the market demand curve. Let's look at Bobbie's Barbershop, the sole supplier of haircuts in Cairo, Nebraska. The table in Fig. 12.2 shows the market demand schedule. At a price of $20, she sells no haircuts. The lower the price, the more haircuts per hour Bobbie can sell. For example, at $12, consumers demand 4 haircuts per hour (row E).

Total revenue (TR) is the price (P) multiplied by the quantity sold (Q). For example, in row D, Bobbie sells 3 haircuts at $14 each, so total revenue is $42. *Marginal revenue* (MR) is the change in total revenue (ΔTR) resulting from a one-unit increase in the quantity sold. For example, if the price falls from $16 (row C) to $14 (row D), the quantity sold increases from 2 to 3 haircuts. Total revenue rises from $32 to $42, so the change in total revenue is $10. Because the quantity sold increases by 1 haircut, marginal revenue equals the change in total revenue and is $10. Marginal revenue is placed between the two rows to emphasize that marginal revenue relates to the *change* in the quantity sold.

Figure 12.2 shows the market demand curve and marginal revenue curve (MR) and also illustrates the calculation we've just made. Notice that at each level of output, marginal revenue is less than price — the marginal revenue curve lies below the demand curve. Why is marginal revenue *less* than price? It is because when the price is lowered to sell one more unit, two opposing forces affect total revenue. The lower price results in a revenue loss, and the increased quantity sold results in a revenue gain. For example, at a price of $16, Bobbie sells 2 haircuts (point C). If she lowers the price to $14, she sells 3 haircuts and has a revenue gain of $14 on the third haircut. But she now receives only $14 on the first two — $2 less than before. As a result, she loses $4 of revenue on the first 2 haircuts. To calculate marginal revenue, she must deduct this amount from the revenue gain of $14. So her marginal revenue is $10, which is less than the price.

FIGURE 12.2   Demand and Marginal Revenue

	Price (P) (dollars per haircut)	Quantity demanded (Q) (haircuts per hour)	Total revenue (TR = P × Q) (dollars)	Marginal revenue (MR = ΔTR/ΔQ) (dollars per haircut)
A	20	0	0	
				18
B	18	1	18	
				14
C	16	2	32	
				10
D	14	3	42	
				 6
E	12	4	48	
				 2
F	10	5	50	

The table shows the demand schedule. Total revenue (TR) is price multiplied by quantity sold. For example, in row C, the price is $16 a haircut, Bobbie sells 2 haircuts and total revenue is $32. Marginal revenue (MR) is the change in total revenue that results from a one-unit increase in the quantity sold. For example, when the price falls from $16 to $14 a haircut, the quantity sold increases by 1 haircut and total revenue increases by $10. Marginal revenue is $10. The demand curve and the marginal revenue curve, MR, are based on the numbers in the table and illustrate the calculation of marginal revenue when the price falls from $16 to $14.

Marginal Revenue and Elasticity

A single-price monopoly's marginal revenue is related to the *elasticity of demand* for its good. The demand for a good can be *elastic* (the elasticity of demand is greater than 1), *inelastic* (the elasticity of demand is less than 1), or *unit elastic* (the elasticity of demand is equal to 1). Demand is *elastic* if a 1 percent fall in price brings a greater than 1 percent increase in the quantity demanded. Demand is *inelastic* if a 1 percent fall in price brings a less than 1 percent increase in the quantity demanded. And demand is *unit elastic* if a 1 percent fall in price brings a 1 percent increase in the quantity demanded. (See Chapter 4, pp. 84–85.)

If demand is elastic, a fall in price brings an increase in total revenue — the increase in revenue from the increase in quantity sold outweighs the decrease in revenue from the lower price — and marginal revenue is positive. If demand is inelastic, a fall in price brings a decrease in total revenue — the increase in revenue from the increase in quantity sold is outweighed by the decrease in revenue from the lower price — and marginal revenue is negative. If demand is unit elastic, total revenue does not change — the increase in revenue from the increase in quantity sold offsets the decrease in revenue from the lower price — and marginal revenue is zero. (The relationship between total revenue and elasticity is explained in Chapter 4, p. 86.)

Figure 12.3 illustrates the relationship between marginal revenue, total revenue, and elasticity. As the price of a haircut gradually falls from $20 to $10, the quantity of haircuts demanded increases from 0 to 5 an hour. Over this output range, marginal revenue is positive (part a), total revenue increases (part b), and the demand for haircuts is elastic. As the price falls from $10 to $0 a haircut, the quantity of haircuts demanded increases from 5 to 10 an hour. Over this output range, marginal revenue is negative (part a), total revenue decreases (part b), and the demand for haircuts is inelastic. When the price is $10 a haircut, marginal revenue is zero, total revenue is a maximum, and the demand for haircuts is unit elastic.

In Monopoly, Demand Is Always Elastic The relationship between marginal revenue and elasticity that you've just discovered implies that a profit-maximizing monopoly never produces an output in the inelastic range of its demand curve. If it did so, it could charge a higher price, produce a smaller quantity, and increase its profit. Let's now look more closely at a monopoly's output and price decision.

FIGURE 12.3 Marginal Revenue and Elasticity

(a) Demand and marginal revenue curves

(b) Total revenue curve

In part (a), the demand curve is *D* and the marginal revenue curve is *MR*. In part (b), the total revenue curve is *TR*. Over the range from 0 to 5 haircuts an hour, a price cut increases total revenue, so marginal revenue is positive — as shown by the blue bars. Demand is elastic. Over the range 5 to 10 haircuts an hour, a price cut decreases total revenue, so marginal revenue is negative — as shown by the red bars. Demand is inelastic. At 5 haircuts an hour, total revenue is maximized and marginal revenue is zero. Demand is unit elastic.

Output and Price Decision

To determine the output level and price that maximize a monopoly's profit, we need to study the behavior of both revenue and costs as output varies. A monopoly faces the same types of technology and cost constraints as a competitive firm. But it faces a different market constraint. The competitive firm is a price taker, whereas the monopoly's output decision influences the price it receives. Let's see how.

Bobbie's revenue, which we studied in Fig. 12.2, is shown again in Table 12.1. The table also contains information on Bobbie's costs and economic profit. Total cost (TC) rises as output increases, and so does total revenue (TR). Economic profit equals total revenue minus total cost. As you can see in the table, the maximum profit ($12) occurs when Bobbie sells 3 haircuts for $14 each. If she sells 2 haircuts for $16 each or 4 haircuts for $12 each, her economic profit will be only $8.

You can see why 3 haircuts is Bobbie's profit-maximizing output by looking at the marginal revenue and marginal cost columns. When Bobbie increases output from 2 to 3 haircuts, her marginal revenue is $10 and her marginal cost is $6. Profit increases by the difference — $4 an hour. If Bobbie increases output yet further, from 3 to 4 haircuts, her marginal revenue is $6 and her marginal cost is $10. In this case, marginal cost exceeds marginal revenue by $4, so profit decreases by $4 an hour. When marginal revenue exceeds marginal cost, profit increases if output increases. When marginal cost exceeds marginal revenue, profit increases if output decreases. When marginal cost and marginal revenue are equal, profit is maximized.

The information set out in Table 12.1 is shown graphically in Fig. 12.4. Part (a) shows Bobbie's total revenue curve (TR) and total cost curve (TC). Economic profit is the vertical distance between TR and TC. Bobbie maximizes her profit at 3 haircuts an hour — economic profit is $42 minus $30, or $12.

A monopoly, like a competitive firm, maximizes profit by producing the output at which marginal cost equals marginal revenue. Figure 12.4(b) shows the market demand curve (D), Bobbie's marginal revenue curve (MR), and her marginal cost curve (MC) and average total cost curve (ATC). Bobbie maximizes her profit by doing 3 haircuts an hour. But what price does she charge for a haircut? To set the price, the monopolist uses the demand curve and finds the highest price at which it can sell the profit-maximizing output. In Bobbie's case, the highest price at which she can sell 3 haircuts an hour is $14.

TABLE 12.1   A Monopoly's Output and Price Decision

Price (P) (dollars per haircut)	Quantity demanded (Q) (haircuts per hour)	Total revenue (TR = P × Q) (dollars)	Marginal revenue (MR = ΔTR/ΔQ) (dollars per haircut)	Total cost (TC) (dollars)	Marginal cost (MC = ΔTC/ΔQ) (dollars per haircut)	Profit (TR – TC) (dollars)
20	0	0		20		−20
			 18		 1	
18	1	18		21		−3
			 14		 3	
16	2	32		24		+8
			 10		 6	
14	**3**	**42**		**30**		**+12**
			 6		 10	
12	4	48		40		+8
			 2		 15	
10	5	50		55		−5

This table gives the information needed to find the profit-maximizing output and price. Total revenue (TR) equals price multiplied by the quantity sold. Profit equals total revenue minus total cost (TC). Profit is maximized when 3 haircuts are sold at a price of $14 each. Total revenue is $42, total cost is $30, and economic profit is $12 ($42 − $30).

FIGURE 12.4   A Monopoly's Output and Price

(a) Total revenue and total cost curves

(b) Demand and marginal revenue and cost curves

In part (a), economic profit is the vertical distance equal to total revenue (*TR*) minus total cost (*TC*) and it is maximized at 3 haircuts an hour. In part (b), economic profit is maximized when marginal cost (*MC*) equals marginal revenue (*MR*). The profit-maximizing output is 3 haircuts an hour. The price is determined by the demand curve (*D*) and is $14 a haircut. Her average total cost is $10 a haircut, so economic profit, the blue rectangle, is $12 — the profit per haircut ($4) multiplied by 3 haircuts.

All firms maximize profit by producing the output at which marginal revenue equals marginal cost. For a competitive firm, price equals marginal revenue, so price also equals marginal cost. For a monopoly, price exceeds marginal revenue, so price also exceeds marginal cost.

A monopoly charges a price that exceeds marginal cost, but does it always make an economic profit? In Bobbie's case, when she produces 3 haircuts an hour, her average total cost is $10 (read from the *ATC* curve) and her price is $14 (read from the *D* curve). Her profit per haircut is $4 ($14 minus $10). Bobbie's economic profit is shown by the blue rectangle, which equals the profit per haircut ($4) multiplied by the number of haircuts (3), for a total of $12.

If firms in a perfectly competitive industry make a positive economic profit, new firms enter. That does not happen in monopoly. Barriers to entry prevent new firms from entering an industry in which there is a monopoly. So a monopoly can make a positive economic profit and continue to do so indefinitely. Sometimes that profit is large, as in the international diamond business.

Bobbie makes a positive economic profit. But suppose that the owner of the shop that Bobbie rents increases Bobbie's rent. If Bobbie pays an additional $12 an hour, her fixed cost increases by $12 an hour. Her marginal cost and marginal revenue don't change, so her profit-maximizing output remains at 3 haircuts an hour. Her profit decreases by $12 an hour to zero. If Bobbie pays more than an additional $12 an hour for her shop rent, she incurs an economic loss. If this situation were permanent, Bobbie would go out of business. But entrepreneurs are a hardy lot, and Bobbie might find another shop where the rent is less.

REVIEW QUIZ

1 What is the relationship between marginal cost and marginal revenue when a single-price monopoly maximizes profit?

2 How does a single-price monopoly determine the price it will charge its customers?

3 What is the relationship between price, marginal revenue, and marginal cost when a single-price monopoly is maximizing profit?

4 Why can a monopoly make a positive economic profit even in the long run?

Single-Price Monopoly and Competition Compared

IMAGINE AN INDUSTRY THAT IS MADE UP OF MANY small firms operating in perfect competition. Then imagine that a single firm buys out all these small firms and creates a monopoly.

What will happen in this industry? Will the price rise or fall? Will the quantity produced increase or decrease? Will economic profit increase or decrease? Will either the original competitive situation or the new monopoly situation be efficient?

These are the questions we're now going to answer. First, we look at the effects of monopoly on the price and quantity produced. Then we turn to the questions about efficiency.

Comparing Output and Price

Figure 12.5 shows the market we'll study. The market demand curve is *D*. The demand curve is the same regardless of how the industry is organized. But the supply side and the equilibrium are different in monopoly and competition. First, let's look at the case of perfect competition.

Perfect Competition Initially, with many small perfectly competitive firms in the market, the market supply curve is *S*. This supply curve is obtained by summing the supply curves of all the individual firms in the market.

In perfect competition, equilibrium occurs where the supply curve and the demand curve intersect. The quantity produced by the industry is Q_C, and the price is P_C. Each firm takes the price P_C and maximizes its profit by producing the output at which its own marginal cost equals the price. Because each firm is a small part of the total industry, there is no incentive for any firm to try to manipulate the price by varying its output.

Monopoly Now suppose that this industry is taken over by a single firm. Consumers do not change, so the demand curve remains the same as in the case of perfect competition. But now the monopoly recognizes this demand curve as a constraint on its sales. The monopoly's marginal revenue curve is *MR*.

The monopoly maximizes profit by producing the quantity at which marginal revenue equals marginal

cost. To find the monopoly's marginal cost curve, first recall that in perfect competition, the industry supply curve is the sum of the supply curves of the firms in the industry. Also recall that each firm's supply curve is its marginal cost curve (see Chapter 11, pp. 240–241). So when the industry is taken over by a single firm, the competitive industry's supply curve becomes the monopoly's marginal cost curve. To remind you of this fact, the supply curve is also labeled *MC*.

The output at which marginal revenue equals marginal cost is Q_M. This output is smaller than the competitive output Q_C. And the monopoly charges the price P_M, which is higher than P_C. We have established that

Compared to a perfectly competitive industry, a single-price monopoly restricts its output and charges a higher price.

We've seen how the output and price of a monopoly compare with those in a competitive industry. Let's now compare the efficiency of the two types of market.

FIGURE 12.5   Monopoly's Smaller Output and Higher Price

A competitive industry produces the quantity Q_C at price P_C. A single-price monopoly produces the quantity Q_M at which marginal revenue equals marginal cost and sells that quantity for the price P_M. Compared to perfect competition, a single-price monopoly restricts output and raises the price.

Efficiency Comparison

When we studied efficiency in perfect competition, (see Chapter 11, pp. 250–251), we discovered that if there are no external costs and benefits, perfect competition is efficient. Along the demand curve, consumers are efficient. Along the supply curve, producers are efficient. And where the curves intersect — the competitive equilibrium — both consumers and producers are efficient. Price, which measures marginal benefit, equals marginal cost.

Monopoly restricts output below the competitive level and is inefficient. If a monopoly increases its output by one unit, consumers' marginal benefit exceeds the monopoly's marginal cost and resource use will be more efficient.

Figure 12.6 illustrates the inefficiency of monopoly and shows the loss of consumer and producer surpluses in a monopoly. In perfect competition (part a), consumers pay P_C for each unit. The marginal benefit to consumers is shown by the demand curve ($D = MB$). This price measures the value of the good to the consumer. Value minus the price paid equals *consumer surplus* (see Chapter 5, p. 105). In Fig. 12.6(a), consumer surplus is shown by the green triangle.

The marginal cost of production (opportunity cost) in perfect competition is shown by the supply curve ($S = MC$). The amount received by the producer in excess of this marginal cost is *producer surplus*. In Fig. 12.6(a), the blue area shows producer surplus.

At the competitive equilibrium, marginal benefit equals marginal cost and the sum of consumer surplus and producer surplus is maximized. Resource use is efficient.

In Fig. 12.6(b), a monopoly restricts output to Q_M and sells that output for P_M. Consumer surplus decreases to the smaller green triangle. Consumers lose partly by having to pay more for the good and partly by getting less of it. Part of the original producer surplus is also lost. The total loss resulting from the smaller monopoly output (Q_M) is the gray triangle. The part of the gray triangle above P_C is the loss of consumer surplus, and the part of the triangle below P_C is a loss of producer surplus. The entire gray triangle measures the loss of consumer surplus plus producer surplus. This loss is called the *deadweight loss*. The smaller output and higher price drive a wedge between marginal benefit and marginal cost and eliminate the producer surplus and the consumer surplus on the output that a competitive industry would have produced but the monopoly does not.

FIGURE 12.6   Inefficiency of Monopoly

(a) Perfect competition

(b) Monopoly

In perfect competition (part a), the quantity Q_C is sold at the price P_C. Consumer surplus is shown by the green triangle. In long-run equilibrium, firms' economic profits are zero and consumer surplus is maximized.

A single-price monopoly (part b) restricts output to Q_M and increases the price to P_M. Consumer surplus is the smaller green triangle. The monopoly takes the darker blue rectangle and creates a deadweight loss (the gray triangle).

Redistribution of Surpluses

You've seen that monopoly is inefficient because marginal benefit exceeds marginal cost and there is deadweight loss — a social loss. But monopoly also brings a *redistribution* of surpluses.

Some of the lost consumer surplus goes to the monopoly. In Fig. 12.6, the monopoly gets the difference between the higher price, P_M, and the competitive price, P_C, on the quantity sold, Q_M. So the monopoly takes the part of the consumer surplus shown by the darker blue rectangle. This portion of the loss of consumer surplus is not a loss to society. It is redistribution from consumers to the monopoly producer.

Rent Seeking

You've seen that monopoly creates a deadweight loss and so is inefficient. But the social cost of monopoly exceeds the deadweight loss because of an activity called rent seeking. **Rent seeking** is any attempt to capture a consumer surplus, a producer surplus, or an economic profit. The activity is not confined to monopoly. But attempting to capture the economic profit of a monopoly is a major form of rent seeking.

You've seen that a monopoly makes its economic profit by diverting part of consumer surplus to itself. Thus the pursuit of an economic profit by a monopolist is rent seeking. It is the attempt to capture consumer surplus.

Rent seekers pursue their goals in two main ways. They might

- Buy a monopoly
- Create a monopoly

Buy a Monopoly To rent seek by buying a monopoly, a person searches for a monopoly that is for sale at a lower price than the monopoly's economic profit. Trading of taxicab licenses is an example of this type of rent seeking. In some cities, taxicabs are regulated. The city restricts both the fares and the number of taxis that can operate so that operating a taxi results in economic profit, or rent. A person who wants to operate a taxi must buy a license from someone who already has one. People rationally devote time and effort to seeking out profitable monopoly businesses to buy. In the process, they use up scarce resources that could otherwise have been used to produce goods and services. The value of this lost production is part of the social cost of monopoly. The amount

paid for a monopoly is not a social cost because the payment is just a transfer of an existing producer surplus from the buyer to the seller.

Create a Monopoly Rent seeking by creating monopoly is mainly a political activity. It takes the form of lobbying and trying to influence the political process. Such influence might be sought by making campaign contributions in exchange for legislative support or by indirectly seeking to influence political outcomes through publicity in the media or more direct contacts with politicians and bureaucrats. An example of a monopoly right created in this way is the government-imposed restrictions on the quantities of textiles that may be imported into the United States. Another is a regulation that limits the number of oranges that may be sold in the United States. These are regulations that restrict output and increase price.

This type of rent seeking is a costly activity that uses up scarce resources. Taken together, firms spend billions of dollars lobbying Congress, state legislators, and local officials in the pursuit of licenses and laws that create barriers to entry and establish a monopoly right. Everyone has an incentive to rent seek, and because there are no barriers to entry into the rent-seeking activity, there is a great deal of competition for new monopoly rights.

Rent-Seeking Equilibrium

Barriers to entry create monopoly. But there is no barrier to entry into rent seeking. Rent seeking is like perfect competition. If an economic profit is available, a new rent seeker will try to get some of it. And competition among rent seekers pushes up the price that must be paid for a monopoly right to the point at which only a normal profit can be made by operating the monopoly. For example, competition for the right to operate a taxi in New York City leads to a price of more than $100,000 for a taxi license, which is sufficiently high to eliminate economic profit for taxi operators and leave them with normal profit.

Figure 12.7 shows a rent-seeking equilibrium. The cost of rent seeking is a fixed cost that must be added to a monopoly's other costs. Rent seeking and rent-seeking costs increase to the point at which no economic profit is made. The average total cost curve, which includes the fixed cost of rent seeking, shifts upward until it just touches the demand curve. Economic profit is zero. It has been lost in rent seeking. Consumer surplus is unaffected. But the deadweight

FIGURE 12.7   Rent-Seeking Equilibrium

With competitive rent seeking, a monopoly uses all its economic profit to prevent another firm from taking its economic rent. The firm's rent-seeking costs are fixed costs. They add to total fixed cost and to average total cost. The *ATC* curve shifts upward until, at the profit-maximizing price, the firm breaks even.

loss of monopoly now includes the original deadweight loss triangle plus the lost producer surplus, shown by the enlarged gray area in the figure.

REVIEW QUIZ

1　Why does a single-price monopoly produce a smaller output and charge a higher price than what would prevail if the industry were perfectly competitive?

2　How does a monopoly transfer consumer surplus to itself?

3　Why is a single-price monopoly inefficient?

4　What is rent seeking and how does it influence the inefficiency of monopoly?

So far, we've considered only a single-price monopoly. But many monopolies do not operate with a single price. Instead, they price discriminate. Let's now see how price-discriminating monopoly works.

Price Discrimination

PRICE DISCRIMINATION — SELLING A GOOD OR service at a number of different prices — is widespread. You encounter it when you travel, go to the movies, get your hair cut, buy pizza, or visit an art museum. Most price discriminators are not monopolies, but monopolies price discriminate when they can do so.

To be able to price discriminate, a monopoly must

1. Identify and separate different buyer types.
2. Sell a product that cannot be resold.

Price discrimination is charging different prices for a single good or service because of differences in buyers' willingness to pay and not because of differences in production costs. So not all price *differences* are price *discrimination*. Some goods that are similar but not identical have different prices because they have different production costs. For example, the cost of producing electricity depends on time of day. If an electric power company charges a higher price during the peak consumption periods from 7:00 to 9:00 in the morning and from 4:00 to 7:00 in the evening than it does at other times of the day, it is not price discriminating.

At first sight, it appears that price discrimination contradicts the assumption of profit maximization. Why would a movie theater allow children to see movies at half price? Why would a hairdresser charge students and senior citizens less? Aren't these firms losing profit by being nice to their customers?

Deeper investigation shows that far from losing profit, price discriminators make a bigger profit than they would otherwise. So a monopoly has an incentive to find ways of discriminating and charging each buyer the highest possible price. Some people pay less with price discrimination, but others pay more.

Price Discrimination and Consumer Surplus

The key idea behind price discrimination is to convert consumer surplus into economic profit. Demand curves slope downward because the value that people place on any good decreases as the quantity consumed of that good increases. When all the units consumed are sold for a single price, consumers benefit. The benefit is the value the consumers get from each unit of the good minus the price actually paid for it. This benefit is *consumer surplus*. Price discrimination is an attempt by a monopoly to capture as much of the consumer surplus as possible for itself.

To extract every dollar of consumer surplus from every buyer, the monopoly would have to offer each individual customer a separate price schedule based on that customer's own willingness to pay. Clearly, such price discrimination cannot be carried out in practice because a firm does not have enough information about each consumer's demand curve.

But firms try to extract as much consumer surplus as possible, and to do so, they discriminate in two broad ways:

- Among units of a good
- Among groups of buyers

Discriminating Among Units of a Good One method of price discrimination charges each buyer a different price on each unit of a good bought. A discount for bulk buying is an example of this type of discrimination. The larger the quantity bought, the larger is the discount — and the lower is the price. (Note that some discounts for bulk arise from lower costs of production for greater bulk. In these cases, such discounts are not price discrimination.)

Discriminating Among Groups of Buyers Price discrimination often takes the form of discriminating between different groups of consumers on the basis of age, employment status, or some other easily distinguished characteristic. This type of price discrimination works when each group has a different average willingness to pay for the good or service.

For example, a face-to-face sales meeting with a customer might bring a large and profitable order. For salespeople and other business travelers, the marginal benefit from a trip is large and the price that such a traveler will pay for a trip is high. In contrast, for a vacation traveler, any of several different trips and even no vacation trip are options. So for vacation travelers, the marginal benefit of a trip is small and the price that such a traveler will pay for a trip is low. Because business travelers are willing to pay more than vacation travelers are, it is possible for an airline to profit by price discriminating between these two groups. Similarly, because students have a lower willingness to pay for a haircut than a working person does, it is possible for a hairdresser to profit by price discriminating between these two groups.

Let's see how an airline exploits the differences in demand by business and vacation travelers and increases its profit by price discriminating.

Profiting by Price Discriminating

Global Air has a monopoly on an exotic route. Figure 12.8 shows the demand curve (*D*) and the marginal revenue curve (*MR*) for travel on this route. It also shows Global Air's marginal cost curve (*MC*) and average total cost curve (*ATC*).

Initially, Global is a single-price monopoly and maximizes its profit by producing 8,000 trips a year (the quantity at which *MR* equals *MC*). The price is $1,200 per trip. The average total cost of producing a trip is $600, so economic profit is $600 a trip. On 8,000 trips, Global's economic profit is $4.8 million a year, shown by the blue rectangle. Global's customers enjoy a consumer surplus shown by the green triangle.

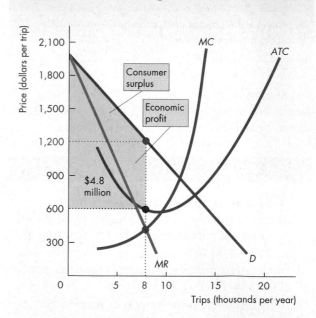

FIGURE 12.8   A Single Price of Air Travel

Global Airlines has a monopoly on an air route. The market demand curve is *D* and marginal revenue curve is *MR*. Global Air's marginal cost curve is *MC* and its average total cost curve is *ATC*. As a single-price monopoly, Global maximizes profit by selling 8,000 trips a year at $1,200 a trip. Its profit is $4.8 million a year — the blue rectangle. Global's customers enjoy a consumer surplus — the green triangle.

Global is struck by the fact that many of its customers are business travelers, and Global suspects they are willing to pay more than $1,200 a trip. So Global does some market research, which tells Global that some business travelers are willing to pay as much as $1,800 a trip. Also, these customers frequently change their travel plans at the last moment. Another group of business travelers is willing to pay $1,600. These customers know a week ahead when they will travel, and they never want to stay over a weekend. Yet another group would pay up to $1,400. These travelers know two weeks ahead when they will travel and don't want to stay away over a weekend.

So Global announces a new fare schedule. No restrictions, $1,800; 7-day advance purchase, no cancellation, $1,600; 14-day advance purchase, no cancellation, $1,400; 14-day advance purchase, must stay over a weekend, $1,200.

Figure 12.9 shows the outcome with this new fare structure and also shows why Global is pleased

with its new fares. It sells 2,000 seats at each of its four prices. Global's economic profit increases by the blue steps in Fig. 12.9. Its economic profit is now its original $4.8 million a year plus an additional $2.4 million from its new higher fares. Consumer surplus has shrunk to the smaller green area.

Perfect Price Discrimination

But Global reckons that it can do even better. It plans to achieve **perfect price discrimination**, which extracts the entire consumer surplus. To do so, Global must get creative and come up with a host of additional fares ranging between $1,200 and $2,000, each of which appeals to a small segment of the business market and that will extract the entire consumer surplus from the business travelers.

With perfect price discrimination, something special happens to marginal revenue. For the perfect price discriminator, the market demand curve becomes the marginal revenue curve. The reason is that when the price is cut to sell a larger quantity, the firm sells only the marginal unit at the lower price. All the other units continue to be sold for the highest price that each buyer is willing to pay. So for the perfect price discriminator, marginal revenue *equals* price and the demand curve becomes the marginal revenue curve.

With marginal revenue equal to price, Global can obtain yet greater profit by increasing output up to the point at which price (and marginal revenue) is equal to marginal cost.

So Global now seeks additional travelers who will not pay as much as $1,200 a trip but who will pay more than marginal cost. More creative pricing comes up with vacation specials and other fares that have combinations of advance reservation, minimum stay, and other restrictions that make these fares unattractive to its existing customers but attractive to a further group of travelers. With all these fares and specials, Global increases sales, extracts the entire consumer surplus, and maximizes economic profit. Figure 12.10 shows the outcome with perfect price discrimination. The dozens of fares paid by the original travelers who are willing to pay between $1,200 and $2,000 have extracted the entire consumer surplus from this group and converted it into economic profit for Global.

The new fares between $900 and $1,200 have attracted 3,000 additional travelers but taken their entire consumer surplus also. Global is earning an economic profit of more than $9 million.

FIGURE 12.9   Price Discrimination

Global revises its fare structure: no restrictions at $1,800, 7-day advance purchase at $1,600, 14-day advance purchase at $1,400, and must stay over a weekend at $1,200. Global sells 2,000 trips at each of its four new fares. Its economic profit increases by $2.4 million a year to $7.2 million a year, which is shown by the original blue rectangle plus the blue steps. Global's customers' consumer surplus shrinks.

FIGURE 12.10 Perfect Price Discrimination

Price (dollars per trip) vs Trips (thousands per year)

Labels on graph: MC, ATC, Increase in economic profit from perfect price discrimination, Increase in output, D = MR

Dozens of fares discriminate among many different types of business traveler, and many new low fares with restrictions appeal to vacation travelers. With perfect price discrimination, Global's demand curve becomes its marginal revenue curve. Economic profit is maximized when the lowest price equals marginal cost. Here, Global sells 11,000 trips and makes an economic profit of $9.35 million a year.

Real-world airlines are just as creative as Global, as you can see in the cartoon!

Would it bother you to hear how little I paid for this flight?

From William Hamilton, "Voodoo Economics," © 1992 by The Chronicle Publishing Company, p.3. Reprinted with permission of Chronicle Books.

Efficiency and Rent Seeking with Price Discrimination

With perfect price discrimination, output increases to the point at which price equals marginal cost — where the marginal cost curve intersects the demand curve. This output is identical to that of perfect competition. Perfect price discrimination pushes consumer surplus to zero but increases producer surplus to equal the sum of consumer surplus and producer surplus in perfect competition. Deadweight loss with perfect price discrimination is zero. So perfect price discrimination achieves efficiency.

The more perfectly the monopoly can price discriminate, the closer its output gets to the competitive output and the more efficient is the outcome.

But there are two differences between perfect competition and perfect price discrimination. First, the distribution of the surplus is different. It is shared by consumers and producers in perfect competition, while the producer gets it all with perfect price discrimination. Second, because the producer grabs the surplus, rent seeking becomes profitable.

People use resources in pursuit of rents, and the bigger the rents, the more resources get used in pursuing them. With free entry into rent seeking, the long-run equilibrium outcome is that rent seekers use up the entire producer surplus.

REVIEW QUIZ

1 What is price discrimination and how is it used to increase a monopoly's profit?
2 Explain how consumer surplus changes when a monopoly price discriminates.
3 Explain how consumer surplus, economic profit, and output change when a monopoly perfectly price discriminates.
4 What are some of the ways that real-world airlines use to price discriminate?

You've seen that monopoly is profitable for the monopolist but costly for other people. It results in inefficiency. Because of these features of monopoly, it is subject to policy debate and regulation. We'll now study the key monopoly policy issues.

Monopoly Policy Issues

MONOPOLY LOOKS BAD WHEN WE COMPARE IT with competition. Monopoly is inefficient, and it captures consumer surplus and converts it into producer surplus or pure waste in the form of rent-seeking costs. If monopoly is so bad, why do we put up with it? Why don't we have laws that crack down on monopoly so hard that it never rears its head? We do indeed have laws that limit monopoly power and regulate the prices that monopolies are permitted to charge. But monopoly also brings some benefits. We begin this review of monopoly policy issues by looking at the benefits of monopoly. We then look at monopoly regulation.

Gains from Monopoly

The main reason why monopoly exists is that it has potential advantages over a competitive alternative. These advantages arise from

■ Incentives to innovation
■ Economies of scale and economies of scope

Incentives to Innovation Invention leads to a wave of innovation as new knowledge is applied to the production process. Innovation may take the form of developing a new product or a lower-cost way of making an existing product. Controversy has raged over whether large firms with market power or small competitive firms lacking such market power are the most innovative. It is clear that some temporary market power arises from innovation. A firm that develops a new product or process and patents it obtains an exclusive right to that product or process for the term of the patent.

But does the granting of a monopoly, even a temporary one, to an innovator increase the pace of innovation? One line of reasoning suggests that it does. Without protection, an innovator is not able to enjoy the profits from innovation for very long. Thus the incentive to innovate is weakened. A contrary argument is that monopolies can afford to be lazy while competitive firms cannot. Competitive firms must strive to innovate and cut costs even though they know that they cannot hang onto the benefits of their innovation for long. But that knowledge spurs them on to greater and faster innovation.

The evidence on whether monopoly leads to greater innovation than competition is mixed. Large firms do more research and development than do small firms. But research and development are inputs into the process of innovation. What matters is not input but output. Two measures of the output of research and development are the number of patents and the rate of productivity growth. On these measures, it is not clear that bigger is better. But as a new process or product spreads through an industry, the large firms adopt the new process or product more quickly than do small firms. So large firms help to speed the process of diffusion of technological change.

Economies of Scale and Scope Economies of scale and economies of scope can lead to natural monopoly. And as you saw at the beginning of this chapter, in a natural monopoly, a single firm can produce at a lower average cost than a number of firms can.

A firm experiences *economies of scale* when an increase in its output of a good or service brings a decrease in the average total cost of producing it (see Chapter 10, pp. 226–227). A firm experiences *economies of scope* when an increase in the *range of goods produced* brings a decrease in average total cost (see Chapter 9, p. 207). Economies of scope occur when different goods can share specialized (and usually costly) capital resources. For example, McDonald's can produce both hamburgers and french fries at a lower average total cost than can two separate firms — a burger firm and a french fries firm — because at McDonald's, hamburgers and french fries share the use of specialized food storage and preparation facilities. A firm that produces a wide range of products can hire specialist computer programmers, designers, and marketing experts whose skills can be used across the product range, thereby spreading their costs and lowering the average total cost of production of each of the goods.

There are many examples in which a combination of economies of scale and economies of scope arise, but not all of them lead to monopoly. Some examples are the brewing of beer, the manufacture of refrigerators and other household appliances, the manufacture of pharmaceuticals, and the refining of petroleum.

Examples of industries in which economies of scale are so significant that they lead to a natural monopoly are becoming rare. Public utilities such as gas, electric power, local telephone service, and garbage collection once were natural monopolies. But technological advances now enable us to separate the *production* of electric power or natural gas from its *distribution*. The provision of water, though, remains a natural monopoly.

A large-scale firm that has control over supply and can influence price — and therefore behaves like the monopoly firm that you've studied in this chapter — can reap these economies of scale and scope. Small, competitive firms cannot. Consequently, there are situations in which the comparison of monopoly and competition that we made earlier in this chapter is not valid. Recall that we imagined the takeover of a large number of competitive firms by a monopoly firm. But we also assumed that the monopoly would use exactly the same technology as the small firms and have the same costs. If one large firm can reap economies of scale and scope, its marginal cost curve will lie below the supply curve of a competitive industry made up of many small firms. It is possible for such economies of scale and scope to be so large as to result in a larger output and lower price under monopoly than a competitive industry would achieve.

Where significant economies of scale and scope exist, it is usually worth putting up with monopoly and regulating its price.

Regulating Natural Monopoly

Where demand and cost conditions create a natural monopoly, a federal, state, or local government agency usually steps in to regulate the prices of the monopoly. By regulating a monopoly, some of the worst aspects of monopoly can be avoided or at least moderated. Let's look at monopoly price regulation.

Figure 12.11 shows the demand curve *D*, the marginal revenue curve *MR*, the long-run average cost curve *ATC*, and the marginal cost curve *MC* for a natural gas distribution company that is a natural monopoly.

The firm's marginal cost is constant at 10 cents per cubic foot. But average total cost decreases as output increases. The reason is that the natural gas company has a large investment in pipelines and so has high fixed costs. These fixed costs are part of the company's average total cost and so appear in the *ATC* curve. The average total cost curve slopes downward because as the number of cubic feet sold increases, the fixed cost is spread over a larger number of units. (If you need to refresh your memory on how the average total cost curve is calculated, look back at Chapter 10, pp. 220–221.)

This one firm can supply the entire market at a lower cost than two firms can because average total cost is falling even when the entire market is supplied. (Refer back to p. 259 if you need a quick refresher on natural monopoly.)

Profit Maximization First, suppose the natural gas company is not regulated and instead maximizes profit. Figure 12.11 shows the outcome. The company produces 2 million cubic feet a day, the quantity at which marginal cost equals marginal revenue. It prices this gas at 20 cents a cubic foot and makes an economic profit of 2 cents a cubic foot, or $40,000 a day.

This outcome is fine for the gas company, but it is inefficient. Gas costs 20 cent a cubic foot when its marginal cost is only 10 cents a cubic foot. Also, the gas company is making a big profit. What can regulation do to improve this outcome?

The Efficient Regulation If the monopoly regulator wants to achieve an efficient use of resources, it must require the gas monopoly to produce the quantity of gas that brings marginal benefit into equality with marginal cost. Marginal benefit is what the consumer is willing to pay and is shown by the demand curve. Marginal cost is shown by the firm's marginal cost curve. You can see in Fig. 12.11 that this outcome occurs if the price is regulated at 10 cents per cubic foot and if 4 million cubic feet per day are produced. The regulation that produces this outcome is called a marginal cost pricing rule. A **marginal cost pricing rule** sets price equal to marginal cost. It maximizes total surplus in the regulated industry. In this example, that surplus is all consumer surplus and it equals the area of the triangle beneath the demand curve and above the marginal cost curve.

The marginal cost pricing rule is efficient. But it leaves the natural monopoly incurring an economic loss. Because average total cost is falling as output increases, marginal cost is below average total cost. And because price equals marginal cost, price is below average total cost. Average total cost minus price is the loss per unit produced. It's pretty obvious that a natural gas company that is required to use a marginal cost pricing rule will not stay in business for long. How can a company cover its costs and, at the same time, obey a marginal cost pricing rule?

One possibility is price discrimination. The company might charge a higher price to some customers but marginal cost to the customers who pay least. Another possibility is to use a two-part price (called a two-part tariff). For example, the gas company might

FIGURE 12.11   Regulating a Natural Monopoly

A natural monopoly is an industry in which average total cost is falling even when the entire market demand is satisfied. A natural gas producer faces the demand curve D. The firm's marginal cost is constant at 10 cents per cubic foot, as shown by the curve labeled MC. Fixed costs are large, and the average total cost curve, which includes average fixed cost, is shown as ATC. A marginal cost pricing rule sets the price at 10 cents per cubic foot. The monopoly produces 4 million cubic feet per day and incurs an economic loss. An average cost pricing rule sets the price at 15 cents per cubic foot. The monopoly produces 3 million cubic feet per day and makes normal profit.

charge a monthly fixed fee that covers its fixed cost and then charge for gas consumed at marginal cost.

But a natural monopoly cannot always cover its costs in these ways. If a natural monopoly cannot cover its total cost from its customers, and if the government wants it to follow a marginal cost pricing rule, the government must give the firm a subsidy. In such a case, the government raises the revenue for the subsidy by taxing some other activity. But as we saw in Chapter 6, taxes themselves generate deadweight loss. Thus the deadweight loss resulting from additional taxes must be subtracted from the efficiency gained by forcing the natural monopoly to adopt a marginal cost pricing rule.

Average Cost Pricing Regulators almost never impose efficient pricing because of its consequences for the firm's profit. Instead, they compromise by permitting the firm to cover its costs and to earn a normal profit. Recall that normal profit is a cost of production and we include it along with the firm's other fixed costs in the average total cost curve. So pricing to cover cost including normal profit means setting price equal to average total cost — called an **average cost pricing rule**.

Figure 12.11 shows the average cost pricing outcome. The natural gas company charges 15 cents a cubic foot and sells 3 million cubic feet per day. This outcome is better for consumers than the unregulated profit-maximizing outcome. The price is 5 cents a cubic foot lower, and the quantity consumed is 1 million cubic feet per day more. And the outcome is better for the producer than the marginal cost pricing rule outcome. The firm earns normal profit. The outcome is inefficient but less so than the unregulated profit-maximizing outcome.

REVIEW QUIZ

1 What are the two main reasons why monopoly is worth tolerating?
2 Can you provide some examples of economies of scale and economies of scope?
3 Why might the incentive to innovate be greater for a monopoly than for a small competitive firm?
4 What is the price that achieves an efficient outcome for a regulated monopoly? And what is the problem with this price?
5 Compare the consumer surplus, producer surplus, and deadweight loss that arise from average cost pricing with those that arise from profit-maximization pricing and marginal cost pricing.

◆ You've now have studied perfect competition and monopoly. *Reading Between the Lines* on pp. 274–275 looks at market power in the market for PC operating systems. In the next chapter, we study markets that lie between the extremes of perfect competition and monopoly and that blend elements of the two.

Software Monopoly

©RALPH NADER, DECEMBER 15, 1999

Consumer Harm in the Microsoft Case

Windows is too expensive. The price for Microsoft Windows depends upon how you buy it. A license for Windows is often bundled with a new PC. That doesn't mean it is free — only that the OEM has paid for the license. ...

Microsoft charges consumers a list price of $109 for an upgrade of Windows 98, which is discounted by retailers to $89 — but to get this price you must already own Windows 95, so it is like a maintenance fee. The list price for a new version of Windows 98 is $209. Yahoo.com sells Windows 98 at a discount for $181.92, nearly half the price of buying a new low end PC, and more than three times the $49.99 price for the well reviewed BeOS. BeOS is a tech-

nologically superior operating system that suffers from a paucity of third party applications, illustrating the significance of the consumer lock-in with Windows.

In addition, Microsoft is steadily tightening the conditions on licenses. Many OEM licenses for Windows are tied to a single machine, and cannot be sold or transferred to another machine, even by the original owner. Business users are facing restrictions on the use of concurrent licenses, requiring them to purchase more copies than before. And for most models of PCs that consumers buy, the OEM has to purchase the license, even if the end user doesn't want the software....

Essence of the Story

■ The price of Microsoft Windows depends upon how you buy it.

■ If you buy Windows installed on a new PC, the price is the license fee paid by the PC maker (called an OEM or original equipment manufacturer).

■ Microsoft is tightening the conditions on OEM licenses by (1) forcing computer makers to pay for a copy of Windows on every machine sold, even if the buyer doesn't want Windows and (2) preventing the transfer of a copy of Windows from one machine to another.

■ If you buy Windows and install it yourself, you pay a higher price.

■ BeOS, a technologically superior operating system to Windows, costs much less than Windows, but few applications have been written for BeOS.

Economic Analysis

■ The market for the Microsoft Windows operating system is not strictly a monopoly.

■ Competing operating systems exist, and there is no legal or natural barrier that prevents other firms from trying to compete with Microsoft.

■ But the existence of a large number of applications that run only on Windows makes it hard for other firms to compete with Microsoft.

■ The high cost and high risk of developing an alternative operating system that supports a large range of applications is a barrier to the entry of new competitors.

■ Operating behind this effective barrier to entry, Microsoft has market power and can price its products like a monopoly.

■ And because it is illegal to resell its software, Microsoft can price discriminate between individual buyers (illustrated in Figure 1) and PC makers (illustrated in Figure 2).

■ In both figures, the demand curve for Windows is *D* and the marginal revenue curve is *MR*.

■ In Figure 1, when Microsoft sells a copy of Windows to an individual user, its marginal cost includes the cost of the CDs, packaging, warehousing, and distribution. In the figure, this marginal cost is slightly increasing.

■ In Figure 2, when Microsoft sells a copy of Windows through a PC maker, its marginal cost is the cost of the CDs only — just a dollar or so — and is constant.

■ In both markets (both figures), Microsoft maximizes profit by producing the quantity at which marginal revenue equals marginal cost and charging the highest price the market will pay for that quantity.

■ The quantity produced is less than the efficient quantity at which marginal cost equals price (and marginal benefit).

You're The Voter

■ How would you suggest that the federal government regulate the market for PC operating systems to achieve an efficient quantity of software?

Figure 1 Windows sold directly to users

Figure 2 Windows sold to PC makers

SUMMARY

KEY POINTS

Market Power (pp. 258–259)

- A monopoly is an industry with a single supplier of a good or service that has no close substitutes and in which barriers to entry prevent competition.
- Barriers to entry may be legal (public franchise, license, patent, copyright, firm owns control of a resource) or natural (created by economies of scale).
- A monopoly might be able to price discriminate when there is no resale possibility.
- Where resale is possible, a firm charges one price.

A Single-Price Monopoly's Output and Price Decision (pp. 260–263)

- A monopoly's demand curve is the market demand curve and a single-price monopoly's marginal revenue is less than price.
- A monopoly maximizes profit by producing the output at which marginal revenue equals marginal cost and by charging the maximum price that consumers are willing to pay for that output.

Single-Price Monopoly and Competition Compared (pp. 264–267)

- A single-price monopoly charges a higher price and produces a smaller quantity than a perfectly competitive industry.
- A single-price monopoly restricts output and creates a deadweight loss.
- Monopoly imposes costs that equal its deadweight loss plus the cost of the resources devoted to rent seeking.

Price Discrimination (pp. 267–270)

- Price discrimination is an attempt by the monopoly to convert consumer surplus into economic profit.
- Perfect price discrimination extracts the entire consumer surplus. Such a monopoly charges a different price for each unit sold and obtains the maximum price that each consumer is willing to pay for each unit bought.

- With perfect price discrimination, the monopoly produces the same output as would a perfectly competitive industry.
- Rent seeking with perfect price discrimination might eliminate the entire consumer surplus and producer surplus.

Monopoly Policy Issues (pp. 271–273)

- A monopoly with large economies of scale and economies of scope can produce a larger quantity at a lower price than a competitive industry can achieve, and monopoly might be more innovative than small competitive firms.
- Efficient regulation requires a monopoly to charge a price equal to marginal cost, but for a natural monopoly, such a price is less than average total cost.
- Average cost pricing is a compromise pricing rule that covers a firm's costs and provides a normal profit but is not efficient. It is more efficient than unregulated profit maximization.

KEY FIGURES AND TABLE

KEY TERMS

PROBLEMS

*1. Minnie's Mineral Springs, a single-price monopoly, faces the demand schedule:

Price (dollars per bottle)	Quantity demanded (bottles per hour)
10	0
8	1
6	2
4	3
2	4
0	5

a. Calculate Minnie's total revenue schedule.
b. Calculate its marginal revenue schedule.

2. Burma Ruby Mines, a single-price monopoly, faces the demand schedule:

Price (dollars per ruby)	Quantity demanded (rubies per day)
1,100	0
900	1
700	2
500	3
300	4

a. Calculate Burma's total revenue schedule.
b. Calculate its marginal revenue schedule.

*3. Minnie's Mineral Springs in problem 1 has the following total cost:

Quantity produced (bottles per hour)	Total cost (dollars)
0	1
1	3
2	7
3	13
4	21
5	31

a. Calculate the marginal cost of producing each output in the table.
b. Calculate the profit-maximizing output and price.
c. Calculate the economic profit.
d. Does Minnie's use resources efficiently? Explain your answer.

4. Burma's Ruby Mines in problem 2 has the following total cost:

Quantity produced (rubies per day)	Total cost (dollars)
1	1,220
2	1,300
3	1,400
4	1,520

a. Calculate the marginal cost of producing each quantity listed in the table.
b. Calculate the profit-maximizing output and price.
c. Calculate the economic profit.
d. Does Burma's Ruby Mines use its resources efficiently? Explain your answer.

*5. The figure illustrates the situation facing the publisher of the only newspaper containing local news in an isolated community.

a. What are the profit-maximizing quantity and price?
b. What is the publisher's daily total revenue?
c. At the price charged, is the demand for newspapers elastic or inelastic? Why?
d. What are consumer surplus and deadweight loss? Mark each on your graph.
e. Might the newspaper try to price discriminate? Explain why or why not.

6. The figure illustrates the situation facing the only coffee shop an isolated community.

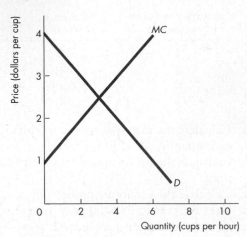

a. What are the profit-maximizing quantity of coffee and price?
b. On the graph mark the coffee shop's profit.
c. What is consumer surplus and deadweight loss?
d. What is the efficient quantity? Explain.
e. Might the coffee shop try to price discriminate? Explain why or why not.

*7. The figure shows the situation facing a natural monopoly that cannot price discriminate.

What quantity will be produced and what will be the deadweight loss if the firm is

a. An unregulated profit maximizer?
b. Regulated to earn only normal profit?
c. Regulated to be efficient?

8. If in problem 7 marginal cost doubles, what now are your answers?

CRITICAL THINKING

1. Study *Reading Between the Lines* on pp. 274–275 and then answer the following questions.
    a. Is it correct to call Microsoft a monopoly?
    b. How would the arrival of a viable alternative operating system to Windows affect Microsoft?
    c. How would you regulate the software industry to ensure that resources are used efficiently?
    d. "Anyone is free to buy stock in Microsoft, so everyone is free to share in Microsoft's economic profit, and the bigger that economic profit, the better for all." Evaluate this statement.

WEB EXERCISES

1. Use the links on the Parkin Web site to find the statement by Ralph Nader about Microsoft.
    a. What are Ralph Nader's main claims about Microsoft?
    b. Do you agree with Ralph Nader? Why or why not?
    c. If some other operating systems are better than Windows, why don't they take off?
    d. Does Ralph Nader identify the main costs to the consumer of Microsoft's practices? Explain why or why not.
2. Use the links on the Parkin Web site to study the market for computer chips.
    a. Is it correct to call Intel a monopoly? Why or why not?
    b. How does Intel try to raise barriers to entry in this market?
3. Use the links on the Parkin Web site to study the story about Heartland Towing of Omaha Nebraska.
    a. Is Heartland Towing a monopoly? Why or why not?
    b. What economic phenomenon does this news article illustrate?
    c. Do you think Heartland Towing ends up earning an economic profit? Why or why not?

MONOPOLISTIC COMPETITION AND OLIGOPOLY

CHAPTER 13

PC War Games

Since the fall of 2000, our newspapers and magazines have been stuffed with advertising by the big-name PC makers announcing yet lower prices and yet better products and value for money. How do firms like PC makers that are locked in fierce competition with each other set their prices, pick their product lines, and choose the quantities to produce? How are the profits of such firms affected by the actions of other firms? ◆ Until recently, only one firm made the chips that drive IBM and compatible PCs: Intel Corporation. During 1994, the prices of powerful personal computers based on Intel's fast Pentium chips nose-dived. The reason: Intel suddenly faced competition from new chip producers such as Advanced Micro Devices, Inc. and Cyrix Corporation. The price of Intel's Pentium processor, set at more than $1,000 when it was launched in 1993, fell to less than $200 by 2001, and the price of a Pentium-based computer fell to less than $1,000. How did competition among a small number of chip makers bring such a rapid fall in the price of chips and computers?

◼ The theories of monopoly and perfect competition do not predict the kind of behavior that we've just described. There are no newspaper ads, best brands, or price wars in perfect competition because each firm produces an identical product and is a price taker. And there are none in monopoly because each monopoly firm has the entire market to itself. To understand advertising and price wars, we need the richer models that are explained in this chapter.

After studying this chapter, you will be able to

- Define and identify monopolistic competition
- Explain how output and price are determined in a monopolistically competitive industry
- Explain why advertising costs are high in a monopolistically competitive industry
- Explain why the price might be sticky in oligopoly
- Explain how price and output are determined when there is one dominant firm and several smaller firms in a market
- Use game theory to make predictions about price wars and competition among a small number of firms

Monopolistic Competition

YOU HAVE STUDIED TWO TYPES OF MARKET structure: perfect competition and monopoly. In perfect competition, a large number of firms produce identical goods, there are no barriers to entry, and each firm is a price taker. In the long run, there is no economic profit. In monopoly, a single firm is protected from competition by barriers to entry and can make an economic profit, even in the long run.

Many real-world markets are competitive but not as fiercely so as perfect competition because firms in these markets possess some power to set their prices as monopolies do. We call this type of market *monopolistic competition*.

Monopolistic competition is a market structure in which

■ A large number of firms compete.
■ Each firm produces a differentiated product.
■ Firms compete on product quality, price, and marketing.
■ Firms are free to enter and exit.

Large Number of Firms

In monopolistic competition, as in perfect competition, the industry consists of a large number of firms. The presence of a large number of firms has three implications for the firms in the industry.

Small Market Share In monopolistic competition, each firm supplies a small part of the total industry output. Consequently, each firm has only limited power to influence the price of its product. Each firm's price can deviate from the average price of other firms by a relatively small amount.

Ignore Other Firms A firm in monopolistic competition must be sensitive to the average market price of the product. But it does not pay attention to any one individual competitor. Because all the firms are relatively small, no one firm can dictate market conditions, and so no one firm's actions directly affect the actions of the other firms.

Collusion Impossible Firms in monopolistic competition would like to be able to conspire to fix a higher price — called collusion. But because there are many firms, collusion is not possible.

Product Differentiation

A firm practices **product differentiation** if it makes a product that is slightly different from the products of competing firms. A differentiated product is one that is a close substitute but not a perfect substitute for the products of the other firms. Some people will pay more for one variety of the product, so when its price rises, the quantity demanded falls but it does not (necessarily) fall to zero. For example, Adidas, Asics, Diadora, Etonic, Fila, New Balance, Nike, Puma, and Reebok all make differentiated running shoes. Other things remaining the same, if the price of Adidas running shoes rises and the prices of the other shoes remain constant, Adidas sells fewer shoes and the other producers sell more. But Adidas shoes don't disappear unless the price rises by a large enough amount.

Competing on Quality, Price, and Marketing

Product differentiation enables a firm to compete with other firms in three areas: product quality, price, and marketing.

Quality The quality of a product is the physical attributes that make it different from the products of other firms. Quality includes design, reliability, the service provided to the buyer, and the buyer's ease of access to the product. Quality lies on a spectrum that runs from high to low. Some firms — Dell Computers is an example — offer high-quality products. They are well designed and reliable, and the customer receives quick and efficient service. Other firms offer a lower-quality product that is less well designed, that might not work perfectly, and that the buyer must travel some distance to obtain.

Price Because of product differentiation, a firm in monopolistic competition faces a downward-sloping demand curve. So, like a monopoly, the firm can set both its price and its output. But there is a tradeoff between the product's quality and price. A firm that makes a high-quality product can charge a higher price than a firm that makes a low-quality product can.

Marketing Because of product differentiation, a firm in monopolistic competition must market its product. Marketing takes two main forms: advertising and packaging. A firm that produces a high-quality product wants to sell it for a suitably high price. To be able to do so, it must advertise and package its product in a way that convinces buyers that they are getting the higher quality for which they are paying a higher price. For example, pharmaceutical companies advertise and package their brand-name drugs to persuade buyers that these items are superior to the lower-priced generic alternatives. Similarly, a low-quality producer uses advertising and packaging to persuade buyers that although the quality is low, the low price more than compensates for this fact.

Entry and Exit

In monopolistic competition, there is free entry and free exit. Consequently, a firm cannot make an economic profit in the long run. When firms make an economic profit, new firms enter the industry. This entry lowers prices and eventually eliminates economic profit. When firms incur economic losses, some firms leave the industry. This exit increases prices and profits and eventually eliminates the economic loss. In long-run equilibrium, firms neither enter nor leave the industry and the firms in the industry make zero economic profit.

Examples of Monopolistic Competition

Figure 13.1 shows 10 industries that are good examples of monopolistic competition. These industries have a large number of firms (shown in parentheses after the name of the industry). In the most concentrated of these industries, canned foods, the largest 4 firms produce only 25 percent of the industry's total sales and the largest 20 firms produce only 65 percent of total sales. The number on the right is the Herfindahl-Hirschman Index. Gas stations, food stores, dry cleaners, and haircutters also all operate in monopolistic competition.

REVIEW QUIZ

1 What are the distinguishing characteristics of monopolistic competition?
2 How do firms in monopolistic competition compete?
3 In addition to the examples in Fig. 13.1, provide some examples of industries near your school that operate in monopolistic competition.

FIGURE 13.1   Examples of Monopolistic Competition

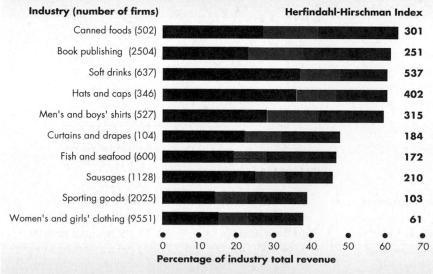

Industry (number of firms) / Herfindahl-Hirschman Index

Industry (number of firms)	HHI
Canned foods (502)	301
Book publishing (2504)	251
Soft drinks (637)	537
Hats and caps (346)	402
Men's and boys' shirts (527)	315
Curtains and drapes (104)	184
Fish and seafood (600)	172
Sausages (1128)	210
Sporting goods (2025)	103
Women's and girls' clothing (9551)	61

Percentage of industry total revenue (0 10 20 30 40 50 60 70)

These industries operate in monopolistic competition. The number of firms in the industry is shown in parentheses after the name of the industry. The red bars show the percentage of industry sales by the largest 4 firms. The green bars show the percentage of industry sales by the next 4 largest firms, and the blue bars show the percentage of industry sales by the next 12 largest firms. So the entire length of the red, green, and blue bar combined shows the percentage of industry sales by the largest 20 firms. The Herfindahl-Hirschman Index is shown on the right.

Source: U.S. Census Bureau.

Output and Price in Monopolistic Competition

WE ARE NOW GOING TO LEARN HOW OUTPUT and price are determined in monopolistic competition. First, we will suppose that the firm has already decided on the quality of its product and on its marketing program. For a given product and a given amount of marketing activity, the firm faces given costs and market conditions.

Figure 13.2 shows how a firm in monopolistic competition determines its price and output. Part (a) deals with the short run, and part (b) deals with the long run. We'll concentrate first on the short run.

Short Run: Economic Profit

The demand curve *D* shows the demand for the firm's product. It is the demand curve for Nautica jackets, not jackets in general. The curve labeled *MR* is the marginal revenue curve associated with the demand curve. It is derived just like the marginal revenue curve of a single-price monopoly that you studied in Chapter 12. The figure also shows the firm's average total cost (*ATC*) and marginal cost (*MC*). These curves are similar to the cost curves that you first encountered in Chapter 10.

Nautica maximizes profit by producing the output at which marginal revenue equals marginal cost. In Fig. 13.2, the output that maximizes Nautica's profit is 150 jackets a day. Nautica charges the maximum price that buyers are willing to pay for this quantity. The demand curve tells us what that maximum price is. Nautica charges $190 a jacket. When Nautica produces 150 jackets a day, its average total cost is $140 a jacket, so Nautica makes a short-run economic profit of $7,500 a day ($50 a jacket multiplied by 150 jackets a day). The blue rectangle shows this economic profit.

FIGURE 13.2   Output and Price in Monopolistic Competition

(a) Short run

(b) Long run

Part (a) shows the short-run outcome. Profit is maximized by producing 150 jackets per day and selling them for a price of $190 per jacket. Average total cost is $140 per jacket, and the firm makes an economic profit (the blue rectangle) of $7,500 a day ($50 per jacket multiplied by 150 jackets).

Economic profit encourages new entrants in the long run, and part (b) shows the long-run outcome. The entry of new firms decreases each firm's demand and shifts the demand curve and marginal revenue curve leftward. When the demand curve has shifted to *D*', the marginal revenue curve is *MR*' and the firm is in long-run equilibrium. The output that maximizes profit is 50 jackets a day, and the price is $145 per jacket. Average total cost is also $145 per jacket, so economic profit is zero.

So far, the firm in monopolistic competition looks just like a single-price monopoly. It produces the quantity at which marginal revenue equals marginal cost and then charges the highest price that buyers are willing to pay for that quantity, determined by the demand curve. The key difference between monopoly and monopolistic competition lies in what happens next.

Long Run: Zero Economic Profit

There is no restriction on entry in monopolistic competition, so economic profit attracts new entrants. As firms enter, each firm has a smaller market share and smaller demand for its product, which means that each firm's demand curve and marginal revenue curve shift leftward. Firms maximize short-run profit by producing the quantity at which marginal revenue equals marginal cost and by charging the highest price that buyers are willing to pay for this quantity. But as the demand for each firm's output decreases, the profit-maximizing quantity and price fall.

Figure 13.2(b) shows the long-run equilibrium. The demand curve for Nautica jackets has shifted leftward to D', and Nautica's marginal revenue curve has shifted leftward to MR'. Nautica produces 50 jackets a day and sells them at a price of $145 each. Nautica's average total cost is also $145 a jacket. So Nautica is making zero economic profit.

When all firms earn zero economic profit, there is no incentive for new firms to enter the industry.

If demand is so low relative to costs that firms are incurring economic losses, exit will occur. As firms leave an industry, the demand for the remaining firms' products increases and their demand curves shift rightward. The exit process ends when all the firms are making zero economic profit.

Monopolistic Competition and Efficiency

When we studied a perfectly competitive industry, we discovered that in some circumstances, such an industry allocates resources efficiently. A key feature of efficiency is that marginal benefit equals marginal cost. Price measures marginal benefit, so efficiency requires price to equal marginal cost. When we studied monopoly, we discovered that such a firm creates an inefficient use of resources because it restricts output to a level at which price exceeds marginal cost. In such

a situation, marginal benefit exceeds marginal cost and production is less than its efficient level.

Monopolistic competition shares this feature of monopoly. Even though there is zero economic profit in long-run equilibrium, the monopolistically competitive industry produces an output at which price equals average total cost but exceeds marginal cost. This outcome means that firms in monopolistic competition always have excess capacity in long-run equilibrium.

Excess Capacity A firm's **capacity output** is the output at which average total cost is a minimum — the output at the bottom of the U-shaped ATC curve. This output is 100 jackets a day in Fig. 13.3. Firms in monopolistic competition always have *excess capacity* in the long run. In Fig. 13.3, Nautica produces 50 jackets a day and has excess capacity of 50 jackets a day. That is, Nautica produces a smaller output than

FIGURE 13.3   Excess Capacity

In long-run equilibrium, entry decreases demand to the point at which the firm makes zero economic profit. Nautica produces 50 jackets a day. A firm's capacity output is the output at which average total cost is a minimum. Nautica's capacity output is 100 jackets a day. Because the demand curve in monopolistic competition slopes downward, the profit-maximizing output in the long-run equilibrium is always less than capacity output. In long-run equilibrium, the firm operates with excess capacity.

that which minimizes average total cost. Consequently, the consumer pays a price that exceeds minimum average total cost. This result arises from the fact that Nautica faces a downward-sloping demand curve. The demand curve slopes downward because of product differentiation, so product differentiation creates excess capacity.

You can see the excess capacity in monopolistic competition all around you. Family restaurants (except for the truly outstanding ones) almost always have some empty tables. You can always get a pizza delivered in less than 30 minutes. It is rare that every pump at a gas station is in use with customers waiting in line. There is always an abundance of realtors ready to help find or sell a home. These industries are examples of monopolistic competition. The firms have excess capacity. They could sell more by cutting their prices, but they would then incur losses.

Because in monopolistic competition, price exceeds marginal cost, this market structure, like monopoly, is inefficient. The marginal cost of producing one more unit of output is less than the marginal benefit to the consumer, determined by the price the consumer is willing to pay. But the inefficiency of monopolistic competition arises from product differentiation — from product variety. Consumers value variety, but it is achievable only if firms make differentiated products. So the loss in efficiency that occurs in monopolistic competition must be weighed against the gain of greater product variety.

REVIEW QUIZ

1 How does a firm in monopolistic competition decide how much to produce and at what price to offer its product for sale?
2 Why can a firm in monopolistic competition earn an economic profit only in the short run?
3 Is monopolistic competition efficient?
4 Why do firms in monopolistic competition operate with excess capacity?

You've seen how the firm in monopolistic competition determines its output and price in the short run and the long run when it produces a given product and undertakes a *given* marketing effort. But how does the firm choose its product quality and marketing effort? We'll now study these decisions.

Product Development and Marketing

WHEN WE STUDIED A FIRM'S OUTPUT AND PRICE decision, we supposed that it had already made its product and marketing decisions. We're now going to study these decisions and the impact they have on the firm's output, price, and economic profit.

Innovation and Product Development

To enjoy economic profits, firms in monopolistic competition must be in a state of continuous product development. The reason is that wherever economic profits are earned, imitators emerge and set up business. So to maintain its economic profit, a firm must seek out new products that will provide it with a competitive edge, even if only temporarily. A firm that manages to introduce a new and differentiated variety will temporarily increase the demand for its product and will be able to increase its price temporarily. The firm will make an economic profit. Eventually, new firms that make close substitutes for the new product will enter and compete away the economic profit arising from this initial advantage. So to restore economic profit, the firm must again innovate.

The decision to innovate is based on the same type of profit-maximizing calculation that you've already studied. Innovation and product development are costly activities, but they also bring in additional revenues. The firm must balance the cost and benefit at the margin. At a low level of product development, the marginal revenue from a better product exceeds the marginal cost. When the marginal dollar of product development expenditure brings in a dollar of revenue, the firm is spending the profit-maximizing amount on product development.

For example, when Eidos Interactive released Tomb Raider: Lost Artifact, it was probably not the best game that Eidos could have created. Rather, it was the game that balanced the marginal benefit and willingness of the consumer to pay for further game enhancements against the marginal cost of these enhancements.

Efficiency and Product Innovation Is product innovation an efficient activity? Does it benefit the consumer? There are two views about these questions. One view is that monopolistic competition brings to market many improved products that bring great benefits to the consumer. Clothing, kitchen and other household appliances, computers, computer programs, cars, and many other products keep getting better every year, and the consumer benefits from these improved products.

But many so-called improvements amount to little more than changing the appearance of a product. And sometimes, the improvement is restricted to a different look in the packaging. In these cases, there is little objective benefit to the consumer.

But regardless of whether a product improvement is real or imagined, its value to the consumer is its marginal benefit, which equals the amount the consumer is willing to pay for the improvement. Whether the amount of product improvement is efficient or not depends on the marginal cost of the improvement. Only if the producers' marginal cost of product improvement equals the consumers' marginal benefit, do we get the efficient amount of product innovation.

Marketing

Some product differentiation is achieved by designing and developing products that are actually different from those of the other firms. But firms also attempt to create a consumer perception of product differentiation even when actual differences are small. Advertising and packaging are the principal means used by firms to achieve this end. An American Express card is a different product from a Visa card. But the actual differences are not the main ones that American Express emphasizes in its marketing. The deeper message is that if you use an American Express card, you are like Tiger Woods (or some other high-profile successful person).

Marketing Expenditures Firms in monopolistic competition incur huge costs to ensure that buyers appreciate and value the differences between their own products and those of their competitors. So a large proportion of the prices that we pay cover the cost of selling a good. And this proportion is increasing. The cost of advertising in newspapers, in magazines, and on radio and television is the main selling cost. But it is not the only one. Selling costs include the cost of shopping malls that look like movie sets, glossy catalogs and brochures, and the salaries, airfares, and hotel bills of salespeople.

The total scale of selling costs is hard to estimate, but some components can be measured. A survey conducted by a commercial agency suggests that for cleaning supplies and toys, around 15 percent of the price of an item is spent on advertising. Figure 13.4 shows some estimates for other industries.

For the U.S. economy as a whole, there are some 20,000 advertising agencies that employ more than 200,000 people and have sales of $45 billion. But these numbers are only part of the total cost of advertising because firms have their own internal advertising departments, the cost of which can only be guessed at.

Marketing efforts affect a firm's profits in two ways: They increase costs, and if they are effective, they change demand. Let's look at these effects.

Selling Costs and Total Costs Selling costs such as advertising expenditures increase the costs of a monopolistically competitive firm above those of a competitive firm or a monopoly. Advertising costs and other selling costs are fixed costs. They do not vary as total output varies. So, just like fixed production costs, advertising costs per unit decrease as production increases.

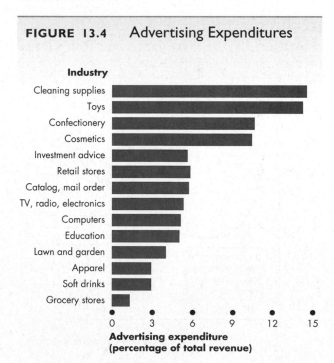

FIGURE 13.4   Advertising Expenditures

Advertising expenditures are a large part of total revenue received by producers of cleaning supplies, toys, confectionery, and cosmetics.

Source: From Schoenfeld & Associates, Lincolnwood, IL. Reported at www.toolkit.cch.com/text/p03_7006.asp. Reported at CCH Business Owner's Toolkit.

Figure 13.5 shows how selling costs and advertising expenditures change a firm's average total cost. The blue curve shows the average total cost of production. The red curve shows the firm's average total cost of production plus advertising. The height of the red area between the two curves shows the average fixed cost of advertising. The *total* cost of advertising is fixed. But the *average* cost of advertising decreases as output increases.

The figure shows that if advertising increases the quantity sold by a large enough amount, it can lower average total cost. For example, if the quantity sold increases from 25 jackets a day with no advertising to 130 jackets a day with advertising, average total cost falls from $170 a jacket to $160 a jacket. The reason is that although the *total* fixed cost has increased, the greater fixed cost is spread over a greater output, so average total cost decreases.

Selling Costs and Demand Advertising and other selling efforts change the demand for a firm's product. But does demand increase or decrease? The most

natural answer is that advertising increases demand. By informing people about the quality of its products or by persuading people to switch from the products of other firms, a firm that advertises expects to increase the demand for its own products.

But all firms in monopolistic competition advertise. If advertising enables a firm to survive, it might increase the number of firms. To the extent that it increases the number of firms, advertising *decreases* the demand faced by any one firm.

Efficiency: The Bottom Line Selling costs that provide consumers with information that they value serve a useful purpose to the consumer and enable a better product choice to be made. But the opportunity cost of the additional services and information must be weighed against the gain to the consumer.

The bottom line on the question of efficiency of monopolistic competition is ambiguous. In some cases, the gains from extra product variety unquestionably offset the selling costs and the extra cost arising from excess capacity. The tremendous varieties of books and magazines, clothing, food, and drinks are examples of such gains. It is less easy to see the gains from being able to buy brand-name drugs that have a chemical composition identical to that of a generic alternative. But some people do willingly pay more for the brand-name alternative.

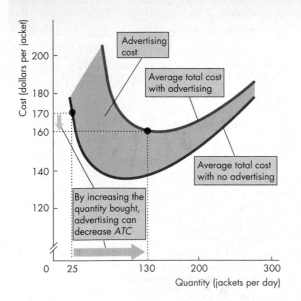

FIGURE 13.5   Selling Costs and Total Cost

Selling costs such as the cost of advertising are fixed costs. When added to the average total cost of production, selling costs increase average total cost by a greater amount at small outputs than at large outputs. If advertising enables sales to increase from 25 jackets a day to 130 jackets a day, average total cost *falls* from $170 to $160 a jacket.

REVIEW QUIZ

1 What are the two main ways, other than by adjusting price, in which a firm in monopolistic competition competes with other firms?
2 Why might product innovation and development be efficient and why might it be inefficient?
3 How does a firm's advertising expenditure influence its cost curves? Does average total cost increase or decrease?
4 How does a firm's advertising expenditure influence the demand for its product? Does demand increase or decrease?
5 Why is it difficult to determine whether monopolistic competition is efficient or inefficient? What is your opinion about the bottom line and why?

Oligopoly

ANOTHER TYPE OF MARKET THAT STANDS BETWEEN the extremes of perfect competition and monopoly is oligopoly. **Oligopoly** is a market structure in which a small number of firms compete.

In oligopoly, the quantity sold by any one firm depends on that firm's price *and* on the other firms' prices and quantities sold. To see why, suppose you run one of the three gas stations in a small town. If you cut your price and your two competitors don't cut theirs, your sales increase, and the sales of the other two firms decrease. With lower sales, the other firms most likely cut their prices too. If they do cut their prices, your sales and profits take a tumble. So before deciding to cut your price, you must predict how the other firms will react and attempt to calculate the effects of those reactions on your own profit.

Several models have been developed to explain the prices and quantities in oligopoly markets. But no one theory has been found that can explain all the different types of behavior that we observe in such markets. The models fall into two broad groups: traditional models and game theory models. We'll look at examples of both types, starting with two traditional models.

The Kinked Demand Curve Model

The kinked demand curve model of oligopoly is based on the assumption that each firm believes that

1. If it raises its price, others will not follow.
2. If it cuts its price, so will the other firms.

Figure 13.6 shows the demand curve (*D*) that a firm believes it faces. The demand curve has a kink at the current price, *P*, and quantity, *Q*. At prices above *P*, a small price rise brings a big decrease in the quantity sold. The other firms hold their current price and the firm has the highest price for the good, so it loses market share. At prices below *P*, even a large price cut brings only a small increase in the quantity sold. In this case, other firms match the price cut, so the firm gets no price advantage over its competitors.

The kink in the demand curve creates a break in the marginal revenue curve (*MR*). To maximize profit, the firm produces the quantity at which marginal cost equals marginal revenue. That quantity, *Q*, is where the marginal cost curve passes through the gap *AB* in the marginal revenue curve. If marginal cost fluctuates between *A* and *B*, like the marginal

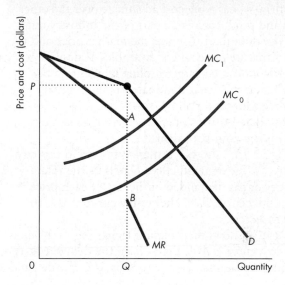

FIGURE 13.6   The Kinked Demand Curve Model

The price in an oligopoly market is *P*. Each firm believes it faces the demand curve *D*. At prices above *P*, a small price rise brings a big decrease in the quantity sold because other firms do not raise their prices. At prices below *P*, even a big price cut brings only a small increase in the quantity sold because other firms also cut their prices. Because the demand curve is kinked, the marginal revenue curve, *MR*, has a break *AB*. Profit is maximized by producing *Q*. The marginal cost curve passes through the break in the marginal revenue curve. Marginal cost changes inside the range *AB* leave the price and quantity unchanged.

cost curves MC_0 and MC_1, the firm does not change its price or its output. Only if marginal cost fluctuates outside the range *AB* does the firm change its price and output. So the kinked demand curve model predicts that price and quantity are insensitive to small cost changes.

A problem with the kinked demand curve model is that the firms' beliefs about the demand curve are not always correct and firms can figure out that they are not correct. If marginal cost increases by enough to cause the firm to increase its price and if all firms experience the same increase in marginal cost, they all increase their prices together. The firm's belief that others will not join it in a price rise is incorrect. A firm that bases its actions on beliefs that are wrong does not maximize profit and might even end up incurring an economic loss.

Dominant Firm Oligopoly

A second traditional model explains a dominant firm oligopoly, which arises when one firm — the dominant firm — has a big cost advantage over the other firms and produces a large part of the industry output. The dominant firm sets the market price and the other firms are price takers. Examples of dominant firm oligopoly are a large gasoline retailer or a big video rental store that dominates its local market.

To see how a dominant firm oligopoly works, suppose that 11 firms operate gas stations in a city. Big-G is the dominant firm.

Figure 13.7 shows the market for gas in this city. In part (a), the demand curve D tells us the total quantity of gas demanded in the city at each price. The supply curve S_{10} is the supply curve of the 10 small suppliers.

Part (b) shows the situation facing Big-G. Its marginal cost curve is MC. Big-G faces the demand curve XD, and its marginal revenue curve is MR. The demand curve XD shows the excess demand not met by the 10 small firms. For example, at a price of $1 a gallon, the quantity demanded is 20,000 gallons, the quantity supplied by the 10 small firms is 10,000 gallons, and the excess quantity demanded is 10,000, measured by the distance AB in both parts of the figure.

To maximize profit, Big-G operates like a monopoly. It sells 10,000 gallons a week, where marginal revenue equals marginal cost, for a price of $1 a gallon. The 10 small firms take the price of $1 a gallon. They behave just like firms in perfect competition. The quantity of gas demanded in the entire city at $1 a gallon is 20,000 gallons, as shown in part (a). Of this amount, Big-G sells 10,000 gallons and the 10 small firms each sell 1,000 gallons.

The traditional theories of oligopoly do not enable us to understand all oligopoly markets and in recent years, economists have developed new models based on game theory. Let's now learn about game theory.

FIGURE 13.7   A Dominant Firm Oligopoly

(a) Ten small firms and market demand

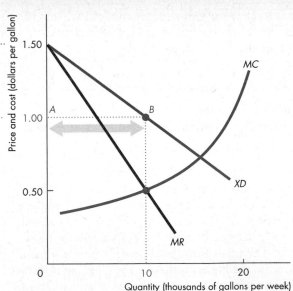

(b) Big-G's price and output decision

The demand curve for gas in a city is D in part (a). There are 10 small competitive firms that together have a supply curve of S_{10}. In addition, there is 1 large firm, Big-G, shown in part (b). Big-G faces the demand curve XD, determined as the market demand D minus the supply of the 10 small firms S_{10} — the demand that is not satisfied by the small firms. Big-G's marginal revenue is MR, and marginal cost is MC. Big-G sets its output to maximize profit by equating marginal cost, MC, and marginal revenue, MR. This output is 10,000 gallons per week. The price at which Big-G can sell this quantity is $1 a gallon. The 10 small firms take this price, and each firm sells 1,000 gallons per week, point A in part (a).

Oligopoly Games

ECONOMISTS THINK ABOUT OLIGOPOLY AS A GAME and to study oligopoly markets they use a set of tools called game theory. **Game theory** is a tool for studying *strategic behavior* — behavior that takes into account the expected behavior of others and the recognition of mutual interdependence. Game theory was invented by John von Neumann in 1937 and extended by von Neumann and Oskar Morgenstern in 1944. Today, it is one of the major research fields in economics.

Game theory seeks to understand oligopoly as well all other forms of economic, political, social, and even biological rivalries by using a method of analysis specifically designed to understand games of all types, including the familiar games of everyday life. We will begin our study of game theory, and its application to the behavior of firms, by thinking about familiar games.

What Is a Game?

What is a game? At first thought, the question seems silly. After all, there are many different games. There are ball games and parlor games, games of chance and games of skill. But what is it about all these different activities that make them games? What do all these games have in common? All games share four features:

- Rules
- Strategies
- Payoffs
- Outcome

Let's see how these common features of games apply to a game called "the prisoners' dilemma." This game, it turns out, captures some of the essential features of oligopoly, and it gives a good illustration of how game theory works and how it generates predictions.

The Prisoners' Dilemma

Art and Bob have been caught red-handed, stealing a car. Facing airtight cases, they will receive a sentence of two years each for their crime. During his interviews with the two prisoners, the district attorney begins to suspect that he has stumbled on the two people who were responsible for a multimillion-dollar bank robbery some months earlier. But this is just a suspicion. The district attorney has no evidence on which he can convict them of the greater crime unless he can get them to confess. The district attorney decides to make the prisoners play a game with the following rules.

Rules Each prisoner (player) is placed in a separate room, and cannot communicate with the other player. Each is told that he is suspected of having carried out the bank robbery and that

> If both of them confess to the larger crime, each will receive a sentence of 3 years for both crimes.
>
> If he alone confesses and his accomplice does not, he will receive an even shorter sentence of 1 year while his accomplice will receive a 10-year sentence.

Strategies In game theory, **strategies** are all the possible actions of each player. Art and Bob each have two possible actions:

- Confess to the bank robbery.
- Deny having committed the bank robbery.

Payoffs Because there are two players, each with two strategies, there are four possible outcomes:

1. Both confess.
2. Both deny.
3. Art confesses and Bob denies.
4. Bob confesses and Art denies.

Each prisoner can work out exactly what happens to him — his *payoff* — in each of these four situations. We can tabulate the four possible payoffs for each of the prisoners in what is called a payoff matrix for the game. A **payoff matrix** is a table that shows the payoffs for every possible action by each player for every possible action by each other player.

Table 13.1 shows a payoff matrix for Art and Bob. The squares show the payoffs for each prisoner — the red triangle in each square shows Art's and the blue triangle shows Bob's. If both prisoners confess (top left), each gets a prison term of 3 years. If Bob confesses but Art denies (top right), Art gets a 10-year sentence and Bob gets a 1-year sentence. If Art confesses and Bob denies (bottom left), Art gets a 1-year sentence and Bob gets a 10-year sentence. Finally, if both of them deny (bottom right), neither can be convicted of the bank robbery charge but both are sentenced for the car theft — a 2-year sentence.

Outcome The choices of both players determine the outcome of the game. To predict that outcome, we use an equilibrium idea proposed by John Nash of Princeton University, (who received the Nobel Prize for Economic Science in 1994 and was the subject of the 2001 movie *A Beautiful Mind*). In **Nash equilibrium**, player *A* takes the best possible action given the action of player *B* and player *B* takes the best possible action given the action of player *A*.

In the case of the prisoners' dilemma, the Nash equilibrium occurs when Art makes his best choice given Bob's choice and when Bob makes his best choice given Art's choice.

To find the Nash equilibrium, we compare all the possible outcomes associated with each choice and eliminate those that are dominated — that are not as good as some other choice. Let's find the Nash equilibrium for the prisoners' dilemma game.

Finding the Nash Equilibrium Look at the situation from Art's point of view. If Bob confesses, Art's best action is to confess because in that case, he is sentenced to 3 years rather than 10 years. If Bob does not confess, Art's best action is still to confess because in that case he receives 1 year rather than 2 years. So Art's best action is to confess.

Now look at the situation from Bob's point of view. If Art confesses, Bob's best action is to confess because in that case, he is sentenced to 3 years rather than 10 years. If Art does not confess, Bob's best action is still to confess because in that case, he receives 1 year rather than 2 years. So Bob's best action is to confess.

Because each player's best action is to confess, each does confess, each gets a 3-year prison term, and the district attorney has solved the bank robbery. This is the Nash equilibrium of the game.

The Dilemma Now that you have found the solution to the prisoners' dilemma, you can better see the dilemma. The dilemma arises as each prisoner contemplates the consequences of denying. Each prisoner knows that if both of them deny, they will receive only a 2-year sentence for stealing the car. But neither has any way of knowing that his accomplice will deny. Each poses the following questions: Should I deny and rely on my accomplice to deny so that we will both get only 2 years? Or should I confess in the hope of getting just 1 year (provided that my accomplice denies) knowing that if my accomplice does confess,

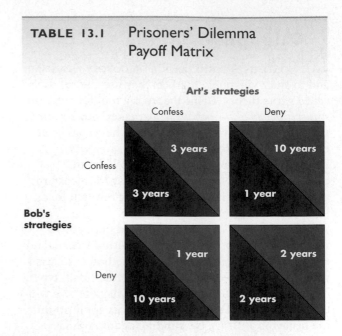

TABLE 13.1   Prisoners' Dilemma Payoff Matrix

	Art's strategies	
	Confess	Deny
Confess	3 years / 3 years	10 years / 1 year
Deny	1 year / 10 years	2 years / 2 years

Each square shows the payoffs for the two players, Art and Bob, for each possible pair of actions. In each square, the red triangle shows Art's payoff and the blue triangle shows Bob's. For example, if both confess, the payoffs are in the top left square. The equilibrium of the game is for both players to confess and each gets a 3-year sentence.

we will both get 3 years in prison? The dilemma is resolved by finding the equilibrium of the game.

A Bad Outcome For the prisoners, the equilibrium of the game, with each confessing, is not the best outcome. If neither of them confesses, each gets only 2 years for the lesser crime. Isn't there some way in which this better outcome can be achieved? It seems that there is not, because the players cannot communicate with each other. Each player can put himself in the other player's place, and so each player can figure out that there is a best strategy for each of them. The prisoners are indeed in a dilemma. Each knows that he can serve 2 years only if he can trust the other to deny. But each prisoner also knows that it is not in the best interest of the other to deny. So each prisoner knows that he must confess, thereby delivering a bad outcome for both.

The firms in an oligopoly are in a similar situation to Art and Bob in the prisoners' dilemma game. Let's see how we can use this game to understand oligopoly.

An Oligopoly Price-Fixing Game

We can use game theory and a game like the prisoners' dilemma to understand price fixing, price wars, and other aspects of the behavior of firms in oligopoly. We'll begin with a price-fixing game.

To understand how oligopolies fix prices, we're going to study a special case of oligopoly called duopoly. **Duopoly** is a market structure in which there are only two producers who compete. You can probably find some examples of duopoly near where you live. Many cities have only two suppliers of milk, two local newspapers, two taxi companies, two car rental firms, two copy centers, or two college bookstores. Duopoly captures the essence of all oligopoly situations. Our goal is to predict the prices charged and the quantities produced by the two firms.

Cost and Demand Conditions Two firms, Trick and Gear, produce switchgears. They have identical costs. Figure 13.8(a) shows their average total cost curve (*ATC*) and marginal cost curve (*MC*). Figure 13.8(b) shows the market demand curve for switchgears (*D*). The two firms produce identical switchgears, so one firm's switchgear is a perfect substitute for the other's. So the market price of each firm's product is identical. The quantity demanded depends on that price — the higher the price, the smaller is the quantity demanded.

This industry is a natural duopoly. Two firms can produce this good at a lower cost than either one firm or three firms can. For each firm, average total cost is at its minimum when production is 3,000 units a week. And when price equals minimum average total cost, the total quantity demanded is 6,000 units a week. So two firms can just produce that quantity.

Collusion We'll suppose that Trick and Gear, enter into a collusive agreement. A **collusive agreement** is an agreement between two (or more) producers to restrict output, raise the price, and increase profits. Such an agreement is illegal in the United States and is undertaken in secret. A group of firms that has entered into a collusive agreement to restrict output and increase prices and profits is called a **cartel**. The strategies that firms in a cartel can pursue are to

■ Comply
■ Cheat

A firm that complies carries out the agreement. A firm that cheats breaks the agreement to its own benefit and to the cost of the other firm.

Because each firm has two strategies, there are four possible combinations of actions for the firms:

1. Both firms comply.
2. Both firms cheat.
3. Trick complies and Gear cheats.
4. Gear complies and Trick cheats.

FIGURE 13.8   Costs and Demand

(a) Individual firm   (b) Industry

The average total cost curve for each firm is *ATC*, and the marginal cost curve is *MC* (part a). Minimum average total cost is $6,000 a unit, and it occurs at a production of 3,000 units a week.

Part (b) shows the market demand curve. At a price of $6,000, the quantity demanded is 6,000 units per week. The two firms can produce this output at the lowest possible average cost. If the market had one firm, it would be profitable for another to enter. If the market had three firms, one would exit. There is room for only two firms in this industry. It is a natural duopoly.

Colluding to Maximize Profits Let's work out the payoffs to the two firms if they collude to make the maximum profit for the cartel by acting like a monopoly. The calculations that the two firms perform are the same calculations that a monopoly performs. (You can refresh your memory of these calculations by looking at Chapter 12, pp. 262–263.) The only thing that the duopolists must do beyond what a monopolist does is to agree on how much of the total output each of them will produce.

Figure 13.9 shows the price and quantity that maximize industry profit for the duopolists. Part (a) shows the situation for each firm, and part (b) shows the situation for the industry as a whole. The curve labeled MR is the industry marginal revenue curve. This marginal revenue curve is like that of a single-price monopoly (Chapter 12, p. 260). The curve labeled MC_I is the industry marginal cost curve if each firm produces the same level of output. That curve is constructed by adding together the outputs of the two firms at each level of marginal cost. That is, at each level of marginal cost, industry output is twice the output of each individual firm. Thus the curve MC_I in part (b) is twice as far to the right as the curve MC in part (a).

To maximize industry profit, the duopolists agree to restrict output to the rate that makes the industry marginal cost and marginal revenue equal. That output rate, as shown in part (b), is 4,000 units a week.

The highest price for which the 4,000 switchgears can be sold is $9,000 each. Trick and Gear agree to charge this price.

To hold the price at $9,000 a unit, production must be not exceed 4,000 units a week. So Trick and Gear must agree on production levels for each of them that total 4,000 units a week. Let's suppose that they agree to split the market equally so that each firm produces 2,000 switchgears a week. Because the firms are identical, this division is the most likely.

The average total cost (ATC) of producing 2,000 switchgears a week is $8,000, so the profit per unit is $1,000 and economic profit is $2 million (2,000 units × $1,000 per unit). The economic profit of each firm is represented by the blue rectangle in Fig. 13.9(a).

We have just described one possible outcome for a duopoly game: The two firms collude to produce the monopoly profit-maximizing output and divide that output equally between themselves. From the industry point of view, this solution is identical to a monopoly. A duopoly that operates in this way is indistinguishable from a monopoly. The economic profit that is made by a monopoly is the maximum total profit that can be made by colluding duopolists.

But with price greater than marginal cost, either firm might think of trying to increase profit by cheating on the agreement and producing more than the agreed amount. Let's see what happens if one of the firms does cheat in this way.

FIGURE 13.9   Colluding to Make Monopoly Profits

(a) Individual firm   **(b) Industry**

The industry marginal cost curve, MC_I in part (b), is the horizontal sum of the two firms' marginal cost curves, MC in part (a). The industry marginal revenue curve is MR. To maximize profit, the firms produce 4,000 units a week (the quantity at which marginal revenue equals marginal cost). They sell that output for $9,000 a unit. Each firm produces 2,000 units a week. Average total cost is $8,000 a unit, so each firm makes an economic profit of $2 million (blue rectangle) — 2,000 units multiplied by $1,000 profit a unit.

One Firm Cheats on a Collusive Agreement To set the stage for cheating on their agreement, Trick convinces Gear that demand has decreased and that it cannot sell 2,000 units a week. Trick tells Gear that it plans to cut its price in order to sell the agreed 2,000 units each week. Because the two firms produce an identical product, Gear matches Trick's price cut but still produces only 2,000 units a week.

In fact, there has been no decrease in demand. Trick plans to increase output, which it knows will lower the price, and Trick wants to ensure that Gear's output remains at the agreed level.

Figure 13.10 illustrates the consequences of Trick's cheating. Part (a) shows Gear (the complier); part (b) shows Trick (the cheat); and part (c) shows the industry as a whole. Suppose that Trick increases output to 3,000 units a week. If Gear sticks to the agreement to produce only 2,000 units a week, total output is 5,000 a week, and given demand in part (c), the price falls to $7,500 a unit.

Gear continues to produce 2,000 units a week at a cost of $8,000 a unit and incurs a loss of $500 a unit, or $1 million a week. This economic loss is represented by the red rectangle in part (a). Trick produces 3,000 units a week at an average total cost of $6,000 each. With a price of $7,500, Trick makes a profit of $1,500 a unit and therefore an economic profit of $4.5 million. This economic profit is the blue rectangle in part (b).

We've now described a second possible outcome for the duopoly game: One of the firms cheats on the collusive agreement. In this case, the industry output is larger than the monopoly output and the industry price is lower than the monopoly price. The total economic profit made by the industry is also smaller than the monopoly's economic profit. Trick (the cheat) makes an economic profit of $4.5 million, and Gear (the complier) incurs an economic loss of $1 million. The industry makes an economic profit of $3.5 million. Thus the industry profit is $0.5 million less than the economic profit a monopoly would make. But the profit is distributed unevenly. Trick makes a bigger economic profit than it would under the collusive agreement, while Gear incurs an economic loss.

A similar outcome would arise if Gear cheated and Trick complied with the agreement. The industry profit and price would be the same, but in this case, Gear (the cheat) would make an economic profit of $4.5 million and Trick (the complier) would incur an economic loss of $1 million.

Let's next see what happens if both firms cheat.

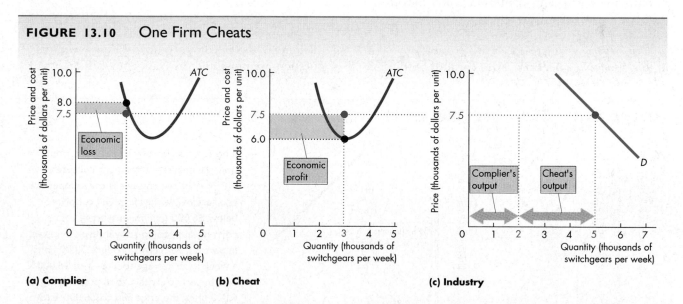

FIGURE 13.10   One Firm Cheats

(a) Complier

(b) Cheat

(c) Industry

One firm, shown in part (a), complies with the agreement and produces 2,000 units. The other firm, shown in part (b), cheats on the agreement and increases its output to 3,000 units. Given the market demand curve, shown in part (c), and with a total production of 5,000 units a week, the price falls to $7,500. At this price, the complier in part (a) incurs an economic loss of $1 million ($500 per unit × 2,000 units), shown by the red rectangle. In part (b), the cheat makes an economic profit of $4.5 million ($1,500 per unit × 3,000 units), shown by the blue rectangle.

Both Firms Cheat Suppose that both firms cheat and that each firm behaves like the cheating firm that we have just analyzed. Each tells the other that it is unable to sell its output at the going price and that it plans to cut its price. But because both firms cheat, each will propose a successively lower price. As long as price exceeds marginal cost, each firm has an incentive to increase its production — to cheat. Only when price equals marginal cost is there no further incentive to cheat. This situation arises when the price has reached $6,000. At this price, marginal cost equals price. Also, price equals minimum average total cost. At a price less than $6,000, each firm incurs an economic loss. At a price of $6,000, each firm covers all its costs and makes zero economic profit (makes normal profit). Also, at a price of $6,000, each firm wants to produce 3,000 units a week, so the industry output is 6,000 units a week. Given the demand conditions, 6,000 units can be sold at a price of $6,000 each.

Figure 13.11 illustrates the situation just described. Each firm, in part (a), produces 3,000 units a week, and its average total cost is a minimum ($6,000 per unit). The market as a whole, in part (b), operates at the point at which the market demand curve (D) intersects the industry marginal cost curve (MC_I). Each firm has lowered its price and increased its output to try to gain an advantage over the other firm. Each has pushed this process as far as it can without incurring an economic loss.

We have now described a third possible outcome of this duopoly game: Both firms cheat. If both firms cheat on the collusive agreement, the output of each firm is 3,000 units a week and the price is $6,000. Each firm makes zero economic profit.

The Payoff Matrix Now that we have described the strategies and payoffs in the duopoly game, we can summarize the strategies and the payoffs in the form of the game's payoff matrix. Then we can find the Nash equilibrium.

Table 13.2 sets out the payoff matrix for this game. It is constructed in the same way as the payoff matrix for the prisoners' dilemma in Table 13.1. The squares show the payoffs for the two firms — Gear and Trick. In this case, the payoffs are profits. (For the prisoners' dilemma, the payoffs were losses.)

The table shows that if both firms cheat (top left), they achieve the perfectly competitive outcome — each firm makes zero economic profit. If both firms comply (bottom right), the industry makes the monopoly profit and each firm earns an economic profit of $2 million. The top right and bottom left squares show what happens if one firm cheats while the other complies. The firm that cheats collects an economic profit of $4.5 million, and the one that complies incurs a loss of $1 million.

Nash Equilibrium in the Duopolists' Dilemma
The duopolists have a dilemma like the prisoners' dilemma. Do they comply or cheat? To answer this question, we must find the Nash equilibrium.

FIGURE 13.11   Both Firms Cheat

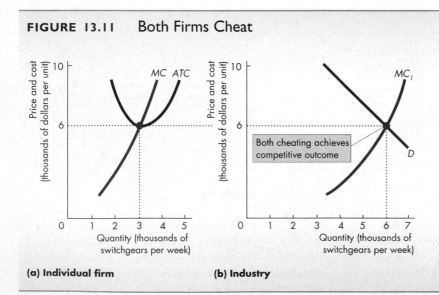

(a) Individual firm

(b) Industry

If both firms cheat by increasing production, the collusive agreement collapses. The limit to the collapse is the competitive equilibrium. Neither firm will cut price below $6,000 (minimum average total cost) because to do so will result in losses. In part (a), both firms produce 3,000 units a week at an average total cost of $6,000 a unit. In part (b), with a total production of 6,000 units, the price falls to $6,000. Each firm now makes zero economic profit because price equals average total cost. This output and price are the ones that would prevail in a competitive industry.

TABLE 13.2 Duopoly Payoff Matrix

Each square shows the payoffs from a pair of actions. For example, if both firms comply with the collusive agreement, the payoffs are recorded in the bottom right square. The red triangle shows Gear's payoff, and the blue triangle shows Trick's. In Nash equilibrium, both firms cheat.

Look at things from Gear's point of view. Gear reasons as follows: Suppose that Trick cheats. If I comply, I will incur an economic loss of $1 million. If I also cheat, I will make zero economic profit. Zero is better than *minus* $1 million, so I'm better off if I cheat. Now suppose Trick complies. If I cheat, I will make an economic profit of $4.5 million, and if I comply, I will make an economic profit of $2 million. A $4.5 million profit is better than a $2 million profit, so I'm better off if I cheat. So regardless of whether Trick cheats or complies, it pays Gear to cheat. Cheating is Gear's best strategy.

Trick comes to the same conclusion as Gear because the two firms face an identical situation. So both firms cheat. The Nash equilibrium of the duopoly game is that both firms cheat. And although the industry has only two firms, they charge the same price and produce the same quantity as those in a competitive industry. Also, as in perfect competition, each firm makes zero economic profit.

This conclusion is not general and will not always arise. We'll see why not first by looking at some other games that are like the prisoners' dilemma. Then we'll broaden the types of games we consider.

Other Oligopoly Games

Firms in oligopoly must decide whether to mount expensive advertising campaigns; whether to modify their product; whether to make their product more reliable and more durable; whether to price discriminate and, if so, among which groups of customers and to what degree; whether to undertake a large research and development (R&D) effort aimed at lowering production costs; and whether to enter or leave an industry.

All of these choices can be analyzed as games that are similar to the one that we've just studied. Let's look at one example: an R&D game.

An R&D Game

Disposable diapers were first marketed in 1966. The two market leaders from the start of this industry have been Procter & Gamble (the maker of Pampers) and Kimberly-Clark (the maker of Huggies). Procter & Gamble has about 40 percent of the total market, and Kimberly-Clark has about 33 percent. When the disposable diaper was first introduced in 1966, it had to be cost-effective in competition with reusable, laundered diapers. A costly research and development effort resulted in the development of machines that could make disposable diapers at a low enough cost to achieve that initial competitive edge. But new firms tried to get into the business and take market share away from the two industry leaders, and the industry leaders themselves battled each other to maintain or increase their own market share.

During the early 1990s, Kimberly-Clark was the first to introduce Velcro closures. And in 1996, Procter & Gamble was the first to introduce "breathable" diapers into the U.S. market.

The key to success in this industry (as in any other) is to design a product that people value highly relative to the cost of producing them. The firm that develops the most highly valued product and also develops the least-cost technology for producing it gains a competitive edge, undercutting the rest of the market, increasing its market share, and increasing its profit. But the R&D that must be undertaken to achieve product improvements and cost reductions is costly. So the cost of R&D must be deducted from the profit resulting from the increased market share that lower costs achieve. If no firm does R&D, every firm can be better off, but if one firm initiates the R&D activity, all must follow.

Table 13.3 illustrates the dilemma (with hypothetical numbers) for the R&D game that Kimberly-Clark and Procter & Gamble play. Each firm has two strategies: Spend $25 million a year on R&D or spend nothing on R&D. If neither firm spends on R&D, they make a joint profit of $100 million: $30 million for Kimberly-Clark and $70 million for Procter & Gamble (bottom right of the payoff matrix). If each firm conducts R&D, market shares are maintained but each firm's profit is lower by the amount spent on R&D (top left square of the payoff matrix). If Kimberly-Clark pays for R&D but Procter & Gamble does not, Kimberly-Clark gains a large part of Procter & Gamble's market. Kimberly-Clark profits, and Procter & Gamble loses (top right square of the payoff matrix). Finally, if Procter & Gamble conducts R&D and Kimberly-Clark does not, Procter & Gamble gains market share from Kimberly-Clark, increasing its profit, while Kimberly-Clark incurs a loss (bottom left square).

TABLE 13.3   Pampers Versus Huggies: An R&D Game

If both firms undertake R&D, their payoffs are those shown in the top left square. If neither firm undertakes R&D, their payoffs are in the bottom right square. When one firm undertakes R&D and the other one does not, their payoffs are in the top right and bottom left squares. The red triangle shows Procter & Gamble's payoff, and the blue triangle shows Kimberly-Clark's. The Nash equilibrium for this game is for both firms to undertake R&D. The structure of this game is the same as that of the prisoners' dilemma.

Confronted with the payoff matrix in Table 13.3, the two firms calculate their best strategies. Kimberly-Clark reasons as follows: If Procter & Gamble does not undertake R&D, we will make $85 million if we do and $30 million if we do not; so it pays us to conduct R&D. If Procter & Gamble conducts R&D, we will lose $10 million if we don't and make $5 million if we do. Again, R&D pays off. Thus conducting R&D is the best strategy for Kimberly-Clark. It pays, regardless of Procter & Gamble's decision.

Procter & Gamble reasons similarly: If Kimberly-Clark does not undertake R&D, we will make $70 million if we follow suit and $85 million if we conduct R&D. It therefore pays to conduct R&D. If Kimberly-Clark does undertake R&D, we will make $45 million by doing the same and lose $10 million by not doing R&D. Again, it pays us to conduct R&D. So for Procter & Gamble, R&D is also the best strategy.

Because R&D is the best strategy for both players, it is the Nash equilibrium. The outcome of this game is that both firms conduct R&D. They make less profit than they would if they could collude to achieve the cooperative outcome of no R&D.

The real-world situation has more players than Kimberly-Clark and Procter & Gamble. A large number of other firms share a small portion of the market, all of them ready to eat into the market share of Procter & Gamble and Kimberly-Clark. So the R&D effort by these two firms not only serves the purpose of maintaining shares in their own battle, but also helps to keep barriers to entry high enough to preserve their joint market share.

Repeated Games and Sequential Games

THE GAMES THAT WE'VE STUDIED ARE PLAYED just once. In contrast, many real-world games are played repeatedly. This feature of games turns out to enable real-world duopolists to cooperate, collude, and earn a monopoly profit.

Another feature of the game that we've studied is that the players move simultaneously. But in many real-world situations, one player moves first and then the other moves—the play is sequential rather than simultaneous. This feature of real-world games creates a large number of possible outcomes.

We're now going to examine these two aspects of strategic decision-making.

A Repeated Duopoly Game

If two firms play a game repeatedly, one firm has the opportunity to penalize the other for previous "bad" behavior. If Gear cheats this week, perhaps Trick will cheat next week. Before Gear cheats this week, won't it take account of the possibility that Trick will cheat next week? What is the equilibrium of this game?

Actually, there is more than one possibility. One is the Nash equilibrium that we have just analyzed. Both players cheat, and each makes zero economic profit forever. In such a situation, it will never pay one of the players to start complying unilaterally because to do so would result in a loss for that player and a profit for the other. But a **cooperative equilibrium** in which the players make and share the monopoly profit is possible.

A cooperative equilibrium might occur if cheating is punished. There are two extremes of punishment. The smallest penalty is called "tit for tat." A *tit-for-tat strategy* is one in which a player cooperates in the current period if the other player cooperated in the previous period but cheats in the current period if the other player cheated in the previous period. The most severe form of punishment is called a trigger strategy. A *trigger strategy* is one in which a player cooperates if the other player cooperates but plays the Nash equilibrium strategy forever thereafter if the other player cheats.

In the duopoly game between Gear and Trick, a tit-for-tat strategy keeps both players cooperating and earning monopoly profits. Let's see why with an example.

Table 13.4 shows the economic profit that Trick and Gear will make over a number of periods under two alternative sequences of events: colluding and cheating with a tit-for-tat response by the other firm.

If both firms stick to the collusive agreement in period 1, each makes an economic profit of $2 million. Suppose that Trick contemplates cheating in period 1. The cheating produces a quick $4.5 million economic profit and inflicts a $1 million economic loss on Gear. But a cheat in period 1 produces a response from Gear in period 2. If Trick wants to get back into a profit-making situation, it must return to the agreement in period 2 even though it knows that Gear will punish it for cheating in period 1. So in period 2, Gear punishes Trick and Trick cooperates. Gear now makes an economic profit of $4.5 million, and Trick incurs an economic loss of $1 million. Adding up the profits over two periods of play, Trick would have made more profit by cooperating — $4 million compared with $3.5 million.

What is true for Trick is also true for Gear. Because each firm makes a larger profit by sticking with the collusive agreement, both firms do so and the monopoly price, quantity, and profit prevail.

In reality, whether a cartel works like a one-play game or a repeated game depends primarily on the

TABLE 13.4	Cheating with Punishment			
	Collude		**Cheat with tit-for-tat**	
Period of play	Trick's profit (millions of dollars)	Gear's profit (millions of dollars)	Trick's profit (millions of dollars)	Gear's profit (millions of dollars)
1	2	2	4.5	−1.0
2	2	2	−1.0	4.5
3	2	2	2.0	2.0
4	.	.	.	.

If duopolists repeatedly collude, each makes an economic profit of $2 million per period of play. If one player cheats in period 1, the other player plays a tit-for-tat strategy and cheats in period 2. The profit from cheating can be made for only one period and must be paid for in the next period by incurring a loss. Over two periods of play, the best that a duopolist can achieve by cheating is an economic profit of $3.5 million, compared to an economic profit of $4 million by colluding.

number of players and the ease of detecting and punishing cheating. The larger the number of players, the harder it is to maintain a cartel.

Games and Price Wars A repeated duopoly game can help us understand real-world behavior and, in particular, price wars. Some price wars can be interpreted as the implementation of a tit-for-tat strategy. But the game is a bit more complicated than the one we've looked at because the players are uncertain about the demand for the product.

Playing a tit-for-tat strategy, firms have an incentive to stick to the monopoly price. But fluctuations in demand lead to fluctuations in the monopoly price, and sometimes, when the price changes, it might seem to one of the firms that the price has fallen because the other has cheated. In this case, a price war will break out. The price war will end only when each firm is satisfied that the other is ready to cooperate again. There will be cycles of price wars and the restoration of collusive agreements. Fluctuations in the world price of oil might be interpreted in this way.

Some price wars arise from the entry of a small number of firms into an industry that had previously been a monopoly. Although the industry has a small number of firms, the firms are in a prisoners' dilemma and they cannot impose effective penalties for price cutting. The behavior of prices and outputs in the computer chip industry during 1995 and 1996 can be explained in this way. Until 1995, the market for Pentium chips for IBM-compatible computers was dominated by one firm, Intel Corporation, which was able to make maximum economic profit by producing the quantity of chips at which marginal cost equaled marginal revenue. The price of Intel's chips was set to ensure that the quantity demanded equaled the quantity produced. Then in 1995 and 1996, with the entry of a small number of new firms, the industry became an oligopoly. If the firms had maintained Intel's price and shared the market, together they could have made economic profits equal to Intel's profit. But the firms were in a prisoners' dilemma. So prices fell toward the competitive level.

Let's now study a sequential game. There are many such games, and the one we'll examine is among the simplest. But it has an interesting implication and it gives you the flavor of this type of game. The sequential game that we'll study is an entry game in a contestable market.

A Sequential Entry Game in a Contestable Market

If two firms play a sequential game, one firm makes a decision at the first stage of the game and the other makes a decision at the second stage.

We're going to study a sequential game in a **contestable market**—a market in which firms can enter and leave so easily that firms in the market face competition from *potential* entrants. Examples of contestable markets are routes served by airlines and by barge companies that operate on the major waterways. These markets are contestable because firms could enter if an opportunity for economic profit arose and could exit with no penalty if the opportunity for economic profit disappeared.

If the Herfindahl-Hirschman Index (p. 202) is used to determine the degree of competition, a contestable market appears to be uncompetitive. But a contestable market can behave as if it were perfectly competitive. To see why, let's look at an entry game for contestable air route.

A Contestable Air Route Agile Air is the only firm operating on a particular route. Demand and cost conditions are such that there is room for only one airline to operate. Wanabe, Inc. is another airline that could offer services on the route.

We describe the structure of a sequential game by using a *game tree* like that in Fig. 13.12. At the first stage, Agile Air must set a price. Once the price is set and advertised, Agile can't change it. That is, once set, Agile's price is fixed and Agile can't react to Wanabe's entry decision. Agile can set its price at the monopoly level or at the competitive level.

At the second stage, Wanabe must decide whether to enter or to stay out. Customers have no loyalty (there are no frequent flyer programs) and they buy from the lowest-price firm. So if Wanabe enters, it sets a price just below Agile's and takes all the business.

Figure 13.12 shows the payoffs from the various decisions (Agile's in the red triangles and Wanabe's in the blue triangles).

To decide on its price, Agile's CEO reasons as follows: Suppose that Agile sets the monopoly price. If Wanabe enters, it earns 90 (think of all payoff numbers as thousands of dollars). If Wanabe stays out it earns nothing. So Wanabe will enter. In this case Agile will lose 50.

FIGURE 13.12   Agile Versus Wanabe: A Sequential Entry Game in a Contestable Market

First stage   **Second stage**   **Payoffs**

Monopoly price — Wanabe — Enter → 90 / −50

Stay out → 0 / 100

Agile

Competitive price — Wanabe — Enter → −10 / −50

Stay out → 0 / 50

If Agile sets the monopoly price, Wanabe makes 90 (thousand dollars) by entering and earns nothing by staying out. So if Agile sets the monopoly price, Wanabe enters.

If Agile sets the competitive price, Wanabe earns nothing if it stays out and incurs a loss if it enters. So if Agile sets the competitive price, Wanabe stays out.

Now suppose that Agile sets the competitive price. If Wanabe stays out, it earns nothing and if it enters, it loses 10, so Wanabe will stay out. In this case, Agile will earn 50.

Agile's best strategy is to set its price at the competitive level and earn 50 (normal profit). The option of earning 100 by setting the monopoly price with Wanabe staying out is not available to Agile. If Agile sets the monopoly price, Wanabe enters, undercuts Agile, and takes all the business.

In this example, Agile sets its price at the competitive level and earns normal profit. A less costly strategy, called **limit pricing**, sets the price at the highest level that inflicts a loss on the entrant. Any loss is big enough to deter entry, so it is not always necessary to set the price as low as the competitive price. In the example of Agile and Wanabe, at the competitive price, Wanabe incurs a loss of 10 if it enters. A smaller loss would still keep Wanabe out.

This game is interesting because it points to the possibility of a monopoly behaving like a competitive industry and serving the consumer interest without regulation. But the result is not general and depends on one crucial feature of the set up of the game: At the second stage, Agile is locked into the price set at the first stage.

If Agile could change its price in the second stage, it would want to set the monopoly price if Wanabe stayed out—100 with the monopoly price beats 50

with the competitive price. But Wanabe can figure out what Agile would do, so the price set at the first stage has no effect on Wanabe. Agile sets the monopoly price and Wanabe might either stay out or enter.

We've looked at two of the many possible repeated and sequential games, and you've seen how these types of game can provide insights into the complex forces that determine prices and profits.

REVIEW QUIZ

1 If a prisoners' dilemma game is played repeatedly, what punishment strategies might the players employ and how does playing the game repeatedly change the equilibrium?
2 If a market is contestable, how does the equilibrium differ from that of a monopoly?

◆ Monopolistic competition and oligopoly are the most common market structures that you encounter in your daily life. *Reading Between the Lines* on pp. 300–301 shows you oligopoly in action and the price war in the market for personal computers.

So far, we've been studying the two big questions: What goods and services are produced and how are they produced? Your next task is to study the forces that determine for whom they are produced.

Oligopoly in Action

INFOWORLD DAILY NEWS, August 20, 2001

A PC Price War

Dell fired the first volley of the PC price war in the Fall of 2000. Since then, PC prices have fallen steadily. Aggressive discounting from chip suppliers such as Intel and Advanced Micro Devices (AMD) has also aided the drop in PC prices.

The fierce campaign for PC market share forced competitors like IBM, Hewlett-Packard, and Compaq to follow suit. The discounting that followed decimated PC gross profit margins, which fell from an industry average of 24.9 percent in the last quarter of 2000 to 19.9 percent on the first quarter of 2001, according to IDC, in Framingham, Mass. Many PC makers, such as Gateway, reported single-digit PC margins for the same time period.

...

Undaunted, Dell apparently will maintain its current course of underselling competitors on all product and service fronts, a company spokesman said.

...

"Dell is displaying our convergence theme," explained UBS Warburg analyst Don Young. "They slashed prices and took down expenses last fall, got a jump on the competition, got a lot of market share. But starting in Q1 2001, and now evident on a broad scale, the competition is responding to Dell's new pricing and Dell's share gains are ending."

"I still think the PC hardware operating margins are converging and falling," Young said. "The companies Dell, HP, IBM, Compaq are more similar today than they've been at any time before. Dell is clearly the best, but its relative advantage is shrinking."

...

Dell is the No. 1 PC maker in the world by units shipped with a 12.9 percent market share, followed by Compaq with an 11.9 percent share, HP with a 7.6 percent share, and IBM with a 6.3 percent share, according to IDC research from the first quarter of 2001.

Essence of the Story

■ On the basis of units shipped during the first quarter of 2001, Dell is the world's largest PC maker (12.9 percent market share); Compaq is second (11.9 percent share); Hewlett Packard is third (7.6 percent share); and IBM is fourth (6.3 percent share).

■ Dell cut its PC prices in the fall of 2000, and since then, PC prices have fallen steadily.

■ IBM, Hewlett-Packard, and Compaq have followed Dell with their own price cuts.

■ Lower chip prices have helped to cut PC prices, but industry average PC gross profit margins fell from an average of 24.9 percent in the last quarter of 2000 to 19.9 percent on the first quarter of 2001.

■ Dell plans to continue to price below its competitors' prices, but its competitive advantage is shrinking.

Economic Analysis

■ The market for personal computers is an example of oligopoly.

■ Figure 1 shows the market shares of the four largest producers that together account for 39 percent of the entire market.

■ During the 1990s, the PC market expanded rapidly and all the producers experienced a high growth rate of total revenue and economic profit.

■ In 2000, the global economy began to grow more slowly and PC makers found their revenues and profits growing slowly.

■ Faced with slow growth in revenues and profits, the PC makers had a choice — either cut price or hold price.

■ Table 1 shows the consequences of these choices for Dell, the largest PC maker, and Compaq, Hewlett Packard (HP), and IBM, the next largest producers.

■ The numbers in Table 1 are gross profit margins (some of which are based on the numbers in the news article).

■ To decide whether to cut price or hold the price, Dell considers what its competitors might do.

■ If Dell's competitors cut price, Dell is better off cutting too. If Dell's competitors hold price, Dell is still better off cutting its price. Cutting price is the best strategy for Dell.

■ Similarly, if Dell cuts price, Dell's competitors are better off cutting too. And if Dell holds its price, its competitors are still better off cutting their prices. Cutting price is the best strategy for Dell's competitors.

■ Because cutting price is the best strategy for both Dell and its competitors, a price-cutting war is the outcome — the Nash equilibrium.

Figure 1 PC market shares in 2001

Table 1 PC market price cutting game

SUMMARY

KEY POINTS

Monopolistic Competition (pp. 280–281)

- Monopolistic competition occurs when a large number of firms compete with each other on product quality, price, and marketing.

Output and Price in Monopolistic Competition (pp. 282–284)

- Firms in monopolistic competition face downward-sloping demand curves and produce the quantity at which marginal revenue equals marginal cost.
- Entry and exit result in zero economic profit and excess capacity in long-run equilibrium.

Product Development and Marketing (pp. 284–286)

- Firms in monopolistic competition innovate and develop new products.
- Advertising expenditures increase total cost, but they might lower average total cost if they increase the quantity sold by enough.
- Advertising expenditures might increase demand, but they might also decrease the demand facing a firm by increasing competition.
- Whether monopolistic competition is inefficient depends on the value we place on product variety.

Oligopoly (pp. 287–288)

- Oligopoly is a market in which a small number of firms compete.
- If rivals match price cuts but do not match price hikes, they face a kinked demand curve and change prices only when large cost changes occur.
- If one firm dominates a market, it acts like a monopoly and the small firms take its price as given and act like perfectly competitive firms.

Oligopoly Games (pp. 289–296)

- Oligopoly is studied by using game theory, which is a method of analyzing strategic behavior.

- In a prisoners' dilemma game, two prisoners acting in their own interest harm their joint interest.
- An oligopoly (duopoly) price-fixing game is a prisoners' dilemma in which the firms might collude or cheat.
- In Nash equilibrium, both firms cheat and output and price are the same as in perfect competition.
- Firms' decisions about advertising and R&D can be studied by using game theory.

Repeated Games and Sequential Games (pp. 297–299)

- In a repeated game, a punishment strategy can produce a cooperative equilibrium in which price and output are the same as in a monopoly.
- In a sequential contestable market game, a small number of firms can behave like firms in perfect competition.

KEY FIGURES AND TABLES

KEY TERMS

PROBLEMS

*1. The figure shows the situation facing Lite and Kool, Inc., a producer of running shoes.

a. What quantity does Lite and Kool produce?
b. What does it charge?
c. How much profit does Lite and Kool make?

2. The figure shows the situation facing the Stiff Shirt, Inc., a producer of shirts.

a. What quantity does the Stiff Shirt produce?
b. What does it charge?
c. How much profit does it make?

*3. A firm in monopolistic competition produces running shoes. If it spends nothing on advertising, it can sell no shoes at $100 a pair, and for each $10 cut in price, the quantity of shoes it can sell increases by 25 pairs a day, so at $20 a

pair, it can sell 200 pairs a day. The firm's total fixed cost is $4,000 a day. Its average variable cost and marginal cost is a constant $20 per pair. If the firm spends $3,000 a day on advertising, it can double the quantity of shoes sold at each price.
a. If the firm doesn't advertise, what is
   (i) The quantity of shoes produced?
   (ii) The price per pair?
   (iii) The firm's economic profit or loss?
b. If the firm does advertise, what is
   (i) The quantity of shoes produced?
   (ii) The price per pair?
   (iii) The firm's economic profit or loss?
c. Will the firm advertise or not? Why?

4. The firm in problem 3 has the same demand and costs as before if it does not advertise. The firm undertakes some quality improvements in its shoes that raise its marginal and average cost to $40 a pair. If the firm spends $3,000 a day on advertising with the new agency, it can double the amount that consumers are willing to pay at each quantity demanded.
a. If the firm hires the new agency, what quantity does it produce and what price does it charge?
b. What is the firm's economic profit or loss?
c. What is the firm's profit in the long run?

*5. A firm with a kinked demand curve experiences an increase in fixed costs. Explain how the firm's price, output, and profit change.

6. A firm with a kinked demand curve experiences an increase in variable cost. Explain how the firm's price, output, and profit change.

*7. An industry with one very large firm and 100 very small firms experiences an increase in the demand for its product. Use the dominant firm model to explain the effects on the price, output, and economic profit of
a. The large firm.
b. A typical small firm.

8. An industry with one very large firm and 100 very small firms experiences an increase in total variable cost. Use the dominant firm model to explain the effects on the price, output, and economic profit of
a. The large firm.
b. A typical small firm.

*9. Consider a game with two players and in which each player is asked a question. The players can answer the question honestly or lie. If both answer honestly, each receives $100. If one answers honestly and the other lies, the liar receives $500 and the honest player gets nothing. If both lie, then each receives $50.
   a. Describe this game in terms of its players, strategies, and payoffs.
   b. Construct the payoff matrix.
   c. What is the equilibrium for this game?

10. Describe the game known as the prisoners' dilemma. In describing the game:
    a. Make up a story that motivates the game.
    b. Work out a payoff matrix.
    c. Describe how the equilibrium of the game is arrived at.

*11. Soapy and Suddies, Inc. are the only producers of soap powder. They collude and agree to share the market equally. If neither firm cheats, each makes $1 million profit. If either firm cheats, the cheat makes a profit of $1.5 million, while the complier incurs a loss of $0.5 million. Neither firm can police the other's actions.
    a. If the game is played once,
       (i)   What is the profit of each firm if both cheat?
       (ii) Describe the best strategy for each firm.
       (iii) Construct the payoff matrix.
       (iv) What is the equilibrium of the game?
    b. If this duopoly game can be played many times, describe some of the strategies that each firm might adopt.

12. Healthy and Energica are the only producers of a new energy drink. The firms collude and agree to share the market equally. If neither firm cheats, each firm makes $4 million profit. If either firm cheats, the cheat makes $6 million profit, while the complier incurs a loss of $1.5 million. Neither firm can police the other's actions.
    a. If the game is played once,
       (i)   What is the payoff matrix?
       (ii) Describe the best strategy for each firm.
       (iii) What is the equilibrium of the game?
    b. If this game can be played many times, what are two strategies that could be adopted?

CRITICAL THINKING

1. Study *Reading Between the Lines* on pp. 296–297 and then answer the following questions.
   a. Why is the PC market an example of oligopoly?
   b. How do you think the price of a PC and the quantity of PCs sold are determined?
   c. Why did Dell begin a price war in the fall of 2000?
   d. What strategic variables other than price do PC makers use?
   e. Why (aside from the fact that it is illegal) is it impossible for PC makers to collude and earn a larger economic profit?

2. Suppose that Netscape and Microsoft each develop their own versions of an amazing new Web browser that allows advertisers to target consumers with great precision. Also, the new browser is easier and more fun to use than existing browsers. Each firm is trying to decide whether to sell the browser or to give it away free. What are the likely benefits from each action and which is likely to occur?

3. Why do Coca-Cola and PepsiCo spend huge amounts on advertising? Do they benefit? Does the consumer benefit? Explain your answer.

WEB EXERCISES

1. Use the links on your Parkin Web site to obtain information about the market for vitamins.
   a. In what type of market are vitamins sold?
   b. What illegal act occurred in the vitamins market during the 1990s?
   c. Describe the actions of BASF and Roche as a game and set out a hypothetical payoff matrix for the game.
   d. Is the game played by BASF and Roche a one-shot game or a repeated game? How do you know which type of game it is?

2. Use the links on your Parkin Web site to obtain information about the market for art and antiques.
   a. What illegal act occurred in the art and antiques auction market during the 1990s?
   b. Describe the game played by Sotheby's and Christie's and set out a payoff matrix.

PART 4

UNDERSTANDING FIRMS AND MARKETS

Managing Change

Our economy is constantly changing. Every year, new goods appear and old ones disappear. New firms are born and old ones die. This process of change is initiated and managed by firms operating in markets. When a new product is invented, just one or two firms sell it initially. For example, when the personal computer first became available, there was an Apple or an IBM. The IBM-PC had just one operating system, DOS, made by Microsoft. One firm, Intel, made the chip that ran the IBM-PC. These are examples of industries in which the producer has market power to determine the price of the product and the quantity produced. The extreme case of a single producer that cannot be challenged by new competitors is *monopoly*, which Chapter 12 explained. ◆ But not all industries with just one producer are monopolies. In many cases, the firm that is first to produce a new good faces severe competition from new rivals. One firm facing potential competition is the case of a *contestable market*. If demand increases and makes space for more than one firm, an industry becomes increasingly competitive. Even with just two rivals, the industry changes its face in a dramatic way. *Duopoly* — the case of just two producers — illustrates this dramatic change. The two firms must pay close attention to each other's production and prices and must predict the effects of their own actions on the actions of the other firm. We call this situation one of *strategic interdependence*. As the number of rivals grows, the industry becomes an *oligopoly*, a market in which a small number of firms devise strategies and pay close attention to the strategies of their competitors. ◆ With the continued arrival of new firms in an industry, the market eventually becomes competitive. Competition might be limited because each firm produces its own special version or brand of a good. This case is called *monopolistic competition* because it has elements of both monopoly and competition. Chapter 13 explored the behavior of firms in all of these types of markets that lie between monopoly at the one extreme and perfect competition at the other. ◆ When competition is extreme — the case that we call *perfect competition* — the market changes again in a dramatic way. Now the firm is unable to influence price. Chapter 11 explained this case. ◆ Often, an industry that is competitive becomes less so as the bigger and more successful firms in the industry begin to swallow up the smaller firms, either by driving them out of business or by acquiring their assets. Through this process, an industry might return to oligopoly or even monopoly. You can see such a movement in the auto and banking industries today. ◆ By studying firms and markets, we gain a deeper understanding of the forces that allocate scarce resources and begin to see the anatomy of the invisible hand. ◆ Many economists have advanced our understanding of these forces and we'll now meet two of them. John von Neumann pioneered the idea of game theory. And Bengt Holmstrom is one of today's leading students of strategic behavior.

PROBING THE IDEAS
Market Power

> "Real life consists of bluffing, of little tactics of deception, of asking yourself what is the other man going to think I mean to do."
>
> JOHN VON NEUMANN, *told to Jacob Bronowski (in a London taxi) and reported in* The Ascent of Man

THE ECONOMIST

JOHN VON NEUMANN *was one of the great minds of the twentieth century. Born in Budapest, Hungary, in 1903, Johnny, as he was known, showed early mathematical brilliance. His first mathematical publication was an article that grew out of a lesson with his tutor, which he wrote at the age of 18! But it was at the age of 25, in 1928, that von Neumann published the article that began a flood of research on game theory — a flood that has still not subsided today. In that article, he proved that in a zero-sum game (like sharing a pie), there exists a best strategy for each player.*

Von Neumann invented the computer and built the first modern practical computer, and he worked on the "Manhattan Project," which developed the atomic bomb at Los Alamos, New Mexico, during World War II.

Von Neumann believed that the social sciences would progress only if they used mathematical tools. But he believed that they needed different tools from those developed from the physical sciences.

THE ISSUES

It is not surprising that firms with market power will charge higher prices than those charged by competitive firms. But how much higher?

This question has puzzled generations of economists. Adam Smith said, "The price of a monopoly is upon every occasion the highest which can be got." But he was wrong. Antoine-Augustin Cournot (see p. 144) first worked out the price a monopoly will charge. It is not the "highest which can be got" but the price that maximizes profit. Cournot's work was not appreciated until almost a century later when Joan Robinson explained how a monopoly sets its price.

Questions about monopoly became urgent and practical during the 1870s, a time when rapid technological change and falling transportation costs enabled huge monopolies to emerge in the United States. Monopolies dominated oil, steel, railroads, tobacco, and even sugar. Industrial empires grew ever larger.

The success of the nineteenth century monopolies led to the creation of our antitrust laws — laws that limit the use of monopoly power. Those laws have been used to prevent monopolies from being set up and to break up existing monopolies. They were used during the 1960s to end a conspiracy between General Electric, Westinghouse, and other firms when they colluded to fix their prices instead of competing with each other. The laws were used during the 1980s to bring greater competition to long-distance telecommunication. But in spite of antitrust laws, near monopolies still exist. Among the most prominent today are those in computer chips and operating systems. Like their forerunners, today's near monopolies make huge profits. But unlike the situation in the nineteenth century, the technological change taking place today is strengthening the forces of competition. Today's information technologies are creating substitutes for services that previously had none. Direct satellite TV is competing with cable, and new phone companies are competing with the traditional phone monopolies.

Then

Ruthless greed, exploitation of both workers and customers — these are the traditional images of monopolies and the effects of their power. These images appeared to be an accurate description during the 1880s, when monopolies stood at their peak of power and influence. One monopolist, John D. Rockefeller, Sr., built his giant Standard Oil Company, which by 1879 was refining 90 percent of the nation's oil and controlling its entire pipeline capacity.

Now

Despite antitrust laws that regulate monopolies, they still exist. One is the monopoly in cable television. In many cities, one firm decides which channels viewers will receive and the price they will pay. During the 1980s, with the advent of satellite technology and specialist cable program producers such as CNN and HBO, the cable companies expanded their offerings. At the same time, they steadily increased prices and their businesses became very profitable. But the very technologies that made cable television profitable are now challenging its market power. Direct satellite TV services are eroding cable's monopoly and bringing greater competition to this market.

Today, many economists who work on microeconomics use the ideas that John von Neumann pioneered. Game theory is the tool of choice. One economist who has made good use of this tool (and many other tools) is Bengt Holmstrom of MIT, whom you can meet on the following pages.

TALKING WITH

BENGT HOLMSTROM *is
Paul A. Samuelson Professor of Economics in
the department of economics and the Sloan
School of Management at the Massachusetts
Institute of Technology. Born in 1949 in
Helsinki, Finland, he studied mathematics
and physics at the University of Helsinki
as an undergraduate and then worked as
an operations researcher before going to
Stanford University as an economics
graduate student. Professor Holmstrom's
research on the way firms use contracts and incentives is recognized as providing a
major advance in our un-
derstanding of the mecha-
nisms that operate inside
firms. Beyond his academic
research, Professor Holm-
strom has provided services
to a number of major corpo-
rations, including Nokia, of which he is currently a director.*

*Michael Parkin talked with Bengt
Holmstrom about his work and the progress
that economists have made in understanding
firms and the markets in which they operate
since the pioneering ideas about the nature of
the firm by Ronald Coase.*

Bengt Holmstrom

**Professor Holmstrom, did you study eco-
nomics as an undergraduate? What drew
you to this subject?**

No. I was a math and physics major as an
undergraduate in Helsinki. I got into economics the way many people do through a
side door from mathematics and operations
research at Stanford Graduate School of
Business.

**How did you get interested in the eco-
nomics of the firm?**

I went from my undergraduate degree to
work as an operations research analyst at a
large conglomerate in Finland. I was hired to
implement a company-wide corporate planning model. This was the early 70s, when
large optimization models were expected to
help firms make better long-term plans and
run operations more centrally.

It didn't take me very long to realize that
this was a misguided belief. The problem was
that the data came from people lower down
that had an apparent incentive to misrepresent
the numbers. Their minds were focused on
outwitting the model. My interest in incentives was entirely driven by this experience.

**One of your most profound insights was
to view the entire firm as an incentive
system. What do you mean when you describe a firm as an incentive system?
What implications follow from this view
of the firm?**

When people talk about incentives, they
tend to think about some explicit reward system like a salesperson's commission or a
stock option for an executive or something
like that.

The key insight has been to understand
that incentives are influenced in an enormous
number of ways, indirectly and implicitly.
For instance, constraints and bureaucratic
rules are very important pieces of the overall
incentive system. There are many different
ways of getting people to do what you think
they should be doing.

Sometimes the best incentive is to pay

no incentive! Incentives can be terribly damaging if they are poorly designed.

The firm as an incentive system is an expression of the fact that you need to think about *all* the possible ways in which you can influence people's actions and then how you orchestrate the instruments that are available. These instruments include promotion incentives, rewards, or even just praise. The narrow view that it's just a matter of paying a bonus of some sort is very misguided.

> *Sometimes the best incentive is to pay no incentive! Incentives can be terribly damaging if they are poorly designed.*

Can you talk about the role of the economist as economic advisor to a firm? One view is that firms are efficient and the task of the economist is to understand why. Another view is that the economist can help firms to become efficient— for example, by devising better incentive mechanisms. Can the economist help firms to become efficient? And are there other roles for the economist as adviser to a firm?

There's a well-known paradox —and tension — in economics. Positive economics deals with figuring out what is optimal —what is the best that can be done — and then using the description of optimal behavior as a predictive tool – as a way of explaining why things are the way they are in the world.

And yet at the same time, nothing is presumably perfect so there is room for innovation — organizational innovation and economic innovation — which leads to the economic advice you're asking about.

There are many roles an economist can play as adviser to a firm. If we really understand things better, maybe we can actually make improvements in them. If nothing else, we can understand that if the constraints change, then a system that's designed in a particular way would need to adapt itself to the new circumstances. For example, a firm might have a centralized organization that's good in one set of circumstances and then suddenly the circumstances change and innovation becomes very important, as we seem to think it is right now. Then that situation calls for changes toward organizational structures that are more suited for innovation.

So you can explain the tradeoff between central control and more flexible, innovative structures so that a firm's managers understand these forces. They then might decide to move in the direction that better achieves their objectives. Or they might realize that the reason why other firms change organizational structures may not be relevant in their case.

The economist can help people understand the variety of organizations so that they can pick the right one for the right set of circumstances. There isn't one organization that's good for everything — quite the contrary. Some activities require one kind of organization; some activities require another kind of organization. Charities, for instance, would not be well run by for-profit firms because they would run away with the money. That's an extreme example. So, non-profit organizations play a very important role in running charities.

Joint stock companies have proven to be an extremely flexible and robust form of organization both for small- and large-scale activities. Their scalability is one reason for their enormous success.

Are there any examples of serious progress that we've made in understanding which types of organizations work best in which circumstances?

I think there are lots. There's a big debate right now about airport security that's a wonderful illustration of the insight that the firm is an incentive system and an example of the possibility of having incentives that are too strong in the wrong place. One view is that profit-making companies that run the airport security checking are too oriented toward profit and too little oriented toward quality, because the quality checks come so infrequently. The standard argument is that if they make a mistake they must pay for it, so they have a strong incentive to deliver high-quality work. But if accidents happen infrequently, that sort of feedback mechanism is just too weak. This is a logical reason for moving in the direction of taking away profit-making incentives from airport security checking.

The very existence of the firm comes from the fact that it is there to remove and restructure incorrect incentives — excessively high-powered incentives that come from the market — and to get people to cooperate. In the market, it can be harder to cooperate because everyone is working for his or her own benefit. This works very well if there are a lot of alternatives to choose — if there's competition. But when there is a small number of traders, or where quality is hard to assess, bringing the activity inside the firm is quite natural.

One firm, Enron, was big news during 2002. What do models of incentive systems tell us about what went wrong with Enron?

I think Enron, like most of these disaster cases, teaches that misplaced incentives lead to potentially big mistakes. It's almost tautological to say that if wrong-doing was done, it was done because the incentives weren't aligned correctly. Now, how much of it was a design flaw within Enron and how much was a flaw of the overall system, is harder to judge. There were certainly regulatory problems — energy production regulations had changed; the energy market had been opened up and arbitrage opportunities created. Some of the activities of Enron that sought to profit from this new regulatory environment were entirely legal.

Then there was financial innovation. It's an old, old idea that it would be nice to remove debts from the balance sheet of a firm to make it look better to investors. And apparently new financial instruments had been created to make off-balance sheet operations possible. Some of them were clearly questionable and perhaps some of them illegal.

But the other problem — and this is a system problem, not just an Enron problem — is that when things are going well and everybody believes that the world is moving forward, it's very hard to question something. You go further and further out on a limb, and then the limb breaks and you learn that that was too much.

> *I don't think that a system that rules out everything that can go wrong is the right system.*

I don't see Enron as catastrophically as most people seem to. I think that we would pay a big price if we never let anybody like Enron try. If you regulate things so that nothing like it ever could have happened, it probably would have also thrown out a lot

of good innovations with it. It's part of the system to learn by having certain things like this happen.

I'm not defending Enron's actions. But I'm trying to give a different angle to the possible response. System design is different from trying to correct individual cases. I don't think that a system that rules out everything that can go wrong is the right system.

Is it important for an academic economist to have professional interests in the "real world"?

I think everybody's different. For me it has been important because I got interested in incentives through non-academic work. That's where I started, and I was just lucky that incentives happened to be a topical issue when I entered the field.

I don't think one could, in any sense, say that everybody must have real-world experience. You have to find your own sources of stimulation and discover what makes you curious and what makes you interested. For some people, that's just being exceedingly theoretical and not thinking about much else. Some are very talented that way; other people desperately need some connection with the real world. For me, that has been very valuable.

Needless to say, the fact that we are all different is extremely important for overall progress.

What advice do you have for a student who is just starting to study economics? Do you think that economics is a good subject in which to major? What other subjects would you urge students to study alongside economics?

I'm a big believer that people do their best work and have their happiest life when they do the things that they are really interested in. With the wonderful undergraduate system that America has, I would advise students to sample broadly and go in the direction they get most excited about. But I think there are many reasons to like economics. It spans a fascinating range of questions. At its heart, economics is about understanding social systems, current and past, and how these systems could be improved for the welfare of the human race. I'm confident that economics has contributed a great deal to the current levels of welfare in the West. And I'm optimistic that the developing world will also benefit from our intellectual progress. As an economist, you can have a really big impact, even if the results are less visible than in the natural sciences like physics. For me, it has been incredibly inspiring.

DEMAND AND SUPPLY IN FACTOR MARKETS

CHAPTER **14**

Many Happy Returns

It may not be your birthday, and even if it is, chances are you are spending most of it working. But at the end of the week or month (or, if you're devoting all your time to college, when you graduate), you will receive the *returns* from your labor. Those returns vary a lot. Demetrio Luna, who spends his days in a small container suspended from the top of Houston's high-rise buildings cleaning windows, makes a happy return of $12 an hour. Katie Couric, who co-anchors a morning news show each weekday, makes a very happy return of more than $16 million a year. Some differences in earnings might seem surprising. For example, your college football coach might earn much more than your economics professor. Why aren't *all* jobs well paid? ◆ Most of us have little trouble spending our pay. But most of us do manage to save some of what we earn. What determines the amount of saving that people do and the returns they make on that saving? ◆ Some people earn their income by supplying natural resources such as oil. What determines the price of a natural resource?

◆ In this chapter, we study the markets for factors of production — labor, capital, natural resources — and learn how their prices and people's incomes are determined. And we'll see in *Reading Between the Lines* at the end of the chapter why universities often pay their football coaches more than they pay professors.

After studying this chapter, you will be able to

■ Explain how firms choose the quantities of labor, capital, and natural resources to employ

■ Explain how people choose the quantities of labor, capital, and natural resources to supply

■ Explain how wages, interest, and natural resource prices are determined in competitive resource markets

■ Explain the concept of economic rent and distinguish between economic rent and opportunity cost

311

Prices and Incomes in Competitive Factor Markets

GOODS AND SERVICES ARE PRODUCED BY USING the four *factors of production—labor, capital, land,* and *entrepreneurship* (we defined these factors of production in Chapter 1, p. 4). Incomes are determined by *factor prices*—the *wage* rate for labor, the *interest* rate for capital, the *rental* rate for land, and the rate of *normal profit* for entrepreneurship—and the quantities of the factors used. In addition to the four factor incomes, a residual income, *economic profit* (or *economic loss*), is paid to (or borne by) firms' owners—sometimes the owner is the entrepreneur and sometimes the owners are the stockholders who provide financial capital.

Factors of production, like goods and services, are traded in markets. Some factors are traded in markets that are competitive and behave like other perfectly competitive markets. Other factors are traded in markets in which there is market power. We focus in this chapter on competitive factor markets to learn how they determine the prices, quantities used, and incomes of factors of production. In an appendix (pp. 337–342), we examine labor markets in which there is market power.

The main tool that we use in this chapter is the demand and supply model. The quantity demanded of a factor of production depends on its price, and the law of demand applies to factors of production just as it does to goods and services. The lower the price of a factor, other things remaining the same, the greater is the quantity demanded. Figure 14.1 shows the demand curve for a factor as the curve labeled *D*.

The quantity supplied of a factor also depends on its price. With a possible exception that we'll identify later in this chapter, the law of supply applies to factors of production. The higher the price of a factor, other things remaining the same, the greater is the quantity supplied of the factor. Figure 14.1 shows the supply curve of a factor as the curve labeled S.

The equilibrium factor price is determined at the point of intersection of the demand and supply curves. In Fig. 14.1, the price is *PF* and the quantity used is *QF*.

The income earned by the factor is its price multiplied by the quantity used. In Fig. 14.1, the factor income equals the area of the blue rectangle. This income is the total income received by the factor. Each person who supplies the factor receives the factor price multiplied by the quantity supplied by that person. A change in demand or supply changes the equilibrium price, quantity, and income.

An increase in demand shifts the demand curve rightward and increases price, quantity, and income. An increase in supply shifts the supply curve rightward and decreases price. The quantity used increases, but income might increase, decrease, or remain constant. The change in income that results from a change in supply depends on the elasticity of demand for the factor. If demand is elastic, income rises; if demand is inelastic, income falls; and if demand is unit elastic, income remains constant (see Chapter 4, p. 86).

The rest of this chapter explores the influences on the demand for and supply of factors of production. It also explains the influences on the elasticities of supply and demand for factors of production. These elasticities have major effects on factor prices, quantities used, and incomes.

We begin with the market for labor. But most of what we will learn about the labor market also applies to the other factor markets that we study later in the chapter.

FIGURE 14.1   Demand and Supply in a Factor Market

The demand curve for a factor of production (D) slopes downward, and the supply curve (S) slopes upward. Where the demand and supply curves intersect, the factor price (PF) and the quantity of the factor used (QF) are determined. The factor income is the product of the factor price and the quantity of the factor, as represented by the blue rectangle.

Labor Markets

FOR MOST OF US, THE LABOR MARKET IS OUR only source of income. And in recent years, many people have had a tough time. But over the years, both wages and the quantity of labor have moved steadily upward. Figure 14.2(a) shows the record since 1961. Using 1996 dollars to remove the effects of inflation, total compensation per hour of work increased by 100 percent, from $12 in 1961 to $24 in 2001. Over the same period, the quantity of labor employed increased by more than 100 percent, from 110 billion hours in 1961 to 230 billion hours in 2001.

Figure 14.2(b) shows why these trends occurred. The demand increased from LD_{61} to LD_{01}, and this increase was much larger than the increase in supply from LS_{61} to LS_{01}.

A lot of diversity lies behind the average wage rate and the aggregate quantity of labor. During the 1980s and 1990s, some wage rates grew much more rapidly than the average and others fell. To understand the trends in the labor market, we must probe the forces that influence the demand for labor and the supply of labor. This chapter studies these forces. We begin on the demand side of the labor market.

The Demand for Labor

The demand for labor is a derived demand. A **derived demand** is a demand for a productive resource that is *derived* from the demand for the goods and services produced by the resource. The derived demand for labor (and the other resources demanded by firms) is driven by the firm's objective, which is to maximize profit.

You learned in Chapters 11, 12, and 13 that a profit-maximizing firm produces the output at which marginal cost equals marginal revenue. This principle holds true for all firms regardless of whether they operate in perfect competition, monopolistic competition, oligopoly, or monopoly.

A firm that maximizes profit hires the quantity of labor that can produce the profit-maximizing output. What is that quantity of labor? And how does it change as the wage rate changes? We can answer these questions by comparing the *marginal* revenue earned by hiring one more worker with the *marginal* cost of that worker. Let's look first at the marginal revenue side of this comparison.

FIGURE 14.2   Labor Market Trends in the United States

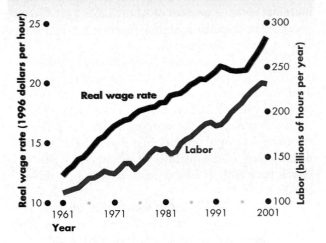

(a) Labor and wage rate

(b) Changes in demand and supply in the labor market

Between 1961 and 2001, the real wage rate doubled and the quantity of labor employed more than doubled. Part (a) shows these increases. Each dot in part (b) shows the real wage rate and the quantity of labor in each year from 1961 to 2001. Part (b) also shows the changes in demand and supply that generated these trends. The demand for labor increased from LD_{61} to LD_{01}, and the supply of labor increased from LS_{61} to LS_{01}. Demand increased by more than supply, so both the wage rate and the quantity of labor employed increased.

Sources: Bureau of Economic Analysis and Bureau of Labor Statistics.

Marginal Revenue Product

The change in total revenue that results from employing one more unit of labor is called the **marginal revenue product** of labor. Table 14.1 shows you how to calculate marginal revenue product for a firm in perfect competition.

The first two columns show the total product schedule for Max's Wash 'n' Wax car wash service. The numbers tell us how the number of car washes per hour varies as the quantity of labor varies. The third column shows the *marginal product of labor* — the change in total product that results from a one-unit increase in the quantity of labor employed. (Look back at p. 215 for a quick refresher on this concept.)

The car wash market in which Max operates is perfectly competitive, and he can sell as many washes as he chooses at $4 a wash, the (assumed) market price. So Max's *marginal revenue* is $4 a wash.

Given this information, we can now calculate *marginal revenue product* (the fourth column). It equals marginal product multiplied by marginal revenue. For example, the marginal product of hiring a second worker is 4 car washes an hour, and because marginal revenue is $4 a wash, the marginal revenue product of the second worker is $16 (4 washes at $4 each).

The last two columns of Table 14.1 show an alternative way to calculate the marginal revenue product of labor. Total revenue is equal to total product multiplied by price. For example, two workers produce 9 washes per hour and generate a total revenue of $36 (9 washes at $4 each). One worker produce 5 washes per hour and generates a total revenue of $20 (5 washes at $4 each). Marginal revenue product, in the sixth column, is the change in total revenue from hiring one more worker. When the second worker is hired, total revenue increases from $20 to $36, an increase of $16. So the marginal revenue product of the second worker is $16, which agrees with our previous calculation.

Diminishing Marginal Revenue Product As the quantity of labor increases, marginal revenue product diminishes. For a firm in perfect competition, marginal revenue product diminishes because marginal product diminishes. For a monopoly (or in monopolistic competition or oligopoly), marginal revenue product diminishes for a second reason. When more labor is hired and total product increases, the firm must cut its price to sell the extra product. So marginal product *and* marginal revenue decrease, both of which bring decreasing marginal revenue product.

TABLE 14.1   Marginal Revenue Product at Max's Wash 'n' Wax

	Quantity of labor (L) (workers)	Total Product (TP) (car washes per hour)	Marginal product (MP = ΔTP/ΔL) (washes per worker)	Marginal revenue product (MRP = MR × MP) (dollars per worker)	Total revenue (TR = P × TP) (dollars)	Marginal revenue product (MRP = ΔTR/ΔL) (dollars per worker)
A	0	0		20	0	
			 5			 20
B	1	5		16	20	
			 4			 16
C	2	9		12	36	
			 3			 12
D	3	12		8	48	
			 2			 8
E	4	14		4	56	
			 1			 4
F	5	15			60	

The car wash market is perfectly competitive, and the price is $4 a wash, so marginal revenue is $4 a wash. Marginal revenue product equals marginal product (column 3) multiplied by marginal revenue. For example, the marginal product of the second worker is 4 washes and marginal revenue is $4 a wash, so the marginal revenue product of the second worker (in column 4) is $16. Alternatively, if Max hires 1 worker (row B), total product is 5 washes an hour and total revenue is $20 (column 5). If he hires 2 workers (row C), total product is 9 washes an hour and total revenue is $36. By hiring the second worker, total revenue rises by $16 — the marginal revenue product of labor is $16.

The Labor Demand Curve

Figure 14.3 shows how the labor demand curve is derived from the marginal revenue product curve. The *marginal revenue product curve* graphs the marginal revenue product of a factor at each quantity of the factor hired. Figure 14.3(a) illustrates the marginal revenue product curve for workers employed by Max. The horizontal axis measures the number of workers that Max hires, and the vertical axis measures the marginal revenue product of labor. The blue bars show the marginal revenue product of labor as Max employs more workers. These bars correspond to the numbers in Table 14.1. The curve labeled *MRP* is Max's marginal revenue product curve.

A firm's marginal revenue product curve is also its demand for labor curve. Figure 14.3(b) shows Max's demand for labor curve (*D*). The horizontal axis measures the number of workers hired — the same as in part (a). The vertical axis measures the wage rate in dollars per hour. In Fig. 14.3(a), when Max increases the quantity of labor employed from 2 workers an hour to 3 workers an hour, his marginal revenue product is $12 an hour. In Fig. 14.3(b), at a wage rate of $12 an hour, Max hires 3 workers an hour.

The marginal revenue product curve is also the demand for labor curve because the firm hires the profit-maximizing quantity of labor. If the wage rate is *less* than marginal revenue product, the firm can increase its profit by employing one more worker. Conversely, if the wage rate is *greater* than marginal revenue product, the firm can increase its profit by employing one fewer worker. But if the wage rate *equals* marginal revenue product, then the firm cannot increase its profit by changing the number of workers it employs. The firm is making the maximum possible profit. Thus the quantity of labor demanded by the firm is such that the wage rate equals the marginal revenue product of labor.

Because the marginal revenue product curve is also the demand curve, and because marginal revenue product diminishes as the quantity of labor employed increases, the demand for labor curve slopes downward. The lower the wage rate, other things remaining the same, the more workers a firm hires.

When we studied firms' output decisions, we discovered that a condition for maximum profit is that marginal revenue equals marginal cost. We've now discovered another condition for maximum profit: Marginal revenue product of a factor equals the factor's price. Let's study the connection between these two conditions.

FIGURE 14.3   The Demand for Labor at Max's Wash 'n' Wax

(a) Marginal revenue product

(b) Demand for labor

Max's Wash 'n' Wax operates in a perfectly competitive car wash market and can sell any quantity of washes at $4 a wash. The blue bars in part (a) represent the firm's marginal revenue product of labor. They are based on the numbers in Table 14.1. The orange line is the firm's marginal revenue product of labor curve. Part (b) shows Max's demand for labor curve. This curve is identical to Max's marginal revenue product curve. Max demands the quantity of labor that makes the wage rate equal to the marginal revenue product of labor. The demand for labor curve slopes downward because marginal revenue product diminishes as the quantity of labor employed increases.

Equivalence of Two Conditions for Profit Maximization

Profit is maximized when, at the quantity of labor hired, *marginal revenue product* equals the wage rate and when, at the output produced, *marginal revenue* equals *marginal cost*.

These two conditions for maximum profit are equivalent. The quantity of labor that maximizes profit produces the output that maximizes profit.

To see the equivalence of the two conditions for maximum profit, first recall that

$$\text{Marginal revenue product} = \text{Marginal revenue} \times \text{Marginal product}.$$

If we call marginal revenue product *MRP*, marginal revenue *MR*, and marginal product *MP*, we have

$$MRP = MR \times MP.$$

If we call the wage rate *W*, the first condition for profit to be maximized is

$$MRP = W.$$

But *MRP* = *MR* × *MP*, so

$$MR \times MP = W.$$

This equation tells us that when profit is maximized, marginal revenue multiplied by marginal product equals the wage rate.

Divide the last equation by *MP* to obtain

$$MR = W \div MP.$$

This equation states that when profit is maximized, marginal revenue equals the wage rate divided by the marginal product of labor.

The wage rate divided by the marginal product of labor equals marginal cost. It costs the firm *W* to hire one more hour of labor. But the labor produces *MP* units of output. So the cost of producing one of those units of output, which is marginal cost, is *W* divided by *MP*.

If we call marginal cost *MC*, then

$$MR = MC,$$

which is the second condition for maximum profit.

Because the first condition for maximum profit implies the second condition, these two conditions are equivalent. Table 14.2 summarizes the calculations you've just done and shows the equivalence of the two conditions for maximum profit.

TABLE 14.2   Two Conditions for Maximum Profit

Symbols

Marginal product	**MP**
Marginal revenue	**MR**
Marginal cost	**MC**
Marginal revenue product	**MRP**
Factor price	**PF**

Two Conditions for Maximum Profit

1. **MR = MC**	2.	**MRP = PF**

Equivalence of Conditions

1.   *MRP/MP* = **MR**   =   **MC** = *PF/MP*

Multiply by *MP* to give

MRP = *MR* × *MP*   *MC* × *MP* = *PF*

Flipping the equation over

2.   *MR* × *MP* = **MRP**   =   **PF** = *MC* × *MP*

The two conditions for maximum profit are that marginal revenue (*MR*) equals marginal cost (*MC*) and that marginal revenue product (*MRP*) equals the wage rate (*W*). These two conditions are equivalent because marginal revenue product (*MRP*) equals marginal revenue (*MR*) multiplied by marginal product (*MP*) and the wage rate (*W*) equals marginal cost (*MC*) multiplied by marginal product (*MP*).

Max's Numbers   Check the numbers for Max's Wash 'n' Wax and confirm that the conditions you've just examined work. Max's profit-maximizing labor decision is to hire 3 workers if the wage rate is $12 an hour. When Max hires 3 hours of labor, marginal product is 3 washes per hour. Max sells the 3 washes an hour for a marginal revenue of $4 a wash. So marginal revenue product is 3 washes multiplied by $4 a wash, which equals $12 per hour. At a wage rate of $12 an hour, Max is maximizing profit.

Equivalently, Max's marginal cost is $12 an hour divided by 3 washes per hour, which equals $4 per wash. At a marginal revenue of $4 a wash, Max is maximizing profit.

You've discovered that the law of demand applies for labor just as it does for goods and services. Other things remaining the same, the lower the wage rate (the price of labor), the greater is the quantity of labor demanded.

Let's now study the influences that change the demand for labor and shift the demand for labor curve.

Changes in the Demand for Labor

The demand for labor depends on three factors:

1. The price of the firm's output
2. The prices of other factors of production
3. Technology

The higher the price of a firm's output, the greater is its demand for labor. The price of output affects the demand for labor through its influence on marginal revenue product. A higher price for the firm's output increases marginal revenue, which, in turn, increases the marginal revenue product of labor. A change in the price of a firm's output leads to a shift in the firm's demand for labor curve. If the price of the firm's output increases, the demand for labor increases and the demand for labor curve shifts rightward.

The other two influences affect the *long-run demand for labor*, which is the relationship between the wage rate and the quantity of labor demanded when all factors of production can be varied. In contrast, the *short-run demand for labor* is the relationship between the wage rate and the quantity of labor demanded when the quantities of the other factors are fixed and labor is the only variable resource. In the long run, a change in the relative price of a factor of production — such as the relative price of labor and capital — leads to a substitution away from the factor whose relative price has increased and toward the factor whose relative price has decreased. So if the price of capital decreases relative to that of using

labor, the firm substitutes capital for labor and increases the quantity of capital demanded.

But the demand for labor might increase or decrease. If the lower price of capital increases the scale of production by enough, the demand for labor increases. Otherwise, the demand for labor decreases.

Finally, a new technology that changes the marginal product of labor changes the demand for labor. For example, the electronic telephone exchange has decreased the demand for telephone operators. This same new technology has increased the demand for telephone engineers. Again, these effects are felt in the long run when the firm adjusts all its resources and incorporates new technologies into its production process. Table 14.3 summarizes the influences on a firm's demand for labor.

We saw in Fig. 14.3 that the demand for labor has increased over time and the demand curve has shifted rightward. We can now give some of the reasons for this increase in demand. Advances in technology and investment in new capital increase the marginal product of labor and increase the demand for labor.

TABLE 14.3   A Firm's Demand for Labor

The Law of Demand
(Movements along the demand curve for labor)

The quantity of labor demanded by a firm

Decreases if:	Increases if:
■ The wage rate increases	■ The wage rate decreases

Changes in Demand
(Shifts in the demand curve for labor)

A firm's demand for labor

Decreases if:	Increases if:
■ The firm's output price decreases	■ The firm's output price increases
■ A new technology decreases the marginal product of labor	■ A new technology increases the marginal product of labor

(Changes in the prices of other factors of production have an ambiguous effect on the demand for labor.)

Market Demand

So far, we've studied the demand for labor by an individual firm. The market demand for labor is the total demand by all firms. The market demand for labor curve is derived (similarly to the market demand curve for any good or service) by adding together the quantities demanded by all firms at each wage rate. Because each firm's demand for labor curve slopes downward, so does the market demand curve.

Elasticity of Demand for Labor

The elasticity of demand for labor measures the responsiveness of the quantity of labor demanded to the wage rate. This elasticity is important because it tells us how labor income changes when the supply of labor changes. An increase in supply (other things remaining the same) brings a lower wage rate. If demand is inelastic, it also brings lower labor income. But if demand is elastic, an increase in supply brings a lower wage rate and an increase in labor income. And if the demand for labor is unit elastic, a change in supply leaves labor income unchanged.

The demand for labor is less elastic in the short run, when only the quantity of labor can be varied, than in the long run, when the quantities of labor and other factors of production can be varied. The elasticity of demand for labor depends on

- The labor intensity of the production process
- The elasticity of demand for the product
- The substitutability of capital for labor

Labor Intensity A labor-intensive production process is one that uses a lot of labor and little capital. Home building is an example. The greater the degree of labor intensity, the more elastic is the demand for labor. To see why, first suppose that wages are 90 percent of total cost. A 10 percent increase in the wage rate increases total cost by 9 percent. Firms will be sensitive to such a large change in total cost, so if the wage rate increases, firms will decrease the quantity of labor demanded by a relatively large amount. But if wages are 10 percent of total cost, a 10 percent increase in the wage rate increases total cost by only 1 percent. Firms will be less sensitive to this increase in cost, so if the wage rate increases in this case, firms will decrease the quantity of labor demanded by a relatively small amount.

The Elasticity of Demand for the Product The greater the elasticity of demand for the good, the larger is the elasticity of demand for the labor used to produce it. An increase in the wage rate increases the marginal cost of producing the good and decreases the supply of it. The decrease in the supply of the good increases the price of the good and decreases the quantity demanded of the good and the quantities of the factors of production used to produce it. The greater the elasticity of demand for the good, the larger is the decrease in the quantity demanded of the good and so the larger is the decrease in the quantities of the factors of production used to produce it.

The Substitutability of Capital for Labor The more easily capital can be used instead of labor in production, the more elastic is the long-run demand for labor. For example, it is easy to use robots rather than assembly-line workers in car factories and grape-picking machines rather than labor in vineyards. So the demand for these types of labor is elastic. At the other extreme, it is difficult (though possible) to substitute computers for newspaper reporters, bank loan officers, and teachers. So the demand for these types of labor is inelastic.

Let's now turn from the demand side of the labor market to the supply side and examine the decisions that people make about how to allocate time between working and other activities.

The Supply of Labor

People can allocate their time to two broad activities: labor supply and leisure. (Leisure is a catch-all term. It includes all activities other than supplying labor.) For most people, leisure is more enjoyable than supplying labor. We'll look at the labor supply decision of Jill, who is like most people. She enjoys her leisure time, and she would be pleased if she didn't have to spend her weekends working a supermarket checkout line.

But Jill has chosen to work weekends. The reason is that she is offered a wage rate that exceeds her *reservation wage*. Jill's reservation wage is the lowest wage at which she is willing to supply labor. If the wage rate exceeds her reservation wage, she supplies some labor. But how much labor does she supply? The quantity of labor that Jill supplies depends on the wage rate.

Substitution Effect Other things remaining the same, the higher the wage rate Jill is offered, at least over a range, the greater is the quantity of labor that she supplies. The reason is that Jill's wage rate is her *opportunity cost of leisure*. If she quits work an hour early to catch a movie, the cost of that extra hour of leisure is the wage rate that Jill forgoes. The higher the wage rate, the less willing Jill is to forgo the income and take the extra leisure time. This tendency for a higher wage rate to induce Jill to work longer hours is a *substitution effect*.

But there is also an *income effect* that works in the opposite direction to the substitution effect.

Income Effect The higher Jill's wage rate, the higher is her income. A higher income, other things remaining the same, induces Jill to increase her demand for most goods. Leisure is one of those goods. Because an increase in income creates an increase in the demand for leisure, it also creates a decrease in the quantity of labor supplied.

Backward-Bending Supply of Labor Curve As the wage rate rises, the substitution effect brings an increase in the quantity of labor supplied while the income effect brings a decrease in the quantity of labor supplied. At low wage rates, the substitution

effect is larger than the income effect, so as the wage rate rises, people supply more labor. But as the wage rate continues to rise, the income effect eventually becomes larger than the substitution effect and the quantity of labor supplied decreases. The labor supply curve is *backward bending*.

Figure 14.4(a) shows the labor supply curves for Jill, Jack, and Kelly. Each labor supply curve is backward bending, but the three people have different reservation wage rates.

Market Supply The market supply of labor curve is the sum of the individual supply curves. Figure 14.4(b) shows the market supply curve (S_M) derived from the supply curves of Jill, Jack, and Kelly (S_A, S_B, and S_C, respectively) in Fig. 14.4(a). At a wage rate of less than $1 an hour, no one supplies any labor. At a wage rate of $1 an hour, Jill works but Jack and Kelly don't. As the wage rate increases and reaches $7 an hour, all three of them are working. The market supply curve S_M eventually bends backward, but it has a long upward-sloping section.

Changes in the Supply of Labor The supply of labor changes when influences other than the wage rate change. The key factors that change the supply of labor and that over the years have increased it are

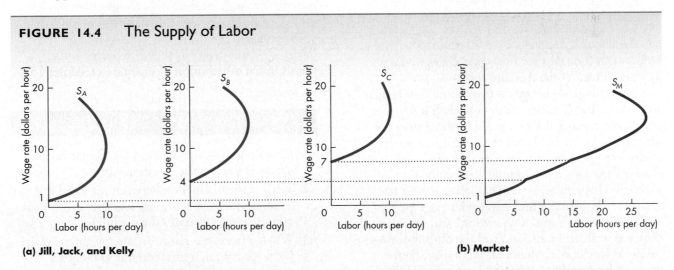

FIGURE 14.4   The Supply of Labor

(a) Jill, Jack, and Kelly

(b) Market

Part (a) shows the labor supply curves of Jill (S_A), Jack (S_B), and Kelly (S_C). Each person has a reservation wage below which she or he will supply no labor. As the wage rises, the quantity of labor supplied increases to a maximum. If the wage continues to rise, the quantity of labor supplied begins to decrease.

Each person's supply curve eventually bends backward.

Part (b) shows how, by adding the quantities of labor supplied by each person at each wage rate, we derive the market supply curve of labor (S_M). The market supply curve has a long upward-sloping region before it bends backward.

1. Adult population
2. Technological change and capital accumulation

An increase in the adult population increases the supply of labor. So does a technological change or increase in capital in home production (of meals, laundry services, and cleaning services). These factors that increase the supply of labor shift the labor supply curve rightward.

Let's now build on what we've learned about the demand for labor and the supply of labor and study labor market equilibrium and the trends in wage rates and employment.

Labor Market Equilibrium

Wages and employment are determined by equilibrium in the labor market. You saw, in Fig. 14.2, that the wage rate and employment have both increased over the years. You can now explain why.

Trends in the Demand for Labor The demand for labor has *increased* because of technological change and capital accumulation, and the demand for labor curve has shifted steadily rightward.

Many people are surprised that technological change and capital accumulation *increase* the demand for labor. They see new technologies *destroying jobs*, not creating them. Downsizing has become a catchword as the computer and information age has eliminated millions of "good" jobs, even those of managers. So how can it be that technological change *creates* jobs and increases the demand for labor?

Technological change destroys some jobs and creates others. But it creates more jobs than it destroys, and *on the average*, the new jobs pay more than the old ones did. But to benefit from the advances in technology, people must acquire new skills and change their jobs. For example, during the past 20 years, the demand for typists has fallen almost to zero. But the demand for people who can type (on a computer rather than a typewriter) and do other things as well has increased. And the output of these people is worth more than that of a typist. So the demand for people with typing (and other) skills has increased.

Trends in the Supply of Labor The supply of labor has increased because of population growth and technological change and capital accumulation in the home. The mechanization of home production of fast-food preparation services (the freezer and the microwave oven) and laundry services (the automatic washer and dryer and wrinkle-free fabrics) has decreased the time spent on activities that once were full-time jobs and have led to a large increase in the supply of labor. As a result, the supply labor curve has shifted steadily rightward, but at a slower pace than the shift in the demand curve.

Trends in Equilibrium Because technological advances and capital accumulation have increased demand by more than population growth and technological change in home production have increased supply, both wage rates and employment have increased. But not everyone has shared in the increased prosperity that comes from higher wage rates. Some groups have been left behind, and some have even seen their wage rates fall. Why?

Two key reasons can be identified. First, technological change affects the marginal productivity of different groups in different ways. High-skilled computer-literate workers have benefited from the information revolution while low-skilled workers have suffered. The demand for the services of the first group has increased, and the demand for the services of the second group has decreased. (Draw a supply and demand figure, and you will see that these changes widen the wage difference between the two groups.) Second, international competition has lowered the marginal revenue product of low-skilled workers and so has decreased the demand for their labor. We look further at skill differences and at trends in the distribution of income in Chapter 15.

REVIEW QUIZ

1 Why do we call the demand for labor a *derived demand*? From what is it derived?

2 What is the distinction between marginal revenue product and marginal revenue? Provide an example that illustrates the distinction.

3 When a firm's marginal revenue product equals the wage rate, marginal revenue also equals marginal cost. Why? Provide a numerical example different from that in the text.

4 What determines the amount of labor that households plan to supply?

5 Describe and explain the trends in wage rates and employment.

Capital Markets

CAPITAL MARKETS ARE THE CHANNELS THROUGH which firms obtain *financial* resources to buy *physical* capital resources. These financial resources come from saving. The "price of capital," which adjusts to make the quantity of capital supplied equal to the quantity demanded, is the interest rate.

For most of us, capital markets are where we make our biggest-ticket transactions. We borrow in a capital market to buy a home. And we lend in capital markets to build up a fund on which to live when we retire. Do the rates of return in capital markets increase as wage rates do?

Figure 14.5(a) answers this question by showing the record since 1960. Measuring interest rates as *real* interest rates, which means that we subtract the loss in the value of money from inflation, returns have fluctuated. They averaged about 2.5 percent a year during the 1960s, became negative during the 1970s, climbed to 9 percent during the mid 1980s, and steadied at around 5 percent during the 1990s and 2000. Over the same period, the quantity of capital employed increased steadily. In 2000, it stood at $24 trillion, three times its 1960 level.

Figure 14.5(b) shows why these trends occurred. Demand increased from KD_{60} to KD_{00}, and this increase was similar to the increase in supply from KS_{60} to KS_{00}. To understand the trends in the capital market, we must again probe the forces of demand and supply. Many of the ideas you've already met in your study of demand and supply in the labor market apply to the capital market as well. But there are some special features of capital. Its main special feature is that in the capital market, people must compare *present* costs with *future* benefits. Let's discover how these comparisons are made by studying the demand for capital.

The Demand for Capital

A firm's demand for *financial* capital stems from its demand for *physical* capital, and the amount that a firm plans to borrow in a given time period is determined by its planned investment — purchases of new capital. This decision is driven by its attempt to maximize profit. As a firm increases the quantity of capital employed, other things remaining the same, the marginal revenue product of capital eventually diminishes. To maximize profit, a firm increases its plant size and uses more capital if the marginal revenue

FIGURE 14.5   Capital Market Trends in the United States

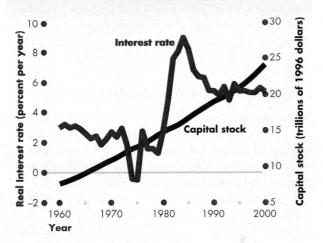

(a) Capital stock and interest rate

(b) Changes in demand and supply in the capital market

The real interest rate (the interest rate adjusted for inflation) fluctuated between a negative return in 1974 and 1975 and a high of 9 percent in 1984. It was steady at 2.5 percent during the 1960s and at about 5 percent during the 1990s and 2000. During the same period, the quantity of capital employed increased. By 2000, it was three times its 1960 level. Part (a) shows these trends. Part (b) shows the changes in demand and supply that have generated the trends. The demand for capital increased from KD_{60} to KD_{00}, and the supply of capital increased from KS_{60} to KS_{00}.

Sources: Bureau of Economic Analysis and Federal Reserve Board.

product of capital exceeds the price of capital. But the marginal revenue product comes in the future, and capital must be paid for in the present. So the firm must convert *future* marginal revenue products into a *present value* so that it can be compared with the price of the new equipment. To make this conversion, we use the technique of discounting.

Discounting and Present Value

Discounting is converting a future amount of money to a present value. And the **present value** of a future amount of money is the amount that, if invested today, will grow to be as large as that future amount when the interest that it will earn is taken into account.

The easiest way to understand discounting and present value is to begin with the relationship between an amount invested today, the interest that it earns, and the amount that it will grow to in the future. The future amount is equal to the present amount (present value) plus the interest it will accumulate in the future. That is,

Future amount = Present value

+ Interest income.

The interest income is equal to the present value multiplied by the interest rate, r, so

Future amount = Present value

+ ($r \times$ Present value)

or

Future amount = Present value $\times (1 + r)$.

If you have $100 today and the interest rate is 10 percent a year ($r = 0.1$), one year from today you will have $110 — the original $100 plus $10 interest. Check that the above formula delivers that answer: $100 \times 1.1 = $110.

The formula that we have just used calculates a future amount one year from today from the present value and an interest rate. To calculate the present value, we just work backward. Instead of multiplying the present value by $(1 + r)$, we divide the future amount by $(1 + r)$. That is,

$$\text{Present value} = \frac{\text{Future amount}}{(1 + r)}.$$

You can use this formula to calculate present value. This calculation of present value is called discounting.

Let's check that we can use the present value formula by calculating the present value of $110 one year from now when the interest rate is 10 percent a year. You'll be able to guess that the answer is $100 because we just calculated that $100 invested today at 10 percent a year becomes $110 in one year. Thus it follows immediately that the present value of $110 in one year's time is $100. But let's use the formula. Putting the numbers into the above formula, we have

$$\text{Present value} = \frac{\$110}{(1 + 0.1)}$$

$$= \frac{\$110}{1.1} = \$100.$$

Calculating the present value of an amount of money one year from now is the easiest case. But we can also calculate the present value of an amount any number of years in the future. As an example, let's see how we calculate the present value of an amount of money that will be available two years from now.

Suppose that you invest $100 today for two years at an interest rate of 10 percent a year. The money will earn $10 in the first year, which means that by the end of the first year, you will have $110. If the interest of $10 is invested, then the interest earned in the second year will be a further $10 on the original $100 plus $1 on the $10 interest. Thus the total interest earned in the second year will be $11. The total interest earned overall will be $21 ($10 in the first year and $11 in the second year). After two years, you will have $121. From the definition of present value, you can see that the present value of $121 two years hence is $100. That is, $100 is the present amount that, if invested at an interest rate of 10 percent a year, will grow to $121 two years from now.

To calculate the present value of an amount of money two years in the future, we use the formula:

$$\text{Present value} = \frac{\text{Amount of money two years in future}}{(1 + r)^2}.$$

Use this formula to calculate the present value of $121 two years from now at an interest rate of 10 percent a year. With these numbers, the formula gives

$$\text{Present value} = \frac{\$121}{(1 + 0.1)^2}$$

$$= \frac{\$121}{(1.1)^2}$$

$$= \frac{\$121}{1.21}$$

$$= \$100.$$

We can calculate the present value of an amount of money n years in the future by using a formula similar to the one we've already used. The general formula is

$$\text{Present value} = \frac{\begin{array}{c}\text{Amount of money}\\ n\text{ years in future}\end{array}}{(1 + r)^n}.$$

For example, if the interest rate is 10 percent a year, $100 to be received 10 years from now has a present value of $38.55. That is, if $38.55 is invested today at 10 percent a year it accumulates to $100 in 10 years.

You've seen how to calculate the present value of an amount of money one year in the future, two years in the future, and n years in the future. Most practical applications of present value calculate the present value of a sequence of future amounts of money that spread over several years. To calculate the present value of a sequence of amounts over several years, we use the formula you have learned and apply it to each year. We then sum the present values for each year to find the present value of the sequence of amounts.

For example, suppose that a firm expects to receive $100 a year for each of the next five years. And suppose that the interest rate is 10 percent per year (0.1 per year). The present value of these five payments of $100 each is calculated by using the following formula

$$PV = \frac{\$100}{1.1} + \frac{\$100}{1.1^2} + \frac{\$100}{1.1^3} + \frac{\$100}{1.1^4} + \frac{\$100}{1.1^5},$$

which equals

$$PV = \$90.91 + \$82.64 + \$75.13 + 68.30$$

$$+ \$62.09$$

$$= \$379.07.$$

You can see that the firm receives $500 over five years. But because the money arrives in the future, it is not worth $500 today. Its present value is only $379.07. And the farther in the future the money arrives, the smaller is its present value. The $100 received one year in the future is worth $90.91 today. And the $100 received five years in the future is worth only $62.09 today.

Let's now see how a firm uses the concept of present value to achieve an efficient use of capital.

The Present Value of a Computer We'll see how a firm decides how much capital to buy by calculating the present value of a new computer.

Tina runs Taxfile, Inc., a firm that sells advice to taxpayers. Tina is considering buying a new computer that costs $10,000. The computer has a life of two years, after which it will be worthless. If Tina buys the computer, she will pay $10,000 now and she expects to generate business that will bring in an additional $5,900 at the end of each of the next two years.

To calculate the present value, PV, of the marginal revenue product of a new computer, Tina calculates

$$PV = \frac{MRP_1}{(1 + r)} + \frac{MRP_2}{(1 + r)^2}.$$

Here, MRP_1 is the marginal revenue product received by Tina at the end of the first year. It is converted to a present value by dividing it by $(1 + r)$, where r is the interest rate (expressed as a proportion). The term MRP_2 is the marginal revenue product received at the end of the second year. It is converted to a present value by dividing it by $(1 + r)^2$.

If Tina can borrow or lend at an interest rate of 4 percent a year, the present value of her marginal revenue product is given by

$$PV = \frac{\$5,900}{(1 + 0.04)} + \frac{\$5,900}{(1 + 0.04)^2}$$

$$PV = \$5,673 + \$5,455$$

$$PV = \$11,128.$$

The present value (PV) of $5,900 one year in the future is $5,900 divided by 1.04 (4 percent as a proportion is 0.04). The present value of $5,900 two years in the future is $5,900 divided by $(1.04)^2$. Tina works out those two present values and then adds them to get the present value of the future flow of marginal revenue product, which is $11,128.

Parts (a) and (b) of Table 14.4 summarize the data and the calculations we've just made. Review these calculations and make sure you understand them.

TABLE 14.4   Net Present Value of an Investment — Taxfile, Inc.

(a) Data

Price of computer	$10,000
Life of computer	2 years
Marginal revenue product	$5,900 at end of each year
Interest rate	4% a year

(b) Present value of the flow of marginal revenue product

$$PV = \frac{MRP_1}{(1 + r)} + \frac{MRP_2}{(1 + r)^2}$$

$$= \frac{\$5,900}{1.04} + \frac{\$5,900}{(1.04)^2}$$

$$= \$5,673 + \$5,455$$

$$= \$11,128.$$

(c) Net present value of investment

$NPV = PV$ of marginal revenue product − Price of computer

$$= \$11,128 - \$10,000$$

$$= \$1,128$$

Tina's Decision to Buy Tina decides whether to buy the computer by comparing the present value of its future flow of marginal revenue product with its purchase price. She makes this comparison by calculating the net present value (*NPV*) of the computer. **Net present value** is the present value of the future flow of marginal revenue product generated by the capital minus the price of the capital. If net present value is positive, the firm buys additional capital. If the net present value is negative, the firm does not buy additional capital. Table 14.4(c) shows the calculation of Tina's net present value of a computer. The net present value is $1,128 — greater than zero — so Tina buys the computer.

Tina can buy any number of computers that cost $10,000 and have a life of two years. But like all other factors of production, capital is subject to diminishing marginal returns. The greater the amount of capital employed, the smaller is its marginal revenue product. So if Tina buys a second computer or a third one, she gets successively smaller marginal revenue products from the additional machines.

Table 14.5(a) sets out Tina's marginal revenue products for one, two, and three computers. The marginal revenue product of one computer (the case just reviewed) is $5,900 a year. The marginal revenue product of a second computer is $5,600 a year, and the marginal revenue product of a third computer is $5,300 a year. Table 14.5(b) shows the calculations of the present values of the marginal revenue products of the first, second, and third computers.

You've seen that with an interest rate of 4 percent a year, the net present value of one computer is positive. At an interest rate of 4 percent a year, the present value of the marginal revenue product of a second computer is $10,562, which exceeds its price by $562. So Tina buys a second computer. But at an interest rate of 4 percent a year, the present value of the marginal revenue product of a third computer is $9,996, which is $4 less than the price of the computer. So Tina does not buy a third computer.

A Change in the Interest Rate We've seen that at an interest rate of 4 percent a year, Tina buys two computers but not three. Suppose that the interest rate is 8 percent a year. In this case, the present value of the first computer is $10,521 (see Table 14.5b), so Tina still buys one machine because it has a positive net present value. At an interest rate of 8 percent a year, the present value of the second computer is $9,986, which is less than $10,000, the price of the computer. So at an interest rate of 8 percent a year, Tina buys only one computer.

Suppose that the interest rate is even higher, 12 percent a year. In this case, the present value of the marginal revenue product of one computer is $9,971 (see Table 14.5b). At this interest rate, Tina buys no computers.

These calculations trace Taxfile's demand schedule for capital, which shows the value of computers demanded by Taxfile at each interest rate. Other things remaining the same, as the interest rate rises, the quantity of capital demanded decreases. The higher the interest rate, the smaller is the quantity of *physical* capital demanded. But to finance the purchase of *physical* capital, firms demand *financial* capital. So the higher the interest rate, the smaller is the quantity of *financial* capital demanded.

TABLE 14.5   Taxfile's Investment Decision

(a) Data

Price of computer	$10,000
Life of computer	2 years
Marginal revenue product:	
Using 1 computer	$5,900 a year
Using 2 computers	$5,600 a year
Using 3 computers	$5,300 a year

(b) Present value of the flow of marginal revenue product

If $r = 0.04$ (4% a year):

Using 1 computer: $PV = \dfrac{\$5,900}{1.04} + \dfrac{\$5,900}{(1.04)^2} = \$11,128$

Using 2 computers: $PV = \dfrac{\$5,600}{1.04} + \dfrac{\$5,600}{(1.04)^2} = \$10,562$

Using 3 computers: $PV = \dfrac{\$5,300}{1.04} + \dfrac{\$5,300}{(1.04)^2} = \$9,996$

If $r = 0.08$ (8% a year):

Using 1 computer: $PV = \dfrac{\$5,900}{1.08} + \dfrac{\$5,900}{(1.08)^2} = \$10,521$

Using 2 computers: $PV = \dfrac{\$5,600}{1.08} + \dfrac{\$5,600}{(1.08)^2} = \$9,986$

If $r = 0.12$ (12% a year):

Using 1 computer: $PV = \dfrac{\$5,900}{1.12} + \dfrac{\$5,900}{(1.12)^2} = \$9,971$

Demand Curve for Capital

The quantity of capital demanded by a firm depends on the marginal revenue product of capital and the interest rate. A firm's demand curve for capital shows the relationship between the quantity of capital demanded by the firm and the interest rate, other things remaining the same. The market demand curve (as in Fig. 14.5) shows the relationship between the total quantity of capital demanded by all firms and the interest rate, other things remaining the same.

Changes in the Demand for Capital Figure 14.5 shows that the market demand for capital has increased steadily over the years. The demand for capital changes when expectations about the future marginal revenue product of capital change. An increase in the expected marginal revenue product of capital increases the demand of capital. Two main factors that change the marginal revenue product of capital and bring changes in the demand by all firms for capital are

1. Population growth
2. Technological change

An increase in the population increases the demand for all goods and services and so increases the demand for the capital that produces them. Advances in technology increase the demand for some types of capital and decrease the demand for other types. For example, the development of diesel engines for railroad transportation decreased the demand for steam engines and increased the demand for diesel engines. In this case, the railroad industry's overall demand for capital did not change much. In contrast, the development of desktop computers increased the demand for office computing equipment, decreased the demand for electric typewriters, and increased the overall demand for capital in the office.

Let's now turn to the supply side of the capital market.

The Supply of Capital

The quantity of capital supplied results from people's saving decisions. The main factors that determine saving are

■ Income
■ Expected future income
■ Interest rate

To see how these factors influence saving, let's see how Aaron makes his saving decisions.

Income Saving is the act of converting *current* income into *future* consumption. When Aaron's income increases, he plans to consume more both now and in the future. But to increase *future* consumption, Aaron must save today. So, other things remaining the same, the higher Aaron's income, the more he saves. The relationship between saving and income is remarkably stable. People tend to save a constant proportion of their income.

Expected Future Income Because a major reason for saving is to increase future consumption, the amount that Aaron saves today depends not only on his current income but also on his *expected future income*. If Aaron's current income is high and his expected future income is low, he will have a high level of saving. But if Aaron's current income is low and his expected future income is high, he will have a low (perhaps even negative) level of saving.

Young people (especially students) usually have low current incomes compared with their expected future income. To smooth out their lifetime consumption, young people consume more than they earn and incur debts and have a negative amount of saving. In middle age, most people's incomes reach their peak. At this stage in life, saving is at its maximum. After retirement, people spend part of the wealth they have accumulated during their working lives and have a negative amount of saving.

Interest Rate A dollar saved today grows into a dollar plus interest tomorrow. The higher the interest rate, the greater is the amount that a dollar saved today becomes in the future. Thus the higher the interest rate, the greater is the opportunity cost of current consumption. With a higher opportunity cost of current consumption, Aaron cuts his current consumption and increases his saving.

Supply Curve of Capital

The supply curve of capital (like that in Fig. 14.5) shows the relationship between the quantity of capital supplied and the interest rate, other things remaining the same. An increase in the interest rate brings an increase in the quantity of capital supplied and a movement along the supply curve. The supply of capital is inelastic in the short run but probably quite elastic in the long run. The reason is that in any given year, the total amount of saving is small relative to the stock of capital in existence. So even a large change in the saving rate brings only a small change in the quantity of capital supplied.

Changes in the Supply of Capital The main influences on the supply of capital are the size and age distribution of the population and the level of income.

Other things remaining the same, an increase in the population or an increase in income brings an increase in the supply of capital. Also, other things remaining the same, the larger the proportion of middle-aged people, the higher is the saving rate. The

reason is that middle-aged people do most of the saving as they build up a pension fund to provide a retirement income. Any one of the factors that increases the supply of capital shifts the supply curve of capital rightward.

Let's now use what we've learned about the demand for and supply of capital and see how the interest rate is determined.

The Interest Rate

Saving plans and investment plans are coordinated through capital markets, and the real interest rate adjusts to make these plans compatible.

Figure 14.6 shows the capital market. Initially, the demand for capital is KD_0, and the supply of capital is KS_0. The equilibrium real interest rate is 6 percent a year, and the quantity of capital is $10 trillion. If the interest rate exceeds 6 percent a year, the quantity of capital supplied exceeds the quantity of capital demanded and the interest rate falls. And if the interest rate is less than 6 percent a year, the

FIGURE 14.6   Capital Market Equilibrium

Initially, the demand for capital is KD_0 and the supply of capital is KS_0. The equilibrium interest rate is 6 percent a year, and the capital stock is $10 trillion. Over time, both demand and supply increase to KD_1 and KS_1. The capital stock increases, but the real interest rate is constant. Demand and supply increase because they are influenced by common factors.

quantity of capital demanded exceeds the quantity of capital supplied and the interest rate rises.

Over time, both the demand for capital and the supply of capital increase. The demand curve shifts rightward to KD_1, and the supply curve also shifts rightward, to KS_1. Both curves shift because the same forces influence both. Population growth increases both demand and supply. Technological advances increase demand and bring higher incomes, which in turn increase supply. Because both demand and supply increase over time, the quantity of capital trends upward and the real interest rate has no trend.

Although the real interest rate does not follow a rising or falling trend, it does fluctuate, as you can see in Fig. 14.5. The reason is that the demand for capital and the supply of capital do not change in lockstep. Sometimes rapid technological change brings an increase in the demand for capital *before* it brings rising incomes that increase the supply of capital. When this sequence of events occurs, the real interest rate rises. The first half of the 1980s was such a time, as you can see in Fig. 14.5(a).

At other times, the demand for capital grows slowly or even decreases temporarily. In this situation, supply outgrows demand and the real interest rate falls. Figure 14.5 shows that the mid-1970s and the period from 1984 through 1991 were two such periods.

REVIEW QUIZ

1 What is discounting and how is it used to calculate a present value? When might you want to calculate a present value to make a decision?
2 How does a firm compare the future marginal revenue product of capital with the current price of capital?
3 What are the main influences on a firm's demand for capital?
4 What are the main influences on the supply of capital?
5 What have been the main trends in the quantity of capital and the real interest rate and how can we explain the trends by using the demand for capital and the supply of capital?

The lessons that we've just learned about capital markets can be used to understand the prices of non-renewable natural resource prices. Let's see how.

Natural Resource Markets

NATURAL RESOURCES, OR WHAT ECONOMISTS CALL *land*, fall into two categories:

■ Renewable
■ Nonrenewable

Renewable natural resources are natural resources that can be used repeatedly. Examples are land (in its everyday sense), rivers, lakes, rain, and sunshine.

Nonrenewable natural resources are natural resources that can be used only once and that cannot be replaced once they have been used. Examples are coal, natural gas, and oil — the so-called hydrocarbon fuels.

The demand for natural resources as inputs into production is based on the same principle of marginal revenue product as the demand for labor (and the demand for capital). But the supply of natural resources is special. Let's look first at the supply of renewable natural resources.

The Supply of a Renewable Natural Resource

The quantity of land and other renewable natural resources available is fixed. The quantity supplied cannot be changed by individual decisions. People can vary the amount of land they own. But when one person buys some land, another person sells it. The aggregate quantity of land supplied of any particular type and in any particular location is fixed, regardless of the decisions of any individual. This fact means that the supply of each particular piece of land is perfectly inelastic. Figure 14.7 illustrates such a supply. Regardless of the rent available, the quantity of land supplied on Chicago's "Magnificent Mile" is a fixed number of square feet.

Because the supply of land is fixed regardless of its price, price is determined by demand. The greater the demand for a specific piece of land, the higher is its price.

Expensive land can be, and is, used more intensively than inexpensive land. For example, high-rise buildings enable land to be used more intensively. However, to use land more intensively, it has to be combined with another factor of production: capital. An increase in the amount of capital per block of land does not change the supply of land itself.

FIGURE 14.7   The Supply of Land

The supply of a given piece of land is perfectly inelastic. No matter what the rent, no more land than the quantity that exists can be supplied.

Although the supply of each type of land is fixed and its supply is perfectly inelastic, each individual firm, operating in competitive land markets, faces an elastic supply of land. For example, Fifth Avenue in New York City has a fixed amount of land, but Doubleday, the bookstore, could rent some space from Saks, the department store. Each firm can rent the quantity of land that it demands at the going rent, as determined in the marketplace. Thus, provided that land markets are competitive, firms are price takers in these markets, just as they are in the markets for other productive resources.

The Supply of a Nonrenewable Natural Resource

The *stock* of a natural resource is the quantity in existence at a given time. This quantity is fixed and is independent of the price of the resource. The *known* stock of a natural resource is the quantity that has been discovered. This quantity increases over time because advances in technology enable ever less accessible sources to be discovered. Both of these *stock* concepts influence the price of a nonrenewable natural resource.

But the influence is indirect. The direct influence on price is the rate at which the resource is supplied for use in production — called the *flow* supply.

The flow supply of a nonrenewable natural resource is *perfectly elastic* at a price that equals the present value of the expected price next period.

To see why, think about the economic choices of Saudi Arabia, a country that possesses a large inventory of oil. Saudi Arabia can sell an additional billion barrels of oil right now and use the income it receives to buy U.S. bonds. Or it can keep the billion barrels in the ground and sell them next year. If it sells the oil and buys bonds, it earns the interest rate on the bonds. If it keeps the oil and sells it next year, it earns the amount of the price increase or loses the amount of the price decrease between now and next year.

If Saudi Arabia expects the price of oil to rise next year by a percentage that equals the current interest rate, the price that it expects next year equals $(1 + r)$ multiplied by this year's price. For example, if this year's price is $12 a barrel and the interest rate is 5 percent ($r = 0.5$), then next year's expected price is $1.05 \times \$12$, which equals $12.60 a barrel.

With the price expected to rise to $12.60 next year, Saudi Arabia is indifferent between selling now for $12 and not selling now but waiting until next year and selling for $12.60. Saudi Arabia expects to make the same return either way. So at $12 a barrel, Saudi Arabia will sell whatever quantity is demanded.

But if Saudi Arabia expects the price to rise next year by a percentage that exceeds the current interest rate, then Saudi Arabia expects to make a bigger return by hanging onto the oil than by selling the oil and buying bonds. So it keeps the oil and sells none. And if Saudi Arabia expects the price to rise next year by a percentage that is less than the current interest rate, the bond gives a bigger return than the oil, so Saudi Arabia sells as much oil as it can.

Recall the idea of discounting and present value. The minimum price at which Saudi Arabia is willing to sell oil is the present value of the expected future price. At this price, it will sell as much oil as buyers demand. So its supply is perfectly elastic.

Price and the Hotelling Principle

Figure 14.8 shows the equilibrium in a natural resource market. Because supply is perfectly elastic at the present value of next period's expected price, the actual price of the natural resource equals the present value of next period's expected price. Also, because

FIGURE 14.8   A Nonrenewable Natural Resource Market

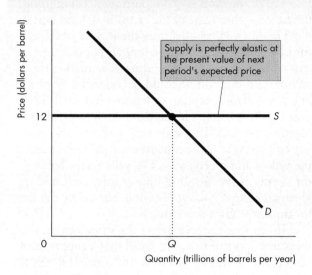

Supply is perfectly elastic at the present value of next period's expected price

The supply of a nonrenewable natural resource is perfectly elastic at the *present value* of next period's expected price. The demand for a nonrenewable natural resource is determined by its marginal revenue product. The price is determined by supply and equals the *present value* of next period's expected price.

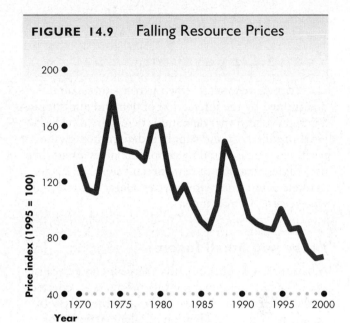

FIGURE 14.9   Falling Resource Prices

The prices of metals (here an average of the prices of aluminum, copper, iron ore, lead, manganese, nickel, silver, tin, and zinc) have tended to fall over time, not rise as predicted by the Hotelling Principle. The reason is that unanticipated advances in technology have decreased the cost of extracting resources and greatly increased the exploitable known reserves.

Source: *International Financial Statistics* (various issues), Washington, DC: International Monetary Fund.

the current price is the present value of the expected future price, the price of the resource is expected to rise at a rate equal to the interest rate.

The proposition that the price of a resource is expected to rise at a rate equal to the interest rate is called the *Hotelling Principle*. It was first realized by Harold Hotelling, a mathematician and economist at Columbia University. But as Fig. 14.9 shows, *actual* prices do not follow the path *predicted* by the Hotelling Principle. Why do the prices of nonrenewable natural resources sometimes fall rather than follow their expected path and increase over time?

The key reason is that the future is unpredictable. Expected technological change is reflected in the price of a natural resource. But a previously unexpected new technology that leads to the discovery or the more efficient use of a nonrenewable natural resource causes its price to fall. Over the years, as technology has advanced, we have become more efficient in our use of nonrenewable natural resources. And we haven't just become more efficient. We've become more efficient than we expected to.

REVIEW QUIZ

1 Why is the supply of a *renewable* natural resource such as land perfectly inelastic?
2 At what price is the flow supply of a nonrenewable natural resource perfectly elastic and why?
3 Why is the price of a nonrenewable natural resource expected to rise at a rate equal to the interest rate?
4 Why do the prices of nonrenewable resources not follow the path predicted by the Hotelling Principle?

People supply resources to earn an income. But some people earn enormous incomes. Are such incomes necessary to induce people to work and supply other resources? Let's now answer this question.

Income, Economic Rent, and Opportunity Cost

YOU'VE NOW SEEN HOW FACTOR PRICES ARE determined by the interaction of demand and supply. And you've seen that demand is determined by marginal productivity and supply is determined by the resources available and by people's choices about their use. The interaction of demand and supply in factor markets determines who receives a large income and who receives a small income.

Large and Small Incomes

A national news anchor earns a large income because she has a high marginal revenue product — reflected in the demand for her services — and the supply of people with the combination of talents needed for this kind of job is small — reflected in the supply. Equilibrium occurs at a high wage rate and a small quantity employed.

People who work at fast-food restaurants earn a low wage rate because they have a low marginal revenue product — reflected in the demand for their services — and many people are able and willing to supply their labor for these jobs. Equilibrium occurs at a low wage rate and a large quantity employed.

If the demand for news anchors increases, their incomes increase by a large amount and the number of news anchors barely changes. If the demand for fast-food workers increases, the number of people doing these jobs increases by a large amount and the wage rate barely changes.

Another difference between a news anchor and a fast-food worker is that if the news anchor were hit with a pay cut, she would probably still supply her services, but if a fast-food worker were hit with a pay cut, he would probably quit. This difference arises from the interesting distinction between economic rent and opportunity cost.

Economic Rent and Opportunity Cost

The total income of a factor of production is made up of its economic rent and its opportunity cost. **Economic rent** is the income received by the owner of a factor of production over and above the amount required to induce that owner to offer the factor for use. Any factor of production can receive an economic rent. The income required to induce the supply of a factor of production is the opportunity cost of using the factor — the value of the factor in its next best use.

Figure 14.10(a) illustrates the way in which a factor income has an economic rent and opportunity cost component. The figure shows the market for a factor of production. It could be *any* factor of production — labor, capital, or land — but we'll suppose that it is labor. The demand curve is D, and the supply curve is S. The wage rate is W, and the quantity employed is C. The income earned is the sum of the yellow and green areas. The yellow area below the supply curve measures opportunity cost, and the green area above the supply curve but below the factor price measures economic rent.

To see why the area below the supply curve measures opportunity cost, recall that a supply curve can be interpreted in two different ways. It shows the quantity supplied at a given price, and it shows the minimum price at which a given quantity is willingly supplied. If suppliers receive only the minimum amount required to induce them to supply each unit of the factor, they will be paid a different price for each unit. The prices will trace the supply curve, and the income received will be entirely opportunity cost — the yellow area in Fig. 14.10(a).

The concept of economic rent is similar to the concept of producer surplus that you met in Chapter 5. Economic rent is the price a person receives for the use of a factor minus the minimum price at which a given quantity of the factor is willingly supplied.

Economic rent is not the same thing as the "rent" that a farmer pays for the use of some land or the "rent" that you pay for your apartment. Everyday "rent" is a price paid for the services of land or a building. *Economic rent* is a component of the income received by any factor of production.

The portion of the factor income that consists of economic rent depends on the elasticity of the supply of the factor. When the supply of a factor is perfectly inelastic, its entire income is economic rent. Most of the income received by Garth Brooks and Pearl Jam is economic rent. Also, a large part of the income of a major-league baseball player is economic rent. When the supply of a factor of production is perfectly elastic, none of its income is economic rent. Most of the income of a babysitter is opportunity cost. In general, when supply is neither perfectly elastic nor perfectly

FIGURE 14.10   Economic Rent and Opportunity Cost

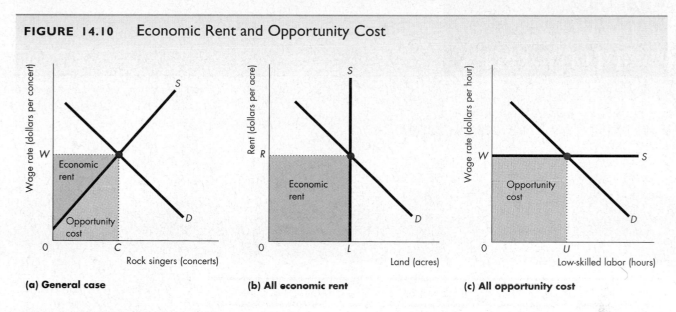

(a) General case

(b) All economic rent

(c) All opportunity cost

When the supply curve of a factor slopes upward — the general case — as in part (a), part of the factor income is economic rent (the green area) and part is opportunity cost (the yellow area). When the supply of a factor is perfectly inelastic (the supply curve is vertical), as in part (b), the entire factor income is economic rent. When the supply of the factor is perfectly elastic, as in part (c), the factor's entire income is opportunity cost.

perfectly inelastic, like that illustrated in Fig. 14.10(a), some part of the factor income is economic rent and the other part is opportunity cost.

Figures 14.10(b) and 14.10(c) show the other two possibilities. Part (b) shows the market for a particular parcel of land in New York City. The quantity of land is fixed in size at *L* acres. Therefore the supply curve of the land is vertical — perfectly inelastic. No matter what the rent on the land is, there is no way of increasing the quantity that can be supplied. Suppose that the demand curve in Fig. 14.10(b) shows the marginal revenue product of this block of land. Then it commands a rent of *R*. The entire income accruing to the owner of the land is the green area in the figure. This income is *economic rent*.

Figure 14.10(c) shows the market for a factor of production that is in perfectly elastic supply. An example of such a market might be that for low-skilled labor in a poor country such as India or China. In those countries, large amounts of labor flock to the cities and are available for work at the going wage rate (in this case, *W*). Thus in these situations, the supply of labor is almost perfectly elastic. The entire income earned by these workers is opportunity cost. They receive no economic rent.

◆ *Reading Between the Lines* on pp. 332–333 looks at the market for college football coaches and compares it with the market for professors.

The next chapter looks at how the market economy distributes income and explains the trends in the distribution of income. The chapter also looks at the efforts by governments to redistribute income and modify the market outcome.

Labor Markets in Action

FORT WORTH STAR-TELEGRAM. NOVEMBER 18, 2001

Who Is Worth More, the Coach or the Prof?

A *Star-Telegram* survey of the conference's 11 public institutions shows that five head football coaches have financial packages exceeding $1 million in guaranteed annual compensation and that more than half the full-time assistant coaches have annual salaries in excess of $100,000.

The survey, based on information and documents provided by the schools in response to public-records requests, found that those head coaches whose annual compensation tops $1 million are Oklahoma's Bob Stoops ($2 million), Kansas State's Bill Snyder ($1.5 million), Texas' Mack Brown ($1.45 million), Nebraska's Frank Solich ($1.1 million) and Texas A&M's R.C. Slocum ($1.02 million).

The survey also found that 53 of the 99 full-time assistant coaches at the 11 schools are receiving more than $100,000 in annual compensation. Eleven are making more than $140,000 a year.

At Oklahoma and Oklahoma State, the survey found, the average salaries of assistant football coaches exceed the average salaries of full professors by more than 50 percent.

Texas' nine full-time assistant coaches are being paid a total of $1.22 million, highest in the Big 12. The annual salaries of the Texas assistant coaches range from $113,668 to $198,640. The average salary of a UT assistant coach, $135,126, is $41,026 more than the average salary of a full professor at the university.

At Oklahoma, eight of the nine assistants make more than $100,000 a year. The average OU assistant's salary, $129,333, is $48,033 more than the average annual salary of the university's full professors.

...

Essence of the Story

■ Five head college football coaches earn more than $1 million a year. They are Oklahoma's Bob Stoops ($2 million), Kansas State's Bill Snyder ($1.5 million), Texas's Mack Brown ($1.45 million), Nebraska's Frank Solich ($1.1 million), and Texas A&M's R.C. Slocum ($1.02 million).

■ Fifty-three of the 99 full-time assistant coaches earn more than $100,000 a year, and 11 earn more than $140,000 a year.

■ At several universities, assistant coaches earn more than the average full professor by between $40,000 and almost $50,000 a year.

Economic Analysis

■ The market for college football coaches and assistant coaches is competitive.

■ The market for professors is also competitive.

■ The demand for both coaches and professors is determined by the marginal revenue product of each group.

■ The marginal revenue product of a coach depends on the coach's ability to win games and the additional revenue that the college or university can raise from its alumni and other contributors when its football team is successful.

■ The marginal revenue product of a professor depends on the ability of the professor to attract students and research funding.

■ For any given quantity of coaches and professors, the marginal revenue product of a professor almost certainly exceeds that of a coach.

■ But the equilibrium wage rate of a coach and that of a professor depend on the marginal revenue product of each group and on the supply of each.

■ The supply of coaches is small and probably inelastic.

■ The supply of professors is large and most likely elastic.

■ The supply of coaches is inelastic because few people have the talent demanded by this specialized activity.

■ The supply of professors is elastic because they are generally well-educated people who can do many alternative jobs.

■ Equilibrium in the market for coaches occurs at a higher wage rate and a much smaller quantity than equilibrium in the market for professors.

■ The figure shows the two markets. Notice that there is a break in the x-axis because the quantity of professors is much greater than that of coaches.

■ The demand for coaches is D_C, and the demand for professors is D_P. The supply of coaches is S_C, and the supply of professors is S_P.

Figure 1 The market for coaches and professors

■ The equilibrium quantity of coaches is 8,000, and the equilibrium quantity of professors is 1 million.

■ The equilibrium wage rate of coaches is $135,000 a year, and the equilibrium wage rate of professors is $94,000 a year.

■ Because the supply of coaches is inelastic, a large part of their income is economic rent. But colleges and universities can't lower the wage rate of coaches because each school faces a perfectly elastic supply at the going market-determined equilibrium wage rate.

■ The figure is based on data for assistant coaches. Head coaches earn 10 times (or more) the wage rate of assistant coaches because the supply of head coaches is even smaller than the supply of assistant coaches.

■ The figure is also based on data for professors on the average. Some professors earn three times (or more) the wage rate of the average professor because the supply of truly outstanding teachers and researchers is smaller than the supply of average teachers and researchers.

333

SUMMARY

KEY POINTS

Prices and Incomes in Competitive Factor Markets (p. 312)

- An increase in the demand for a factor of production increases the factor's price and total income; a decrease in the demand for a factor of production decreases its price and total income.
- An increase in the supply of a factor of production increases the quantity used but decreases its price and might increase or decrease its total income depending on whether demand is elastic or inelastic.

Labor Markets (pp. 313–320)

- The demand for labor is determined by the marginal revenue product of labor.
- The demand for labor increases if the price of the firm's output rises or if technological change and capital accumulation increase marginal product.
- The elasticity of demand for labor depends on the labor intensity of production, the elasticity of demand for the product, and the ease with which labor can be substituted for capital.
- The quantity of labor supplied increases as the real wage rate increases, but at high wage rates, the supply curve eventually bends backward.
- The supply of labor increases as the population increases and with technological change and capital accumulation.
- Wage rates and employment increase because demand increases by more than supply.

Capital Markets (pp. 321–327)

- To make an investment decision, a firm compares the *present value* of the marginal revenue product of capital with the price of capital.
- Population growth and technological change increase the demand for capital.
- The higher the interest rate, the greater is the amount of saving and the quantity of capital supplied.
- The supply of capital increases as incomes increase.
- Capital market equilibrium determines the real interest rate.

Land and Nonrenewable Natural Resource Markets (pp. 327–329)

- The demand for natural resources is determined by marginal revenue product.
- The supply of land is inelastic.
- The supply of nonrenewable natural resources is perfectly elastic at a price equal to the present value of the expected future price.
- The price of nonrenewable natural resources is expected to rise at a rate equal to the interest rate but fluctuates and sometimes falls.

Incomes, Economic Rent, and Opportunity Cost (pp. 330–331)

- Economic rent is the income received by the owner of a factor of production over and above the amount needed to induce the owner to supply the factor for use.
- The rest of a factor's income is an opportunity cost.
- When the supply of a factor is perfectly inelastic, its entire income is made up of economic rent, and when supply is perfectly elastic, the entire income is made up of opportunity cost.

KEY FIGURES AND TABLES

KEY TERMS

PROBLEMS

*1. The figure illustrates the market for blueberry pickers.

a. What is the wage rate paid to blueberry pickers?
b. How many blueberry pickers get hired?
c. What is the income received by blueberry pickers?

2. In problem 1, if the demand for blueberry pickers decreases by 100 a day,
    a. What is the new wage rate paid to the pickers?
    b. How many pickers get laid off?
    c. What is the total income paid to pickers?

🖥 *3. Wanda owns a fish shop. She employs students to sort and pack the fish. Students can pack the following amounts of fish in an hour:

Number of students	Quantity of fish (pounds)
1	20
2	50
3	90
4	120
5	145
6	165
7	180
8	190

Wanda can sell her fish for 50¢ a pound, and the wage rate of packers is $7.50 an hour.
    a. Calculate the marginal product of the students and draw the marginal product curve.

b. Calculate the marginal revenue product of the students and draw the marginal revenue product curve.
    c. Find Wanda's demand for labor curve.
    d. How many students does Wanda employ?

4. Larry makes gourmet ice cream in small batches. He employs workers who can produce the following quantities in a day:

Number of workers	Quantity of ice cream (batches)
1	4
2	10
3	18
4	24
5	29
6	33
7	36
8	38

Larry can sell ice cream for $25 a batch, and the wage rate of his workers is $100 a day.
    a. Calculate the marginal product of the workers and draw the marginal product curve.
    b. Calculate the marginal revenue product of the workers and draw the marginal revenue product curve.
    c. Find Larry's demand for labor curve.
    d. How much ice cream does Larry sell?

*5. Back at Wanda's fish shop described in problem 3, the price of fish falls to 33.33¢ a pound but fish packers' wages remain at $7.50 an hour.
    a. What happens to the student's marginal product?
    b. What happens to Wanda's marginal revenue product?
    c. What happens to her demand for labor curve?
    d. What happens to the number of students that she employs?

6. Back at Larry's ice cream making plant described in problem 4, the price of ice cream falls to $20 a batch but the wage rate remains at $100 a day.
    a. What happens to the student's marginal product?
    b. What happens to Larry's marginal revenue product?
    c. What happens to his demand for labor curve?
    d. What happens to the number of workers that he employs?

*7. Back at Wanda's fish shop described in problem 3, packers' wages increase to $10 an hour but the price of fish remains at 50¢ a pound.
   a. What happens to marginal revenue product?
   b. What happens to Wanda's demand for labor curve?
   c. How many students does Wanda employ?

8. Back at Larry's ice cream-making plant described in problem 4, the wage rate rises to $125 a day but the price of ice cream remains at $25 a batch.
   a. What happens to marginal revenue product?
   b. What happens to Larry's demand for labor curve?
   c. How many workers does Larry employ?

*9. Using the information provided in problem 3, calculate Wanda's marginal revenue, marginal cost, and marginal revenue product. Show that when Wanda is making maximum profit, marginal cost equals marginal revenue and marginal revenue product equals the wage rate.

10. Using the information provided in problem 4, calculate Larry's marginal revenue, marginal cost, and marginal revenue product. Show that when Larry is making maximum profit, marginal cost equals marginal revenue and marginal revenue product equals the wage rate.

*11. Greg has found an oil well in his backyard. A geologist estimates that a total of 10 million barrels can be pumped for a pumping cost of a dollar a barrel. The price of oil is $20 a barrel. How much oil does Greg sell each year? If you can't predict how much he will sell, what extra information would you need to be able to do so?

12. Orley has a wine cellar in which he keeps choice wines from around the world. What does Orley expect to happen to the prices of the wines he keeps in his cellar? Explain your answer. How does Orley decide which wine to drink and when to drink it?

*13. Use the figure in problem 1 and show on the figure the blueberry pickers':
   a. Economic rent.
   b. Opportunity cost.

14. Use the figure in problem 1 and the information in problem 2 and show on the figure the blueberry pickers':
   a. Economic rent.
   b. Opportunity cost.

CRITICAL THINKING

1. Study *Reading Between the Lines* on pp. 328–329 and answer the following questions:
   a. What determines the marginal revenue product of a college football coach?
   b. Do you think a head coach has a higher marginal revenue product than an assistant coach? Why or why not?
   c. What determines the marginal revenue product of a professor?
   d. Do you think a professor of economics has a higher marginal revenue product than a professor of English? Why or why not?
   e. Why does a coach earn a higher wage rate than a professor, on the average?
   f. Explain what would happen to a university that decided to pay coaches and professors the same wage rate.

2. "We are running out of natural resources and must take urgent action to conserve our precious reserves." "There is no shortage of resources that the market cannot cope with." Debate these two views. List the pros and cons for each.

3. Why do we keep finding new reserves of oil? Why don't we do a once-and-for-all big survey that catalogs the earth's entire inventory of natural resources?

WEB EXERCISES

1. Use the link on your Parkin Web site and read the article on "Trends in Hours of Work Since the Mid 1970s."
   a. What are the trends in hours of work since the mid-1970s?
   b. Are the trends for men the same as those for women? What are the similarities and differences?
   c. Do you think the trends arise from changes on the demand side of the labor market or from changes on the supply side?
   d. What additional information would you need to be sure about your answer to part (c)?

Labor Unions

After studying this appendix, you will be able to

- **Explain why union workers earn more than nonunion workers**
- **Explain how a labor market works in a monopsony**
- **Explain the effects of a minimum wage law in a monopsony**

Market Power in the Labor Market

JUST AS A MONOPOLY FIRM CAN RESTRICT OUTPUT and raise price, so a monopoly owner of a resource can restrict supply and raise the price of the resource.

The main source of market power in the labor market is the labor union. A **labor union** is an organized group of workers that aims to increase wages and influence other job conditions.

There are two main types of union: craft unions and industrial unions. A *craft union* is a group of workers who have a similar range of skills but work for many different firms in many different industries and regions. Examples are the carpenters' union and the electrical workers union (IBEW). An *industrial union* is a group of workers who have a variety of skills and job types but work for the same firm or industry. The United Auto Workers (UAW) and the Steelworkers Union are examples of industrial unions.

Most unions are members of the AFL-CIO, which was created in 1955 when the American Federation of Labor (AFL), founded in 1886 to organize craft unions, and the Congress of Industrial Organizations (CIO), founded in 1938 to organize industrial unions, combined.

Unions vary enormously in size. Craft unions are the smallest, and industrial unions are the biggest. Union strength peaked in the 1950s, when 35 percent of the nonagricultural work force belonged to unions. That percentage has declined steadily since 1955 and is now only 12 percent.

A labor union can operate an open shop, a closed shop, or a union shop. An *open shop* is an arrangement in which workers can be employed without joining the union — there is no union restriction on who can work in the "shop," or firm. A *closed shop* is an arrangement in which only union members can be employed by a firm. Closed shops have been illegal since the passage of the Taft-Hartley Act in 1947. A *union shop* is an arrangement by which a firm can hire nonunion workers but in order for such workers to remain employed, they must join the union within a brief period specified by the union. Union shops are illegal in the 20 states that have passed right-to-work laws. A *right-to-work law* allows an individual to work in any firm without joining a union.

Unions negotiate with employers or their representatives in a process called *collective bargaining*. The main weapons available to the union and the employer in collective bargaining are the strike and the lockout. A *strike* is a group decision by the workers to refuse to work under prevailing conditions. A *lockout* is a firm's refusal to operate its plant and employ its workers. Each party uses the threat of a strike or a lockout to try to get an agreement in its own favor. Sometimes, when the two parties in the collective bargaining process cannot agree on the wage rate or other conditions of employment, they agree to submit their disagreement to binding arbitration. *Binding arbitration* is a process in which a third party — an arbitrator — determines wages and other employment conditions on behalf of the negotiating parties.

Although they are not labor unions in a legal sense, professional associations act in ways similar to labor unions. A *professional association* is an organized group of professional workers such as lawyers, dentists, or physicians (an example of which is the American Medical Association — AMA). Professional associations control entry into the professions and license practitioners, ensuring the adherence to minimum standards of competence. But they also influence the compensation and other labor market conditions of their members.

Unions' Objectives and Constraints

A union has three broad objectives that it strives to achieve for its members:

1. To increase compensation
2. To improve working conditions
3. To expand job opportunities

Each of these objectives contains a series of more detailed goals. For example, in seeking to increase members' compensation, a union operates on a variety of fronts: wage rates, fringe benefits, retirement pay, and such things as vacation allowances. In seeking to improve working conditions, a union is concerned with occupational health and safety as well as the environmental quality of the workplace. In seeking to expand job opportunities, a union tries to get greater job security for existing union members and to find ways of creating additional jobs for them.

A union's ability to pursue its objectives is restricted by two sets of constraints — one on the supply side of the labor market and the other on the demand side. On the supply side, the union's activities are limited by how well it can restrict nonunion workers from offering their labor in the same market as union labor. The larger the fraction of the work force controlled by the union, the more effective the union can be in this regard. It is difficult for unions to operate in markets where there is an abundant supply of willing nonunion labor. For example, the market for farm labor in southern California is very tough for a union to organize because of the ready flow of nonunion, often illegal, labor from Mexico. At the other extreme, unions in the construction industry can better pursue their goals because they can influence the number of people who can obtain skills as electricians, plasterers, and carpenters. The professional associations of dentists and physicians are best able to restrict the supply of dentists and physicians. These groups control the number of qualified workers by controlling either the examinations that new entrants must pass or entrance into professional degree programs.

On the demand side of the labor market, the union faces a tradeoff that arises from firms' profit-maximizing decisions. Because labor demand curves slope downward, anything a union does that increases the wage rate or other employment costs decreases the quantity of labor demanded.

Let's see how unions operate in competitive labor markets.

A Union in a Competitive Labor Market

When a union operates in an otherwise competitive labor market, it seeks to increase wages and other compensation and to limit employment reductions by increasing demand for the labor of its members. That is, the union tries to take actions that shift the demand curve for its members' labor rightward.

Figure A14.1 illustrates a competitive labor market that a union enters. The demand curve is D_C, and the supply curve is S_C. Before the union enters the market, the wage rate is $7 an hour and 100 hours of labor are employed.

Now suppose that a union is formed to organize the workers in this market. The union can attempt to increase wages in this market in two ways. It can try to restrict the supply of labor, or it can try to stimulate the demand for labor. First, look at what happens if the union has sufficient control over the supply of labor to be able to artificially restrict that supply below its competitive level — to S_U. If that is all the union is able to do, employment falls to 85 hours of labor and the wage rate rises to $8 an hour. The union simply picks its preferred position along the

FIGURE A14.1   A Union in a Competitive Labor Market

In a competitive labor market, the demand curve is D_C and the supply curve is S_C. Competitive equilibrium occurs at a wage rate of $7 an hour with 100 hours employed. By restricting employment below the competitive level, the union shifts the supply of labor to S_U. If the union can do no more than that, the wage rate will increase to $8 an hour but employment will fall to 85 hours. If the union can increase the demand for labor (by increasing the demand for the good produced by union members or by raising the price of substitute labor) and shift the demand curve to D_U, then it can increase the wage rate still higher, to $9 an hour, and achieve employment of 90 hours.

demand curve that defines the tradeoff it faces between employment and the wage rate.

You can see that if the union can only restrict the supply of labor, it raises the wage rate but decreases the number of jobs available. Because of this outcome, unions try to increase the demand for labor and shift the demand curve rightward. Let's see what they might do to achieve this outcome.

How Unions Try to Change the Demand for Labor

Unless a union can take actions that change the demand for the labor that it represents, it has to accept the fact that a higher wage rate can be obtained only at the price of lower employment.

The union tries to operate on the demand for labor in two ways. First, it tries to make the demand for union labor inelastic. Second, it tries to increase the demand for union labor. Making the demand for labor less elastic does not eliminate the tradeoff between employment and the wage rate. But it does make the tradeoff less unfavorable. If a union can make the demand for labor less elastic, it can increase the wage rate at a lower cost in terms of lost employment opportunities. But if the union can increase the demand for labor, it might even be able to increase both the wage rate and the employment opportunities of its members. Some of the methods used by the unions to change the demand for the labor of its members are to

■ Increase the marginal product of union members
■ Encourage import restrictions
■ Support minimum wage laws
■ Support immigration restrictions
■ Increase demand for the good produced

Unions try to increase the marginal product of their members, which in turn increases the demand for their labor, by organizing and sponsoring training schemes, by encouraging apprenticeship and other on-the-job training activities, and by professional certification.

One of the best examples of import restrictions is the support by the United Auto Workers union (UAW) for import restrictions on foreign cars.

Unions support minimum wage laws to increase the cost of employing low-skilled labor. An increase in the wage rate of low-skilled labor leads to a decrease in the quantity demanded of low-skilled

labor and to an increase in demand for high-skilled union labor, a substitute for low-skilled labor.

Restrictive immigration laws decrease the supply of low-skilled workers and increase their wage rate. As a result, the demand for high-skilled union labor increases.

Because the demand for labor is a derived demand, an increase in the demand for the good produced by union labor increases the demand for union labor. The garment workers' union urging us to buy union-made clothes and the UAW asking us to buy only American cars made by union workers are examples of attempts by unions to increase the demand for union labor.

Figure A14.1 illustrates the effects of an increase in the demand for the labor of a union's members. If the union can also take steps that increase the demand for labor to D_U, it can achieve an even bigger increase in the wage rate with a smaller fall in employment. By maintaining the restricted labor supply at S_U, the union increases the wage rate to $9 an hour and achieves an employment level of 90 hours of labor.

Because a union restricts the supply of labor in the market in which it operates, its actions increase the supply of labor in nonunion markets. Workers who can't get union jobs must look elsewhere for work. This increase in the supply of labor in nonunion markets lowers the wage rate in those markets and further widens the union-nonunion differential.

The Scale of Union-Nonunion Wage Differentials

We have seen that unions can influence the wage rate by restricting the supply of labor and increasing the demand for labor. How much of a difference to wage rates do unions make in practice?

Union wage rates are, on the average, 30 percent higher than nonunion wage rates. In mining and financial services, union and nonunion wages are similar. In services, manufacturing, and transportation, the differential is between 11 and 19 percent. In wholesale and retail trades, the differential is 28 percent, and in construction, it is 65 percent.

But these union-nonunion wage differentials don't give a true measure of the effects of unions. In some industries, union wages are higher than nonunion wages because union members do jobs that involve greater skill. Even without a union, those workers would receive a higher wage. To calculate the effects of unions, we have to examine the wages of unionized and nonunionized workers who do nearly identical work. The evidence suggests that after allowing for skill differentials, the union-nonunion wage differential lies between 10 percent and 25 percent. For example, airline pilots who belong to the Airline Pilots' Union earn about 25 percent more than nonunion pilots with the same level of skill.

Let's now look at monopsony.

Monopsony

A MARKET IN WHICH THERE IS A SINGLE BUYER IS called **monopsony**. This market type is unusual, but it does exist. With the growth of large-scale production over the last century, large manufacturing plants such as coal mines, steel and textile mills, and car manufacturers became the major employer in some regions, and in some places a single firm employed almost all the labor. Today, in some parts of the country, managed health care organizations are the major employer of health care professionals. These firms have market power.

In monopsony, the employer determines the wage rate and pays the lowest wage at which it can attract the labor it plans to hire. A monopsony makes a bigger profit than a group of firms that compete with each other for their labor. Let's find out how they achieve this outcome.

Like all firms, a monopsony has a downward-sloping marginal revenue product curve, which is *MRP* in Fig. A14.2. This curve tells us the extra revenue the monopsony receives by selling the output produced by an extra hour of labor. The supply of labor curve is *S*. This curve tells us how many hours are supplied at each wage rate. It also tells us the minimum wage for which a given quantity of labor is willing to work.

A monopsony recognizes that to hire more labor, it must pay a higher wage; equivalently, by hiring less labor, it can pay a lower wage. Because a monopsony controls the wage rate, the marginal cost of labor exceeds the wage rate. The marginal cost of labor is shown by the curve *MCL*. The relationship between the marginal cost of labor curve and the supply curve is similar to the relationship between the marginal cost and average cost curves that you studied in Chapter 10. The supply curve is like the average cost of labor curve. In Fig. A14.2, the firm can hire 49 hours of labor for a wage rate of just below $4.90 an hour. The firm's total labor cost is $240. But suppose

that the firm hires 50 hours of labor. It can hire the 50th hour of labor for $5 an hour. The total cost of labor is now $250 an hour. So hiring the 50th hour of labor increases the cost of labor from $240 to $250, which is a $10 increase. The marginal cost of labor is $10 an hour. The curve *MCL* shows the $10 marginal cost of hiring the 50th hour of labor.

To calculate the profit-maximizing quantity of labor to hire, the firm sets the marginal cost of labor equal to the marginal revenue product of labor. That is, the firm wants the cost of the last worker hired to equal the extra total revenue brought in. In Fig. A14.2, this outcome occurs when the monopsony employs 50 hours of labor. What is the wage rate that the monopsony pays? To hire 50 hours of labor, the firm must pay $5 an hour, as shown by the supply of labor curve. So each worker is paid $5 an hour. But the marginal revenue product of labor is $10 an hour, which means that the firm makes an economic profit of $5 on the last hour of labor that it hires. Compare this outcome with that in a competitive labor market.

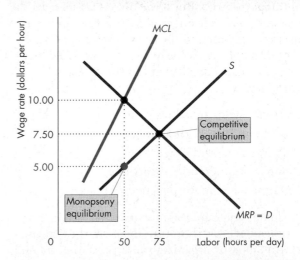

FIGURE A14.2   A Monopsony Labor Market

A monopsony is a market structure in which there is a single buyer. A monopsony in the labor market has value of marginal revenue product curve *MRP* and faces a labor supply curve *S*. The marginal cost of labor curve is *MCL*. Making the marginal cost of labor equal to marginal revenue product maximizes profit. The monopsony hires 50 hours of labor and pays the lowest wage for which that labor will work, which is $5 an hour.

If the labor market shown in Fig. A14.2 were competitive, equilibrium would occur at the point of intersection of the demand curve and the supply curve. The wage rate would be $7.50 an hour, and 75 hours of labor a day would be employed. So compared with a competitive labor market, a monopsony decreases both the wage rate and employment.

The ability of a monopsony to cut the wage rate and employment and make an economic profit depends on the elasticity of labor supply. If the supply of labor is highly elastic, a monopsony has little power to cut the wage rate and employment to boost its profit.

Monopsony Tendencies

Today, monopsony is rare. Workers can commute long distances to a job, so most people have more than one potential employer. But firms that are dominant employers in isolated communities do face an upward-sloping supply of labor curve and so have a marginal cost of labor that exceeds the wage rate. But in such situations, there is also, usually, a union. Let's see how unions and monopsonies interact.

Monopsony and a Union

In Chapter 12, we discovered that in monopoly, a firm can determine the market price. We've now seen that in monopsony — a market with a single buyer — the buyer can determine the price. Suppose that a union operates in a monopsony labor market. A union is like a monopoly. If the union (monopoly seller) faces a monopsony buyer, the situation is called **bilateral monopoly**. In bilateral monopoly, the wage rate is determined by bargaining.

In Fig. A14.2, if the monopsony is free to determine the wage rate and the level of employment, it hires 50 hours of labor for a wage rate of $5 an hour. But suppose that a union represents the workers. The union agrees to maintain employment at 50 hours but seeks the highest wage rate the employer can be forced to pay. That wage rate is $10 an hour — the wage rate that equals the marginal revenue product of labor. The union might not be able to get the wage rate up to $10 an hour. But it won't accept $5 an hour. The monopsony firm and the union bargain over the wage rate, and the result is an outcome between $10 an hour and $5 an hour.

The outcome of the bargaining depends on the costs that each party can inflict on the other as a result of a failure to agree on the wage rate. The firm can shut down the plant and lock out its workers, and the workers can shut down the plant by striking. Each party knows the other's strength and knows what it will lose if it does not agree to the other's demands. If the two parties are equally strong and they realize it, they will split the gap between $5 and $10 and agree to a wage rate of $7.50 an hour. If one party is stronger than the other — and both parties know that — the agreed wage will favor the stronger party. Usually, an agreement is reached without a strike or a lockout. The threat is usually enough to bring the bargaining parties to an agreement. When a strike or lockout does occur, it is usually because one party has misjudged the costs each party can inflict on the other.

Minimum wage laws have interesting effects in monopsony labor markets. Let's study these effects.

Monopsony and the Minimum Wage

In a competitive labor market, a minimum wage that exceeds the equilibrium wage decreases employment (see Chapter 6, pp. 127–128). In a monopsony labor market, a minimum wage can *increase* both the wage rate and employment. Let's see how.

Figure A14.3 shows a monopsony labor market in which the wage rate is $5 an hour and 50 hours of

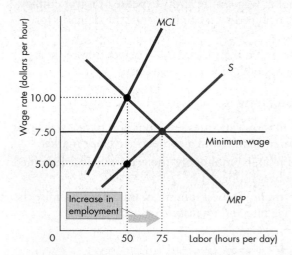

FIGURE A14.3   Minimum Wage Law in Monopsony

In a monopsony labor market, the wage rate is $5 an hour and 50 hours are hired. If a minimum wage law increases the wage rate to $7.50 an hour, employment increases to 75 hours.

labor are employed. A minimum wage law is passed that requires employers to pay at least $7.50 an hour.

The monopsony in Fig. A14.3 now faces a perfectly elastic supply of labor at $7.50 an hour up to 75 hours. Above 75 hours, a wage above $7.50 an hour must be paid to hire additional hours of labor. Because the wage rate is a fixed $7.50 an hour up to 75 hours, the marginal cost of labor is also constant at $7.50 up to 75 hours. Beyond 75 hours, the marginal cost of labor rises above $7.50 an hour. To maximize profit, the monopsony sets the marginal cost of labor equal to the marginal revenue product of labor. That is, the monopsony hires 75 hours of labor at $7.50 an hour. The minimum wage law has made the supply of labor perfectly elastic and made the marginal cost of labor the same as the wage rate up to 75 hours. The law has not affected the supply of labor curve or the marginal cost of labor at employment levels above 75 hours. The minimum wage law has succeeded in raising the wage rate by $2.50 an hour and increasing the amount of labor employed by 25 hours.

SUMMARY

KEY POINTS

Market Power in the Labor Market (pp. 337–340)

- In competitive labor markets, unions obtain higher wages only at the expense of lower employment but they try to influence the demand for labor.
- Union workers earn 10–25 percent more than comparable nonunion workers.

Monopsony (pp. 340–342)

- A monopsony hires less labor and pays a wage rate lower than that in a competitive labor market.
- In bilateral monopoly, the wage rate is determined by bargaining.
- In monopsony, a minimum wage law can raise the wage rate and increase employment.

KEY TERMS

Bilateral monopoly, 341
Labor union, 337
Monopsony, 340

PROBLEMS

*1. A monopsony gold-mining firm operates in an isolated part of the Amazon basin. The table shows the firm's labor supply schedule (columns 1 and 2) and total product schedule (columns 2 and 3). The price of gold is $1.40 a grain.

Wage rate (dollars per day)	Number of workers	Quantity produced (grains per day)
5	0	0
6	1	10
7	2	25
8	3	45
9	4	60
10	5	70
11	6	75

a. What wage rate does the company pay?
b. How many workers does the gold mine hire?
c. What is the marginal revenue product at the quantity of labor employed?

2. A monopsony logging firm operates in an isolated part of the Alaska. The following table shows the firm's labor supply schedule (columns 1 and 2) and total product schedule (columns 2 and 3). The price of logs is $2 a ton.

Wage rate (dollars per day)	Number of workers	Quantity produced (tons per day)
5	0	0
6	1	9
7	2	17
8	3	24
9	4	30
10	5	35
11	6	39
12	7	42

a. What wage rate does the company pay?
b. How many workers does the gold mine hire?
c. What is the marginal revenue product at the quantity of labor employed?

Rags and Riches

Six percent of adults, some 375,000 people, experienced homelessness in Los Angeles County during the past five years. In this same part of the nation is Beverly Hills, with its mansions that are home to some fabulously wealthy movies stars. Los Angeles is not unusual. In New York City, where Donald Trump is building a luxury apartment tower with a penthouse priced at $13 million, more than 20,000 people, 9,000 of whom are children, seek a bed in a shelter for the homeless every night. Extreme poverty and extreme wealth exist side by side in every major city in the United States and in most parts of the world ◆ How many rich and poor people are there in the United States? How are income and wealth distributed? And are the rich getting richer and the poor getting poorer? ◆ What causes inequality in the distribution of economic well-being? ◆ How much redistribution does the government do to limit extreme poverty?

◆ In this chapter, we study economic inequality — its extent, its sources, and the things governments do to make it less extreme. We begin by looking at some facts about economic inequality in the United States. We end, in *Reading Between the Lines*, by returning to California and looking at the changing gap between the rich and poor in that state.

After studying this chapter, you will be able to

- Describe the inequality in income and wealth in the United States in 2000 and the trends in inequality
- Explain the features of the labor market that contribute to economic inequality
- Describe the scale of income redistribution by governments

Measuring Economic Inequality

THE MOST COMMONLY USED MEASURE OF ECO-nomic inequality is the distribution of annual income. The Census Bureau defines income as **money income**, which equals *market income* plus cash payments to households by government. **Market income** equals wages, interest, rent, and profit earned in factor markets and before paying income taxes.

The Distribution of Income

Figure 15.1 shows the distribution of annual income across the 106 million households in the United States in 2000. Note that the *x*-axis measures household income and the *y*-axis is percentage of households.

The most common household income, called the *mode* income, was received by the 7 percent of the households whose incomes fell between $10,000 and $15,000. The midpoint of this range — $12,500 a year — is marked on the figure.

The income that separated the households into two equal groups, called the *median* income, was $42,148. One half of U.S. households had an income greater than this amount, and the other half had an income less than this amount.

The average household money income in 2000, called the *mean* income, was $57,045. This number equals total household income, a bit more than $6 trillion, divided by the 106 million households.

You can see in Fig. 15.1 that the mode income is less than the median income and the median income is less than the mean income. This feature of the distribution of income tells us that there are more households with low incomes than with high incomes. And some of the high incomes are very high.

The income distribution in Fig. 15.1 is called a *positively skewed* distribution, which means that it has a long tail of high values. This distribution shape contrasts with a *bell-shaped* distribution such as the distribution of people's heights. In a bell-shaped distribution, the mean, median, and mode are all equal.

Another way of looking at the distribution of income is to measure the percentage of total income received by each given percentage of households. Data are reported for five groups — called *quintiles* or fifth shares — each consisting of 20 percent of households.

FIGURE 15.1   The Distribution of Income in the United States in 2000

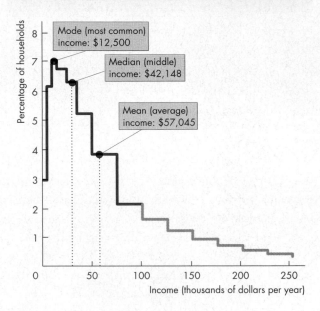

The distribution of income is positively skewed. The mode (most common) income is less than the median (middle) income, which in turn is less than the mean (average) income. The shape of the distribution above $100,000 is an indication rather than a precise measure, and the distribution goes up to several million dollars a year.

Source: U.S. Bureau of the Census, "Money Income in the United States: 2000," *Current Population Reports*, P-60-200 (Washington, D.C.: U.S. Government Printing Office, 2001).

Figure 15.2 shows the distribution based on these shares in 2000. The poorest 20 percent of households received 3.6 percent of total income; the second poorest 20 percent received 8.9 percent of total income; the middle 20 percent received 14.8 percent of total income; the next highest 20 percent received 23.1 percent of total income; and the highest 20 percent received 49.6 percent of total income.

The distribution of income in Fig. 15.1 and the quintile shares in Fig. 15.2 tell us that income is distributed unequally. But we need a way of comparing the distribution of income in different periods and using different measures. A neat graphical tool called the *Lorenz curve* enables us to make such comparisons.

FIGURE 15.2   U.S. Quintile Shares in 2000

In 2000, the poorest 20 percent of households received 3.6 percent of total income; the second poorest 20 percent received 8.9 percent; the middle 20 percent received 14.8 percent; the next highest 20 percent received 23.1 percent; and the highest 20 percent received 49.6 percent.

Source: U.S. Bureau of the Census, "Money Income in the United States: 2000," *Current Population Reports*, P-60-200 (Washington, D.C.: U.S. Government Printing Office, 2001).

Households (percentage)	Income (percentage of total income)
Lowest 20	3.6
Second 20	8.9
Middle 20	14.8
Next highest 20	23.1
Highest 20	49.6

The Income Lorenz Curve

The income **Lorenz curve** graphs the cumulative percentage of income against the cumulative percentage of households. Figure 15.3 shows the income Lorenz curve using the quintile shares from Fig. 15.2. The table shows the percentage of income of each quintile group. For example, row *A* tells us that the lowest quintile of households receives 3.6 percent of total income. The table also shows the *cumulative* percentages of households and income. For example, row *B* tells us that the lowest two quintiles (lowest 40 percent) of households receive 12.5 percent of total

FIGURE 15.3   The Income Lorenz Curve in 2000

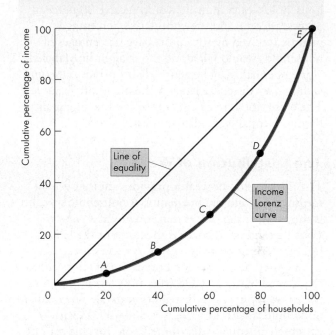

	Households		Income	
	Percentage	Cumulative **percentage**	**Percentage**	Cumulative **percentage**
A	Lowest 20	20	3.6	3.6
B	Second 20	40	8.9	12.5
C	Middle 20	60	14.8	27.3
D	Next highest 20	80	23.1	50.4
E	Highest 20	100	49.6	100.0

The cumulative percentage of income is graphed against the cumulative percentage of households. Points A through E on the Lorenz curve correspond to the rows of the table. If incomes were distributed equally, each 20 percent of households would receive 20 percent of total income and the Lorenz curve would fall along the line of equality. The Lorenz curve shows that income is unequally distributed.

Source: U.S. Bureau of the Census, "Money Income in the United States: 2000," *Current Population Reports*, P-60-200(Washington, D.C.: U.S. Government Printing Office, 2001).

income (3.6 percent for the lowest quintile and 8.9 percent for the next lowest). The Lorenz curve graphs the cumulative income shares against the cumulative household percentages.

If income were distributed equally across all the households, each quintile would receive 20 percent of total income and the cumulative percentages of income received by the cumulative percentages of households would fall along the straight line labeled "Line of equality." The actual distribution of income is shown by the curve labeled "Income Lorenz curve." The closer the Lorenz curve is to the line of equality, the more equal is the distribution.

The Distribution of Wealth

The distribution of wealth provides another way of measuring economic inequality. A household's wealth is the value of the things that it owns at a *point in time*. In contrast, income is the amount that the household receives over a given *period of time*.

Figure 15.4 shows the Lorenz curve for wealth in the United States in 1998 (the most recent year for which we have wealth distribution data). The median household wealth in 1998 was $60,700. Wealth is extremely unequally distributed, and for this reason, the data are grouped by seven unequal groups of households. The poorest 40 percent of households own only 0.2 percent of total wealth (row *A'* in the table in Fig. 15.4). The richest 20 percent of households own 83.4 percent of total wealth. Because this group owns almost all the wealth, we need to break the group into smaller bits. That is what rows *E'* through *G'* do. You can see that the richest 1 percent of households own 38.1 percent of total wealth.

Figure 15.4 shows the income Lorenz curve (from Fig. 15.3) alongside the wealth Lorenz curve. You can see that the Lorenz curve for wealth is much farther away from the line of equality than the Lorenz curve for income is, which means that the distribution of wealth is much more unequal than the distribution of income.

Wealth Versus Income

We've seen that wealth is much more unequally distributed than income. Which distribution provides the better description of the degree of inequality? To answer this question, we need to think about the connection between wealth and income.

Wealth is a stock of assets, and income is the flow of earnings that results from the stock of wealth. Suppose that a person owns assets worth $1 million

FIGURE 15.4   Lorenz Curves for Income and Wealth

	Households			Wealth	
	Percentage	Cumulative percentage		Percentage	Cumulative percentage
A	Lowest 40	40	A'	0.2	0.2
B	Next 20	60	B'	4.5	4.7
C	Next 20	80	C'	11.9	16.6
D	Next 10	90	D'	12.5	29.1
E	Next 5	95	E'	11.5	40.6
F	Next 4	99	F'	21.3	61.9
G	Highest 1	100	G'	38.1	100.0

The cumulative percentage of wealth is graphed against the cumulative percentage of households. Points *A* through *G* on the Lorenz curve for wealth correspond to the rows of the table. By comparing the Lorenz curves for income and wealth, we can see that wealth is distributed much more unequally than income.

Sources: U.S. Bureau of the Census, "Money Income in the United States: 2000," *Current Population Reports*, P-60-200 (Washington, D.C.: U.S. Government Printing Office, 2001); and Edward N. Wolff, "Recent Trends in Wealth Ownership, 1938–1998," Jerome Levy Economics Institute Working Paper No. 300, April 2000.

— has a wealth of $1 million. If the rate of return on assets is 5 percent a year, then this person receives an income of $50,000 a year from those assets. We can describe this person's economic condition by using either the wealth of $1 million or the income of $50,000. When the rate of return is 5 percent a year, $1 million of wealth equals $50,000 of income in perpetuity. Wealth and income are just different ways of looking at the same thing.

But in Fig. 15.4, the distribution of wealth is more unequal than the distribution of income. Why? It is because the wealth data do not include the value of human capital, while the income data measure income from all wealth, including human capital.

Table 15.1 illustrates the consequence of omitting human capital from the wealth data. Lee has twice the wealth and twice the income of Peter. But Lee's human capital is less than Peter's — $200,000 compared with $499,000. And Lee's income from human capital of $10,000 is less than Peter's income from human capital of $24,950. Lee's nonhuman capital is larger than Peter's — $800,000 compared with $1,000. And Lee's income from nonhuman capital of $40,000 is larger than Peter's income from nonhuman capital of $50.

When Lee and Peter are surveyed by the Census Bureau in a national wealth and income survey, their incomes are recorded as $50,000 and $25,000, respectively, which implies that Lee is twice as well off as Peter. And their tangible assets are recorded as $800,000 and $1,000, respectively, which implies that Lee is 800 times as wealthy as Peter.

Because the national survey of wealth excludes human capital, the income distribution is a more accurate measure of economic inequality than the wealth distribution.

Annual or Lifetime Income and Wealth?

A typical household's income changes over time. It starts out low, grows to a peak when the household's workers reach retirement age, and then falls after retirement. Also, a typical household's wealth changes over time. Like income, it starts out low, grows to a peak at the point of retirement, and falls after retirement.

Suppose we look at three households that have identical lifetime incomes. One household is young, one is middle-aged, and one is retired. The middle-aged household has the highest income and wealth, the retired household has the lowest, and the young household falls in the middle. The distributions of

TABLE 15.1	Capital, Wealth, and Income			
	Lee		Peter	
	Wealth	Income	Wealth	Income
Human capital	200,000	10,000	499,000	24,950
Other capital	800,000	40,000	1,000	50
Total	$1,000,000	$50,000	$500,000	$25,000

When wealth is measured to include the value of human capital as well as other forms of capital, the distribution of income and the distribution of wealth display the same degree of inequality.

annual income and wealth in a given year are unequal, but the distributions of lifetime income and wealth are equal. So some of the inequality in annual income arises because different households are at different stages in the life cycle. But we can see *trends* in the income distribution using annual income data.

Trends in Inequality

Figure 15.5 shows how the distribution of income has changed since 1970. The precise definitions and methods used by the Census Bureau to measure the distribution of income change from time to time, and a major change occurred in 1992, which makes the data before that year not comparable with data after that year. For this reason, Fig. 15.5 shows a break in the data in 1992. Despite this break in the series, some trends are clearly visible. These trends are

- The share of income received by the richest 20 percent of households has increased.
- The share of income received by all four other groups of households has decreased.

No one knows for sure why these trends have occurred, and a large amount of research has been done to try to explain them.

The most likely explanation is one that we'll explore and explain in the next section: Higher-income groups have gained and lower-income groups have lost because the technological change of the past few decades has increased the productivity of highly skilled workers and decreased the productivity of lower-skilled workers. The increase in international mobility and competition is another possible explanation.

FIGURE 15.5   Trends in the Distribution
of Income: 1970–2000

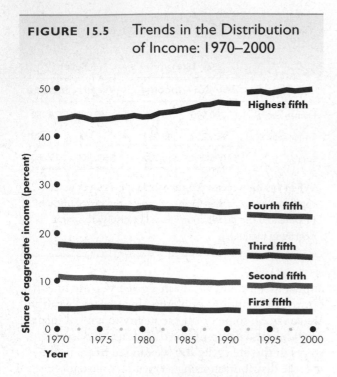

The distribution of income in the United States became more unequal between 1970 and 2000. The percentage of income earned by the highest fifth increased steadily through the 1970s and 1980s and sharply during the 1990s. A change in definitions makes the numbers after 1992 not comparable with those before 1992. But despite the break in the data, the trends are still visible.

Source: U.S. Bureau of the Census, "Money Income in the United States: 2000," *Current Population Reports*, P-60-200 (Washington, D.C.: U.S. Government Printing Office, 2001).

Who Are the Rich and the Poor?

The highest incomes in America are earned by high-profile movie stars, sports stars, and television personalities and by less well known but very highly paid chief executives of large corporations. The lowest incomes are earned by people who scratch a living doing seasonal work on farms. But aside from these extremes, what are the characteristics of people who earn high incomes and people who earn low incomes?

Five characteristics stand out:

- Education
- Type of household
- Size of household
- Age of householder
- Race

Education The median income per person in the United States in 2000 was $21,971. Education brought the largest spread around this median. A person who had not completed grade 9 lived in a household in which the average income per person was less than $10,000 in 2000. At the other extreme, and again on the average, a person with a doctoral degree or a professional degree (such as a medical or law degree) lived in a household in which the average income per person was more than $45,000. Just completing high school raises average income by more than $5,000 per person per year. And getting a bachelor's degree adds another $15,000 per person per year.

Type of Household The Census Bureau divides households into *family households* and *non-family households*. Most non-family households are single people who live alone. These households have higher incomes per person than do family households. Men living alone received more than $37,000 on the average in 2000. Women living alone received $26,000 on the average. The poorest household type is a single mother. The income per person in such a household averaged $11,520 in 2000.

Size of Household On the average, the greater the number of people in a household, the smaller is the income per person. In 2000, on the average, a one-person household received almost $31,000 per person, while a household with seven or more people received only $8,321 per person.

Age of Householder The oldest and youngest households have lower incomes than middle-aged households. In 2000, when a householder was aged between 45 and 64, income per person was around $27,000 on the average. When the householder was between 25 and 34 or over 65, the average income per person was around $20,000. And for householders under 25, the average income per person was only $15,000.

Race White households had an average income per person in 2000 of $23,415, while black households had an average income per person of just over $15,000. Households of Hispanic origin were even worse off, with an average income per person of only $12,000.

Figure 15.6 provides a quick visual summary of the numbers that we've just described. The figure also shows the small effect that region of residence has on income per person. Incomes were highest in 2000

FIGURE 15.6   The Distribution of Income by Selected Household Characteristics in 2000

Median money income per person in 2000 was $21,971. Education is the single biggest factor affecting income distribution, but type of household, household size, age, and race play roles. Region of residence is not a very important source of inequality.

Source: U.S. Bureau of the Census, *Current Population Survey*, Detailed Tables.

(and in most other years) in the Northeast. But incomes in the West and the Midwest were close to those in the Northeast and a bit higher than incomes in the South.

Poverty

Households at the low end of the income distribution are so poor that they are considered to be living in poverty. **Poverty** is a situation in which a household's income is too low to be able to buy the quantities of food, shelter, and clothing that are deemed necessary. Poverty is a relative concept. Millions of people living in Africa and Asia survive on incomes of less than $400 a year. In the United States, the poverty level is calculated each year by the Social Security Administration. In 2000, the poverty level for a four-person household was an income of $17,761. In that year, 31.1 million Americans — 11.3 percent of the population — lived in households that had incomes below the poverty level. Many of these households benefited from Medicare and Medicaid, two government programs that aid the poorest households and lift some of them above the poverty level.

The distribution of poverty by race is unequal: 9.4 percent of white Americans live in poor households compared to 21.2 percent of Hispanic-origin Americans and 31.3 percent of African Americans. Poverty is also influenced by household status. Almost 25 percent of households in which the householder is a female and no husband is present are below the poverty level.

Despite the widening of the income distribution, poverty rates are falling.

REVIEW QUIZ

1 Which is distributed more unequally, income or wealth? Why? Which is the better measure?

2 Has the distribution of income become more equal or more unequal? Which quintile share has changed most?

3 What are the main characteristics of people who earn large incomes and small incomes?

4 What is poverty and how does its incidence vary across the races?

The Sources of Economic Inequality

WE'VE DESCRIBED ECONOMIC INEQUALITY IN THE United States. Our task now is to explain it. We began this task in Chapter 14 by learning about the forces that influence demand and supply in the markets for labor, capital, and land. We're now going to deepen our understanding of these forces.

Inequality arises from unequal labor market outcomes and from unequal ownership of capital. We'll begin by looking at labor markets and two features of them that contribute to differences in income:

- Human capital
- Discrimination

Human Capital

A clerk in a law firm earns less than a tenth of the amount earned by the attorney he assists. An operating room assistant earns less than a tenth of the amount earned by the surgeon she works with. A bank teller earns less than a tenth of the amount earned by the bank's CEO. These differences in earnings arise from differences in human capital. We can explain these differences by using a model of competitive labor markets.

We'll study a model economy with two levels of human capital, which we'll call high-skilled labor and low-skilled labor. The low-skilled labor might represent the law clerk, the operating room assistant, or the bank teller, and the high-skilled labor might represent the attorney, the surgeon, or the bank's CEO. We'll first look at the demand side of the markets for these two types of labor.

The Demand for High-Skilled and Low-Skilled Labor High-skilled workers can perform tasks that low-skilled labor would perform badly or perhaps cannot perform at all. Imagine an untrained person doing open-heart surgery. High-skilled labor has a higher marginal revenue product than low-skilled labor. As we learned in Chapter 14, a firm's demand for labor curve is the same as the marginal revenue product of labor curve.

Figure 15.7(a) shows the demand curves for high-skilled and low-skilled labor. The demand curve for high-skilled labor is D_H, and that for low-skilled labor is D_L. At any given level of employment, firms

are willing to pay a higher wage rate to a high-skilled worker than to a low-skilled worker. The gap between the two wage rates measures the marginal revenue product of skill; for example, at an employment level of 2,000 hours, firms are willing to pay $12.50 for a high-skilled worker and only $5 for a low-skilled worker, a difference of $7.50 an hour. Thus the marginal revenue product of skill is $7.50 an hour.

The Supply of High-Skilled and Low-Skilled Labor High-skilled labor contains more human capital than low-skilled labor, and human capital is costly to acquire. The opportunity cost of acquiring human capital includes actual expenditures on such things as tuition and room and board and also costs in the form of lost or reduced earnings while the skill is being acquired. When a person goes to school full time, that cost is the total earnings forgone. But some people acquire skills on the job — on-the-job training. Usually, a worker undergoing on-the-job training is paid a lower wage than one doing a comparable job but not undergoing training. In such a case, the cost of acquiring the skill is the difference between the wage paid to a person not being trained and that paid to a person being trained.

The position of the supply curve of high-skilled labor reflects the cost of acquiring human capital. Figure 15.7(b) shows two supply curves: one for high-skilled labor and the other for low-skilled labor. The supply curve for high-skilled labor is S_H, and that for low-skilled labor is S_L.

The high-skilled labor supply curve lies above the low-skilled labor supply curve. The vertical distance between the two supply curves is the compensation that high-skilled labor requires for the cost of acquiring the skill. For example, suppose that the quantity of low-skilled labor supplied is 2,000 hours at a wage rate of $5 an hour. This wage rate compensates the low-skilled workers mainly for their time on the job. To induce high-skilled workers to supply 2,000 hours of labor, firms must pay a wage rate of $8.50 an hour. This wage rate for high-skilled labor is higher than that for low-skilled labor because high-skilled workers must be compensated not only for the time on the job but also for the time and other costs of acquiring the skill.

Wage Rates of High-Skilled and Low-Skilled Labor To work out the wage rates of high-skilled and low-skilled labor, we have to bring together the effects of skill on the demand for and supply of labor.

FIGURE 15.7   Skill Differentials

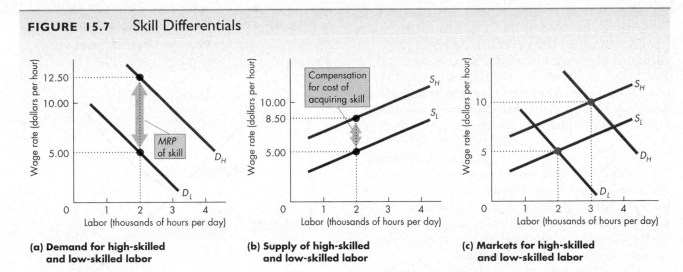

(a) Demand for high-skilled and low-skilled labor

(b) Supply of high-skilled and low-skilled labor

(c) Markets for high-skilled and low-skilled labor

Part (a) illustrates the marginal revenue product of skill. Low-skilled workers have a marginal revenue product that gives rise to the demand curve marked D_L. High-skilled workers have a higher marginal revenue product than low-skilled labor. Therefore the demand curve for high-skilled labor, D_H, lies to the right of D_L. The vertical distance between these two curves is the marginal revenue product of the skill.

Part (b) shows the effects of the cost of acquiring skills on the supply curves of labor. The supply curve for low-skilled labor is S_L. The supply curve for high-skilled labor is S_H. The vertical distance between these two curves is the required compensation for the cost of acquiring a skill.

Part (c) shows the equilibrium employment and the wage differential. Low-skilled workers earn a wage rate of $5 an hour, and 2,000 hours of low-skilled labor are employed. High-skilled workers earn a wage rate of $10 an hour, and 3,000 hours of high-skilled labor are employed. The wage rate for high-skilled labor always exceeds that for low-skilled labor.

Figure 15.7(c) shows the demand curves and the supply curves for high-skilled and low-skilled labor. These curves are exactly the same as those plotted in parts (a) and (b). Equilibrium occurs in the market for low-skilled labor where the supply and demand curves for low-skilled labor intersect. The equilibrium wage rate is $5 an hour, and the quantity of low-skilled labor employed is 2,000 hours. Equilibrium in the market for high-skilled labor occurs where the supply and demand curves for high-skilled labor intersect. The equilibrium wage rate is $10 an hour, and the quantity of high-skilled labor employed is 3,000 hours.

As you can see in part (c), the equilibrium wage rate of high-skilled labor is higher than that of low-skilled labor. There are two reasons why this occurs: First, high-skilled labor has a higher marginal revenue product than low-skilled labor, so at a given wage rate, the quantity of high-skilled labor demanded exceeds that of low-skilled labor. Second, skills are costly to acquire, so at a given wage rate, the quantity of high-skilled labor supplied is less than that of low-skilled labor. The wage differential (in this case, $5 an hour)

depends on both the marginal revenue product of the skill and the cost of acquiring it. The higher the marginal revenue product of the skill, the larger is the vertical distance between the demand curves. The more costly it is to acquire a skill, the larger is the vertical distance between the supply curves. The higher the marginal revenue product of the skill and the more costly it is to acquire, the larger is the wage differential between high-skilled and low-skilled labor.

Do Education and Training Pay? Rates of return on high school and college education have been estimated to be in the range of 5–10 percent a year after allowing for inflation, which suggest that a college degree is a better investment than almost any other that a person can undertake.

Inequality Explained by Human Capital Differences Human capital differences help to explain some of the inequality that we've described above. They also help to explain some of the trends in the distribution of income that occurred during the 1990s.

You saw in Fig. 15.6 that high-income households tend to be better educated, middle-aged, male headed, and white. Human capital differences are correlated with these household characteristics. Education contributes directly to human capital. Age contributes indirectly to human capital because older workers have more experience than younger workers. Human capital differences can also explain a small part of the inequality associated with sex and race. A larger proportion of men (25 percent) than women (20 percent) have completed four years of college, and a larger proportion of whites (24 percent) than blacks (13 percent) have completed a bachelor's degree or higher. These differences in education levels among the sexes and the races are becoming smaller, but they have not yet been eliminated.

Interruptions to a career reduce the effectiveness of job experience in contributing to human capital. Historically, job interruptions have been more common for women than for men because women's careers have been interrupted for bearing and rearing children. This factor is a possible source of lower wages, on the average, for women. Although maternity leave and day-care facilities are making career interruptions for women less common, this factor remains a problem for many women.

Trends in Inequality Explained by Human Capital Trends You saw in Fig. 15.5 that high-income households have earned an increasing share of total income while low-income households have earned a decreasing share. Human capital differences are a possible explanation for this trend, and Fig. 15.8 illustrates this explanation. The supply of low-skilled labor (part a) and that of high-skilled labor (part b) are S, and initially, the demand in each market is D_0. The low-skilled wage rate is $5 an hour, and the high-skilled wage rate is $10 an hour.

Information technologies such as computers and laser scanners are *substitutes* for low-skilled labor: they perform tasks that previously were performed by low-skilled labor. The introduction of these technologies has decreased the demand for low-skilled labor (part a), decreased the number of low-skilled jobs, and lowered the wage rate of low-skilled workers.

These same technologies require high-skilled labor to design, program, and run them. High-skilled labor and the information technologies are *complements*. So the introduction of these technologies has increased the demand for high-skilled labor (part b), increased the number of high-skilled jobs, and raised the wage rate of high-skilled workers.

FIGURE 15.8 Explaining the Trend in Income Distribution

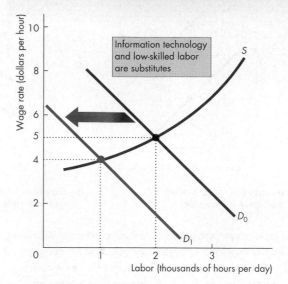

(a) A decrease in demand for low-skilled labor

(b) An increase in demand for high-skilled labor

Low-skilled labor in part (a) and information technologies are substitutes. When these technologies were introduced, the demand for low-skilled labor decreased and the quantity of this type of labor and its wage rate decreased. High-skilled labor in part (b) and information technologies are complements. When these technologies were introduced, the demand for high-skilled labor increased and the quantity of this type of labor and its wage rate increased.

Discrimination

Human capital differences can explain some of the economic inequality that we observe. But it can't explain all of it. Discrimination is another possible source of inequality.

Suppose that black females and white males have identical abilities as investment advisors. Figure 15.9 shows the supply curves of black females, S_{BF} (in part a), and of white males, S_{WM} (in part b). The marginal revenue product of investment advisors shown by the two curves labeled MRP in parts (a) and (b) is the same for both groups.

If everyone is free of race and sex prejudice, the market determines a wage rate of $40,000 a year for investment advisors. But if the customers are prejudiced against women and minorities, this prejudice is reflected in the wage rate and employment.

Suppose that the perceived marginal revenue product of the black females, when discriminated against, is MRP_{DA}. Suppose that the perceived marginal revenue product for white males, the group discriminated in favor of, is MRP_{DF}. With these MRP curves, black females earn $20,000 a year and only 1,000 black females work as investment advisors. White males earn $60,000 a year, and 3,000 of them work as investment advisors.

Counteracting Forces Economists disagree about whether prejudice actually causes wage differentials, and one line of reasoning implies that it does not. In the example you've just studied, customers who buy from white men pay a higher service charge for investment advice than do the customers who buy from black women. This price difference acts as an incentive to encourage people who are prejudiced to buy from the people against whom they are prejudiced. This force could be strong enough to eliminate the effects of discrimination altogether. Suppose, as is true in manufacturing, that a firm's customers never meet its workers. If such a firm discriminates against women or minorities, it can't compete with firms who hire these groups because its costs are higher than those of the nonprejudiced firms. Only firms that do not discriminate survive in a competitive industry.

Whether because of discrimination or from some other source, women and visible minorities do earn lower incomes than white males. Another possible source of lower wage rates of women arises from differences in the relative degree of specialization of women and men.

FIGURE 15.9   Discrimination

(a) Black females

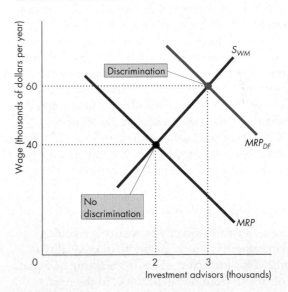

(b) White males

With no discrimination, the wage rate is $40,000 a year and 2,000 of each group are hired. With discrimination against blacks and women, the marginal revenue product curve in part (a) is MRP_{DA} and that in part (b) is MRP_{DF}. The wage rate for black women falls to $20,000 a year, and only 1,000 are employed. The wage rate for white men rises to $60,000 a year, and 3,000 are employed.

Differences in the Degree of Specialization

Couples must choose how to allocate their time between working for a wage and doing jobs in the home, such as cooking, cleaning, shopping, organizing vacations, and, most important, bearing and rearing children. Let's look at the choices of Bob and Sue.

Bob might specialize in earning an income and Sue in taking care of the home. Or Sue might specialize in earning an income and Bob in taking care of the home. Or both of them might earn an income and share home production jobs.

The allocation they choose depends on their preferences and on the earning potential of each of them. The choice of an increasing number of households is for each person to diversify between earning an income and doing some home chores. But in most households, Bob will specialize in earning an income and Sue will both earn an income and bear a larger share of the task of running the home. With this allocation, Bob will probably earn more than Sue. If Sue devotes time and effort to ensuring Bob's mental and physical well-being, the quality of Bob's market labor will be higher than it would be if he were diversified. If the roles were reversed, Sue would be able to supply market labor that earns more than Bob.

To test whether the degree of specialization accounts for earnings differences between the sexes, economists have compared the incomes of never-married men and women. They have found that, on the average, with equal amounts of human capital, the wages of these two groups are the same.

We've examined some sources of inequality in the labor market. Let's now look at the way inequality arises from unequal ownership of capital.

Unequal Ownership of Capital

You've seen that inequality in wealth (excluding human capital) is much greater than inequality in income. This inequality arises from saving and transfers of wealth from one generation to the next.

The higher a household's income, the more that household tends to save and pass on to the next generation. Saving is not always a source of increased inequality. If a household saves to redistribute an uneven income over its life cycle and enable consumption to fluctuate less than income, saving decreases inequality. If a lucky generation that has a high income saves a large part of that income and leaves capital to a succeeding generation that is unlucky, this act of saving also decreases the degree of inequality. But two features of intergenerational transfers of wealth lead to increased inequality: People can't inherit debts, and marriage tends to concentrate wealth.

Can't Inherit Debt Although a person may die in debt — with negative wealth — a debt can't be forced onto the next generation of a family. So inheritance only adds to a future generation's wealth; it cannot decrease it.

Most people inherit nothing or a very small amount. A few people inherit an enormous fortune. As a result, intergenerational transfers make the distribution of income persistently more unequal than the distribution of ability and job skills. A household that is poor in one generation is more likely to be poor in the next. A household that is wealthy in one generation is more likely to be wealthy in the next. And marriage reinforces this tendency.

Marriage and Wealth Concentration People tend to marry within their own socioeconomic class — a phenomenon called *assortative mating*. In everyday language, "like attracts like." Although there is a good deal of folklore that "opposites attract," perhaps such Cinderella tales appeal to us because they are so rare in reality. Wealthy people seek wealthy partners.

Because of assortative mating, wealth becomes more concentrated in a small number of families and the distribution of wealth becomes more unequal.

REVIEW QUIZ

1 What role does human capital play in accounting for income inequality?
2 What role might discrimination play in accounting for income inequality?
3 What are the possible reasons for income inequality by sex and race?
4 What are the possible reasons for income inequality by age group?
5 Does inherited wealth make the distribution of income less equal or more equal?
6 Why does wealth inequality persist across generations?

Next, we're going to see how taxes and government programs redistribute income and decrease the degree of economic inequality.

Income Redistribution

THE THREE MAIN WAYS IN WHICH GOVERNMENTS in the United States redistribute income are

- Income taxes
- Income maintenance programs
- Subsidized services

Income Taxes

Income taxes may be progressive, regressive, or proportional. A **progressive income tax** is one that taxes income at an average rate that increases with income. A **regressive income tax** is one that taxes income at an average rate that decreases with income. A **proportional income tax** (also called a *flat-rate income tax*) is one that taxes income at a constant average rate, regardless of the level of income.

The tax rates that apply in the United States are composed of two parts: federal and state taxes. Some cities, such as New York City, also have an income tax. There is variety in the detailed tax arrangements in the individual states, but the tax system, at both the federal and state levels, is progressive. The poorest working households receive money from the government through an earned income tax credit. The middle-income households pay 15 percent of each additional dollar they earn, and successively higher-income households pay 28 percent and 31 percent of each additional dollar earned.

Income Maintenance Programs

Three main types of programs redistribute income by making direct payments (in cash, services, or vouchers) to people in the lower part of the income distribution. They are

- Social security programs
- Unemployment compensation
- Welfare programs

Social Security Programs The main social security program is OASDHI — Old Age, Survivors, Disability, and Health Insurance. Monthly cash payments to retired or disabled workers or their surviving spouses and children are paid for by compulsory payroll taxes on both employers and employees. In 2002, total social security expenditure was budgeted at $630 billion, and the standard monthly social security check for a married couple was $817.

The other component of social security is Medicare, which provides hospital and health insurance for the elderly and disabled.

Unemployment Compensation To provide an income to unemployed workers, every state has established an unemployment compensation program. Under these programs, a tax is paid that is based on the income of each covered worker and such a worker receives a benefit when he or she becomes unemployed. The details of the benefits vary from state to state.

Welfare Programs The purpose of welfare is to provide incomes for people who do not qualify for social security or unemployment compensation. They are

1. Supplementary Security Income (SSI) program, designed to help the neediest elderly, disabled, and blind people
2. Temporary Assistance for Needy Households (TANF) program, designed to help households that have inadequate financial resources
3. Food Stamp program, designed to help the poorest households obtain a basic diet
4. Medicaid, designed to cover the costs of medical care for households receiving help under the SSI and TANF programs

Subsidized Services

A great deal of redistribution takes place in the United States through the provision of subsidized services — services provided by the government at prices below the cost of production. The taxpayers who consume these goods and services receive a transfer in kind from the taxpayers who do not consume them. The two most important areas in which this form of redistribution takes place are education — both kindergarten through grade 12 and college and university — and health care.

In 2001–2002, students enrolled in the University of California system paid annual tuition fees of $3,702. The cost of providing a year's education at the University of California was more than $15,000. So households with a member enrolled in one of these institutions received a benefit from the government of more than $11,000 a year.

Government provision of health-care services has grown to equal the scale of private provision. Programs such as Medicaid and Medicare bring high-quality and high-cost health care to millions of people who earn too little to buy such services themselves.

The Scale of Income Redistribution

A household's *market income* tells us what a household earns in the absence of government redistribution. You've seen that market income is *not* the official basis for measuring the distribution of income that we used in Figs. 15.1 through 15.6. The Census Bureau's measure is *money income* (market income plus cash transfers from the government). But market income is the correct starting point for measuring the scale of income redistribution.

We begin with market income and then subtract taxes and add the amounts received in benefits. The result is the distribution of income after taxes and benefits. The data available on benefits exclude the value of subsidized services such as college, so the resulting distribution might understate the total amount of redistribution from the rich to the poor.

Figure 15.10 shows the scale of redistribution based on the calculations just described. In part (a), the blue Lorenz curve describes the market distribution of income and the green Lorenz curve shows the distribution of income after all taxes and benefits, including Medicaid and Medicare benefits. (The Lorenz curve based on money income in Fig. 15.3 lies between the two curves in Fig. 15.10.)

The distribution after taxes and benefits is less unequal than the market distribution. In 2000, the lowest 20 percent of households received only 1.1 percent of market income but 4.6 percent of income after taxes and benefits. The highest 20 percent of households received 55.1 percent of market income but only 46.7 percent of income after taxes and benefits.

Figure 15.10(b) highlights the percentage of total income redistributed among the five groups. In 2000, the share of total income received by the lowest 60 percent of households increased. The share of total income received by the fourth quintile barely changed. And the share of total income received by the highest quintile fell by 8.4 percent.

The Big Tradeoff

The redistribution of income creates what has been called the **big tradeoff**, a tradeoff between equity and

FIGURE 15.10   Income Redistribution

(a) Income distribution before and after redistribution

(b) The scale of redistribution

Redistribution reduces the degree of inequality that the market generates. In 2000, the 20 percent of households with the lowest incomes received net benefits that increased their share of total income from 1.1 percent of market income to 4.6 percent after taxes and redistribution. The 20 percent of households with the highest incomes paid taxes that decreased their share from 55.1 percent of market income to 46.7 percent of income after taxes and redistribution.

Source: U.S. Bureau of the Census, "Money Income in the United States: 2000," *Current Population Reports*, P-60-200 (Washington, D.C.: U.S. Government Printing Office, 2001).

efficiency. The big tradeoff arises because redistribution uses scarce resources and weakens incentives.

A dollar collected from a rich person does not translate into a dollar received by a poor person. Some of it gets used up in the process of redistribution. Tax-collecting agencies such as the Internal Revenue Service and welfare-administering agencies (as well as tax accountants and lawyers) use skilled labor, computers, and other scarce resources to do their work. The bigger the scale of redistribution, the greater is the opportunity cost of administering it.

But the cost of collecting taxes and making welfare payments is a small part of the total cost of redistribution. A bigger cost arises from the inefficiency — deadweight loss — of taxes and benefits. Greater equality can be achieved only by taxing productive activities such as work and saving. Taxing people's income from their work and saving lowers the after-tax income they receive. This lower after-tax income makes them work and save less, which in turn results in smaller output and less consumption not only for the rich who pay the taxes but also for the poor who receive the benefits.

It is not only taxpayers who face weaker incentives to work. Benefit recipients also face weaker incentives. In fact, under the welfare arrangements that prevailed before the 1996 reforms, the weakest incentives to work were those faced by households that benefited from welfare. When a welfare recipient got a job, benefits were withdrawn and eligibility for programs such as Medicaid ended, so the household in effect paid a tax of more than 100 percent on its earnings. This arrangement locked poor households in a welfare trap.

So the scale and methods of income redistribution must pay close attention to the incentive effects of taxes and benefits. Let's close this chapter by looking at one way in which lawmakers are tackling the big tradeoff today.

A Major Welfare Challenge Young women who have not completed high school, have a child (or children), live without a partner, and more likely are black or Hispanic than white are among the poorest people in the United States today. These young women and their children present a major welfare challenge.

First, their numbers are large. In 2000, there were 12.5 million single-mother families. This number is 16 percent of families. In 1997 (the most recent year with census data), single mothers were owed $26 billion in child support. Of this amount, $10 billion was not paid and 30 percent of the women received no support from their children's fathers.

The long-term solution to the problem of these people is education and job training — acquiring human capital. The short-term solutions are enforcing child support payments by absent fathers and former spouses and providing welfare.

Welfare must be designed to minimize the disincentive to pursue the long-term goal of becoming self-supporting. The current welfare program in the United States tries to walk this fine line.

Passed in 1996, the Personal Responsibility and Work Opportunities Reconciliation Act strengthened the Office of Child Support Enforcement and increased the penalties for nonpayment of support. The act also created the Temporary Assistance for Needy Households (TANF) program. TANF is a block grant paid to the states, which administer payments to individuals. It is not an open-ended entitlement program. An adult member of a household receiving assistance must either work or perform community service, and there is a five-year limit for assistance.

REVIEW QUIZ

1 How do governments in the United States redistribute income?
2 How large is the scale of redistribution in the United States?
3 What is one of the major welfare challenges today and how is it being tackled in the United States?

◆ We've examined economic inequality in the United States, and we've seen how inequality arises. And we've seen that inequality has been increasing. *Reading Between the Lines* on pp. 358–359 looks at the increasing inequality in California during the 1990s.

Your task in the following chapters is to look more closely at government actions that modify the outcome of the market economy. We look at sources of market failure and the ways in which government actions aim to overcome it. We also look at what has been called the *political marketplace* and the potential for it to fail too.

Trends in Inequality

SAN JOSE MERCURY NEWS, MAY 10, 2001

Income Gap Increasing in California

During the boom economy of the mid-to-late 1990s, the income gap between California's rich and poor narrowed slightly, with those earning low incomes gaining some ground. But over the entire decade, the gap widened, according to a new study by ... the Public Policy Institute of California, a nonpartisan, nonprofit San Francisco research organization. ...

Deborah Reed, an economist who is one of the authors, says she worries that as the income gap widens, the bar to succeed keeps being raised and poorer residents have less opportunity than those who earn more.

The income gap decreased in the mid-1990s, according to the study, which looked at data from the March Current Population Survey collected by the U.S. Census Bureau.

But for the entire decade, the income gap in California increased by 13 percent. ...

The study quantifies the income gap by looking at inflation-adjusted change in family income for families at different economic levels. In California, families at the 90th percentile — the point at which just 10 percent of the families have higher incomes — saw their income grow 58 percent in the three decades between 1969 and 1999, from $86,140 to $135,850.

By contrast, family income at the 10th percentile dropped 14 percent, from $15,810 in 1969 to $13,600 in 1999. ...

California's gap is wider than the rest of the nation's, according to the report, in part because the region is attracting a disproportionate number of low-income immigrants. ...

Bob Brownstein, policy director at Working Partnerships USA, a labor union-backed research organization in San Jose, said the income gap has widened mostly because the structure of the economy has changed.

"We've had nothing but immigration over the past 200 years," he said. "But certain economic structures were able to take immigrants and move them into the upper income. You could graduate from high school in 1950 and get a good-paying union job and eventually buy a house."

The magnitude of immigration in recent years, however, is greater, Reed said. Combine that with the higher value placed on education in people's earning power and the new immigrant has a tougher road to travel than in the past.

Essence of the Story

■ The March 2001 *Current Population Survey* shows that during the 1990s, the gap between high-income families and low-income families in California widened by 13 percent.

■ Adjusted for inflation, the incomes of families at the 90th percentile increased from $86,140 in 1969 to $135,850 in 1999, a 58 percent increase.

■ The incomes of families at the 10th percentile *decreased* from $15,810 in 1969 to $13,600 in 1999, a 14 percent decrease.

■ Deborah Reed says the income gap is wider in California than in the rest of the nation because of immigration.

■ Bob Brownstein says that immigration is not new and the wider gap results from a changed structure of the economy.

Economic Analysis

■ In this chapter, we look at quintile income shares, which are shares of fifths of the population. A percentile is a 100th part.

■ The lowest quintile runs from the first to the 20th percentile, so the income at the 10th percentile is the income in the middle of the lowest quintile.

■ The highest quintile runs from the 80th to the 100th percentile, and the income at the 90th percentile is the income in the middle of the highest quintile.

■ In 1969, the income gap was $86,140 minus $15,810, which is $70,330.

■ In 1999, the income gap was $135,850 minus $13,600, which is $122,250.

■ Both Deborah Reed and Bob Brownstein are correct about the possible reasons for the widening gap and for why California's gap is wider than that for the United States on the average. And they don't really disagree with each other.

■ Immigration alone can explain why the wage rate of low-skilled workers might fall.

■ In Figure 1, the demand for low-skilled labor in California in 1990 is D_{90} and the supply of labor is S_{90}. By 1999, demand has increased to D_{99} and supply has increased to S_{99}.

■ Because supply increases by more than demand, the quantity of labor has increased but the wage rate has fallen.

■ The supply of low-skilled labor has increased partly because of immigration. The demand for low-skilled labor has increased but by less than supply for the reasons that we identify in the chapter: New technologies are a substitute for low-skilled labor. In Bob Brownstein's words, "the structure of the economy has changed."

■ In Figure 2, the demand for high-skilled labor in California in 1990 is D_{90} and the supply of labor is S_{90}. By 1999, demand has increased to D_{99} and supply has increased to S_{99}.

■ Because demand increases by more than supply, the quantity of labor has increased and the wage rate has risen.

■ The supply of high-skilled labor has increased slowly because the new technologies

require a higher level of education to complement them.

■ The demand for high-skilled labor has increased by a large

amount because the new technologies that have changed the structure of the economy have increased the marginal revenue product of highly educated workers.

Figure 1 A market for low-skilled labor

Supply increases by more than demand and the wage rate falls

Figure 2 A market for high-skilled labor

Demand increases by more than supply and the wage rate rises

SUMMARY

KEY POINTS

Measuring Economic Inequality (pp. 344–349)

- In 2000, the mode money income was $12,500 a year, the median money income was $42,148, and the mean money income was $57,045.
- The income distribution is positively skewed.
- In 2000, the poorest 20 percent of households received 3.6 percent of total income, and the wealthiest 20 percent received 49.6 percent of total income.
- Wealth is distributed more unequally than income because the wealth data exclude the value of human capital.
- Since 1970, the share of income received by the richest 20 percent of households has increased and the share of income received by all four other groups of households has decreased.
- Education, type of household, size of household, age of householder, and race all influence household income.

The Sources of Economic Inequality (pp. 350–354)

- Inequality arises from differences in human capital.
- Inequality might arise from discrimination.
- Inequality between men and women might arise from differences in the degree of specialization.
- Intergenerational transfers of wealth lead to increased inequality because people can't inherit debts and assortative mating tends to concentrate wealth.

Income Redistribution (pp. 355–357)

- Governments redistribute income through progressive income taxes, income maintenance programs, and subsidized services.

- Redistribution increases the share of total income received by the lowest 60 percent of households and decreases the share of total income received by the highest quintile. The share of the fourth quintile barely changes.
- Because the redistribution of income weakens incentives, it creates a tradeoff between equity and efficiency.
- Effective redistribution seeks to support the long-term solution to low income, which is education and job training — acquiring human capital.

KEY FIGURES

KEY TERMS

PROBLEMS

*1. The table shows money income shares in the United States in 1967.

Households	Money income (percent of total)
Lowest 20%	4.0
Second 20%	10.8
Third 20%	17.3
Fourth 20%	24.2
Highest 20%	43.7

a. What is money income?
b. Draw a Lorenz curve for the United States in 1967 and compare with the Lorenz curve in 2000 shown in Figure 15.3.
c. Was U.S. money income distributed more equally or less equally in 2000 than it was in 1967?
d. Can you think of some reasons for the differences in the distribution of money income in the United States in 1967 and 2000?

2. The table shows money income shares in Sweden in 1992.

Households	Money income (percent of total)
Lowest 20%	6.7
Second 20%	12.2
Third 20%	17.6
Fourth 20%	24.5
Highest 20%	39.0

a. Draw the Lorenz curve for money income in Sweden in 1992.
b. Was money income distributed more equally or less equally in the United States in 2000 than in Sweden in 1992?
c. Use the information provided in problem 1 on the distribution of money income in the United States in 1967. Was money income distributed more equally or less equally in the United States in 1967 than in Sweden in 1992?
d. Can you think of some reasons for the differences in the distribution of money income in the United States and Sweden?

*3. The following figure shows the demand for and supply of low-skilled labor.

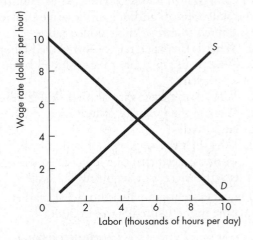

High-skilled workers have twice the marginal product of low-skilled workers. (The marginal product at each employment level is twice the marginal product of a low-skilled worker.) But the cost of acquiring the skill adds $2 an hour to the wage that must be offered to attract high-skilled labor. What is
a. The wage rate of low-skilled labor?
b. The quantity of low-skilled labor employed?
c. The wage rate of high-skilled labor?
d. The quantity of high-skilled labor employed?

4. The following figure shows the demand for and supply of low-skilled labor.

The marginal productivity of a high-skilled worker is $8 an hour greater than that of a low-skilled worker. (The marginal product at each employment level is $8 greater than that of a low-skilled worker.) The cost of acquiring the skill adds $6 an hour to the wage that must be offered to attract high-skilled labor.

a. What is the wage rate of low-skilled labor?
b. What is the quantity of low-skilled labor employed?
c. What is the wage rate of high-skilled labor?
d. What is the quantity of high-skilled labor employed?
e. Why does the wage rate of a high-skilled worker exceed that of a low-skilled worker by exactly the cost of acquiring the skill?

*5. The table shows the distribution of market income in the United States in 2000.

Households	Market income (percent of total)
Lowest 20%	1.1
Second 20%	7.1
Third 20%	13.9
Fourth 20%	22.8
Highest 20%	55.1

a. What is the definition of market income?
b. Draw the Lorenz curve for the distribution of market income.
c. Compare the distribution of market income with the distribution of money income shown in Fig. 15.3. Which distribution is more unequal and why?

6. Use the information provided in problem 5 and in Fig. 15.3.
a. What is the percentage of total income that is redistributed from the highest income group?
b. What are the percentages of total income that are redistributed to the lower income groups?
c. Describe the effects of increasing the amount of income redistribution in the United States to the point at which the lowest income group receives 15 percent of total income and the highest income group receives 30 percent of total income.

CRITICAL THINKING

1. Study *Reading Between the Lines* on pp. 358–359 and then
a. Describe the main facts about the changes in the distribution of income in California reported in the news article.
b. Is the distribution of income more unequal or less unequal in California than in the rest of the United States?
c. Why, according to the news article, is California different from the rest of the nation?
d. Do you think the author of the news article has identified the relevant factors at work? Explain why or why not using the ideas that you have learned in this chapter.
e. What policy issues are raised by the news article?
f. How do you think the tax system and the welfare system should be changed to influence the distribution of income in California?

WEB EXERCISES

1. Use the link on your Parkin Web site to obtain data on income distribution and poverty for your own state. Then
a. Describe the main facts about the income distribution and poverty in your state.
b. Compare the situation in your state with that in the rest of the country.
c. Why do you think your state is performing better or worse (as the case may be) than the nation as a whole?

2. Use the link on your Parkin Web site to download the World Bank's Deininger and Squire Data Set on income distribution in a large number of countries.
a. Which country in the data set has the most unequal distribution?
b. Which country in the data set has the most equal distribution?
c. Can you think of reasons that might explain the differences in income distribution in the two countries you've identified?

UNDERSTANDING FACTOR MARKETS

For Whom?

During the past 35 years, the rich have been getting richer and the poor poorer. This trend is new. From the end of World War II until 1965, the poor got richer at a faster pace than the rich and the gap between rich and poor narrowed a bit. What are the forces that generate these trends? The answer to this question is the forces of demand and supply in factor markets. These forces determine wages, interest rates, and the prices of land and natural resources. These forces also determine people's incomes. ◆ The three categories of resources are human, capital, and natural. Human resources include labor, human capital, and entrepreneurship. The income of labor and human capital depends on wage rates and employment levels, which are determined in labor markets. The income from capital depends on interest rates and the amount of capital, which are determined in capital markets. The income from natural resources depends on prices and quantities that are determined in natural resource markets. Only the return to entrepreneurship is not determined directly in a market. That return is normal profit plus economic profit, and it depends on how successful each entrepreneur is in the business that he or she runs. ◆ The chapters in this part study the forces at play in factor markets and explain how those forces have led to changes in the distribution of income. ◆ The overview of all the factor markets in Chapter 14 explained how the demand for factors of production results from the profit-maximizing decisions of firms. You studied these decisions from a different angle in Chapters 9–13, where you learned how firms choose their profit-maximizing output and price. Chapter 14 explained how a firm's profit-maximizing decisions determine its demand for productive factors. It also explained how factor supply decisions are made and how equilibrium in factor markets determines factor prices and the incomes of owners of factors of production. ◆ Some of the biggest incomes earned by superstars are a surplus that we call *economic rent*. ◆ Chapter 14 used labor resources and the labor market as its main example. But it also looked at some special features of capital markets and natural resource markets. ◆ Chapter 15 studied the distribution of income. This chapter took you right back to the fundamentals of economics and answered one of the big economic questions: Who gets to consume the goods and services that are produced? ◆ Many outstanding economists have advanced our understanding of factor markets and the role they play in helping to resolve the conflict between the demands of humans and the resources available. One of them is Thomas Robert Malthus, whom you can meet on the following page. You can also enjoy the insights of Janet Currie, a professor of economics at UCLA and a prominent contemporary labor economist.

PROBING THE IDEAS
Running Out of Resources

"The passion between the sexes has appeared in every age to be so nearly the same, that it may always be considered, in algebraic language, as a given quantity."

THOMAS
ROBERT
MALTHUS
An Essay on the Principle of Population

THOMAS ROBERT MALTHUS *(1766–1834), an English clergyman and economist, was an extremely influential social scientist. In his best-selling* Essay on the Principle of Population, *published in 1798, he predicted that population growth would outstrip food production and said that wars, famine, and disease were inevitable unless population growth was held in check by what he called "moral restraint." By "moral restraint," he meant marrying at a late age and living a celibate life. He married at the age of 38 a wife of 27, marriage ages that he recommended for others. Malthus's ideas were regarded as too radical in their day. And they led Thomas Carlyle, a contemporary thinker, to dub economics the "dismal science." But the ideas of Malthus had a profound influence on Charles Darwin, who got the key idea that led him to the theory of natural selection from reading the* Essay on the Principle of Population. *And David Ricardo and the classical economists were strongly influenced by Malthus's ideas.*

Is there a limit to economic growth, or can we expand production and population without effective limit? Thomas Malthus gave one of the most influential answers to these questions in 1798. He reasoned that population, unchecked, would grow at a geometric rate — 1, 2, 4, 8, 16 … — while the food supply would grow at an arithmetic rate — 1, 2, 3, 4, 5 … . To prevent the population from outstripping the available food supply, there would be periodic wars, famines, and plagues. In Malthus's view, only what he called moral restraint could prevent such periodic disasters.

As industrialization proceeded through the nineteenth century, Malthus's idea came to be applied to all natural resources, especially those that are exhaustible.

Modern-day Malthusians believe that his basic idea is correct and that it applies not only to food but also to every natural resource. In time, these prophets of doom believe, we will be reduced to the subsistence level that Malthus predicted. He was a few centuries out in his predictions but not dead wrong.

One modern-day Malthusian is ecologist Paul Ehrlich, who believes that we are sitting on a "population bomb." Governments must, says Ehrlich, limit both population growth and the resources that may be used each year.

In 1931, Harold Hotelling developed a theory of natural resources with different predictions from those of Malthus. The Hotelling Principle is that the relative price of an exhaustible natural resource will steadily rise, bringing a decline in the quantity used and an increase in the use of substitute resources.

Julian Simon (who died in 1998) challenged both the Malthusian gloom and the Hotelling Principle. He believed that people are the "ultimate resource" and predicted that a rising population lessens the pressure on natural resources. A bigger population provides a larger number of resourceful people who can work out more efficient ways of using scarce resources. As these solutions are found, the prices of exhaustible resources actually fall. To demonstrate his point, in 1980, Simon bet Ehrlich that the prices of five metals — copper, chrome, nickel, tin, and tungsten — would fall during the 1980s. Simon won the bet!

Then

No matter whether it is agricultural land, an exhaustible natural resource, or the space in the center of Chicago, and no matter whether it is 1998 or, as shown here, 1892, there is a limit to what is available, and we persistently push against that limit. Economists see urban congestion as a consequence of the value of doing business in the city center relative to the cost. They see the price mechanism, bringing ever-higher rents and prices of raw materials, as the means of allocating and rationing scarce natural resources. Malthusians, in contrast, explain congestion as the consequence of population pressure, and they see population control as the solution.

Now

In Tokyo, the pressure on space is so great that in some residential neighborhoods, a parking space costs $1,700 a month. To economize on this expensive space — and to lower the cost of car ownership and hence boost the sale of new cars — Honda, Nissan, and Toyota, three of Japan's big car producers, have developed a parking machine that enables two cars to occupy the space of one. The most basic of these machines costs a mere $10,000 — less than 6 months' parking fees.

Malthus developed his ideas about population growth in a world in which women played a limited role in the economy. Malthus did not consider the opportunity cost of women's time a factor to be considered in predicting trends in the birth rate and population growth. But today, the opportunity cost of women's time is a crucial factor because women play an expanded role in the labor force. One woman who has made significant contributions to our knowledge of labor markets is Janet Currie of UCLA. You can meet Professor Currie on the following pages.

365

TALKING WITH

JANET CURRIE *is a professor of economics at the University of California, Los Angeles. Born in 1960 in Kingston, Canada, she attended the University of Toronto, where she received her B.A. and M.A. in economics before moving to Princeton University, where she completed her Ph.D. in 1988. Professor Currie's research examines a wide range of public programs — medical, nutritional, educational, and housing — on (mainly) poor families. She has provided valuable assessments of the short-term and long-term effects of the Head Start program (enriched preschool for children in poor households) and Medicaid (government provided health insurance for poor mothers and their children).*

Janet Currie

Michael Parkin talked with Janet Currie about her work and the progress that economists have made in understanding how public policies can influence the distribution of income and economic well-being as well as the supply of labor and human capital.

Professor Currie, what attracted you to economics?

I was attracted to economics because it addresses questions of broad human interest (such as poverty and inequality) with intellectual rigor. Some may view the economic paradigm as restrictive (does everyone really maximize utility all the time?), but it provides a set of tools that yield powerful predictions about human behavior, and it can be tested. For example, the "Law of Demand" (people consume less of a good when the price goes up) can be adopted to think about why many eligible people do not participate in social programs that might benefit them.

Why are there still relatively few women in our field?

Like other scientific careers, that of an economist requires an initial investment in mathematical skills. Mathematics is the language of science, and it is difficult to become a scientist if you don't speak the language. Undergraduate programs in economics may be partially to blame for not preparing students adequately for graduate work in the field. Many programs are aimed more at preparing students for careers in law or business. While this may be what the majority of undergraduate economics students want, we should also serve those who may go on to study economics in graduate school.

Difficulties in combining work and family are also an issue, but economics is not unique in requiring women to devote a lot of time to their careers at precisely the point when traditionally women would spend most time with their families. However, supports such as maternity leave and child care are improving, and making it easier for younger women to "do it all."

Could you briefly describe Head Start and summarize your main conclusions about its effects?

Head Start is a preschool program for disadvantaged three- to five-year-old children. In a series of studies comparing Head Start children to siblings who did not attend, I find evidence of lasting effects of Head Start in terms of schooling attainment and reductions in criminal activity. These findings are important because, while everyone would like to believe that investments in children pay off, there was little prior evidence of longer-term effects of Head Start.

You asked in a recent paper "Are public housing projects good for kids?" What's the answer?

The title of this paper is intentionally provocative. Given all the negative publicity about some housing projects, most people assume that public housing must be bad for children. However, the key question is not whether kids in public housing do worse than other kids (they do) but whether they do better than they would have done in the absence of the program. For example, without the program, some children might have become homeless or had to move many times. It turns out that on average, public housing programs do improve the housing available to poor families, and have some positive effects in terms of schooling attainments.

In another paper, published in 1998, you summarized what we know and need to know about the effects of welfare programs on children. What, in a nutshell, do we know? What do we still need to know? And how would we set about finding the needed answers?

One striking conclusion from this review of welfare programs is that the available evidence suggests that in-kind programs are more effective than traditional welfare programs, which give cash to parents. This might account for the growing proportion of aid to poor families that is given in the form of specific in-kind benefits (e.g. Head Start, medical insurance, housing assistance). However, the evidence is far from complete. We need a lot more information about effects of programs on children, since anti-poverty programs are often justified in terms of their possible beneficial effects on children. We also need more information about longer-term effects of programs. For example, does it matter at what age the benefits are received?

In terms of how to find out what we need to know, I am a big supporter of social experiments, since a real random-assignment, treatment-control design provides more convincing answers than most statistical studies. On the other hand, it isn't possible to mount an experiment for every question. Much more could be done with existing data if more of it was made available to researchers, and if governments were more willing to allow linkages of different data sources.

What are some of the social experiments that have provided convincing answers? And how could economists do better work if governments were more willing to allow linkages of different data sources?

The great thing about a well-designed experiment is that anyone can understand the results. For example, in a drug trial, we randomly assign people to a treatment group that gets the drug, and a control group that gets a placebo. Because of the random assignment, the two groups are the same on average, so that

> *"The great thing about a well-designed experiment is that anyone can understand the results."*

any *ex poste* differences in how they do can be attributed to the treatment. Social experiments like the "Moving to Opportunity" project also rely on random assignment. In this experiment, the treatment consisted of giving a voucher to families in public housing projects that allowed the families to move into a low-poverty neighborhood and gave them some assistance in relocating. The initial results indicate that the experiment had an effect on youth crime, as well as on criminal victimization. So far, there are no positive effects on schooling attainment or parental employment, but it is possible that these will emerge in the followup that is currently being conducted.

Another interesting experiment involves Early Head Start, a program that extends Head Start benefits to infants and toddlers. This program has demonstrated short-term effects of the program on cognitive test scores. Again, it will be necessary to do

367

some long-term followup in order to see whether these benefits are retained.

The downside of experiments is that they are very expensive, relative to a statistical study, and cannot be used to answer questions other than those they were designed to address. Some of my work on the effects of Medicaid expansions provides an example of what can be done by linking various types of data. The U.S. government collects a good deal of survey data about health insurance and health care utilization. Because my co-author, Jon Gruber, was working in Washington, we were able to get state identifiers so that we could link information about Medicaid income cutoffs in each state to the individual-level records. This enabled us to ask how changing the income cutoffs affected health care utilization. In recent years, the government has been unwilling to release geographic identifiers, so that it is not possible to do a similar study of more recent health insurance expansions.

A few years ago, you stuck out your neck on the never-to-end minimum wage issue. What, according to your work, is the effect of the minimum wage on youth employment?

We found compelling evidence that youths affected by minimum wage legislation were less likely to be employed than those who were not (because they had wages either above or below the affected group). There are some obvious methodological flaws with some of the work arguing that minimum wages actually increase employment (such as failures to properly control for increases in demand, which might be driving increases in employment even at the higher minimum wages). However, much of the work (my own included) ignores an important question, which is whether we actually want to increase employment among youths. If higher minimum wages reduced employment but increased schooling, perhaps this would be a good outcome.

You've studied the effects of restrictions on the use of public funds for abortion. What did you discover?

Many people have argued that restrictions on abortion may cause more unwanted children to be born and hence worsen infant and child outcomes. The basic idea of my paper was that if this were true, then one ought to be able to see the effect in the distribution of birthweights. That is, if children who would have been aborted are more likely to be of low birthweight (because their mothers did not take care of themselves), then one should see more

> *""...economists are increasingly contributing to debate (and frequently having the last word) on questions that used to be considered far outside their scope."*

low birthweight infants in areas that adopt abortion restrictions. We did not, however, find this effect. In hindsight, it is not obvious that children who are born as a result of abortion restrictions ought to be less healthy than average, since the majority of women seeking abortions are young and non-poor.

What advice do you have for a student who is just starting to study economics? Do you think that economics is good subject in which to major? What other subjects would you urge students to study along side economics?

I have never regretted choosing economics as a major. Economics gives one the tools to study a vast array of social issues in a rigourous manner. Not surprisingly, economists are increasingly contributing to debate (and frequently having the last word) on questions that used to be considered far outside their scope. Economic concepts such as "opportunity cost," "selection bias," and cost-benefit analysis are central to the discussion of a vast array of policy issues.

Students who want to leave open the option of graduate work in economics should make sure they take enough mathematics courses to get them through a good graduate program.

PUBLIC GOODS AND TAXES

CHAPTER 16

Government: The Solution or the Problem?

In 2000, the federal, state, and local governments in the United States employed 19.8 million people and spent $3 trillion. Independent government agencies employed yet another million people. Do we need this much government? Is government, as conservatives sometimes suggest, too big? Is government "the problem"? Or, despite its enormous size, is government too small to do all the things it must attend to? Is government, as liberals sometimes suggest, not contributing enough to economic life? ◆ After the terrorist attacks on New York and Washington on September 11, 2001, almost everyone agreed that the government needed to step up the scope and quality of domestic security. What determines the scale on which the government provides a public service such as domestic security? And why can't the market provide the security that people demand? To pay for the things they provide, governments collect taxes. What determines the types and scale of the taxes that we pay?

◆ We begin our study of government by describing the areas in which the market economy fails to achieve an efficient allocation of resources. We then explain what determines the scale of government provision of public services and the taxes that pay for them.

After studying this chapter, you will be able to

- **Explain how government arises from market failure and redistribution**

- **Distinguish between public goods and private goods, explain the free-rider problem, and explain how the quantity of public goods is determined**

- **Explain why most of the government's revenue comes from income taxes, why income taxes are progressive, and why some goods are taxed at a much higher rate than others**

The Economic Theory of Government

THE ECONOMIC THEORY OF GOVERNMENT explains the purpose of governments, the economic choices that governments make, and the consequences of those choices.

Governments exist for two major reasons. First, they establish and maintain property rights and set the rules for the redistribution of income and wealth. Property rights are the foundation on which all market activity takes place. They replace stealing with a rule-based and law-enforced system for redistributing income and wealth.

Second, governments provide a nonmarket mechanism for allocating scarce resources when the market economy results in *inefficiency* — a situation called **market failure.** When market failure occurs, too many of some things and too few of some other things are produced. By reallocating resources, it is possible to make some people better off while making no one worse off. So people support government activity that modifies the market outcome and corrects market failure.

We're going to study four economic problems that are dealt with by government or public choices:

- Public goods
- Taxes and redistribution
- Monopoly
- Externalities

Public Goods

Some goods and services are consumed either by everyone or by no one. Examples are national defense, law and order, and sewage and waste disposal services. National defense systems cannot isolate individuals and refuse to protect them. Airborne diseases from untreated sewage do not favor some people and hit others. A good or service that is consumed either by everyone or by no one is called a *public good.*

The market economy fails to deliver the efficient quantity of public goods because of a free-rider problem. Everyone tries to free ride on everyone else because the good is available to all whether they pay for it or not. We'll study public goods and the free-rider problem later in this chapter. We'll study the factors that influence the scale of provision of public goods. We'll also study the taxes that pay for them.

Taxes and Redistribution

You saw in Chapter 15 that the market economy delivers an unequal distribution of income and wealth and that income support systems and progressive income taxes influence the distribution.

Taxes play a dual role: They pay for public goods, and they redistribute income. In this chapter, we'll look further at taxes and explain why the income tax is progressive and why some goods are taxed at high rates and others at lower rates.

Monopoly

Monopoly and *rent seeking* prevent the allocation of resources from being efficient. Every business tries to maximize profit, and when a monopoly exists, it can increase profit by restricting output and keeping the price high. For example, some years ago, AT&T had a monopoly on long-distance telephone services and the quantity of long-distance services was much smaller and the price much higher than they are today. After the power of government was used to break up AT&T, the quantity of long-distance calls exploded.

Some monopolies arise from *legal barriers to entry* — barriers to entry created by governments — but a major activity of government is to regulate monopoly and to enforce laws that prevent cartels and other restrictions on competition. We study these regulations and laws in Chapter 17.

Externalities

When a chemical factory (legally) dumps its waste into a river and kills the fish, it imposes a cost — called an *external cost* — on the members of a fishing club who fish downstream. When a homeowner fills her garden with spring bulbs, she generates an external benefit for all the passers-by. External costs and benefits are not usually taken into account by the people whose actions create them. The chemical factory does not take the fishing club's wishes into account when it decides whether to dump waste into the river. The homeowner does not take her neighbors' views into account when she decides to fill her garden with flowers. We study externalities in Chapter 18.

Before we begin to study each of these problems from which government activity arises, let's look at the arena in which governments operate: the "political marketplace."

Public Choice and the Political Marketplace

Government is a complex organization made up of millions of individuals, each with his or her own economic objectives. Government policy is the outcome of the choices made by these individuals. To analyze these choices, economists have developed a *public choice theory* of the political marketplace. The actors in the political marketplace are

- Voters
- Politicians
- Bureaucrats

Figure 16.1 illustrates the choices and interactions of these actors. Let's look at each in turn.

Voters Voters are the consumers in the political marketplace. In the markets for goods and services, people express their preferences by their willingness to pay. In the political marketplace, they express their preferences by their votes, campaign contributions, and lobbying activity. Public choice theory assumes that people support the policies they believe will make them better off and oppose the policies that they believe will make them worse off. It is voters' *perceptions* rather than reality that guide their choices.

Politicians Politicians are the entrepreneurs of the political marketplace. Public choice theory assumes that the objective of a politician is to get elected and to remain in office. Votes to a politician are like economic profit to a firm. To get enough votes, politicians propose policies that they expect will appeal to a majority of voters.

Bureaucrats Bureaucrats are the hired officials in government departments. They are the producers or firms in the political marketplace. Public choice theory assumes that bureaucrats aim to maximize their own utility and that to achieve this objective, they try to maximize the budgets of their departments.

The bigger the budget of a department, the greater is the prestige of its chief and the larger is the opportunity for promotion for people farther down the bureaucratic ladder. So all the members of a department have an interest in maximizing the department's budget. To maximize their budgets, bureaucrats devise programs that they expect will appeal to politicians and they help politicians to explain their programs to voters.

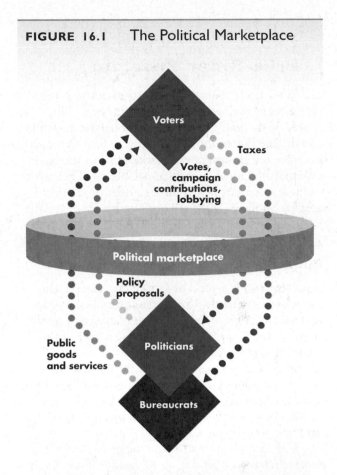

FIGURE 16.1   The Political Marketplace

Voters express their demands for policies by voting, making campaign contributions, and lobbying. Politicians propose policies to appeal to a majority of voters. Bureaucrats try to maximize the budgets of their departments. A political equilibrium emerges in which no group can improve its position by making a different choice.

Political Equilibrium

Voters, politicians, and bureaucrats make choices to best further their own objectives. But each group is constrained by the preferences of the other groups and by what is technologically feasible. The outcome that results from the choices of voters, politicians, and bureaucrats is a **political equilibrium**, which is a situation in which all their choices are compatible and in which no group can improve its position by making a different choice. Let's see how voters, politicians, and bureaucrats interact to determine the quantity of public goods.

Public Goods and the Free-Rider Problem

WHY DOES THE GOVERNMENT PROVIDE GOODS and services such as national defense and public health? Why don't we buy our national defense from North Pole Protection, Inc., a private firm that competes for our dollars in the marketplace in the same way that McDonald's and Coca-Cola do? The answer to these questions lies in the free-rider problem created by public goods. Let's explore this problem. We begin by looking at the nature of a public good.

Public Goods

A **public good** is a good or service that can be consumed simultaneously by everyone and from which no one can be excluded. The first feature of a public good is called nonrivalry. A good is *nonrival* if the consumption by one person does not decrease the consumption by another person. An example is watching a television show. The opposite of nonrival is rival. A good is *rival* if the consumption by one person decreases the consumption by another person. An example is eating a hotdog.

The second feature of a public good is that it is nonexcludable. A good is *nonexcludable* if it is impossible, or extremely costly, to prevent someone from benefiting from a good. An example is national defense. It would be difficult to exclude someone from being defended. The opposite of nonexcludable is excludable. A good is *excludable* if it is possible to prevent a person from enjoying the benefits of a good. An example is cable television. Cable companies can ensure that only those people who have paid the fee receive programs.

Figure 16.2 classifies goods according to these two criteria and gives examples of goods in each category. National defense is a *pure* public good. One person's consumption of the security provided by our national defense system does not decrease the security of someone else — defense is nonrival. And the military cannot select those whom it will protect and those whom it will leave exposed to threats — defense is nonexcludable.

Many goods have a public element but are not pure public goods. An example is a highway. A highway is nonrival until it becomes congested. One more car on a highway with plenty of space does not reduce

FIGURE 16.2   Public Goods and Private Goods

	Rival	**Nonrival**
Excludable	**Pure private goods** Food Car House	**Excludable and nonrival** Cable television Bridge Highway
Non-excludable	**Nonexcludable and rival** Fish in the ocean Air	**Pure public goods** Lighthouse National defense

A pure public good (bottom right) is one for which consumption is nonrival and from which it is impossible to exclude a consumer. Pure public goods pose a free-rider problem. A pure private good (top left) is one for which consumption is rival and from which consumers can be excluded. Some goods are nonexcludable but are rival (bottom left), and some goods are nonrival but are excludable (top right).

Source: Adapted from and inspired by E. S. Savas, *Privatizing the Public Sector* (Chatham, N.J.: Chatham House Publishers, 1982), p. 34.

anyone else's consumption of transportation services. But once the highway becomes congested, one extra vehicle lowers the quality of the service available to everyone else — it becomes rival like a private good. Also, users can be excluded from a highway by tollgates. Another example is fish in the ocean. Ocean fish are rival because a fish taken by one person is not available for anyone else. Ocean fish are also nonexcludable because it is difficult to prevent people from catching them.

The Free-Rider Problem

Public goods create a free-rider problem. A **free rider** is a person who consumes a good without paying for it. Public goods create a *free-rider problem* because the quantity of the good that a person is able to consume is not influenced by the amount the person pays for the good. So no one has an incentive to pay for a public good. Let's look more closely at the free-rider problem by studying an example.

The Benefit of a Public Good

Suppose that for its defense, a country must launch some surveillance satellites. The benefit provided by a satellite is the *value* of its services. The *value* of a *private* good is the maximum amount that a person is willing to pay for one more unit, which is shown by the person's demand curve. The value of a *public* good is the maximum amount that all the *people* are willing to pay for one more unit of it.

To calculate the value placed on a public good, we use the concepts of total benefit and marginal benefit. *Total benefit* is the dollar value that a person places on a given level of provision of a public good. The greater the quantity of a public good, the larger is a person's total benefit. *Marginal benefit* is the increase in total benefit that results from a one-unit increase in the quantity of a public good.

Figure 16.3 shows the marginal benefit that arises from defense satellites for a society with just two members, Lisa and Max. Lisa's and Max's marginal benefits are graphed as MB_L and MB_M, respectively, in parts (a) and (b) of the figure. The marginal benefit from a public good is similar to the marginal utility from a private good — its magnitude diminishes as the quantity of the good increases. For Lisa, the marginal benefit from the first satellite is $80 and that from the second is $60. By the time five satellites are deployed, Lisa's marginal benefit is zero. For Max, the marginal utility from the first satellite is $50 and that from the second is $40. By the time five satellites are deployed, Max perceives only $10 worth of marginal benefit.

Part (c) shows the economy's marginal benefit curve, *MB*. An individual's marginal benefit curve for a public good is similar to the individual's demand curve for a private good. But the economy's marginal benefit curve for a public good is different from the market demand curve for a *private* good. To obtain the market demand curve for a private good, we sum the quantities demanded by all individuals at each price — we sum the individual demand curves *horizontally* (see Chapter 7, p. 159). But to find the economy's marginal benefit curve of a *public* good, we sum the marginal benefits of each individual at each quantity — we sum the individual marginal benefit curves *vertically*. The resulting marginal benefit for the economy made up of Lisa and Max is the economy's marginal benefit curve graphed in part (c) — the curve *MB*. Lisa's marginal benefit from the first satellite gets added to Max's marginal benefit from the first satellite because they *both* consume the first satellite.

FIGURE 16.3   Benefits of a Public Good

(a) Lisa's marginal benefit

(b) Max's marginal benefit

(c) Economy's marginal benefit

The marginal benefit to the economy at each quantity of the public good is the sum of the marginal benefits of all individuals. The marginal benefit curves are MB_L for Lisa, MB_M for Max, and *MB* for the economy.

The Efficient Quantity of a Public Good

An economy with two people would not buy any satellites — because the total benefit would fall far short of the cost. But an economy with 250 million people might. To determine the efficient quantity, we need to take the cost as well as the benefit into account.

The cost of a satellite is based on technology and the prices of the resources used to produce it (just like the cost of producing sweaters, which you studied in Chapter 10).

Figure 16.4 sets out the benefits and costs. The second and third columns of the table show the total and marginal benefits. The next two columns show the total and marginal cost of producing satellites. The final column shows net benefit. Total benefit, *TB*, and total cost, *TC*, are graphed in part (a) of the figure.

The efficient quantity is the one that maximizes *net benefit* — total benefit minus total cost — and occurs when two satellites are provided.

The fundamental principles of marginal analysis that you have used to explain how consumers maximize utility and how firms maximize profit can also be used to calculate the efficient scale of provision of a public good. Figure 16.4(b) shows this alternative approach. The marginal benefit curve is *MB*, and the marginal cost curve is *MC*. When marginal benefit exceeds marginal cost, net benefit increases if the quantity produced increases. When marginal cost exceeds marginal benefit, net benefit increases if the quantity produced decreases. Marginal benefit equals marginal cost with two satellites. So making marginal cost equal to marginal benefit maximizes net benefit and uses resources efficiently.

Private Provision

We have now worked out the quantity of satellites that maximizes net benefit. Would a private firm — North Pole Protection, Inc. — deliver that quantity? It would not. To do so, it would have to collect $15 billion to cover its costs — or $60 from each of the 250 million people in the economy. But no one would have an incentive to buy his or her "share" of the satellite system. Everyone would reason as follows: The number of satellites provided by North Pole Protection, Inc., is not affected by my $60. But my own private consumption is greater if I free ride and do not pay my share of the cost of the satellite system. If I do not pay, I enjoy the same level of security and I can buy more private goods. Therefore I will spend my $60 on other goods and free ride on the public good. This is the free-rider problem.

If everyone reasons the same way, North Pole Protection has zero revenue and so provides no satellites. Because two satellites is the efficient level, private provision is inefficient.

Public Provision

Suppose there are two political parties, the Hawks and the Doves, that agree with each other on all issues except for the quantity of satellites. The Hawks would like to provide four satellites at a total cost of $50 billion, with total benefits of $50 billion and a net benefit of zero, as shown in Fig. 16.4(a). The Doves would like to provide one satellite at a cost of $5 billion, a benefit of $20 billion, and a net benefit of $15 billion — see Fig. 16.4(a).

Before deciding on their policy proposals, the two political parties do a "what-if" analysis. Each party reasons as follows: If each party offers the satellite program it wants — Hawks four satellites and Doves one satellite — the voters will see that they will get a net benefit of $15 billion from the Doves and zero net benefit from the Hawks, and the Doves will win the election.

Contemplating this outcome, the Hawks realize that they are too hawkish to get elected. They must scale back their proposal to two satellites at a total cost of $15 billion. Total benefit is $35 billion, and net benefit is $20 billion. So if the Doves stick with one satellite, the Hawks will win the election.

Contemplating this outcome, the Doves realize that they must match the Hawks. They too propose to provide two satellites. If the two parties offer the same number of satellites, the voters are indifferent between the parties. They flip coins to decide their votes, and each party receives around 50 percent of the vote.

The result of the politicians' "what-if" analysis is that each party offers two satellites, so regardless of who wins the election, this is the quantity of satellites installed. And this quantity is efficient. It maximizes the perceived net benefit of the voters. Thus in this example, competition in the political marketplace results in the efficient provision of a public good. But for this outcome to occur, voters must be well informed and evaluate the alternatives. As you will see below, they do not always have an incentive to achieve this outcome.

FIGURE 16.4   The Efficient Quantity of a Public Good

(a) Total benefit and total cost

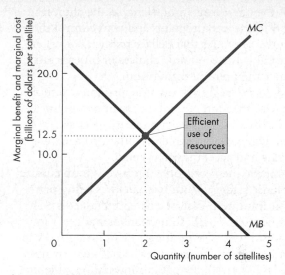

(b) Marginal benefit and marginal cost

Quantity (number of satellites)	Total benefit (billions of dollars)	Marginal benefit (billions of dollars per satellite)	Total cost (billions of dollars)	Marginal cost (billions of dollars per satellite)	Net benefit (billions of dollars)
0	0		0		0
		20		5	
1	20		5		15
		15		10	
2	**35**		**15**		**20**
		10		15	
3	45		30		15
		5		20	
4	50		50		0
		0		25	
5	50		75		−25

Net benefit — the vertical distance between total benefit, *TB* and total cost, *TC* — is maximized when two satellites are installed (part a) and where marginal benefit, *MB*, equals marginal cost, *MC* (part b). The Doves would like one satellite, and the Hawks would like four. But each party recognizes that its only hope of being elected is to provide two satellites — the quantity that maximizes net benefit and so leaves no room for the other party to improve on.

The Principle of Minimum Differentiation In the example we've just studied, both parties propose identical policies. This tendency toward identical policies is an example of the **principle of minimum differentiation**, which is the tendency for competitors to make themselves identical to appeal to the maximum number of clients or voters. This principle not only describes the behavior of political parties but also explains why fast-food restaurants cluster in the same block and even why new auto models have similar features. If McDonald's opens a restaurant in a new location, it is likely that Burger King will open next door to McDonald's rather than a mile down the road. If Chrysler designs a new van with a sliding door on the driver's side, most likely Ford will too.

The Role of Bureaucrats

We have analyzed the behavior of politicians but not that of the bureaucrats who translate the choices of the politicians into programs and who control the day-to-day activities that deliver public goods. Let's now see how the economic choices of bureaucrats influence the political equilibrium.

To do so, we'll stick with the previous example. We've seen that competition between two political parties delivers the efficient quantity of satellites. But will the Defense Department — the Pentagon — cooperate and accept this outcome?

Suppose the Pentagon's objective is to maximize the defense budget. With two satellites being provided at minimum cost, the defense budget is $15 billion (see Fig. 16.4). To increase its budget, the Pentagon might do two things. First, it might try to persuade the politicians that two satellites cost more than $15 billion. As Fig. 16.5 shows, if possible, the Pentagon would like to convince Congress that two satellites cost $35 billion — the entire benefit. Second, and pressing its position even more strongly, the Pentagon might argue for more satellites. It might press for four satellites and a budget of $50 billion. In this situation, total benefit and total cost are equal and net benefit is zero.

The Pentagon wants to maximize its budget, but won't the politicians prevent it from doing so because the Pentagon's preferred outcome costs votes? They will if voters are well informed and know what is best for them. But voters might be rationally ignorant. In this case, well-informed interest groups might enable the Pentagon to achieve its objective.

Rational Ignorance

A principle of public choice theory is that it is rational for a voter to be ignorant about an issue unless that issue has a perceptible effect on the voter's income. **Rational ignorance** is the decision *not* to acquire information because the cost of doing so exceeds the expected benefit. For example, each voter knows that he or she can make virtually no difference to the defense policy of the U.S. government. Each voter also knows that it would take an enormous amount of time and effort to become even moderately well informed about alternative defense technologies. So voters remain relatively uninformed about the technicalities of defense issues. (Though we are using

FIGURE 16.5   Bureaucratic Overprovision

The goal of a bureaucracy is to maximize its budget. A bureaucracy that maximizes its budget will seek to increase its budget so that its total cost equals total benefit and then to use its budget to expand output and expenditure. Here, the Pentagon tries to get $35 billion to provide two satellites. It would like to increase the quantity of satellites to four with a budget of $50 billion.

defense policy as an example, the same applies to all aspects of government economic activity.)

All voters are consumers of national defense. But not all voters are producers of national defense. Only a small number are in this latter category. Voters who own or work for firms that produce satellites have a direct personal interest in defense because it affects their incomes. These voters have an incentive to become well informed about defense issues and to operate a political lobby aimed at furthering their own interests. In collaboration with the defense bureaucracy, these voters exert a larger influence than do the relatively uninformed voters who only consume this public good.

When the rationality of the uninformed voter and special interest groups are taken into account, the political equilibrium provides public goods in excess of the efficient quantity. So in the satellite example, three or four satellites might be installed rather than the efficient quantity, which is two satellites.

Two Types of Political Equilibrium

We've seen that two types of political equilibrium are possible: efficient and inefficient. These two types of political equilibrium correspond to two theories of government:

- Public interest theory
- Public choice theory

Public Interest Theory Public interest theory predicts that governments make choices that achieve efficiency. This outcome occurs in a perfect political system in which voters are fully informed about the effects of policies and refuse to vote for outcomes that can be improved upon.

Public Choice Theory Public choice theory predicts that governments make choices that result in inefficiency. This outcome occurs in political markets in which voters are rationally ignorant and base their votes only on issues that they know affect their own net benefit. Voters pay more attention to their interests as producers than their interests as consumers, and public officials also act in their own best interest. The result is *government failure* that parallels market failure.

Why Government Is Large and Grows

Now that we know how the quantity of public goods is determined, we can explain part of the reason for the growth of government. Government grows in part because the demand for some public goods increases at a faster rate than the demand for private goods. There are two possible reasons for this growth:

- Voter preferences
- Inefficient overprovision

Voter Preferences The growth of government can be explained by voter preferences in the following way. As voters' incomes increase (as they do in most years), the demand for many public goods increases more quickly than income. (Technically, the *income elasticity of demand* for many public goods is greater than 1 — see Chapter 4, pp. 90–91.) These goods include public health, education, national defense, highways, airports, and air-traffic control systems. If politicians did not support increases in expenditures on these items, they would not get elected.

Inefficient Overprovision Inefficient overprovision might explain the *size* of government but not its *growth rate*. It (possibly) explains why government is *larger* than its efficient scale, but it does not explain why governments use an increasing proportion of total resources.

Voters Strike Back

If government grows too large relative to the value that voters place on public goods, there might be a voter backlash against government programs and a large bureaucracy. Electoral success during the 1990s at the state and federal levels required politicians of all parties to embrace smaller, leaner, and more efficient government. The September 11 attacks have led to a greater willingness to pay for security but have probably not lessened the desire for lean government.

Another way in which voters — and politicians — can try to counter the tendency of bureaucrats to expand their budgets is to privatize the production of public goods. Government *provision* of a public good does not automatically imply that a government-operated bureau must *produce* the good. Garbage collection (a public good) is often done by a private firm, and experiments are being conducted with private fire departments and even private prisons.

REVIEW QUIZ

1 What is the free-rider problem and why does it make the private provision of a public good inefficient?

2 Under what conditions will competition for votes among politicians result in an efficient quantity of a public good?

3 How do rationally ignorant voters and budget-maximizing bureaucrats prevent competition in the political marketplace from producing the efficient quantity of a public good? Do they result in too much or too little public provision of public goods?

We've now seen how voters, politicians, and bureaucrats interact to determine the quantity of a public good. But public goods are paid for with taxes. Taxes also redistribute income. How does the political marketplace determine the taxes we pay?

Taxes

TAXES GENERATE THE FINANCIAL RESOURCES that provide public goods. Taxes also redistribute income. Governments use five types of taxes:

- Income taxes
- Social Security taxes
- Sales taxes
- Property taxes
- Excise taxes

Figure 16.6 shows the relative amounts raised by these five types of tax in 1999 (the most recent year for which data on state and local government are available at the time of writing). Income taxes raised 51 percent of tax revenues in 1999. Social Security taxes are the next biggest revenue source, and they raised 24 percent of total taxes. State sales taxes raise 12 percent of total taxes, and local government property taxes raise about 10 percent of total taxes. Finally, excise taxes raise a small amount of government revenue. Although they raise a small amount of revenue, excise taxes have a big impact on some markets, as you'll discover later in this chapter. Let's take a closer look at each type of tax.

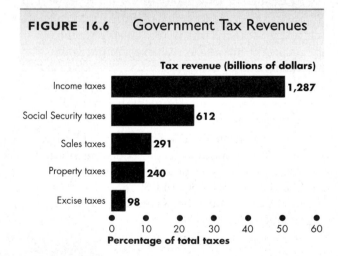

FIGURE 16.6   Government Tax Revenues

More than half of government revenues come from income taxes. Almost a quarter comes from Social Security taxes. Excise taxes bring in a small amount of revenue, but these taxes have big effects on a small number of markets.

Sources: U.S. Census Bureau and *Economic Report of the President*, 2002.

Income Taxes

Income taxes are paid on personal incomes and corporate profits. In 1999, the personal income tax raised $879 billion for the federal government and another $189 billion for state and local governments. Corporate profits taxes raised $185 billion for the federal government and $34 billion for the state governments. We'll look first at the effects of personal income taxes and then at corporate profits taxes.

Personal Income Tax   The amount of income tax that a person pays depends on her or his *taxable income*, which equals total income minus a *personal exemption* and a *standard deduction* or other allowable deductions. In 2000, the personal exemption was $2,800 and the standard deduction was $4,400 for a single person. So for such a person, taxable income equals total income minus $7,200.

The *tax rate* (percent) depends on the income level and for a single person increases according to the following scale:

$0 to $26,250	15 percent
$26,251 to $63,550	28 percent
$63,551 to $132,600	31 percent
$132,601 to $288,350	36 percent
Over $288,350	39.6 percent

The percentages in this list are marginal tax rates. A **marginal tax rate** is the percentage of an additional dollar of income that is paid in tax. For example, if taxable income increases from $25,000 to $25,001, the additional tax paid is 15 cents and the marginal tax rate is 15 percent. If income increases from $288,350 to $288,351, the additional tax paid is 39.6 cents and the marginal tax rate is 39.6 percent.

The **average tax rate** is the percentage of income that is paid in tax. Let's calculate the average tax rate for a single person who earns $50,000 in a year. Tax is zero on the first $7,200 plus $3,938 (15 percent) on the next $26,250, plus $4,634 (28 percent) on the remaining $16,550. Total tax is $8,572, which is 17.1 percent of $50,000. The average tax rate is 17.1 percent.

If the marginal tax rate exceeds the average tax rate, the average tax rate increases as income increases and the tax is a *progressive tax* (see p. 355). The personal income tax is a progressive tax. To see this feature of the income tax, calculate the average tax rate for someone whose income is $100,000 a year. Tax is zero on the first $7,200 plus $3,938 (15 percent) on the next $26,250, plus $10,444 (28 percent) on the next $37,300, plus $9,068 (31 percent) on the remaining $29,250. Total taxes equal $23,449, which is 23.4 percent of $100,000. The average tax rate is 23.4 percent.

The Effect of Income Taxes Figure 16.7 shows how the income tax affects labor markets. Part (a) shows the market for low-wage workers, and part (b) shows the market for high-wage workers. These labor markets are competitive, and with no income taxes, they work just like all the other competitive markets you have studied. The demand curves are *LD*, and the supply curves are *LS* (in both parts of the figure). Both groups work 40 hours a week. Low-wage workers earn $9.50 an hour, and high-wage workers earn $175 an hour. What happens when an income tax is introduced?

If low-wage workers are willing to supply 40 hours a week for $9.50 an hour when there is no tax, then they are willing to supply that same quantity in the face of a 15 percent tax only if the wage rises by

enough to provide an after-tax wage rate of $9.50 an hour. That is, they want to get the $9.50 an hour they received before plus enough to pay 15 percent of their income to the government. So the supply of labor decreases because the amount received from work is lowered by the amount of income tax paid. The acceptable wage rate at each level of employment rises by the amount of the tax that must be paid. For low-wage workers who face a tax rate of 15 percent, the supply curve shifts to *LS + tax*. The equilibrium wage rate rises to $10 an hour, but the after-tax wage rate falls to $8.50 an hour. Employment falls to 36 hours a week.

For high-wage workers who face a tax rate of 39.6 percent, the supply curve shifts to *LS + tax*. The equilibrium wage rate rises to $200 an hour, and the after-tax wage rate falls to $121 an hour. Employment falls to 32 hours a week. The decrease in employment of high-wage workers is larger than that of low-wage workers because of the different marginal tax rates that each type of worker faces.

FIGURE 16.7   The Effects of Income Taxes

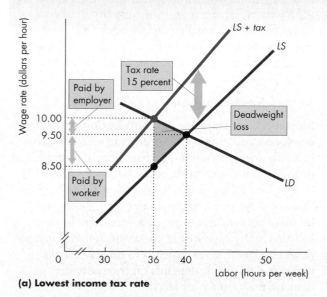

(a) Lowest income tax rate

(b) Highest income tax rate

The demand for labor is *LD*, and with no income taxes, the supply of labor is *LS* (both parts). In part (a), low-wage workers earn $9.50 an hour and each works 40 hours a week. In part (b), high-wage workers earn $175 an hour and each works 40 hours a week. An income tax decreases the supply of labor, and the labor supply curve shifts leftward. For low-wage workers in part (a), whose marginal tax rate is 15 percent,

supply decreases to *LS + tax*. Employment falls to 36 hours a week. For high-wage workers in part (b), whose marginal tax rate is 39.6 percent, supply decreases to *LS + tax*. Employment falls to 32 hours a week. The deadweight loss from the high marginal tax rate on high-wage workers is much larger than that from the low marginal tax rate on low-wage workers.

Notice that the income tax is paid by both the employer and the worker. In the case of a low-wage worker, the employer pays an extra 50 cents an hour and the worker pays $1 an hour. In the case of a high-wage worker, the employer pays an extra $25 an hour and the worker pays $54 an hour. The exact split depends on the elasticities of demand and supply.

Notice also the difference in the *deadweight loss* for the two groups. The deadweight loss is larger for the high-wage workers than for the low-wage workers.

Why Do We Have a Progressive Income Tax? We have a progressive income tax because it is part of the political equilibrium. A majority of voters support it, so politicians who also support it get elected.

The economic model that predicts progressive income taxes is called the *median voter* model. The core idea of the median voter model is that political parties pursue policies that are most likely to attract the support of the median voter. The median voter is the one in the middle — one half of the population lies on one side and one half on the other. Let's see how the median voter model predicts a progressive income tax.

Imagine that government programs benefit everyone equally and are paid for by a proportional income tax. Everyone pays the same percentage of their income in tax. In this situation, there is a redistribution from high-income voters to low-income voters. Everyone benefits equally, but because they have higher incomes, the high-income voters pay a larger amount of taxes.

Is this situation the best one possible for the median voter? It is not. Suppose that instead of using a proportional tax, the marginal tax rate is lowered for low-income voters and increased for high-income voters — a progressive tax. Low-income voters are now better off, and high-income voters are worse off. Low-income voters will support this change, and high income voters will oppose it. But there are many more low-income voters than high-income voters, so the low-income voters win.

The median voter is a low-income voter. In fact, because the distribution of income is skewed, the median voter has a smaller income than the average income (see Fig. 15.1 on p. 344). This fact raises an interesting question: Why doesn't the median voter support taxes that skim off all income above the average and redistribute it to everyone with a below-average income? Such a tax would be so progressive that it would result in equal incomes after taxes and redistribution.

The answer is that high taxes discourage work and saving and the median voter would be worse off with such radical redistribution than under the arrangements that prevail today. (See the big tradeoff in Chapter 5, p. 113.)

Let's now look at corporate profits taxes.

Corporate Profits Tax In popular discussions of taxes, corporate profits taxes are seen as a free source of revenue for the government. Taxing people is bad, but taxing corporations is just fine.

It turns out that taxing corporations is very inefficient. We use an inefficient tax because it redistributes income in favor of the median voter, just like the personal income tax. Let's see why taxing corporate profits is inefficient.

First, the tax is misnamed. It is only partly a tax on economic profit. It is mainly a tax on the income from capital. Taxing the income from capital works like taxing the income from labor except for two critical differences: The supply of capital is highly (perhaps perfectly) elastic, and the quantity of capital influences the productivity of labor and wage income. Because the supply of capital is highly elastic, the tax is fully borne by firms and the quantity of capital decreases. With a smaller capital stock than we would otherwise have, the productivity of labor and wage income are lower than they would otherwise be.

Social Security Taxes

Social Security taxes are the contributions paid by employers and employees to provide social security benefits, unemployment compensation, and health and disability benefits to workers (see Chapter 15, p. 355).

Unions lobby to get employers to pay a bigger share of these taxes, and employers' organizations lobby to get workers to pay a bigger share of them. But this lobbying effort is not worth much, for who *really* pays these taxes depends in no way on who writes the checks. It depends on the elasticities of demand and supply for labor.

Figure 16.8 shows you why. The demand curve, LD, and the supply curve, LS, are identical in the two parts of the figure. With no Social Security tax, the quantity of labor employed is QL^* and the wage rate is W^*.

A Social Security tax is now introduced. In part (a), the employee pays the tax, and in part (b), the employer pays. When the employee pays, supply decreases and the supply of labor curve shifts leftward to *LS* + *tax*. The vertical distance between the supply curve *LS* and the new supply curve *LS* + *tax* is the amount of the tax. The wage rate rises to *WC*, after-tax wages fall to *WT*, and employment decreases to QL_0.

When the employer pays (in part b), demand decreases and the demand for labor curve shifts leftward to *LD* − *tax*. The vertical distance between the demand curve *LD* and the new demand curve *LD* − *tax* is the amount of the tax. The wage rate falls to *WT*, but the cost of labor rises to *WC* and employment decreases to QL_0.

So regardless of which side of the market is taxed, the outcome is identical. If the demand for labor is perfectly inelastic or if the supply of labor is perfectly elastic, the employer pays the entire tax. And if the demand for labor is perfectly elastic or if the supply of labor is perfectly inelastic, the employee pays the entire tax. These cases are like those for the sales tax that you studied in Chapter 6 (pp. 129–132).

Sales Taxes

Sales taxes are the taxes levied by states on a wide range of goods and services. We studied the effects of these taxes in Chapter 6. There is one feature of these taxes, though, that we need to note. They are *regressive*. The reason they are regressive is that saving increases with income and sales taxes are paid only on the part of income that is spent.

Suppose, for example, that the sales tax rate is 8 percent. A family that earns $20,000 and spends $18,000 on goods and services pays $1,440 (8 percent of $18,000) in sales tax. The family's taxes are 7.2 percent of its income. A family that earns $100,000 and spends $60,000 on goods and services pays $4,800 (8 percent of 60,000) in sales taxes. So this family's taxes are only 4.8 percent of its income.

If the sales tax is regressive, why does the median voter support it? It is the entire tax code that matters, not an individual tax. So a regressive sales tax is voted for only as part of an overall tax regime that is progressive.

Property Taxes

Property taxes are collected by local governments and are used to provide local public goods. A **local public good** is a public good that is consumed by all the people who live in a particular area. Examples of local public goods are parks, museums, and safe neighborhoods.

There is a much closer connection between property taxes paid and benefits received than in the case

FIGURE 16.8   Social Security Tax

(a) Tax on employees

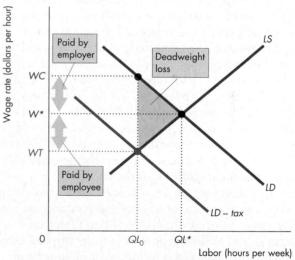

(b) Tax on employers

The labor demand curve is *LD*, and the supply curve is *LS*. With no Social Security tax, the quantity of labor employed is QL^* and the wage rate is W^* (in both parts). In part (a), employees pay a Social Security tax. Supply decreases, and the supply of labor curve shifts leftward to *LS* + *tax*. The wage rate rises to *WC*, after-tax wages fall to *WT*, and employment decreases to QL_0. In part (b), employers pay a Social Security tax. Demand decreases, and the demand for labor curve shifts leftward to *LD* − *tax*. The wage rate falls to *WT*, but the cost of labor rises to *WC* and employment decreases to QL_0. The outcome is identical in the two cases.

of federal and state taxes. This close connection makes property taxes similar to a price for local services. Because of this connection, property taxes change both the demand for and supply of property in a neighborhood. A higher tax decreases supply, but improved local public goods increase demand. So some neighborhoods have high taxes and high-quality local government services, and other neighborhoods have low taxes and low-quality services. Both types of neighborhoods can exist in the political equilibrium.

Excise Taxes

An **excise tax** is a tax on the sale of a particular commodity. The total amount raised by these taxes is small, but they have a big impact on some markets. Let's study the effects of an excise tax by considering the tax on gasoline shown in Fig. 16.9. The demand curve is D, and the supply curve is S. If there is no tax on gasoline, its price is 60¢ a gallon and 400 million gallons of gasoline a day are bought and sold.

Now suppose that a tax is imposed on gasoline at the rate of 60¢ a gallon. As a result of the tax, the supply of gasoline decreases and the supply curve shifts leftward. The magnitude of the shift is such that the vertical distance between the original and the new supply curve is the amount of the tax. The new supply curve is the red curve, $S + tax$. The new supply curve intersects the demand curve at 300 million gallons a day and $1.10 a gallon. Sellers receive 50¢, the price at which they are willing to supply 300 million gallons a day. This situation is the new equilibrium after the imposition of the tax.

The excise tax creates a deadweight loss made up of the loss of consumer surplus and producer surplus. The dollar value of that loss is $30 million a day. Because 300 million gallons of gasoline are sold each day and the tax is 60¢ a gallon, total revenue from the gasoline tax is $180 million a day (300 million gallons multiplied by 60¢ a gallon). So to raise tax revenue of $180 million dollars a day by using the gasoline tax, a deadweight loss of $30 million a day — one sixth of the tax revenue — is incurred.

One of the main influences on the deadweight loss arising from a tax is the elasticity of demand for the product. The demand for gasoline is fairly inelastic. As a consequence, when a tax is imposed, the quantity demanded falls by a smaller percentage than the percentage rise in price.

To see the importance of the elasticity of demand, let's consider a different commodity: orange

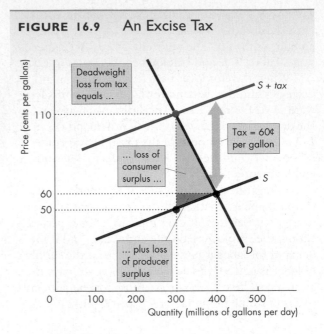

FIGURE 16.9   An Excise Tax

The demand curve for gasoline is D, and the supply curve is S. In the absence of any taxes, gasoline sells for 60¢ a gallon and 400 million gallons a day are bought and sold. With a tax of 60¢ a gallon, the supply curve shifts leftward to become the curve $S + tax$. The new equilibrium price is $1.10 a gallon, and 300 million gallons a day are bought and sold. The excise tax creates a deadweight loss represented by the gray triangle. The tax revenue collected is 60¢ a gallon on 300 million gallons, which is $180 million a day. The deadweight loss is $30 million a day. That is, to raise tax revenue of $180 million a day, a deadweight loss of $30 million a day is incurred.

juice. So that we can make a quick and direct comparison, let's assume that the orange juice market is exactly as big as the market for gasoline. Figure 16.10 illustrates this market. The demand curve for orange juice is D, and the supply curve is S. Orange juice is not taxed, and so the price of orange juice is 60¢ a gallon — where the supply curve and the demand curve intersect — and the quantity of orange juice traded is 400 million gallons a day.

Now suppose that the government contemplates abolishing the gasoline tax and taxing orange juice instead. The demand for orange juice is more elastic than the demand for gasoline. It has many good substitutes in the form of other fruit juices. The government wants to raise $180 million a day so that its

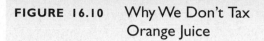

FIGURE 16.10   Why We Don't Tax Orange Juice

The demand curve for orange juice is *D,* and the supply curve is *S*. The price is 60¢ a gallon, and 400 million gallons of juice a day are traded. To raise $180 million of tax revenue, a tax of 90¢ a gallon is imposed. This tax shifts the supply curve to *S + tax*. The price rises to $1.30 a gallon, and the quantity falls to 200 million gallons a day. The deadweight loss, the gray triangle, equals $90 million a day. The deadweight loss from taxing orange juice is larger than that from taxing gasoline (Fig. 16.9) because the demand for orange juice is more elastic than the demand for gasoline.

total revenue is not affected by this tax change. The government's economists, armed with their statistical estimates of the demand and supply curves for orange juice that appear in Fig. 16.10, work out that a tax of 90¢ a gallon will do the job. With such a tax, the supply curve shifts leftward to become the curve labeled *S + tax*. This new supply curve intersects the demand curve at a price of $1.30 a gallon and at a quantity of 200 million gallons a day. The price at which suppliers are willing to produce 200 million gallons a day is 40¢ a gallon. The government collects a tax of 90¢ a gallon on 200 million gallons a day, so it collects a total revenue of $180 million a day — exactly the amount that it requires.

But what is the deadweight loss in this case? The answer can be seen by looking at the gray triangle in Fig. 16.10. The magnitude of that deadweight loss is $90 million. Notice how much bigger the deadweight loss is from taxing orange juice than from taxing gasoline. In the case of orange juice, the deadweight loss is one half the revenue raised, while in the case of gasoline, it is only one sixth. What accounts for this difference? The supply curves are identical in each case, and the examples were also set up to ensure that the initial no-tax prices and quantities were identical. The difference between the two cases is the elasticity of demand: In the case of gasoline, the quantity demanded falls by only 25 percent when the price almost doubles. In the case of orange juice, the quantity demanded falls by 50 percent when the price only slightly more than doubles.

You can see why taxing orange juice is not on the political agenda of any of the major parties. Vote-seeking politicians seek out taxes that benefit the median voter. Other things being equal, this means that they try to minimize the deadweight loss of raising a given amount of revenue. Equivalently, they tax items with poor substitutes more heavily than items with close substitutes.

REVIEW QUIZ

1 How do income taxes influence employment and efficiency? Why are income taxes progressive?
2 Can Congress make employers pay a larger share of the Social Security tax?
3 Why do some neighborhoods have high taxes and high-quality services and others have low taxes and low-quality services?
4 Why does the government impose excise taxes at high rates on goods that have a low elasticity of demand?

◆ *Reading Between the Lines* on pp. 384–385 looks at the changing scale of provision of domestic security services brought about by the increased awareness of terrorism. In the next two chapters, we are going to look at government economic actions in the face of monopolies and externalities.

An Increase in Demand for a Public Good

C N N . C O M , DECEMBER 22, 2001

Bush Expected to Seek $15 Billion More for Domestic Security

President Bush is expected to seek at least $15 billion in new spending for domestic security needs in his 2003 budget, a financial request that would fund everything from local police to baggage-screening equipment.

The budget may include money for vaccines and items such as communications equipment for hospitals and public health agencies to better coordinate their response to a terrorist attack, congressional aides say.

In Congress, "there will be a strong desire to spend more than that," said Rich Meade, Republican staff director of the House Budget Committee.

Congress approved $20 billion in spending earmarked for domestic security in the 2002 budget. About half of that was requested prior to the September 11 terrorist attacks.

Homeland Security Director Tom Ridge told The Washington Post for a story in Saturday's editions that the White House has settled on "substantial increases in spending" for domestic security. The budget request will focus on helping police and health-care professionals respond to possible attacks, said Ridge, who was Pennsylvania's governor before taking the security position.

Ridge "is developing a national strategy for homeland security," a White House spokesman said Saturday. "As part of that, Gov. Ridge is assessing our needs for combating terror, and responding to any attacks that may come." ...

The House committee's staff surveyed government agencies for their antiterrorism budget requests and came up with at least $15 billion in proposals, said Meade.

There is broad agreement that hospitals and public health agencies need help getting communications equipment and other technology so they can quickly identify attack victims and respond appropriately, said Bill Hoagland, the GOP staff director of the Senate Budget Committee. ...

Another big-ticket item: baggage-screening equipment for airports. The government would need $6 billion to buy all the machines that are necessary, Hoagland said.

Bush's budget request is expected to set off a struggle in Congress to increase the spending and define what can be classified as a security need. ...

Essence of the Story

■ President Bush is expected to request at least $15 billion in new spending for domestic security in the 2003 budget.

■ Congress approved spending $20 billion on domestic security in the 2002 budget and is likely to want to spend more than the President requests.

■ Congress increased spending on domestic security by almost $10 billion following the September 11 terrorist attacks.

■ There is broad agreement that more should be spent on communications equipment and other technology for hospitals and public health agencies and baggage-screening equipment for airports.

Economic Analysis

■ After the terrorist attacks of September 11, 2001, U.S. citizens and politicians revised their assessment of the benefit of domestic security.

■ Domestic security is a public good, and its efficient provision requires that its marginal benefit equal its marginal cost.

■ The total cost and marginal cost curve of domestic security did not change on September 11, 2001. Figure 1 shows an example of the total cost curve, TC, and Fig. 2 shows an example of the marginal cost curve, MC.

■ But the terrorist attacks changed the assessment of total benefit and marginal benefit. Before September 11, 2001, the benefit curves were TB_0 in Fig. 1 and MB_0 in Fig. 2.

■ The efficient quantity of domestic security was 10 units (an index number), and expenditure on this public good was $10 billion a year (on the y-axis in Fig.1).

■ Soon after the attacks, total benefit and marginal benefit increased to TB_1 in Fig. 1 and MB_1 in Fig. 2.

■ The efficient quantity increased to 15 (an assumed value) in Fig. 2, and expenditure in the 2002 budget increased to $20 billion (on the y-axis in Fig. 1).

■ As people assessed the benefits of domestic security more closely, the total benefit and marginal benefit increased yet further, to TB_2 in Fig. 1 and MB_2 in Fig. 2.

■ The efficient quantity increased to 20 (an assumed value) in Fig. 2, and expenditure in the 2003 budget increased to $40 billion (on the y-axis in Fig. 1).

■ We don't know by how much the quantity of domestic security will increase because we don't know the slope of the MC curve. But because opportunity cost increases when the quantity produced increases, we do know that the percentage increase in the quantity of domestic security will be smaller than the percentage increase in expenditure on it.

■ We don't know that the efficient quantity of domestic security will be provided. Possibly, there will be an overprovision as the bureaus responsible seek the largest possible budget.

Figure 1 Total benefit and total cost

Figure 2 Marginal benefit and marginal cost

385

SUMMARY

KEY POINTS

The Economic Theory of Government
(pp. 370–371)

- Government exists to provide public goods, regulate monopoly, cope with externalities, and reduce economic inequality.
- Public choice theory explains how voters, politicians, and bureaucrats interact in a political marketplace.

Public Goods and the Free-Rider Problem (pp. 372–377)

- A public good is a good or service that is consumed by everyone and that is *nonrival* and *nonexcludable*.
- A public good creates a *free rider* problem: No one has an incentive to pay their share of the cost of providing a public good.
- The efficient level of provision of a public good is that at which net benefit is maximized. Equivalently, it is the level at which marginal benefit equals marginal cost.
- Competition between political parties, each of which tries to appeal to the maximum number of voters, can lead to the efficient scale of provision of a public good and to both parties proposing the same policies — the principle of minimum differentiation.
- Bureaucrats try to maximize their budgets, and if voters are rationally ignorant, producer interests might result in voting to support taxes that provide public goods in quantities that exceed those that maximize net benefit.

Taxes (pp. 378–383)

- Government revenue comes from income taxes, Social Security taxes, sales taxes, property taxes, and excise taxes.
- Income taxes decrease employment and create a deadweight loss.

- Taxes can be progressive (the average tax rate rises with income), proportional (the average tax rate is constant), or regressive (the average tax rate falls with income).
- Income taxes are progressive because this arrangement is in the interest of the median voter.
- Social Security taxes are paid by the employer and the employee (and sales taxes are paid by the buyer and the seller) in amounts that depend on the elasticities of demand and supply.
- Property taxes change both demand and supply and can result in high-tax/high-quality service areas and low-tax/low-quality service areas.
- Excise taxes at high rates on gasoline, alcoholic beverages, and tobacco products create a smaller deadweight loss than would taxes on items with more elastic demands.

KEY FIGURES

KEY TERMS

PROBLEMS

*1. You are provided with the following information about a sewage disposal system that a city of 1 million people is considering installing.

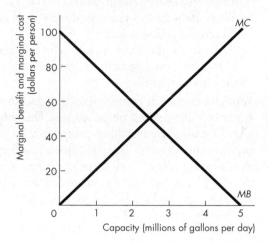

a. What is the capacity that achieves maximum net benefit?
b. How much will each person have to pay in taxes to pay for the efficient capacity level?
c. What is the political equilibrium if voters are well informed?
d. What is the political equilibrium if voters are rationally ignorant and bureaucrats achieve the highest attainable budget?

2. You are provided with the following information about a mosquito control program.

Quantity (square miles sprayed per day)	Marginal cost (dollars per day)	Marginal benefit (dollars per day)
0	0	0
1	1,000	5,000
2	2,000	4,000
3	3,000	3,000
4	4,000	2,000
5	5,000	1,000

a. What is the quantity of spraying that achieves maximum net benefit?
b. What is the total tax revenue needed to pay for the efficient quantity of spraying?

c. What is the political equilibrium if voters are well informed?
d. What is the political equilibrium if voters are rationally ignorant and bureaucrats achieve the highest attainable budget?

*3. An economy has two groups of people, A and B. The population consists of 80 percent A-types and 20 percent B-types. A-types have a perfectly elastic supply of labor at a wage rate of $10 an hour. B-types have a perfectly inelastic supply of labor, and their equilibrium wage rate is $100 an hour.
a. What kinds of tax arrangements do you think this economy will adopt?
b. Analyze the labor market in this economy and explain what will happen to the wage rates and employment levels of the two groups when the taxes you predict in your answer to part (a) are introduced.

4. Suppose that in the economy described in problem 3, the proportion of A-types is 20 percent and the proportion of B-types is 80 percent. Everything else remains the same.
a. Now what kinds of tax arrangements do you think the economy will adopt?
b. Analyze the labor market in this economy and explain what will happen to the wage rates and employment levels of the two groups when the taxes you predict in your answer to part (a) are introduced.
c. Compare the economy in problem 3 with the economy in this problem. Which economy more closely resembles our actual economy?

*5. An economy has a competitive labor market, which is described by the following demand and supply schedule:

Wage rate (dollars per hour)	Quantity demanded (hours per week)	Quantity supplied (hours per week)
20	0	50
16	15	40
12	30	30
8	45	20
4	60	10
0	75	0

a. What are the equilibrium wage rate and hours of work done?

b. If a $4 Social Security tax is imposed on employers, what is
  (i)   The new wage rate?
  (ii) The new number of hours worked?
  (iii) The after-tax wage rate?
  (iv) The tax revenue?
  (v)   The deadweight loss?

6. In the economy described in problem 5, the Social Security tax on employers is eliminated and a new Social Security tax of $4 is imposed on employees.
  a. What is the new wage rate?
  b. What is the new number of hours worked?
  c. What is the after-tax wage rate?
  d. What is the tax revenue?
  e. What is the deadweight loss?
  f. Compare the situation in problem 5 with that in this problem and explain the similarities and differences in the two situations.

*7. A competitive market for cookies has the following demand and supply schedule:

Price (dollars per pound)	Quantity demanded (pounds per month)	Quantity supplied (pounds per month)
7	0	8
6	1	7
5	2	6
4	3	5
3	4	4
2	5	3
1	6	2
0	7	0

  a. Find the equilibrium price and quantity.
  b. If cookies are taxed $2.00 a pound:
    (i)   What is the new price of cookies?
    (ii) What is the new quantity bought?
    (iii) What is the tax revenue?
    (iv) What is the deadweight loss?

8. In the competitive market for cookies in problem 7, the government wants to change the tax to the rate that brings in the greatest possible amount of revenue.
  a. What is that tax rate?
  b. What is the new price of cookies?
  c. What is the new quantity bought?
  d. What is the tax revenue?
  e. What is the deadweight loss?

CRITICAL THINKING

1. Study *Reading Between the Lines* on pp. 384–385 and then answer the following:
  a. Describe some of the items included in domestic security and explain whether they are public goods or private goods.
  b. Why might the provision of domestic security exceed the efficient level?
  c. Can you think of any reasons why the provision of domestic security might be less than the efficient level?

2. Your city council is contemplating upgrading its system for controlling traffic signals. The council believes that by installing computers, it can improve the speed of the traffic flow. The bigger the computer the council buys, the better job it can do. The mayor and the other elected officials who are working on the proposal want to determine the scale of the system that will win them the most votes. The city bureaucrats want to maximize the budget. Suppose that you are an economist who is observing this public choice. Your job is to calculate the quantity of this public good that uses resources efficiently.
  a. What data would you need to reach your own conclusions?
  b. What does the public choice theory predict will be the quantity chosen?
  c. How could you, as an informed voter, attempt to influence the choice?

WEB EXERCISES

1. Use the links on your Parkin Web site and read the article on demand revealing processes.
  a. What is a demand revealing process and what is its purpose?
  b. Why might using a demand revealing process deliver a more efficient level of public goods than our current political system?
  c. Why might our current political system deliver a more efficient level of public goods than would a demand revealing process?

REGULATION AND ANTITRUST LAW

CHAPTER 17

Public Interest or Special Interests?

When you consume water or local telephone service, you usually buy from a regulated monopoly. Why are the industries that produce these items regulated? How are they regulated? Do the regulations work in the interest of all consumers and producers — the public interest — or do they serve the interests of particular groups of consumers or producers — special interests? ◆ Cable TV has been on a regulatory roller coaster. It was initially regulated, but in 1984, it was deregulated. After deregulation, the profits of cable TV firms soared, and in 1992, Congress reregulated the industry, only to deregulate it yet again in 1996. Why has cable TV been deregulated, reregulated, and then deregulated again? ◆ Some years ago, PepsiCo and 7-Up wanted to merge. Coca-Cola and Dr Pepper also wanted to merge. But the government blocked these mergers with its antitrust laws. It used these same laws to break up the American Telephone and Telegraph Company (AT&T). This action brought competition into the market for long-distance telephone service and permitted previously struggling firms such as MCI and Sprint to expand and flourish. The government has also used its antitrust laws to punish Archer Daniels Midland for price fixing, to permit Boeing and McDonnell Douglas to merge their aircraft-building businesses, and to permit mergers of big banks. These same laws were used to charge Microsoft with monopolizing the markets for computer operating systems and web browsers. And, as you will see in *Reading Between the Lines* at the end of the chapter, similar laws in Europe have been used to fine companies for fixing the price of vitamins. What are antitrust laws? How have they evolved over the years? How are they used today? Do they serve the public interest or the special interests of producers?

◆ This chapter studies these questions.

After studying this chapter, you will be able to

- Define regulation and antitrust law

- Distinguish between the public interest and capture theories of regulation

- Explain how regulation affects prices, outputs, profits, and the distribution of the gains from trade between consumers and producers

- Explain how antitrust law has been applied in a number of landmark cases and how it is used today

Market Intervention

THE GOVERNMENT INTERVENES IN MONOPOLY and oligopoly markets to influence prices, quantities produced, and the distribution of the gains from economic activity. It intervenes in two main ways:

- Regulation
- Antitrust law

Regulation

Regulation consists of rules administered by a government agency to influence economic activity by determining prices, product standards and types, and the conditions under which new firms may enter an industry.

To implement its regulations, the government establishes agencies to oversee the regulations and ensure their enforcement. The first national regulatory agency to be set up in the United States was the Interstate Commerce Commission (ICC), established in 1887. Over the years since then, up to the late 1970s, regulation of the economy grew until, at its peak, almost a quarter of the nation's output was produced by regulated industries. Regulation applied to banking and financial services, telecommunications, gas and electric utilities, railroads, trucking, airlines and buses, many agricultural products, and even haircutting and braiding. Since the late 1970s, there has been a tendency to deregulate the U.S. economy.

Deregulation is the process of removing restrictions on prices, product standards and types, and entry conditions. In recent years, deregulation has occurred in domestic air transportation, telephone service, interstate trucking, and banking and financial services. Cable TV was deregulated in 1984, reregulated in 1992, and deregulated again in 1996.

Antitrust Law

An **antitrust law** is a law that regulates and prohibits certain kinds of market behavior, such as monopoly and monopolistic practices. Antitrust law is enacted by Congress and enforced through the judicial system. Lawsuits under the antitrust laws may be initiated either by government agencies or by injured private parties.

The main thrust of antitrust law is the prohibition of monopoly practices of restricting output to achieve higher prices and profits. The first antitrust law — the Sherman Act — was passed in 1890. Successive acts and amendments have strengthened and refined the body of antitrust law. Antitrust law (like all law) depends as much on the decisions of the courts and of the Supreme Court as on the statutes passed by Congress. Over the 100 years since the passage of the Sherman Act, there have been some interesting changes in the courts' interpretation of the law and in how vigorously the law has been enforced. We'll study these changes later in this chapter.

To understand why the government intervenes in the markets for goods and services and to work out the effects of its interventions, we need to identify the gains and losses that government actions can create. These gains and losses are the consumer surplus and producer surplus associated with different output levels and prices. We first study the economics of regulation.

Economic Theory of Regulation

THE ECONOMIC THEORY OF REGULATION IS part of the broader theory of public choice that is explained in Chapter 16. Here, we apply public choice theory to regulation. We'll examine the demand for government actions, the supply of those actions, and the political equilibrium that emerges.

Demand for Regulation

People and firms demand regulation that makes them better off. They express this demand through political activity: voting, lobbying, and making campaign contributions. But engaging in political activity is costly, so people demand political action only if the benefit that they individually receive from such action exceeds their individual costs in obtaining it.

The four main factors that affect the demand for regulation are

1. Consumer surplus per buyer
2. Number of buyers
3. Producer surplus per firm
4. Number of firms

The larger the consumer surplus per buyer that results from regulation, the greater is the demand for regulation by buyers. Also, as the number of buyers increases, so does the demand for regulation. But numbers alone do not necessarily translate into an effective political force. The larger the number of buyers, the greater is the cost of organizing them, so the demand for regulation does not increase proportionately with the number of buyers.

The larger the producer surplus per firm that arises from a particular regulation, the larger is the demand for that regulation by firms. Also, as the number of firms that might benefit from some regulation increases, so does the demand for that regulation. But again, large numbers do not necessarily mean an effective political force. The larger the number of firms, the greater is the cost of organizing them.

For a given consumer or producer surplus, the smaller the number of households or firms that share the surplus, the larger is the demand for the regulation that creates the surplus.

Supply of Regulation

Politicians and bureaucrats supply regulation. According to public choice theory, politicians choose policies that appeal to a majority of voters, thereby enabling themselves to achieve and maintain office. Bureaucrats support policies that maximize their budgets (see Chapter 16, p. 376). Given these objectives of politicians and bureaucrats, the supply of regulation depends on three factors:

1. Consumer surplus per buyer
2. Producer surplus per firm
3. The number of voters benefited

The larger the consumer surplus per buyer or the producer surplus per firm generated and the larger the number of people affected by a regulation, the greater is the tendency for politicians to supply that regulation.

If a regulation benefits a large number of people by enough for it to be noticed and if the recipients know the source of the benefits, that regulation appeals to politicians and is supplied. If a regulation benefits a large number of people but by too small an amount per person to be noticed, that regulation does not appeal to politicians and is not supplied.

If a regulation benefits a *small* number of people but by a large amount per person, that regulation also appeals to politicians, as long as its costs are spread widely and are not easily identified.

Political Equilibrium

In equilibrium, the regulation that exists is such that no interest group finds it worthwhile to use additional resources to press for changes and no group of politicians finds it worthwhile to offer different regulations. Being in a political equilibrium is not the same thing as everyone being in agreement. Lobby groups will devote resources to trying to change regulations that are already in place. Others will devote resources to maintaining the existing regulations. But no one will find it worthwhile to *increase* the resources they are devoting to such activities. Also, political parties might not agree with each other. Some support the existing regulations, and others propose different regulations. In equilibrium, no one wants to change the proposals that they are making.

What will a political equilibrium look like? The answer depends on whether the regulation serves the public interest or the interest of the producer. Let's look at these two possibilities.

Public Interest Theory The **public interest theory** is that regulations are supplied to satisfy the demand of consumers and producers to maximize the sum of consumer surplus and producer surplus — that is, to attain efficiency. Public interest theory implies that the political process relentlessly seeks out deadweight loss and introduces regulations that eliminate it. For example, where monopoly practices exist, the political process will introduce price regulations to ensure that outputs increase and prices fall to their competitive levels.

Capture Theory The **capture theory** is that the regulations are supplied to satisfy the demand of producers to maximize producer surplus — that is, to maximize economic profit. The key idea of capture theory is that the cost of regulation is high and only those regulations that increase the surplus of small, easily identified groups and that have low organization costs are supplied by the political process. Such regulations are supplied even if they impose costs on others, provided that those costs are spread thinly and widely enough that they do not decrease votes.

The predictions of the capture theory are less clear-cut than those of the public interest theory. The capture theory predicts that regulations benefit cohesive interest groups that have large and visible benefits and imposes small costs on everyone else. Those costs per person are so small that no one finds it worthwhile to incur the cost of organizing an interest group to avoid them.

Whichever theory of regulation is correct, according to public choice theory, the political system delivers the amounts and types of regulations that best further the electoral success of politicians. Because producer-oriented and consumer-oriented regulation are in conflict with each other, the political process can't satisfy both groups in any particular industry. Only one group can win. This makes the regulatory actions of government a bit like a unique product — for example, a painting by Leonardo da Vinci. There is only one original, and it will be sold to just one buyer. Normally, a unique commodity is sold at auction; the highest bidder takes the prize. Equilibrium in the regulatory process is similar: The suppliers satisfy the demands of the highest bidder. If a producer demand offers a bigger return to the politicians, either directly through votes or indirectly through campaign contributions, then the producers' interests will be served. If the consumer demand translates into a larger number of votes, then the consumers' interests will be served by regulation.

REVIEW QUIZ

1 How do consumers and producers express their demand for regulation? What are their objectives? What are the costs of expressing a demand for regulation?

2 When politicians and bureaucrats supply regulation, what are they trying to achieve? Do politicians and bureaucrats have the same objectives?

3 What is a political equilibrium? When does the political equilibrium achieve allocative efficiency? When does the political equilibrium serve the interests of producers? When do the bureaucrats win?

We have now completed our study of the *theory* of regulation in the marketplace. Let's turn our attention to the regulations that exist in our economy today. Which theory of regulation best explains these real-world regulations? Which regulations are in the public interest and which are in the interest of producers?

Regulation and Deregulation

THE PAST 20 YEARS HAVE SEEN BIG CHANGES IN the way the U.S. economy is regulated. We're going to examine some of these changes. To begin, we'll look at what is regulated and at the scope of regulation. Then we'll turn to the regulatory process and examine how regulators control prices and other aspects of market behavior. Finally, we'll tackle the more difficult and controversial questions: Why do we regulate some things but not others? Who benefits from the regulations that we have — consumers or producers?

The Scope of Regulation

The first federal regulatory agency, the Interstate Commerce Commission (ICC), was set up in 1887 to control prices, routes, and the quality of service of interstate railroads. Its scope was later extended to trucking lines, bus lines, water carriers, and, in more recent years, oil pipelines. Following the establishment of the ICC, the federal regulatory environment remained static until the years of the Great Depression. Then, in the 1930s, more agencies were established: the Federal Power Commission, the Federal Communications Commission, the Securities and Exchange Commission, the Federal Maritime Commission, the Federal Deposit Insurance Corporation, and, in 1938, the Civil Aeronautical Agency, which was replaced in 1940 by the Civil Aeronautics Board. There was a further lull until the establishment during the 1970s of the Copyright Royalty Tribunal and the Federal Energy Regulatory Commission. In addition to these, there are many state and local regulatory commissions.

In the mid-1970s, almost one quarter of the economy was subject to some form of regulation. Heavily regulated industries — those subject both to price regulation and to regulation of entry of new firms — were electricity, natural gas, telephones, airlines, highway freight services, and railroads.

During the 1980s and 1990s, a deregulation process stimulated competition in broadcasting, telecommunications, banking and finance, and all forms of transportation (air, rail, and road, passengers and freight.)

What exactly do regulatory agencies do? How do they regulate?

The Regulatory Process

Though regulatory agencies vary in size and scope and in the detailed aspects of economic life that they control, all agencies have features in common.

First, the bureaucrats who are the key decision makers in a regulatory agency are appointed by the administration or Congress in the case of federal agencies and by state and local governments. In addition, all agencies have a permanent bureaucracy made up of experts in the industry being regulated and often recruited from the regulated firms. Agencies have financial resources, voted by Congress or state or local legislatures, to cover the costs of their operations.

Second, each agency adopts a set of practices or operating rules for controlling prices and other aspects of economic performance. These rules and practices are based on well-defined physical and financial accounting procedures, but they are extremely complicated in practice and hard to administer.

In a regulated industry, individual firms are usually free to determine the technology that they will use. But they are not free to determine the prices at which they will sell their output, the quantities that they will sell, or the markets that they will serve. The regulatory agency grants certification to a company to serve a particular market and with a particular line of products, and it determines the level and structure of prices that will be charged. In some cases, the agency also determines the scale of output permitted.

To analyze the way in which regulation works, it is convenient to distinguish between the regulation of natural monopoly and the regulation of cartels. Let's begin with the regulation of natural monopoly.

Natural Monopoly

Natural monopoly was defined in Chapter 12 (p. 258) as an industry in which one firm can supply the entire market at a lower price than two or more firms can. Examples of natural monopoly include local distribution of cable television signals, electricity and gas, and urban rail services. For these activities, most of the costs are fixed and the larger the output, the lower is its average total cost. It is much more expensive to have two or more competing sets of wires, pipes, and train lines serving every neighborhood than it is to have a single set. (What is a natural monopoly changes over time as technology changes. With the introduction of fiber-optic cables, telephone companies and cable TV companies can compete with each other in both markets, so what was once a

natural monopoly is becoming a more competitive industry. Direct satellite TV is also beginning to break the cable TV monopoly.)

Let's consider the example of cable TV, which is shown in Fig. 17.1. The demand curve for cable TV is *D*. The cable TV company's marginal cost curve is *MC*. That marginal cost curve is (assumed to be) horizontal at $10 per household per month — that is, the cost of providing each additional household with a month of cable programming is $10. The cable company has a heavy investment in satellite receiving dishes, cables, and control equipment and so has high fixed costs. These fixed costs are part of the company's average total cost curve, shown as *ATC*. The average total cost curve slopes downward because as the number of households served increases, the fixed

FIGURE 17.1   Natural Monopoly: Marginal Cost Pricing

A natural monopoly is a firm that can supply the entire market at a lower price than two or more firms can. A cable TV operator faces the demand curve *D*. The firm's marginal cost is constant at $10 per household per month, as shown by the curve labeled *MC*. Fixed costs are large, and the average total cost curve, which includes average fixed cost, is shown as *ATC*. A marginal cost pricing rule sets the price at $10 a month, with 8 million households being served. The consumer surplus is shown as the green area. The firm incurs a loss on each household, indicated by the red arrow. To remain in business, the firm must price discriminate, use a two-part tariff, or receive a subsidy.

cost is spread over a larger number of households. (If you need to refresh your memory on how the average total cost curve is calculated, take a quick look back at Chapter 10, p. 220.)

Regulation in the Public Interest How will cable TV be regulated according to the public interest theory? In the public interest theory, regulation maximizes total surplus (the sum of consumer surplus and producer surplus), which occurs if marginal cost equals price. As you can see in Fig. 17.1, that outcome occurs if the price is regulated at $10 per household per month and if 8 million households are served. Such a regulation is called a marginal cost pricing rule. A **marginal cost pricing rule** sets price equal to marginal cost. It maximizes total surplus in the regulated industry.

A natural monopoly that is regulated to set price equal to marginal cost incurs an economic loss. Because its average total cost curve is falling, marginal cost is below average total cost. Because price equals marginal cost, price is below average total cost. Average total cost minus price is the loss per unit produced. It's obvious that a company that is required to use a marginal cost pricing rule will not stay in business for long. How can a company cover its costs and, at the same time, obey a marginal cost pricing rule?

One possibility is price discrimination (see Chapter 12, pp. 267-270). Another possibility is to use a two-part price (called a two-part tariff). For example, local telephone companies can charge consumers a monthly fee for being connected to the telephone system and then charge a price equal to marginal cost for each local call. A cable TV operator can charge a one-time connection fee that covers its fixed cost and then charge a monthly fee equal to marginal cost.

If a natural monopoly cannot cover its total cost from its customers, and if the government wants it to follow a marginal cost pricing rule, the government must give the firm a subsidy. In such a case, the government raises the revenue for the subsidy by taxing some other activity. But as we saw in Chapter 16, taxes themselves generate deadweight loss.

The deadweight loss that results from additional taxes must be subtracted from the efficiency gained by forcing the natural monopoly to adopt a marginal cost pricing rule.

It is possible that deadweight loss will be minimized by permitting the natural monopoly to charge a higher price than marginal cost rather than by taxing some other sector of the economy to subsidize the natural monopoly. Such a pricing arrangement is called an average cost pricing rule. An **average cost pricing rule** sets price equal to average total cost. Figure 17.2 shows the average cost pricing solution. The cable TV operator charges $15 a month and serves 6 million households. A deadweight loss arises, which is shown by the gray triangle in the figure.

The marginal cost pricing rule and the average cost pricing rule that we've just examined are easier to state than to implement. The major obstacle to implementing them is that the regulator knows less than the regulated firm about the cost of production.

The regulator does not directly observe the firm's costs and doesn't know how hard the firm is trying to minimize cost. For this reason, regulators use one of two practical rules:

- Rate of return regulation
- Price cap regulation

Let's see whether these rules deliver an outcome that is in the public interest or the private interest.

FIGURE 17.2   Natural Monopoly: Average Cost Pricing

Average cost pricing sets the price equal to average total cost. The cable TV operator charges $15 a month and serves 6 million households. In this situation, the firm breaks even — average total cost equals price. Deadweight loss, shown by the gray triangle, is generated. Consumer surplus is reduced to the green area.

Rate of Return Regulation Under **rate of return regulation**, a regulated firm must justify its price by showing that the price enables it to earn a specified target percent return on its capital. The target rate of return is determined with reference to what is normal in competitive industries. This rate of return is part of the opportunity cost of the natural monopoly and part of the firm's average total cost.

If the regulator was able to observe the firm's total cost and also know that the firm had minimized total cost, it would accept only a price proposal from the firm that was equivalent to average cost pricing.

The outcome would be like that in Fig. 17.2, where the regulated price is $15 a month and 6 million households are served. In this case, rate of return regulation would result in a price that favors the consumer and prevents the producer from maximizing economic profit. The monopoly will have failed to capture the regulator, and the outcome will be closer to that predicted by the public interest theory of regulation.

But the managers of a regulated firm might not minimize cost. And if the firm is regulated to achieve a target rate of return, the managers have an incentive to inflate costs and raise price. One way to inflate the firm's costs is to spend on inputs that are not strictly required for the production of the good. On-the-job luxury in the form of sumptuous office suites, limousines, free baseball tickets (disguised as public relations expenses), company jets, lavish international travel, and entertainment are all ways in which managers can inflate costs.

Managers also have an incentive to use more capital than the efficient amount because the more capital they use, the larger is the total return they are permitted to earn. And they have an incentive to make larger-than-required charges for depreciation and losses from bad debts.

If the cable TV operator in our example manages to persuade the regulator that its true average total cost curve is that shown as *ATC (inflated)* in Fig. 17.3, then the regulator, applying the normal rate of return principle, will accept the firm's proposed price of $20 a month. In this example, the price and quantity will be the same as those under unregulated monopoly.

Price Cap Regulation For the reason we've just examined, rate of return regulation is increasingly being replaced by price cap regulation. A **price cap regulation** is a price ceiling — a rule that specifies the highest price the firm is permitted to set. This type of

FIGURE 17.3   Natural Monopoly: Inflating Cost

If the cable TV operator is able to inflate its costs to *ATC (inflated)* and persuade the regulator that these are genuine minimum costs of production, rate of return regulation results in a price of $20 a month — the profit-maximizing price. To the extent that the producer can inflate costs above average total cost, the price rises, output decreases, and deadweight loss increases. The profit is captured by the managers, not the shareholders (owners) of the firm.

regulation gives a firm an incentive to operate efficiently and keep costs under control. Price cap regulation has become common for the electricity and telecommunications industries and is replacing rate of return regulation.

To see how a price cap works, let's suppose that the cable TV operator in our example is subject to this type of regulation. Figure 17.4 shows what happens.

Without regulation, the firm maximizes profit by serving 4 million households and charging a price of $20 a month. If a price cap is set at $15 a month, the firm is permitted to sell any quantity it chooses at that price or at a lower price. At 4 million households, the firm now incurs an economic loss. It can decrease the loss by *increasing* output to 6 million households. But at more than 6 million households, the firm incurs losses. So the profit-maximizing quantity is 6 million households — the same as with average cost pricing.

FIGURE 17.4   Price Cap Regulation of Natural Monopoly

If the cable TV operator is subject to a price cap regulation, the price cap limits the price that may be charged. At all quantities less than 6 million, the firm incurs a loss. At all quantities greater than 6 million, the firm also incurs a loss. Only at an output of 6 million can the firm break even and earn a normal rate of return. The firm has an incentive to keep costs as low as possible and to produce the quantity demanded at the price cap.

Notice that a price cap lowers the price and increases output. This outcome is in sharp contrast to the effect of a price ceiling in a competitive market that you studied in Chapter 6 (pp. 122–125). The reason is that in an unregulated monopoly, the equilibrium output is less than the competitive equilibrium output and the price cap regulation replicates the conditions of a competitive market.

In Fig. 17.4, the price cap delivers average cost pricing. In practice, the regulator might set the cap too high. For this reason, price cap regulation is often combined with **earnings sharing regulation**, under which profits that rise above a target level must be shared with the firm's customers.

The regulator might alternatively set the price too low. If this occurs, there can be a shortage like that faced by the California power industry in 2001. We examine California power regulation in a special feature on the Economics Place Web site.

Public Interest or Capture in Natural Monopoly Regulation?

It is not clear whether natural monopoly regulation produces prices and quantities that more closely correspond with the predictions of capture theory or with public interest theory. But one thing is clear: Price regulation does not require natural monopolies to use the marginal cost pricing rule. If it did, most natural monopolies would make losses and receive hefty government subsidies to enable them to remain in business.

There is an exception. Many telephone companies use marginal cost pricing. They cover their total cost by charging a flat fee each month for being connected to their system and then permit each call to be made at its marginal cost — zero.

A test of whether natural monopoly regulation is in the public interest or the interest of the producer is to examine the rates of return earned by regulated natural monopolies. If those rates of return are significantly higher than those in the rest of the economy, then, to some degree, the regulator might have been captured by the producer. If the rates of return in the regulated monopoly industries are similar to those in the rest of the economy, then we cannot tell for sure whether the regulator has been captured or not because we cannot know the extent to which costs have been inflated by the managers of the regulated firms.

Table 17.1 shows the rates of return in regulated natural monopolies as well as the economy's average rate of return in the 1960s and 1970s. In the 1960s, rates of return in regulated natural monopolies were somewhat below the economy average; in the 1970s, those returns exceeded the economy average. Overall, the rates of return achieved by regulated natural monopolies were not very different from those in the rest of the economy. We can conclude from these data either that natural monopoly regulation does, to some degree, serve the public interest or that natural monopoly managers inflate their costs by amounts sufficiently large to disguise the fact that they have captured the regulator and that the public interest is not being served.

A final test of whether regulation of natural monopoly is in the public interest or the interest of producers is to study the changes in consumer surplus and producer surplus following deregulation. Microeconomists have researched this issue, and their conclusions are summarized in Table 17.2. In the case of railroad deregulation, which occurred during the

TABLE 17.1   Rates of Return in Regulated Monopolies

Industry	Years 1962–69	1970–77
Electricity	3.2	6.1
Gas	3.3	8.2
Railroad	5.1	7.2
Average of above	3.9	7.2
Economy average	6.6	5.1

Source: Paul W. MacAvoy, *The Regulated Industries and the Economy* (New York: W.W. Norton, 1979), pp. 49–60.

1980s, both consumers and producers gained — and by large amounts. The gains from deregulation of telecommunications and cable television were smaller and accrued only to the consumer. These findings suggest that railroad regulation hurts everyone, while regulation of telecommunications and cable television hurts only the consumer.

We've now examined the regulation of natural monopoly. Let's next turn to regulation in oligopoly — the regulation of cartels.

TABLE 17.2   Gains from Deregulating Natural Monopolies

Industry	Consumer surplus	Producer surplus	Total surplus
	(billions of 1990 dollars)		
Railroads	8.5	3.2	11.7
Telecommunications	1.2	0.0	1.2
Cable television	0.8	0.0	0.8
Total	10.5	3.2	13.7

Source: Clifford Winston, "Economic Deregulation: Days of Reckoning for Microeconomists," *Journal of Economic Literature,* Vol. 31, September 1993, pp. 1263–1289, and the author's calculations.

Cartel Regulation

A *cartel* is a collusive agreement among a number of firms that is designed to restrict output and achieve a higher profit for the cartel's members. Cartels are illegal in the United States and in most other countries. But international cartels can sometimes operate legally, such as the international cartel of oil producers known as OPEC (the Organization of Petroleum Exporting Countries).

Illegal cartels can arise in oligopoly industries. An oligopoly is a market structure in which a small number of firms compete with each other. We studied oligopoly (and duopoly — two firms competing for a market) in Chapter 13. There, we saw that if firms manage to collude and behave like a monopoly, they can set the same price and sell the same total quantity as a monopoly firm would. But we also discovered that in such a situation, each firm will be tempted to cheat, increasing its own output and profit at the expense of the other firms. The result of such cheating on the collusive agreement is the unraveling of the monopoly equilibrium and the emergence of a competitive outcome with zero economic profit for producers. Such an outcome benefits consumers at the expense of producers.

How is oligopoly regulated? Does regulation prevent monopoly practices or does it encourage those practices? According to the public interest theory, oligopoly is regulated to ensure a competitive outcome. According to the capture theory, oligopoly regulators are captured by the firms and the regulation enables the firms to earn economic profit and operate against the public interest.

Let's look at these two possible outcomes in the oligopoly market for trucking tomatoes from the San Joaquin Valley to Los Angeles, illustrated in Fig. 17.5. The market demand curve for trips is *D*. The industry marginal cost curve — and the competitive supply curve — is *MC*.

If this industry is regulated in the public interest, the price will be set so that marginal benefit equals marginal cost. This price will be $20 a trip, and there will be 300 trips a week. A price cap regulation at $20 a trip could achieve this outcome.

How would this industry be regulated according to the capture theory? Regulation that is in the producer interest will maximize profit. To find the outcome in this case, we need to determine the price and quantity when marginal cost equals marginal revenue. The marginal revenue curve is *MR*. So marginal cost equals marginal revenue at 200 trips a week. The price of a trip is $30.

One way of achieving this outcome is to place an output limit on each firm in the industry. If there are 10 trucking companies, an output limit of 20 trips per company ensures that the total number of trips in a week is 200. Penalties can be imposed to ensure that no single producer exceeds its output limit.

All the firms in the industry would support this type of regulation because it helps to prevent cheating and to maintain a monopoly outcome. Each firm knows that without effectively enforced production quotas, every firm has an incentive to increase output. (For each firm, price exceeds marginal cost, so a greater output brings a larger profit.) So each firm wants a method of preventing output from rising

FIGURE 17.5   Collusive Oligopoly

Ten trucking firms transport tomatoes from the San Joaquin Valley to Los Angeles. The demand curve is *D*, and the industry marginal cost curve is *MC*. Under competition, the *MC* curve is the industry supply curve. If the industry is competitive, the price of a trip will be $20 and 300 trips will be made each week. Producers will demand regulation that restricts entry and limits output to 200 trips a week, where industry marginal revenue (*MR*) is equal to industry marginal cost (*MC*). This regulation raises the price to $30 a trip and results in each producer making maximum profit — as if it is a monopoly.

above the industry profit-maximizing level, and the quotas enforced by regulation achieve this end. With this type of cartel regulation, the regulator enables a cartel to operate legally and in its own best interest.

Public Interest or Capture in Cartel Regulation?

What does cartel regulation do in practice? Some regulation has benefited the producer. When the Interstate Commerce Commission regulated trucking, producers persistently earned economic profits. Also, by forming a strong labor union, truck drivers captured a large part of the producer surplus.

Some regulation has benefited both the producer and the consumer. When the Civil Aeronautics Board regulated the airlines, they earned economic profits. But they competed on quality, which increased costs and eventually eroded profits.

Table 17.3 provides some evidence in support of the conclusion that regulation increased profits in trucking and airlines. If regulation ensured a competitive outcome, rates of return in regulated oligopolies would be no higher than those in the economy as a whole. As the numbers in Table 17.3 show, rates of return in airlines and trucking were close to twice the economy average rate of return in the 1960s. In the 1970s, the rate of return in trucking remained higher than the economy average (although by a smaller margin than had prevailed in the 1960s). Airline rates of return in the 1970s fell to below the economy average. The overall picture that emerges from examining data on rates of return is mixed. The regulation of oligopoly does not always result in higher profit, but there are many situations in which it does.

TABLE 17.3   Rates of Return in Regulated Oligopolies

| | Years | |
Industry	1962–69	1970–77
Airlines	12.8	3.0
Trucking	13.6	8.1
Economy average	6.6	5.1

Source: Paul W. MacAvoy, The Regulated Industries and the Economy (New York: W.W. Norton, 1978), pp. 49–60.

Further evidence on cartel and oligopoly regulation can be obtained from the performance of prices and profit following deregulation. If, following deregulation, prices and profit fall, then, to some degree, the regulation must have been serving the interest of the producer.

In contrast, if, following deregulation, prices and profits remain constant or increase, then the regulation may be presumed to have been serving the public interest. Because there has been a substantial amount of deregulation in recent years, we can use this test of oligopoly regulation to see which of the two theories better fits the facts.

The evidence is mixed, but in the cases of the airlines and trucking, the two main oligopolies that have been deregulated, prices fell and there was a large increase in the volume of business. Table 17.4 summarizes the estimated effects of deregulation of airlines and trucking on consumer surplus, producer surplus, and total surplus. Most of the gains were in consumer surplus. In the case of the airlines, there was a gain in producer surplus as well.

But the table shows that in the trucking industry, producer surplus decreased by almost $5 billion a year. This outcome implies that regulation of the trucking industry benefited the producer by restricting competition and enabling prices to be higher than their competitive levels.

Making Predictions

Most industries have a few producers and many consumers. In this situation, public choice theory predicts that regulation protects producer interests and that politicians are rewarded with campaign contributions rather than votes. But there are situations in which the consumer interest has prevailed. There are also cases in which the balance has switched from producer to consumer, as seen in the deregulation process that began in the late 1970s.

Deregulation has occurred for three main reasons. First, economists have become more confident and vocal in predicting gains from deregulation. Second, a large increase in energy prices in the 1970s increased the cost of regulation borne by consumers. These price hikes made route regulation in the transportation sector extremely costly and changed the balance in favor of consumers in the political equilibrium. Third, technological change ended some natural monopolies. New technologies enabled small producers to offer low-cost long-distance telephone services. These producers wanted a share of the business — and profit — of AT&T. Furthermore, as communication technology improves, the cost of communication falls and the cost of organizing larger groups of consumers also falls.

If this line of reasoning is correct, there will be more public interest regulation and deregulation in the future.

TABLE 17.4   Gains from Deregulating Oligopolies

Industry	Consumer surplus	Producer surplus	Total surplus
	(billions of 1990 dollars)		
Airlines	11.8	4.9	16.7
Trucking	15.4	−4.8	10.6
Total	27.2	0.1	27.3

Source: Clifford Winston, "Economic Deregulation: Days of Reckoning for Microeconomists," *Journal of Economic Literature,* Vol. 31, September 1993, pp. 1263–1289, and the author's calculations.

REVIEW QUIZ

1 When did regulation begin in the United States, what was regulated, and when did regulation reach its peak?
2 Why does natural monopoly need to be regulated?
3 What pricing rule enables a natural monopoly to operate in the public interest and why is that rule difficult to implement?
4 How does rate of return regulation work and what problems does it create?
5 How does price cap regulation work and what problems is it designed to overcome?
6 How might cartels be regulated in the public interest?

Let's now leave regulation and turn to the other method of intervention in markets: antitrust law.

Antitrust Law

ANTITRUST LAW PROVIDES AN ALTERNATIVE WAY in which the government may influence the marketplace. As in the case of regulation, antitrust law can be formulated in the public interest, to maximize total surplus, or in private interests, to maximize the surplus of special interest groups such as producers.

The Antitrust Laws

The first antitrust law, the Sherman Act, was passed in 1890 in an atmosphere of outrage and disgust at the actions and practices of J.P. Morgan, John D. Rockefeller, and W.H. Vanderbilt — the so-called robber barons. Ironically, the most lurid stories of the actions of these great American capitalists are not of their monopolization and exploitation of consumers but of their sharp practices against each other. Nevertheless, monopolies did emerge — for example, the control of the oil industry by John D. Rockefeller.

A wave of mergers at the beginning of the twentieth century produced stronger antitrust laws. The Clayton Act of 1914 supplemented the Sherman Act, and the Federal Trade Commission, an agency charged with enforcing the antitrust laws, was created.

Table 17.5 summarizes the two main provisions of the Sherman Act. Section 1 of the act is precise: Conspiring with others to restrict competition is illegal. But Section 2 is general and imprecise. Just what is an "attempt to monopolize"? The Clayton Act and its two amendments, the Robinson-Patman Act of 1936 and the Celler-Kefauver Act of 1950, which

TABLE 17.5	The Sherman Act of 1890

Section 1:

Every contract, combination in the form of trust or otherwise, or conspiracy, in restraint of trade or commerce among the several States, or with foreign nations, is hereby declared to be illegal.

Section 2:

Every person who shall monopolize, or attempt to monopolize, or combine or conspire with any other person or persons, to monopolize any part of the trade or commerce among the several States, or with foreign nations, shall be deemed guilty of a felony.

TABLE 17.6	The Clayton Act and Its Amendments
Clayton Act	1914
Robinson-Patman Act	1936
Celler-Kefauver Act	1950

These acts prohibit the following practices *only if* they substantially lessen competition or create monopoly:

1. Price discrimination
2. Contracts that require other goods to be bought from the same firm (called *tying arrangements*)
3. Contracts that require a firm to buy all its requirements of a particular item from a single firm (called *requirements contracts*)
4. Contracts that prevent a firm from selling competing items (called *exclusive dealing*)
5. Contracts that prevent a buyer from reselling a product outside a specified area (called *territorial confinement*)
6. Acquiring a competitor's shares or assets
7. Becoming a director of a competing firm

outlaw specific practices, provided greater precision. Table 17.6 describes these practices and summarizes the main provisions of these three acts.

Landmark Antitrust Cases

The real force of any law arises from its interpretation. The interpretation of the antitrust laws has been clear on price fixing (Section 1 of the Sherman Act) but less clear on attempts to monopolize (Section 2 of the Sherman Act and the Clayton Act), and rulings have fluctuated between favoring producers and consumers. Table 17.7 summarizes the landmark cases.

Price Fixing Court decisions have made *any* price fixing deal a violation of Section 1 of the Sherman Act. Taking someone's life is a serious offense. But it is not always a violation of the murder law. In contrast, price-fixing is always a violation of the antitrust law. Accidents and other involuntary causes of death are recognized as reasons not to convict someone of murder. But if the Justice Department can prove the existence of price fixing, a defendant can offer no acceptable excuse.

A 1927 case against Trenton Potteries Company and others first established this hard line, which is known as the *per se* interpretation of the law. The court ruled that an agreement between Trenton Potteries and others to fix the prices of sanitary pottery violated the Sherman Act even if the prices themselves were reasonable. Price fixing *per se* (in and of itself) is a violation of the law.

In 1961, General Electric, Westinghouse, and other electrical component manufacturers were found guilty of a price-fixing conspiracy. This case was the first one in which the executives (rather than the company itself) were fined and jailed.

The Archer Daniels Midland (ADM) case is another illustration of this strict interpretation of the law. In 1996, ADM, a major producer of agricultural products, was fined $100 million for conspiring with foreign producers to fix prices.

Attempts to Monopolize The most important early antitrust cases were those involving the American Tobacco Company and Standard Oil Company. In 1911, these two companies were found guilty of violations under the Sherman Act and ordered to divest themselves of large holdings in other companies. The breakup of John D. Rockefeller's Standard Oil Company resulted in the creation of the oil companies that today are household names, such as Amoco, Chevron, Exxon, and Sohio.

In finding these companies to be in violation of the provisions of the Sherman Act, the Supreme Court enunciated the "rule of reason." The "rule of reason" states that monopoly arising from mergers and agreements among firms is not necessarily illegal. Only if there is an unreasonable restraint of trade does the arrangement violate the provisions of the Sherman Act.

TABLE 17.7   Landmark Antitrust Cases

Case	Year	Verdict and consequence
1. Price Fixing		
Trenton Potteries Company	1927	Guilty: Agreement to fix prices was *per se* a violation of the Sherman Act, regardless of whether the prices themselves are "reasonable."
General Electric, Westinghouse, and others	1961	Guilty: Price-fixing conspiracy; executives fined and jailed.
Archer Daniels Midland	1996	Guilty: Price-fixing conspiracy; fined $100 million. Three company executives fined $350,000; two jailed for 3 years and one for 30 months.
2. Attempts to Monopolize?		
American Tobacco Co. and Standard Oil Co.	1911	Guilty: Ordered to divest themselves of large holdings in other companies; "rule of reason" enunciated — only *unreasonable* combinations guilty under Sherman Act.
U.S. Steel Co.	1920	Not guilty: Although U.S. Steel had a very large market share (near monopoly), mere "size alone is not an offense"; application of the "rule of reason."
Alcoa	1945	Guilty: Too big — had too large a share of the market.
Aspen Skiing	1985	Guilty: Owner of three of the four downhill ski facilities refused to offer an all-Aspen ticket and share revenues on a use basis with the owner of the other facility.
Spectrum Sports	1993	Not guilty: Although Spectrum Sports was the national distributor of sorbothane (used in athletic products), no evidence was present that the company had attempted to monopolize the relevant market.

The "rule of reason" was widely regarded as removing the force of the Sherman Act itself. This view was reinforced in 1920 when U.S. Steel Company was acquitted of violations under the act even though it had a very large (more than 50 percent) share of the U.S. steel market. Applying the "rule of reason," the court declared that "size alone is not an offense."

In a case that some people interpreted as challenging the "rule of reason," the *Alcoa* case, decided in 1945, Alcoa was judged to be in violation of the antitrust law because it was too big. It had too large a share of the aluminum market. This relatively tough interpretation of the law continued through the late 1960s.

Of the many other cases concerning the attempt to monopolize, we look at two interesting and relatively recent ones. During the 1970s, the Aspen Skiing Company, which owned three of the four downhill ski facilities in Aspen, offered an all-Aspen ticket and shared the revenues with Aspen Highlands Skiing Corporation, which owned the fourth facility. Revenues were split on the basis of a survey of users. In 1977, Aspen Skiing refused to offer the all-Aspen ticket unless Aspen Highlands agreed to accept a low fixed share of the revenue. The all-Aspen ticket was not offered, and Aspen Highlands lost business. The court held that the Aspen Skiing Company was attempting to monopolize.

When Spectrum Sports became the national distributor of sorbothane athletic products (sorbothane is a shock absorber), some injured companies alleged that Spectrum had attempted to monopolize. The court held that Spectrum could not be held to have attempted to monopolize in the absence of evidence that it had engaged in monopoly practices.

A Recent Showcase: The United States Versus Microsoft

Microsoft was charged with specific violations of the antitrust laws, and in 1998, a high-profile trial of these charges began.

The Case Against Microsoft The claims against Microsoft are that the firm

1. Possesses monopoly power in the market for PC operating systems.
2. Uses below-cost pricing (called predatory pricing) and tying arrangements to achieve a monopoly in the market for web browsers.
3. Uses other anticompetitive practices to strengthen its monopoly in these two markets.

Microsoft, it is claimed, operates behind barriers to entry that arise from economies of scale and network economies. Microsoft's average total cost falls as production increases (economies of scale) because the costs of developing software are large but are a fixed cost while the marginal cost of one copy of Windows is small. The benefit to Windows users increases as the number of users increases (network economies) because with more users, the range of Windows applications expands.

When Microsoft entered the Internet browser market with Internet Explorer (IE), it offered the browser for a zero price. This is viewed as predatory pricing — an attempt to drive out the competition and monopolize a market. Microsoft now has integrated IE with Windows, which means that no one using this operating system needs a separate browser such as Netscape Communicator or Opera. Microsoft's critics claim that this practice is illegal product tying.

Microsoft's Response Microsoft challenges all these claims. It says that although Windows dominates today, it is vulnerable to new operating systems. It also claims that integrating Internet Explorer with Windows provides a product of greater consumer value. It is not tying; it is one product.

Microsoft is still the subject of court challenges by several states and will be the subject of ongoing investigation. Keep track of developments!

Merger Rules

The Federal Trade Commission (FTC) uses guidelines to determine which mergers it will examine and possibly block. The Herfindahl-Hirschman Index (HHI), is one of the guidelines (see Chapter 9, pp. 204–205). A market in which the HHI is less than 1,000 is regarded as competitive. An index between 1,000 and 1,800 indicates a moderately concentrated market, and a merger in this market that would increase the index by 100 points is challenged by the FTC. An index above 1,800 indicates a concentrated market, and a merger in this market that would increase the index by 50 points is challenged. Figure 17.6(a) summarizes these guidelines.

The FTC used these guidelines to analyze two recently proposed mergers in the market for soft drinks. In 1986, PepsiCo announced its intention to buy 7-Up for $380 million. A month later, Coca-Cola said it would buy Dr Pepper for $470 million. Whether this market is concentrated depends on how it is defined. The market for all soft drinks, which

FIGURE 17.6   The HHI Merger Guidelines

Competitive	Moderately concentrated	Concentrated

Challenge merger if index rises by more than:

100 points   50 points

0   1,000   1,800   3,000   4,000

Herfindahl-Hirschman Index (HHI)

(a) The merger guidelines

No mergers

Pepsi / 7-Up

Coke / Dr Pepper

Both mergers

0   1,000   2,000   3,000   4,000

Herfindahl-Hirschman Index (HHI)

(b) Product mergers in soft drinks

The FTC scrutinizes proposed mergers if the HHI exceeds 1,000. Proposed mergers between producers of carbonated soft drinks were blocked in 1986 by application of these guidelines.

includes carbonated drinks marketed by these four companies plus fruit juices and bottled water, has an HHI of 120, so it is highly competitive. But the market for carbonated soft drinks is highly concentrated. Coca-Cola has a 39 percent share, PepsiCo has 28 percent, Dr Pepper is next with 7 percent, then comes 7-Up with 6 percent. One other producer, RJR, has a 5 percent market share. So the five largest firms in this market have an 85 percent market share. If we assume that the other 15 percent of the market consists of 15 firms, each with a 1 percent market share, the Herfindahl-Hirschman index is

$$HHI = 39^2 + 28^2 + 7^2 + 6^2 + 5^2 + 15 = 2,430.$$

With an HHI of this magnitude, a merger that increases the index by 50 points is examined by the FTC. Figure 17.6(b) shows how the HHI would have

changed with the mergers. The PepsiCo and 7-Up merger would have increased the index by more than 300 points, the Coca-Cola and Dr Pepper merger would have increased it by more than 500 points, and both mergers together would have increased the index by almost 800 points. The FTC decided to define the market narrowly and, with increases of these magnitudes, blocked the mergers.

Public or Special Interest?

It is clear from the historical contexts in which antitrust law has evolved that its intent has been to protect and pursue the public interest and restrain the profit-seeking and anticompetitive actions of producers. But it is also clear from the above brief history of antitrust legislation and cases that, from time to time, the interest of the producer has had an influence on the way in which the law has been interpreted and applied. Nevertheless, the overall thrust of antitrust law appears to have been directed toward achieving efficiency and therefore to serving the public interest.

REVIEW QUIZ

1 What are the four acts of Congress that make up our antitrust laws? When were these laws enacted?
2 When is price fixing not a violation of the antitrust laws?
3 What is an attempt to monopolize an industry?
4 Under what circumstances is a merger unlikely to be approved?
5 Name three antitrust cases that involve price fixing. What did the court decide?

◆ We have reviewed the public interest and capture theories of government intervention. And we've seen that regulators do sometimes get captured by the regulated and work against the interest of consumers. But this outcome does not always occur.

In *Reading Between the Lines*, on pp. 404–405, you can see a recent example of antitrust law being used to penalize price fixing in an attempt to protect the public interest.

Fixing Vitamin Prices

THE WALL STREET JOURNAL, NOVEMBER 22, 2001

EU Levies $755.1 Million Fine in Vitamin Price-Fixing Case

The European Commission fined eight companies a record 855.2 million euros ($755.1 million) for allegedly fixing vitamin prices, but let one drug maker almost completely off the hook for turning on its former partners.

The supposed ringleader of the price-fixing cartel, Roche Holding AG of Switzerland, was fined 462 million euros, or 2.6% of world-wide sales in 1999.

Under the commission's rules, fines start at 20 million euros per offense and increase by 10% for each additional year of illegal activity. The figures in that formula are subject to mitigating or aggravating factors.

The commission said although it would have been justified in fining Roche as much as 962 million euros, the sum was reduced because Roche cooperated in the investigation by, among other things, willingly giving the commission documents for which it asked.

Roche was the "prime mover and main beneficiary" of the scheme to fix prices on 12 separate vitamins in the 1990s, the commission said. BASF AG of Germany was another "paramount" player, the commission said, and was fined 296.2 million euros. Fines for the six other companies ranged from 5 million euros to 37.1 million euros.

...

Mario Monti, the commissioner responsible for antitrust policy, ... said the eight companies operated the "most damaging series of cartels the commission has ever investigated" in terms of harm to consumers. But the commission didn't impose the maximum penalty possible under the law: 10% of a company's annual sales during the last year in which the cartel operated. Altogether, that could have run into the billions of euros.

Mr. Monti insisted the commission wasn't letting the companies off lightly. But he lamented the fact that under European Union law, there are no criminal sanctions for price-fixing, as there are in the U.S. "We're working to make penalties more and more effective and more and more deterrent," he said.

In the 1999 U.S. case, Roche paid a fine of $500 million, and a former executive went to prison.

...

Amelia Torres, a spokeswoman for Mr. Monti, said the commission had wide discretion on the final amount of the fine, in part because it wanted to maintain "a certain degree of uncertainty" so companies didn't calculate likely fines into their business plans. However, Roche said it had already figured the fine into its spending plans back in 1999.

Essence of the Story

■ Price fixing is illegal in the European Union but not subject to criminal sanctions.

■ Under European Commission (EC) rules, fines start at 20 million euros per offense and increase by 10 percent for each additional year of illegal activity.

■ In 2001, the EC fined eight companies for allegedly fixing vitamin prices.

■ The largest fine imposed was on Roche of Switzerland (462 million euros — 2.6 percent of its 1999 worldwide sales).

■ The EC could have fined Roche 962 million euros but reduced the fine because Roche cooperated in the investigation.

■ Roche said that it had budgeted for the fine in its spending plans.

Economic Analysis

- In the United States, price fixing is a criminal offense that can be punished by a combination of fines and imprisonment.

- In the European Union (EU), price fixing is illegal but subject only to a fine.

- The formula for a fine is a fixed amount per violation per year. For the firm, the fine is a fixed cost.

- Even when the EC uses discretion to keep the firm guessing about the scale of the fine, the firm can figure out the maximum fine and can compare paying the fine with the alternative of not engaging in price fixing.

- If the profit that results from price fixing minus the fine exceeds the profit from not price fixing, it is rational, but illegal, for a firm to price fix.

- Figure 1 shows the situation that Roche of Switzerland faces.

- The demand curve for Roche's products depends on the prices set by its competitors.

- When Roche's competitors engage in price fixing, the demand curve for Roche's products is D and its marginal revenue curve is MR.

- Roche's average total cost curve is ATC, and its marginal cost curve is MC.

- Roche maximizes profit by selling 3 billion items a year (where $MC = MR$) at a price of $6 per item.

- Roche's economic profit, shown by the sum of the two blue rectangles, is $6 billion a year. (Roche's actual economic profit in 2000 was about $5 billion.)

- Because Roche pays a price-fixing fine, which is about $0.4 billion, its ATC curve shifts upward to $ATC + fine$.

- Even if Roche paid a price-fixing fine of $4 billion, ten times as large as the one imposed, its ATC curve would shift upward to $ATC + fine^*$ and the firm would still make an economic profit.

- Figure 2 illustrates the alternative of competing without price fixing. Competition from other producers decreases the demand for Roche's products to D_{comp}. The price is driven down to the point at which economic profit is eliminated and the firm earns normal profit (included in ATC).

- The U.S. antitrust law is more powerful than the EU law and makes it harder for firms to use price fixing as a business strategy.

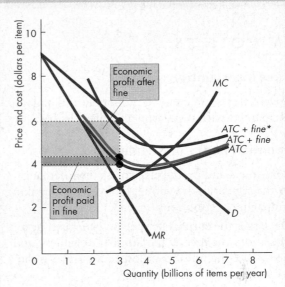

Figure 1 Roche in 2000

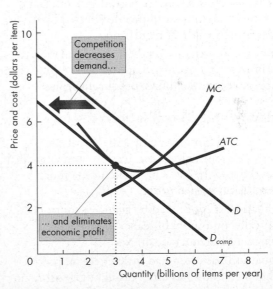

Figure 2 Roche in competition

405

SUMMARY

KEY POINTS

Market Intervention (p. 390)

- Governments intervene in monopoly and oligopoly markets with regulation and antitrust law.

Economic Theory of Regulation (pp. 390–392)

- Consumers and producers express their demand for the regulation by voting, lobbying, and making campaign contributions.
- The larger the surplus per person generated by a regulation, the greater the number of gainers, and the smaller the number of losers, the larger is the demand for the regulation.
- Regulation is supplied by politicians, who pursue votes, and bureaucrats, who pursue large budgets.
- The larger the surplus per person generated and the larger the number of people affected by it, the larger is the supply of regulation.
- Public interest theory predicts that regulation maximizes total surplus. Capture theory predicts that regulation maximizes producer surplus.

Regulation and Deregulation (pp. 392–399)

- Federal regulation began in 1887 (with the Interstate Commerce Commission) and expanded until the mid-1970s, since which time much deregulation has occurred.
- Regulation is conducted by agencies controlled by politically appointed bureaucrats and staffed by a permanent bureaucracy of experts.
- Regulation has often had little effect on profits, and deregulation has often brought gains for consumers and producers.

Antitrust Law (pp. 400–403)

- Antitrust law is an alternative way in which the government can control monopoly and monopolistic practices.
- The first antitrust law, the Sherman Act, was passed in 1890, and the law was strengthened in 1914 when the Clayton Act was passed and the Federal Trade Commission was created.

- All price-fixing agreements are violations of the Sherman Act, and no acceptable excuse exists.
- The first landmark cases (against the American Tobacco Company and Standard Oil Company) established the "rule of reason," which holds that an attempt to monopolize is illegal but monopoly itself is not illegal.
- The Federal Trade Commission uses guidelines to determine which mergers to investigate and possibly block on the basis of the Herfindahl-Hirschman Index.
- The intent of antitrust law is to protect the public interest. This intent has been served most of the time. But sometimes the interest of the producer has influenced the interpretation and application of the law.

KEY FIGURES AND TABLES

KEY TERMS

PROBLEMS

*1. Elixir Springs, Inc., is an unregulated natural monopoly that bottles Elixir, a unique health product with no substitutes. The total fixed cost incurred by Elixir Springs is $150,000, and its marginal cost is 10¢ a bottle. The figure illustrates the demand for Elixir.

a. What is the price of a bottle of Elixir?
b. How many bottles does Elixir Springs sell?
c. Does Elixir Springs maximize total surplus or producer surplus?

2. Cascade Springs, Inc., is a natural monopoly that bottles water from a spring in the Rocky Mountains. Its total fixed cost is $80,000, and its marginal cost is 5 cents a bottle. The figure illustrates the demand for Cascade Springs water.

a. What is the price of Cascade Springs water?
b. How many bottles does Cascade Springs sell?

c. Does Cascade Springs maximize total surplus or producer surplus?

*3. The government imposes a marginal cost pricing rule on Elixir Springs in problem 1.
a. What is the price of a bottle of Elixir?
b. How many bottles does Elixir Springs sell?
c. What is Elixir Springs' producer surplus?
d. What is the consumer surplus?
e. Is the regulation in the public interest? Explain.

4. The government imposes a marginal cost pricing rule on Cascade Springs in problem 2.
a. What is the price of Cascade Springs water?
b. How many bottles does Cascade Springs sell?
c. What is the economic profit?
d. What is the consumer surplus?
e. Is the regulation in the public interest? Explain.

*5. The government imposes an average cost pricing rule on Elixir Springs in problem 1.
a. What is the price of a bottle of Elixir?
b. How many bottles does Elixir Springs sell?
c. What is Elixir Springs' producer surplus?
d. What is the consumer surplus?
e. Is the regulation in the public interest? Explain.

6. The government imposes an average cost pricing rule on Cascade Springs in problem 2.
a. What is the price of Cascade Springs water?
b. How many bottles does Cascade Springs sell?
c. What is the economic profit?
d. What is the consumer surplus?
e. Is the regulation in the public interest or in the private interest?

*7. Two airlines share an international route. The figure shows the demand curve for trips on this route and the marginal cost curve that each firm faces. This air route is regulated.

a. What is the price of a trip and what is the number of trips per day if the regulation is in the public interest?
b. What is the price of a trip and what is the number of trips per day if the regulation is in the producer's interest?
c. What is the deadweight loss in part (b)?
d. What do you need to know to predict whether the regulation will be in the public interest or the producer's interest?

8. Two phone companies offer local calls in an area. The figure shows the demand curve for calls and the marginal costs curves of each firm. These firms are regulated.

a. What is the price of a call and what is the number of calls per day if the regulation is in the public interest?
b. What is the price of a call and what is the number of calls per day if the regulation is in the producer's interest?
c. What is the deadweight loss in part (b)?
d. What do you need to know to predict whether the regulation will be in the public interest or the producer's interest?

*9. Explain the difference between regulation and antitrust law. To what situations does each apply? Give an example of the use of each.

10. Describe the difference between the ways in which the two parts of the Sherman Act have been applied. Why do you think one part has been interpreted more strictly than the other?

CRITICAL THINKING

1. After you have studied *Reading Between the Lines* on pp. 404–405, answer the following questions:
   a. What did Roche and BASF do that is illegal?
   b. Would their actions have been illegal if they had been carried out in the United States?
   c. How does the European Commission try to discourage price fixing? Do you think this method works?
   d. What changes would you recommend to the EU law and why?

WEB EXERCISES

1. Use the link on your Parkin Web site to visit the FTC and read the press release on the consent order for the AOL–Time Warner merger.
   a. What conditions did the FTC impose when it approved the merger?
   b. What are the markets in which AOL–Time Warner operates? Which of these markets, if any, are competitive and in which of them, if any, might AOL–Time Warner be a monopoly?
   c. Who benefits from the AOL–Time Warner merger? Draw a diagram that illustrates the directions of the changes in price, output, producer surplus, and consumer surplus that you think resulted from the merger.

2. Use the link on your Parkin Web site to visit the FTC and read the press release on the charge that Intel Corporation has abused its monopoly position.
   a. What does the FTC say that Intel did in violation of the antitrust law?
   b. Do you agree with the FTC? Why or why not?
   c. Draw a figure that illustrates how Intel benefited and others lost from its actions.

3. Use the link on your Parkin Web site to read about the order issued by the court to break up Microsoft.
   a. What exactly did the court order?
   b. How do you think the software industry would have changed if the breakup order had been implemented?

Greener and Smarter

We burn huge quantities of fossil fuels — coal, natural gas, and oil — that cause acid rain and possibly global warming. We use chlorofluoro-carbons (CFCs) that may damage the earth's ozone layer, expose us to additional ultraviolet rays, and increase the risk of skin cancer. We dump toxic waste into rivers, lakes, and oceans. These environmental issues are simultaneously everybody's problem and nobody's problem. How can we take account of the damage that we cause others every time we turn on our heating or air conditioning systems? ◆ Almost every day, we hear about a new discovery — in medicine, engineering, chemistry, physics, or even economics. The advance of knowledge seems boundless. And more and more people are learning more and more of what is already known. The stock of knowledge is increasing, apparently without bound. We are getting smarter. But are we getting smarter fast enough? Are we spending enough on research and education? Do enough people remain in school for long enough? And do we work hard enough at school? Would we be better off if we spent more on research and education?

◆ In this chapter, we study the problems that arise because many of our actions create externalities. They affect other people, for ill or good, in ways that we do not usually take into account when we make our own economic choices. We study two big areas — pollution and knowledge — in which externalities are especially important. Externalities are a major source of *market failure*. When market failure occurs, we must either live with the inefficiency it creates or try to achieve greater efficiency by making some *public choices*. This chapter studies these choices.

After studying this chapter, you will be able to

- Explain how property rights can sometimes be used to overcome externalities
- Explain how emission charges, marketable permits, and taxes can be used to achieve efficiency in the face of external costs
- Explain how subsidies can be used to achieve efficiency in the face of external benefits
- Explain how scholarships, below-cost tuition, and research grants make the quantity of education and invention more efficient
- Explain how patents increase economic efficiency

409

Externalities in Our Lives

A COST OR BENEFIT THAT ARISES FROM PRODUC-tion and falls on someone other than the producer or a cost or benefit that arises from consumption and falls on someone other than the consumer is called an **externality**. Let's review the range of externalities, classify them, and look at some everyday examples.

An externality can arise from either *production* or *consumption* and it can be either a **negative externality**, which imposes an external cost, or a **positive externality**, which provides an external benefit. So there are four types of externalities:

- Negative production externalities
- Positive production externalities
- Negative consumption externalities
- Positive consumption externalities

Negative Production Externalities

When the U.S. Open tennis tournament is being played at Flushing Meadows, New York, players, spectators, and television viewers around the world share a negative production externality that many New Yorkers experience every day: the noise of air-planes taking off from Kennedy Airport. Aircraft noise imposes a large cost on millions of people who live under the approach paths to airports in every major city.

Logging and the clearing of forests are the source of another negative production externality. These activities destroy the habitat of wildlife and influence the amount of carbon dioxide in the atmosphere, which has a long-term effect on temperature. Everyone living and future generations bear these external costs. Pollution, which we examine in the next section, is another an example of this type of externality.

Positive Production Externalities

To produce orange blossom honey, Honey Run Honey of Chico, California, locates beehives next to an orange orchard. The honeybees collect pollen and nectar from the orange blossoms to make the honey. At the same time, they transfer pollen between the blossoms, which helps to fertilize the blossoms. Two positive production externalities are present in this example: Honey Run Honey gets a positive produc-tion externality from the owner of the orange orchard, and the orange grower gets a positive production externality from Honey Run.

Negative Consumption Externalities

Negative consumption externalities are a source of irritation for most of us. Smoking tobacco in a con-fined space creates fumes that many people find unpleasant and that pose a health risk. So smoking in restaurants and on airplanes generates a negative externality. To avoid this negative externality, many restaurants and all airlines ban smoking. But while a smoking ban avoids a negative consumption external-ity for most people, it imposes a negative consump-tion externality on smokers. The majority imposes a cost on the minority — the smokers who would pre-fer to enjoy the consumption of tobacco while dining or taking a plane trip.

Noisy parties and outdoor rock concerts are other examples of negative consumption externalities. They are also examples of the fact that a simple ban on an activity is not a solution. Banning noisy parties avoids the external cost on sleep-seeking neighbors, but it results in the sleepers imposing an external cost on the fun-seeking partygoers.

Permitting dandelions to grow in lawns, not picking up leaves in the fall, and allowing a dog to bark loudly or to foul a neighbor's lawn are other sources of negative consumption externalities.

Positive Consumption Externalities

When you get a flu vaccination, you lower your risk of getting infected this winter. But if you avoid the flu, your neighbor who didn't get vaccinated has a better chance of avoiding it too. Flu vaccination generates positive consumption externalities.

When the owner of an historic building restores it, everyone who sees the building gets pleasure from it. Similarly, when someone erects a spectacular house — such as those built by Frank Lloyd Wright during the 1920s and 1930s — or another exciting building — such as the Chrysler Building and the Empire State Building in New York or the Wrigley Building in Chicago — an external consumption benefit flows to everyone who has an opportunity to view it. Educa-tion, which we examine in this chapter, is another example of this type of externality.

Negative Externalities: Pollution

POLLUTION IS NOT A NEW PROBLEM AND IS NOT restricted to rich industrial countries. Preindustrial towns and cities in Europe had sewage disposal problems that created cholera epidemics and plagues that killed millions. London's air in the Middle Ages was dirtier than that of Los Angeles today. Some of the worst pollution today is found in Russia and China. Nor is the desire to find solutions to pollution new. The development in the fourteenth century of garbage and sewage disposal is an example of early attempts to tackle pollution.

Popular discussions of pollution usually pay little attention to economics. They focus on physical aspects of the problem, not on the costs and benefits. A common assumption is that if people's actions cause *any* pollution, those actions must cease. In contrast, an economic study of pollution emphasizes costs and benefits. An economist talks about the efficient amount of pollution. This emphasis on costs and benefits does not mean that economists, as citizens, do not share the same goals as others and value a healthy environment. Nor does it mean that economists have the right answers and everyone else has the wrong ones (or vice versa). The starting point for an economic analysis of pollution is the demand for a pollution-free environment.

The Demand for a Pollution-Free Environment

The demand for a pollution-free environment is greater today than it has ever been. We express this demand by joining organizations that lobby for antipollution regulations and policies. We vote for politicians who support the policies that we want to see implemented. We buy "green" products, even if we pay a bit more to do so. And we pay higher housing costs and commuting costs to live in pleasant neighborhoods.

The demand for a pollution-free environment has grown for two main reasons. First, as our incomes increase, we demand a larger range of goods and services, and one of these "goods" is a pollution-free environment. We value clean air, unspoiled natural scenery, and wildlife, and we are willing and able to pay for them.

Second, as our knowledge of the effects of pollution grows, we are able to take measures that reduce those effects. For example, now that we know how sulfur dioxide causes acid rain and how clearing rain forests destroys natural stores of carbon dioxide, we are able, in principle, to design measures that limit these problems.

Let's look at the range of pollution problems that have been identified and the actions that create those problems.

The Sources of Pollution

Economic activity pollutes air, water, and land, and these individual areas of pollution interact through the *ecosystem*.

Air Pollution Sixty percent of our air pollution comes from road transportation and industrial processes. Only 16 percent arises from electric power generation.

A common belief is that air pollution is getting worse. In many developing countries, air pollution *is* getting worse. But air pollution in the United States is getting less severe for most substances. Figure 18.1 shows the trends in the concentrations of six air pollutants. Lead has been almost eliminated from our air. Sulfur dioxide, carbon monoxide, and suspended particulates have been reduced to around a half of their 1980 levels. And even the more stubborn ozone and nitrogen dioxide are at around 70 percent of their 1980 levels.

These reductions in levels of air pollution are even more impressive when they are compared with the level of economic activity. Between 1970 and 2000, total production in the United States increased by 158 percent. During this same period, vehicle miles traveled increased by 143 percent, energy consumption increased by 45 percent, and the population increased by 36 percent. While all this economic activity was on the increase, air pollution from all sources *decreased* by 29 percent.

While the facts about the sources and trends in air pollution are not in doubt, there is disagreement about the *effects* of air pollution. The least controversial is *acid rain* caused by sulfur dioxide and nitrogen oxide emissions from coal- and oil-fired generators of electric utilities. Acid rain begins with air pollution, and it leads to water pollution and damages vegetation.

More controversial are airborne substances (suspended particulates) such as lead from leaded gasoline. Some scientists believe that in sufficiently large

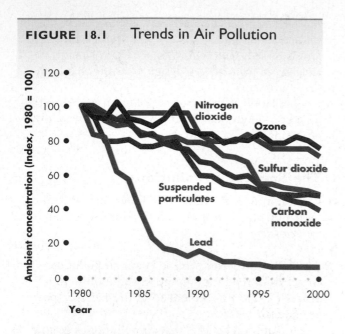

FIGURE 18.1   Trends in Air Pollution

Lead has almost been eliminated from our air; concentrations of carbon monoxide, sulfur dioxide, and suspended particulates have decreased to about 50 percent of their 1980 levels; and nitrogen dioxide and ozone have fallen to about 70 percent of their 1980 levels.

Source: U.S. Environmental Protection Agency, *National Air Quality and Emissions Trends Report, 1999 and 2000.*

concentrations, these substances (189 of which have currently been identified) cause cancer and other life-threatening conditions.

Even more controversial is *global warming,* which some scientists believe results from the carbon dioxide emissions. The earth's average temperature has increased over the past 100 years, but most of the increase occurred *before* 1940. Determining what causes changes in the earth's temperature and isolating the effect of carbon dioxide from other factors are proving to be difficult.

Equally controversial is the problem of *ozone layer depletion.* There is no doubt that a hole in the ozone layer exists over Antarctica and that the ozone layer protects us from cancer-causing ultraviolet rays from the sun. But how our industrial activity influences the ozone layer is simply not understood at this time.

One air pollution problem has almost been eliminated: lead from gasoline. In part, this happened because the cost of living without leaded gasoline, it turns out, is not high. But sulfur dioxide and the so-called greenhouse gases are a much tougher problem

to tackle. Their alternatives are costly or have pollution problems of their own. The major sources of these pollutants are road vehicles and electric utilities. Road vehicles can be made "greener" in a variety of ways. One is with new fuels, and some alternatives being investigated are alcohol, natural gas, propane and butane, and hydrogen. Another way of making cars and trucks "greener" is to change the chemistry of gasoline. Refiners are working on reformulations of gasoline that reduce tailpipe emissions. Similarly, electric power can be generated in cleaner ways by harnessing solar power, tidal power, or geothermal power. While technically possible, these methods are more costly than conventional carbon-fueled generators. Another alternative is nuclear power. This method is good for air pollution but creates a potential long-term problem for land and water pollution because there is no known entirely safe method of disposing of spent nuclear fuel.

Water Pollution The largest sources of water pollution are the dumping of industrial waste and treated sewage in lakes and rivers and the runoff from fertilizers. A more dramatic source is the accidental spilling of crude oil into the oceans such as the *Exxon Valdez* spill in Alaska in 1989.

There are two main alternatives to polluting the waterways and oceans. One is the chemical processing of waste to render it inert or biodegradable. The other, in wide use for nuclear waste, is to use land sites for storage in secure containers.

Land Pollution Land pollution arises from dumping toxic waste products. Ordinary household garbage does not pose a pollution problem unless contaminants from dumped garbage seep into the water supply. This possibility increases as landfills reach capacity and less suitable landfill sites are used. It is estimated that 80 percent of existing landfills will be full by 2010. Some regions (New York, New Jersey, and other East Coast states) and some countries (Japan and the Netherlands) are seeking less costly alternatives to landfill, such as recycling and incineration. Recycling is an apparently attractive alternative, but it requires an investment in new technologies to be effective. Incineration is a high-cost alternative to landfill, and it produces air pollution. Furthermore, these alternatives are not free, and they become efficient only when the cost of using landfill is high.

We've seen that the demand for a pollution-free environment has grown, and we've described the range of pollution problems. Let's now look at the economics of these problems. The starting point is the distinction between private costs and social costs.

Private Costs and Social Costs

A *private cost* of production is a cost that is borne by the producer of a good or service. *Marginal cost* is the cost of producing an *additional unit* of a good or service. So **marginal private cost** (*MC*) is the cost of producing an additional unit of a good or service that is borne by the producer of that good or service.

You've seen that an *external cost* is a cost of producing a good or service that is *not* borne by the producer but borne by other people. A **marginal external cost** is the cost of producing an additional unit of a good or service that falls on people other than the producer.

Marginal social cost (*MSC*) is the marginal cost incurred by the entire society — by the producer and by everyone else on whom the cost falls — and is the sum of marginal private cost and marginal external cost. That is,

$$MSC = MC + \text{Marginal external cost.}$$

We express costs in dollars. But we must always remember that a cost is an opportunity cost — what we give up to get something. A marginal external cost is what someone other than the producer of a good or service must give up when the producer makes one more unit of the item. Something real, such as a clean river or clean air, is given up.

Valuing an External Cost Economists use market prices to put a dollar value on the cost of pollution. For example, suppose that there are two similar rivers, one polluted and the other clean. Five hundred identical homes are built along the side of each river. The homes on the clean river rent for $2,500 a month, and those on the polluted river rent for $1,500 a month. If the pollution is the only detectable difference between the two rivers and the two locations, the rent decrease of $1,000 per month is the cost of the pollution. For the 500 homes, the external cost is $500,000 a month.

External Cost and Output Figure 18.2 shows an example of the relationship between output and cost in a chemical industry that pollutes. The marginal cost curve, *MC*, describes the private marginal cost

borne by the firms that produce the chemical. Marginal cost increases as the quantity of chemical produced increases. If the firms dump waste into a river, they impose an external cost that increases with the amount of the chemical produced. The marginal social cost curve, *MSC*, is the sum of marginal private cost and marginal external cost. For example, when output is 4,000 tons per month, marginal private cost is $100 a ton, marginal external cost is $125 a ton, and marginal social cost is $225 a ton.

In Fig. 18.2, when the quantity of chemicals produced increases, the amount of pollution increases and the external cost of pollution increases.

Figure 18.2 shows the relationship between the quantity of chemicals produced and the amount of pollution created, but it doesn't tell us how much pollution gets created. That quantity depends on how the market for chemicals operates. First, we'll see what happens when the industry is free to pollute.

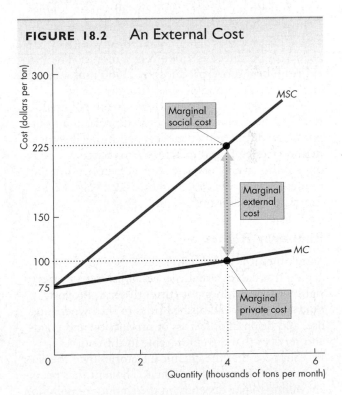

FIGURE 18.2   An External Cost

The *MC* curve shows the private marginal cost borne by the factories that produce a chemical. The *MSC* curve shows the sum of marginal private cost and marginal external cost. When output is 4 tons of chemicals per month, marginal private cost is $100 a ton, marginal external cost is $125 a ton, and marginal social cost is $225 a ton.

Production and Pollution: How Much?

When an industry is unregulated, the amount of pollution it creates depends on the market equilibrium price and quantity of the good produced. In Fig. 18.3, the demand curve for a pollution-creating chemical is *D*. This curve also measures the marginal benefit, *MB*, to the buyers of the chemical. The supply curve is *S*. This curve also measures the marginal private cost, *MC*, of the producers. The supply curve is the marginal private cost curve because when firms make their production and supply decisions, they consider only the costs that they will bear. Market equilibrium occurs at a price of $100 a ton and a quantity of 4,000 tons a month.

This equilibrium is inefficient. You learned in Chapter 5 that the allocation of resources is efficient when marginal benefit equals marginal cost. But we must count all the costs — private and external — when we compare marginal benefit and marginal cost. So with an external cost, the allocation is efficient when marginal benefit equals marginal *social* cost. This outcome occurs when the quantity of chemicals produced is 2,000 tons a month. The market equilibrium overproduces by 2,000 tons a month and creates a deadweight loss, the gray triangle.

How can the people who live by the polluted river get the chemical factories to decrease their output of chemicals and create less pollution? If some method can be found to achieve this outcome, everyone — the owners of the chemical factories and the residents of the riverside homes — can gain. Let's explore some solutions.

Property Rights

Sometimes it is possible to reduce the inefficiency arising from an externality by establishing a property right where one does not currently exist. **Property rights** are legally established titles to the ownership, use, and disposal of factors of production and goods and services that are enforceable in the courts.

Suppose that the chemical factories own the river and the 500 homes alongside it. The rent that people are willing to pay depends on the amount of pollution. Using the earlier example, people are willing to pay $2,500 a month to live alongside a pollution-free river but only $1,500 a month to live with the pollution created by 4,000 tons of chemicals a month. If the factories produce this quantity, they lose $1,000 a month for each home and a total of $500,000 a month.

FIGURE 18.3 Inefficiency with an External Cost

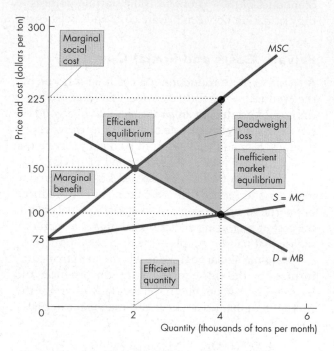

The market supply curve is the marginal private cost curve, *S* = *MC*. The demand curve is the marginal benefit curve, *D* = *MB*. Market equilibrium at a price of $100 a ton and 4,000 tons a month is inefficient because marginal social cost exceeds marginal benefit. The efficient quantity is 2,000 tons a month. The gray triangle shows the deadweight loss created by the pollution externality.

The chemical factories are now confronted with the cost of their pollution — forgone rent from the people who live by the river.

Figure 18.4 illustrates the outcome by using the same example as in Fig. 18.3. With property rights in place, the *MC* curve no longer measures all the costs that the factories face in producing the chemical. It excludes the pollution costs that they must now bear. The *MSC* curve now becomes the marginal private cost curve *MC*. All the costs fall on the factories, so the market supply curve is based on all the marginal costs and is the curve labeled *S* = *MC* = *MSC*.

Market equilibrium now occurs at a price of $150 a ton and a quantity of 2,000 tons a month. This outcome is efficient. The factories still produce some pollution, but it is the efficient quantity.

FIGURE 18.4   Property Rights Achieve an Efficient Outcome

Price equals marginal social cost and marginal benefit

Efficient market equilibrium

$S = MC = MSC$

Cost of pollution borne by polluter

MC excluding pollution cost

$D = MB$

With property rights, the marginal cost curve that excludes pollution costs shows only part of the producers' marginal cost. The marginal private cost curve includes the cost of pollution, and the supply curve is $S = MC = MSC$. Market equilibrium is at a price of $150 a ton and a quantity of 2,000 tons a month and is efficient because marginal social cost equals marginal benefit.

The Coase Theorem

Does it matter how property rights are assigned? Does it matter whether the polluter or the victim of the pollution owns the resource that might be polluted? Until 1960, everyone — including economists who had thought long and hard about the problem — thought that it did matter. But in 1960, Ronald Coase had a remarkable insight, now called the Coase theorem.

The **Coase theorem** is the proposition that if property rights exist, if only a small number of parties are involved, and if transactions costs are low, then private transactions are efficient. There are no externalities because the transacting parties take all the costs and benefits into account. Furthermore, it doesn't matter who has the property rights.

Application of the Coase Theorem In the example that we've just studied, the factories own the river and the homes. Suppose that instead, the residents own their homes and the river. Now the factories must pay a fee to the homeowners for the right to dump their waste. The greater the quantity of waste dumped into the river, the more the factories must pay. So again, the factories face the opportunity cost of the pollution they create. The quantity of chemicals produced and the amount of waste dumped are the same whoever owns the homes and the river. If the factories own them, they bear the cost of pollution because they receive a lower income from home rents. And if the residents own the homes and the river, the factories bear the cost of pollution because they must pay a fee to the homeowners. In both cases, the factories bear the cost of their pollution and dump the efficient amount of waste into the river.

The Coase solution works only when transactions costs are low. **Transactions costs** are the opportunity costs of conducting a transaction. For example, when you buy a house, you incur a series of transactions costs. You might pay a realtor to help you find the best place and a lawyer to run checks that assure you that the seller owns the property and that after you've paid for it, the ownership has been properly transferred to you.

In the example of the homes alongside a river, the transactions costs that are incurred by a small number of chemical factories and a few homeowners might be low enough to enable them to negotiate the deals that produce an efficient outcome. But in many situations, transactions costs are so high that it would be inefficient to incur them. In these situations, the Coase solution is not available.

Suppose, for example, that everyone owns the airspace above their homes up to, say, 10 miles. If someone pollutes your airspace, you can charge a fee. But to collect the fee, you must identify who is polluting your airspace and persuade them to pay you. Imagine the costs of negotiating and enforcing agreements with the 50 million people who live in your part of the United States (and perhaps in Canada or Mexico) and the several thousand factories that emit sulfur dioxide and create acid rain that falls on your property! In this situation, we use public choices to cope with externalities. But the transactions costs that block a market solution are real costs, so attempts by the government to deal with externalities offer no easy solution. Let's look at some of these attempts.

Government Actions in the Face of External Costs

The three main methods that governments use to cope with externalities are

- Taxes
- Emission charges
- Marketable permits

Taxes The government can use taxes as an incentive for producers to cut back on pollution. Taxes used in this way are called **Pigovian taxes**, in honor of Arthur Cecil Pigou, the British economist who first worked out this method of dealing with externalities during the 1920s.

By setting the tax rate equal to the marginal external cost, firms can be made to behave in the same way as they would if they bore the cost of the externality directly. To see how government actions can change market outcomes in the face of externalities, let's return to the example of the chemical factories and the river.

Assume that the government has assessed the marginal external cost accurately and imposes a tax on the factories that exactly equals this cost. Figure 18.5 illustrates the effects of this tax.

The demand curve and marginal benefit curve, $D = MB$, and the firms' marginal cost curve, MC, are the same as in Fig. 18.3. The pollution tax equals the marginal external cost of the pollution. We add this tax to the marginal cost to find the market supply curve. This curve is the one labeled $S = MC + tax = MSC$. This curve is the market supply curve because it tells us the quantities supplied at each price given the firms' marginal cost and the tax they must pay. This curve is also the marginal social cost curve because the pollution tax has been set equal to the marginal external cost.

Demand and supply now determine the market equilibrium price at $150 a ton and the equilibrium quantity at 2,000 tons a month. At this scale of chemical production, the marginal social cost is $150 and the marginal benefit is $150, so the outcome is efficient. The firms incur a marginal cost of $88 a ton and pay a tax of $62 a ton. The government collects tax revenue of $124,000 a month.

Emission Charges Emission charges are an alternative to a tax for confronting a polluter with the external cost of pollution. The government sets a price per unit of pollution. The more pollution a firm creates, the more it

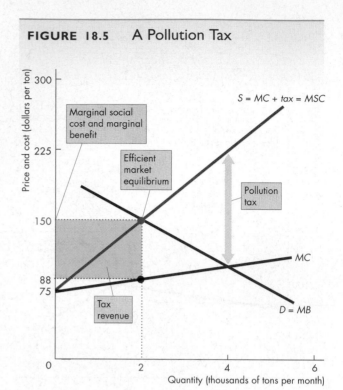

FIGURE 18.5   A Pollution Tax

A pollution tax is imposed equal to the marginal external cost of pollution. The supply curve becomes the marginal private cost curve, MC, plus the tax — $S = MC + tax$. Market equilibrium is at a price of $150 a ton and a quantity of 2,000 tons a month and is efficient because marginal social cost equals marginal benefit. The government collects a tax revenue shown by the purple rectangle.

pays in emission charges. This method of dealing with pollution externalities has been used only modestly in the United States but is common in Europe where, for example, France, Germany, and the Netherlands make water polluters pay a waste disposal charge.

To work out the emission charge that achieves efficiency, the government needs a lot of information about the polluting industry that, in practice, is rarely available.

Marketable Permits Instead of taxing or imposing emission charges on polluters, each potential polluter might be assigned a permitted pollution limit. Each firm knows its own costs and benefits of pollution, and making pollution limits marketable is a clever way of using this private information that is unknown to the government. The government issues each firm a permit to emit a certain amount of pollution, and firms can buy and sell these permits. Firms that have a low marginal cost of reducing pollution sell their permits, and firms that have a high marginal cost of reducing pollution buy permits. The market in permits determines the price at which firms trade permits. And firms buy or sell permits until their marginal cost of pollution equals the market price.

This method of dealing with pollution provides an even stronger incentive than do emission charges to find technologies that pollute less because the price of a permit to pollute rises as the demand for permits increases.

The Market for Emission Permits in the United States Trading in lead pollution permits became common during the 1980s, and this marketable permit program has been rated a success. It enabled lead to be virtually eliminated from the atmosphere of the United States (see Fig. 18.1). But this success might not easily translate to other situations because lead pollution has some special features. First, most lead pollution came from a single source: leaded gasoline. Second, lead in gasoline is easily monitored. Third, the objective of the program was clear: to eliminate lead in gasoline.

The Environmental Protection Agency is now considering using marketable permits to promote efficiency in the control of chlorofluorocarbons, the gases that are believed to damage the ozone layer.

REVIEW QUIZ

1 What is the distinction between a negative production externality and a negative consumption externality?

2 What is the distinction between private cost and social cost?

3 How does an externality prevent a competitive market from allocating resources efficiently?

4 How can an externality be eliminated by assigning property rights? How does this method of coping with an externality work?

5 How do taxes help us to cope with externalities? At what level must a pollution tax be set if it is to induce firms to produce the efficient quantity of pollution?

6 How do emission charges and marketable pollution permits work?

Positive Externalities: Knowledge

KNOWLEDGE COMES FROM EDUCATION AND research. To study the economics of knowledge, we must distinguish between private and social benefits.

Private Benefits and Social Benefits

A *private benefit* is a benefit that the consumer of a good or service receives. *Marginal benefit* is the benefit from an *additional unit* of a good or service. So a **marginal private benefit** (*MB*) is the benefit from an additional unit of a good or service that the consumer of that good or service receives.

The *external benefit* from a good or service is the benefit that someone other than the consumer receives. A **marginal external benefit** is the benefit from an additional unit of a good or service that people other than the consumer enjoy.

Marginal social benefit (*MSB*) is the marginal benefit enjoyed by society — by the consumer of a good or service (marginal private benefit) plus the marginal benefit enjoyed by others (the marginal external benefit). That is,

$$MSB = MB + \text{Marginal external benefit.}$$

Figure 18.6 shows an example of the relationship between marginal private benefit, marginal external benefit, and marginal social benefit. The marginal benefit curve, *MB*, describes the marginal private benefit — such as expanded job opportunities and higher incomes — enjoyed by college graduates. Marginal private benefit decreases as the quantity of education increases.

But college graduates generate external benefits. On the average, they tend to be better citizens. Their crime rates are lower, and they are more tolerant of the views of others. A society with a large number of college graduates can support activities such as high-quality newspapers and television channels, music, theater, and other organized social activities.

In the example in Fig. 18.6, the marginal external benefit is $15,000 per student per year when 15 million students enroll in college. The marginal social benefit curve, *MSB*, is the sum of marginal private benefit and marginal external benefit. For example, when 15 million students a year enroll in college, the marginal private benefit is $10,000 per student and

FIGURE 18.6 An External Benefit

FIGURE 18.6 An External Benefit

The *MB* curve shows the marginal private benefit enjoyed by the people who receive a college education. The *MSB* curve shows the sum of marginal private benefit and marginal external benefit. When 15 million students attend college, marginal private benefit is $10,000 per student, marginal external benefit is $15,000 per student, and marginal social benefit is $25,000 per student.

FIGURE 18.7 Inefficiency with an External Benefit

The market demand curve is the marginal private benefit curve, *D = MB*. The supply curve is the marginal cost curve, *S = MC*. Market equilibrium at a tuition of $15,000 a year and 7.5 million students is inefficient because marginal social benefit exceeds marginal cost. The efficient quantity is 15 million students. The gray triangle shows the deadweight loss created because too few students enroll in college.

the marginal external benefit is $15,000 per student, so the marginal social benefit is $25,000 per student.

When people make schooling decisions, they ignore its external benefits and consider only its private benefits. So if education were provided by private schools that charged full-cost tuition, we would produce too few college graduates.

Figure 18.7 illustrates the underproduction if the government left education to the private market. The supply curve is the marginal cost curve of the private schools, *S = MC*. The demand curve is the marginal private benefit curve, *D = MB*. Market equilibrium occurs at a tuition of $15,000 per student per year and 7.5 million students per year. At this equilibrium, marginal social benefit is $38,000 per student, which exceeds marginal cost by $23,000. There are too few students in college. The efficient number is 15 million, where marginal social benefit

equals marginal cost. The gray triangle shows the deadweight loss.

Underproduction similar to that in Fig. 18.7 would occur in grade school and high school if an unregulated market produced it. When children learn basic reading, writing, and number skills, they receive the private benefit of increased earning power. But even these basic skills bring the external benefit of developing better citizens.

External benefits also arise from the discovery of new knowledge. When Isaac Newton worked out the formulas for calculating the rate of response of one variable to another — calculus — everyone was free to use his method. When a spreadsheet program called VisiCalc was invented, Lotus Corporation and Microsoft were free to copy the basic idea and create 1-2-3 and Excel. When the first shopping mall was built and found to be a successful way of arranging retailing, everyone was free to copy the idea, and malls spread like mushrooms.

Once someone has discovered how to do something, others can copy the basic idea. They do have to work to copy an idea, so they face an opportunity cost. But they do not usually have to pay the person who made the discovery to use it. When people make decisions, they ignore its external benefits and consider only its private benefits.

When people make decisions about the quantity of education or the amount of research to undertake, they balance the marginal private cost against the marginal private benefit. They ignore the external benefit. As a result, if we left education and research to unregulated market forces, we would get too little of these activities.

To get closer to producing the efficient quantity of a good or service that generates an external benefit, we make public choices, through governments, to modify the market outcome.

Government Actions in the Face of External Benefits

Four devices that governments can use to achieve a more efficient allocation of resources in the presence of external benefits are

- Public provision
- Private subsidies
- Vouchers
- Patents and copyrights

Public Provision Under **public provision**, a public authority that receives its revenue from the government produces the good or service. The education services produced by the public universities, colleges, and schools are examples of public provision.

Figure 18.8(a) shows how public provision might overcome the underproduction that arises in Fig. 18.7. Public provision cannot lower the cost of production, so marginal cost is the same as before. Marginal

---

FIGURE 18.8   Public Provision or Private Subsidy to Achieve an Efficient Outcome

(a) Public provision

(b) Private subsidy

In part (a), marginal social benefit equals marginal cost with 15 million students enrolled in college, the efficient quantity. Tuition is set at $10,000 per student, and the taxpayers cover the other $15,000 of marginal cost per student. In part (b),

with a subsidy of $15,000 per student, the supply curve is S = MC − subsidy. The equilibrium price is $10,000, and the market equilibrium is efficient with 15 million students enrolled in college. Marginal social benefit equals marginal cost.

private benefit and marginal external benefit are also the same as before.

The efficient quantity occurs where marginal social benefit equals marginal cost. In Fig. 18.8(a), this quantity is 15 million students. Tuition is set to ensure that the efficient number of students enrolls. That is, tuition is set at the level that equals the marginal private benefit at the efficient quantity. In Fig. 18.8(a), tuition is $10,000 a year. The rest of the cost of the public university is borne by the taxpayers and, in this example, is $15,000 per student per year.

Private Subsidies A **subsidy** is a payment that the government makes to private producers. By making the subsidy depend on the level of output, the government can induce private decision makers to consider external benefits when they make their choices.

Figure 18.8(b) shows how a subsidy to private colleges works. In the absence of a subsidy, the marginal cost curve is the market supply curve of private college education, $S = MC$. The marginal benefit is the demand curve, $D = MB$. In this example, the government provides a subsidy to colleges of $15,000 per student per year. We must subtract the subsidy from the marginal cost of education to find the colleges' supply curve. That curve is $S = MC - subsidy$ in the figure. The equilibrium tuition (market price) is $10,000 a year, and the equilibrium quantity is 15 million students. To educate 15 million students, colleges incur a marginal cost of $25,000 a year. The marginal social benefit is also $25,000 a year. So with marginal cost equal to marginal social benefit, the subsidy has achieved an efficient outcome. The tuition and the subsidy just cover the colleges' marginal cost.

Vouchers A **voucher** is a token that the government provides to households, which they can use to buy specified goods or services. Food stamps are examples of vouchers. The vouchers (stamps) can be spent only on food and are designed to improve the diet and health of extremely poor families.

School vouchers have been advocated as a means of improving the quality of education and have been used in Cleveland and Milwaukee.

A school voucher allows parents to choose the school their children will attend and to use the voucher to pay part of the cost. The school cashes the vouchers to pay its bills. A voucher could be provided to a college student in a similar way, and although technically not a voucher, a federal Pell Grant has a similar effect.

FIGURE 18.9   Vouchers Achieve an Efficient Outcome

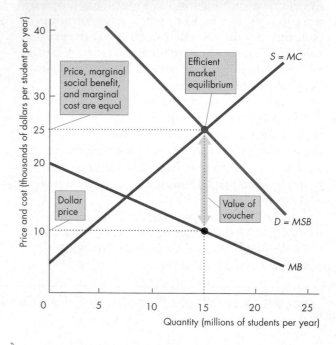

With vouchers, buyers are willing to pay MB plus the value of the voucher, so the demand curve becomes the marginal social benefit curve, $D = MSB$. Market equilibrium is efficient with 15 million students enrolled in college because price, marginal social benefit, and marginal cost are equal. The tuition consists of the dollar price of $10,000 and the value of the voucher.

Because vouchers can be spent only on a specified item, they increase the willingness to pay for that item and so increase the demand for it. Figure 18.9 shows how a voucher system works. The government provides vouchers worth $15,000 per student per year. Parents (or students) use these vouchers to supplement the dollars they pay for college education. The marginal social benefit curve becomes the demand for college education, $D = MSB$. The market equilibrium occurs at a price of $25,000 per student per year, and 15 million students attend college. Each student pays $10,000 tuition, and schools collect an additional $15,000 per student from the voucher.

If the government estimates the value of the external benefit correctly and makes the value of the voucher equal the marginal external benefit, the outcome from the voucher scheme is efficient.

Marginal cost equals marginal social benefit, and the deadweight loss is eliminated.

Vouchers are similar to subsidies, but their advocates say that they are more efficient than subsidies because the consumer can monitor school performance more effectively than the government can.

Patents and Copyrights Knowledge might be an exception to the principle of diminishing marginal benefit. Additional knowledge (about the right things) makes people more productive. And there seems to be no tendency for the additional productivity from additional knowledge to diminish.

For example, in just 15 years, advances in knowledge about microprocessors have given us a sequence of processor chips that has made our personal computers increasingly powerful. Each advance in knowledge about how to design and manufacture a processor chip has brought apparently ever larger increments in performance and productivity. Similarly, each advance in knowledge about how to design and build an airplane has brought apparently ever larger increments in performance: Orville and Wilbur Wright's 1903 Flyer was a one-seat plane that could hop a farmer's field. The Lockheed Constellation, designed in 1949, was an airplane that could fly 120 passengers from New York to London, but with two refueling stops in Newfoundland and Ireland. The latest version of the Boeing 747 can carry 400 people nonstop from Los Angeles to Sydney, Australia, or New York to Tokyo (flights of 7,500 miles that take 13 hours). Similar examples can be found in agriculture, biogenetics, communications, engineering, entertainment, and medicine.

One reason why the stock of knowledge increases without diminishing returns is the sheer number of different techniques that can in principle be tried. Paul Romer explains this fact. "Suppose that to make a finished good, 20 different parts have to be attached to a frame, one at a time. A worker could proceed in numerical order, attaching part one first, then part two.... Or the worker could proceed in some other order, starting with part 10, then adding part seven.... With 20 parts, ... there are [more] different sequences ... than the total number of seconds that have elapsed since the big bang created the universe, so we can be confident that in all activities, only a very small fraction of the possible sequences have ever been tried."[1]

Think about all the processes, all the products, and all the different bits and pieces that go into each, and you can see that we have only begun to scratch around the edges of what is possible.

Because knowledge is productive and generates external benefits, it is necessary to use public policies to ensure that those who develop new ideas have incentives to encourage an efficient level of effort. The main way of providing the right incentives uses the central idea of the Coase theorem and assigns property rights — called **intellectual property rights** — to creators. The legal device for establishing intellectual property rights is the patent or copyright. A **patent** or **copyright** is a government-sanctioned exclusive right granted to the inventor of a good, service, or productive process to produce, use, and sell the invention for a given number of years. A patent enables the developer of a new idea to prevent others from benefiting freely from an invention for a limited number of years.

Although patents encourage invention and innovation, they do so at an economic cost. While a patent is in place, its holder has a monopoly. And monopoly is another source of inefficiency (which is explained in Chapter 12). But without a patent, the effort to develop new goods, services, or processes is diminished and the flow of new inventions is slowed. So the efficient outcome is a compromise that balances the benefits of more inventions against the cost of temporary monopoly in newly invented activities.

REVIEW QUIZ

1 What is special about knowledge that creates external benefits?
2 How might governments use public provision, private subsidies, and vouchers to achieve an efficient amount of education?
3 How might governments use public provision, private subsidies, vouchers, and patents and copyrights to achieve an efficient amount of research and development?

◆ *Reading Between the Lines* on pp. 422–423 looks at the pollution created by generating electricity and the debate over whether the regulation of power utilities is too lax or too severe.

---

[1] Paul Romer, "Ideas and Things," in *The Future Surveyed*, supplement to *The Economist*, September 11, 1993, pp. 71–72.

The Air Pollution Debate

THE NEW YORK TIMES, March 21, 2002

Study Ranking Utility Polluters Aims to Sway Emissions Debate

As debate flares anew over White House plans to revise air pollution regulations, a study that ranks the biggest air polluters in the power industry is expected to be issued today.

The study was conducted by two environmental organizations and a large New Jersey utility and uses government data. It contends that a handful of companies accounts for at least half of the industry's most noxious emissions, including those that contribute to smog, acid rain and possibly global warming. Moreover, the study shows a wide disparity in the relative level of emissions produced by power plants, a gap that the authors say reflects the level of investment that companies have made toward improving their environmental performance.

The report's release is timed to sway the current discussion about revisions to air pollution rules.

One author, David Gardiner, said such changes could end up protecting the biggest polluters and removing incentives for the industry as a whole to reduce its rate of emissions.

"The very large disparity between the cleanest and the dirtiest companies," said Mr. Gardiner, one of the report's lead authors and the former director of climate change policy in the Clinton administration, "demonstrates that a large number of companies are relatively clean, and a relatively small number are responsible for the vast portion of emissions. It shows that clean electricity is both possible and profitable."

...

The study relies primarily on data that companies provided to the E.P.A. and the Energy Department for 2000. It details which corporations are the largest polluters and the relative emission levels of various pollutants by companies. In gross terms, the biggest polluters tend to be the companies that have the most power plants and that generate the most electricity.

The three largest electricity companies in the United States — American Electric Power, the Southern Company and the Tennessee Valley Authority — together accounted for 17 percent to 24 percent of total industry emissions of the four pollutants tracked in the study. Those are sulfur dioxide and nitrogen oxides, which contribute to acid rain and haze; mercury, which is toxic to humans; and carbon dioxide, which is widely linked to global warming.

...

Essence of the Story

■ A new study finds that a few companies account for most of the electricity industry's emissions.

■ The three largest companies account for 17 percent to 24 percent of total industry emissions of sulfur dioxide, nitrogen oxides, mercury, and carbon dioxide.

■ These emissions contribute to smog, acid rain and possibly global warming.

■ The study shows a wide gap in emissions levels between the cleanest and dirtiest companies.

■ The companies with the cleanest plants have invested most in improving their environmental performance.

Economic Analysis

■ In producing electricity, there is a tradeoff between the private cost of production and the social cost.

■ The cheapest fuels and production technologies are very dirty.

■ These dirty technologies are not used in the United States today. But they are used in China and Russia (among other countries) where air pollution is a serious problem.

■ The United States, in contrast, has achieved a high standard of air quality. But is the standard high enough? Or is it too high?

■ To answer this question, we need to consider the economics of pollution from producing electricity.

■ Figure 1 shows the demand for electricity and its marginal benefit as the curve $D = MB$.

■ The curve MC shows the marginal cost of producing electricity in dirty plants.

■ With an unregulated and competitive market, the quantity produced is 6 megawatt hours.

■ Because the plants are dirty, a pollution problem arises. The curve MSC shows the marginal social cost of producing electricity.

■ The vertical distance between the MC curve and the MSC curve is the marginal external cost.

■ Taking the marginal external cost into account, we can find the efficient quantity of electricity to produce and the efficient amount of pollution.

■ In Fig. 1, the efficient quantity is 4 megawatt hours. Notice that at the efficient quantity, we still have pollution, but a smaller amount than with the unregulated outcome.

■ Figure 2 focuses on the overall cost of pollution — its deadweight loss.

■ If production is cut to 4 megawatt hours, the deadweight loss disappears and we have the efficient outcome.

■ If power companies are regulated to use a more costly but cleaner technology, the MC curve shifts upward, the cost of electricity rises, the quantity produced decreases, and the deadweight loss shrinks.

Figure 1 Efficient and unregulated outcomes compared

Figure 2 Cost of pollution

■ If the additional cost imposed by regulation on the power companies is less than the marginal external cost, production and pollution move toward but remain above their efficient levels.

■ If the additional cost imposed by regulation on the power companies exceeds the marginal external cost, production and pollution move below their efficient levels.

423

SUMMARY

KEY POINTS

Externalities in Our Lives (p. 410)

- An externality can arise from either a production activity or a consumption activity.
- A negative externality imposes an external cost.
- A positive externality provides an external benefit.

Negative Externalities: Pollution (pp. 411–417)

- External costs are costs of production that fall on people other than the producer of a good or service. Marginal social cost equals marginal private cost plus marginal external cost.
- Producers take account only of marginal private cost and produce more than the efficient quantity when there is a marginal external cost.
- Sometimes it is possible to overcome a negative externality by assigning a property right.
- When property rights cannot be assigned, governments might overcome externalities by using taxes, emission charges, or marketable permits.

Positive Externalities: Knowledge (pp. 417–421)

- External benefits are benefits that are received by people other than the consumer of a good or service. Marginal social benefit equals marginal private benefit plus marginal external benefit.
- External benefits from education arise because better-educated people tend to be better citizens, commit fewer crimes, and support social activities.
- External benefits from research arise because once someone has worked out a basic idea, others can copy it.
- Vouchers or subsidies to schools or the provision of public education below cost can achieve a more efficient provision of education.

- Patents and copyrights create intellectual property rights and an incentive to innovate. But they do so by creating a temporary monopoly, the cost of which must be balanced against the benefit of more inventive activity.

KEY FIGURES

KEY TERMS

PROBLEMS

🖥 *1. The table provides information about costs and benefits arising from the production of pesticide that pollutes a lake used by a trout farmer.

Total product of pesticide (tons per week)	Pesticide producer's MC	Trout farmer's MC from pesticide production	Marginal benefit of pesticide
		(dollars per ton)	
0	0	0	250
1	5	33	205
2	15	67	165
3	30	100	130
4	50	133	100
5	75	167	75
6	105	200	55
7	140	233	40

a. If no one owns the lake and if there is no regulation of pollution, what is the quantity of pesticide produced per week and what is the marginal cost of pollution borne by the trout farmer?

b. If the trout farm owns the lake, how much pesticide is produced per week and what does the pesticide producer pay the farmer per ton?

c. If the pesticide producer owns the lake, and if a pollution-free lake rents for $1,000 a week, how much pesticide is produced per week and how much rent per week does the farmer pay the factory for the use of the lake?

d. Compare the quantities of pesticide produced in your answers to (b) and (c) and explain the relationship between these quantities.

2. The table at the top of the next column provides information about the costs and benefits of steel smelting that pollutes the air of a city.

a. With no property rights in the city's air and no regulation of pollution, what is the quantity of steel produced per week and what is the marginal cost of pollution borne by the citizens?

b. If the city owns the steel plant, how much steel is produced per week and what does the city charge the steel producer per ton?

Total product of steel (tons per week)	Steel producer's MC	Marginal External cost	Marginal benefit of steel
	(dollars per ton)		
0	0	0	1,200
10	100	15	1,100
20	200	25	1,000
30	300	50	900
40	400	100	800
50	500	200	700
60	600	300	600
70	700	400	500
80	800	500	400

c. If the steel firm owns the city, and if the residents of a pollution-free city are willing to pay $15,000 a week in property taxes, how much steel is produced per week and how much are the citizens willing to pay in property taxes to live in the polluted city?

d. Compare the quantities of steel produced in your answers to (b) and (c) and explain the relationship between these quantities.

*3. Back at the pesticide plant and trout farm described in problem 1, suppose that no one owns the lake and that the government introduces a pollution tax.

a. What is the tax per ton of pesticide produced that achieves an efficient outcome?

b. Explain the connection between your answer to (a) and the answer to problem 1.

4. Back at the steel smelter and city in problem 2, suppose that the city government introduces a pollution tax.

a. What is the tax per ton of steel produced that will achieve an efficient outcome?

b. Explain the connection between your answer to (a) and the answer to problem 2.

*5. Using the information provided in problem 1, suppose that no one owns the lake and that the government issues two marketable pollution permits, one to the farmer and one to the factory. Each may pollute the lake by the same amount, and the total amount of pollution is the efficient amount.

a. What is the quantity of pesticide produced?

b. What is the market price of a pollution permit? Who buys and who sells a permit?

c. What is the connection between your answer and the answers to problems 1 and 3?

6. Using the information given in problem 2, suppose that the city government issues two marketable pollution permits, one to the city government and one to the smelter. Each may pollute the air by the same amount, and the total is the efficient amount.
   a. How much steel is produced?
   b. What is the market price of a permit? Who buys and who sells a permit?
   c. What is the connection between your answer and the answers to problems 2 and 4?

*7. The marginal cost of educating a student is $4,000 a year and is constant. The figure shows the marginal private benefit curve.

   a. With no government involvement and if the schools are competitive, how many students are enrolled and what is the tuition?
   b. The external benefit from education is $2,000 per student per year and is constant. If the government provides the efficient amount of education, how many school places does it offer and what is the tuition?

8. A technological advance cuts the marginal cost of educating a student to $2,000 a year. The marginal private benefit is the same as that in problem 7. The external benefit from education increases to $4,000 per student per year.
   a. With no government involvement and if the schools are competitive, how many students are enrolled and what is the tuition?
   b. If the government provides the efficient amount of education, how many school places does it offer and what is the tuition?
   c. Compare the outcomes in problem 8 with those in problem 7. Explain the differences.

CRITICAL THINKING

After you have studied *Reading Between the Lines* on pp. 422–423, answer the following questions:
   a. Which electric power companies create most of the air pollution in the electricity industry in the United States?
   b. What are the pros and cons of stiffening the regulations that power utilities face?
   c. If a technological advance lowers the cost of producing electricity but leaves the marginal external pollution cost unchanged, would the adoption of this technology in an unregulated market increase or decrease pollution? Explain using a figure like those on p. 423.

WEB EXERCISES

1. Use the links on your Parkin Web site to get two viewpoints on global warming. Then answer these questions:
   a. What are the benefits and costs of greenhouse gas emissions?
   b. Do you think environmentalists are correct in the view that greenhouse gas emissions must be cut or do you think the costs of reducing greenhouse gas emissions exceed the benefits?
   c. If greenhouse gas emissions are to be reduced, should firms be assigned production limits or marketable permits?

2. To decrease the amount of overfishing of southern bluefin tuna in its territorial waters, the government of Australia introduced private property rights with an allocation of Individual Transferable Quotas (ITQs). To check out the effects of this system, use the link on your Parkin Web site to read the review by John Coombs of Colby College, Maine. Also look at the Greenpeace view. Then answer the following questions:
   a. Would the introduction of ITQs in the United States help to replenish U.S. fish stocks?
   b. Explain why ITQs give a disincentive to overfish.
   c. Why does Greenpeace oppose ITQs?

UNDERSTANDING MARKET FAILURE AND GOVERNMENT

We, the People, ...

Thomas Jefferson knew that creating a government of the people, by the people, and for the people was a huge enterprise and one that could easily go wrong. Creating a constitution that made despotic and tyrannical rule impossible was relatively easy. The founding fathers did their best to practice sound economics. They designed a sophisticated system of incentives—of carrots and sticks—to make the government responsive to public opinion and to limit the ability of individual special interests to gain at the expense of the majority. But they were not able to create a constitution that effectively blocks the ability of special interest groups to capture the consumer and producer surpluses that result from specialization and exchange. ◆ We have created a system of government to deal with four economic problems. The market economy would produce too small a quantity of those public goods and services that we must consume together, such as national defense and air-traffic control. It enables monopoly to restrict production and charge too high a price. It produces too large a quantity of some goods and services, the production of which creates pollution. And it generates a distribution of income and wealth that most people believe is too unequal. So we need a government to help cope with these economic

problems. But as the founding fathers knew would happen, when governments get involved in the economy, people try to steer the government's actions in directions that bring personal gains at the expense of the general interest. ◆ The four chapters in this part explained the problems with which the market has a hard time coping. Chapter 16 overviewed the entire range of problems and studied one of these problems, public goods, more deeply. Chapter 17 studied antitrust law and the regulation of natural monopoly. And Chapter 18 dealt with externalities. It examined the external costs imposed by pollution and the external benefits that come from education and research. It described some of the ways in which externalities can be dealt with. And it explained that one way of coping with externalities is to strengthen the market and "internalize" the externalities rather than to intervene in the market. ◆ Many economists have thought long and hard about the problems discussed in this part. But none has had as profound an effect on our ideas in this area as Ronald Coase, whom you can meet on the following page. You can also meet Joel Slemrod of the University of Michigan, another major contributor to our understanding of the role of government and taxes in our economy.

PROBING THE IDEAS
Externalities and Property Rights

THE ECONOMIST	THE ISSUES

"The question to be decided is: is the value of fish lost greater or less than the value of the product which contamination of the stream makes possible?"

RONALD H.
COASE
*The Problem of
Social Cost*

RONALD COASE *(1910–), was born in England and educated at the London School of Economics, where he was deeply influenced by his teacher, Arnold Plant, and by the issues of his youth: communist central planning versus free markets. Professor Coase has lived in the United States since 1951. He first visited America as a 20-year-old on a traveling scholarship during the depths of the Great Depression. It was on this visit, and before he had completed his bachelor's degree, that he conceived the ideas that 60 years later were to earn him the 1991 Nobel Prize for Economic Science. He discovered and clarified the significance of transaction costs and property rights for the functioning of the economy. Ronald Coase has revolutionized the way we think about property rights and externalities and has opened up the growing field of law and economics.*

As knowledge accumulates, we are becoming more sensitive to environmental externalities. We are also developing more sensitive methods of dealing with them. But all the methods involve a public choice.

Urban smog, which is both unpleasant and dangerous to breathe, forms when sunlight reacts with emissions from the tailpipes of automobiles. Because of this external cost of auto exhaust, we set emission standards and tax gasoline. Emission standards increase the cost of a car, and gasoline taxes increase the cost of the marginal mile traveled. The higher costs decrease the quantity demanded of road transportation and so decrease the amount of pollution it creates. Is the value of cleaner urban air worth the higher cost of transportation? The public choices of voters, regulators, and lawmakers answer this question.

Acid rain, which imposes a cost on everyone who lives in its path, falls from sulfur-laden clouds produced by electric utility smokestacks. This external cost is being tackled with a market solution. This solution is marketable permits, the price and allocation of which are determined by the forces of supply and demand. Private choices determine the demand for pollution permits, but a public choice determines the supply.

As cars stream onto an urban freeway during the morning rush hour, the highway clogs and becomes an expensive parking lot. Each rush hour traveler imposes external costs on all the others. Today, road users bear private congestion costs but do not face a share of the external congestion costs that they create. But a market solution to this problem is now technologically feasible. It is a solution that charges road users a fee similar to a toll that varies with time of day and

428

degree of congestion. Confronted with the social marginal cost of their actions, each road user makes a choice and the market for highway space is efficient. Here, a public choice to use a market solution leaves the final decision about the degree of congestion to private choices.

Chester Jackson, a Lake Erie fisherman, recalls that when he began fishing on the lake, boats didn't carry drinking water. Fishermen drank from the lake. Speaking after World War II, Jackson observed, "Can't do that today. Those chemicals in there would kill you." Farmers used chemicals, such as the insecticide DDT that got carried into the lake by runoff. Industrial waste and trash were also dumped in the lake in large quantities. As a result, Lake Erie became badly polluted during the 1940s and became incapable of sustaining a viable fish stock.

Today, Lake Erie supports a fishing industry, just as it did in the 1930s. No longer treated as a garbage dump for chemicals, the lake is regenerating its ecosystem. Fertilizers and insecticides are now recognized as products that have potential externalities, and their external effects are assessed by the Environmental Protection Agency before new versions are put into widespread use. Dumping industrial waste into rivers and lakes is now subject to much more stringent regulations and penalties. Lake Erie's externalities have been dealt with by one of the methods available: government regulation.

Joel Slemrod, whom you can meet on the following pages, has done much to improve our understanding of public policy and the role of taxes in our economy.

429

TALKING WITH

JOEL SLEMROD *is the Paul W. McCracken Collegiate Professor of Business Economics and Public Policy, and Director of the Office of Tax Policy Research, at the University of Michigan. Born in 1951 in Newark, New Jersey, he was an undergraduate at Princeton University and a graduate student at Harvard.*

Professor Slemrod is one of the world's leading experts on the economics of taxation. He has written more than 100 articles, edited nine major books covering all aspects of taxation — one of which is Does Atlas Shrug? The Economic Consequences of Taxing the Rich *(Harvard University Press, 2000) — and he is coauthor of* Taxing Ourselves: A Citizen's Guide to the Great Debate Over Tax Reform *(MIT Press, 2000).*

Professor Slemrod has been a consultant to the U.S. Department of the Treasury, the Canadian Department of Finance, the New Zealand Department of Treasury, the South Africa Ministry of Finance, the World Bank, and the OECD. He is a member of the Congressional Budget Office Panel of Economic Advisers, and has testified before the Congress on taxation issues. His views on taxation

Joel Slemrod

have appeared in The New York Times, The Wall Street Journal, Business Week, *and* The Economist, *as well as on National Public Radio's* Talk of the Nation.

Michael Parkin talked with Joel Slemrod about his work and the progress that economists have made in understanding how taxes influence behavior and the distribution of income and wealth.

Professor Slemrod, what attracted you to the economics of taxation?

One thing that attracted me was the inspiration of a wonderful professor I had at Princeton whose name is James Ohls. Once I got interested in economics I found taxation especially fascinating because to me it's about all aspects of the economy. It's about housing because of the tax subsidies to owner-occupied housing; it's about charity because of the tax deductibility of charitable donations; it's about research and development because of the R&D credit. It's a way in for looking at many different aspects of economics. Another thing I like is that it touches on many aspects of human behavior beyond the usual things that economists study about how people change their behavior when prices change. It's about honesty — I study tax evasion; it's about procrastination — I study the process of filing tax returns; and it's about trust — whether people change their tax compliance behavior depending on whether they trust the government and feel good about what the government is doing with their money.

Do governments do enough to make people feel good about what they are doing with their money — to make the benefits of programs match the costs of

the taxes that pay for them? And do economists do enough?

As a practical matter, this happens through the political system when voters choose among candidates and parties that stand for different levels and compositions of public spending. The role of the economist in this process is to inform the debate so that election decisions are made with a clear view of the cost of different ways of raising revenue and the benefits of different public projects.

One role of the tax economist is to point out that, because we have to raise taxes in ways that distort the economy, the true cost of raising a dollar is generally more than a dollar, so when you're doing benefit-cost calculations about whether to build a bridge or expand a public park, you should be comparing the benefits — your estimated benefits of these things — not to the dollars raised but something more than that related to how distortionary taxes are.

You edited a book with the intriguing title _Does Atlas Shrug?_ What does the title mean? And does Atlas shrug? What's the main thrust of the articles in this book?

The title of the book comes from a novel written by Ayn Rand in 1957 called _Atlas Shrugged_. The novel opens in the United States when the country is in disrepair, nothing's working, and the economy is shattered. Over the hundreds of pages of this novel, you learn that the reason for these hard times is that the talented people in the country, which Ayn Rand calls the prime movers, are on strike. They believe that their contributions are not appreciated, and the tax system and other aspects of government policy make it not worth their while to contribute to the economy.

Ayn Rand believed that, in the 1950s at least, the U.S. economy was creating a lot of disincentives for talented people to work harder and to be entrepreneurs. So, the point of _Does Atlas Shrug?_ is to study the economic consequences of taxing the richest. We assembled more than a dozen economists to try to quantify just how much talented, high-income people do respond to the different aspects of the tax sys-

tem — is it true that _Atlas shrugs_? That is, is it true that high-income people work less, save less, and are less likely to become entrepreneurs because of the tax system that the United States and most other countries have?

The main thrust of the book is hard to concisely summarize because it reports the views of several economists studying different aspects of this question. But I can summarize what _I_ think the overall answer is.

Atlas shrugs in different ways. The timing responses to taxation seem very large. High-income people certainly take notice and respond when the tax rates are going to change — say, January 1st of the next year — and they move up or postpone behavior to take advantage of the changing tax rate. Financial decisions are also fairly responsive — firms for example will change whether they raise their money through borrowing or issuing shares, depending on the tax consequences.

The bulk of the evidence suggests that regarding decisions about savings and labor supply — what I call real decisions — Atlas doesn't shrug all that much. There isn't that much compelling evidence that saving rates respond to taxes, nor does labor supply with the possible exception of the labor supply participation decision of married women.

What about the real cost of minimizing taxes? This is a real effect of high tax rates. Do we know how costly this is?

A lot of my research has been on exactly this question. How do you get a quantitative estimate of the cost of complying with the tax system, which includes the forms individuals and businesses have to fill out, but also includes the value of the resources that people voluntarily put into finding ways to lower their tax liability, such as hiring a good accountant or spending Saturday afternoon in the library going through books about the tax system. My own best estimate for the United States federal income tax system is that this cost is about 10 percent of the revenue raised, and that's non-trivial.

I know that some of my best students end up in jobs finding ways to reduce other people's taxes, either by designing tax-efficient financial instruments or identifying other kinds of tax planning opportunities, and that is part of the resource cost of collecting taxes.

Ten percent of total income tax revenue in 2002 is about $150 billion. That's a huge cost. Do you have suggestions about how we could revise the tax system to reduce it?

I don't think there's any question that the U.S. tax system and probably the tax system of most industrialized countries could and should be a lot simpler. And that would certainly reduce the resource costs. The issue is what you give up in making the tax system simpler. One of the things you give up is being able to use the tax system as a vehicle for instituting scores of subsidy programs that really have nothing to

The issue is what you give up in making the tax system simpler. … you must settle for rough justice.

do with raising revenue, but just have found their way into the tax system for one reason or another. The other thing you give up is any attempt to fine-tune the horizontal equity of the tax system — getting the right taxes for a family of given circumstances. Instead, you must settle for rough justice.

The issue is what you give up in making the tax system simpler. … you must settle for rough justice.

Couldn't the first problem be handled with explicit subsidies rather than implicit subsidies through the tax systems?

Perhaps. For example, the U.S. tax system provides a subsidy for owner-occupied housing. We could eliminate this subsidy, but the question is whether the United States would then offer explicit subsidies to owner-occupied housing delivered by a department other than the Internal Revenue Service. Maybe, but maybe not.

Sometimes when these subsidies are in the tax system they're hidden from the public eye. If they

became explicit subsidies, some of the ones that aren't worth doing might disappear. It's hard to know whether that would happen.

Another consequence of running subsidies through the tax system is that they inevitably take on a different form than they otherwise would. For example, tax deductions deliver a subsidy at a rate that depends on a person's marginal tax rate. It doesn't strike me that you would get that arrangement if you started from scratch. If you wanted to subsidize charity, for example, would you have a higher subsidy rate for a higher income family? Probably not, but that's what you get by having the subsidy through a tax deduction.

Another problem is that it is difficult to deliver subsidies to people whose income is so low that they fall below the filing threshold — they obviously don't get any subsidy if they're not filing income tax.

What advice do you have for a student who is just starting to study economics? Is economics a good subject in which to major? What other subjects go well alongside economics?

Economics is a wonderful subject to study if you like to read the front page of the newspaper and if you have a quantitative mind. So much of what is in the newspapers is about economics, and economics is a way to understand and learn more about many aspects of the world and do so in a rigorous and often quantitative way. That's what attracted me to economics — I came to college thinking I might be a math major, but I wasn't good enough to be a great mathematician. I saw that I could use my math and quantitative talent to study the sorts of issues that are always contentious all over the world.

Unlike physicists and chemists, economists can't easily do controlled experiments. We have to observe the world and draw conclusions from it and that always means that we're making statistical statements. I think if you want to be an economist it is important to have a good background both in math and statistics, and a curiosity about what makes the world tick.

MEASURING GDP AND ECONOMIC GROWTH

CHAPTER 19

An Economic Barometer

Did our economy go into recession in 2001, and if it did, was the recession a severe or a mild one? Many U.S. and foreign corporations wanted to know the answer to this question at the beginning of 2002. AOL wanted to know whether to expand its server network or delay for a while. Amazon.com wanted to know whether to increase its warehousing facilities. To assess the severity of a recession and to make big decisions about business expansion, firms such as AOL and Amazon use forecasts of GDP. What exactly *is* GDP and how can we use it to tell us whether we are in a recession or how rapidly our economy is expanding? ◆ To reveal the rate of growth or shrinkage of GDP, we must remove the effects of inflation and assess how *real* GDP is changing. How do we remove the inflation component of GDP to reveal *real* GDP? ◆ Some countries are rich while others are poor. How do we compare economic well-being in one country with that in another? How can we make international comparisons of GDP?

◆ In this chapter, you will find out how economic statisticians measure GDP, real GDP, and the economic growth rate. You will also learn about the limitations of these measures. In *Reading Between the Lines* at the end of the chapter, we'll look at real GDP during the 2001 recession.

After studying this chapter, you will be able to

- Define GDP and use the circular flow model to explain why GDP equals aggregate expenditure and aggregate income
- Explain the two ways of measuring GDP
- Explain how we measure *real* GDP and the GDP deflator
- Explain how we use real GDP to measure economic growth and describe the limitations of our measure

Gross Domestic Product

WHAT EXACTLY IS GDP, HOW IS IT CALCULATED, what does it mean, and why do we care about it? You are going to discover the answers to these questions in this chapter. First, what *is* GDP?

GDP Defined

GDP, or **gross domestic product**, is the market value of all the final goods and services produced within a country in a given time period. This definition has four parts:

- Market value
- Final goods and services
- Produced within a country
- In a given time period

We'll examine each in turn.

Market Value To measure total production, we must add together the production of apples and oranges, computers and popcorn. Just counting the items doesn't get us very far. For example, which is the greater total production: 100 apples and 50 oranges, or 50 apples and 100 oranges?

GDP answers this question by valuing items at their *market values* — at the prices at which each item is traded in markets. If the price of an apple is 10 cents, the market value of 50 apples is $5. If the price of an orange is 20 cents, the market value of 100 oranges is $20. By using market prices to value production, we can add the apples and oranges together. The market value of 50 apples and 100 oranges is $5 plus $20, or $25.

Final Goods and Services To calculate GDP, we value the *final goods and services* produced. A **final good** (or service) is an item that is bought by its final user during a specified time period. It contrasts with an **intermediate good** (or service), which is an item that is produced by one firm, bought by another firm, and used as a component of a final good or service.

For example, a Ford SUV is a final good, but a Firestone tire on the SUV is an intermediate good. A Dell computer is a final good, but an Intel Pentium chip inside it is an intermediate good.

If we were to add the value of intermediate goods and services produced to the value of final goods and services, we would count the same thing many times — a problem called *double counting*. The value of an SUV already includes the value of the tires, and the value of a Dell PC already includes the value of the Pentium chip inside it.

Some goods can be an intermediate good in some situations and a final good in other situations. For example, the ice cream that you buy on a hot summer day is a final good, but the ice cream that a diner buys and uses to make sundaes is an intermediate good. The sundae is the final good. So whether a good is an intermediate good or a final good depends on what it is used for, not on what it is.

Produced Within a Country Only goods and services that are produced *within a country* count as part of that country's GDP. Nike Corporation, a U.S. firm, produces sneakers in Vietnam, and the market value of those shoes is part of Vietnam's GDP, not part of U.S. GDP. Toyota, a Japanese firm, produces automobiles in Georgetown, Kentucky, and the value of this production is part of U.S. GDP, not part of Japan's GDP.

In a Given Time Period GDP measures the value of production *in a given time period* — normally either a quarter of a year — called the quarterly GDP data — or a year — called the annual GDP data. Some components of GDP are measured for a period as short as a month, but we have no reliable monthly GDP data.

Businesses, such as AOL and Amazon, and governments use the quarterly GDP data to keep track of the short-term evolution of the economy. They use the annual GDP data to examine long-term trends and changes in production and the standard of living.

GDP measures not only the value of total production but also total income and total expenditure. The equality between the value of total production and total income is important because it shows the direct link between productivity and living standards. Our standard of living rises when our incomes rise and we can afford to buy more goods and services. But we must produce more goods and services if we are to be able to buy more goods and services.

Rising incomes and a rising value of production go together. They are two aspects of the same phenomenon — increasing productivity. To see why, we study the circular flow of expenditure and income.

GDP and the Circular Flow of Expenditure and Income

Figure 19.1 illustrates the circular flow of expenditure and income. The economy consists of households, firms, governments, and the rest of the world (the purple diamonds), which trade in factor markets, goods (and services) markets, and financial markets. We focus first on households and firms.

Households and Firms Households sell and firms buy the services of labor, capital, and land in factor markets. For these factor services, firms pay income to households: wages for labor services, interest for the use of capital, and rent for the use of land. A fourth factor of production, entrepreneurship, receives profit.

Firms' retained earnings — profits that are not distributed to households — are part of the household sector's income. You can think of retained

earnings as being income that households save and lend back to firms. Figure 19.1 shows the total income — *aggregate income* — received by households, including retained earnings, by the blue dots labeled *Y*.

Firms sell and households buy consumer goods and services — such as inline skates and haircuts — in the markets for goods and services. The total payment for these goods and services is **consumption expenditure**, shown by the red dots labeled *C*.

Firms buy and sell new capital equipment — such as computer systems, airplanes, trucks, and assembly line equipment — in the goods market. Some of what firms produce is not sold but is added to inventory. For example, if GM produces 1,000 cars and sells 950 of them, the other 50 cars remain in GM's inventory of unsold cars, which increases by 50 cars. When a firm adds unsold output to inventory, we can think of the firm as buying goods from

---

FIGURE 19.1   The Circular Flow of Expenditure and Income

Billions of dollars in 2001
C = 7,064
I = 1,634
G = 1,840
X – M = –330
Y = 10,208
C = 7,064
S =   944
T = 2,200
Y = 10,208

In the circular flow of expenditure and income, households make consumption expenditures (*C*); firms make investment expenditures (*I*); governments purchase goods and services (*G*); and the rest of the world purchases net exports (*X – M*) — (red flows). Households receive income (*Y*) from firms (blue flow).

Aggregate income (blue flow) equals aggregate expenditure (red flows). Households use their income to consume, (*C*), save (*S*), and pay net taxes (*T*). Firms borrow to finance their investment expenditures, and governments and the rest of the world borrow to finance their deficits or lend their surpluses (green flows).

Source: U.S. Department of Commerce, Bureau of Economic Analysis (March 2002).

itself. The purchase of new plant, equipment, and buildings and the additions to inventories are **investment**, shown by the red dots labeled *I*.

Governments Governments buy goods and services, called **government purchases**, from firms. In Fig. 19.1, government purchases of goods and services are shown as the red flow *G*. Governments use taxes to pay for their purchases. Figure 19.1 shows taxes as net taxes by the green dots labeled *T*. **Net taxes** are equal to taxes paid to governments minus transfer payments received from governments and minus interest payments on the governments' debt. *Transfer payments* are cash transfers from governments to households and firms such as social security benefits, unemployment compensation, and subsidies.

Rest of the World Firms sell goods and services to the rest of the world, **exports**, and buy goods and services from the rest of the world, **imports**. Exports (*X*) minus imports (*M*) are called **net exports**, which Fig. 19.1 shows by the red flow *X* − *M*.

If net exports are positive (if exports exceed imports), there is a net flow of goods and services from U.S. firms to the rest of the world. If net exports are negative (if imports exceed exports), there is net flow of goods and services from the rest of the world to U.S. firms.

GDP Equals Expenditure Equals Income Gross domestic product can be determined in two ways: By the total expenditure on goods and services or by the total income earned producing goods and services.

The total expenditure — *aggregate expenditure* — is the sum of the red flows in Fig. 19.1. Aggregate expenditure equals consumption expenditure plus investment plus government purchases plus net exports.

Aggregate income earned producing goods and services is equal to the total amount paid for the factors of production used — wages, interest, rent, and profit. This amount is shown by the blue flow in Fig. 19.1. Because firms pay out as incomes (including retained profits) everything they receive from the sale of their output, income (the blue flow) equals expenditure (the sum of the red flows). That is,

$$Y = C + I + G + X - M.$$

The table in Fig. 19.1 shows the numbers for 2001. You can see that the sum of the expenditures is $10,208 billion, which also equals aggregate income.

Because aggregate expenditure equals aggregate income, these two methods of valuing GDP give the same answer. So

GDP equals aggregate expenditure and equals aggregate income.

The circular flow model is the foundation on which the national economic accounts are built.

Financial Flows

The circular flow model also enables us to see the connection between the expenditure and income flows and flows through the financial markets that finance deficits and pay for investment. These flows are shown in green in Fig. 19.1. Household **saving** (*S*) is the amount that households have left after they have paid their taxes and bought their consumption goods and services. Government borrowing finances a government budget deficit. (Government lending arises when the government has a budget surplus.) And foreign borrowing pays for a deficit with the rest of the world. These financial flows are the sources of the funds that firms use to pay for their investment in new capital. Let's look a bit more closely at how investment is financed.

How Investment Is Financed

Investment adds to the stock of capital and is one of the determinants of the rate at which production grows. Investment is financed from three sources:

1. Private saving
2. Government budget surplus
3. Borrowing from the rest of the world

Private saving is the green flow labeled *S* in Fig. 19.1. Notice that households' income is consumed, saved, or paid in taxes. That is,

$$Y = C + S + T.$$

But you've seen that *Y* also equals the sum of the components of aggregate expenditure. That is,

$$Y = C + I + G + X - M.$$

By using these two equations, you can see that

$$I + G + X - M = S + T.$$

Now subtract *G* and *X* from both sides of the last equation and add *M* to both sides to obtain

$$I = S + (T - G) + (M - X).$$

In this equation, $(T - G)$ is the government budget surplus and $(M - X)$ is borrowing from the rest of the world.

If taxes (T) exceed government purchases (G), the government has a budget surplus equal to $(T - G)$, and this surplus contributes toward paying for investment. If taxes are less than government purchases, the government has a budget deficit equal to $(T - G)$, which is now negative. This deficit subtracts from the sources that finance investment.

If we import (M) more than we export (X), we borrow an amount equal to $(M - X)$ from the rest of the world. So part of the rest of the world's saving finances investment in the United States. If we export more than we import, we lend an amount equal to $(X - M)$ to the rest of the world. So part of U.S. saving is used to finance investment in other countries.

The sum of private saving, S, and government saving, $(T - G)$ is called **national saving**. So investment is financed by national saving and foreign borrowing.

Every year since the early 1980s, the United States has borrowed from the rest of the world — total foreign borrowing of more that $1.5 trillion over that period. In 2001, the United States increased its international debt by $330 billion.

Gross and Net Domestic Product

What does the "gross" in GDP mean? Gross means before accounting for the depreciation of capital. The opposite of gross is net, which means after accounting for the depreciation of capital. To understand what the depreciation of capital is and how it affects aggregate expenditure and income, we need to expand the accounting framework that we use and distinguish between flows and stocks.

Flows and Stocks in Macroeconomics A **flow** is a quantity per unit of time. The water that is running from an open faucet into a bathtub is a flow. So are the number of CDs that you buy during a month, and the amount of income that you earn during a month. GDP is a flow — the value of the goods and services produced in a country *during a given time period*. Saving and investment are also flows.

A **stock** is a quantity that exists at a point in time. The water in a bathtub is a stock. So are the number of CDs that you own, and the amount of money in your savings account. The two key stocks in macroeconomics are wealth and capital. And the

flows of saving and investment change these stocks. Let's see how.

Wealth and Saving **Wealth** is the value of all the things that people own. What people own, a stock, is related to what they earn, a flow. People earn an income, which is the amount they receive during a given time period from supplying the services of resources. Income that is left after paying taxes is either consumed or saved. *Consumption expenditure* is the amount spent on consumption goods and services. *Saving* is the amount of income remaining after consumption expenditures are met. So saving adds to wealth.

For example, suppose that at the end of the school year, you have $250 in a savings account and some textbooks that are worth $300. That's all you own. Your wealth is $550. Suppose that you take a summer job and earn an income of $5,000. You are extremely careful and spend only $1,000 through the summer on consumption goods and services. At the end of the summer, when school starts again, you have $4,250 in your savings account. Your wealth is now $4,550. Your wealth has increased by $4,000, which equals your saving of $4,000. Your saving of $4,000 equals your income of $5,000 minus your consumption expenditure of $1,000.

National wealth and national saving work just like this personal example. The wealth of a nation at the start of a year equals its wealth at the start of the previous year plus its saving during the year. Its saving equals its income minus its consumption expenditure.

Capital and Investment *Capital* is the plant, equipment, buildings, and inventories of raw materials and semifinished goods that are used to produce other goods and services. The amount of capital in the economy exerts a big influence on GDP.

Two flows change the stock of capital: investment and depreciation. *Investment*, the purchase of new capital, increases the stock of capital. (Investment includes additions to inventories.) **Depreciation** is the decrease in the stock of capital that results from wear and tear and obsolescence. Another name for depreciation is **capital consumption**. The total amount spent on purchases of new capital and on replacing depreciated capital is called **gross investment**. The amount by which the stock of capital increases is called **net investment**. Net investment equals gross investment minus depreciation.

FIGURE 19.2   Capital and Investment

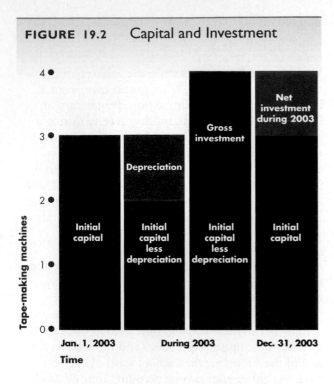

Tom's Tapes has a capital stock at the end of 2003 that equals its capital stock at the beginning of the year plus its net investment. Net investment is equal to gross investment less depreciation. Tom's gross investment is the 2 new machines bought during the year, and its depreciation is the 1 machine that Tom's scrapped during the year. Tom's net investment is 1 machine.

Figure 19.2 illustrates these concepts. On January 1, 2003, Tom's Tapes, Inc., had 3 machines. This quantity was its initial capital. During 2003, Tom's scrapped an older machine. This quantity is its depreciation. After depreciation, Tom's stock of capital was down to 2 machines. But also during 2003, Tom's bought 2 new machines. This amount is its gross investment. By December 31, 2003, Tom's Tapes had 4 machines, so its capital had increased by 1 machine. This amount is Tom's net investment. Tom's net investment equals its gross investment (the purchase of 2 new machines) minus its depreciation (1 machine scrapped).

The example of Tom's Tapes can be applied to the economy as a whole. The nation's capital stock decreases because capital depreciates and increases because of gross investment. The change in the nation's capital stock from one year to the next equals its net investment.

Back to the Gross in GDP We can now see the distinction between gross domestic product and net domestic product. On the income side of the flows that measure GDP, a firm's *gross* profit is its profit *before* subtracting *depreciation*. A firm's gross profit is part of aggregate income, so depreciation is counted as part of gross income and GDP. Similarly, on the expenditure side of the flows that measure GDP, *gross investment* includes depreciation, so depreciation is counted as part of aggregate expenditure, and total expenditure is a gross measure.

Net domestic product excludes depreciation. Like GDP, it can be viewed as the sum of incomes or expenditures. Net income includes firms' *net* profits — profits *after* subtracting depreciation. And net expenditure includes *net* investment, which also excludes depreciation.

The Short Term Meets the Long Term The flows and stocks that you've just studied influence GDP growth and fluctuations. One of the reasons why GDP grows is that the capital stock grows. Investment adds to capital, so GDP grows because of investment. But investment fluctuates, which brings fluctuations to GDP. So capital and investment along with wealth and saving are part of the key to understanding both the growth and the fluctuations of GDP.

Investment and saving interact with income and consumption expenditure in a circular flow of expenditure and income. In this circular flow, income equals expenditure, which also equals the value of production. This equality is the foundation on which a nation's economic accounts are built and from which its GDP is measured.

REVIEW QUIZ

1 Define GDP and distinguish between a final good and an intermediate good. Provide examples.
2 Why does GDP equal aggregate income and also equal aggregate expenditure?
3 How is U.S. investment financed? What determines national saving?
4 What is the distinction between gross and net?

Let's now see how the ideas that you've just studied are used in practice. We'll see how GDP and its components are measured in the United States today.

Measuring U.S. GDP

THE BUREAU OF ECONOMIC ANALYSIS (BEA) uses the concepts that you met in the circular flow model to measure GDP and its components in the *National Income and Product Accounts*. Because the value of aggregate output equals aggregate expenditure and aggregate income, there are two approaches available for measuring GDP, and both are used. They are

- The expenditure approach
- The income approach

The Expenditure Approach

The *expenditure approach* measures GDP as the sum of consumption expenditure (*C*), investment (*I*), government purchases of goods and services (*G*), and net exports of goods and services (*X – M*), corresponding to the red flows in the circular flow model in Fig. 19.1. Table 19.1 shows the result of this approach for 2001. The table uses the terms in the *National Income and Product Accounts*.

Personal consumption expenditures are the expenditures by households on goods and services produced in the United States and in the rest of the world. They include goods such as CDs and books and services such as banking and legal advice. They do *not* include the purchase of new homes, which is counted as part of investment. But they do include the purchase of consumer durable goods, which technically are capital like homes.

Gross private domestic investment is expenditure on capital equipment and buildings by firms and expenditure on new homes by households. It also includes the change in business inventories.

Government purchases of goods and services are the purchases of goods and services by all levels of government. This item includes expenditures on national defense and garbage collection. But it does *not* include *transfer payments* because they are not purchases of goods and services.

Net exports of goods and services are the value of exports minus the value of imports. This item includes computers that IBM sells to Volkswagen, the German auto producer (a U.S. export), and Japanese DVD players that Circuit City buys from Sony (a U.S. import).

Table 19.1 shows the relative magnitudes of the four items of aggregate expenditure.

TABLE 19.1 GDP: The Expenditure Approach

Item	Symbol	Amount in 2001 (billions of dollars)	Percentage of GDP
Personal consumption expenditures	*C*	7,064	69.2
Gross private domestic investment	*I*	1,634	16.0
Government purchases of goods and services	*G*	1,840	18.0
Net exports of goods and services	*X – M*	–330	–3.2
Gross domestic product	**Y**	**10,208**	**100.0**

The expenditure approach measures GDP as the sum of personal consumption expenditures (*C*), gross private domestic investment (*I*), government purchases of goods and services (*G*), and net exports (*X – M*). In 2001, GDP measured by the expenditure approach was $10,208 billion. Two thirds of aggregate expenditure is on personal consumption goods and services.

Source: U.S. Department of Commerce, Bureau of Economic Analysis.

The Income Approach

The *income approach* measures GDP by summing the incomes that firms pay households for the factors of production they hire — wages for labor, interest for capital, rent for land, and profits for entrepreneurship. Let's see how the income approach works.

The *National Income and Product Accounts* divide incomes into five categories:

1. Compensation of employees
2. Net interest
3. Rental income
4. Corporate profits
5. Proprietors' income

Compensation of employees is the payment for labor services. It includes net wages and salaries (called "take-home pay") that workers receive plus taxes withheld on earnings plus fringe benefits such as social security and pension fund contributions.

Net interest is the interest households receive on loans they make minus the interest households pay on their own borrowing.

Rental income is the payment for the use of land and other rented resources.

Corporate profits are the profits of corporations, some of which are paid to households in the form of dividends and some of which are retained by corporations as undistributed profits. They are all income.

Proprietors' income is a mixture of the previous four items. The BEA cannot split the income earned by the owner-operator of a business into compensation for labor, payment for the use of capital, and profit, so the BEA lumps them into this single category.

Table 19.2 shows these five incomes and their relative magnitudes.

The sum of the incomes is called *net domestic income at factor cost*. The term *factor cost* is used because it is the cost of the factors of production used to produce final goods. When we sum all the expenditures on final goods, we arrive at a total called *domestic product at market prices*. Market prices and factor cost would be the same except for indirect taxes and subsidies.

An *indirect tax* is a tax paid by consumers when they buy goods and services. (In contrast, a *direct tax* is a tax on income.) State sales taxes and taxes on alcohol, gasoline, and tobacco products are indirect taxes. Because of indirect taxes, consumers pay more for some goods and services than producers receive. Market price exceeds factor cost. For example, if the sales tax is 7 percent, when you buy a $1 chocolate bar you pay $1.07. The factor cost of the chocolate bar including profit is $1. The market price is $1.07.

A *subsidy* is a payment by the government to a producer. Payments made to grain growers and dairy farmers are subsidies. Because of subsidies, consumers pay less for some goods and services than producers receive. Factor cost exceeds market price.

To get from factor cost to market price, we add indirect taxes and subtract subsidies. Making this adjustment brings us one step closer to GDP, but it does not quite get us there.

The final step is to add depreciation (or capital consumption). You can see the reason for this adjustment by recalling the distinction between gross and net profit and between gross and net investment. Total income is a net number because it includes firms' net profits, which exclude depreciation. Total expenditure is a gross number because it includes gross investment. So to get from total income to GDP, we must add depreciation to total income.

TABLE 19.2   GDP: The Income Approach

Item	Amount in 2001 (billions of dollars)	Percentage of GDP
Compensation of employees	6,010	58.9
Net interest	554	5.4
Rental income	143	1.4
Corporate profits	767	7.5
Proprietors' income	744	7.3
Indirect taxes less subsidies	639	6.3
Capital consumption (depreciation)	1,351	13.2
Gross domestic product	**10, 208**	**100.0**

The sum of all incomes equals net domestic income at factor cost. GDP equals net domestic income at factor cost plus indirect taxes less subsidies plus capital consumption (depreciation). In 2001, GDP measured by the income approach was $10,208 billion. The compensation of employees — labor income — was by far the largest part of aggregate income.

Source: U.S. Department of Commerce, Bureau of Economic Analysis.

REVIEW QUIZ

1 What is the expenditure approach to measuring GDP?

2 What is the income approach to measuring GDP?

3 What adjustments must be made to total income to make it equal GDP?

You now know how GDP is defined and measured. The dollar value of GDP can change because either prices change or the volume of goods and services produced changes. You are next going to learn how we unscramble these two sources of change in GDP to reveal changes in the volume of goods and services produced — changes in what we call *real* GDP.

Real GDP and the Price Level

You've seen that GDP measures total expenditure on final goods and services in a given period. In 2001, GDP was $10,208 billion. The year before, in 2000, GDP was $9,873 billion. Because GDP in 2001 was greater than in 2000, we know that one or two things must have happened during 2001:

- We produced more goods and services in 2001 than in 2000.
- We paid higher prices for our goods and services in 2001 than we paid in 2000.

Producing more goods and services contributes to an improvement in our standard of living. Paying higher prices means that our cost of living has increased but our standard of living has not. So it matters a great deal why GDP has increased.

You're now going to learn how economists at the Bureau of Economic Analysis split GDP into two parts. One part tells us the change in production, and the other part tells us the change in prices. The method that is used has changed in recent years, and you are going to learn about the new method.

We measure the change in production by using a number that we call real GDP. **Real GDP** is the value of final goods and services produced in a given year when valued at constant prices. By comparing the value of the goods and services produced at constant prices, we can measure the change in the volume of production.

Calculating Real GDP

Table 19.3 shows the quantities produced and the prices in 2002 for an economy that produces only two goods: balls and bats. The first step toward calculating real GDP is to calculate **nominal GDP**, which is the value of the final goods and services produced in a given year valued at the prices that prevailed in that same year. Nominal GDP is just a more precise name for GDP that we use when we want to be emphatic that we are not talking about real GDP.

Nominal GDP Calculation To calculate nominal GDP in 2002, sum the expenditures on balls and bats in 2002 as follows:

Expenditure on balls = 100 balls × $1   = $100.
Expenditure on bats = 20 bats × $5   = $100.
Nominal GDP in 2002 = $100 + $100 = $200.

Table 19.4 shows the quantities produced and the prices in 2003. The quantity of balls produced increased to 160, and the quantity of bats produced increased to 22. The price of a ball fell to 50¢, and the price of a bat increased to $22.50. To calculate nominal GDP in 2003, we sum the expenditures on balls and bats in 2003 as follows:

Expenditure on balls = 160 balls × $0.50 = $80.
Expenditure on bats = 22 bats × $22.50 = $495.
Nominal GDP in 2003 = $80 + $495   = $575.

To calculate real GDP, we choose one year, called the *base year*, against which to compare the other years. In the United States today, the base year is 1996. The choice of the base year is not important. It is just a common reference point. We'll use 2002 as the base year. By definition, real GDP equals nominal GDP in the base year. So real GDP in 2002 is $200.

Base-Year Prices Value of Real GDP The base-year prices method of calculating real GDP, which is the traditional method, values the quantities produced in a year at the prices of the base year. Table 19.5 shows the prices for 2002 and the quantities in 2003 (based on the information in Tables 19.3 and 19.4).

TABLE 19.3	GDP Data for 2002	
Item	**Quantity**	**Price**
Balls	100	$1.00
Bats	20	$5.00

TABLE 19.4	GDP Data for 2003	
Item	**Quantity**	**Price**
Balls	160	$0.50
Bats	22	$22.50

TABLE 19.5	2003 Quantities and 2002 Prices	
Item	Quantity	Price
Balls	160	$1.00
Bats	22	$5.00

The value of the 2003 quantities at the 2002 prices is calculated as follows:

Expenditure on balls = 160 balls × $1.00 = $160.
Expenditure on bats = 22 bats × $5.00   = $110.
Value of the 2003 quantities at 2002 prices = $270.

Using the traditional base-year prices method, $270 would be recorded as real GDP in 2003.

Chain-Weighted Output Index Calculation The **chain-weighted output index** method, which is the new method of calculating real GDP, uses the prices of two adjacent years to calculate the real GDP growth rate. So to find the real GDP growth rate in 2003, we compare the quantities produced in 2002 and 2003 by using both the 2002 prices and the 2003 prices. We then average the two sets of numbers in a special way that we'll now describe.

To compare the quantities produced in 2002 and 2003 at 2003 prices, we need to calculate the value of 2002 quantities at 2003 prices. Table 19.6 summarizes these quantities and prices. The value of the 2002 quantities at the 2003 prices is calculated as follows:

Expenditure on balls = 100 balls × $0.50   = $50.
Expenditure on bats = 20 bats × $22.50   = $450.
Value of the 2002 quantities at 2003 prices = $500.

We now have two comparisons between 2002 and 2003. At the 2002 prices, the value of production

TABLE 19.6	2002 Quantities and 2003 Prices	
Item	Quantity	Price
Balls	100	$0.50
Bats	20	$22.50

increased from $200 in 2002 to $270 in 2003. The increase in value is $70, and the percentage increase is ($70 ÷ $200) × 100, which is 35 percent.

At the 2003 prices, the value of production increased from $500 in 2002 to $575 in 2003. The increase in value is $75, and the percentage increase is ($75 ÷ $500) × 100, which is 15 percent.

The new method of calculating real GDP uses the average of these two percentage increases. The average of 35 percent and 15 percent is (35 + 15) ÷ 2, which equals 25 percent. Real GDP is 25 percent greater in 2003 than in 2002. Real GDP in 2002 is $200, so real GDP in 2003 is $250.

Chain Linking The calculation that we've just described is repeated each year. Each year is compared with its preceding year. So in 2004, the calculations are repeated but using the prices and quantities of 2003 and 2004. Real GDP in 2004 equals real GDP in 2003 increased by the calculated percentage change in real GDP for 2004. For example, suppose that real GDP for 2004 is calculated to be 20 percent greater than that in 2003. You know that real GDP in 2003 is $250. So real GDP in 2004 is 20 percent greater than this value and is $300. In every year, real GDP is valued in base-year (2002) dollars.

By applying the calculated percentage change to the real GDP of the preceding real GDP, each year is linked back to the dollars of the base year like the links in a chain.

Calculating the Price Level

You've seen how real GDP is used to reveal the change in the quantity of goods and services produced. We're now going to see how we can find the change in prices that increases our cost of living.

The average level of prices is called the **price level**. One measure of the price level is the **GDP deflator**, which is an average of current year prices expressed as a percentage of base-year prices. We calculate the GDP deflator by using nominal GDP and real GDP in the formula:

GDP deflator = (Nominal GDP ÷ Real GDP) × 100.

You can see why the GDP deflator is a measure of the price level. If nominal GDP rises but real GDP remains unchanged, it must be that the price level has risen. The formula gives a higher value for the GDP deflator. The larger the nominal GDP for a

TABLE 19.7   Calculating the GDP Deflator

Year	Nominal GDP	Real GDP	GDP Deflator
2002	$200	$200	100
2003	$575	$250	230

given real GDP, the higher is the price level and the larger is the GDP deflator.

Table 19.7 shows how the GDP deflator is calculated. In 2002, the deflator is 100. In 2003, it is 230, which equals nominal GDP of $575 divided by real GDP of $250 and then multiplied by 100.

Deflating the GDP Balloon

You can think of GDP as a balloon that is blown up by growing production and rising prices. In Fig. 19.3, the GDP deflator lets the inflation air out of the nominal GDP balloon — the contribution of rising prices — so that we can see what has happened to *real* GDP. The red balloon for 1991 shows real GDP

in that year. The green balloon shows *nominal* GDP in 2001. The red balloon for 2001 shows real GDP for that year. To see real GDP in 2001, we *deflate* nominal GDP using the GDP deflator.

> **R E V I E W   Q U I Z**
>
> 1 What is the distinction between nominal GDP and real GDP?
> 2 What is the traditional method of calculating real GDP?
> 3 What is the new method of calculating real GDP?
> 4 How is the GDP deflator calculated?

You now know how to calculate real GDP and the GDP deflator. Your next task is to learn how to use real GDP to calculate economic growth and to make economic welfare comparisons. We also look at some limitations of real GDP as a measure of economic welfare and as a tool for comparing living standards across countries.

FIGURE 19.3   The U.S. GDP Balloon

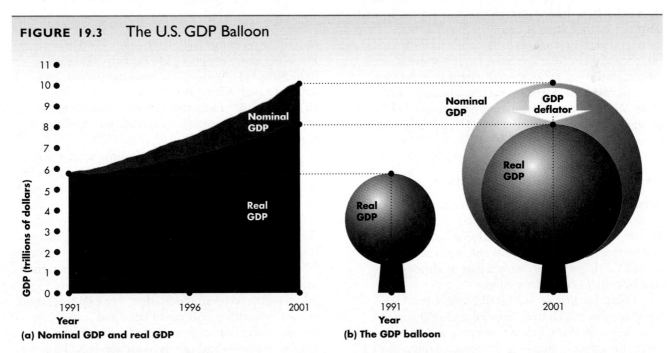

(a) Nominal GDP and real GDP

(b) The GDP balloon

Part of the rise in GDP comes from inflation and part from increased production — an increase in real GDP. The GDP deflator lets some air out of the GDP balloon so that we can see the extent to which production has increased.

Source: U.S. Department of Commerce, Bureau of Economic Analysis (March 2002).

Measuring Economic Growth

WE USE ESTIMATES OF REAL GDP TO CALCULATE the economic growth rate. The **economic growth rate** is the percentage change in the quantity of goods and services produced from one year to the next. To calculate the economic growth rate, we use the formula:

$$\text{Economic growth rate} = \frac{\text{Real GDP this year} - \text{Real GDP last year}}{\text{Real GDP last year}} \times 100.$$

For example, real GDP was $9,334 billion in 2001 and $9,224 billion in 2000. So the economic growth rate (percent per year) during 2001 was:

$$\text{Economic growth rate} = \frac{(\$9,334 - \$9,224)}{\$9,224} \times 100$$

$$= 1.2 \text{ percent per year.}$$

We want to measure the economic growth rate so that we can make

- Economic welfare comparisons
- International comparisons
- Business cycle forecasts

Although the real GDP growth rate is used for these three purposes, it is not a perfect measure for any of them. Nor is it a totally misleading measure. We'll evaluate the limitations of real GDP and its growth rate in each of the three cases.

Economic Welfare Comparisons

Economic welfare is a comprehensive measure of the general state of economic well-being. Economic welfare improves when the production of *all* the goods and services grows. The goods and services that make up real GDP growth are only a part of all the items that influence economic welfare.

Today, because of real GDP growth, real GDP per person in the United States of $33,000 is twice what it was in 1966. But are we twice as well off? Does this growth of real GDP provide a full and accurate measure of the change in economic welfare?

It does not. The reason is that economic welfare depends on many other factors that are not measured by real GDP or that are not measured accurately by real GDP. Some of these factors are

- Overadjustment for inflation
- Household production
- Underground economic activity
- Health and life expectancy
- Leisure time
- Environment quality
- Political freedom and social justice

Overadjustment for Inflation The price indexes that are used to measure inflation give an upward-biased estimate of true inflation. (You will learn about the sources of this bias on p. 469.) If we overestimate the rise in prices, we underestimate the growth of real GDP. When car prices rise because cars have gotten better (safer, more fuel efficient, more comfortable), the GDP deflator counts the price increase as inflation. So what is really an increase in production is counted as an increase in price rather than an increase in real GDP. It is deflated away by the wrongly measured higher price level. The magnitude of this bias is probably less than 1 percentage point a year, but its exact magnitude is not known.

Household Production An enormous amount of production takes place every day in our homes. Preparing meals, cleaning the kitchen, changing a light bulb, cutting the grass, washing the car, and helping a high school student with homework are all examples of productive activities that do not involve market transactions and are not counted as part of GDP.

If these activities grew at the same rate as real GDP, not measuring them would not be a problem. But it is likely that market production, which is part of GDP, is increasingly replacing household production, which is not part of GDP. Two trends point in this direction. One is the number of people who have jobs, which has increased from 60 percent in 1970 to 67 percent in 2001. The other is the trend in the purchase of traditionally home-produced goods and services in the market. For example, more and more families now eat in fast-food restaurants — one of the fastest-growing industries in the United States — and use day-care services. This trend means that an increasing proportion of food preparation and child care that were part of household production are now measured as part of GDP. So real GDP grows more rapidly than does real GDP plus home production.

Underground Economic Activity The *underground economy* is the part of the economy that is purposely hidden from the view of the government to avoid taxes and regulations or because the goods and services being produced are illegal. Because underground economic activity is unreported, it is omitted from GDP.

The underground economy is easy to describe, even if it is hard to measure. It includes the production and distribution of illegal drugs, production that uses illegal labor that is paid less than the minimum wage, and jobs done for cash to avoid paying income taxes. This last category might be quite large and includes tips earned by cab drivers, hairdressers, and hotel and restaurant workers.

Estimates of the scale of the underground economy range between 9 and 30 percent of GDP ($800 billion to $2,800 billion) in the United States and much more in some countries. It is particularly large in some Eastern European countries that are making a transition from communist economic planning to a market economy.

Provided that the underground economy is a reasonably stable proportion of the total economy, the growth rate of real GDP still gives a useful estimate of changes in economic welfare. But sometimes, production shifts from the underground economy to the rest of the economy, and sometimes it shifts the other way. The underground economy expands relative to the rest of the economy if taxes become especially high or if regulations become especially restrictive. And the underground economy shrinks relative to the rest of the economy if the burdens of taxes and regulations are eased. During the 1980s, when tax rates were cut, there was an increase in the reporting of previously hidden income and tax revenues increased. So some part (but probably a very small part) of the expansion of real GDP during the 1980s represented a shift from the underground economy rather than an increase in production.

Health and Life Expectancy Good health and a long life — the hopes of everyone — do not show up in real GDP, at least not directly. A higher real GDP does enable us to spend more on medical research, health care, a good diet, and exercise equipment. And as real GDP has increased, our life expectancy has lengthened — from 70 years at the end of World War II to approaching 80 years today. Infant deaths and death in childbirth, two fearful scourges of the nineteenth century, have almost been eliminated.

But we face new health and life expectancy problems every year. AIDS and drug abuse are taking young lives at a rate that causes serious concern. When we take these negative influences into account, we see that real GDP growth overstates the improvements in economic welfare.

Leisure Time Leisure time is an economic good that adds to our economic welfare. Other things being equal, the more leisure we have, the better off we are. Our working time is valued as part of GDP, but our leisure time is not. Yet from the point of view of economic welfare, that leisure time must be at least as valuable to us as the wage that we earn on the last hour worked. If it was not, we would work instead of taking the leisure. Over the years, leisure time has steadily increased. The workweek has become shorter, more people take early retirement, and the number of vacation days has increased. These improvements in economic well-being are not reflected in real GDP.

Environment Quality Economic activity directly influences the quality of the environment. The burning of hydrocarbon fuels is the most visible activity that damages our environment. But it is not the only example. The depletion of exhaustible resources, the mass clearing of forests, and the pollution of lakes and rivers are other major environmental consequences of industrial production.

Resources that are used to protect the environment are valued as part of GDP. For example, the value of catalytic converters that help to protect the atmosphere from automobile emissions are part of GDP. But if we did not use such pieces of equipment and instead polluted the atmosphere, we would not count the deteriorating air that we were breathing as a negative part of GDP.

An industrial society possibly produces more atmospheric pollution than an agricultural society does. But pollution does not always increase as we become wealthier. Wealthy people value a clean environment and are willing to pay for one. Compare the pollution that was discovered in East Germany in the late 1980s with pollution in the United States. East Germany, a poor country, polluted its rivers, lakes, and atmosphere in a way that is unimaginable in the United States or in wealthy West Germany.

Political Freedom and Social Justice Most people in the Western world value political freedoms such as those provided by the U.S. Constitution. And they value social justice or fairness — equality of opportunity and of access to social security safety nets that protect people from the extremes of misfortune.

A country might have a very large real GDP per person but have limited political freedom and equity. For example, a small elite might enjoy political liberty and extreme wealth while the vast majority are effectively enslaved and live in abject poverty. Such an economy would generally be regarded as having less economic welfare than one that had the same amount of real GDP but in which political freedoms were enjoyed by everyone. Today, China has rapid real GDP growth but limited political freedoms, while Russia has slow real GDP growth and an emerging democratic political system. Economists have no easy way to determine which of these countries is better off.

The Bottom Line Do we get the wrong message about the growth in economic welfare by looking at the growth of real GDP? The influences that are omitted from real GDP are probably important and could be large. Developing countries have a larger underground economy and a larger amount of household production than do developed countries. So as an economy develops and grows, part of the apparent growth might reflect a switch from underground to regular production and from home production to market production. This measurement error overstates the rate of economic growth and the improvement in economic welfare.

Other influences on living standards include the amount of leisure time available, the quality of the environment, the security of jobs and homes, and the safety of city streets. It is possible to construct broader measures that combine the many influences that contribute to human happiness. Real GDP will be one element in those broader measures, but it will by no means be the whole of them.

International Comparisons

All the problems we've just reviewed affect economic welfare of every country, so to make international comparisons of economic welfare, factors additional to real GDP must be used. But real GDP comparisons are major components of international welfare comparisons, and two special problems arise in making these comparisons. First, the real GDP of one country must be converted into the same currency units as the real GDP of the other country. Second, the same prices must be used to value the goods and services in the countries being compared. Let's look at these two problems by using a striking example, a comparison of the United States and China.

In 1992 (the most recent year for which we can make this comparison), real GDP per person in the United States was $24,408. The official Chinese statistics published by the International Monetary Fund say that real GDP per person in China in 1992 was 2,028 yuan. (The yuan is the currency of China.) On the average, during 1992, $1 U.S. was worth 5.762 yuan. If we use this exchange rate to convert Chinese yuan into U.S. dollars, we get a value of $352.

The official comparison of China and the United States makes China look extremely poor. In 1992, real GDP per person in the United States was 69 times that in China.

Figure 19.4 shows the official story of real GDP in China from 1980 to 1998. Figure 19.4 also shows another story based on an estimate of real GDP per person that is much larger than the official measure. Let's see how this alternative measurement is made.

GDP in the United States is measured by using prices that prevail in the United States. China's GDP is measured by using prices that prevail in China. But the relative prices in the two countries are very different. Some goods that are expensive in the United States cost very little in China. These items get a small weight in China's real GDP. If, instead of using China's prices, all the goods and services produced in China are valued at the prices prevailing in the United States, then a more valid comparison can be made of GDP in the two countries. Such a comparison uses prices called *purchasing power parity prices.*

Robert Summers and Alan Heston, economists in the Center for International Comparisons at the University of Pennsylvania, have used purchasing power parity prices to construct real GDP data for more than 100 countries. These data, which are published in the Penn World Table (PWT), tell a remarkable story about China. The PWT data use 1985 as the base year, so they are measured in 1985 dollars. According to the PWT, in 1992, real GDP per person in the United States was 12 times that of China, not the 69 times shown in the official data.

Figure 19.4 shows the PWT view of China's real GDP and compares it with the official view. The difference in the two views arises from the prices used. The official statistics use Chinese prices, while the PWT data use purchasing power parity prices.

Another China scholar, Thomas Rawski of the University of Pittsburgh, doubts both sets of data

FIGURE 19.4   Two Views of Real GDP in China

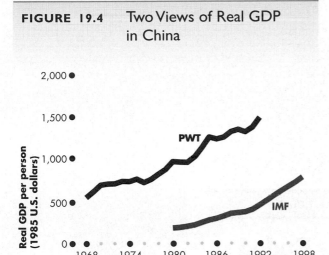

According to the official statistics of the International Monetary Fund (IMF) and the World Bank, China is a poor developing country. But according to an alternative view, Penn World Table (PWT), which is based on purchasing power parity prices, China's real GDP is more than 6 times the official view. Yet other China scholars think that even the official numbers are too big. So there is much uncertainty about China's real GDP.

Sources: World Economic Outlook, 2001 (Washington, D.C.: International Monetary Fund); The Penn World Table (Mark 5.6).

shown in Fig. 19.4. He believes that the growth rate of China's real GDP has been exaggerated for some years and that even the official data overstate real GDP in China.

U.S. real GDP is measured pretty reliably. But China's is not. The alternative measures of China's real GDP are unreliable, and the truth about GDP in China is not known. But China is expanding, and many businesses are paying close attention to the prospects of expanding their activities in China and other fast-growing Asian economies.

Business Cycle Forecasts

If policymakers plan to raise interest rates to slow an expansion that they believe is too strong, they look at the latest estimates of real GDP. But suppose that for the reasons that we've just discussed, real GDP is mismeasured. Does this mismeasurement hamper our ability to identify the phases of the business cycle? It

does not. The reason is that although the omissions from real GDP do change over time, they probably do not change in a systematic way with the business cycle. So inaccurate measurement of real GDP does not necessarily cause a wrong assessment of the phase of the business cycle.

The fluctuations in economic activity measured by real GDP tell a reasonably accurate story about the phase of the business cycle that the economy is in. When real GDP grows, the economy is in a business cycle expansion; when real GDP shrinks (for two quarters), the economy is in a recession. Also, as real GDP fluctuates, so do production and jobs.

But real GDP fluctuations probably exaggerate or overstate the fluctuations in total production and economic welfare. The reason is that when business activity slows in a recession, household production increases and so does leisure time. When business activity speeds up in an expansion, household production and leisure time decrease. Because household production and leisure time increase in a recession and decrease in an expansion, real GDP fluctuations tend to overstate the fluctuations in total production and in economic welfare. But the directions of change of real GDP, total production, and economic welfare are probably the same.

REVIEW QUIZ

1 Does real GDP measure economic welfare? If not, why not?

2 Does real GDP measure total production of goods and services? If not, what are the main omissions?

3 How can we make valid international comparisons of real GDP?

4 Does the growth of real GDP measure the economic growth rate accurately?

5 Do the fluctuations in real GDP measure the business cycle accurately?

◆ You've now studied the methods used to measure GDP, economic growth, and the price level. And you've learned about some of the limitations of these measures. *Reading Between the Lines* on pp. 448–449 looks at real GDP in the recent U.S. slowdown.

Your next task is to learn how we measure employment and unemployment and inflation.

Real GDP in 2001

LOS ANGELES TIMES, NOVEMBER 1, 2001

Economic Expansion Has Ended

The U.S. economy shrank from July through September for the first such contraction since 1993, the Commerce Department said Wednesday. The decline ended the longest economic expansion in American history and almost surely signals an economy in recession.

The gross domestic product, the value of all goods and services produced in the United States, contracted at a 0.4% annual rate. Though it was a milder decline than many analysts had predicted, there was little celebration.

...

The country has been unable to muster better than a 1.5% growth rate during the last year, a far cry from the glory days of 1997 through the middle of 2000, when it regularly posted 4%-plus rates. The economy has expanded every year since 1991, the longest stretch of growth since the country began keeping records in the mid-19th century.

...

Some elements of the economy held up better than expected during the last quarter. Consumer spending rose at a 1.2% rate rather than falling, as many analysts had predicted. But the increase, less than half the 2.5% rate of the previous quarter, appeared to have been largely the product of steep price cuts by business.

...

Consumer willingness to spend did not translate into business readiness to invest and maintain inventories. Business investment dropped at an 11.9% annual rate from July through September, following a 14.6% decline in the previous quarter.

Corporate America's decision to shrink inventories accounted for virtually all of the decline in GDP from July through September, according to government statistics. Companies reduced their stock of goods on hand by $50.4 billion during the third quarter, following declines of $38.3 billion in the second quarter and $27.1 billion in the first quarter.

Both imports and exports fell sharply in the latest quarter, a sign of economic weakness both here and abroad, according to analysts. Government figures showed imports fell 15.2% after slipping 8.4% in the previous quarter.

Exports plunged 16.6%, after an 11.9% fall the previous quarter.

...

Essence of the Story

■ GDP grew from 1993 through 2000, the longest stretch of growth since records began in the mid-19th century.

■ The GDP growth rate in 2000 was 1.5 percent compared with 4 percent or more a year from 1997 through mid–2000.

■ GDP shrank at a 0.4 percent annual rate during the third quarter (July–September) of 2001, for the first decrease since 1993.

■ During the third quarter of 2001 and expressed at annual rates, consumer spending *rose* by 1.2 percent, business investment fell by 11.9 percent, imports fell by 15.2 percent, and exports fell by 16.6 percent. Business inventories fell by $50.4 billion.

Economic Analysis

■ This news article reports the real GDP numbers for the third quarter of 2001.

■ The data for this quarter were the first to show a decrease in real GDP since the recession of the early 1990s.

■ The National Bureau of Economic Research says that the U.S. economy went into recession some time in March 2001, but this assessment is based on employment, disposable income, and industrial production rather than on real GDP.

■ Figure 1 shows the real GDP growth rate (annualized) quarter by quarter from the first quarter of 1995 to the fourth quarter of 2001.

■ You can see the spectacular growth rates of the 1990s, and you can see a slowing of the growth rate during 2000.

■ Figure 2 shows the components of real GDP. You can see that most of the growth of real GDP comes from consumption growth and that, during 2000 and 2001, investment, shown by the red bars, decreased.

■ Viewed from the perspective of 2002, the 2001 recession looks mild.

■ Figure 3 emphasizes the mildness of the 2001 recession. In the third quarter of 2001, real GDP was only 0.3 percent below the level of March 2001, the month in which the NBER says the economy was at a business cycle peak.

■ At a similar point in the average of the previous six recessions, real GDP was 1.3 percent below its peak.

Figure 1 Real GDP growth rates: 1995–2001

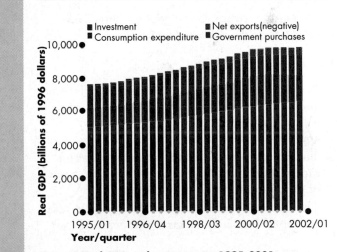

Figure 2 Real GDP and components: 1995–2001

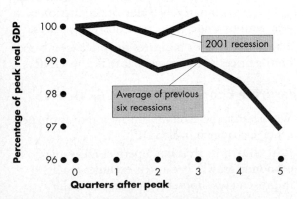

Figure 3 Where is the 2001 recession?

449

SUMMARY

KEY POINTS

Gross Domestic Product (pp. 434–438)

- GDP, or gross domestic product, is the market value of all the final goods and services produced in a country during a given period.
- A final good is an item that is bought by its final user during a specified time period, and contrasts with an intermediate good, which is a component of a final good.
- GDP is calculated by using the expenditure and income totals in the circular flow of expenditure and income.
- Aggregate expenditure on goods and services equals aggregate income and GDP.

Measuring U.S. GDP (pp. 439–440)

- Because aggregate expenditure, aggregate income, and the value of aggregate production are equal, we can measure GDP by using the expenditure approach or the income approach.
- The expenditure approach sums consumption expenditure, investment, government purchases of goods and services, and net exports.
- The income approach sums wages, interest, rent, and profit (and indirect taxes and depreciation).

Real GDP and the Price Level (pp. 441–443)

- Real GDP is measured by a chain-weighted output index that compares the value of production each year with its value at the previous year's prices.
- The GDP deflator measures the price level based on the prices of the items that make up GDP.

Measuring Economic Growth (pp. 444–447)

- We measure the economic growth rate as the percentage change in real GDP.
- Real GDP growth is not a perfect measure of economic growth because it excludes quality improvements, household production, the underground economy, environmental damage, health and life expectancy, leisure time, political freedom, and social justice.
- The growth rate of real GDP gives a good indication of the phases of the business cycle.

KEY FIGURES AND TABLES

KEY TERMS

PROBLEMS

*1. The figure at the bottom of the page shows the flows of expenditure and income on Lotus Island. During 2002, A was $20 million, B was $60 million, C was $24 million, D was $30 million, and E was $6 million. Calculate
   a. Aggregate expenditure.
   b. Aggregate income.
   c. GDP.
   d. Government budget deficit.
   e. Household saving.
   f. Government saving.
   g. National saving.
   h. Borrowing from the rest of the world.

2. In problem 1, during 2003, A was $25 million, B was $100 million, C was $30 million, D was $30 million, and E was –$10 million. Calculate the quantities in problem 1 during 2003.

*3. Martha owns a copy shop that has 10 copiers. One copier wears out each year and is replaced. In addition, this year Martha will expand her business to 14 copiers. Calculate Martha's initial capital stock, depreciation, gross investment, net investment, and final capital stock.

4. Wendy operates a weaving shop with 20 looms. One loom wears out each year and is replaced. But this year, Wendy will expand her business to 24 looms. Calculate Wendy's initial capital stock, depreciation, gross investment, net investment, and final capital stock.

*5. The transactions in Ecoland last year were

Item	Dollars
Wages paid to labor	800,000
Consumption expenditure	600,000
Taxes	250,000
Transfer payments	50,000
Profits	200,000
Investment	250,000
Government purchases	200,000
Exports	300,000
Saving	300,000
Imports	250,000

   a. Calculate Ecoland's GDP.
   b. Did you use the expenditure approach or the incomes approach to make this calculation?
   c. How is investment financed?

6. The transactions in Highland last year were

Item	Dollars
Wages paid to labor	400,000
Consumption expenditure	350,000
Net taxes	125,000
Profits	140,000
Investment	150,000
Government purchases	130,000
Exports	120,000
Saving	135,000
Imports	140,000

   a. Calculate Highland's GDP.
   b. What extra information do you need to calculate net domestic product at factor cost?
   c. Where does Highland get the funds to finance its investment?

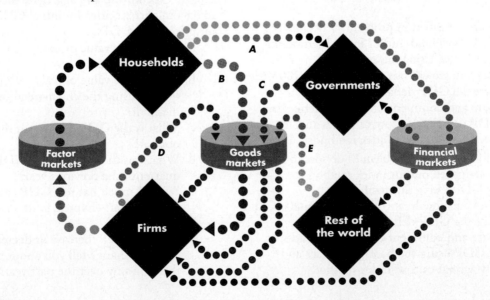

*7. Bananaland produces only bananas and sunscreen. The base year is 2002, and the tables give the quantities produced and prices.

| | Quantity | |
Good	2002	2003
Bananas	1,000 bunches	1,100 bunches
Sunscreen	500 bottles	525 bottles

| | Price | |
Good	2002	2003
Bananas	$2 a bunch	$3 a bunch
Sunscreen	$10 a bottle	$8 a bottle

Calculate Bananaland's
a. Nominal GDP in 2002 and 2003.
b. Real GDP in 2003 using the base-year prices method.

8. Sea Island produces only lobsters and crabs. The base year is 2003, and the tables give the quantities produced and the prices.

| | Quantity | |
Good	2003	2004
Lobsters	1,000	1,100
Crabs	500	525

| | Price | |
Good	2003	2004
Lobsters	$20 each	$25 each
Crabs	$10 each	$12 each

Calculate Sea Island's
a. Nominal GDP in 2003 and 2004.
b. Real GDP in 2004 using the base-year prices method.

*9. Bananaland (described in problem 7) decides to use the chain-weighted output index method to calculate real GDP. Using this method:
a. Calculate the growth rate of real GDP in 2003.
b. Calculate the GDP deflator in 2003.
c. Compare and comment on the differences in real GDP using the base-year prices and chain-weighted output index methods.

10. Sea Island (described in problem 8) decides to use the chain-weighted output index method to calculate real GDP. Using this method:
a. Calculate the growth rate of real GDP in 2004.
b. Calculate the GDP deflator in 2004.
c. Compare and comment on the differences in real GDP using the base-year prices and chain-weighted output index methods.

CRITICAL THINKING

Study *Reading Between the Lines* on pp. 448–449 and then answer the following questions:
a. In how many quarters did real GDP shrink during 2001?
b. How would you describe the growth of real GDP in 2001 compared to that in 2000 and the years between 1996 and 1999?
c. Which component of aggregate expenditure was the largest during 2001?
d. Which component of aggregate expenditure grew fastest during 2001?
e. What happened to business inventories during 2001?
f. Where, in the circular flow, do changes in business inventories appear?
g. What happened to net exports during 2001? Did the United States increase or decrease its net borrowing from the rest of the world during that year?
h. Compare and comment on the recession of 2001 and the average of the six previous recessions.

WEB EXERCISES

Use the link on your Parkin Web site to visit the Bureau of Economic Analysis. There you can obtain all the available data on GDP and the components of aggregate expenditure and aggregate income. You will find data in current price (nominal GDP) and constant prices (real GDP).
a. What is the value of nominal GDP in the current quarter?
b. What is the value of real GDP in the current quarter using the chain-weighted index method?
c. What is the GDP deflator in the current quarter?
d. What was the value of real GDP in the same quarter of the previous year?
e. By how much has real GDP changed over the past year? (Express your answer as a percentage.)
f. Did real GDP increase or decrease and what does the change tell you about the state of the economy over the past year?

MONITORING CYCLES, JOBS, AND THE PRICE LEVEL

Vital Signs

The U.S. economy went into recession during March 2001. What exactly is a recession, who decides when it begins and ends, and what criteria are used to make these decisions? ◆ Each month, we chart the course of the unemployment rate as a measure of U.S. economic health. How do we measure the unemployment rate? What does it tell us? Is it a reliable vital sign for the economy? ◆ We also chart every month the number of people working, the number of hours they work, and the wages they receive. Are most new jobs full time or part time? And are they high-wage jobs or low-wage jobs? ◆ As the U.S. economy went into recession in 2001, these questions about the health of the labor market became of vital importance to millions of American families. We put the spotlight on the labor market during the 2001 recession in *Reading Between the Lines* at the end of this chapter. ◆ Having a good job that pays a decent wage is only half of the equation that translates into a good standard of living. The other half is the cost of living. We track the cost of the items that we buy with another number that is published every month, the Consumer Price Index, or CPI. What is the CPI? How is it calculated? And does it provide a reliable guide to the changes in our cost of living?

◇ These are the questions we study in this chapter. We begin by looking at the way in which a recession is identified and dated.

After studying this chapter, you will be able to

- Explain how we date business cycles
- Define the unemployment rate, the labor force participation rate, the employment-to-population ratio, and aggregate hours
- Describe the sources of unemployment, its duration, the groups most affected by it, and how it fluctuates over a business cycle
- Explain how we measure the price level and the inflation rate using the CPI

The Business Cycle

WE DEFINED THE BUSINESS CYCLE IN CHAPTER 1 as the periodic but irregular up-and-down movement in production and jobs. A business cycle has two phases — expansion and recession — and two turning points — peak and trough. The National Bureau of Economic Research (NBER) Business Cycle Dating Committee identifies and dates the phases of the cycle in the United States. The NBER defines the phases and turning points of the cycle as follows.

A **recession** is a significant decline in activity spread across the economy, lasting more than a few months, visible in industrial production, employment, real income, and wholesale-retail trade. A recession begins just after the economy reaches a **peak** of activity and ends as the economy reaches its **trough**. Between trough and peak, the economy is in an **expansion**.[1]

Real GDP is the broadest measure of economic activity, and another popular working definition of a recession is a decrease in real GDP that lasts for at least two quarters. But we don't measure real GDP each month, so the NBER does not use the real GDP numbers. Instead, it looks at employment, which is the broadest *monthly* indicator of economic activity, along with other monthly measures that include personal income, sales of manufactures, and industrial production.

The NBER Dating Committee waits until it sees a large enough decline before declaring that a recession has begun and until it sees a large enough expansion before declaring that a recession has ended.

Business Cycle Dates

Each recession, expansion, and turning point has been dated by the NBER, which has identified 16 recessions and expansions since 1920. Table 20.1 lists the dates of their peaks and troughs, and on the average, recessions have lasted for just over a year and real GDP has fallen from peak to trough by more than 6 percent. Expansions have lasted for almost 4 years on the average, and real GDP has increased from trough to peak by an average of 22 percent.

But the averages hide huge variations from one cycle to another. The Great Depression, which began

with a recession that ran from August 1929 to March 1933, was the most severe contraction of economic activity ever experienced. Over a 43-month period, real GDP shrank by 33 percent. The second most severe recession was also in the 1930s. Another relatively severe fall in real GDP occurred at the end of World War II in 1945. The only other recession that comes close to these is that of 1974–1975, which resulted from a fourfold rise in the price of oil, lasted for 16 months, and saw real GDP fall by 5 percent. The other recessions since 1950, including the 2001–2002 recession, have been much milder than those of the 1930s. The biggest expansion occurred during World War II, but the longest was in the 1990s. Other big expansions were in the 1960s and 1980s. There is no correlation between the length of an expansion and the length of the preceding recession.

Figure 20.1 shows the range of variation across the different recessions and expansions. Figure 20.1

TABLE 20.1	Business Cycle Reference Dates
Trough	**Peak**
March 1919	January 1920
July 1921	May 1923
July 1924	October 1926
November 1927	August 1929
March 1933	May 1937
June 1938	February 1945
October 1945	November 1948
October 1949	July 1953
May 1954	August 1957
April 1958	April 1960
February 1961	December 1969
November 1970	November 1973
March 1975	January 1980
July 1980	July 1981
November 1982	July 1990
March 1991	March 2001

Sixteen cycles between 1920 and 2001 had average recessions that lasted for a bit more than a year and expansions that had average lengths of almost 4 years. Recessions have been getting shorter and expansions longer.

Source: National Bureau of Economic Research.

---

[1] "The NBER's Business-Cycle Dating Procedure," January 10, 2002, NBER Web site (www.nber.org). (Boldfacing of key terms added.)

FIGURE 20.1   Business Cycle Patterns

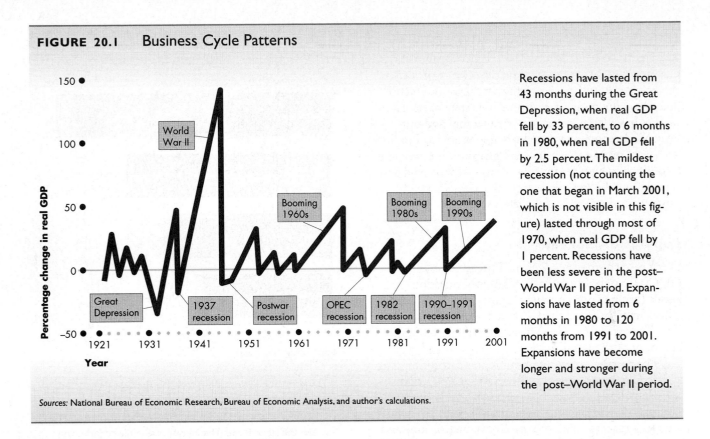

Recessions have lasted from 43 months during the Great Depression, when real GDP fell by 33 percent, to 6 months in 1980, when real GDP fell by 2.5 percent. The mildest recession (not counting the one that began in March 2001, which is not visible in this figure) lasted through most of 1970, when real GDP fell by 1 percent. Recessions have been less severe in the post–World War II period. Expansions have lasted from 6 months in 1980 to 120 months from 1991 to 2001. Expansions have become longer and stronger during the post–World War II period.

Sources: National Bureau of Economic Research, Bureau of Economic Analysis, and author's calculations.

shows the total percentage change in real GDP during successive recessions and expansions. The figure also shows that expansions last much longer than recessions. Expansions are the normal state of the economy. Recessions are relatively short-lived interruptions of that normal process.

The 2001–2002 Recession

The NBER identified March 2001 as the month in which the most recent recession began. But as you will see in *Reading Between the Lines* on pp. 470–471, the recession looks like the mildest ever experienced. Of the major indicators of recession that the NBER committee considers, only employment peaked in March 2001. Industrial production had already peaked in the summer of 2000. Manufacturing trade sales fluctuated erratically during 2001 and had no clear direction. Personal incomes continued to rise and eventually peaked in the fall of 2001.

Another interesting aspect of the 2001 recession is that as the year progressed and real GDP data became available, this broadest of indicators of economic performance showed only a one-quarter dip. Real GDP continued to rise during the second quarter of 2001,

fell in the third quarter, and then rose again in the fourth quarter. A recession would usually see a two-quarter or longer-lasting decrease in real GDP.

At the beginning of 2002, most people thought that the recession was almost over. Others were less optimistic. And a small number of economists were even saying that the real recession had not yet begun. They pointed to large debts, failing corporations such as Enron, overvalued stocks, and a low saving rate as signs of a further deterioration of economic performance in the near future. With our current level of understanding of the causes of the business cycle, no one could be sure which of these visions of the future would turn out to be correct.

REVIEW QUIZ

1 What are the phases of the business cycle?
2 How do we know when a recession has begun?
3 How do we know when a recession has ended?
4 Have recessions been getting worse?
5 What was unusual about the 2001 recession?

Jobs and Wages

YOU HAVE SEEN THAT EMPLOYMENT IS ONE OF the key features of the economy that helps the NBER determine the onset of recession. The state of the labor market has a large impact on our incomes and our lives. We become concerned when jobs are hard to find and more relaxed when they are plentiful. But we want a good job, which means that we want a well-paid and interesting job. You are now going to learn how economists track the health of the labor market.

Population Survey

Every month, the U.S. Census Bureau surveys 60,000 households and asks a series of questions about the age and job market status of its members. This survey is called the Current Population Survey. The Census Bureau uses the answers to describe the anatomy of the labor force.

Figure 20.2 shows the population categories used by the Census Bureau and the relationships among the categories. It divides the population into two groups: the working-age population and others who are too young to work or who live in institutions and are unable to work. The **working-age population** is the total number of people aged 16 years and over who are not in jail, a hospital, or some other form of institutional care. The Census Bureau divides the working-age population into two groups: those in the labor force and those not in the labor force. It also divides the labor force into two groups: the employed and the unemployed. So the **labor force** is the sum of the employed and the unemployed.

To be counted as employed in the Current Population Survey, a person must have either a full-time job or a part-time job. To be counted as *un*employed, a person must be available for work and must be in one of three categories:

1. Without work but has made specific efforts to find a job within the previous four weeks
2. Waiting to be called back to a job from which he or she has been laid off
3. Waiting to start a new job within 30 days

Anyone surveyed who satisfies one of these three criteria is counted as unemployed. People in the working-age population who are neither employed nor unemployed are classified as not in the labor force.

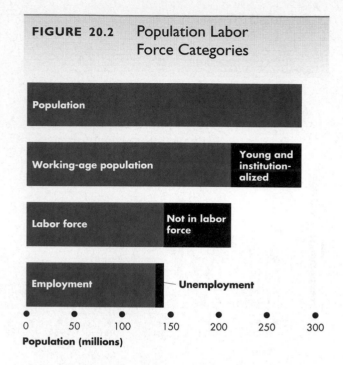

FIGURE 20.2   Population Labor Force Categories

The total population is divided into the working-age population and the young and institutionalized. The working-age population is divided into those in the labor force and those not in the labor force. The labor force is divided into the employed and the unemployed.

Source: Bureau of Labor Statistics, 2002.

In 2001, the population of the United States was 284.8 million. There were 73 million people under 16 years of age or living in institutions. The working-age population was 211.8 million. Of this number, 69.5 million were not in the labor force. Most of these people were in school full time or had retired from work. The remaining 142.3 million people made up the U.S. labor force. Of these, 134 million were employed and 8.3 million were unemployed.

Three Labor Market Indicators

The Census Bureau calculates three indicators of the state of the labor market, which are shown in Fig. 20.3. They are

■ The unemployment rate
■ The labor force participation rate
■ The employment-to-population ratio

The Unemployment Rate The amount of unemployment is an indicator of the extent to which people who want jobs can't find them. The **unemployment rate** is the percentage of the people in the labor force who are unemployed. That is,

$$\text{Unemployment rate} = \frac{\text{Number of people unemployed}}{\text{Labor force}} \times 100$$

and

$$\text{Labor force} = \frac{\text{Number of people employed} + \text{Number of people unemployed}}{}.$$

In 2001, the number of people employed was 134 million and the number unemployed was 8.3 million. By using the above equations, you can verify that the labor force was 142.3 million (134 million plus 8.3 million) and the unemployment rate was 5.8 percent (8.3 million divided by 142.3 million, multiplied by 100).

Figure 20.3 shows the unemployment rate (the orange line) and two other labor market indicators between 1961 and 2001. The average unemployment rate has been 6 percent, and it reached peak values at the end of the recessions of 1974, 1982, and 1990–1991.

The Labor Force Participation Rate The number of people who join the labor force is an indicator of the willingness of people of working age to take jobs. The **labor force participation rate** is the percentage of working-age population who are members of the labor force. That is,

$$\text{Labor force participation rate} = \frac{\text{Labor force}}{\text{Working-age population}} \times 100.$$

In 2001, the labor force was 142.3 million and the working-age population was 211.8 million. By using the above equation, you can calculate the labor force participation rate. It was 67.2 percent (142.3 million divided by 211.8 million, multiplied by 100).

Figure 20.3 shows the labor force participation rate (graphed in red and plotted on the left-hand scale). It has followed an upward trend and has increased from 59 percent during the early 1960s to 67 percent during the 1990s. It has also had some mild fluctuations. They result from unsuccessful job seekers becoming discouraged workers. **Discouraged workers** are people who are available and willing to work but have not made specific efforts to find a job within the previous four weeks. These workers often temporarily leave the labor force during a recession and reenter during an expansion and become active job seekers.

FIGURE 20.3   Employment, Unemployment, and the Labor Force: 1961–2001

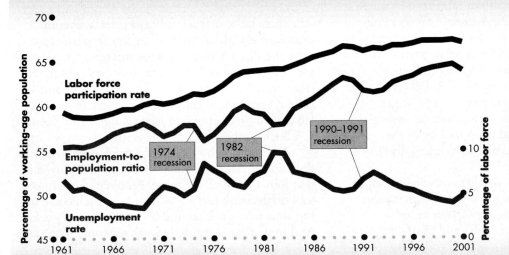

The unemployment rate increases in recessions and decreases in expansions. The labor force participation rate and the employment-to-population ratio have upward trends and fluctuate with the business cycle. The employment-to-population ratio fluctuates more than the labor force participation rate and reflects cyclical fluctuations in the unemployment rate. Fluctuations in the labor force participation rate arise mainly because of discouraged workers.

Source: Bureau of Labor Statistics, 2002.

The Employment-to-Population Ratio The number of people of working age who have jobs is an indicator of both the availability of jobs and the degree of match between people's skills and jobs. The **employment-to-population ratio** is the percentage of people of working age who have jobs. That is,

$$\text{Employment-to-population ratio} = \frac{\text{Number of people employed}}{\text{Working-age population}} \times 100.$$

In 2001, employment was 134 million and the working-age population was 211.8 million. By using the above equation, you can calculate the employment-to-population ratio. It was 63.3 percent (134 million divided by 211.8 million, multiplied by 100).

Figure 20.3 shows the employment-to-population ratio (graphed in blue and plotted against the left-hand scale). It increased from 55 percent during the early 1960s to 64 percent in 2000. The increase in the employment-to-population ratio means that the U.S. economy has created jobs at a faster rate than the working-age population has grown. This labor market indicator also fluctuates, and its fluctuations coincide with but are opposite to those in the unemployment rate. It falls during a recession and increases during an expansion.

Why have the labor force participation rate and the employment-to-population ratio increased? The main reason is an increase in the number of women in the labor force. Figure 20.4 shows this increase. Between 1961 and 2001, the female labor force participation rate increased from 38 percent to 60 percent. Shorter work hours, higher productivity, and an increased emphasis on white-collar jobs have expanded the job opportunities and wages available to women. At the same time, technological advances have increased productivity in the home and freed up women's time to take jobs outside the home.

Figure 20.4 also shows another remarkable trend in the U.S. labor force: The labor force participation rate and the employment-to-population ratio for men have *decreased*. Between 1961 and 2001, the male labor force participation rate decreased from 83 percent to 74 percent. It decreased because increasing numbers of men were remaining in school longer and because some were retiring earlier.

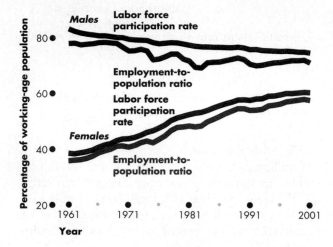

The upward trends in the labor force participation rate and the employment-to-population ratio are accounted for mainly by the increasing participation of women in the labor market. The male labor force participation rate and employment-to-population ratio have decreased.

Source: Bureau of Labor Statistics, 2002.

Aggregate Hours

The three labor market indicators that we've just examined are useful signs of the health of the economy and directly measure what matters to most people: jobs. But these three indicators don't tell us the quantity of labor used to produce real GDP, and we cannot use them to calculate the productivity of labor. The productivity of labor is significant because it influences the wages people earn.

The reason why the number of people employed does not measure the quantity of labor employed is that jobs are not all the same. People in part-time jobs might work just a few hours a week. People in full-time jobs work around 35 to 40 hours a week. And some people regularly work overtime. For example, a 7-11 store might hire six students who work for three hours a day each. Another 7-11 store might hire two full-time workers who work nine hours a day each. The number of people employed in these two stores is eight, but the total hours worked by six of the eight is the same as the total hours worked by the other two. To determine the total amount of labor used to produce real GDP, we measure labor in hours rather than in jobs. **Aggregate hours** are the total number of hours worked by all the people employed, both full time and part time, during a year.

Figure 20.5(a) shows aggregate hours in the U.S. economy from 1961 to 2001. Like the employment-to-population ratio, aggregate hours have an upward trend. But aggregate hours have not grown as quickly as has the number of people employed. Between 1961 and 2001, the number of people employed in the U.S. economy increased by 160 percent. During that same period, aggregate hours increased by a bit more than 100 percent. Why the difference? Because average hours per worker decreased.

Figure 20.5(b) shows average hours per worker. After hovering at almost 39 hours a week during the early 1960s, average hours per worker decreased to about 34 hours a week during the 1990s. This shortening of the average workweek arose partly because of a decrease in the average hours worked by full-time workers but mainly because the number of part-time jobs increased faster than the number of full-time jobs.

Fluctuations in aggregate hours and average hours per worker line up with the business cycle. Figure 20.5 highlights the past three recessions, during which aggregate hours decreased and average hours per worker decreased more quickly than trend.

Real Wage Rate

The **real wage rate** is the quantity of goods and services that an hour's work can buy. It is equal to the money wage rate (dollars per hour) divided by the price level. If we use the GDP deflator to measure the price level, the real wage rate is expressed in 1996 dollars because the GDP deflator is 100 in 1996. The real wage rate is a significant economic variable because it measures the reward for labor.

What has happened to the real wage rate in the United States? Figure 20.6 answers this question. It shows three measures of the average hourly real wage rate in the U.S. economy between 1961 and 2001.

The first measure of the real wage rate is the Department of Labor's calculation of the average hourly earnings of private manufacturing nonsupervisory workers. This measure increased to $11.80 in 1978 (in 1996 dollars) and then remained almost

FIGURE 20.5 Aggregate Hours: 1961–2001

(a) Aggregate hours

(b) Average weekly hours per person

Aggregate hours (part a) measure the total labor used to produce real GDP more accurately than does the number of people employed because an increasing proportion of jobs are part time. Between 1961 and 2001, aggregate hours increased by an average of 1.9 percent a year. Fluctuations in aggregate hours coincide with the business cycle. Aggregate hours have increased at a slower rate than the number of jobs because the average workweek has shortened (part b).

Source: Bureau of Labor Statistics, and the author's calculations.

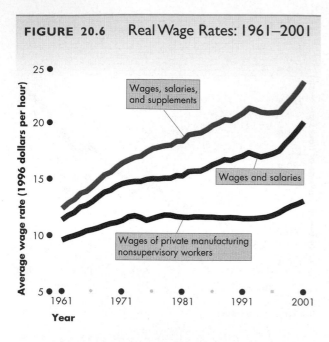

FIGURE 20.6   Real Wage Rates: 1961–2001

The average hourly real wage rate of private manufacturing nonsupervisory workers peaked in 1978, was constant through 1993, then increased again through 2001. Broader measures of hourly real wage rates increased, but all show a growth slowdown during the 1970s.

Sources: Bureau of Economic Analysis, Bureau of Labor Statistics, and the author's calculations.

constant at around $11.60 for 15 years. From the mid-1990s, the real wage rate increased again and reached $13.10 in 2001.

The second measure of the real wage rate is calculated by dividing total wages and salaries in the *National Income and Product Accounts* by aggregate hours. This measure is broader than the first and includes the incomes of all types of labor, whether their rate of pay is calculated by the hour or not. This broader measure did not stop growing after 1978, but its growth rate slowed during the mid-1970s and remained low through the early 1980s. It then speeded up during the late 1980s, sagged during the early 1990s, and then grew very rapidly after 1996.

Fringe benefits such as pension contributions and the payment by employers of health insurance premiums have become an increasing part of labor compensation. Figure 20.6 shows a third measure of

the hourly real wage rate that reflects this trend. It is *total labor compensation* — wages, salaries, and supplements — divided by aggregate hours. This measure is the most comprehensive one available, and it shows that the real wage rate has increased. But it also shows that no matter how we measure the wage rate, its growth rate slowed during the 1970s.

The constant average wage rate of manufacturing nonsupervisory workers and the slowdown in the growth rate of the broader measures of the average wage rate coincided with a slowdown in productivity growth — in the growth rate of real GDP per hour of work. The true extent of the slowdown in productivity growth and the slowdown in real wage growth can be determined only if the price level and inflation rate are measured accurately.

The measures of real wages described in Fig. 20.6 are based on the official measure of inflation. Some economists think that inflation has been overestimated, perhaps by as much as 1 percent a year. If this assessment is correct, real wage rates have grown more rapidly than those shown in Fig. 20.6.

REVIEW QUIZ

1 What are the trends in the unemployment rate, the labor force participation rate, and the employment-to-population ratio?

2 How do the unemployment rate, the labor force participation rate, and the employment-to-population ratio fluctuate over the business cycle?

3 Has the female labor force participation rate been similar to or different from the male labor force participation rate?

4 How have aggregate hours changed since 1961?

5 How did average hourly real wage rates change during the 1990s?

You've now seen how we measure employment, unemployment, and real wage rate. Your next task is to study the anatomy of unemployment and see why it never disappears, even at full employment.

Unemployment and Full Employment

How do people become unemployed, and how does a period of unemployment end? How long do people remain unemployed on the average? Who is at greatest risk of becoming unemployed? Let's answer these questions by looking at the anatomy of unemployment.

The Anatomy of Unemployment

People become unemployed if they

1. Lose their jobs and search for another job.
2. Leave their jobs and search for another job.
3. Enter or reenter the labor force to search for a job.

People end a spell of unemployment if they

1. Are hired or recalled.
2. Withdraw from the labor force.

People who are laid off, either permanently or temporarily, from their jobs are called **job losers**. Some job losers become unemployed, but some immediately withdraw from the labor force. People who voluntarily quit their jobs are called **job leavers**. Like job losers, some job leavers become unemployed and search for a better job while others withdraw from the labor force temporarily or permanently retire from work. People who enter or reenter the labor force are called **entrants** and **reentrants**. Entrants are mainly people who have just left school. Some entrants get a job right away and are never unemployed, but many spend time searching for their first job, and during this period, they are unemployed. Reentrants are people who have previously withdrawn from the labor force. Most of these people are formerly discouraged workers. Figure 20.7 shows these labor market flows.

Let's see how much unemployment arises from the three different ways in which people can become unemployed.

The Sources of Unemployment Figure 20.8 shows unemployment by reason for becoming unemployed. Job losers are the biggest source of unemployment. On the average, they account for around half of total

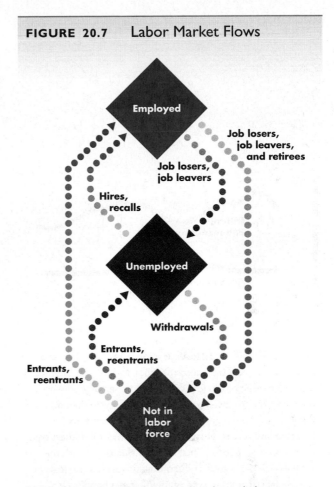

FIGURE 20.7   Labor Market Flows

Unemployment results from employed people losing or leaving their jobs (job losers and job leavers) and from people entering the labor force (entrants and reentrants). Unemployment ends because people get hired or recalled or because they withdraw from the labor force.

unemployment. Also, their number fluctuates a great deal. At the trough of the recession of 1990–1991, on any given day, more than 5 million of the 9.4 million unemployed were job losers. In contrast, at the business cycle peak in March 2001, only 3.3 million of the 6 million unemployed were job losers.

Entrants and reentrants also make up a large component of the unemployed, and their number fluctuates but more mildly than the fluctuations in the number of job losers.

Job leavers are the smallest and most stable source of unemployment. On any given day, fewer than 1 million people are unemployed because they

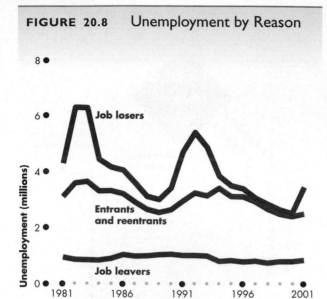

FIGURE 20.8   Unemployment by Reason

Everyone who is unemployed is a job loser, a job leaver, or an entrant or reentrant into the labor force. Most unemployment results from job loss. The number of job losers fluctuates more closely with the business cycle than do the numbers of job leavers and entrants and reentrants. Entrants and reentrants are the second most common type of unemployed people. Their number fluctuates with the business cycle because of discouraged workers. Job leavers are the least common type of unemployed people.

Source: Bureau of Labor Statistics, 2002.

FIGURE 20.9   Unemployment by Duration

Close to a business cycle peak in 2000, when the unemployment rate was 4 percent, 45 percent of unemployment lasted for less than 5 weeks and 30 percent lasted for 5 to 14 weeks. So 75 percent of unemployment lasted for less than 15 weeks and 25 percent lasted for 15 weeks or more.

Close to a business cycle trough in 1992, when the unemployment rate was 7.8 percent, 35 percent of unemployment lasted for less than 5 weeks and 29 percent lasted for 5 to 14 weeks. So 64 percent of unemployment lasted for less than 15 weeks, and 36 percent lasted for 15 weeks or more.

Source: Bureau of Labor Statistics, 2002.

are job leavers. The number of job leavers is remarkably constant, although to the extent that it fluctuates, it does so in line with the business cycle: A slightly larger number of people leave their jobs in good times than in bad times.

The Duration of Unemployment   Some people are unemployed for a week or two, and others are unemployed for periods of a year or more. The longer the spell of unemployment, the greater the personal cost to the unemployed. The average duration of unemployment varies over the business cycle. Figure 20.9 compares the duration of unemployment close to a business cycle peak in 2000, when the unemployment rate was low, with that close to a business cycle trough in 1992, when the unemployment rate was high. In 2000, when the unemployment rate hit a

low of 4 percent, 45 percent of the unemployed were in that situation for less than 5 weeks and only 11 percent of the unemployed were jobless for longer than 27 weeks. In 1992, when unemployment approached 8 percent, only 35 percent of the unemployed found a new job in less than 5 weeks and 20 percent were unemployed for more than 27 weeks. At both low and high unemployment rates, about 30 percent of the unemployed take between 5 weeks and 14 weeks to find a job.

The Demographics of Unemployment   Figure 20.10 shows unemployment rates for different demographic groups. The figure shows that high unemployment rates occur among young workers and also among blacks. In the business cycle trough in 1992, the unemployment rate of black teenage males was 42 percent.

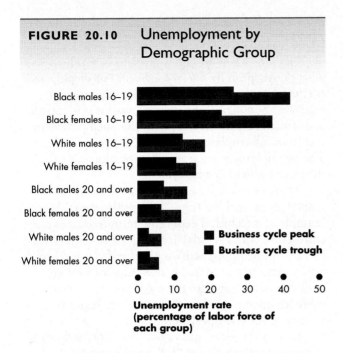

FIGURE 20.10   Unemployment by Demographic Group

Black males 16–19
Black females 16–19
White males 16–19
White females 16–19
Black males 20 and over
Black females 20 and over
White males 20 and over
White females 20 and over

■ Business cycle peak
■ Business cycle trough

0   10   20   30   40   50

Unemployment rate (percentage of labor force of each group)

Black teenagers experience unemployment rates that average twice those of white teenagers, and teenage unemployment rates are much higher than those for people aged 20 years and over. Even in a business cycle trough, when unemployment is at its highest rate, only 6 percent of whites aged 20 years and over are unemployed.

Source: Bureau of Labor Statistics, 2002.

Even in 2000, when the unemployment rate was 4 percent, the black teenage unemployment rates were more than 20 percent. The unemployment rates for white teenagers are less than half those of black teenagers. The racial differences also exist for workers aged 20 years and over. The highest unemployment rates that whites 20 years and over experience are lower than the lowest rates experienced by the other groups.

Why are teenage unemployment rates so high? There are three reasons. First, young people are still in the process of discovering what they are good at and trying different lines of work. So they leave their jobs more frequently than do older workers. Second, firms sometimes hire teenagers on a short-term trial basis. So the rate of job loss is higher for teenagers than for other people. Third, most teenagers are not in the labor force but are in school. This fact means that the percentage of the teenage population that is unemployed is much lower than the percentage of the teenage labor force that is unemployed. In 2000,

for example, 1 million teenagers were unemployed and 7 million were employed. So the teenage unemployment rate (all races) was 14 percent. But 12 million teenagers were in school. If we considered being in school as the equivalent of having a job and measured teenage unemployment as a percentage of the teenage labor force plus the school population, we would record that 6 percent of teenagers are unemployed.

Types of Unemployment

Unemployment is classified into three types that are based on its origins. They are

■ Frictional
■ Structural
■ Cyclical

Frictional Unemployment **Frictional unemployment** is the unemployment that arises from normal labor turnover — from people entering and leaving the labor force and from the ongoing creation and destruction of jobs. Frictional unemployment is a permanent and healthy phenomenon in a dynamic, growing economy.

The unending flow of people into and out of the labor force and the processes of job creation and job destruction create the need for people to search for jobs and for businesses to search for workers. Always there are businesses with unfilled jobs and people seeking jobs. Look in your local newspaper, and you will see that there are always some jobs being advertised. Businesses don't usually hire the first person who applies for a job, and unemployed people don't usually take the first job that comes their way. Instead, both firms and workers spend time searching out what they believe will be the best match available. By this process of search, people can match their own skills and interests with the available jobs and find a satisfying job and a good income. While these unemployed people are searching, they are frictionally unemployed.

The amount of frictional unemployment depends on the rate at which people enter and reenter the labor force and on the rate at which jobs are created and destroyed. During the 1970s, the amount of frictional unemployment increased as a consequence of the postwar baby boom that began during the 1940s. By the late 1970s, the baby boom had created a bulge in the number of people leaving school. As these people entered the labor force, the amount of frictional unemployment increased.

The amount of frictional unemployment is influenced by unemployment compensation. The greater the number of unemployed people covered by unemployment insurance and the more generous the unemployment benefit they receive, the longer is the average time taken in job search and the greater is the amount of frictional unemployment. In the United States in 1996, 36 percent of the unemployed received unemployment benefit. And the average benefit check was $160 a week. Canada and Western Europe have more generous benefits than those in the United States and have higher unemployment rates.

Structural Unemployment **Structural unemployment** is the unemployment that arises when changes in technology or international competition change the skills needed to perform jobs or change the locations of jobs. Structural unemployment usually lasts longer than frictional unemployment because workers must usually retrain and possibly relocate to find a job. For example, when a steel plant in Gary, Indiana, is automated, some jobs in that city are destroyed. Meanwhile, new jobs for security guards, life-insurance salespeople, and retail clerks are created in Chicago, Indianapolis, and other cities. The unemployed former steelworkers remain unemployed for several months until they move, retrain, and get one of these jobs. Structural unemployment is painful, especially for older workers for whom the best available option might be to retire early or take a lower-skilled, lower-paying job.

At some times the amount of structural unemployment is modest. At other times it is large, and at such times, structural unemployment can become a serious long-term problem. It was especially large during the late 1970s and early 1980s. During those years, oil price hikes and an increasingly competitive international environment destroyed jobs in traditional U.S. industries, such as auto and steel, and created jobs in new industries, such as electronics and bioengineering, as well as in banking and insurance. Structural unemployment was also present during the early 1990s as many businesses and governments "downsized."

Cyclical Unemployment **Cyclical unemployment** is the fluctuating unemployment over the business cycle. Cyclical unemployment increases during a recession and decreases during an expansion. An autoworker who is laid off because the economy is in a recession and who gets rehired some months later when the expansion begins has experienced cyclical unemployment.

Full Employment

There is always *some* unemployment — someone looking for a job or laid off and waiting to be recalled. So what do we mean by *full employment*? **Full employment** occurs when there is no cyclical unemployment or, equivalently, when all the unemployment is frictional and structural. The divergence of the unemployment rate from full employment is cyclical unemployment. The unemployment rate at full employment is called the **natural rate of unemployment**.

There can be a lot of unemployment at full employment, and the term "full employment" is an example of a technical economic term that does not correspond with everyday language. The term "natural rate of unemployment" is another technical economic term whose meaning does not correspond with everyday language. For most people — especially for unemployed workers — there is nothing *natural* about unemployment.

So why do economists call a situation with a lot of unemployment one of "full employment"? And why is the unemployment at full employment called "natural"?

The reason is that the economy is a complex mechanism that is always changing. In 2001, the U.S. economy employed 134 million people. More than 2.5 million workers retired during that year, and more than 3 million new workers entered the labor force. All these people worked in some 20 million businesses that produced goods and services valued at more than $10 trillion. Some of these businesses downsized and failed, and others expanded. This process of change creates frictions and dislocations that are unavoidable. And they create unemployment.

There is not much controversy about the existence of a natural rate of unemployment. Nor is there much disagreement that it changes. The natural rate of unemployment arises from the existence of frictional and structural unemployment, and it fluctuates because the frictions and the amount of structural change fluctuate. But economists don't agree about the size of the natural rate of unemployment and the extent to which it fluctuates. Some economists believe that the natural rate of unemployment fluctuates frequently and that at times of rapid demographic and technological change, the natural rate of unemployment can be high. Others think that the natural rate of unemployment changes slowly.

FIGURE 20.11   Unemployment and Real GDP

(a) Real GDP

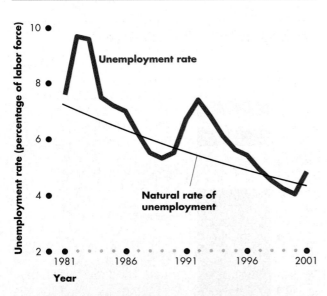

(b) Unemployment rate

As real GDP fluctuates around potential GDP (part a), the unemployment rate fluctuates around the natural rate of unemployment (part b). In the deep recession of 1982, the unemployment rate reached almost 10 percent. In the milder recession of 1990–1991, the unemployment rate peaked at less than 8 percent. The natural rate of unemployment decreased during the 1980s and 1990s.

Sources: Bureau of Economic Analysis, Bureau of Labor Statistics, International Monetary Fund, and the author's calculations.

Real GDP and Unemployment Over the Cycle

The quantity of real GDP at full employment is called **potential GDP.** You will study the forces that determine potential GDP in Chapter 22 (pp. 510–512). Over the business cycle, real GDP fluctuates around potential GDP and the unemployment rate fluctuates around the natural rate of unemployment. Figure 20.11 illustrates these fluctuations in the United States between 1981 and 2001 — real GDP in part (a) and the unemployment rate in part (b).

When the economy is at full employment, the unemployment rate equals the natural rate of unemployment and real GDP equals potential GDP. When the unemployment rate is less than the natural rate of unemployment, real GDP is greater than potential GDP. And when the unemployment rate is greater than the natural rate of unemployment, real GDP is less than potential GDP.

Figure 20.11(b) shows one view of the natural rate of unemployment. Keep in mind that economists do not know the magnitude of the natural rate of unemployment and the natural rate shown in the figure is only one estimate. In Fig. 20.11(b), the natural rate of unemployment is 7.6 percent in 1981 and it falls steadily through the 1980s and 1990s to 4.3 percent by 2001. This estimate of the natural rate of unemployment in the United States is one that many, but not all, economists would accept.

REVIEW QUIZ

1   What are the categories of people who become unemployed?
2   Define frictional unemployment, structural unemployment, and cyclical unemployment and provide an example of each type of unemployment.
3   What is the natural rate of unemployment?
4   How might the natural unemployment rate change and what factors might make it change?
5   How does the unemployment rate fluctuate over the business cycle?

Your final task in this chapter is to learn about another vital sign that gets monitored every month, the Consumer Price Index (CPI). What is the CPI, how do we measure it, and what does it mean?

The Consumer Price Index

THE BUREAU OF LABOR STATISTICS (BLS) calculates the Consumer Price Index every month. The **Consumer Price Index (CPI)** is a measure of the average of the prices paid by urban consumers for a fixed "basket" of consumer goods and services. What you learn in this section will help you to make sense of the CPI and relate it to your own economic life. The CPI tells you what has happened to the value of the money in your pocket.

Reading the CPI Numbers

The CPI is defined to equal 100 for a period called the **reference base period**. Currently, the reference base period is 1982–1984. That is, for the average of the 36 months from January 1982 through December 1984, the CPI equals 100.

In December 2001, the CPI was 176.7. This number tells us that the average of the prices paid by urban consumers for a fixed market basket of consumer goods and services was 76.7 percent higher in December 2001 than it was on the average during 1982–1984.

In December 2000, the CPI was 174.0. Comparing the December 2001 CPI with the December 2000 CPI tells us that the index of the prices paid by urban consumers for a fixed basket of consumer goods and services increased during 2001 by 2.7 — from 174.0 to 176.7.

Constructing the CPI

Constructing the CPI is a huge operation that costs millions of dollars and involves three stages:

- Selecting the CPI basket
- Conducting the monthly price survey
- Calculating the CPI

The CPI Basket   The first stage in constructing the CPI is to select what is called the *CPI basket*. This "basket" contains the goods and services represented in the index and the relative importance attached to each of them. The idea is to make the relative importance of the items in the CPI basket the same as that in the budget of an average urban household. For example, because people spend more on housing than on bus rides, the CPI places more weight on the price of housing than on the price of bus rides.

The BLS uses two baskets and calculates two CPIs. One, called CPI-U, measures the average price paid by *all* urban households. The other, called CPI-W, measures the average price paid by urban wage earners and clerical workers. Here, we will focus on CPI-U, the broader measure.

To determine the spending patterns of households and to select the CPI basket, the BLS conducts a Consumer Expenditure Survey. This survey is costly and so is undertaken infrequently. Today's CPI basket is based on data gathered in a Consumer Expenditure Survey of 1993–1995. Before 1998, the CPI basket was based on a 1982–1984 Consumer Expenditure Survey. The BLS plans more frequent updates of the CPI basket in the future.

Until recently, the time period covered by the Consumer Expenditure Survey was also the reference base period. But when the BLS switched to the 1993–1995 basket, it decided to retain 1982–1984 as the reference base period.

Figure 20.12 shows the CPI basket at the end of 2001. The basket contains around 80,000 goods and

FIGURE 20.12   The CPI Basket

Apparel (4 percent)
Other goods and services (5 percent)
Education and communication (5 percent)
Recreation (6 percent)
Medical care (6 percent)
Food and beverages (16 percent)
Transportation (18 percent)
Housing (40 percent)

The CPI basket consists of the items that an average urban household buys. It consists mainly of housing (40 percent), transportation (18 percent), and food and beverages (16 percent). All other items add up to 26 percent of the total.

Sources: United States Census Bureau, and Bureau of Labor.

services arranged in the eight large groups shown in the figure. The most important item in a household's budget is housing, which accounts for 40 percent of total expenditure. Transportation comes next at 18 percent. Third in relative importance are food and beverages at 16 percent. These three groups account for almost three quarters of the average household budget. Medical care and recreation each take 6 percent, and education and communication take 5 percent. Another 5 percent is spent on other goods and services, and apparel (clothing and footwear) takes 4 percent.

The BLS breaks down each of these categories into smaller ones. For example, the education and communication category breaks down into textbooks and supplies, tuition, telephone services, and personal computer services.

As you look at the relative importance of the items in the CPI basket, remember that they apply to the *average* household. *Individual* households are spread around the average. Think about your own expenditure and compare the basket of goods and services you buy with the CPI basket.

The Monthly Price Survey Each month, BLS employees check the prices of the 80,000 goods and services in the CPI basket in 30 metropolitan areas. Because the CPI aims to measure price *changes*, it is important that the prices recorded each month refer to exactly the same item. For example, suppose the price of a box of jelly beans has increased but a box now contains more beans. Has the price of jelly beans increased? The BLS employee must record the details of changes in quality or packaging so that price changes can be isolated from other changes.

Once the raw price data are in hand, the next task is to calculate the CPI.

Calculating the CPI The CPI calculation has three steps:

1. Find the cost of the CPI basket at base period prices.
2. Find the cost of the CPI basket at current period prices.
3. Calculate the CPI for the base period and the current period.

We'll work through these three steps for a simple example. Suppose the CPI basket contains only two goods and services: oranges and haircuts. We'll construct an annual CPI rather than a monthly CPI with the reference base period 2000 and the current period 2001.

Table 20.2 shows the quantities in the CPI basket and the prices in the base period and current period.

Part (a) contains the data for the base period. In that period, consumers bought 10 oranges at $1 each and 5 haircuts at $8 each. To find the cost of the CPI basket in the base period prices, multiply the quantities in the CPI basket by the base period prices. The cost of oranges is $10 (10 at $1 each), and the cost of haircuts is $40 (5 at $8 each). So total expenditure in the base period on the CPI basket is $50 ($10 + $40).

Part (b) contains the price data for the current period. The price of an orange increased from $1 to $2, which is a 100 percent increase ($1 ÷ $1 × 100 = 100). The price of a haircut increased from $8 to $10, which is a 25 percent increase ($2 ÷ $8 × 100 = 25).

The CPI provides a way of averaging these price increases by comparing the cost of the basket rather than the price of each item. To find the cost of the CPI basket in the current period, 2001, multiply the quantities in the basket by their 2001 prices. The cost of oranges is $20 (10 at $2 each), and the cost of haircuts is $50 (5 at $10 each) So total expenditure on the fixed CPI basket at current period prices is $70 ($20 + $50).

TABLE 20.2   The CPI:
A Simplified Calculation

(a) The cost of the CPI basket at base period prices: 2000

Item	CPI basket Quantity	Price	Cost of CPI Basket
Oranges	10	$1.00	$10
Haircuts	5	$8.00	$40
Cost of CPI basket at base period prices			$50

(b) The cost of the CPI basket at current period prices: 2001

Item	CPI basket Quantity	Price	Cost of CPI Basket
Oranges	10	$2.00	$20
Haircuts	5	$10.00	$50
Cost of CPI basket at current period prices			$70

You've now taken the first two steps toward calculating the CPI: calculating the cost of the CPI basket in the base period and the current period. The third step uses the numbers you've just calculated to find the CPI for 2000 and 2001.

The formula for the CPI is

$$\text{CPI} = \frac{\text{Cost of CPI basket at current period prices}}{\text{Cost of CPI basket at base period prices}} \times 100.$$

In Table 20.2, you have established that in 2000, the cost of the CPI basket was \$50 and in 2001, it was \$70. You also know that the base period is 2000. So the cost of the CPI basket at base year prices is \$50. If we use these numbers in the CPI formula, we can find the CPI for 2000 and 2001. For 2000, the CPI is

$$\text{CPI in 2000} = \frac{\$50}{\$50} \times 100 = 100.$$

For 2001, the CPI is

$$\text{CPI in 2000} = \frac{\$70}{\$50} \times 100 = 140.$$

The principles that you've applied in this simplified CPI calculation apply to the more complex calculations performed every month by the BLS.

Measuring Inflation

A major purpose of the CPI is to measure *changes* in the cost of living and in the value of money. To measure these changes, we calculate the **inflation rate**, which is the percentage change in the price level from one year to the next. To calculate the inflation rate, we use the formula:

$$\frac{\text{Inflation}}{\text{rate}} = \frac{(\text{CPI this year} - \text{CPI last year})}{\text{CPI last year}} \times 100.$$

We can use this formula to calculate the inflation rate in 2001. The CPI in December 2001 was 176.4, and the CPI in December 2000 was 170.0. So the inflation rate during 2001 was

$$\text{Inflation rate} = \frac{(176.7 - 174.0)}{174.0} \times 100 = 1.6.$$

Figure 20.13 shows the CPI and the inflation rate in the United States during the 30 years between 1971 and 2001. The two parts of the figure are related.

FIGURE 20.13   The CPI and the Inflation Rate

(a) CPI: 1971-2001

(b) Inflation rate: 1971-2001

In part (a), the CPI (the price level) has increased every year. In part (b), the inflation rate has averaged 5 percent a year. During the 1970s and early 1980s, the inflation rate was high and sometimes exceeded 10 percent a year. But after 1985, the inflation rate fell to an average of 3 percent a year.

Figure 20.13 shows that when the price *level* in part (a) rises rapidly, the inflation rate in part (b) is high, and when the price level in part (a) rises slowly, the inflation rate in part (b) is low. Notice in part (a) that the CPI increased every year during this period. During the late 1970s and 1980, the CPI was increasing rapidly, but its rate of increase slowed during the 1980s and 1990s.

The CPI is not a perfect measure of the price level, and changes in the CPI probably overstate the inflation rate. Let's look at the sources of bias.

The Biased CPI

The main sources of bias in the CPI are

- New goods bias
- Quality change bias
- Commodity substitution bias
- Outlet substitution bias

New Goods Bias If you want to compare the price level in 2003 with that in 1973, you must somehow compare the price of a computer today with that of a typewriter in 1973. Because a PC is more expensive than a typewriter was, the arrival of the PC puts an upward bias into the CPI and its inflation rate.

Quality Change Bias Cars, CD players, and many other items get better every year. Part of the rise in the prices of these items is a payment for improved quality and is not inflation. But the CPI counts the entire price rise as inflation and so overstates inflation.

Commodity Substitution Bias Changes in relative prices lead consumers to change the items they buy. For example, if the price of beef rises and the price of chicken remains unchanged, people buy more chicken and less beef. Suppose they switch from beef to chicken on a scale that provides the same amount of protein and the same enjoyment as before and their expenditure is the same as before. The price of protein has not changed. But because it ignores the substitution of chicken for beef, the CPI says the price of protein has increased.

Outlet Substitution Bias When confronted with higher prices, people use discount stores more frequently and convenience stores less frequently. This phenomenon is called *outlet substitution*. The CPI surveys do not monitor outlet substitutions.

The Magnitude of the Bias

You've reviewed the sources of bias in the CPI. But how big is the bias? This question was tackled in

1996 by a Congressional Advisory Commission on the Consumer Price Index chaired by Michael Boskin, an economics professor at Stanford University. This commission said that the CPI overstates inflation by 1.1 percentage points a year. That is, if the CPI reports that inflation is 3.1 percent a year, most likely inflation is actually 2 percent a year.

Some Consequences of the Bias

The bias in the CPI distorts private contracts and increases government outlays. Many private agreements, such as wage contracts, are linked to the CPI. For example, a firm and its workers might agree to a three-year wage deal that increases the wage rate by 2 percent a year *plus* the percentage increase in the CPI. Such a deal ends up giving the workers more real income than the firm intended.

Close to a third of federal government outlays, including Social Security checks, are linked directly to the CPI. And while a bias of 1 percent a year seems small, accumulated over a decade it adds up to almost a trillion dollars of additional expenditures.

Reducing the Bias To reduce the bias in the CPI, the BLS has decided to undertake consumer spending surveys at more frequent intervals and to revise the basket that is used for calculating the CPI every two years.

REVIEW QUIZ

1 What is the CPI and how is it calculated?
2 How do we calculate the inflation rate and what is the relationship between the CPI and the inflation rate?
3 What are the four main ways in which the CPI is an upward-biased measure of the price level?
4 What problems arise from the CPI bias?

◆ You've now completed your study of the measurement of macroeconomic performance. Your task in the following chapters is to learn what determines that performance and how policy actions might improve it.

Unemployment in the 2001 Recession

THE NEW YORK TIMES, JANUARY 5, 2002

Nation's Unemployment Rate Rises to 5.8%

The unemployment rate continued to creep upward last month, though fewer Americans lost their jobs than in any of the previous three months.

The Labor Department reported yesterday that the economy lost 124,000 jobs in December, the smallest decline since August. The unemployment rate rose two-tenths of a percentage point, to 5.8 percent, a level it last reached in April 1995.

Economists said the numbers suggested the job market might be stabilizing after severe cutbacks caused by the terrorist attacks and the recession. They also said they saw other promising signs, like a rise in the number of hours worked per week in manufacturing, and a wave of hiring in education and health care.

But most experts continued to paint a gloomy picture of the economy. "The overall report was quite weak," Lynn Reaser, chief economist for the Bank of America, said. Job losses are still high, and several forecasters expect the unemployment rate to climb as high as 6.5 percent in the first half of the year.

...

Some of the worst job losses in December occurred in the travel industry, where the hangover from Sept. 11 continues. Travel lost 32,000 jobs last month, for a five-month total of 273,000. Employment in retail sales also fell, by 77,000 on a seasonally adjusted basis, as a result of retailers' pessimism about holiday shopping.

...

Half the increase in hours worked came from overtime. That could mean employers are working their existing employees harder as an interim measure before hiring more workers, said Diane Swonk, chief economist of Bank One in Chicago. "The overtime is what you want to see," she said. "It is income, and income is important."

...

Last month, consumer confidence rose to levels unseen since the summer. Bigger paychecks helped to keep spending strong. Hourly wages for nonfarm workers edged up to $14.65 from $14.56.

...

Essence of the Story

■ The unemployment rate increased from 5.6 percent in November 2001 to 5.8 percent in December 2001, its highest since April 1995.

■ The number *employed* decreased by 124,000, the smallest decrease since August 2001.

■ The worst job losses occurred in travel (32,000 jobs) and retail sales (77,000 jobs).

■ Education and health care jobs increased.

■ Some forecasters expect unemployment to climb to 6.5 percent in the first half of 2002.

■ Average weekly hours in manufacturing increased. A half of the increase came from overtime.

■ Wage rates increased by 9 cents an hour to $14.65 an hour.

Economic Analysis

■ The National Bureau of Economic Research says that the U.S. economy went into recession in March 2001.

■ During a recession, employment decreases, average weekly hours decrease, aggregate hours decrease, and the unemployment rate increases.

■ This news article described some of these changes in December 2001, when the recession was 9 months old.

■ At 9 months, a recession is almost over if it is of usual length. The average length of the last six recessions is 11 months.

■ The figures tell an interesting story about the 2001 recession. Figure 1 shows that this recession is one in which the number *employed* decreased in the months after the business cycle peak by more than usual.

■ But Figure 2 shows that average weekly hours fell by less than usual. This feature is noted in the news article and attributed to increased overtime.

■ Figures 3 and 4 show that aggregate hours and the unemployment rate were on track with the average of the previous recessions.

■ The forecasters who expected unemployment to climb to 6.5 percent in the first half of 2002 were predicting a worse than average recession.

■ But if the 2001 recession remained average, the unemployment rate would peak at about 6.1 percent in February 2002.

■ The increase in the average hourly wage rates was *really* greater than reported because the price level *fell* in December 2001 and the increase in the *real wage rate* was equivalent to a 15 cent, or 1 percent, increase.

■ The news article suggests that aside from the recession, the labor market was doing a lot of job *reallocation* — job cuts in travel and retail sales and job creation in education and health — which might increase the structural unemployment rate.

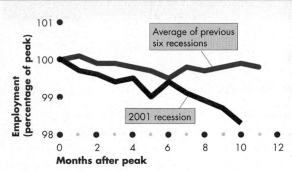

Figure 1 During the 2001 recession employment fell by more than usual ...

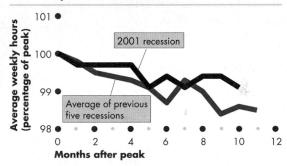

Figure 2 ... but average weekly hours fell by less than usual ...

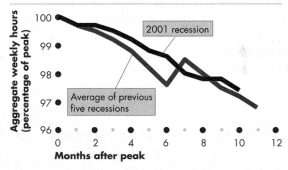

Figure 3 ... and aggregate hours worked were on track

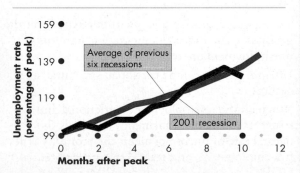

Figure 4 The unemployment rate also was on track

471

SUMMARY

KEY POINTS

The Business Cycle (pp. 454–455)

- A recession is a significant decline in activity spread across the economy and lasting more than a few months.
- Another definition of recession is a decrease in real GDP that lasts for at least two quarters.
- The NBER has identified 16 recessions and expansions since 1920.

Jobs and Wages (pp. 456–460)

- The unemployment rate has averaged 6 percent. It increases in recessions and decreases in expansions.
- The labor force participation rate and the employment-to-population ratio have an upward trend and fluctuate with the business cycle.
- The labor force participation rate has increased for females and decreased for males.
- Aggregate hours have an upward trend, and they fluctuate with the business cycle.
- Real hourly wage rates grow but their growth rates slowed during the 1970s.

Unemployment and Full Employment (pp. 461–465)

- People are constantly entering and leaving the state of unemployment.
- The duration of unemployment fluctuates over the business cycle. But the demographic patterns of unemployment are constant.
- Unemployment can be frictional, structural, and cyclical.
- When all the unemployment is frictional and structural, the unemployment rate equals the natural rate of unemployment, the economy is at full employment, and real GDP equals potential GDP.
- Over the business cycle, real GDP fluctuates around potential GDP and the unemployment rate fluctuates around the natural rate of unemployment.

The Consumer Price Index (pp. 466–469)

- The Consumer Price Index (CPI) is a measure of the average of the prices paid by urban consumers for a fixed basket of consumer goods and services.
- The CPI is defined to equal 100 for a reference base period — currently 1982–1984.
- The inflation rate is the percentage change in the CPI from one year to the next.
- Changes in the CPI probably overstate the inflation rate because of the bias that arises from new goods, quality changes, commodity substitution, and outlet substitution.
- The bias in the CPI distorts private contracts and increases government outlays.

KEY FIGURES

KEY TERMS

PROBLEMS

*1. The Bureau of Labor Statistics reported the following data for December 2000:

Labor force: 141,544,000

Employment: 135,888,000

Working-age population: 210,743,000

Calculate for that month the

a. Unemployment rate.

b. Labor force participation rate.

c. Employment-to-population ratio.

2. The Bureau of Labor Statistics reported the following data for December 2001:

Labor force: 142,314,000

Employment: 134,055,000

Working-age population: 212,927,000

Calculate for that month the

a. Unemployment rate.

b. Labor force participation rate.

c. Employment-to-population ratio.

*3. During 2000, the working-age population increased by 1,911,000, employment increased by 1,375,000, and the labor force increased by 1,311,000. Use these numbers and the data in problem 1 to calculate the change in unemployment and the change in the number of people not in the labor force during 2000.

4. During 2001, the working-age population increased by 2,184,000, employment decreased by 1,833,000, and the labor force increased by 770,000. Use these numbers and the data in problem 2 to calculate the change in unemployment and the change in the number of people not in the labor force during 2001.

*5. In August 2000, the unemployment rate was 4.1 percent. In August 2001, the unemployment rate was 4.9 percent. Use this information to predict what happened between August 2000 and August 2001 to the numbers of

a. Job losers and job leavers.

b. Labor force entrants and reentrants.

6. In January 2001, the unemployment rate was 4.2 percent. In January 2002, the unemployment rate was 5.6 percent. Use these data to predict what happened in 2002 to the numbers of

a. Job losers and job leavers.

b. Labor force entrants and reentrants.

*7. In July 2002, in the economy of Sandy Island, 10,000 people were employed, 1,000 were unemployed, and 5,000 were not in the labor force. During August 2002, 80 people lost their jobs, 20 people quit their jobs, 150 people were hired or recalled, 50 people withdrew from the labor force, and 40 people entered or reentered the labor force. Calculate for July 2002

a. The labor force.

b. The unemployment rate.

c. The working-age population.

d. The employment-to-population ratio.

And calculate for the end of August 2002

e. The number of people unemployed.

f. The number of people employed.

g. The labor force.

h. The unemployment rate.

8. In July 2003, in the economy of Sandy Island, 11,000 people were employed, 900 were unemployed, and 5,000 were not in the labor force. During August 2002, 40 people lost their jobs, 10 people quit their jobs, 180 people were hired or recalled, 20 people withdrew from the labor force, and 60 people entered or reentered the labor force. Calculate for July 2003

a. The labor force.

b. The unemployment rate.

c. The working-age population.

d. The employment-to-population ratio.

And calculate for the end of August 2003

e. The number of people unemployed.

f. The number of people employed.

g. The labor force.

h. The unemployment rate.

*9. A typical family on Sandy Island consumes only juice and cloth. Last year, which was the base year, the family spent $40 on juice and $25 on cloth. In the base year, juice was $4 a bottle and cloth was $5 a length. This year, juice is $4 a bottle and cloth is $6 a length. Calculate

a. The basket used in the CPI.

b. The CPI in the current year.

c. The inflation rate in the current year.

10. A typical family on Lizard Island consumes only mangoes and nuts. In the base year, the family spent $60 on nuts and $10 on mangoes. In the base year, mangoes were $1 each and nuts were $3 a bag. This year, mangoes are $1.50 each and nuts are $4 a bag. Calculate

a. The basket used in the CPI.

b. The CPI in the current year.

c. The inflation rate in the current year.

CRITICAL THINKING

1. Study *Reading Between the Lines* on pp. 470–471 and then answer the following questions:
   a. Describe the indicators of economic performance to which the NBER Business Cycle Dating Committee paid most attention when it declared that a recession began in March 2001.
   b. Explain how the 2001 recession compares with the average of the six previous recessions.
   c. Do you think the NBER committee is correct in its determination of the starting date of recession in 2001? Explain why you think the committee got it right or wrong.

2. Thinking about the economy of Sandy Island in problems 7 and 8:
   a. In what phase of its business cycle was Sandy Island during 2003?
   b. What do you predict would be happening to real GDP on Sandy Island? Why?
   c. What do you predict would be happening to standard of living on Sandy Island? Why?

3. Describe the main features of the labor market at the peak of the business cycle.

4. Describe the main features of the labor market at the trough of the business cycle.

5. You've seen in this chapter that the average workweek has shortened over the years. Do you think that shorter work hours are a problem or a benefit? Do you expect the average workweek to keep getting shorter? Why or why not?

6. An increasing number of jobs are part-time jobs. Can you think of some reasons for this trend? Who benefits from part time jobs, the employer or the worker or both? Explain with examples.

7. You've seen that the CPI is biased and overstates the true inflation rate. It would be a simple matter to adjust the CPI for the known average bias. Yet we continue to keep a flawed measure of inflation in place. Why do you think we don't adjust the CPI for the known average bias so that its measure of the inflation rate is more accurate? Explain who gains from the biased measure and who loses from it. Try to think of reasons why those who lose have not persuaded those who win to adopt a more accurate measure.

WEB EXERCISES

1. Use the link on your Parkin Website to review the Federal Reserve's *Beige Book*. In which phase of the business cycle is the economy in your region? How does your region compare to the nation as a whole?

2. Use the link on your Parkin Website to visit the Website of the Bureau of Labor Statistics and find labor market data for your own state.
   a. What have been the trends in employment, unemployment, and labor force participation in your own state during the past two years?
   b. On the basis of what you know about your own region, how would you set about explaining these trends?
   c. Try to identify those industries that have expanded most and those that have shrunk.
   d. What are the problems with your own regional labor market that you think need state government action to resolve?
   e. What actions do you think your state government must take to resolve these problems? Answer this question by using the demand and supply model of the labor market and predict the effects of the actions you prescribe.
   f. Compare the labor market performance of your own state with that of the nation as a whole.
   g. If your state is performing better than the national average, to what do you attribute the success? If your region is performing worse than the national average, to what do you attribute its problems? What federal actions are needed in your state labor market?

3. Use the link on your Parkin Website to visit the Website of the Bureau of Labor Statistics and find CPI data for your own region.
   a. What have been the trends in the CPI in your region during the past two years?
   b. Compare the CPI performance of your own region with that of the nation as a whole.
   c. On the basis of what you know about your own region, how would you set about explaining its deviation from the national average?

AGGREGATE SUPPLY AND AGGREGATE DEMAND

CHAPTER 21

Production and Prices

During the 10 years from 1991 to 2001, U.S. real GDP increased by 40 percent. Expanding at this pace, real GDP doubles every 20 years. What forces bring persistent and rapid expansion of real GDP? ◆ Expanding real GDP brings a rising standard of living. Inflation — rising prices — brings a rising cost of living. Because of inflation, you need $2 today to buy what $1 bought in 1980. What causes inflation? ◆ Our economy expands and prices rise at an uneven pace. They ebb and flow over the business cycle. After 10 years of rapid expansion, our economy came to a grinding halt in 2001. Why do we have a business cycle? ◆ Because our economy fluctuates, the government and the Federal Reserve try to smooth its path. How do the policy actions of the government and the Federal Reserve affect production and prices?

◼ To answer these questions, we need a *model* of real GDP and the price level. Our main task in this chapter is to study such a model: the *aggregate supply–aggregate demand model*. Our second task is to use the aggregate supply–aggregate demand (or *AS-AD*) model to answer the questions we've just posed. You'll discover that this model enables us to understand the forces that make our economy expand, that bring inflation, and that cause business cycle fluctuations. At the end of the chapter, we'll use the *AS-AD* model to understand the forces that brought rapid economic growth during the 1990s and recession in 2001.

After studying this chapter, you will be able to

- ◼ **Explain what determines aggregate supply**
- ◼ **Explain what determines aggregate demand**
- ◼ **Explain macroeconomic equilibrium**
- ◼ **Explain the effects of changes in aggregate supply and aggregate demand on economic growth, inflation, and the business cycle**
- ◼ **Explain U.S. economic growth, inflation, and business cycles by using the *AS-AD* model**

Aggregate Supply

THE AGGREGATE SUPPLY–AGGREGATE DEMAND model enables us to understand three features of macroeconomic performance:

- Growth of potential GDP
- Inflation
- Business cycle fluctuations

The model uses the concepts of *aggregate* supply and *aggregate* demand to determine *real GDP* and the *price level* (the GDP deflator). We begin by looking at the limits to production that influence aggregate supply.

Aggregate Supply Fundamentals

The *quantity of real GDP supplied* (Y) depends on

1. The quantity of labor (L)
2. The quantity of capital (K)
3. The state of technology (T)

The influence of these three factors on the quantity of real GDP supplied is described by the **aggregate production function**, which is written as the equation:

$$Y = F(L, K, T).$$

In words, the quantity of real GDP supplied is determined by (is a function F of) the quantities of labor and capital and of the state of technology. The larger is L, K, or T, the greater is Y.

At any given time, the quantity of capital and the state of technology are fixed. They depend on decisions that were made in the past. The population is also fixed. But the quantity of labor is not fixed. It depends on decisions made by people and firms about the supply of and demand for labor.

The labor market can be in any one of three states: at full employment, above full employment, or below full employment.

Even at full employment, there are always some people looking for jobs and some firms looking for people to hire. The reason is that there is a constant churning of the labor market. Every day, some jobs are destroyed as businesses reorganize or fail. Some jobs are created as new businesses start up or existing ones expand. Some workers decide, for any of a thousand personal reasons, to quit their jobs. And other people decide to start looking for a job. This constant churning in the labor market prevents unemployment from ever disappearing. The unemployment rate at full employment is called the **natural rate of unemployment**.

Another way to think about full employment is as a state of the labor market in which the quantity of labor demanded equals the quantity supplied. Firms demand labor only if it is profitable to do so. And the lower the wage rate, which is the cost of labor, the greater is the quantity of labor demanded. People supply labor only if doing so is the most valuable use of their time. And the higher the wage rate, which is the return to labor, the greater is the quantity of labor supplied. The wage rate that makes the quantity of labor demanded equal to the quantity of labor supplied is the equilibrium wage rate. At this wage rate, there is full employment. (You can study the labor market at full employment further in Chapter 22 on pp. 507–512.)

The quantity of real GDP at full employment is *potential GDP*, which depends on the full-employment quantity of labor, the quantity of capital, and the state of technology. Over the business cycle, employment fluctuates around full employment and real GDP fluctuates around potential GDP.

To study aggregate supply in different states of the labor market, we distinguish two time frames:

- Long-run aggregate supply
- Short-run aggregate supply

Long-Run Aggregate Supply

The economy is constantly bombarded by events that move real GDP away from potential GDP and, equivalently, move employment away from full employment. Following such an event, forces operate to take real GDP back toward potential GDP and restore full employment. The **macroeconomic long run** is a time frame that is sufficiently long for these forces to have done their work so that real GDP equals potential GDP and full employment prevails.

The **long-run aggregate supply curve** is the relationship between the quantity of real GDP supplied and the price level in the long run when real GDP equals potential GDP. Figure 21.1 shows this relationship as the vertical line labeled *LAS*. Along the long-run aggregate supply curve, as the price level changes, real GDP remains at potential GDP, which in Fig. 21.1 is $10 trillion. The long-run aggregate supply curve is always vertical and is located at potential GDP.

FIGURE 21.1   Long-Run Aggregate Supply

The long-run aggregate supply curve (*LAS*) shows the relationship between potential GDP and the price level. Potential GDP is independent of the price level, so the *LAS* curve is vertical at potential GDP.

The long-run aggregate supply curve is vertical because potential GDP is independent of the price level. The reason for this independence is that a movement along the *LAS* curve is accompanied by a change in *two* sets of prices: the prices of goods and services — the price level — and the prices of productive resources. A 10 percent increase in the prices of goods and services is matched by a 10 percent increase in the money wage rate and other resource prices. That is, the price level, wage rate, and other resource prices all change by the same percentage, and *relative prices* and the *real wage rate* remain constant. When the price level changes but relative prices and the real wage rate remain constant, real GDP remains constant.

Production at a Pepsi Plant   You can see why real GDP remains constant when all prices change by the same percentage by thinking about production decisions at a Pepsi bottling plant. The plant is producing the quantity of Pepsi that maximizes profit. The plant

can increase production but only by incurring a higher *marginal cost* (see Chapter 2, p. 35). So the firm has no incentive to change production.

Short-Run Aggregate Supply

The **macroeconomic short run** is a period during which real GDP has fallen below or risen above potential GDP. At the same time, the unemployment rate has risen above or fallen below the natural rate of unemployment.

The **short-run aggregate supply curve** is the relationship between the quantity of real GDP supplied and the price level in the short run when the money wage rate, the prices of other resources, and potential GDP remain constant. Figure 21.2 shows a short-run aggregate supply curve as the upward-sloping curve labeled *SAS*. This curve is based on the short-run aggregate supply schedule, and each point on the aggregate supply curve corresponds to a row of the aggregate supply schedule. For example, point *A* on the short-run aggregate supply curve and row *A* of the schedule tell us that if the price level is 100, the quantity of real GDP supplied is $9 trillion.

At point *C*, the price level is 110 and the quantity of real GDP supplied is $10 trillion, which equals potential GDP. If the price level is higher than 110, real GDP exceeds potential GDP; if the price level is below 110, real GDP is less than potential GDP.

Back at the Pepsi Plant   You can see why the short-run aggregate supply curve slopes upward by returning to the Pepsi bottling plant. The plant produces the quantity that maximizes profit. If the price of Pepsi rises and the money wage rate and other costs don't change, the *relative price* of Pepsi rises and the firm has an incentive to increase production. The higher relative price of Pepsi covers the higher marginal cost of producing more Pepsi, so the firm increases production.

Similarly, if the price of Pepsi falls and the money wage rate and other costs don't change, the lower relative price is not sufficient to cover the marginal cost of Pepsi, so the firm decreases production.

Again, what's true for Pepsi bottlers is true for the producers of all goods and services. So when the price level rises and the money wage rate and other resource prices remain constant, the quantity of real GDP supplied increases.

FIGURE 21.2   Short-Run Aggregate Supply

	Price Level (GDP deflator)	Real GDP (trillions of 1996 dollars)
A	100	9.0
B	105	9.5
C	110	10.0
D	115	10.5
E	120	11.0

The short-run aggregate supply curve shows the relationship between the quantity of real GDP supplied and the price level when the money wage rate, other resource prices, and potential GDP remain the same. The short-run aggregate supply curve, SAS, is based on the schedule in the table. This curve is upward-sloping because firms' costs increase as the rate of output increases, so a higher price is needed, relative to the prices of productive resources, to bring forth an increase in the quantity produced.

On the SAS curve, when the price level is 110, real GDP equals potential GDP. If the price level is greater than 110, real GDP exceeds potential GDP; if the price level is below 110, real GDP is less than potential GDP.

Movements Along the *LAS* and *SAS* Curves

Figure 21.3 summarizes what you've just learned about the *LAS* and *SAS* curves. When the price level, the money wage rate, and other resource prices rise by the same percentage, relative prices remain constant and real GDP remains at potential GDP. There is a *movement along* the *LAS* curve.

When the price level rises but the money wage rate and other resource prices remain the same, the quantity of real GDP supplied increases and there is a *movement along* the *SAS* curve.

Let's next study the influences that bring changes in aggregate supply.

FIGURE 21.3   Movements Along the Aggregate Supply Curves

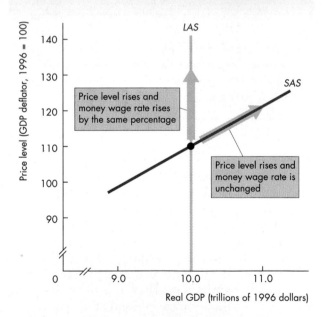

A rise in the price level with no change in the money wage rate and other resource prices brings an increase in the quantity of real GDP supplied and a movement along the short-run aggregate supply curve, SAS.

A rise in the price level with equal percentage increases in the money wage rate and other resource prices keeps the quantity of real GDP supplied constant at potential GDP and brings a movement along the long-run aggregate supply curve, LAS.

Changes in Aggregate Supply

You've just seen that a change in the price level brings a movement along the aggregate supply curves but does not change aggregate supply. Aggregate supply changes when influences on production plans other than the price level change. Let's begin by looking at factors that change potential GDP.

Changes in Potential GDP When potential GDP changes, both long-run aggregate supply and short-run aggregate supply change. Potential GDP changes for three reasons:

1. Change in the full-employment quantity of labor
2. Change in the quantity of capital
3. Advance in technology

An increase in the full-employment quantity of labor, an increase in the quantity of capital, or an advance in technology increases potential GDP. And an increase in potential GDP changes both the long-run aggregate supply and short run aggregate supply.

Figure 21.4 shows these effects of a change in potential GDP. Initially, the long-run aggregate supply curve is LAS_0 and the short-run aggregate supply curve is SAS_0. If an increase in the quantity of capital or a technological advance increases potential GDP to $11 trillion, long-run aggregate supply increases and the long-run aggregate supply curve shifts rightward to LAS_1. Short-run aggregate supply also increases, and the short-run aggregate supply curve shifts rightward to SAS_1.

Let's look more closely at the influences on potential GDP and the aggregate supply curves.

A Change in the Full-Employment Quantity of Labor

A Pepsi bottling plants that employs 100 workers bottles more Pepsi than an otherwise identical plant that employs 10 workers. The same is true for the economy as a whole. The larger the quantity of labor employed, the greater is GDP.

Over time, potential GDP increases because the labor force increases. But (with constant capital and technology) *potential* GDP increases only if the full-employment quantity of labor increases. Fluctuations in employment over the business cycle bring fluctuations in real GDP. But these changes in real GDP are fluctuations around potential GDP. They are not changes in potential GDP and long-run aggregate supply.

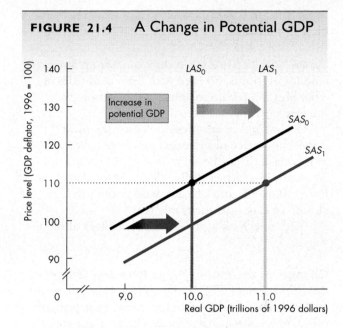

FIGURE 21.4   A Change in Potential GDP

An increase in potential GDP increases both long-run aggregate supply and short-run aggregate supply and shifts both aggregate supply curves rightward from LAS_0 to LAS_1 and from SAS_0 to SAS_1.

A Change in the Quantity of Capital

A Pepsi bottling plant with two production lines bottles more Pepsi than an otherwise identical plant that has only one production line. For the economy, the larger the quantity of capital, the more productive is the labor force and the greater is its potential GDP. Potential GDP per person in the capital-rich United States is vastly greater than that in capital-poor China and Russia.

Capital includes *human capital*. One Pepsi plant is managed by an economics major with an MBA and has a labor force with an average of 10 years of experience. This plant produces a much larger output than an otherwise identical plant that is managed by someone with no business training or experience and that has a young labor force that is new to bottling. The first plant has a greater amount of human capital than the second. For the economy as a whole, the larger the quantity of *human capital* — the skills that people have acquired in school and through on-the-job training — the greater is potential GDP.

An Advance in Technology A Pepsi plant that has pre–computer age machines produces less than one that uses the latest robot technology. Technological change enables firms to produce more from any given amount of inputs. So even with fixed quantities of labor and capital, improvements in technology increase potential GDP.

Technological advances are by far the most important source of increased production over the past two centuries. Because of technological advances, one farmer in the United States today can feed 100 people and one autoworker can produce almost 14 cars and trucks in a year.

Let's now look at the effects of changes of money wages.

Changes in the Money Wage Rate and Other Resource Prices

When the money wage rate or the money prices of other resources such as the price of oil change, short-run aggregate supply changes but long-run aggregate supply does not change.

Figure 21.5 shows the effect on aggregate supply of an increase in the money wage rate. Initially, the short-run aggregate supply curve is SAS_0. A rise in the money wage rate *decreases* short-run aggregate supply and shifts the short-run aggregate supply curve leftward to SAS_2.

The money wage rate (and other resource prices) affect short-run aggregate supply because they influence firms' costs. The higher the money wage rate, the higher are firms' costs and the smaller is the quantity that firms are willing to supply at each price level. So an increase in the money wage rate decreases short-run aggregate supply.

A change in the money wage rate does not change long-run aggregate supply because on the *LAS* curve, the change in the money wage rate is accompanied by an equal percentage change in the price level. With no change in *relative* prices, firms have no incentive to change production and GDP remains constant at potential GDP.

In Fig. 21.5, the vertical distance between the original *SAS* curve and the new *SAS* curve is determined by the percentage change in the money wage rate. That is, the percentage increase in the price level between point *A* and point *B* equals the percentage increase in the money wage rate.

Because potential GDP does not change when the money wage rate changes, long-run aggregate supply does not change. The long-run aggregate supply curve remains at *LAS*.

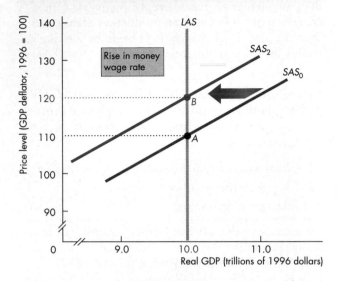

FIGURE 21.5   A Change in the Money Wage Rate

A rise in the money wage rate decreases short-run aggregate supply and shifts the short-run aggregate supply curve leftward from SAS_0 to SAS_2. A rise in the money wage rate does not change potential GDP, so the long-run aggregate supply curve does not shift.

REVIEW QUIZ

1   If the price level rises and if the money wage rate also rises by the same percentage, what happens to the quantity of real GDP supplied? Along which aggregate supply curve does the economy move?

2   If the price level rises and the money wage rate remains constant, what happens to the quantity of real GDP supplied? Along which aggregate supply curve does the economy move?

3   If potential GDP increases, what happens to aggregate supply? Is there a shift of or a movement along the *LAS* curve and the *SAS* curve?

4   If the money wage rate rises and potential GDP remains the same, what happens to aggregate supply? Is there a shift of or a movement along the *LAS* curve and the *SAS* curve?

Aggregate Demand

THE QUANTITY OF REAL GDP DEMANDED IS the sum of the real consumption expenditure (C), investment (I), government expenditures (G), and exports (X) minus imports (M). That is,

$$Y = C + I + G + X - M.$$

The *quantity of real GDP demanded* is the total amount of final goods and services produced in the United States that people, businesses, governments, and foreigners plan to buy.

These buying plans depend on many factors. Some of the main ones are

- The price level
- Expectations
- Fiscal policy and monetary policy
- The world economy

We first focus on the relationship between the quantity of real GDP demanded and the price level. To study this relationship, we keep all other influences on buying plans the same and ask: How does the quantity of real GDP demanded vary as the price level varies?

The Aggregate Demand Curve

Other things remaining the same, the higher the price level, the smaller is the quantity of real GDP demanded. This relationship between the quantity of real GDP demanded and the price level is called **aggregate demand**. Aggregate demand is described by an *aggregate demand schedule* and an *aggregate demand curve*.

Figure 21.6 shows an aggregate demand curve (*AD*) and an aggregate demand schedule. Each point on the *AD* curve corresponds to a row of the schedule. For example, point C' on the *AD* curve and row C' of the schedule tell us that if the price level is 110, the quantity of real GDP demanded is $10 trillion.

The aggregate demand curve slopes downward for two reasons:

- Wealth effect
- Substitution effects

Wealth Effect When the price level rises but other things remain the same, *real* wealth decreases. Real

FIGURE 21.6 Aggregate Demand

	Price Level (GDP deflator)	Real GDP (trillions of 1996 dollars)
A'	90	11.0
B'	100	10.5
C'	110	10.0
D'	120	9.5
E'	130	9.0

The aggregate demand curve (*AD*) shows the relationship between the quantity of real GDP demanded and the price level. The aggregate demand curve is based on the aggregate demand schedule in the table. Each point A' through E' on the curve corresponds to the row in the table identified by the same letter. Thus when the price level is 110, the quantity of real GDP demanded is $10 trillion, shown by point C' in the figure. A change in the price level with all other influences on aggregate buying plans remaining the same brings a change in the quantity of real GDP demanded and a movement along the *AD* curve.

wealth is the amount of money in the bank, bonds, stocks, and other assets that people own, measured not in dollars but in terms of the goods and services that this money, bonds, and stock will buy.

People save and hold money, bonds, and stocks for many reasons. One reason is to build up funds for education expenses. Another reason is to build up enough funds to meet possible medical or other big bills. But the biggest reason is to build up enough funds to provide a retirement income.

If the price level rises, real wealth decreases. People then try to restore their wealth. To do so, they must increase saving and, equivalently, decrease current consumption. Such a decrease in consumption is a decrease in aggregate demand.

Maria's Wealth Effect You can see how the wealth effect works by thinking about Maria's buying plans. Maria lives in Moscow, Russia. She has worked hard all summer and saved 20,000 rubles (the ruble is the currency of Russia), which she plans to spend attending graduate school when she has finished her economics degree. So Maria's wealth is 20,000 rubles. Maria has a part-time job, and her income from this job pays her current expenses. The price level in Russia rises by 100 percent, and now Maria needs 40,000 rubles to buy what 20,000 once bought. To try to make up some of the fall in value of her savings, Maria saves even more and cuts her current spending to the bare minimum.

Substitution Effects When the price level rises and other things remain the same, interest rates rise. The reason is related to the wealth effect that you've just studied. A rise in the price level decreases the real value of the money in people's pockets and bank accounts. With a smaller amount of real money around, banks and other lenders can get a higher interest rate on loans. But faced with higher interest rates, people and businesses delay plans to buy new capital and consumer durable goods and cut back on spending.

This substitution effect involves substituting goods in the future for goods in the present and is called an *intertemporal* substitution effect — a substitution across time. Saving increases to increase future consumption.

To see this intertemporal substitution effect more clearly, think about your own plan to buy a new computer. At an interest rate of 5 percent a year, you might borrow $2,000 and buy the new computer. But at an interest rate of 10 percent a year, you might decide that the payments would be too high. You don't abandon your plan to buy the computer, but you decide to delay your purchase.

A second substitution effect works through international prices. When the U.S. price level rises and other things remain the same, U.S.-made goods and services become more expensive relative to foreign-made goods and services. This change in *relative prices* encourages people to spend less on U.S.-made items and more on foreign-made items. For example, if the U.S. price level rises relative to the Canadian price level, Canadians buy fewer U.S.-made cars (U.S. exports decrease) and Americans buy more Canadian-made cars (U.S. imports increase). U.S. GDP decreases.

Maria's Substitution Effects In Moscow, Russia, Maria makes some substitutions. She was planning to trade in her old motor scooter and get a new one. But with a higher price level and faced with higher interest rates, she decides to make her old scooter last one more year. Also, with the prices of Russian goods sharply increasing, Maria substitutes a low-cost dress made in Malaysia for the Russian-made dress she had originally planned to buy.

Changes in the Quantity of Real GDP Demanded When the price level rises and other things remain the same, the quantity of real GDP demanded decreases — a movement up the aggregate demand curve as shown by the arrow in Fig. 21.6. When the price level falls and other things remain the same, the quantity of real GDP demanded increases — a movement down the aggregate demand curve.

We've now seen how the quantity of real GDP demanded changes when the price level changes. How do other influences on buying plans affect aggregate demand?

Changes in Aggregate Demand

A change in any factor that influences buying plans other than the price level brings a change in aggregate demand. The main factors are

- Expectations
- Fiscal policy and monetary policy
- The world economy

Expectations An increase in expected future income increases the amount of consumption goods (especially big-ticket items such as cars) that people plan to buy today and increases aggregate demand.

An increase in the expected future inflation rate increases aggregate demand because people decide to buy more goods and services at today's relatively lower prices.

An increase in expected future profit increases the investment that firms plan to undertake today and increases aggregate demand.

Fiscal Policy and Monetary Policy The government's attempt to influence the economy by setting and changing taxes, making transfer payments, and purchasing goods and services is called **fiscal policy**. A tax cut or an increase in transfer payments — for example, unemployment benefits or welfare payments — increases aggregate demand. Both of these influences operate by increasing households' *disposable* income. **Disposable income** is aggregate income minus taxes plus transfer payments. The greater the disposable income, the greater is the quantity of consumption goods and services that households plan to buy and the greater is aggregate demand.

Government purchases of goods and services are one component of aggregate demand. So if the government spends more on spy satellites, schools, and highways, aggregate demand increases.

Monetary policy consists of changes in interest rates and in the quantity of money in the economy. The quantity of money is determined by the Federal Reserve (the Fed) and the banks (in a process described in Chapters 27 and 28). An increase in the quantity of money in the economy increases aggregate demand. To see why money affects aggregate demand, imagine that the Fed borrows the army's helicopters, loads them with millions of new $10 bills, and sprinkles them like confetti across the nation. People gather the newly available money and plan to spend some of it. So the quantity of goods and services demanded increases. But people don't plan to spend all the new money. They plan to save some of it and lend it to others through the banks. Interest rates fall, and with lower interest rates, people plan to buy more consumer durables and firms plan to increase their investment.

The World Economy Two main influences that the world economy has on aggregate demand are the foreign exchange rate and foreign income. The *foreign exchange rate* is the amount of a foreign currency that you can buy with a U.S. dollar. Other things remaining the same, a rise in the foreign exchange

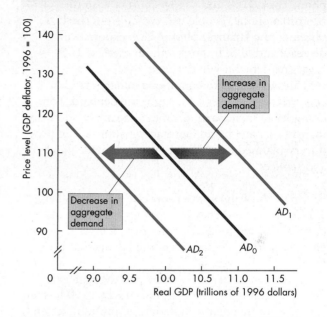

FIGURE 21.7 Changes in Aggregate Demand

Aggregate demand

Decreases if:

- Expected future income, inflation, or profits decrease
- Fiscal policy decreases government purchases, increases taxes, or decreases transfer payments
- Monetary policy decreases the quantity of money and increases interest rates
- The exchange rate increases or foreign income decreases

Increases if:

- Expected future income, inflation, or profits increase
- Fiscal policy increases government purchases, decreases taxes, or increases transfer payments
- Monetary policy increases the quantity of money and decreases interest rates
- The exchange rate decreases or foreign income increases

rate decreases aggregate demand. To see how the foreign exchange rate influences aggregate demand, suppose that $1 exchanges for 100 Japanese yen. A Fujitsu phone (made in Japan) costs 12,500 yen, and an equivalent Motorola phone (made in the United States) costs $110. In U.S. dollars, the Fujitsu phone costs $125, so people around the world buy the cheaper U.S. phone. Now suppose the exchange rate rises to 125 yen. At 125 yen per dollar, the Fujitsu phone costs $100 and is now cheaper than the Motorola phone. People will switch from the U.S. phone to the Japanese phone. U.S. exports will decrease and U.S. imports will increase, so U.S. aggregate demand will decrease.

An increase in foreign income increases U.S. exports and increases U.S. aggregate demand. For example, an increase in income in Japan and Germany increases Japanese and German consumers' and producers' planned expenditures on U.S.-made goods and services.

Shifts of the Aggregate Demand Curve When aggregate demand changes, the aggregate demand curve shifts. Figure 21.7 shows two changes in aggregate demand and summarizes the factors that bring about such changes.

Aggregate demand increases and the aggregate demand curve shifts rightward from AD_0 to AD_1 when expected future income, inflation, or profit increases; government purchases of goods and services increase; taxes are cut; transfer payments increase; the quantity of money increases and interest rates fall; the foreign exchange rate falls; or foreign income increases.

Aggregate demand decreases and the aggregate demand curve shifts leftward from AD_0 to AD_2 when expected future income, inflation, or profit decreases; government purchases of goods and services decrease; taxes increase; transfer payments decrease; the quantity of money decreases and interest rates rise; the foreign exchange rate rises; or foreign income decreases.

REVIEW QUIZ

1 What does the aggregate demand curve show, what factors change, and what factors remain the same when there is a movement along the aggregate demand curve?

2 Why does the aggregate demand curve slope downward?

3 How do changes in expectations, fiscal policy and monetary policy, and the world economy change aggregate demand and the aggregate demand curve?

Macroeconomic Equilibrium

THE PURPOSE OF THE AGGREGATE SUPPLY–aggregate demand model is to explain changes in real GDP and the price level. To achieve this purpose, we combine aggregate supply and aggregate demand and determine macroeconomic equilibrium. There is a macroeconomic equilibrium for each of the time frames for aggregate supply: a long-run equilibrium and a short-run equilibrium. Long-run equilibrium is the state toward which the economy is heading. Short-run equilibrium is the normal state of the economy as it fluctuates around potential GDP.

We'll begin our study of macroeconomic equilibrium by looking first at the short run.

Short-Run Macroeconomic Equilibrium

The aggregate demand curve tells us the quantity of real GDP demanded at each price level, and the short-run aggregate supply curve tells us the quantity of real GDP supplied at each price level. **Short-run macroeconomic equilibrium** occurs when the quantity of real GDP demanded equals the quantity of real GDP supplied. That is, short-run macroeconomic equilibrium occurs at the point of intersection of the *AD* curve and the *SAS* curve. Figure 21.8 shows such an equilibrium at a price level of 110 and real GDP of $10 trillion (points *C* and *C'*).

To see why this position is the equilibrium, think about what happens if the price level is something other than 110. Suppose, for example, that the price level is 120 and that real GDP is $11 trillion (at point *E* on the *SAS* curve). The quantity of real GDP demanded is less than $11 trillion, so firms are unable to sell all their output. Unwanted inventories pile up, and firms cut both production and prices. Production and prices are cut until firms can sell all their output. This situation occurs only when real GDP is $10 trillion and the price level is 110.

Now suppose the price level is 100 and real GDP is $9 trillion (at point *A* on the *SAS* curve). The quantity of real GDP demanded exceeds $9 trillion, so firms are unable to meet the demand for their output. Inventories decrease, and customers clamor for goods and services. So firms increase production and raise prices. Production and prices

FIGURE 21.8   Short-Run Equilibrium

Short-run macroeconomic equilibrium occurs when real
GDP demanded equals real GDP supplied — at the intersection of the aggregate demand curve (*AD*) and the short-
run aggregate supply curve (*SAS*). Here, such an equilibrium
occurs at points *C* and *C'*, where the price level is 110 and
real GDP is $10 trillion. If the price level is 120 and real
GDP is $11 trillion (point *E*), firms will not be able to sell
all their output. They will decrease production and cut
prices. If the price level is 100 and real GDP is $9 trillion
(point *A*), people will not be able to buy all the goods and
services they demand. Firms will increase production and
raise their prices. Only when the price level is 110 and real
GDP is $10 trillion can firms sell all that they produce and
can people buy all the goods and services they demand.
This is the short-run macroeconomic equilibrium.

increase until firms can meet demand. This situation
occurs only when real GDP is $10 trillion and the
price level is 110.

In short-run equilibrium, the money wage rate is
fixed. It does not adjust to bring full employment. So
in the short run, real GDP can be greater than or less
than potential GDP. But in the long run, the money
wage rate does adjust and real GDP moves toward
potential GDP. We are going to study this adjustment
process. But first, let's look at the economy in long-
run equilibrium.

Long-Run Macroeconomic Equilibrium

Long-run macroeconomic equilibrium occurs when
real GDP equals potential GDP — equivalently,
when the economy is on its *long-run* aggregate supply
curve. Figure 21.9 shows the long-run macroeconomic equilibrium, which occurs at the intersection
of the *AD* curve and the *LAS* curve (the blue curves).
Long-run macroeconomic equilibrium comes about
because the money wage rate adjusts. Potential GDP
and aggregate demand determine the price level, and
the price level influences the money wage rate. In
long-run equilibrium, the money wage rate has
adjusted to put the (green) *SAS* curve through the
long-run equilibrium point.

We'll look at this money wage adjustment
process later in this chapter. But first, let's see how
the *AS-AD* model helps us to understand economic
growth and inflation.

FIGURE 21.9   Long-Run Equilibrium

In long-run macroeconomic equilibrium, real GDP equals
potential GDP. So long-run equilibrium occurs where the
aggregate demand curve *AD* intersects the long-run aggregate demand curve *LAS*. In the long run, aggregate demand
determines the price level and has no effect on real GDP.
The money wage rate adjusts in the long run, so the *SAS*
curve intersects the *LAS* curve at the long-run equilibrium
price level.

Economic Growth and Inflation

Economic growth occurs because over time, the quantity of labor grows, capital is accumulated, and technology advances. These changes increase potential GDP and shift the *LAS* curve rightward. Figure 21.10 shows such a shift. The growth rate of potential GDP is determined by the pace at which labor grows, capital is accumulated, and technology advances.

Inflation occurs when, over time, aggregate demand increases by more than long-run aggregate supply. That is, inflation occurs if the *AD* curve shifts rightward by more than the rightward shift in the *LAS* curve. Figure 21.10 shows such shifts.

If aggregate demand increased at the same pace as long-run aggregate supply, we would experience real GDP growth with no inflation.

In the long run, the main influence on aggregate demand is the growth rate of the quantity of money.

At times when the quantity of money increases rapidly, aggregate demand increases quickly and the inflation rate is high. When the growth rate of the quantity of money slows, other things remaining the same, the inflation rate eventually decreases.

Our economy experiences growth and inflation, like those shown in Fig. 21.10. But it does not experience *steady* growth and *steady* inflation. Real GDP fluctuates around potential GDP in a business cycle, and inflation fluctuates. When we study the business cycle, we ignore economic growth. By doing so, we can see the business cycle more clearly.

The Business Cycle

The business cycle occurs because aggregate demand and short-run aggregate supply fluctuate but the money wage rate does not adjust quickly enough to keep real GDP at potential GDP. Figure 21.11 shows three types of short-run macroeconomic equilibrium.

In part (a), there is a below full-employment equilibrium. A **below full-employment equilibrium** is a macroeconomic equilibrium in which potential GDP exceeds real GDP. The amount by which potential GDP exceeds real GDP is called a **recessionary gap**. This name reminds us that a gap has opened up between potential GDP and real GDP either because the economy has experienced a recession or because real GDP, while growing, has grown more slowly than potential GDP.

The below full-employment equilibrium shown in Fig. 21.11(a) occurs where the aggregate demand curve AD_0 intersects short-run aggregate supply curve SAS_0 at a real GDP of $9.8 trillion and a price level of 110. Potential GDP is $10 trillion, so the recessionary gap is $0.2 trillion. The U.S. economy was in a situation similar to that shown in Fig. 21.11(a) during the early 1980s, again during the early 1990s, and in 2001. In those years, real GDP was less than potential GDP.

Figure 21.11(b) is an example of *long-run equilibrium*, in which real GDP equals potential GDP. In this example, the equilibrium occurs where the aggregate demand curve AD_1 intersects the short-run aggregate supply curve SAS_1 at an actual and potential GDP of $10 trillion. The U.S. economy was in a situation such as that shown in Fig. 21.11(b) in 1998.

Figure 21.11(c) shows an above full-employment equilibrium. An **above full-employment equilibrium**

FIGURE 21.10   Economic Growth and Inflation

Economic growth is the persistent increase in potential GDP. Economic growth is shown as an ongoing rightward shift of the *LAS* curve. Inflation is the persistent rise in the price level. Inflation occurs when aggregate demand increases by more than the increase in long-run aggregate supply.

is a macroeconomic equilibrium in which real GDP exceeds potential GDP. The amount by which real GDP exceeds potential GDP is called an **inflationary gap**. This name reminds us that a gap has opened up between real GDP and potential GDP and that this gap creates inflationary pressure.

The above full-employment equilibrium shown in Fig. 21.11(c) occurs where the aggregate demand curve AD_2 intersects the short-run aggregate supply curve SAS_2 at a real GDP of \$10.2 trillion and a price level of 110. There is an inflationary gap of

\$0.2 trillion. The U.S. economy was in a situation similar to that depicted in Fig. 21.11(c) in 1999 and 2000.

The economy moves from one type of equilibrium to another as a result of fluctuations in aggregate demand and in short-run aggregate supply. These fluctuations produce fluctuations in real GDP and the price level. Figure 21.11(d) shows how real GDP fluctuates around potential GDP.

Let's now look at some of the sources of these fluctuations around potential GDP.

FIGURE 21.11   The Business Cycle

(a) Below full-employment equilibrium

(b) Long-run equilibrium

(c) Above full-employment equilibrium

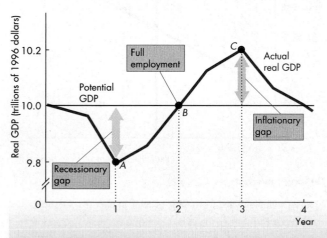

(d) Fluctuations in real GDP

Part (a) shows a below full-employment equilibrium in year 1; part (b) shows a long-run equilibrium in year 2; and part (c) shows an above full-employment equilibrium in year 3. Part (d) shows how real GDP fluctuates around potential GDP in a business cycle. In year 1, a recessionary gap exists and the economy is at point A (in parts a and d). In year 2, the economy is in long-run equilibrium and the economy is at point B (in parts b and d). In year 3, an inflationary gap exists and the economy is at point C (in parts c and d).

Fluctuations in Aggregate Demand

One reason real GDP fluctuates around potential GDP is that aggregate demand fluctuates. Let's see what happens when aggregate demand increases.

Figure 21.12(a) shows an economy in long-run equilibrium. The aggregate demand curve is AD_0, the short-run aggregate supply curve is SAS_0, and the long-run aggregate supply curve is LAS. Real GDP equals potential GDP at $10 trillion, and the price level is 110.

Now suppose that the world economy expands and that the demand for U.S.-made goods increases in Japan and Europe. The increase in U.S. exports increases aggregate demand in the United States and the aggregate demand curve shifts rightward from AD_0 to AD_1 in Fig. 21.12(a).

Faced with an increase in demand, firms increase production and raise prices. Real GDP increases to $10.5 trillion, and the price level rises to 115. The economy is now in an above full-employment equilibrium. Real GDP exceeds potential GDP, and there is an inflationary gap.

The increase in aggregate demand has increased the prices of all goods and services. Faced with higher prices, firms have increased their output rates. At this stage, prices of goods and services have increased but wage rates have not changed. (Recall that as we move along a short-run aggregate supply curve, the money wage rate is constant.)

The economy cannot produce in excess of potential GDP forever. Why not? What are the forces at work that bring real GDP back to potential GDP?

Because the price level has increased and the money wage rate is unchanged, workers have experienced a fall in the buying power of their wages and firms' profits have increased. In these circumstances, workers demand higher wages and firms, anxious to maintain their employment and output levels, meet those demands. If firms do not raise the money wage rate, they will either lose workers or have to hire less productive ones.

As the money wage rate rises, the short-run aggregate supply curve begins to shift leftward. In Fig. 21.12(b), the short-run aggregate supply curve moves

FIGURE 21.12   An Increase in Aggregate Demand

(a) Short-run effect

(b) Long-run effect

An increase in aggregate demand shifts the aggregate demand curve from AD_0 to AD_1. In short-run equilibrium, real GDP increases to $10.5 trillion and the price level rises to 115. In this situation, an inflationary gap exists. In the long run, the money wage rate rises and the short-run aggregate supply

curve shifts leftward from SAS_0 to SAS_1 in part (b). As short-run aggregate supply decreases, the SAS curve shifts and intersects the aggregate demand curve AD_1 at higher price levels and real GDP decreases. Eventually, the price level rises to 125 and real GDP decreases to $10 trillion — potential GDP.

from SAS_0 toward SAS_1. The rise in the wage rate and the shift in the SAS curve produce a sequence of new equilibrium positions. Along the adjustment path, real GDP decreases and the price level rises. The economy moves up along its aggregate demand curve as shown by the arrowheads in the figure.

Eventually, the money wage rate rises by the same percentage as the price level. At this time, the aggregate demand curve AD_1 intersects SAS_1 at a new long-run equilibrium. The price level has risen to 125, and real GDP is back where it started, at potential GDP.

A decrease in aggregate demand has similar but opposite effects to those of an increase in aggregate demand. That is, a decrease in aggregate demand shifts the aggregate demand curve leftward. Real GDP decreases to less than potential GDP, and a recessionary gap emerges. Firms cut prices. The lower price level increases the purchasing power of wages and increases firms' costs relative to their output prices because the wage rate remains unchanged. Eventually, the money wage rate falls and the short-run aggregate supply curve shifts rightward. But the wage rate changes slowly, so real GDP slowly returns to potential GDP and the price level falls slowly.

Let's now work out how real GDP and the price level change when aggregate supply changes.

Fluctuations in Aggregate Supply

Fluctuations in short-run aggregate supply can bring fluctuations in real GDP around potential GDP. Suppose that initially real GDP equals potential GDP. Then there is a large but temporary rise in the price of oil. What happens to real GDP and the price level?

Figure 21.13 answers this question. The aggregate demand curve is AD_0, the short-run aggregate supply curve is SAS_0, and the long-run aggregate supply curve is LAS. Real GDP is $10 trillion, which equals potential GDP, and the price level is 110. Then the price of oil rises. Faced with higher energy and transportation costs, firms decrease production. Short-run aggregate supply decreases, and the short-run aggregate supply curve shifts leftward to SAS_1. The price level rises to 120, and real GDP decreases to $9.5 trillion. Because real GDP decreases, the economy experiences recession. Because the price level increases, the economy experiences inflation. A combination of recession and inflation, called **stagflation**, actually occurred in the United States in the mid-1970s and early 1980s. But events like this are not common.

FIGURE 21.13   A Decrease in Aggregate Supply

An increase in the price of oil decreases short-run aggregate supply and shifts the short-run aggregate supply curve from SAS_0 to SAS_1. Real GDP falls from $10 trillion to $9.5 trillion, and the price level increases from 110 to 120. The economy experiences stagflation.

REVIEW QUIZ

1 Does economic growth result from increases in aggregate demand, short-run aggregate supply, or long-run aggregate supply?

2 Does inflation result from increases in aggregate demand, in short-run aggregate supply, or in long-run aggregate supply?

3 Describe three types of short-run macroeconomic equilibrium.

4 How do fluctuations in aggregate demand and short-run aggregate supply bring fluctuations in real GDP around potential GDP?

Let's put our new knowledge of aggregate supply and aggregate demand to work and see how we can explain recent U.S. macroeconomic performance.

U.S. Economic Growth, Inflation, and Cycles

THE ECONOMY IS CONTINUALLY CHANGING. If you imagine the economy as a video, then an aggregate supply–aggregate demand figure such as Fig. 21.13 is a freeze-frame. We're going to run the video — an instant replay — but keep our finger on the freeze-frame button and look at some important parts of the previous action. Let's run the video from 1960.

Figure 21.14 shows the economy in 1960 at the point of intersection of its aggregate demand curve, AD_{60}, and short-run aggregate supply curve, SAS_{60}. Real GDP was $2.4 trillion, and the GDP deflator was 22 (less than a fifth of its 2001 level). In 1960, real GDP equaled potential GDP — the economy was on its long-run aggregate supply curve, LAS_{60}.

By 2001, the economy had reached the point marked by the intersection of aggregate demand curve AD_{01} and short-run aggregate supply curve SAS_{01}. Real GDP was $9.3 trillion, and the GDP deflator was 109. The LAS_{01} curve assumes that potential GDP in 2001 was also $9.3 trillion.

The path traced by the blue and red dots in Fig. 21.14 shows three key features:

- Economic growth
- Inflation
- Business cycles

Economic Growth

Over the years, real GDP grows — shown in Fig. 21.14 by the rightward movement of the dots. The faster real GDP grows, the larger is the horizontal distance between successive dots. The forces that generate economic growth are those that increase potential GDP. Potential GDP grows because the quantity of labor grows, we accumulate physical capital and human capital, and our technologies advance.

These forces that bring economic growth were strongest during the 1960s and 1990s. During the late 1970s, economic growth was slow.

FIGURE 21.14   Aggregate Supply and Aggregate Demand: 1960–2001

Each point shows the GDP deflator and real GDP in a given year. In 1960 the aggregate demand curve, AD_{60}, and the short-run aggregate supply curve, SAS_{60}, determined these variables. Each point is generated by the gradual shifting of the AD and SAS curves. By 2001, the curves were AD_{01} and SAS_{01} Real GDP grew, and the price level increased. Real GDP grew quickly and inflation was moderate during the 1960s; real GDP growth sagged in 1974–1975 and again in 1982. Inflation was rapid during the 1970s but slowed after the 1982 recession. The period from 1982 to 1989 was one of strong, persistent expansion. A recession began in 1991, and a further strong and sustained expansion then followed. The 2001 recession is not visible in the GDP data for that year.

Source: Bureau of Economic Analysis and author's assumptions.

Inflation

The price level rises over the years — shown in Fig. 21.14 by the upward movement of the points. The larger the rise in the price level, the larger is the vertical distance between successive dots in the figure. The main force generating the persistent increase in the price level is a tendency for aggregate demand to increase at a faster pace than the increase in long-run aggregate supply. All of the factors that increase aggregate demand and shift the aggregate demand curve influence the pace of inflation. But one factor — the growth of the quantity of money — is the main source of *persistent* increases in aggregate demand and persistent inflation.

Business Cycles

Over the years, the economy grows and shrinks in cycles — shown in Fig. 21.14 by the wavelike pattern made by the points, with the recessions highlighted. The cycles arise because both the expansion of short-run aggregate supply and the growth of aggregate demand do not proceed at a fixed, steady pace. Although the economy has cycles, recessions do not usually follow quickly on the heels of their predecessors; "double-dip" recessions like the one in the cartoon are rare.

The Evolving Economy: 1960–2001

During the 1960s, real GDP growth was rapid and inflation was low. This was a period of rapid increases in aggregate supply and of moderate increases in aggregate demand.

The mid-1970s were years of rapid inflation and recession — of stagflation. The major source of these developments was a series of massive oil price increases that decreased short-run aggregate supply and rapid increases in the quantity of money that increased aggregate demand. Recession occurred because short-run aggregate supply decreased at a faster pace than aggregate demand increased.

The rest of the 1970s saw high inflation — the price level increased quickly — and only moderate growth in real GDP. By 1980, inflation was a major problem and the Fed decided to take strong action against it. It permitted interest rates to rise to previously unknown levels. Consequently, aggregate demand decreased. By 1982, the decrease in aggregate demand put the economy in a deep recession.

"Please stand by for a series of tones. The first indicates the official end of the recession, the second indicates prosperity, and the third the return of the recession."

During the years 1983–1990, capital accumulation and steady technological advance resulted in a sustained increase in potential GDP. Wage growth was moderate, and short-run aggregate supply increased. Aggregate demand growth kept pace with the growth of aggregate supply. Sustained but steady growth in aggregate supply and aggregate demand kept real GDP growing and inflation steady. The economy moved from a recession with real GDP less than potential GDP in 1982 to above full employment in 1990. It was in this condition when a decrease in aggregate demand led to the 1991 recession. The economy again embarked on a path of expansion through 2001. The expansion took real GDP to a level that probably exceeded potential GDP and took employment to above full employment during 1998.

◆ The *AS-AD* model explains economic growth, inflation, and the business cycle. The *AS-AD* model enables us to keep our eye on the big picture, but it lacks detail. It does not tell us as much as we need to know about the deeper forces that lie behind aggregate supply and aggregate demand. The chapters that follow begin to fill in the details. We begin with the supply side and study the forces that make our economy grow. But before you embark on this next stage, take a look at *Reading Between the Lines* on pp. 492–493, which gives you a look at the U.S. economy during the 1990s and in 2000 and 2001.

Aggregate Supply and Aggregate Demand in Action

THE WASHINGTON POST, THURSDAY, JANUARY 31, 2002

Numbers Point to Economic Recovery
Recession May Have Been Mildest Yet

By JOHN M. BERRY

Powered by soaring auto sales and a sharp increase in government spending, the U.S. economy resumed growing in the final three months of last year, albeit at a meager 0.2 percent annual rate, the Commerce Department reported yesterday.

The unexpectedly strong number, an initial estimate that will be revised in coming months, suggests that the U.S. recession that began last spring may have already ended. If so, it will have been the mildest on record. ...

"The worst is over. We're on the road to recovery," said Bill Cheney, chief economist at John Hancock Financial Services Inc. in Boston. ...

In the July-September period last year, the nation's output of goods and services, or gross domestic product, declined at a 1.3 percent annual rate — primarily because of the shock of the Sept. 11 terrorist attacks. Economic growth had already slowed to a crawl before the attacks; afterward, economic activity virtually halted for a few weeks as fearful consumers hunkered down, travelers canceled plans and businesses laid off thousands of workers.

But that third-quarter drop in GDP was offset by modest growth in the other three quarters of 2001, so the GDP level ended the year slightly higher than at the end of 2000. ...

While consumer and government spending rose strongly in the fourth quarter, business spending on exports, new plants, housing construction, and equipment and software all declined. Purchases of high-tech equipment — particularly computers — which had been falling sharply for a year, stabilized in the fourth quarter, however, suggesting to some analysts that the worst is over for that hard-hit sector. ...

Yesterday's report also painted a very tame picture of inflation. ... The ... GDP price index fell 0.3 percent, the first decline in nearly half a century. ...

Essence of the Story

■ Real GDP increased in the fourth quarter (October–December) of 2001 at a rate of 0.2 percent a year, and the GDP deflator fell.

■ Consumption expenditure (auto sales) and government purchases were the two fastest-growing items of expenditure.

■ Exports; business spending on new plant, equipment, and software; and housing construction all declined, but purchases of computers, which had been falling for a year, stabilized.

■ If the recession that began in March 2001 was over by the end of 2001, it had been the mildest on record.

■ Real GDP decreased during the third quarter (July–September) of 2001 at a rate of 1.3 percent a year.

■ The shock of the September 11 terrorist attacks was the primary cause of the decrease, but economic growth had already slowed before then.

Economic Analysis

■ U.S. real GDP grew spectacularly between 1991 and 2001, by 3.3 percent a year, and the price level rose by only 2 percent a year.

■ Growth slowed, and in the third quarter of 2001, real GDP shrank.

■ But most forecasters were optimistic that the recession would be over by early 2002 and growth would resume.

■ Figure 1 explains the growth and low inflation of the 1990s in terms of changes in aggregate supply and aggregate demand.

■ In 1991, real GDP was $6.7 trillion and the price level was 92 at the intersection of the aggregate demand curve, AD_{91} and the short-run aggregate supply curve, SAS_{91}. Potential GDP in 1991 was $6.9 trillion, so long-run aggregate supply was at LAS_{91} and there was a recessionary gap.

■ During the 1990s, extraordinary technological change and capital accumulation, particularly in the new high-tech economy, brought a rapid growth in potential GDP and the LAS curve shifted rightward to LAS_{01} by 2001.

■ Aggregate demand increased by more than potential GDP. With rising stock prices, consumers felt wealthier, decreased saving, and increased consumption. Low interest rates and steady money growth sustained this increase in aggregate demand. The AD curve shifted rightward to AD_{01}.

■ The money wage rate increased, and the short-run aggregate supply curve shifted leftward from SAS_{91} to SAS_{01}.

■ By 2001, real GDP was $9.3 trillion and the price level was 109. Real GDP was slightly greater than potential GDP (but by too little to be seen in Figure 1).

■ Figure 2 zooms in on the economy in 2001 and shows the events that brought a decrease in real GDP during the second quarter.

■ At its peak, real GDP was $9.34 trillion at the intersection of AD_{Q2} and SAS_{Q2} and was greater than potential GDP.

■ Aggregate demand decreased in the third quarter to AD_{Q3}, and a rise in the money wage rate brought a decrease in short-run aggregate supply to SAS_{Q3}. Real GDP

fell below potential GDP to $9.31 trillion, but the price level rose slightly.

■ During the fourth quarter of 2001 (not shown in the figure), aggregate demand increased but so did aggregate supply. So real GDP increased again, and the price level fell slightly.

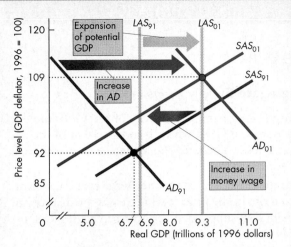

Figure 1 The 1990s expansion

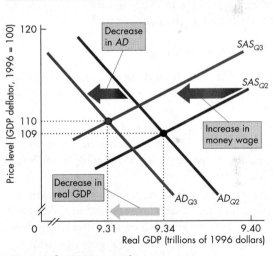

Figure 2 The 2001 recession

You're The Voter

■ Do you think the Fed should lower interest rates further to end recession? Explain your answer.

■ Do you think the federal government should implement a stimulus package to end recession? Explain your answer.

SUMMARY

KEY POINTS

Aggregate Supply (pp. 476–480)

- In the long run, the quantity of real GDP supplied is potential GDP, which is independent of the price level. The long-run aggregate supply curve is vertical.
- In the short run, the money wage rate is constant, so a rise in the price level increases the quantity of real GDP supplied. The short-run aggregate supply curve is upward sloping.
- A change in potential GDP changes both long-run and short-run aggregate supply. A change in the money wage rate and other resource prices change only short-run aggregate supply.

Aggregate Demand (pp. 481–484)

- A rise in the price level decreases the quantity of real GDP demanded, other things remaining the same.
- The reason is that the higher price level decreases the quantity of *real* money, raises the interest rate, and raises the price of domestic goods compared with foreign goods.
- Changes in expected future income, inflation, and profits; changes in fiscal policy and monetary policy; and changes in world real GDP and the foreign exchange rate change aggregate demand.

Macroeconomic Equilibrium (pp. 484–489)

- In the short run, real GDP and the price level are determined by aggregate demand and short-run aggregate supply.
- In the long run, real GDP equals potential GDP and aggregate demand determines the price level and the money wage rate.
- Economic growth occurs because potential GDP increases.
- Inflation occurs because aggregate demand grows more quickly than potential GDP.
- Business cycles occur because aggregate demand and aggregate supply fluctuate.

U.S. Economic Growth, Inflation, and Cycles (pp. 490–491)

- Potential GDP grew fastest during the 1960s and 1990s and slowest during the 1970s.
- Inflation persists because aggregate demand grows faster than potential GDP.
- Business cycles occur because aggregate supply and aggregate demand change at an uneven pace.

KEY FIGURES

KEY TERMS

PROBLEMS

*1. The following events occur that influence the economy of Toughtimes:
   - A deep recession hits the world economy.
   - Oil prices rise sharply.
   - Businesses expect huge losses in the near future.

   a. Explain the separate effects of each of these events on real GDP and the price level in Toughtimes, starting from a position of long-run equilibrium.

   b. Explain the combined effects of these events on real GDP and the price level in Toughtimes, starting from a position of long-run equilibrium.

   c. Explain what the Toughtimes government and the Fed can do to overcome the problems faced by the economy.

2. The following events occur that influence the economy of Coolland:
   - There is a strong expansion in the world economy.
   - Businesses expect huge profits in the near future.
   - The government cuts its purchases.

   a. Explain the separate effects of each of these events on real GDP and the price level in Coolland, starting from a position of long-run equilibrium.

   b. Explain the combined effects of these events on real GDP and the price level in Coolland, starting from a position of long-run equilibrium.

   c. Explain why the Coolland government or central bank might want to take action to influence the Coolland economy.

*3. The economy of Mainland has the following aggregate demand and supply schedules:

Price level	Real GDP demanded	Real GDP supplied in the short run
	(billions of 1996 dollars)	
90	450	350
100	400	400
110	350	450
120	300	500
130	250	550
140	200	600

   a. In a figure, plot the aggregate demand curve and the short-run aggregate supply curve.

   b. What are the values of real GDP and the price level in Mainland in a short-run macroeconomic equilibrium?

   c. Mainland's potential GDP is $500 billion. Plot the long-run aggregate supply curve in the figure in part (a).

4. The economy of Miniland has the following aggregate demand and supply schedules:

Price level	Real GDP demanded	Real GDP supplied in the short run
	(billions of 1996 dollars)	
90	600	150
100	500	200
110	400	250
120	300	300
130	200	350
140	100	400

   a. In a figure, plot the aggregate demand curve and the short-run aggregate supply curve.

   b. What are the values of real GDP and the price level in Miniland in a short-run macroeconomic equilibrium?

   c. Miniland's potential GDP is $250 billion. Plot the long-run aggregate supply curve in the figure in part (a).

*5. In problem 3, aggregate demand increases by $100 billion. How do real GDP and the price level change in the short run?

6. In problem 4, aggregate demand decreases by $150 billion. How do real GDP and the price level change in the short run?

*7. In problem 3, aggregate supply decreases by $100 billion. What now is the short-run macroeconomic equilibrium?

8. In problem 4, aggregate supply increases by $150 billion. What now is the short-run macroeconomic equilibrium?

*9. In the economy shown in the figure on the next page, initially the short-run aggregate supply is SAS_0 and aggregate demand is AD_0. Then some events change aggregate demand, and the aggregate demand curve shifts rightward to AD_1. Later, some other events change aggregate supply, and the short-run aggregate supply curve shifts leftward to SAS_1.

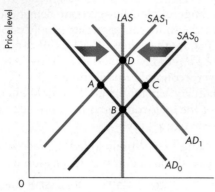

a. What is the equilibrium point after the change in aggregate demand?
b. What is the equilibrium point after the change in aggregate supply?
c. What events could have changed aggregate demand from AD_0 to AD_1?
d. What events could have changed aggregate supply from SAS_0 to SAS_1?

10. In the economy shown in the figure, initially long-run aggregate supply is LAS_0, short-run aggregate supply is SAS_0, and aggregate demand is AD. Then some events change aggregate supply, and the aggregate supply curves shift rightward to LAS_1 and SAS_1.

a. What is the equilibrium point after the change in aggregate supply?
b. What events could have changed long-run aggregate supply from LAS_0 to LAS_1?
c. What events could have changed short-run aggregate supply from SAS_0 to SAS_1?
d. After the increase in aggregate supply, is real GDP greater than or less than potential GDP?
e. What change in aggregate demand will make real GDP equal to potential GDP?

CRITICAL THINKING

1. After you have studied the account of the U.S. economy since 1991 in *Reading Between the Lines* on pp. 492–493,
   a. Describe the main features of U.S. economic growth since 1991.
   b. In which periods did the United States have a recessionary gap and in which did it have an inflationary gap?
   c. Use the *AS-AD* model to show the changes in aggregate demand and aggregate supply that brought the increase in real GDP and fall in the price level in the fourth quarter of 2001.
   d. Use the *AS-AD* model to show the changes in aggregate demand and aggregate supply that would occur if the Federal Reserve cut interest rates again.
   e. Use the *AS-AD* model to show the changes in aggregate demand and aggregate supply that would occur if the federal government implemented its proposed fiscal stimulus package.

WEB EXERCISES

1. Use the links on your Parkin Web site to find data on recent changes in and forecasts of real GDP and the price level in the United States.
   a. What is your forecast of next year's real GDP?
   b. What is your forecast of next year's price level?
   c. What is your forecast of the inflation rate?
   d. What is your forecast of the growth rate of real GDP?
   e. Do you think there will be a recessionary gap or an inflationary gap next year?
2. Use the links on your Parkin Web site to find data on recent changes in and forecasts of real GDP and the price level in Japan.
   a. What is your forecast of next year's real GDP?
   b. What is your forecast of next year's price level?
   c. What is your forecast of the inflation rate?
   d. What is your forecast of the growth rate of real GDP?
   e. Compare and contrast the forecasts for the U.S. and Japanese economies.

UNDERSTANDING THE THEMES OF MACROECONOMICS

The Big Picture

Macroeconomics is a large and controversial subject that is interlaced with political ideological disputes. And it is a field in which charlatans as well as serious thinkers have much to say. This page is a map that looks back at the road you've just traveled and forward at the path you will take from here. ◆ You began your study of macroeconomics with the core questions of the subject. What are the causes of:

- Economic growth?
- Business cycles?
- Unemployment?
- Inflation?

In Chapter 19, you learned how we measure the economy's output and the price level. These measures are used to calculate the rate of economic growth, business cycle fluctuations, and inflation. You discovered that making these measurements is not straightforward and that small measurement errors can have a big effect on our perceptions about how we are doing. ◆ In Chapter 20, you learned how we measure the state of the labor market — the levels of employment and unemployment and wages. And in Chapter 21, you studied the macroeconomic version of supply and demand — *aggregate supply* and *aggregate demand*. You saw that the aggregate supply–aggregate demand model is the big picture model. It explains both the long-term trends in economic growth and inflation and the short-term

business cycle fluctuations in production, jobs, and inflation. ◆ The chapters that lie ahead of you look behind aggregate supply and aggregate demand. First, in Chapters 22 through 24, you study aggregate supply and economic growth. This material is so central to the oldest question in macroeconomics that Adam Smith tried to answer. You'll begin in Chapter 22 by looking at the economy at full employment and study the forces that determine potential GDP and make it change. In Chapter 23, you will study the role played by saving and investment in increasing the amount of capital and creating economic growth. Then, in Chapter 24, you will study the growth process and the roles of capital accumulation and technological change in bringing about economic growth. ◆ Second, in Chapters 25 through 31, you will study aggregate demand, inflation, and deflation. This material is central to the macroeconomics that Keynes developed as a response to the Great Depression. Here you will learn about economic fluctuations and the policies that might limit their severity. ◆ Before continuing your study of macroeconomics, spend a few minutes with John Maynard Keynes and Jean Baptiste Say, the leading scholars who developed this subject. And spend a few minutes with one of today's leading macroeconomists, Robert Barro of Harvard University.

PROBING THE IDEAS
Macroeconomic Revolutions

JOHN MAYNARD KEYNES, *born in England in 1883, was one of the outstanding minds of the twentieth century. He wrote on probability as well as economics, represented Britain at the Versailles peace conference at the end of World War I, was a master speculator on international financial markets (an activity he conducted from bed every morning and which made and lost him several fortunes), and played a prominent role in creating the International Monetary Fund. He was a member of the Bloomsbury Group, a circle of outstanding artists and writers that included E. M. Forster, Bertrand Russell, and Virginia Woolf. Keynes was a controversial and quick-witted figure. A critic once complained that Keynes had changed his opinion on some matter, to which Keynes retorted: "When I discover I am wrong, I change my mind. What do you do?"*

THE ISSUES

During the Industrial Revolution, as technological change created new jobs and destroyed old ones, people began to wonder whether the economy could create enough jobs and sufficient demand to buy all the things that the new industrial economy could produce.

Jean-Baptiste Say argued that production creates incomes that are sufficient to buy everything that is produced — supply creates its own demand — an idea that came to be called *Say's Law.*

Say and Keynes would have had a lot to disagree about. Jean-Baptiste Say, born in Lyon, France, in 1767 (he was 9 years old when Adam Smith's *Wealth of Nations* was published), suffered the wrath of Napoleon for his views on government and the economy. In today's world, Say would be leading a radical conservative charge for a smaller and leaner government. Say was the most famous economist of his era on both sides of the Atlantic. His book, *Traité d'économie politique (A Treatise in Political Economy),* published in 1803, became a best-selling university economics textbook in both Europe and North America.

As the Great Depression of the 1930s became more severe and more prolonged, Say's Law looked less and less relevant. John Maynard Keynes revolutionized macroeconomic thinking by turning Say's Law on its head, arguing that production does not depend on supply. Instead, it depends on what people are willing to buy — on demand. Or as Keynes put it, production depends on *effective demand.* It is possible, argued Keynes, for people to refuse to spend all of their incomes. If businesses fail to spend on new capital the amount that people plan to save, demand might be less than supply. In this situation, resources might go unemployed and remain unemployed indefinitely.

The influence of Keynes persists even today, more than 60 years after the publication of his main work. But during the past 20 years, Nobel Laureate Robert E. Lucas, Jr., with significant contributions from a list of outstanding macroeconomists too long to name, has further revolutionized macroeconomics. Today, we know a lot about economic growth, unemployment, inflation, and business cycles. And we know how to use fiscal policy and monetary policy to improve macroeconomic performance. But we don't yet have all the answers. Macroeconomics remains a field of lively controversy and exciting research.

In 1776, James Hargreaves, an English weaver and carpenter, developed a simple hand-operated machine called a spinning jenny (pictured here). Using this machine, a person could spin 80 threads at once. Thousands of hand-wheel spinners, operators of machines that could spin only one thread, lost their jobs. They protested by wrecking spinning jennies. In the long run, the displaced hand-wheel spinners found work, often in factories that manufactured the machines that had destroyed their previous jobs. From the earliest days of the Industrial Revolution to the present day, people have lost their jobs as new technologies have automated what human effort had previously been needed to accomplish.

Advances in computer technology have made it possible for us to dial our own telephone calls to any part of the world and get connected in a flash. A task that was once performed by telephone operators, who made connections along copper wires, is now performed faster and more reliably by computers along fiber-optic cables. Just as the Industrial Revolution transformed the textile industry, so today's Information Revolution is transforming the telecommunications industry. In the process, the mix of jobs is changing. There are fewer jobs for telephone operators but more jobs for telephone systems designers, builders, managers, and marketers. In the long run, as people spend the income they earn in their changing jobs, supply creates its own demand, just as Say predicted. But does supply create its own demand in the short run, when displaced workers are unemployed?

Robert Barro, whom you can meet on the following pages, is one of the most distinguished macroeconomists. He has contributed to our understanding of economic growth, inflation, and the business cycle and played a significant role in the contemporary macroeconomic revolution.

TALKING WITH

ROBERT J. BARRO *is Robert C. Waggoner Professor of Economics at Harvard University and a senior fellow at the Hoover Institution of Stanford University. Born in 1944 in New York City, he was a physics undergraduate at the California Institute of Technology and an economics graduate student at Harvard. Professor Barro is one of the world's leading economists and has done research on every aspect of macroeconomics, with a focus in recent years on economic growth. In addition to his many scholarly books and articles, he writes extensively for a wider audience. His book,*

Getting it Right: Markets and Choices in a Free Society *(MIT Press, 1996) explains, in non-technical language, the importance of property rights and free markets for achieving economic growth and a high standard of living. A new book,* Nothing Is Sacred: Economic Ideas for the New Millennium *(MIT Press, 2002), expands on these ideas. And his regular articles in* Business Week *and the* Wall Street Journal *provide an accessible analysis of an incredible range of current economic issues.*

Robert J. Barro

Michael Parkin talked with Robert Barro about his work and the progress that economists have made in understanding macroeconomic performance since the pioneering work of Keynes.

Professor Barro, your first degree was in physics. Why did you switch to economics when you went to graduate school?

For me, economics provided an ideal combination of technical analysis with applications to social problems and policies. Physics — or really mathematics — provided a strong background for economic theory and econometrics, but it was not until later in graduate school that I thought I acquired good economic insights. Overall, the transition from physics to economics was a relatively easy one for me, and I have never regretted the choice to switch fields. (Perhaps it also helped that, after taking courses from the great Richard Feynman at Caltech, I recognized that I would never be an outstanding theoretical physicist.)

Your recent research has focused on the determinants of economic growth. What do we know about determinants of growth? And what do we still need to discover?

A lot of progress has been made over the last decade in attaining an empirical understanding of the determinants of economic growth. There are no "silver bullets" for growth, but there are a number of favorable policies, institutions, and national characteristics that have been identified.

For example, growth is stimulated by a strong rule of law, high levels of human capital in the forms of education and health, low levels of non-productive government spending (and associated taxes), international openness, low fertility rates, and macroeconomic stability (including low and stable inflation). Given these and other factors, growth tends to be higher if a country starts off poorer. That is, convergence — in the sense of the poor tending to grow faster than the rich — holds in a conditional sense, when one holds constant an array of policies

> *There are no "silver bullets" for growth, but there are a number of favorable policies, institutions, and national characteristics that have been identified.*

and national characteristics. However, convergence does not apply in an absolute sense because the poorest countries tend to have the worst policies and characteristics (which explains why they are observed to be poor).

Is there anything that rich countries can do to help poor countries grow faster? Or does successful economic growth come only from self-help?

Mostly economic growth has to come from internal improvements in institutions and policies and from domestic accumulations of human and physical capital. There is no evidence that the rich countries can help through welfare programs, such as foreign aid and debt relief. On the contrary, there is some evidence that, because of the low quality of governance in most developing countries, foreign aid goes mainly to increased government spending and corruption. In the bad old days, the rich countries also provided governance (though not aimed especially at the interests of the governed). However, no one wants to return to the era of colonialism.

You've identified international openness as a characteristic that encourages growth. Is this an area in which the rich countries might do more by opening themselves to free trade with poor countries? Or is it enough for poor countries to just get on with opening their doors?

The rich countries could help to spur economic development by opening themselves more to trade in goods and services, technology, and financial transactions. Protectionist policies, notably in agriculture and textiles, are harmful to developing countries as well as to consumers in rich countries. President Bush's policies have been disgraceful in this area, notably in his protectionism during 2002 for steel and agriculture.

Inflation has been subdued in the United States for most of the 1990s and 2000s. Is this now a problem of the past that we can stop worrying about?

I am optimistic that the monetary authorities of the United States and many other countries have become committed to price stability and have learned that high inflation does not stimulate growth. Central banks seem also to have learned a lot about the mechanics of achieving price stability. One worry, however, is that monetary authorities — including the Federal Reserve — will become overconfident

> *I am optimistic that the monetary authorities of the United States and many other countries have become committed to price stability and have learned that high inflation does not stimulate growth.*

and will come to believe that they can fine-tune the real economy without losing price stability. For example, the Fed's sharp reductions in interest rates during the 2001 recession may have stimulated too much and could lead eventually to higher inflation.

How do economic growth and inflation interact? Why can't a country grow faster by keeping demand growth strong and inflating?

Inflation is inversely related to economic growth over the medium term — for example, periods of five years or more. This relationship is particularly evident at high inflation rates — say, above 10-15% per year — but probably also applies for more moderate inflation. The likely reason for the inverse relation is that high and volatile inflation makes it difficult for the price system to operate efficiently. It is possible that unanticipated monetary stimulus expands the real economy in the short run. However, this short-term benefit is not worth the cost over the medium

501

and long term. Moreover, the stimulus works mainly when it comes as a surprise, and it is hard to be surprising in a systematic way.

Some years ago, you worked on the business cycle. What is your current view on the nature and causes of aggregate fluctuations? Are they primarily an efficient response to the uneven pace of technical change, or are they primarily the consequence of market failure and demand fluctuations?

Many factors are sources of business cycles, and economists have not been very successful at isolating the precise causes. Influences that seem to matter include variations in the rate of technological progress, shifts in the terms of trade, fiscal effects (particularly important during wartime), and monetary fluctuations. In some countries, shifts in labor relations and in regulatory policies are important. Other countries are influenced by major changes in the quality of governance, such as the recent deterioration of public institutions in Argentina.

I do not think that we know what portion of fluctuations represents efficient responses to shocks as opposed to excess volatility associated with market failure. We do know that many observed fluctuations stem from failures of government policy and institutions, so it is inappropriate to think of governments as typically smoothing out the excesses of the private sector.

What remains in today's macroeconomics of the contribution of Keynes?

Probably Keynesian economics is most influential today in analyses that stress the real effects of monetary policy — either as sources of business fluctuations or as ways to smooth out the cycle. This situation is ironic because Keynes himself deemphasized monetary shocks as a source of fluctuations. He stressed the excesses of the private economy — including the amplifying effects of multipliers and the sensitivity of investment to shifting expectations — and the potentially beneficial role of offsetting fiscal policies.

Empirically, the multiplier seems to have existed only in the mind of Keynes.

What advice do you have for a student who is just starting to study economics? Is it a good subject in which to major? If so, what other subjects would you urge students to study alongside economics? Or is the path that you followed, starting with physics (or perhaps math) and then moving to economics for graduate school more effective?

Economics is an excellent field for an undergraduate to study whether one chooses to become an economist or — more likely — if one goes into other fields, such as business or law. Economists have found the framework or methodology that makes economics the core social science, and its impact has been felt greatly by other fields, such as political science, law, and history. These days, economic reasoning is being applied to the study of an array of social topics, including marriage and fertility, crime, democracy, and legal structure. As another example, I am currently participating in a project that involves the interactions between economics and religion (see www.wcfia.harvard.edu/religion for a description). Partly this work is about how economic development and government policies affect religiosity and partly about how religious beliefs and participation influence economic and political outcomes. So, perhaps in the future economics will also be important for studies in theology. No doubt, many economists (including me) have imperialistic tendencies, but this is because they have a great product to sell. As to

> *Economists have found the framework or methodology that makes economics the core social science ...*

other complementary subjects to study, the most valuable one is probably mathematics, which provides many of the useful tools to carry out theoretical and empirical inquiries.

THE ECONOMY AT FULL EMPLOYMENT

CHAPTER 22

Production and Jobs

Over time, we become more productive and our incomes grow. For each hour we worked in 2001, we earned twice what we earned in 1961. We even became more productive during the recession of 2001 as production and jobs shrank. What makes production and incomes grow? Why did productivity grow during a recession? ◆ Our population also grows every year. How does population size influence employment, wage rates, and potential GDP? ◆ We hear a lot about the need to increase our national saving to invest in new capital, the importance of education, and the need to support science and technology. How do capital accumulation, education, and advances in technology influence employment, wage rates, and potential GDP? ◆ You know that when we talk about full employment, we don't mean there is *no* unemployment. But what determines the amount of unemployment when the economy is at full employment?

◆ We'll answer these questions in this chapter. We'll discover how changes in population, capital, and technology influence production, jobs, and incomes over long periods of time. We'll learn about the forces that create unemployment when the economy is at full employment. And in *Reading Between the Lines* at the end of this chapter, we'll explain why productivity grows even in a recession.

After studying this chapter, you will be able to

- **Describe the relationship between the quantity of labor employed and real GDP**

- **Explain what determines the demand for labor and the supply of labor and how labor market equilibrium determines employment, the real wage rate, and potential GDP**

- **Explain how an increase in the population, an increase in capital, and an advance in technology change employment, the real wage rate, and potential GDP**

- **Explain what determines unemployment when the economy is at full employment**

503

Real GDP and Employment

To produce more output, we must use more inputs. We can increase real GDP by employing more labor, increasing the quantity of capital, or developing technologies that are more productive. In the short term, the quantity of capital and the state of technology are fixed. So to increase real GDP in the short term, we must increase the quantity of labor employed. Let's look at the relationship between real GDP and the quantity of labor employed.

Production Possibilities

When you studied the limits to production in Chapter 2 (see p. 32), you learned about the *production possibilities frontier*, which is the boundary between those combinations of goods and services that can be produced and those that cannot. We can think about the production possibilities frontier for any pair of goods or services when we hold the quantities of all other goods and services constant. Let's think about the production possibilities frontier for two special items: real GDP and the quantity of leisure time.

Real GDP is a measure of the final goods and services produced in the economy in a given time period (see p. 434). We measure real GDP as a number of 1996 dollars, but the measure is a *real* one. Real GDP is not a pile of dollars. It is a pile of goods and services. Think of it as a number of big shopping carts filled with goods and services. Each cart contains some of each kind of different goods and services produced, and one cartload of items costs $1 trillion. To say that real GDP is $10 trillion means that real GDP is 10 very big shopping carts of goods and services.

The quantity of leisure time is the number of hours we spend not working. It is the time we spend playing or watching sports, seeing movies, and hanging out with friends. Leisure time is a special type of good or service.

Each hour that we spent pursuing fun could have been spent working. So when the quantity of leisure time increases by one hour, the quantity of labor employed decreases by one hour. If we spent all our time having fun rather than working, we would not produce anything. Real GDP would be zero. The more leisure time we forgo to work, the greater is the quantity of labor employed and the greater is real GDP.

The relationship between leisure time and real GDP is a *production possibilities frontier (PPF)*. Figure 22.1(a) shows an example of this frontier. The economy has 450 billion hours of leisure time available. If people use all these hours to pursue leisure, no labor is employed and real GDP is zero. As people forgo leisure and work more, real GDP increases. If people spent 200 billion hours working and took 250 billion hours in leisure, real GDP would be $10 trillion at point *A*. If people spent all the available hours working, real GDP would be $15 trillion.

The bowed-out *PPF* displays increasing opportunity cost. In this case, the opportunity cost of a given amount of real GDP is the amount of leisure time forgone to produce it. As real GDP increases, each additional unit of real GDP costs an increasing amount of forgone leisure. The reason is that we use the most productive labor first, and as we use more labor, we use increasingly less productive labor.

The Production Function

The **production function** is the relationship between real GDP and the quantity of labor employed when all other influences on production remain the same. The production function shows how real GDP varies as the quantity of labor employed varies, other things remaining the same.

Because one more hour of labor employed means one less hour of leisure, the production function is like a mirror image of the leisure time–real GDP *PPF*. Figure 22.1(b) shows the production function for the economy whose *PPF* is shown in Fig. 22.1(a). You can see that when the quantity of labor employed is zero, real GDP is also zero. And as the quantity of labor employed increases, so does real GDP. When 200 billion labor hours are employed, real GDP is $10 trillion (at point *A*).

A decrease in leisure hours and the corresponding increases in the quantity of labor employed and real GDP bring a movement along the production possibilities frontier and along the production function. The arrows along the *PPF* and the production function in Fig. 22.1 show these movements. Such movements occurred when employment and real GDP surged during World War II.

But the increase in real GDP during World War II changed for an additional reason. Labor became more productive. Let's study the influences on the productivity of labor.

FIGURE 22.1   Production Possibilities and the Production Function

(a) Production possibility frontier

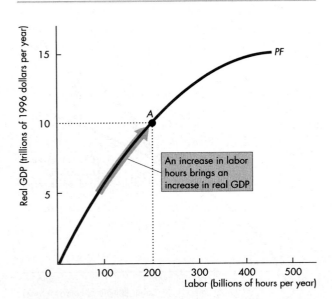

(b) Production function

On the production possibilities frontier in part (a), if we enjoy 450 billion hours of leisure, we produce no real GDP. If we forgo 200 billion hours of leisure time to work and spend 250 billion hours of leisure time, we produce a real GDP of $10 trillion, at point A.

At point A on the production function in part (b), we use 200 billion hours of labor to produce $10 trillion of real GDP.

Changes in Productivity

When we talk about *productivity*, we usually mean labor productivity. **Labor productivity** is real GDP per hour of labor. Three factors influence labor productivity:

- Physical capital
- Human capital
- Technology

Physical Capital   A farm worker equipped with only a stick and primitive tools can cultivate almost no land and grow barely enough food to feed a single family. A farmer equipped with a steel plow pulled by an animal can cultivate more land and produce enough food to feed a small village. A farmer equipped with a modern tractor, plow, and harvester can cultivate thousands of acres and produce enough food to feed hundreds of people.

By using physical capital on our farms and in our factories, shops, and offices, we enormously increase labor productivity. And the more physical capital we use, the greater is our labor productivity, other things remaining the same.

Human Capital   An economy's **human capital** is the knowledge and skill that people have obtained from education and on-the-job training.

The average college graduate has a greater amount of human capital than the average high school graduate possesses. Consequently, the college graduate is able to perform some tasks that are beyond the ability of the high school graduate. The college graduate is more productive. For the nation as a whole, the greater the amount of schooling its citizens complete, the greater is its real GDP, other things remaining the same.

Regardless of how much schooling a person has completed, not much production is accomplished on the first day at work. Learning about the new work environment consumes the newly hired worker. But as time passes and experience accumulates, the worker becomes more productive. We call this on-the-job education activity **learning-by-doing**.

Learning-by-doing can bring incredible increases in labor productivity. The more experienced the labor force, the greater is its labor productivity, and other things remaining the same, the greater is real GDP.

World War II provides a carefully documented example of the importance of this source of increase in labor productivity. In the shipyards that produced the transport vessels called Liberty ships, labor productivity increased by an astonishing 30 percent purely as a result of learning-by-doing.

Technology A student equipped with a pen can complete a readable page of writing in perhaps 10 minutes. This same task takes 5 minutes with a typewriter and 2 minutes with a computer. Traveling on foot from New York to Los Angeles takes a person (a fit person!) more than 100 days. In a car, the trip takes a comfortable 5 days. And in an airplane, the trip takes 5 hours. These are examples of the enormous impact of technology on productivity. Imagine the profound effect of these advances in technology on the productivity of a movie director who works in both New York and Los Angeles!

Shifts in the Production Function

Any influence on production that increases labor productivity shifts the production function upward. Real GDP increases at each level of labor hours. In Fig. 22.2(a), the production function is initially PF_0. Then an increase in physical capital and human capital or an advance in technology occurs. The production function shifts upward to PF_1.

At each quantity of labor employed, real GDP is greater on the new production function than it was on the original one. For example, at 200 billion hours, real GDP increases from $10 trillion (point A) to $11 trillion (point B).

Figure 22.2(b) shows how the production function in the United States shifted upward between 1981 and 2001. Along the production function PF_{01}, labor productivity is 45 percent greater than that on PF_{81}. Labor productivity in the United States increased by almost 2 percent a year.

FIGURE 22.2 An Increase in Labor Productivity

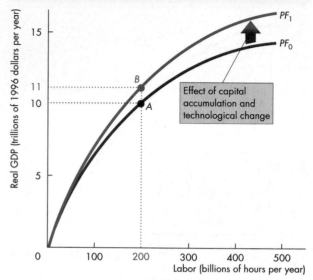

(a) An increase in labor productivity

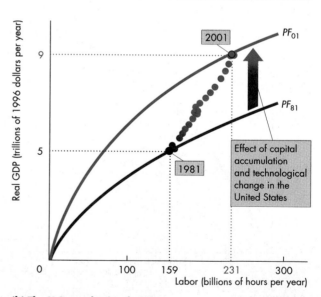

(b) The U.S. production function

On PF_0 in part (a), 200 billion labor hours produce a real GDP of $10 trillion (point A). An increase in capital or an advance in technology increases labor productivity and shifts the production function upward to PF_1. Now, 200 billion labor hours produce a real GDP of $11 trillion (point B). U.S. real GDP has increased (part b) because labor productivity and the quantity of labor have increased.

The Labor Market and Aggregate Supply

YOU'VE SEEN THAT IN A GIVEN YEAR, WITH A given amount of physical and human capital and given technology, real GDP depends on the quantity of labor hours employed. To produce more real GDP, we must employ more labor hours. The labor market determines the quantity of labor hours employed and the quantity of real GDP supplied. We'll learn how by studying

- The demand for labor
- The supply of labor
- Labor market equilibrium
- Aggregate supply

The Demand for Labor

The **quantity of labor demanded** is the number of labor hours hired by all the firms in the economy. The **demand for labor** is the relationship between the quantity of labor demanded and the real wage rate when all other influences on firms' hiring plans remain the same. The **real wage rate** is the quantity of goods and services that an hour of labor earns. In contrast, the **money wage rate** is the number of dollars that an hour of labor earns. A real wage rate is equal to a money wage rate divided by the price of a good. For the economy as a whole, the average real wage rate equals the average money wage rate divided by the price level multiplied by 100. So we express the real wage rate in constant dollars. (Today, we express this real wage rate in 1996 dollars.)

The *real* wage rate influences the quantity of labor demanded because what matters to firms is not the number of dollars they pay (money wage rate) but how much output they must sell to earn those dollars.

We can represent the demand for labor as either a demand schedule or a demand curve. The table in Fig. 22.3 shows part of a demand for labor schedule. It tells us the quantity of labor demanded at three different real wage rates. For example, if the real wage rate falls from $40 an hour to $35 an hour, the quantity of labor demanded increases from 150 billion hours a year to 200 billion hours a year. (You can find these numbers in rows *A* and *B* of the table.)

The demand for labor curve is *LD*. Points *A*, *B*, and *C* on the curve correspond to rows *A*, *B*, and *C* of the demand schedule.

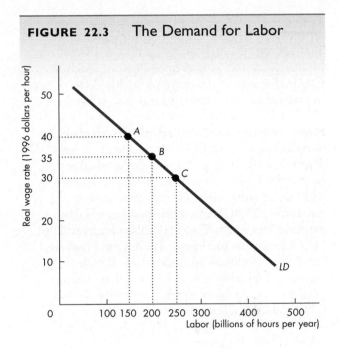

FIGURE 22.3   The Demand for Labor

	Real wage rate (1996 dollars per hour)	Quantity of labor demanded (billions of hours per year)
A	40	150
B	35	200
C	30	250

The table shows part of a demand for labor schedule. Points A, B, and C on the demand for labor curve correspond to the rows of the table. The lower the real wage rate, the greater is the quantity of labor demanded.

Why does the quantity of labor demanded *increase* as the real wage rate *decreases*? That is, why does the demand for labor curve slope downward? To answer these questions, we must learn about the marginal product of labor.

The Marginal Product of Labor The **marginal product of labor** is the additional real GDP produced by an additional hour of labor when all other influences on production remain the same. The marginal product of labor is governed by the **law of diminishing returns**, which states that as the quantity of labor increases, other things remaining the same, the marginal product of labor decreases.

The Law of Diminishing Returns Diminishing returns arise because the amount of capital is fixed. Two people operating one machine are not twice as productive as one person operating one machine. Eventually, as more labor hours are hired, workers get in each other's way and output increases barely at all.

Marginal Product Calculation We calculate the marginal product of labor as the change in real GDP divided by the change in the quantity of labor employed. Figure 22.4(a) shows some calculations, and Fig. 22.4(b) shows the marginal product curve.

In Fig. 22.4(a), when the quantity of labor employed increases from 100 billion hours to 200 billion hours, an increase of 100 billion hours, real GDP increases from $6 trillion to $10 trillion, an increase of $4 trillion, or $4,000 billion. The marginal product of labor equals the increase in real GDP ($4,000 billion) divided by the increase in the quantity of labor employed (100 billion hours), which is $40 an hour.

When the quantity of labor employed increases from 200 billion hours to 300 billion hours, an increase of 100 billion hours, real GDP increases from $10 trillion to $13 trillion, an increase of $3 trillion, or $3,000 billion. The marginal product of labor equals $3,000 billion divided by 100 billion hours, which is $30 an hour.

In Fig. 22.4(b), as the quantity of labor employed increases, the marginal product of labor diminishes. Between 100 billion and 200 billion hours (at 150 billion hours), marginal product is $40 an hour. And between 200 billion and 300 billion hours (at 250 billion hours), marginal product is $30 an hour.

The diminishing marginal product of labor limits the demand for labor.

Diminishing Marginal Product and the Demand for Labor Firms are in business to maximize profits. Each hour of labor that a firm hires increases output and adds to costs. Initially, an extra hour of labor produces more output than the real wage that the labor costs. Marginal product exceeds the real wage rate. But each additional hour of labor produces less additional output than the previous hour — the marginal product of labor diminishes.

As a firm hires more labor, eventually the extra output from an extra hour of labor is exactly what that hour of labor costs. At this point, marginal product equals the real wage rate. Hire one less hour and marginal product exceeds the real wage rate. Hire one

FIGURE 22.4 Marginal Product and the Demand for Labor

(a) Calculating marginal product

(b) The marginal product curve

Between 100 billion and 200 billion hours, the marginal product of labor is $40 an hour. Between 200 billion and 300 billion hours, the marginal product of labor is $30 an hour. At point A on the MP curve, the marginal product of labor is $40 an hour at 150 billion hours (the midpoint between 100 billion and 200 billion). The MP curve is the demand for labor curve.

more hour and the real wage rate exceeds the marginal product. In either case, profit is less.

Because marginal product diminishes as the quantity of labor employed increases, the lower the real wage rate, the greater is the quantity of labor that a firm can profitably hire. The marginal product curve is the same as the demand for labor curve.

You might gain a clearer understanding of the demand for labor by looking at an example.

The Demand for Labor in a Soda Factory

Suppose that when a soda factory employs one additional hour of labor, output increases by 11 bottles. Marginal product is 11 bottles an hour. If the money wage rate is $5.50 an hour and soda sells for 50¢ a bottle, the real wage rate is 11 bottles an hour. (We calculate the real wage rate for the soda factory as the money wage rate of $5.50 an hour divided by a price of 50¢ a bottle, which equals a real wage rate of 11 bottles an hour.) Because marginal product diminishes, we know that if the firm did not hire this hour of labor, marginal product would exceed 11 bottles. Because the firm can hire the hour of labor for a real wage rate of 11 bottles, it just pays it to do so.

If the price of soda remains at 50¢ a bottle and the money wage rate falls to $5.00 an hour, the real wage rate falls to 10 bottles an hour and the firm increases the quantity of labor demanded.

Similarly, if the money wage rate remains at $5.50 an hour and the price of soda rises to 55¢ a bottle, the real wage rate falls to 10 bottles an hour and the firm increases the quantity of labor demanded.

When the firm pays a real wage rate equal to the marginal product of labor, it is maximizing profit.

Changes in the Demand for Labor When the marginal product of labor changes, the demand for labor changes and the demand for labor curve shifts. You've seen that an increase in capital (both physical and human) and an advance in technology that increases productivity shift the production function upward. These same forces increase the demand for labor and shift the demand for labor curve rightward.

The Supply of Labor

The **quantity of labor supplied** is the number of labor hours that all the households in the economy plan to work. The **supply of labor** is the relationship between the quantity of labor supplied and the real wage rate when all other influences on work plans remain the same.

We can represent the supply of labor as a supply schedule or a supply curve. The table in Fig. 22.5 shows a supply of labor schedule. It tells us the quantity of labor supplied at different real wage rates. For example, if the real wage rate rises from $15 an hour (row *A*) to $35 an hour (row *B*), the quantity of labor supplied increases from 150 billion hours a year to 200 billion hours a year. The curve *LS* is a supply of labor curve. Points *A*, *B*, and *C* on the curve correspond to rows *A*, *B*, and *C* of the supply schedule.

The *real* wage rate influences the quantity of labor supplied because what matters to people is not the number of dollars they earn (the money wage rate) but what those dollars will buy.

FIGURE 22.5   The Supply of Labor

	Real wage rate (1996 dollars per hour)	Quantity of labor supplied (billions of hours per year)
A	15	150
B	35	200
C	55	250

The table shows part of a supply of labor schedule. Points *A*, *B*, and *C* on the supply of labor curve correspond to the rows of the table. The higher the real wage rate, the greater is the quantity of labor supplied.

The quantity of labor supplied increases as the real wage rate increases for two reasons:

- Hours per person increase
- Labor force participation increases

Hours per Person In choosing how many hours to work, a household considers the opportunity cost of not working. This opportunity cost is the real wage rate. The higher the real wage rate, the greater is the opportunity cost of taking leisure and not working. And as the opportunity cost of taking leisure rises, so, other things remaining the same, the more the household chooses to work.

But other things don't remain the same. The higher the real wage rate, the greater is the household's income. And the higher the household's income, the more it wants to consume. One item that it wants to consume more of is leisure.

So a rise in the real wage rate has two opposing effects. By increasing the opportunity cost of leisure, it makes the household want to consume less leisure and to work more. And by increasing the household's income, it makes the household want to consume more leisure and to work fewer hours. For most households, the opportunity cost effect is stronger than the income effect. So the higher the real wage rate, the greater is the amount of work that the household chooses to do.

Labor Force Participation Some people have productive opportunities outside the labor force. These people choose to work only if the real wage rate exceeds the value of these other productive activities. For example, a parent might spend time caring for her or his child. The alternative is day care. The parent will choose to work only if he or she can earn enough per hour to pay the cost of child care and have enough left to make the work effort worthwhile. The higher the real wage rate, the more likely it is that a parent will choose to work and so the greater is the labor force participation rate.

Labor Supply Response The quantity of labor supplied increases as the real wage rate rises. But the quantity of labor supplied is not highly responsive to the real wage rate. A large percentage change in the real wage rate brings a small percentage change in the quantity of labor supplied.

Let's now see how the labor market determines employment, the real wage rate, and potential GDP.

Labor Market Equilibrium and Potential GDP

The forces of supply and demand operate in labor markets just as they do in the markets for goods and services. The price of labor is the real wage rate. A rise in the real wage rate eliminates a shortage of labor by decreasing the quantity demanded and increasing the quantity supplied. A fall in the real wage rate eliminates a surplus of labor by increasing the quantity demanded and decreasing the quantity supplied. If there is neither a shortage nor a surplus, the labor market is in equilibrium.

In macroeconomics, we study the economy-wide labor market to determine the total quantity of labor employed and the average real wage rate.

Labor Market Equilibrium Figure 22.6(a) shows a labor market in equilibrium. The demand curve *LD* and the supply curve *LS* are the same as those in Fig. 22.3 and Fig. 22.5, respectively.

If the real wage rate exceeds $35 an hour, the quantity of labor supplied exceeds the quantity demanded and there is a surplus of labor. In this situation, the real wage rate falls.

If the real wage rate is less than $35 an hour, the quantity of labor demanded exceeds the quantity supplied and there is a shortage of labor. In this situation, the real wage rate rises.

If the real wage rate is $35 an hour, the quantity of labor demanded equals the quantity supplied and there is neither a shortage nor a surplus of labor. In this situation, the labor market is in equilibrium and the real wage rate remains constant. The equilibrium level of employment is 200 billion hours a year. This equilibrium level of employment is *full-employment*.

Potential GDP You've seen that the quantity of real GDP depends on the quantity of labor employed. The production function tells us how much real GDP a given amount of employment can produce. At the equilibrium level of employment, the economy is at full employment. And the level of real GDP at full employment is *potential GDP*. So the equilibrium level of employment produces potential GDP.

Figure 22.6(b) shows potential GDP. The equilibrium level of employment in Fig. 22.6(a) is 200 billion hours. The production function in Fig. 22.6(b) tells us that 200 billion hours of labor can produce a real GDP of $10 trillion. This amount is potential GDP.

FIGURE 22.6   The Labor Market and Potential GDP

(a) The labor market

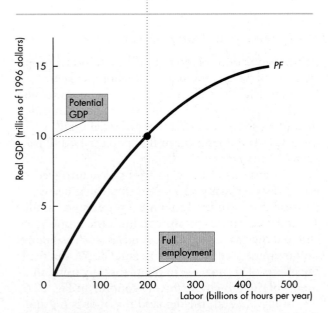

(b) Potential GDP

Full employment occurs (part a) when the quantity of labor demanded equals the quantity of labor supplied. The real wage rate is $35 an hour, and employment is 200 billion hours a year. Part (b) shows potential GDP. It is the quantity of real GDP determined by the production function at the full-employment quantity of labor.

Aggregate Supply

The **long-run aggregate supply curve** is the relationship between the quantity of real GDP supplied and the price level when real GDP equals potential GDP. Figure 22.7 shows this relationship as the vertical *LAS* curve. Along the long-run aggregate supply curve, as the price level changes, the money wage rate changes to keep the real wage rate at the full-employment equilibrium level in Fig. 22.6(a). With no change in the real wage rate and no change in employment, real GDP remains at potential GDP.

The **short-run aggregate supply curve** is the relationship between the quantity of real GDP supplied and the price level when the money wage rate and potential GDP remain constant. Figure 22.7 shows a short-run aggregate supply curve as the upward-sloping *SAS* curve. Along the short-run aggregate supply curve, as the price level rises, the money wage rate remains fixed, so the real wage rate *falls*. In Fig. 22.6,

FIGURE 22.7   The Aggregate Supply Curves

A rise in the price level accompanied by a rise in the money wage rate that keeps the real wage rate at its full-employment equilibrium level keeps the quantity of real GDP supplied constant at potential GDP. There is a movement along the *LAS* curve. A rise in the price level with no change in the money wage rate lowers the real wage rate and brings an increase in employment and in the quantity of real GDP supplied. There is a movement along the *SAS* curve.

when the real wage rate falls, the quantity of labor demanded increases and real GDP increases.

When the economy is at a point on its short-run aggregate supply curve above potential GDP, the real wage rate is below the full-employment equilibrium level. And when the economy is at a point on the short-run aggregate supply curve below potential GDP, the real wage rate is above the full-employment equilibrium level. In both cases, the quantity of labor that firms employ departs from the quantity that households would like to supply.

Production is efficient in the sense that the economy operates on its production possibilities frontier. But production is inefficient in the sense that the economy operates at the wrong point on the frontier. When the real wage rate is below the full-employment equilibrium, people do too much work and produce too much real GDP. When the real wage rate is above the full-employment equilibrium, people do too little work and produce too little real GDP.

When the real wage rate has departed from its full-employment equilibrium level, the resulting shortage or surplus of labor brings market forces into play that move the real wage rate and quantity of labor employed back toward their full-employment levels.

REVIEW QUIZ

1 Why does a rise in the real wage rate bring a decrease in the quantity of labor demanded, other things remaining the same?
2 Why does a rise in the real wage rate bring an increase in the quantity of labor supplied, other things remaining the same?
3 What happens in the labor market if the real wage rate is above or below the full-employment level?
4 How is potential GDP determined?
5 What is the relationship between full-employment equilibrium in the labor market and long-run aggregate supply?
6 What is the relationship between the labor market and short-run aggregate supply?

You have studied the forces that determine full-employment and potential GDP. Let's now look at *changes* in full-employment equilibrium.

Changes in Potential GDP

REAL GDP WILL INCREASE IF

1. The economy recovers from recession.
2. Potential GDP increases.

Recovery from recession means that the economy moves along the leisure time–real GDP *PPF* from a point at which real GDP and employment are too low to the full-employment equilibrium point. Equivalently, the economy moves along the short-run aggregate supply curve. Economists have a lot to say about such a move. And you can learn about this type of short-term change in real GDP in Chapters 25–29.

Increasing potential GDP means expanding production possibilities. We're going to study such an expansion in the rest of this chapter and in Chapters 23 and 24. We begin this process here by examining two influences on potential GDP:

■ An increase in population
■ An increase in labor productivity

An Increase in Population

As the population increases and the additional people reach working age, the supply of labor increases. With more labor available, the economy's production possibilities expand. But does the expansion of production possibilities mean that potential GDP increases? And does it mean that potential GDP *per person* increases?

The answers to these questions have intrigued economists for many years. And they cause heated political debate today. In China, for example, families are under enormous pressure to limit the number of children they have. In other countries, such as France, the government encourages large families. We can study the effects of an increase in population by using the model of the full-employment economy in Fig. 22.8.

In Fig. 22.8(a), the demand for labor is LD and initially the supply of labor is LS_0. At full employment, the real wage rate is $35 an hour and the level of employment is 200 billion hours a year. In Fig. 22.8(b), the production function (PF) shows that with 200 billion hours of labor employed, potential GDP is $10 trillion. We're now going to work out what happens when the population increases.

An increase in the population increases the number of people of working age, and the supply of labor

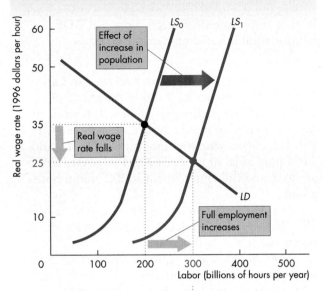

FIGURE 22.8   The Effects of an Increase in Population

(a) The labor market

(b) Potential GDP

An increase in population increases the supply of labor. In part (a), the real wage rate falls, and the full-employment quantity of labor increases. In part (b), the increase in full employment increases potential GDP. Because the marginal product of labor diminishes, the increased population increases potential GDP but potential GDP per hour of work decreases.

increases. The labor supply curve shifts rightward to LS_1. At a real wage rate of $35 an hour, there is now a surplus of labor. So the real wage rate falls. In this example, it falls until it reaches $25 an hour. At $25 an hour, the quantity of labor demanded equals the quantity of labor supplied. Equilibrium employment increases to 300 billion hours a year.

Figure 22.8(b) shows the effect of the increase in equilibrium employment on real GDP. As the full-employment quantity of labor increases from 200 billion hours to 300 billion hours, potential GDP increases from $10 trillion to $13 trillion.

So at full employment, an increase in population increases employment, increases potential GDP, and lowers the real wage rate.

An increase in population also decreases potential GDP per hour of work. You can see this decrease by dividing potential GDP by total labor hours. Initially, with potential GDP at $10 trillion and labor hours at 200 billion, potential GDP per hour of work was $50. With the increase in population, potential GDP is $13 trillion and labor hours are 300 billion. Potential GDP per hour of work is $43.33. Diminishing returns are the source of the decrease in potential GDP per hour of work.

You've seen that an increase in population increases potential GDP and decreases potential GDP per work hour. Some people challenge this conclusion and argue that people are the ultimate economic resource. They claim that a larger population brings forth a greater amount of scientific discovery and technological advance. Consequently, according to this argument, an increase in population never takes place in isolation. It is always accompanied by an increase in labor productivity. Let's now look at the effects of this influence on potential GDP.

An Increase in Labor Productivity

We've seen that three factors increase labor productivity:

■ An increase in physical capital
■ An increase in human capital
■ An advance in technology

Saving and investment increase the quantity of physical capital over time. In Chapter 23, we study the factors that influence the decisions that determine how quickly capital grows. Education and on-the-job training and experience increase human capital. Research and development efforts bring advances in technology. In Chapter 24, we study how all these forces interact to determine the growth rate of potential GDP.

Here, we study the *effects* of an increase in physical capital, an increase in human capital, or an advance in technology on the labor market and potential GDP. We'll see how potential GDP, employment, and the real wage rate change when any of these three influences on labor productivity changes.

An Increase in Physical Capital

If the quantity of physical capital increases, labor productivity increases. With labor being more productive, the economy's production possibilities expand. How does such an expansion of production possibilities change the real wage rate, employment, and potential GDP?

The additional capital increases the real GDP that each quantity of labor can produce. It also increases the marginal product of labor and so increases the demand for labor. Some physical capital replaces some types of labor. So the demand for those types of labor decreases when capital increases. But an increase in physical capital creates a demand for the types of labor that build, sell, and maintain the additional capital. The increases in demand for labor are always larger than the decreases in demand, and the economy-wide demand for labor increases.

With an increase in the economy-wide demand for labor, the real wage rate rises and the quantity of labor supplied increases. Equilibrium employment increases.

Potential GDP now increases for two reasons. First, a given level of employment produces more real GDP. Second, equilibrium employment increases.

An Increase in Human Capital

If the quantity of human capital increases, labor productivity increases. Again, with labor being more productive, the economy's production possibilities expand. And this expansion of production possibilities changes the equilibrium real wage rate, employment, and potential GDP in a similar manner to the effects of a change in physical capital.

An Advance in Technology

As technology advances, labor productivity increases. And exactly as in the case of an increase in capital, the economy's production possibilities expand. Again, just as in the case of an increase in capital, the new technology increases the real GDP that each quantity of labor can produce and increases the marginal product of labor and the demand for labor.

With an increase in the demand for labor, the real wage rate rises, the quantity of labor supplied increases, and equilibrium employment increases. And again, potential GDP increases because a given level of employment produces more real GDP and because equilibrium employment increases.

Illustrating the Effects of an Increase in Labor Productivity

Figure 22.9 shows the effects of an increase in labor productivity that results from an increase in capital or an advance in technology. In part (a), the demand for labor initially is LD_0 and the supply of labor is LS. The real wage rate is $35 an hour, and full employment is 200 billion hours a year.

In part (b), the production function initially is PF_0. With 200 billion hours of labor employed, potential GDP is $10 trillion.

Now an increase in capital or an advance in technology increases the productivity of labor. In Fig. 22.9(a), the demand for labor increases and the demand curve shifts rightward to LD_1. In Fig. 22.9(b), the productivity of labor increases and the production function shifts upward to PF_1.

In Fig. 22.9(a), at the original real wage rate of $35 an hour, there is now a shortage of labor. So the real wage rate rises. In this example, it keeps rising until it reaches $45 an hour. At $45 an hour, the quantity of labor demanded equals the quantity of labor supplied and full employment increases to 225 billion hours a year.

Figure 22.9(b) shows the effects of the increase in full employment combined with the new production function on potential GDP. As full employment increases from 200 billion hours to 225 billion hours, potential GDP increases from $10 trillion to $15 trillion.

Potential GDP per hour of work also increases. You can see this increase by dividing potential GDP by total labor hours. Initially, with potential GDP at $10 trillion and labor hours at 200 billion, potential GDP per hour of work was $50. With the increase in labor productivity, potential GDP is $15 trillion and labor hours are 225 billion, so potential GDP per hour of work is $66.67.

We've just studied the effects of a change in population and an increase in labor productivity separately. In reality, these changes occur together. We can see the combined effects by examining an episode in the life of the U.S. economy.

FIGURE 22.9   The Effects of an Increase in Labor Productivity

(a) The labor market

(b) Potential GDP

An increase in labor productivity shifts the demand for labor curve rightward from LD_0 to LD_1 (part a) and the production function upward from PF_0 to PF_1 (part b). The real wage rate rises to $45 an hour, and full employment increases from 200 billion to 225 billion hours. Potential GDP increases from $10 trillion to $15 trillion.

Population and Productivity in the United States

The U.S. economy was close to full employment in 2001. It was also close to full employment 20 years earlier, in 1981. We're going to compare these two years and look at the forces that moved the economy from one full-employment equilibrium to another.

In 1981, real GDP in the United States was $5 trillion, employment was 159 billion hours, and the real wage rate was $18 an hour. (We are using 1996 dollars.)

By 2001, real GDP had increased to $9.3 trillion, labor hours had increased to 231 billion, and the real wage rate had risen to $24 an hour. (Again, we are using 1996 dollars.)

The factors that you've just studied — an increase in population, increases in physical and human capital, and advances in technology — brought these changes.

Population Increase   In 1981, the U.S. working-age population was 170 million. By 2001, this number had increased to 212 million. The 2001 working-age population was 25 percent larger than the 1981 working-age population. Recall that labor hours were 159 billion in 1981. A 25 percent increase would take labor hours in 2001 to 198 billion. But labor hours actually increased to 231 billion. Why? The increased labor productivity increased the real wage rate, which increased the quantity of labor supplied by increasing the labor force participation rate.

Capital Increase   In 1981, the capital stock in the United States was estimated to be $15 trillion (in 1996 dollars). By 2001, the capital stock had increased to $25 trillion. This increase in capital increased labor productivity. But the increase in capital was not the only influence on labor productivity. Technological advances also occurred.

Technological Advances   In 1981, we were just getting into the information revolution. Personal computers had just arrived. They were slow, had little memory, and had no hard drive, much less the CD-ROM and DVD drives of today. The Internet existed as a tool used by academic researchers for e-mail and file transfers, but no one had imagined the World Wide Web. Telephones couldn't remember numbers or record messages. Communication was slower and more costly than it was to become by 2001.

FIGURE 22.10   Full Employment in the United States: 1981 and 2001

(a) The labor market

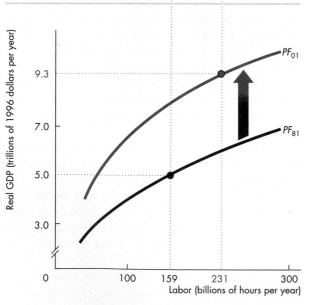

(b) The U.S. production function in 1981 and 2001

In 1981, the real wage rate was $18 an hour and the quantity of labor employed was 159 billion hours (part a). Potential GDP was $5 trillion on PF_{81} (part b). By 2001, the real wage rate was $24 an hour and 231 billion hours of labor were employed. Potential GDP had increased to $9.3 trillion on PF_{01}.

Production processes were beginning to be computerized but on a limited scale. Banks equipped with ATMs were in the future. Supermarkets with laser scanners were only a dream. Robots in automaking factories and coal mines were still unknown. The biotechnology sector had yet to be developed. The combined effects of capital accumulation and technological advance have made our farms and factories, shops and offices more productive.

Figure 22.10 shows these effects along with the effects of the increase in population that occurred. In 1981, the demand for labor curve was LD_{81}, the supply of labor curve was LS_{81}, the full-employment real wage rate was $18, and 159 billion hours of labor were employed. The production function in 1981 was PF_{81}. With 159 billion hours of labor employed, real GDP (and potential GDP) was $5 trillion.

By 2001, the increase in population had increased the working-age population by 25 percent. This increase in population increased the supply of labor and shifted the labor supply curve rightward to LS_{01}.

The accumulation of capital and advances in technology increased labor productivity. The demand for labor increased, and the demand for labor curve shifted rightward to LD_{01}. And the production function shifted upward to PF_{01}.

The real wage rate increased to $24, and employment increased to 231 billion hours. At this quantity of labor, real GDP (and potential GDP) increased to $9.3 trillion.

So in the United States, the effects of an increase in capital and advances in technology that increase labor productivity have been larger than the effects of increases in population.

REVIEW QUIZ

1 When the population increases but nothing else changes, why does real GDP per hour of work decrease?

2 How does an increase in capital change the real wage rate, full employment, and potential GDP?

3 How do advances in technology change the real wage rate, full employment, and potential GDP?

4 If, as some people suggest, capital accumulation and technological change always accompany an increase in population, is it possible for potential GDP per hour of work to decrease?

Unemployment at Full Employment

SO FAR, WE'VE FOCUSED ON THE FORCES THAT determine the real wage rate, the quantity of labor employed, and potential GDP. And we've studied the effects of changes in population, capital, and technology on these variables. We're now going to bring unemployment into the picture.

In Chapter 20 (p. 456), we learned how unemployment is measured. We described how people become unemployed — they lose jobs, leave jobs, and enter or reenter the labor force — and we classified unemployment — it can be frictional, structural, and cyclical. We also learned that we call the unemployment rate at full employment the *natural rate of unemployment.*

But measuring, describing, and classifying unemployment do not *explain* it. Why is there always some unemployment? Why does its rate fluctuate? Why was the unemployment rate lower during the 1960s and the late 1990s than during the 1980s and early 1990s?

The forces that make the unemployment rate fluctuate around the natural rate take some time to explain, and we study these forces in Chapters 25–31. Here, we look at the churning economy and the reasons why we have unemployment at full employment.

Unemployment is ever present for two broad reasons:

- Job search
- Job rationing

Job Search

Job search is the activity of looking for an acceptable vacant job. There are always some people who have not yet found a suitable job and who are actively searching for one. The reason is that the labor market is in a constant state of change. The failure of existing businesses destroys jobs. The expansion of existing businesses and the startup of new businesses that use new technologies and develop new markets create jobs. As people pass through different stages of life, some enter or reenter the labor market. Others leave their jobs to look for better ones, and still others retire. This constant churning in the labor market

means that there are always some people looking for jobs, and these people are the unemployed.

The amount of job search depends on a number of factors, one of which is the real wage rate. In Figure 22.11, when the real wage rate is $35 an hour, the economy is at full-employment equilibrium. The amount of job search that takes place at this wage rate generates unemployment at the natural rate. If the real wage rate is above the full-employment equilibrium — for example, at $45 an hour — there is a surplus of labor. At this higher real wage rate, more job search takes place and unemployment exceeds the natural rate. If the real wage rate is below the full-employment equilibrium — for example, at $25 an hour — there is a shortage of labor. At this real wage rate, less job search takes place and unemployment falls below the natural rate.

The market forces of supply and demand move the real wage rate toward the full-employment equilibrium. And these same forces move the amount of

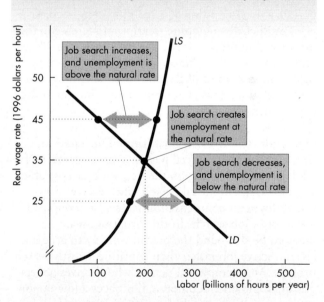

FIGURE 22.11   Job Search Unemployment

When the real wage rate is at its full-employment level — $35 an hour in this example — job search puts unemployment at the natural rate. If the real wage rate is above the full-employment level, there is a surplus of labor. Job search increases, and unemployment rises above the natural rate. If the real wage rate is below the full-employment level, there is a shortage of labor. Job search decreases, and unemployment falls below the natural rate.

job search toward the level that creates unemployment at the natural rate.

But other influences on the amount of job search bring changes, over time, in the natural rate of unemployment. The main sources of these changes are

- Demographic change
- Unemployment compensation
- Structural change

Demographic Change An increase in the proportion of the population that is of working age brings an increase in the entry rate into the labor force and an increase in the unemployment rate. This factor has been important in the U.S. labor market in recent years. The bulge in the birth rate that occurred from the late 1940s through the late 1950s increased the proportion of new entrants into the labor force during the 1970s and brought an increase in the unemployment rate.

As the birth rate declined, the bulge moved into higher age groups, and the proportion of new entrants declined during the 1980s. During this period, the natural rate of unemployment decreased.

Another demographic trend is an increase in the number of households with two paid workers. When one of these workers becomes unemployed, it is possible, with income still flowing in, to take longer to find a new job. This factor might have increased frictional unemployment.

Unemployment Compensation The length of time that an unemployed person spends searching for a job depends, in part, on the opportunity cost of job search. An unemployed person who receives no unemployment compensation faces a high opportunity cost of job search. In this situation, search is likely to be short and the person is likely to accept a less attractive job rather than continue a costly search process. An unemployed person who receives generous unemployment compensation faces a low opportunity cost of job search. In this situation, search is likely to be prolonged. The unemployed worker will continue to search for an ideal job.

The extension of unemployment compensation to larger groups of workers during the late 1960s and 1970s lowered the opportunity cost of job search. Consequently, the amount of job search and the natural rate of unemployment increased during those years.

Structural Change Labor market flows and unemployment are influenced by the pace and direction of technological change. Sometimes, technological change brings a *structural slump*, a condition in which some industries die and some regions suffer while other industries are born and other regions flourish. When these events occur, labor turnover is high — the flows between employment and unemployment increase and the number of unemployed people increases. The decline of industries in the "Rust Belt" and the rapid expansion of industries in the "Sun Belt" illustrate the effects of technological change and were a source of the increase in unemployment during the 1970s and early 1980s. While these changes were taking place, the natural rate of unemployment increased.

Job Rationing

You've learned that markets *allocate* scarce resources by adjusting the market price to make buying plans and selling plans agree. Another word that has a meaning similar to "allocate" is "ration." Markets *ration* scarce resources by adjusting prices. In the labor market, the real wage rate rations employment and therefore rations jobs. Changes in the real wage rate keep the number of people seeking work and the number of jobs available in balance.

But the real wage rate is not the only possible instrument for rationing jobs. And in some industries, the real wage rate is set above the market equilibrium level. **Job rationing** is the practice of paying a real wage rate above the equilibrium level and then rationing jobs by some method.

Two reasons why the real wage rate might be set above the equilibrium level are

- Efficiency wage
- Minimum wage

Efficiency Wage It is costly for a firm to pay its workers more than the market wage rate. But doing so also brings benefits. An **efficiency wage** is a real wage rate that is set above the full-employment equilibrium wage rate that balances the costs and benefits of this higher wage rate to maximize the firm's profit.

The cost of paying a higher wage is direct. It is the addition to the firm's wage bill. The benefits of paying a higher wage rate are indirect.

First, a firm that pays a high wage rate can attract the most productive workers. Second, the firm can get greater productivity from its work force if it threatens to fire those who do not perform at the desired standard. The threat of losing a well-paid job stimulates greater work effort. Third, workers are less likely to quit their jobs, so the firm faces a lower rate of labor turnover and lower training costs. Fourth, the firm's recruiting costs are lower. The firm always faces a steady stream of available new workers.

Faced with benefits and costs, a firm offers a wage rate that balances productivity gains from the higher wage rate against its additional cost. This wage rate maximizes the firm's profit and is the efficiency wage.

Minimum Wage A **minimum wage** is the lowest wage rate at which a firm may legally hire labor. If the minimum wage is set *below* the equilibrium wage, the minimum wage has no effect. The minimum wage and market forces are not in conflict. But if a minimum wage is set *above* the equilibrium wage, the minimum wage is in conflict with the market forces and does have some effects on the labor market.

The minimum wage in the United States is set by the federal government's Fair Labor Standards Act. The federal minimum wage increases from time to time and has fluctuated between 35 percent and more than 50 percent of the average wage of production workers. It was last set in 1997 at $5.15 an hour. Some state governments have passed state minimum wage laws that exceed the federal minimum.

Job Rationing and Unemployment

Regardless of the reason, if the real wage rate is set above the equilibrium level, the natural rate of unemployment increases. The above-equilibrium real wage rate decreases the quantity of labor demanded and increases the quantity of labor supplied. So even at full employment, the quantity of labor supplied exceeds the quantity of labor demanded.

The surplus of labor is an addition to the amount of unemployment. The unemployment that results from a nonmarket wage rate and job rationing increases the natural rate of unemployment because it is added to the job search that takes place at full-employment equilibrium.

Economists broadly agree that efficiency wages can create persistent unemployment. And most economists believe that the minimum wage contributes to unemployment, especially among low-skilled young workers. But David Card of the University of California at Berkeley and Alan Krueger of Princeton University have challenged this view. And the challenge has been rebutted.

Card and Krueger say that an increase in the minimum wage works like an efficiency wage. It makes workers more productive and less likely to quit. Most economists remain skeptical about this suggestion. If higher wages make workers more productive and reduce labor turnover, why don't firms freely pay the wage rates that encourage the correct work habits? Daniel Hamermesh of the University of Texas at Austin says that firms anticipate increases in the minimum wage and cut employment *before* they occur. Looking for the effects of an increase in the minimum wage *after* it has occurred misses its effects. Finis Welch of Texas A&M University and Kevin Murphy of the University of Chicago say that regional differences in economic growth and not changes in the minimum wage explain the facts that Card and Krueger found.

REVIEW QUIZ

1 Why does the economy experience unemployment at full employment?

2 Why does the natural rate of unemployment fluctuate?

3 What is job rationing and why does it occur?

4 How does an efficiency wage influence the real wage rate, employment, and unemployment?

5 How does the minimum wage create unemployment?

◆ In this chapter, you've seen how the economy operates at full employment. *Reading Between the Lines* on pp. 520–521 looks at productivity gains in the United States during the 2001 recession. In the next two chapters, we study the rate of growth of the full-employment economy. In Chapter 23, we study decisions by firms to increase the amount of capital they employ and the decisions by households about the amount to save to finance capital accumulation. Then in Chapter 24, we study the interactions of capital accumulation, technological change, and population growth in the process of economic growth.

Productivity and Real Wages in the United States

THE WASHINGTON POST, NOVEMBER 8, 2001

U.S. Productivity Rises 2.7%

JOHN M. BERRY

Despite the slump in U.S. economic growth this year, many companies have continued to become more efficient by reducing their use of labor faster than their production has declined, the Labor Department reported yesterday.

Productivity — the amount of goods and services produced for each hour worked — rose at a 2.7 percent annual rate in the July-September period at businesses other than farms. That was up from the 2.2 percent rate for the spring quarter, the department said.

...

Analysts said that's good news because rising productivity is ultimately the source of increases in the American standard of living.

"The rise in productivity was far better than usual for a recession period, emphasizing that U.S. productivity growth has improved permanently since the mid-1990s thanks to high [business investment in new plants and equipment] and rapid technological innovation," said Maury N. Harris, chief economist at UBS Warburg in New York.

...

The third-quarter productivity gain was the result of a decline in the number of hours worked, which fell at a 3.6 percent annual rate, and a smaller decline in output, which fell at a 1 percent rate.

...

Essence of the Story

■ During the third quarter of 2001, aggregate hours fell at a 3.6 percent annual rate and real GDP fell at a 1 percent annual rate, so labor productivity — real GDP per hour worked — increased at a 2.7 percent annual rate.

■ Analysts are reported to have said that the productivity increase is good news because rising productivity is the source of increases in the standard of living.

■ Maury N. Harris, chief economist at UBS Warburg in New York said, "The rise in productivity was far better than usual for a recession period, emphasizing that U.S. productivity growth has improved permanently since the mid-1990s."

Economic Analysis

■ The analyst quoted in this news article is confusing the permanent gains in labor productivity that come from capital accumulation and technological change with a temporary increase in labor productivity that almost always occurs during a recession.

■ The permanent improvement in productivity since the mid-1990s that Maury N. Harris is talking about is unrelated to the productivity increase that occurred during 2001.

■ Technological change and capital accumulation, especially in the new technology sectors of the economy, have brought permanent gains in productivity, output, and earnings.

■ We illustrate these permanent gains by an upward shift of the production function like that in Figure 22.10(b) on p. 516.

■ What happened in the 2001 recession (and what happens in most recessions) results from the law of diminishing returns working in reverse.

■ The law of diminishing returns says that as more labor is employed, its marginal product decreases. Going in the opposite direction, the same law says that as *less* labor is employed, its marginal product *increases*.

■ Figure 1 shows the production function, *PF*, and Fig. 2 shows the demand for labor curve, *LD*, during 2001.

■ During the second quarter of 2001, 231 billion labor hours produced $9.322 trillion of real GDP. Aggregate hours decreased to 223 billion, and real GDP fell to $9.310 trillion during the third quarter.

■ Figure 1 shows this change as a movement along the production function.

■ Figure 2 shows the effects of the decrease in employment in the labor market. As aggregate hours fell from 231 billion to 223 billion, there was a movement along the demand for labor curve. The real wage rate and marginal product of labor increased from $18 to $18.50 an hour.

Figure 1 Production function

Figure 2 Labor market

SUMMARY

KEY POINTS

Real GDP and Employment (pp. 504–506)

- To produce real GDP, we must forgo leisure time.
- As the quantity of labor increases, real GDP increases.
- Labor productivity increases if the amount of physical capital or human capital increases or if technology advances.

The Labor Market and Aggregate Supply (pp. 507–512)

- The quantity of labor demanded increases as the real wage rate falls, other things remaining the same.
- The diminishing marginal product of labor is the reason the quantity of labor demanded increases as the real wage rate falls.
- The quantity of labor supplied increases as the real wage rate rises, other things remaining the same.
- At full-employment equilibrium, the quantity of labor demanded equals the quantity of labor supplied.
- Potential GDP is real GDP produced by the full-employment quantity of labor.
- Along the long-run aggregate supply curve, the real wage rate is constant at its full-employment level. Along the short-run aggregate supply curve, the real wage rate, employment, and real GDP change.

Changes in Potential GDP (pp. 512–516)

- An increase in population increases the supply of labor, lowers the real wage rate, increases the quantity of labor employed, and increases potential GDP. It decreases potential GDP per hour of work.
- An increase in capital or an advance in technology increases labor productivity. It shifts the production function upward and the demand for labor curve rightward. The real wage rate rises, the quantity of labor employed increases, and potential GDP increases.

Unemployment at Full Employment (pp. 517–519)

- The unemployment rate at full employment is the natural rate of unemployment.
- Unemployment is ever present because of job search and job rationing.
- Job-search unemployment is influenced by demographic change, unemployment compensation, and structural change.
- Job-rationing unemployment arises from efficiency wages and the minimum wage.

KEY FIGURES

KEY TERMS

PROBLEMS

*1. Robinson Crusoe lives on a desert island on the equator. He has 12 hours of daylight every day to allocate between leisure and work. The table shows seven alternative combinations of leisure and real GDP in Crusoe's economy:

Possibility	Leisure (hours per day)	Real GDP (dollars per day)
A	12	0
B	10	10
C	8	18
D	6	24
E	4	28
F	2	30
G	0	30

a. Make a graph of Crusoe's *PPF* for leisure and real GDP.
b. Make a table and a graph of Crusoe's production function.
c. Find the marginal product of labor for Crusoe at different quantities of labor.

2. The people of Nautica have 100 hours every day to allocate between leisure and work. The table shows the opportunity cost of real GDP in terms of leisure time forgone in the economy of Nautica:

Possibility	Leisure (hours per day)	Opportunity cost of leisure (dollars of real GDP per hour)
A	0	0
B	20	5
C	40	10
D	60	15
E	80	20
F	100	25

a. Make a table and a graph of Nautica's *PPF* for leisure and real GDP.
b. Make a table and a graph of Nautica's production function.
c. Find the marginal product of labor for Nautica at different quantities of labor.

*3. Use the information provided in problem 1 about Robinson Crusoe's economy. Also, use the information that Crusoe must earn $4.50

an hour. If he earns less than this amount, he does not have enough food on which to live. He has no interest in earning more than $4.50 an hour. At a real wage rate of $4.50 an hour, Crusoe is willing to work any number of hours between zero and the total available to him.
a. Make a table that shows Crusoe's demand for labor schedule and draw Crusoe's demand for labor curve.
b. Make a table that shows Crusoe's supply of labor schedule and draw Crusoe's supply of labor curve.
c. What are the full-employment equilibrium real wage rate and quantity of labor in Crusoe's economy?
d. Find Crusoe's potential GDP.

4. Use the information provided in problem 2 about the economy of Nautica. Also, use the information that the people of Nautica are willing to work 10 hours a day for a real wage rate of $10 an hour. And for each 50¢ an hour *increase* in the real wage, they are willing to work an *additional* hour a day.
a. Make a table that shows Nautica's demand for labor schedule and draw Nautica's demand for labor curve.
b. Make a table that shows Nautica's supply of labor schedule and draw Nautica's supply of labor curve.
c. Find the full-employment equilibrium real wage rate and quantity of labor in Nautica's economy.
d. Find Nautica's potential GDP.

*5. Robinson Crusoe, whose economy is described in problems 1 and 3, gets a bright idea. He diverts a stream and increases his food production by 50 percent. That is, each hour that he works produces 50 percent more real GDP than before.
a. Make a table that shows Crusoe's new production function and new demand for labor schedule.
b. Find the new full-employment equilibrium real wage rate and quantity of labor in Crusoe's economy.
c. Find Crusoe's new potential GDP.
d. Explain and interpret the results you obtained in parts (a), (b), and (c).

6. Nautica's economy, described in problems 2 and 4, experiences a surge in its population. The supply of labor increases, and 30 more hours are supplied at each real wage rate.
   a. Make a table that shows Nautica's new supply of labor schedule.
   b. Find the new full-employment equilibrium real wage rate and quantity of labor in Nautica's economy.
   c. Find Nautica's new potential GDP.
   d. Explain and interpret the results you obtained parts in (a), (b), and (c).

 *7. The figure describes the labor market on Cocoa Island. In addition (not shown in the figure), a survey tells us that when Cocoa Island is at full employment, people spend 1,000 hours a day in job search.

a. Find the full-employment equilibrium real wage rate and quantity of labor employed.
b. Find potential GDP on Cocoa Island. (Hint: The demand for labor curve tells you the *marginal* product of labor. How do we calculate the marginal product of labor?)
c. Calculate the natural rate of unemployment on Cocoa Island.

8. On Cocoa Island described in the figure and in problem 7, the government introduces a minimum wage of $4 an hour.
   a. Find the new equilibrium real wage rate and quantity of labor employed.
   b. What now is potential GDP on Cocoa Island?
   c. Calculate the new natural rate of unemployment on Cocoa Island.
   d. How much of the unemployment results from the minimum wage?

CRITICAL THINKING

1. Study the news article about labor productivity during the 2001 recession in the United States in *Reading Between the Lines* on pp. 520–521 and then
   a. Explain why Maury N. Harris is not correct.
   b. By drawing diagrams similar to the two figures on p. 521, explain what Maury N. Harris is talking about and contrast it with what happened during the 2001 recession.
   c. When the recession ends and recovery begins, what do you think will happen to labor productivity? Will it increase or decrease? Why?

2. You are working for the President's Council of Economic Advisors and must write a memo for the President that provides a checklist of policy initiatives that will increase potential GDP. Be as imaginative as possible, but justify each of your suggestions with reference to the concepts and tools that you have learned about in this chapter.

WEB EXERCISES

1. Use the links on your Parkin Web site to obtain information about the economy of Russia during the 1990s. Try to figure out what happened to the production possibilities frontier and production function and to the demand for labor and supply of labor in Russia during the 1990s. Tell a story about the Russian economy during those years using only the concepts and tools that you have learned about in this chapter.

2. Use the links on your Parkin Web site to obtain information about the economy of China during the 1990s. Try to figure out what happened to the production possibilities frontier and production function and to the demand for labor and supply of labor in China during the 1990s. Tell a story about the Chinese economy during those years using only the concepts and tools that you have learned about in this chapter.

CAPITAL, INVESTMENT, AND SAVING

CHAPTER 23

Illusion or Real?

In 1999, a stock market boom increased the paper wealth of American families by an astonishing $5.6 trillion, or 63 percent of real GDP. On paper and on the average, each adult American had $26,500 more at the end of 1999 than at the beginning of that year. In the same year, income exceeded consumption expenditure by only $1.3 trillion, or 16 percent of real GDP. On the average, each adult American saved $6,400. Which of these numbers tells us what Americans truly saved during 1999? Was the additional $26,500 of wealth an illusion or real? Was only the additional $6,400 real saving? You will learn the answer in this chapter. ◆ Saving is important because it pays for investment in new capital. And capital makes our labor more productive and increases our incomes and living standards. How do businesses make their investment decisions? How do people make their saving decisions? And how do capital markets coordinate investment and saving plans?

◆ In this chapter, we study the decisions that determine the amount of capital in the economy and the return — the interest rate — that capital earns. When you have completed your study of this topic, you will be ready to learn about the forces that make potential GDP grow, which you'll study in Chapter 24. We begin by looking at some facts about investment, capital, and interest rates in the United States and around the world.

After studying this chapter, you will be able to

■ Describe the growth and fluctuations of investment and the capital stock and the real interest rate

■ Explain how business investment decisions are made

■ Explain how household saving decisions are made

■ Explain how investment and saving interact to determine the real interest rate

■ Explain how government influences the real interest rate, saving, and investment

■ Explain what determines international borrowing and lending

Capital and Interest

POTENTIAL GDP DEPENDS ON THE QUANTITIES of our productive resources, and the growth rate of potential GDP depends on how rapidly our resources grow. One resource that grows is the economy's **capital stock** — the total quantity of plant, equipment, buildings, and inventories. The capital stock includes business capital such as communication satellites and computers as well as the inventories that businesses carry. It includes houses and apartments. And it includes government-owned *social infrastructure capital* such as the justice system that establishes and enforces property rights, highways, dams and canals, schools, state universities, and national defense systems.

Investment decisions determine the size of the capital stock. The purchase of new capital, called **gross investment**, increases the capital stock. The wearing out and scrapping of capital, called **depreciation**, decreases the capital stock. The capital stock changes by the amount of **net investment,** which equals gross investment minus depreciation (see Chapter 19, p. 437). So net investment tell us how the capital stock is increasing.

We begin by looking at the facts about investment and the capital stock.

Investment and Capital

Figure 23.1(a) shows gross investment and depreciation. In recession years such as 1982, 1991, and 2001, gross investment decreases, and in expansion years, it grows quickly. Depreciation also grows and fluctuates, but it does not line up neatly with the business cycle. In Fig. 23.1(a), the vertical distance between the two lines shows net investment (gross investment minus depreciation). Net investment fluctuates like gross investment.

Figure 23.1(b) provides a more direct view of net investment, which fluctuates with the business cycle, and the capital stock, which grows steadily every year. The capital stock increased from $15 trillion in 1981 to $25 trillion in 2001. The growth rate of the capital stock slows during a recession, but the capital stock has grown every year because net investment has always been positive. When net investment increases during an expansion, the capital stock grows at about 3 percent a year, but on the average, the capital stock grows at around 2.5 percent per year.

FIGURE 23.1   Investment and the Capital Stock in the United States: 1981–2001

(a) Investment

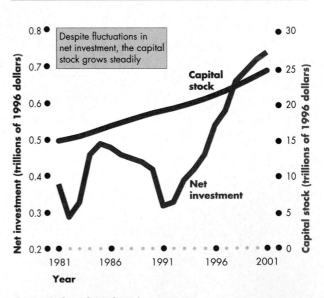

(b) Capital stock and net investment

Net investment fluctuated between $0.3 trillion a year in a recession and $0.7 trillion a year in an expansion. The capital stock grew steadily to $25 trillion in 2001.

Source: Bureau of Economic Analysis.

Saving

Saving finances investment, and Fig. 23.2 shows you the amount of saving in the United States from 1981 to 2001. **Personal saving**, which is personal disposable income minus consumption expenditure, is a small part of total saving, and it has been falling. In 2000 and 2001, personal saving almost dried up. **Business saving**, which is the retained profits of firms plus pension funds that result from payroll deductions, is the largest component of saving and has been growing. **Government saving**, which is the government's budget surplus, has fluctuated and is negative when the government runs a budget deficit.

You can see in Fig. 23.2 that total saving in the United States has increased over the years. And you can see in Fig. 23.1 that investment has increased. Which of the two has increased more? Figure 23.3 answers this question. This figure graphs investment minus saving. You can see that in 1982 and 1991, recession years, investment and saving were almost equal. In every other year, investment exceeded saving, and during the 1990s, the gap increased.

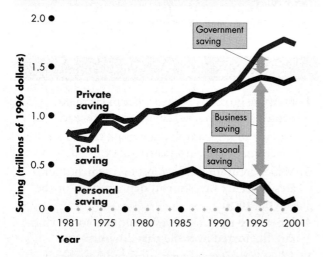

FIGURE 23.2   Saving in the United States: 1981–2001

Personal saving in the United States is a small and decreasing part of total saving. Business saving is the largest part of total saving. Government saving was negative when the government had a budget deficit and positive when the government had a budget surplus.

Source: Bureau of Economic Analysis.

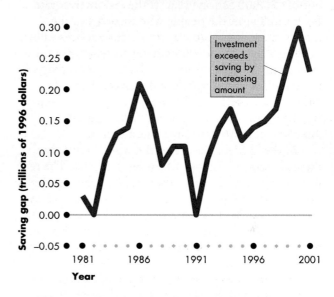

FIGURE 23.3   The Gap Between Investment and Saving in the United States: 1981–2001

Investment exceeded saving every year between 1981 and 2001 except for 1982 and 1991, both recession years.

Source: Bureau of Economic Analysis.

Interest Rates

When we studied the labor market in Chapter 20, we discovered that over the years, both the quantity of labor and the real wage rate per hour of labor have increased. We've seen that the capital stock has grown steadily over time. But what has happened to the return on capital? Has it grown also? To find out, we must first define the return on capital.

The return on capital is the **real interest rate**, which is equal to the *nominal* interest rate adjusted for inflation. The nominal interest rate is the interest rate expressed in terms of money.

The real interest rate is approximately equal to the nominal interest rate minus the inflation rate.[1]

---

[1] The *exact* real interest rate formula allows for the change in the purchasing power of the interest as well as the amount of the loan. The exact formula is: Real interest rate = (Nominal interest rate − Inflation rate) ÷ (1 + Inflation rate/100). If the nominal interest rate is 10 percent and the inflation rate is 4 percent, the real interest rate is (10 − 4) ÷ (1 + 0.04) = 5.77 percent. The lower the inflation rate, the better is the approximation.

For example, if the nominal interest rate is 10 percent a year and the inflation rate is 4 percent a year, the real interest rate (approximately) is 6 percent a year. To see why, think about the following example. You borrow $1,000 for one year. If the real interest rate is 6 percent a year, the people who loaned you the money must be able to buy goods and services valued in today's prices at $1,060 when you repay them. But after a year in which prices rise by 4 percent, they will need $1,100 to buy goods and services that today cost $1,060. So if you pay them $1,100, you are paying them only $1,060 in today's prices and the *real* interest paid is $60 — 6 percent a year.

In the U.S economy and the world economy, there are thousands of different interest rates. The real interest rate at which homebuyers and risky businesses can borrow is higher than the rate at which large corporations can borrow. And large corporations pay a higher interest rate than the U.S. government pays. But all real interest rates tend to move up and down together.

One real interest rate that fluctuates with many others is the real interest rate at which big U.S. corporations borrow. This rate is higher than that at which the U.S government can borrow but lower than the rate that you must pay on a bank loan or credit card balance. But all three interest rates move up and down in the same way.

Figure 23.4 shows the real interest rate paid by big U.S. corporations from 1981 through 2001. The average real interest rate during these years was almost 6 percent a year. The real interest rate does not rise steadily the way the real wage rate rises. It fluctuates around a constant level. Three subperiods are striking:

1. The early 1980s: rising real interest rate
2. The later 1980s: falling real interest rate
3. The 1990s: steady real interest rate

The 1980s began with a deep recession that resulted from large oil price hikes by the oil-producing nations combined with large interest rate hikes by the Federal Reserve and other banks around the world. As the 1980s progressed, real GDP grew. Like the 1980s, the 1990s began in recession, but then the economy went into a long expansion that became rapid by the end of the 1990s. Real GDP growth then slowed in 2000 and came to a near halt in 2001. We'll learn in this chapter *why* and *how* these events influenced the real interest rate.

FIGURE 23.4   The Real Interest Rate: 1981–2001

The real interest rate (here, the rate at which big U.S. corporations can borrow) increased sharply between 1981 and 1984 and then decreased through 1989. It was relatively steady at between 5 percent and 6 percent a year during the 1990s.

Sources: Federal Reserve Board and Bureau of Economic Analysis.

REVIEW QUIZ

1 How are gross investment, net investment, depreciation, and the capital stock related?
2 Provide some examples of private capital and of government social infrastructure capital.
3 Which item fluctuates most and which fluctuates least: net investment, depreciation, or the capital stock?
4 How have the U.S. investment rate and saving rate fluctuated over the past 20 years?
5 What is the return on capital and how has it changed over the past 20 years?

We are now going to study businesses' investment decisions and learn what determines the demand for new capital.

Investment Decisions

INVESTMENT CONSISTS OF PRIVATE INVESTMENT and government investment. We'll look at the role of government later in this chapter and first focus on private investment decisions.

How does Amazon.com decide how much to spend on servers, software, and warehouses? How does AT&T decide how much to spend on fiber-optic cables? Business investment decisions are influenced by

- The expected profit rate
- The real interest rate

To decide whether to invest in a new Internet book-distribution system, Amazon.com compares the expected profit rate with the real interest rate. The real interest rate is the opportunity cost of an investment. Let's look more closely at the expected profit rate and the real interest rate.

The Expected Profit Rate

Other things remaining the same, the greater the expected profit rate from new capital, the greater is the amount of investment.

Imagine that Amazon.com is trying to decide whether to build a new Internet book-distribution system that will operate for one year and then be scrapped and replaced by an even better system. Amazon.com expects net revenue of $120 million from operating the system. Net revenue is equal to total revenue from sales minus the cost of labor and materials. The firm's expected profit from this investment is $20 million, which equals $120 million (net revenue) minus $100 million (cost of the system). The expected *profit rate* is 20 percent a year — ($20 million ÷ $100 million) × 100.

Of the many influences on the expected profit rate, the three that stand out are

1. The phase of the business cycle
2. Advances in technology
3. Taxes

The phase of the business cycle influences the expected profit rate because sales fluctuate over the business cycle. In an expansion, an increase in sales brings a higher profit rate. In a recession, a decrease in sales brings a lower profit rate.

As technologies advance, profit expectations change. When a new technology first becomes available, firms expect to be on a learning curve and so expect a modest profit rate from the new technology. But as firms gain experience with a new technology, they expect costs to fall and the profit rate to increase.

It is the *after-tax* profit rate that a firm receives, so changes in tax rates influence the firm's after-tax profit rate. Firms go to extreme lengths to avoid taxes, and for multinational firms, the decision about *where* to invest often turns on the effect of taxes on profit.

The Real Interest Rate

Other things remaining the same, the lower the real interest rate, the greater is the amount of investment.

The funds used to finance investment might be borrowed, or they might be the financial resources of the firm's owners (the firm's retained earnings). But regardless of the source of the funds, the opportunity cost of the funds is the real interest rate. The real interest paid on borrowed funds is an obvious cost. The real interest rate is also the cost of using retained earnings because these funds could be loaned to another firm. The real interest income forgone is the opportunity cost of using retained earnings to finance an investment project.

In the Amazon.com example, the expected profit rate is 20 percent a year. So it is profitable for Amazon to invest as long as the real interest rate is less than 20 percent a year. That is, at real interest rates below 20 percent a year, Amazon.com will invest in the new system, and at real interest rates in excess of 20 percent a year, it will not. Some projects are profitable at high real interest rates, but other projects are profitable only at low real interest rates. Consequently, the higher the real interest rate, the smaller is the number of projects that are worth undertaking and the smaller is the amount of investment.

We summarize the influences on investment decisions in an investment demand curve.

Investment Demand

If the real interest rate rises, other things remaining the same, investment decreases. The table in Fig. 23.5 shows an example of this relationship. It lists the amounts of investment that occur at three real interest rates and with three expected profit rates. The relationship between investment and the real interest rate, other things remaining the same, is called **investment demand**.

Figure 23.5(a) shows an investment demand curve when the expected profit rate is average. Each point (*A* through *C*) on the investment demand curve corresponds to a row in the table. If the real interest rate is 6 percent a year, investment is $1 trillion. A change in the real interest rate brings a movement along the investment demand curve. If the real interest rate rises to 8 percent a year, investment decreases to $0.8 trillion; there is a movement up the investment demand curve. If the real interest rate falls to 4 percent a year, investment increases to $1.2 trillion; there is a movement down the investment demand curve.

Figure 23.5(b) shows how the investment demand curve depends on the expected rate of profit. When firms expect an average profit rate, investment demand is ID_0, the same as in part (a). But when the expected profit rate increases, investment demand increases and the investment demand curve shifts rightward to ID_1. When the expected profit rate decreases, investment demand decreases and the investment demand curve shifts leftward to ID_2. Fluctuations in the expected profit rate are the main source of fluctuations in investment demand.

Let's now see how the investment demand curve helps us to understand the changes in investment in the United States.

FIGURE 23.5 Investment Demand

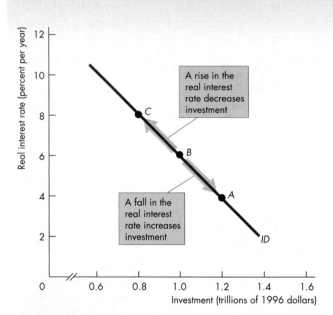

(a) The effect of a change in the real interest rate

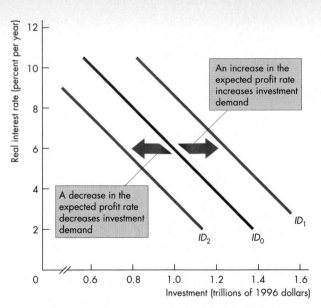

(b) The effect of a change in the expected profit rate

		Investment (trillions of 1996 dollars)		
	Real interest rate (percent per year)	**Expected profit rate**		
		Low	Average	High
A	4	1.0	1.2	1.4
B	6	0.8	1.0	1.2
C	8	0.6	0.8	1.0

The table shows the amount of investment for three different expected profit rates — low, average, and high — and three different interest rates. For example, when the real interest rate is 6 percent a year and the expected profit rate is average, investment is $1.0 trillion. Part (a) shows the investment demand curve, *ID*, for an average expected profit rate. A change in the interest rate brings a movement along the investment demand curve. A change in profit expectations rate shifts the investment demand curve, shown in part (b). A high expected profit rate shifts the curve rightward to ID_1, and a low expected profit rate shifts it leftward to ID_2.

Investment Demand in the United States

Fluctuations in the real interest rate and in the expected profit rate bring fluctuations in investment. Figure 23.6 shows the relative importance of these two factors in the United States. The blue dots show *gross* investment and the real interest rate each year from 1981 to 2001. The curves labeled ID_0, ID_1, ID_2, and ID_3 are four U.S. investment demand curves.

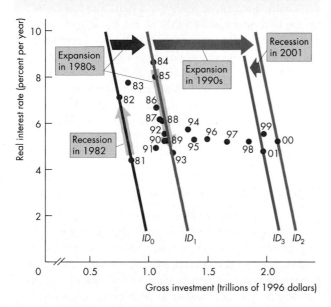

FIGURE 23.6   Investment Demand in the United States: 1981–2001

The blue dots show gross investment and the real interest rate in the United States for each year between 1981 and 2001. The downward sloping curves are investment demand curves. During the 1982 recession, a rising real interest rate decreased investment along the investment demand curve ID_0. During the 1980s expansion, investment demand increased and by 1984, the investment demand curve had shifted rightward to ID_1. A falling real interest rate increased investment in 1985 and 1986 as the 1980s expansion continued. Investment demand decreased slightly during the 1991 recession (not shown in the figure) and then increased during the 1990s expansion. By 2000, the investment demand curve had shifted rightward to ID_2. Investment demand decreased during the 2001 recession and the investment demand curve shifted leftward to ID_3.

Source: Figures 23.1, 23.4, and the author's assumptions.

During the early 1980s, the investment demand curve was ID_0. A rise in the interest rate in the recession of 1982 brought a decrease in investment and a movement up along the investment demand curve. The expected profit rate increased during the expansion of 1983 and 1984, and investment demand increased. The investment demand curve shifted rightward to ID_1. Between 1984 and 1989, the real interest rate fell and there was a movement down along the investment demand curve ID_1.

During the 1991 recession, investment demand decreased slightly (not shown in the figure). By 1994, as the expansion of the 1990s began to pick up speed, the expected profit rate increased and investment demand increased each year. By 2000, the investment demand curve had shifted rightward to ID_2. A fall in the expected profit rate in the 2001 recession brought a decrease in investment demand in that year, and the investment demand curve shifted leftward to ID_3.

You can see in Fig. 23.6 that investment fluctuates for two reasons: The real interest rate changes, which brings movements along an investment demand curve, and the expected profit rate changes, which shifts the investment demand curve. The real interest rate effects are smaller than the expected profit effects. That is, the movements along the investment demand curve are less important than the shifts of the investment demand curve in determining changes in net investment.

REVIEW QUIZ

1 Use the investment demand curve to illustrate what happens to investment if the real interest rate falls and other things remain the same; and if the real interest rate rises and other things remain the same.

2 Use the investment demand curve to illustrate what happens to investment if the expected profit rate increases and other things remain the same; and if the expected profit rate decreases and other things remain the same.

3 In which years have changes in the real interest rate changed U.S. net investment?

Next, we study the decisions that create the funds that finance investment: saving decisions.

Saving Decisions

PRIVATE INVESTMENT IS FINANCED BY NATIONAL saving and by borrowing from the rest of the world (see Chapter 19, pp. 436–437). **National saving** is the sum of private saving and government saving. We first study private saving. Later in the chapter, we'll see how government actions influence saving decisions.

Households must decide how to allocate their *disposable income* between saving and consumption. Of the many factors that influence a household's saving decision, the more important ones are

- The real interest rate
- Disposable income
- Wealth
- Expected future income

The Real Interest Rate

Other things remaining the same, the lower the real interest rate, the smaller is the amount of saving and the greater is the amount of consumption. The real interest rate is the opportunity cost of consumption. A dollar consumed is a dollar not saved, so the interest that could have been earned on that saving is forgone. This opportunity cost arises regardless of whether a person is a lender or a borrower. For a lender, saving less this year means receiving less interest next year. For a borrower, saving less this year means paying less off a loan this year and paying more interest next year.

You can see why the real interest rate influences saving by thinking about student loans. If the real interest rate on student loans jumped to 20 percent a year, students would save more (buying cheaper food and finding lower-rent accommodations) to pay off their loans as quickly as possible. If the real interest rate on student loans fell to 1 percent a year, students would save less and take out larger loans.

Disposable Income

The greater a household's disposable income, other things remaining the same, the greater is its saving. For example, suppose a student works during the summer and earns a disposable income of $10,000. She spends the entire $10,000 on consumption during the year and saves nothing. When she graduates as an economics major, her disposable income jumps to $20,000 a year. She now saves $4,000 and spends $16,000 on consumption. The increase in disposable income of $10,000 has increased saving by $4,000.

Wealth

A household's *wealth* equals its assets (what it *owns*) minus its debts (what it *owes*). The purchasing power of a household's wealth is the *real* value of its wealth. It is the quantity of goods and services that the household's wealth can buy. The greater a household's real wealth, other things remaining the same, the less is its saving.

Patty is a department store executive who earns a disposable income of $30,000 a year. She has been saving and now has $15,000 in the bank and no debts. That is, Patty's wealth is $15,000. Patty's colleague, Tony, also earns a disposable income of $30,000, but he has no money in the bank. Tony's wealth is zero. Patty decides that this year, she will take a vacation and save only $1,000. But Tony decides to skip a vacation and save $5,000. With greater wealth and other things the same, Patty saves less than Tony.

Expected Future Income

The lower a household's expected future income, other things remaining the same, the greater is its saving. That is, if two households have the same disposable income in the current year, the household with the larger expected future income will spend a larger portion of current disposable income on consumption goods and services and saves less.

Look at Patty and Tony again. Patty has just been promoted and will receive a $10,000 pay raise next year. Tony has just been told that he will be fired at the end of the year. On receiving this news, Patty buys a new car — increases her consumption and decreases her saving. Tony sells his car and takes the bus — decreases his consumption and increases his saving.

A young household expects to have a higher future income for some years and then to have a lower income during retirement. Because of this life-cycle income pattern, young people and retired people save least, and middle-aged people save most.

Saving plans interact with investment plans to determine the real interest rate and the amount of investment and saving. Before we can understand these interactions, we need to learn about the saving supply curve.

Saving Supply

If the real interest rate rises, other things remaining the same, saving increases. The relationship between saving and the real interest rate, other things remaining the same, is called **saving supply**.

Figure 23.7 illustrates saving supply. The table shows a saving supply schedule, and the graph shows the saving supply curve. The points *A* through *C* on the saving supply curve *SS* in Fig. 23.7(a) correspond to the rows of the table. For example, point *B* indicates that when the real interest rate is 6 percent a year, saving is $1.0 trillion. If the real interest rate rises from 6 percent a year to 8 percent a year, saving

increases from $1 trillion to $1.1 trillion and there is a movement along the saving supply curve from *B* to *C*.

Along the saving supply curve, all influences on saving except the interest rate remain the same. A change in any other influence on saving changes saving supply and shifts the saving supply curve. An increase in disposable income, a decrease in wealth, or a decrease in expected future income increases saving supply and shifts the saving supply curve rightward from SS_0 to SS_1. Changes in these factors in the opposite direction decrease saving and shift the saving supply curve leftward from SS_0 to SS_2.

Let's now see how the saving supply curve helps us to understand changes in saving in the United States.

FIGURE 23.7   Saving Supply

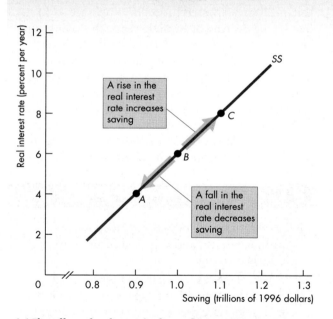

(a) The effect of a change in the real interest rate

(b) The effects of other influences on saving

Part (a) shows the saving supply curve. Points *A* through *C* on the saving supply curve correspond to the rows in the table. Along the saving supply curve, the real interest rate changes but all other influences on saving remain the same. Part (b) shows the effects of all influences on saving other than the interest rate. An increase in disposable income (or a decrease in wealth or a decrease in expected future income) increases saving and shifts the saving supply curve rightward from SS_0 to SS_1. A decrease in disposable income (or an increase in wealth or an increase in expected future income) decreases saving and shifts the saving supply curve leftward from SS_0 to SS_2.

	Real interest rate (percent per year)	Saving (trillions of 1996 dollars)
A	4	0.9
B	6	1.0
C	8	1.1

Saving Supply in the United States

Fluctuations in the real interest rate, disposable income, wealth, and expected future income change saving. Figure 23.8 shows the relative importance of these factors in the United States. The blue dots show net private saving and the real interest rate each year from 1981 to 2001. The curves labeled SS_0, SS_1, SS_2, and SS_3 are four U.S. saving supply curves.

The saving supply curve shows that when the real interest rate rises, saving increases. For example, between 1981 and 1984, the real interest rate rose and saving increased. But a large change in the real interest rate brings only a small change in saving.

Although changes in the real interest rate bring changes in saving, most of the changes in saving result from changes in the three factors that shift the saving supply curve.

During the 19232 recession, disposable income decreased and the saving supply curve shifted leftward to SS_1. But in most years, disposable income increases and shifts the saving supply curve rightward.

Increases in wealth and expected future income decrease saving. During the 1980s and more strongly during the second half of the 1990s, people increasingly expected continued rapid economic expansion. As a result, expected future incomes increased. At the same time, a booming stock market increased wealth. The result of these increases in wealth and expected future income was an increase in consumption expenditure that almost equaled the increase in disposable income. So saving barely changed during some years.

In some years, such as 1998, a rising stock market and rising expected future income were so strong that saving decreased. In these years, the saving supply curve shifts leftward (not shown in the figure).

But on the average, rising disposable income increases saving supply, and the forces that generate a rightward shift in the saving supply curve have been stronger than the forces that generate a leftward shift. So by 2000, the saving supply curve had shifted rightward to SS_2. The recession of 2001 decreased saving supply and the SS curve shifted leftward to SS_3.

FIGURE 23.8 Saving Supply in the United States: 1981–2001

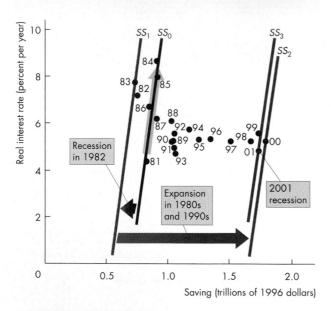

The curve SS_0 is an estimate of the saving supply curve for 1981. A decrease in disposable income shifted the supply curve leftward to SS_1 in the 1982 recession. But generally rising disposable income increased saving supply, and by 2000 the supply curve had shifted rightward to SS_2. In the 2001 recession, saving supply decreased to SS_3. In some years, rising stock prices and rising expected future income encouraged consumption and decreased saving supply.

Sources: Bureau of Economic Analysis, Figure 23.4, and the author's assumptions.

REVIEW QUIZ

1 How do the real interest rate, disposable income, wealth, and expected future income influence saving?
2 If the real interest rate falls and other things remain the same, what happens to saving? If the real interest rate rises and other things remain the same, what happens to saving? How would you illustrate these events using a saving supply curve?
3 How has the U.S. saving supply curve shifted in recent years and what have been the main causes of the shifts?

We've now studied the decisions that determine investment and saving and seen that both sets of decisions depend on the real interest rate. Next, we're going to see how the real interest rate, investment, and saving are simultaneously determined.

Equilibrium in the World Economy

WE ARE NOW GOING TO SEE HOW INVESTMENT decisions and saving decisions determine the real interest rate. To do so, we study the global economy, not the national economy. The reason is that there is a single world capital market. Capital is free to roam the globe and seek the highest possible real rate of return. In 2001, for example, loans from the rest of the world to the United States were around $900 billion. So the saving of one country is not always used to finance the investment of that country.

Real interest rates are not the same in every country because some countries are riskier than others. The riskier the country, the higher is the real interest rate. But interest rates in different countries move up and down together. If two countries with equal risk had different interest rates, people would borrow in the country with a low interest rate and lend in the country with a high interest rate. There would be a shortage of loans in the low-interest-rate country, and the interest rate would rise. Similarly, there would be a surplus of loans in the high-interest-rate country and the interest rate would fall. Interest rates would quickly become equal in the two countries.

Determining the Real Interest Rate

Figure 23.9 shows how global investment and global saving determine the real interest rate. The *ID* curve is the world investment demand curve. The *SS* curve is the world saving supply curve. The higher the real interest rate, the greater is the amount of saving and the smaller is the amount of investment.

In Fig. 23.9, when the real interest rate exceeds 6 percent a year, saving exceeds investment. Borrowers have an easy time finding the loans they want, but lenders are unable to lend all the funds they have available. The real interest rate falls. The interest rate continues to fall until saving equals investment.

Alternatively, when the interest rate is less than 6 percent a year, saving is less than investment. Borrowers can't find the loans they want, but lenders are able to lend all the funds they have available. So the real interest rate rises and continues to rise until saving equals investment.

Regardless of whether there is a surplus or a shortage of saving, the real interest rate changes and is

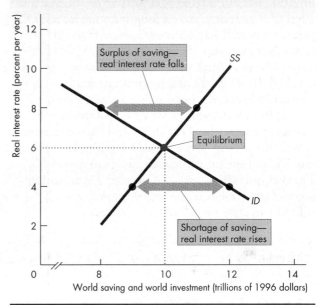

FIGURE 23.9   Equilibrium in the World Capital Market

Real interest rate (percent per year)	Investment	Saving
	(trillions of 1996 dollars)	
4	12	9
6	10	10
8	8	11

The table shows world investment and saving at three interest rates, and the figure shows the world investment demand curve, *ID*, and world saving supply curve, *SS*. If the real interest rate were 4 percent a year, investment would exceed saving and the real interest rate would rise. If the real interest rate were 8 percent a year, saving would exceed investment and the real interest rate would fall. When the real interest rate is 6 percent a year, investment equals saving and the real interest rate is at its equilibrium.

pulled toward an equilibrium level. In Fig. 23.9, this equilibrium is 6 percent a year. At this interest rate, there is neither a surplus nor a shortage of saving. Investors can get the funds they demand, and savers can lend all the funds they have available. The plans of savers and investors are consistent with each other.

Let's use the global saving supply and investment demand curves to explain changes in the real interest rate in the world economy.

Explaining Changes in the Real Interest Rate

In 2001, the real interest rate paid by the biggest and safest U.S. corporations on long-term loans was 4.8 percent a year. It had been even lower than this rate, at 4.4 percent a year, 20 years earlier, in 1981. But during the next three years, the real interest rate climbed. In 1984, the real interest rate paid by big companies reached a peak at 8.7 percent a year.

Figure 23.10 explains why the real interest rate increased during the early 1980s and then decreased again. In 1981 (in part a), the saving supply curve was SS_0 and the investment demand curve was ID_{81}. The real interest rate was 4.4 percent a year, and saving and investment in the world economy was $4.4 trillion (measured in 1996 U.S. dollars).

Between 1981 and 1984, world investment demand increased from ID_{81} to ID_{84}. The increase in investment demand resulted from a rise in expected profit rates as the U.S. economy recovered from recession. During these same years, there was no change in saving supply. The saving supply curve remained at SS_0. The result was a rise in the real interest rate associated with a movement along the given saving supply curve.

Figure 23.10(b) takes up the story at this point. As the global economy expanded during the rest of the 1980s, disposable income increased, which brought a strong increase in saving supply. Expectations of rising profit increased investment demand, but not by as much as the increase in saving supply. So by 1991, the investment demand curve had shifted rightward to

---

FIGURE 23.10   Explaining Changes in the Real Interest Rate

(a) Expansion from 1982 recession

(b) Expansion through 1980s and 1990s

In 1981 (part a), world saving supply was SS_0, world investment demand was ID_{81}, and the real interest rate was 4.4 percent a year. The recovery of the U.S. economy from recession increased expected profit rates, which increased world investment demand. The investment demand curve shifted rightward to ID_{84}, and the real interest rate rose to 8.7 percent a year.

Between 1984 and 1991 (part b), rising disposable income increased saving supply by more than the increase in investment demand. Investment demand increased to ID_{91}, and saving supply increased to SS_{91}. The real interest rate fell. After 1991, saving supply and investment demand increased by similar amounts, so investment and saving increased but the real interest rate didn't change much.

Sources: World Economic Outlook (Washington D.C.: International Monetary Fund, October 2001); *International Financial Statistics Yearbook* (Washington D.C.: International Monetary Fund, 2001); Federal Reserve Board, and the author's assumptions.

ID_{91}. Because the increase in saving supply exceeded the increase in investment demand, the real interest rate fell. By 1991, the real interest rate had fallen to 5 percent a year. Investment and saving in the global economy had increased by \$1 trillion to \$5.7 trillion.

Through the 1990s, investment demand and saving supply increased at a similar pace. The increase in investment demand was driven by the promise of increased profits resulting from the technologies of the new economy. Rising disposable income had a strong positive influence on saving supply, but rising stock prices that brought increased wealth counteracted the effect of rising disposable income and kept the increase in saving supply in check.

Another factor at work, which we examine in the next part of this chapter, was the gradual decrease in government deficits, which brought an increase in government saving.

The combination of similar increases in investment demand and saving supply saw a huge increase in global investment and saving from \$5.7 trillion in 1991 to \$7.3 trillion in 2001. At the same time, the real interest rate barely moved.

So far in our study of investment, saving, and

REVIEW QUIZ

1 How is the real interest rate determined?

2 Why is the real interest rate determined in the *world* capital market rather than in the capital market of a single country?

3 What factors increased investment demand and left saving supply unchanged in 1981–1984? What was the effect on the real interest rate?

4 What were the trends in global investment demand, saving supply, and the real interest rate during the second half of the 1980s? Can you explain the trends?

5 What were the trends in global investment demand, saving supply, and the real interest rate during the 1990s? Can you explain the trends?

the real interest rate, we've ignored government saving. We're now going to bring government saving into the picture.

The Role of Government

PART OF THE CAPITAL STOCK ARISES FROM GOVernment investment. And investment is financed by total saving, which is made up of private saving plus government saving. So government actions influence investment demand, saving supply, and the real interest rate. To complete our study of the forces that determine the quantity of capital and the real interest rate, we must investigate the role played by governments.

But because the real interest rate is determined in the *world* capital market, it is the *aggregate* investment and *aggregate* saving of all governments that matters, not the investment and saving of one government.

Most governments are tiny, and many U.S. corporations have a bigger impact on the world capital market than do some governments. Even the biggest governments have a relatively small impact on the world capital market. For example, the saving of the U.S. government is less than 1 percent of world saving.

But governments in total are large. The saving of world total government is close to 10 percent of world total saving. And the direction of world total government saving is *negative*.

Let's see why government saving is negative and how government investment and saving influence total investment demand, saving supply, and the real interest rate.

Government Budgets

You learned in Chapter 19 (p. 436) that GDP equals the sum of consumption expenditure, C, investment, I, government purchases, G, and net exports. We'll ignore net exports for the moment and consider only a closed economy (such as the world economy). So in a closed economy,

$$GDP = C + I + G.$$

GDP also equals the sum of consumption expenditure, saving, S, and net taxes, T. That is,

$$GDP = C + S + T.$$

By combining these two ways of looking at GDP, you can see that

$$I = S + T - G.$$

- If net taxes, *T*, exceed government purchases, *G*, the government has a budget surplus and government saving is positive.
- If government purchases exceed net taxes, the government has a budget deficit and government saving is negative.

When the government has a budget surplus, it contributes toward financing investment. Its saving must be added to private saving. But when the government has a budget deficit, it competes with businesses for private saving. In this situation, government saving must be subtracted from private saving.

Government saving can influence the world capital market in two ways, one direct and one indirect. We'll begin with the direct effect.

Direct Effect of Government Saving

Figure 23.11 shows the direct effect of government saving for the case in which government saving is negative — governments have a deficit. The investment demand curve, *ID*, is the same as that in Fig. 23.9. The *private* saving supply curve, *PS*, shows the relationship between private saving and the real interest rate. The saving supply curve, *SS*, shows the sum of private saving and government saving.

The horizontal distance between the private saving curve and the world saving supply curve is government saving. In Fig. 23.11, government saving is a negative $2 trillion. That is, the governments of all the nations have a total budget deficit of $2 trillion. (This number is larger than the actual total government deficit in the world economy in 2001.)

The effect of negative government saving, which is also called *dissaving*, is to decrease world saving supply and increase the real interest rate. Investment decreases. In Fig. 23.11, with a government deficit of $2 trillion, the world saving supply curve shifts leftward and the real interest rate rises from 6 percent to 7 percent a year. Investment decreases from $10 trillion to $9 trillion.

Investment does not decrease by the full amount of the government deficit because the higher real interest rate induces an increase in private saving. In Fig. 23.11, private saving increases by $1 trillion to $11 trillion. In reality, the increase in private saving might be quite small, at least in the short term.

The tendency for a government budget deficit to decrease investment is called a **crowding-out effect**. By raising the real interest rate, the government deficit crowds out private investment.

FIGURE 23.11   A Crowding-Out Effect

The world investment demand curve is *ID*, and the world private saving supply curve is *PS*. With balanced government budgets, the real interest rate is 6 percent a year and investment equals saving at $10 trillion a year. A government budget deficit is negative government saving (dissaving). We subtract the government deficit from private saving to determine the world saving supply curve *SS*. The real interest rate rises, investment decreases (is crowded out), and private saving increases.

A government surplus has the opposite effect to what we've just seen. It increases world saving supply, lowers the real interest rate, and stimulates investment.

Indirect Effect of Government Saving

Government saving has an indirect effect on the world capital market because it influences private saving. In the crowding-out story we've just told, the *quantity of private saving* changes because the real interest rate changes. There is a movement along the *PS* curve. But private saving supply does not change. That is, the *PS* curve does not shift. The indirect effect arises from the possibility that a change in government saving changes private saving supply and shifts the *PS* curve. In an extreme version of this effect, private saving changes to offset the government deficit and the deficit has no effect on the real interest rate or investment. Let's look at this extreme case.

The Ricardo-Barro Effect So named because it was first suggested by the English economist David Ricardo in the eighteenth century and refined by Robert J. Barro of Harvard University during the 1980s, the Ricardo-Barro effect holds that a government budget deficit has no effect on the real interest rate or investment. Another way of stating this view is to say that financing government purchases by taxes and financing them by borrowing are equivalent.

The reasoning behind the Ricardo-Barro effect is the following. A government that runs a deficit must sell bonds to pay for the goods and services that are not paid for by taxes. And the government must pay interest on those bonds. It must also collect more taxes *in the future* to pay the interest on the larger quantity of bonds that are outstanding. Taxpayers are rational and have good foresight. They can see that their taxes will be higher in the future and so their disposable income will be smaller. With a smaller expected future disposable income, saving increases. And if taxpayers want to neutralize the effects of the government deficit on their own consumption plans, they increase their saving by the same amount that the government is dissaving through its deficit.

Figure 23.12 shows this outcome. Initially, the government has a balanced budget — neither a deficit nor a surplus — so the world saving supply curve SS is the private saving supply curve PS_0. With investment demand ID, the real interest rate is 6 percent a year and investment and saving are $10 trillion.

Governments now run deficits that total $2 trillion. But these deficits induce an increase in private saving. In Fig. 23.12, the increase in private saving equals the government deficit. So the private saving supply curve shifts rightward to PS_1. But the world saving supply curve SS remains unchanged, and the real interest rate remains at 6 percent a year. Investment also remains at $10 trillion a year. Private saving increases to $12 trillion.

The outcome shown in Fig. 23.12 is extreme and probably does not actually occur. Taxpayers probably respond in the *direction* suggested by Ricardo and Barro but not in the *amount* they suggest. So the effect of government deficits probably lies between the two cases shown in Figs. 23.11 and 23.12. That is, a government deficit increases the real interest rate and partly crowds out private investment, but it also induces a partial increase in private saving in anticipation of lean times later when taxes rise to pay the interest on a rising debt.

FIGURE 23.12   A Ricardo-Barro Effect

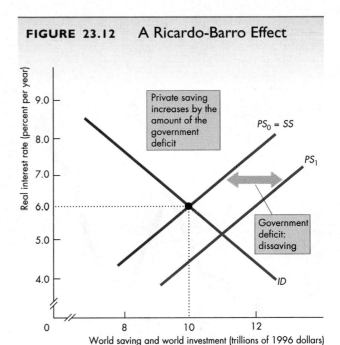

The world investment demand curve is *ID*, and initially, the world saving supply curve *SS* is the private saving supply curve, PS_0. With balanced government budgets, the real interest rate is 6 percent a year and investment equals saving at $10 trillion a year. A government budget deficit induces an increase in private saving to PS_1, but the world saving supply curve remains at *SS*. The real interest rate, investment, and *total* saving remain constant.

Government Deficits Today

Government deficits were large during the early 1990s but fell through the decade, and by 2000, the global government budget was roughly in balance. Figure 23.13 shows the sum of the government budget deficits and surpluses for the world's most advanced economies from 1983 through 2001.

In the early 1980s, the deficit was 5 percent of global GDP. The deficit fell through 1989, then increased through 1992. For the rest of the 1990s, the deficit decreased, and by 2000, the advanced economies had a balanced government sector budget.

The government budget deficits shown in Fig. 23.13 represent negative government saving. So the direct impact of government saving on world saving supply was negative for most of the 1980s and 1990s. By 2000, government saving was exerting no direct impact on world saving supply.

FIGURE 23.13   Government Surpluses and Deficits

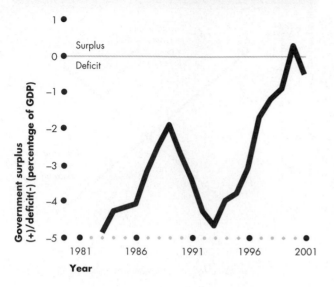

Government budget deficits in the advanced economies were 5 percent of GDP in 1983. The deficit decreased through 1989, increased through 1992, and then decreased to almost zero by 2001.

Source: World Economic Outlook (Washington D.C.: International Monetary Fund, October 2001).

But the indirect effect of government saving on world saving supply depends on the strength of the Ricardo-Barro effect.

REVIEW QUIZ

1 How is world saving supply influenced by private saving, taxes, and government purchases?
2 How does an increase in the aggregate budget deficit of all governments change private saving, investment, and the real interest rate?

So far, we've looked at investment and saving in the world economy. Next we look at the national economy.

Saving and Investment in the National Economy

SAVING SUPPLY AND INVESTMENT DEMAND IN THE world economy determine the world real interest rate. At the equilibrium real interest rate, world saving equals world investment.

Although saving and investment are equal in the world economy, they are not equal in a national economy. In a nation, investment is financed by *national* saving plus borrowing from the rest of the world (see Chapter 19, p. 437). Nations in which investment exceeds national saving borrow from the rest of the world, and nations in which national saving exceeds investment lend to the rest of the world. For the world as a whole, international borrowing equals international lending.

But as you also learned in Chapter 19, a nation's international lending equals its net exports. So a nation that has a net export surplus is also one that lends to the rest of the world. A nation whose imports exceed its exports has negative net exports and borrows from the rest of the world. Whether a nation has a surplus or deficit in its international trade depends on whether its national saving exceeds or falls short of its investment.

Let's take a closer look at the role played by national saving and investment decisions and see how they determine international borrowing. There are two channels of influence to consider.

First, each nation contributes to world saving and investment and so influences the world real interest rate. The larger the country, the greater is that influence. For example, investment and saving decisions in the United States, the European Union, and Japan have a big impact on world investment demand and world saving supply. So they have a big influence on the world real interest rate. The investment and saving of other nations individually have a small impact on world investment demand and world saving supply. So they have a negligible influence on the world real interest rate.

Second, a nation's saving and investment decisions, along with the world real interest rate, determine the amount the nation borrows from or lends to the rest of the world. They also, equivalently, determine a nation's net exports.

Figure 23.14 shows the determination of a nation's international borrowing and net exports. The nation's investment demand curve is *ID*, and its saving supply curve (including any government saving) is *SS*. The world real interest rate is 6 percent a year. At this real interest rate, investment is $1.5 trillion and saving is $1 trillion. International borrowing fills the gap between the nation's investment and saving. In the example in Fig. 23.13, investment exceeds saving, so the nation borrows from the rest of the world. If, at the world real interest rate, saving exceeds investment, the nation lends to the rest of the world.

International Borrowing and Lending in the World Today

You can now see why the United States has been a borrower from the rest of the world for the past 20 years. It is because U.S. national saving has been less than U.S. investment.

U.S. international borrowing has increased over the past few years because U.S. investment has increased and U.S. national saving has decreased.

Japan is one of the big lenders on the world capital market. Japan is a mirror image of the United States. The reason is that a relatively high volume of saving has exceeded the investment that this depressed economy has undertaken. So Japan has lent its excess of saving over investment to the rest of the world.

Government Deficit and International Borrowing

The greater the amount of government saving, other things remaining the same, the greater is national saving. And the greater the national saving, the smaller is international borrowing (or the larger is international lending). So an increase in a government's deficit decreases national saving and increases international borrowing.

When the U.S. government had a large deficit during the 1980s, this deficit contributed to U.S. international borrowing. And as the government deficit shrank during the 1990s, the government contributed to a decrease in U.S. international borrowing. Despite this contribution, international borrowing has increased. The reason is that private saving has shrunk.

Because the capital market is a global market, a U.S. government deficit does not crowd out U.S.

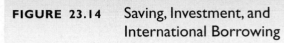

FIGURE 23.14   Saving, Investment, and International Borrowing

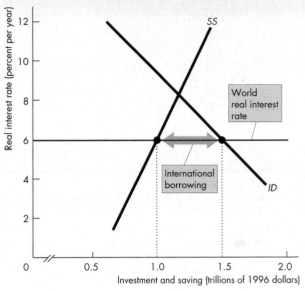

A nation's investment demand curve is *ID*, and its saving supply curve (including government saving) is *SS*. The world real interest rate is 6 percent a year. At this interest rate, investment demand, which is $1.5 trillion, exceeds saving, which is $1 trillion. The nation borrows $0.5 trillion from the rest of the world.

investment. But it does influence our standard of living because it increases interest payments that we must make to the rest of the world.

REVIEW QUIZ

1 If, in a country, investment exceeds saving at the world real interest rate, does that country have positive or negative net exports?
2 Does an increase in a government's deficit crowd out investment?

◆ *Reading Between the Lines* on pp. 542–543 returns to the question posed at the beginning of this chapter and examines two views of saving in the United States. Your task in the next chapter is to see how investment and saving bring economic growth.

Saving in the United States

LOS ANGELES TIMES, JANUARY 7, 2002

Saving Rate Misleading, Study Says

Measures of personal saving by Americans may be extraordinarily low, but that does not necessarily mean households are putting too little aside for retirement, according to a new study by two economists.

"The recent decline in personal saving rates does not in itself indicate that households are ill-prepared to finance their retirement or handle unexpected expenses," said economists Marshall Reinsdorf and Maria Perozek, of the Commerce Department's Bureau of Economic Analysis and the Federal Reserve Board, respectively. ...

The widely watched saving rate, published monthly by the bureau in its income and spending report, stood at only 0.9% of disposable personal income in November, or less than a penny from each after-tax dollar of income. That was up from 0.2% in October. For 2000, it was only 1.0%, down from 2.4% in 1999. ...

But some economists have long expressed skepticism about the government numbers. The data don't include the value of some assets most people would think of as savings, including capital gains on stock investments.

However, the study shows that, even after adjusting the bureau's data to accommodate some of the criticisms, saving is down sharply in recent years. ...

To get an idea of household balance sheets, however, the authors instead advised looking to a separate measure, household net worth, based on quarterly data in the Federal Reserve's "flow of funds" accounts. That measure tracks asset values held by households, including gains in home prices and stocks held.

"The change in net worth is useful for answering questions about the aggregate value of household wealth, which is an indicator of the future consumption possibilities of the household sector," Reinsdorf and Perozek wrote. ...

And, even by that measure, households have been hit hard by the decline in stock prices recently. According to the Federal Reserve Board's latest data, released in December, household net worth fell by $1.192 trillion in the third quarter of 2001 to $38.701 trillion, its third drop in the last four quarters.

Compared with the third quarter of 2000, household wealth fell by $3.810 trillion.

Though homes added more than $270 million to household balance sheets in the third quarter, declining stocks and mutual fund shares subtracted $1.562 trillion from household wealth.

Essence of the Story

■ Marshall Reinsdorf of the Bureau of Economic Analysis (BEA) and Maria Perozek of the Federal Reserve Board (Fed) have compared two measures of saving.

■ One measure, published monthly by the BEA, is based on income and consumption data.

■ The other measure, published quarterly by the Fed, is based on the value of household assets and includes home prices and stock prices.

■ Reinsdorf and Perozek show that, on both measures, saving is down.

■ According to the BEA data, personal saving in November 2001 was less than a penny per after-tax dollar of income.

■ According to the Fed data, household net worth fell by $1.192 trillion in the third quarter of 2001, its third drop in the last four quarters, and was $3.810 trillion less than its level a year earlier.

Economic Analysis

■ You learned in Chapter 4 that the income that households earn, Y, is either spent on consumption goods and services, C, saved, S, or paid in taxes, T. That is,

$$Y = C + S + T.$$

■ By subtracting C and T from both sides of this equation, we get the first measure of saving:

$$S = Y - T - C.$$

■ Disposable income is $Y - T$, so this definition is the one that the BEA uses: Saving equals disposable income minus consumption expenditure.

■ You also learned in Chapter 4 that saving is an addition to the stock of wealth. That is,

$$S = \text{Change in wealth.}$$

■ The change in the value of the assets that people own minus the amounts that they owe, a number that we call *net worth*, measures the change in wealth and is the Fed's alternative measure of saving.

■ Figure 1 shows the two measures for private saving in billions of 1996 dollars, and Figure 2 shows the two measures as percentages of real GDP.

■ The income-based measure barely fluctuates, but the wealth-based measure fluctuates a lot.

■ On the average, the wealth-based measure exceeds the income-based measure over the period shown in the figures, and by a large margin.

■ On the average, the income minus consumption measure of saving is $1.7 trillion a year, or 15 percent of real GDP. In contrast, the change in wealth-based measure of saving is $2.3 trillion a year, or 27 percent of real GDP.

■ Income minus consumption is the correct measure of saving. The change in wealth-based measure of saving is based on unfulfilled hopes about *future* earnings.

You're The Voter

■ What do you think the federal government should do about the low U.S. saving rate?

■ Can you think of any tax reforms that might increase saving?

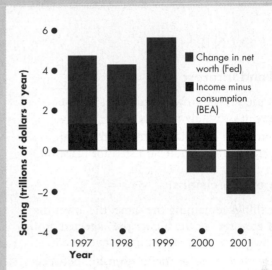

Figure 1 Two measures of private saving

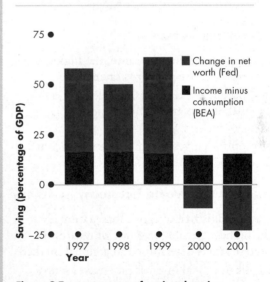

Figure 2 Two measures of national saving

■ How do you think Social Security and Medicare might influence personal saving?

■ Would you vote for tax incentives, a cut in Social Security, neither, or both, and why?

SUMMARY

KEY POINTS

Capital and Interest (pp. 526–528)

- The capital stock grows steadily because net investment is usually positive.
- The return on capital is the real interest rate — the nominal interest rate adjusted for inflation.

Investment Decisions (pp. 529–531)

- Other things remaining the same, the lower the real interest rate or the higher the expected profit rate, the greater is the amount of investment.
- Investment demand is the relationship between investment and the real interest rate, other things remaining the same. Investment demand changes when the expected profit rate changes.

Saving Decisions (pp. 532–534)

- Other things remaining the same, the higher the real interest rates, the greater is saving.
- Saving supply is the relationship between saving and the real interest rate, other things remaining the same.
- Saving supply changes when disposable income, wealth, or expected future income changes.

Equilibrium in the World Economy (pp. 535–537)

- Because capital is free to move internationally to seek the highest possible real rate of return, the real interest rate is determined in a global market.
- The equilibrium real interest rate makes global saving equal to global investment.

The Role of Government (pp. 537–540)

- National saving equals private saving plus government saving.

- Government saving equals net taxes minus government purchases.
- A government budget deficit might increase the real interest rate and crowd out private investment.
- A government budget deficit might also increase private saving supply because it decreases expected future disposable income.

Saving and Investment in the National Economy (pp. 540–541)

- In the national economy, foreign borrowing fills the gap between national saving and investment.
- An increase in the government budget deficit decreases national saving and increases foreign borrowing, but it does not decrease investment.

KEY FIGURES

KEY TERMS

PROBLEMS

*1. A cellular phone assembly plant costs $10 million and has a life of one year. The firm will have to hire labor at a cost of $3 million and buy parts and fuel at a cost of a further $3 million. If the firm builds the plant, it will be able to produce cellular telephones that will sell for a total revenue of $17 million. Does it pay the firm to invest in this new production line at the following real interest rates:
   a. 5 percent a year?
   b. 10 percent a year?
   c. 15 percent a year?

2. A natural gas deposit contains gas that can be pumped out in one year and sold for a total revenue of $40 million. It will take a $36 million investment in equipment and pipelines to access the gas and deliver it to the buyers. Does it pay to undertake this investment at the following real interest rates:
   a. 5 percent a year?
   b. 10 percent a year?
   c. 15 percent a year?

*3. In 1999, the Batman family (Batman and Robin) had a disposable income of $50,000, wealth of $100,000, and an expected future income of $50,000 a year. At an interest rate of 4 percent a year, the Batmans would save $10,000. At an interest rate of 6 percent a year, they would save $12,500. And at an interest rate of 8 percent a year, they would save $15,000.
   a. Draw a graph of the Batman family's saving supply curve for 1999.
   b. In 2000, everything remained the same as the year before except that the Batmans expected their future income to rise to $60,000 a year. Show the influence of this change on the Batman family's saving supply curve.
   c. In 2001, everything remained the same as the year before except that the Batmans' disposable income increased to the $60,000 a year they expected it would the year before. The Batmans now expect their income to remain at $60,000 a year. Show the influence of this change on the Batman family's saving supply curve.

4. It is now 2002, and the Batman family has wealth of $120,000. Its disposable income is $60,000, and its expected future income is also $60,000 a year. The Batmans will save $15,000 at an interest rate of 6 percent a year. If the interest rate falls to 4 percent a year, they will cut their saving to $10,000. And if the interest rate rises to 8 percent a year, they will increase their saving to $20,000.
   a. Draw a graph of the Batman family's saving supply curve for 2002.
   b. In 2002, the stock market boomed and the Batmans' wealth increased by 50 percent. Indicate the direction of influence of this change on the Batman family's saving supply curve.
   c. In 2003, the stock market crashed and the Batmans' wealth was wiped out. Indicate the direction of influence of this change on the Batman family's saving supply curve.

*5. The year is 3053. The economy of Planet Earth, which is isolated from all other planets, has the following saving supply and investment demand:

Real interest rate (percent per year)	Saving	Investment (trillions of 3050 dollars)
4	2	7
5	6	6
6	10	5
7	14	4
8	18	3

Planet Earth's government budget is balanced.
   a. What is the equilibrium real interest rate?
   b. What is equilibrium investment?
   c. What is equilibrium saving?

6. The year is 3053. The economy of Alpha Centauri, which is isolated from all other planets, has the following saving supply and investment demand:

Real interest rate (percent per year)	Saving	Investment (trillions of 3050 zips)
4	1	16
5	3	13
6	5	10
7	7	7
8	9	4

Alpha Centauri's government budget is balanced.
a. What is the equilibrium real interest rate?
b. What is equilibrium investment?
c. What is equilibrium saving?

*7. The government of Planet Earth spends big on a space program and incurs a deficit of 5 trillion dollars. But the citizens of Planet Earth have a long memory and remember the Ricardo-Barro principle and they apply it to their saving and spending decisions.
a. What is the new equilibrium real interest rate?
b. What are the new equilibrium investment and saving?

8. The government of Alpha Centauri spends big on a space program and incurs a deficit of 5 trillion zips. The citizens of Alpha Centauri have never heard of David Ricardo and Robert Barro, so they keep spending as if there were no government deficit.
a. What is the new equilibrium real interest rate?
b. What are the new equilibrium investment and saving?

*9. The space programs of Alpha Centauri and Planet Earth pay off. The Alpha Centaurians and the Earth people discover each other and begin to pursue intergalactic economic trade, borrowing, and lending. They establish a common currency: 1 zip equals 1 dollar. They terminate their government deficits and return to the levels of saving and investment described in problems 5 and 6.
a. What is the real interest rate in the galactic economy?
b. What is the level of galactic investment?
c. What is the level of galactic saving?
b. Do investment and saving on Alpha Centauri increase or decrease?

10. In the galactic economy consisting of Alpha Centauri and Planet Earth described in problem 9,
a. Do investment and saving on Planet Earth increase or decrease?
b. Do investment and saving on Alpha Centauri increase or decrease?
c. Which planet borrows from the other and how much?

CRITICAL THINKING

1. Study *Reading Between the Lines* on pp. 542–543 and then answer the following questions:
a. What has happened to the saving rate in the United States during the past few years?
b. How does the way we measure saving influence your answer to part (a)?
c. What are the main reasons you can think of that might account for the patterns that you describe in your answer to parts (a) and (b)?
d. What are the likely effects of a decrease in U.S. saving supply? Explain the effects on national saving, investment, the world real interest rate, and U.S. international borrowing and lending.
e. If the U.S. saving rate increases during the 2000s, how will that change influence the U.S. and world quantity of capital by 2010?

2. Suppose the U.S. government cuts the tax rate on business profits.
a. How do you think this tax cut will influence firms' investment plans?
b. How will the tax cut influence private saving decisions?
c. How will the tax cut influence the real interest rate?
d. How will the tax cut influence U.S. international borrowing?
For each part (a) through (d), draw a figure to illustrate the effects. Then go on to think about and answer the following questions:
e. Who would benefit from such a tax cut?
f. Who would pay for such a tax cut?
g. On balance, do you favor or oppose such a tax cut? Why?

WEB EXERCISES

1. Use the link on your Parkin Web site to get data on government budget deficits.
a. What are the trends in deficits? Are they the same as or different from that in Fig. 23.13 on p. 540?
b. What influence do you expect the deficits to have on the real interest rate and investment next year?

ECONOMIC GROWTH — CHAPTER 24

Transforming People's Lives

Real GDP *per person* in the United States more than doubled between 1961 and 2001. If you live in a dorm, chances are it was built during the 1960s and equipped with two electrical outlets, one for a desk lamp and one for a bedside lamp. Today, with the help of a power bar (or two), your room bulges with a personal computer, television and VCR or DVD player, stereo system, microwave, refrigerator, coffeemaker, and toaster — the list goes on. What has brought about this growth in production, incomes, and living standards? ◆ We see even greater economic growth if we look at modern Asia. On the banks of the Li River in Southern China, Songman Yang breeds cormorants, amazing birds that he trains to fish and to deliver their catch to a basket on his simple bamboo raft. Songman's work, the capital equipment and technology he uses, and the income he earns are similar to those of his ancestors going back some 2,000 years. Yet all around Songman, in China's bustling cities, people are participating in an economic miracle. They are creating businesses, investing in new technologies, developing local and global markets, and transforming their lives. Why are incomes in China growing so rapidly?

◆ In this chapter, we study the forces that make real GDP grow, that make some countries grow faster than others, and that make our own growth rate sometimes slow down and sometimes speed up.

After studying this chapter, you will be able to

- Describe the long-term growth trends in the United States and other countries and regions
- Identify the main sources of long-term real GDP growth
- Explain the productivity growth slowdown in the United States during the 1970s and the speedup during the 1990s
- Explain the rapid economic growth rates being achieved in Asia
- Explain the theories of economic growth

Long-Term Growth Trends

THE LONG-TERM GROWTH TRENDS THAT WE study in this chapter are the trends in *potential GDP*. We are interested in long-term growth primarily because it brings rising incomes *per person*. So we begin by looking at some facts about the level and the growth rate of real GDP per person in the United States and around the world. Let's look first at real GDP per person in the United States over the past hundred years.

Growth in the U.S. Economy

Figure 24.1 shows real GDP per person in the United States for the hundred years from 1901 to 2001. In the middle of the graph are two extraordinary events: the Great Depression of the 1930s and World War II of the 1940s. The fall in real GDP during the depression and the bulge during the war obscure any changes in the long-term growth trend that might have occurred within these years.

For the century as a whole, the average growth rate was 2.1 percent a year. But from 1901 to the onset of the Great Depression in 1929, the average growth rate was only 1.4 percent a year. Between 1930 and 1950, averaging out the depression and the war, the long-term growth rate was 2.2 percent a year. Then, after World War II, the average growth rate was 2.1 percent a year. Growth was especially rapid during the 1960s and late 1990s and slower during the period from 1973 to 1983.

Figure 24.1 shows the productivity growth slowdown of the 1973–1983 in a longer perspective. It also shows that productivity growth slowdowns have occurred before. The early years of the 1900s and the mid-1950s had even slower growth than we had during the 1970s and 1980s. The rapid growth of the 1960s and 1990s is not unusual either. The 1920s were years of similarly rapid growth.

A major goal of this chapter is to explain why our economy grows and why the long-term growth rate varies. Another goal is to explain variations in the economic growth rate across countries. Let's look at some facts about growth rates.

FIGURE 24.1 A Hundred Years of Economic Growth in the United States

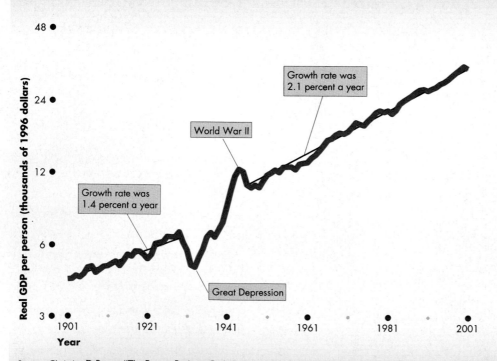

During the 100 years from 1901 to 2001, real GDP per person in the United States grew by 2.1 percent a year, on the average. The growth rate was greater after World War II than before the Great Depression.

Sources: Christina D. Romer, "The Prewar Business Cycle Reconsidered: New Estimates of Gross National Product, 1869–1908," *Journal of Political Economy,* Vol. 97 1989; Bureau of Economic Analysis; and author's calculations to link these two sources.

Real GDP Growth in the World Economy

Figure 24.2 shows real GDP per person in the United States and in other countries between 1961 and 2001. Part (a) looks at the seven richest countries — known as the G7 nations. Among these nations, the United States has the highest real GDP per person. In 2001, Canada had the second-highest real GDP per person, ahead of Japan and France, Germany, Italy, and the United Kingdom (collectively the Europe Big 4).

Before the 1990s, the other six members of the G7 had grown faster than the United States. Japan had grown fastest and overtook Europe in the mid-1980s. But during the 1990s, the Japanese economy stagnated while Europe's continued to expand, so by 2001, these nations had similar levels of real GDP per person.

Not all countries are growing faster than, and catching up with, the United States. Figure 24.2(b) looks at some of these. Western Europe (other than the Big 4) grew faster than the United States before 1975, slowed to the U.S. growth rate during the 1980s, and fell farther behind during the 1990s. After a brief period of catch-up, the former Communist countries of Central Europe have fallen increasingly behind the United States, and by 2001, they were as far behind as they had been 30 years earlier.

Africa and Central and South America have grown more slowly than the United States. Real GDP per person in Central and South America slipped from a comparative high of 30 percent of the U.S. level of real GDP per person in 1980 to 23 percent in 2001. Africa slipped from 8 percent of the U.S. level of real GDP per person in 1960 to 6 percent in 2001.

FIGURE 24.2   Economic Growth Around the World: Catch-Up or Not?

(a) Catch-up?

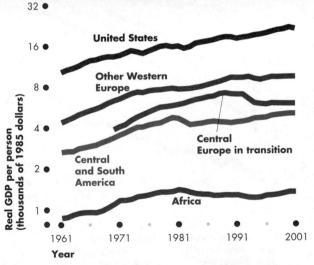

(b) No catch-up?

Real GDP per person has grown throughout the world economy. Among the rich industrial countries (part a), real GDP growth has been faster in Canada, the Europe Big 4 (France, Germany, Italy, and the United Kingdom), and Japan than in the United States, and these countries have narrowed the gap. The most spectacular growth was in Japan during the 1960s. Real GDP per person in Canada became close to the U.S. level during the 1980s but slipped back during the 1990s. Among a wider range of countries (part b), there is little sign of catch-up. The gaps between the levels of real GDP per person in the United States, other Western European countries, and Central and South America have remained constant. The gaps between the United States and Central Europe and Africa have widened.

Sources: 1960–1992: Robert Summers and Alan Heston, New Computer Diskette (Mark 5.6a), January 15, 1995 , distributed by the National Bureau of Economic Research to update "The Penn World Table: An Expanded Set of International Comparisons, 1950–1988," *Quarterly Journal of Economics*, May 1991, 327–368. 1993-2001; and *World Economic Outlook* (Washington, D.C.: International Monetary Fund, October 2001).

A group of Asian economies provides a strong contrast to the persistent gaps between the United States and other economies shown in Fig. 24.2(b). Hong Kong, Korea, Singapore, and Taiwan have experienced spectacular growth, which you can see in Fig. 24.3. During the 1960s, real GDP per person in these economies ranged from 10 to 25 percent of that in the United States. But by 2001, two of them, Hong Kong and Singapore, had almost caught up with the United States and the other two were close behind.

Figure 24.3 shows that China is also catching up, but more slowly and from a very long way behind. China's real GDP per person increased from 5 percent of the U.S. level in 1961 to 15 percent in 2001.

The four small Asian economies shown in Fig. 24.3 are like fast trains running on the same track at similar speeds and with a roughly constant gap between them. Hong Kong is the lead train and runs about 15 years in front of Korea, which is the last train. Real GDP per person in Korea in 2001 was similar to that in Hong Kong in 1986, 15 years earlier. Between 1961 and 2001, Hong Kong transformed itself from a poor developing economy into one of the world's richest economies.

China is now doing what Hong Kong has done. If China continues its rapid growth, the world economy will become a dramatically different place because China is equivalent to more than 200 countries of the size of Hong Kong. Whether China will continue on its current path of rapid growth is impossible to predict.

FIGURE 24.3 Catch-Up in Asia

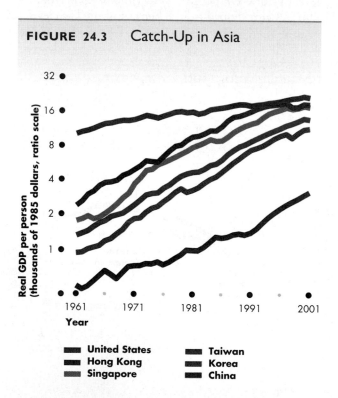

Catch-up has occurred in five economies in Asia. After starting out in 1960 with real GDP per person as low as 10 percent of that in the United States, Hong Kong, Korea, Singapore, and Taiwan have substantially narrowed the gap between them and the United States. And from being a very poor developing country in 1960, China now has a real GDP per person that equals that of Hong Kong in 1960. China is growing at a rate that is enabling it to continue to catch up with the United States.

Sources: See Fig. 24.2.

REVIEW QUIZ

1 What has been the average economic growth rate in the United States over the past 100 years? In which periods was growth the most rapid and in which periods was it the slowest?

2 Describe the gaps between the levels of real GDP per person in the United States and other countries. For which countries are the gaps narrowing? For which countries are the gaps widening? And for which countries are the gaps remaining unchanged?

3 Compare the growth rates and levels of real GDP per person in Hong Kong, Korea, Singapore, Taiwan, China, and the United States. How far is China behind the other Asian economies?

The facts about economic growth in the United States and around the world raise some big questions that we're now going to answer. We'll study the causes of economic growth in three stages. First, we'll look at the preconditions for growth and the activities that sustain it. Second, we'll learn how economists measure the relative contributions of the sources of growth — an activity called *growth accounting*. And third, we'll study three theories of economic growth that seek to explain how the influences on growth interact to determine the growth rate. Let's take our first look at the causes of economic growth.

The Causes of Economic Growth: A First Look

MOST HUMAN SOCIETIES HAVE LIVED FOR CEN-turies and even thousands of years, like Songman Yang, with no economic growth. The key reason is that they have lacked some fundamental social institutions and arrangements that are essential preconditions for economic growth. Let's see what these preconditions are.

Preconditions for Economic Growth

The most basic precondition for economic growth is an appropriate *incentive* system. Three institutions are crucial to the creation of incentives:

1. Markets
2. Property rights
3. Monetary exchange

Markets enable buyers and sellers to get information and to do business with each other, and market prices send signals to buyers and sellers that create incentives to increase or decrease the quantities demanded and supplied. Markets enable people to specialize and trade and to save and invest. But markets need property rights and monetary exchange.

Property rights are the social arrangements that govern the ownership, use, and disposal of factors of production and goods and services. They include the rights to physical property (land, buildings, and capital equipment), to financial property (claims by one person against another), and to intellectual property (such as inventions). Clearly established and enforced property rights give people an assurance that a capricious government will not confiscate their income or savings.

Monetary exchange facilitates transactions of all kinds, including the orderly transfer of private property from one person to another. Property rights and monetary exchange create incentives for people to specialize and trade, to save and invest, and to discover new technologies.

No unique political system is necessary to deliver the preconditions for economic growth. Liberal democracy, founded on the fundamental principle of the rule of law, is the system that does the best job. It provides a solid base on which property rights can be established and enforced. But authoritarian political systems have sometimes provided an environment in which economic growth has occurred.

Early human societies, based on hunting and gathering, did not experience economic growth, because they lacked these preconditions. Economic growth began when societies evolved the three key institutions that create incentives. But the presence of an incentive system and the institutions that create it does not guarantee that economic growth will occur. It permits economic growth but does not make that growth inevitable.

The simplest way in which growth happens when the appropriate incentive system exists is that people begin to specialize in the activities at which they have a comparative advantage and trade with each other. You saw in Chapter 2 how everyone can gain from such activity. By specializing and trading, everyone can acquire goods and services at the lowest possible cost. Equivalently, people can obtain a greater volume of goods and services from their labor.

As an economy moves from one with little specialization to one that reaps the gains from specialization and exchange, its production and consumption grow. Real GDP per person increases, and the standard of living rises.

But for growth to be persistent, people must face incentives that encourage them to pursue three activities that generate ongoing economic growth:

- Saving and investment in new capital
- Investment in human capital
- Discovery of new technologies

These three sources of growth, which interact with each other, are the primary sources of the extraordinary growth in productivity during the past 200 years. Let's look at each in turn.

Saving and Investment in New Capital

Saving and investment in new capital increase the amount of capital per worker and increase real GDP per hour of labor — labor productivity. Labor productivity took the most dramatic upturn when the amount of capital per worker increased during the Industrial Revolution. Production processes that use hand tools can create beautiful objects, but production methods that use large amounts of capital per worker, such as auto plant assembly lines, are much more productive. The accumulation of capital on farms, in textile factories, in iron foundries and steel mills, in coal mines, on building sites, in chemical plants, in auto plants, in banks and insurance companies, and in shopping malls has added incredibly to the productivity of our economy. The next time you see a movie set in the Old West or colonial times, look carefully at the small amount of capital around. Try to imagine how productive you would be in such circumstances compared with your productivity today.

Investment in Human Capital

Human capital — the accumulated skill and knowledge of human beings — is the most fundamental source of economic growth. It is a source of both increased productivity and technological advance.

The development of one of the most basic human skills — writing — was the source of some of the earliest major gains in productivity. The ability to keep written records made it possible to reap ever-larger gains from specialization and exchange. Imagine how hard it would be to do any kind of business if all the accounts, invoices, and agreements existed only in people's memories.

Later, the development of mathematics laid the foundation for the eventual extension of knowledge about physical forces and chemical and biological processes. This base of scientific knowledge was the foundation for the technological advances of the Industrial Revolution 200 years ago and of today's information revolution.

But much human capital that is extremely productive is much more humble. It takes the form of millions of individuals learning and repetitively doing simple production tasks and becoming remarkably more productive in the tasks.

One carefully studied example illustrates the importance of this kind of human capital. Between 1941 and 1944 (during World War II), U.S. shipyards produced some 2,500 units of a cargo ship, called the Liberty Ship, to a standardized design. In 1941, it took 1.2 million person-hours to build one ship. By 1942, it took 600,000 person-hours, and by 1943, it took only 500,000. Not much change occurred in the capital employed during these years. But an enormous amount of human capital was accumulated. Thousands of workers and managers learned from experience and accumulated human capital that more than doubled their productivity in two years.

Discovery of New Technologies

Saving and investment in new capital and the accumulation of human capital have made a large contribution to economic growth. But technological change — the discovery and the application of new technologies and new goods — has made an even greater contribution.

People are many times more productive today than they were a hundred years ago. We are not more productive because we have more steam engines per person and more horse-drawn carriages per person. Rather, it is because we have engines and transportation equipment that use technologies that were unknown a hundred years ago and that are more productive than the old technologies were. Technological change makes an enormous contribution to our increased productivity. It arises from formal research and development programs and from informal trial and error, and it involves discovering new ways of getting more out of our resources.

To reap the benefits of technological change, capital must increase. Some of the most powerful and far-reaching fundamental technologies are embodied in human capital — for example, language, writing, and mathematics. But most technologies are embodied in physical capital. For example, to reap the benefits of the internal combustion engine, millions of horse-drawn carriages and horses had to be replaced by automobiles; more recently, to reap the benefits of computerized word processing, millions of typewriters had to be replaced by PCs and printers.

REVIEW QUIZ

1 What economic activities that lead to economic growth do markets, property rights, and monetary exchange facilitate?
2 How do saving and investment in new capital, the growth of human capital, and the discovery of new technologies generate economic growth?
3 Provide some examples of how human capital has created new technologies that are embodied in both human and physical capital.

What is the quantitative contribution of the sources of economic growth? To answer this question, economists use growth accounting.

Growth Accounting

THE QUANTITY OF REAL GDP SUPPLIED (Y) depends on three factors:

- The quantity of labor (L)
- The quantity of capital (K)
- The state of technology (T)

The purpose of **growth accounting** is to calculate how much real GDP growth results from growth of labor and capital and how much is attributable to technological change.

The key tool of growth accounting is the **aggregate production function**, which is written as the equation:

$$Y = F(L, K, T).$$

In words, the quantity of real GDP supplied is determined by (is a function F of) the quantities of labor and capital and of the state of technology. The larger is L, K, or T, the greater is Y. And the faster L and K grow and the faster T advances, the faster Y grows.

So understanding what makes labor and capital grow and technology advance is the key to understanding economic growth. Labor growth depends primarily on population growth. And the growth rate of capital and the pace of technological advance determine the growth rate of labor productivity.

Labor Productivity

Labor productivity is real GDP per hour of labor. It is calculated by dividing real GDP by aggregate labor hours. That is, labor productivity equals Y divided by L.

Labor productivity determines how much income an hour of labor generates. Figure 24.4 shows labor productivity for the period 1961–2001. Productivity growth was most rapid during the 1960s. It slowed down in 1973 and remained low for about 10 years. Productivity growth then speeded up again in what has been called the new economy of the 1990s.

Why did productivity grow fastest during the 1960s and late 1990s? Why did it slow down in 1973 and then speed up again after 1983?

Growth accounting answers these questions by dividing the growth in labor productivity into two components and then measuring the contribution of each. The components are:

- Growth in capital per hour of labor
- Technological change

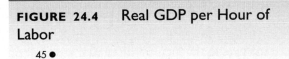

FIGURE 24.4 Real GDP per Hour of Labor

Real GDP divided by aggregate hours equals real GDP per hour of labor, which is a broad measure of productivity. During the 1960s and late 1990s, the productivity growth rate was high. It slowed between 1973 and 1983.

Sources: Bureau of Economic Analysis, Bureau of Labor Statistics, and author's calculations.

Capital is physical capital. Technological change includes everything that contributes to labor productivity growth that is not included in growth in capital per hour. In particular, technological change includes human capital growth. Human capital growth and technological change are intimately related. Technology advances because knowledge advances. And knowledge is part of human capital. So "technological change" is a broad catchall concept.

The analytical engine of growth accounting is a relationship called the productivity curve. Let's learn about this relationship and see how it is used.

The Productivity Curve

The **productivity curve** is a relationship that shows how real GDP per hour of labor changes as the amount of capital per hour of labor changes with a given state of technology. Figure 24.5 illustrates the productivity curve. Capital per hour of labor is measured on the x-axis, and real GDP per hour of labor is measured on the *y*-axis. The figure shows *two* productivity curves. One is the curve labeled PC_0, and the other is the curve labeled PC_1.

An increase in the quantity of capital per hour of labor increases real GDP per hour of labor, which is shown by a movement along a productivity curve. For example, on PC_0, when capital per hour of labor is $30, real GDP per hour of labor is $20. If capital per hour of labor increases to $60, real GDP per hour of labor increases to $25.

Technological change increases the amount of GDP per hour of labor that can be produced by a given amount of capital per hour of labor. Technological change shifts the productivity curve upward. For example, if capital per hour of labor is $30 and a technological change increases real GDP per hour of labor from $20 to $25, the productivity curve shifts upward from PC_0 to PC_1 in Fig. 24.5. Similarly, if capital per hour of labor is $60, the same technological change increases real GDP per hour of labor from $25 to $32 and shifts the productivity curve upward from PC_0 to PC_1.

To calculate the contributions of capital growth and technological change to productivity growth, we need to know the shape of the productivity curve. The shape of the productivity curve reflects a fundamental economic law — the law of diminishing returns. The **law of diminishing returns** states that as the quantity of one input increases with the quantities of all other inputs remaining the same, output increases but by ever smaller increments. For example, in a factory that has a given amount of capital, as more labor is hired, production increases. But each *additional* hour of labor produces less *additional* output than the previous hour produced. Two typists working with one computer type fewer than twice as many pages per day as one typist working with one computer.

Applied to capital, the law of diminishing returns states that if a given number of hours of labor use more capital (with the same technology), the *additional* output that results from the *additional* capital gets smaller as the amount of capital increases. One typist working with two computers types fewer than twice as many pages per day as one typist working with one computer. More generally, one hour of labor working with $40 of capital produces less than twice the output of one hour of labor working with $20 of capital. But how much less? The answer is given by the *one third rule*.

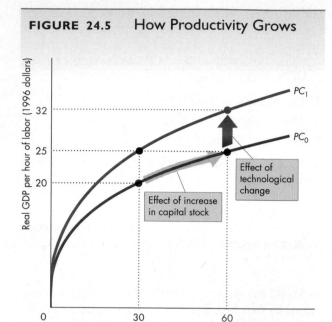

FIGURE 24.5   How Productivity Grows

Productivity is measured by real GDP per hour of labor, and it can grow for two reasons: (1) Capital per hour of labor increases, and (2) technological advances occur. The productivity curve, PC_0, shows the effects of an increase in capital per hour of labor on productivity. Here, when capital per hour of labor increases from $30 to $60, real GDP per hour of labor increases from $20 to $25 along the productivity curve PC_0. Technological advance shifts the productivity curve upward. Here, an advance in technology shifts the productivity curve from PC_0 to PC_1. When capital per hour of labor is $60, real GDP per hour of labor increases from $25 to $32.

The One Third Rule   Robert Solow of MIT estimated a U.S. productivity curve and discovered the **one third rule**, that on the average, with no change in technology, a 1 percent increase in capital per hour of labor brings a *one third of 1 percent* increase in real GDP per hour of labor. This one third rule is used to calculate the contributions of an increase in capital per hour of labor and technological change to the growth of real GDP. Let's do such a calculation.

Suppose that capital per hour of labor grows by 3 percent a year and real GDP per hour of labor grows by 2.5 percent a year. The one third rule tells us that capital growth has contributed one third of 3 percent, which is 1 percent. The rest of the 2.5 percent growth of real GDP per hour of labor comes from technological change. That is, technological change has contributed 1.5 percent, which is the 2.5 percent growth of real GDP per hour of labor minus the estimated 1 percent contribution of capital growth.

Accounting for the Productivity Growth Slowdown and Speedup

We can use the one third rule to study U.S. productivity growth and the productivity growth slowdown. Figure 24.6 tells the story, starting in 1961.

Booming Sixties In 1961, capital per hour of labor was $72 and real GDP per hour of labor was $22 at the point marked 61 on PC_0. During the next 12 years, real GDP per hour of labor expanded by 32 percent, to $29. At the same time, capital per hour of labor increased by 18 percent, to $85. With no change in technology, the economy would have moved to point A on PC_0 in Fig. 24.6, where real GDP per hour of labor has increased by 6 percent (1/3 of 18 percent). But rapid technological change shifted the productivity curve upward to PC_1, and the economy moved to the point marked 73 on that curve.

Slowdown During the 10 years from 1973 to 1983, real GDP per hour of labor expanded by 14 percent, to $33. At the same time, capital per hour of labor increased by 19 percent, to $101. With no change in technology, the economy would have moved to point B on PC_1 in Fig. 24.6, where real GDP per hour of labor has increased by 6.3 percent (1/3 of 19 percent). But a small amount of technological change shifted the productivity curve upward to PC_2, and the economy moved to the point marked 83 on that curve. So the productivity growth slowdown occurred because the contribution of technological change to real GDP growth slowed.

Growth Again During the 18 years from 1983 to 2001, real GDP per hour of labor expanded by 21 percent, to $40. At the same time, capital per hour of labor increased by 7 percent, to $108. With no change in technology, the economy would have moved to point C on PC_2 in Fig. 24.6, where real GDP per hour of labor has increased by 2.3 percent (1/3 of 7 percent). But a return of more rapid technological change shifted the productivity curve

FIGURE 24.6   Growth Accounting and the Productivity Growth Slowdown

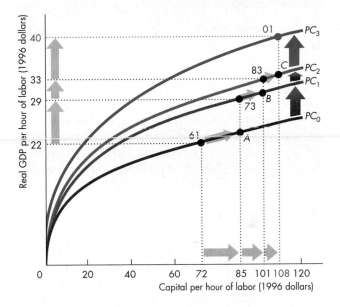

Between 1961 and 1973, which was a period of rapid productivity growth, capital per hour of labor increased from $72 to $85, and technological progress shifted the productivity curve upward from PC_0 to PC_1. Between 1973 and 1983, when potential GDP grew slowly, capital per hour of labor increased from $85 to $101 and the productivity curve barely shifted, to PC_2. The effect of technological change was offset by oil price shocks. Between 1983 and 2001, capital per hour of labor increased from $101 to $108, and technological progress shifted the productivity curve upward from PC_2 to PC_3. Although productivity growth was not as rapid as that in the 1960s, the productivity growth rate did increase.

Sources: Bureau of Economic Analysis, Bureau of Labor Statistics, and the author's calculations.

upward to PC_3, and the economy moved to the point marked 01 on that curve. Although technological change resumed, its pace was slower than that during the 1960s.

The growth accounting exercise that we've just worked through suggests that the so-called new economy of the late 1990s was not such a spectacular or unusual growth phenomenon.

Technological Change During the Productivity Growth Slowdown

Technological change did not stop during the productivity growth slowdown. But its focus changed from increasing productivity to coping with

- Energy price shocks
- The environment

Energy Price Shocks Energy price increases that occurred in 1973–1974 and in 1979–1980 diverted research efforts toward saving energy rather than increasing productivity. Airplanes became more fuel efficient, but they didn't operate with smaller crews. Real GDP per gallon of fuel increased faster, but real GDP per hour of labor increased more slowly.

The Environment The 1970s saw an expansion of laws and resources devoted to protecting the environment and improving the quality of the workplace. The benefits of these actions — cleaner air and water and safer factories — are not counted as real GDP. So the growth of these benefits is not measured as part of productivity growth.

Achieving Faster Growth

Growth accounting tells us that to achieve faster economic growth, we must either increase the growth rate of capital per hour of labor or increase the pace of technological advance (which includes improving human capital). The main suggestions for achieving these objectives are

- Stimulate saving
- Stimulate research and development
- Target high-technology industries
- Encourage international trade
- Improve the quality of education

Stimulate Saving Saving finances investment, which brings capital accumulation. So stimulating saving can stimulate economic growth. The East Asian economies have the highest growth rates and the highest saving rates. Some African economies have the lowest growth rates and the lowest saving rates.

Tax incentives can increase saving. Individual Retirement Accounts (IRAs) are a tax incentive to save. Economists claim that a tax on consumption rather than income provides the best saving incentive.

Stimulate Research and Development Everyone can use the fruits of *basic* research and development efforts. For example, all biotechnology firms can use advances in gene-splicing technology. Because basic inventions can be copied, the inventor's profit is limited, and the market allocates too few resources to this activity.

Governments can direct public funds toward financing basic research, but this solution is not foolproof. It requires a mechanism for allocating the public funds to their highest-valued use. The National Science Foundation is one possibly efficient channel for allocating public funds to universities to finance and stimulate basic research.

Target High-Technology Industries Some people say that by providing public funds to high-technology firms and industries, a country can become the first to exploit a new technology and can earn above-average profits for a period while others are busy catching up. This strategy is risky and just as likely to use resources inefficiently as to speed growth.

Encourage International Trade Free international trade stimulates growth by extracting all the available gains from specialization and exchange. The fastest-growing nations today are those with the fastest-growing exports and imports.

Improve the Quality of Education The free market produces too little education because it brings benefits beyond those valued by the people who receive the education. By funding basic education and by ensuring high standards in basic skills such as language, mathematics, and science, governments can contribute to a nation's growth potential. Education can also be stimulated and improved by using tax incentives to encourage improved private provision.

REVIEW QUIZ

1 Explain how the one third rule isolates the contributions of capital growth and technological change to productivity growth.
2 Explain how growth accounting gives us information about the factors that contributed to the productivity growth slowdown of the 1970s. Why did the slowdown occur?

Growth Theories

WE'VE SEEN THAT REAL GDP GROWS WHEN the quantities of labor and capital (which includes human capital) grow and when technology advances. Does this mean that the growth of labor and capital and technological advances *cause* economic growth? It might. But there are other possibilities. *One* of these factors might be the cause of real GDP growth, and the others might be the *effect*. We must try to discover how the influences on economic growth interact with each other to make some economies grow quickly and others grow slowly. And we must probe the reasons why a country's long-term growth rate sometimes speeds up and sometimes slows down.

Growth theories are designed to study the interactions among the several factors that contribute to growth and to disentangle cause and effect. They are also designed to enable us to study the way the different factors influence each other.

Growth theories are also designed to be universal. They are not theories about the growth of poor countries only or rich countries only. They are theories about why and how poor countries become rich and rich countries continue to get richer.

We're going to study three theories of economic growth, each of which gives some insights into the process of economic growth. But none provides a definite answer to the basic questions: What causes economic growth and why do growth rates vary? Economics has some way to go before it can provide a definite answer to these most important of questions. The three growth theories we study are

- Classical growth theory
- Neoclassical growth theory
- New growth theory

Classical Growth Theory

Classical growth theory is the view that real GDP growth is temporary and that when real GDP per person rises above the subsistence level, a population explosion eventually brings real GDP per person back to the subsistence level. Adam Smith, Thomas Robert Malthus, and David Ricardo, the leading economists of the late eighteenth century and early nineteenth century, proposed this theory, but the view is most closely associated with the name of Malthus and is sometimes called the *Malthusian theory*.

Many people today are Malthusians! They say that if today's global population of 6.2 billion explodes to 11 billion by 2200, we will run out of resources and return to a primitive standard of living. We must act, say the Malthusians, to contain the population growth.

The Basic Classical Idea To understand classical growth theory, let's transport ourselves back to the world of 1776, when Adam Smith is first explaining the idea. Most of the 2.5 million people who live in the newly independent United States of America work on farms or on their own land and perform their tasks using simple tools and animal power. They earn an average of 2 shillings (a bit less than 12 dollars in today's money) for working a 10-hour day.

Then advances in farming technology bring new types of plows and seeds that increase farm productivity. As farm productivity increases, farm production increases and some farm workers move from the land to the cities, where they get work producing and selling the expanding range of farm equipment. Incomes rise, and the people seem to be prospering. But will the prosperity last? Classical growth theory says it will not.

Advances in technology — in both agriculture and industry — lead to an investment in new capital, which makes labor more productive. More and more businesses start up and hire the now more productive labor. The greater demand for labor raises the real wage rate and increases employment.

At this stage, economic growth has occurred and everyone has benefited from it. Real GDP has increased, and the real wage rate has increased. But the classical economists believe that this new situation can't last because it will induce a population explosion.

Classical Theory of Population Growth When the classical economists were developing their ideas about population growth, an unprecedented population explosion was under way. In Britain and other Western European countries, improvements in diet and hygiene had lowered the death rate while the birth rate remained high. For several decades, population growth was extremely rapid. For example, after being relatively stable for several centuries, the population of Britain increased by 40 percent between 1750 and 1800 and by a further 50 percent between 1800 and 1830. Meanwhile, an estimated 1 million people (about 20 percent of the 1750 population) left Britain for America and Australia before 1800, and outward migration continued on a similar scale through the nineteenth century. These facts are the empirical basis for the classical theory of population growth.

To explain the high rate of population growth, the classical economists used the idea of a **subsistence real wage rate**, which is the minimum real wage rate needed to maintain life. If the actual real wage rate is less than the subsistence real wage rate, some people cannot survive and the population decreases. In classical theory, when the real wage rate exceeds the subsistence real wage rate, the population grows. But a rising population brings diminishing returns to labor. So labor productivity eventually decreases. This dismal implication led to economics being called the *dismal science*. The dismal implication is that no matter how much technological change occurs, real wage rates are always pushed back toward the subsistence level.

Classical Theory and the Productivity Curve
Figure 24.7 illustrates the classical growth theory using the productivity curve. Initially, the productivity curve is PC_0. Subsistence real GDP is $20 an hour, shown by the horizontal line in the graph. The economy starts out at point A, with $60 of capital per hour of labor and $20 of real GDP per hour of labor, the subsistence level. Because real GDP is at the subsistence level, the population is constant.

Then a technological advance occurs, which shifts the productivity curve upward to PC_1. The economy now moves to point B on PC_1, and real GDP per hour of labor rises to $30. Now earning more than the subsistence wage, people have more children and live longer. The population grows.

A growing population means that labor hours grow, so capital per hour of labor falls. As capital per hour of labor falls, there is a movement down along the productivity curve PC_1. Real GDP per hour of labor falls and keeps falling as long as the population grows and capital per hour of labor falls.

This process ends when real GDP per hour of labor is back at the subsistence level at point C on productivity curve PC_1. The population stops growing and capital per hour of labor stops falling.

Repeated advances in technology play out in the same way as the advance that we've just studied. No matter how productive our economy becomes, population growth lowers capital per hour of labor and drives real GDP per hour of labor toward the subsistence level. Living standards temporarily improve while the population is expanding, but when the

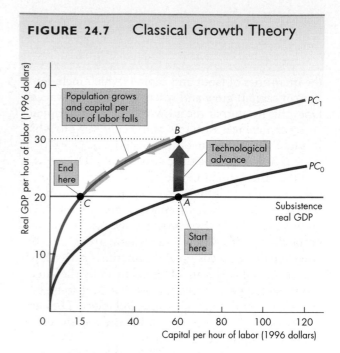

FIGURE 24.7 Classical Growth Theory

The economy starts out at point A with capital per hour of labor of $60 and real GDP per hour of labor of $20 — the subsistence level — on productivity curve PC_0. A technological advance increases productivity and shifts the productivity curve upward to PC_1. The economy moves to point B. The population now grows, and both capital and real GDP per hour of labor fall. The process ends at point C when real GDP per hour of labor is back at its subsistence level.

population expansion ends, the standard of living is back at the subsistence level.

Classical Theory and Capital Accumulation
In the story you've just worked through, the total quantity of capital didn't change. Suppose that people save and invest, so capital grows. Doesn't a growing quantity of capital prevent the dismal conclusion of classical theory? It does not. *Anything* that raises real GDP per hour of labor above the subsistence level triggers a population explosion that eventually wipes out the gains from greater productivity.

The dismal conclusion of classical growth theory is a direct consequence of the assumption that the population explodes if real GDP per hour of labor exceeds the subsistence level. To avoid this conclusion, we need a different view of population growth.

The neoclassical growth theory that we'll now study provides a different view.

Neoclassical Growth Theory

Neoclassical growth theory is the proposition that that real GDP per person grows because technological change induces a level of saving and investment that makes capital per hour of labor grow. Growth ends only if technological change stops.

Robert Solow of MIT suggested the most popular version of neoclassical growth theory in the 1950s. But Frank Ramsey of Cambridge University in England first developed this theory in the 1920s.

Neoclassical theory's big break with its classical predecessor is its view about population growth. So we'll begin our account of neoclassical theory by examining its views about population growth.

The Neoclassical Economics of Population Growth
The population explosion of eighteenth century Europe that created the classical theory of population eventually ended. The birth rate fell, and while the population continued to increase, its rate of increase became moderate. This slowdown in population growth seemed to make the classical theory less relevant. It also eventually led to the development of a modern economic theory of population growth.

The modern view is that although the population growth rate is influenced by economic factors, the influence is not a simple and mechanical one like that proposed by the classical economists. Key among the economic influences on population growth is the opportunity cost of a woman's time. As women's wage rates increase and their job opportunities expand, the opportunity cost of having children increases. Faced with a higher opportunity cost, families choose to have fewer children and the birth rate falls.

A second economic influence works on the death rate. The technological advance that brings increased productivity and increased incomes brings advances in health care that extends lives.

These two opposing economic forces influence the population growth rate. As incomes increase, both the birth rate and the death rate decrease. It turns out that these opposing forces almost offset each other, so the rate of population growth is independent of the rate of economic growth.

This modern view of population growth and the historical trends that support it contradict the views of the classical economists. They also call into question the modern doomsday conclusion that the planet will one day be swamped with too many people to feed.

Neoclassical growth theory adopts this modern view of population growth. Forces other than real GDP and its growth rate determine population growth.

Technological Change
In the neoclassical theory, the rate of technological change influences the rate of economic growth but economic growth does not influence the pace of technological change. It is assumed that technological change results from chance. When we get lucky, we have rapid technological change, and when bad luck strikes, the pace of technological advance slows.

Target Rate of Return and Saving
The key assumption in the neoclassical growth theory concerns saving. Other things remaining the same, the higher the real interest rate, the greater is the amount that people save. To decide how much to save, people compare the real interest rate with a *target rate of return*. If the real interest rate exceeds the target rate of return, saving is sufficient to make capital per hour of labor grow. If the target rate of return exceeds the real interest rate, saving is not sufficient to maintain the current level of capital per hour of labor, so capital per hour of labor shrinks. And if the real interest rate equals a target rate of return, saving is just sufficient to maintain the quantity of capital per hour of labor at its current level.

The Basic Neoclassical Idea
To understand neoclassical growth theory, imagine the world of the mid-1950s, when Robert Solow is explaining his idea. Americans are enjoying post–World War II prosperity. Income per person is around $12,000 a year in today's money. The population is growing at about 1 percent a year. People are saving and investing about 20 percent of their incomes, enough to keep the quantity of capital per hour of labor constant. Income per person is growing, but not by much.

Then technology begins to advance at a more rapid pace across a range of activities. The transistor revolutionizes an emerging electronics industry. New plastics revolutionize the manufacture of household appliances. The interstate highway system revolutionizes road transportation. Jet airliners start to replace piston-engine airplanes and speed air transportation.

These technological advances bring new profit opportunities. Businesses expand, and new businesses are created to exploit the newly available profitable technologies. Investment and saving increase. The economy enjoys new levels of prosperity and growth. But will the prosperity last? And will the growth last? Neoclassical growth theory says that the *prosperity* will last but the *growth* will not last unless technology keeps advancing.

According to the neoclassical growth theory, the prosperity will persist because there is no classical population growth to induce lower wages.

But growth will stop if technology stops advancing, for two related reasons. First, high profit rates that result from technological change bring increased saving and capital accumulation. But second, capital accumulation eventually results in diminishing returns that lower the real interest rate, and that eventually decrease saving and slow the rate of capital accumulation.

Neoclassical Theory and the Productivity Curve

Figure 24.8 illustrates the neoclassical growth theory using the productivity curve. Initially, the productivity curve is PC_0 and the economy is at point A, with $60 of capital per hour of labor and real GDP of $20 an hour.

The slope of the productivity curve measures the real interest rate. If the quantity of capital is small, the PC curve is steep and the real interest rate is high. If the quantity of capital is large, the PC curve becomes less steep and the real interest rate is low. A straight line with a slope equal to the target rate of return illustrates the target rate of return.

At point A on productivity curve PC_0, the slope of the PC curve equals the slope of the target rate of return line. If the quantity of capital per hour of labor were less than $60, the real interest rate would exceed the target rate of return and capital per hour of labor would grow. If the quantity of capital per hour of labor were greater than $60, the real interest rate would be less than the target rate of return and capital per hour of labor would shrink. But when the quantity of capital per hour of labor is $60, the real interest rate equals the target rate of return and capital per hour of labor is constant.

Now a technological advance occurs that shifts the productivity curve upward to PC_1. The economy now moves to point B on PC_1, and real GDP per hour of labor rises to $30. It is at this point in the classical theory that forces kick in to drive real GDP back to the subsistence level. But in the neoclassical theory, no such forces operate. Instead, at point B, the real interest rate exceeds the target rate of return.

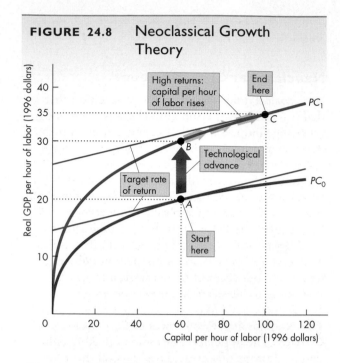

FIGURE 24.8 Neoclassical Growth Theory

The economy starts on productivity curve PC_0 at point A. The slope of the productivity curve measures the real interest rate so at point A the real interest rate equals the target rate of return. A technological advance shifts the productivity curve upward to PC_1 and the economy moves to point B. The real interest rate exceeds the target rate of return, and the quantity of capital per hour of labor rises — a movement upward along the productivity curve PC_1. Growth ends when the real interest rate again equals the target rate of return at point C.

(You can see why by comparing the slopes of PC_1 at point B and the target rate of return line.)

With a high real interest rate available, saving and investment increase and the quantity of capital per hour of labor rises. There is a movement up along the productivity curve PC_1, and real GDP per hour of labor increases.

This growth process eventually ends because, as the quantity of capital per hour of labor increases, the real interest rate falls. At point C, where the process ends, the real interest rate again equals the target rate of return.

Throughout the process you've just studied, real GDP per hour of labor grows but the growth rate gradually decreases and growth eventually ends.

But if another advance in technology occurs, the process you've just seen repeats. Ongoing advances in technology constantly increase the real interest rate, inducing the saving that increases capital per hour of labor. The growth process persists as long as technology advances. And the growth rate fluctuates because technological progress occurs at a variable rate.

A Problem with Neoclassical Growth Theory

All economies have access to the same technologies, and capital is free to roam the globe seeking the highest available real interest rate. Given these facts, neoclassical growth theory implies that growth rates and income levels per person around the globe will converge. While there is some sign of convergence among the rich countries, as Fig. 9.2(a) shows, convergence is slow, and it does not appear to be imminent for all countries, as Fig. 9.2(b) shows.

New growth theory attempts to overcome this shortcoming of neoclassical growth theory. It also attempts to explain how the rate of technological change is determined.

New Growth Theory

New growth theory holds that real GDP per person grows because of the choices people make in the pursuit of profit and that growth can persist indefinitely. Paul Romer of Stanford University developed this theory during the 1980s, but the ideas go back to work by Joseph Schumpeter during the 1930s and 1940s.

The theory begins with two facts about market economies:

- Discoveries result from choices.
- Discoveries bring profit and competition destroys profit.

Discoveries and Choices When people discover a new product or technique, they think of themselves as being lucky. They are right. But the pace at which new discoveries are made — and at which technology advances — is not determined by chance. It depends on how many people are looking for a new technology and how intensively they are looking.

Discoveries and Profits Profit is the spur to technological change. The forces of competition squeeze profits, so to increase profit, people constantly seek either lower-cost methods of production or new and better

products for which people are willing to pay a higher price. Inventors can maintain a profit for several years by taking out a patent or copyright. But eventually, a new discovery is copied, and profits disappear.

Two further facts play a key role in the new growth theory:

- Discoveries are a public capital good.
- Knowledge is capital that is not subject to the law of diminishing returns.

Discoveries Are a Public Capital Good Economists call a good a *public good* when no one can be excluded from using it and when one person's use does not prevent others from using it. National defense is one example of a public good. Knowledge is another.

When in 1992, Marc Andreesen and his friend Eric Bina developed a browser they called Mosaic, they laid the foundation for Netscape Navigator and Internet Explorer, two pieces of capital that have increased productivity unimaginably.

While patents and copyrights protect the inventors or creators of new products and production processes and enable them to reap the returns from their innovative ideas, once a new discovery has been made, everyone can benefit from its use. And one person's use of a new discovery does not prevent others from using it. Your use of a Web browser doesn't prevent someone else from using that same code simultaneously.

Because knowledge is a public good, as the benefits of a new discovery spread, free resources become available. These resources are free because nothing is given up when they are used. They have a zero opportunity cost. Knowledge is even more special because it is not subject to diminishing returns.

Knowledge Capital not Subject to Diminishing Returns Production is subject to diminishing returns when one resource is fixed and the quantity of another resource changes. Adding labor to a fixed amount of equipment, or adding equipment to a fixed amount of labor both bring diminishing marginal product — diminishing returns.

But increasing the stock of knowledge makes labor and machines more productive. Knowledge capital does not bring diminishing returns.

The fact that knowledge capital does *not* experience diminishing returns is the central novel proposition of the new growth theory. And the implication of this simple and appealing idea is astonishing. The new growth theory has no growth-stopping mechanism like those of the other two theories. As physical capital accumulates, the real interest rate falls. But the incentive to innovate and earn a higher profit becomes stronger. So innovation occurs, which increases the real interest rate. Real GDP per hour of labor grows indefinitely as people find new technologies that yield a higher real interest rate.

The growth rate depends on people's ability to innovate and the real interest rate. Over the years, the ability to innovate has changed. The invention of language and writing (the two most basic human capital tools) and later the development of the scientific method and the establishment of universities and research institutions brought huge increases in the real interest rate. Today, a deeper understanding of genes is bringing profit in a growing biotechnology industry. And astonishing advances in computer technology are creating an explosion of profit opportunities in a wide range of information age industries.

New Growth Theory and the Productivity Curve
Figure 24.9 illustrates new growth theory. Like Fig. 24.8, which illustrates neoclassical growth theory, Fig. 24.9 contains a productivity curve and a target rate of return curve.

But unlike in neoclassical theory, in the new growth theory, the productivity curve never stands still. The pursuit of profit means that technology is always advancing and human capital is always growing. The result is an ever upward-shifting PC curve. As physical capital is accumulated, diminishing returns lower its rate of return. But ever-advancing productivity counteracts this tendency and keeps the rate of return above the target rate of return.

Advancing technology and human capital growth keep the PC curve shifting upward from PC_0 to PC_1 to PC_2 and beyond. As the productivity curve shifts upward, capital and real GDP per hour of labor rise together along the line labeled as the Ak line in the figure.

The new growth theory implies that although the productivity curve shows diminishing returns, if capital is interpreted more broadly as physical capital, human capital, and the technologies they embody, then real GDP per hour of labor grows at the same rate as the growth in capital per hour of labor. Real GDP per hour of labor is proportional to capital per hour of labor.

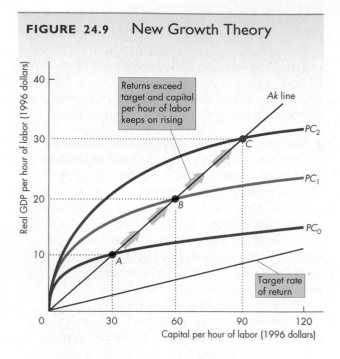

FIGURE 24.9 New Growth Theory

In new growth theory, economic growth results from incentives to innovate and from capital that does not experience diminishing returns. The productivity curve, PC, keeps shifting upward, and real GDP per hour of labor and capital per hour of labor grow along the Ak line.

Capital is k, real GDP is y, and real GDP is related to capital by the equation:

$$y = Ak.$$

In Fig 24.9, $A = (1/3)$. When capital per hour of labor is $30, real GDP per hour of labor is $10 at point A. People look for yet more profit and accumulate yet more capital. The economy expands to point B, with capital per hour of labor of $60 and real GDP per hour of labor of $20. In pursuit of further profit, technology keeps advancing and capital per hour of labor rises to $90 with real GDP per hour of labor of $30, at point C. Real GDP per hour of labor and capital per hour of labor increase without limit.

A Perpetual Motion Economy The new growth theory sees the economy as a perpetual motion machine, which Fig. 24.10 illustrates. Insatiable wants lead us to pursue profit, innovate, and create new and better products. New firms start up and old firms go out of business. As firms start up and die, jobs are

FIGURE 24.10   A Perpetual Motion Machine

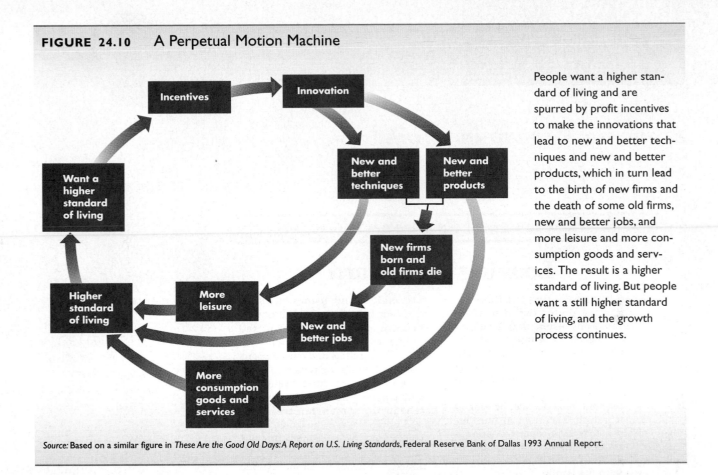

People want a higher standard of living and are spurred by profit incentives to make the innovations that lead to new and better techniques and new and better products, which in turn lead to the birth of new firms and the death of some old firms, new and better jobs, and more leisure and more consumption goods and services. The result is a higher standard of living. But people want a still higher standard of living, and the growth process continues.

Source: Based on a similar figure in *These Are the Good Old Days: A Report on U.S. Living Standards*, Federal Reserve Bank of Dallas 1993 Annual Report.

created and destroyed. New and better jobs lead to more leisure and more consumption. But our insatiable wants are still there, so the process continues, going round and round a circle of wants, profits, innovation, and new products.

Sorting Out the Theories

Which theory is correct? Probably none, but they all teach us something of value. The classical theory reminds us that our physical resources are limited and that with no advances in technology, we must eventually hit diminishing returns. Neoclassical theory reaches the same conclusion, but not because of a population explosion. Instead, it emphasizes diminishing returns to capital and reminds us that we cannot keep growth going just by accumulating physical capital. We must also advance technology and accumulate human capital. We must become more creative in our use of scarce resources. New growth theory emphasizes the possible capacity of human resources to innovate at a pace that offsets diminishing returns.

REVIEW QUIZ

1 What is the key idea of classical growth theory that leads to the dismal outcome?
2 What, according to the neoclassical growth theory, is the fundamental cause of economic growth?
3 What is the key proposition of the new growth theory that makes growth persist?

◆ Economic growth is the single most decisive factor influencing a country's living standard. But another is the extent to which the country fully employs its scarce resources. In the next part, we study economic fluctuations and recessions. But before embarking on this new topic, take a look at *Reading Between the Lines* on pp. 564–565 and see how economic growth is transforming the economy of China.

Economic Growth in China

THE WASHINGTON POST, JANUARY 28, 2002

Looking Homeward

When Zhongren Jing left China to study in the United States in 1989, he didn't know when, or if, he'd ever return. Government tanks had just crushed peaceful student demonstrations in Beijing's Tiananmen Square, and Jing had lost faith in China's hard-line rulers.

Over the next decade, he earned a doctorate in sociology at the University of Maryland, landed a research job at a Georgetown consulting firm and settled in the Washington suburbs with his family.

But a year and a half ago Jing, 47, was on a plane to China, lured back by new opportunities in a rapidly changing country. He joined a Shanghai venture capital firm started by a former classmate, and he helps manage its investments.

...

Since 1978, when China opened up to the outside world, tens of thousands of students have left to pursue graduate study in the United States. After earning their degrees, the majority found jobs here, obtained residency or citizenship and settled with their families. Until recently, there were few incentives to return to China, where economic opportunities were limited and living standards lagged far behind the United States. The flight of China's best and brightest sparked worries of "brain drain," as U.S. universities and corporations absorbed China's top talent.

But many of those brains are looking homeward. Chinese students are studying abroad in increasingly large numbers and most will likely stay abroad for years, if not a lifetime. But experts say the return of U.S.-trained Chinese to China, which began with a trickle in the mid-1990s, is quickly accelerating. Of the 320,000 Chinese students who have studied abroad in the past two decades, about 140,000 have returned and the figure is growing by 13 percent a year, according to the Chinese news agency Xinhua. More overseas Chinese are expected to return as China's increasingly free-market economy expands.

...

Returnees are being lured back to China with aggressive pro-business policies. Local governments are courting U.S.-trained Chinese with grants, tax breaks and facilities for start-up companies....

Essence of the Story

■ During the past 20 years, 320,000 Chinese students have studied abroad and about 140,000 have returned to China.

■ Today, more Chinese students who study abroad are returning to China, and the number is growing by 13 percent a year.

■ China's increasingly free market and expanding economy are providing an incentive to return.

■ Aggressive probusiness policies are also providing a stronger incentive to return.

■ Local governments are offering U.S.-trained Chinese graduates grants, tax breaks, and facilities for start-up companies.

Economic Analysis

■ Starting around 1981, China began to open up its economy to international investment and trade and permitted its citizens to seek graduate education abroad.

■ At the same time, private enterprise increasingly replaced state-owned enterprise as the method of production.

■ Although it is a stretch, let's assume that the productivity curve in China after 1981 became the same as that in the United States.

■ Using this assumption, Fig. 1 shows the positions of China and the United States on the productivity curves for 1981 and 2001.

■ In 1981, the United States had $95 of capital per hour of labor and produced $32 of real GDP per hour of labor.

■ By 2001, the United States had $108 of capital per hour of labor and produced $40 of real GDP per hour of labor. Capital per hour of labor had increased by 13 percent, and real GDP per hour of labor had increased by 28 percent.

■ China is too far behind the United States to see the changes in China in Fig. 1.

■ But Fig. 2 zooms in on China and shows the incredibly large changes that have occurred in that economy.

■ In 1981, China had 3 cents of capital per hour of labor and produced $2 of real GDP per hour of labor. (The values are in 1996 U.S. dollars.)

■ By 2001, China had 40 cents of capital per hour of labor and produced $6.25 of real GDP per hour of labor. Capital per hour of labor had increased by 1,500 percent, and real GDP per hour of labor had increased by 152 percent.

■ These data for China in 2001 are based on official Chinese statistics. Some scholars think that the official data exaggerate China's real GDP and growth rate.

■ Based on the official data, China is converging on the United States but has a long way to go. At the current rate of convergence, real GDP per person will be equal in the two countries in the mid-2040s.

■ But the population of China is 4.5 times that of the United States, so at current growth rates, the two countries will have the same real GDP in 2010.

Figure 1 Productivity curves in China and the United States

Figure 2 Zoom in on the productivity curves in China

■ After 2010, China will have the world's largest economy, and it will become larger every year.

You're The Voter

■ Do you think the United States can learn any lessons from China to make the U.S. economy grow faster?

■ What effects do you think the Chinese policies described in the news article will have on China's growth rate?

■ Can you think of any tax reforms that might increase the U.S. growth rate? Would you vote for these reforms? Why or why not?

SUMMARY

KEY POINTS

Long-Term Growth Trends (pp.548–550)

- Between 1901 and 2001, real GDP per person in the United States grew at an average rate of 2 percent a year. Growth was rapid during the 1960s and late 1990s.
- The real GDP gap between the United States and Central and South America has persisted. The gaps between the United States and Hong Kong, Korea, Taiwan, and China have narrowed. The gaps between the United States and Africa and Central Europe have widened.

**The Causes of Economic Growth:
A First Look** (pp. 551–552)

- Economic growth requires an *incentive* system created by markets, property rights, and monetary exchange.
- Economic growth occurs when people save, invest in physical and human capital, and discover new technologies.

Growth Accounting (pp. 553–556)

- Growth accounting measures the contributions of capital accumulation and technological change to productivity growth.
- Growth accounting uses the productivity curve and the one third rule: A 1 percent increase in capital per hour of labor brings a one third of 1 percent increase in real GDP per hour of labor.
- During the productivity growth slowdown of the 1970s, technological change made no contribution to real GDP growth.
- It might be possible to achieve faster growth by stimulating saving, stimulating research and development, targeting high-technology industries, encouraging more international trade, and improving the quality of education.

Growth Theories (pp. 557–563)

- In classical theory, when a technological advance increases real GDP per person above the *subsistence* level, a population explosion brings diminishing returns to labor and real GDP per person returns to the subsistence level.
- In neoclassical growth theory, when a technological advance increases saving and investment, an increase in the capital stock brings diminishing returns to capital and eventually, without further technological change, the capital stock and real GDP per person stop growing.
- In new growth theory, when technological advances increase saving and investment, an increase in the capital stock *does not* bring diminishing returns to capital and growth persists indefinitely.

KEY FIGURES

KEY TERMS

PROBLEMS

💻 *1. The following information has been discovered about the economy of Longland. The economy's productivity curve is

Capital per hour of labor (1996 dollars per hour)	Real GDP per hour of labor (1996 dollars per hour)
10	3.80
20	5.70
30	7.13
40	8.31
50	9.35
60	10.29
70	11.14
80	11.94

Does this economy conform to the one third rule? If so, explain why. If not, explain why not and explain what rule, if any, it does conform to. Explain how you would do the growth accounting for this economy.

2. The following information has been discovered about the economy of Flatland. The economy's productivity curve is

Capital per hour of labor (1996 dollars per hour)	Real GDP per hour of labor (1996 dollars per hour)
20	6.00
40	7.50
60	8.44
80	9.14
100	9.72
120	10.20
140	10.62
160	11.00

Does this economy conform to the one third rule? If so, explain why. If not, explain why not and explain what rule, if any, it does conform to. Explain how you would do the growth accounting for this economy.

💻 *3. In Longland, described in problem 1, capital per hour of labor in 1999 was $40 and real GDP per hour of labor was $8.31. In 2001, capital per hour of labor was $50 and real GDP per hour of labor was $10.29 an hour.
   a. Does Longland experience diminishing returns? Explain why or why not.

b. Use growth accounting to find the contribution of the change in capital between 1999 and 2001 to the growth of productivity in Longland.
   c. Use growth accounting to find the contribution of technological change between 1999 and 2001 to the growth of productivity in Longland.

4. In Flatland, described in problem 2, capital per hour of labor in 1999 was $60 and real GDP per hour of labor was $8.44. In 2001, capital per hour of labor was $120 and real GDP per hour of labor was $12.74 an hour.
   a. Does Flatland experience diminishing returns? Explain why or why not.
   b. Use growth accounting to find the contribution of the change in capital between 1999 and 2001 to the growth of productivity in Flatland.
   c. Use growth accounting to find the contribution of technological change between 1999 and 2001 to the growth of productivity in Flatland.

💻 *5. The following information has been discovered about the economy of Cape Despair. Subsistence real GDP is $15 an hour. Whenever real GDP per hour rises above this level, the population grows, and when real GDP per hour of labor falls below this level, the population falls. The productivity curve in Cape Despair is as follows:

Capital per hour of labor (1996 dollars per hour)	Real GDP per hour of labor (1996 dollars per hour)
20	8
40	15
60	21
80	26
100	30
120	33
140	35
160	36

Initially, the population of Cape Despair is constant, and real GDP is at its subsistence level. Then a technological advance shifts the productivity curve upward by $7 at each level of capital per hour of labor.
   a. What are the initial capital per hour of labor and real GDP per hour of labor?

b. What happens to real GDP per hour of labor immediately following the technological advance?

c. What happens to the population growth rate following the technological advance?

d. What is the eventual quantity of capital per hour of labor in Cape Despair?

6. Martha's Island is an economy that behaves according to the neoclassical growth model. The economy has no growth, a target rate of return of 10 percent a year, and the following productivity curve:

Capital per hour of labor (1996 dollars per hour)	Real GDP per hour of labor (1996 dollars per hour)
40	16
80	30
120	42
160	52
200	60
240	66
280	70
320	72

A technological advance shifts the productivity curve upward.

a. What is the initial capital per hour of labor on Martha's Island?

b. What is the initial real GDP per hour of labor?

c. What happens to the return from capital immediately following the technological advance?

d. What happens to the return on capital and the quantity of capital per hour of labor?

*7. Romeria is a country that behaves according to the predictions of new growth theory. The target rate is 3 percent a year. A technological advance increases the demand for capital and raises the real interest rate to 5 percent a year. Describe the events that happen in Romeria and contrast them with the events in Martha's Island in problem 6.

8. Suppose that in Romeria, described in problem 7, technological advance slows and the real interest rate falls to 3 percent a year. Describe what happens in Romeria.

CRITICAL THINKING

1. After studying *Reading Between the Lines* on pp. 564–565, answer the following questions:

a. What is China doing to attract educated citizens back to China after they complete their graduate studies abroad?

b. Is real GDP per hour of labor in China growing because capital per hour of labor is increasing, because of other factors, or both? How would you determine the contribution of each factor?

c. Is China narrowing the gap between real GDP per person in China and real GDP per person in the United States?

d. At the current rate of convergence, how long will it take for real GDP per person in China to equal that in the United States?

2. Is faster economic growth always a good thing? Argue the case for faster growth and the case for slower growth and then reach a conclusion on whether growth should be increased or decreased.

WEB EXERCISES

1. Use the links on your Parkin Web site to obtain data on real GDP per person for the United States, China, South Africa, and Mexico since 1960.

a. Draw a graph of the data.

b. Which country has the lowest real GDP per person and which has the highest?

c. Which country has experienced the fastest growth rate since 1960 and which the slowest?

d. Explain why the growth rates in these four countries are ranked in the order you have discovered.

e. Return to the Penn World Table Web site and obtain data for any four other countries that interest you. Describe and explain the patterns that you find for these countries.

2. Write a memo to your member of Congress in which you set out the policies you believe the U.S. government must follow to speed up the growth rate of real GDP in the United States.

UNDERSTANDING AGGREGATE SUPPLY AND ECONOMIC GROWTH

Expanding the Frontier

Economics is about how we cope with scarcity. We cope by making choices that balance marginal benefits and marginal costs so that we use our scarce resources efficiently. ◆ These choices determine how much work we do; how hard we work at school to learn the mental skills that form our human capital and that determine the kinds of jobs we get and the incomes we earn; and how much we save for future big-ticket expenditures. These choices also determine how much businesses and governments spend on new capital — on auto assembly lines, computers and fiber cables for improved Internet services, shopping malls, highways, bridges, and tunnels; and how intensively existing capital and natural resources are used and therefore how quickly they wear out or are used up. Most significant of all, these choices determine the problems that scientists, engineers, and other inventors work on to develop new technologies. ◆ All the choices we've just described determine two vital measures of economic performance:

- Real GDP
- Economic growth

Real GDP is determined by the quantity of labor, the quantity of capital, and the state of technological knowledge. And economic growth — the growth rate of real GDP — is determined by growth in the quantity of labor, capital accumulation, and technological advances. ◆ Economic growth, maintained at a steady rate over a number of decades, is the single most powerful influence on any society. It brings a transformation that continues to amaze thoughtful people. Economic growth that is maintained at a rapid rate can transform a society in years, not decades. Such transformations are taking place right now in many Asian countries. These transformations are economic miracles. ◆ The three chapters in this part studied the miracle of rapid economic growth and the forces that shape our capacity to produce goods and services. ◆ Chapter 22 explained how potential GDP and the full-employment quantity of labor, employment, and unemployment are determined by equilibrium in the labor market. ◆ Chapter 23 explained how capital accumulation results from saving and investment decisions that are coordinated in a global capital market. Some countries don't save enough to pay for the capital they accumulate; others save more than they need. And the international capital market moves savings to the places in which they obtain the highest available real interest rate. ◆ Chapter 24 studied the process of economic growth in the fast-growing economies of Asia and the United States. It explained how growth is influenced by technological change and the incentives that stimulate it. ◆ Modern ideas about economic growth owe much to two economists, Joseph Schumpeter and Paul Romer, whom you can meet on the following pages.

"Economic progress, in capitalist society, means turmoil."

JOSEPH
SCHUMPETER
*Capitalism,
Socialism, and
Democracy*

570

THE ECONOMIST

JOSEPH SCHUMPETER, *the son of a textile factory owner, was born in Austria in 1883. He moved from Austria to Germany during the tumultuous 1920s when those two countries experienced hyperinflation. In 1932, in the depths of the Great Depression, he came to the United States and became a professor of economics at Harvard University.*

This creative economic thinker wrote about economic growth and development, business cycles, political systems, and economic biography. He was a person of strong opinions who expressed them strongly and delighted in verbal battles.

Schumpeter has become the unwitting founder of modern growth theory. He saw the development and diffusion of new technologies by profit-seeking entrepreneurs as the source of economic progress. But he saw economic progress as a process of creative destruction — the creation of new profit opportunities and the destruction of currently profitable businesses. For Schumpeter, economic growth and the business cycle were a single phenomenon.

When Schumpeter died, in 1950, he had achieved his self-expressed life ambition: He was regarded as the world's greatest economist.

THE ISSUES

Technological change, capital accumulation, and population growth all interact to produce economic growth. But what is cause and what is effect? And can we expect productivity and income per person to keep growing?

The classical economists of the eighteenth and nineteenth centuries believed that technological advances and capital accumulation were the engines of growth. But they also believed that no matter how successful people were at inventing more productive technologies and investing in new capital, they were destined to live at the subsistence level. These economists based their conclusion on the belief that productivity growth causes population growth, which in turn causes productivity to decline. These classical economists believed that whenever economic growth raises incomes above the subsistence level, the population will increase. They went on to reason that the increase in population brings diminishing returns that lower productivity. As a result, incomes must always return to the subsistence level. Only when incomes are at the subsistence level is population growth held in check.

A new approach, called neoclassical growth theory, was developed by Robert Solow of MIT, during the 1950s. Solow, who was one of Schumpeter's students, received the Nobel Prize for Economic Science for this work.

Solow challenged the conclusions of the classical economists. But the new theories of economic growth developed during the 1980s and 1990s went further. They stand the classical belief on its head. Today's theory of population growth is that rising income slows the population growth rate because it increases the opportunity cost of having children and lowers the opportunity cost of investing in children and equipping them with more human capital, which makes them more productive. Productivity and income grow because technology advances, and the scope for further productivity growth, which is stimulated by the search for profit, is practically unlimited.

THEN

In 1830, a strong and experienced farm worker could harvest three acres of wheat in a day. The only capital employed was a scythe to cut the wheat, which had been used since Roman times, and a cradle on which the stalks were laid, which had been invented by Flemish farmers in the fifteenth century. With newly developed horse-drawn plows, harrows, and planters, farmers could plant more wheat than they could harvest. But despite big efforts, no one had been able to make a machine that could replicate the swing of a scythe. Then in 1831, 22-year-old Cyrus McCormick built a machine that worked. It scared the horse that pulled it, but it did in a matter of hours what three men could accomplish in a day. Technological change has increased productivity on farms and brought economic growth. Do the facts about productivity growth mean that the classical economists, who believed that diminishing returns would push us relentlessly back to a subsistence living standard, were wrong?

NOW

Today's technologies are expanding our horizons beyond the confines of our planet and are expanding our minds. Geosynchronous satellites bring us global television, voice and data communication, and more accurate weather forecasts, which, incidentally, increase agricultural productivity. In the foreseeable future, we might have superconductors that revolutionize the use of electric power, virtual reality theme parks and training facilities, pollution-free hydrogen cars, wristwatch telephones, and optical computers that we can talk to. Equipped with these new technologies, our ability to create yet more dazzling technologies increases. Technological change begets technological change in an (apparently) unending process and makes us ever more productive and brings ever higher incomes.

Today's revolution in the way economists think about economic growth has been led by Paul Romer, a professor of economics at Stanford University, whom you can meet on the following pages.

571

TALKING WITH

PAUL ROMER *is Professor of Economics at the Graduate School of Business at Stanford University and the Royal Bank Fellow of the Canadian Institute for Advanced Research. Born in 1955 in Denver, Colorado, he earned his B.S. in Mathematics (1977) and his Ph.D. in Economics (1983) from the University of Chicago.*

Professor Romer has transformed the way economists think about economic growth. He believes that sustained economic growth arises from competition among firms. Firms try to increase their profits by devoting resources to creating new products and developing new ways of making existing products.

Michael Parkin talked with Professor Romer about his work, how he was influenced by Joseph Schumpeter and Robert Solow, and the insights economic growth offers us.

Professor Romer, why did you decide to become an economist?

As an undergraduate, I studied math and physics and was interested in becoming a cosmologist. During my senior year, I concluded that job prospects in physics were not very promising, so I decided to go to law school. I was an undergraduate at the University of Chicago, where the law and economics movement first emerged. In the fall of my senior year, I took my first economics course to prepare for law school. My economics professor, Sam Peltzman, presented a simple piece of economic analysis that changed my life. He argued that the demand for economists was likely to grow for decades. The government, which employs economists, would grow in size. Businesses that deal with the government would want their own economists. The legal profession that serves businesses would also need more economists. Because of all these demands, many students would want to take economics courses. This meant that there would be many job openings for economists at universities. Moreover, he claimed, being a professor of economics was a lot like being a cosmologist and far more fun than being a lawyer. I could take fragmentary bits of evidence and try to make sense of them using mathematical equations. So I tore up my law school applications, applied to graduate school in economics, and never looked back.

What are the truly important lessons about the causes of economic growth?

As a physics major, I felt that the description economists used for growth violated a basic law of physics: the conservation of mass. Economists seemed to be saying that GDP, the output of a nation, was a bunch of stuff that was "produced" and that the quantity of stuff produced has grown steadily over time and will continue to do so. But this can't be right. We have the same amount of stuff, or elements from the periodic table, that we had 100,000 years ago because there are many more people now. In terms of kilograms of matter per person, we know that we are vastly poorer than our ancestors were 100,000 years ago. Yet we clearly have a higher standard of living. How could this be? This basic question indicates that thinking about growth as a production process that generates stuff is a dead-end. Instead,

Paul Romer

economic growth has to be about rearranging the fixed amount of matter that we have to work with and making new combinations that seem a lot more valuable. The key insight is that economic growth comes from increases in value, not increases in the amount of matter.

Can you give us an example of an increase in value?

For tens of thousands of years, we treated iron oxide, ordinary rust, like dirt. When we lived in caves, we learned how to use it as a pigment for decorating cave walls. We took the low-value dirt and put it to the higher-valued use of making cave paintings. Later, we learned how to extract the iron from iron ore to make bridges and rails. Later still, we learned how to arrange the iron atoms together with carbon atoms and make steel. Recently, we learned how to take iron oxide and put it on magnetic tape and use it to store sound and pictures. The iron, oxygen, and carbon atoms have always been here. We have a higher standard of living because we have learned how to arrange these atoms in ways that we find more valuable.

What kind of policy implications does this kind of thinking lead to?

Policy makers must encourage institutions to become more efficient at discovering new recipes to rearrange matter. Consider the transistor as an example. We take silicon and mix it with a few impurities and some metal in just the right way, and we get a computer chip worth thousands of times what the raw ingredients were worth. Research grants, subsidies for education, and institutions like the nonprofit private

> *We take silicon and mix it with a few impurities and some metal in just the right way, and we get a computer chip worth thousands of times what the raw ingredients were worth.*

university encourage the production of new recipes or ideas. But so do venture capitalists who help new-technology startups, competitive markets that allow the firms with better instructions or ideas to quickly displace existing firms, and labor laws that let inefficient firms lay off workers when more efficient new firms come on the scene. We must let firms like Digital Electronics or Wang Computers shrink, maybe even fail, if we want to make room for new firms like Intel to enter the scene and thrive.

Were the classical economists wrong in their view that population growth and diminishing returns are the dominant long-term influences on production and incomes? Or is the current global population explosion part of a process that will ultimately prove them correct?

Classical economists like Malthus and Ricardo were right when they argued that we have a fixed amount of natural resources to work with. Malthus pointed out that resource scarcity will lead to falling standards of living if we continue to work with the same set of recipes or instructions for using our resources. Where he went wrong was in assuming that there was little scope for us to find new recipes for taking resources such as land, water, carbon dioxide, nitrogen, and sunshine and converting them into carbohydrates and proteins that we can eat.

The classical economists got half of the story right. We do live in a world with scarce resources. They missed the other half. There is an incomprehensibly large number of different formulas we can use to recombine these scarce resources into things we value, such as protein or entertainment.

Scarcity is a very important part of economics and our lives. For example, we know that there is an absolute limit on the number of people who can live on the earth. One way or another, we know that the rate of population growth will slow down. It's only a question of how and when. But will this ultimately lead to a period when standards of living fall as Malthus predicted? I doubt it. As countries get rich, population growth slows. As a larger fraction of the worldwide population becomes educated, these people will help us to discover new things, like plants that are more efficient at taking carbon dioxide out of the atmosphere, and more efficient distribution systems. Thus standards of living for all humans will continue to improve.

573

During the past decade, China and several other economies in East Asia have experienced rapid, unheralded growth rates. Why?

These countries took some of the recipes, formulas, and instructions for generating value that already existed in the advanced countries of the world and put them to use within their borders. It's the same process that the Japanese followed after the Meiji restoration at the end of the last century. These countries noticed that other people in the world knew a lot about how to create value and realized that by trading with these people, they could share in the gains.

What lessons from East Asia can, in principle, be applied in Africa and Central Europe?

The basic insight is that there are huge potential gains from trade. Poor countries can supply their natural and human resources. Rich countries can supply their know-how. When these are combined, everyone can be better off. The challenge is for a country to arrange its laws and institutions so that both sides can profitably engage in trade. If there are barriers to trade or if the government cannot protect basic property rights and prevent crime, trade can't take place. For example, the Japanese have been able to borrow many ideas about manufacturing and design and even to improve on some of these ideas. But because they have barriers that limit entry of foreign firms into the retail sector, they still waste vast quantities of resources on a very inefficient distribution system.

What does today's thinking about economic growth owe to Joseph Schumpeter and Robert Solow?

Schumpeter worked at a time before most economists had learned to work with equations. He coined the phrase "creative destruction," which describes the process by which companies like Wang shrink or go out of business when new firms come in. He also described in words how important monopoly profits are in the process of innovation. There were many other economists, including Alfred Marshall, who described these same issues in verbal terms and also struggled to express these ideas in terms of equations.

Robert Solow was part of the post–World War II generation of economists who truly mastered the use of equations and wrote eloquently using both words

574

and equations. As a result, his ideas have been far more influential than Schumpeter's. Many economists in the 1950s were trying to get a grasp on the economic effects of knowledge, formulas, recipes, and instructions. Solow called these things "technology" and gave us a wonderfully concise and workable way to think about how technology interacts with other economic inputs such as capital and labor. He also linked the methods that he and several economists were using to measure technology with this framework for thinking about the behavior of the economy as a whole. His work on growth was a masterful piece of invention, synthesis, and exposition.

Recent economists have taken Solow's mathematical framework and extended it to bring in some of the elements that Schumpeter described in words, like creative destruction and monopoly power. One of the great things about ideas is that they build on each other. In Isaac Newton's famous phrase, those of us working on growth today are "able to see farther because we stand on the shoulders of giants." Newton was another person who was pretty good with equations and could turn a good phrase.

Is economics a worthwhile subject to major in? What can one do with an economics degree?

Economics is an excellent training ground for developing mathematical and verbal skills. But students should supplement the courses in economics with courses in mathematics and science that force them to practice working with equations, graphs, and numbers. There is no substitute for such practice. Innate ability is far less important than most students think.

> *If you can learn how to write readable prose and use the basic tools of mathematics, you can do almost anything.*

They should also take courses that force them to write, revise, and edit. I took an English course in college that taught me the basics of how to edit, and it is one of the best investments I made. You can't tell what you will end up doing or what skills you will need later in life. But if you can learn how to write readable prose and use the basic tools of mathematics, you can do almost anything.

EXPENDITURE MULTIPLIERS

CHAPTER 25

Economic Amplifier or Shock Absorber?

Erykah Badu sings into a microphone in a barely audible whisper. Increasing in volume, through the magic of electronic amplification, her voice fills Central Park. ◆ Michael Bloomberg, the mayor of New York, and a secretary are being driven to a business meeting along one of the city's less well-repaired streets. The car's wheels bounce and vibrate over some of the worst potholes in the nation, but its passengers are completely undisturbed and the secretary's notes are written without a ripple, thanks to the car's efficient shock absorbers. ◆ Investment and exports fluctuate like the volume of Erykah Badu's voice and the uneven surface of a New York City street. How does the economy react to those fluctuations? Does it react like a limousine, absorbing the shocks and providing a smooth ride for the economy's passengers? Or does it behave like an amplifier, blowing up the fluctuations and spreading them out to affect the many millions of participants in an economic rock concert?

◆ You will explore these questions in this chapter. You will learn how a recession or an expansion begins when a change in investment or exports induces an amplified change in aggregate expenditure and real GDP. And you'll learn the crucial role played by business inventories in the transition from expansion to recession and back to expansion. *Reading Between the Lines* at the end of the chapter looks at the role played by business inventories during the 2001 recession.

After studying this chapter, you will be able to

- Explain how expenditure plans and real GDP are determined when the price level is fixed

- Explain the expenditure multiplier

- Explain how recessions and expansions begin

- Explain the relationship between aggregate expenditure and aggregate demand

- Explain how the multiplier gets smaller as the price level changes

Fixed Prices and Expenditure Plans

MOST FIRMS ARE LIKE YOUR LOCAL SUPERMARKET. They set their prices, advertise their products and services, and sell the quantities their customers are willing to buy. If they persistently sell a greater quantity than they plan to and are constantly running out of inventory, they eventually raise their prices. And if they persistently sell a smaller quantity than they plan to and have inventories piling up, they eventually cut their prices. But in the very short term, their prices are fixed. They hold the prices they have set, and the quantities they sell depend on demand, not supply.

The Aggregate Implications of Fixed Prices

Fixed prices have two immediate implications for the economy as a whole:

1. Because each firm's price is fixed, the *price level* is fixed.
2. Because demand determines the quantities that each firm sells, *aggregate demand* determines the aggregate quantity of goods and services sold, which equals real GDP.

So to understand the fluctuations in real GDP when the price level is fixed, we must understand aggregate demand fluctuations. The aggregate expenditure model explains fluctuations in aggregate demand by identifying the forces that determine expenditure plans.

Expenditure Plans

Aggregate expenditure has four components:

1. Consumption expenditure
2. Investment
3. Government purchases of goods and services
4. Net exports (exports *minus* imports)

These four components of aggregate expenditure sum to real GDP (see Chapter 19, pp. 435–436). **Aggregate planned expenditure** is equal to *planned* consumption expenditure plus *planned* investment plus *planned* government purchases of good and services plus *planned* exports minus *planned* imports.

In the very short term, *planned* investment, *planned* government purchases, and *planned* exports are fixed. But *planned* consumption expenditure and *planned* imports are not fixed. They depend on the level of real GDP itself.

A Two-Way Link Between Aggregate Expenditure and GDP Because real GDP influences consumption expenditure and imports, and because consumption expenditure and imports are components of aggregate expenditure, there is a two-way link between aggregate expenditure and GDP. Other things remaining the same,

- An increase in real GDP increases aggregate expenditure, and
- An increase in aggregate expenditure increases real GDP.

You are going to learn how this two-way link between aggregate expenditure and real GDP determines real GDP when the price level is fixed. The starting point is to consider the first piece of the two-way link: the influence of real GDP on planned consumption expenditure and saving.

Consumption Function and Saving Function

Several factors influence consumption expenditure and saving. The more important ones are

- Real interest rate
- Disposable income
- Wealth
- Expected future income

Chapter 23 (see pp. 532–534) explains how these factors influence consumption expenditure and saving. The second factor, **disposable income**, is aggregate income minus taxes plus transfer payments. And aggregate income equals real GDP. So to explore the two-way link between real GDP and planned consumption expenditure, we focus on the relationship between consumption expenditure and disposable income when the other factors are constant.

Consumption and Saving Plans The table in Fig. 25.1 shows an example of the relationship among planned consumption expenditure, planned saving, and disposable income. It lists the consumption expenditure and the saving that people plan to undertake at each level of disposable income. Notice that at each level of disposable income, consumption expenditure plus saving always equals disposable income. The reason is that households can only consume or save their disposable income. So planned consumption plus planned saving always equals disposable income.

The relationship between consumption expenditure and disposable income, other things remaining the same, is called the **consumption function**. The relationship between saving and disposable income, other things remaining the same, is called the **saving function**. Let's beginning by studying the consumption function.

FIGURE 25.1   Consumption Function and Saving Function

(a) Consumption function

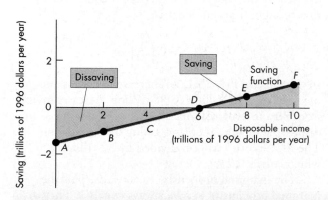

(b) Saving function

	Disposable income	Planned consumption expenditure	Planned saving
		(trillions of 1996 dollars per year)	
A	0	1.5	−1.5
B	2	3.0	−1.0
C	4	4.5	−0.5
D	6	6.0	0
E	8	7.5	0.5
F	10	9.0	1.0

The table shows consumption expenditure and saving plans at various levels of disposable income. Part (a) of the figure shows the relationship between consumption expenditure and disposable income (the consumption function). The height of the consumption function measures consumption expenditure at each level of disposable income. Part (b) shows the relationship between saving and disposable income (the saving function). The height of the saving function measures saving at each level of disposable income. Points A through F on the consumption and saving functions correspond to the rows in the table. The height of the 45° line in part (a) measures disposable income. So along the 45° line, consumption expenditure equals disposable income. Consumption expenditure plus saving equals disposable income. When the consumption function is above the 45° line, saving is negative (dissaving occurs). When the consumption function is below the 45° line, saving is positive. At the point where the consumption function intersects the 45° line, all disposable income is consumed and saving is zero.

Consumption Function Figure 25.1(a) shows a consumption function. The *y*-axis measures consumption expenditure and the *x*-axis measures disposable income. Along the consumption function, the points labeled *A* through *F* correspond to the rows of the table. For example, point *E* shows that when disposable income is $8 trillion, consumption expenditure is $7.5 trillion. Along the consumption function, as disposable income increases, consumption expenditure also increases.

At point *A* on the consumption function, consumption expenditure is $1.5 trillion even though disposable income is zero. This consumption expenditure is called *autonomous consumption*, and it is the amount of consumption expenditure that would take place in the short run even if people had no current income. Consumption expenditure in excess of this amount is called *induced consumption*, which is expenditure that is induced by an increase in disposable income.

45° Line Figure 25.1(a) also contains a 45° line, the height of which measures disposable income. At each point on this line, consumption expenditure equals disposable income. In the range over which the consumption function lies above the 45° line — between *A* and *D* — consumption expenditure exceeds disposable income. In the range over which the consumption function lies below the 45° line — between *D* and *F* — consumption expenditure is less than disposable income. And at a point at which the consumption function intersects the 45° line — at point *D* — consumption expenditure equals disposable income.

Saving Function Figure 25.1(b) shows a saving function. The *x*-axis is exactly the same as that in part (a). The *y*-axis measures saving. Again, the points marked *A* through *F* correspond to the rows of the table. For example, point *E* shows that when disposable income is $8 trillion, saving is $0.5 trillion. Along the saving function, as disposable income increases, saving also increases. At disposable income less than $6 trillion (point *D*), saving is negative. Negative saving is called *dissaving*. At disposable income greater than $6 trillion, saving is positive, and at $6 trillion, saving is zero.

Notice the connection between the two parts of Fig. 25.1. When consumption expenditure exceeds disposable income in part (a), saving is negative in

part (b). When disposable income exceeds consumption expenditure in part (a), saving is positive in part (b). And when consumption expenditure equals disposable income in part (a), saving is zero in part (b).

When saving is negative (when consumption expenditure exceeds disposable income), past savings are used to pay for current consumption. Such a situation cannot last forever, but it can occur if disposable income falls temporarily.

Marginal Propensities to Consume and Save

The extent to which consumption expenditure changes when disposable income changes depends on the marginal propensity to consume. The **marginal propensity to consume** (*MPC*) is the fraction of a *change* in disposable income that is consumed. It is calculated as the *change* in consumption expenditure (ΔC) divided by the *change* in disposable income (ΔYD) that brought it about. That is,

$$MPC = \frac{\Delta C}{\Delta YD}.$$

In the table in Fig. 25.1, when disposable income increases from $6 trillion to $8 trillion, consumption expenditure increases from $6 trillion to $7.5 trillion. The $2 trillion increase in disposable income increases consumption expenditure by $1.5 trillion. The *MPC* is $1.5 trillion divided by $2 trillion, which equals 0.75.

The **marginal propensity to save** (*MPS*) is the fraction of a *change* in disposable income that is saved. It is calculated as the *change* in saving (ΔS) divided by the *change* in disposable income (ΔYD) that brought it about. That is,

$$MPS = \frac{\Delta S}{\Delta YD}.$$

In the table in Fig. 25.1, an increase in disposable income from $6 trillion to $8 trillion increases saving from zero to $0.5 trillion. The $2 trillion increase in disposable income increases saving by $0.5 trillion. The *MPS* is $0.5 trillion divided by $2 trillion, which equals 0.25.

The marginal propensity to consume plus the marginal propensity to save always equals 1. They sum to 1 because consumption expenditure and saving exhaust disposable income. Part of each dollar increase in disposable income is consumed, and the remaining part is saved. You can see that these two marginal propensities sum to 1 by using the equation:

$$\Delta C + \Delta S = \Delta YD.$$

Divide both sides of the equation by the change in disposable income to obtain

$$\frac{\Delta C}{\Delta YD} + \frac{\Delta S}{\Delta YD} = 1.$$

$\Delta C/\Delta YD$ is the marginal propensity to consume (MPC), and $\Delta S/\Delta YD$ is the marginal propensity to save (MPS), so

$$MPC + MPS = 1.$$

Slopes and Marginal Propensities

The slopes of the consumption function and the saving function are the marginal propensities to consume and save. Figure 25.2(a) shows the MPC as the slope of the consumption function. A $2 trillion increase in disposable income from $6 trillion to $8 trillion is the base of the red triangle. The increase in consumption expenditure that results from this increase in disposable income is $1.5 trillion and is the height of the triangle. The slope of the consumption function is given by the formula "slope equals rise over run" and is $1.5 trillion divided by $2 trillion, which equals 0.75 — the MPC.

Figure 25.2(b) shows the MPS as the slope of the saving function. A $2 trillion increase in disposable income from $6 trillion to $8 trillion (the base of the red triangle) increases saving by $0.5 trillion (the height of the triangle). The slope of the saving function is $0.5 trillion divided by $2 trillion, which equals 0.25 — the MPS.

Other Influences on Consumption Expenditure and Saving

You've seen that a change in disposable income leads to changes in consumption expenditure and saving. A change in disposable income brings movements along the consumption function and saving function.

Along the consumption function and saving function, all other influences on consumption expenditure and saving (such as the real interest rate, wealth, and expected future income) are fixed. A change in any of these other influences shifts both the consumption function and the saving function.

FIGURE 25.2 Marginal Propensities to Consume and Save

(a) Consumption function

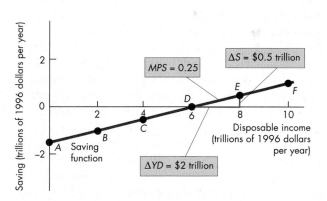

(b) Saving function

The marginal propensity to consume, MPC, is equal to the change in consumption expenditure divided by the change in disposable income, other things remaining the same. It is measured by the slope of the consumption function. In part (a), the MPC is 0.75. The marginal propensity to save, MPS, is equal to the change in saving divided by the change in disposable income, other things remaining the same. It is measured by the slope of the saving function. In part (b), the MPS is 0.25.

When the real interest rate falls or when wealth or expected future income increases, consumption expenditure increases and saving decreases. Figure 25.3 shows the effects of these changes on the consumption function and the saving function. The consumption function shifts upward from CF_0 to CF_1, and the saving function shifts downward from SF_0 to SF_1. Such shifts commonly occur during the expansion phase of the business cycle because, at such a time, expected future income increases.

When the real interest rate rises or when wealth or expected future income decreases, consumption decreases and saving increases. Figure 25.3 also shows the effects of these changes on the consumption function and the saving function. The consumption function shifts downward from CF_0 to CF_2, and the saving function shifts upward from SF_0 to SF_2. Such shifts often occur when a recession begins because, at such a time, expected future income decreases.

We've studied the theory of the consumption function. Let's now see how that theory applies to the U.S. economy.

The U.S. Consumption Function

Figure 25.4 shows the U.S. consumption function. Each point identified by a blue dot represents consumption expenditure and disposable income for a particular year. (The dots are for the years 1961–2001. Five of the years are identified in the figure.) The line labeled CF_0 is an estimate of the U.S. consumption function in 1961 and the line labeled CF_1 is an estimate of the U.S. consumption function in 2001.

The slope of the consumption function in Fig. 25.4 is 0.9, which means that a $1 trillion increase in disposable income brings a $0.9 trillion increase in consumption expenditure. This slope, which is an estimate of the marginal propensity to consume, is an assumption that is at the upper end of the range of values that economists have estimated for the marginal propensity to consume.

The consumption function shifts upward over time as other influences on consumption expenditure change. Of these other influences, the real interest rate and wealth fluctuate and so bring upward and downward shifts in the consumption function. But rising expected future income brings a steady upward shift in the consumption function. As the consumption function shifts upward, autonomous consumption expenditure increases.

FIGURE 25.3   Shifts in the Consumption and Saving Functions

(a) Consumption function

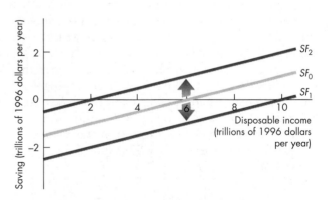

(b) Saving function

A fall in the real interest rate, an increase in wealth, or an increase in expected future income increases consumption expenditure and decreases saving. It shifts the consumption function upward from CF_0 to CF_1 and shifts the saving function downward from SF_0 to SF_1. A rise in the real interest rate or a decrease in either wealth or expected future income shifts the consumption function downward from CF_0 to CF_2 and shifts the saving function upward from SF_0 to SF_2.

FIGURE 25.4   The U.S. Consumption Function

Each blue dot shows consumption expenditure and disposable income for a particular year. The lines CF_{61} and CF_{01} are estimates of the U.S. consumption function in 1961 and 2001, respectively. Here, the (assumed) marginal propensity to consume is 0.9.

Consumption as a Function of Real GDP

You've seen that consumption expenditure changes when disposable income changes. Disposable income changes when either real GDP changes or net taxes change. If tax rates don't change, real GDP is the only influence on disposable income. So consumption depends not only on disposable income but also on real GDP. We use this link between consumption and real GDP to determine equilibrium expenditure. But before we do so, we need to look at one further component of aggregate expenditure: imports. Like consumption expenditure, imports also are influenced by real GDP.

Import Function

U.S. imports are determined by many factors, but in the short run, one factor dominates: U.S. real GDP.

Other things remaining the same, the greater the U.S. real GDP, the larger is the quantity of U.S. imports.

The relationship between imports and real GDP is determined by the marginal propensity to import. The **marginal propensity to import** is the fraction of an increase in real GDP that is spent on imports. It is calculated as the change in imports divided by the change in real GDP that brought it about, other things remaining the same. For example, if a $1 trillion increase in real GDP increases imports by $0.25 trillion, the marginal propensity to import is 0.25.

In recent years, since the North American Free Trade Agreement (NAFTA) was implemented, U.S. imports have surged. For example, between 1991 and 2001, real GDP increased by $2,657 billion and imports increased by $861 billion. If no factors other than real GDP influenced imports during the 1990s, these numbers would imply a marginal propensity to import of 0.32. But other factors, such as NAFTA, increased imports, so the marginal propensity to import is smaller than 0.32. The marginal propensity to import is probably as large as 0.2, and it has been increasing as the global economy has become more integrated.

REVIEW QUIZ

1 Which components of aggregate expenditure are influenced by real GDP?

2 Define the marginal propensity to consume. What is your estimate of your own marginal propensity to consume? After you graduate, will it change? Why or why not?

3 How do we calculate the effects of real GDP on consumption expenditure and imports by using the marginal propensity to consume and the marginal propensity to import?

Real GDP influences consumption expenditure and imports. But consumption expenditure and imports along with investment, government purchases, and exports influence real GDP. Your next task is to study this second piece of the two-way link between aggregate expenditure and real GDP and see how all the components of aggregate planned expenditure interact to determine real GDP.

Real GDP with a Fixed Price Level

YOU ARE NOW GOING TO DISCOVER HOW AGGREgate expenditure plans interact to determine real GDP when the price level is fixed. First, we will study the relationship between aggregate planned expenditure and real GDP. Second, we'll learn about the key distinction between *planned* expenditure and *actual*

expenditure. And third, we'll study equilibrium expenditure, a situation in which aggregate planned expenditure and actual expenditure are equal.

The relationship between aggregate planned expenditure and real GDP can be described by either an aggregate expenditure schedule or an aggregate expenditure curve. The *aggregate expenditure schedule* lists aggregate planned expenditure generated at each level of real GDP. The *aggregate expenditure curve* is a graph of the aggregate expenditure schedule.

FIGURE 25.5   Aggregate Expenditure

Aggregate planned expenditure is the sum of planned consumption expenditure, investment, government purchases of goods and services, and exports minus imports. For example, in row B of the table, when real GDP is $8 trillion, planned consumption expenditure is $5.6 trillion, planned investment is $1.5 trillion, planned government purchases of goods and services are $1.8 trillion, planned exports are $1.7 trillion, and planned imports are $1.6 trillion. So when real GDP is $8 trillion, aggregate planned expenditure is $9 trillion ($5.6 + $1.5 + $1.8 + $1.7 − $1.6). The schedule shows that aggregate planned expenditure increases as real GDP increases. This relationship is graphed as the aggregate expenditure curve AE. The components of aggregate expenditure that increase with real GDP are consumption expenditure and imports. The other components — investment, government purchases, and exports — do not vary with real GDP.

	Real GDP (Y)	Consumption expenditure (C)	Investment (I)	Government purchases (G)	Exports (X)	Imports (M)	Aggregate planned expenditure (AE = C + I + G + X − M)
				(trillions of 1992 dollars)			
	0	0	1.5	1.8	1.7	0.0	5.0
A	7	4.9	1.5	1.8	1.7	1.4	8.5
B	8	5.6	1.5	1.8	1.7	1.6	9.0
C	9	6.3	1.5	1.8	1.7	1.8	9.5
D	10	7.0	1.5	1.8	1.7	2.0	10.0
E	11	7.7	1.5	1.8	1.7	2.2	10.5
F	12	8.4	1.5	1.8	1.7	2.4	11.0

Planned expenditure

Aggregate Planned Expenditure and Real GDP

The table in Fig. 25.5 sets out an aggregate expenditure schedule together with the components of aggregate planned expenditure. To calculate aggregate planned expenditure at a given real GDP, we add the various components together. The first column of the table shows real GDP, and the second column shows the consumption expenditure generated by each level of real GDP. A $1 trillion increase in real GDP generates a $0.7 trillion increase in consumption expenditure — the *MPC* is 0.7.

The next two columns show investment and government purchases of goods and services. Investment depends on the real interest rate and the expected rate of profit (see Chapter 23, pp. 529–531). At a given point in time, these factors generate a particular level of investment. Suppose this level of investment is $1.5 trillion. Also, suppose that government purchases of goods and services are $1.8 trillion.

The next two columns show exports and imports. Exports are influenced by events in the rest of the world, prices of foreign-made goods and services relative to the prices of similar U.S.-made goods and services, and foreign exchange rates. But they are not directly affected by U.S. real GDP. Exports are a constant $1.7 trillion. Imports increase as U.S. real GDP increases. A $1 trillion increase in U.S. real GDP generates a $0.2 trillion increase in imports — the marginal propensity to import is 0.2.

The final column shows aggregate planned expenditure — the sum of planned consumption expenditure, investment, government purchases of goods and services, and exports minus imports.

Figure 25.5 plots an aggregate expenditure curve. Real GDP is shown on the *x*-axis, and aggregate planned expenditure is shown on the *y*-axis. The aggregate expenditure curve is the red line *AE*. Points *A* through *F* on that curve correspond to the rows of the table. The *AE* curve is a graph of aggregate planned expenditure (the last column) plotted against real GDP (the first column).

Figure 25.5 also shows the components of aggregate expenditure. The constant components — investment (*I*), government purchases of goods and services (*G*), and exports (*X*) — are shown by the horizontal lines in the figure. Consumption expenditure (*C*) is the vertical gap between the lines labeled *I + G + X* and *I + G + X + C*.

To construct the *AE* curve, subtract imports (*M*) from the *I + G + X + C* line. Aggregate expenditure is expenditure on U.S.-made goods and services. But the components of aggregate expenditure — *C*, *I*, and *G* — include expenditure on imported goods and services. For example, if you buy a new cell phone, your expenditure is part of consumption expenditure. But if the cell phone is a Nokia made in Finland, your expenditure on it must be subtracted from consumption expenditure to find out how much is spent on goods and services produced in the United States — on U.S. real GDP. Money paid to Nokia for cell phone imports from Finland does not add to aggregate expenditure in the United States.

Because imports are only a part of aggregate expenditure, when we subtract imports from the other components of aggregate expenditure, aggregate planned expenditure still increases as real GDP increases, as you can see in Fig. 25.5.

Consumption expenditure minus imports, which varies with real GDP, is called **induced expenditure**. The sum of investment, government purchases, and exports, which does not vary with real GDP, is called **autonomous expenditure**. Consumption expenditure and imports can also have an autonomous component — a component that does not vary with real GDP. Another way of thinking about autonomous expenditure is that it would be the level of aggregate planned expenditure if real GDP were zero.

In Fig. 25.5, autonomous expenditure is $5 trillion — aggregate planned expenditure when real GDP is zero. For each $1 trillion increase in real GDP, induced expenditure increases by $0.5 trillion.

The aggregate expenditure curve summarizes the relationship between aggregate *planned* expenditure and real GDP. But what determines the point on the aggregate expenditure curve at which the economy operates? What determines *actual* aggregate expenditure?

Actual Expenditure, Planned Expenditure, and Real GDP

Actual aggregate expenditure is always equal to real GDP, as we saw in Chapter 19 (p. 436). But aggregate *planned* expenditure is not necessarily equal to actual aggregate expenditure and therefore is not necessarily equal to real GDP. How can actual expenditure and planned expenditure differ from each other? Why don't expenditure plans get implemented? The reason is that firms might end up with greater inventories than planned or with smaller inventories than planned. People carry out their consumption expenditure plans, the government implements its planned purchases of goods and services, and net exports are as planned. Firms carry out their plans to purchase new buildings, plant, and equipment. But one component of investment is the change in firms' inventories of goods. If aggregate planned expenditure is less than real GDP, firms don't sell all the goods they produce

and they end up with inventories they hadn't planned. If aggregate planned expenditure exceeds real GDP, firms sell more than they produce and inventories decrease below the level that firms had planned.

Equilibrium Expenditure

Equilibrium expenditure is the level of aggregate expenditure that occurs when aggregate *planned* expenditure equals real GDP. Equilibrium expenditure is a

---

FIGURE 25.6   Equilibrium Expenditure

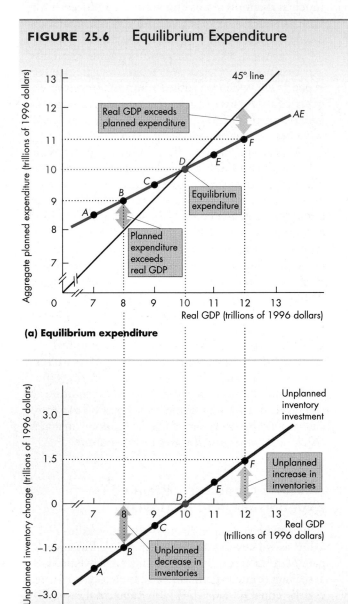

(a) Equilibrium expenditure

(b) Unplanned inventory changes

	Real GDP (Y)	Aggregate planned expenditure (AE)	Unplanned inventory change (Y – AE)
		(trillions of 1996 dollars)	
A	7	8.5	−1.5
B	8	9.0	−1.0
C	9	9.5	−0.5
D	10	10.0	0
E	11	10.5	0.5
F	12	11.0	1.0

The table shows expenditure plans at different levels of real GDP. When real GDP is $10 trillion, aggregate planned expenditure equals real GDP.

Part (a) of the figure illustrates equilibrium expenditure, which occurs when aggregate planned expenditure equals real GDP at the intersection of the 45° line and the AE curve. Part (b) of the figure shows the forces that bring about equilibrium expenditure. When aggregate planned expenditure exceeds real GDP, inventories decrease — for example, at point B in both parts of the figure. Firms increase production, and real GDP increases.

When aggregate planned expenditure is less than real GDP, inventories increase — for example, at point F in both parts of the figure. Firms decrease production, and real GDP decreases. When aggregate planned expenditure equals real GDP, there are no unplanned inventory changes and real GDP remains constant at equilibrium expenditure.

level of aggregate expenditure and real GDP at which everyone's spending plans are fulfilled. When the price level is fixed, equilibrium expenditure determines real GDP. When aggregate planned expenditure and actual aggregate expenditure are unequal, a process of convergence toward equilibrium expenditure occurs. And throughout this convergence process, real GDP adjusts. Let's examine equilibrium expenditure and the process that brings it about.

Figure 25.6(a) illustrates equilibrium expenditure. The table sets out aggregate planned expenditure at various levels of real GDP. These values are plotted as points *A* through *F* along the *AE* curve. The 45° line shows all the points at which aggregate planned expenditure equals real GDP. Thus where the *AE* curve lies above the 45° line, aggregate planned expenditure exceeds real GDP; where the *AE* curve lies below the 45° line, aggregate planned expenditure is less than real GDP; and where the *AE* curve intersects the 45° line, aggregate planned expenditure equals real GDP. Point *D* illustrates equilibrium expenditure. At this point, real GDP is $10 trillion.

Convergence to Equilibrium

What are the forces that move aggregate expenditure toward its equilibrium level? To answer this question, we must look at a situation in which aggregate expenditure is away from its equilibrium level. Suppose that in Fig. 25.6, real GDP is $8 trillion. With real GDP at $8 trillion, actual aggregate expenditure is also $8 trillion. But aggregate *planned* expenditure is $9 trillion, point *B* in Fig. 25.6(a). Aggregate planned expenditure exceeds *actual* expenditure. When people spend $9 trillion and firms produce goods and services worth $8 trillion, firms' inventories fall by $1 trillion, point *B* in Fig. 25.6(b). Because the change in inventories is part of investment, *actual* investment is $1 trillion less than *planned* investment.

Real GDP doesn't remain at $8 trillion for very long. Firms have inventory targets based on their sales. When inventories fall below target, firms increase production to restore inventories to the target level. To increase inventories, firms hire additional labor and increase production. Suppose that they increase production in the next period by $1 trillion. Real GDP increases by $1.0 trillion to $9.0 trillion. But again, aggregate planned expenditure exceeds real GDP. When real GDP is $9.0 trillion, aggregate planned expenditure is $9.5 trillion, point *C* in Fig.

25.6(a). Again, inventories decrease, but this time by less than before. With real GDP of $9.0 trillion and aggregate planned expenditure of $9.5 trillion, inventories decrease by $0.5 trillion, point *C* in Fig. 25.6(b). Again, firms hire additional labor, and production increases; real GDP increases yet further.

The process that we've just described — planned expenditure exceeds real GDP, inventories decrease, and production increases to restore inventories — ends when real GDP has reached $10 trillion. At this real GDP, there is equilibrium. Unplanned inventory changes are zero. Firms do not change their production.

You can do an experiment similar to the one we've just done but starting with a level of real GDP greater than equilibrium expenditure. In this case, planned expenditure is less than actual expenditure, inventories pile up, and firms cut production. As before, real GDP keeps on changing (decreasing this time) until it reaches its equilibrium level of $10.0 trillion.

REVIEW QUIZ

1 What is the relationship between aggregate planned expenditure and real GDP at expenditure equilibrium?

2 How does equilibrium expenditure come about? What adjusts to achieve equilibrium?

3 If real GDP and aggregate expenditure are less than their equilibrium levels, what happens to firms' inventories? How do firms change their production? And what happens to real GDP?

4 If real GDP and aggregate expenditure are greater than equilibrium expenditure, what happens to firms' inventories? How do firms change their production? And what happens to real GDP?

We've learned that when the price level is fixed, real GDP is determined by equilibrium expenditure. And we have seen how unplanned changes in inventories and the production response they generate bring a convergence toward equilibrium. We're now going to study *changes* in equilibrium and discover an economic amplifier called the *multiplier*.

The Multiplier

INVESTMENT AND EXPORTS CAN CHANGE FOR many reasons. A fall in the real interest rate might induce firms to increase their planned investment. A wave of innovation, such as occurred with the spread of multimedia computers in the 1990s, might increase expected future profits and lead firms to increase their planned investment. An economic boom in Western Europe and Japan might lead to a large increase in their expenditure on U.S.-produced goods and services — on U.S. exports. These are all examples of increases in autonomous expenditure.

When autonomous expenditure increases, aggregate expenditure increases, and so does equilibrium expenditure and real GDP. But the increase in real GDP is *larger* than the change in autonomous expenditure. The **multiplier** is the amount by which a change in autonomous expenditure is magnified or multiplied to determine the change in equilibrium expenditure and real GDP.

It is easiest to get the basic idea of the multiplier if we work with an example economy in which there are no income taxes and no imports. So we'll first assume that these factors are absent. Then, when you understand the basic idea, we'll bring these factors back into play and see what difference they make to the multiplier.

The Basic Idea of the Multiplier

Suppose that investment increases. The additional expenditure by businesses means that aggregate expenditure and real GDP increase. The increase in real GDP increases disposable income, and with no income taxes, real GDP and disposable income increase by the same amount. The increase in disposable income brings an increase in consumption expenditure. And the increased consumption expenditure adds even more to aggregate expenditure. Real GDP and disposable income increase further, and so does consumption expenditure. The initial increase in investment brings an even bigger increase in aggregate expenditure because it induces an increase in consumption expenditure. The magnitude of the increase in aggregate expenditure that results from an increase in autonomous expenditure is determined by the *multiplier*.

The table in Fig. 25.7 sets out an aggregate planned expenditure schedule. Initially, when real

GDP is $9 trillion, aggregate planned expenditure is $9.25 trillion. For each $1 trillion increase in real GDP, aggregate planned expenditure increases by $0.75 trillion. This aggregate expenditure schedule is shown in the figure as the aggregate expenditure curve AE_0. Initially, equilibrium expenditure is $10 trillion. You can see this equilibrium in row B of the table and in the figure where the curve AE_0 intersects the 45° line at the point marked B.

Now suppose that autonomous expenditure increases by $0.5 trillion. What happens to equilibrium expenditure? You can see the answer in Fig. 25.7. When this increase in autonomous expenditure is added to the original aggregate planned expenditure, aggregate planned expenditure increases by $0.5 trillion at each level of real GDP. The new aggregate expenditure curve is AE_1. The new equilibrium expenditure, highlighted in the table (row D'), occurs where AE_1 intersects the 45° line and is $12 trillion (point D'). At this real GDP, aggregate planned expenditure equals real GDP.

The Multiplier Effect

In Fig. 25.7, the increase in autonomous expenditure of $0.5 trillion increases equilibrium expenditure by $2 trillion. That is, the change in autonomous expenditure leads, like Erykah Badu's electronic equipment, to an amplified change in equilibrium expenditure. This amplified change is the *multiplier effect* — equilibrium expenditure increases by *more than* the increase in autonomous expenditure. The multiplier is greater than 1.

Initially, when autonomous expenditure increases, aggregate planned expenditure exceeds real GDP. As a result, inventories decrease. Firms respond by increasing production so as to restore their inventories to the target level. As production increases, so does real GDP. With a higher level of real GDP, *induced expenditure* increases. Thus equilibrium expenditure increases by the sum of the initial increase in autonomous expenditure and the increase in induced expenditure. In this example, induced expenditure increases by $1.5 trillion, so equilibrium expenditure increases by $2 trillion.

Although we have just analyzed the effects of an *increase* in autonomous expenditure, the same analysis applies to a decrease in autonomous expenditure. If initially the aggregate expenditure curve is AE_1, equilibrium expenditure and real GDP are $12 trillion. A decrease in autonomous expenditure of $0.5 trillion

FIGURE 25.7   The Multiplier

Real GDP (Y)	Aggregate planned expenditure			
	Original (AE₀)		New (AE₁)	
	(trillions of 1996 dollars)			
9	A	9.25	A'	9.75
10	B	10.00	B'	10.50
11	C	10.75	C'	11.25
12	D	11.50	D'	12.00
13	E	12.25	E'	12.75

A $0.5 trillion increase in autonomous expenditure shifts the AE curve upward by $0.5 trillion from AE₀ to AE₁. Equilibrium expenditure increases by $2 trillion from $10 trillion to $12 trillion. The increase in equilibrium expenditure is 4 times the increase in autonomous expenditure, so the multiplier is 4.

shifts the aggregate expenditure curve downward by $0.5 trillion to AE_0. Equilibrium expenditure decreases from $12 trillion to $10 trillion. The decrease in equilibrium expenditure ($2 trillion) is larger than the decrease in autonomous expenditure that brought it about ($0.5 trillion). The multiplier is 4.

Why Is the Multiplier Greater Than 1?

We've seen that equilibrium expenditure increases by more than the increase in autonomous expenditure. This makes the multiplier greater than 1. How come? Why does equilibrium expenditure increase by more than the increase in autonomous expenditure?

The multiplier is greater than 1 because induced expenditure increases — an increase in autonomous expenditure *induces* further increases in expenditure. Each time NASA launches a space shuttle, it spends $450 million. If NASA increases its program by one flight, aggregate expenditure and real GDP immediately increase by $450 million. But that is not the end of the story. Astronauts and engineers now have more income, and they spend part of the extra income on cars, microwave ovens, vacations, and a host of other goods and services. Real GDP now rises by the initial $450 million plus the extra consumption expenditure induced by the $450 million increase in income. The producers of cars, microwave ovens, vacations, and other goods and services now have increased incomes, and they, in turn, spend part of the increase in their incomes on consumption goods and services. Additional income induces additional expenditure, which creates additional income.

We have seen that a change in autonomous expenditure has a multiplier effect on real GDP. But how big is the multiplier effect?

The Size of the Multiplier

Suppose that the economy is in a recession. Profit prospects start to look better, and firms are making plans for large increases in investment. The world economy is also heading toward expansion, and exports are increasing. The question on everyone's lips is: How strong will the expansion be? This is a hard question to answer. But an important ingredient in the answer is working out the size of the multiplier.

The *multiplier* is the amount by which a change in autonomous expenditure is multiplied to determine the change in equilibrium expenditure that it generates. To calculate the multiplier, we divide the change in equilibrium expenditure by the change in autonomous expenditure. Let's calculate the multiplier for the example in Fig. 25.7. Initially, equilibrium expenditure is $10 trillion. Then autonomous expenditure increases by $0.5 trillion, and equilibrium expenditure increases by $2 trillion, to $12 trillion.

The multiplier is

$$\text{Multiplier} = \frac{\text{Change in equilibrium expenditure}}{\text{Change in autonomous expenditure}}$$

$$= \frac{\$2 \text{ trillion}}{\$0.05 \text{ trillion}} = 4.$$

The Multiplier and the Marginal Propensities to Consume and Save

What determines the magnitude of the multiplier? The answer is the marginal propensity to consume. The larger is the marginal propensity to consume, the larger is the multiplier. To see why, let's do a calculation.

Aggregate expenditure and real GDP change because consumption expenditure changes and investment changes. The change in real GDP (ΔY) equals the change in consumption expenditure (ΔC) plus the change in investment (ΔI). That is,

$$\Delta Y = \Delta C + \Delta I.$$

But the change in consumption expenditure is determined by the change in real GDP and the marginal propensity to consume. It is

$$\Delta C = MPC \times \Delta Y.$$

Now substitute $MPC \times \Delta Y$ for ΔC in the previous equation to give

$$\Delta Y = MPC \times \Delta Y + \Delta I.$$

Now, solve for ΔY as

$$(1 - MPC) \times \Delta Y = \Delta I$$

and rearrange

$$\Delta Y = \frac{\Delta I}{(1 - MPC)}.$$

Finally, divide both sides of this equation by ΔI to give

$$\text{Multiplier} = \frac{\Delta Y}{\Delta I} = \frac{1}{(1 - MPC)}.$$

Using the numbers for Fig. 25.7, MPC is 0.75, so the multiplier is

$$\text{Multiplier} = \frac{1}{(1 - 0.75)} = \frac{1}{0.25} = 4.$$

There is another formula for the multiplier. Because the marginal propensity to consume (MPC)

plus the marginal propensity to save (MPS) sum to 1, the term $(1 - MPC)$ equals MPS. So another formula for the multiplier is

$$\text{Multiplier} = \frac{1}{MPS}.$$

Again using the numbers in Fig. 25.7, we have

$$\text{Multiplier} = \frac{1}{0.25} = 4.$$

Because the marginal propensity to save (MPS) is a fraction — a number between 0 and 1 — the multiplier is greater than 1.

Figure 25.8 illustrates the multiplier process. Autonomous expenditure increases by $0.5 trillion. At this time, real GDP increases by $0.5 trillion (the green bar in round 1). This increase in real GDP induces more consumption expenditure in round 2. Induced expenditure increases by 0.75 times the increase in real GDP, so the increase in real GDP of $0.5 trillion induces a further increase in expenditure of $0.375 trillion. This change in induced expenditure (the green bar in round 2) when added to the previous increase in expenditure (the blue bar in round 2) increases real GDP by $0.875 trillion. The round 2 increase in real GDP induces a round 3 increase in consumption expenditure. The process repeats through successive rounds. Each increase in real GDP is 0.75 times the previous increase. The cumulative increase in real GDP gradually approaches $2 trillion.

So far, we've ignored imports and income taxes. Let's now see how these two factors influence the multiplier.

Imports and Income Taxes

The multiplier is determined, in general, not only by the marginal propensity to consume but also by the marginal propensity to import and by the marginal tax rate. Imports make the multiplier smaller than it otherwise would be. To see why, think about what happens following an increase in investment. An increase in investment increases real GDP, which in turn increases consumption expenditure. But part of the increase in investment and consumption expenditure is expenditure on imported goods and services, not U.S.-produced goods and services. Only expenditure on U.S.-produced goods and services increases U.S. real GDP. The larger is the marginal propensity to import, the smaller is the change in U.S. real GDP.

FIGURE 25.8   The Multiplier Process

Autonomous expenditure increases by $0.5 trillion. In round 1, real GDP increases by the same amount. With a marginal propensity to consume of 0.75, each additional dollar of real GDP induces an additional 0.75 of a dollar of consumption expenditure. The round 1 increase in real GDP induces an increase in consumption expenditure of $0.375 trillion in round 2. At the end of round 2, real GDP has increased by $0.875 trillion. The extra $0.375 trillion of real GDP in round 2 induces a further increase in consumption expenditure of $0.281 trillion in round 3. Real GDP increases yet further to $1.156 trillion. This process continues with real GDP increasing by ever-smaller amounts. When the process comes to an end, real GDP has increased by a total of $2 trillion.

Income taxes also make the multiplier smaller than it otherwise would be. Again, think about what happens following an increase in investment. An increase in investment increases real GDP. But because income taxes increase, disposable income increases by less than the increase in real GDP. Consequently, consumption expenditure increases by less than it would if taxes had not changed. The larger is the marginal tax rate, the smaller is the change in disposable income and real GDP.

The marginal propensity to import and the marginal tax rate together with the marginal propensity to consume determine the multiplier. And their combined influence depends on the slope of the *AE* curve. The multiplier is equal to $1 \div (1 - \text{Slope of the } AE \text{ curve})$.

Figure 25.9 compares two situations. In Fig. 25.9(a), there are no imports and no taxes. The slope of the *AE* curve equals the marginal propensity to consume, which is 0.75, and the multiplier is 4. In Fig. 25.9(b), imports and income taxes decrease the slope of the *AE* curve to 0.5. The multiplier is 2.

Over time, the value of the multiplier changes as tax rates change and as the marginal propensity to consume and the marginal propensity to import change. These ongoing changes make the multiplier hard to predict. But they do not change the fundamental fact that an initial change in autonomous expenditure leads to a magnified change in aggregate expenditure and real GDP.

The math note on pp. 598–599 shows the effects of taxes, imports, and the *MPC* on the multiplier.

Now that we've studied the multiplier and the factors that influence its magnitude, let's use what we've learned to gain some insights into business cycle turning points.

Business Cycle Turning Points

At business cycle turning points, the economy moves from expansion to recession or from recession to expansion. Economists understand these turning points as seismologists understand earthquakes. They know quite a lot about the forces and mechanisms that produce them, but they can't predict them. The forces that bring business cycle turning points are the swings in autonomous expenditure such as investment and exports. The mechanism that gives momentum to the economy's new direction is the multiplier. Let's use what we've now learned to examine these turning points.

An Expansion Begins An expansion is triggered by an increase in autonomous expenditure that increases aggregate planned expenditure. At the moment the economy turns the corner into expansion, aggregate planned expenditure exceeds real GDP. In this situation, firms see their inventories taking an unplanned dive. The expansion now begins. To meet their inventory targets, firms increase production, and real GDP begins to increase. This

FIGURE 25.9   The Multiplier and the Slope of the *AE* Curve

(a) Multiplier is 4

Imports and income taxes make the *AE* curve less steep and reduce the value of the multiplier. In part (a), with no imports and income taxes, the slope of the *AE* curve is 0.75 (the marginal propensity to consume) and the multiplier is 4.

(b) Multiplier is 2

But with imports and income taxes, the slope of the *AE* curve is less than the marginal propensity to consume. In part (b), the slope of the *AE* curve is 0.5. In this case, the multiplier is 2.

initial increase in real GDP brings higher incomes that stimulate consumption expenditure. The multiplier process kicks in, and the expansion picks up speed.

A Recession Begins   The process we've just described works in reverse at a business cycle peak. A recession is triggered by a decrease in autonomous expenditure that decreases aggregate planned expenditure. At the moment the economy turns the corner into recession, real GDP exceeds aggregate planned expenditure. In this situation, firms see unplanned inventories piling up. The recession now begins. To lower their inventories, firms cut production, and real GDP begins to decrease. This initial decrease in real GDP brings lower incomes that cut consumption expenditure. The multiplier process kicks in, and the recession takes hold.

The 2001 Recession   The NBER has declared March 2001 as the start of the most recent recession. During 2000, the year before the recession, business

inventories built up by $50 billion. But through 2001, inventories decreased. The decrease in inventories during the first part of 2001 was almost certainly a planned inventory run-down. But the continued decrease in inventories during the final part of 2001 might have had an unplanned component. *Reading Between the Lines* on pp. 596–597 looks at this episode.

REVIEW QUIZ

1   What is the multiplier? What does it determine? Why does it matter?
2   How do the marginal propensity to consume, the marginal propensity to import, and the marginal tax rate influence the multiplier?
3   How do fluctuations in autonomous expenditure influence real GDP? If autonomous expenditure decreases, which phase of the business cycle does the economy enter?

The economy's potholes are changes in investment and exports. And the economy does not operate like the shock absorbers on Michael Bloomberg's car. While the price level is fixed, the effects of the economic potholes are not smoothed out. Instead, they are amplified like Erykah Badu's voice. But we've considered only the adjustments in spending that occur in the very short term when the price level is fixed. What happens after a long enough time lapse for the price level to change? Let's answer this question.

The Multiplier and the Price Level

WHEN FIRMS CAN'T KEEP UP WITH SALES AND their inventories fall below target, they increase production, but at some point, they raise their prices. Similarly, when firms find unwanted inventories piling up, they decrease production, but eventually they cut their prices. So far, we've studied the macroeconomic consequences of firms changing their production levels when their sales change, but we haven't looked at the effects of price changes. When individual firms change their prices, the economy's price level changes.

To study the simultaneous determination of real GDP and the price level, we use the *aggregate supply–aggregate demand model*, which is explained in Chapter 21. But to understand how aggregate demand adjusts, we need to work out the connection between the aggregate supply–aggregate demand model and the equilibrium expenditure model that we've used in this chapter. The key to understanding the relationship between these two models is the distinction between the aggregate *expenditure* and aggregate *demand* and the related distinction between the aggregate *expenditure curve* and the aggregate *demand curve*.

Aggregate Expenditure and Aggregate Demand

The aggregate expenditure curve is the relationship between the aggregate planned expenditure and real GDP, all other influences on aggregate planned expenditure remaining the same. The aggregate demand curve is the relationship between the aggregate quantity of goods and services demanded and the price level, all other influences on aggregate demand remaining the same. Let's explore the links between these two relationships.

Aggregate Expenditure and the Price Level

When the price level changes, aggregate planned expenditure changes and the quantity of real GDP demanded changes. The aggregate demand curve slopes downward. Why? There are two main reasons:

- Wealth effect
- Substitution effects

Wealth Effect Other things remaining the same, the higher the price level, the smaller is the purchasing power of people's real wealth. For example, suppose you have $100 in the bank and the price level is 110. If the price level rises to 130, your $100 buys fewer goods and services. You are less wealthy. With less wealth, you will probably want to try to spend a bit less and save a bit more. The higher the price level, other things remaining the same, the lower is aggregate planned expenditure.

Substitution Effects A rise in the price level today, other things remaining the same, makes current goods and services more expensive relative to future goods and services and results in a delay in purchases — an *intertemporal substitution*. A rise in the price level, other things remaining the same, makes U.S.-produced goods more expensive relative to foreign-produced goods and services. As a result, U.S. imports increase and U.S. exports decrease — an *international substitution*.

When the price level rises, each of these effects reduces aggregate planned expenditure at each level of real GDP. As a result, when the price level *rises*, the aggregate expenditure curve shifts *downward*. A fall in the price level has the opposite effect. When the price level *falls*, the aggregate expenditure curve shifts *upward*.

Figure 25.10(a) shows the shifts of the *AE* curve. When the price level is 110, the aggregate expenditure curve is AE_0, which intersects the 45° line at point *B*. Equilibrium expenditure is $10 trillion. If the price level increases to 130, the aggregate expenditure curve shifts downward to AE_1, which intersects the 45° line at point *A*. Equilibrium expenditure is

$9 trillion. If the price level decreases to 90, the aggregate expenditure curve shifts upward to AE_2, which intersects the 45° line at point C. Equilibrium expenditure is $11 trillion.

We've just seen that when the price level changes, other things remaining the same, the aggregate expenditure curve shifts and the equilibrium expenditure changes. And when the price level changes, other things remaining the same, there is a movement along the aggregate demand curve.

Figure 25.10(b) shows the movements along the aggregate demand curve. At a price level of 110, the aggregate quantity of goods and services demanded is $10 trillion — point B on the AD curve. If the price level rises to 130, the aggregate quantity of goods and services demanded decreases to $9 trillion. There is a movement up along the aggregate demand curve to point A. If the price level falls to 90, the aggregate quantity of goods and services demanded increases to $11 trillion. There is a movement down along the aggregate demand curve to point C.

Each point on the aggregate demand curve corresponds to a point of equilibrium expenditure. The equilibrium expenditure points A, B, and C in Fig. 25.10(a) correspond to the points A, B, and C on the aggregate demand curve in Fig. 25.10(b).

A change in the price level, other things remaining the same, shifts the aggregate expenditure curve and brings a movement along the aggregate demand curve. A change in any other influence on aggregate planned expenditure shifts *both* the aggregate expenditure curve and the aggregate demand curve. For example, an increase in investment or in exports increases both aggregate planned expenditure and aggregate demand and shifts both the AE curve and the AD curve. Figure 25.11 illustrates the effect of such an increase.

Initially, the aggregate expenditure curve is AE_0 in part (a) and the aggregate demand curve is AD_0 in part (b). The price level is 110, real GDP is $10 trillion, and the economy is at point A in both parts of Fig. 25.11. Now suppose that investment increases by $1 trillion. At a constant price level of 110, the aggregate expenditure curve shifts upward to AE_1. This curve intersects the 45° line at an equilibrium expenditure of $12 trillion (point B). This equilibrium expenditure of $12 trillion is the aggregate quantity of goods and services demanded at a price level of 110, as shown by point B in part (b). Point B lies on a new aggregate demand curve. The aggregate demand curve has shifted rightward to AD_1.

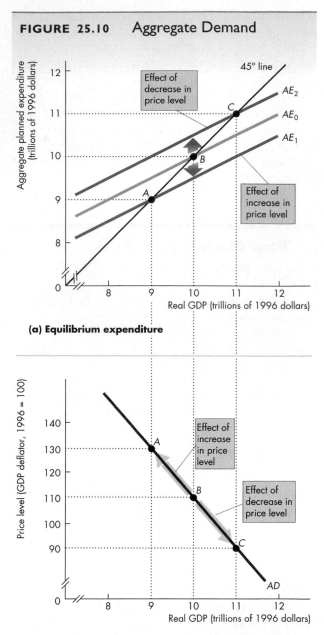

FIGURE 25.10   Aggregate Demand

(a) Equilibrium expenditure

(b) Aggregate demand

A change in the price level *shifts* the AE curve and results in a *movement along* the AD curve. When the price level is 110, the AE curve is AE_0 and equilibrium expenditure is $10 trillion at point B. When the price level rises to 130, the AE curve is AE_1 and equilibrium expenditure is $9 trillion at point A. When the price level falls to 90, the AE curve is AE_2 and equilibrium expenditure is $11 trillion at point C. Points A, B, and C on the AD curve in part (b) correspond to the equilibrium expenditure points A, B, and C in part (a).

FIGURE 25.11   A Change in Aggregate Demand

A $1 trillion increase in investment increases aggregate planned expenditure ...

(a) Aggregate expenditure

... and increases aggregate demand. The multiplier in this example is 2

(b) Aggregate demand

The price level is 110. When the aggregate expenditure curve is AE_0 (part a), the aggregate demand curve is AD_0 (part b). An increase in autonomous expenditure shifts the AE curve upward to AE_1. In the new equilibrium, real GDP is $12 trillion (at point B). Because the quantity of real GDP demanded at a price level of 110 increases to $12 trillion, the AD curve shifts rightward to AD_1.

But how do we know by how much the *AD* curve shifts? The multiplier determines the answer. The larger the multiplier, the larger is the shift in the aggregate demand curve that results from a given change in autonomous expenditure. In this example, the multiplier is 2. A $1 trillion increase in investment produces a $2 trillion increase in the aggregate quantity of goods and services demanded at each price level. That is, a $1 trillion increase in autonomous expenditure shifts the aggregate demand curve rightward by $2 trillion.

A decrease in autonomous expenditure shifts the aggregate expenditure curve downward and shifts the aggregate demand curve leftward. You can see these effects by reversing the change that we've just described. If the economy is initially at point *B* on the aggregate expenditure curve AE_1, the aggregate demand curve is AD_1. A decrease in autonomous expenditure shifts the aggregate planned expenditure curve downward to AE_0. The aggregate quantity of goods and services demanded falls from $12 trillion to $10 trillion, and the aggregate demand curve shifts leftward to AD_0.

Let's summarize what we have just discovered:

If some factor other than a change in the price level increases autonomous expenditure, the *AE* curve shifts upward and the *AD* curve shifts rightward.

The size of the *AD* curve shift depends on the change in autonomous expenditure and the multiplier.

Equilibrium Real GDP and the Price Level

In Chapter 21, we learned that aggregate demand and short-run aggregate supply determine equilibrium real GDP and the price level. We've now put aggregate demand under a more powerful microscope and have discovered that a change in investment (or in any component of autonomous expenditure) changes aggregate demand and shifts the aggregate demand curve. The magnitude of the shift depends on the multiplier. But whether a change in autonomous expenditure results ultimately in a change in real GDP, a change in the price level, or a combination of the two depends on aggregate supply. There are two time frames to consider: the short run and the long run. First we'll see what happens in the short run.

An Increase in Aggregate Demand in the Short Run Figure 25.12 describes the economy. Initially, in part (a), the aggregate expenditure curve is AE_0 and equilibrium expenditure is $10 trillion — point A. In part (b), aggregate demand is AD_0 and the short-run aggregate supply curve is SAS. (Chapter 21, pp. 477–480 explains the SAS curve.) Equilibrium is at point A, where the aggregate demand and short-run aggregate supply curves intersect. The price level is 110, and real GDP is $10 trillion.

Now suppose that investment increases by $1 trillion. With the price level fixed at 110, the aggregate expenditure curve shifts upward to AE_1. Equilibrium expenditure increases to $12 trillion — point B in part (a). In part (b), the aggregate demand curve shifts rightward by $2 trillion, from AD_0 to AD_1. How far the aggregate demand curve shifts is determined by the multiplier when the price level is fixed. But with this new aggregate demand curve, the price level does not remain fixed. The price level rises, and as it does, the aggregate expenditure curve shifts downward. The short-run equilibrium occurs when the aggregate expenditure curve has shifted downward to AE_2 and the new aggregate demand curve, AD_1, intersects the short-run aggregate supply curve. Real GDP is $11.3 trillion, and the price level is 123 (at point C).

When price level effects are taken into account, the increase in investment still has a multiplier effect on real GDP, but the multiplier is smaller than it would be if the price level were fixed. The steeper the slope of the short-run aggregate supply curve, the larger is the increase in the price level and the smaller is the multiplier effect on real GDP.

An Increase in Aggregate Demand in the Long Run Figure 25.13 illustrates the long-run effect of an increase in aggregate demand. In the long run, real GDP equals potential GDP and there is full employment. Potential GDP is $10 trillion, and the long-run aggregate supply curve is LAS. Initially, the economy is at point A in parts (a) and (b).

Investment increases by $1 trillion. In Fig. 25.13, the aggregate expenditure curve shifts to AE_1 and the aggregate demand curve shifts to AD_1. With no change in the price level, the economy would move to point B and real GDP would increase to $12 trillion. But in the short run, the price level rises to 123 and real GDP increases to only $11.3 trillion. With the higher price level, the AE curve shifts from AE_1 to

FIGURE 25.12   The Multiplier in the Short Run

An increase in investment increases aggregate planned expenditure ...

... but the price level rises, which decreases aggregate planned expenditure

(a) Aggregate expenditure

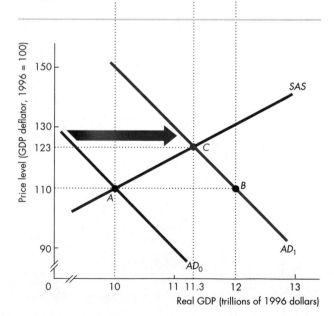

(b) Aggregate demand

An increase in investment shifts the AE curve from AE_0 to AE_1 and the AD curve from AD_0 to AD_1. The price level rises, and the higher price level shifts the AE curve downward from AE_1 to AE_2. The economy moves to point C in both parts. In the short run, when prices are flexible, the multiplier effect is smaller than when the price level is fixed.

FIGURE 25.13 The Multiplier in the Long Run

(a) Aggregate expenditure

(b) Aggregate demand

Starting from point A, an increase in investment shifts the AE curve to AE_1 and the AD curve to AD_1. In the short run, the economy moves to point C. In the long run, the money wage rate rises, and the SAS curve shifts to SAS_1. As the price level rises, the AE curve shifts back to AE_0, and the economy moves to point A'. In the long run, the multiplier is zero.

AE_2. The economy is now in a short-run equilibrium at point C in both part (a) and part (b). Real GDP now exceeds potential GDP. The labor force is more than fully employed, and shortages of labor increase the money wage rate. The higher money wage rate increases firms' costs, which decreases short-run aggregate supply and shifts the SAS curve leftward to SAS_1. The price level rises further, and real GDP decreases. There is a movement along AD_1, and the AE curve shifts downward from AE_2 toward AE_0. When the money wage rate and the price level have increased by the same percentage, real GDP is again equal to potential GDP and the economy is at point A'. In the long run, the multiplier is zero.

REVIEW QUIZ

1 How does a change in the price level influence the AE curve and the AD curve?

2 If autonomous expenditure increases with no change in the price level, what happens to the AE curve and the AD curve? Which curve shifts by an amount that is determined by the multiplier and why?

3 How does an increase in autonomous expenditure change real GDP in the short-run? Does real GDP change by the same amount as the change in aggregate demand? Why or why not?

4 How does real GDP change in the long run when autonomous expenditure increases? Does real GDP change by the same amount as the change in aggregate demand? Why or why not?

◆ You are now ready to build on what you've learned about aggregate expenditure fluctuations and study the roles of fiscal policy and monetary policy in smoothing the business cycle. In Chapter 26, we study fiscal policy — government purchases, taxes, and the deficit. In Chapters 27 and 28, we study monetary policy — interest rates and the quantity of money. But before you leave the current topic, look at *Reading Between the Lines* on pages 596–597 and see the model you've studied in this chapter in action in the U.S. economy during the 2001 recession.

Inventories in Recession

THE SAN FRANCISCO CHRONICLE, DECEMBER 1, 2001

Bad Numbers, Good Tidings

The Commerce Department revised its third-quarter gross domestic product estimate sharply downward yesterday, to a 1.1 percent falloff from a 0.4 percent drop, but many economists still expect a recovery in the first half of 2002.

Sharply lower business inventories accounted for the downward shift. Companies cut $60.1 billion from their stockpiles in the July through September period, a number not fully captured in preliminary data.

While the closet cleaning had a negative impact on GDP, it is actually a positive for the economy because businesses are now in a position to increase their inventories when the recovery begins, economists said yesterday.

The inventory number "is the ray of hope in the report, because it implies that the adjustment is behind us and firms are getting a better handle on production and demand," said Cary Leahey, senior economist at Deutsche Banc in New York.

The 1.1 percent decline is the biggest quarterly drop in GDP since the first quarter of 1991. The National Bureau of Economic Research earlier this week pegged the official beginning of the recession to March 2001. ...

Consumer spending, the largest component of the GDP report, rose a meager 1.1 percent during the third quarter, in large part because retailers have cut prices on commodities ranging from clothing to automobiles. ...

Essence of the Story

■ The Commerce Department's revised real GDP estimate for the third quarter of 2001 showed a fall of 1.1 percent.

■ This decrease is the biggest quarterly fall in real GDP since the first quarter of 1991.

■ Consumer spending *increased* by 1.1 percent during the third quarter, helped by price cuts on a wide range of items.

■ A decrease in business inventories of $60.1 billion accounted for the decrease in real GDP.

■ Many economists said that the inventory decrease meant that real GDP would increase during the first half of 2002.

Economic Analysis

■ We can interpret the changes in expenditure and real GDP that occurred during 2001 by using the *AE* model.

■ If we look at the second half of 2001 as a whole, real GDP barely changed. But the components changed by the amounts shown in Table 1. (Note that the numbers don't sum to the change in real GDP because there is a statistical discrepancy in chain-weighted data.)

■ The changes in consumption expenditure and net exports must have been changes in autonomous expenditure because real GDP didn't change.

■ The changes in business fixed investment and government purchases were also changes in autonomous expenditure.

■ Summing the changes in consumption expenditure, business fixed investment, government purchases, and net exports, you can see that autonomous expenditure *increased* by $90 billion.

■ The decrease in business inventories might have been a planned decrease, an unplanned decrease, or (most likely) a combination of the two.

■ If the entire decrease in inventories was planned, then autonomous expenditure remained (roughly) constant during the second half of 2001.

■ With constant autonomous expenditure, the *AE* curve didn't change and equilibrium real GDP didn't change.

■ But if the decrease in inventory was unplanned, aggregate planned expenditure increased by the $90 billion that we've calculated and the *AE* curve shifted upward. The figure shows this interpretation of the events of 2001.

■ In June 2001, the *AE* curve was AE_0 in part (a). By December 2001, an increase in autonomous expenditure had increased aggregate planned expenditure and the *AE* curve was AE_1.

■ But the increase in planned expenditure was offset by an unplanned decrease in inventories (part b).

■ In this interpretation, a multiplier process would begin to increase real GDP during 2002.

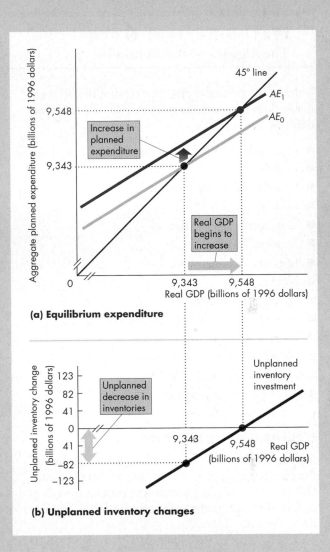

(a) Equilibrium expenditure

(b) Unplanned inventory changes

Item	Change during second half of 2001 (billions of 1996 dollars)
Consumption expenditure	+110
Business fixed investment	−73
Government purchases	+41
Net exports	+12
Business inventories	−82
Real GDP	+1

Table 1 Changes in components of real GDP

Mathematical Note
The Algebra of the Multiplier

THIS NOTE EXPLAINS THE MULTIPLIER IN GREATER detail than that presented on p. 588. We begin by defining the symbols we need:

- Aggregate planned expenditure, AE
- Real GDP, Y
- Consumption expenditure, C
- Investment, I
- Government purchases, G
- Exports, X
- Imports, M
- Net taxes, T
- Disposable income, YD
- Autonomous consumption expenditure, a
- Marginal propensity to consume, b
- Marginal propensity to import, m
- Marginal tax rate, t
- Autonomous expenditure, A

Aggregate Expenditure

Aggregate planned expenditure (AE) is the sum of the planned amounts of consumption expenditure (C), investment (I), government purchases (G), and exports (X) minus the planned amount of imports (M). That is,

$$AE = C + I + G + X - M.$$

Consumption Function Consumption expenditure (C) depends on disposable income (YD), and we write the consumption function as

$$C = a + bYD.$$

Disposable income (YD) equals real GDP minus net taxes ($Y - T$). So if we replace YD with ($Y - T$), the consumption function becomes:

$$C = a + b(Y - T).$$

Net taxes equal real GDP (Y) multiplied by the marginal tax rate (t). That is,

$$T = tY.$$

Use this equation in the previous one to obtain

$$C = a + b(1 - t)Y.$$

This equation describes consumption expenditure as a function of real GDP.

Import Function Imports depend on real GDP, and the import function is

$$M = mY.$$

Aggregate Expenditure Curve Use the consumption function and the import function to replace C and M in the aggregate planned expenditure equation. That is,

$$AE = a + b(1 - t)Y + I + G + X - mY.$$

Collect the terms on the right side of the equation that involve Y to obtain:

$$AE = (a + I + G + X) + [b(1 - t) - m]Y.$$

Autonomous expenditure (A) is ($a + I + G + X$), and the slope of the AE curve is $[b(1 - t) - m]$. So the equation for the AE curve, which is shown in Fig. 1, is

$$AE = A + [b(1 - t) - m]Y.$$

Figure 1 The AE curve

Equilibrium Expenditure

Equilibrium expenditure occurs when aggregate planned expenditure (AE) equals real GDP (Y). That is,

$$AE = Y.$$

In Fig. 2, the scales of the x-axis (real GDP) and the y-axis (aggregate planned expenditure) are identical, so the 45° line shows the points at which aggregate planned expenditure equals real GDP.

Figure 2 shows the point of equilibrium expenditure at the intersection of the AE curve and the 45° line.

To calculate equilibrium expenditure and real GDP, we solve the equations for the AE curve and the 45° line for the two unknown quantities AE and Y. So starting with

$$AE = A + [b(1 - t) - m]Y$$

$$AE = Y,$$

replace AE with Y in the AE equation to obtain

$$Y = A + [b(1 - t) - m]Y.$$

The solution for Y is

$$Y = \frac{1}{1 - [b(1 - t) - m]}A.$$

The Multiplier

The multiplier equals the change in equilibrium expenditure and real GDP (Y) that results from a change in autonomous expenditure (A) divided by the change in autonomous expenditure.

A change in autonomous expenditure (ΔA) changes equilibrium expenditure and real GDP (ΔY) by

$$\Delta Y = \frac{1}{1 - [b(1 - t) - m]}\Delta A.$$

$$\text{Multiplier} = \frac{1}{1 - [b(1 - t) - m]}.$$

The size of the multiplier depends on the slope of the AE curve, $b(1 - t) - m$. The larger the slope, the larger is the multiplier. So the multiplier is larger:

- The greater the marginal propensity to consume (b)
- The smaller the marginal tax rate (t)
- The smaller the marginal propensity to import (m)

An economy with no imports and no marginal taxes has $m = 0$ and $t = 0$. In this special case, the multiplier equals $1/(1 - b)$. If b is 0.75, then the multiplier is 4, as shown in Fig. 3.

In an economy with $b = 0.75$, $t = 0.2$, and $m = 0.1$, the multiplier is $1 \div [1 - 0.75(1 - 0.2) - 0.1]$, which equals 2. Make up some more examples to show the effects of b, t, and m on the multiplier.

Figure 2 Equilibrium expenditure

Figure 3 The multiplier

SUMMARY

KEY POINTS

Fixed Prices and Expenditure Plans
(pp. 576–581)

- When the price level is fixed, expenditure plans determine real GDP.
- Consumption expenditure is determined by disposable income, and the marginal propensity to consume (*MPC*) determines the change in consumption expenditure brought about by a change in disposable income. Real GDP determines disposable income.
- Imports are determined by real GDP, and the marginal propensity to import determines the change in imports brought about by a change in real GDP.

Real GDP with a Fixed Price Level (pp. 582–585)

- Aggregate *planned* expenditure depends on real GDP.
- Equilibrium expenditure occurs when aggregate planned expenditure equals actual expenditure and real GDP.

The Multiplier (pp. 586–591)

- The multiplier is the magnified effect of a change in autonomous expenditure on real GDP.
- The multiplier is influenced by the marginal propensity to consume, the marginal propensity to import, and the marginal income tax rate.

The Multiplier and the Price Level (pp. 591–595)

- The aggregate demand curve is the relationship between the quantity of real GDP demanded and the price level, other things remaining the same.
- The aggregate expenditure curve is the relationship between aggregate planned expenditure and real GDP, other things remaining the same.
- At a given price level, there is a given aggregate expenditure curve. A change in the price level changes aggregate planned expenditure and shifts the aggregate expenditure curve. A change in the price level also creates a movement along the aggregate demand curve.
- A change in autonomous expenditure that is not caused by a change in the price level shifts the aggregate expenditure curve and shifts the aggregate demand curve. The magnitude of the shift of the aggregate demand curve depends on the multiplier and on the change in autonomous expenditure.
- The multiplier decreases as the price level changes, and the long-run multiplier is zero.

KEY FIGURES

KEY TERMS

PROBLEMS

f. What is the multiplier?

*1. You are given the following information about the economy of Heron Island:

Disposable income (millions of dollars per year)	Consumption expenditure (millions of dollars per year)
0	5
10	10
20	15
30	20
40	25

Calculate Heron Island's:
a. Marginal propensity to consume.
b. Saving at each level of disposable income.
c. Marginal propensity to save.

2. You are given the following information about the economy of Spendthrift Island:

Disposable income (millions of dollars per year)	Saving (millions of dollars per year)
0	−10
50	−5
100	0
150	5
200	10
250	15
300	20

a. Calculate the marginal propensity to save.
b. Calculate consumption at each level of disposable income.
c. Calculate the marginal propensity to consume.
d. Why is the island called "spendthrift"?

*3. Turtle Island has no imports or exports, the people of Turtle Island pay no incomes taxes, and the price level is fixed. The figure illustrates the components of aggregate planned expenditure on Turtle Island. On Turtle Island,
a. What is autonomous expenditure?
b. What is the marginal propensity to consume?
c. What is aggregate planned expenditure when real GDP is $6 billion?
d. If real GDP is $4 billion, what is happening to inventories?
e. If real GDP is $6 billion, what is happening to inventories?

4. The spreadsheet lists the components of aggregate planned expenditure in Spice Bay. The numbers are in billions of cloves, the currency of Spice Bay.

	A	B	C	D	E	F	G
1		Y	C	I	G	X	M
2	a	100	110	50	60	60	15
3	b	200	170	50	60	60	30
4	c	300	230	50	60	60	45
5	d	400	290	50	60	60	60
6	e	500	350	50	60	60	75
7	f	600	410	50	60	60	90

In Spice Bay,
a. What is autonomous expenditure?
b. What is the marginal propensity to consume?
c. What is aggregate planned expenditure when real GDP is 200 billion cloves?
d. If real GDP is 200 billion cloves, what is happening to inventories?
e. If real GDP is 500 billion cloves, what is happening to inventories?
f. What is the multiplier in Spice Bay?

*5. You are given the following information about the economy of Zeeland: Autonomous consumption expenditure is $100 billion, and the marginal propensity to consume is 0.9. Investment is $460 billion, government purchases of goods and services are $400 billion, and net taxes are a constant $400 billion — they do not vary with income.

a. What is the consumption function?

b. What is the equation that describes the aggregate expenditure curve?

c. Calculate equilibrium expenditure.

d. If investment falls to $360 billion, what is the change in equilibrium expenditure and what is the size of the multiplier?

6. You are given the following information about the economy of Antarctica: Autonomous consumption expenditure is $1 billion, and the marginal propensity to consume is 0.9. Investment is $5 billion, government purchases of goods and services are $4 billion, and net taxes are a constant $4 billion — they do not vary with income.

a. What is the consumption function?

b. What is the equation that describes the aggregate expenditure curve?

c. Calculate equilibrium expenditure.

d. If investment falls to $3 billion, what is the change in equilibrium expenditure and what is the size of the multiplier?

*7. Suppose that in problem 5, the price level is 100 and real GDP equals potential GDP.

a. If investment increases by $100 billion, what happens to the quantity of real GDP demanded?

b. In the short run, does real GDP increase by more than, less than, or the same amount as the increase in the quantity of real GDP demanded?

c. In the long run, does real GDP increase by more than, less than, or the same amount as the increase in the quantity of real GDP demanded?

d. In the short run, does the price level in Zeeland rise, fall, or remain unchanged?

e. In the long run, does the price level in Zeeland rise, fall, or remain unchanged?

8. Suppose that in problem 6, the price level is 100 and real GDP equals potential GDP.

a. If investment increases by $1 billion, what happens to the quantity of real GDP demanded?

b. In the long run, does real GDP increase by more than, less than, or the same amount as the increase in the quantity of real GDP demanded?

c. In the short run, does the price level in Antarctica rise, fall, or remain unchanged?

CRITICAL THINKING

1. Study *Reading Between the Lines* on pp. 596–597 and then answer the following questions:

a. If the 2001 changes in inventories were part of *planned* investment, what role did they play in shifting the *AE* curve and changing equilibrium expenditure? Use a figure similar to that on p. 587 to answer this question.

b. If the 2001 changes in inventories were part of *unplanned* investment, what role did they play in shifting the *AE* curve and changing equilibrium expenditure? Use a figure similar to that on p. 587 to answer this question.

c. What do you think will happen to real GDP, aggregate expenditure, and inventory investment in 2002? What clues do you get from the news article?

d. Is a run-down of business inventories a cause or a consequence of recession?

WEB EXERCISES

1. Use the links on your Parkin Web site to obtain data on real GDP per person and consumption as a percentage of real GDP for the United States, China, South Africa, and Mexico since 1960.

a. In a spreadsheet, multiply your real GDP data by the consumption percentage and divide by 100 to obtain data on real consumption expenditure per person.

b. Make graphs like Fig. 25.4 to show the relationship between consumption and real GDP for these four countries.

c. On the basis of the numbers you've obtained, in which country do you expect the multiplier to be largest (other things remaining the same)?

d. What other data would you need to be able to calculate the multipliers for these countries?

2. You are a research assistant in the office of the President's Council of Economic Advisors. Draft a note for the President that explains the power and limitations of the multiplier. The President wants only 250 words of crisp, clear, jargon-free explanation together with a lively example.

FISCAL POLICY — CHAPTER 26

Balancing Acts on Capitol Hill

In 2003, the federal government planned to spend 18 cents of every dollar that Americans earned, and it planned to collect almost as much in taxes. What are the effects of government spending on the economy? Does a dollar spent by the government on goods and services have the same effect as a dollar spent by someone else? Does it create jobs, or does it destroy them? What are the effects of taxes on the economy? Do they harm employment and economic growth? ◆ For many years during the 1980s and 1990s, the government had a large budget deficit and ran up a debt. Your share of that debt is about $12,000. Does it matter if the government doesn't balance its books? What are the effects of an ongoing government deficit and accumulating debt? Do they slow economic growth? Do they impose a burden on future generations — on you and your children? What must be done to balance the budget? Can spending cuts do it, or must taxes be increased? Or can spending be cut so severely that taxes can also be cut?

◆ These are the fiscal policy issues that you will study in this chapter. We'll begin by describing the federal budget and the process of creating it. We'll also look at the recent history of the federal budget. We'll then use the multiplier analysis of Chapter 25, aggregate supply and aggregate demand of Chapter 21, the full-employment economy of Chapter 22, and the capital market of Chapter 23 to study the effects of the budget on the economy. In *Reading Between the Lines* at the end of the chapter, we look at the President's 2003 budget proposals. And in a special feature on the Economics Place Web site, we examine the stimulus package (Tax Act) signed into law in March 2002.

After studying this chapter, you will be able to

- Describe the federal budget process
- Describe the recent history of federal expenditures, tax revenues, and the budget deficit
- Distinguish between automatic and discretionary fiscal policy
- Define and explain the fiscal policy multipliers
- Explain the effects of fiscal policy in both the short run and the long run
- Distinguish between and explain the demand-side and supply-side effects of fiscal policy

603

The Federal Budget

THE ANNUAL STATEMENT OF THE EXPENDITURES and tax revenues of the government of the United States together with the laws and regulations that approve and support those expenditures and taxes make up the **federal budget**. The federal budget has two purposes:

1. To finance the activities of the federal government
2. To stabilize the economy

The first purpose of the federal budget was its only purpose before the Great Depression years of the 1930s. The second purpose arose as a reaction to the Great Depression. The use of the federal budget to achieve macroeconomic objectives such as full employment, sustained economic growth, and price level stability is called **fiscal policy**. It is on this second purpose that we focus in this chapter.

The Institutions and Laws

Fiscal policy is made by the President and Congress on an annual timeline that is shown in Figure 26.1 for the 2003 budget.

The Roles of the President and Congress

The President *proposes* a budget to Congress each February and, after Congress has passed the budget acts in September, either signs those acts into law or vetoes the *entire* budget bill. He does not have the veto power to eliminate specific items in a budget bill and approve others — known as a *line-item veto*. Many state governors have long had line-item veto authority, and Congress attempted to grant these powers to the President of the United States in 1996. But in a 1998 Supreme Court ruling, the line-item veto for the President was declared unconstitutional. Although the President proposes and ultimately approves the budget, the task of making the tough decisions on spending and taxes rests with Congress.

Congress begins its work on the budget with the President's proposal. The House of Representatives and the Senate develop their own budget ideas in their respective House and Senate Budget Committees. Formal conferences between the two houses eventually resolve differences of view, and a series of spending acts and an overall budget act are usually passed by both houses before the start of the fiscal year. A

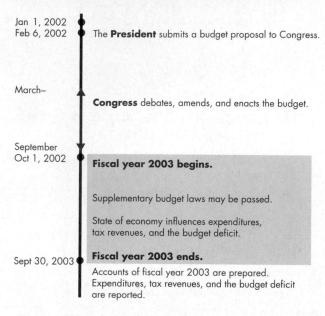

FIGURE 26.1   The Federal Budget Timeline in Fiscal 2003

Jan 1, 2002 Feb 6, 2002	The **President** submits a budget proposal to Congress.
March–	**Congress** debates, amends, and enacts the budget.
September Oct 1, 2002	**Fiscal year 2003 begins.** Supplementary budget laws may be passed. State of economy influences expenditures, tax revenues, and the budget deficit.
Sept 30, 2003	**Fiscal year 2003 ends.** Accounts of fiscal year 2003 are prepared. Expenditures, tax revenues, and the budget deficit are reported.

The federal budget process begins with the President's proposals in February. Congress debates and amends these proposals and enacts a budget before the start of the fiscal year on October 1. The President signs the budget acts into law or vetoes the entire budget bill. Throughout the fiscal year, Congress might pass supplementary budget laws. The budget outcome is calculated after the end of the fiscal year.

fiscal year is a year that runs from October 1 to September 30 in the next calendar year. *Fiscal* 2003 is the fiscal year that *begins* on October 1, 2002.

During a fiscal year, Congress often passes supplementary budget laws, and the budget outcome is influenced by the evolving state of the economy. For example, if a recession begins, tax revenues fall and welfare payments increase.

The Employment Act of 1946 Fiscal policy operates within the framework of the landmark **Employment Act of 1946** in which Congress declared that

> ... it is the continuing policy and responsibility of the Federal Government to use all practicable means ... to coordinate and utilize all its plans, functions, and resources ... to promote maximum employment, production, and purchasing power.

This act recognized a role for government actions to keep unemployment low, keep the economy expanding, and keep inflation in check. The *Full Employment and Balanced Growth Act of 1978*, more commonly known as the *Humphrey-Hawkins Act*, went farther than the 1946 employment act and set a specific target of 4 percent for the unemployment rate. But this target has never been treated as an unwavering policy goal. Under the 1946 act, the President must describe the current economic situation and the policies he believes are needed in an annual *Economic Report of the President*, which the Council of Economic Advisers writes.

The Council of Economic Advisers The President's Council of Economic Advisers was established in 1946 by the Employment Act. The Council consists of a chairperson and two other members, all of whom are economists on a one- or two-year leave from their regular university or public service jobs. In 2003, the chair of President Bush's Council of Economic Advisers was Gregory Mankiw of Harvard University. The **Council of Economic Advisers** monitors the economy and keeps the President and the public well informed about the current state of the economy and the best available forecasts of where it is heading. This economic intelligence activity is one source of data that informs the budget-making process.

Let's look at the most recent federal budget.

Highlights of the 2003 Budget

Table 26.1 shows the main items in the federal budget proposed by President Bush for 2003. The numbers are projected amounts for the fiscal year beginning on October 1, 2002 — fiscal 2003. Notice the three main parts of the table: *Tax revenues* are the government's receipts, *expenditures* are the government's outlays, and the *deficit* is the amount by which the government's expenditures exceed its tax revenues.

Tax Revenues Tax revenues were projected to be $2,080 billion in fiscal 2003. These revenues come from four sources:

1. Personal income taxes
2. Social insurance taxes
3. Corporate income taxes
4. Indirect taxes

The largest source of revenue is *personal income taxes*, which in 2003 are expected to be $987 billion. These taxes are paid by individuals on their incomes. The second largest source is *social insurance taxes*. These taxes are paid by workers and their employers to finance the government's social insurance programs. Third in size are *corporate income taxes*. These taxes are paid by companies on their profits. Finally, the smallest source of federal revenue is what are called *indirect taxes*. These taxes are on the sale of gasoline, alcoholic beverages, and a few other items.

Expenditures Expenditures are classified in three categories:

1. Transfer payments
2. Purchases of goods and services
3. Debt interest

The largest item of expenditure, *transfer payments*, are payments to individuals, businesses, other levels of government, and the rest of the world. In 2003, this item is expected to be $1,307 billion. It includes Social Security benefits, Medicare and Medicaid, unemployment checks, welfare payments, farm subsidies, grants to state and local governments, aid to developing countries, and dues to international

TABLE 26.1	Federal Budget in Fiscal 2003
Item	Projections (billions of dollars)
Tax Revenues	**2,080**
Personal income taxes	987
Social insurance taxes	787
Corporate income taxes	195
Indirect taxes	111
Expenditures	**2,158**
Transfer payments	1,307
Purchases of goods and services	625
Debt interest	226
Deficit	**78**

Source: Budget of the United States Government, Fiscal Year 2003, Table 14.1, Federal Transactions in the National Income and Product Accounts.

organizations such as the United Nations. Transfer payments, especially those for Medicare and Medicaid, are sources of persistent growth in government expenditures and are a major source of concern and political debate.

Purchases of goods and services are expenditures on final goods and services, and in 2003, they are expected to total $625 billion. These expenditures, which include those on national defense, homeland security, research on cures for AIDS, computers for the Internal Revenue Service, government cars and trucks, federal highways, and dams, have decreased in recent years. This component of the federal budget is *government purchases of goods and services* that appears in the circular flow of expenditure and income and in the National Income and Product Accounts (see Chapter 19, pp. 435–436).

Debt interest is the interest on the government debt. In 2003, this item is expected to be $226 billion — about 10 percent of total expenditure. This interest payment is large because the government has a debt of about $3 trillion, which has arisen from many years of budget deficits during the 1970s, 1980s, and 1990s.

Surplus or Deficit The government's budget balance is equal to tax revenues minus expenditures.

Budget balance = Tax revenues − Expenditures.

If tax revenues exceed expenditures, the government has a **budget surplus**. If expenditures exceed tax revenues, the government has a **budget deficit**. If tax revenues equal expenditures, the government has a **balanced budget**. In fiscal 2003, with projected expenditures of $2,158 billion and tax revenues of $2,080 billion, the government projected a budget deficit of $78 billion.

Big numbers like these are hard to visualize and hard to compare over time. To get a better sense of the magnitude of taxes, spending, and the deficit, we often express them as percentages of GDP. Expressing them in this way lets us to see how large government is relative to the size of the economy and also helps us to study *changes* in the scale of government over time.

How typical is the federal budget of 2003? Let's look at the recent history of the budget.

The Budget in Historical Perspective

Figure 26.2 shows the government's tax revenues, expenditures, and budget surplus or deficit since 1983. Through 1997, there was a budget deficit. The federal government began running a deficit in 1970, and the 1983 deficit shown in the figure was the highest on record at 5.2 percent of GDP. The deficit declined through 1989 but climbed again during the 1990–1991 recession. During the 1990s

---

FIGURE 26.2 The Budget Surplus and Deficit

The figure records the federal government's expenditures, tax revenues, and budget surplus/deficit from 1983 through 2003. During the 1980s, a large and persistent budget deficit arose from the combination of a decrease in tax revenues and an increase in expenditures. In 1998, rising revenues and falling expenditures (as percentages of GDP) created a budget surplus, but a deficit emerged again in 2002 as expenditure on security increased.

Source: Budget of the United States Government, Fiscal Year 2003, Table 14.2, Federal Transactions in the National Income and Product Accounts.

expansion, the deficit gradually shrank, and in 1998, the first surplus since 1969 emerged. But by 2002, the budget was again in deficit.

Why did the budget deficit grow during the 1980s and vanish in the late 1990s? The answer lies in the changes in expenditures and tax revenues. But which components of expenditures and tax revenues changed to swell and then shrink the deficit? Let's look at tax revenues and expenditures in a bit more detail.

Tax Revenues Figure 26.3(a) shows the components of tax revenues as percentages of GDP between 1983 and 2003. Cuts in corporate and personal income taxes lowered total tax revenues between 1983 and 1986. The decline resulted from tax cuts that had been passed during 1981. From 1986 through 1991, tax revenues did not change much as a percentage of GDP. Personal income tax payments increased through the 1990s but fell after 2000.

FIGURE 26.3   Federal Government Tax Revenues and Expenditures

(a) Tax revenues

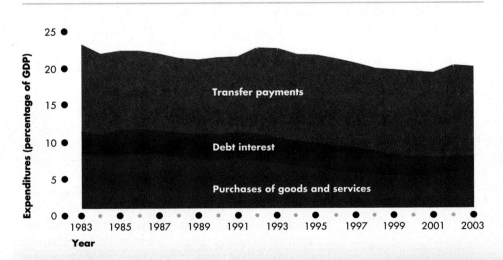

(b) Expenditures

In part (a), revenues from personal and corporate income taxes as a percentage of GDP were approximately constant during the 1980s and increased during the 1990s. The other components of tax revenues remained steady.

In part (b), purchases of goods and services as a percentage of GDP decreased. Transfer payments increased during the early 1990s. Debt interest held steady during the 1980s and decreased during the 1990s as the deficit shrank and interest rates fell. Purchases of security-related goods and services increased sharply in 2002.

Source: Budget of the United States Government, Fiscal Year 2003, Table 14.2, Federal Transactions in the National Income and Product Accounts.

Expenditures Figure 26.3(b) shows the components of government expenditures as percentages of GDP between 1983 and 2003. Total expenditures decreased slightly through 1989, increased during the early 1990s, decreased steadily until 2001, and then increased again. Purchases of goods and services decreased through 2001. They increased when expenditures on security-related goods and services increased sharply in 2002 in the wake of the attacks that occurred on September 11, 2001. Debt interest was a constant percentage of GDP during the 1980s and fell slightly during the late 1990s and 2000s. To understand the role of debt interest, we need to see the connection between the government budget surplus or deficit and government debt.

Surplus, Deficit, and Debt The government borrows when it has a deficit and makes repayments when it has a surplus. **Government debt** is the total amount that the government has borrowed. It is the sum of past deficits minus the sum of past surpluses. A government budget deficit increases government debt. And a persistent budget deficit feeds itself. The deficit leads to increased borrowing; increased borrowing leads to larger interest payments; and larger interest payments lead to a larger deficit. That is the story of the increasing deficit during the 1970s and 1980s.

Figure 26.4 shows the story of two definitions of government debt since 1942. Gross debt includes the amounts that the government owes to future generations in social security payments. Net debt is the debt held by the public and it excludes social security obligations.

As a percentage of GDP, government debt was at an all-time high at the end of World War II. Budget surpluses and rapid economic growth lowered the debt-to-GDP ratio through 1974. Small deficits increased the debt-to-GDP ratio slightly through the 1970s, and large deficits increased it dramatically during the 1980s and through the 1990–1991 recession. The growth rate of the debt-to-GDP ratio slowed as the economy expanded during the mid-1990s and began to fall when the government budget went into surplus in the late 1990s.

Debt and Capital Businesses and individuals incur debts to buy capital — assets that yield a return. In fact, the main point of debt is to enable people to buy assets that will earn a return that exceeds the

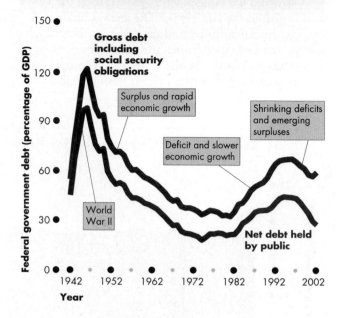

Gross and net government debt (the accumulation of past budget deficits less past budget surpluses) was at its highest at the end of World War II. Debt as a percentage of GDP fell through 1974 but then started to increase. After a further brief decline during the late 1970s, it exploded during the 1980s and continued to increase through 1995, after which it began to fall.

Source: Budget of the United States Government, Fiscal Year 2003, Table 7.1, Federal Debt.

interest paid on the debt. The government is similar to individuals and businesses in this regard. Much government expenditure is on public assets that yield a return. Highways, major irrigation schemes, public schools and universities, public libraries, and the stock of national defense capital all yield a social rate of return that probably far exceeds the interest rate the government pays on its debt.

But total government debt, which is almost $6 trillion, is more than four times the value of the public capital stock. So some government debt has been incurred to finance public consumption expenditure and transfer payments, which do not have a social return. Future generations bear the cost of this debt.

How does the U.S. government budget balance compare with those in other countries?

The U.S. Government Budget in Global Perspective

Figure 26.5 places the U.S. government budget in a global perspective in 2001. In that year, almost all countries had budget deficits. Summing the deficits of all the governments, the world as a whole had a deficit of 1.5 percent of world GDP — a total government deficit of about $700 billion.

The government of Japan had the largest deficit, as a percentage of GDP. The developing countries also had large deficits on the average. Of the other advanced industrial countries, Italy and France had the largest deficits. Germany and the entire European Union also had deficits.

The few surpluses were in the newly industrialized economies of Asia (Hong Kong, Korea, Singapore, and Taiwan), the United Kingdom, Canada, and the United States. And Canada and the United States had the largest surpluses.

State and Local Budgets

The *total government* sector of the United States includes state and local governments as well as the federal government. In 2001, when federal government expenditures were $1,900 billion, state and local expenditures were almost $1,300 billion. Most of these expenditures were on public schools, colleges, and universities ($480 billion), local police and fire services, and roads.

It is the total government sector that influences the aggregate economy. But state and local budgets are not designed, as the federal budget is, with the specific goal of stabilizing the aggregate economy. Sometimes, when the aggregate economy needs an injection of additional expenditures, state and local governments cut their expenditures and deficits. Such changes in expenditures occurred during the 1990–1991 recession when many states both cut their expenditures and increased taxes.

FIGURE 26.5 Government Budgets Around the World in 2001

Governments in most countries had budget deficits in 2001. The largest ones were in Japan, followed by the developing countries, Italy, and France. The United States, Canada, and a few other economies had surpluses.

Source: World Economic Outlook, October 2001 (Washington, D.C.: International Monetary Fund).

Now that you know what the federal budget is and what the main items of revenue and expenditure are, it is time to study the *effects* of fiscal policy. We'll begin by learning about its effects on expenditure plans when the price level is fixed. You will see that fiscal policy has multiplier effects like the expenditure multipliers explained in Chapter 25. Then we'll study the influences of fiscal policy on both aggregate demand and aggregate supply and look at its short-run and long-run effects on real GDP and the price level.

Fiscal Policy Multipliers

FISCAL POLICY ACTIONS CAN EITHER BE AUTO-matic or discretionary. **Automatic fiscal policy** is a change in fiscal policy that is triggered by the state of the economy. For example, an increase in unemployment triggers an *automatic* increase in payments to the unemployed. A fall in incomes triggers an *automatic* decrease in tax revenues. That is, this type of fiscal policy adjusts automatically. **Discretionary fiscal policy** is a policy action that is initiated by an act of Congress. It requires a change in tax laws or in some spending program. For example, an increase in the income tax rate and an increase in defense spending are discretionary fiscal policy actions. That is, discretionary fiscal policy is a deliberate policy action.

We begin by studying the effects of *discretionary* changes in government spending and taxes. To focus on the essentials, we'll initially study a model economy that is simpler than the one in which we live. In our model economy, there is no international trade and the taxes are all lump sum. **Lump-sum taxes** are taxes that do not vary with real GDP. The government fixes them, and they change when the government changes them. But they do not vary automatically with the state of the economy.

The main example of a lump-sum tax is the *property tax*. This tax varies across individuals and depends on the value of the property a person occupies. But unlike the income tax, it does not change simply because a person's income changes.

We use lump-sum taxes in our model economy because they make the principles we are studying easier to understand. Once we've grasped the principles, we'll explore our real economy with its international trade and income taxes — taxes that *do* vary with real GDP.

Like our real economy, the model economy we study is bombarded by spending fluctuations. Business investment in new building, plant and equipment, and inventories fluctuates because of swings in profit expectations and interest rates. These fluctuations set up multiplier effects that begin a recession or an expansion. If a recession takes hold, unemployment increases and incomes fall. If an expansion becomes too strong, inflationary pressures build up. To minimize the effects of these swings in spending, the government might change either its purchases of goods and services or taxes. By changing either of these items, the government can influence aggregate expenditure and real GDP. But it also changes its budget deficit or surplus. An alternative fiscal policy action is to change both purchases and taxes together so that the budget balance does not change. We are going to study the initial effects of these discretionary fiscal policy actions in the very short run when the price level is fixed. Each of these actions creates a multiplier effect on real GDP. These multipliers are

■ The government purchases multiplier
■ The lump-sum tax multiplier

The Government Purchases Multiplier

The **government purchases multiplier** is the magnification effect of a change in government purchases of goods and services on equilibrium aggregate expenditure and real GDP.

Government purchases are a component of aggregate expenditure. So when government purchases change, aggregate expenditure and real GDP change. The change in real GDP induces a change in consumption expenditure, which brings a further change in aggregate expenditure. A multiplier process ensues. This multiplier process is like the one described in Chapter 25 (pp. 586–589). Let's look at an example.

Cape Canaveral Multiplier Before the National Aeronautics and Space Administration (NASA) built a major spacecraft-launching facility at Cape Canaveral in Florida in the 1960s, the Cape was a quiet place. The injection of government purchases to build the launching and research facility created jobs in the region. Because construction workers and NASA workers spent most of their incomes locally, consumption expenditure increased. Retail stores and hotels and motels opened and hired yet more people and, in the process, created yet bigger incomes. These incomes were also spent in the area, so spending and incomes rose still further. Eventually, expenditures and incomes stopped rising but remained at their new higher levels.

The Size of the Multiplier Table 26.2 illustrates the government purchases multiplier with a numerical example. The first data column lists various possible levels of real GDP. Our task is to find equilibrium expenditure and the change in real GDP when government purchases change. The second column

TABLE 26.2   The Government Purchases Multiplier

	Real GDP (Y)	Taxes (T)	Disposable income (Y – T)	Consumption expenditure (C)	Investment (I)	Initial government purchases (G)	Initial aggregate planned expenditure (AE = C + I + G)	New government purchases (G')	New aggregate planned expenditure (AE' = C + I + G')
					(trillions of dollars)				
A	9	2	7	5.25	2	2	9.25	2.5	9.75
B	10	2	8	6.00	2	2	10.00	2.5	10.50
C	11	2	9	6.75	2	2	10.75	2.5	11.25
D	12	2	10	7.50	2	2	11.50	2.5	12.00
E	13	2	11	8.25	2	2	12.25	2.5	12.75

shows taxes. They are fixed at $2 trillion, regardless of the level of real GDP. (This is an assumption that keeps your attention on the key idea and makes the calculations easier to do.) The third column calculates disposable income. Because taxes are a lump sum, disposable income equals real GDP minus the $2 trillion of taxes. For example, in row B, real GDP is $10 trillion and disposable income is $8 trillion. The next column shows consumption expenditure. In this example, the *marginal propensity to consume* is 0.75. That is, a $1 increase in disposable income brings a 75-cent increase in consumption expenditure. Check this fact by calculating the increase in consumption expenditure when disposable income increases by $1 trillion from row B to row C. Consumption expenditure increases by $0.75 trillion. The next column shows investment, which is a constant of $2 trillion. The next column shows the initial level of government purchases, which is $2 trillion. Aggregate planned expenditure is the sum of consumption expenditure, investment, and government purchases.

Equilibrium expenditure and real GDP occur when aggregate planned expenditure equals actual expenditure. In this example, equilibrium expenditure is $10 trillion (highlighted in row B of the table.)

The final two columns of the table show what happens when government purchases increase by $0.5 trillion, to $2.5 trillion. Aggregate planned expenditure increases by $0.5 trillion at each level of real GDP. At the initial real GDP of $10 trillion (row B), aggregate planned expenditure increases to $10.5 trillion.

Because aggregate planned expenditure now exceeds real GDP, inventories decrease and firms increase production. Output, incomes, and expenditure increase. Increased incomes induce a further increase in expenditure. But the induced increase in aggregate planned expenditure is less than the increase in income, and eventually, a new equilibrium is reached. The new equilibrium is at a real GDP of $12 trillion (highlighted in row D).

A $0.5 trillion increase in government purchases has increased equilibrium expenditure and real GDP by $2 trillion. So the government purchases multiplier is 4. The size of the multiplier depends on the marginal propensity to consume, which in this example is 0.75. The following formula shows the connection between the government purchases multiplier and the marginal propensity to consume (MPC):

$$\text{Government purchases multiplier} = \frac{1}{1 - MPC}.$$

Let's check this formula by using the numbers in the above example. The marginal propensity to consume is 0.75, so the government purchases multiplier is 4.

Figure 26.6 illustrates the government purchases multiplier. Initially, aggregate planned expenditure is shown by the curve labeled AE_0. The points on this curve, labeled A through E, correspond with the rows of Table 26.2. This aggregate expenditure curve intersects the 45° line at the equilibrium level of real GDP, which is $10 trillion.

When government purchases increase by $0.5 trillion, the aggregate expenditure curve shifts

FIGURE 26.6   The Government
Purchases Multiplier

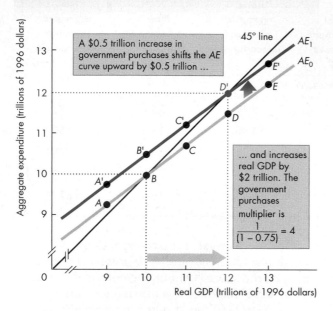

Initially, the aggregate expenditure curve is AE_0, and real GDP is $10 trillion (at point B). An increase in government purchases of $0.5 trillion increases aggregate planned expenditure at each level of real GDP by $0.5 trillion. The aggregate expenditure curve shifts upward from AE_0 to AE_1 — a parallel shift.

At the initial real GDP of $10 trillion, aggregate planned expenditure is now $10.5 trillion. Because aggregate planned expenditure is greater than real GDP, inventories are run down, firms increase production, and real GDP increases.

The new equilibrium is reached when real GDP is $12 trillion — the point at which the AE_1 curve intersects the 45° line (at point D'). In this example, the government purchases multiplier is 4.

upward by that amount to AE_1. With this new aggregate expenditure curve, equilibrium real GDP increases to $12 trillion. The increase in real GDP is 4 times the increase in government purchases. The government purchases multiplier is 4.

You've seen that in the very short term, when the price level is fixed, an increase in government purchases increases real GDP. But to produce more output, more people must be employed, so in the short term, an increase in government purchases can create jobs.

Increasing its purchases of goods and services is one way in which the government can try to stimulate the economy. A second way is to increase real GDP in the very short run is by decreasing lump-sum taxes. Let's see how this action works.

The Lump-Sum Tax Multiplier

The **lump-sum tax multiplier** is the magnification effect of a change in lump-sum taxes on equilibrium aggregate expenditure and real GDP. An *increase* in taxes *decreases* disposable income, which *decreases* consumption expenditure. The amount by which consumption expenditure initially changes is determined by the marginal propensity to consume. In our example, the marginal propensity to consume is 0.75, so a $1 tax cut increases disposable income by $1 and increases aggregate expenditure initially by 75 cents.

This initial change in aggregate expenditure has a multiplier just like the government purchases multiplier. We've seen that the government purchases multiplier is $1/(1 - MPC)$. Because a tax *increase* leads to a *decrease* in expenditure, the lump-sum tax multiplier is *negative*. And because a change in lump-sum taxes changes aggregate expenditure initially by only MPC multiplied by the tax change, the lump-sum tax multiplier is

$$\text{Lump-sum tax multiplier} = \frac{-MPC}{1-MPC}.$$

In our example, the marginal propensity to consume is 0.75, so the lump-sum tax multiplier is

$$\text{Lump-sum taxes multiplier} = \frac{-\dfrac{3}{4}}{1 - \dfrac{3}{4}} = -3.$$

Figure 26.7 illustrates the lump-sum tax multiplier. Initially, the aggregate expenditure curve is AE_0 and equilibrium expenditure is $10 trillion. Taxes increase by $1 trillion, and disposable income falls by that amount. With a marginal propensity to consume of 0.75, aggregate expenditure decreases initially by $0.75 trillion and the aggregate expenditure curve shifts downward by that amount to AE_1. Equilibrium expenditure and real GDP fall by $3 trillion, to $7 trillion. The lump-sum tax multiplier is –3.

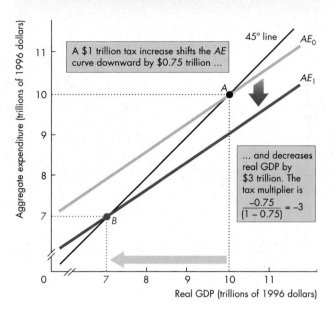

FIGURE 26.7   The Lump-Sum Tax Multiplier

A $1 trillion tax increase shifts the *AE* curve downward by $0.75 trillion ...

... and decreases real GDP by $3 trillion. The tax multiplier is $\dfrac{-0.75}{(1-0.75)} = -3$

Initially, the aggregate expenditure curve is AE_0 and equilibrium expenditure is $10 trillion. The marginal propensity to consume is 0.75. An increase in lump-sum taxes of $1 trillion decreases disposable income by $1 trillion. The decrease in aggregate expenditure is found by multiplying this change in disposable income by the marginal propensity to consume and is $1 trillion $\times$ 0.75 = $0.75 trillion. The aggregate expenditure curve shifts *downward* by this amount to AE_1. Equilibrium expenditure decreases by $3 trillion, from $10 trillion to $7 trillion. The lump-sum tax multiplier is –3.

Lump-Sum Transfer Payments The lump-sum tax multiplier also tells us the effects of a change in lump-sum transfer payments. Transfer payments are like negative taxes, so an increase in transfer payments works like a decrease in taxes. Because the tax multiplier is negative, a decrease in taxes increases expenditure. An increase in transfer payments also increases expenditure. So the lump-sum transfer payments multiplier is positive. It is

$$\text{Lump-sum transfer payments multiplier} = \frac{MPC}{1-MPC}.$$

Induced Taxes and Entitlement Spending

In the examples we've studied so far, taxes are lump-sum taxes. But in reality, net taxes (taxes minus transfer payments) vary with the state of the economy.

On the revenue side of the budget, tax laws define tax *rates* to be paid, not tax *dollars* to be paid. Tax *dollars* paid depend on tax *rates* and incomes. But incomes vary with real GDP, so tax *revenues* depend on real GDP. Taxes that vary with real GDP are called **induced taxes.** When the economy expands, induced taxes increase because real GDP increases. When the economy is in a recession, induced taxes decrease because real GDP decreases.

On the outlay side of the budget, the government creates programs that entitle suitably qualified people and businesses to receive benefits. The spending on such programs is called **entitlement spending,** and it results in transfer payments that depend on the economic state of individual citizens and businesses. When the economy is in a recession, unemployment is high, the number of people, firms, and farms experiencing economic hardship increases. Entitlement spending increases. When the economy expands, entitlement spending decreases.

Induced taxes and entitlement payments decrease the multiplier effects of changes in government purchases and lump-sum taxes. The reason is that they weaken the link between real GDP and disposable income and so dampen the effect of a change in real GDP on consumption expenditure. When real GDP increases, induced taxes increase and entitlement payments decrease, so disposable income does not increase by as much as the increase in real GDP. As a result, consumption expenditure does not increase by as much as it otherwise would have done and the multiplier effect is reduced.

The extent to which induced taxes and entitlement payments decrease the multiplier depends on the *marginal tax rate*. The marginal tax rate is the proportion of an additional dollar of real GDP that flows to the government in net taxes (taxes minus transfer payments). The higher the marginal tax rate, the larger is the proportion of an additional dollar of real GDP that is paid to the government and the smaller is the induced change in consumption expenditure. The smaller the change in consumption expenditure induced by a change in real GDP, the smaller is the multiplier effect of a change in government purchases or lump-sum taxes.

International Trade and Fiscal Policy Multipliers

Not all expenditure in the United States is on U.S.-produced goods and services. Some of it is on imports — on foreign-produced goods and services. Imports affect the fiscal policy multipliers in the same way that they influence the investment multiplier, as explained in Chapter 25 (see pp. 588–591). The extent to which an additional dollar of real GDP is spent on imports is determined by the *marginal propensity to import*. Expenditure on imports does not generate U.S. real GDP and does not lead to an increase in U.S. consumption expenditure. The larger the marginal propensity to import, the smaller are the government purchases and lump-sum tax multipliers.

The math note on pp. 624–625 explains the details of the effects of induced taxes and transfer payments and imports on the fiscal policy multipliers.

So far, we've studied *discretionary* fiscal policy. Let's now look at *automatic* stabilizers.

Automatic Stabilizers

Automatic stabilizers are mechanisms that stabilize real GDP without explicit action by the government. Their name is borrowed from engineering and conjures up images of shock absorbers, thermostats, and sophisticated devices that keep airplanes and ships steady in turbulent air and seas. But automatic fiscal stabilizers do not actually stabilize. They just make the fluctuations less severe. These stabilizers operate because income taxes and transfer payments fluctuate with real GDP. If real GDP begins to decrease, tax revenues fall and transfer payments rise and the government's budget deficit changes. Let's look at the budget deficit over the business cycle.

Budget Deficit Over the Business Cycle   Figure 26.8 shows the business cycle and fluctuations in the budget deficit between 1981 and 2001. Part (a) shows the fluctuations of real GDP around potential GDP. Part (b) shows the federal budget deficit. Both parts highlight recessions by shading those periods. By comparing the two parts of the figure, you can see the relationship between the business cycle and the budget deficit. As a rule, when the economy is in an expansion the budget deficit declines. (In the figure, a declining deficit means a deficit that is getting closer to zero.) As the expansion slows before the recession begins, the budget deficit increases. It continues to

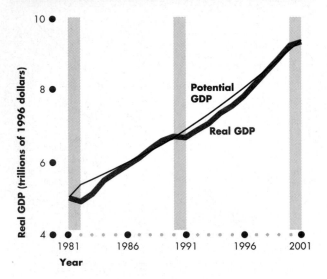

FIGURE 26.8   The Business Cycle and the Budget Deficit

(a) Growth and recessions

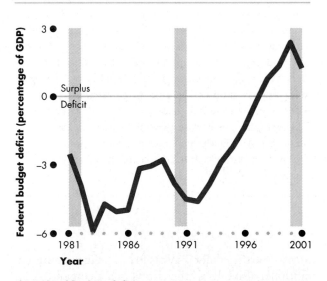

(b) Federal budget deficit

As real GDP fluctuates around potential GDP (part a), the budget deficit fluctuates (part b). During a recession (shaded years), tax revenues decrease, transfer payments increase, and the budget deficit increases. The deficit also increases *before* a recession as real GDP growth slows and *after* a recession before real GDP growth speeds up.

Sources: Figure 5.11(a) and Figure 26.2.

increase during the recession and for a period after the recession is over. Then, when the expansion is well under way, the budget deficit declines again.

The budget deficit fluctuates with the business cycle because both tax revenues and expenditures fluctuate with real GDP. As real GDP increases during an expansion, tax revenues increase and transfer payments decrease, so the budget deficit automatically decreases. As real GDP decreases during a recession, tax revenues decrease and transfer payments increase, so the budget deficit automatically increases.

Fluctuations in investment and exports have a multiplier effect on real GDP. But fluctuations in tax revenues (and the budget deficit) act as an automatic stabilizer. They decrease the swings in disposable income and make the multiplier effect smaller. They dampen both expansions and recessions.

Cyclical and Structural Balances   Because the government budget balance fluctuates with the business cycle, we need a method of measuring the balance that tells us whether it is a temporary cyclical phenomenon or a persistent phenomenon. A temporary and cyclical surplus or deficit vanishes when full employment returns. A persistent surplus or deficit requires government action to remove it.

To determine whether the budget balance is persistent or temporary and cyclical, economists have developed the concepts of the structural budget balance and the cyclical budget balance. The **structural surplus or deficit** is the budget balance that would occur if the economy were at full employment and real GDP were equal to potential GDP. The **cyclical surplus or deficit** is the actual surplus or deficit minus the structural surplus or deficit. That is, the cyclical surplus or deficit is the part of the budget balance that arises purely because real GDP does not equal potential GDP.

For example, suppose that the budget deficit is $100 billion. And suppose that economists have determined that there is a structural deficit of $25 billion. Then there is a cyclical deficit of $75 billion.

Figure 26.9 illustrates the concepts of the cyclical surplus or deficit and the structural surplus or deficit. The blue curve shows government expenditures. The expenditures curve slopes downward because transfer payments, a component of government expenditures, decreases as real GDP increases. The green curve shows tax revenues. The tax revenues curve slopes upward because most components of tax revenues increase as incomes and real GDP increase.

FIGURE 26.9   Cyclical and Structural Surpluses and Deficits

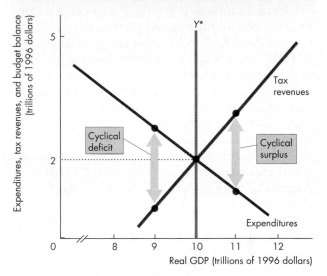

(a) Cyclical deficit and cyclical surplus

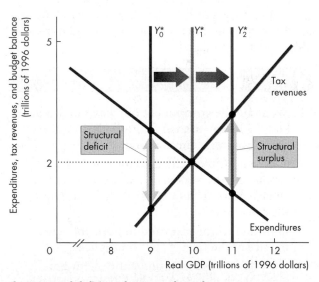

(b) Structural deficit and structural surplus

In part (a), potential GDP is $10 trillion. When real GDP is less than potential GDP, the budget is in a *cyclical deficit*. When real GDP exceeds potential GDP, the budget is in a *cyclical surplus*. The government has a *balanced budget* when real GDP equals potential GDP.

In part (b), when potential GDP is $9 trillion, there is a *structural deficit*. But when potential GDP is $11 trillion, there is a *structural surplus*.

In Fig. 26.9(a), potential GDP is $10 trillion. If real GDP equals potential GDP, the government has a *balanced budget*. Expenditures and tax revenues each equal $2 trillion. If real GDP is less than potential GDP, expenditures exceed tax revenues and there is a *cyclical deficit*. If real GDP is greater than potential GDP, expenditures are less than tax revenues and there is a *cyclical surplus*.

In Fig. 26.9(b), potential GDP grows but the tax revenue curve and the expenditure curve do not change. When potential GDP is $9 trillion ($Y_0^*$), there is a *structural deficit*. When potential GDP grows to $10 trillion($Y_1^*$), there is a *structural balance* of zero (neither a deficit nor a surplus). And when potential GDP grows to $11 trillion($Y_2^*$), there is a *structural surplus*.

The U.S. federal budget was in a structural deficit starting in the mid-1970s and continuing through the mid-1990s. That is, even if the economy had been at full employment, the budget would have been in deficit. Worse, the structural deficit was so large that even at the peak of a business cycle, the budget was in deficit. The budget surplus that emerged at the end of the 1990s was at least partly a cyclical surplus and as the economy slowed during 2001, a deficit emerged.

REVIEW QUIZ

1 What are the government purchases multiplier and the lump-sum tax multiplier? How do these multiplier effects work?

2 Which multiplier effect is larger, that of a change in government purchases or that of a change in lump-sum taxes? Why is one larger than the other?

3 How do income taxes and imports influence the size of the fiscal policy multipliers?

4 How do income taxes and entitlement programs work as automatic stabilizers to dampen the business cycle?

5 How do we tell whether a budget deficit needs government action to remove it?

Your next task is to see how, with the passage of more time and with some price level adjustments, these multiplier effects change.

Fiscal Policy Multipliers and the Price Level

WE'VE SEEN HOW REAL GDP RESPONDS TO changes in fiscal policy when the price level is fixed and all the adjustments that take place are in spending, income, and production. The period over which this response occurs is very short. Once production starts to change, regardless of whether it increases or decreases, prices also start to change. The price level and real GDP change together, and the economy moves to a new short-run equilibrium.

To study the simultaneous changes in real GDP and the price level, we use the *AS-AD* model of Chapter 21. In the long run, both the price level and the money wage rate respond to fiscal policy. As these further changes take place, the economy gradually moves toward a new long-run equilibrium. We also use the *AS-AD* model to study these adjustments.

We begin by looking at the effects of fiscal policy on aggregate demand and the aggregate demand curve.

Fiscal Policy and Aggregate Demand

You learned about the relationship between aggregate demand, aggregate expenditure, and equilibrium expenditure in Chapter 25 (pp. 591–595). You are now going to use what you learned there to work out what happens to aggregate demand, the price level, real GDP, and jobs when fiscal policy changes. We'll start by looking at the effects of a change in fiscal policy on aggregate demand.

Figure 26.10 shows the effects of an increase in government purchases on aggregate demand. Initially, the aggregate expenditure curve is AE_0 in part (a), and the aggregate demand curve is AD_0 in part (b). The price level is 110, real GDP is $10 trillion, and the economy is at point A in both parts of the figure. Now suppose that the government increases its purchases by $0.5 trillion. At a constant price level of 110, the aggregate expenditure curve shifts upward to AE_1. This curve intersects the 45° line at an equilibrium expenditure of $12 trillion at point B. This amount is the aggregate quantity of goods and services demanded at a price level of 110, as shown by point B in part (b). Point B lies on a new aggregate demand curve. The aggregate demand curve has shifted rightward to AD_1.

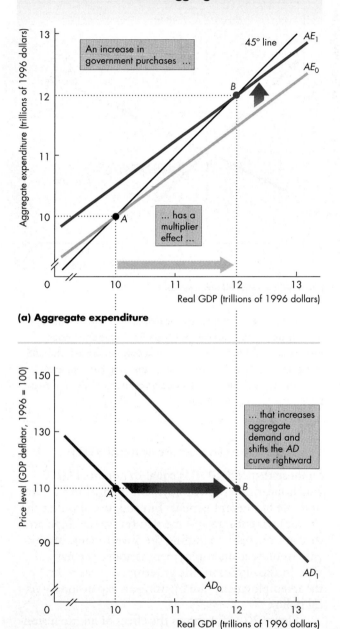

FIGURE 26.10 Government Purchases and Aggregate Demand

(a) Aggregate expenditure

(b) Aggregate demand

The price level is 110, aggregate planned expenditure is AE_0 (part a), and aggregate demand is AD_0 (part b). An increase in government purchases shifts the AE curve to AE_1 and increases equilibrium real GDP to $12 trillion. The aggregate demand curve shifts rightward to AD_1.

The government purchases multiplier determines the distance by which the aggregate demand curve shifts rightward. The larger the multiplier, the larger is the shift in the aggregate demand curve resulting from a given change in government purchases. In this example, a $0.5 trillion increase in government purchases produces a $2 trillion increase in the aggregate quantity of goods and services demanded at each price level. The multiplier is 4. So the $0.5 trillion increase in government purchases shifts the aggregate demand curve rightward by $2 trillion.

Figure 26.10 shows the effects of an increase in government purchases. But a similar effect occurs for *any* expansionary fiscal policy. An **expansionary fiscal policy** is an increase in government purchases or a decrease in taxes. But the distance of the aggregate demand curve shifts is smaller for a decrease in taxes than for an increase in government purchases of the same size.

Figure 26.10 can also be used to illustrate the effects of a **contractionary fiscal policy** — a decrease in government purchases or an increase in taxes. In this case, start at point B in each part of the figure and decrease government purchases or increase taxes. Aggregate demand decreases and the aggregate demand curve shifts from AD_1 to AD_0.

Equilibrium GDP and the Price Level in the Short Run We've seen how an increase in government purchases increases aggregate demand. Let's now see how it changes real GDP and the price level. Figure 26.11(a) describes the economy. Aggregate demand is AD_0, and the short-run aggregate supply curve is *SAS*. (Check back to Chapter 21, pp. 477–480, to refresh your understanding of the *SAS* curve.) Equilibrium is at point A, where the aggregate demand and short-run aggregate supply curves intersect. The price level is 110, and real GDP is $10 trillion.

An increase in government purchases of $0.5 trillion shifts the aggregate demand curve rightward from AD_0 to AD_1. While the price level is fixed at 110, the economy moves toward point B and real GDP increases toward $12 trillion. But during the adjustment process, the price level does not remain constant. It gradually rises, and the economy moves along the short-run aggregate supply curve to the point of intersection of the short-run aggregate supply curve and the new aggregate demand curve — point C. The price level rises to 123, and real GDP increases to only $11.3 trillion.

FIGURE 26.11 Fiscal Policy, Real GDP, and the Price Level

(a) Fiscal policy with unemployment

(b) Fiscal policy with full employment

An increase in government purchases shifts the AD curve from AD_0 to AD_1 (part a). With a fixed price level, the economy would have moved to point B. But the price level rises, and in the short run, the economy moves to point C. The price level increases to 123, and real GDP increases to $11.3 trillion.

At point C, real GDP exceeds potential GDP and unemployment is below the natural rate (part b). The money wage rate rises, and short-run aggregate supply decreases. The SAS curve shifts leftward to SAS_1, and in the long run, the economy moves to point A'. The price level rises to 150, and real GDP returns to $10 trillion.

When we take the price level effect into account, the increase in government purchases still has a multiplier effect on real GDP, but the effect is smaller than it would be if the price level remained constant. Also, the steeper the slope of the short-run aggregate supply curve, the larger is the increase in the price level, the smaller is the increase in real GDP, and the smaller is the government purchases multiplier. But the multiplier is not zero.

In the long run, real GDP equals potential GDP — the economy is at full-employment equilibrium. When real GDP equals potential GDP, an increase in aggregate demand has the same short-run effect as we've just worked out, but its long-run effect is different. The increase in aggregate demand raises the price level but leaves real GDP unchanged at potential GDP.

To study this case, let's see what happens if the government embarks on an expansionary fiscal policy when real GDP equals potential GDP.

Fiscal Expansion at Potential GDP

Suppose that real GDP is equal to potential GDP, which means that unemployment is equal to the natural rate of unemployment. But suppose also that the unemployment rate and the natural rate are high and that most people, including the government, mistakenly think that unemployment is above the natural rate. In this situation, the government tries to lower the unemployment rate by using an expansionary fiscal policy.

Figure 26.11(b) shows the effect of an expansionary fiscal policy when real GDP equals potential GDP. In this example, potential GDP is $10 trillion. Aggregate demand increases, and the aggregate demand curve shifts rightward from AD_0 to AD_1. The short-run equilibrium, point C, is an above full-employment equilibrium. Now the money wage rate begins to rise, and short-run aggregate supply decreases. The SAS curve shifts leftward from SAS_0 to SAS_1. The economy moves up along the aggregate demand curve AD_1 toward point A'.

When all the wage and price adjustments have occurred, the price level is 150 and real GDP is again at potential GDP of $10 trillion. The multiplier is zero. There has been only a temporary increase in real GDP, but a permanent rise in the price level.

Limitations of Fiscal Policy

Because the short-run fiscal policy multipliers are not zero, expansionary fiscal policy can be used to increase real GDP and decrease the unemployment rate in a recession. Contractionary fiscal policy can also be used, if the economy is overheating, to decrease real GDP and help to keep inflation in check. But two factors limit the use of fiscal policy.

First, the legislative process is slow, which means that it is difficult to take fiscal policy actions in a timely way. The economy might be able to benefit from fiscal stimulation right now, but it will take Congress many months, perhaps more than a year, to act. By the time the action is taken, the economy might need an entirely different fiscal medicine. Most economists think that the 2002 stimulus package illustrates this problem. The economy went into recession in March 2001 and it was not until March 2002 that the long debated stimulus package was eventually signed into law.

Second, potential GDP (and the related natural rate of unemployment) are not known with much precision. So fiscal stimulation might occur too close to full employment, in which case it will increase the price level and push the inflation rate upward.

REVIEW QUIZ

1 How do changes the price level influence the multiplier effects of fiscal policy on real GDP?
2 What are the long-run effects of fiscal policy on real GDP and the price level when real GDP equals potential GDP?

So far, we've ignored any potential effects of fiscal policy on aggregate supply. Yet many economists believe that the supply-side effects of fiscal policy are the biggest. Let's now look at these effects.

Supply-Side Effects of Fiscal Policy

FISCAL POLICY HAS IMPORTANT EFFECTS ON THE supply side of the economy that we'll now examine. In particular, we'll look at its effects on

- Potential GDP
- Economic growth

Fiscal Policy and Potential GDP

Potential GDP depends on the full-employment quantity of labor (see Chapter 22, pp. 510–512). Income taxes — taxes on labor income — influence potential GDP and aggregate supply by changing the full-employment quantity of labor. The income tax weakens the incentive to work and drives a wedge between the take-home wage of workers and the cost of labor to firms. The result is a smaller quantity of labor and a lower potential GDP.

Taxes and the Labor Market Figure 26.12 shows a labor market. The demand for labor is LD, and the supply of labor is LS. With no income tax, the real wage rate is $30 an hour and 250 billion hours of labor per year are employed.

An income tax weakens the incentive to work and decreases the supply of labor. The reason is that for each dollar of before-tax earnings, workers must pay the government an amount determined by the income tax code. So workers look at the after-tax wage rate when they decide how much labor to supply.

When an income tax is imposed, the supply curve shifts leftward to $LS + tax$. The amount of income tax payable is measured by the vertical distance between the LS curve and the $LS + tax$ curve. With this smaller supply of labor, the *before-tax* wage rate rises to $35 an hour, but the *after-tax* wage rate falls to $20 an hour.

The quantity of labor employed decreases to 200 billion hours a year. Because the quantity of labor decreases, so does potential GDP.

In this example, the tax rate is high — $15 tax on a $35 wage rate, about 43 percent. A lower tax rate would have a smaller negative effect on employment and potential GDP. And a tax cut would increase the supply of labor, increase equilibrium employment, and increase potential GDP.

FIGURE 26.12   The Income Tax in the Labor Market

The demand for labor curve is *LD*, and the supply of labor curve is *LS*. With no income tax, the real wage rate is $30 an hour and employment is 250 billion hours. An income tax shifts the supply of labor curve leftward to *LS + tax*. The before-tax wage rate rises to $35 an hour, the after-tax wage rate falls to $20 an hour, and the quantity of labor employed decreases. With less labor, potential GDP falls.

FIGURE 26.13   Two Views of the Supply-Side Effects of Fiscal Policy

A tax cut increases aggregate demand and shifts the *AD* curve from AD_0 to AD_1. If the supply-side effect of the tax cut is small, the *SAS* curve shifts from SAS_0 to SAS_1. Real GDP increases and the price level rises. If the supply-side effect of a tax cut is large, the *SAS* curve shifts to SAS_2. Real GDP increases, and the price level remains constant. A larger supply-side effect might lower the price level.

Supply Effects and Demand Effects We can combine these supply effects with the demand effects of fiscal policy in the previous section. A tax cut increases aggregate demand. But it increases the incentive to work, so it also increases potential GDP and aggregate supply. The resulting changes in real GDP and the price level depend on the relative strengths of the demand and supply effects.

Figure 26.13 shows the possibilities. If a tax cut has a small supply-side effect, the short-run aggregate supply curve shifts to SAS_1. The increase in aggregate demand exceeds the increase in short-run aggregate supply. The price level rises and real GDP increases. But the price level rises by *less* and real GDP increases by *more* than would occur if there were no supply-side effects.

If a tax cut has a large supply-side effect, the short-run aggregate supply curve shifts to SAS_2. In this particular case, the increase in aggregate supply equals the increase in aggregate demand. So the price level remains constant and real GDP increases by

a large amount. A yet larger increase in aggregate supply would have brought a fall in the price level.

The general point is that a tax cut that strengthens incentives increases real GDP by more than an equal-size expansionary fiscal policy that does not change incentives or that weakens them.

Fiscal Policy and Economic Growth

Fiscal policy can influence economic growth by changing the incentive to save, invest in new capital, and develop the new technologies. These incentive effects work similarly to those that you've just examined in the labor market. The higher the income tax rate, other things remaining the same, the smaller is the quantity of saving and investment and the fewer are the resources devoted to innovation. So high income taxes can slow the pace of capital accumulation and technological change, and slow the growth rate of potential GDP. And a tax cut can strengthen these incentives and speed economic growth.

Second, fiscal policy can influence economic growth and the well-being of future generations by crowding out investment and by increasing foreign debt. Less investment means a smaller capital stock and smaller output both in the present and future. Increased foreign debt means larger interest payments to the rest of the world stretching out into the future.

Figure 26.14 (based on Fig. 23.14, p. 541) shows the effects in the capital market if the government increases purchases or cuts taxes. Investment demand is ID. Initially, the real interest rate, which is determined in the global market for financial capital, is R_0 and saving supply is SS_0. Investment is $1.5 trillion, saving is $1 trillion, and international borrowing, borrowing from the rest of the world, is $0.5 trillion.

Now the government tries to stimulate aggregate demand by increasing its purchases and/or by cutting taxes. These actions decrease government saving and the saving supply curve shifts leftward to SS_1.

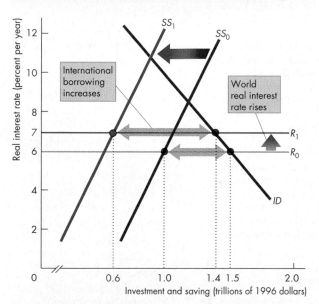

FIGURE 26.14 Crowding Out and International Borrowing

Investment demand is ID. Initially, saving supply is SS_0 and the world real interest rate is R_0. Investment is $1.5 trillion, saving is $1 trillion, and international borrowing is $0.5 trillion. A fiscal stimulus package decreases government saving and shifts the saving supply curve leftward to SS_1. Lower U.S. saving lowers global saving, increases the world real interest rate and crowds out some investment. Foreign borrowing increases.

What happens next depends on the strength of the Ricardo-Barro effect (see pp. 539–540). If that effect is strong, private saving changes to offset the change in government saving and the fiscal policy action has no effect in the capital markets. But this outcome is extreme and, most economists believe, unlikely.

More likely is that the decrease in government saving decreases national saving, so the new saving supply curve lies between SS_1 and SS_0.

Because the United States is a large part of the global economy, the decrease in U.S. saving decreases world saving by an amount that is sufficient to increase the world real interest rate. In Fig. 26.14, the world real interest rate rises to 7 percent, shown by the line R_1. The higher interest rate crowds out some U.S. investment, which falls to $1.4 trillion. The higher interest rate also induces a small increase in national saving. But international borrowing increases.

The increase in international borrowing means that U.S. residents incur an increased international debt and must commit to higher annual interest payments to the rest of the world. For the United States, the burden of international debt is not currently a serious problem. But it could become serious if it were to persist. For some countries, such as Argentina, the problem is overwhelming.

REVIEW QUIZ

1 How does the income tax affect potential GDP?
2 Because a tax cut increases both aggregate supply and aggregate demand, can we tell whether it increases or decreases real GDP and the price level?
3 How does an increase in government purchases or a tax cut change investment, international borrowing, and the well-being of future generations?

◆ You've seen how fiscal policy influences the way real GDP fluctuates around its trend and how it influences potential GDP. *Reading Between the Lines* on pp. 622–623 looks further at the 2003 budget and President Bush's fiscal policy. Your next task is to study the other main arm of macroeconomic policy: monetary policy. We begin in the next chapter by describing the monetary system of a modern economy.

A Budget Deficit in Fiscal 2003

THE BOSTON GLOBE, JANUARY 12, 2002

White House Sees Red on Horizon

President Bush will propose a federal deficit for the coming fiscal year while the government focuses on defense, homeland security, and the economy, the White House budget director said yesterday.

In an interview, budget chief Mitchell Daniels used no dollar figure, but said the shortfall would be less than 1 percent the size of the US economy. Since the economy is about $10 trillion, that suggests a deficit of about $100 billion or less.

"The budget we propose, because it fights a war, addresses our emergency, and will propose a growth package to combat recession, will be very slightly in deficit," Daniels said.

Bush said earlier this week that his election-year budget may not be balanced. Analysts of both parties have predicted red ink.

Daniels said Bush would propose big spending increases for the Pentagon and a roughly $15 billion boost — about double this year's total — for domestic security programs like public health, airline safety, and local law enforcement. There also will be an economic stimulus package of tax cuts and unemployment aid similar to the GOP plan that died in the Senate last month, Daniels said.

...

Democrats have blamed the $1.35 trillion, 10-year tax cut that Bush pushed through Congress last spring for the budget's crashing return to deficits, while Republicans have pointed to the recession and the costs of battling terrorism.

...

Bush will send his budget to Congress on Feb. 4. His fiscal 2003 spending plan, for the year starting Oct. 1, will be the first to exceed $2 trillion, as well as the first to forecast a deficit since the budget President Clinton proposed in February 1997.

Essence of the Story

■ President Bush will send his fiscal 2003 budget to Congress on February 4, 2002.

■ The 2003 budget will be the first ever to exceed $2 trillion, and the first deficit budget — estimated at $100 billion — since 1997.

■ The administration said that it would be a budget to fight a war, address a national emergency, stimulate growth, and combat recession.

■ Defense spending would increase by $15 billion, and spending on domestic security programs, public health, airline safety, and local law enforcement would all increase.

■ Tax cuts would stimulate the economy.

■ Democrats said that the deficit arose from the $1.35 trillion, 10-year tax cut enacted by Congress in 2001 rather than recession and the costs of fighting terrorism.

Economic Analysis

■ We can interpret the proposed fiscal policy changes in the 2003 budget by using the aggregate expenditure model and the *AS-AD* model.

■ To determine the effects of the budget proposals on the *AE* curve and the *AD* curve, we must distinguish between induced changes and discretionary changes in tax revenues and expenditures.

■ Table 1 shows this breakdown for the changes in 2003.

■ Tax revenues are predicted to fall in 2003 by $120 billion and expenditures to rise by $17 billion because of the state of the economy — slower real GDP growth than previously expected. These are induced fiscal actions.

■ Legislation already passed by Congress was expected to lower tax revenues by $83 billion and increase expenditure by $62 billion in 2003.

■ The 2003 budget was expected to lower tax revenues by $73 billion and increase expenditures by $59 billion.

■ Democrats can use these numbers to support the claim that deficit arose from previously enacted tax cuts because the tax cuts of $83 billion almost equal the deficit of $80 billion. But without the spending increases and with the tax cuts, there would still be a deficit.

■ Figure 1 shows the effect of the 2003 budget on the *AE* curve and expenditure equilibrium. Without the 2003 discretionary fiscal actions, the *AE* curve would be AE_0. The 2003 budget changes increase aggregate planned expenditure, and the *AE* curve becomes AE_1.

Figure 1 Equilibrium expenditure

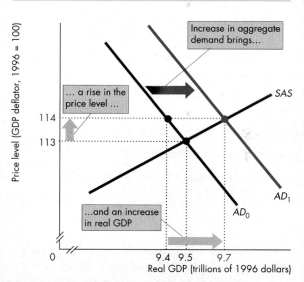

Figure 2 The 2003 budget and the *AD* curve

■ Figure 2 shows the effects on aggregate demand. The 2003 budget changes increase aggregate demand from AD_0 to AD_1.

■ Real GDP and the price level will be higher in 2003 than they would have been without the budget changes in taxes and expenditures. If real GDP exceeds potential GDP, inflation will occur.

■ Over the longer term, supply-side effects of the tax cuts might bring an increase in aggregate supply.

	Tax revenues	Expenditures	Surplus(+) Deficit(−)
		(billions of dollars)	
2002 baseline	2,324	1,990	334
Induced	−120	17	−137
Discretionary			
Past legislation	−83	62	−145
2003 budget	−73	59	−132
Total changes	−276	138	−414
2003 budget	2,048	2,128	−80

Table 1 2003 budget

623

Mathematical Note
The Algebra of the Fiscal Policy Multipliers

THIS MATHEMATICAL NOTE DERIVES FORMULAS FOR the fiscal policy multipliers. We begin by defining the symbols we need:

- Aggregate planned expenditure, AE
- Real GDP, Y
- Consumption expenditure, C
- Investment, I
- Government purchases, G
- Exports, X
- Imports, M
- Net taxes, T
- Autonomous consumption expenditure, a
- Lump-sum taxes, T_a
- Lump-sum transfer payments, T_r
- Marginal propensity to consume, b
- Marginal propensity to import, m
- Marginal tax rate, t
- Autonomous expenditure, A

Equilibrium Expenditure

Aggregate planned expenditure is

$$AE = C + I + G + X - M.$$

The consumption function is

$$C = a + b(Y - T).$$

Net taxes equals lump-sum taxes minus lump-sum transfer payments plus induced taxes, which is

$$T = T_a - T_r + tY.$$

Use the last equation in the consumption function to give consumption expenditure as a function of GDP:

$$C = a - bT_a + bT_r + b(1 - t)Y.$$

The import function is

$$M = mY.$$

Use the consumption function and the import function to replace C and M in the aggregate planned expenditure equation to obtain

$$AE = a - bT_a + bT_r + b(1-t)Y + I + G + Y - mY.$$

Collect the terms on the right side of the equation that involve Y to obtain

$$AE = [a - bT_a + bT_r + I + G + X] + [b(1 - t) - m]Y.$$

Autonomous expenditure (A) is given by

$$A = a - bT_a + bT_r + I + G + X.$$

So

$$AE = A + [b(1 - t) - m]Y.$$

Equilibrium expenditure occurs when aggregate planned expenditure (AE) equals real GDP (Y). That is,

$$AE = Y.$$

To calculate equilibrium expenditure, we solve the equation

$$Y = A + [b(1 - t) - m]Y$$

to obtain

$$Y = \frac{1}{1 - [b(1 - t) - m]}A.$$

Government Purchases Multiplier

The government purchases multiplier equals the change in equilibrium expenditure (Y) that results from a change in government purchases (G) divided by the change in government purchases. Because autonomous expenditure is equal to

$$A = a - bT_a + bT_r + I + G + X,$$

the change in autonomous expenditure equals the change in government purchases. That is,

$$\Delta A = \Delta G.$$

The government purchases multiplier is found by working out the change in Y that results from the change in A. You can see from the solution for Y that

$$\Delta Y = \frac{1}{1 - [b(1 - t) - m]}\Delta G.$$

The government purchases multiplier equals

$$\frac{1}{1 - [b(1 - t) - m]}.$$

In an economy in which $t = 0$ and $m = 0$, the government purchases multiplier is $1/(1 - b)$. With $b = 0.75$, the government purchases multiplier equals 4, as part (a) of the figure shows. Make up some examples and use the above formula to show how b, m, and t influence the government purchases multiplier.

Lump-Sum Tax Multiplier

The lump-sum tax multiplier equals the change in equilibrium expenditure (Y) that results from a change in lump-sum taxes (T_a) divided by the change in lump-sum taxes. Because autonomous expenditure is equal to

$$A = a - bT_a + bT_r + I + G + X,$$

the change in autonomous expenditure equals *minus b* multiplied by the change in lump-sum taxes. That is,

$$\Delta A = -b\Delta T_a.$$

You can see from the solution for equilibrium expenditure Y that

$$\Delta Y = \frac{-b}{1 - [b(1 - t) - m]}\Delta T_a.$$

The lump-sum tax multiplier equals

$$\frac{-b}{1 - [b(1 - t) - m]}.$$

In an economy in which $t = 0$ and $m = 0$, the lump-sum tax multiplier is $-b/(1 - b)$. With $b = 0.75$, the lump-sum tax multiplier equals -3, as part (b) of the figure shows. Make up some examples and use the above formula to show how b, m, and t influence the lump-sum tax multiplier.

Lump-Sum Transfer Payments Multiplier

The lump-sum transfer payments multiplier equals the change in equilibrium expenditure (Y) that results from a change in lump-sum transfer payments (T_r) divided by the change in lump-sum transfer payments. Because autonomous expenditure is equal to

$$A = a - bT_a + bT_r + I + G + X,$$

the change in lump-sum transfer payments changes autonomous expenditure such that

$$\Delta A = b\Delta T_r.$$

Because transfer payments are like negative taxes, the lump-sum transfer payments multiplier equals minus the lump-sum tax multiplier. The lump-sum transfer payments multiplier equals

$$\frac{b}{1 - [b(1 - t) - m]}.$$

In an economy in which $t = 0$ and $m = 0$, the lump-sum transfer payments multiplier is $b/(1 - b)$. With $b = 0.75$, the lump-sum transfer payments multiplier equals 3, as part (c) of the figure shows. Make up some examples and use the above formula to show how b, m, and t influence the lump-sum transfer payments multiplier.

(a) Government purchases multiplier

(b) Lump-sum tax multiplier

(c) Lump-sum transfer payments multiplier

SUMMARY

KEY POINTS

The Federal Budget (pp. 604–609)

- The federal budget finances the activities of the government and is used to stabilize real GDP.
- Federal tax revenues come from personal income taxes, social insurance taxes, corporate income taxes, and indirect taxes. Federal expenditures include transfer payments, purchases of goods and services, and debt interest.
- When tax revenues exceed government expenditures, the government has a budget surplus.

Fiscal Policy Multipliers (pp. 610–616)

- Fiscal policy actions are discretionary or automatic.
- Government purchases, taxes, and transfer payments have multiplier effects on real GDP.
- Induced taxes and transfer payments and imports make the fiscal policy multipliers smaller.
- Income taxes and entitlement payments act as automatic stabilizers.

Fiscal Policy Multipliers and the Price Level (pp. 616–619)

- An expansionary fiscal policy increases aggregate demand and shifts the aggregate demand curve rightward. It increases real GDP and raises the price level. (A contractionary fiscal policy has the opposite effects.)
- Price level changes dampen fiscal policy multiplier effects.
- At potential GDP, an expansionary fiscal policy raises the price level but leaves real GDP unchanged. The fiscal policy multipliers are zero.

Supply-Side Effects of Fiscal Policy (pp. 619–621)

- Fiscal policy has supply-side effects because the increases in taxes weaken the incentives to work, and decrease potential GDP.
- A tax cut increases both aggregate demand and aggregate supply. Real GDP increases, but the price level might rise, fall, or remain the same.

- An increase in government purchases or a tax cut decreases government saving, crowds out investment, and increases foreign borrowing.

KEY FIGURES

KEY TERMS

PROBLEMS

*1. In the economy of Zap, the marginal propensity to consume is 0.9. Investment is $50 billion, government purchases of goods and services are $40 billion, and lump-sum taxes are $40 billion. Zap has no exports and no imports.

a. The government cuts its purchases of goods and services to $30 billion. What is the change in equilibrium expenditure?

b. What is the value of the government purchases multiplier?

c. The government continues to purchase $40 billion of goods and services and cuts lump-sum taxes to $30 billion. What is the change in equilibrium expenditure?

d. What is the value of the lump-sum tax multiplier?

e. The government simultaneously cuts both its purchases of goods and services and taxes to $30 billion. What is the change in equilibrium expenditure? Why does equilibrium expenditure decrease?

2. In the economy of Zip, the marginal propensity to consume is 0.8. Investment is $60 billion, government purchases of goods and services are $50 billion, and lump-sum taxes are $60 billion. Zap has no exports and no imports.

a. The government increases its purchases of goods and services to $60 billion. What is the change in equilibrium expenditure?

b. What is the value of the government purchases multiplier?

c. The government continues to purchase $60 billion of goods and services and increases lump-sum taxes to $70 billion. What is the change in equilibrium expenditure?

d. What is the value of the lump-sum tax multiplier?

e. The government simultaneously increases both its purchases of goods and services and taxes by $10 billion. What is the change in equilibrium expenditure? Why does equilibrium expenditure increase?

*3. Suppose that the price level in the economy of Zap as described in problem 1 is 100. The economy is also at full employment.

a. If the government of Zap increases its purchases of goods and services by $10 billion, what happens to the quantity of real GDP demanded?

b. How does Zap's aggregate demand curve change? Draw a two-part diagram that is similar to Fig. 26.10 to illustrate the change in both the *AE* curve and the *AD* curve.

c. In the short run, does equilibrium real GDP increase by more than, less than, or the same amount as the increase in the quantity of real GDP demanded?

d. In the long run, does equilibrium real GDP increase by more than, less than, or the same amount as the increase in the quantity of real GDP demanded?

e. In the short run, does the price level in Zap rise, fall, or remain unchanged?

f. In the long run, does the price level in Zap rise, fall, or remain unchanged?

4. Suppose that the price level in the economy of Zip as described in problem 2 is 100. The economy is also at full employment.

a. If the government of Zip decreases its purchases of goods and services by $5 billion, what happens to the quantity of real GDP demanded?

b. How does Zip's aggregate demand curve change? Draw a two-part diagram that is similar to Fig. 26.10 to illustrate the change in both the *AE* curve and the *AD* curve.

c. In the short run, does equilibrium real GDP decrease by more than, less than, or the same amount as the increase in the quantity of real GDP demanded?

d. In the short run, does the price level in Zip rise, fall, or remain unchanged?

e. Why does real GDP decrease by a smaller amount than the decrease in aggregate demand?

*5. The figure shows expenditures and tax revenues of the government of Dreamland. Potential GDP is $40 million.

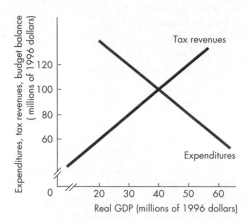

a. What is the government's budget balance if real GDP equals potential GDP?
b. Does Dreamland have a structural surplus or deficit if its real GDP is $40 million? What is its size? Explain why.
c. What is the government's budget balance if real GDP is $30 million?
d. If Dreamland's real GDP is $30 million, does Dreamland have a structural surplus or deficit? What is its size? Explain why.
e. If Dreamland's real GDP is $50 million, does Dreamland have a structural surplus or deficit? What is its size? Explain why.

6. In problem 5, if Dreamland's real GDP is $50 million,
a. What is the government's budget balance?
b. Does Dreamland have a structural surplus? What is its size? Explain why.
c. What is the government's budget balance if potential GDP is $30 million?
d. If Dreamland's potential GDP is $30 million, does Dreamland have a structural surplus or deficit? What is its size? Explain why.
e. What would Dreamland's real GDP have to be for it to have neither a structural deficit/surplus nor a cyclical deficit/surplus if its potential GDP is $40 million?

CRITICAL THINKING

1. Study *Reading Between the Lines* on pp. 622–623 and then
   a. Describe the main features of President Bush's 2003 budget proposals.
   b. Explain why it can be argued that previously enacted tax cuts have brought about the 2003 deficit.
   c. Do you think the 2003 budget should be balanced? If so, do you think spending should fall or taxes should rise?
   d. Suppose the government were to cut expenditures and turn its deficit into a surplus. What do you predict would be the short-run and long-run effects of such an action?

2. Think about the supply-side effects of 2003 budget.
   a. What would be the main effects of lower income tax rates on the level of potential GDP?
   b. How would lower income taxes influence the real wage rate and the real interest rate?
   c. What are the main costs of lower income taxes?

WEB EXERCISES

1. Use the link on your Parkin Web site to visit the National Center for Policy Analysis Idea House. Click on "Dick Armey Flat Tax" and "The Liberal Case for a Flat Tax." When you have studied these two pages, answer the following questions:
   a. What are the main features of Dick Armey's plan?
   b. What is the liberal case for a flat tax?
   c. Why do you think a flat tax is usually associated with conservatives rather than liberals?

2. Use the link on your Parkin Web site to visit the U.S. government budget Web site. Use the information that you can find on this site to describe the main features of the budget for the current fiscal year. Analyze the demand side and supply-side effects of the current year's budget.

MONEY

Money Makes the World Go Around

Money, like fire and the wheel, has been around for a long time. And it has taken many forms. Money was wampum (beads made from shells) for North American Indians, whale's teeth for Fijians, and tobacco for early American colonists. Cakes of salt served as money in Ethiopia and Tibet. Today, when we want to buy something, we use coins or bills, write a check, or present a credit card. Tomorrow, we'll use a "smart card" that keeps track of spending and that our pocket computer can read. Are all these things money? ◆ When we deposit some coins or notes into a bank, is that still money? And what happens when the bank lends the money we've deposited to someone else? How can we get our money back if it has been lent out? Does lending by banks create money? ◆ In Argentina, the quantity of money increased rapidly during the late 1980s and so did prices. To break the cycle of rising prices, Argentina decided to use the U.S. dollar as its money. What are the effects of a rapidly increasing quantity of money?

◆ In this chapter, we study the functions of money, the banks that create it, and the effects of money on the economy.

After studying this chapter, you will be able to

- Define money and describe its functions
- Explain the economic functions of banks and other depository institutions
- Describe some financial innovations that have changed the way we use money today
- Explain how banks create money
- Explain the effects of the quantity of money on the the price level and real GDP, and explain the quantity theory of money

What Is Money?

WHAT DO WAMPUM, TOBACCO, AND NICKELS AND dimes have in common? Why are they all examples of money? To answer these questions, we need a definition of money. **Money** is any commodity or token that is generally acceptable as a means of payment. A **means of payment** is a method of settling a debt. When a payment has been made, there is no remaining obligation between the parties to a transaction. So what wampum, tobacco, and nickels and dimes have in common is that they have served (or still do serve) as the means of payment. But money has three other functions:

- Medium of exchange
- Unit of account
- Store of value

Medium of Exchange

A *medium of exchange* is an object that is generally accepted in exchange for goods and services. Money acts as such a medium. Without money, it would be necessary to exchange goods and services directly for other goods and services — an exchange called **barter**. For example, if you want to buy a hamburger, you might offer the paperback novel you've just finished reading in exchange for it. Barter requires a *double coincidence of wants*, a situation that occurs when Erika wants to buy what Kazia wants to sell and Kazia wants to buy what Erika wants to sell. To get your hamburger, you must find someone who's selling hamburgers and who wants your paperback novel. Money guarantees a double coincidence of wants because people with something to sell will always accept money in exchange for it. Money acts as a lubricant that smoothes the mechanism of exchange.

Unit of Account

A *unit of account* is an agreed measure for stating the prices of goods and services. To get the most out of your budget, you have to figure out whether seeing one more movie is worth its opportunity cost. But that cost is not dollars and cents. It is the number of ice-cream cones, sodas, or cups of coffee that you must give up. It's easy to do such calculations when all these goods have prices in terms of dollars and cents (see Table 27.1). If a movie costs $6 and a six-pack of soda costs $3, you know right away that

TABLE 27.1	The Unit of Account Function of Money Simplifies Price Comparisons	
Good	**Price in money units**	**Price in units of another good**
Movie	$6.00 each	2 six-packs of soda
Soda	$3.00 per six-pack	2 ice-cream cones
Ice cream	$1.50 per cone	3 packs of jelly beans
Jelly beans	$0.50 per pack	2 cups of coffee
Coffee	$0.25 per cup	1 local phone call

Money as a unit of account: The price of a movie is $6 and the price of a cup of coffee is 25¢, so the opportunity cost of a movie is 24 cups of coffee ($6.00 ÷ 25¢ = 24).

No unit of account: You go to a movie theater and learn that the price of a movie is 2 six-packs of soda. You go to a candy store and learn that a pack of jelly beans costs 2 cups of coffee. But how many cups of coffee does seeing a movie cost you? To answer that question, you go to the convenience store and find that a six-pack of soda costs 2 ice-cream cones. Now you head for the ice-cream shop, where an ice-cream cone costs 3 packs of jelly beans. Now you get out your pocket calculator: 1 movie costs 2 six-packs of soda, or 4 ice-cream cones, or 12 packs of jelly beans, or 24 cups of coffee!

seeing one more movie costs you 2 six-packs of soda. If jelly beans are 50¢ a pack, one more movie costs 12 packs of jelly beans. You need only one calculation to figure out the opportunity cost of any pair of goods and services.

But imagine how troublesome it would be if your local movie theater posted its price as 2 six-packs of soda, and if the convenience store posted the price of a six-pack of soda as 2 ice-cream cones, and if the ice-cream shop posted the price of an ice-cream cone as 3 packs of jelly beans, and if the candy store priced a pack of jelly beans as 2 cups of coffee! Now how much running around and calculating would you have to do to figure out how much that movie is going to cost you in terms of the soda, ice cream, jelly beans, or coffee that you must give up to see it? You get the answer for soda right away from the sign posted on the movie theater. But for all the other goods, you're going to have to visit many different stores to establish the price of each commodity in terms of another and then calculate prices in units that are relevant for your own decision. Cover up the column labeled "Price in money units" in Table 27.1 and see how hard it is to figure out the number of local phone calls it costs to see one movie. It's enough to make a person swear off movies! You can see how much simpler it is if all the prices are expressed in dollars and cents.

Store of Value

Money is a *store of value* in the sense that can be held and exchanged later for goods and services. If money were not a store of value, it could not serve as a means of payment.

Money is not alone in acting as a store of value. A physical object such as a house, a car, a work of art, or a computer can act as a store of value.

The most reliable and useful stores of value are items that have a stable value. The more stable the value of a commodity or token, the better it can act as a store of value and the more useful it is as money. No store of value has a completely stable value. The value of a house, a car, or a work of art fluctuates over time. The value of the commodities and tokens that are used as money also fluctuate over time. And when there is inflation, their values persistently fall.

Because inflation brings a falling value of money, a low inflation rate is needed to make money as useful as possible as a store of value.

Money in the United States Today

In the United States today, money consists of

- Currency
- Deposits at banks and other depository institutions

Currency The bills and coins that we use in the United States today are known as **currency**. Bills are money because the government declares them so with the words "This note is legal tender for all debts, public and private." You can see these words on every dollar bill.

Deposits Deposits at banks and other depository institutions such as savings and loan associations are also money. Deposits are money because they can be converted into currency and because they are used to settle debts.

Official Measures of Money The two main official measures of money in the United States today are known as M1 and M2. Figure 27.1 shows the items that make up these two measures. **M1** consists of currency and traveler's checks plus checking deposits owned by individuals and businesses. M1 does *not* include currency held by banks, and it does not include currency and checking deposits owned by the U.S. government. **M2** consists of M1 plus time deposits, savings deposits, and money market mutual funds and other deposits. You can see that M2 is almost five times as large as M1. You can also see that currency is a small part of our money.

FIGURE 27.1   Two Measures of Money

	$ billions in 2001
M2	**5,449**
Money market mutual funds and other deposits	967
Savings deposits	2,304
Time deposits	970
M1	**1,177**
Checking deposits	590
Currency and traveler's checks	588

M1
- Currency held outside banks and traveler's checks
- Checking deposits at commercial banks, savings and loan associations, savings banks, and credit unions

M2
- M1
- Time deposits
- Savings deposits
- Money market mutual funds and other deposits

Source: The Federal Reserve Board.

Are M1 and M2 Really Money? Money is the means of payment. So the test of whether an asset is money is whether it serves as a means of payment. Currency passes the test. But what about deposits? Checking deposits are money because they can be transferred from one person to another by writing a check. Such a transfer of ownership is equivalent to handing over currency. Because M1 consists of currency plus checking deposits and each of these is a means of payment, *M1 is money.*

But what about M2? Some of the savings deposits in M2 are just as much a means of payment as the checking deposits in M1. You can use the ATM at the grocery store checkout or gas station and transfer funds directly from your savings account to pay for your purchase. But other savings deposits are not means of payment. These deposits are known as *liquid assets.* **Liquidity** is the property of being instantly convertible into a means of payment with little loss in value. Because most of the deposits in M2 are quickly and easily converted into currency or checking deposits, they are operationally similar to M1, but they are not means of payment.

Deposits Are Money but Checks Are Not In defining money, we include, along with currency, deposits at banks and other depository institutions. But we do not count the checks that people write as money. Why are deposits money and checks not?

To see why deposits are money but checks are not, think about what happens when Colleen buys some roller-blades for $200 from Rocky's Rollers. When Colleen goes to Rocky's shop, she has $500 in her deposit account at the Laser Bank. Rocky has $1,000 in his deposit account — at the same bank, as it happens. The total deposits of these two people are $1,500. Colleen writes a check for $200. Rocky takes the check to the bank right away and deposits it. Rocky's bank balance rises from $1,000 to $1,200, and Colleen's balance falls from $500 to $300. The total deposits of Colleen and Rocky are still the same as before: $1,500. Rocky now has $200 more than before, and Colleen has $200 less.

This transaction has transferred money from Colleen to Rocky. The check itself was never money. There wasn't an extra $200 worth of money while the check was in circulation. The check instructs the bank to transfer money from Colleen to Rocky.

If Colleen and Rocky use different banks, there is an extra step. Rocky's bank credits the check to

Rocky's account and then takes the check to a check-clearing center. The check is then sent to Colleen's bank, which pays Rocky's bank $200 and then debits Colleen's account $200. This process can take a few days, but the principles are the same as when two people use the same bank.

Credit Cards Are Not Money So checks are not money. But what about credit cards? Isn't having a credit card in your wallet and presenting the card to pay for your roller-blades the same thing as using money? Why aren't credit cards somehow valued and counted as part of the quantity of money?

When you pay by check, you are frequently asked to prove your identity by showing your driver's license. It would never occur to you to think of your driver's license as money. It's just an ID card. A credit card is also an ID card but one that lets you take out a loan at the instant you buy something. When you sign a credit card sales slip, you are saying, "I agree to pay for these goods when the credit card company bills me." Once you get your statement from the credit card company, you must make at least the minimum payment due. To make that payment, you need money — you need to have currency or a checking deposit to pay the credit card company. So although you use a credit card when you buy something, the credit card is not the *means of payment* and it is not money.

REVIEW QUIZ

1 What makes something money? What functions does money perform? Why do you think packs of chewing gum don't serve as money?
2 What are the problems that arise when a commodity is used as money?
3 What are the main components of money in the United States today?
4 What are the official measures of money? Are all the measures really money?
5 Why are checks and credit cards not money?

We've seen that the main component of money in the United States is deposits at banks and other depository institutions. Let's take a closer look at these institutions.

Depository Institutions

A FIRM THAT TAKES DEPOSITS FROM HOUSEHOLDS and firms and makes loans to other households and firms is called a **depository institution**. The deposits of three types of depository institution make up the nation's money:

■ Commercial banks
■ Thrift institutions
■ Money market mutual funds

Commercial Banks

A **commercial bank** is a firm that is licensed by the Comptroller of the Currency (at the U.S. Treasury) or by a state agency to receive deposits and make loans. Close to 13,000 commercial banks operate in the United States today. A commercial bank's business is summarized in its balance sheet.

A bank's *balance sheet* lists its assets, liabilities, and net worth. *Assets* are what the bank *owns, liabilities* are what the bank *owes*, and *net worth*, which is equal to assets minus liabilities, is the value of the bank to its stockholders — its owners. A bank's balance sheet is described by the equation:

$$\text{Liabilities} + \text{Net worth} = \text{Assets.}$$

Among a bank's liabilities are the deposits that are part of the nation's money. Your deposit at the bank is a liability to your bank (and an asset to you) because the bank must repay your deposit whenever you decide to take your money out of the bank.

Profit and Prudence: A Balancing Act The aim of a bank is to maximize the net worth of its stockholders. To achieve this objective, the interest rate at which a bank lends exceeds that rate at which it borrows. But a bank must perform a delicate balancing act. Lending is risky, and the more a bank ties up its deposits in high-risk, high-interest rate loans, the bigger is its chance of not being able to repay its depositors. And if depositors perceive a high risk of not being repaid, they withdraw their funds and create a crisis for the bank. So a bank must be prudent in the way it uses its deposits, balancing security for the depositors against profit for its stockholders.

Reserves and Loans To achieve security for its depositors, a bank divides its funds into two parts: reserves and loans. **Reserves** are the cash in a bank's vault plus its deposits at Federal Reserve banks. (We'll study the Federal Reserve banks in Chapter 28.) The cash in a bank's vaults is a reserve to meet its depositors' demands for currency. This cash keeps the ATM replenished every time you and your friends raid it for money for a midnight pizza. The account of a bank at the Federal Reserve is similar to your own bank account. Commercial banks use these accounts to receive and make payments. A commercial bank deposits cash into or draws cash out of its account at the Federal Reserve and writes checks on that account to settle debts with other banks.

If a bank kept all its deposits as reserves, it wouldn't make any profit. In fact, it keeps only a small fraction of its funds in reserves and lends the rest. A bank has three types of assets:

1. *Liquid assets* are U.S. government Treasury bills and commercial bills. These assets are the banks' first line of defense if they need cash. Liquid assets can be sold and instantly converted into cash with virtually no risk of loss. Because they are virtually risk free, they have a low interest rate.

2. *Investment securities* are longer-term U.S. government bonds and other bonds. These assets can be sold quickly and converted into cash but at prices that fluctuate. Because their prices fluctuate, these assets are riskier than liquid assets, but they also have a higher interest rate.

3. *Loans* are commitments of fixed amounts of money for agreed-upon periods of time. Most banks' loans are made to corporations to finance the purchase of capital equipment and inventories and to households — personal loans — to finance consumer durable goods, such as cars or boats. The outstanding balances on credit card accounts are also bank loans. Loans are the riskiest assets of a bank because they cannot be converted into cash until they are due to be repaid. And some borrowers default and never repay. Because they are the riskiest of a bank's assets, loans carry the highest interest rate.

Commercial bank deposits are one component of the nation's money. But thrift institutions and money market mutual funds also take deposits that form part — an increasing part — of the nation's money. We'll now describe the other institutions whose deposits form part of the nation's money.

Thrift Institutions

The **thrift institutions** are

- Savings and loan associations
- Savings banks
- Credit unions

Savings and Loan Association A **savings and loan association** (S&L) is a depository institution that receives checking deposits and savings deposits and that makes personal, commercial, and home-purchase loans.

Savings Bank A **savings bank** is a depository institution that accepts savings deposits and makes mostly mortgage loans. Some savings banks (called *mutual* savings banks) are owned by their depositors.

Credit Union A **credit union** is a depository institution owned by a social or economic group such as a firm's employees that accepts savings deposits and makes mostly consumer loans.

Money Market Mutual Funds

A **money market mutual fund** is a fund operated by a financial institution that sells shares in the fund and holds liquid assets such as U.S. Treasury bills or short-term commercial bills.

Money market mutual fund shares act like bank deposits. Shareholders can write checks on their money market mutual fund accounts. But there are restrictions on most of these accounts. For example, the minimum deposit accepted might be $2,500, and the smallest check a depositor is permitted to write might be $500.

The Economic Functions of Depository Institutions

All depository institutions make a profit from the spread between the interest rate they pay on deposits and the interest rate at which they lend. Why can depository institutions get deposits at a low interest rate and lend at a higher one? What services do they perform that make their depositors willing to put up with a low interest rate and their borrowers willing to pay a higher one?

Depository institutions provide four main services that people are willing to pay for:

- Creating liquidity
- Minimizing the cost of obtaining funds
- Minimizing the cost of monitoring borrowers
- Pooling risk

Creating Liquidity Depository institutions create liquidity. *Liquid assets* are those that are easily convertible into money with little loss of value. Some of the liabilities of depository institutions are themselves money; others are highly liquid assets that are easily converted into money.

Depository institutions create liquidity by borrowing short and lending long. *Borrowing short* means taking deposits but standing ready to repay them on short notice (and even on no notice in the case of checking deposits). *Lending long* means making loan commitments for a prearranged, and often quite long, period of time. For example, when a person makes a deposit with a savings and loan association, that deposit can be withdrawn at any time. But the S&L makes a lending commitment for perhaps more than 20 years to a homebuyer.

Minimizing the Cost of Obtaining Funds Finding someone from whom to borrow can be a costly business. Imagine how troublesome it would be if there were no depository institutions. A firm that was looking for $1 million to buy a new factory would probably have to hunt around for several dozen people from whom to borrow to acquire enough funds for its capital project. Depository institutions lower the costs of this search. The firm that needs $1 million can go to a single depository institution to obtain those funds. The depository institution has to borrow from a large number of people, but it's not doing that just for this one firm and the million dollars it wants to borrow. The depository institution can establish an organization that is capable of raising funds from a large number of depositors and can spread the cost of this activity over a large number of borrowers.

Minimizing the Cost of Monitoring Borrowers Lending money is a risky business. There's always a danger that the borrower will not repay. Most of the money that is lent gets used by firms to invest in projects that they hope will return a profit. But sometimes those hopes are not fulfilled. Checking up on the activities of a borrower and ensuring that the best possible decisions are being made for making a profit and avoiding a loss are costly and specialized activities. Imagine how costly it would be if each household that lent money to a firm had to incur the costs of monitoring that firm directly. By depositing funds with a depository institution, households avoid those costs. The depository institution performs the monitoring activity by using specialized resources that have a much lower cost than what the households would incur if they had to undertake the activity individually.

Pooling Risk As we noted above, lending money is risky. There is always a chance of not being repaid — of default. Lending to a large number of different individuals can reduce the risk of default. In such a situation, if one person defaults on a loan, it is a nuisance but not a disaster. In contrast, if only one person borrows and that person defaults on the loan, the entire loan is a write-off. Depository institutions enable people to pool risk in an efficient way. Thousands of people lend money to any one institution, and, in turn, the institution relends the money to hundreds, perhaps thousands, of individual firms. If any one firm defaults on its loan, that default is spread across all the people who deposited money with the institution, and no individual depositor is left exposed to a high degree of risk.

REVIEW QUIZ

1 What are the functions of commercial banks, savings and loan associations, savings banks, credit unions, and money market mutual funds? What functions do they have in common and how do they differ from each other?

2 What is liquidity and how do depository institutions create it?

3 How do depository institutions lower the cost of borrowing and lending and of monitoring borrowers?

4 How do depository institutions pool risks?

We are interested in banks and other depository institutions because they *create* money. But these firms are highly regulated, and this regulation limits their ability to create money. So next, we'll examine these regulations. We'll also look at the deregulation and innovation that have occurred in the financial sector during the past 20 years.

Financial Regulation, Deregulation, and Innovation

DEPOSITORY INSTITUTIONS ARE HIGHLY REGU-lated firms. But regulation is not static, and during the 1980s, some important changes in their regulation as well as deregulation took place. Also, the institutions are not static. In their pursuit of profit, they constantly seek lower-cost ways of obtaining funds, monitoring borrowers, pooling risk, and creating liquidity. They also are inventive in seeking ways to avoid the costs imposed on them by financial regulation. Let's look at regulation, deregulation, and innovation in the financial sector in recent years.

Financial Regulation

Depository institutions face two types of regulation:

■ Deposit insurance
■ Balance sheet rules

Deposit Insurance The deposits of most depository institutions are insured by the Federal Deposit Insurance Corporation (FDIC). The FDIC is a federal agency that receives its income from compulsory insurance premiums paid by commercial banks and other depository institutions. The FDIC operates two separate insurance funds: the Bank Insurance Fund (BIF), which insures deposits in commercial banks, and the Saving Association Insurance Fund (SAIF), which insures the deposits of S&Ls, savings banks, and credit unions. Each of these funds insures deposits of up to $100,000.

The existence of deposit insurance provides protection for depositors in the event that a depository institution fails. But it also weakens the incentive for the owner of a depository institution to make safe investments and loans. Some economists believe that deposit insurance played an important role in creating a crisis for S&Ls during the 1980s. Depositors did not worry about risk because their deposits were insured. The S&L owners made high-risk loans because they knew they were making a one-way bet. If their loans paid off, they made a high rate of return. If they failed and could not meet their obligations to the depositors, the insurance fund would step in. Bad loans were good business!

Because of this type of problem, all depository institutions face regulation of their balance sheets.

Balance Sheet Rules The most important balance sheet regulations are

- Equity capital requirements
- Reserve requirements
- Deposit rules
- Lending rules

Equity capital requirements are the minimum amount of an owner's own financial resources — called *equity capital* — that must be put into a depository institution. This amount must be sufficiently large to discourage owners from making loans that are too risky.

Reserve requirements are rules setting out the minimum percentages of deposits that must be held in currency or other safe, liquid assets. These minimum percentages vary across the different types of depository institutions and deposits; they are largest for checking deposits and smallest for long-term savings deposits.

Deposit rules are restrictions on the different types of deposits that an institution may accept. These are the rules that historically have created the sharpest distinctions between the various institutions. For example, in the past, commercial banks provided checking accounts while other institutions provided only savings accounts.

Lending rules are restrictions on the proportions of different types of loans that a depository institution may make. Like deposit rules, these rules also helped to create distinctions between the institutions. Before 1980, commercial banks were the only institutions that were permitted to make commercial loans, and S&Ls and savings banks were restricted to making mostly mortgage loans to homebuyers.

Deregulation in the 1980s

In 1980, Congress passed the Depository Institutions' Deregulation and Monetary Control Act (DIDMCA). The DIDMCA removed many of the distinctions between commercial banks and other depository institutions. It permitted nonbank depository institutions to compete with commercial banks in a wider range of lending business. At the same time, it permitted the payment of interest on checking deposits so that NOW accounts and ATS accounts could be offered by all deposit-taking institutions — banks

and nonbanks.[1] It also extended the powers of the Federal Reserve to place reserve requirements on all depository institutions. Despite the general direction of deregulation, this move brought a greater measure of central control over the financial system than had previously existed and represented a strengthening of the Fed's control.

The ability of S&Ls and savings banks to compete for lending business with commercial banks was further strengthened in 1982 with the passage of the Garn–St. Germain Depository Institutions Act. This legislation further eased restrictions on the scale of commercial lending that S&Ls and savings banks could undertake.

Deregulation in the 1990s

The most significant deregulation during the 1990s was the Riegle–Neal Interstate Banking and Branching Efficiency Act of 1994. This law permits U.S. banks for the first time to establish branches in any state.

This new law brought large changes in the structure of the banking industry. The most visible was the wave of mergers of large banks and the appearance on the American banking scene of some major international banks. These changes will make the U.S. banking industry more efficient.

Financial Innovation

The development of new financial products — of new ways of borrowing and lending — is called **financial innovation**. The aim of financial innovation is to lower the cost of deposits or to increase the return from lending or, more simply, to increase the profit from financial intermediation. There are three main influences on financial innovation:

- Economic environment
- Technology
- Regulation

The pace of financial innovation was remarkable during the 1980s and 1990s, and all three of these forces played a role.

---

[1]A NOW account is a Negotiable Order of Withdrawal account; "negotiable order of withdrawal" is another name for a check. An ATS account is an Automatic-Transfer Savings account — a savings account that is linked to a checking account. Funds are automatically transferred between the two accounts.

Economic Environment Some of the innovation was a response to high inflation and high interest rates. An important example is the development of variable interest rate mortgages. Traditionally, house purchases were financed by mortgage loans at a guaranteed interest rate. Rising interest rates brought rising borrowing costs for S&Ls, and because they were committed to fixed interest rates on their mortgages, the industry incurred severe losses. The creation of variable interest rate mortgages has taken some of the risk out of long-term lending for house purchases.

Technology Other financial innovations resulted from technological change, most notably that associated with the decreased cost of computing and long-distance communication. The spread in the use of credit cards and the development of international financial markets — for example, the increased importance of Eurodollars — are consequences of technological change.[2]

Regulation A good deal of financial innovation takes place to avoid regulation. For example, Regulation Q, which prevented banks from paying interest on checking deposits, gave the impetus to devising new types of deposits on which checks could be written and interest paid, thereby getting around the regulation.

Deregulation, Innovation, and Money

Deregulation and financial innovation that have led to the development of new types of deposit accounts have brought important changes in the composition of the nation's money. In 1960, M1 consisted of only currency and checking deposits at commercial banks. In the 1990s, new types of checking deposits expanded while traditional checking deposits declined. Similar changes have taken place in the composition of M2. Savings deposits have declined, while time deposits and money market mutual funds have expanded.

---

[2]Eurodollars are U.S. dollar bank accounts held in other countries, mainly in Europe. They were "invented" during the 1960s when the Soviet Union wanted the security and convenience of holding funds in U.S. dollars but was unwilling to place deposits in U.S. banks.

REVIEW QUIZ

1 Is everyone free to open a bank, take deposits, and make loans with no restrictions on these activities? What are the main restrictions that regulators impose on banks? Why?
2 Did the financial deregulation of the 1980s make commercial banks more like or less like other depository institutions?
3 What are the main factors that stimulate depository institutions constantly to develop new financial products and services?
4 What have deregulation and financial innovation done to the composition of the nation's money?

We're now ready to learn how banks create money. In the following section, we'll use the term "banks" to refer to all the institutions whose deposits are part of the nation's money. Let's see how money gets created.

How Banks Create Money

BANKS CREATE MONEY. BUT THIS DOESN'T MEAN that they have smoke-filled back rooms in which counterfeiters are busily working. Remember, most money is deposits, not currency. What banks create is deposits, and they do so by making loans. But the amount of deposits they can create is limited by their reserves.

Reserves: Actual and Required

We've seen that banks don't have $100 in bills for every $100 that people have deposited with them. In fact, a typical bank today has reserves of $6 for every $100 of deposits. But there's no need for panic. These reserve levels are adequate for ordinary business needs.

The fraction of a bank's total deposits that are held in reserves is called the **reserve ratio**. The reserve ratio changes when a bank's customers make a deposit or withdrawal. Making a deposit increases the reserve ratio, and making a withdrawal decreases the reserve ratio.

The **required reserve ratio** is the ratio of reserves to deposits that banks are required, by regulation, to hold. A bank's *required reserves* are equal to its deposits multiplied by the required reserve ratio. Actual reserves minus required reserves are **excess reserves**. Whenever banks have excess reserves, they are able to create money.

To see how banks create money, we'll look at two model banking systems. In the first, there is only one bank; in the second, there are many banks.

Creating Deposits by Making Loans in a One-Bank Economy

In the model banking system that we'll study first, there is only one bank, and its required reserve ratio is 25 percent. That is, for each dollar deposited, the bank keeps 25¢ in reserves and lends the rest. Figure 27.2(a) shows the balance sheet of One-and-Only Bank. On January 1, its deposits are $400 million, and its reserves are 25 percent of this amount: $100 million. Its loans are equal to deposits minus reserves and are $300 million.

The story begins with Al Capone, who has decided to end his career of crime. He has been holding all his money in currency and has a nest egg of $1 million. On January 2, Al decides to put his $1 million on deposit at the One-and-Only Bank. On the day that Al makes his deposit, the One-and-Only Bank's balance sheet changes. Figure 27.2(b) shows the new situation. The bank now has $101 million in reserves and $401 million in deposits. It still has loans of $300 million.

The bank now has *excess reserves*. With reserves of $101 million, the bank would like to have deposits of $404 million and loans of $303 million. Because it is the only bank, the manager knows that the reserves will remain at $101 million. That is, she knows that when she makes a loan, the amount lent remains on deposit at the One-and-Only Bank. She knows, for example, that all the suppliers of Sky's-the-Limit Construction are also depositors of One-and-Only. So she knows that if she makes the loan that Sky's-the-Limit has just requested, the deposit she lends will never leave One-and-Only. When Sky's-the-Limit uses part of its new loan to pay $100,000 to I-Dig-It Excavating Company for some excavations, the One-and-Only Bank simply moves the funds from Sky's-the-Limit's checking account to I-Dig-It's checking account.

FIGURE 27.2   Creating Money at the One-and-Only Bank

(a) Balance sheet on January 1

Assets (millions of dollars)		Liabilities (millions of dollars)	
Reserves	$100	Deposits	$400
Loans	$300		
Total	$400	Total	$400

(b) Balance sheet on January 2

Assets (millions of dollars)		Liabilities (millions of dollars)	
Reserves	$101	Deposits	$401
Loans	$300		
Total	$401	Total	$401

(c) Balance sheet on January 3

Assets (millions of dollars)		Liabilities (millions of dollars)	
Reserves	$101	Deposits	$404
Loans	$303		
Total	$404	Total	$404

In part (a), the One-and-Only Bank has deposits of **$400 million**, loans of **$300 million**, and reserves of **$100 million**. The bank's required reserve ratio is 25 percent. When the bank receives a deposit of **$1** million in part (b), it has excess reserves. It lends **$3** million and creates a further **$3** million of deposits. Deposits increase by **$3** million, and loans increase by **$3** million in part (c).

So on January 3, the manager of One-and-Only calls Sky's-the-Limit and offers to lend the maximum that she can. How much does she lend? She lends $3 million. When the $3 million is lent, One-and-Only's balance sheet changes to the one shown in Fig. 27.2(c). Loans increase by $3 million to $303 million. The loan shows up in Sky's-the-Limit's deposit initially, and total deposits increase to $404 million — $400 million plus Al Capone's deposit of $1 million plus the newly created deposit of $3 million. The bank now has no excess reserves and has reached the limit of its ability to create money.

The Deposit Multiplier

The **deposit multiplier** is the amount by which an increase in bank reserves is multiplied to calculate the increase in bank deposits. That is,

$$\text{Deposit multiplier} = \frac{\text{Change in deposits}}{\text{Change in reserves}}.$$

In the example we've just worked through, the deposit multiplier is 4. The $1 million increase in reserves created a $4 million increase in deposits. The deposit multiplier is linked to the required reserve ratio by the following equation:

$$\text{Deposit multiplier} = \frac{1}{\text{Required reserve ratio}}.$$

In the example, the required reserve ratio is 25 percent, or 0.25. That is,

$$\text{Deposit multiplier} = \frac{1}{0.25}$$
$$= 4.$$

Creating Deposits by Making Loans with Many Banks

If you told the loan officer at your own bank that she creates money, she wouldn't believe you. Bankers see themselves as lending the money they receive from others, not as creating money. But in fact, even though each bank lends only what it receives, the banking *system* creates money. To see how, let's look at another example.

Figure 27.3 is going to keep track of what is happening in the process of money creation by a banking system in which each bank has a required reserve ratio of 25 percent. The process begins when Art decides to decrease his currency holding and put $100,000 on deposit. Now Art's bank has $100,000 of new deposits and $100,000 of additional reserves. With a required reserve ratio of 25 percent, the bank keeps $25,000 on reserve and lends $75,000 to Amy. Amy writes a check for $75,000 to buy a copy-shop franchise from Barb. At this point, Art's bank has a new deposit of $100,000, new loans of $75,000, and new reserves of $25,000. You can see this situation in Fig. 27.3 as the first row of the running tally.

For Art's bank, that is the end of the story. But it's not the end of the story for the entire banking system. Barb deposits her check for $75,000 in another bank. Its deposits and reserves increase by $75,000. This bank puts 25 percent of its increase in deposits ($18,750) into reserve and lends $56,250 to Bob. Bob then writes a check to Carl to pay off a business loan. The current state of play is seen in Fig. 27.3. Now total reserves of the banking system have increased by $43,750 ($25,000 plus $18,750), total loans have increased by $131,250 ($75,000 plus $56,250), and total deposits have increased by $175,000 ($100,000 plus $75,000).

When Carl takes his check to his bank, its deposits and reserves increase by $56,250, $14,063 of which it keeps in reserve and $42,187 of which it lends. This process continues until there are no excess reserves in the banking system. But the process takes a lot of further steps. Figure 27.3 shows one additional step. It also shows the final tallies: Reserves increase by $100,000, loans increase by $300,000, and deposits increase by $400,000.

The sequence in Fig. 27.3 shows the first four stages of the process. To figure out the entire process, look closely at the numbers in the figure. At each stage, the loan is 75 percent (0.75) of the previous loan and the deposit is 0.75 of the previous deposit. Call that proportion L ($L = 0.75$). The complete sequence is

$$1 + L + L^2 + L^3 + \dots.$$

Remember, L is a fraction, so at each stage in this sequence, the amount of new loans gets smaller. The total number of loans made at the end of the process is the above sum, which is[3]

$$\frac{1}{(1 - L)}.$$

---

[3] Both here and in the expenditure multiplier process in Chapter 25, pp. 588–589, the sequence of values is called a convergent geometric series. To find the sum of a series such as this, begin by calling the sum S. Then write out the sum as

$$S = 1 + L + L^2 + L^3 + \dots$$

Multiply by L to get

$$LS = L + L^2 + L^3 + \dots$$

and then subtract the second equation from the first to get

$$S(I - L) = 1$$

or

$$S = \frac{1}{(1 - L)}.$$

FIGURE 27.3   The Multiple Creation of Bank Deposits

The sequence	The running tally		
	Reserves	**Loans**	**Deposits**
Deposit $100,000			
Reserve $25,000 / Loan $75,000	$25,000	$75,000	$100,000
Deposit $75,000			
Reserve $18,750 / Loan $56,250	$43,750	$131,250	$175,000
Deposit $56,250			
Reserve $14,063 / Loan $42,187	$57,813	$173,437	$231,250
Deposit $42,187			
Reserve $10,547 / Loan $31,640	$68,360	$205,077	$273,437
and so on ...	$100,000	$300,000	$400,000

When a bank receives deposits, it keeps 25 percent in reserves and lends 75 percent. The amount lent becomes a new deposit at another bank. The next bank in the sequence keeps 25 percent and lends 75 percent, and the process continues until the banking system has created enough deposits to eliminate its excess reserves. The running tally tells us the amounts of deposits and loans created at each stage. At the end of the process, an additional $100,000 of reserves creates an additional $400,000 of deposits.

If we use the numbers from the example, the total increase in deposits is

$$\$100,000 + 75,000 + 56,250 + 42,187 + \ldots$$
$$= \$100,000(1 + 0.75 + 0.5625 + 0.42187 + \ldots)$$
$$= \$100,000(1 + 0.75 + 0.75^2 + 0.75^3 + \ldots$$
$$= \$100,000 \times \frac{1}{(1 - 0.75)}$$
$$= \$100,000 \times \frac{1}{(0.25)}$$
$$= \$100,000 \times 4$$
$$= \$400,000.$$

By using the same method, you can check that the totals for reserves and loans are the ones shown in Fig. 27.3.

So even though each bank lends only the money it receives, the banking system as a whole does create money by making loans. The amount created is exactly the same in a multibank system as in a one-bank system.

The Deposit Multiplier in the United States The deposit multiplier in the United States works in the same way as the deposit multiplier we've just worked out for a model economy. But the deposit multiplier in the United States differs from the one we've just calculated for three reasons. First, the required reserve ratio of U.S. banks is smaller than the 25 percent we used here. Second, U.S. banks sometimes choose to hold excess reserves. Third, not all the loans made by banks return to them in the form of reserves. Some of the loans remain outside the banks and are held as currency. The smaller required reserve ratio makes the U.S. multiplier larger than the multiplier in the above example. But the other two factors make the U.S. multiplier smaller.

Now that we know what money is and how banks create it, let's see how the amount of money created by the banks influences the economy. We'll discover that this influence is powerful.

Money, Real GDP, and the Price Level

You now know that in a modern economy such as that of the United States today, most of the money is bank deposits. You've seen that banks actually create money by making loans. Does the quantity of money created by the banking and financial system matter? What effect does money have? Does it matter whether the quantity of money increases quickly or slowly? How does the quantity of money influence real GDP, the price level, and the inflation rate? Can a country increase its real GDP just by increasing the quantity of money?

We're going to answer these questions first by using the aggregate supply–aggregate demand model, which explains how money affects real GDP and the price level in the short run. Then we're going to study a theory called the quantity theory of money, which explains how money growth influences inflation in the long run. We'll also look at some historical and international evidence about the relationship between money growth and inflation.

The Short-Run Effects of a Change in the Quantity of Money

Figure 27.4 illustrates the aggregate supply–aggregate demand model that explains how real GDP and the price level are determined in the short run. (Chapter 21, pp. 476–489, explains the aggregate supply–aggregate demand model.) We are going to use this model to study the short-run effects of a change in the quantity of money on real GDP and the price level. Potential GDP is $10 trillion, and the long-run aggregate supply curve is *LAS*. The short-run aggregate supply curve is *SAS*. Initially, the aggregate demand curve is AD_0. Equilibrium real GDP is $9.8 trillion, and the price level is 107 at the intersection of the AD_0 curve and the *SAS* curve. The economy is below full employment.

FIGURE 27.4   Short-Run Effects of a Change in the Quantity of Money

Initially, the economy is at a below full-employment equilibrium. Real GDP is $9.8 trillion, which is less than potential GDP. An increase in the quantity of money increases aggregate demand and shifts the aggregate demand curve rightward from AD_0 to AD_1. The price level rises to 110, and real GDP increases to $10 trillion. The increase in the quantity of money increases real GDP to potential GDP.

Banks, flush with excess reserves, make loans, and the loans create money. This increase results from the process of money creation we've just studied. With more money in their bank accounts and more loans, people plan to increase their consumption expenditure and businesses plan to increase their investment. Aggregate demand increases, and the aggregate demand curve shifts rightward to AD_1. A new equilibrium emerges at the intersection point of AD_1 and SAS. Real GDP increases to $10 trillion, and the price level rises to 110. Real GDP now equals potential GDP, and the economy is at full employment. This increase in the quantity of money has increased both real GDP and the price level.

Now imagine the reverse situation. Real GDP is initially $10 trillion, and the price level is 110 at the intersection point of AD_1 and SAS in Fig. 27.4. The quantity of money *decreases*. With *less* money in their bank accounts, people and businesses plan to decrease their expenditures. Aggregate demand decreases, and the aggregate demand curve shifts leftward to AD_0. A recession occurs as real GDP shrinks to $9.8 trillion and the price level falls to 107.

These influences of the quantity of money on real GDP and the price level are *short-run* effects. In the long run, a change in the quantity of money, perhaps surprisingly, has no effect on real GDP. All its effects are on the price level. Let's see why this outcome occurs.

The Long-Run Effects of a Change in the Quantity of Money

Figure 27.5 explains how real GDP and the price level are determined in both the short run and the long run. Again, potential GDP is $10 trillion and the long-run aggregate supply curve is LAS. The short-run aggregate supply curve is SAS_1. Initially, the aggregate demand curve is AD_1. Equilibrium real GDP is $10 trillion, and the price level is 110. So real GDP equals potential GDP, and there is full employment.

Now suppose the quantity of money increases. Aggregate demand increases, and the aggregate demand curve shifts rightward to AD_2 in Fig. 27.5. The new short-run equilibrium is at the intersection point of AD_2 and SAS_1. The price level rises to 113, and real GDP increases to $10.2 trillion. This short-run adjustment has put real GDP above potential GDP and has decreased unemployment below the

FIGURE 27.5   Long-Run Effects of a Change in the Quantity of Money

Real GDP equals potential GDP. An increase in the quantity of money shifts the aggregate demand curve from AD_1 to AD_2. In the short run, the price level rises to 113 and real GDP increases to $10.2 trillion. Real GDP exceeds potential GDP, and the money wage rate rises. Short-run aggregate supply decreases, and the SAS curve shifts leftward from SAS_1 to SAS_2. Real GDP returns to potential GDP, and the price level rises to 121. In the long run, the increase in the quantity of money increases the price level and has no effect on real GDP.

natural rate. A shortage of labor makes the money wage rate rise. As the money wage rate rises, short-run aggregate supply decreases and the SAS curve shifts leftward toward SAS_2. As short-run aggregate supply decreases, the price level rises to 121 and real GDP decreases back to potential GDP at $10 trillion.

Thus from one full-employment equilibrium to another, an increase in the quantity of money increases the price level and has no effect on real GDP. This relationship between the quantity of money and the price level at full employment is made more precise by the quantity theory of money, which tells us about the quantitative link between money growth and inflation.

The Quantity Theory of Money

The **quantity theory of money** is the proposition that in the long run, an increase in the quantity of money brings an equal percentage increase in the price level. The original basis of the quantity theory of money is a concept known as *the velocity of circulation* and an equation called *the equation of exchange*.

The **velocity of circulation** is the average number of times a dollar of money is used annually to buy the goods and services that make up GDP. GDP is equal to the price level (P) multiplied by real GDP (Y). That is,

$$GDP = PY.$$

Call the quantity of money M. The velocity of circulation, V, is determined by the equation:

$$V = PY/M.$$

For example, if GDP is $6.0 trillion and the quantity of money is $3 trillion, the velocity of circulation is 2.

On the average, each dollar of money circulates twice in its use to purchase the final goods and services that make up GDP; that is, each dollar of money is used twice in a year to buy GDP.

Figure 27.6 shows the velocity of circulation of both M1 and M2, the two main official measures of money, since 1961. You can see that the velocity of circulation of M1 increased through 1980 and fluctuated during the 1980s and 1990s. In contrast, the velocity of circulation of M2 has been remarkably stable. The reason why the velocity of M1 has increased is that deregulation and financial innovation have created new types of deposits and payments technologies that are substitutes for M1. As a result, the quantity of M1 per dollar of GDP has decreased, and equivalently, the velocity of circulation of M1 has increased. The reason why the velocity of M2 has been almost constant is that the new types of deposits that have replaced M1 are part of M2. So the ratio of M2 to GDP and the velocity of circulation of M2 have been much more stable.

FIGURE 27.6   The Velocity of Circulation in the United States: 1961–2001

The velocity of circulation of M1 has increased over the years because deregulation and financial innovation have created M1 substitutes. The velocity of circulation of M2 has been relatively stable because the M1 substitutes that have resulted from deregulation and financial innovation are new types of deposits that are part of M2.

Sources: The Federal Reserve Board and Bureau of Economic Analysis.

The **equation of exchange** states that the quantity of money (M) multiplied by the velocity of circulation (V) equals GDP, or

$$MV = PY.$$

Given the definition of the velocity of circulation, this equation is always true — it is true by definition. With M equal to $3 trillion and V equal to 2, MV is equal to $6.0 trillion, the value of GDP.

The equation of exchange becomes the quantity theory of money by making two assumptions:

1. The velocity of circulation is not influenced by the quantity of money.
2. Potential GDP is not influenced by the quantity of money.

If these two assumptions are true, the equation of exchange tells us that a change in the quantity of money brings about an equal proportional change in the price level. You can see why by solving the equation of exchange for the price level. Dividing both sides of the equation by real GDP (Y) gives

$$P = (V/Y)M.$$

In the long run, real GDP, Y, equals potential GDP, so if potential GDP and velocity are not influenced by the quantity of money, the relationship between the change in the price level (ΔP) and the change in the quantity of money (ΔM) is

$$\Delta P = (V/Y)\Delta M.$$

Divide this equation by the previous one, $P = (V/Y)M$, to get

$$\Delta P/P = \Delta M/M.$$

($\Delta P/P$) is the proportional increase in the price level, and ($\Delta M/M$) is the proportional increase in the quantity of money. So this equation is the quantity theory of money: In the long run, the percentage increase in the price level equals the percentage increase in the quantity of money.

The Quantity Theory and the AS-AD Model

The quantity theory of money can be interpreted in terms of the *AS-AD* model. The aggregate demand curve is a relationship between the quantity of real GDP demanded (Y) and the price level (P), other things remaining constant. We can obtain such a

relationship from the equation of exchange:

$$MV = PY.$$

Dividing both sides of this equation by real GDP (Y) gives

$$P = MV/Y.$$

This equation may be interpreted as describing an aggregate demand curve. In Chapter 21 (p. 481), you saw that the aggregate demand curve slopes downward. As the price level increases, the quantity of real GDP demanded decreases. The above equation also shows such a relationship between the price level and the quantity of real GDP demanded. For a given quantity of money (M) and a given velocity of circulation (V), the higher the price level (P), the smaller is the quantity of real GDP demanded (Y).

In general, when the quantity of money changes, the velocity of circulation might also change. But the quantity theory asserts that velocity is not influenced by the quantity of money. If this assumption is correct, an increase in the quantity of money increases aggregate demand and shifts the aggregate demand curve upward by the same amount as the percentage change in the quantity of money.

The quantity theory of money also asserts that real GDP, which in the long run equals potential GDP, is not influenced by the quantity of money. This assertion is true in the *AS-AD* model in the long run when the economy is on its long-run aggregate supply curve. Figure 27.5 shows the quantity theory result in the *AS-AD* model. Initially, the economy is on the long-run aggregate supply curve *LAS* and at the intersection of the aggregate demand curve AD_1 and the short-run aggregate supply curve SAS_1. A 10 percent increase in the quantity of money shifts the aggregate demand curve from AD_1 to AD_2. This shift, measured by the vertical distance between the two demand curves, is 10 percent. In the long run, wages rise (also by 10 percent) and shift the *SAS* curve leftward to SAS_2. A new long-run equilibrium occurs at the intersection of AD_2 and SAS_2. Real GDP remains at potential GDP of $10 trillion, and the price level rises to 121. The new price level is 10 percent higher than the initial one ($121 - 110 = 11$, which is 10 percent of 110).

So the *AS-AD* model predicts the same outcome as the quantity theory of money. The *AS-AD* model also predicts a less precise relationship between the quantity of money and the price level in the short run than in the long run. For example, Fig. 27.4 shows that if we start out at a below-full employment equilibrium, an increase in the quantity of money increases real GDP. In this case, a 10 percent increase in the quantity of money increases the price level from 107 to 110 — a 2.8 percent increase. That is, the price level increases by a smaller percentage than the percentage increase in the quantity of money.

How good a theory is the quantity theory of money? Let's answer this question by looking at some historical and international data.

Historical Evidence on the Quantity Theory of Money

The percentage increase in the price level is the inflation rate, and the percentage increase in the quantity of money is the money growth rate. So the quantity theory predictions can be cast in terms of money growth and inflation. The quantity theory predicts that at a given potential GDP and in the long run, the inflation rate will equal the money growth rate. But over time, potential GDP expands. Taking this expansion into account, the quantity theory predicts that in the long run, the inflation rate will equal the money growth rate minus the growth rate of potential GDP.

We can test the quantity theory of money by looking at the historical relationship between money growth and inflation in the United States. Figure 27.7 shows two views of this relationship for the years between 1931 and 2001. In both parts of the figure, the inflation rate is the percentage change in the GDP deflator and the money growth rate is the growth rate of M2. Part (a) shows year-to-year changes in money and the price level. These changes show the short-run relationship between money growth and inflation. Part (b) shows decade average changes. These changes average out the year-to-year fluctuations and enable us to see the long-run relationship between the variables. If the quantity theory is a reasonable guide to reality, there should be a strong correlation between inflation and money growth in the decade average data and a weak correlation in the year-to-year data.

That is what the data show. The year-to-year fluctuations in money growth and inflation, which contain short-run influences (in part a), show a weak correlation, and the decade average fluctuations in money growth and inflation (in part b) show a stronger correlation. The burst of inflation after World War II resulted from the strong burst of money growth during the war. The low inflation of the 1960s was associated with a low money growth rate. The inflation speed up during the 1970s came from a speed up in money growth. And the falling inflation of the 1980s and low inflation of the 1990s came from a slowing of money growth. Money growth increased during the late 1990s, a predictor of higher inflation.

International Evidence on the Quantity Theory of Money

Another way to test the quantity theory of money is to look at the cross-country data. Figure 27.8(a) shows the relationship between money growth and inflation in 60 countries during the 1980s. Figure 27.8(b) shows the relationship for 13 regions and countries that cover the entire world during the 1990s. By looking at a decade average, we again smooth out the short-run effects of money growth and focus on the long-run effects. These data show that rapid money growth is associated with high inflation. Evidence from Argentina in *Reading Between the Lines* on pp. 648–649 reinforces this conclusion.

Correlation, Causation, and Other Influences

Both the historical evidence for the United States and the international data tell us that in the long run, money growth and inflation are correlated. But the correlation between money growth and inflation does not tell us that money growth causes inflation. Money growth might cause inflation; inflation might cause money growth; or some third variable might simultaneously cause inflation and money growth.

According to the quantity theory and according to the *AS-AD* model, causation runs from money growth to inflation. But neither theory denies the possibility that at different times and places, causation might run in the other direction or that some third factor might be the root cause of both rapid money growth and inflation. One possible third factor is a large and persistent government budget deficit that gets financed by creating money.

Some occasions provide an opportunity to test our assumptions about causation. One of these is World War II and the years immediately following it. Rapid money growth during the war years was accompanied by controls that held prices down

FIGURE 27.7   Money Growth and Inflation in the United States: 1961–2001

(a) Year-to-year change in the money supply and the price level

Year-to-year fluctuations in money growth and inflation (part a) are loosely correlated, but decade average fluctuations in money growth and inflation (part b) are closely correlated. The burst of inflation after World War II and again during the 1970s were caused by rapid money growth. The slowing of inflation during the 1980s and low inflation of the 1990s came from slower money growth. The increase in money growth during the late 1990s predicts higher inflation in the near future.

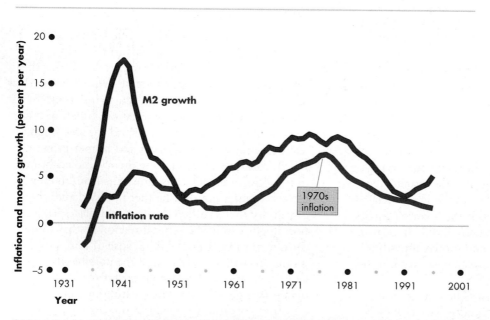

(b) Decade average change in the money supply and the price level

Sources: The Federal Reserve Board and the Bureau of Economic Analysis.

FIGURE 27.8   Money Growth and Inflation in the World Economy

(a) 60 countries during the 1980s

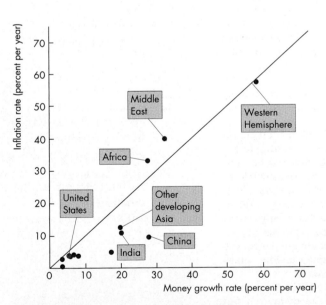

(b) 13 regions and countries during the 1990s

Inflation and money growth in 60 countries in part (a) and in the low-inflation countries in part (b) show a clear positive relationship.

Sources: The Federal Reserve Bank of St. Louis, *Review*, May/June 1988, p. 15 and International Monetary Fund.

during the war but allowed them to rise immediately after the war. The inflationary consequence of wartime money growth was delayed by price controls but not avoided. And the wartime money growth caused the postwar inflation. The late 1960s and 1970s provide another test. Rapid money growth began during the 1960s that caused higher inflation during the 1970s. The combination of historical and international correlations between money growth and inflation and independent evidence about the direction of causation leads to the conclusion that the quantity theory is correct in the long run. It explains the long-term fundamental source of inflation. It also implies that the only way to slow inflation, in the long run, is to slow money growth.

But the quantity theory is not correct in the short run. To understand the short-term fluctuations in inflation, the joint effects of a change in the quantity of money on real GDP, the velocity of circulation, and the price level must be explained. The *AS-AD* model provides this explanation, and points to other factors that influence the inflation rate independently of the money growth rate in the short run.

REVIEW QUIZ

1 Do the short-run effects of an increase in the quantity of money on the price level and real GDP differ from the long-run effects? What are the differences? Why are there different effects?

2 What is the quantity theory of money? Are the predictions of the quantity theory in conflict with the predictions of the *AS-AD* model?

3 Do the long-run historical evidence and the international evidence on the relationship between money growth and inflation support the quantity theory?

◆Before you leave the subject of this chapter, look at *Reading Between the Lines* on pp. 648–649 and see how rapid money growth has brought inflation in Argentina. In the next chapter, we'll learn how the Fed influences the quantity of money and interest rates in its attempt to steer the course of the economy. Then, in Chapter 29, we'll return to the problem of inflation and explore more deeply its causes, its consequences, and ways of keeping it under control.

The Quantity Theory of
Money in Argentina

THE WASHINGTON POST, JANUARY 6, 2002

Argentines Prepare To Face Fallout
of Economic 'D-Day'

BUENOS AIRES, Jan. 5 — Enter a bustling, warehouse-style superstore and the first impression is of a coming storm. A 31-year-old music teacher wearing a black Paris Opera T-shirt is stocking up on light bulbs and Diet Coke. A woman, jittery and arguing with her accountant husband, wheels around a cart brimming with enough coffee and beef to last a month. But the line of people at the register — desperate to buy computers, stereos and televisions — is the tip-off that the disaster here is manmade.

With the announcement Friday that Argentina's bankrupt government will devalue the peso and end its decade-old parity with the U.S. dollar, a latent panic began to resurface today, the fear of hyperinflation.

Ten years ago, when annual inflation reached 5,000 percent, people would rush down the aisles of supermarkets, desperate to grab goods before clerks could stamp on higher prices. Imported goods such as computers and VCRs were often scarce or expensive or both. Now, with financial collapse about to break the peso-dollar peg that tamed inflation, Argentina's unprecedented era of monetary stability is coming to an end.

And many fear inflation will return.

"I'm broke, but I'm still buying before D-Day — Devaluation Day," said Paula Cardoso, 57, a chain-smoking librarian who picked out a Sony television for $275. She, like so many, feared the prices of imported electronics would be the first to rise. "We had 10 years of stability, but the party is over, my friend. We're going back to the old Argentina. Just you wait."...

Inflation has become part of national mythology, a boogeyman story passed down from generation to generation.

"My father told me all about those years — about getting to the grocery store in the morning because he didn't know what prices would be like after he got out of work," said Jorge Villegas, 22, a college student who spent most of his savings today on a $950 Compaq computer at Carrefour, a French chain similar to Wal-Mart, in the upper-middle class Palermo neighborhood.

"I was going to wait a few months before I bought the computer, but now, I didn't think I could afford to wait," he said.

...

Essence of the Story

■ In January 2002, Argentines were stocking up on all types of goods: light bulbs, Diet Coke, coffee, beef, computers, stereos, and televisions.

■ The reason was that they feared hyperinflation.

The government had announced that it would devalue the peso and end its 10-year-long fixed link with the U.S. dollar.

■ Ten years earlier, the inflation rate had been 5,000 percent a year.

Economic Analysis

■ Argentina has long suffered from a high inflation rate.

■ During the 1970s, its average inflation rate was 130 percent a year. During the 1980s, the inflation rate climbed to an average of 570 percent a year. And in 1989, the inflation rate exceeded 3,000 percent a year.

■ To appreciate an inflation rate of 3,000 percent a year, translate it to a monthly inflation rate. Every month, on the average, prices rise by 33 percent. Table 1 shows what happens to the price of a coffee that in January was $3.00 a cup. After six months, the price is $12.50!

■ When people expect prices to rise rapidly, they expect the money they hold to fall in value rapidly. So they spend and hold goods rather than money.

■ Figure 1 shows the inflation record in Argentina from 1971 through 2001.

■ During the 1970s and 1980s, when the inflation rate was high, the money growth rate in Argentina was also high — as predicted by the quantity theory of money.

■ The very high inflation rate of 1989–1990 created a crisis of confidence in the ability of Argentina to achieve a stable value of money.

■ To instill confidence, the government adopted a U.S. dollar standard. One unit of the national currency was defined to be worth one U.S. dollar.

■ For a decade, this arrangement kept money growth and inflation in check and Argentina had a stable price level.

■ But other problems — slow economic growth, a high unemployment rate, and government budget deficits — led the Argentine government to abandon the fixed link with the U.S. dollar in 2001.

■ With a return to the monetary system of the 1980s, people feared a return to the inflation of the 1980s, so they spent their money on a wide range of goods.

■ The increased spending increased the velocity of circulation of money and increased the inflation rate by more than the increase in the money growth rate.

Figure 1 Inflation in Argentina

Month	Price of coffee (dollars per cup)
January	3.00
February	4.00
March	5.30
April	7.00
May	9.49
June	12.50

Table 1 A 33-percent-a-year inflation

KEY POINTS

What Is Money? (pp. 630–632)

- Money is the means of payment, a medium of exchange, a unit of account, and a store of value.
- M1 consists of currency, travelers' checks, and checking deposits owned by individuals and businesses. M2 consists of M1 plus savings deposits, time deposits, and money market mutual funds.

Depository Institutions (pp. 633–635)

- Commercial banks, S&Ls, savings banks, credit unions, and money market mutual funds are depository institutions whose liabilities are money.
- Depository institutions provide four main economic services: They create liquidity, minimize the cost of obtaining funds, minimize the cost of monitoring borrowers, and pool risks.

Financial Regulation, Deregulation, and Innovation (pp. 635–637)

- Financial regulation to protect depositors includes deposit insurance and balance sheet rules such as minimum equity capital rules, required reserves, and deposit and lending rules.
- Deregulation during the 1980s removed the distinctions between banks and nonbank depository institutions.
- The search for profit leads to the creation of new types of deposits and loans, which change the composition of the nation's money.

How Banks Create Money (pp. 637–641)

- Banks create money by making loans.
- The total quantity of deposits that can be supported by a given amount of reserves (the deposit multiplier) is determined by the required reserve ratio.

Money, Real GDP, and the Price Level (pp. 641–647)

- An increase in the quantity of money increases aggregate demand and, in the short run, increases both the price level and real GDP.
- In the long run, an increase in the quantity of money increases the price level and brings no change in real GDP.
- Like the *AS-AD* model, the quantity theory of money predicts no long-run relationship between money, the price level, and real GDP.

KEY FIGURES

KEY TERMS

PROBLEMS

*1. In the United States today, money includes which of the following items?
   a. Federal Reserve banknotes in the Bank of America's cash machines
   b. Your Visa card
   c. The quarters inside public phones
   d. U.S. dollar bills in your wallet
   e. The check you have just written to pay for your rent
   f. The loan you took out last August to pay for your school fees

2. Which of the following items are money? Which are deposit money?
   a. Checking deposits at Citicorp
   b. Yahoo! stock held by individuals
   c. An American Express traveler's check
   d. State of Florida securities
   e. NOW accounts
   Explain your answer by referring to the three basic functions of money.

*3. Sara withdraws $1,000 from her savings account at the Lucky S&L, keeps $50 in cash, and deposits the balance in her checking account at the Bank of Illinois. What is the immediate change in M1 and M2?

4. Monica takes $10,000 from her money market mutual fund and puts the funds into her savings account at the Bank of Alaska. What is the immediate change in M1 and M2?

*5. The commercial banks in Zap have

Reserves	$250 million
Loans	$1,000 million
Deposits	$2,000 million
Total assets	$2,500 million

   a. Construct the commercial banks' balance sheet. If you are missing any assets, call them "other assets"; if you are missing any liabilities, call them "other liabilities."
   b. Calculate the banks' reserve ratio.
   c. If banks hold no excess reserves, calculate the deposit multiplier.

6. The commercial banks in Zip have

Reserves	$250 million
Loans	$3,750 million
Deposits	$4,000 million
Total assets	$4,200 million

   a. Construct the commercial banks' balance sheet. If you are missing any assets, call them "other assets"; if you are missing any liabilities, call them "other liabilities."
   b. Calculate the banks' reserve ratio.
   c. If banks hold no excess reserves, calculate the deposit multiplier.

*7. An immigrant arrives in New Transylvania with $1,200. The $1,200 is deposited in a bank. All the banks in New Transylvania have a required reserve ratio of 10 percent, and they have no excess reserves when the immigrant arrives.
   a. What is the initial increase in the quantity of money in New Transylvania?
   b. What is the initial increase in the quantity of bank deposits when the immigrant arrives?
   c. How much does the immigrant's bank lend initially?
   d. Set out the transactions that take place and calculate the amount lent and the amount of deposits created if all the funds lent are returned to the banking system in the form of deposits.
   e. By how much has the quantity of money increased after the banks have made 2 loans?
   f. What is the total increase in the quantity of money, in bank loans, and in bank deposits?

8. An Internet thief in Chicago steals $1 million from a bank in Buenos Aires, Argentina. He transfers the funds to bank account in Chicago. The Chicago bank has a required reserve ratio of 5 percent, and it has no excess reserves when the transfer occurs.
   a. What is the initial increase in the quantity of money in the United States?
   b. What is the initial increase in the quantity of bank deposits when the theft occurs?
   c. How much does the thief's bank lend out?
   d. Set out the transactions that take place and calculate the amount lent and the amount of deposits created if all the funds lent are returned to the banking system in the form of deposits.
   e. By how much has the quantity of money increased after the banks have made 2 loans?
   f. What is the total increase in the quantity of money, in bank loans, and in bank deposits?

*9. Slowcon is a country in which the quantity theory of money operates in the long run but not in the short run. Slowcon has some unemployment when banks begin to make new loans and increase the quantity of money.
   a. What is the effect of the banks' actions on aggregate demand?
   b. What are the effects of the banks' actions on real GDP and the price level in the short run?
   c. What are the effects of the banks' actions on real GDP and the price level in the long run?

10. Banks in Japan make bad loans that don't get repaid, and several banks fail. The banks' customers lose their deposits.
   a. What is the effect of the bank failures on the quantity of money?
   b. What is the effect of the bank failures on aggregate demand?
   c. What are the effects of the bank failures on real GDP and the price level in the short run?
   d. What are the effects of the bank failures on real GDP and the price level in the long run?

*11. Quantecon is a country in which the quantity theory of money operates. The country has a constant population, capital stock, and technology. In year 1, real GDP was $400 million, the price level was 200, and the velocity of circulation of money was 20. In year 2, the quantity of money was 20 percent higher than in year 1.
   a. What was the quantity of money in year 1?
   b. What was the quantity of money in year 2?
   c. What was the price level in year 2?
   d. What was the level of real GDP in year 2?
   e. What was the velocity of circulation in year 2?

12. In Quantecon described in problem 11, in year 3, the quantity of money falls to one fifth of its year 2 level.
   a. What is the quantity of money in year 3?
   b. What is the price level in year 3?
   c. What is the level of real GDP in year 3?
   d. What is the velocity of circulation in year 3?
   e. If it takes more than one year for the full quantity theory effect to occur, what do you predict happens in Quantecon in year 3 to real GDP? Why?

CRITICAL THINKING

1. Study *Reading Between the Lines* on pp. 648–649 and then answer the following questions:
   a. How has Argentina coped with the problem of finding a stable unit of account?
   b. What happened to the velocity of circulation of money in Argentina in 2001?
   c. How do people protect themselves from a falling value of money in Argentina?

2. Rapid inflation in Brazil caused the cruzeiro to lose its ability to function as money. Which of these commodities do you think would be most likely to take the place of the cruzeiro in the Brazilian economy? Explain why.
   a. Tractor parts
   b. Packs of cigarettes
   c. Loaves of bread
   d. Impressionist paintings
   e. Baseball trading cards

WEB EXERCISES

1. Use the link on your Parkin Web site to visit Mark Bernkopf's Central Banking Resource Center and read the short article on electronic cash and "The End of Cash" by James Gleick (first published in the *New York Times Magazine* on June 16, 1996). Then answer the following questions:
   a. What is e-cash?
   b. Mark Bernkopf asks, "Will 'e-cash' enable private currencies to overturn the ability of governments to make monetary policy?" Do you think it will? Why or why not?
   c. When you buy an item on the Internet and pay by using a form of e-cash, are you using money? Explain why or why not.
   d. In your opinion, is the concern about e-cash a real concern or hype?

2. Use the link on your Parkin Web site to visit the Federal Reserve, the BLS, and BEA. Obtain the M1, M2, CPI, and GDP deflator data for the past ten years. Do these data confirm or contradict the quantity theory of money? Explain your answer using both the quantity theory of money and the *AS-AD* model.

MONETARY POLICY — CHAPTER 28

Temple of Secrets

In 1987, William Greider's book *Secrets of the Temple: How the Federal Reserve Runs the Country* made the *New York Times* best-seller list. This book lets its reader in on some secrets of a mysterious Fed. What exactly is the Fed? What tools does it possess? And how does it use them? ◆ One thing the Fed does is manage the nation's money. What determines the amount of money floating around the economy and how does the Fed influence it? ◆ Through 2001, as the U.S. economy slowed to a near standstill, the Fed, anxious to keep the economy expanding, cut interest rates 11 times from more than 6 percent at the start of the year to less than 2 percent at the year's end. ◆ A year earlier, in 2000, the Fed was more concerned about inflation than recession and it raised interest rates. How does the Fed change interest rates? How do interest rates influence the economy? How do lower interest rates fight recession? How do higher interest rates keep inflation in check?

◆ In this chapter, you'll discover the answers to these questions. In *Reading Between the Lines* at the end of the chapter, you'll see how the Fed tried to fight off recession with repeated interest rate cuts through 2001.

After studying this chapter, you will be able to

- Describe the structure of the Federal Reserve System (the Fed), and the tools used by the Fed to conduct monetary policy

- Explain what an open market operation is, how it works, and how it changes the quantity of money

- Explain what determines the demand for money

- Explain how the Fed influences interest rates

- Explain how the Fed's actions influence spending plans, real GDP, and the price level

653

The Federal Reserve System

THE CENTRAL BANK OF THE UNITED STATES IS the **Federal Reserve System**. A **central bank** is a bank's bank and a public authority that regulates a nation's depository institutions and controls the quantity of money. As the banks' bank, the Fed provides banking services to commercial banks such as the Bank of America. A central bank is not a citizens' bank. That is, the Fed does not provide general banking services for businesses and individual citizens.

The Fed's Goals and Targets

The Fed conducts the nation's **monetary policy**, which means that it adjusts the quantity of money in circulation. The Fed's goals are to keep inflation in check, maintain full employment, moderate the business cycle, and contribute toward achieving long-term growth. Complete success in the pursuit of these goals is impossible, and the Fed's more modest goal is to improve the performance of the economy and to get closer to the goals than a hands-off approach would achieve. Whether the Fed succeeds in improving economic performance is a matter on which there is a range of opinion.

In pursuit of its ultimate goals, the Fed pays close attention to interest rates and pays special attention to one interest rate, the **federal funds rate**, which is the interest rate that the banks charge each other on overnight loans of reserves. The Fed sets a target for the federal funds rate that is consistent with its ultimate goals and then takes actions to achieve its target.

This chapter examines the tools available to the Fed in its conduct of monetary policy and looks at the effects of the Fed's actions on the economy. We begin by describing the structure of the Fed.

The Structure of the Fed

The key elements in the structure of the Federal Reserve System are

- The Board of Governors
- The Regional Federal Reserve Banks
- The Federal Open Market Committee

The Board of Governors The Board of Governors has seven members, who are appointed by the President of the United States and confirmed by the Senate, each for a 14-year term. The terms are staggered so that one seat on the board becomes vacant every two years. The President appoints one of the board members as chairman for a term of four years, which is renewable.

The Federal Reserve Banks There are 12 Federal Reserve banks, one for each of 12 Federal Reserve districts shown in Fig. 28.1. These Federal Reserve banks provide check clearing services to commercial banks and other depository institutions, hold the reserve accounts of commercial banks, lend reserves to banks, and issue the bank notes that circulate as currency.

One of the district banks, the Federal Reserve Bank of New York (known as the New York Fed), occupies a special place in the Federal Reserve System because it implements the policy decisions of the Federal Open Market Committee.

The Federal Open Market Committee The **Federal Open Market Committee** (FOMC) is the main policy-making organ of the Federal Reserve System. The FOMC consists of the following voting members:

- The chairman and the other six members of the Board of Governors
- The president of the Federal Reserve Bank of New York
- The presidents of the other regional Federal Reserve banks (of whom, on a yearly rotating basis, only four vote)

The FOMC meets approximately every six weeks to review the state of the economy and to decide the actions to be carried out by the New York Fed.

The Fed's Power Center

A description of the formal structure of the Fed gives the impression that power in the Fed resides with the Board of Governors. In practice, it is the chairman of the Board of Governors who has the largest influence on the Fed's monetary policy actions, and some remarkable individuals have held this position. One of these is Alan Greenspan, the current chairman, who was appointed by President Reagan in 1987, reappointed by President Bush in 1992, and again

FIGURE 28.1   The Federal Reserve System

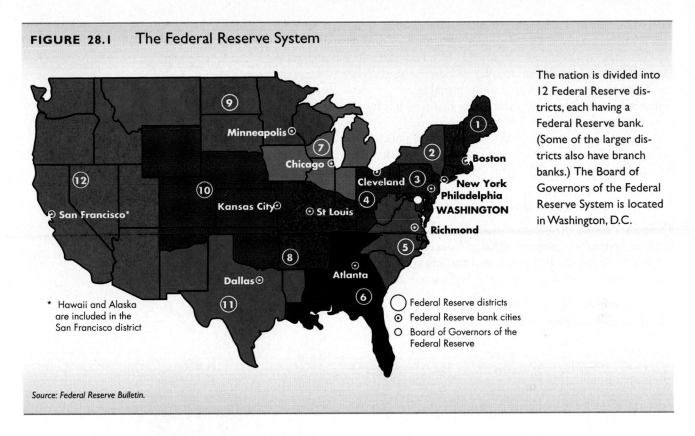

The nation is divided into 12 Federal Reserve districts, each having a Federal Reserve bank. (Some of the larger districts also have branch banks.) The Board of Governors of the Federal Reserve System is located in Washington, D.C.

* Hawaii and Alaska are included in the San Francisco district

○ Federal Reserve districts
◉ Federal Reserve bank cities
○ Board of Governors of the Federal Reserve

Source: Federal Reserve Bulletin.

by President Clinton in 1996 and 2000. Another is Paul Volcker, who was appointed in 1979 by President Carter and reappointed in 1983 by President Reagan. Volcker eradicated inflation but at the cost of one of the most severe postwar recessions.

The chairman's power and influence stem from three sources. First, it is the chairman who controls the agenda and who dominates the meetings of the FOMC. Second, day-to-day contact with a large staff of economists and other technical experts provides the chairman with detailed background briefings on monetary policy issues. Third, the chairman is the spokesperson for the Fed and the main point of contact of the Fed with the President and government and with foreign central banks and governments.

The Fed's Policy Tools

The Federal Reserve System has many responsibilities, but we'll examine its single most important one: regulating the amount of money floating around in the United States. How does the Fed control the quantity of money? It does so by adjusting the reserves of the banking system. It is also by adjusting the reserves of the banking system and by standing ready

to make loans to banks that the Fed is able to prevent bank failures. The Fed uses three main policy tools to achieve its objectives:

- Required reserve ratios
- Discount rate
- Open market operations

Required Reserve Ratios All depository institutions in the United States are required to hold a minimum percentage of deposits as reserves. This minimum percentage is known as a *required reserve ratio*. The Fed determines a required reserve ratio for each type of deposit. In 2002, banks were required to hold minimum reserves equal to 3 percent of checking deposits up to $42.8 million and 10 percent of these deposits in excess of $42.8 million. The required reserves on other types of deposits were zero.

Discount Rate The **discount rate** is the interest rate at which the Fed stands ready to lend reserves to depository institutions. A change in the discount rate is proposed to the FOMC by the Board of Directors of at least one of the 12 Federal Reserve banks and is approved by the Board of Governors.

Open Market Operations An **open market operation** is the purchase or sale of government securities — U.S. Treasury bills and bonds — by the Federal Reserve System in the open market. When the Fed conducts an open market operation, it makes a transaction with a bank or some other business but it does not transact with the federal government.

Figure 28.2 summarizes the structure and policy tools of the Fed. To understand how the tools work, we need to know about the Fed's balance sheet.

The Fed's Balance Sheet

Table 28.1 shows the balance sheet of the Federal Reserve System for February 2001. The assets on the left side are what the Fed owns, and the liabilities on the right side are what it owes. The Fed's assets are

1. Gold and foreign exchange
2. U.S. government securities
3. Loans to banks

Gold and foreign exchange are the Fed's holdings of international reserves, which consist of deposits at other central banks and an account called Special Drawing Rights, which the Fed holds at the International Monetary Fund.

The Fed's major assets are its holdings of U.S. government securities. These securities are mainly short-term Treasury bills and bonds.

When the banks are short of reserves, they can borrow reserves from the Fed. These borrowed reserves are an asset, "loans to banks," in the Fed's balance sheet.

The Fed's assets are the backing for its liabilities:

1. Federal Reserve notes in circulation
2. Banks' deposits

The Federal Reserve notes in circulation are the dollar bills that we use in our daily transactions. Some of these bills are held by the public; others are in the tills and vaults of banks and other financial institutions. Banks' deposits are the deposits of depository institutions and part of their reserves.

You might be wondering why Federal Reserve notes are considered a liability of the Fed. When bank notes were invented, they gave their owner a claim on the gold reserves of the issuing bank. Such notes were *convertible paper money.* The holder of such a note could convert the note on demand into gold (or some other commodity such as silver) at a guaranteed price. So when a bank issued a note, it was holding itself

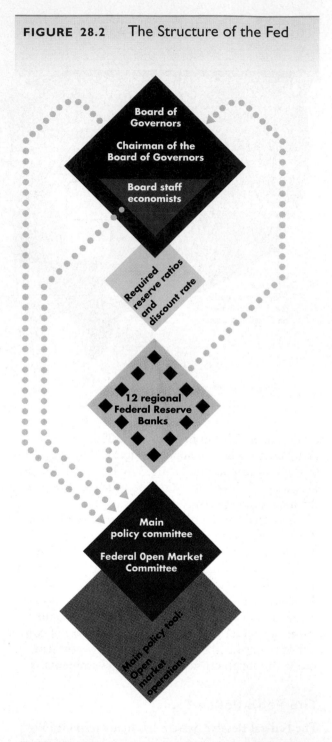

FIGURE 28.2   The Structure of the Fed

Board of Governors

Chairman of the Board of Governors

Board staff economists

Required reserve ratios and discount rate

12 regional Federal Reserve Banks

Main policy committee

Federal Open Market Committee

Main policy tool: Open market operations

The Board of Governors sets required reserve ratios and, on the proposal of the 12 Federal Reserve banks, sets the discount rate. The Board of Governors and presidents of the regional Federal Reserve banks sit on the FOMC to determine open market operations.

TABLE 28.1   The Fed's Balance Sheet, February 2002

Assets (billions of dollars)		Liabilities (billions of dollars)	
Gold and foreign exchange	47	Federal Reserve notes	609
U.S. government securities	569	Banks' deposits	15
Loans to banks	30	Other assets (net)	22
Total assets	646	Total liabilities	646

Source: Federal Reserve Board.

liable to convert that note into gold or silver. Modern bank notes are nonconvertible. A *nonconvertible note* is a bank note that is not convertible into any commodity and that obtains its value by government fiat — hence the term "fiat money." Such notes are the legal liability of the bank that issues them, and they are backed by holdings of securities and loans. Federal Reserve notes are backed by the Fed's holdings of U.S. government securities.

The Fed's liabilities together with coins in circulation (coins are issued by the Treasury and are not liabilities of the Fed) make up the monetary base. That is, the **monetary base** is the sum of Federal Reserve notes, coins, and banks' deposits at the Fed. The monetary base is so called because it acts like a base that supports the nation's money supply. The larger the monetary base, the greater is the quantity of money.

REVIEW QUIZ

1 What is the central bank of the United States and what functions does it perform?
2 Who appoints the Fed board members and chairman and for how long do they serve?
3 Can you name the Fed's three policy tools?
4 What is the Federal Open Market Committee and what are its main functions?
5 How often does the FOMC meet?

Next, we're going to see how the Fed controls the quantity of money. We'll see how the Fed's monetary policy instruments change the monetary base and how changes in the monetary base change the quantity of money.

Controlling the Quantity of Money

THE FED CONSTANTLY MONITORS AND ADJUSTS the quantity of money in the economy. To change the quantity of money, the Fed can use any of its three tools: required reserve ratios, discount rate, and open market operations. Required reserve ratios are changed infrequently. The discount rate and open market operations are used more frequently. Let's see how these tools work.

How Required Reserve Ratios Work

When the Fed *increases* the required reserve ratio, the banks must hold more reserves. To increase their reserves, the banks must *decrease* their lending, which *decreases* the quantity of money. When the Fed *decreases* the required reserve ratio, the banks may hold less reserves. To decrease their reserves, the banks *increase* their lending, which *increases* the quantity of money.

How the Discount Rate Works

When the Fed *increases* the discount rate, banks must pay a higher price for any reserves that they borrow from the Fed. Faced with the higher cost of reserves, the banks try to get by with smaller reserves. But with a given required reserve ratio, banks must also *decrease* their lending to decrease their borrowed reserves. So the quantity of money *decreases*. When the Fed *decreases* the discount rate, banks pay a lower price for any reserves that they borrow from the Fed. Faced with lower cost of reserves, banks are willing to borrow more reserves and *increase* their lending. So the quantity of money *increases*.

How an Open Market Operation Works

When the Fed *buys* securities in an open market operation, bank reserves *increase*, banks *increase* their lending, and the quantity of money *increases*. When the Fed *sells* securities in an open market operation, bank reserves *decrease*, banks *decrease* their lending, and the quantity of money *decreases*. Open market operations are used more frequently than the other two tools and are the most complex in their operation. So we'll study this tool in greater detail than the other two.

The key to understanding how an open market operation works is to see how it changes the reserves of the banking system. We'll trace the effects of an open market operation when the Fed *buys* securities.

The Fed Buys Securities Suppose the Fed buys $100 million of U.S. government securities in the open market. There are two cases to consider: when the Fed buys from a commercial bank and when it buys from the public (a person or business that is not a commercial bank). The outcome is essentially the same in both cases, but you might need to be convinced of this fact, so we'll study the two cases. We'll start with the simpler case, in which the Fed buys from a commercial bank.

Buys from Commercial Bank When the Fed buys $100 million of securities from the Manhattan Commercial Bank, two things happen:

1. The Manhattan Commercial Bank has $100 million less in securities, and the Fed has $100 million more in securities.
2. The Fed pays for the securities by crediting the Manhattan Commercial Bank's deposit account at the Fed with $100 million.

Figure 28.3(a) shows the effects of these actions on the balance sheets of the Fed and the Manhattan Commercial Bank. Ownership of the securities passes from the commercial bank to the Fed, so the bank's assets decrease by $100 million and the Fed's assets increase by $100 million, as shown by the blue arrow running from the Manhattan Commercial Bank to the Fed. The Fed pays for the securities by crediting the Manhattan Commercial Bank's deposit account — its reserves — at the Fed with $100 million, as shown by the green arrow running from the Fed to the Manhattan Commercial Bank. This action increases the monetary base and increases the reserves of the banking system.

The Fed's assets increase by $100 million, and its liabilities also increase by $100 million. The commercial bank's total assets remain constant, but their composition changes. Its holdings of government securities decrease by $100 million, and its deposits at the Fed increase by $100 million. So the bank has additional reserves, which it can use to make loans.

We've just seen that when the Fed buys government securities from a bank, the bank's reserves increase. But what happens if the Fed buys government securities from the public — say, from Goldman Sachs, a financial services company?

FIGURE 28.3   The Fed Buys Securities in the Open Market

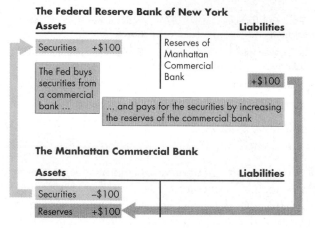

(a) The Fed buys securities from a commercial bank

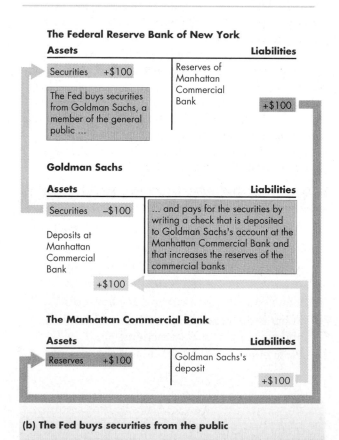

(b) The Fed buys securities from the public

Buys from Public When the Fed buys $100 million of securities from Goldman Sachs, three things happen:

1. Goldman Sachs has $100 million less in securities, and the Fed has $100 million more in securities.
2. The Fed pays for the securities with a check for $100 million drawn on itself, which Goldman Sachs deposits in its account at the Manhattan Commercial Bank.
3. The Manhattan Commercial Bank collects payment of this check from the Fed, and $100 million is deposited in Manhattan's deposit account at the Fed.

Figure 28.3(b) shows the effects of these actions on the balance sheets of the Fed, Goldman Sachs, and the Manhattan Commercial Bank. Ownership of the securities passes from Goldman Sachs to the Fed, so Goldman Sachs's assets decrease by $100 million and the Fed's assets increase by $100 million, as shown by the blue arrow running from Goldman Sachs to the Fed. The Fed pays for the securities with a check payable to Goldman Sachs, which Goldman Sachs deposits in the Manhattan Commercial Bank. This payment increases Manhattan's reserves by $100 million, as shown by green arrow running from the Fed to Manhattan Commercial Bank. It also increases Goldman Sachs's deposit at the Manhattan Commercial Bank by $100 million, as shown by the red arrow running from the Manhattan Commercial Bank to Goldman Sachs. Just as when the Fed buys from a bank, this action increases the monetary base and increases the reserves of the banking system.

Again, the Fed's assets increase by $100 million, and its liabilities also increase by $100 million. Goldman Sachs has the same total assets as before, but their composition has changed. It now has more money and fewer securities. The Manhattan Commercial Bank's total assets increase, and so do its liabilities. Its deposits at the Fed — its reserves — increase by $100 million, and its deposit liability to Goldman Sachs increases by $100 million. Because its reserves have increased by the same amount as its deposits, the bank has excess reserves, which it can use to make loans.

We've studied what happens when the Fed *buys* government securities from either a bank or the public. When the Fed *sells* securities, all the transactions and events you've just studied work in reverse. (Trace the process again but with the Fed selling and the banks or public buying securities.)

The effects of an open market operation on the balance sheets of the Fed and the banks that we've just described are not the end of the story — they are just the beginning.

A change in bank reserves that results from an open market operation has ripple effects through the economy. First, it has a multiplier effect on the quantity of money. Second, it changes interest rates. Third, it changes aggregate expenditure and real GDP.

We are going to study these ripple effects in the rest of this chapter. We begin by studying the multiplier effect of an open market operation on the quantity of money. To do so, we build on the link between bank reserves and bank deposits that you studied in Chapter 27, pp. 638–640. But first we must learn about a related link between bank reserves and the monetary base.

Bank Reserves, the Monetary Base, and the Money Multiplier

An open market purchase that increases bank reserves also increases the monetary base. The increase in the monetary base equals the amount of the open market purchase, and initially it equals the increase in bank reserves. To see why, recall that the *monetary base* is the sum of Federal Reserve notes, coins, and banks' deposits at the Fed. An open market purchase increases the banks' deposits at the Fed — part of banks' reserves — by the amount of the open market purchase. Nothing else changes, so the monetary base increases by the amount of the open market purchase.

But when the banks use the new reserves to make loans, bank deposits and currency held outside the banks increase. An increase in currency held outside the banks is called a **currency drain**. A currency drain does not change the monetary base. Bank reserves decrease, currency increases, and the monetary base remains the same. But a currency drain decreases the amount of money that banks can create from a given increase in the monetary base.

The amount of money that banks can create from a given increase in the monetary base is determined by the **money multiplier**, which is the amount by which a change in the monetary base is multiplied to determine the resulting change in the quantity of money. Let's now look at the money multiplier.

The Multiplier Effect of an Open Market Operation

Figure 28.4 shows the multiplier effect of an open market purchase of securities from the banks. Initially, the banks' reserves increase, but the quantity of money does not change. But the banks have excess reserves, and the following sequence of events takes place:

- Banks lend excess reserves.
- The quantity of money increases.
- New deposits are used to make payments.
- Some of new money is held as currency — a *currency drain*.
- Some of the new money remains on deposit in banks.
- Banks' required reserves increase.
- Excess reserves decrease but remain positive.

The sequence repeats in a series of rounds, but each round begins with a smaller quantity of excess reserves than did the previous one. The process continues until excess reserves have finally been eliminated.

Figure 28.5 keeps track of the magnitudes of the increases in reserves, loans, deposits, currency, and money that result from an open market operation of $100,000. In this figure, the *currency drain* is 33.33 percent and the *required reserve ratio* is 10 percent. These numbers are assumed to keep the arithmetic simple.

The Fed buys $100,000 of securities from the banks. The banks' reserves increase by this amount, but deposits do not change. The banks have excess reserves of $100,000, and they lend those reserves. When the banks lend $100,000 of excess reserves, $66,667 remains in the banks as deposits and $33,333 drains off and is held outside the banks as currency. The quantity of money has now increased by $100,000 — the increase in deposits plus the increase in currency holdings.

The increased bank deposits of $66,667 generates an increase in required reserves of 10 percent of

---

FIGURE 28.4   A Round in the Multiplier Process Following an Open Market Purchase

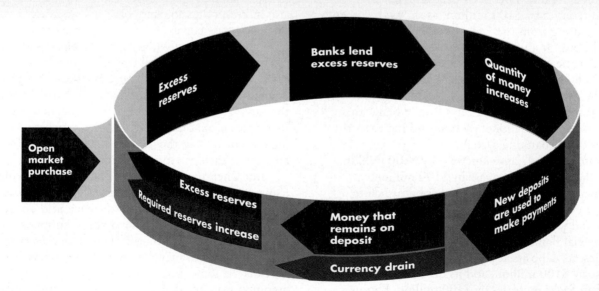

An open market purchase increases bank reserves and creates excess reserves. Banks lend the excess reserves, and new loans are used to make payments. Households and firms receiving payments keep some of the receipts in the form of currency — a currency drain — and place the rest on deposit in banks. The increase in bank deposits increases banks' reserves but also increases banks' required reserves. Required reserves increase by less than actual reserves, so the banks still have some excess reserves, though less than before. The process repeats until excess reserves have been eliminated.

FIGURE 28.5 The Multiplier Effect of an Open Market Purchase

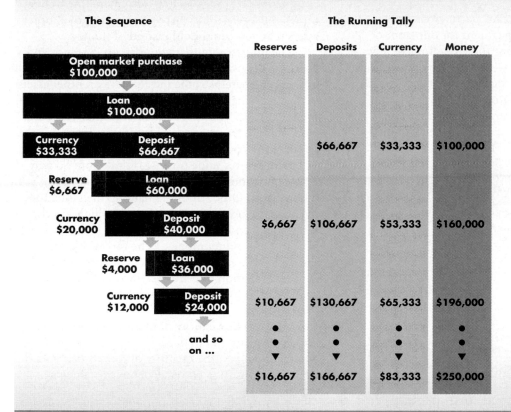

When the Fed provides the banks with $100,000 of additional reserves in an open market operation, the banks lend those reserves. Of the amount lent, $33,333 (33.33 percent) leaves the banks in a currency drain and $66,667 remains on deposit. With additional deposits, required reserves increase by $6,667 (10 percent required reserve ratio) and the banks lend $60,000. Of this amount, $20,000 leaves the banks in a currency drain and $40,000 remains on deposit. The process repeats until the banks have created enough deposits to eliminate their excess reserves. An additional $100,000 of reserves creates $250,000 of money.

that amount, which is $6,667. Actual reserves have increased by the same amount as the increase in deposits: $66,667. So the banks now have excess reserves of $60,000. At this stage, we have gone around the circle shown in Fig. 28.4 once. The process we've just described repeats but begins with excess reserves of $60,000. Figure 28.5 shows the next two rounds. At the end of the process, the quantity of money has increased by a multiple of the increase in the monetary base. In this case, the increase is $250,000, which is 2.5 times the increase in the monetary base.

An open market *sale* works similarly to an open market purchase, but it *decreases* the quantity of money. (Trace the process again but with the Fed selling and the banks or public buying securities.)

When the Fed undertakes an open market operation, it is trying to influence the course of the economy. But the Fed's influence is indirect. You've now studied the initial effect of the Fed's actions, which is to change the quantity of money.

REVIEW QUIZ

1 What happens when the Fed buys securities in the open market?
2 What happens when the Fed sells securities in the open market?
3 What do the banks do when they have excess reserves and how do their actions influence the quantity of money?
4 What do the banks do when they are short of reserves and how do their actions influence the quantity of money?

When the Fed changes the quantity of money, it sets off a ripple effect, the next part of which is a change in interest rates. Why do interest rates change when the quantity of money changes? We'll discover the answer by studying the demand for money.

The Demand for Money

THERE IS NO LIMIT TO THE AMOUNT OF MONEY we would like to *receive* in payment for our labor or as interest on our savings. But there *is* a limit to how big an inventory of money — the money that we hold in our wallet or in a deposit account at the bank — we would like to hold onto and not either spend or use to buy assets that generate an income. The demand for money is the demand for the inventory of money that people plan to hold.

The Influences on Money Holding

The quantity of money that people plan to hold depends on four main factors:

- The price level
- The interest rate
- Real GDP
- Financial innovation

The Price Level The quantity of money measured in dollars is *nominal money*. The quantity of nominal money demanded is proportional to the price level, other things remaining the same. If the price level rises by 10 percent, people hold 10 percent more nominal money than before, other things remaining the same. If you hold $20 to buy your weekly movies and soda, you will increase your money holding to $22 if the prices of movies and soda — and your wage rate — increase by 10 percent.

The quantity of money measured in constant dollars (for example, in 1996 dollars) is *real money*. Real money is equal to nominal money divided by the price level and is the quantity of money measured in terms of what it will buy. In the above example, when the price level rises by 10 percent and you increase your money holding by 10 percent, your *real* money holding is constant. Your $22 at the new price level buys the same quantity of goods and is the same quantity of *real money* as your $20 at the original price level. The quantity of real money demanded is independent of the price level.

The Interest Rate A fundamental principle of economics is that as the opportunity cost of something increases, people try to find substitutes for it. Money is no exception. The higher the opportunity cost of holding money, other things remaining the same, the lower is the quantity of real money demanded. But what is the opportunity cost of holding money? It is the interest rate that you can earn by holding money minus the interest rate that you must forgo on other assets that you could hold instead of money.

The interest rate that you earn on currency and checking deposits is zero. So the opportunity cost of holding these items is the interest rate on other assets such as a savings bond or Treasury bill. By holding money instead, you forgo the interest that you otherwise would have received. This forgone interest is the opportunity cost of holding money.

Money loses value because of inflation. So why isn't the inflation rate part of the cost of holding money? It is: Other things remaining the same, the higher the expected inflation rate, the higher is the interest rate and the higher, therefore, is the opportunity cost of holding money. (The forces that make the interest rate change to reflect changes in the expected inflation rate are described in Chapter 29, pp. 692–693.)

Real GDP The quantity of money that households and firms plan to hold depends on the amount they are spending, and the quantity of money demanded in the economy as a whole depends on aggregate expenditure — real GDP.

Again, suppose that you hold an average of $20 to finance your weekly purchases of movies and soda. Now imagine that the prices of these goods and of all other goods remain constant but that your income increases. As a consequence, you now spend more and you also keep a larger amount of money on hand to finance your higher volume of expenditure.

Financial Innovation Technological change and the arrival of new financial products change the quantity of money held. The major financial innovations are the widespread use of

1. Daily interest checking deposits
2. Automatic transfers between checking and savings deposits
3. Automatic teller machines
4. Credit cards

These innovations have occurred because of the development of computing power that has lowered the cost of calculations and record keeping.

We summarize the effects of the influences on money holding by using a demand for money curve.

The Demand for Money Curve

The demand for money curve is the relationship between the quantity of real money demanded and the interest rate when all other influences on the amount of money that people wish to hold remain the same.

Figure 28.6 shows a demand for money curve, MD. When the interest rate rises, everything else remaining the same, the opportunity cost of holding money rises and the quantity of real money demanded decreases — there is a movement up along the demand for money curve. Similarly, when the interest rate falls, the opportunity cost of holding money falls, and the quantity of real money demanded increases — there is a movement down along the demand for money curve.

When any influence on money holding other than the interest rate changes, there is a change in the demand for money and the demand for money curve shifts. Let's study these shifts.

Shifts in the Demand for Money Curve

A change in real GDP or financial innovation changes the demand for money and shifts the demand curve for real money.

Figure 28.7 illustrates the change in the demand for money. A decrease in real GDP decreases the demand for money and shifts the demand curve leftward from MD_0 to MD_1. An increase in real GDP has the opposite effect: It increases the demand for money and shifts the demand curve rightward from MD_0 to MD_2.

The influence of financial innovation on the demand for money curve is more complicated. It might increase the demand for some types of deposits, decrease the demand for others, and decrease the demand for currency.

We'll look at the effects of changes in real GDP and financial innovation by studying the demand for money in the United States.

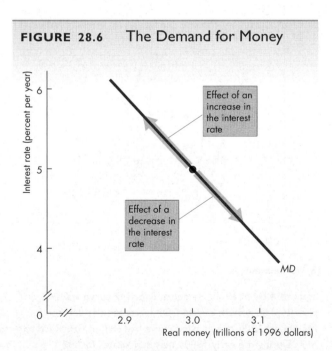

FIGURE 28.6 The Demand for Money

The demand for money curve, MD, shows the relationship between the quantity of money that people plan to hold and the interest rate, other things remaining the same. The interest rate is the opportunity cost of holding money. A change in the interest rate brings a movement along the demand curve.

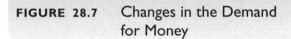

FIGURE 28.7 Changes in the Demand for Money

A decrease in real GDP decreases the demand for money. The demand curve shifts leftward from MD_0 to MD_1. An increase in real GDP increases the demand for money. The demand curve shifts rightward from MD_0 to MD_2. Financial innovation generally decreases the demand for money.

The Demand for Money in the United States

Figure 28.8 shows the relationship between the interest rate and the quantity of real money demanded in the United States between 1970 and 2001. Each dot shows the interest rate and the amount of real money held in a given year. In 1970, the demand for M1 (shown in part a) was MD_0. During the early 1970s, the spread of credit cards decreased the demand for M1 (currency and checking deposits) and this financial innovation shifted the demand for M1 curve leftward to MD_1. But over the years, real GDP growth increased the demand for M1, and by 1994, the demand for M1 curve had shifted rightward to MD_2.

Further financial innovation arising from a continued increase in the use of credit cards and the

spread of ATMs decreased the demand for M1 and shifted the demand curve leftward again.

In 1970, the demand for M2 (shown in part b) was MD_0. The spread of credit cards that decreased the demand for M1 during the period did not decrease demand for M2. The reason is that many new financial products were M2 deposits. So from 1970 through 1989, the demand for M2 increased and the demand for M2 curve shifted rightward to MD_1. But between 1989 and 1994, innovations in financial products that compete with deposits of all kinds occurred and the demand for M2 decreased. The demand for M2 curve shifted leftward to MD_2. Finally, after 1994, the expanding economy brought rising real GDP. The demand for M2 increased again, and the demand curve shifted rightward to MD_3.

FIGURE 28.8   The Demand for Money in the United States

(a) M1 demand

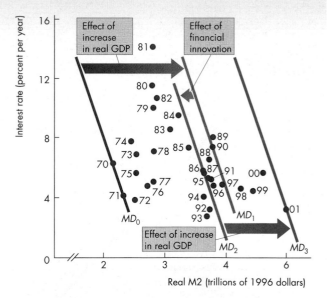

(b) M2 demand

The dots show the quantity of real money and the interest rate in each year between 1970 and 2001. In 1970, the demand for M1 was MD_0 in part (a). The demand for M1 decreased during the early 1970s because of financial innovation, and the demand curve shifted leftward to MD_1. But real GDP growth increases the demand for M1 and by 1994, the demand curve had shifted rightward to MD_2. Further financial innovation decreased the demand for M1 during the 1990s and 2000s and shifted the demand curve leftward

Sources: Bureau of Economic Analysis and Federal Reserve Board.

again to MD_3. In 1970, the demand for M2 curve was MD_0 in part (b). The growth of real GDP increased the demand for M2, and by 1989, the demand curve had shifted rightward to MD_1. During the early 1990s, new substitutes for M2 decreased the demand for M2 and the demand curve shifted leftward to MD_2. But during the late 1990s, rapid growth of real GDP increased the demand for M2. By 2001, the demand curve had shifted rightward to MD_3.

1 What are the main influences on the quantity of real money that people and businesses plan to hold?

2 What does the demand for money curve show?

3 How does an increase in the interest rate change the quantity of money demanded and how would you show the effect by using the demand for money curve?

4 How does an increase in real GDP change the demand for money and how would you show the effect by using the demand for money curve?

5 How have financial innovations changed the demand for M1 and the demand for M2?

We now know what determines the demand for money. And we've seen that a key factor is the interest rate — the opportunity cost of holding money. But what determines the interest rate? Let's find out.

Interest Rate Determination

AN INTEREST RATE IS THE PERCENTAGE YIELD ON a financial security such as a *bond* or a *stock*. The higher the price of a financial security, other things remaining the same, the lower is the interest rate. An example will make this relationship clear. Suppose the federal government sells a bond that promises to pay $10 a year. If the price of the bond is $100, the interest rate is 10 percent per year — $10 is 10 percent of $100. If the price is $50, the interest rate is 20 percent — $10 is 20 percent of $50. And if the price is $200, the interest rate is 5 percent — $10 is 5 percent of $200.

You've just seen the link between the price of a bond and the interest rate. People divide their wealth between bonds (along with other interest-bearing financial assets) and money, and the amount they hold as money depends on the interest rate. We can study these forces that determine the interest rate in either the market for bonds or the market for money.

Because the Fed can influence the *quantity of money*, we focus on the market for money.

Money Market Equilibrium

The interest rate is determined by the supply of money and the demand for money. The quantity of money supplied is determined by the actions of the banking system and the Fed. On any given day, the quantity of money is fixed. The *real* quantity of money supplied is equal to the nominal quantity supplied divided by the price level. At a given moment in time, there is a particular price level, and so the quantity of real money supplied is a fixed amount. In Fig. 28.9, the quantity of real money supplied is $3.0 trillion and the supply of money curve is *MS*.

FIGURE 28.9   Money Market Equilibrium

Money market equilibrium occurs when the interest rate has adjusted to make the quantity of money demanded equal to the quantity supplied. Here, equilibrium occurs at an interest rate of 5 percent. At interest rates above 5 percent, the quantity of money demanded is less than the quantity supplied, so people buy bonds and the interest rate falls. At interest rates below 5 percent, the quantity of money demanded exceeds the quantity supplied, so people sell bonds and the interest rate rises. Only at 5 percent is the quantity of money in existence willingly held.

On any given day, all the influences on the demand for money except for the interest rate are constant. That is, real GDP and the price level are given. But the interest rate fluctuates daily. And the lower the interest rate, the greater is the quantity of money demanded. In Fig. 28.9, the demand for money curve is *MD*.

When the quantity of money supplied equals the quantity of money demanded, the money market is in equilibrium. Figure 28.9 illustrates money market equilibrium. Equilibrium is achieved by changes in the interest rate. If the interest rate is too high, people demand a smaller quantity of money than the quantity supplied. They are holding too much money. In this situation, they try to get rid of money by buying bonds. As they do so, the price of a bond rises and the interest rate falls toward the equilibrium rate. Conversely, if the interest rate is too low, people demand a larger quantity of money than the quantity supplied. They are holding too little money. In this situation, they try to get more money by selling bonds. The supply of bonds increases, the price of a bond falls, and the interest rate rises toward the equilibrium rate. Only when the interest rate is at the level at which the quantity of money demanded equals the quantity supplied do people willingly hold the money and take no actions that change the interest rate.

Changing the Interest Rate

Suppose that the economy is overheating and the Fed fears inflation. It decides to take action to decrease aggregate demand and spending. To do so, it wants to raise interest rates and discourage borrowing and expenditure on goods and services. What does the Fed do?

The Fed sells securities in the open market. As it does so, it mops up bank reserves and induces the banks to cut their lending. The banks make a smaller quantity of new loans each day until the stock of loans outstanding has fallen to a level that is consistent with the new lower level of reserves. The quantity of money decreases.

Suppose that the Fed undertakes open market operations on a sufficiently large scale to decrease the quantity of money from $3.0 trillion to $2.9 trillion in Fig. 28.10. As a consequence, the supply of money curve shifts leftward, from MS_0 to MS_1. The demand for money curve is *MD*. With an interest rate of 5 percent, and with $2.9 trillion of money in the economy, firms and households are now holding less money than they wish to hold. They attempt to increase their

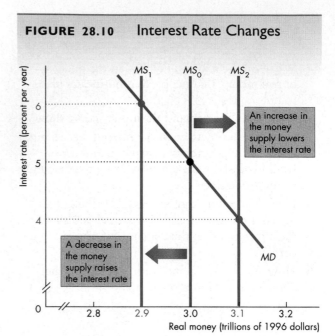

FIGURE 28.10   Interest Rate Changes

An open market sale of securities shifts the money supply curve leftward to MS_1, and the interest rate rises to 6 percent. An open market purchase of securities shifts the money supply curve rightward to MS_2, and the interest rate falls to 4 percent.

money holding by selling financial assets. As they do so, the price of a bond falls and the interest rate rises. When the interest rate has increased to 6 percent, people are willing to hold the smaller $2.9 trillion of money that the Fed and the banks have created.

Conversely, suppose that the Fed fears recession and decides to stimulate spending by increasing the quantity of money. If the Fed increases the quantity of real money to $3.1 trillion, the supply of money curve shifts rightward from MS_0 to MS_2. Equilibrium occurs when the interest rate has fallen to 4 percent.

REVIEW QUIZ

1 How is the short-term interest rate determined?
2 What do people do if they are holding more money than they plan to hold and what happens to the interest rate?
3 What actions does the Fed take if it wants to increase the interest rate? What actions does it take if it wants to decrease the interest rate?

Monetary Policy, Real GDP, and the Price Level

YOU HAVE SEEN HOW THE FED CAN CHANGE THE interest rate. We're now going to look at the wider effects of the Fed's actions on the economy. We'll begin with an overview of the ripple effects of the Fed's actions.

Ripple Effects of Monetary Policy

If the Fed increases the interest rate, three events follow:

■ Investment and consumption expenditure decrease.
■ The dollar rises, and net exports decrease.
■ A multiplier process unfolds.

Investment and Consumption The real interest rate is the *opportunity cost* of the funds used to finance investment and the purchase of big-ticket consumer items. So when the real interest rate rises, expenditure on these items falls. In the long run, the real interest rate is determined by demand and supply in the global capital market (Chapter 23, pp. 535–537). But in the short run, the Fed raises the real interest rate by raising the nominal interest rate.

The Dollar and Net Exports A rise in the interest rate, other things remaining the same, means that the U.S. interest rate rises relative to the interest rates in other countries. Some people will want to move funds into the United States from other countries to take advantage of the higher interest rate they can now earn on their U.S. bank deposits and bonds. When money is moved into the United States, people buy dollars and sell other currencies, such as Japanese yen or British pounds. With more dollars demanded, the price of the dollar rises on the foreign exchange market.

The higher price of the dollar means that foreigners must now pay more for U.S.-made goods and services. So the quantity demanded and the expenditure on U.S.-made items decrease. U.S. exports decrease. Similarly, the higher dollar means that Americans now pay less for foreign-made goods and services. So the quantity demanded and the expenditure on foreign-made items increase. U.S. imports increase.

The Multiplier Process Taking these effects together, investment, consumption expenditure, and net exports are all interest-sensitive components of expenditure. So a rise in the interest rate brings a decrease in aggregate expenditure.

You already know the rest of the story, because it is the same as that of the fiscal policy multipliers (see Chapter 26, pp. 610–612). The decrease in expenditure decreases incomes, and the decrease in income induces a decrease in consumption expenditure. The decreased consumption expenditure lowers aggregate expenditure. Real GDP and disposable income decrease further, and so does consumption expenditure. Real GDP growth slows, and the inflation rate slows.

If the Fed lowers the interest rate, the events that we've just described occur in the opposite directions, so real GDP growth and the inflation rate speed up.

Figure 28.11 summarizes the process that we've just described. It begins with the Fed's open market

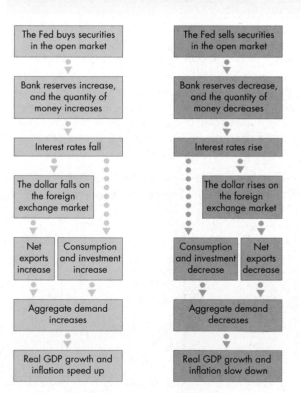

FIGURE 28.11 Ripple Effects of the Fed's Actions

The Fed's open market operations change the quantity of money and the interest rate. Expenditure plans change, and so does aggregate demand. Eventually, the Fed's open market operation has ripple effects that change real GDP and the price level.

operations that change the quantity of money and the interest rate and ends with the effects on real GDP and the price level.

Monetary Policy in the AS-AD Model

We've described the broad outline of how the Fed's actions influence the economy. Let's now see how monetary policy might be used to stabilize real GDP.

The Fed Tightens to Fight Inflation In Fig. 28.12, part (a) shows the money market, part (b) shows investment demand, and part (c) shows aggregate demand and aggregate supply. Initially, the interest rate is 5 percent a year and the quantity of investment is $2 trillion. At this level of investment (and given the other components of aggregate expenditure not shown in the figure), aggregate demand is AD_0 in part (c). The aggregate supply curve is SAS, so equilibrium real GDP is $10.2 trillion, which exceeds potential GDP.

The Fed now conducts an open market sale that increases the interest rate to 6 percent a year. The quantity of investment decreases to $1.9 trillion. Other interest-sensitive expenditure items (not shown in the figure) also decrease. The result is a decrease in aggregate demand to $AD_0 - \Delta I$.

With a decrease in aggregate demand, real GDP, aggregate expenditure, and aggregate income decrease. The decrease in income induces a further decrease in

consumption expenditure, and aggregate demand decreases further. The aggregate demand curve shifts farther leftward to AD_1.

The Fed's actions have eliminated an inflation threat and brought real GDP to equal potential GDP at $10 trillion and the price level to 110. In reality, because real GDP is growing and the price level is rising, the Fed's actions would slow real GDP growth and slow inflation rather than decrease real GDP and the price level as they do in this example.

The Fed Eases to Fight Recession Figure 28.13 is similar to Fig. 28.12. The starting point is the same in parts (a) and (b). The interest rate is 5 percent a year, and investment is $2 trillion. But the starting point is different in part (c). Now, at the level of investment (and other components of aggregate expenditure), aggregate demand is AD_0 in part (c). The aggregate supply curve is SAS, so equilibrium real GDP is $9.8 trillion, which is less than potential GDP.

The Fed now conducts an open market purchase that lowers the interest rate to 4 percent a year. Investment increases to $2.1 trillion. Other interest-sensitive expenditure items (not shown in the figure) also increase. The result is an increase in aggregate demand to $AD_0 + \Delta I$.

With an increase in aggregate demand, real GDP, aggregate expenditure, and aggregate income increase. The increase in income induces a further increase in consumption expenditure, and aggregate demand

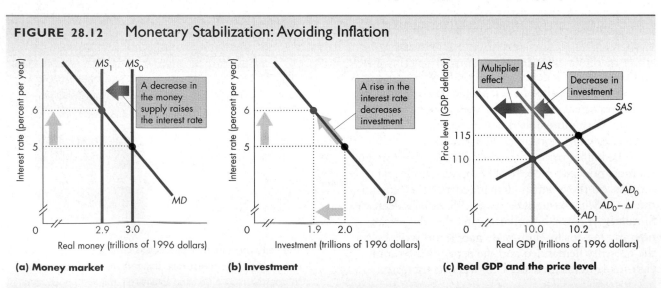

FIGURE 28.12   Monetary Stabilization: Avoiding Inflation

(a) Money market

(b) Investment

(c) Real GDP and the price level

Real GDP is $10.2 trillion, which exceeds potential GDP of $10 trillion in part (c). The Fed raises the interest rate

(part a), investment decreases (part b), and aggregate demand decreases with a multiplier effect (part c).

FIGURE 28.13   Monetary Stabilization: Avoiding Recession

(a) Money market

(b) Investment

(c) Real GDP and the price level

Real GDP is $9.8 trillion, which is below potential GDP of $10 trillion in part (c). The Fed lowers the interest rate (part a), investment increases (part b), and aggregate demand increases with a multiplier effect (part c).

increases further. The aggregate demand curve shifts farther rightward to AD_1.

The Fed's actions have eliminated a recession and brought real GDP to equal potential GDP at $10 trillion and the price level to 110.

The Size of the Multiplier Effect The size of the multiplier effect of monetary policy depends on the sensitivity of expenditure plans to the interest rate. The larger the effect of a change in the interest rate on aggregate expenditure, the greater is the multiplier effect and the smaller is the change in the interest rate that achieves the Fed's objective.

Limitations of Monetary Stabilization Policy

Monetary policy has an advantage over fiscal policy because it cuts out the law-making time lags. The FOMC meets eight times a year and uses conference calls between its scheduled meetings if the need arises. Actions that change the quantity of money are taken daily by the New York Fed. So monetary policy is a continuous policy process and is not subject to the long decision lag and the need to create a broad political consensus that confront fiscal policy.

But monetary policy shares the other limitation of fiscal policy: Estimating potential GDP is hard, so policy might stimulate demand or hold back demand when no action is needed. And monetary policy

suffers an additional limitation: Its effects are long drawn out, indirect, and depend on how private decisions respond to a change in the interest rate. These responses are hard to forecast and vary from one situation to another in unpredictable ways. So the effects of successful monetary policy are harder to forecast than the effects of fiscal policy.

REVIEW QUIZ

1 Which components of expenditure are sensitive to the real interest rate?
2 Sketch the ripple effects of the Fed's actions from an open market operation to a change in real GDP and the price level.
3 Use the *AS-AD* model to show the effects of the Fed's attempt to avoid the 2001 recession.

You have now learned a great deal about the Fed, the monetary policy actions it can take, and the effects of those actions. Most of the "secrets of the temple" have been revealed. But you are possibly thinking, "All this sounds nice in theory, but does it really happen? Does the Fed actually do the things we've learned about in this chapter?" Indeed, it does happen, sometimes with dramatic effect, as you will now see.

The Fed in Action

To see the Fed in action, we'll do two things. First, we'll look at the fluctuations in short-term interest rates in the United States since 1971 and see how the Fed has influenced those fluctuations. Second, we'll focus on two episodes in the life of the Fed. One is the early 1980s, when the Fed was struggling to eradicate a stubborn inflation. The other is the period since a stock market crash of 1987 during which the Fed has tried to keep inflation in check without killing economic growth.

You've seen that the immediate effect of the Fed's actions is a change in the short-term interest rate. Figure 28.14 shows the course of three short-term interest rates since 1971. The federal funds rate — the interest rate that the banks charge each other on overnight loans of reserves — is the immediate target of the Fed's monetary policy. The 3-month Treasury bill rate is the interest rate paid by the federal government on 3-month loans, and the 6-month commercial bill rate is the interest rate paid by large corporations on 6-month loans.

Notice how closely these three interest rates move together. Because the short-term rates all move up and down together, the Fed is effectively able to influence all these rates.

Are short-term interest rate changes a response to changes in the quantity of money, as the theory we've just studied predicts? Mostly they are. Between 1970 and 1990, the rises and falls in the interest rate were exactly matched by decreases and increases in the supply of money relative to the demand for money. After 1990, the relationship between money and interest rates became weaker because the demand for M2 decreased as new substitute ways of holding wealth, such as bond and equity mutual funds, became more popular. These funds grew quickly during the 1990s, and their growth disturbed the traditional relationship between M2 and short-term interest rates. Consequently, after 1990, the Fed began to pay less attention to M2.

Do the Fed's own actions move interest rates? Two episodes in the life of the Fed show that they do.

Paul Volcker's Fed At the start of Paul Volcker's term of office as chairman of the Fed, which began in August 1979, the United States was locked in the grip of double-digit inflation. Volcker ended that inflation. He did so by forcing interest rates sharply upward from 1979 through 1981. This increase in

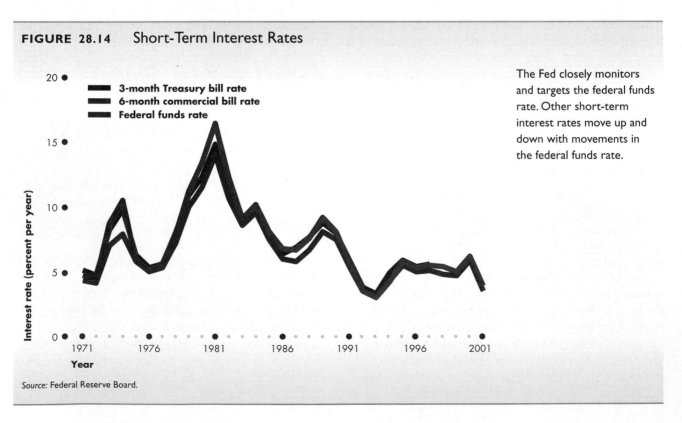

FIGURE 28.14   Short-Term Interest Rates

The Fed closely monitors and targets the federal funds rate. Other short-term interest rates move up and down with movements in the federal funds rate.

- 3-month Treasury bill rate
- 6-month commercial bill rate
- Federal funds rate

Interest rate (percent per year)

Year

Source: Federal Reserve Board.

interest rates resulted from the Fed using open market operations (purchases) and increases in the discount rate to keep the banks short of reserves, which in turn held back the growth in the supply of loans and of money relative to the growth in their demand.

As we saw in Fig. 28.10, to increase interest rates, the Fed has to cut the quantity of money. In practice, because the economy is growing and because prices are rising, a *slowdown* in the growth of nominal money is enough to increase interest rates. It is not necessary to actually *cut* the nominal quantity of money.

When Volcker became chairman of the Fed, the money growth was more than 8 percent a year. Volcker slowed down money growth to 6.5 percent in 1981. As a result, interest rates increased. The Treasury bill rate increased from 10 percent to 14 percent a year. The rate at which big corporations borrow increased from 9 percent to 14 percent a year. Mortgage rates — the rates at which home buyers borrow — increased from 11 percent to 15 percent a year. The economy went into recession. The money growth slowdown and interest rate hike cut the growth rate of aggregate demand. Real GDP fell, and the inflation rate slowed down.

Alan Greenspan's Fed Alan Greenspan became Fed chairman in August 1987. In the two preceding years, money growth had been at a rapid pace, interest rates had tumbled, and the stock market had boomed. Then, suddenly and with no warning, stock prices fell, bringing fears of recession. This was Alan Greenspan's first test as Fed chairman.

The Fed's immediate reaction to the new situation was to emphasize the flexibility and sensitivity of the financial system and to make reserves plentiful to avoid any fear of a banking crisis. But as the months passed, it became increasingly clear that the economy was not heading for recession. Real GDP growth was strong, unemployment fell, and the fears that emerged were of inflation, not recession.

Seeking to avoid an upturn in inflation, the Fed slowed money growth and, just as Paul Volcker had done eight years earlier, forced interest rates sharply upward. The slowdown in money growth had the effect implied by the model that you have been studying in this chapter. Interest rates increased throughout 1988. As 1989 advanced, concern about inflation remained, but renewed fears of recession returned, and interest rates were gradually lowered.

By 1990, recession had become a reality. At first, the Fed adopted a neutral position and waited for signs of recovery. But as the months passed and recovery seemed elusive, the Fed eventually began to cut interest rates. During 1991, interest rates fell by three percentage points as the Fed tried to stimulate spending.

By mid-1991, the recovery had begun and real GDP expanded. This expansion was to become one of the longest and strongest in history. The Fed helped to keep the expansion alive and to hold inflation in check. It did so by trying to anticipate unwanted deviations in either direction.

Through 1992 and 1993, the Fed permitted rapid money growth and kept interest rates low. During 1994, the Fed slowed money growth and pushed interest rates upward. It permitted interest rates to fall again during 1996 and then kept them steady through 1999.

By 2000, the Fed's main concern was to hold inflation in check. So it increased interest rates. But by the end of 2000 and through 2001, a different type of risk threatened. The U.S. economy was moving into recession. The Fed saw no risk of rising inflation but a large risk of recession, so it began to cut interest rates. Through 2001, the Fed cut the interest rate on 11 occasions, and by the end of 2001, the federal funds rate was at its lowest level since the early 1960s.

The terrorist attacks of September 11, 2001, complicated the Fed's task and probably encouraged the Fed to keep cutting the interest rate. As 2002 began, the Fed became increasingly confident that the recession was over, but it was not ready to begin the process of raising the interest rate.

REVIEW QUIZ

1 To which interest rates does the Fed pay the closest attention?
2 What was the main challenge of the Volcker Fed and how was the challenge met?
3 What was the main challenge of the Greenspan Fed and how was the challenge met?

◆ You've seen that most of the time, the Fed is fighting either recession or inflation. *Reading Between the Lines* on pp. 672–673 looks at the Fed in action during 2001 as it sought to fight recession. And the next chapter takes a deeper look at the causes, consequences, and challenges of avoiding or curing inflation.

The Fed Fights Recession

THE BOSTON GLOBE, December 12, 2001

Fed Cuts Interest Rates for 11th Time

Bank Lowers Key Fees to 40-Year Low in Push to Rejuvenate Economy

The Federal Reserve cut short-term interest rates by a quarter percentage point yesterday, the 11th reduction this year, as the US central bank continued its campaign to lift the country out of recession.

The banks' policy making Federal Open Market Committee lowered the federal funds rate charged on overnight loans between banks to 1.75 percent, the lowest rate since the John F. Kennedy administration.

In a brief statement that accompanied the announcement, the Fed said that although it saw signs that the weakness in the US economy was abating, those signs were "preliminary and tentative."

"Economic activity remains soft, with underlying inflation likely to edge lower from relatively modest levels," the Fed said.

Although the rate cut was widely anticipated, Wayne Ayers, chief economist at FleetBoston Financial Corp., noted that "what was more significant was that the Fed left the door open to do another cut, or two."

"In past recessions the Fed has demonstrated it is willing to push the real inflation-adjusted interest rate to zero," Ayers said. "It's not there yet, so there's still room to cut."

According to Ayers, this leaves open the possibility for another cut in January, "and maybe one more after that."

The action by Fed chairman Alan Greenspan and his colleagues at the central bank comes at a time when the US economy is generating mixed messages.

...

This year's aggressive interest rate reductions by the Fed, which have slashed benchmark rates by 4.5 percent to their lowest level in 40 years, has proven to be an effective strategy, according to Ayers.

...

This latest cut is unlikely to further reduce mortgage rates, according to Chris Probyn, chief international economist at State Street Corp. It will, however, cut borrowing costs for businesses and consumers who have loans pegged to variable rates like the prime rate, which banks are expected to reduce by a quarter point to 4.75 percent.

"Anyone with loans tied to short-term interest rates will benefit," Probyn said.

As for the larger economic picture, the cuts will probably serve as a mitigant rather than a cure, Probyn said. "The root causes of this downturn are in the capital markets, which are not as affected by this kind of cut," he said. "But it is still an entirely appropriate action for the Fed to be taking, even though it's not necessarily curative."

...

Essence of the Story

■ In December 2001, the FOMC cut the federal funds rate for the eleventh time in the year.

■ The December cut was 0.25 percent, making the new rate 1.75 percent, the lowest rate since the Kennedy administration.

■ The Fed said that it saw signs that the U.S. economy was recovering, but weakly.

■ The rate cut was widely anticipated.

■ Wayne Ayers, chief economist at FleetBoston Financial Corp., said that the Fed had left the door open to make another cut or two and that the real interest rate was still positive.

■ Chris Probyn, chief international economist at State Street Corp., said that the rate cut lowers borrowing costs that are pegged to variable interest rates but does not affect interest rates in the capital markets.

Economic Analysis

■ To lower the short-term interest rate, the Fed conducted open market purchases that increased the quantity of money.

■ Figure 1 shows the events in the money market (the market for M2 money) during 2001.

■ The demand for real M2 was *MD*, and this demand curve was unchanged during 2001 because real GDP was approximately constant.

■ In January 2001, the money supply curve was MS_0, at a quantity of real M2 of $4.6 trillion (1996 dollars). The interest rate (the interest rate on 3-month Treasury bills) was 5.3 percent a year.

■ During 2001, the quantity of real M2 was increased by $0.4 trillion to $5 trillion ($MS_1$ in Figure 1) — an increase of 8.7 percent.

■ The increase in the supply of money lowered the interest rate to 1.7 percent a year by December 2001.

■ The Fed has the power to lower the interest rate on short-term assets such as Treasury bills. But it has little direct influence on the interest rates on long-term loans, as noted by Chris Probyn in the news article.

■ Figure 2 shows the roughly constant interest rates on corporate and government long-term bonds.

■ The long-term interest rates are determined by investment demand and saving supply in global capital markets (Chapter 23) and by long-term inflation expectations (Chapter 29).

You're The Voter

■ Do you think the Fed did a good job during 2000 and 2001?

■ Do you think the Fed should have done anything differently? If so, what?

Figure 1 The money market in 2001

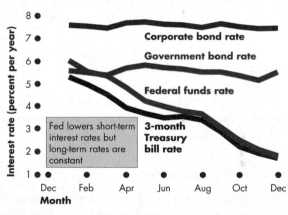

Figure 2 Interest rates in 2001

SUMMARY

KEY POINTS

The Federal Reserve System (pp. 654–657)

- The Federal Reserve System is the central bank of the United States.
- The Fed influences the economy by setting the required reserve ratio for banks, by setting the discount rate — the interest rate at which it is willing to lend reserves to the banking system, and by open market operations.

Controlling the Money Supply (pp. 657–661)

- By buying government securities in the market (an open market purchase), the Fed is able to increase the monetary base and the reserves available to banks.
- An expansion of bank lending follows an open market purchase and the quantity of money increases.
- By selling government securities, the Fed is able to decrease the monetary base and bank reserves and decrease the quantity of money.

The Demand for Money (pp. 662–665)

- The quantity of money demanded is the amount of money that people plan to hold.
- The quantity of real money equals the quantity of nominal money divided by the price level.
- The quantity of real money demanded depends on the interest rate and real GDP. A higher interest rate induces a smaller quantity of real money demanded.

Interest Rate Determination (pp. 665–666)

- Changes in interest rates achieve equilibrium in the markets for money and financial assets.
- Money market equilibrium achieves an interest rate (and an asset price) that makes the quantity of real money available willingly held.
- If the quantity of real money is increased by the actions of the Fed, the interest rate falls and the prices of financial assets rise.

Monetary Policy, Real GDP, and the Price Level (pp. 667–669)

- When the Fed raises interest rates, investment, consumption expenditure, and net exports decrease and a multiplier effect brings a greater decrease in aggregate demand.
- When the Fed lowers interest rates, investment, consumption expenditure, and net exports increase and a multiplier effect brings a greater increase in aggregate demand.
- The size of the multiplier effect of monetary policy depends on the sensitivity of spending plans to the interest rate.

The Fed in Action (pp. 670–671)

- The Fed targets the federal funds rate, but all short-term rates fluctuate together and the Fed influences all short-term interest rates.
- The Fed battled inflation during the 1980s and has alternated between fighting inflation and recession during the 1990s and 2000s.

KEY FIGURES

KEY TERMS

PROBLEMS

*1. You are given the following information about the economy of Nocoin: The banks have deposits of $300 billion. Their reserves are $15 billion, two thirds of which is in deposits with the central bank. There are $30 billion notes outside the banks. There are no coins! Calculate
   a. The monetary base.
   b. The quantity of money.
   c. The banks' reserve ratio.
   d. The currency drain as a percentage of the quantity of money.

2. You are given the following information about the economy of Fredzone: The people and businesses in Fredzone have bank deposits of $500 billion and hold $100 billion in notes and coins. The banks hold deposits at the Fredzone Fed of $5 billion, and they keep $5 billion in notes and coins in their vaults and ATM machines. Calculate
   a. The monetary base.
   b. The quantity of money.
   c. The banks' reserve ratio.
   d. The currency drain as a percentage of the quantity of money.

*3. Suppose that in problem 1, the Bank of Nocoin, the central bank, undertakes an open market purchase of securities of $0.5 billion.
   a. What happens to the quantity of money?
   b. Explain why the change in the quantity of money is not equal to the change in the monetary base.
   c. Calculate the money multiplier.

4. Suppose that in problem 2, the Fredzone Fed undertakes an open market sale of securities of $1 billion.
   a. What happens to the quantity of money?
   b. Explain why the change in the quantity of money is not equal to the change in the monetary base.
   c. Calculate the money multiplier.

*5. The spreadsheet provides information about the demand for money in Minland. Column A is the interest rate, R. Columns B, C, and D show the quantity of money demanded at three different levels of real GDP. Y_0 is $10 billion, Y_1 is

$20 billion, and Y_2 is $30 billion. The quantity of money is $3 billion. Initially, real GDP is $20 billion.

	A	B	C	D
1	R	Y_0	Y_1	Y_2
2	7	1.0	1.5	2.0
3	6	1.5	2.0	2.5
4	5	2.0	2.5	3.0
5	4	2.5	3.0	3.5
6	3	3.0	3.5	4.0
7	2	3.5	4.0	4.5
8	1	4.0	4.5	5.0

What happens in Minland
   a. If the interest rate exceeds 4 percent a year?
   b. If the interest rate is less than 4 percent a year?
   c. If the interest rate equals 4 percent a year?

6. The Minland economy in problem 5 experiences a severe recession. Real GDP decreases to $10 billion. The Minland Fed takes no actions to change the quantity of money.
   a. What happens in Minland if the interest rate is 4 percent a year?
   b. What is the equilibrium interest rate in Minland?
   c. Compared with the situation on problem 5, does the interest rate in Minland rise or fall? Why?

*7. The Minland economy in problem 5 experiences a severe business cycle. Real GDP increses to $30 billion and then decreases to $10 billion. The Minland Fed takes no actions to change the quantity of money. What happens to the interest rate in Minland
   a. During the expansion phase of the cycle?
   b. During the recession phase of the cycle?

8. Financial innovation in Minland changes the demand for money. People now plan to hold $0.5 billion less than the numbers provided in the spreadsheet in problem 5.
   a. What happens to the interest rate if the Minland Fed takes no actions?
   b. What happens to the interest rate if the Minland Fed decreases the quantity of money by $0.5 billion? Explain.

*9. The figure shows the demand for money in Upland.
   a. In the figure, draw the supply of money curve if the interest rate is 3 percent a year.
   b. Suppose that the Upland Fed wants to lower the interest rate by 1 percentage point. By how much must it change the quantity of real money? Draw the new supply of money curve.

Suppose that to change the quantity of money in part (b) of the problem, the Upland Fed uses open market operations. Does it make an open market purchase or an open market sale of securities?

10. In Upland, in problem 9, a new smart card replaces currency and the demand for money changes. Also, the new smart card causes business to boom. Real GDP increases.
    a. Draw a new demand for money curve that is consistent with the events just described.
    b. Suppose that the Upland Fed wants to prevent the interest rate from changing. What must it do to the quantity of money? Draw the new supply of money curve.
    c. Does the Upland Fed make an open market purchase or an open market sale of securities?

*11. Starting from above full-employment equilibrium, briefly explain with the aid of the *AS-AD* model the short-run effect on the price level and real GDP of an open market sale. Does such an action help to avoid inflation? Does it lower real GDP in the long run?

12. Starting from unemployment equilibrium, briefly explain with the aid of the *AS-AD* model the short-run effect on the price level and real GDP of an open market purchase. Does such an action help to avoid inflation? Does it increase real GDP in the long run?

CRITICAL THINKING

1. Study *Reading Between the Lines* on pp. 672–673 and then answer the following questions:
   a. Why did the Fed repeatedly lower the interest rate during 2001?
   b. What does the Fed look at when it is deciding whether to change interest rates?
   c. What are the risks from the Fed's raising interest rates and from the Fed's not raising interest rates? Which is more risky in your opinion and why?
   d. When the Fed does raise interest rates, what actions does it take?

2. What did the Volcker Fed do to bring inflation under control? What were the main side effects of the Fed's policy actions? Do you think the Fed acted appropriately? Why or why not?

WEB EXERCISES

1. Use the link on your Parkin Web site to visit the Federal Reserve Board and obtain the latest data on M1, M2, and some short-term interest rates. Then answer the following questions.
   a. Is the Fed trying to slow the economy or speed it up? How can you tell which?
   b. What open market operations do you think the Fed has undertaken during the past month?
   c. Skim the latest minutes of the FOMC, which you can find at the Fed's Web site, and see whether you can discover the open market operations that are planned.
   d. In light of the Fed's recent actions, what ripple effects do you expect over the coming months?

2. Use the link on your Parkin Web site to visit the Federal Reserve Board and look at the current economic conditions described in the Beige Book. On the basis of current forecasts by the Fed, do you predict that the Fed will raise interest rates, lower interest rates, or hold interest rates steady? Write a brief summary of your predictions and reasons.

From Rome to Rio de Janeiro

At the end of the third century A.D., Roman Emperor Diocletian struggled to contain an inflation that raised prices by more than 300 percent a year. At the end of the twentieth century, Brazil's president, Fernando Henrique Cardoso, struggled to contain an inflation that hit a rate of 40 percent *per month* — or 5,600 percent a year. ◆ Today, the United States has remarkable price stability, but during the 1970s, the U.S. price level more than doubled — an inflation of more than 100 percent over the decade. Why do inflation rates vary? And why do serious inflations break out from time to time? ◆ Will inflation increase so our savings buy less? Or will inflation decrease so our debts are harder to repay? To make good decisions, we need good forecasts of inflation, and not for just next year but for many years into the future. How do people try to forecast inflation? And how do expectations of inflation influence the economy? ◆ Does the Fed face a tradeoff between inflation and unemployment? And does a low unemployment rate signal a rising inflation rate? How does inflation affect the interest rate?

◆ We'll answer these questions in this chapter. We'll begin by reviewing what inflation is and how it is measured. And we'll end, in *Reading Between the Lines*, by returning to links between inflation and unemployment in the United States today.

After studying this chapter, you will be able to

■ **Distinguish between inflation and a one-time rise in the price level**

■ **Explain how demand-pull inflation is generated**

■ **Explain how cost-push inflation is generated**

■ **Describe the effects of inflation**

■ **Explain the short-run and long-run relationships between inflation and unemployment**

■ **Explain the short-run and long-run relationships between inflation and interest rates**

Inflation and the Price Level

WE DON'T HAVE MUCH INFLATION TODAY, BUT during the 1970s, inflation was a major problem. **Inflation** is a process in which the *price level is rising* and *money is losing value.*

If the price level rises persistently, then people need more and more money to make transactions. Incomes rise, so firms must pay out more in wages and other payments to owners of factors of production. And prices rise, so consumers must take more money with them when they go shopping. But the value of money gets smaller and smaller.

A change in one price is not inflation. For example, if the price of a hot dog jumps to $25 and all other money prices fall slightly so that the price level remains constant, there is no inflation. Instead, the relative price of a hot dog has increased. If the price of a hot dog and all other prices rise by a similar percentage, there is inflation.

But a one-time jump in the price level is not inflation. Instead, inflation is an ongoing *process.* Figure 29.1 illustrates this distinction. The red line shows the price level rising continuously. That is inflation. The blue line shows a one-time jump in the price level. This economy is not experiencing inflation. Its price level is constant most of the time.

Inflation is a serious problem, and preventing inflation is the main task of monetary policy and the actions of the Fed. We are going to learn how inflation arises and see how we can avoid the situation shown in the cartoon. But first, let's see how we calculate the inflation rate.

"I told you the Fed should have tightened."

© The New Yorker Collection 1997
Robert Mankoff from cartoonbank.com. All rights reserved.

FIGURE 29.1   Inflation Versus a One-Time Rise in the Price Level

Along the red line, an economy experiences inflation because the price level is rising persistently. Along the blue line, an economy experiences a one-time rise in the price level.

To measure the inflation *rate,* we calculate the annual percentage change in the price level. For example, if this year's price level is 126 and last year's price level was 120, the inflation rate is

$$\text{Inflation rate} = \frac{126 - 120}{120} \times 100$$

$$= 5 \text{ percent per year.}$$

This equation shows the connection between the *inflation rate* and the *price level.* For a given price level last year, the higher the price level in the current year, the higher is the inflation rate. If the price level is *rising*, the inflation rate is *positive.* If the price level rises at a *faster* rate, the inflation rate *increases.* Also, the higher the new price level, the lower is the value of money and the higher is the inflation rate.

Inflation can result from either an increase in aggregate demand or a decrease in aggregate supply. These two sources of impulses are called

- Demand-pull
- Cost-push

We'll first study a demand-pull inflation.

Demand-Pull Inflation

AN INFLATION THAT RESULTS FROM AN INITIAL increase in aggregate demand is called **demand-pull inflation**. Demand-pull inflation can arise from *any* factor that increases aggregate demand, such as an

1. Increase in the quantity of money
2. Increase in government purchases
3. Increase in exports

Initial Effect of an Increase in Aggregate Demand

Suppose that last year the price level was 110 and real GDP was $10 trillion. Potential GDP was also $10 trillion. Figure 29.2(a) illustrates this situation. The aggregate demand curve is AD_0, the short-run aggregate supply curve is SAS_0, and the long-run aggregate supply curve is LAS.

In the current year, aggregate demand increases to AD_1. Such a situation arises if, for example, the

Fed loosens its grip on the quantity of money, or the government increases its purchases of goods and services, or exports increase.

With no change in potential GDP, and with no change in the money wage rate, the long-run aggregate supply curve and the short-run aggregate supply curve remain at LAS and SAS_0, respectively.

The price level and real GDP are determined at the point where the aggregate demand curve AD_1 intersects the short-run aggregate supply curve. The price level rises to 113, and real GDP increases above potential GDP to $10.5 trillion. The economy experiences a 2.7 percent rise in the price level (a price level of 113 compared with 110 in the previous year) and a rapid expansion of real GDP. Unemployment falls below its natural rate. The next step in the unfolding story is a rise in the money wage rate.

Money Wage Rate Response

Real GDP cannot remain above potential GDP forever. With unemployment below its natural rate, there is a shortage of labor. In this situation, the

---

FIGURE 29.2 A Demand-Pull Rise in the Price Level

(a) Initial effect

(b) Wages adjust

In part (a), the aggregate demand curve is AD_0, the short-run aggregate supply curve is SAS_0, and the long-run aggregate supply curve is LAS. The price level is 110, and real GDP is $10 trillion, which equals potential GDP. Aggregate demand increases to AD_1. The price level rises to 113, and real GDP

increases to $10.5 trillion. In part (b), starting from above full employment, the money wage rate begins to rise and the short-run aggregate supply curve shifts leftward toward SAS_1. The price level rises further, and real GDP returns to potential GDP.

money wage rate begins to rise. As it does so, short-run aggregate supply decreases and the *SAS* curve starts to shift leftward. The price level rises further, and real GDP begins to decrease.

With no further change in aggregate demand — that is, the aggregate demand curve remains at AD_1 — this process ends when the short-run aggregate supply curve has shifted to SAS_1 in Fig. 29.2(b). At this time, the price level has increased to 121 and real GDP has returned to potential GDP of $10 trillion, the level from which it started.

A Demand-Pull Inflation Process

The process we've just studied eventually ends when, for a given increase in aggregate demand, the money wage rate has adjusted enough to restore the real wage rate to its full-employment level. We've studied a one-time rise in the price level like that described in Fig. 29.1. For inflation to proceed, aggregate demand must persistently increase.

The only way in which aggregate demand can persistently increase is if the quantity of money persistently increases. Suppose the government has a budget deficit that it finances by selling bonds. Also suppose that the Fed buys some of these bonds. When the Fed buys bonds, it creates more money. In this situation, aggregate demand increases year after year. The aggregate demand curve keeps shifting rightward. This persistent increase in aggregate demand puts continual upward pressure on the price level. The economy now experiences demand-pull inflation.

Figure 29.3 illustrates the process of demand-pull inflation. The starting point is the same as that shown in Fig. 29.2. The aggregate demand curve is AD_0, the short-run aggregate supply curve is SAS_0, and the long-run aggregate supply curve is *LAS*. Real GDP is $10 trillion, and the price level is 110. Aggregate demand increases, shifting the aggregate demand curve to AD_1. Real GDP increases to $10.5 trillion, and the price level rises to 113. The economy is at an above full-employment equilibrium. There is a shortage of labor, and the money wage rate rises. The short-run aggregate supply curve shifts to SAS_1. The price level rises to 121, and real GDP returns to potential GDP.

But the Fed increases the quantity of money again, and aggregate demand continues to increase. The aggregate demand curve shifts rightward to AD_2. The price level rises further to 125, and real GDP

FIGURE 29.3   A Demand-Pull Inflation Spiral

Each time the quantity of money increases, aggregate demand increases, and the aggregate demand curve shifts rightward from AD_0 to AD_1 to AD_2, and so on. Each time real GDP goes above potential GDP, the money wage rate rises and the short-run aggregate supply curve shifts leftward from SAS_0 to SAS_1 to SAS_2, and so on. The price level rises from 110 to 113, 121, 125, 133, and so on. There is a perpetual demand-pull inflation. Real GDP fluctuates between $10 trillion and $10.5 trillion.

again exceeds potential GDP at $10.5 trillion. Yet again, the money wage rate rises and decreases short-run aggregate supply. The *SAS* curve shifts to SAS_2, and the price level rises further, to 133. As the quantity of money continues to grow, aggregate demand increases and the price level rises in an ongoing demand-pull inflation process.

The process you have just studied generates inflation — an ongoing process of a rising price level.

Demand-Pull Inflation in Kalamazoo   You may better understand the inflation process that we've just described by considering what is going on in an individual part of the economy, such as a Kalamazoo soda-bottling plant. Initially, when aggregate demand increases, the demand for soda increases and the price of soda rises. Faced with a higher price, the soda plant works overtime and increases production. Conditions are good for workers in Kalamazoo, and the soda factory finds it hard to hang onto its best people. To do so, it offers a higher money wage rate. As the wage rate rises, so do the soda factory's costs.

What happens next depends on what happens to aggregate demand. If aggregate demand remains constant (as in Fig. 29.2b), the firm's costs are increasing, but the price of soda is not increasing as quickly as its costs. Production is scaled back. Eventually, the money wage rate and costs increase by the same percentage as the rise in the price of soda. In real terms, the soda factory is in the same situation as it was initially — before the increase in aggregate demand. The plant produces the same amount of soda and employs the same amount of labor as before the increase in demand.

But if aggregate demand continues to increase, so does the demand for soda and the price of soda rises at the same rate as wages. The soda factory continues to operate above full employment, and there is a persistent shortage of labor. Prices and wages chase each other upward in an unending spiral.

Demand-Pull Inflation in the United States A demand-pull inflation like the one you've just studied occurred in the United States during the 1960s. In 1960, inflation was a moderate 2 percent a year, but its rate increased slowly to 3 percent by 1966. Then, in 1967, a large increase in government purchases on the Vietnam War and an increase in spending on social programs, together with an increase in the growth rate of the quantity of money, increased aggregate demand more quickly. Consequently, the rightward shift of the aggregate demand curve speeded up and the price level increased more quickly. Real GDP moved above potential GDP, and the unemployment rate fell below its natural rate.

With unemployment below its natural rate, the money wage rate started to rise more quickly and the short-run aggregate supply curve shifted leftward. The Fed responded with a further increase in the money growth rate, and a demand-pull inflation spiral unfolded. By 1970, the inflation rate had reached 5 percent a year.

For the next few years, aggregate demand grew even more quickly and the inflation rate kept rising. By 1975, the inflation rate had almost reached 10 percent a year.

REVIEW QUIZ

1 How does demand-pull inflation begin? What are the initial effects of demand-pull inflation on real GDP?
2 When real GDP moves above potential GDP, what happens to the money wage rate and short-run aggregate supply? How do real GDP and the price level respond?
3 What must happen to create a demand-pull inflation spiral?

Next, let's see how shocks to aggregate supply can create cost-push inflation.

Cost-Push Inflation

AN INFLATION THAT RESULTS FROM AN INITIAL increase in costs is called **cost-push inflation**. The two main sources of increases in costs are

1. An increase in money wage rates
2. An increase in the money prices of raw materials

At a given price level, the higher the cost of production, the smaller is the amount that firms are willing to produce. So if money wage rates rise or if the prices of raw materials (for example, oil) rise, firms decrease their supply of goods and services. Aggregate supply decreases, and the short-run aggregate supply curve shifts leftward.[1] Let's trace the effects of such a decrease in short-run aggregate supply on the price level and real GDP.

Initial Effect of a Decrease in Aggregate Supply

Suppose that last year the price level was 110 and real GDP was $10 trillion. Potential real GDP was also $10 trillion. Figure 29.4 illustrates this situation. The aggregate demand curve was AD_0, the short-run

---

[1] Some cost-push forces, such as an increase in the price of oil accompanied by a decrease in the availability of oil, can also decrease long-run aggregate supply. We'll ignore such effects here and examine cost-push factors that change only short-run aggregate supply.

FIGURE 29.4   A Cost-Push Rise in the Price Level

Initially, the aggregate demand curve is AD_0, the short-run aggregate supply curve is SAS_0, and the long-run aggregate supply curve is LAS. A decrease in aggregate supply (for example, resulting from a rise in the world price of oil) shifts the short-run aggregate supply curve to SAS_1. The economy moves to the point where the short-run aggregate supply curve SAS_1 intersects the aggregate demand curve AD_0. The price level rises to 117, and real GDP decreases to $9.5 trillion. The economy experiences stagflation.

aggregate supply curve was SAS_0, and the long-run aggregate supply curve was LAS. In the current year, the world's oil producers form a price-fixing organization that strengthens their market power and increases the relative price of oil. They raise the price of oil, and this action decreases short-run aggregate supply. The short-run aggregate supply curve shifts leftward to SAS_1. The price level rises to 117, and real GDP decreases to $9.5 trillion. The combination of a rise in the price level and a fall in real GDP is called *stagflation.*

This event is a one-time rise in the price level, like that in Fig. 29.1. It is not inflation. In fact, a supply shock on its own cannot cause inflation. Something more must happen to enable a one-time supply shock, which causes a one-time rise in the price level, to be converted into a process of money growth and ongoing inflation. The quantity of

money must persistently increase. And it often does increase, as you will now see.

Aggregate Demand Response

When real GDP falls, unemployment rises above its natural rate. In such a situation, there is usually an outcry of concern and a call for action to restore full employment. Suppose that the Fed increases the quantity of money. Aggregate demand increases. In Fig. 29.5, the aggregate demand curve shifts rightward to AD_1. The increase in aggregate demand has restored full employment. But the price level rises to 121, a 10 percent increase over the initial price level.

A Cost-Push Inflation Process

The oil producers now see the prices of everything that they buy increase by 10 percent. So they increase the price of oil again to restore its new high relative price. Figure 29.6 continues the story.

FIGURE 29.5   Aggregate Demand Response to Cost-Push

Following a cost-push increase in the price level, real GDP is below potential GDP and unemployment is above its natural rate. If the Fed responds by increasing aggregate demand to restore full employment, the aggregate demand curve shifts rightward to AD_1. The economy returns to full employment but the price level rises to 121.

The short-run aggregate supply curve now shifts to SAS_2, and another bout of stagflation ensues. The price level rises further, to 129, and real GDP decreases to $9.5 trillion. Unemployment increases above its natural rate. If the Fed responds yet again with an increase in the quantity of money, aggregate demand increases and the aggregate demand curve shifts to AD_2. The price level rises even higher — to 133 — and full employment is again restored. A cost-push inflation spiral results. But if the Fed does not respond, the economy remains below full employment.

You can see that the Fed has a dilemma. If it increases the quantity of money to restore full employment, it invites another oil price hike that will call forth yet a further increase in the quantity of money.

Inflation will rage along at a rate decided by the oil-exporting nations. If the Fed keeps the lid on money growth, the economy operates with a high level of unemployment.

Cost-Push Inflation in Kalamazoo What is going on in the Kalamazoo soda-bottling plant when the economy is experiencing cost-push inflation? When the oil price increases, so do the costs of bottling soda. These higher costs decrease the supply of soda, increasing its price and decreasing the quantity produced. The soda plant lays off some workers. This situation will persist until either the Fed increases aggregate demand or the price of oil falls. If the Fed increases aggregate demand, the demand for soda increases and so does its price. The higher price of soda brings higher profits, and the bottling plant increases its production. The soda factory rehires the laid-off workers.

Cost-Push Inflation in the United States A cost-push inflation like the one you've just studied occurred in the United States during the 1970s. It began in 1974 when the Organization of Petroleum Exporting Countries (OPEC) raised the price of oil fourfold. The higher oil price decreased aggregate supply, which caused the price level to rise more quickly and real GDP to shrink. The Fed then faced a dilemma: Would it increase the quantity of money and accommodate the cost-push forces, or would it keep aggregate demand growth in check by limiting money growth? In 1975, 1976, and 1977, the Fed repeatedly allowed the quantity of money to grow quickly and inflation proceeded at a rapid rate. In 1979 and 1980, OPEC was again able to push oil prices higher. On that occasion, the Fed decided not to respond to the oil price hike with an increase in the quantity of money. The result was a recession but also, eventually, a fall in inflation.

FIGURE 29.6   A Cost-Push Inflation Spiral

When a cost increase decreases short-run aggregate supply from SAS_0 to SAS_1, the price level rises to 117 and real GDP decreases to $9.5 trillion. The Fed responds with an increase in the quantity of money. The aggregate demand curve shifts from AD_0 to AD_1, the price level rises to 121, and real GDP returns to $10 trillion. A further cost increase occurs, which shifts the short-run aggregate supply curve again, this time to SAS_2. Stagflation is repeated, and the price level rises to 129. The Fed responds again, and the cost-price inflation spiral continues.

REVIEW QUIZ

1 How does cost-push inflation begin? What are the initial effects of a cost-push rise in the price level?

2 What is stagflation and why does cost-push inflation cause stagflation?

3 What must the Fed do to convert a one-time rise in the price level into a freewheeling cost-push inflation?

Effects of Inflation

REGARDLESS OF WHETHER INFLATION IS DEMAND-pull or cost-push, the failure to correctly *anticipate* it results in unintended consequences. These unintended consequences impose costs in both labor markets and capital markets. Let's examine these costs.

Unanticipated Inflation in the Labor Market

Unanticipated inflation has two main consequences for the operation of the labor market:

■ Redistribution of income
■ Departure from full employment

Redistribution of Income Unanticipated inflation redistributes income between employers and workers. Sometimes employers gain at the expense of workers, and sometimes they lose. If an unexpected increase in aggregate demand increases the inflation rate, then the money wage rate will not have been set high enough. Profits will be higher than expected, and real wages will buy fewer goods than expected. In this case, employers gain at the expense of workers. But if aggregate demand is expected to increase at a rapid rate and it fails to do so, workers gain at the expense of employers. With a high inflation rate anticipated, the money wage rate is set too high and profits are squeezed. Redistribution between employers and workers creates an incentive for both firms and workers to try to forecast inflation correctly.

Departures from Full Employment Redistribution brings gains to some and losses to others. But departures from full employment impose costs on everyone. To see why, let's return to the soda-bottling plant.

If the bottling plant and its workers do not anticipate inflation but inflation occurs, the money wage rate does not rise to keep up with inflation. The real wage rate falls, and the firm tries to hire more labor and increase production. But because the real wage rate has fallen, the firm has a hard time attracting the labor it wants to employ. It pays overtime rates to its existing work force, and because it runs its plant at a faster pace, it incurs higher plant maintenance and parts replacement costs. But also, because the real wage rate has fallen, workers begin to quit the bottling

plant to find jobs that pay a real wage rate that is closer to one that prevailed before the outbreak of inflation. This labor turnover imposes additional costs on the firm. So even though its production increases, the firm incurs additional costs and its profits do not increase as much as they otherwise would. The workers incur additional costs of job search, and those who remain at the bottling plant wind up feeling cheated. They've worked overtime to produce the extra output, and when they come to spend their wages, they discover that prices have increased so their wages buy a smaller quantity of goods and services than expected.

If the bottling plant and its workers anticipate a high inflation rate that does not occur, they increase the money wage rate by too much and the real wage rate rises. At the higher real wage rate, the firm lays off some workers and the unemployment rate increases. The workers who keep their jobs gain, but those who become unemployed lose. Also, the bottling plant loses because its output and profits fall.

Unanticipated Inflation in the Market for Financial Capital

Unanticipated inflation has two consequences for the operation of the market for financial capital:

■ Redistribution of income
■ Too much or too little lending and borrowing

Redistribution of Income Unanticipated inflation redistributes income between borrowers and lenders. Sometimes borrowers gain at the expense of lenders, and sometimes they lose. When inflation is unexpected, interest rates are not set high enough to compensate lenders for the falling value of money. In this case, borrowers gain at the expense of lenders. But if inflation is expected and then fails to occur, interest rates are set too high. In this case, lenders gain at the expense of borrowers. Redistributions of income between borrowers and lenders create an incentive for both groups to try to forecast inflation correctly.

Too Much or Too Little Lending and Borrowing If the inflation rate turns out to be either higher or lower than expected, the interest rate does not incorporate a correct allowance for the falling value of money and the real interest rate is either lower or higher than it otherwise would be. When the real interest rate turns out to be too low, which occurs when inflation is *higher* than expected, borrowers wish they had borrowed more and lenders wish they had lent less. Both groups would have made different lending and borrowing decisions with greater foresight about the inflation rate. When the real interest rate turns out to be too high, which occurs when inflation is *lower* than expected, borrowers wish they had borrowed less and lenders wish they had lent more. Again, both groups would have made different lending and borrowing decisions with greater foresight about the inflation rate.

So unanticipated inflation imposes costs regardless of whether the inflation turns out to be higher or lower than anticipated. The presence of these costs gives everyone an incentive to forecast inflation correctly. Let's see how people go about this task.

Forecasting Inflation

Inflation is difficult to forecast for two reasons. First, there are several sources of inflation — the demand-pull and cost-push sources you've just studied. Second, the speed with which a change in either aggregate demand or aggregate supply translates into a change in the price level varies. This speed of response also depends, as you will see below, on the extent to which the inflation is anticipated.

Because inflation is costly and difficult to forecast, people devote considerable resources to improving inflation forecasts. Some people specialize in forecasting, and others buy forecasts from specialists. The specialist forecasters are economists who work for public and private macroeconomic forecasting agencies and for banks, insurance companies, labor unions, and large corporations. The returns these specialists make depend on the quality of their forecasts, so they have a strong incentive to forecast as accurately as possible. The most accurate forecast possible is the one that is based on all the relevant information and is called a **rational expectation**.

A rational expectation is not necessarily a correct forecast. It is simply the best forecast available. It will often turn out to be wrong, but no other forecast that could have been made with the information available could be predicted to be better.

You've seen the effects of inflation when people fail to anticipate it. And you've seen why it pays to try to anticipate inflation. Let's now see what happens if inflation is correctly anticipated.

Anticipated Inflation

In the demand-pull and cost-push inflations that we studied earlier, the money wage rate is sticky. When aggregate demand increases, either to set off a demand-pull inflation or to accommodate cost-push inflation, the money wage rate does not change immediately. But if people correctly anticipate increases in aggregate demand, they will adjust the money wage rate so as to keep up with anticipated inflation.

In this case, inflation proceeds with real GDP equal to potential GDP and unemployment at its natural rate. Figure 29.7 explains why. Suppose that last year the price level was 110 and real GDP was $10 trillion, which is also potential GDP. The aggregate demand curve was AD_0, the aggregate supply curve was SAS_0, and the long-run aggregate supply curve was LAS.

Suppose that potential GDP does not change, so the LAS curve does not shift. Also suppose that aggregate demand is expected to increase and that the expected aggregate demand curve for this year is AD_1. In anticipation of this increase in aggregate demand, the money wage rate rises and the short-run aggregate supply curve shifts leftward. If the money wage rate rises by the same percentage as the price level rises, the short-run aggregate supply curve for next year is SAS_1.

If aggregate demand turns out to be the same as expected, the aggregate demand curve is AD_1. The short-run aggregate supply curve, SAS_1, and AD_1 determine the actual price level at 121. Between last year and this year, the price level increased from 110 to 121 and the economy experienced an inflation rate of 10 percent, the same as the inflation rate that was anticipated. If this anticipated inflation is ongoing, in the following year aggregate demand increases (as anticipated) and the aggregate demand curve shifts to AD_2. The money wage rate rises to reflect the anticipated inflation, and the short-run aggregate supply curve shifts to SAS_2. The price level rises by a further 10 percent to 133.

What has caused this inflation? The immediate answer is that because people expected inflation, the wage rate was increased and prices increased. But the expectation was correct. Aggregate demand was expected to increase, and it did increase. Because aggregate demand was *expected* to increase from AD_0 to AD_1, the short-run aggregate supply curve shifted from SAS_0 to SAS_1. Because aggregate demand actually did increase by the amount that was expected, the actual aggregate demand curve shifted from AD_0

to AD_1. The combination of the anticipated and actual shifts of the aggregate demand curve rightward produced an increase in the price level that was anticipated.

Only if aggregate demand growth is correctly forecasted does the economy follow the course described in Fig. 29.7. If the expected growth rate of aggregate demand is different from its actual growth rate, the expected aggregate demand curve shifts by an amount that is different from the actual aggregate demand curve. The inflation rate departs from its expected level, and to some extent, there is unanticipated inflation.

FIGURE 29.7 Anticipated Inflation

Potential real GDP is $10 trillion. Last year, aggregate demand was AD_0, and the short-run aggregate supply curve was SAS_0. The actual price level was the same as the expected price level — 110. This year, aggregate demand is expected to increase to AD_1. The rational expectation of the price level changes from 110 to 121. As a result, the money wage rate rises and the short-run aggregate supply curve shifts to SAS_1. If aggregate demand actually increases as expected, the actual aggregate demand curve AD_1 is the same as the expected aggregate demand curve. Real GDP is $10 trillion and the actual price level is 121. The Inflation is correctly anticipated. Next year, the process continues with aggregate demand increasing as expected to AD_2 and the money wage rate rising to shift the short-run aggregate supply curve to SAS_2. Again, real GDP remains at $10 trillion, and the price level rises, as anticipated, to 133.

Unanticipated Inflation

When aggregate demand increases by *more* than expected, there is some unanticipated inflation that looks just like the demand-pull inflation that you studied earlier. Some inflation is expected, and the money wage rate is set to reflect that expectation. The SAS curve intersects the LAS curve at the expected price level. Aggregate demand then increases but by more than expected. So the AD curve intersects the SAS curve at a level of real GDP that exceeds potential GDP. With real GDP above potential GDP and unemployment below its natural rate, the money wage rate rises. So the price level rises further. If aggregate demand increases again, a demand-pull inflation spiral unwinds.

When aggregate demand increases by *less* than expected, there is some unanticipated inflation that looks like the cost-push inflation that you studied earlier. Again, some inflation is expected, and the money wage rate is set to reflect that expectation. The SAS curve intersects the LAS curve at the expected price level. Aggregate demand then increases but by less than expected. So the AD curve intersects the SAS curve at a level of real GDP below potential GDP. Aggregate demand increases to restore full employment. But if aggregate demand is expected to increase by more than it actually does, the money wage rate again rises, short-run aggregate supply again decreases, and a cost-push spiral unwinds.

We've seen that only when inflation is unanticipated does real GDP depart from potential GDP. When inflation is anticipated, real GDP remains at potential GDP. Does this mean that an anticipated inflation has no costs?

The Costs of Anticipated Inflation

The costs of an anticipated inflation depend on its rate. At a moderate rate of 2 or 3 percent a year, the cost is probably small. But as the anticipated inflation rate rises, so does its cost, and an anticipated inflation at a rapid rate can be extremely costly.

Anticipated inflation decreases potential GDP and slows economic growth. These adverse consequences arise for three major reasons:

- Transactions costs
- Tax effects
- Increased uncertainty

Transactions Costs The first transactions costs are known as the "shoe leather costs." These are costs that arise from an increase in the velocity of circulation of money and an increase in the amount of running around that people do to try to avoid incurring losses from the falling value of money.

When money loses value at a rapid anticipated rate, it does not function well as a store of value and people try to avoid holding money. They spend their incomes as soon as they receive them, and firms pay out incomes — wages and dividends — as soon as they receive revenue from their sales. The velocity of circulation increases. During the 1920s in Germany, when inflation reached *hyperinflation* levels (rates more than 50 percent a month), wages were paid and spent twice in a single day!

The range of estimates of the shoe leather costs is large. Some economists put them at close to zero. Others estimate them to be as much as 2 percent of GDP for a 10 percent inflation. For a rapid inflation, these costs are much more.

The shoe leather costs of inflation are just one of several transactions costs that are influenced by the inflation rate. At high anticipated inflation rates, people seek alternatives to money as means of payment and use tokens and commodities or even barter, all of which are less efficient than money as a means of payment. For example, in Israel during the 1980s, when inflation reached 1,000 percent a year, the U.S. dollar started to replace the increasingly worthless shekel. Consequently, people had to keep track of the exchange rate between the shekel and the dollar hour by hour and had to engage in many additional and costly transactions in the foreign exchange market.

Because anticipated inflation increases transactions costs, it diverts resources from producing goods and services and it decreases potential GDP. The faster the anticipated inflation rate, the greater is the decrease in potential GDP and the farther leftward does the *LAS* curve shift.

Tax Consequences Anticipated inflation interacts with the tax system and creates serious distortions in incentives. Its major effect is on real interest rates.

Anticipated inflation swells the dollar returns on investments. But dollar returns are taxed, so the effective tax rate rises. This effect becomes serious at even modest inflation rates. Let's consider an example.

Suppose the real interest rate is 4 percent a year and the tax rate is 50 percent. With no inflation, the nominal interest rate is also 4 percent a year and 50 percent of this rate is taxable. The real *after-tax* interest rate is 2 percent a year (50 percent of 4 percent). Now suppose the inflation rate is 4 percent a year and the nominal interest rate is 8 percent a year. (See Chapter 23, p. 527.) The *after-tax* nominal rate is 4 percent a year (50 percent of 8 percent). Now subtract the 4 percent inflation rate from this amount, and you see that the *after-tax real interest rate* is zero! The true tax rate on interest income is 100 percent.

The higher the inflation rate, the higher is the effective tax rate on income from capital. And the higher the tax rate, the higher is the interest rate paid by borrowers and the lower is the after-tax interest rate received by lenders.

With a low after-tax real interest rate, the incentive to save is weakened and the saving rate falls. With a high cost of borrowing, the amount of investment decreases. And with a fall in saving and investment, the pace of capital accumulation slows and so does the long-term growth rate of real GDP.

Increased Uncertainty When the inflation rate is high, there is increased uncertainty about the long-term inflation rate. Will inflation remain high for a long time, or will price stability be restored? This increased uncertainty makes long-term planning difficult and gives people a shorter-term focus. Investment falls, and so the growth rate slows.

But this increased uncertainty also misallocates resources. Instead of concentrating on the activities at which they have a comparative advantage, people find it more profitable to search for ways of avoiding the losses that inflation inflicts. As a result, inventive talent that might otherwise work on productive innovations works on finding ways of profiting from the inflation instead.

The implications of inflation for economic growth have been estimated to be enormous. Peter Howitt of Brown University, building on work by Robert Barro of Harvard University, has estimated that if inflation is lowered from 3 percent a year to zero, the growth rate of real GDP will rise by between 0.06 and 0.09 percentage point a year. These numbers might seem small, but they are growth rates. After 30 years, real GDP would be 2.3 percent higher and the present value of all the future output would by 85 percent of current GDP — $8.5 trillion! In the rapid anticipated inflations of Brazil and Russia, the costs are much greater than the numbers given here.

You've seen that an increase in aggregate demand that is not fully anticipated increases both the price level and real GDP. It also decreases unemployment. Similarly, a decrease in aggregate demand that is not fully anticipated decreases the price level and real GDP. It also increases unemployment. Do these relationships mean that there is a tradeoff between inflation and unemployment? Does low unemployment always bring inflation and does low inflation bring high unemployment? We explore these questions.

Inflation and Unemployment: The Phillips Curve

THE AGGREGATE SUPPLY–AGGREGATE DEMAND model focuses on the price level and real GDP. Knowing how these two variables change, we can work out what happens to the inflation rate and the unemployment rate. But the model does not place inflation and unemployment at center stage.

A more direct way of studying inflation and unemployment uses a relationship called the Phillips curve. The Phillips curve approach uses the same basic ideas as the *AS-AD* model, but it focuses directly on inflation and unemployment. The Phillips curve is so named because New Zealand economist A.W. Phillips popularized it. A **Phillips curve** is a curve that shows a relationship between inflation and unemployment. There are two time frames for Phillips curves:

- The short-run Phillips curve
- The long-run Phillips curve

The Short-Run Phillips Curve

The **short-run Phillips curve** is a curve that shows the tradeoff between inflation and unemployment, holding constant:

1. The expected inflation rate
2. The natural unemployment rate

You've just seen what determines the expected inflation rate. The natural rate of unemployment and the factors that influence it are explained in Chapter 22, pp. 517–519.

Figure 29.8 shows a short-run Phillips curve, *SRPC*. Suppose that the expected inflation rate is 10 percent a year and the natural rate of unemployment is 6 percent, point *A* in the figure. A short-run Phillips curve passes through this point. If inflation rises above its expected rate, unemployment falls

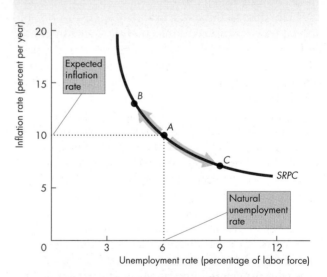

FIGURE 29.8 A Short-Run Phillips Curve

The short-run Phillips curve (*SRPC*) shows the relationship between inflation and unemployment at a given expected inflation rate and a given natural unemployment rate. With an expected inflation rate of 10 percent a year and a natural unemployment rate of 6 percent, the short-run Phillips curve passes through point *A*. An unanticipated increase in aggregate demand lowers unemployment and increases inflation — a movement up the short-run Phillips curve. An unanticipated decrease in aggregate demand increases unemployment and lowers inflation — a movement down the short-run Phillips curve.

below its natural rate. This joint movement in the inflation rate and the unemployment rate is illustrated as a movement up along the short-run Phillips curve from point *A* to point *B* in the figure. Similarly, if inflation falls below its expected rate, unemployment rises above its natural rate. In this case, there is movement down along the short-run Phillips curve from point *A* to point *C*.

This negative relationship between inflation and unemployment along the short-run Phillips curve is explained by the aggregate supply–aggregate demand model. Figure 29.9 shows the connection between the two approaches. Initially, the aggregate demand curve is AD_0, the short-run aggregate supply curve is SAS_0, and the long-run aggregate supply curve is *LAS*. Real GDP is $10 trillion, and the price level is 100. Aggregate demand is expected to increase, and the aggregate demand curve is expected to shift rightward to AD_1. Anticipating this increase in aggregate demand, the money wage rate rises, which shifts the short-run aggregate supply curve to SAS_1. What happens to actual inflation and real GDP depends on the *actual* change in aggregate demand.

First, suppose that aggregate demand actually increases by the amount expected, so the aggregate demand curve shifts to AD_1. The price level rises from 100 to 110, and the inflation rate is an anticipated 10 percent a year. Real GDP remains at potential GDP, and unemployment remains at its natural rate — 6 percent. The economy moves to point *A* in Fig. 29.9, and it can equivalently be described as being at point *A* on the short-run Phillips curve in Fig. 29.8.

Alternatively, suppose that aggregate demand is expected to increase to AD_1 but actually increases by more than expected, to AD_2. The price level now rises to 113, a 13 percent inflation rate. Real GDP increases above potential GDP, and unemployment falls below its natural rate. We can now describe the economy as moving to point *B* in Fig. 29.9 or as being at point *B* on the short-run Phillips curve in Fig. 29.8.

Finally, suppose that aggregate demand is expected to increase to AD_1 but actually remains at AD_0. The price level now rises to 107, a 7 percent inflation rate. Real GDP falls below potential GDP, and unemployment rises above its natural rate. We can now describe the economy as moving to point *C* in Fig. 29.9 or as being at point *C* on the short-run Phillips curve in Fig. 29.8.

FIGURE 29.9   AS-AD and the Short-Run Phillips Curve

If aggregate demand is expected to increase and shift the aggregate demand curve from AD_0 to AD_1, then the money wage rate rises by an amount that shifts the short-run aggregate supply curve from SAS_0 to SAS_1. The price level rises to 110, a 10 percent rise, and the economy is at point *A* in this figure and at point *A* on the short-run Phillips curve in Fig. 29.8. If, with the same expectations, aggregate demand increases and shifts the aggregate demand curve from AD_0 to AD_2, the price level rises to 113, a 13 percent rise, and the economy is at point *B* in this figure and at point *B* on the short-run Phillips curve in Fig. 29.8. If, with the same expectations, aggregate demand does not change, the price level rises to 107, a 7 percent rise, and the economy is at point *C* in this figure and at point *C* on the short-run Phillips curve in Fig. 29.8.

The short-run Phillips curve is like the short-run aggregate supply curve. A movement along the *SAS* curve that brings a higher price level and an increase in real GDP is equivalent to a movement along the short-run Phillips curve that brings an increase in the inflation rate and a decrease in the unemployment rate. (Similarly, a movement along the *SAS* curve that brings a lower price level and a decrease in real GDP is equivalent to a movement along the short-run Phillips curve that brings a decrease in the inflation rate and an increase in the unemployment rate.)

The Long-Run Phillips Curve

The **long-run Phillips curve** shows the relationship between inflation and unemployment when the actual inflation rate equals the expected inflation rate. The long-run Phillips curve is vertical at the natural unemployment rate. In Fig. 29.10, it is the vertical line *LRPC*. The long-run Phillips curve tells us that any anticipated inflation rate is possible at the natural unemployment rate. This proposition is consistent with the *AS-AD* model, which predicts that when inflation is anticipated, real GDP equals potential GDP and unemployment is at its natural rate.

When the expected inflation rate changes, the short-run Phillips curve shifts but the long-run Phillips curve does not shift. If the expected inflation rate is 10 percent a year, the short-run Phillips curve is $SRPC_0$. If the expected inflation rate falls to 7 percent a year, the short-run Phillips curve shifts

downward to $SRPC_1$. The distance by which the short-run Phillips curve shifts downward when the expected inflation rate falls is equal to the change in the expected inflation rate.

To see why the short-run Phillips curve shifts when the expected inflation rate changes, let's do a thought experiment. There is full employment, and a 10 percent a year anticipated inflation is raging. The Fed now begins an attack on inflation by slowing money growth. Aggregate demand growth slows, and the inflation rate falls to 7 percent a year. At first, this decrease in inflation is *un*anticipated, so the money wage rate continues to rise at its original rate. The short-run aggregate supply curve shifts leftward at the same pace as before. Real GDP decreases, and unemployment increases. In Fig. 29.10, the economy moves from point *A* to point *C* on $SRPC_0$.

If the actual inflation rate remains steady at 7 percent a year, this rate eventually comes to be expected. As this happens, wage growth slows and the short-run aggregate supply curve shifts leftward less quickly. Eventually, it shifts leftward at the same pace at which the aggregate demand curve is shifting rightward. The actual inflation rate equals the expected inflation rate, and full employment is restored. Unemployment is back at its natural rate. In Fig. 29.10, the short-run Phillips curve has shifted from $SRPC_0$ to $SRPC_1$ and the economy is at point *D*.

An increase in the expected inflation rate has the opposite effect to that shown in Fig. 29.10. Another important source of shifts in the Phillips curve is a change in the natural rate of unemployment.

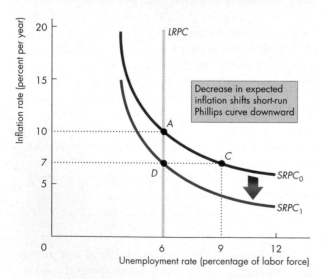

FIGURE 29.10 Short-Run and Long-Run Phillips Curves

The long-run Phillips curve is *LRPC*. A fall in expected inflation from 10 percent a year to 7 percent a year shifts the short-run Phillips curve downward from $SRPC_0$ and $SRPC_1$. The new short-run Phillips curve intersects the long-run Phillips curve at the new expected inflation rate — point *D*. With the original expected inflation rate (of 10 percent a year), a fall in the actual inflation rate to 7 percent a year increases the unemployment rate to 9 percent, at point *C*.

Changes in the Natural Rate of Unemployment

The natural rate of unemployment changes for many reasons (see Chapter 22, pp. 517–519). A change in the natural rate of unemployment shifts both the short-run and long-run Phillips curves. Figure 29.11 illustrates such shifts. If the natural rate of unemployment increases from 6 percent to 9 percent, the long-run Phillips curve shifts from $LRPC_0$ to $LRPC_1$, and if expected inflation is constant at 10 percent a year, the short-run Phillips curve shifts from $SRPC_0$ to $SRPC_1$. Because the expected inflation rate is constant, the short-run Phillips curve $SRPC_1$ intersects the long-run curve $LRPC_1$ (point *E*) at the same inflation rate at which the short-run Phillips curve $SRPC_0$ intersects the long-run curve $LRPC_0$ (point *A*).

The U.S. Phillips Curve

Figure 29.12(a) is a scatter diagram of inflation and unemployment since 1960. We can interpret the data in terms of the shifting short-run Phillips curve in Fig. 29.12(b). During the 1960s, the short-run Phillips curve was $SRPC_0$ with a natural rate of unemployment of 4.5 percent and an expected inflation rate of 2 percent a year (point A). During the early 1970s, the short-run Phillips curve was $SRPC_1$ with a natural rate of unemployment of 5 percent and an expected inflation rate of 6 percent a year (point B). During the late 1970s, the natural unemployment rate increased to 8 percent (point C) and the short-run Phillips curve was $SRPC_2$. And briefly in 1975 and again in 1981, the expected inflation rate surged to 8 percent a year (point D) and the short-run Phillips curve was $SRPC_3$. During the 1980s and 1990s, the expected inflation rate and the natural rate of unemployment decreased and the short-run Phillips curve shifted leftward. By the early 1990s, it was back at $SRPC_1$. And by the mid-1990s, it was again $SRPC_0$.

FIGURE 29.12 Phillips Curves in the United States

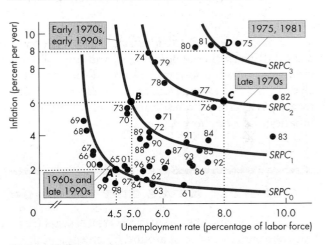

(a) Time sequence

(b) Four Phillips curves

In part (a), each dot represents the combination of inflation and unemployment for a particular year in the United States. Part (b) interprets the data with a shifting short-run Phillips curve. The black dots A, B, C, and D show the combination of the natural rate of unemployment and the expected inflation rate in different periods. The short-run Phillips curve was $SRPC_0$ during the 1960s and the late 1990s and early 2000s. It was $SRPC_1$ during the early 1970s and early 1990s, $SRPC_2$ during the late 1970s, and $SRPC_3$ (briefly) in 1975 and 1981.

Source: Bureau of Labor Statistics and the author's calculations and assumptions.

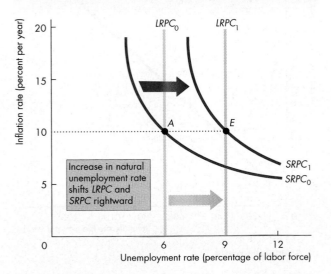

FIGURE 29.11 A Change in the Natural Unemployment Rate

A change in the natural unemployment rate shifts both the short-run and long-run Phillips curves. Here, the natural unemployment rate increases from 6 percent to 9 percent, and the two Phillips curves shift right to $SRPC_1$ and $LRPC_1$. The new long-run Phillips curve intersects the new short-run Phillips curve at the expected inflation rate — point E.

REVIEW QUIZ

1 How would you use the Phillips curve to illustrate an unanticipated change in the inflation rate?

2 What are the effects of an unanticipated increase in the inflation rate on the unemployment rate?

3 If the expected inflation rate increases by 10 percentage points, how does the short-run Phillips curve and the long-run Phillips curve change?

4 If the natural unemployment rate increases, what happens to the short-run Phillips curve, the long-run Phillips curve, and the expected inflation rate?

5 Does the United States have a stable short-run Phillips curve? Explain why or why not.

6 Does the United States have a stable long-run Phillips curve?

So far, we've studied the effects of inflation on real GDP, real wages, employment, and unemployment. But inflation lowers the value of money and changes the real value of the amounts borrowed and repaid. As a result, interest rates are influenced by inflation. Let's see how.

Interest Rates and Inflation

TODAY, BUSINESSES IN THE UNITED STATES CAN borrow at interest rates of around 6 percent a year. Businesses in Russia pay interest rates of 60 percent a year, and those in Turkey pay 80 percent a year. Although U.S. interest rates have never been as high as these two cases, U.S. businesses faced interest rates of 16 percent or higher during the 1980s. Why do interest rates vary so much both across countries and over time? Part of the answer is because risk differences make *real interest rates* vary across countries. High-risk countries pay higher interest rates than do low-risk countries. But another part of the answer is that the inflation rate varies.

Figure 29.13 shows that the higher the inflation rate, the higher is the nominal interest rate. This proposition is true for the United States over time in part (a) and the world in 2000 in part (b).

FIGURE 29.13   Inflation and the Interest Rate

(a) United States

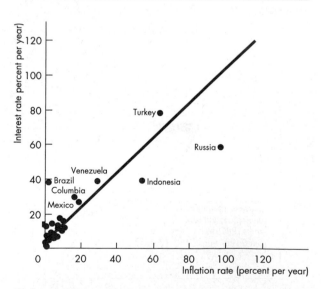

(b) Around the world

Other things remaining the same, the higher the inflation rate, the higher is the nominal interest rate. Part (a) shows this relationship between nominal interest rates and the inflation rate in the United States, and part (b) shows the relationship across a number of countries in 2000.

Sources: Federal Reserve Board, Bureau of Labor Statistics, and International Monetary Fund.

How Interest Rates Are Determined

The *real* interest rate is determined by investment demand and saving supply in the global market for financial capital. Investment demand and saving supply depend on the real interest rate. And the real interest rate adjusts to make investment plans and saving plans equal. (Chapter 23, pp. 535–537, explains the forces that determine the equilibrium real interest rate. National real interest rates vary around the world-average real interest rate because of national differences in risk.)

A *nominal* interest rate is determined by the demand for money and the supply of money in each nation's money market. The demand for money depends on the nominal interest rate, and the supply of money is determined by the central bank's monetary policy — the Fed's monetary policy in the United States. And the nominal interest rate adjusts to make the quantity of money demanded equal to the quantity supplied. (Chapter 28, pp. 665–666, explains the forces that determine the equilibrium nominal interest rate.)

Why Inflation Influences the Nominal Interest Rate

Because the real interest rate is determined in the global capital market and nominal interest rates are determined in each nation's money market, there is no tight and mechanical link between the two interest rates. But on the average, and other things remaining the same, a 1 percentage point rise in the inflation rate leads to a 1 percentage point rise in the nominal interest rate. Why? The answer is that the capital market and the money market are closely interconnected. The investment, saving, and demand for money decisions that people make are connected and the result is that the equilibrium nominal interest rate approximately equals the real interest rate plus the expected inflation rate.

To see why this relationship between the real interest rate and the nominal interest rate arises, think about the investment, saving, and demand for money decisions that people make. Imagine first that there is no inflation. Investment equals saving at a real interest rate of 6 percent a year. The demand for money equals the supply of money at a nominal interest rate of 6 percent a year. Walt Disney Corporation is willing to pay an interest rate of 6 percent a year to get the funds it needs to pay for its global investment in new theme parks. Sue and thousands of people like

her are willing to save and lend Disney the amount it needs for its theme parks if they can get a *real* return of 6 percent a year. (Sue is saving to buy a new car.) And Disney, Sue, and everyone else are willingly holding the quantity of (real) money supplied by the Fed.

Now imagine that the inflation rate is a steady and expected 4 percent a year. All dollar amounts, including theme park profits and car prices, are rising by 4 percent a year. If Disney was willing to pay a 6 percent interest rate when there was no inflation, it is now willing to pay a 10 percent interest rate. Its profits are rising by 4 percent a year, so it is *really* paying only 6 percent. Similarly, if Sue was willing to lend at a 6 percent interest rate when there was no inflation, she is now willing to lend only if she gets a 10 percent interest rate. The price of the car Sue is planning on buying is rising by 4 percent a year, so she is *really* getting only a 6 percent interest rate.

Because borrowers are willing to pay the higher rate and lenders are willing to lend only if they receive the higher rate when inflation is anticipated, the *nominal interest rate* increases by an amount equal to the expected inflation rate. The *real interest rate* remains constant.

At a nominal interest rate of 10 percent a year, people are willing to hold the quantity of (real) money supplied by the Fed. This quantity is less than that with zero inflation. The price level rises by more than the quantity of money, and the real quantity of money decreases because of the increase in inflation.

REVIEW QUIZ

1 What is the relationship between the real interest rate, the nominal interest rate, and the inflation rate?

2 Why does inflation change the nominal interest rate?

◆ Before leaving this chapter, take a look at *Reading Between the Lines* on pp. 694–695, which looks at the current low inflation and unemployment in the United States and gives you a look at today's short-run Phillips curve.

Your task in the next chapter is to focus on the business cycle. What causes cycles in economic activity and what brought the recession of 2001?

The U.S. Phillips Curve in 2000–2001

PITTSBURGH POST-GAZETTE, July 27, 2000

Links More Tenuous Between Inflation, Jobless Rates

Federal Reserve Chairman Alan Greenspan last week took aim at the favorite theory of anyone who thinks U.S. interest rates have to rise just because the jobless rate is close to a 30-year low.

That theory holds that at a certain point unemployment goes too low for the economy's good, driving up wage demands and, ultimately, inflation. Some economists say the figure is as high as 6 percent, some say 5 percent. The Fed chairman said the relationship between unemployment and inflation is tenuous at best.

Such a theory may have been "very useful" at one time, but "is probably going to fail in the years ahead as a useful indicator," Greenspan told the Senate Banking Committee in his twice-yearly economic report card.

His comments may give a clue to how the Fed will deal with future developments in the U.S. labor market. If unemployment sticks near 4 percent, Greenspan probably will continue to resist the once automatic reaction of Fed Governor Lawrence Meyer and other members of the policy-setting Open Market Committee to raise rates in an effort to curtail consumer and business borrowing and slow growth. ...

That evidence doesn't support Meyer and other so-called hawks on the Fed. Unemployment dropped below 5 percent in 1996, a level many of them thought would lead directly to higher prices.

Still, consumer price inflation, not including food and energy items, has held below 3 percent the entire time. ...

In a speech last month, Meyer dismissed "the broader interpretation of the New Economy concept" — meaning the notion that there's no link between low unemployment and accelerating inflation.

A jobless rate of 4 percent or so is probably too low, he said. And if the level of unemployment that leads to accelerating inflation "turns out to be closer to 5 percent, then the task is more demanding," and more workers might have to lose their jobs to bring the economy back into balance, he suggested. ...

But Greenspan can marshal some reasons Meyer's theory hasn't held true: Higher worker productivity has allowed companies to make do with fewer workers.

Also, inflation expectations remain low, so workers are less likely to demand outsized wage increases. ...

Essence of the Story

- Federal Reserve Chairman Alan Greenspan challenged the view that U.S. interest rates must rise if the unemployment rate gets too low.

- He said the relationship between unemployment and inflation is weak and not very useful.

- Federal Reserve Governor Lawrence Meyer and other members of Federal Open Market Committee say that if the unemployment rate goes too low, inflation will increase.

- Economists differ on what that unemployment rate is. Some say it is as high as 6 percent, and some say 5 percent. But most say that 4 percent is too low.

- The unemployment rate fell below 5 percent in 1996, but the inflation rate remained below 3 percent a year.

- Inflation expectations remain low, so workers are less likely to demand outsized wage increases.

Economic Analysis

■ This news article is about the U.S. Phillips curve.

■ During 2000, when the news article was written, the unemployment rate fluctuated between 3.9 percent and 4.1 percent and was 4.0 percent on the average.

■ Inflation did not take off at this low average unemployment rate. But the inflation rate did edge upward slightly from 2.5 percent a year in January 2000 to 3.8 percent a year in July 2000.

■ We can interpret the data in 2000 as being on the long-run Phillips curve for that year.

■ Figure 1 shows the long-run Phillips curve for 2000. The natural unemployment rate was 4 percent, and the expected inflation rate increased (along with the actual inflation rate) from 2.5 percent to 3.8 percent a year.

■ Starting in December 2000, the unemployment rate increased almost every month. By December 2001, it had reached 5.8 percent.

■ Through this same period, the inflation rate

decreased almost every month. In January 2001, the inflation rate was 3.8 percent a year, and by December 2001, it had fallen to 1.6 percent a year.

■ Figure 2 shows how we can interpret the data for 2001. The natural unemployment rate remained at 4 percent, so the long-run Phillips curve did not shift.

■ The expected inflation rate remained constant at (an approximate guess) 4 percent a year, so the short-run Phillips curve did not shift.

■ As 2001 unfolded, the economy moved downward along its short-run Phillips curve.

■ The data for 2000 and 2001 are consistent with the view that there is a tradeoff between unemployment and inflation.

■ But during 2000 when Alan Greenspan was speaking, because the unemployment rate was constant, we could see only the long-run tradeoff.

■ The fact that the natural unemployment rate and expected inflation rate remained constant

Figure 1 In 2000

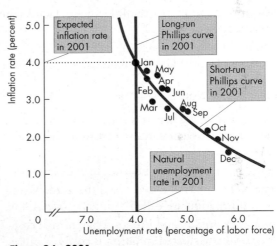

Figure 2 In 2001

through 2001 enables us to see the short-run tradeoff during that year.

■ We cannot predict future changes in the natural unemployment rate and expected inflation rate, and the short-

run tradeoff shifts in ways that we can't predict.

■ For this reason, Alan Greenspan is correct when he says the tradeoff has limited usefulness for policy.

SUMMARY

KEY POINTS

Inflation and the Price Level (p. 678)

- Inflation is a process of persistently rising prices and falling value of money.

Demand-Pull Inflation (pp. 679–681)

- Demand-pull inflation arises from increasing aggregate demand.
- Its main sources are increases in the quantity of money or in government purchases.

Cost-Push Inflation (pp. 681–683)

- Cost-push inflation can result from any factor that decreases aggregate supply.
- Its main sources are increasing wage rates and increasing prices of key raw materials.

Effects of Inflation (pp. 684–688)

- Inflation is costly when it is unanticipated because it creates inefficiencies and redistributes income and wealth.
- People try to anticipate inflation to avoid its costs.
- Forecasts of inflation based on all the available relevant information are called rational expectations.
- A moderate anticipated inflation has a small cost. But a rapid anticipated inflation is costly because it decreases potential GDP and slows growth.

Inflation and Unemployment: The Phillips Curve (pp. 688–692)

- The short-run Phillips curve shows the tradeoff between inflation and unemployment when the expected inflation rate and the natural rate of unemployment are constant.
- The long-run Phillips curve, which is vertical, shows that when the actual inflation rate equals the expected inflation rate, the unemployment rate equals the natural rate of unemployment.

- Unexpected changes in the inflation rate bring movements along the short-run Phillips curve.
- Changes in expected inflation shift the short-run Phillips curve.
- Changes in the natural rate of unemployment shift both the short-run and long-run Phillips curves.

Interest Rates and Inflation (pp. 692–693)

- The higher the expected inflation rate, the higher is the nominal interest rate.
- As the anticipated inflation rate rises, borrowers willingly pay a higher interest rate and lenders successfully demand a higher interest rate.
- The nominal interest rate adjusts to equal the real interest rate plus the expected inflation rate.

KEY FIGURES

KEY TERMS

PROBLEMS

*1. The figure shows an economy's long-run aggregate supply curve *LAS*; three aggregate demand curves AD_0, AD_1, and AD_2; and three short-run aggregate supply curves SAS_0, SAS_1, and SAS_2. The economy starts out on the curves AD_0 and SAS_0. Some events then occur that generate a demand-pull inflation.
   a. List the events that might cause a demand-pull inflation.
   b. Using the figure, describe the initial effects of a demand-pull inflation.
   c. Using the figure, describe what happens as a demand-pull inflation spiral unwinds.

2. The economy, described in problem 1, starts out on the curves AD_0 and SAS_0. Some events then occur that generate a cost-push inflation.
   a. List the events that might cause a cost-push inflation.
   b. Using the figure, describe the initial effects of a cost-push inflation.
   c. Using the figure, describe what happens as a cost-push inflation spiral unwinds.

*3. The economy, described in problem 1, starts out on the curves AD_0 and SAS_0. Some events then occur that generate a perfectly anticipated inflation.
   a. List the events that might cause a perfectly anticipated inflation.
   b. Using the figure, describe the initial effects of an anticipated inflation.
   c. Using the figure, describe what happens as an anticipated inflation proceeds.

4. In the economy described in problem 1, suppose that people anticipate deflation (a falling price level) but aggregate demand turns out to not change.
   a. What happens to the short-run and long-run aggregate supply curves? (Draw some new curves if you need to.)
   b. Using the figure, describe the initial effects of an anticipated deflation.
   c. Using the figure, describe what happens as it becomes obvious to everyone that the anticipated deflation is not going to occur.

*5. An economy has an unemployment rate of 4 percent and an inflation rate of 5 percent at point *A* in the figure. Some events then occur that move the economy to point *D*.

   a. Describe the events that could move the economy from point *A* to point *D*.
   b. Draw in the diagram the economy's short-run and long-run Phillips curves when the economy is at point *A*.
   c. Draw in the diagram the economy's short-run and long-run Phillips curves when the economy is at point *D*.

6. The economy, described in problem 5, is initially at point *B*. Some events occur that move the economy from point *B* to point *C*.
   a. Describe the events that could move the economy from point *B* to point *C*.
   b. Draw in the diagram the economy's short-run and long-run Phillips curves when the economy is at point *B*.
   c. Draw in the diagram the economy's short-run and long-run Phillips curves when the economy is at point *C*.

*7. In the economy described in problem 5, some events occur that move the economy in a clockwise loop from *A* to *B* to *D* to *C* and back to *A*.
   a. Describe the events that could create this sequence.
   b. Draw in the figure the sequence of the economy's short-run and long-run Phillips curves.
   c. Has the economy experienced demand-pull inflation, cost-push inflation, anticipated inflation, or none of these?

8. In the economy described in problem 5, some events occur that move the economy in a counterclockwise loop from *A* to *C* to *D* to *B* and back to *A*.
   a. Describe the events that could create this sequence.
   b. Draw in the figure the sequence of the economy's short-run and long-run Phillips curves.
   c. Has the economy experienced demand-pull inflation, cost-push inflation, anticipated inflation, or none of these?

*9. An economy with a natural rate of unemployment of 4 percent and an expected inflation rate of 6 percent a year has the following inflation and unemployment history:

Year	Inflation rate (percent per year)	Unemployment rate (percent)
1999	10	2
2000	8	3
2001	6	4
2002	4	5
2003	2	6

   a. Draw a figure that shows the economy's short-run and long-run Phillips curves.
   b. If the actual inflation rate rises from 6 percent a year to 8 percent a year, what is the change in the unemployment rate? Explain why it occurs.

10. For the economy described in problem 9, the natural rate of unemployment rises to 5 percent and the expected inflation rate falls to 5 percent. Draw the new short-run and long-run Phillips curves in a figure.

CRITICAL THINKING

1. Study *Reading Between the Lines* on pp. 694–695 and then answer the following questions:
   a. What does Alan Greenspan say about the tradeoff between inflation and unemployment?
   b. What does Federal Reserve Governor Lawrence Meyer say about the tradeoff between inflation and unemployment?
   c. Whom do you think is correct, Greenspan or Meyer, and why?
   d. Do you think the evidence of 2000 and 2001 is consistent with the view that the natural rate of unemployment is 6 percent? Explain why or why not.

2. In light of what you have learned in this chapter, what do you think the Fed should do during the next few months to keep the economy expanding and to keep inflation in check?

WEB EXERCISES

1. Use the links on your Parkin Web site to obtain data on the growth rate of the quantity of money and the inflation rate in the United States since 2000.
   a. Calculate the average growth rate of the quantity of money since 2000.
   b. Calculate the average inflation rate since 2000.
   c. Make a graph of the growth rate of the quantity of money and the inflation rate since 2000.
   d. Interpret your graph and explain what it tells you about the forces that generate inflation and the relationship between money growth and inflation.

2. Use the links on your Parkin Web site to obtain data on the inflation rate and the unemployment rate in Canada during the 1990s and 2000s.
   a. Make a graph using the data you've obtained that is similar to Fig. 29.12.
   b. Describe the similarities and the differences in relationship between inflation and unemployment found in the United States and in Canada.

UNDERSTANDING AGGREGATE DEMAND AND INFLATION

PART 9

Money Chasing Goods

Aggregate demand fluctuations bring recessions and expansions. If aggregate demand expands more rapidly than long-run aggregate supply, we get inflation. So understanding the forces that determine aggregate demand helps us to understand both the business cycle and inflation. ◆ It took economists a long time to achieve this knowledge, and we still don't know enough about aggregate demand to be able to forecast it more than a few months ahead. But we do know the basic factors that influence aggregate demand. And we know a lot about how those factors interact to send shock waves rippling through the economy. ◆ Fundamentally, aggregate demand is a monetary phenomenon. The quantity of money is the single most significant influence on aggregate demand. This insight was first outlined more than 200 years ago by David Hume, a Scottish philosopher and close friend of Adam Smith. Said Hume, "In every Kingdom into which money begins to flow in greater abundance than formerly, every thing takes a new face: labor and industry gain life; the merchant becomes more enterprising, the manufacturer more diligent and skilful, and even the farmer follows his plow with greater alacrity and attention." Milton Friedman and other economists known as *monetarists* also emphasize the central role of money. Money lies at the center of Keynes' theory of aggregate demand as well. But Keynes also called attention to the power of independent changes in government purchases, taxes, and business investment to influence aggregate demand. In the modern world, we also recognize the effect of changes in exports on aggregate demand. ◆ The chapters in this part explain the factors that influence aggregate demand and help you to understand how they interact to bring multiplier effects on aggregate expenditure. Chapter 25 explained the effects of changes in business investment and the multiplier effect they have on consumption expenditure and aggregate expenditure. This chapter also explained how changes in business inventories trigger changes in production and incomes. Chapter 26 looked at fiscal policy and applied the model of Chapter 25 to study the effects of changes in government purchases and taxes. Chapter 27 brought money into the picture and explained exactly what money is and how banks create it. Chapter 28 showed how the Fed controls the quantity of money and thereby influences interest rates and expenditure. Chapter 29 returned to the aggregate supply–aggregate demand framework and explained inflation. It showed how the trends in inflation are determined by the trend in the money supply and how fluctuations in aggregate demand bring fluctuations in inflation, employment, and unemployment. ◆ Many economists have developed the insights you've learned in these chapters. One of the truly outstanding ones is Milton Friedman, whom you can meet on the next page. Another, and one of today's leading macroeconomists, is Michael Woodford of Princeton University, whom you can also meet on the following pages.

"Inflation is always and everywhere a monetary phenomenon."

MILTON
FRIEDMAN
*The Counter-
Revolution in
Monetary
Theory*

700

THE ECONOMIST

MILTON FRIEDMAN *was born into a poor immigrant family in New York City in 1912. He was an undergraduate at Rutgers and graduate student at Columbia University during the Great Depression. Today, Professor Friedman is a Senior Fellow at the Hoover Institution at Stanford University. But his reputation was built between 1946 and 1983, when he was a leading member of the "Chicago School," an approach to economics developed at the University of Chicago and based on the views that free markets allocate resources efficiently and that stable and low money supply growth delivers macroeconomic stability.*

Friedman has advanced our understanding of the forces that determine aggregate demand and clarified the effects of the quantity of money and for this work, he was awarded the (much overdue, in the opinion of his many admirers) 1977 Nobel Prize for Economic Science.

By reasoning from basic economic principles, Friedman predicted that persistent demand stimulation would not increase output but would cause inflation. When output growth slowed and inflation broke out in the 1970s, Friedman seemed like a prophet, and for a time, his policy prescription, known as monetarism, was embraced around the world.

THE ISSUES

The combination of history and economics has taught us a lot about the causes of inflation. Severe inflation — hyperinflation — arises from a breakdown of the normal fiscal policy processes at times of war or political upheaval. Tax revenues fall short of government spending, and newly printed money fills the gap between them. As inflation increases, the quantity of money that is needed to make payments increases, and a shortage of money can even result. So the rate of money growth increases yet further, and prices rise yet faster. Eventually, the monetary system collapses. Such was the experience of Germany during the 1920s and Brazil during the 1990s.

In earlier times, when commodities were used as money, inflation resulted from the discovery of new sources of money. The most recent occurrence of this type of inflation was at the end of the nineteenth century when gold, then used as money, was discovered in Australia, the Klondike, and South Africa.

In modern times, inflation has resulted from increases in the money supply that has accommodated increases in costs. The most dramatic such inflations occurred during the 1970s when the Fed and other central banks around the world accommodated oil price increases.

To avoid inflation, money supply growth must be held in check. But at times of severe cost pressure, central banks feel a strong tug in the direction of avoiding recession and accommodating the cost pressure.

Yet some countries have avoided inflation more effectively than others have. One source of success is central bank independence. In low-inflation countries, such as Germany and Japan, the central bank decides how much money to create and at what level to set interest rates, and does not take instructions from the government. In high-inflation countries, such as the United Kingdom and Italy, the central bank takes direct orders from the government about interest rates and money supply growth. The architects of the new monetary system for the European Community based on the euro noticed this connection between central bank independence and inflation and modeled the constitution for the European Central Bank on the independent German central bank.

THEN

When inflation is especially rapid, as it was in Germany in 1923, money becomes almost worthless. In Germany at that time, bank notes were more valuable as fire kindling than as money, and the sight of people burning Reichmarks was a common one. To avoid having to hold money for too long, wages were paid and spent twice a day. Banks took deposits and made loans, but at interest rates that compensated both depositors and the bank for the falling value of money — interest rates that could exceed 100 percent a month. The price of a dinner would increase during the course of an evening, making lingering over coffee a very expensive pastime.

NOW

In 1994, Brazil had a computer-age hyperinflation, an inflation rate that was close to 50 percent a month. Banks installed ATMs on almost every street corner and refilled them several times an hour. Brazilians tried to avoid holding currency. As soon as they were paid, they went shopping and bought enough food to get them through to the next payday. Some shoppers filled as many as six carts on a single monthly trip to the supermarket. Also, instead of using currency, Brazilians used credit cards whenever possible. But they paid their card balances off quickly because the interest rate on unpaid balances was 50 percent a month. Only at such a high interest rate did it pay banks to lend to cardholders, because banks themselves were paying interest rates of 40 percent a month to induce depositors to keep their money in the bank.

Many economists today are working on aggregate demand and inflation. One distinguished contributor, whom you can meet on the following pages, is Michael Woodford of Princeton University.

701

TALKING WITH

MICHAEL WOODFORD *is Harold H. Helm '20 Professor of Economics and Banking at Princeton University. Born in 1955 in Chicopee, Massachusetts, he was an undergraduate at the University of Chicago and a doctoral student at the Yale Law School before pursuing his doctorate in economics at the Massachusetts Institute of Technology. Professor Woodford's research on money and monetary policy has challenged much traditional thinking, and his ideas about a (future) world without money are attracting a great deal of interest. His advanced text,* Interest and Prices: Foundations of a Theory of Monetary Policy *is being published by Princeton University Press.*

Michael Parkin talked with Michael Woodford about his work and the progress that economists have made in designing effective monetary policy rules.

Michael Woodford

Why, after completing law school, did you decide to become an economist?

Almost every class in law school was full of economic reasoning. I became fascinated by economic analysis, and thought that I would have to get a better foundation in economics in order to think clearly about legal issues. In the end I found that I liked economics enough to become an economist.

I am able to address questions of public policy, which is what had originally drawn me to law, but in a way that also allows me to indulge a taste for thinking about what

the world might be like or should be like, and not simply the way that it already is.

In a world as rapidly changing as ours is, I think that the perspective provided by economics is essential for understanding which kinds of laws and rules make sense.

You are a supporter of rules for monetary policy. Why are rules so important?

In my view, rules are important not because central bankers can't be relied upon to take the public interest to heart, or because they don't know what they're doing, but because the effects of monetary policy depend critically upon what the private sector expects about future policy, and hence about the future course of the economy. Thus effective monetary policy depends more on the successful *management of expectations* than on any direct consequences of the current level of interest rates.

In order to steer people's expectations about future monetary policy in the way that it would like, a central bank needs to communicate details about how policy will be conducted in the future. The best way to do this is by being explicit about the *rule* that guides its decision making. The central bank also needs to establish a reputation for actually following the rule.

Following the rule means *not* always doing what might seem best in given current conditions. What is best for the economy now will be independent of what people may have expected in the past. But if the central bank doesn't feel bound to follow through on its prior commitments, people will learn that they don't mean anything. Then those commitments will not shape people's expectations in the desired way.

There is actually a strong parallel between monetary policy rules and the law, and the desirability of rules is an example of the perspective that I gained from the study of law. A judge doesn't simply seek to determine, in each individual case, what outcome would do the most good, given the individual circumstances. Instead, the judge makes a decision based on rules established either by precedent or by statute. Because the law is rule-based, people are able to forecast more accurately the consequences of their contemplated actions.

A central banker is often portrayed as the captain of the economic ship, steering it skillfully between the rocks of inflation and unemployment in a choppy sea. But a ship's captain doesn't need to care about how the ocean will interpret his actions. So the parallel isn't a good one. In my view, the role of a central banker is more similar to that of a judge than to that of a ship's captain. Both central bankers and judges

> *"Following the rule means* not *always doing what might seem best in given current conditions."*

care enormously about the effects of their decisions on the expectations of people whose behavior depends on expected future decisions.

The rule that you favor is different from that suggested by Milton Friedman. What is wrong with the Friedman rule?

Friedman's rule involves a target for the growth rate of some definition of the quantity of money. I don't think that the best monetary rule involves a target of any kind for the growth rate of a monetary aggregate. Friedman's rule is not the worst sort of rule, as simple rules go, but we can do better.

Just a century ago, no one had any idea how to establish a reasonably predictable monetary standard except by guaranteeing the convertibility of money into a precious metal such as gold. We didn't have the surprisingly modern concept of index numbers and today's routinely calculated price indexes like the CPI that enable us to measure, to a decent approximation, the purchasing power of the dollar.

We now understand that pegging the value of money to something like gold is a cruder solution to the problem than is necessary. We don't need to leave the value of money hostage to the vagaries of the gold

market simply in order to maintain confidence that a dollar means *something*.

Friedman recognizes the value of a well-managed fiat currency, but supposes that there is unlikely to be much predictability to the value of money unless the central bank is committed to a fixed target growth path for the quantity of money. But that again is a more indirect solution to the problem of maintaining a stable and predictable value for money than is necessary.

And there is a potentially large cost of such a crude approach when the relation between one's favorite monetary aggregate and the value of money shifts over time. A focus on stabilizing a monetary aggregate means less stability than would otherwise have been possible in the purchasing power of money.

So what would be a good monetary rule?

First, there should be a clearly defined target in terms of variables that policymakers actually care about, such as the inflation rate, rather than an "intermediate target" such as a monetary aggregate. Second, the central bank should be as clear as possible about the decision making process through which it determines the level of interest rates that is believed to be consistent with achieving the target.

"Inflation targeting," as currently practiced in the United Kingdom, Canada, and New Zealand, is an example of the general approach that I would advocate. But I think that central banks of an inflation-targeting country could do a better job of explaining the procedures used to determine the interest rate that is judged to be consistent with the inflation target— they could be more transparent.

And all of these countries could better explain to the public the ways in which variables other than inflation are also taken into consideration. I'm not sure that inflation targeting needs to be *stricter,* in the sense that considerations other than inflation should be more scrupulously ruled out. But I think that it is desirable to make it more of a *rule.*

One of the most intriguing issues that you've worked on is the question of what determines the price level in a "cashless economy." How would we control inflation in such a world?

One advantage of the approach to monetary policy that I've just mentioned is that the form of policy rule that is appropriate need not change much at all if we were to progress to a "cashless economy." As long as the central bank can still control the overnight interest rates—the federal funds rate in the United States—the *rule* for adjusting the interest rate need not change. Yet there might no longer be any meaning to a target path for a monetary aggregate in such a world.

The critical question is whether a central bank would still be able to control overnight interest rates in such a world. Some argue that central banks only control interest rates in the interbank market for reserves because the private sector cannot supply a good substitute for reserves and the central bank is therefore a monopoly supplier. They then worry that if private substitutes for reserves were available, central banks would lose control of the interest rate.

But this line of reasoning assumes, as do most textbooks (even the good ones!), that central banks can change the interest rate *only* by changing the *opportunity cost* of holding reserves, which should only be possible in the presence of market power. But central banks can change the overnight interest rate *without* changing the opportunity cost of holding reserves. Indeed, the Bank of Canada already does so. It pays interest on reserves and maintains a fixed difference between the interest rate on reserves and the discount rate—the rate at which it stands willing to lend reserves to the banks. The overnight rate fluctuates inside the range of these two rates, so by changing the interest rate on reserves, the Bank of Canada controls the overnight rate but doesn't change the opportunity cost of holding reserves.

Every central bank, including the Fed, would have to adjust the interest rate in a way similar to this in a "cashless economy."

Where do you stand on the sources of aggregate fluctuations? Are they primarily an efficient response to the uneven pace of technical change, or are they primarily the consequence of market failure and demand fluctuations?

I don't think that they are primarily an *efficient* response to variations in technical progress or to other real disturbances of that kind. I think that there are important distortions that often result in *inefficient* responses of the economy to real disturbances,

and this is why monetary policy matters. But I do think that real disturbances are important—for example, I don't think that exogenous variations in monetary policy have been responsible for too much of the economic instability in the U.S. economy in recent decades—and I think that their supply-side effects are important, too.

The important issue, to my mind, is not whether the disturbances are thought to have more to do with supply or demand factors; it is whether the economy can be relied upon to respond efficiently to them, regardless of the nature of monetary policy. I don't think that that occurs automatically. The goal of good monetary policy is to bring about such a world: one in which monetary policy is not itself a source of disturbances, and in which the responses to real disturbances are efficient ones. The first part simply requires that monetary policy be systematic, but the second part depends upon the choice of a monetary policy rule of the right sort.

What advice do you have for a student who is just starting to study economics? Is it a good subject in which to major? What other subjects would you urge students to study alongside economics?

I think economics is an excellent major for students with many different interests. Most people who study economics are probably looking for an edge in the business world, and economics is valuable for that. But it's also an extremely valuable background for people interested in careers in law, government, or public policy. And of course, for some of us, the subject is interesting in its own right. I find that the challenges just get deeper the farther I get into the subject.

Probably the most important other subject for someone thinking of actually becoming an economist is mathematics. This is often the determining factor as to how well a student will do in graduate study, because the research literature is a good deal more mathematical than many people suspect from their undergraduate economics courses. But economics is not a branch of mathematics. It's a subject that seeks to understand people and social institutions, and so all sorts of other subjects—history, politics, sociology, psychology, moral and political philosophy—are useful background for an economist, too. I don't at all regret the amount of time I spent in liberal arts courses as an undergraduate.

THE BUSINESS CYCLE — CHAPTER 30

Must What Goes Up Always Come Down?

The 1990s were years of rapid expansion for the U.S. economy — so much so that people began to talk of a "new economy," an economy fueled by information technologies in which recession was a disease that had been cured. But then came the 2001 recession, which was mild in comparison with its predecessors but a recession nonetheless. ◆ Like the 1990s, the 1920s were years of expansion and unprecedented prosperity. After the horrors of World War I (1914–1918), Americans were back at work, producing such technological marvels as cars and airplanes, telephones and vacuum cleaners. Houses and apartments were being built at a frantic pace. Then, almost without warning, in October 1929, came a devastating stock market crash. Overnight, the values of stocks and shares trading on Wall Street fell by 30 percent. During the next four years, there followed the most severe economic contraction in recorded history. By 1933, real GDP had fallen by 30 percent, unemployment had increased to 25 percent of the labor force, and employment was down 20 percent. ◆ Our economy has experienced 16 recessions since 1920 and 10 since the end of World War II in 1945. Most of these recessions were short lived and were followed by another, much longer spell of expansion.

◆ What causes a repeating sequence of recessions and expansions in our economy? Must what goes up always come down? This chapter explores these questions.

After studying this chapter, you will be able to

- Distinguish among the different theories of the business cycle
- Explain the Keynesian and monetarist theories of the business cycle
- Explain the new classical and new Keynesian theories of the business cycle
- Explain real business cycle theory
- Describe the origins of, and the mechanisms at work during, the expansion of the 1990s, the recession of 2001, and the Great Depression

Cycle Patterns, Impulses, and Mechanisms

YOU'VE LOOKED AT THE BUSINESS CYCLE AT SEVeral points in your study of macroeconomics. You met it first in Chapter 1, which defines the phases of the cycle and describes its history. You saw in Chapter 20 how unemployment fluctuates over the business cycle. In Chapter 21, you learned about a framework for studying the business cycle: the *AS-AD* model. In Chapter 25, you focused on business cycle turning points and the inventory changes and multiplier effects that operate as the economy swings from expansion to recession and back to expansion. In Chapter 26, you studied the ways in which fiscal policy influences and is influenced by the business cycle. Finally, you saw in Chapters 27 through 29 how money influences economic fluctuations and how inflation and the business cycle intertwine.

You've also looked at another type of economic fluctuation: the productivity growth slowdown of the 1970s. This slowdown is not classified as a business cycle event, but it has some similarities. It is part of an overall process of economic growth, the pace of which fluctuates. The processes of growth and of the business cycle are intimately connected. In fact, according to one view, they are all manifestations of the same phenomenon.

This chapter brings all these strands in your previous study of macroeconomics together and gives you an opportunity both to review what you have learned and to put it to work in a focused way in interpreting and making sense of particular episodes in our economic history. We'll get moving by first returning to the facts about the business cycle and looking at the complex patterns it makes.

Business Cycle Patterns

The *business cycle* is an irregular and nonrepeating up-and-down movement of business activity that takes place around a generally rising trend and that shows great diversity. Each recession, expansion, and turning point has been dated by the National Bureau of Economic Research (NBER). The NBER has identified 16 recessions and expansions since 1920. On the average, recessions have lasted for just over a year, and real GDP has fallen from peak to trough by more than 6 percent. On the average, expansions have

lasted for almost 4 years, and real GDP has increased from trough to peak by 22 percent. But these averages hide huge variations from one cycle to another.

Table 30.1 shows the range of variation. You can see that the Great Depression was much more severe than anything that followed it. Over a 43-month period (August 1929 to March 1933), real GDP shrank by 32.6 percent. The second most severe recession was also in the 1930s. Another relatively severe recession occurred at the end of World War II, in 1945. The only other recession that comes close to these is that of 1974–1975, which resulted from a fourfold rise in the price of oil, lasted for 16 months, and saw real GDP fall by 4.9 percent. The other recessions since 1950, including the most recent 2001 recession, have been much milder than those of the 1930s. The biggest expansion occurred during World War II. The other two big expansions were in the 1960s and 1990s. There is no correlation between the length of an expansion and the length of the preceding recession.

With this enormous diversity of experience, there is no simple explanation for the business cycle. Also, there is no currently available way of forecasting when the next turning point will come. But there is a body of theory about the business cycle that helps us to understand its causes. A good place to begin studying this theory is to distinguish the possible ways in which cycles can be created.

Cycle Impulses and Mechanisms

Cycles are a widespread physical phenomenon. In a tennis match, the ball cycles from one side of the court to the other and back again. Every day, the earth cycles from day to night and back to day. A child on a rocking horse creates a cycle as the horse swings back and forth.

The tennis ball cycle is the simplest. It is caused by the actions of the players. Each time the ball changes direction (at each turning point), the racket (an outside force) is applied. The day-night-day cycle is the most subtle. This cycle is caused by the rotation of the earth. No new force is applied each day to make the sun rise and set. It happens because of the design of the objects that interact to create the cycle. Nothing happens at a turning point (sunrise and sunset) that is any different from what is happening at other points except that the sun comes into or goes out of view. The child's rocking horse cycle is a combination of these two cases. To start the horse rocking, some outside force must be exerted (as in the tennis ball cycle). But once the horse is rocking, the to-and-fro cycle continues for some time with no further force being applied (as in the day-night-day cycle). The rocking horse cycle eventually dies out unless the horse is pushed again, and each time the horse is pushed, the cycle temporarily becomes more severe.

The economy is a bit like all three of these examples. It can be hit by shocks (like a tennis ball) that send it in one direction or another, it can cycle indefinitely (like the turning of day into night), and it can cycle in swings that get milder until another shock sets off a new burst of bigger swings (like a rocking horse). While none of these analogies is perfect, they all contain some insights into the business cycle. Different theories of the cycle emphasize different

outside forces (different tennis rackets) and different cycle mechanisms (different solar system and rocking horse designs).

Although there are several different theories of the business cycle, they all agree about one aspect of the cycle: the central role played by investment and the accumulation of capital.

The Central Role of Investment and Capital

Whatever the shocks are that hit the economy, they hit one crucial variable: investment. Recessions begin when investment in new capital slows down, and they turn into expansions when investment speeds up. Investment and capital interact like the spinning earth and the sun to create an ongoing cycle.

TABLE 30.1   Business Cycle Dates Since 1920

Business cycle dates		Duration in months				
Peak	Trough	Contraction (previous peak to trough)	Expansion (trough to peak)	Cycle (trough from previous trough)	Cycle (peak from previous peak)	Fall in real GDP (peak to trough, percent)
January 1920	July 1921	18	22	28	40	8.7
May 1923	July 1924	14	27	36	41	4.1
October 1926	November 1927	13	21	40	34	2.0
August 1929	March 1933	43	50	64	93	32.6
May 1937	June 1938	13	80	63	93	18.2
February 1945	October 1945	8	37	88	45	11.0
November 1948	October 1949	11	45	48	56	1.5
July 1953	May 1954	10	39	55	49	3.2
August 1957	April 1958	8	24	47	32	3.3
April 1960	February 1961	10	106	34	116	1.2
December 1969	November 1970	11	36	117	47	1.0
November 1973	March 1975	16	58	52	74	4.9
January 1980	July 1980	6	12	64	18	2.5
July 1981	November 1982	16	92	28	108	3.0
July 1990	March 1991	8	120	100	128	1.4
March 2001						

Sources: National Bureau of Economic Research, Bureau of Economic Analysis, and the author's calculations.

In an expansion, investment proceeds at a rapid rate and the capital stock grows quickly. But rapid capital growth means that the amount of capital per hour of labor is growing. Equipped with more capital, labor becomes more productive. But the *law of diminishing returns* begins to operate. The law of diminishing returns states that as the quantity of capital increases, with the quantity of labor remaining the same, the gain in productivity from the additional units of capital eventually diminishes. Diminishing returns to capital bring a fall in the profit rate, and with a lower profit rate, the incentive to invest weakens. As a result, investment eventually falls. When it falls by a large amount, recession begins.

In a recession, investment is low and the capital stock grows slowly. In a deep recession, the capital stock might actually fall. Slow capital growth (or even a falling capital stock) means that the amount of capital per hour of labor is falling. With a low amount of capital per hour of labor, businesses begin to see opportunities for profitable investment and the pace of investment eventually picks up. As it does so, recession turns into expansion.

The *AS-AD* Model

Investment and capital are a crucial part of the business cycle mechanism, but they are just one part. To study the broader business cycle mechanism, we need a broader framework. That framework is the *AS-AD* model of Chapter 21. All the theories of the business cycle can be described in terms of the *AS-AD* model. Theories differ both in what they identify as the impulse and in the cycle mechanism. But all theories can be thought of as making assumptions about the factors that make either aggregate supply or aggregate demand fluctuate and assumptions about how they interact with each other to create a business cycle. Business cycle impulses can affect either the supply side or the demand side of the economy or both. But there are no pure supply-side theories. We will classify all theories of the business cycle as either

- Aggregate demand theories
- Real business cycle theory

We'll study the aggregate demand theories first. Then we'll study real business cycle theory, which is a more recent approach that isolates a shock that has both aggregate supply and aggregate demand effects.

Aggregate Demand Theories of the Business Cycle

THREE TYPES OF AGGREGATE DEMAND THEORY OF the business cycle have been proposed:

- Keynesian theory
- Monetarist theory
- Rational expectations theories

Keynesian Theory

The **Keynesian theory of the business cycle** regards volatile expectations as the main source of economic fluctuations. This theory is distilled from Keynes's *General Theory of Employment, Interest, and Money*. We'll explore the Keynesian theory by looking at its main impulse and the mechanism that converts that impulse into a real GDP cycle.

Keynesian Impulse The *impulse* in the Keynesian theory of the business cycle is *expected future sales and profits*. A change in expected future sales and profits changes the demand for new capital and changes the level of investment.

Keynes had a sophisticated theory about *how* expected sales and profits are determined. He reasoned that these expectations would be volatile because most of the events that shape the future are unknown and impossible to forecast. So, he reasoned, news or even rumors about future tax rate changes, interest rate changes, advances in technology, global economic and political events, or any other of the thousands of relevant factors that influence sales and profits change expectations in ways that can't be quantified but that have large effects.

To emphasize the volatility and diversity of sources of changes in expected sales and profits, Keynes described these expectations as *animal spirits*. In using this term, Keynes was not saying that expectations are irrational. Rather, he meant that because future sales and profits are impossible to forecast, it might be rational to take a view about them based on rumors, guesses, intuition, and instinct. Further, it might be rational to *change* one's view of the future, perhaps radically, in light of scraps of new information.

Keynesian Cycle Mechanism In the Keynesian theory, once a change in animal spirits has changed investment, a cycle mechanism begins to operate that has two key elements. First, the initial change in investment has a multiplier effect. The change in investment changes *aggregate* expenditure, real GDP, and disposable income. The change in disposable income changes consumption expenditure, and aggregate demand changes by a multiple of the initial change in investment. (This mechanism is described in detail in Chapter 25, pp. 586–590.) The aggregate demand curve shifts rightward in an expansion and leftward in a recession.

The second element of the Keynesian cycle mechanism is the response of real GDP to a change in aggregate demand. The short-run aggregate supply curve is horizontal (or nearly so). With a horizontal *SAS* curve, swings in aggregate demand translate into swings in real GDP with no changes in the price level. But the short-run aggregate supply curve depends on the money wage rate. If the money wage rate is fixed (sticky), the *SAS* curve does not move. And if the money wage rate changes, the *SAS* curve shifts. In the Keynesian theory, the response of the money wage rate to changes in aggregate demand are *asymmetric*.

On the downside, when aggregate demand decreases and unemployment rises, the money wage rate does not change. It is completely rigid in the downward direction. With a decrease in aggregate demand and no change in the money wage rate, the economy gets stuck in a below full-employment equilibrium. There are no natural forces operating to restore full employment. The economy remains in that situation until animal spirits are lifted and investment increases again.

On the upside, when aggregate demand increases and unemployment falls below its natural rate, the money wage rate rises quickly. It is flexible in the upward direction. At above full employment, the horizontal *SAS* curve plays no role and only the vertical *LAS* curve is relevant. With an increase in aggregate demand and an accompanying rise in the money wage rate, the price level rises quickly to eliminate the shortages and bring the economy back to full employment. The economy remains in that situation until animal spirits fall and investment and aggregate demand decrease.

Figures 30.1 and 30.2 illustrate the Keynesian theory of the business cycle by using the aggregate

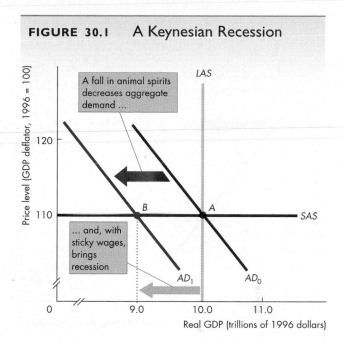

FIGURE 30.1   A Keynesian Recession

The economy is operating at point *A* at the intersection of the long-run aggregate supply curve, *LAS*; the short-run aggregate supply curve, *SAS*; and the aggregate demand curve, AD_0. A Keynesian recession begins when a fall in animal spirits causes investment demand to decrease. Aggregate demand decreases, and the *AD* curve shifts leftward to AD_1. With a sticky money wage rate, real GDP decreases to $9 trillion and the price level does not change. The economy moves to point *B*.

supply–aggregate demand model. In Fig. 30.1, the economy is initially at full employment (point *A*) on the long-run aggregate supply curve, *LAS*; the aggregate demand curve, AD_0; and the short-run aggregate supply curve, *SAS*. A fall in animal spirits decreases investment, and a multiplier process decreases aggregate demand. The aggregate demand curve shifts leftward to AD_1. With a fixed money wage rate, real GDP falls to $9 trillion and the economy moves to point *B*. Unemployment has increased, and there is a surplus of labor, but the money wage rate does not fall, and the economy remains at point *B* until some force moves it away.

That force is shown in Fig. 30.2. Here, starting out at point *B*, a rise in animal spirits increases investment. The multiplier process kicks in, and aggregate demand increases. The *AD* curve shifts to AD_2, and real GDP begins to increase. An expansion

FIGURE 30.2   A Keynesian Expansion

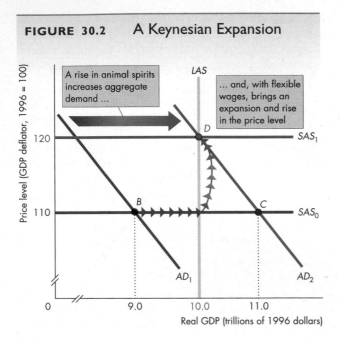

> A rise in animal spirits increases aggregate demand ...

> ... and, with flexible wages, brings an expansion and rise in the price level

Starting at point B, a Keynesian expansion begins when a rise in animal spirits causes investment demand to increase. Aggregate demand increases, and the AD curve shifts rightward to AD_2. If the money wage rate is sticky, real GDP increases to $10 trillion. But the economy does not go all the way to point C. When full employment is reached, the money wage rate rises and the SAS curve shifts upward toward SAS_1. The price level rises as the economy heads toward point D.

is underway. As long as real GDP remains below potential GDP ($10 trillion in this example), the money wage rate and the price level remain constant. But real GDP never increases to point C, the point of intersection of SAS_0 and AD_2. The reason is that once real GDP exceeds potential GDP and unemployment falls below its natural rate, the money wage rate begins to rise and the SAS curve starts to shift upward toward SAS_1. As the money wage rate rises, the price level also rises and real GDP growth slows. The economy follows a path like the one shown by the arrows connecting point B, the initial equilibrium, with point D, the final equilibrium.

The Keynesian business cycle is mainly like a tennis match. It is caused by outside forces — animal spirits — that change direction and set off a process that ends at an equilibrium that must be hit again by the outside forces to disturb it.

Monetarist Theory

The **monetarist theory of the business cycle** regards fluctuations in the quantity of money as the main source of economic fluctuations. This theory is distilled from the writings of Milton Friedman and several other economists. We'll explore the monetarist theory, as we did the Keynesian theory, by looking first at its main impulse and second at the mechanism that creates a cycle in real GDP.

Monetarist Impulse The *impulse* in the monetarist theory of the business cycle is the *growth rate of the quantity of money*. A speedup in money growth brings expansion, and a slowdown in money growth brings recession. The source of the change in the growth rate of the quantity of money is the monetary policy actions of the Fed.

Monetarist Cycle Mechanism In the monetarist theory, once the Fed has changed the money growth rate, a cycle mechanism begins to operate that, like the Keynesian mechanism, first affects aggregate demand. When the money growth rate increases, the quantity of real money in the economy increases and interest rates fall. The foreign exchange rate also falls — the dollar loses value on the foreign exchange market. These initial financial market effects begin to spill over into other markets. Investment and exports increase, and consumers spend more on durable goods. These initial changes in expenditure have a multiplier effect, just as investment has in the Keynesian theory. Through these mechanisms, a speedup in money growth shifts the aggregate demand curve rightward and brings an expansion. Similarly, a slowdown in money growth shifts the aggregate demand curve leftward and brings a recession.

The second element of the monetarist cycle mechanism is the response of aggregate supply to a change in aggregate demand. The short-run aggregate supply curve is upward-sloping. With an upward-sloping SAS curve, swings in aggregate demand translate into swings in both real GDP and the price level. But monetarists believe that real GDP deviations from full-employment are temporary in both directions.

In monetarist theory, the money wage rate is only *temporarily sticky*. When aggregate demand decreases and unemployment rises, the money wage rate eventually begins to fall. As the money wage rate falls, so does the price level, and after a period of adjustment, full employment is restored. When aggregate demand increases and unemployment falls below its natural rate, the money wage rate begins to rise. As the money wage rate rises, so does the price level, and through a period of adjustment, real GDP returns to potential GDP and the unemployment rate returns to the natural rate.

Figure 30.3 illustrates the monetarist theory. In part (a), the economy is initially at full employment (point A) on the long-run aggregate supply curve, LAS; the aggregate demand curve, AD_0; and the short-run aggregate supply curve, SAS_0. A slowdown in the money growth rate decreases aggregate demand, and the aggregate demand curve shifts leftward to AD_1.

Real GDP decreases to $9.5 trillion, and the economy goes into recession (point B). Unemployment increases, and there is a surplus of labor. The money wage rate begins to fall. As the money wage falls, the short-run aggregate supply curve starts to shift rightward toward SAS_1. The price level falls, and real GDP begins to expand as the economy moves to point C, its new full-employment equilibrium.

Figure 30.3(b) shows the effects of the opposite initial money shock — a speedup in money growth. Here, starting out at point C, a rise in the money growth rate increases aggregate demand and shifts the AD curve to AD_2. Both real GDP and the price level increase as the economy moves to point D, the point of intersection of SAS_1 and AD_2. With real GDP above

---

FIGURE 30.3   A Monetarist Business Cycle

(a) Recession

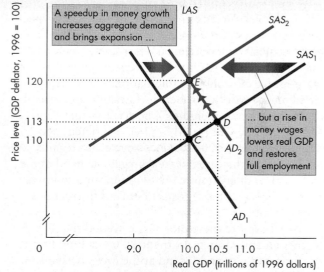

(b) Expansion

A monetarist recession begins when a slowdown in money growth decreases aggregate demand. The AD curve shifts leftward from AD_0 to AD_1 (in part a). With a sticky money wage rate, real GDP decreases to $9.5 trillion and the price level falls to 117 as the economy moves from point A to point B. With a surplus of labor, the money wage rate falls and the SAS curve shifts rightward to SAS_1. The price level falls further, and real GDP returns to potential GDP at point C.

Starting at point C (part b), a monetarist expansion begins when an increase in money growth increases aggregate demand and shifts the AD curve rightward to AD_2. With a sticky money wage rate, real GDP rises to $10.5 trillion, the price level rises to 113, and the economy moves to point D. With a shortage of labor, the money wage rate rises and the SAS curve shifts toward SAS_2. The price level rises, and real GDP decreases to potential GDP as the economy heads toward point E.

potential GDP and unemployment below its natural rate, the money wage rate begins to rise and the *SAS* curve starts to shift leftward toward SAS_2. As the money wage rate rises, the price level also rises and real GDP decreases. The economy moves from point *D* to point *E*, its new full-employment equilibrium.

The monetarist business cycle is like a rocking horse. It needs an outside force to get it going, but once going, it rocks back and forth (but just once). It doesn't matter in which direction the force initially hits. If it is a money growth slowdown, the economy cycles with a recession followed by expansion. If it is a money growth speedup, the economy cycles with an expansion followed by recession.

Rational Expectations Theories

A *rational expectation* is a forecast that is based on all the available relevant information (see Chapter 29, p. 685). Rational expectations theories of the business cycle are theories based on the view that the money wage rate is determined by a rational expectation of the price level. Two distinctly different rational expectations theories of the cycle have been proposed. A **new classical theory of the business cycle** regards *unanticipated* fluctuations in aggregate demand as the main source of economic fluctuations. This theory is based on the work of Robert E. Lucas, Jr. and several other economists, including Thomas J. Sargent and Robert J. Barro (see pp. 712–714). A different **new Keynesian theory of the business cycle** also regards *unanticipated* fluctuations in aggregate demand as the main source of economic fluctuations but also leaves room for *anticipated* aggregate demand fluctuations to play a role.

We'll explore these theories, as we did the Keynesian and monetarist theories, by looking first at the main impulse and second at the cycle mechanism.

Rational Expectations Impulse The *impulse* that distinguishes the rational expectations theories from the other aggregate demand theories of the business cycle is the *unanticipated change in aggregate demand.* A larger than anticipated increase in aggregate demand brings an expansion, and a smaller than anticipated increase in aggregate demand brings a recession. Any factor that influences aggregate demand — for example, fiscal policy, monetary policy, or developments in the world economy that influence exports — whose change is not anticipated can bring a change in real GDP.

Rational Expectations Cycle Mechanisms To describe the rational expectations cycle mechanisms, we'll deal first with the new classical version. When aggregate demand decreases, if the money wage rate doesn't change, real GDP and the price level both decrease. The fall in the price level increases the *real* wage rate, and employment decreases and unemployment rises. In the new classical theory, these events occur only if the decrease in aggregate demand is not anticipated. If the decrease in aggregate demand *is* anticipated, the price level is expected to fall and both firms and workers will agree to a lower money wage rate. By doing so, they can prevent the real wage rate from rising and avoid a rise in the unemployment rate.

Similarly, if firms and workers anticipate an increase in aggregate demand, they expect the price level to rise and will agree to a higher money wage rate. By doing so, they can prevent the real wage rate from falling and avoid a fall in the unemployment rate below the natural rate.

Only fluctuations in aggregate demand that are unanticipated and not taken into account in wage agreements bring changes in real GDP. *Anticipated* changes in aggregate demand change the price level, but they leave real GDP and unemployment unchanged and do not create a business cycle.

New Keynesian economists, like new classical economists, believe that the money wage rate is influenced by rational expectations of the price level. But new Keynesians emphasize the long-term nature of most wage contracts. They say that *today's* money wage rate is influenced by *yesterday's* rational expectations. These expectations, which were formed in the past, are based on old information that might now be known to be incorrect. After they have made a long-term wage agreement, both firms and workers might anticipate a change in aggregate demand, which they expect will change the price level. But because they are locked into their agreement, they are unable to change the money wage rate. So the money wage rate is sticky in the new Keynesian theory, and with sticky money wages, even an *anticipated* change in aggregate demand changes real GDP.

New classical economists believe that long-term contracts are renegotiated when conditions change to make them outdated. So they do not regard long-term contracts as an obstacle to money wage flexibility, provided that both parties to an agreement recognize the changed conditions. If both firms and workers expect the price level to change, they will change the agreed money wage rate to reflect that shared expectation. In this situation, anticipated changes in aggregate demand change the money wage rate and the price level and leave real GDP unchanged.

The distinctive feature of both versions of the rational expectations theory of the business cycle is the role of unanticipated changes in aggregate demand. Figure 30.4 illustrates its effect on real GDP and the price level.

Potential GDP is $10 trillion, and the long-run aggregate supply curve is LAS. Aggregate demand is expected to be EAD. Given potential GDP and EAD, the money wage rate is set at the level that is expected to bring full employment. At this money wage rate, the short-run aggregate supply curve is SAS. Imagine

that initially aggregate demand equals expected aggregate demand, so there is full employment, and the economy is at point A. Real GDP is $10 trillion, and the price level is 110. Then, unexpectedly, aggregate demand turns out to be less than expected, and the aggregate demand curve shifts leftward to AD_0 (in Fig. 30.4a). Many different aggregate demand shocks, such as a slowdown in the money growth rate or a collapse of exports, could have caused this shift. A recession begins. Real GDP decreases to $9.5 trillion, and the price level falls to 107. The economy moves to point B. Unemployment increases, and there is a surplus of labor. But aggregate demand is expected to be at EAD, so the money wage rate doesn't change and the short-run aggregate supply curve remains at SAS.

FIGURE 30.4   A Rational Expectations Business Cycle

(a) Recession

(b) Expansion

The economy is expected to be at point A at the intersection of the long-run aggregate supply curve, LAS; the short-run aggregate supply curve, SAS; and the *expected* aggregate demand curve, EAD. A rational expectations recession begins when an unanticipated fall in aggregate demand shifts the AD curve leftward to AD_0. With money wage rates based on the expectation that aggregate demand will be EAD, real GDP falls to $9.5 trillion and the price level falls to 107 as the economy moves to point B. As long as aggregate demand is *expected* to

be EAD, there is no change in the money wage rate.

A rational expectations expansion begins when an unanticipated rise in aggregate demand shifts the AD curve rightward from AD_0 to AD_1. With money wage rates based on the expectation that aggregate demand will be EAD, real GDP increases to $10.5 trillion and the price level rises to 113 as the economy moves to point C. Again, as long as aggregate demand is *expected* to be EAD, there is no change in the money wage rate.

The recession ends when aggregate demand increases again to its expected level. And a larger shock that takes aggregate demand to a level that exceeds *EAD* brings an expansion. In Fig. 30.4(b), the aggregate demand curve shifts rightward to AD_1. Such an increase in aggregate demand might be caused by a speedup in the money growth rate or an export boom. Real GDP now increases to $10.5 trillion, and the price level rises to 113. The economy moves to point *C*. Unemployment is now below the natural rate. But aggregate demand is expected to be at *EAD*, so the money wage rate doesn't change and the short-run aggregate supply curve remains at *SAS*.

Fluctuations in aggregate demand between AD_0 and AD_1 around expected aggregate demand *EAD* bring fluctuations in real GDP and the price level between points *B* and *C*.

The two versions of the rational expectations theory differ in their predictions about the effects of a change in expected aggregate demand. The new classical theory predicts that as soon as expected aggregate demand changes, the money wage rate also changes, so the *SAS* curve shifts. The new Keynesian theory predicts that the money wage rate changes only gradually when new contracts are made, so the *SAS* curve moves only slowly. This difference between the two theories is crucial for policy. According to the new classical theory, anticipated policy actions change the price level only and have no effect on real GDP and unemployment. The reason is that when policy is expected to change, the money wage rate changes, so the *SAS* curve shifts and offsets the effects of the policy action on real GDP. In contrast, in the new Keynesian theory, because the money wage rate changes only when new contracts are made, even anticipated policy actions change real GDP and can be used in an attempt to stabilize the cycle.

Like the monetarist business cycle, these rational expectations cycles are similar to rocking horses. They need an outside force to get them going, but once they are going, the economy rocks around its full employment point. The new classical horse rocks faster and comes to rest more quickly than the new Keynesian horse.

AS-AD General Theory

All the theories of the business cycle that we've considered can be viewed as particular cases of the more general *AS-AD* theory. In this more general theory,

the impulses of both the Keynesian and monetarist theories can change aggregate demand. A multiplier effect makes aggregate demand change by more than any initial change in one of its components. The money wage rate can be viewed as responding to changes in the expected price level. Even if the money wage is flexible, it will change only to the extent to which price level expectations change. As a result, the money wage rate will adjust gradually.

Although in all three types of business cycle theory that we've considered, the cycle is caused by fluctuations in aggregate demand, the possibility that an occasional aggregate supply shock might occur is not ruled out. A recession could occur because aggregate supply falls. For example, a widespread drought that cuts agricultural production could cause a recession in an economy that has a large agricultural sector. But the aggregate demand theories of the cycle regard aggregate supply shocks as rare rather than normal events. Aggregate demand fluctuations are the normal ongoing sources of fluctuations.

REVIEW QUIZ

1 What, according to Keynesian theory, causes the business cycle? What are the roles of *animal spirits*, the multiplier, and the sticky money wage rate in this theory?

2 What, according to monetarist theory, causes the business cycle? What are the roles of the Fed and money growth in this theory?

3 What, according to new classical theory and new Keynesian theory, causes the business cycle? What are the roles of rational expectations and unanticipated fluctuations in aggregate demand in these theories?

4 What are the differences between the new classical theory and the new Keynesian theory concerning the money wage rate over the business cycle?

A new theory of the business cycle challenges the mainstream and traditional aggregate demand theories that you've just studied. It is called the real business cycle theory. Let's look at this new theory of the business cycle.

Real Business Cycle Theory

THE NEWEST THEORY OF THE BUSINESS CYCLE, known as **real business cycle theory** (or RBC theory), regards random fluctuations in productivity as the main source of economic fluctuations. These productivity fluctuations are assumed to result mainly from fluctuations in the pace of technological change, but they might also have other sources, such as international disturbances, climate fluctuations, or natural disasters. The origins of real business cycle theory can be traced to the rational expectations revolution set off by Robert E. Lucas, Jr., but the first demonstrations of the power of this theory were given by Edward Prescott and Finn Kydland and by John Long and Charles Plosser. Today, real business cycle theory is part of a broad research agenda called *dynamic general equilibrium analysis*, and hundreds of young macroeconomists do research on this topic.

Like our study of the aggregate demand theories, we'll explore RBC theory by looking first at its impulse and then at the mechanism that converts that impulse into a cycle in real GDP.

The RBC Impulse

The *impulse* in RBC theory is the *growth rate of productivity that results from technological change.* RBC theorists believe this impulse to be generated mainly by the process of research and development that leads to the creation and use of new technologies.

Most of the time, technological change is steady and productivity grows at a moderate pace. But sometimes productivity growth speeds up, and occasionally productivity *decreases* — labor becomes less productive, on the average.

A period of rapid productivity growth brings a strong business cycle expansion, and a *decrease* in productivity triggers a recession.

It is easy to understand why technological change brings productivity growth. But how does it *decrease* productivity? All technological change eventually increases productivity. But if initially, technological change makes a sufficient amount of existing capital, especially human capital, obsolete, productivity

---

FIGURE 30.5   The Real Business Cycle Impulse

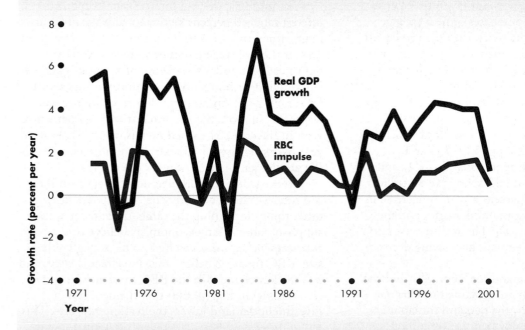

The real business cycle is caused by changes in technology that bring fluctuations in the growth rate of productivity. The fluctuations in productivity growth shown here are calculated by using growth accounting (the one third rule) to remove the contribution of capital accumulation to productivity growth. Productivity fluctuations are correlated with real GDP fluctuations. Economists are not sure what the productivity variable actually measures or what causes it to fluctuate.

Source: Bureau of Economic Analysis and the author's calculations.

temporarily decreases. At such a time, more jobs are destroyed than created and more businesses fail than start up.

To isolate the RBC theory impulse, economists use growth accounting, which is explained in Chapter 24, pp. 553–556. Figure 30.5 shows the RBC impulse for the United States from 1971 through 2001. You can see that fluctuations in productivity growth are correlated with real GDP fluctuations. But this RBC impulse variable is a catch-all, and no one knows what it actually measures or what causes it to fluctuate.

The RBC Mechanism

According to RBC theory, two immediate effects follow from a change in productivity that gets an expansion or a contraction going:

1. Investment demand changes.
2. The demand for labor changes.

We'll study these effects and their consequences during a recession. In an expansion, they work in the direction opposite to what is described here.

Technological change makes some existing capital obsolete and temporarily decreases productivity. Firms expect the future profits to fall and see their labor productivity falling. With lower profit expectations, they cut back their purchases of new capital, and with lower labor productivity, they plan to lay off some workers. So the initial effect of a temporary fall in productivity is a decrease in investment demand and a decrease in the demand for labor.

Figure 30.6 illustrates these two initial effects of a decrease in productivity. Part (a) shows investment demand, ID, and saving supply, SS (both of which are explained in Chapter 23, pp. 529–531 and 532–534). Initially, investment demand is ID_0, and the equilibrium investment and saving are $2 trillion at a real interest rate of 6 percent a year. A decrease in productivity decreases investment demand, and the ID curve shifts leftward to ID_1. The real interest rate falls to 4 percent, and investment and saving decrease to $1.7 trillion.

Part (b) shows the demand for labor, LD, and the supply of labor, LS (which are explained in Chapter 22, pp. 507–511). Initially, the demand for labor is LD_0, and equilibrium employment is 200 billion hours a year at a real wage rate of $35 an hour. The decrease in productivity decreases the demand for labor, and the LD curve shifts leftward to LD_1.

Before we can determine the new level of employment and real wage rate, we need to take a ripple effect into account — the key ripple effect in RBC theory.

The Key Decision: When to Work? According to RBC theory, people decide *when* to work by doing a cost-benefit calculation. They compare the return from working in the current period with the *expected* return from working in a later period. You make such a comparison every day in school. Suppose your goal in this course is to get an A. To achieve this goal, you work pretty hard most of the time. But during the few days before the midterm and final exams, you work especially hard. Why? Because you believe that the return from studying close to the exam is greater than the return from studying when the exam is a long time away. So during the term, you take time off for the movies and other leisure pursuits, but at exam time, you work every evening and weekend.

Real business cycle theory says that workers behave like you. They work fewer hours, sometimes zero hours, when the real wage rate is temporarily low, and they work more hours when the real wage rate is temporarily high. But to properly compare the current wage rate with the expected future wage rate, workers must use the real interest rate. If the real interest rate is 6 percent a year, a real wage of $1 an hour earned this week will become $1.06 a year from now. If the real wage rate is expected to be $1.05 an hour next year, today's real wage of $1 looks good. By working longer hours now and shorter hours a year from now, a person can get a 1 percent higher real wage. But suppose the real interest rate is 4 percent a year. In this case, $1 earned now is worth $1.04 next year. Working fewer hours now and more next year is the way to get a 1 percent higher real wage.

So the when-to-work decision depends on the real interest rate. The lower the real interest rate, other things remaining the same, the smaller is the supply of labor. Many economists believe this *intertemporal substitution* effect to be of negligible size. RBC theorists believe that the effect is large, and it is the key element in the RBC mechanism.

You saw in Fig. 30.6(a) that the decrease in investment demand lowers the real interest rate. This fall in the real interest rate lowers the return to current work and decreases the supply of labor. In Fig. 30.6(b), the labor supply curve shifts leftward to LS_1. The effect of a productivity shock on the demand for

FIGURE 30.6   Capital and Labor Markets in a Real Business Cycle

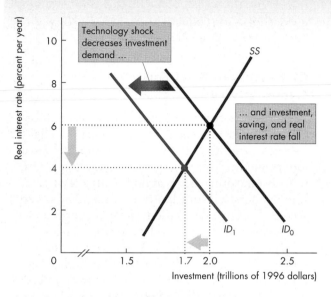

(a) Investment, saving, and interest rate

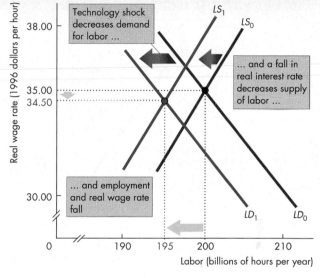

(b) Labor and wage rate

Saving supply is SS (part a), and initially, investment demand is ID_0. The real interest rate is 6 percent a year, and saving and investment are $2 trillion. In the labor market (part b), the demand for labor is LD_0 and the supply of labor is LS_0. The real wage rate is $35 an hour, and employment is 200 billion hours. A technological change temporarily decreases productivity, and both investment demand and the demand for

labor decrease. The two demand curves shift leftward to ID_1 and LD_1. In part (a), the real interest rate falls to 4 percent a year and investment and saving decrease. In part (b), the fall in the real interest rate decreases the supply of labor (the when-to-work decision) and the supply curve shifts leftward to LS_1. Employment decreases to 195 billion hours, and the real wage rate falls to $34.50 an hour. A recession is underway.

labor is larger than the effect of the fall in the real interest rate on the supply of labor. That is, the LD curve shifts farther leftward than does the LS curve. As a result, the real wage rate falls to $34.50 an hour and the level of employment decreases to 195 billion hours. A recession has begun and is intensifying.

Real GDP and the Price Level The next part of the RBC story traces the consequences of the changes you've just seen for real GDP and the price level. With a decrease in employment, aggregate supply decreases, and with a decrease in investment, aggregate demand decreases. Figure 30.7 illustrates these effects, using the AS-AD model. Initially, the long-run aggregate supply curve is LAS_0, and the aggregate demand curve is AD_0. The price level is 110, and real GDP is $10 trillion. There is no short-run aggregate supply curve in this figure because in RBC theory, the SAS curve has no meaning. The labor market

moves relentlessly toward its equilibrium, and the money wage rate adjusts freely (either upward or downward) to ensure that the real wage rate keeps the quantity of labor demanded equal to the quantity supplied. In RBC theory, unemployment is always at the natural rate, and the natural rate fluctuates over the business cycle because the amount of job search fluctuates.

The decrease in employment decreases total production, and aggregate supply decreases. The LAS curve shifts leftward to LAS_1. The decrease in investment decreases aggregate demand, and the AD curve shifts leftward to AD_1. The price level falls to 107, and real GDP decreases to $9.8 trillion. The economy has gone through a recession.

What Happened to Money? The name *real* business cycle theory is no accident. It reflects the central prediction of the theory. Real things, not nominal or monetary things, cause the business cycle. If the

FIGURE 30.7   *AS-AD* in a Real Business Cycle

Initially, the long-run aggregate supply curve is LAS_0, and the aggregate demand curve is AD_0. Real GDP is $10 trillion (which equals potential GDP), and the price level is 110. There is no *SAS* curve in RBC theory because the money wage rate is flexible. The technological change described in Fig. 30.6 temporarily decreases potential GDP, and the *LAS* curve shifts leftward to LAS_1. The fall in investment demand decreases aggregate demand, and the *AD* curve shifts leftward to AD_1. Real GDP falls to $9.8 trillion, and the price level falls to 107. The economy has gone into recession.

quantity of money changes, aggregate demand changes. But if there is no real change — with no change in the use of resources and no change in potential GDP — the change in the quantity of money changes only the price level. In real business cycle theory, this outcome occurs because the aggregate supply curve is the *LAS* curve, which pins real GDP down at potential GDP, so when *AD* changes, only the price level changes.

Cycles and Growth   The shock that drives the business cycle of RBC theory is the same as the force that generates economic growth: technological change. On the average, as technology advances, productivity grows. But it grows at an uneven pace. You saw this fact when you studied growth accounting in Chapter 24, pp. 553–556. There, we focused on slow-changing trends in productivity growth. Real business cycle theory uses the same idea but says that there are frequent shocks to productivity that are mostly positive but that are occasionally negative.

Criticisms of Real Business Cycle Theory

RBC theory is controversial, and when economists discuss it, they often generate more heat than light. Its detractors claim that its basic assumptions are just too incredible. Money wages *are* sticky, they claim, so to assume otherwise is at odds with a clear fact. Intertemporal substitution is too weak, they say, to account for large fluctuations in labor supply and employment with small real wage rate changes.

But what really kills the RBC story, say most economists, is an implausible impulse. Technology shocks are not capable of creating the swings in productivity that growth accounting reveals. These swings in productivity are caused by something, they concede, but they are as likely to be caused by *changes in aggregate demand* as by technology. If the fluctuations in productivity are caused by aggregate demand fluctuations, then the traditional aggregate demand theories are needed to explain them. Fluctuations in productivity do not cause the cycle but are caused by it!

Building on this theme, the critics point out that the so-called productivity fluctuations that growth accounting measures are correlated with changes in the growth rate of money and other indicators of changes in aggregate demand.

Defense of Real Business Cycle Theory

The defenders of RBC theory claim that the theory works. It explains the macroeconomic facts about the business cycle and is consistent with the facts about economic growth. In effect, a single theory explains *both growth and cycles*. The growth accounting exercise that explains slowly changing trends also explains the more frequent business cycle swings. Its defenders also claim that RBC theory is consistent with a wide range of *micro*economic evidence about labor supply decisions, labor demand and investment demand decisions, and information on the distribution of income between labor and capital.

RBC theorists acknowledge that money and the business cycle are correlated. That is, rapid money growth and expansion go together, and slow money growth and recession go together. But, they argue, causation does not run from money to real GDP as the traditional aggregate demand theories state. Instead, they view causation as running from real GDP to money — so-called reverse causation. In a recession, the initial fall in investment demand that lowers the interest rate decreases the demand for bank loans and lowers the profitability of banking. So banks increase their reserves and decrease their loans. The quantity of bank deposits and hence the quantity of money decrease. This reverse causation is responsible for the correlation between money growth and real GDP, according to real business cycle theory.

Its defenders also argue that the RBC view is significant because it at least raises the possibility that the business cycle is efficient. The business cycle does not signal an economy that is misbehaving; it is business as usual. If this view is correct, it means that policy designed to smooth the cycle is misguided. Only by taking out the peaks can the troughs be smoothed out. But peaks are bursts of investment to take advantage of new technologies in a timely way. So smoothing the cycle means delaying the benefits of new technologies.

REVIEW QUIZ

1 What, according to real business cycle theory, causes the business cycle? What is the role of fluctuations in the rate of technological change?

2 How, according to real business cycle theory, does a fall in productivity growth influence investment demand, the real interest rate, the demand for labor, the supply of labor, employment, and the real wage rate?

3 How, according to real business cycle theory, does a fall in productivity growth influence long-run aggregate supply, aggregate demand, real GDP, and the price level?

You've now reviewed the main theories of the business cycle. Your next task is to examine some actual business cycles. We'll focus on two episodes: expansions and recessions during the 1990s and 2000s and the Great Depression of the 1930s.

Expansion and Recession During the 1990s and 2000s

IN THE THEORIES OF THE BUSINESS CYCLE THAT you've studied, recessions and expansions can be triggered by a variety of forces, some on the aggregate demand side and some on the aggregate supply side. We'll study the events and the processes at work during two recent episodes:

■ The U.S. expansion of the 1990s
■ The U.S. recession of 2001

The U.S. Expansion of the 1990s

From March 1991 through March 2001, the U.S. economy enjoyed 120 months of uninterrupted expansion, the longest period of sustained expansion in the nation's history and more than a year longer than the previous all-time record of the 1960s. Real GDP grew by 40 percent during this period. What caused this long and strong expansion?

Productivity Growth in the Information Age
The most significant feature of the 1990s was an explosion in the use of the computer. The growth of the Internet is the single most visible consequence of this explosion. But it is just one of many transformations of economic life that occurred during the 1990s.

The personal computer changed the way we write, keep financial and other records, and communicate with each other. The microprocessor that is at the heart of the PC has also, in other specialized forms, revolutionized the way we listen to music, drive a car, use a camera, get cash from the bank, make a microwave dinner, and check out at the supermarket. It has revolutionized even more the way firms produce goods and services.

All this technological change created profit opportunities but required a large amount of investment to realize those profits. Also, most of the world shared in this technological revolution. And its global nature brought a large increase in U.S. exports.

The increase in investment and exports, with their multiplier effects on consumption expenditure, brought a large and persistent increase in aggregate demand.

The hot pace of technological change brought a correspondingly large increase in aggregate supply by increasing capital and increasing productivity.

Fiscal Policy and Monetary Policy The expansion of the 1990s was to some degree made possible by the fiscal policy and monetary policy that accompanied it. The expansion was not caused by these policies, but they encouraged sustained real GDP growth.

Aggregate Demand and Aggregate Supply During the Expansion Figure 30.8 shows the 1990s expansion using the *AS-AD* model. In 1991, the economy was on aggregate demand curve AD_{91} and short-run aggregate supply curve SAS_{91} with real GDP at \$6.6 trillion and the GDP deflator at 79. The long-run aggregate supply curve was LAS_{91}, and potential GDP exceeded real GDP. There was a recessionary gap. By 2001, capital accumulation, increased labor hours, and technological change had increased potential GDP to \$9.3 trillion and the long-run aggregate supply curve had shifted to LAS_{01}. The large increase in investment demand and exports with their multiplier effects increased aggregate demand, and the aggregate demand curve shifted to AD_{01}.

The increase in potential GDP increased short-run aggregate supply, but a higher money wage rate decreased short-run aggregate supply. The net effect of these effects was a small decrease in short-run aggregate supply to SAS_{01}. Real GDP increased to \$9.3 trillion — equal to potential GDP — and the price level increased to 109.

A Real Business Cycle Expansion Phase The description of the expansion of the 1990s that we've just reviewed looks exactly like the events that real business cycle theory predicts. A strong and sustained burst of technological change brought rising productivity. The result was an increase in investment demand, an increase in the demand for labor, and an increase in the supply of labor. The real interest rate increased, and the real wage rate increased but only slightly.

The increases in the demand for labor and supply of labor brought a falling unemployment rate. The lower unemployment rate is a lower *natural* rate and not a sign that the economy is overheating.

The U.S. Recession of 2001

The 2001 recession was the mildest recession on record. It turned out to be so mild through 2001 that it barely qualified as a recession. If the NBER dating

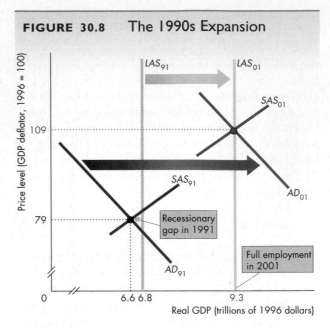

FIGURE 30.8 The 1990s Expansion

In 1991, the economy was on its aggregate demand curve, AD_{91}, and its short-run aggregate supply curve, SAS_{91}, with real GDP at \$6.6 trillion and a GDP deflator of 79. Potential GDP exceeded real GDP and there was a recessionary gap. Technological advances increased both aggregate demand and aggregate supply. The aggregate demand curve shifted to AD_{01}, and the long-run aggregate supply curve shifted to LAS_{01}. But a higher money wage rate shifted the short-run aggregate supply curve to SAS_{01}. The result of these shifts was an increase in real GDP to \$9.3 trillion (equal to potential GDP) and an increase in the price level to 109.

committee ever felt tempted to cancel a recession, this one was a prime candidate!

Absence of External Shocks The recession did not originate from any clearly visible external shocks. The huge shock of the September 11 attacks, while they strongly influenced the economy in the final part of 2001, could not have been at work at the onset of the recession.

Fiscal Policy There were no major fiscal policy shocks to trigger the recession. On the contrary, six months after the recession began, government purchases increased to strengthen defense and security in the wake of September 11. Tax revenues decreased and the deficit increased as the normal automatic stabilizers began to operate (see Chapter 26, p. 614).

Monetary Policy There were no major monetary policy shocks to trigger the recession, although the Fed had raised interest rates very slightly and held the M2 money growth rate steady during 2000.

Real Business Cycle Effects The real business cycle impulse (see Fig. 30.5, p. 715) pointed downward strongly during 2001. The growth rate of productivity arising from technological change and other factors slowed from 1.7 percent in 2000 to 0.5 percent in 2001. This slowdown would have been enough to slow real GDP growth rate but not to bring the economy to a full-blown recession.

The exact technological events that brought a slowing of the pace of productivity growth are hard to identify with certainty. But it seems likely that much of the slowdown came in the overgrown "dot-com" sector. Judging by the movements in stock prices, it was the high-tech sector generally that was hit hardest during the slowdown.

Whatever the exact source of the productivity growth slowdown, it hit investment hard. Business investment fell, and this was the major source of the decrease in aggregate demand. No other component of aggregate demand fell.

Labor Market and Productivity Although real GDP barely fell, employment and aggregate hours did fall and the unemployment rate increased. Labor productivity increased, and so did the real wage rate.

The tendency for labor productivity and the real wage rate to rise during a recession is not unusual. But the strength of these effects during the 2001 recession were unusual.

The money wage rate rose by 4 percent during 2001, and the real wage rate rose by 3.4 percent. The slowdown in productivity growth and the strong rise in the money wage rate decreased short-run aggregate supply during 2001.

Aggregate Demand and Aggregate Supply Figure 30.9 illustrates the 2001 recession in terms of the shifting aggregate demand and aggregate supply curves. In the first quarter of 2001, the economy was on aggregate demand curve AD_{Q1} and short-run aggregate supply curve SAS_{Q1} with real GDP at $9.34 trillion and the GDP deflator at 109.2. In the second quarter of 2001, the short-run aggregate supply curve had shifted to SAS_{Q2} and the aggregate demand curve had shifted to AD_{Q2}. Real GDP had decreased

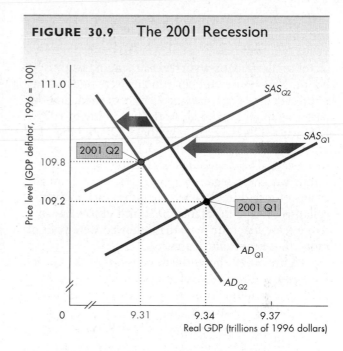

FIGURE 30.9   The 2001 Recession

In the first quarter of 2001, the economy was on its aggregate demand curve, AD_{Q1}, and its short-run aggregate supply curve, SAS_{Q1}, with real GDP at $9.34 trillion and a GDP deflator of 109.2. A rise in the money wage rate decreased aggregate supply and shifted the SAS curve to SAS_{Q2}. A fall in investment decreased aggregate demand and shifted the AD curve to AD_{Q2}. The combination of a decrease in both aggregate supply and aggregate demand put the economy into a mild recession.

to $9.31 trillion. The GDP deflator had increased to 109.8.

REVIEW QUIZ

1 What factors brought the long and strong expansion in the United States during the 1990s?
2 What factors contributed to the recession of 2001?

You've now seen how business cycle theory can be used to interpret the expansion of the 1990s and the recession of 2001. But can we use business cycle theory to explain the greatest of recessions — the Great Depression? Let's find out.

The Great Depression

THE LATE 1920S WERE YEARS OF ECONOMIC boom. New houses and apartments were built on an unprecedented scale, new firms were created, and the nation's capital expanded. At the beginning of 1929, U.S. real GDP exceeded potential GDP and the unemployment rate was a low 3.2 percent. But as that eventful year unfolded, increasing signs of economic weakness began to appear. The most dramatic events occurred in October when the stock market collapsed, losing more than one third of its value in two weeks. The four years that followed were years of monstrous economic depression.

Figure 30.10 shows the dimensions of the Great Depression. On the eve of the Great Depression in 1929, the economy was on aggregate demand curve AD_{29} and short-run aggregate supply curve SAS_{29}. Real GDP was $822 billion (1996 dollars), and the GDP deflator was 12.6.

In 1930, there was a widespread expectation that the price level would fall, and the money wage rate fell. With a lower money wage rate, the short-run aggregate supply curve shifted from SAS_{29} to SAS_{30}. But increased pessimism and uncertainty decreased investment and the demand for consumer durables, and aggregate demand decreased to AD_{30}. In 1930, real GDP decreased to $752 billion (a 9 percent decrease) and the GDP deflator fell to 12.2 (a 3 percent fall).

In a normal recession, the economy might have remained below full employment for a year or so and then started to expand. But the recession of 1930 was not a normal one. In 1930 and the next two years, the economy was further bombarded with huge negative demand shocks (the sources of which we'll look at in a moment). The aggregate demand curve shifted leftward all the way to AD_{33}. With a depressed economy, the price level was expected to fall, and wages fell in line with those expectations. The money wage fell from 55¢ an hour in 1930 to 44¢ an hour by 1933. As a result of lower wages, the aggregate supply curve shifted from SAS_{30} to SAS_{33}. But the size of the shift of the short-run aggregate supply curve was much less than the decrease in aggregate demand. As a result, the aggregate demand curve and the short-run aggregate supply curve intersected in 1933 at a real GDP of $603 billion (a decrease of 29 percent from 1929) and a GDP deflator of 9.4 (a decrease of 24 percent from 1929).

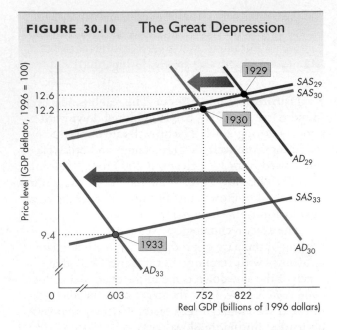

FIGURE 30.10   The Great Depression

In 1929, real GDP was $822 billion and the GDP deflator was 12.6 — at the intersection of AD_{29} and SAS_{29}. Increased pessimism and uncertainty resulted in a decrease in investment, and aggregate demand decreased to AD_{30}. Capital increased and wages decreased, so the short-run aggregate supply curve shifted to SAS_{30}. Real GDP and the price level fell. In the next three years, decreases in the quantity of money and investment decreased aggregate demand, shifting the aggregate demand curve to AD_{33}. Again, to some degree, the decrease in aggregate demand was anticipated, so the money wage rate fell and the short-run aggregate supply curve shifted to SAS_{33}. By 1933, real GDP had fallen to $603 billion (71 percent of its 1929 level) and the GDP deflator had fallen to 9.4 (76 percent of its 1929 level).

Although the Great Depression brought enormous hardship, the distribution of that hardship was uneven. Twenty-five percent of the work force had no jobs at all. Also at that time, there were virtually no organized social security and unemployment programs in place. So for many families, there was virtually no income. But the pocketbooks of those who kept their jobs barely noticed the Great Depression. It is true that wages fell from 57¢ an hour in 1929 to 44¢ an hour in 1933. But at the same time, the price level fell by a larger percentage, so real wages actually increased. Thus people who had jobs became better off during the Great Depression.

You can begin to appreciate the magnitude of the Great Depression if you compare it with the two recessions that we studied earlier in this chapter. Between mid-1990 and mid-1991, real GDP fell by 1.6 percent. During 2001, real GDP barely fell at all. A hypothetical 2003 Great Depression would lower real GDP by 30 percent, to its 1992 level.

Why the Great Depression Happened

The late 1920s were years of economic boom, but they were also years of increasing uncertainty. The main source of increased uncertainty was international. The world economy was going through tumultuous times. The patterns of world trade were changing as Britain, the traditional economic power-house of the world, began its period of relative economic decline and new economic powers such as Japan began to emerge. International currency fluctuations and the introduction of restrictive trade policies (see Chapter 32) by many countries further increased the uncertainty faced by firms. There was also domestic uncertainty arising from the fact that there had been such a strong boom in recent years, especially in the capital goods sector and housing. No one believed that this boom would last forever, but many people thought it had a lot farther to run, and there was great uncertainty about how demand would change.

This environment of uncertainty led to a slow-down in consumer spending, especially on new homes and household appliances. By the fall of 1929, the uncertainty had reached a critical level and contributed to the stock market crash. The stock market crash, in turn, heightened people's fears about economic prospects in the foreseeable future. Fear fed fear. Investment collapsed. The building industry almost disappeared. An industry that had been operating flat out just two years earlier was now building virtually no new houses and apartments. It was this drop in investment and a drop in consumer spending on durables that led to the initial leftward shift of the aggregate demand curve from AD_{29} to AD_{30} in Fig. 30.10.

At this stage, what became the Great Depression was no worse than many previous recessions had been. What distinguishes the Great Depression from previous recessions are the events that followed between 1930 and 1933. But economists, even to this day, have not come to agreement on how to interpret those events. One view, argued by Peter Temin,[1] is that spending continued to fall for a wide variety of reasons — including a continuation of increasing pessimism and uncertainty. According to Temin's view, the continued contraction resulted from a collapse of expenditure that was independent of the decrease in the quantity of money. The investment demand curve shifted leftward. Milton Friedman and Anna J. Schwartz have argued that the continuation of the contraction was almost exclusively the result of the subsequent worsening of financial and monetary conditions.[2] According to Friedman and Schwartz, it was a severe cut in the quantity of money that lowered aggregate demand, prolonging the contraction and deepening the depression.

Although there is disagreement about the causes of the contraction phase of the Great Depression, the disagreement is not about the elements at work but about the degree of importance attached to each. Everyone agrees that increased pessimism and uncertainty lowered investment demand, and everyone agrees that there was a massive contraction of the quantity of real money. Temin and his supporters assign primary importance to the fall in autonomous expenditure and secondary importance to the fall in the quantity of money. Friedman and Schwartz and their supporters assign primary responsibility to the quantity of money and regard the other factors as being of limited importance.

Let's look at the contraction of aggregate demand a bit more closely. Between 1930 and 1933, nominal money decreased by 20 percent. This decrease in the quantity of money was not directly induced by the Fed's actions. The *monetary base* (currency in circulation and bank reserves) hardly fell at all. But the bank deposits component of money suffered an enormous collapse. It did so primarily because a large number of banks failed. Before the Great Depression, fueled by increasing stock prices and booming business conditions, bank loans expanded. But after the stock market crash and the downturn, many borrowers found themselves in hard economic times. They

---

[1] Peter Temin, *Did Monetary Forces Cause the Great Depression?* (New York: W.W. Norton, 1976).
[2] Milton Friedman and Anna J. Schwartz developed this explanation in *A Monetary History of the United States: 1867–1960* (Princeton, N.J.: Princeton University Press, 1963), Chapter 22.

could not pay the interest on their loans, and they could not meet the agreed repayment schedules. Banks had deposits that exceeded the realistic value of the loans that they had made. When depositors withdrew funds from the banks, the banks lost reserves. Many of them simply couldn't meet their depositors' demands to be repaid.

Bank failures feed on themselves and create additional failures. Seeing banks fail, people become anxious to protect themselves and so take their money out of the banks. Such were the events of 1930. The quantity of notes and coins in circulation increased, and the volume of bank deposits declined. But the very action of taking money out of the bank to protect one's wealth accentuated the process of banking failure. Banks were increasingly short of cash and unable to meet their obligations.

What role did the stock market crash of 1929 play in producing the Great Depression? It certainly created an atmosphere of fear and panic and probably also contributed to the overall air of uncertainty that dampened investment spending. It also reduced the wealth of stockholders, encouraging them to cut back on their consumption spending. But the direct effect of the stock market crash on consumption, although a contributing factor to the Great Depression, was not the major source of the drop in aggregate demand. It was the collapse in investment arising from increased uncertainty that brought the 1930 decline in aggregate demand.

The stock market crash was a predictor of severe recession. It reflected the expectations of stockholders concerning future profit prospects. As those expectations became pessimistic, people sold their stocks. There were more sellers than buyers, and the prices of stocks were bid lower and lower. That is, the behavior the stock market was a consequence of expectations about future profitability, and those expectations were lowered as a result of increased uncertainty.

Can It Happen Again?

Because we have an incomplete understanding of the causes of the Great Depression, we cannot be sure whether such an event will happen again. The economic turmoil of the 1920s that preceded the Depression certainly can happen again. But there are some significant differences between the current economy and that of the 1930s that make a severe depression much less likely today than it was 60 years ago. The

most significant features of the economy that make severe depression less likely today are

- Bank deposit insurance
- The Fed's role as lender of last resort
- Taxes and government spending
- Multi-income families

Let's examine each of these in turn.

Bank Deposit Insurance As a result of the Great Depression, the federal government established, in the 1930s, the Federal Deposit Insurance Corporation (FDIC). The FDIC insures bank deposits for up to $100,000 per deposit, so most depositors need no longer fear bank failure. If a bank fails, the FDIC pays the deposit holders. With federally insured bank deposits, the key event that turned a fairly ordinary recession into the Great Depression is most unlikely to occur. It was the fear of bank failure that caused people to withdraw their deposits from banks. The aggregate consequence of these individually rational acts was to cause the very bank failures that were feared. With deposit insurance, most depositors have nothing to lose if a bank fails and so have no incentive to take actions that are likely to give rise to that failure.

Some recent events reinforce this conclusion. With massive failures of S&Ls in the 1980s and with bank failures in New England in 1990 and 1991, there was no tendency for depositors to panic and withdraw their funds in a self-reinforcing run on similar institutions.

Lender of Last Resort The Fed is the lender of last resort in the U.S. economy. If a single bank is short of reserves, it can borrow reserves from other banks. If the entire banking system is short of reserves, banks can borrow from the Fed. By making reserves available (at a suitable interest rate), the Fed is able to make the quantity of reserves in the banking system respond flexibly to the demand for those reserves. Bank failure can be prevented or at least contained to cases in which bad management practices are the source of the problem. Widespread failures of the type that occurred in the Great Depression can be prevented.

It is now generally agreed that the Fed made a serious mistake in its handling of monetary policy during the Great Depression. With one eye on the international situation, the Fed *increased* the discount rate sharply from 1.5 percent to 3.5 percent just when the banks needed to borrow more. It was only long after the event, when Friedman and Schwartz examined the contraction years of the Great Depression, that economists came to realize that the Fed would have had to *decrease* the discount rate and *increase* the monetary base to have prevented the intensification of the contraction. Now that this lesson has been learned and there is such widespread agreement about the matter, there is at least some chance that the mistake will not be repeated.

The last time the Fed was confronted by a similar problem, although on a much smaller scale, was in October 1987. At that time, a severe stock market crash triggered fears of a new Great Depression. The Fed Chairman, Alan Greenspan, told the U.S. banking and financial community that the Fed had both the ability and the intent to maintain calm financial conditions and to supply sufficient reserves to ensure that the banking system did not begin to contract.

Taxes and Government Spending The government sector was a much smaller part of the economy in 1929 than it is today. On the eve of that earlier recession, government purchases of goods and services were less than 9 percent of GDP. Today, government purchases exceed 20 percent of GDP. Government transfer payments were less than 6 percent of GDP in 1929. Today, they exceed 15 percent of GDP.

A larger level of government purchases of goods and services means that when recession hits, a large component of aggregate demand does not decline. But government transfer payments are the most sensitive economic stabilizer. When the economy goes into recession and depression, more people qualify for unemployment compensation and social security. As a consequence, although disposable income decreases, the extent of the decrease is moderated by the existence of such programs. Consumption expenditure, in turn, does not decline by as much as it would in the absence of such government programs. The limited decline in consumption spending further limits the overall decrease in aggregate expenditure, thereby limiting the magnitude of an economic downturn.

Multi-Income Families At the time of the Great Depression, families with more than one wage earner were much less common than they are today. The labor force participation rate in 1929 was around 55 percent. Today, it is 67 percent. So even if the unemployment rate increased to around 25 percent today, close to 50 percent of the adult population would actually have

jobs. During the Great Depression, less than 40 percent of the adult population had work. Multi-income families have greater security than single-income families. The chance of both (or all) income earners in a family losing their jobs simultaneously is much lower than the chance of a single earner losing work. With greater family income security, family consumption is likely to be less sensitive to fluctuations in family income that are seen as temporary. So when aggregate income falls, it might not induce a cut in consumption. For example, during the OPEC recession, as real GDP fell, personal consumption expenditure actually increased. In 1990–1991, when real GDP fell by $30 billion, consumption expenditure fell by only $13 billion.

For the four reasons we have just reviewed, it appears that the economy has better shock-absorbing characteristics today than it had in the 1920s and 1930s. Even if there is a collapse of confidence, leading to a fall in investment, today's shock absorbers will not translate that initial shock into the large and prolonged fall in real GDP and rise in unemployment that occurred more than 60 years ago.

Because the economy is now more immune to severe recession than it was in the 1930s, even a stock market crash of the magnitude that occurred in 1987 had barely noticeable effects on spending. A crash of a similar magnitude in 1929 resulted in the near collapse of housing investment and consumer durable purchases. In the period following the 1987 stock market crash, investment and spending on durable goods hardly changed.

None of this is to say that there might not be a deep recession or even a Great Depression in the twenty-first century. But it would take a very severe shock to trigger one.

◆ We have now completed our study of the business cycle. Before you leave this topic, take a look at *Reading Between the Lines* on pp. 726–727, which provides a further examination of the U.S. economy during the expanding 1990s and recession of 2001.

We have also completed our study of the science of macroeconomics and learned about the influences on long-term economic growth and inflation as well as the business cycle. We have discovered that these issues pose huge policy challenges. How can we speed up the rate of economic growth while at the same time keep inflation low and avoid big swings of the business cycle? Our task in the next chapter is to study these macroeconomic policy challenges and the debate that surrounds them.

The Most Recent U.S. Business Cycle

THE NEW YORK TIMES, November 27, 2001

Economists Make It Official: U.S. Is In Recession

The group of economists that tracks business cycles made official today what has been apparent to laid-off workers and struggling businesses for months: the longest economic expansion on record gave way earlier this year to the first recession in a decade and the 10th since World War II.

The group, the National Bureau of Economic Research's business-cycle dating committee, said the recession began in March, months before the terrorist attacks on Sept. 11 or the sharp rise in unemployment.

The group's statement put a headstone on a remarkable period of economic vibrancy. The last decade included the emergence of the stock market as a national sport, the appearance (and subsequent disappearance) of huge federal budget surpluses, a heated debate about the merits of globalization and a surge of optimism about the potential of a technology-driven "new economy." ...

"The committee is satisfied that the total contraction in the economy is sufficient to merit the determination that a recession is under way," it said. ...

Barring any new terrorist attacks, economists expect this downturn to be over in the first half of 2002. ...

But there is considerable disagreement about how robust a rebound can be expected, with some analysts predicting that growth will remain lackluster for a year or two after the recession officially ends. ...

"The official recession could be pretty short," said James W. Paulsen, chief investment strategist at Wells Capital Management, an investment firm. "But the real issue isn't when ... do you get back to a sustainable growth rate of 3 to 4 percent, and on that count I think there's going to be disappointment."

Consumers have sated themselves on big-ticket purchases and pushed their savings rates to almost zero, leaving them an unlikely engine of economic recovery, Mr. Paulsen said. ...

Mr. Paulsen said it could be well into 2003 before the economy was really back on track....

Essence of the Story

■ The National Bureau of Economic Research's business-cycle dating committee said that a recession began in March 2001.

■ The 2001 recession was the tenth since World War II and followed a decade of strong expansion.

■ The expansion of the 1990s saw stock market trading become a popular activity, converted a federal budget deficit into a surplus, generated debate about the merits of globalization, and brought optimism about a technology-driven "new economy."

■ Most economists expected the recession to be over in the first half of 2002.

■ Some economists said that in the next expansion, consumer spending would grow slowly at first and that rapid growth would not begin until 2003.

Economic Analysis

■ The recession that the National Bureau of Economic Research's business-cycle dating committee says began in March 2001 has been one of the mildest on record.

■ Although employment decreased and unemployment increased, real GDP barely changed and it ended 2001 at a higher level than that at the beginning of the year.

■ Figure 1 shows the 2001 recession as a slowdown rather than a decrease in real GDP.

■ The figure also enables you to compare the 2001 recession with its predecessor of 1991. In the 1991 recession, real GDP decreased by 1.5 percent from peak to trough. In 2001, real GDP fell only in the second quarter and by only 0.3 percent.

■ The figure also provides a view of the expansion of the 1990s.

■ As the news article notes, this expansion created an optimism about a technology-driven "new economy." The figure helps to assess this optimism by showing and comparing potential GDP and real GDP.

■ Estimating potential GDP is an imprecise science. The data plotted here are from the International Monetary Fund's *World Economic Outlook* and are based on official U.S. estimates.

■ The most striking feature of the potential GDP line is the near constancy of its growth rate. Along that line, the economy expands at an average rate of 3 percent a year.

■ The "new economy" did not bring an increase in the growth rate of potential GDP.

■ Far from being a new economy, the economy behaved in much the same way as it always behaves in an expansion.

■ In contrast to the constant growth rate of potential GDP, actual real GDP grows at a fluctuating rate.

■ Starting out in the trough of the 1991 recession, real GDP was about 3 percent below potential GDP.

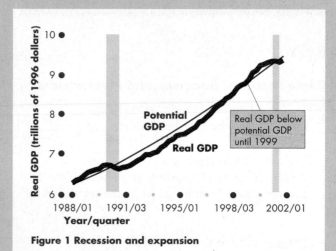

Figure 1 Recession and expansion

■ Real GDP grew at a rate close to that of potential GDP, but the gap didn't narrow much until after 1996.

■ Then, from 1996 through 2000, real GDP grew faster than potential GDP and a recessionary gap was transformed into an inflationary gap.

■ The growth rate of potential GDP remained at 3 percent a year from 1996 through 2000, but real GDP grew at 4 percent a year.

■ A recessionary gap of –2.4 percent in 1996 became an inflationary gap of 2 percent in 2000.

■ Following the 1991 recession, it took eight years for real GDP to return to potential GDP.

■ If the 2001 recession remains on track, real GDP will be much closer to potential GDP than it was during the early 1990s and will return to potential GDP more rapidly.

■ But another recession could strike at any time to move the economy below potential GDP again.

■ The forces that trigger recession are detectable only after the event.

SUMMARY

KEY POINTS

Cycle Patterns, Impulses, and Mechanisms (pp. 706–708)

- Since 1920, there have been 16 recessions and expansions.
- The Great Depression was the most severe contraction of real GDP, and the post–World War II recessions have been milder than the prewar recessions.

Aggregate Demand Theories of the Business Cycle (pp. 708–714)

- Keynesian business cycle theory identifies volatile expectations about future sales and profits as the main source of economic fluctuations.
- Monetarist business cycle theory identifies fluctuations in the quantity of money as the main source of economic fluctuations.
- Rational expectations theory identifies unanticipated fluctuations in aggregate demand as the main source of economic fluctuations.

Real Business Cycle Theory (pp. 715–719)

- In real business cycle (RBC) theory, economic fluctuations are caused by fluctuations in the influence of technological change on productivity growth.
- A temporary slowdown in the pace of technological change decreases investment demand and both the demand for labor and supply of labor.

Expansion and Recession During the 1990s and 2000s (pp. 719–721)

- The 1990s expansion resulted from a large increase in the rate of productivity growth that increased investment demand and the demand for and supply of labor and that increased both aggregate demand and aggregate supply.

- The 2001 recession was accompanied by a slowdown in the growth rate of productivity from technological change, which was probably concentrated in the high-tech sectors.

The Great Depression (pp. 722–725)

- The Great Depression started with increased uncertainty, which brought a fall in investment (especially in housing) and spending on consumer durables.
- There followed a near total collapse of the financial system. Banks failed, and the quantity of money decreased, resulting in a continued fall in aggregate demand.
- The Great Depression itself produced a series of reforms that make a repeat of such a depression much less likely.

KEY FIGURES

KEY TERMS

PROBLEMS

*1. The figure shows the economy of Virtual Reality. When the economy is in a long-run equilibrium, it is at points *B*, *F*, and *J*. When a recession occurs in Virtual Reality, the economy moves away from these points to one of the other points identified in each of the three parts of the figure.

a. If the Keynesian theory is the correct explanation for the recession, to which points does the economy move?

b. If the monetarist theory is the correct explanation for the recession, to which points does the economy move?

c. If the new classical rational expectations theory is the correct explanation for the recession, to which points does the economy move?

d. If the new Keynesian rational expectations theory is the correct explanation for the recession, to which points does the economy move?

e. If real business cycle theory is the correct explanation for the recession, to which points does the economy move?

2. The figure also shows the economy of Vital Signs. When the economy is in a long-run equilibrium, it is at points *A*, *E*, and *I*. When an expansion occurs in Vital Signs, the economy moves away from these points to one of the other points identified in each of the three parts of the figure.

a. If the Keynesian theory is the correct explanation for the recession, to which points does the economy move?

b. If the monetarist theory is the correct explanation for the recession, to which points does the economy move?

c. If the new classical rational expectations theory is the correct explanation for the recession, to which points does the economy move?

d. If the new Keynesian rational expectations theory is the correct explanation for the recession, to which points does the economy move?

e. If real business cycle theory is the correct explanation for the recession, to which points does the economy move?

(a) Labor market

(b) AS-AD

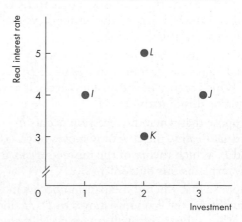

(c) Investment

*3. Suppose that when the recession occurs in Virtual Reality, the economy moves to *D*, *G*, and *K*. Which theory of the business cycle, if any, explains this outcome?

4. Suppose that when the expansion occurs in Vital Signs, the economy moves to *D*, *H*, and *L*. Which theory of the business cycle, if any, explains this outcome?

*5. Suppose that when the recession occurs in Virtual Reality, the economy moves to *C*, *G*, and *K*. Which theory of the business cycle, if any, explains this outcome?

6. Suppose that when the expansion occurs in Vital Signs, the economy moves to *C*, *H*, and *L*. Which theory of the business cycle, if any, explains this outcome?

*7. Suppose that when the recession occurs in Virtual Reality, the economy moves to *D*, *H*, and *K*. Which theory of the business cycle, if any, explains this outcome?

8. Suppose that when the expansion occurs in Vital Signs, the economy moves to *D*, *G*, and *L*. Which theory of the business cycle, if any, explains this outcome?

*9. Suppose that when the recession occurs in Virtual Reality, the economy moves to *C*, *H*, and *K*. Which theory of the business cycle, if any, explains this outcome?

10. Suppose that when the expansion occurs in Vital Signs, the economy moves to *C*, *G*, and *L*. Which theory of the business cycle, if any, explains this outcome?

*11. Suppose that when the recession occurs in Virtual Reality, the economy moves to *D*, *G*, and *L*. Which theory of the business cycle, if any, explains this outcome?

12. Suppose that when the expansion occurs in Vital Signs, the economy moves to *C*, *H*, and *K*. Which theory of the business cycle, if any, explains this outcome?

*13. Suppose that when the recession occurs in Virtual Reality, the economy moves to *C*, *G*, and *L*. Which theory of the business cycle, if any, explains this outcome?

14. Suppose that when the expansion occurs in Vital Signs, the economy moves to *D*, *H*, and *K*. Which theory of the business cycle, if any, explains this outcome?

CRITICAL THINKING

1. Study *Reading Between the Lines* on pp. 726–727 and then answer the following questions:
   a. What is the consensus view about the likely length of the 2001 recession?
   b. Why might the recovery from recession be weak?
   c. What does the performance of the real GDP growth rate of the 1990s tell us about the "new economy"?
   d. Can you interpret the 1990s expansion and 2001 recession using Keynesian, monetarist, new classical, new Keynesian, and real business cycle ideas?

2. Describe the changes in real GDP, employment and unemployment, and the price level that occurred during the Great Depression years of 1929–1933.

WEB EXERCISES

1. Use the links on your Parkin Web site to obtain data on the current state of the U.S. economy.
   a. List all of the features of the U.S. economy during the current year that you can think of that are consistent with a pessimistic outlook for the next two years.
   b. List all of the features of the U.S. economy during the current year that you can think of that are consistent with an optimistic outlook for the next two years.
   c. How do you think the U.S. economy is going to evolve over the next year or two? Explain your predictions, drawing on the pessimistic and optimistic factors that you have listed in the previous two questions and on your knowledge of macroeconomic theory.

2. Use the links on your Parkin Web site to obtain data on the current state of the global economy. How do you think the global economy is going to evolve over the next year or two? Explain your predictions, drawing on the pessimistic and optimistic factors that you have listed in the previous two questions and on your knowledge of macroeconomic theory.

MACROECONOMIC POLICY CHALLENGES

31

What Can Policy Do?

From 1991 through 1999, the U.S. economy performed well. Real GDP expanded, unemployment fell, the inflation rate was steady, and a federal government budget deficit turned into a surplus. ◆ But by 2000, growth was slowing, and in 2001, growth stopped and unemployment turned upward. ◆ The United States was not alone in facing a growth slowdown. Every other major country in the so-called Group of Seven saw its economy slow. ◆ Presidents and finance ministers began to talk of stimulus packages. And some people talked about a concerted global stimulus package. But not everyone agreed that the economy needed government stimulation. ◆ What can and should policy makers do to achieve a desirable macroeconomic performance?

◆ In this chapter, we're going to study the challenges of achieving sustainable long-term growth, low unemployment, and avoiding inflation. We're also going to review the alternative views on these issues. At the end of the chapter, you will have a deeper understanding of the macroeconomic policy problems facing the U.S. economy and the global economy today and of the debates that surround us concerning those problems.

After studying this chapter, you will be able to

■ Describe the goals of macroeconomic policy

■ Describe the main features of fiscal policy and monetary policy since 1961

■ Explain how fiscal policy and monetary policy influence long-term economic growth

■ Distinguish between and evaluate fixed-rule and feedback-rule policies to stabilize the business cycle

■ Evaluate fixed-rule and feedback-rule policies to contain inflation and explain why lowering inflation usually brings recession

Policy Goals

MACROECONOMIC POLICY GOALS FALL INTO TWO big categories: domestic and international. We will study international macroeconomic policy issues in Chapters 32 and 33. Here, we focus on domestic policy. The four main domestic macroeconomic policy goals are to

- Achieve the highest sustainable rate of potential GDP growth
- Smooth out avoidable business cycle fluctuations
- Maintain low unemployment
- Maintain low inflation

Potential GDP Growth

Rapid sustained real GDP growth can make a profound contribution to economic well-being. With a growth rate of 2 percent a year, it takes more than 30 years for production to double. With a growth rate of 5 percent a year, production more than doubles in just 15 years. And with a growth rate of 10 percent a year, as some Asian countries are achieving, production doubles in just 7 years. The limits to *sustainable* growth are determined by the availability of natural resources, by environmental considerations, and by the willingness of people to save and invest in new capital and new technologies rather than consume everything they produce.

How fast can the economy grow over the long term? Between 1990 and 2000, through one complete business cycle, potential GDP grew at a rate of 3 percent a year in the United States. But the U.S. population grows at about 1 percent a year, so the growth rate of real GDP per person was 2 percent a year, which means that output per person would double every 70 years.

Most economists believe that the U.S. economy can maintain a long-term growth rate of potential GDP of 2.5 percent a year. This growth rate would double output per person every 48 years. A few economists believe that with the right policies, sustainable growth of 5 percent a year is possible. This growth rate would double output per person every 18 years, increase it more than sixfold over 48 years, and increase it more than twelvefold in 70 years. So increasing the long-term growth rate is of critical importance.

The Business Cycle

Potential GDP probably does not grow at a constant rate. Fluctuations in the pace of technological advance and in the pace of investment in new capital bring fluctuations in potential GDP. So some fluctuations in real GDP represent fluctuations in potential GDP. But when real GDP grows less quickly than potential GDP, output is lost, and when real GDP grows more quickly than potential GDP, bottlenecks arise. Keeping real GDP growth steady and equal to potential GDP growth avoids these problems.

It is not known how smooth real GDP growth can be made. Real business cycle theory regards all the fluctuations in real GDP as fluctuations in potential GDP. The aggregate demand theories regard most of the fluctuations in real GDP as being avoidable deviations from potential GDP.

Unemployment

When real GDP growth slows, unemployment rises above the natural rate of unemployment. The higher the unemployment rate, the longer is the time taken by unemployed people to find jobs. Productive labor is wasted, and there is a slowdown in the accumulation of human capital. If high unemployment persists, serious psychological and social problems arise for the unemployed workers and their families.

When real GDP growth speeds up, unemployment decreases and falls below the natural rate of unemployment. The lower the unemployment rate, the harder it becomes for expanding industries to get the labor they need to keep growing. If extremely low unemployment persists, serious bottlenecks and production dislocations occur.

Keeping unemployment at its natural rate avoids both of these problems. But just what is the natural rate of unemployment? Assessments vary. The actual average unemployment rate over the most recent business cycle — 1990 to 2000 — was 5.6 percent. Most economists think the natural rate of unemployment has fallen in recent years and would put it at around 5 percent today. Real business cycle theorists believe that the natural rate fluctuates and always equals the actual unemployment rate.

If the natural rate of unemployment becomes high, then a goal of policy becomes lowering the natural rate itself. This goal is independent of smoothing the business cycle.

Inflation

When inflation fluctuates unpredictably, money becomes less useful as a measuring rod for conducting transactions. In extreme cases, money becomes useless and is abandoned as the means of payment. Borrowers and lenders and employers and workers must take on extra risks. Keeping the inflation rate steady and predictable avoids these problems.

What is the most desirable inflation rate? Some economists say that the *rate* of inflation doesn't matter much as long as the rate is *predictable*. But most economists believe that price stability, which they translate as an inflation rate of between 0 and 3 percent a year, is desirable. The reason why zero is not the target is that some price increases are due to quality improvements — a measurement bias in the price index — so a *measured* inflation rate of between 0 and 3 percent a year is equivalent to price stability.

The Two Core Policy Indicators: Real GDP Growth and Inflation

Although macroeconomic policy pursues the four goals we've just considered, the goals are not independent ones. Three of these goals — increasing the real GDP growth rate, smoothing the business cycle, and maintaining low unemployment — are linked together. Real GDP growth tells us directly about the long-term goal of high sustainable growth and the business cycle. It also has a strong link to unemployment. If growth becomes too rapid, unemployment falls below its natural rate, and if growth becomes too slow, unemployment rises above its natural rate. So keeping real GDP growing steadily at its maximum sustainable rate is equivalent to avoiding business fluctuations and keeping unemployment at its natural rate.

There are some connections between real GDP growth and inflation, but over the long run, these two variables are largely independent. So two variables, real GDP growth and inflation, are the core policy targets.

Policy performance, judged by the two core policy targets — real GDP growth and inflation — is shown in Fig. 31.1. Here the red line shows real GDP growth. Real GDP growth averaged 4 percent a year during the 1960s, but after 1970, the growth rate fell to less than 2.5 percent a year. Real GDP growth has fluctuated between a high of 6.8 percent in 1984 and a low of –2.1 percent in 1982. The height of the green shaded area shows inflation. The inflation rate was low during the 1960s, exploded during the 1970s, and then fell through the 1980s. During the 1990s, inflation returned to its 1960s level.

FIGURE 31.1 Macroeconomic Performance: Real GDP and Inflation

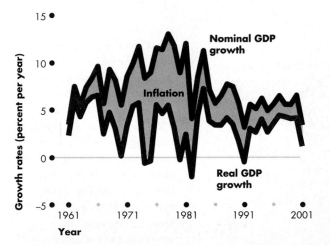

Real GDP growth and inflation fluctuate a great deal, and during the 1970s, inflation (the height of the green shaded area) mushroomed and real GDP growth slowed. This macroeconomic performance falls far short of the goals of a high and stable real GDP growth rate and low and predictable inflation.

Source: Bureau of Economic Analysis.

REVIEW QUIZ

1 Why does macroeconomic policy try to achieve the highest sustainable rate of potential GDP growth, small business cycle fluctuations, low inflation, and low unemployment?

2 Can stabilization policy keep the unemployment rate below its natural rate?

3 Why are real GDP growth and inflation the two core policy indicators?

We've examined the policy goals. Let's now look at the policy tools and the way they have been used.

Policy Tools and Performance

THE TOOLS THAT ARE USED TO TRY TO ACHIEVE macroeconomic performance objectives are fiscal policy and monetary policy.

Fiscal policy, which is described in Chapter 26, is the use of the federal budget to achieve macroeconomic objectives. The detailed fiscal policy tools are tax rates, benefit rates, and government purchases of goods and services. These tools work by influencing aggregate supply and aggregate demand in the ways explained in Chapter 21.

Monetary policy, which is described in Chapter 28, is the adjustment of the quantity of money in circulation and interest rates by the Federal Reserve (the Fed) to achieve macroeconomic objectives. These tools work by changing aggregate demand.

How have these policy tools been used in the United States? Let's answer this question by summarizing the main directions of fiscal and monetary policy over the years since 1960.

Fiscal Policy Since 1961

Figure 31.2 summarizes fiscal policy since 1961. It shows federal government revenues, expenditures, and the budget balance as percentages of GDP. So that you can see the political context of fiscal policy, the figure also shows the terms of administrations, the names of the incumbent Presidents, and the majority parties in the Senate and the House of Representatives.

Fiscal policy was mildly expansionary during the Kennedy years and strongly expansionary during the later Johnson years when the Vietnam War buildup occurred. During Nixon's presidency, spending growth was kept moderate. But under the pressure of the first OPEC oil shock, spending soared during Ford's presidency. The Carter years began with spending cuts, but then spending climbed to a new high. During the first Reagan term, spending continued to increase at first but it was later held in check, and then during the second Reagan term, spending was cut. During the term of the first President Bush, government spending took an increased percentage of GDP but taxes took a smaller percentage. As the 1991 recession

---

FIGURE 31.2   The Fiscal Policy Record: A Summary

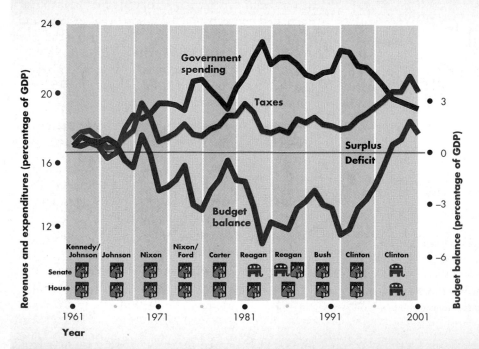

Fiscal policy is summarized here by the performance of government spending, taxes, and the budget balance as percentages of GDP. From 1961 through the early 1990s, spending was on an upward trend, taxes were roughly constant, and a large budget deficit emerged. During the rest of the 1990s and 2000s, spending decreased, taxes increased, and the budget moved into surplus. Cycles in spending and taxes have resulted in cycles in the deficit that often have been expansionary in the year before an election and contractionary in the year after an election.

Sources: Budget of the United States Government, Fiscal Year 2003, Table 14.2, Federal Transactions in the National Income and Product Accounts, and The Congressional Record.

intensified and the 1992 election drew closer, tax cuts became the rage, especially in Congress, and revenues decreased. But a tax bill in 1993 increased taxes, so revenues increased during the Clinton presidency. At the same time, spending was held in check and decreased as a percentage of GDP.

The budget balance tells an interesting story. During the terms of Johnson, Nixon, and Ford and the first Reagan term, the budget deficit decreased in the immediate postelection year and increased as the next election approached. Through the Clinton years, the deficit decreased and was replaced by a surplus.

Monetary Policy Since 1961

Figure 31.3 shows three broad measures of monetary policy. They are the growth rate of M2, the federal funds rate, and the real federal funds rate. The M2 growth rate tells us how monetary policy was influencing an important determinant of aggregate demand. The federal funds rate tells us how the Fed was acting to change money growth. And the real federal funds rate tells us how the Fed was acting on the opportunity cost of short-term funds that influences spending plans.

Figure 31.3 also identifies the terms of office of the presidents and Fed chairmen. The Fed has had five chairmen during this period. Notice that the term of a Fed chairman does not coincide with the term of a President. William McChesney Martin was a long-serving chairman, whose term began in 1951. He retired in 1969 and was replaced by Arthur Burns, who served until 1977. William Miller had the shortest term and was replaced by Paul Volcker in 1979. The next chairman, Alan Greenspan, was appointed by President Reagan in 1987 and has served under four Presidents, including the second President Bush.

First, let's look at some of the monetary policy trends. During the 1960s, the M2 growth rate averaged 7 percent a year and ranged between a low of 4 percent in 1969 and a high of 9 percent in 1967. It then increased to an average of 10 percent a year between 1970 and 1983 and hit a peak of 14 percent in 1976. M2 growth fell steadily from 12 percent in 1983 to less than 1 percent in 1994 but then increased in 1995. The federal funds rate trended upward from 1960 through 1981 and then trended downward. It fell during the early 1990s but then began to rise again through 1995. It then remained

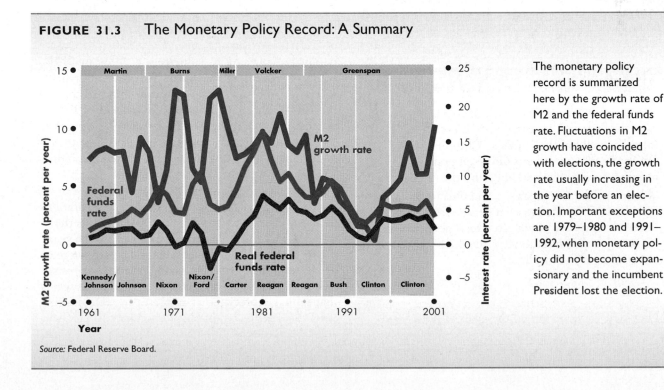

FIGURE 31.3   The Monetary Policy Record: A Summary

The monetary policy record is summarized here by the growth rate of M2 and the federal funds rate. Fluctuations in M2 growth have coincided with elections, the growth rate usually increasing in the year before an election. Important exceptions are 1979–1980 and 1991–1992, when monetary policy did not become expansionary and the incumbent President lost the election.

Source: Federal Reserve Board.

steady until 2001, when it was cut sharply. The real federal funds rate fell through 1975 and then increased and remained high through most of the 1980s. Since the early 1960s, the real federal funds rate has followed the same path as the federal funds rate.

The general upward trend in M2 growth brought the 1970s inflation, which brought rising *nominal* interest rates but, at first, falling real interest rates. The subsequent sharp downward trend in M2 growth brought falling inflation and falling nominal interest rates but was accompanied by high real interest rates. M2 growth increased during the late 1990s and remained high through 2002.

There is a tendency for the peaks and troughs in M2 growth to coincide with the opposite turning points in the federal funds rate. Notice also a remarkable fact about the monetary policy cycles: There is a tendency for the federal funds rate to rise and the M2 growth rate to decrease immediately following an election and for the federal funds rate to fall and the M2 growth rate to increase as the next election approaches. Usually, the incumbent President or his party's successor has won the election. There are two exceptions. In 1980, M2 growth increased but not as quickly as the demand for money. Interest rates increased, the economy slowed, and Jimmy Carter lost his reelection bid. In 1992, M2 growth slowed, interest rates rose, and George Bush lost his reelection bid. A coincidence? Perhaps, but Presidents take a keen interest in what the Fed is up to.

REVIEW QUIZ

1 What were the main features and effects of fiscal policy during the terms of each President from Kennedy in the 1960s to Clinton in the 1990s? To what problems did fiscal policy respond during the late 1960s and the 1970s?

2 What were the main features and effects of monetary policy during each decade from the 1960s through the 1990s? In which periods was monetary policy inflationary? In which periods was it used to fight inflation?

Now that we've examined the goals of policy and the policy actions of the past, we're going to look at ways in which policy might be used better to achieve its goals.

Long-Term Growth Policy

THE SOURCES OF THE LONG-TERM GROWTH OF potential GDP, which are explained in Chapter 24 (pp. 551–552), are the accumulation of physical and human capital and the advance of technology. Chapter 24 briefly examines the range of policies that might achieve faster growth. Here, we probe more deeply into the problem of boosting the long-term growth rate.

Monetary policy can contribute to long-term growth by keeping the inflation rate low. (Chapter 29, pp. 686–687, explains some connections between inflation and growth.) Fiscal policy and other policies can also contribute to growth by influencing the private decisions on which long-term growth depends in three areas. All growth policies increase

■ National saving
■ Investment in human capital
■ Investment in new technologies

National Saving

National saving equals private saving plus government saving. Figure 31.4 shows the private and government components of national saving since 1961. During the 1960s and 1970s, national saving (the blue line) fluctuated around an average of 20 percent of GDP. There then began a steady slide that saw national saving sink to 16 percent of GDP in 1993 before beginning to rise again. Government saving (the green line) was on a downward trend all through the 1960s and 1970s. It was positive before 1975, became negative (government dissaving) during the 1980s, and returned to positive in 1997. Private saving (the pale green shaded area) increased through 1984, when it peaked at 21 percent of GDP.

The data you have just examined are for *gross* saving. Each year, national wealth grows by the amount of *net* saving, which equals gross saving minus the value of the capital that is scrapped during the year. Figure 31.4 shows U.S. net saving as a percentage of GDP. You can see that net saving (the red line) was followed a falling trend through 1993. The reason is that capital depreciated at an increasing rate. During the 1960s, depreciation ranged between 10 percent and 14 percent of GDP. This percentage edged upward and was around 12 percent by the mid-1990s. In the 1982 recession, it reached 14 percent of GDP. As a

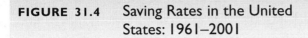

FIGURE 31.4   Saving Rates in the United States: 1961–2001

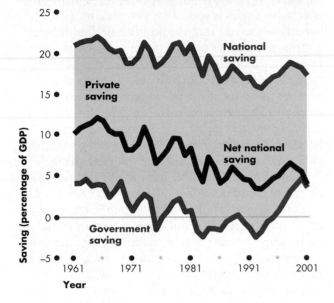

The U.S. national saving (the green line) peaked in 1979 and has fallen since that year. Both government saving and private saving have contributed to the fall. U.S. net national saving (the red line) has fallen even faster than national saving and has been on a downward trend since the mid-1960s. It hit an all-time low of 2.4 percent of GDP in 1993. It has increased since then but has begun to fall again.

Source: Bureau of Economic Analysis.

result of the fall in gross saving and the increase in the depreciation rate, net saving in the United States sank to an all-time low of 2.4 percent of GDP in 1993. Between 1993 and 1998, the net saving rate increased and then began to fall again.

U.S. investment, one of the engines of growth, is not limited by U.S. saving. The reason is that foreign saving can be harnessed to finance U.S. investment. But boosting the U.S. saving rate can help to bring faster real GDP growth for two reasons. First, the U.S. economy is a significant proportion of the world economy, so an increase in U.S. saving would increase world saving and bring lower real interest rates around the world. With lower real interest rates, investment would be boosted everywhere. The U.S. economy and the world economy could grow faster. Second, with more U.S. saving, there might be an increase in

domestic investment in high-risk–high-return new technologies that could boost U.S. growth.

How can national saving be increased? The two points of attack are

- Increasing government saving
- Increasing private saving

Increasing Government Saving   Government saving was negative between 1975 and 1996, and its average during the 1990s was –1.3 percent of GDP. But government saving increased after 1992 as the federal budget deficit was gradually eliminated and replaced by a surplus. Maintaining a federal budget surplus will be hard work and will be achieved only by resisting tax cuts and increases in expenditures on Social Security, Medicaid, and Medicare.

Increasing Private Saving   Private saving has fallen from its peak of the mid-1980s, but even in the low years of 1992 and 1993, private saving was the same percentage of GDP it had been in 1960. The main way in which government actions can boost private saving is by increasing the after-tax rate of return on saving. This is what government policy has sought to do, but on only one type of asset: individual retirement accounts (IRAs). By putting their savings into IRAs, people can avoid income tax on their interest income. But they cannot use their IRAs (without tax penalties) until they reach the age of 59. Also, there are limits (that were relaxed somewhat in 1997) to the amount that can be accumulated tax-free in an IRA.

Private saving probably could be stimulated more effectively by cutting taxes on interest income and capital gains across the board and replacing the lost government revenue from such a tax cut with a national consumption tax or a national sales tax. Whether such restructuring of taxes is politically feasible or desirable is a question that goes beyond the scope of macroeconomics.

Private Saving and Inflation   Inflation erodes the value of money and other financial assets such as bonds, and uncertainty about future inflation discourages saving. So another policy that increases the saving rate is a monetary policy that preserves stable prices and minimizes uncertainty about the future value of money. Chapter 29 (pp. 686–687) spells out the broader connection between inflation and real GDP and explains why low inflation brings greater output and faster growth.

Investment in Human Capital

The accumulation of human capital plays a crucial role in economic growth, and two areas are relevant: schooling and on-the-job experience. Economic research shows that both schooling and on-the-job training pay. That is, on the average, the greater the number of years a person remains in school and the greater the number of years of work experience, the higher are that person's earnings. Furthermore, schooling and on-the-job experience yield one of the highest rates of return available.

If education and on-the-job training yield higher earnings, why does the government need a policy to increase investment in human capital? Why can't people simply be left to get on with making their own decisions about how much human capital to acquire? The answer is that the *social* returns to human capital probably exceed the *private* returns. The extra productivity that comes from the *interactions* of well-educated and experienced people exceeds what each individual could achieve alone. So, left to ourselves, we would probably accumulate too little human capital. Let's look at some aspects of education and training policies.

Education and Training Policies Governments attempt to increase human capital by subsidizing schooling. They also help to set the standards of achievement for the school system.

The United States has achieved a high standard on some dimensions of schooling but not on all dimensions. For example, in 1996, 63 percent of high school graduates enrolled in postsecondary education (one of the highest percentages in the world) but 13 percent of high school students dropped out and did not graduate.

The Goals 2000: Educate America Act of 1994 and the current administration's education initiatives are examples of attempts to improve the quality of schooling. The 1994 Act paid special attention to improving each child's state of preparation for school and performance in school, especially in mathematics and science, two areas in which U.S. schoolchildren are not leading the world. A further feature of Goals 2000 is to improve college access, especially for adults who can benefit from retraining.

The scope for government training programs is limited, but the government can set an example as an employer, and it can encourage best-practice training programs for workers.

Investment in New Technologies

Investment in new technologies is the third area in which policy can influence economic growth. As Chapter 24 (pp. 561–562) explains, investment in new technologies is special for two reasons. First, it appears not to run into the problem of diminishing returns that plagues other types of capital and other factors of production. Second, the benefits of new technologies spill over to influence all parts of the economy, not just the firms undertaking the investment. For these reasons, increasing the rate of investment in new technologies is a promising way of boosting long-term growth. But how can government policy influence the pace of technological change?

Government can fund and provide tax incentives for research and development activities. Through the National Science Foundation, the public universities, and various research establishments, governments fund a large amount of basic research. Also, the federal government encourages business research with a Research and Experiment Tax Credit (R&E credit). This credit is available to firms that spend more on research and development than some threshold amount. The idea is to stimulate more expenditure on these activities than would occur otherwise. There is some evidence that the R&E credit is a cost-effective way of boosting research.

REVIEW QUIZ

1 Why do long-term growth policies focus on increasing saving and increasing investment in human capital and new technologies?
2 What have been the trends in the U.S. net saving since the mid-1970s?
3 What actions can the government take that might increase the saving rate?
4 What actions can the government take that might increase investment in human capital?
5 What actions can the government take that might increase investment in new technologies?

We've seen how government might use its fiscal and monetary policies to influence long-term growth. How can it influence the business cycle and unemployment? Let's now address this question.

Business Cycle and Unemployment Policy

MANY DIFFERENT FISCAL AND MONETARY POLICIES can be pursued to stabilize the business cycle and cyclical unemployment. But all these polices fall into three broad categories:

- Fixed-rule policies
- Feedback-rule policies
- Discretionary policies

Fixed-Rule Policies

A **fixed-rule policy** specifies an action to be pursued independently of the state of the economy. An everyday example of a fixed rule is a stop sign. It says, "Stop regardless of the state of the road ahead — even if no other vehicle is trying to use the road." One fixed-rule policy, proposed by Milton Friedman, is to keep the quantity of money growing at a constant rate year in and year out, regardless of the state of the economy, to make the *average* inflation rate zero. Another fixed-rule policy is to balance the federal budget. Fixed rules are rarely followed in practice, but they have some merits in principle, and later in this chapter, we will study how they would work if they were pursued.

Feedback-Rule Policies

A **feedback-rule policy** specifies how policy actions respond to changes in the state of the economy. A yield sign is an everyday feedback rule. It says, "Stop if another vehicle is attempting to use the road ahead, but otherwise, proceed." A macroeconomic feedback-rule policy is one that changes the money supply, interest rates, or even tax rates in response to the state of the economy. Some feedback rules guide the actions of policy makers. For example, the Fed's Federal Open Market Committee used a feedback rule when it kept pushing interest rates ever higher through 1994 in response to persistently falling unemployment and strong real GDP growth. Other feedback-rule policies are automatic. Examples are the automatic increase in tax revenues and decrease in transfer payments during an expansion and the automatic decrease in tax revenues and increase in transfer payments during a recession.

Discretionary Policies

A **discretionary policy** responds to the state of the economy in a possibly unique way that uses all the information available, including perceived lessons from past "mistakes." An everyday discretionary policy occurs at an unmarked intersection. Each driver uses discretion in deciding whether to stop and how slowly to approach the intersection. Most macroeconomic policy actions have an element of discretion because every situation is to some degree unique. For example, through 1998, the Fed cut interest rates several times to maintain economic growth in the face of a sagging Asian economy. The Fed might have delayed cutting interest rates until it was sure that lower interest rates were needed and then cut them in larger increments. The Fed used discretion based on lessons it had learned from earlier expansions. But despite the fact that all policy actions have an element of discretion, they can be regarded as modifications of a basic feedback-rule policy.

We'll study the effects of business cycle policy by comparing the performance of real GDP and the price level under a fixed rule and a feedback rule. Because the business cycle can result from demand shocks or supply shocks, we need to consider these two cases. We'll begin by studying demand shocks.

Stabilizing Aggregate Demand Shocks

We'll study an economy that starts out at full employment and has no inflation. Figure 31.5 illustrates this situation. The economy is on aggregate demand curve AD_0 and short-run aggregate supply curve *SAS*. These curves intersect at point *A* on the long-run aggregate supply curve, *LAS*. The GDP deflator is 110, and real GDP is $10 trillion. Now suppose that there is an unexpected and temporary decrease in aggregate demand. Let's see what happens.

Perhaps investment decreases because of a wave of pessimism about the future, or perhaps exports decrease because of a recession in the rest of the world. Regardless of the origin of the decrease in aggregate demand, the aggregate demand curve shifts leftward, to AD_1 in Fig. 31.5. Aggregate demand curve AD_1 intersects the short-run aggregate supply curve, *SAS*, at point *B* where the GDP deflator is 105 and real GDP is $9.5 trillion. The economy is in a recession. Real GDP is less than potential GDP, and unemployment is above its natural rate.

FIGURE 31.5   A Decrease in
Aggregate Demand

The economy starts out at full employment on aggregate demand curve AD_0 and short-run aggregate supply curve SAS, the two curves intersecting on the long-run aggregate supply curve, LAS, at point A. Real GDP is $10 trillion, and the GDP deflator is 110. A fall in aggregate demand (due to pessimism about future profits, for example) unexpectedly shifts the aggregate demand curve to AD_1. Real GDP decreases to $9.5 trillion, and the GDP deflator falls to 105. The economy is in a recession at point B.

Suppose that the decrease in aggregate demand from AD_0 to AD_1 is temporary. As confidence in the future improves, firms' investment picks up, or as economic expansion proceeds in the rest of the world, exports gradually increase. As a result, the aggregate demand curve gradually returns to AD_0, but it takes some time to do so.

We are going to work out how the economy responds under two alternative policies during the period in which aggregate demand gradually increases to its original level: a fixed rule and a feedback rule.

Fixed Rule: Monetarism   The fixed rule that we'll study here is one in which government purchases of goods and services, taxes, and the quantity of money remain constant. Neither fiscal policy nor monetary policy responds to the depressed economy. This is the

rule advocated by monetarists. A **monetarist** is an economist who believes that fluctuations in the quantity of money are the main source of economic fluctuations — the monetarist theory of the business cycle (see Chapter 30, pp. 710–712).

Figure 31.6(a) illustrates the response of the economy under a fixed rule when the decrease in aggregate demand to AD_1 is *temporary*. Starting from the recession at point B, aggregate demand gradually returns to its original level and the aggregate demand curve shifts rightward to AD_0. Real GDP and the GDP deflator gradually increase as the economy returns to point A. Throughout this process, real GDP growth is more rapid than usual but beginning from below potential GDP. Throughout the adjustment, unemployment remains above its natural rate.

Figure 31.6(b) illustrates the response of the economy under a fixed rule when the decrease in aggregate demand to AD_1 is *permanent*. Again starting from the recession point B and with unemployment above its natural rate, the money wage rate falls. Short-run aggregate supply decreases and the SAS curve shifts rightward to SAS_1. Real GDP gradually increases toward $10 trillion and the GDP deflator falls toward 95, at point C. Again, throughout the adjustment, real GDP is less than potential GDP and unemployment exceeds its natural rate.

Let's contrast the adjustment under a fixed-policy rule with that under a feedback-rule policy.

Feedback Rule: Keynesian Activism   The feedback rule that we'll study is one in which government purchases of goods and services increase, tax rates decrease, and the quantity of money increases when real GDP falls below potential GDP. In other words, both fiscal policy and monetary policy become expansionary when real GDP is less than potential GDP. When real GDP exceeds potential GDP, both policies operate in reverse, becoming contractionary. This rule is advocated by Keynesian activists. A **Keynesian activist** is an economist who believes that fluctuations in aggregate demand combined with sticky wages (and/or sticky prices) are the main source of economic fluctuations — the Keynesian and new Keynesian theories of the business cycle (see Chapter 30, pp. 708–710 and pp. 712–714).

Figure 31.6(c) illustrates the response of the economy under this feedback-rule policy. Starting from the recession at point B, the expansionary fiscal and monetary policies shift the aggregate demand

FIGURE 31.6   Two Stabilization Policies: Aggregate Demand Shock

(a) Fixed rule: temporary demand shock   **(b) Fixed rule: permanent demand shock**   **(c) Feedback rule**

Aggregate demand is AD_1 and the economy is in a recession at point B. Real GDP is \$9.5 trillion, and the GDP deflator is 105. In part (a), the aggregate demand shock is temporary and a fixed-rule policy is pursued. Aggregate demand gradually increases to AD_0, real GDP increases to \$10 trillion, and the GDP deflator increases to 110 at point A. In part (b), the aggregate demand shock is permanent and a fixed-rule policy is pursued. Aggregate demand remains at AD_1. Eventually the

money wage rate falls and the SAS curve shifts to SAS_1. The price level falls to 105, and real GDP increases to \$10 trillion at point C. In part (c), a feedback rule is pursued. With the economy in recession, expansionary fiscal and monetary policies increase aggregate demand and shift the aggregate demand curve from AD_1 to AD_0. Real GDP increases to \$10 trillion, and the GDP deflator increases to 110 at point A.

curve immediately to AD_0 and the economy moves back to point A. As other influences increase aggregate demand, fiscal and monetary policies become contractionary to hold the aggregate demand curve steady at AD_0. Real GDP is held steady at \$10 trillion, and the GDP deflator remains at 110.

The Two Rules Compared   Under a fixed-rule policy, the economy goes into a recession and stays there for as long as it takes for aggregate demand to increase again under its own steam. Only gradually does the aggregate demand curve return to its original position and the recession come to an end.

Under a feedback-rule policy, the economy is pulled out of its recession by the policy action. Once back at potential GDP, real GDP is held there by a gradual, policy-induced decrease in aggregate demand that exactly offsets the increase in aggregate demand coming from private spending decisions.

The price level and real GDP decrease and increase by exactly the same amounts under the two policies, but real GDP stays below potential GDP for longer with a fixed rule than it does with a feedback rule.

So Feedback Rules Are Better?   Isn't it obvious that a feedback rule is better than a fixed rule? Can't the government and the Fed use feedback rules to keep the economy close to full employment with a stable price level? Of course, unforecasted events — such as a collapse in business confidence — will hit the economy from time to time. But by responding with a change in tax rates, spending, interest rates, and the quantity of money, can't the government and the Fed minimize the damage from such a shock? It appears to be so from our analysis, and the Fed did a pretty good job during the ten years between 1992 and 2002.

Despite the apparent superiority of a feedback rule, many economists remain convinced that a fixed rule stabilizes aggregate demand more effectively than a feedback rule does. These economists assert that fixed rules are better than feedback rules because

- Potential GDP is not known.
- Policy lags are longer than the forecast horizon.
- Feedback-rule policies are less predictable than fixed-rule policies.

Let's look at these assertions.

Knowledge of Potential GDP To decide whether a feedback policy needs to stimulate or retard aggregate demand, it is necessary to determine whether real GDP is currently above or below potential GDP. But potential GDP is not known with certainty. It depends on a large number of factors, one of which is the level of employment when unemployment is at its natural rate. But uncertainty and disagreement exist about how the labor market works, so we can only estimate the natural rate of unemployment. As a result, there is uncertainty about the *direction* in which a feedback policy should be pushing the level of aggregate demand.

Policy Lags and the Forecast Horizon The effects of policy actions taken today are spread out over the next two years or even more. But no one is able to forecast accurately that far ahead. The forecast horizon of the policy makers is less than 1 year. Further, it is not possible to predict the precise timing and magnitude of the effects of policy actions. So a feedback policy that reacts to today's economy may be inappropriate for the state of the economy at that uncertain future date when the policy's effects are felt.

For example, suppose that today the economy is in recession. The Fed reacts with an increase in the money growth rate. When the Fed steps on the monetary accelerator, the first reaction is a fall in interest rates. Some time later, lower interest rates produce an increase in investment and the purchases of consumer durable goods. Some time still later, this increase in expenditure increases income; higher income in turn induces higher consumption expenditure. Later yet, the higher expenditure increases the demand for labor, and eventually, the money wage rate and prices rise. The industries and regions in which spending increases occur vary, and so does the impact on employment. It can take from nine months to two years for an initial action by the Fed to cause a change in real GDP, employment, and the inflation rate.

By the time the Fed's actions are having their maximum effect, the economy has moved on to a new situation. Perhaps a world economic slowdown has added a new negative effect on aggregate demand that is offsetting the Fed's expansionary actions. Or perhaps a boost in business confidence has increased aggregate demand yet further, adding to the Fed's own expansionary policy. Whatever the situation, the Fed can take the appropriate actions today only if it can forecast those future shocks to aggregate demand.

To smooth the fluctuations in aggregate demand, the Fed needs to take actions today that are based on a forecast of what will be happening over a period stretching two or more years into the future. It is no use taking actions a year from today to influence the situation that then prevails. By then it will be too late.

If the Fed is good at economic forecasting and bases its policy actions on its forecasts, then the Fed can deliver the type of aggregate-demand-smoothing performance that we assumed in the model economy that we studied earlier in this chapter. But if the Fed takes policy actions that are based on today's economy rather than on the forecasted economy a year into the future, then those actions will often be inappropriate ones.

When unemployment is high and the Fed puts its foot on the accelerator, it speeds the economy back to full employment. But the Fed might not be able to see far enough ahead to know when to ease off the accelerator and gently tap the brake, holding the economy at its full-employment point. Usually, the Fed keeps its foot on the accelerator for too long, and after the Fed has taken its foot off the accelerator pedal, the economy races through the full-employment point and starts to experience shortages and inflationary pressures. Eventually, when inflation increases and unemployment falls below its natural rate, the Fed steps on the brake and pushes the economy back below full employment.

According to advocates of fixed rules, the Fed's own reactions to the current state of the economy are one of the major sources of fluctuations in aggregate demand and the major factor that people have to forecast to make their own economic choices.

During recent years, the Fed has tried to avoid the problems just described. In 1994, it increased interest rates early in the expansion and by small increments. In 1995, after real GDP growth slowed but before any signs of recession were on the horizon, the Fed began to cut interest rates. In 1997, before inflation turned seriously upward, the Fed hit the monetary brake. And in 1998, while the economy expanded strongly, the Fed cut interest rates to avoid the effects of the Asian recession. But the Fed was far too late in its 2001 interest rate cuts to deal with the recession that began in March of that year. The Fed would have needed to start the cutting a year earlier to have been effective.

The problems for fiscal policy feedback rules are more severe than those for monetary policy because of the lags in the implementation of fiscal policy. The Fed can take actions relatively quickly, but before a fiscal policy action can be taken, the entire legislative process must be completed. So even before a fiscal policy action is implemented, the economy may have moved on to a new situation that calls for a different feedback policy from the one that is in the legislative pipeline.

Predictability of Policies To make decisions about long-term contracts for employment (wage contracts) and for borrowing and lending, people have to anticipate the future course of prices — the future inflation rate. To forecast the inflation rate, it is necessary to forecast aggregate demand. And to forecast aggregate demand, it is necessary to forecast the policy actions of the government and the Fed.

If the government and the Fed stick to rock-steady, fixed rules for tax rates, spending programs, and money growth, then policy itself cannot be a contributor to unexpected fluctuations in aggregate demand.

In contrast, when a feedback rule is being pursued, there is more scope for the policy actions to be unpredictable. The main reason is that feedback rules are not written down for all to see. Rather, they have to be inferred from the behavior of the government and the Fed.

So with a feedback policy, it is necessary to predict the variables to which the government and Fed react and the extent to which they react. Consequently, a feedback rule for fiscal and monetary policies can create more unpredictable fluctuations in aggregate demand than a fixed rule can.

Economists disagree about whether those bigger fluctuations offset the potential stabilizing influence of the predictable changes the Fed makes. No agreed measurements have been made to settle this dispute. Nevertheless, the unpredictability of the Fed in its pursuit of feedback policies is an important fact of economic life. And the Fed does not always go out of its way to make its reactions clear. Even in Congressional testimony, Federal Reserve Board chairmen are reluctant to make the Fed's actions and intentions entirely plain. (It has been suggested that two former chairmen of the Federal Reserve Board, the pipe-puffing Arthur Burns and the cigar-puffing Paul Volcker, carried their own smokescreens around with them, as if to exemplify the Fed's mysteriousness and unpredictability. The nonsmoking Alan Greenspan seems to be running a more open and predictable Fed.)

It is not surprising that the Fed seeks to keep *some* of its actions behind a smokescreen. First, the Fed wants to maintain as much freedom of action as possible and so does not want to state with too great a precision the feedback rules that it will follow in any given circumstances. Second, the Fed is part of a political process and, although legally independent of the federal government, is not immune to subtle influence. For at least these two reasons, the Fed does not specify feedback rules as precisely as the one we've analyzed in this chapter. As a result, the Fed cannot deliver an economic performance that has the stability that we generated in the model economy.

To the extent to which the Fed's actions are discretionary and unpredictable, they lead to unpredictable fluctuations in aggregate demand. These fluctuations, in turn, produce fluctuations in real GDP, employment, and unemployment.

If it is difficult for the Fed to pursue a predictable feedback stabilization policy, it is probably impossible for Congress to do so. The stabilization policy of Congress is formulated in terms of spending programs and tax laws. Because these programs and laws are the outcome of a political process that is constrained only by the Constitution, there can be no effective way in which a predictable feedback fiscal policy can be adhered to.

We reviewed three reasons why feedback-rule policies might not be more effective than fixed-rule policies in controlling aggregate demand. But there is a fourth reason why some economists prefer fixed rules: Not all shocks to the economy are on the demand side. Let's now see how aggregate supply fluctuations affect the economy under a fixed rule and a feedback rule. We will also see why the economists who believe that aggregate supply fluctuations are the dominant ones also favor a fixed rule rather than a feedback rule.

Stabilizing Aggregate Supply Shocks

Real business cycle theorists believe that fluctuations in real GDP (and in employment and unemployment) are caused not by fluctuations in aggregate demand but by fluctuations in productivity growth. According to real business cycle theory, there is no useful distinction between long-run aggregate supply and short-run aggregate supply. Because the money wage rate is flexible, the labor market is always in equilibrium and unemployment is always at its natural rate. So the vertical long-run aggregate supply curve is also the short-run aggregate supply curve. Fluctuations occur because of shifts in the long-run aggregate supply curve. Normally, the long-run aggregate supply curve shifts rightward — the economy expands. But the pace at which the long-run aggregate supply curve shifts rightward varies. Also, on occasion, the long-run aggregate supply curve shifts leftward, bringing a decrease in aggregate supply and a decrease in real GDP.

If the real business cycle theory is correct, economic policy that influences the aggregate demand curve has no effect on real GDP. But it does affect the price level. If a feedback-rule policy is used to increase aggregate demand every time real GDP decreases, and if the real business cycle theory is correct, the feedback-rule policy will make price level fluctuations more severe than they otherwise would be.

Figure 31.7 illustrates these alternative policy responses to a decrease in aggregate supply. The economy starts out at point A on aggregate demand curve AD_0 and long-run aggregate supply curve LAS_0 at a GDP deflator of 110 and with real GDP equal to $10 trillion. Now suppose that the long-run aggregate supply curve shifts to LAS_1. A decrease in long-run aggregate supply can occur as a result of a severe drought or other natural catastrophe or perhaps as the result of a disruption of international trade such as the OPEC embargo of the 1970s.

Fixed Rule With a fixed rule, the decrease in the long-run aggregate supply has no effect on the policies of the Fed or the government and no effect on aggregate demand. The aggregate demand curve remains AD_0. Real GDP decreases to $9.5 trillion, and the GDP deflator increases to 120 at point B.

Feedback Rule Now suppose that the Fed and the government use feedback rules. In particular, suppose that when real GDP decreases, the Fed increases the quantity of money and Congress enacts a tax cut to increase aggregate demand. In this example, the money growth and tax cut shift the aggregate demand curve to AD_1. The policy goal is to bring real GDP back to $10 trillion. But the long-run aggregate supply curve has shifted, and so potential GDP has decreased to $9.5 trillion. The increase in aggregate demand cannot bring forth an increase in output if the economy does not have the capacity to produce that output. So real GDP stays at $9.5 trillion, and

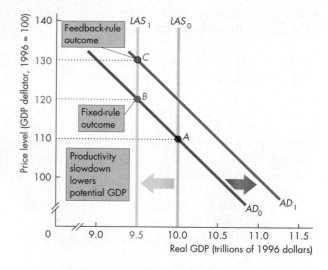

FIGURE 31.7 Responding to a Productivity Growth Slowdown

Initially the economy is at point A. A productivity growth slowdown shifts the long-run aggregate supply curve from LAS_0 to LAS_1. Real GDP decreases to $9.5 trillion, and the GDP deflator rises to 120 at point B. With a fixed rule, there is no change in the quantity of money, taxes, or government spending. Aggregate demand stays at AD_0, and that is the end of the matter. With a feedback rule, the Fed increases the money supply and the Congress cuts taxes or increases spending, intending to increase real GDP. Aggregate demand shifts to AD_1, but the result is an increase in the price level — the GDP deflator rises to 130 — with no change in real GDP, at point C.

the price level rises still further — the GDP deflator rises to 130 at point C. You can see that in this case the attempt to stabilize real GDP using a feedback-rule policy has no effect on real GDP but generates a substantial price level increase.

We've now seen some of the shortcomings of using feedback rules for stabilization policy. Some economists believe that these shortcomings are serious and want to constrain Congress and the Fed so that they use fixed rules. Others, regarding the potential advantages of feedback rules as greater than their costs, advocate the continued use of such policies but with an important modification that we'll now look at.

Natural Rate Policies

The business cycle and unemployment policies we've considered have been directed at smoothing the business cycle and minimizing *cyclical unemployment*. It is also possible to pursue policies aimed at lowering the natural rate of unemployment. But there are no costless ways of lowering the natural rate of unemployment. Let's look at two possible ways.

One policy tool is unemployment compensation. To lower the natural rate of unemployment, the government might lower the unemployment compensation rate, or shorten the period for which compensation is paid, or restrict compensation to people who undertake training programs that increase the likelihood of their finding jobs. With lower compensation, an unemployed person would spend less time looking for a job and would accept a job even it was not a good match for the person's skills. But such a policy might create hardship and have a cost that exceeds the cost of a high natural rate of unemployment.

The government might lower the minimum real wage rate. It could achieve a cut in the minimum wage either by holding the minimum money wage rate constant and letting inflation cut the minimum real wage rate or by cutting the minimum money wage rate. A lower minimum wage increases the quantity of labor demanded and lowers unemployment. Again, the government faces a tradeoff.

REVIEW QUIZ

1 What is a fixed-rule fiscal policy and what is a fixed-rule monetary policy? Can you provide two examples of fixed rules in everyday life (other than those in the text)?

2 What is a feedback fiscal policy and what is a feedback monetary policy? When might a feedback policy be used? Can you provide two examples of feedback rules in everyday life (other than those in the text)?

3 Why do some economists say that feedback rules do not necessarily deliver a better macroeconomic performance than fixed rules?

We've studied growth policy and business cycle and unemployment policy. Let's now study inflation policy.

Anti-Inflation Policy

THERE ARE TWO INFLATION POLICY PROBLEMS. In times of price level stability, the problem is to prevent inflation from breaking out. In times of inflation, the problem is to reduce its rate and restore price stability. Preventing inflation from breaking out means avoiding both demand-pull and cost-push forces. Avoiding demand-pull inflation is the flip side of avoiding demand-driven recession and is achieved by stabilizing aggregate demand. So the business cycle and unemployment policy we've just studied is also an anti-inflation policy. But avoiding cost-push inflation raises some special issues that we need to consider. So we will look at two issues for inflation policy:

- Avoiding cost-push inflation
- Slowing inflation

Avoiding Cost-Push Inflation

Cost-push inflation is inflation that has its origins in cost increases (see Chapter 29, pp. 681–683). In 1973–1974 and again in 1979, the world oil price exploded. Cost shocks such as these become inflationary if they are accommodated by an increase in the quantity of money. Such an increase in the quantity of money can occur if a monetary policy feedback rule is used. A fixed-rule policy for the quantity of money makes cost-push inflation impossible. Let's see why.

Figure 31.8 shows the economy at full employment. Aggregate demand is AD_0, short-run aggregate supply is SAS_0, and long-run aggregate supply is LAS. Real GDP is \$10 trillion, and the GDP deflator is 110 at point A. Now suppose that OPEC tries to gain a temporary advantage by increasing the price of oil. The short-run aggregate supply curve shifts leftward from SAS_0 to SAS_1.

Monetarist Fixed Rule Figure 31.8(a) shows what happens if the Fed follows a fixed rule for monetary policy and the government follows a fixed rule for fiscal policy. Suppose that the fixed rule is for zero money growth and no change in taxes or government purchases of goods and services. With these fixed rules, the Fed and the government pay no attention to the fact that there has been an increase in the price of oil. No policy actions are taken. The short-run

FIGURE 31.8   Responding to an OPEC Oil Price Increase

(a) Fixed rule

(b) Feedback rule

The economy starts out at point A on AD_0 and SAS_0, with a GDP deflator of 110 and real GDP of $10 trillion. OPEC forces up the price of oil, and the short-run aggregate supply curve shifts to SAS_1. Real GDP decreases to $9.5 trillion, and the GDP deflator increases to 120 at point B. With a fixed-rule policy (part a), the Fed makes no change to aggregate demand. The economy stays in a recession at point B until

the price of oil falls again and the economy returns to its original position. With a feedback-rule policy (part b), the Fed injects additional money and the aggregate demand curve shifts to AD_1. Real GDP returns to $10 trillion (potential GDP), but the GDP deflator increases to 125 at point C. The economy is set for another round of cost-push inflation.

aggregate supply curve has shifted to SAS_1, but the aggregate demand curve remains at AD_0. The GDP deflator rises to 120, and real GDP decreases to $9.5 trillion at point B. The economy has experienced *stagflation*. With unemployment above its natural rate, the money wage rate will eventually fall. Also, the low level of real GDP and low sales will probably bring a fall in the price of oil. These events shift the short-run aggregate supply curve back to SAS_0. The GDP deflator will fall to 110, and real GDP will increase to $10 trillion. But this adjustment might take a long time.

Keynesian Feedback Rule   Figure 31.8(b) shows what happens if the Fed and government operate a feedback rule. The starting point A is the same as before — the economy is on SAS_0 and AD_0 with a GDP deflator of 110 and real GDP of $10 trillion. OPEC raises the price of oil, and the short-run aggregate supply curve shifts to SAS_1. Real GDP decreases to $9.5 trillion, and the price level rises to 120 at point B.

A feedback rule is followed. With potential GDP perceived to be $10 trillion and with actual real GDP at $9.5 trillion, the Fed pumps money into the economy and the government increases its spending and lowers taxes. Aggregate demand increases, and the aggregate demand curve shifts rightward to AD_1. The price level rises to 125, and real GDP returns to $10 trillion at point C. The economy moves back to full employment but at a higher price level. The economy has experienced *cost-push inflation*.

The Fed responded in the way we've just described to the first wave of OPEC price increases in the mid-1970s. OPEC saw the same advantage in forcing up the price of oil again. A new rise in the price of oil decreased aggregate supply, and the short-run aggregate supply curve shifted leftward once more. If the Fed had chased it with an increase in aggregate demand, the economy would have been in a free-wheeling inflation. Realizing this danger, the Fed did *not* respond to the second wave of OPEC price increases in the early 1980s as it had done before.

Instead, the Fed held firm and even slowed the growth of aggregate demand to further dampen the inflation consequences of OPEC's actions.

Incentives to Push Up Costs You can see that there are no checks on the incentives to push up *nominal* costs if the Fed accommodates price hikes. If some group sees a temporary gain from pushing up the price at which they are selling their resources and if the Fed always accommodates the increase to prevent unemployment and slack business conditions from emerging, then cost-push elements will have a free rein. But when the Fed pursues a fixed-rule policy, the incentive to attempt to steal a temporary advantage from a price increase is severely weakened. The cost of higher unemployment and lower output is a consequence that each group will have to face and recognize.

So a fixed rule can deliver steady inflation, while a feedback rule, in the face of cost-push pressures, leaves inflation free to rise at the whim of whichever group believes a temporary advantage to be available from pushing up its price.

Slowing Inflation

So far, we've concentrated on *avoiding* inflation. But often the problem is not to avoid inflation but to tame it. The United States was in such a situation during the late 1970s and early 1980s. How can inflation, once it has set in, be cured? We'll look at two cases:

■ A surprise inflation reduction
■ A credible announced inflation reduction

A Surprise Inflation Reduction We'll use two equivalent approaches to study the problem of lowering inflation: the aggregate supply–aggregate demand model and the Phillips curve. The *AS-AD* model tells us about real GDP and the price level, while the Phillips curve, which is explained in Chapter 29 (pp. 688–690), lets us keep track of inflation and unemployment.

Figure 31.9 illustrates the economy at full employment with inflation raging at 10 percent a year. In part (a), the economy is on aggregate demand curve AD_0 and short-run aggregate supply curve SAS_0. Real GDP is $10 trillion, and the GDP deflator is 110. With real GDP equal to potential GDP on the *LAS* curve, the economy is at full employment. Equivalently, in part (b), the economy is on its long-run Phillips curve, *LRPC*, and short-run Phillips

curve, $SRPC_0$. The inflation rate of 10 percent a year is anticipated, so unemployment is at its natural rate, 6 percent of the labor force.

Next year, aggregate demand is *expected* to increase and the aggregate demand curve in Fig. 31.9(a) is expected to shift rightward from AD_0 to AD_1. In expectation of this increase in aggregate demand, the money wage rate increases and shifts the short-run aggregate supply curve from SAS_0 to SAS_1. If expectations are fulfilled, the GDP deflator rises to 121 — a 10 percent inflation — and real GDP remains at potential GDP. In part (b), the economy remains at its original position — unemployment is at its natural rate, and the inflation rate is 10 percent a year.

Now suppose that no one is expecting the Fed to change its policy but the Fed actually tries to slow inflation. It raises interest rates and slows money growth. Aggregate demand growth slows, and the aggregate demand curve (in part a) shifts rightward from AD_0, not to AD_1 as people expect, but only to AD_2.

With no change in the expected inflation rate, the money wage rate rises by the same amount as before and the short-run aggregate supply curve shifts leftward from SAS_0 to SAS_1. Real GDP decreases to $9.5 trillion, and the GDP deflator rises to 118.8 — an inflation rate of 8 percent a year. In Fig. 31.9(b), the economy moves along the short-run Phillips curve $SRPC_0$ as unemployment rises to 9 percent and inflation falls to 8 percent a year. The Fed's policy has succeeded in slowing inflation, but at the cost of recession. Real GDP is below potential GDP, and unemployment is above its natural rate.

A Credible Announced Inflation Reduction
Suppose that instead of simply slowing down the growth of aggregate demand, the Fed announces its intention ahead of its action and in a credible and convincing way so that its announcement is believed. That is, the Fed's policy is anticipated. Because the lower level of aggregate demand is expected, the money wage rate increases at a pace that is consistent with the lower level of aggregate demand. The short-run aggregate supply curve (in Fig. 31.9a) shifts leftward from SAS_0 but only to SAS_2. Aggregate demand increases by the amount expected, and the aggregate demand curve shifts from AD_0 to AD_2. The GDP deflator rises to 115.5 — an inflation rate of 5 percent a year — and real GDP remains at potential GDP.

In Fig. 31.9(b), the lower expected inflation rate shifts the short-run Phillips curve downward to $SRPC_1$,

FIGURE 31.9   Lowering Inflation

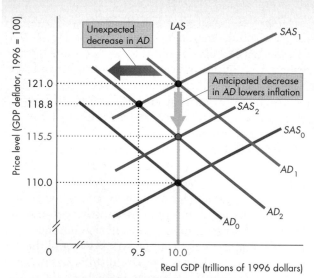

(a) Aggregate demand and aggregate supply

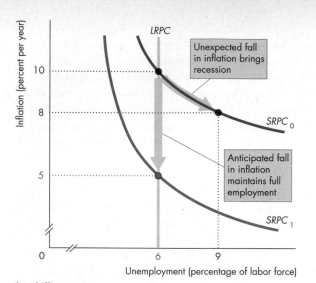

(b) Phillips curves

In part (a), the aggregate demand curve is expected to shift and actually shifts to AD_1. The short-run aggregate supply curve shifts to SAS_1. The GDP deflator rises to 121, but real GDP remains at $10 trillion. Inflation is 10 percent a year, and this inflation rate is anticipated. Part (b) shows this same situation. Unemployment is at the natural rate of 6 percent, and inflation is 10 percent a year. An unexpected slowdown in aggregate demand growth shifts the aggregate demand curve from AD_0 to AD_2. Real GDP decreases to $9.5 trillion,

and inflation slows to 8 percent (GDP deflator is 118.8). Unemployment rises to 9 percent as the economy slides down $SRPC_0$. An anticipated, credible, announced slowdown in aggregate demand growth shifts the aggregate demand curve from AD_0 to AD_2. The short-run aggregate supply curve shifts from SAS_0 to SAS_2. The short-run Phillips curve shifts to $SRPC_1$. Inflation slows to 5 percent, real GDP remains at $10 trillion, and unemployment remains at its natural rate of 6 percent.

and inflation falls to 5 percent a year, while unemployment remains at its natural rate of 6 percent.

A credible announced inflation reduction lowers inflation but with no accompanying recession or increase in unemployment.

Inflation Reduction in Practice

When the Fed in fact slowed inflation in 1981, we paid a high price. The Fed's policy action was unpredicted. It occurred in the face of a money wage rate that had been set at too high a level to be consistent with the growth of aggregate demand that the Fed subsequently allowed. The consequence was recession — a decrease in real GDP and a rise in unemployment. Could the Fed have lowered inflation without causing recession by telling people far enough ahead of time that it did indeed plan to lower inflation?

The answer appears to be no. The main reason is that people expect the Fed to behave in line with its record, not with its stated intentions. How many times have you told yourself that it is your firm intention to take off 10 unwanted pounds or to keep within your budget and put a few dollars away for a rainy day, only to discover that, despite your very best intentions, your old habits win out in the end?

To form expectations of the Fed's actions, people look at the Fed's past *actions*, not its stated intentions. On the basis of such observations — called Fed-watching — they try to work out what the Fed's policy is, to forecast its future actions, and to forecast the effects of those actions on aggregate demand and inflation. The Greenspan Fed, like the Volcker Fed that preceded it, has built a reputation for being anti-inflationary. That reputation is valuable because it helps the Fed to contain inflation and lowers the cost of eliminating inflation if it temporarily returns. The reason is that with a low expected inflation rate, the short-run Phillips curve is in a favorable position (like $SRPC_1$ in Fig. 31.9b). The Fed's actions during the 1990s were designed to keep inflation expectations low and prevent the gains made during the 1980s recession from being eroded.

Balancing the Inflation and Real GDP Objective: The Taylor Rule

John Taylor, formerly an economics professor at Stanford University and now Undersecretary of the Treasury for International Affairs in the Bush administration, has suggested a policy feedback rule that he says would deliver a better performance than what the Fed has achieved.

The idea is to target inflation but to also be explicit about the extent to which the Fed will adjust the federal funds rate in response to both inflation and deviations of real GDP from potential GDP. By being explicit and always following the same rule, Fed watching becomes a simpler task and smaller forecasting errors might be made, which translates into smaller deviations of real GDP from potential GDP, and smaller deviations of the unemployment rate from its natural rate.

If the Fed followed the Taylor rule, it would set a target inflation rate of 2 percent a year. It would then, each month, set a target for the federal funds rate equal to 2 percent plus one half of the amount by which the inflation rate exceeds 2 percent a year, plus one half of the percentage gap between real GDP and potential GDP. And the Fed would move the actual federal funds rate gradually toward the target rate.

Figure 31.10 shows the federal funds rate and the rate if the Taylor rule were followed. You can see that the Fed's actual policy is similar to the Taylor rule. So if the Fed announced that it is using the Taylor rule, it would not be changing the way it acts, but by being explicit about the formula that determines the federal funds rate, it would take the mystery and unpredictability out of its policy actions.

But you can also see that the Fed's actions have not exactly followed the Taylor rule. During the 1970s, the Fed was following the rule almost exactly, but during the 1980s, 1990s, and 2000s, the Fed has set the federal funds rate higher than the Taylor rule. The reason could be that the Fed has a lower target inflation rate or places less weight on real GDP fluctuations than does the Taylor rule.

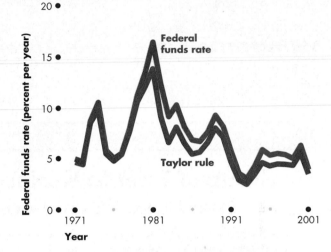

FIGURE 31.10   The Federal Funds Rate and the Taylor Rule

The green line shows the federal funds rate between 1971 and 2001. The red line shows what the federal funds rate would have been if the Fed had followed the Taylor rule and adjusted the federal funds rate to place equal emphasis on achieving low inflation and full employment.

Sources: Federal Reserve, International Monetary Fund, Bureau of the Census, and author's calculations.

REVIEW QUIZ

1 Why does a fixed rule provide more effective protection against a cost-push inflation than a feedback rule?
2 Why does a recession usually result as inflation is being tamed?
3 How does establishing a reputation of being an inflation fighter improve the Fed's ability to maintain low inflation and to lower the cost of fighting inflation?

◆ *Reading Between the Lines* on pp. 750–751 looks at the global stabilization challenge in 2002 as the world economy stands on the edge of recession.

You've now completed your study of macroeconomics. In the remaining chapters, we shift our focus to the international economy.

READING BETWEEN THE LINES

Stabilization in a Global Economy

THE NEW YORK TIMES, NOVEMBER 6, 2001

Group of 7 Set to Explore Ways to Recharge World Economy

WASHINGTON Treasury Secretary Paul H. O'Neill said he and his counterparts from the world's leading industrial nations would explore fresh ways of stimulating their economies when they gathered here this weekend. But European and Japanese leaders played down expectations that wealthy countries would act in concert to address the worsening global slump....

The United States and its peers were suffering a synchronized slump even before Sept. 11. They have now entered a period of severe weakness, with both the United States and Japan likely to experience recessions this year and Europe growing at a negligible rate.

American officials have urged their Japanese and European counterparts for years to overhaul their economies and reduce the cost of money so they can grow as rapidly as the United States. The idea that Europe and Japan need to fuel their economies has become even more pressing now, with the United States unable to serve as a locomotive as it did through much of the 1990's. ...

It is unclear, though, whether the Group of 7 can muster a consensus for forceful action. Though Gordon Brown, Britain's chancellor of the exchequer, said his country would support doing "whatever we have to do" to revive growth, his German counterpart damped expectations.

"A concerted economic stimulus package is out of the question," Hans Eichel, the German finance minister, said in Berlin before departing for Washington. "The attacks affected the U.S. in a different way to the rest of the world. Therefore, such a package is not relevant to Europe."

Japanese officials also signaled that they are not eager to take decisive new steps. "If there is a shift in the international economic situation, then we may have to consider" fresh measures, Finance Minister Masajuro Shiokawa said. "But we can't decide what to do so soon."

Copyright © 2001 by The New York Times Co.
Reprinted by permission.

Essence of the Story

■ At the end of 2001, the Group of Seven (G7) was in a synchronized slowdown, with the United States and Japan in recession and Europe growing very slowly.

■ Treasury Secretary Paul H. O'Neill said that he and his G7 counterparts would try to find ways to coordinate stimulation policies to counter the global slowdown.

■ American officials have said for some time that Japan and Europe should lower interest rates to grow as rapidly as the United States.

■ Opinions differed among the G7 finance ministers.

■ Gordon Brown of Britain supported efforts to revive growth.

■ Hans Eichel of Germany said that a stimulus package was out of the question and "not relevant to Europe."

■ Masajuro Shiokawa of Japan did not believe that further stimulus was needed.

750

Economic Analysis

■ During 2001, real GDP growth slowed in the United States and in the other G7 nations (Canada, France, Germany, Italy, Japan, and the United Kingdom).

■ Figure 1 shows this growth slowdown and places it in the context of the 30 years from 1971 through 2001.

■ You can see that in 2001, the growth rate of real GDP was similar in the United States to the average growth rate of the other G7 nations.

■ You can also see that during the 1990s, the U.S. growth rate exceeded that of the average of the other G7 nations.

■ Over the entire 30 years shown in the figure, the U.S. growth rate is 3.1 percent a year, compared to 2.8 percent a year for the other G7 members.

■ One reason for slower growth in the other G7 nations is that many of them have placed greater emphasis on keeping inflation in check.

■ Figure 2 shows the inflation record over the same period. You can see that during the 1990s, U.S. inflation, although not high, was higher than the average inflation of the other G7 nations. Also, the U.S. inflation rate was rising during the late 1990s.

■ Judging whether stimulus is needed and how much turns in part on the estimated degree of slack in the economy.

■ Figure 3 shows the *World Economic Outlook*'s estimates of output gaps — the deviation of real GDP from potential GDP as a percentage of potential GDP.

■ These data suggest that the 2001 recession in the United States was too shallow to need much stimulus and that the trend in the rest of the G7 has been toward closing the output gap.

■ Paying due attention to long-term price level stability, as the Germans and Japanese do, would lead to the view that stimulus was not required in 2002.

Figure 1 Real GDP growth rates

Figure 2 Inflation rates

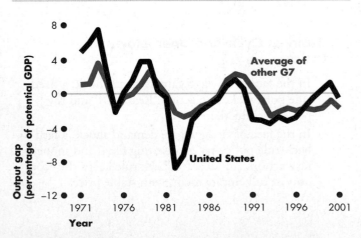

Figure 3 Output gaps

SUMMARY

KEY POINTS

Policy Goals (pp. 732–733)

- The goals of macroeconomic policy are to achieve the highest sustainable rate of potential GDP growth, smooth the business cycle, maintain low unemployment, and maintain low inflation.

Policy Tools and Performance (pp. 734–736)

- Fiscal policy was expansionary during the Kennedy years, in the late 1960s and early 1970s, and during the Reagan 1980s. It was contractionary during the Carter and Clinton years.
- The M2 growth rate increased during the 1970s, peaked in 1976, and then fell.

Long-Term Growth Policy (pp. 736–738)

- Policies to increase the long-term growth rate focus on increasing saving and investment in human capital and new technologies.
- To increase saving, government saving must increase or incentives for private saving must be strengthened by increasing after-tax returns.
- Human capital investment might be increased with improved education and by improving on-the-job training programs.
- Investment in new technologies can be encouraged by tax incentives.

Business Cycle and Unemployment Policy (pp. 739–745)

- In the face of an aggregate demand shock, a fixed-rule policy takes no action. Real GDP and the price level fluctuate.
- In the face of an aggregate demand shock, a feedback-rule policy takes offsetting fiscal and monetary action. An ideal feedback rule keeps the economy at full employment, with stable prices.

- Some economists say that a feedback rule creates fluctuations because it requires greater knowledge of the economy than we have, operates with time lags that extend beyond the forecast horizon, and introduces unpredictability about policy reactions.
- In the face of a productivity growth slowdown, both rules have the same effect on output. A feedback rule brings a higher inflation rate than does a fixed rule.

Anti-Inflation Policy (pp. 745–749)

- A fixed rule minimizes the threat of cost-push inflation. A feedback rule validates cost-push inflation and leaves the price level and inflation rate free to move to wherever they are pushed.
- Inflation can be tamed, at little or no cost in terms of lost output or excessive unemployment, by slowing the growth of aggregate demand in a credible and predictable way. But usually, when inflation is slowed down, a recession occurs.

KEY FIGURES

KEY TERMS

PROBLEMS

*1. A productivity growth slowdown has occurred. Explain its possible origins and describe a policy package that is designed to speed up growth again.

2. A nation is experiencing a falling saving rate. Explain its possible origins and describe a policy package that is designed to increase the saving rate.

*3. The economy shown in the figure is initially on aggregate demand curve AD_0 and short-run aggregate supply curve SAS. Then aggregate demand decreases, and the aggregate demand curve shifts leftward to AD_1.

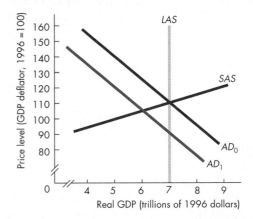

a. What is the initial equilibrium real GDP and price level?

b. If the decrease in aggregate demand is temporary and the government follows a fixed-rule fiscal policy, what happens to real GDP and the price level? Trace the immediate effects and the adjustment as aggregate demand returns to its original level.

c. If the decrease in aggregate demand is temporary and the government follows a feedback-rule fiscal policy, what happens to real GDP and the price level? Trace the immediate effects and the adjustment as aggregate demand returns to its original level.

d. If the decrease in aggregate demand is permanent and the government follows a fixed-rule fiscal policy, what happens to real GDP and the price level?

e. If the decrease in aggregate demand is permanent and the government follows a feedback-rule fiscal policy, what happens to real GDP and the price level?

4. The economy shown in the figure is initially on aggregate demand curve AD and short-run aggregate supply curve SAS_0. Then short-run aggregate supply decreases, and the short-run aggregate supply curve shifts leftward to SAS_1.

a. What is the initial equilibrium real GDP and price level?

b. What type of event could have caused the decrease in short-run aggregate supply?

c. If the government follows a fixed-rule monetary policy, what happens to real GDP and the price level? Trace the immediate effects and the adjustment as aggregate demand and short-run aggregate supply return to their original level.

d. If the government follows a feedback-rule monetary policy, what happens to real GDP and the price level? Trace the immediate effects and the adjustment as aggregate demand and short-run aggregate supply respond to the policy action.

*5. The economy is experiencing 10 percent inflation and 7 percent unemployment. Real GDP growth has sagged to 1 percent a year. The stock market has crashed.

a. Explain how the economy might have gotten into its current state.

b. Set out policies for the Fed and Congress to pursue that will lower inflation, lower unemployment, and speed real GDP growth.

c. Explain how and why your proposed policies will work.

6. The inflation rate has fallen to less than 1 percent a year, and the unemployment rate has decreased to less then 4 percent. Real GDP is growing at almost 5 percent a year. The stock market is at a record high.
   a. Explain how the economy might have gotten into its current state.
   b. Set out policies for the Fed and Congress to pursue that will maintain low inflation, low unemployment, and rapid real GDP growth.
   c. Explain how and why your proposed policies will work.

*7. When the economies of Indonesia, Korea, Thailand, Malaysia, and the Philippines entered into recession in 1997, the International Monetary Fund (IMF) made loans but only on condition that the recipients of the loans increase interest rates, raise taxes, and cut government purchases.
   a. Would you describe the IMF prescription as a feedback-rule policy or a fixed-rule policy?
   b. What do you predict the effects of the IMF policies would be?
   c. Do you have any criticisms of the IMF policies? What would you have required these countries to do? Why?

8. As the United States economy continued to expand and its stock market soared to new record levels during 1998, the Fed cut interest rates.
   a. Would you describe the Fed's actions as a feedback-rule policy or a fixed-rule policy?
   b. What do you predict the effects of the Fed's policies would be?
   c. Do you have any criticisms of the Fed's policies? What monetary policy would you have pursued? Why?

1. Study *Reading Between the Lines* on pp. 750–751 and then
   a. Describe the views of Treasury Secretary Paul H. O'Neill on the needs of the global economy in 2002.
   b. Has the United States had a higher or a lower average growth rate than the rest of the G7 nations? To what would you attribute the difference?
   c. Has the United States had a higher or a lower average inflation rate than the rest of the G7 nations? To what would you attribute the difference?
   d. Has the United States had a more or less stable business cycle than the rest of the G7 nations? To what would you attribute the difference?

2. Suppose the economy is booming and inflation is beginning to rise, but it is widely agreed that a massive recession is just around the corner. Weigh the advantages and disadvantages of Congress pursuing a fixed rule and a feedback rule for *fiscal* policy.

3. Suppose the economy is in a recession and inflation is falling. It is widely agreed that a strong recovery is just around the corner. Weigh the advantages and disadvantages of the Fed pursuing a fixed-rule policy and a feedback-rule policy.

1. Use the link on your Parkin Web site to review the 2002 *Economic Report of the President*.
   a. Review Chapter 1, "Restoring Prosperity."
   b. Write a summary and critique of this chapter.

2. Use the link on your Parkin Web site to review the latest *World Economic Outlook*.
   a. What are the major macroeconomic stabilization policy problems in the world today?
   b. What is the general direction in which policy actions are pushing the global economy?

UNDERSTANDING STABILIZATION PROB- LEMS AND POLICIES

Boom and Bust

To cure a disease, doctors must first understand how the disease responds to different treatments. It helps to understand the mechanisms that operate to cause the disease, but sometimes, a workable cure can be found even before the full story of the causes has been told. ◆ Curing economic ills is similar to curing our medical ills. We need to understand how the economy responds to the treatments we might prescribe for it. And sometimes, we want to try a cure even though we don't fully understand the reasons for the problem we're trying to control. ◆ You've seen how the pace of capital accumulation and technological change determine the long-term growth trend. You've learned how fluctuations around the long-term trend can be generated by changes in aggregate demand and aggregate supply. And you've learned about the key sources of fluctuations in aggregate demand and aggregate supply. ◆ The two chapters in this part have built on everything you've studied in macroeconomics. The central tool they use is the *AS-AD* model. But they use it to explain the big picture or grand vision that different schools of thought hold concerning the way the economy operates and what is important. ◆ In Chapter 30, we learned about alternative visions of the business cycle. All of these visions can be translated into the *AS-AD* model. And doing so helps us to compare and contrast the competing visions. But one theory of the cycle, the new *real business cycle (RBC)* theory, is more at home with the demand and supply model of microeconomics (Chapter 3) than the *AS-AD* model. Most economists have not embraced the real business cycle approach. It is an extreme view. But the method that real business cycle theory uses is here to stay. This method is to build a (mathematical) model of the entire economy and then see, in a computer simulation, what kind of cycle the model creates. The economy on the computer is then calibrated to the real economy, and the cycles are compared. The computer model can be treated with a variety of "medications" and their effects observed. This new style of business cycle research cannot be explained in detail without using advanced mathematical ideas. But Chapter 30 explained the economics that underlies it and showed you the type of model that real business cycle theorists use. ◆ Chapter 31 described the policy debate and explained the alternative approaches that have been proposed to speed growth, smooth the business cycle, and contain inflation. Again, the *AS-AD* model was the workhorse that was used to compare the effects of alternative policy strategies. ◆ The economist you're going to meet on the following page, Irving Fisher, developed ideas about business cycles that have never been in the mainstream but that are becoming fashionable today. Frederic S. Mishkin has helped to refine modern business cycle theory and has worked as the director of research at the New York Fed.

PROBING THE IDEAS
Business Cycles

THE ECONOMIST

IRVING FISHER *(1867-1947) ranks among the greatest American-born economists. The son of a Congregational minister who died as Irving was finishing high school, he paid his way through Yale and earned enough to keep his mother and younger brother by tutoring his fellow students.*

Irving Fisher came to economics by way of mathematics. He was Yale's first Ph.D. student in pure economics, but in the math department!

The contributions that Fisher made to economics cover the entire subject. He is best known for his work on the quantity theory of money (Chapter 27, pp. 701–704) and the relation between interest rates and inflation (Chapter 29, pp. 750–751). But he also wrote on the business cycle. He believed that the Great Depression was caused because the fall in the price level increased the real burden of debts. He wrote from experience. He had borrowed heavily to buy stocks in the rising market of the late 1920s and lost a fortune of perhaps 10 million dollars in the crash of 1929.

THE ISSUES

Economic activity has fluctuated between boom and bust for as long as we've had records. And understanding the sources of economic fluctuations has turned out to be difficult. One reason is that there are no simple patterns. Every new episode of the business cycle is different from its predecessor in some way. Some cycles are long and some short, some are mild and some severe, some begin in the United States and some abroad. We never know with any certainty when the next turning point (down or up) is coming or what will cause it. A second reason is that the apparent waste of resources during a recession or a depression seems to contradict the very foundation of economics: Resources are limited and people have unlimited wants—there is scarcity. A satisfactory theory of the business cycle must explain why scarce resources don't *always* get fully employed.

One theory is that recessions result from insufficient aggregate demand. The solution is to increase government spending, cut taxes, and cut interest rates. But demand stimulation must not be overdone. Countries that stimulate aggregate demand too much, such as Brazil, find their economic growth rates sagging, unemployment rising, and inflation accelerating.

Today's new theory, real business cycle theory, predicts that fluctuations in aggregate demand have *no* effect on output and employment and change only the price level and inflation rate. But this theory ignores the *real* effects of financial collapse of the type that occurred in the 1930s. If banks fail on a large scale and people lose their wealth, other firms also begin to fail and jobs are destroyed. Unemployed people cut their spending, and output falls yet further. Demand stimulation might not be called for, but action to ensure that sound banks survive certainly is.

While economists are trying to understand the sources of the business cycle, the government and the Fed are doing the best they can to moderate the cycle. In the years since World War II, there appears to have been some success. Although the business cycle has not disappeared, it has become much less severe.

THEN

What happens to the economy when people lose confidence in banks? They withdraw their funds. These withdrawals feed on themselves, creating a snowball of withdrawals and, eventually, panic. Short of funds with which to repay depositors, banks call in loans and previously sound businesses are faced with financial distress. They close down and lay off workers. And recession deepens and turns into depression. Bank failures and the resulting decline in the nation's supply of money and credit were a significant factor in deepening and prolonging the Great Depression. But they taught us the importance of stable financial institutions and gave rise to the establishment of federal deposit insurance to prevent future financial collapse.

Now

How can a building designed as a shop have no better use than to be boarded up and left empty? Not enough aggregate demand, say the Keynesians. Not so, say the real business cycle theorists. Technological change has reduced the building's current productivity as a shop to zero. But its expected future productivity is sufficiently high that it is not efficient to refit the building for some other purpose.

All unemployment, whether of buildings or people, can be explained in a similar way. For example, how can it be that during a recession, a person trained as a shop clerk is without work? Not enough aggregate demand is one answer. Another is that the current productivity of shop clerks is low but their expected future productivity is sufficiently high that it does not pay an unemployed clerk to retrain for a job that is currently available.

It is now over 70 years since the Great Depression began. Although we've had many recessions since then, none of them compare with the severity of that event. Some credit for avoiding another major depression must go to the Federal Reserve Board and the monetary policy it has pursued. Next you can meet Professor Frederic Mishkin of Columbia University and former director of research and executive vice-president at the Federal Reserve Bank of New York.

757

TALKING WITH

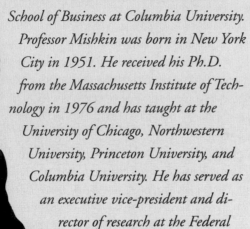

FREDERIC S. MISHKIN *is the Alfred Lerner Professor of Banking and Financial Institutions in the Graduate School of Business at Columbia University. Professor Mishkin was born in New York City in 1951. He received his Ph.D. from the Massachusetts Institute of Technology in 1976 and has taught at the University of Chicago, Northwestern University, Princeton University, and Columbia University. He has served as an executive vice-president and director of research at the Federal Reserve Bank of New York.*

Professor Mishkin's research focuses on monetary policy and its impact on financial markets and the aggregate economy.

Frederic S. Mishkin

Michael Parkin talked with Professor Mishkin about his work, the role the Fed plays in monetary policy, and the legacy of Irving Fisher.

Why are you an economist?

The Great Depression was the most important event in my father's life, and we talked about it continually at the dinner table. We also talked about the stock market. These discussions piqued my interest in economics. When I went to college, I thought of becoming a physicist, but I realized that economics has many of same attributes. Both disciplines demand thinking logically and are consistently based on models. The real-world problems that were implicit in the study of economics proved much more interesting to me then. I realized that economics was my calling, and in fact, it was one of the best choices I've ever made.

What are the most basic principles that you find yourself repeatedly returning to in your professional life, and especially in your life as the director of research at the New York Fed?

A key principle is that incentives are everything. Particularly in today's world, where you need creativity, you cannot motivate people to do good research by just commanding them. You instead need to motivate them by saying, "Do your own work, figure it out yourself, but, on the other hand, I'm going to give you the right incentives." A second principle is the concept of backward induction. If you think about where you want to be and work backwards, you are frequently way ahead of the game. Not only are these two concepts extremely useful in thinking about real-world economic problems, they were absolutely invaluable to me when I managed the New York Fed's research group

> *A key principle is that incentives are everything.*

of 150 people. We had an annual evaluation process followed by a salary review, and promotions were determined by how well people were doing and how well they responded to incentives.

Does the work of Federal Reserve banks directly contribute to the quality of the monetary policy that is developed?

In economics we never really have answers, but we are able to understand things better through research that initiates debate and makes good policy outcomes more likely. Many of the new ideas that are published in the academic journals have helped to guide policy makers. I stressed the value of basic research when I was research director at the Federal Reserve Bank of New York and emphasized our need to be at the very frontier of ideas. We also had to make decisions from day to day that involved much more nitty-gritty research. For example, we had to forecast the economy and tried to understand what was going on in the inflation process.

We have enjoyed the longest uninterrupted expansion in U.S. economic history, the 2001 recession was the mildest on record, and there is little sign of serious inflation on the horizon. To what do you attribute this successful run? What part do you think the Fed can take credit for, and where else would you allocate credit, if anywhere?

There's a fair amount of credit due to the Fed, but I'm going to use an adage that my mother always said to me, "It's better to be lucky than good, but it's even better to be good and lucky." The Fed has been both good and lucky. The "good" part is that the Fed has acted in accordance with the results of economic research that indicates that good monetary policy is forward looking. There are lags from monetary policy to inflation on the order of two to three years. This indicates that monetary policy actions today have little effect on today's inflation but are highly relevant to what will happen to future inflation. The Fed must look to the future if it is to promote a stable economic environment in which we have very low inflation. In February 1994, when the Fed started to raise interest rates, unemployment was close to the 7 percent range and inflation pressures were nonexistent. Yet, looking several years down the road, the Fed realized that if it did not start to raise interest rates and tighten monetary policy, then we would eventually have an overheated economy with inflation out of control. The preemptive policy of raising interest rates was extremely successful because it helped the inflation rate to stay very low, and the economy continued to grow at a sustainable pace. Similarly, the Fed began to lower interest rates early in 2000 when there were suspicions that the economy might weaken, even though it was not clear at the time that the economy had entered a recession. Another benefit of pursuing a preemptive policy is that markets and businesses understand that the central bank will be serious about controlling inflation. That produces a much more stable environment because businesses

> *Monetary policy actions today have little effect on today's inflation but are highly relevant to what will happen to future inflation.*

know they can't solve their problems by just raising prices. Instead, they have to be efficient and keep costs low. The Fed has also been "lucky." Even if the Fed did the right thing during the business cycle expansion, there still was a possibility that the economy would overheat a little bit and a little bit of inflation would occur. Luckily, this never happened.

The traditional categories for discussing policy involve terms such as *rules*, *discretion*, and *fixed rules* versus *feedback rules*. Is that language of use in thinking about Fed policy?

I think that there's a problem with the dichotomy between rules and discretion. One part of the literature views rules as being critical to solving problems such as time inconsistency. Trying to do what looks good right now but not worrying about the future may result in a sequence of policies that lead to poor outcomes in the long run. You have to avoid the temptation to do what looks like the right thing today and ignore the long run. That's one of the reasons why people feel that rules are important. On the other hand, the criticism of rules is that they are too rigid, particularly for dealing with unexpected events. Rules can, in that situation, lead to a very bad outcome. An alternative is to pursue a policy that is basically constrained discretion. It's rulelike, but without a rigid rule. For example, inflation-targeting regimes that have been pursued in many countries throughout the world in recent years are neither a rule nor discretion. They are, instead, constrained discretion. My view is that a good monetary policy should always be rulelike; but, on the other hand, the idea of putting in fixed rules is probably not a good idea.

For the past 15 years the real business cycle research agenda has downplayed the role of money. How do you evaluate the recent real business cycle research program?

The real business cycle literature takes the view that monetary policy is not important to the actual short-term business cycle. I think that monetary policy is more important to the business cycle than real business cycle models give credit for. There is evidence that monetary policy has been important. For example, during the early 1980s, the Federal Reserve took very active steps to get inflation under control and the result was a quite severe recession, but eventually the tight monetary policy produced the right outcome, which was low inflation. I would also characterize the Great Depression as a period where monetary policy performed very poorly and contributed to the most severe economic contraction in U.S. history. I think monetary policy actions were extremely important during that episode and extremely important during the period 1980 to 1982. On the other hand, real business cycle literature points out that the degree of control that monetary policy authorities can exert on the business cycle is indeed limited, and I am quite sympathetic to this view. The idea that the monetary authorities are able to tweak the business cycle at every turn is just not correct because the actual degree of certainty as to what will happen as a result of certain monetary policy actions is by no means clear. The real business cycle literature has made people aware that monetary policy cannot be fully in control of what happens in the business cycle. On the other hand, I think that it's overstretching to say that monetary policy actions don't have real effects.

How can students help themselves to be more able to address interesting, real problems?

It is critical to get students to apply what they learn in class to their everyday lives. I tell my students that they must be reading newspapers such as *The Wall Street Journal, The Financial Times,* or *The New York Times* for business and financial news. I also tell students that they actually can use economic principles such as adverse selection and moral hazard to solve real-world problems every day. For example, if somebody's a rich person and is thinking about getting married, he or she faces an adverse selection problem: Does the other person love me because I'm wealthy rather than because I'm a lovable person?

In addition to having managed the research group, I participated in the management committee of the bank. I was able to actively contribute to the management of the bank because I could use economic principles to discuss what I thought would be sensible solutions to problems. Economics is wonderful training for being able to solve many problems that hit you every day.

What, for you, is the legacy of Irving Fisher?

Irving Fisher is one of the extraordinary American economists. He's famous for the quantity theory of money, which is extremely useful in thinking about the importance of money to the economy. He was a pioneer whose work on interest rates is still valuable today in thinking about how to conduct monetary policy. He also did path-breaking work for which he was not famous. For example, his paper "The Debt Deflation Theory of the Great Depression" has led to a much better understanding of financial crises in today's world.

What can an undergraduate gain from taking an economics course?

Economics is an important part of a liberal arts education and is essential for law and MBA students. When I was manager of the research group, one of the things that was really striking was how useful economic concepts were in helping me to be effective. I could go back to my MBA students and show them that many of these concepts were ones that I actually used in practice to make me a better manager.

Economics is not only useful in helping people become professionals, but also extremely useful in terms of making them better educated citizens. Yes, I do want to train people to help them be successful directly in their careers, but I also want to make them more successful, generally, as people. I think economics is a very powerful tool in achieving that.

TRADING WITH
THE WORLD

Silk Routes and Sucking Sounds

Since ancient times, people have expanded their trading as far as technology allowed. Marco Polo opened up the silk route between Europe and China in the thirteenth century. Today, container ships laden with cars and electronics and Boeing 747s stuffed with farm-fresh foods ply sea and air routes, carrying billions of dollars worth of goods. Why do people go to such great lengths to trade with those in other nations? ◆ In 1994, the United States entered into a free trade agreement with Canada and Mexico — the North American Free Trade Agreement, or NAFTA. Some people predicted a "giant sucking sound" as jobs were transferred from high-wage Michigan to low-wage Mexico. Can we compete with a country that pays its workers a fraction of U.S. wages? Are there any industries, besides perhaps the Hollywood movie industry, in which we have an advantage? ◆ The United States imports lumber from Canada for homebuilding. But U.S. lumber producers say that Canadian producers receive an unfair subsidy from their government, so the United States has imposed a tariff on Canadian lumber imports. Do tariffs benefit the importing country?

◈ In this chapter, we're going to learn about international trade and discover how *all* nations can gain from trading with other nations. We'll discover that all nations can compete, no matter how high their wages. We'll also explain why, despite the fact that international trade brings benefits to all, governments restrict trade.

After studying this chapter, you will be able to

- ■ **Describe the trends and patterns in international trade**

- ■ **Explain comparative advantage and explain why all countries can gain from international trade**

- ■ **Explain why international trade restrictions reduce the volume of imports and exports and reduce our consumption possibilities**

- ■ **Explain the arguments that are used to justify international trade restrictions and show how they are flawed**

- ■ **Explain why we have international trade restrictions**

Patterns and Trends in International Trade

THE GOODS AND SERVICES THAT WE BUY FROM people in other countries are called **imports**. The goods and services that we sell to people in other countries are called **exports**. What are the most important things that we import and export? Most people would probably guess that a rich nation such as the United States imports raw materials and exports manufactured goods. Although that is one feature of U.S. international trade, it is not its most important feature. The vast bulk of our exports *and* imports is manufactured goods. We sell foreigners earth-moving equipment, airplanes, supercomputers, and scientific equipment, and we buy televisions, VCRs, blue jeans, and T-shirts from them. Also, we are a major exporter of agricultural products and raw materials. We also import and export a huge volume of services.

Trade in Goods

Manufactured goods account for 50 percent of our exports and 60 percent of our imports. Industrial materials (raw materials and semimanufactured items) account for 17 percent of our exports and for 20 percent of our imports, and agricultural products account for only 7 percent of our exports and 3 percent of our imports. Our largest individual export and import items are capital goods and automobiles.

But goods account for only 74 percent of our exports and 83 percent of our imports. The rest of our international trade is in services.

Trade in Services

You may be wondering how a country can "export" and "import" services. Here are some examples.

If you take a vacation in France and travel there on an Air France flight from New York, you import transportation services from France. The money you spend in France on hotel bills and restaurant meals is also classified as the import of services. Similarly, the money spent by a French student on vacation in the United States is a U.S. export of services to France.

When we import TV sets from South Korea, the owner of the ship that transports them might be Greek and the company that insures them might be British.

The payments that we make for the transportation and insurance are imports of services. Similarly, when an American shipping company transports California wine to Tokyo, the transportation cost is an export of a service to Japan. Our international trade in these types of services is large and growing.

Geographical Patterns of International Trade

The United States has trading links with every part of the world, but Canada is our biggest trading partner. In 2001, 21 percent of our exports went to Canada and 18 percent of our imports came from Canada. Japan is our second biggest trading partner, accounting for 10 percent of exports and 14 percent of imports in 2000. The regions in which our trade is largest are the European Union — 36 percent of our exports and 32 percent of our imports in 2001 — and Latin America — 28 percent of exports and 22 percent of imports in 2001.

Trends in the Volume of Trade

In 1960, we exported less than 5 percent of total output and imported 4 1/2 percent of the goods and services that we bought. In 2001, we exported 11 percent of total output and imported 15 percent of the goods and services that we bought.

On the export side, capital goods, automobiles, food, and raw materials have remained large items and held a roughly constant share of total exports. But the composition of imports has changed. Food and raw material imports have fallen steadily. Imports of fuel increased dramatically during the 1970s but fell during the 1980s. Imports of machinery have grown and today approach 50 percent of total imports.

Net Exports and International Borrowing

The value of exports minus the value of imports is called **net exports**. In 2001, U.S. net exports were a negative $348 billion. Our imports were $348 billion more than our exports. When we import more than we export, as we did in 2001, we borrow from foreigners or sell some of our assets to them. When we export more than we import, we make loans to foreigners or buy some of their assets.

The Gains from International Trade

THE FUNDAMENTAL FORCE THAT GENERATES international trade is *comparative advantage*. And the basis of comparative advantage is divergent *opportunity costs*. You met these ideas in Chapter 2 (pp. 40–43), when we learned about the gains from specialization and exchange between Tom and Nancy.

Tom and Nancy each specialize in producing just one good and then trade with each other. Most nations do not go to the extreme of specializing in a single good and importing everything else. But nations can increase the consumption of all goods if they redirect their scarce resources toward the production of those goods and services in which they have a comparative advantage.

To see how this outcome occurs, we'll apply the same basic ideas that we learned in the case of Tom and Nancy to trade among nations. We'll begin by recalling how we can use the production possibilities frontier to measure opportunity cost. Then we'll see how divergent opportunity costs bring comparative advantage and gains from trade for countries as well as for individuals even though no country completely specializes in the production of just one good.

Opportunity Cost in Farmland

Farmland (a fictitious country) can produce grain and cars at any point inside or along its production possibilities frontier, *PPF*, shown in Fig. 32.1. (We're holding constant the output of all the other goods that Farmland produces.) The Farmers (the people of Farmland) are consuming all the grain and cars that they produce, and they are operating at point *A* in the figure. That is, Farmland is producing and consuming 15 billion bushels of grain and 8 million cars each year. What is the opportunity cost of a car in Farmland?

We can answer that question by calculating the slope of the production possibilities frontier at point *A*. The magnitude of the slope of the frontier measures the opportunity cost of one good in terms of the other. To measure the slope of the frontier at point *A*, place a straight line tangential to the frontier at point *A* and calculate the slope of that straight line. Recall that the formula for the slope of a line is the change in the value of the variable measured on the *y*-axis divided by the change in the value of the variable

measured on the *x*-axis as we move along the line. Here, the variable measured on the *y*-axis is billions of bushels of grain, and the variable measured on the *x*-axis is millions of cars. So the slope is the change in the number of bushels of grain divided by the change in the number of cars.

As you can see from the red triangle at point *A* in Fig. 32.1, if the number of cars produced increases by 2 million, grain production decreases by 18 billion bushels. Therefore the magnitude of the slope is 18 billion divided by 2 million, which equals 9,000. To get one more car, the people of Farmland must give up 9,000 bushels of grain. So the opportunity cost of 1 car is 9,000 bushels of grain. Equivalently, 9,000 bushels of grain cost 1 car. For the people of Farmland, these opportunity costs are the prices they face. The price of a car is 9,000 bushels of grain, and the price of 9,000 bushels of grain is 1 car.

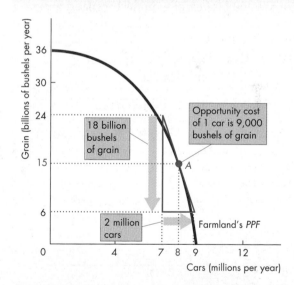

FIGURE 32.1   Opportunity Cost in Farmland

Farmland produces and consumes 15 billion bushels of grain and 8 million cars a year. That is, it produces and consumes at point A on its production possibilities frontier. Opportunity cost is equal to the magnitude of the slope of the production possibilities frontier. The red triangle tells us that at point A, 18 billion bushels of grain must be forgone to get 2 million cars. That is, at point A, 2 million cars cost 18 billion bushels of grain. Equivalently, 1 car costs 9,000 bushels of grain or 9,000 bushels cost 1 car.

Opportunity Cost in Mobilia

Figure 32.2 shows the production possibilities frontier of Mobilia (another fictitious country). Like the Farmers, the Mobilians consume all the grain and cars that they produce. Mobilia consumes 18 billion bushels of grain a year and 4 million cars, at point A'.

Let's calculate the opportunity costs in Mobilia. At point A', the opportunity cost of a car is equal to the magnitude of the slope of the red line tangential to Mobilia's *PPF*. You can see from the red triangle that the magnitude of the slope of Mobilia's *PPF* is 6 billion bushels of grain divided by 6 million cars, which equals 1,000 bushels of grain per car. To get one more car, the Mobilians must give up 1,000 bushels of grain. So the opportunity cost of 1 car is 1,000 bushels of grain, or equivalently, the opportunity cost of 1,000 bushels of grain is 1 car. These are the prices faced in Mobilia.

Comparative Advantage

Cars are cheaper in Mobilia than in Farmland. One car costs 9,000 bushels of grain in Farmland but only 1,000 bushels of grain in Mobilia. But grain is

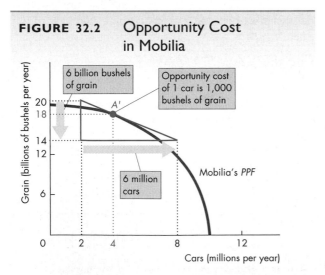

FIGURE 32.2   Opportunity Cost in Mobilia

Mobilia produces and consumes 18 billion bushels of grain and 4 million cars a year at point A' on its production possibilities frontier. Opportunity cost is equal to the magnitude of the slope of the production possibilities frontier. The red triangle tells us that at point A', 6 billion bushels of grain must be forgone to get 6 million cars. That is, at point A', 6 million cars cost 6 billion bushels of grain. Equivalently, 1 car costs 1,000 bushels of grain or 1,000 bushels cost 1 car.

cheaper in Farmland than in Mobilia — 9,000 bushels of grain cost only 1 car in Farmland, while that same amount of grain costs 9 cars in Mobilia.

Mobilia has a comparative advantage in car production. Farmland has a comparative advantage in grain production. A country has a **comparative advantage** in producing a good if it can produce that good at a lower opportunity cost than any other country. Let's see how opportunity cost differences and comparative advantage generate gains from international trade.

The Gains from Trade: Cheaper to Buy Than to Produce

If Mobilia bought grain for what it costs Farmland to produce it, then Mobilia could buy 9,000 bushels of grain for 1 car. That is much lower than the cost of growing grain in Mobilia, for there it costs 9 cars to produce 9,000 bushels of grain. If the Mobilians can buy grain at the low Farmland price, they will reap some gains.

If the Farmers can buy cars for what it costs Mobilia to produce them, they will be able to obtain a car for 1,000 bushels of grain. Because it costs 9,000 bushels of grain to produce a car in Farmland, the Farmers would gain from such an opportunity.

In this situation, it makes sense for Mobilians to buy their grain from Farmers and for Farmers to buy their cars from Mobilians. But at what price will Farmland and Mobilia engage in mutually beneficial international trade?

The Terms of Trade

The quantity of grain that Farmland must pay Mobilia for a car is Farmland's **terms of trade** with Mobilia. Because the United States exports and imports many different goods and services, we measure the terms of trade in the real world as an index number that averages the terms of trade over all the items we trade.

The forces of international supply and demand determine the terms of trade. Figure 32.3 illustrates these forces in the Farmland-Mobilia international car market. The quantity of cars *traded internationally* is measured on the *x*-axis. On the *y*-axis, we measure the price of a car. This price is expressed as the *terms of trade*: bushels of grain per car. If no international trade takes place, the price of a car in

FIGURE 32.3   International Trade in Cars

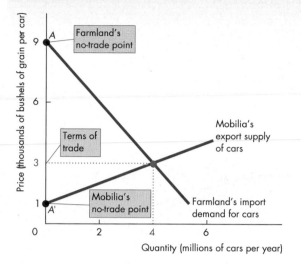

Farmland's import demand curve for cars is downward sloping, and Mobilia's export supply curve of cars is upward sloping. With no international trade, the price of a car is 9,000 bushels of grain in Farmland (point A) and 1,000 bushels of grain in Mobilia (point A'). With free international trade, the price (terms of trade) is determined where the export supply curve intersects the import demand curve: 3,000 bushels of grain per car. At that price, 4 million cars a year are imported by Farmland and exported by Mobilia. The value of grain exported by Farmland and imported by Mobilia is 12 billion bushels a year, the quantity required to pay for the cars imported.

The international market in cars determines the equilibrium terms of trade (price) and quantity traded. This equilibrium occurs where the import demand curve intersects the export supply curve. In this case, the equilibrium terms of trade are 3,000 bushels of grain per car. Mobilia exports and Farmland imports 4 million cars a year. Notice that the terms of trade are lower than the initial price in Farmland but higher than the initial price in Mobilia.

Balanced Trade

The number of cars exported by Mobilia — 4 million a year — is exactly equal to the number of cars imported by Farmland. How does Farmland pay for its cars? The answer is by exporting grain. How much grain does Farmland export? You can find the answer by noticing that for 1 car, Farmland must pay 3,000 bushels of grain. So for 4 million cars, Farmland pays 12 billion bushels of grain. Farmland's exports of grain are 12 billion bushels a year, and Mobilia imports this same quantity of grain.

Mobilia exchanges 4 million cars for 12 billion bushels of grain each year, and Farmland exchanges 12 billion bushels of grain for 4 million cars. Trade is balanced. For each country, the value received from exports equals the value paid out for imports.

Changes in Production and Consumption

We've seen that international trade makes it possible for Farmers to buy cars at a lower price than they can produce them and sell their grain for a higher price. International trade also enables Mobilians to sell their cars for a higher price and buy grain for a lower price. Everyone gains. How is it possible for *everyone* to gain? What are the changes in production and consumption that accompany these gains?

An economy that does not trade with other economies has identical production and consumption possibilities. Without trade, the economy can consume only what it produces. But with international trade, an economy can consume different quantities of goods from those that it produces. The production possibilities frontier describes the limit of what a country can produce, but it does not describe the limits to what it can consume. Figure 32.4 will help you to see the distinction between production possibilities and consumption possibilities when a country trades with other countries.

Farmland is 9,000 bushels of grain, its opportunity cost, indicated by point A in the figure. Again, if no trade takes place, the price of a car in Mobilia is 1,000 bushels of grain, its opportunity cost, indicated by point A' in the figure. The no-trade points A and A' in Fig. 32.3 correspond to the points identified by those same letters in Figs. 32.1 and 32.2. The lower the price of a car (terms of trade), the greater is the quantity of cars that the Farmers are willing to import from the Mobilians. This fact is illustrated by the downward-sloping curve, which shows Farmland's import demand for cars.

The Mobilians respond in the opposite direction. The higher the price of a car, the greater is the quantity of cars that Mobilians are willing to export to Farmers. This fact is reflected in Mobilia's export supply of cars — the upward-sloping line in Fig. 32.3.

FIGURE 32.4   Expanding Consumption Possibilities

(a) Farmland

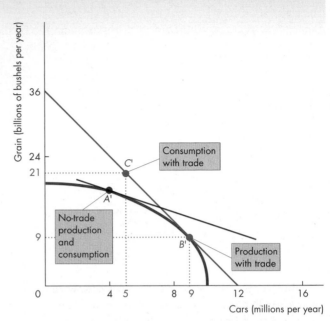

(b) Mobilia

With no international trade, the Farmers produce and consume at point A and the opportunity cost of a car is 9,000 bushels of grain (the slope of the black line in part a). Also, with no international trade, the Mobilians produce and consume at point A' and the opportunity cost of 1,000 bushels of grain is 1 car (the slope of the black line in part b). Goods can be exchanged internationally at a price of 3,000 bushels of grain for 1 car along the red line in each part of the figure. In part (a), Farmland decreases its production of cars and increases its production of grain, moving from A to B. It

exports grain and imports cars, and it consumes at point C. The Farmers have more of both cars and grain than they would if they produced all their own consumption goods — at point A. In part (b), Mobilia increases car production and decreases grain production, moving from A' to B'. Mobilia exports cars and imports grain, and it consumes at point C'. The Mobilians have more of both cars and grain than they would if they produced all their own consumption goods — at point A'.

First of all, notice that the figure has two parts: part (a) for Farmland and part (b) for Mobilia. The production possibilities frontiers that you saw in Figs. 32.1 and 32.2 are reproduced here. The slopes of the two black lines in the figure represent the opportunity costs in the two countries when there is no international trade. Farmland produces and consumes at point A, and Mobilia produces and consumes at A'. Cars cost 9,000 bushels of grain in Farmland and 1,000 bushels of grain in Mobilia.

Consumption Possibilities The red line in each part of Fig. 32.4 shows the country's consumption possibilities with international trade. These two red

lines have the same slope, and the magnitude of that slope is the opportunity cost of a car in terms of grain on the world market: 3,000 bushels per car. The *slope* of the consumption possibilities line is common to both countries because its magnitude equals the *world* price. But the position of a country's consumption possibilities line depends on the country's production possibilities. A country cannot produce outside its production possibilities curve, so its consumption possibilities curve touches its production possibilities curve. So Farmland could choose to consume at point B with no international trade or, with international trade, at any point on its red consumption possibilities line.

Free Trade Equilibrium With international trade, the producers of cars in Mobilia can get a higher price for their output. As a result, they increase the quantity of car production. At the same time, grain producers in Mobilia get a lower price for their grain, and so they reduce production. Producers in Mobilia adjust their output by moving along their production possibilities frontier until the opportunity cost in Mobilia equals the world price (the opportunity cost in the world market). This situation arises when Mobilia is producing at point *B'* in Fig. 32.4(b).

But the Mobilians do not consume at point *B'*. That is, they do not increase their consumption of cars and decrease their consumption of grain. Instead, they sell some of their car production to Farmland in exchange for some of Farmland's grain. They trade internationally. But to see how that works out, we first need to check in with Farmland to see what's happening there.

In Farmland, producers of cars now get a lower price and producers of grain get a higher price. As a consequence, producers in Farmland decrease car production and increase grain production. They adjust their outputs by moving along the production possibilities frontier until the opportunity cost of a car in terms of grain equals the world price (the opportunity cost on the world market). They move to point *B* in part (a). But the Farmers do not consume at point *B*. Instead, they trade some of their additional grain production for the now cheaper cars from Mobilia.

The figure shows us the quantities consumed in the two countries. We saw in Fig. 32.3 that Mobilia exports 4 million cars a year and Farmland imports those cars. We also saw that Farmland exports 12 billion bushels of grain a year and Mobilia imports that grain. So Farmland's consumption of grain is 12 billion bushels a year less than it produces, and its consumption of cars is 4 million a year more than it produces. Farmland consumes at point *C* in Fig. 32.4(a).

Similarly, we know that Mobilia consumes 12 billion bushels of grain more than it produces and 4 million cars fewer than it produces. Mobilia consumes at point *C'* in Fig. 32.4(b).

Calculating the Gains from Trade

You can now literally see the gains from trade in Fig. 32.4. Without trade, Farmers produce and consume at *A* (part a) — a point on Farmland's production possibilities frontier. With international trade, Farmers consume at point *C* in part (a) — a point *outside* the production possibilities frontier. At point *C*, Farmers are consuming 3 billion bushels of grain a year and 1 million cars a year more than before. These increases in consumption of both cars and grain, beyond the limits of the production possibilities frontier, are the Farmers' gains from international trade.

Mobilians also gain. Without trade, they consume at point *A'* in part (b) — a point on Mobilia's production possibilities frontier. With international trade, they consume at point *C'* — a point outside their production possibilities frontier. With international trade, Mobilia consumes 3 billion bushels of grain a year and 1 million cars a year more than they would without trade. These are the gains from international trade for Mobilia.

Gains for All

Trade between the Farmers and the Mobilians does not create winners and losers. It creates only winners. Farmers selling grain and Mobilians selling cars face an increased demand for their products because the net demand by foreigners is added to domestic demand. With an increase in demand, the price rises.

Farmers buying cars and Mobilians buying grain face an increased supply of these products because the net foreign supply is added to domestic supply. With an increase in supply, the price falls.

Gains from Trade in Reality

The gains from trade that we have just studied between Farmland and Mobilia in grain and cars occur in a model economy — in a world economy that we have imagined. But these same phenomena occur every day in the real global economy.

Comparative Advantage in the Global Economy
We buy TVs and VCRs from Korea, machinery from Europe, and fashion goods from Hong Kong. In exchange, we sell machinery, grain and lumber, airplanes, computers and financial services. All this international trade is generated by comparative advantage, just like the international trade between Farmland and Mobilia in our model economy. All international trade arises from comparative advantage, even when trade is in similar goods such as tools and machines. At first thought, it seems puzzling that countries exchange manufactured goods. Why doesn't each developed country produce all the manufactured goods its citizens want to buy?

Trade in Similar Goods Why does the United States produce automobiles for export and at the same time import large quantities of automobiles from Canada, Japan, Korea, and Western Europe? Wouldn't it make more sense to produce all the cars that we buy here in the United States? After all, we have access to the best technology available for producing cars. Autoworkers in the United States are surely as productive as their fellow workers in Canada, Western Europe, and Asian countries. So why does the United States have a comparative advantage in some types of cars and Japan and Europe in others?

Diversity of Taste and Economies of Scale The first part of the answer is that people have a tremendous diversity of taste. Let's stick with the example of cars. Some people prefer a sports car, some prefer a limousine, some prefer a regular, full-size car, some prefer a sport utility vehicle, and some prefer a mini-van. In addition to size and type of car, there are many other dimensions in which cars vary. Some have low fuel consumption, some have high performance, some are spacious and comfortable, some have a large trunk, some have four-wheel drive, some have front-wheel drive, some have a radiator grill that looks like a Greek temple, others resemble a wedge. People's preferences across these many dimensions vary. The tremendous diversity in tastes for cars means that people value variety and are willing to pay for it in the marketplace.

The second part of the answer to the puzzle is *economies of scale* — the tendency for the average cost to be lower, the larger the scale of production. In such situations, larger and larger production runs lead to ever lower average costs. Production of many goods, including cars, involves economies of scale. For example, if a car producer makes only a few hundred (or perhaps a few thousand) cars of a particular type and design, the producer must use production techniques that are much more labor-intensive and much less automated than those employed to make hundreds of thousands of cars in a particular model. With short production runs and labor-intensive production techniques, costs are high. With very large production runs and automated assembly lines, production costs are much lower. But to obtain lower costs, the automated assembly lines have to produce a large number of cars.

It is the combination of diversity of taste and economies of scale that determines opportunity cost, produces comparative advantages, and generates such

a large amount of international trade in similar commodities. With international trade, each car manufacturer has the whole world market to serve. Each producer can specialize in a limited range of products and then sell its output to the entire world market. This arrangement enables large production runs on the most popular cars and feasible production runs even on the most customized cars demanded by only a handful of people in each country.

The situation in the market for cars is also present in many other industries, especially those producing specialized equipment and parts. For example, the United States exports computer central processor chips but imports memory chips, exports mainframe computers but imports PCs, exports specialized video equipment but imports VCRs. International trade in similar but slightly different manufactured products is profitable.

REVIEW QUIZ

1 What is the fundamental source of the gains from international trade?
2 In what circumstances can countries gain from international trade?
3 What determines the goods and services that a country will export?
4 What determines the goods and services that a country will import?
5 What is a comparative advantage and what role does it play in determining the amount and type of international trade that occurs?
6 How can it be that all countries gain from international trade and that there are no losers?
7 Provide some examples of comparative advantage in today's world.
8 Why does the United States both export and import automobiles?

You've now seen how free international trade brings gains for all. But trade is not free in our world. We'll now take a brief look at the history of international trade restrictions and also work out the effects of international trade restrictions. We'll see that free trade brings the greatest possible benefits and that international trade restrictions are costly.

International Trade Restrictions

GOVERNMENTS RESTRICT INTERNATIONAL TRADE to protect domestic industries from foreign competition by using two main tools:

1. Tariffs
2. Nontariff barriers

A **tariff** is a tax that is imposed by the importing country when an imported good crosses its international boundary. A **nontariff barrier** is any action other than a tariff that restricts international trade. Examples of nontariff barriers are quantitative restrictions and licensing regulations limiting imports. First, let's look at tariffs.

The History of Tariffs

U.S. tariffs today are modest in comparison with their historical levels. Figure 32.5 shows the average tariff rate — total tariffs as a percentage of total imports. You can see in this figure that this average

reached a peak of 20 percent in 1933. In that year, three years after the passage of the Smoot-Hawley Act, one third of our imports was subject to a tariff and on those imports the tariff rate was 60 percent. The average tariff in Fig. 32.5 for 1933 is 60 percent multiplied by 0.33, which equals 20 percent. Today, the average tariff rate is about 4 percent.

The reduction in tariffs after World War II followed the signing in 1947 of the **General Agreement on Tariffs and Trade** (GATT). From its formation, GATT organized a series of "rounds" of negotiations that resulted in a steady process of tariff reduction. One of these, the Kennedy Round that began in the early 1960s, resulted in large tariff cuts starting in 1967. Another, the Tokyo Round, resulted in further tariff cuts in 1979. The final round, the Uruguay Round, started in 1986 and was completed in 1994.

The Uruguay Round was the most ambitious and comprehensive of the rounds and led to the creation of the **World Trade Organization** (WTO). Membership of the WTO brings greater obligations for countries to observe the GATT rules. The United States signed the Uruguay Round agreements, and Congress ratified them in 1994.

FIGURE 32.5   U.S. Tariffs: 1930–2000

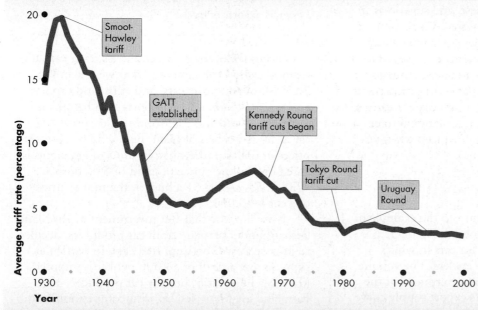

The Smoot-Hawley Act, which was passed in 1930, took U.S. tariffs to a peak average rate of 20 percent in 1933. (One third of imports was subject to a tariff rate of 60 percent.) Since the establishment of GATT in 1947, tariffs have steadily declined in a series of negotiating rounds, the most significant of which are identified in the figure. Tariffs are now as low as they have ever been.

Sources: U.S. Bureau of the Census, *Historical Statistics of the United States, Colonial Times to 1970,* Bicentennial Edition, Part 1 (Washington, D.C., 1975); Series U-212: updated from *Statistical Abstract of the United States:* various editions.

In addition to the agreements under the GATT and the WTO, the United States is a party to the **North American Free Trade Agreement** (NAFTA), which became effective on January 1, 1994, and under which barriers to international trade between the United States, Canada, and Mexico will be virtually eliminated after a 15-year phasing-in period.

In other parts of the world, trade barriers have virtually been eliminated among the member countries of the European Union, which has created the largest unified tariff-free market in the world. In 1994, discussions among the Asia-Pacific Economic group (APEC) led to an agreement in principle to work toward a free-trade area that embraces China, all the economies of East Asia and the South Pacific, Chile, Peru, Mexico, and the United States and Canada. These countries include the fastest-growing economies and hold the promise of heralding a global free-trade area.

The effort to achieve freer trade underlines the fact that trade in some goods is still subject to a high tariff. Textiles and footwear are among the goods that face the highest tariffs, and rates on these items average more than 10 percent. Some individual items face a tariff much higher than the average. For example, when you buy a pair of blue jeans for $20, you pay about $5 more than you would if there were no tariffs on textiles. Other goods that are protected by tariffs are agricultural products, energy and chemicals, minerals, and metals. The meat, cheese, and sugar that you consume cost significantly more because of protection than they would with free international trade.

The temptation for governments to impose tariffs is a strong one. First, tariffs provide revenue to the government. Second, they enable the government to satisfy special interest groups in import-competing industries. But, as we'll see, free international trade brings enormous benefits that are reduced when tariffs are imposed. Let's see how.

How Tariffs Work

To see how tariffs work, let's return to the example of trade between Farmland and Mobilia. Figure 32.6 shows the international market for cars in which these two countries are the only traders. The volume of trade and the price of a car are determined at the point of intersection of Mobilia's export supply curve of cars and Farmland's import demand curve for cars.

FIGURE 32.6   The Effects of a Tariff

Farmland imposes a tariff on car imports from Mobilia. The tariff increases the price that Farmers have to pay for a car. It shifts the supply curve of cars in Farmland leftward. The vertical distance between the original supply curve and the new one is the amount of the tariff, $4,000 per car. The price of a car in Farmland increases, and the quantity of cars imported decreases. The government of Farmland collects a tariff revenue of $4,000 per car — a total of $8 billion on the 2 million cars imported. Farmland's exports of grain decrease because Mobilia now has a lower income from its exports of cars.

In Fig. 32.6, these two countries trade cars and grain in exactly the same way that we saw in Fig. 32.3. Mobilia exports cars, and Farmland exports grain. The volume of car imports into Farmland is 4 million a year, and the world market price of a car is 3,000 bushels of grain. Figure 32.6 expresses prices in dollars rather than in units of grain and is based on a money price of grain of $1 a bushel. With grain costing $1 a bushel, the money price of a car is $3,000.

Now suppose that the government of Farmland, perhaps under pressure from car producers, decides to impose a tariff on imported cars. In particular, suppose that a tariff of $4,000 per car is imposed. (This is a huge tariff, but the car producers of Farmland are pretty fed up with competition from Mobilia.) What happens?

- The supply of cars in Farmland decreases.
- The price of cars in Farmland rises.
- The quantity of cars imported by Farmland decreases.
- The government of Farmland collects the tariff revenue.
- Resource use is inefficient.
- The *value* of exports changes by the same amount as the *value* of imports, and trade remains balanced.

Change in the Supply of Cars Farmland cannot buy cars at Mobilia's export supply price. It must pay that price plus the $4,000 tariff. So the supply curve in Farmland shifts leftward. The new supply curve is that labeled "Mobilia's export supply of cars plus tariff." The vertical distance between Mobilia's original export supply curve and the new supply curve is the tariff of $4,000 a car.

Rise in Price of Cars A new equilibrium occurs where the new supply curve intersects Farmland's import demand curve for cars. That equilibrium is at a price of $6,000 a car, up from $3,000 with free trade.

Fall in Imports Car imports fall from 4 million to 2 million cars a year. At the higher price of $6,000 a car, domestic car producers increase their production. Domestic grain production decreases as resources are moved into the expanding car industry.

Tariff Revenue Total expenditure on imported cars by the Farmers is $6,000 a car multiplied by the 2 million cars imported ($12 billion). But not all of that money goes to the Mobilians. They receive $2,000 a car, or $4 billion for the 2 million cars. The difference — $4,000 a car, or a total of $8 billion for the 2 million cars — is collected by the government of Farmland as tariff revenue.

Inefficiency The people of Farmland are willing to pay $6,000 for the marginal car imported. But the opportunity cost of that car is $2,000. So there is a gain from trading an extra car. In fact, there are gains — willingness to pay exceeds opportunity cost — all the way up to 4 million cars a year. Only when 4 million cars are being traded is the maximum price that a Farmer is willing to pay equal to the minimum price that is acceptable to a Mobilian. Restricting trade reduces the gains from trade.

Trade Remains Balanced With free trade, Farmland was paying $3,000 a car and buying 4 million cars a year from Mobilia. The total amount paid to Mobilia for imports was $12 billion a year. With a tariff, Farmland's imports have been cut to 2 million cars a year and the price paid to Mobilia has also been cut to only $2,000 a car. The total amount paid to Mobilia for imports has been cut to $4 billion a year. Doesn't this fact mean that Farmland now has a balance of trade surplus? It does not.

The price of cars in Mobilia has fallen. But the price of grain remains at $1 a bushel. So the relative price of cars has fallen, and the relative price of grain has increased. With free trade, the Mobilians could buy 3,000 bushels of grain for one car. Now they can buy only 2,000 bushels for a car. With a higher relative price of grain, the quantity demanded by the Mobilians decreases and Mobilia imports less grain. But because Mobilia imports less grain, Farmland exports less grain. In fact, Farmland's grain industry suffers from two sources. First, there is a decrease in the quantity of grain sold to Mobilia. Second, there is increased competition for inputs from the now-expanded car industry. The tariff leads to a contraction in the scale of the grain industry in Farmland.

It seems paradoxical at first that a country imposing a tariff on cars hurts its own export industry, lowering its exports of grain. It may help to think of it this way: Mobilians buy grain with the money they make from exporting cars to Farmland. If they export fewer cars, they cannot afford to buy as much grain. In fact, in the absence of any international borrowing and lending, Mobilia must cut its imports of grain by exactly the same amount as the loss in revenue from its export of cars. Grain imports into Mobilia are cut back to a value of $4 billion, the amount that can be paid for by the new lower revenue from Mobilia's car exports. Trade is still balanced. The tariff cuts imports and exports by the same amount. The tariff has no effect on the *balance* of trade, but it reduces the *volume* of trade.

The result that we have just derived is perhaps one of the most misunderstood aspects of international economics. On countless occasions, politicians and others call for tariffs to remove a balance of trade deficit or argue that lowering tariffs would produce a balance of trade deficit. They reach this conclusion by failing to work out all the implications of a tariff.

Let's now look at nontariff barriers.

Nontariff Barriers

The two main forms of nontariff barrier are

1. Quotas
2. Voluntary export restraints

A **quota** is a quantitative restriction on the import of a particular good, which specifies the maximum amount of the good that may be imported in a given period of time. A **voluntary export restraint** (VER) is an agreement between two governments in which the government of the exporting country agrees to restrain the volume of its own exports.

Quotas are especially prominent in textiles and agriculture. Voluntary export restraints are used to regulate trade between Japan and the United States.

How Quotas and VERs Work

To see how a quota works, suppose that Farmland imposes a quota that restricts its car imports to 2 million cars a year. Figure 32.7 shows the effects of this action. The quota is shown by the vertical red line at 2 million cars a year. Because it is illegal to exceed the quota, car importers buy only that quantity from Mobilia, for which they pay $2,000 a car. But because the import supply of cars is restricted to 2 million cars a year, people in Farmland are willing to pay $6,000 per car. This is the price of a car in Farmland.

The value of imports falls to $4 billion, exactly the same as in the case of the tariff. So with lower incomes from car exports and with a higher relative price of grain, Mobilians cut back on their imports of grain in exactly the same way that they did under a tariff.

The key difference between a quota and a tariff lies in who collects the gap between the import supply price and the domestic price. In the case of a tariff, it is the government of the importing country. In the case of a quota, it goes to the person who has the right to import under the import quota regulations.

A voluntary export restraint is like a quota arrangement in which quotas are allocated to each exporting country. The effects of a VER are similar to those of a quota but differ from them in that the gap between the domestic price and the export price is captured not by domestic importers but by the foreign exporter. The government of the exporting country has to establish procedures for allocating the restricted volume of exports among its producers.

FIGURE 32.7   The Effects of a Quota

Farmland imposes a quota of 2 million cars a year on car imports from Mobilia. That quantity appears as the vertical line labeled "Quota." Because the quantity of cars supplied by Mobilia is restricted to 2 million, the price at which those cars will be traded increases to $6,000. Importing cars is profitable because Mobilia is willing to supply cars at $2,000 each. There is competition for import quotas.

REVIEW QUIZ

1 What happens to a country's consumption possibilities when it opens itself up to international trade and trades freely at world market prices?
2 What do international trade restrictions do to the gains from international trade?
3 Which is best for a country: restricted trade, no trade, or free trade? Why?
4 What does a tariff on imports do to the volume of imports and the volume of exports?
5 In the absence of international borrowing and lending, how do tariffs and other international trade restrictions influence the total value of imports and exports and the balance of trade?

We're now going to look at some commonly heard arguments for restricting international trade and see why they are almost never correct.

The Case Against Protection

FOR AS LONG AS NATIONS AND INTERNATIONAL trade have existed, people have debated whether a country is better off with free international trade or with protection from foreign competition. The debate continues, but for most economists, a verdict has been delivered and is the one you have just seen. Free trade promotes prosperity for all; protection is inefficient. We've seen the most powerful case for free trade in the example of how Farmland and Mobilia both benefit from their comparative advantage. But there is a broader range of issues in the free trade versus protection debate. Let's review these issues.

Three arguments for restricting international trade are

- The national security argument
- The infant-industry argument
- The dumping argument

Let's look at each in turn.

The National Security Argument

The national security argument for protection is that a country must protect the industries that produce defense equipment and armaments and those on which the defense industries rely for their raw materials and other intermediate inputs. This argument for protection does not withstand close scrutiny.

First, it is an argument for international isolation, for in a time of war, there is no industry that does not contribute to national defense. Second, if the case is made for boosting the output of a strategic industry, it is more efficient to achieve this outcome with a subsidy to the firms in the industry financed out of taxes. Such a subsidy would keep the industry operating at the scale judged appropriate, and free international trade would keep the prices faced by consumers at their world market levels.

The Infant-Industry Argument

The so-called **infant-industry argument** for protection is that it is necessary to protect a new industry to enable it to grow into a mature industry that can compete in world markets. The argument is based on the idea of *dynamic comparative advantage*, which can arise from *learning-by-doing* (see Chapter 2).

Learning-by-doing is a powerful engine of productivity growth, and comparative advantage does evolve and change because of on-the-job experience. But these facts do not justify protection.

First, the infant-industry argument is valid only if the benefits of learning-by-doing *not only* accrue to the owners and workers of the firms in the infant industry but also *spill over* to other industries and parts of the economy. For example, there are huge productivity gains from learning-by-doing in the manufacture of aircraft. But almost all of these gains benefit the stockholders and workers of Boeing and other aircraft producers. Because the people making the decisions, bearing the risk, and doing the work are the ones who benefit, they take the dynamic gains into account when they decide on the scale of their activities. In this case, almost no benefits spill over to other parts of the economy, so there is no need for government assistance to achieve an efficient outcome.

Second, even if the case is made for protecting an infant industry, it is more efficient to do so by a subsidy to the firms in the industry, with the subsidy financed out of taxes.

The Dumping Argument

Dumping occurs when a foreign firm sells its exports at a lower price than its cost of production. Dumping might be used by a firm that wants to gain a global monopoly. In this case, the foreign firm sells its output at a price below its cost to drive domestic firms out of business. When the domestic firms have gone, the foreign firm takes advantage of its monopoly position and charges a higher price for its product. Dumping is usually regarded as a justification for temporary countervailing tariffs.

But there are powerful reasons to resist the dumping argument for protection. First, it is virtually impossible to detect dumping because it is hard to determine a firm's costs. As a result, the test for dumping is whether a firm's export price is below its domestic price. But this test is a weak one because it can be rational for a firm to charge a low price in markets in which the quantity demanded is highly sensitive to price and a higher price in a market in which demand is less price-sensitive.

Second, it is hard to think of a good that is produced by a natural *global* monopoly. So even if all the domestic firms were driven out of business in some industry, it would always be possible to find several and usually many alternative foreign sources of supply and to buy at prices determined in competitive markets.

Third, if a good or service were a truly global natural monopoly, the best way of dealing with it would be by regulation — just as in the case of domestic monopolies. Such regulation would require international cooperation.

The three arguments for protection that we've just examined have an element of credibility. The counterarguments are in general stronger, however, so these arguments do not make the case for protection. But they are not the only arguments that you might encounter. The many other arguments that are commonly heard are quite simply wrong. They are fatally flawed. The most common of them are that protection:

■ Saves jobs
■ Allows us to compete with cheap foreign labor
■ Brings diversity and stability
■ Penalizes lax environmental standards
■ Protects national culture
■ Prevents rich countries from exploiting developing countries

Saves Jobs

The argument that protection saves jobs goes as follows: When we buy shoes from Brazil or shirts from Taiwan, U.S. workers in these industries lose their jobs. With no earnings and poor prospects, these workers become a drain on welfare and spend less, causing a ripple effect of further job losses. The proposed solution to this problem is to ban imports of cheap foreign goods and protect U.S. jobs. The proposal is flawed for the following reasons.

First, free trade does cost some jobs, but it also creates other jobs. It brings about a global rationalization of labor and allocates labor resources to their highest-valued activities. Because of international trade in textiles, tens of thousands of workers in the United States have lost jobs as textile mills and other factories have closed. But tens of thousands of workers in other countries have gotten jobs because textile mills have opened there. And tens of thousands of U.S. workers have gotten better-paying jobs than textile workers because other export industries have expanded and created more jobs than have been destroyed.

Second, imports create jobs. They create jobs for retailers that sell imported goods and firms that service those goods. They also create jobs by creating incomes in the rest of the world, some of which are spent on imports of U.S.-made goods and services.

Although protection does save particular jobs, it does so at inordinate cost. For example, textile jobs are protected in the United States by quotas imposed under an international agreement called the Multifiber Arrangement. The U.S. International Trade Commission (ITC) has estimated that because of quotas, 72,000 jobs exist in textiles that would otherwise disappear and annual clothing expenditure in the United States is $15.9 billion or $160 per family higher than it would be with free trade. Equivalently, the ITC estimates that each textile job saved costs $221,000 a year.

Allows Us to Compete with Cheap Foreign Labor

With the removal of tariffs in U.S. trade with Mexico, people said we would hear a "giant sucking sound" as jobs rushed to Mexico (shown in the cartoon). Let's see what's wrong with this view.

The labor cost of a unit of output equals the wage rate divided by labor productivity. For example, if a U.S. autoworker earns $30 an hour and produces 15 units of output an hour, the average labor cost of a

"I don't know what the hell happened — one minute I'm at work in Flint, Michigan, then there's a giant sucking sound and suddenly here I am in Mexico."

unit of output is $2. If a Mexican auto assembly worker earns $3 an hour and produces 1 unit of output an hour, the average labor cost of a unit of output is $3. Other things remaining the same, the higher a worker's productivity, the higher is the worker's wage rate. High-wage workers have high productivity. Low-wage workers have low productivity.

Although high-wage U.S. workers are more productive, on the average, than low-wage Mexican workers, there are differences across industries. U.S. labor is relatively more productive in some activities than in others. For example, the productivity of U.S. workers in producing movies, financial services, and customized computer chips is relatively higher than their productivity in the production of metals and some standardized machine parts. The activities in which U.S. workers are relatively more productive than their Mexican counterparts are those in which the United States has a *comparative advantage*. By engaging in free trade, increasing our production and exports of the goods and services in which we have a comparative advantage and decreasing our production and increasing our imports of the goods and services in which our trading partners have a comparative advantage, we can make ourselves and the citizens of other countries better off.

Brings Diversity and Stability

A diversified investment portfolio is less risky than one that has all the eggs in one basket. The same is true for an economy's production. A diversified economy fluctuates less than an economy that produces only one or two goods.

But big, rich, diversified economies such as those of the United States, Japan, and Europe do not have this type of stability problem. Even a country such as Saudi Arabia that produces only one good (in this case, oil) can benefit from specializing in the activity at which it has a comparative advantage and then investing in a wide range of other countries to bring greater stability to its income and consumption.

Penalizes Lax Environmental Standards

Another argument for protection is that many poorer countries, such as Mexico, do not have the same environmental policies that we have and, because they are willing to pollute and we are not, we cannot compete with them without tariffs. So if they want free trade with the richer and "greener" countries, they must clean up their environments to our standards.

This argument for international trade restrictions is weak. First, not all poorer countries have significantly lower environmental standards than the United States has. Many poor countries and the former communist countries of Eastern Europe do have bad environmental records. But some countries enforce strict laws. Second, a poor country cannot afford to be as concerned about its environment as a rich country can. The best hope for a better environment in Mexico and in other developing countries is rapid income growth through free trade. As their incomes grow, developing countries will have the *means* to match their desires to improve their environment. Third, poor countries have a comparative advantage at doing "dirty" work, which helps rich countries achieve higher environmental standards than they otherwise could.

Protects National Culture

The national culture argument for protection is not heard much in the United States, but it is a commonly heard argument in Canada and Europe.

The expressed fear is that free trade in books, magazines, movies, and television programs means U.S. domination and the end of local culture. So, the reasoning continues, it is necessary to protect domestic "culture" industries from free international trade to ensure the survival of a national cultural identity.

Protection of these industries is common and takes the form of nontariff barriers. For example, local content regulations on radio and television broadcasting and in magazines is often required.

The cultural identity argument for protection has no merit, and it is one more example of rent seeking. Writers, publishers, and broadcasters want to limit foreign competition so that they can earn larger economic profits. There is no actual danger to national culture. In fact, many of the creators of so-called American cultural products are not Americans but the talented citizens of other countries, ensuring the survival of their national cultural identities in Hollywood! Also, if national culture is in danger, there is no surer way of helping it on its way out than by impoverishing the nation whose culture it is. And protection is an effective way of doing just that.

Prevents Rich Countries from Exploiting Developing Countries

Another argument for protection is that international trade must be restricted to prevent the people of the rich industrial world from exploiting the poorer people of the developing countries, forcing them to work for slave wages.

Wage rates in some developing countries are indeed very low. But by trading with developing countries, we increase the demand for the goods that these countries produce and, more significantly, we increase the demand for their labor. When the demand for labor in developing countries increases, the wage rate also increases. So, far from exploiting people in developing countries, trade improves their opportunities and increases their incomes.

We have reviewed the arguments that are commonly heard in favor of protection and the counter-arguments against them. There is one counterargument to protection that is general and quite overwhelming. Protection invites retaliation and can trigger a trade war. The best example of a trade war occurred during the Great Depression of the 1930s when the Smoot-Hawley tariff was introduced in the United States. Country after country retaliated with its own tariff, and in a short period, world trade had almost disappeared. The costs to all countries were large and led to a renewed international resolve to avoid such self-defeating moves in the future. They also led to the creation of GATT and are the impetus behind NAFTA, APEC, and the European Union.

REVIEW QUIZ

1 Can we achieve national security goals, stimulate the growth of new industries, or restrain foreign monopoly by restricting international trade?

2 Can we save jobs, compensate for low foreign wages, make the economy more diversified, compensate for costly environmental policies, protect national culture, or protect developing countries from being exploited by restricting international trade?

3 Is there any merit to the view that we should restrict international trade for any reason? What is the main argument against international trade restrictions?

Why Is International Trade Restricted?

WHY, DESPITE ALL THE ARGUMENTS AGAINST protection, is trade restricted? There are two key reasons:

- Tariff revenue
- Rent seeking

Tariff Revenue

Government revenue is costly to collect. In the developed countries such as the United States, a well-organized tax collection system is in place that can generate billions of dollars of income tax and sales tax revenues. This tax collection system is made possible by the fact that most economic transactions are done by firms that must keep properly audited financial records. Without such records, the revenue collection agencies (the Internal Revenue Service in the United States) would be severely hampered in the work. Even with audited financial accounts, some proportion of potential tax revenue is lost. Nonetheless, for the industrialized countries, the income tax and sales taxes are the major sources of revenue and the tariff plays a very small role.

But governments in developing countries have a difficult time collecting taxes from their citizens. Much economic activity takes place in an informal economy with few financial records. So only a small amount of revenue is collected from income taxes and sales taxes. The one area in which economic transactions are well recorded and audited is in international trade. So this activity is an attractive base for tax collection in these countries and is used much more extensively than in the developed countries.

Rent Seeking

Rent seeking is the major reason why international trade is restricted. **Rent seeking** is lobbying and other political activity that seek to capture the gains from trade. Free trade increases consumption possibilities *on the average*, but not everyone shares in the gain and some people even lose. Free trade brings benefits to some and imposes costs on others, with total benefits exceeding total costs. It is the uneven distribution of costs and benefits that is the principal source of impediment to achieving more liberal international trade.

Returning to our example of trade in cars and grain between Farmland and Mobilia, the benefits from free trade accrue to all the producers of grain and to those producers of cars who would not have to bear the costs of adjusting to a smaller car industry. Those costs are transition costs, not permanent costs. The costs of moving to free trade are borne by those car producers and their employees who have to become grain producers. The number of people who gain will, in general, be enormous in comparison with the number who lose. The gain per person will therefore be rather small. The loss per person to those who bear the loss will be large. Because the loss that falls on those who bear it is large, it will pay those people to incur considerable expense to lobby against free trade. On the other hand, it will not pay those who gain to organize to achieve free trade. The gain from trade for any one individual is too small for that individual to spend much time or money on a political organization to achieve free trade. The loss from free trade will be seen as being so great by those bearing that loss that they *will* find it profitable to join a political organization to prevent free trade. Each group is optimizing — weighing benefits against costs and choosing the best action for themselves. The anti-free-trade group will, however, undertake a larger quantity of political lobbying than the pro-free-trade group.

Compensating Losers

If, in total, the gains from free international trade exceed the losses, why don't those who gain compensate those who lose so that everyone is in favor of free trade? To some degree, such compensation does take place. When Congress approved the NAFTA deal with Canada and Mexico, it set up a $56 million fund to support and retrain workers who lost their jobs because of the new trade agreement. During the first six months of the operation of NAFTA, only 5,000 workers applied for benefits under this scheme.

The losers from freer international trade are also compensated indirectly through the normal unemployment compensation arrangements. But only limited attempts are made to compensate those who lose from free international trade. The main reason why full compensation is not attempted is that the costs of identifying all the losers and estimating the value of their losses would be enormous. Also, it would never be clear whether a person who has fallen on hard times is suffering because of free trade or for other reasons, perhaps reasons that are largely under the

control of the individual. Furthermore, some people who look like losers at one point in time may, in fact, wind up gaining. The young autoworker who loses his job in Michigan and becomes a computer assembly worker in Minneapolis resents the loss of work and the need to move. But a year or two later, looking back on events, he counts himself fortunate. He has made a move that has increased his income and given him greater job security.

It is because we do not, in general, compensate the losers from free international trade that protectionism is such a popular and permanent feature of our national economic and political life.

REVIEW QUIZ

1 What are the two main reasons for imposing tariffs on imports?

2 What type of country most benefits from the revenue from tariffs? Provide some examples of such countries.

3 Does the United States need to use tariffs to raise revenue for the government? Explain why or why not.

4 If international trade restrictions are costly, why do we use them? Why don't the people who gain from trade organize a political force that is strong enough to ensure that their interests are protected?

◆ You've now seen how free international trade enables all nations to gain from specialization and trade. By producing goods in which we have a comparative advantage and trading some of our production for that of others, we expand our consumption possibilities. Placing impediments on that trade restricts the extent to which we can gain from specialization and trade. By opening our country up to free international trade, the market for the things that we sell expands and the relative price rises. The market for the things that we buy also expands, and the relative price falls.

Reading Between the Lines on pp. 778–779 looks at a recent example of an international trade dispute between the United States and Canada — the softwood lumber dispute. This dispute provides a clear example of the economic cost of restricting international trade.

Tariffs in Action

THE NEW YORK TIMES, October 31, 2001

U.S. Imposes a Second Duty On Canadian Lumber Imports

The Commerce Department accused Canadian lumber producers of unfair trade practices today and imposed a double-digit duty on their exports to the United States.

The department said today that it would impose antidumping duties averaging 12.6 percent on imports of softwood lumber, flooring and siding from six Canadian producers. The duties, which range from 5.9 percent to 17.2 percent, are the second imposed in the last three months.

A countervailing duty of 17.3 percent was imposed on Aug. 17. Canadian lumber, used mainly in housing, has about a third of the American market. Imports last year were valued at $6.38 billion, the Commerce Department said.

The latest duty is a response to complaints by American producers that Canadian companies have flouted international trade rules by exporting lumber at prices below their production costs, a practice known as dumping.

The earlier countervailing duty, the Commerce Department said, was intended to offset the benefits of subsidies to Canadian sawmills, such as low fees for harvesting trees in government-owned forests.

Both duties are preliminary, with final determinations expected next March after further discussions with the affected parties.

American homebuilders and other lumber users criticized the antidumping duty, saying it raised the cost of material at a time of weakening demand. Michael Carliner, chief economist at the National Association of Home Builders in Washington, said today that the pain that it caused the customer was greater than the benefit to producers in the United States.

...

Essence of the Story

■ American lumber producers say that Canadian producers are dumping — exporting lumber to the United States at prices below the cost of production.

■ The Commerce Department agreed with the U.S. producers and imposed a countervailing duty of 17.3 percent on Canadian lumber used in housing.

■ Michael Carliner, chief economist at the National Association of Home Builders, said that the pain that the tariff caused the home buyer was greater than the benefit it brought to U.S. lumber producers.

Economic Analysis

■ Figure 1 shows the U.S. market for softwood lumber.

■ The demand curve of U.S. buyers of softwood lumber is D.

■ There are two supply curves: the supply curve of the Canadian producers, S_C, and the supply curve of U.S. producers, S_{US}.

■ With no tariff, the quantity of softwood lumber bought in the United States is QC_0. Of this amount, QP_0 is produced in the United States and the rest is imported from Canada, as shown by the arrow in Fig. 1.

■ Now the United States puts a 19 percent tariff on the import of softwood lumber. Canadian lumber is now supplied to the U.S. market at the original supply price, $100, plus the tariff, $19, so the supply curve of lumber from Canada shifts to become $S_C + tariff$.

■ With the tariff, the quantity of softwood lumber bought in the United States is QC_1. Of this amount, QP_1 is produced in the United

States and the rest is imported from Canada, as shown by the arrow in Fig. 1.

■ The tariff decreases U.S. consumption and imports and increases U.S. production.

■ Figure 2 shows the winners and the losers in the United States.

■ The winners include U.S lumber producers, who gain additional producer surplus, which is shown by the blue area in Fig. 2.

■ Another winner is the U.S. government, which collects additional revenue, shown by the purple area in Fig. 2.

■ The sum of the blue, red, purple, and gray areas is the loss of consumer surplus that results from the tariff.

■ A Canadian subsidy has no influence on the effects of the tariff. A deadweight loss arises — the decrease in consumer surplus exceeds the increase in producer surplus — regardless of whether Canadian softwood lumber producers receive a subsidy.

Figure 1 Tariffs and imports

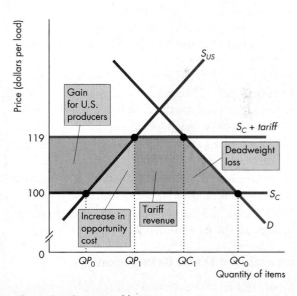

Figure 2 Winners and losers

You're The Voter

■ Do you support or oppose the tariff on Canadian softwood lumber?

■ Write a report to your member of Congress explaining why you support or oppose the tariff.

779

SUMMARY

KEY POINTS

Patterns and Trends in International Trade
(p. 762)

- Large flows of trade take place between countries, most of which is in manufactured goods exchanged among rich industrialized countries.
- Since 1960, the volume of U.S. trade has more than doubled.

The Gains from International Trade
(pp. 763–768)

- Comparative advantage is the fundamental source of the gains from trade.
- Comparative advantage exists when opportunity costs between countries diverge.
- By increasing its production of goods in which it has a comparative advantage and then trading some of the increased output, a country can consume at points outside its production possibilities frontier.
- In the absence of international borrowing and lending, trade is balanced as prices adjust to reflect the international supply of and demand for goods.
- The world price balances the production and consumption plans of the trading parties. At the equilibrium price, trade is balanced.
- Comparative advantage explains the international trade that takes place in the world.
- But trade in similar goods arises from economies of scale in the face of diversified tastes.

International Trade Restrictions
(pp. 769–772)

- Countries restrict international trade by imposing tariffs and quotas.
- International trade restrictions raise the domestic price of imported goods, lower the volume of imports, and reduce the total value of imports.
- They also reduce the total value of exports by the same amount as the reduction in the value of imports.

The Case Against Protection
(pp. 773–776)

- Arguments that protection is necessary for national security, to protect infant industries, and to prevent dumping are weak.
- Arguments that protection saves jobs, allows us to compete with cheap foreign labor, makes the economy diversified and stable, protects national culture, and is needed to offset the costs of environmental policies are fatally flawed.

Why Is International Trade Restricted?
(pp. 776–777)

- Trade is restricted because tariffs raise government revenue and because protection brings a small loss to a large number of people and a large gain per person to a small number of people.

KEY FIGURES

KEY TERMS

PROBLEMS

🖥 *1. The table provides information about Virtual Reality's production possibilities.

TV sets (per day)		Computers (per day)
0	and	36
10	and	35
20	and	33
30	and	30
40	and	26
50	and	21
60	and	15
70	and	8
80	and	0

a. Calculate Virtual Reality's opportunity cost of a TV set when it produces 10 sets a day.

b. Calculate Virtual Reality's opportunity cost of a TV set when it produces 40 sets a day.

c. Calculate Virtual Reality's opportunity cost of a TV set when it produces 70 sets a day.

d. Using the answers to parts (a), (b), and (c), sketch the relationship between the opportunity cost of a TV set and the quantity of TV sets produced in Virtual Reality.

2. The table provides information about Vital Sign's production possibilities.

TV sets (per day)		Computers (per day)
0	and	18.0
10	and	17.5
20	and	16.5
30	and	15.0
40	and	13.0
50	and	10.5
60	and	7.5
70	and	4.0
80	and	0

a. Calculate Vital Sign's opportunity cost of a TV set when it produces 10 sets a day.

b. Calculate Vital Sign's opportunity cost of a TV set when it produces 40 sets a day.

c. Calculate Vital Sign's opportunity cost of a TV set when it produces 70 sets a day.

d. Using the answers to parts (a), (b), and (c), sketch the relationship between the opportunity cost of a TV set and the quantity of TV sets produced in Virtual Reality.

🖥 *3. Suppose that with no international trade, Virtual Reality in problem 1 produces and consumes 10 TV sets a day and Vital Signs produces and consumes 60 TV sets a day. Now suppose that the two countries begin to trade with each other.

a. Which country exports TV sets?

b. What adjustments are made to the amount of each good produced by each country?

c. What adjustments are made to the amount of each good consumed by each country?

d. What can you say about the terms of trade (the price of a TV set expressed as computers per TV set) under free trade?

4. Suppose that with no international trade, Virtual Reality in problem 1 produces and consumes 50 TV sets a day and Vital Signs produces and consumes 20 TV sets a day. Now suppose that the two countries begin to trade with each other.

a. Which country exports TV sets?

b. What adjustments are made to the amount of each good produced by each country?

c. What adjustments are made to the amount of each good consumed by each country?

d. What can you say about the terms of trade (the price of a TV set expressed as computers per TV set) under free trade?

🖥 *5. Compare the total quantities of each good produced in problems 1 and 2 with the total quantities of each good produced in problems 3 and 4.

a. Does free trade increase or decrease the total quantities of TV sets and computers produced in both cases? Why?

b. What happens to the price of a TV set in Virtual Reality in the two cases? Why does it rise in one case and fall in the other?

c. What happens to the price of a computer in Vital Signs in the two cases? Why does it rise in one case and fall in the other?

6. Compare the international trade in problem 3 with that in problem 4.

a. Why does Virtual Reality export TV sets in one of the cases and import them in the other case?

b. Do the TV producers or the computer producers gain in each case?

c. Do consumers gain in each case?

*7. The figure depicts the international market for soybeans.

a. If the two countries did not engage in international trade, what would be the prices of soybeans in the two countries?

b. What is the world price of soybeans if there is free trade between these countries?

c. What quantities of soybeans are exported and imported?

d. What is the balance of trade?

8. If the country in problem 7 that imports soybeans imposes a tariff of $2 per bushel, what is the world price of soybeans and what quantity of soybeans gets traded internationally? What is the price of soybeans in the importing country? Calculate the tariff revenue.

*9. The importing country in problem 7 imposes a quota of 300 million bushels on imports of soybeans.

a. What is the price of soybeans in the importing country?

b. What is the revenue from the quota?

c. Who gets this revenue?

10. The exporting country in problem 7 imposes a VER of 300 million bushels on its exports of soybeans.

a. What is the world price of soybeans now?

b. What is the revenue of soybean growers in the exporting country?

c. Which country gains from the VER?

CRITICAL THINKING

1. Study *Reading Between the Lines* on pp. 778–779 and then answer the following questions.

a. Why did the United States impose a tariff on softwood lumber imports from Canada?

b. What are the effects of the tariff on softwood lumber?

c. Who are the winners and who are the losers from the tariff on softwood lumber?

d. Modify the figures on page 433 to show the effects of a Canadian subsidy to softwood lumber producers on the consumer surplus, producer surplus, and deadweight loss in the United States.

WEB EXERCISES

1. Visit your Parkin Web site and study the Web *Reading Between the Lines* on steel dumping, and then answer the following questions.

a. What is the argument in the news article for limiting steel imports?

b. Evaluate the argument. Is it correct or incorrect in your opinion? Why?

c. Would you vote to eliminate steel imports? Why or why not?

d. Would you vote differently if you lived in another steel-producing country? Why or why not?

2. Use the links on your Parkin Web site to visit the Public Citizen Global Trade Watch and the State of Arizona Department of Commerce Web sites. Review the general message provided by the two sites about NAFTA and then answer the following questions.

a. What is the message that the Public Citizen Global Trade Watch wants to give?

b. What is the message that the State of Arizona Department of Commerce wants to give?

c. Which message do you think is correct and why?

d. Would you vote to maintain NAFTA? Why or why not?

INTERNATIONAL FINANCE

¥€$!

The yen (¥), the euro (€), and the dollar ($) are the world's three big currencies. The yen (the currency of Japan) and the dollar (the currency of the United States) have been around for a long time. The euro is the new currency of 12 members of the European Union and it came into everyday use as notes and coins on January 1, 2002. Most of the world's international trade and finance are conducted using these three currencies. ◆ In 1971, one U.S. dollar bought 360 Japanese yen. In 2001, it bought 121 yen, and six years earlier, it had bought only 84 yen. One Argentine peso was worth one U.S. dollar in 2001. But in 2002, its value crashed to 33 U.S. cents. ◆ Why do currency exchange rates fluctuate? Is there anything we can do or should do to stabilize the value of the dollar? ◆ In 1988, Americans owned foreign assets equal in value to the assets that foreigners owned in the United States. Before 1988, American ownership of foreign assets exceeded foreign ownership of U.S. assets. But every year since 1988, the balance has tipped increasingly the other way. Foreign entrepreneurs such as Australian-born Rupert Murdoch and Sony's Akio Mori have roamed the United States with giant virtual shopping carts and loaded them up with such items as Twentieth Century Fox, the Rockefeller Center, and MGM. Why have foreigners been buying more U.S. real estate and businesses than Americans have been buying abroad?

◇ In this chapter, you're going to discover why the U.S. economy has become attractive for foreign investors, what determines the amount of international borrowing and lending, and why the dollar fluctuates against other currencies. At the end of the chapter, in Reading Between the Lines, we'll return to the crash of the Argentine peso in 2002.

After studying this chapter, you will be able to

- Explain how international trade is financed
- Describe a country's balance of payments accounts
- Explain what determines the amount of international borrowing and lending
- Explain why the United States changed from being a lender to being a borrower in the mid-1980s
- Explain how the foreign exchange value of the dollar is determined
- Explain why the foreign exchange value of the dollar fluctuates

Financing International Trade

WHEN SONY STORES IN THE UNITED STATES imports CD players from Japan, it does not pay for them with U.S. dollars — it uses Japanese yen. And when a French construction company buys an earth mover from Caterpillar, Inc., it uses U.S. dollars. Whenever we buy things from another country, we use the currency of that country to make the transaction. It doesn't make any difference what the item being traded is; it might be a consumption good or a capital good, a building, or even a firm.

We're going to study the markets in which money — different types of currency — is bought and sold. But first we're going to look at the scale of international trading, borrowing and lending and at the way in which we keep our records of these transactions. Such records are called the balance of payments accounts.

Balance of Payments Accounts

A country's **balance of payments accounts** records its international trading, borrowing, and lending. There are in fact three balance of payments accounts:

1. Current account
2. Capital account
3. Official settlements account

The **current account** records payments for imports of goods and services from abroad, receipts from exports of goods and services sold abroad, net interest income paid abroad, and net transfers (such as foreign aid payments). The *current account balance* equals the sum of exports minus imports, net interest income, and net transfers.

The **capital account** records foreign investment in the United States minus U.S. investment abroad. (This account also has a statistical discrepancy that arises from errors and omissions in measuring capital transactions.)

The **official settlements account** records the change in **U.S. official reserves**, which are the government's holdings of foreign currency. If U.S. official reserves *increase*, the official settlements account balance is *negative*. The reason is that holding foreign money is like investing abroad. U.S. investment abroad is a minus item in the capital account and in the official settlements account.

The sum of the balances on the three accounts always equals zero. That is, to pay for our current account deficit, either we must borrow more from abroad than we lend abroad or our official reserves must decrease to cover the shortfall.

Table 33.1 shows the U.S. balance of payments accounts in 2001. Items in the current account and capital account that provide foreign currency to the United States have a plus sign; items that cost the United States foreign currency have a minus sign. The table shows that in 2001, U.S. imports exceeded U.S. exports and the current account had a deficit of $417 billion. How do we pay for imports that exceed the value of our exports? That is, how do we pay for our current account deficit? We pay by borrowing from the rest of the world. The capital account tells us by how much. We borrowed $895 billion (foreign investment in the United States) but made loans of $435 billion (U.S. investment abroad). Our *net* foreign borrowing

TABLE 33.1 U.S. Balance of Payments Accounts in 2001

Current account	Billions of dollars
Imports of goods and services	−1,352
Exports of goods and services	+1,005
Net interest income	−19
Net transfers	−51
Current account balance	−417

Capital account	
Foreign investment in the United States	+895
U.S. investment abroad	−434
Statistical discrepancy	−39
Capital account balance	+422

Official settlements account	
Official settlements account balance	−5

Source: Bureau of Economic Analysis.

was $895 billion minus $434 billion, which equals $461 billion. There is almost always a statistical discrepancy between our capital account and current account transactions and in 2001, the discrepancy was –$39 billion. Combining the discrepancy with the measured net foreign borrowing gives a capital account balance of $422 billion.

Our capital account balance plus our current account balance equals the change in official U.S. reserves. In 2001, our capital account balance of $422 billion plus our current balance of –$417 billion equals $5 billion. Our reserves *increased* in 2001 by $5 billion. This amount appears in Table 33.1 as –$5 billion. Recall that when our reserves *increase* we record this as a negative number in our international accounts because an increase in our reserves is like making a loan to the rest of the world — the government increases its deposits in foreign central banks.

The numbers in Table 33.1 give a snapshot of the balance of payments accounts in 2001. Figure 33.1 puts that snapshot into perspective by showing the balance of payments between 1981 and 2001. Because the economy grows and the price level rises, changes in the dollar value of the balance of payments do not convey much information. To remove

the influences of growth and inflation, Fig. 33.1 shows the balance of payments as a percentage of nominal GDP.

As you can see, the capital account balance is almost a mirror image of the current account balance. The official settlements balance is very small in comparison with the balances on these other two accounts. A large current account deficit (and capital account surplus) emerged during the 1980s but declined from 1987 to 1991. It then increased every year through 2000 and decreased again in the 2001 recession.

You might find it easier to understand the balance of payments accounts and the way in which they are linked together if you think about the income and expenditure, borrowing and lending, and bank account of an individual.

Individual Analogy An individual's current account records the income from supplying the services of factors of production and the expenditure on goods and services. Consider, for example, Joanne. She worked in 2002 and earned an income of $25,000. Joanne has $10,000 worth of investments that earned her an interest income of $1,000. Joanne's current account shows an income of $26,000. Joanne spent

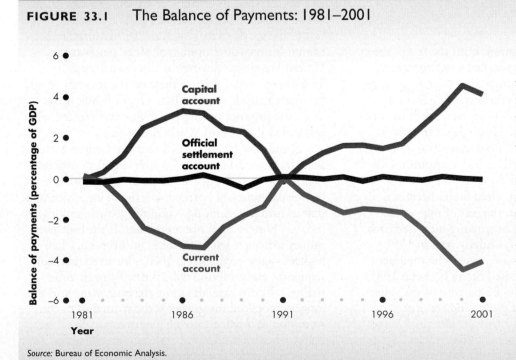

FIGURE 33.1   The Balance of Payments: 1981–2001

During the 1980s, a large current account deficit arose. That deficit decreased in the late 1980s but increased again through 2000. It decreased slightly in the 2001 recession. The capital account balance mirrors the current account balance. When the current account balance is negative, the capital account balance is positive — we borrow from the rest of the world. Fluctuations in the official settlements balance are small in comparison with fluctuations in the current account balance and the capital account balance.

Source: Bureau of Economic Analysis.

$18,000 buying goods and services for consumption. She also bought a new house, which cost her $60,000. So Joanne's total expenditure was $78,000. The difference between her expenditure and her income is $52,000 ($78,000 minus $26,000). This amount is Joanne's current account deficit.

To pay for expenditure of $52,000 in excess of her income, Joanne has to use the money that she has in the bank or she has to take out a loan. In fact, Joanne took out a mortgage of $50,000 to help buy her house. This mortgage was the only borrowing that Joanne did, so her capital account surplus was $50,000. With a current account deficit of $52,000 and a capital account surplus of $50,000, Joanne is still $2,000 short. She got that $2,000 from her own bank account. Her cash holdings decreased by $2,000.

Joanne's income from her work is analogous to a country's income from its exports. Her income from her investments is analogous to a country's interest income from foreigners. Her purchases of goods and services, including her purchase of a house, are analogous to a country's imports. Joanne's mortgage — borrowing from someone else — is analogous to a country's borrowing from the rest of the world. The change in Joanne's bank account is analogous to the change in the country's official reserves.

Borrowers and Lenders, Debtors and Creditors

A country that is borrowing more from the rest of the world than it is lending to it is called a **net borrower**. Similarly, a **net lender** is a country that is lending more to the rest of the world than it is borrowing from it.

The United States is a net borrower, but it has not always been in this situation. Throughout the 1960s and most of the 1970s, the United States was a net lender to the rest of the world. It had a surplus on its current account and a deficit on its capital account. It was not until 1983 that the United States became a significant net borrower from the rest of the world. Between 1983 and 1987, its borrowing increased each year. It then decreased and was briefly zero in 1991, after which it started to increase again. The total net foreign borrowing by the United States between 1983 and 2001 was $2.8 trillion — 28 percent of the value of the nation's production of goods and services.

Most countries are net borrowers like the United States. But a small number of countries, including Japan and oil-rich Saudi Arabia, are net lenders.

A net borrower might be reducing its net assets held in the rest of the world, or it might be going deeper into debt. A nation's total stock of foreign investment determines whether it is a debtor or creditor. A **debtor nation** is a country that during its entire history has borrowed more from the rest of the world than it has lent to it. It has a stock of outstanding debt to the rest of the world that exceeds the stock of its own claims on the rest of the world. A **creditor nation** is a country that during its entire history has invested more in the rest of the world than other countries have invested in it.

At the heart of the distinction between a net borrower/net lender and a debtor/creditor nation is the distinction between flows and stocks, which you have encountered many times in your study of macroeconomics. Borrowing and lending are flows — amounts borrowed or lent per unit of time. Debts are stocks — amounts owed at a point in time. The flow of borrowing and lending changes the stock of debt.

The United States was a debtor nation through the nineteenth century as we borrowed from Europe to finance our westward expansion, railroads, and industrialization. We paid off our debt and became a creditor nation for most of the twentieth century. But following a string of current account deficits, we became a debtor nation again in 1989.

Since 1989, total stock of U.S. borrowing from the rest of the world has exceeded U.S. lending to the rest of the world. The largest debtor nations are the capital-hungry developing countries (such as the United States was during the nineteenth century). The international debt of these countries grew from less than a third to more than a half of their gross domestic product during the 1980s and created what was called the "Third World debt crisis."

Should we be concerned that the United States is a net borrower? The answer to this question depends mainly on what the net borrower is doing with the borrowed money. If borrowing is financing investment that in turn is generating economic growth and higher income, borrowing is not a problem. If the borrowed money is being used to finance consumption, then higher interest payments are being incurred, and consequently, consumption will have to be reduced. In this case, the more the borrowing and the longer it goes on, the greater is the reduction in consumption that will eventually be necessary. We'll see below whether the United States is borrowing for investment or for consumption.

Current Account Balance

What determines a country's current account balance and net foreign borrowing? You've seen that net exports (NX) is the main item in the current account. We can define the current account balance (CAB) as:

$$CAB = NX + \text{Net interest income} + \text{Net transfers}.$$

We can study the current account balance by looking at what determines net exports because the other two items are small and do not fluctuate much.

Net Exports

Net exports are determined by the government budget and private saving and investment. To see how net exports are determined, we need to recall some of the things that we learned about the *National Income and Product Accounts* in Chapter 4. Table 33.2 will refresh your memory and summarize some calculations.

Part (a) lists the national income variables that are needed, with their symbols. Part (b) defines three balances. **Net exports** is exports of goods and services minus imports of goods and services.

The **government sector surplus or deficit** is equal to net taxes minus government purchases of goods and services. If that number is positive, a government sector surplus is lent to other sectors; if that number is negative, a government deficit must be financed by borrowing from other sectors. The government sector deficit is the sum of the deficits of the federal, state, and local governments.

The **private sector surplus or deficit** is saving minus investment. If saving exceeds investment, a private sector surplus is lent to other sectors. If investment exceeds saving, a private sector deficit is financed by borrowing from other sectors.

Part (b) also shows the values of these balances for the United States in 2001. As you can see, net exports were –$330 billion, a deficit of $330 billion. The government sector's revenue from net taxes was $2,200 billion, and it purchased $1,840 billion worth of goods and services. The government sector surplus was $360 billion. The private sector saved $940 billion and invested $1,634 billion, so it had a deficit of $690 billion.

Part (c) shows the relationship among the three balances. From the *National Income and Product Accounts*, we know that real GDP, Y, is the sum of consumption expenditure (C), investment, government purchases, and net exports. It also equals the

TABLE 33.2 Net Exports, the Government Budget, Saving, and Investment

	Symbols and equations	United States in 2001 (billions of dollars)
(a) Variables		
Exports*	X	10,050
Imports*	M	13,080
Government purchases	G	1,840
Net taxes	T	2,200
Investment	I	1,634
Saving	S	944
(b) Balances		
Rest of world	$X - M$	$10,050 - 13,080 = -330$
Government sector	$T - G$	$2,200 - 1,840 = 360$
Private sector	$S - I$	$944 - 1,634 = -690$
(c) Relationship among balances		
National accounts	$Y = C + I + G + X - M$	
	$= C + S + T$	
Rearranging:	$X - M = S - I + T - G$	
Net exports	$X - M$	–330
equals:		
Government sector	$T - G$	360
plus		
Private sector	$S - I$	–690

Source: Bureau of Economic Analysis.

* The *National Income and Product Accounts* measures of exports and imports are slightly different from the balance of payments accounts measures in Table 33.1 on p. 784.

sum of consumption expenditure, saving, and taxes. Rearranging these equations tells us that net exports is the sum of the government sector deficit and the private sector deficit. In the United States in 2001, the government sector had a surplus of $360 billion and the private sector had a deficit of $690 billion. The government sector deficit plus the private sector deficit equals net exports of –$330 billion.

The Three Sector Balances

You've seen that net exports equal the sum of the government balance and the private balance. How do these three sector balances fluctuate over time? Figure 33.2 answers this question. It shows the government sector balance (the red line), net exports (the blue line), and the private sector balance (the green line).

You can see that there is a strong tendency for the private sector balance and the government sector balance to move in opposite directions. During the 1980s, when the government went into deeper deficit, the private sector went into a larger surplus.

FIGURE 33.2   The Three Sector Balances

The private sector balance and the government sector balance tend to move in opposite directions. Net exports respond to the *sum* of the government sector and private sector balances. When the private sector and the government sector together are in deficit, that deficit is financed by net foreign borrowing.

Source: Bureau of Economic Analysis.

And since 1997, as the government sector has gone into a surplus, the private sector has gone into a deepening deficit.

The relationship between net exports and the other two sector balances is not a strong one. Sometimes, when the government sector balance becomes increasingly negative (a larger deficit), as it did during the first half of the 1980s, net exports become negative. But through the 1990s and into the 2000s, net exports did not follow the government sector balance closely. Net exports respond to the *sum* of the government sector and private sector balances. When the private sector and the government sector together are in deficit, that deficit is financed by net foreign borrowing.

Is U.S. Borrowing for Consumption or Investment?

In 2001, net exports were a negative $330 billion and we borrowed this amount from abroad. Did we borrow for consumption or investment? In 2001, private investment in buildings, plant, and equipment was $1,634 billion. Government investment in defense equipment and public structures such as highways and dams was $318 billion. All this investment added to the nation's capital, and much of it increased productivity. Government also spends on education and health care services, which increase *human capital*. Our international borrowing is financing private and public investment, not consumption.

The Exchange Rate

WHEN WE BUY FOREIGN GOODS OR INVEST IN another country, we have to obtain some of that country's currency to make the transaction. When foreigners buy U.S.-produced goods or invest in the United States, they have to obtain some U.S. dollars. We get foreign currency, and foreigners get U.S. dollars in the foreign exchange market. The **foreign exchange market** is the market in which the currency of one country is exchanged for the currency of another. The foreign exchange market is not a place like a downtown flea market or a produce market. The market is made up of thousands of people — importers and exporters, banks, and specialists in the buying and selling of foreign exchange, called foreign exchange brokers. The foreign exchange market opens on Monday morning in Hong Kong, which is still Sunday evening in New York. As the day advances, markets open in Singapore, Tokyo, Frankfurt, London, New York, Chicago, and San Francisco. As the West Coast markets close, Hong Kong is only an hour away from opening for the next day of business. The sun barely sets on the foreign exchange market. Dealers around the world are in continual contact by telephone, and on a typical day, $1.5 trillion changes hands.

The price at which one currency exchanges for another is called a **foreign exchange rate**. For example, in January 2002, one U.S. dollar bought 132 Japanese yen. The exchange rate was 132 yen per dollar.

Figure 33.3 shows the exchange rate of the U.S. dollar in terms of the Japanese yen between 1982 and 2002. Over this period, the dollar has mostly depreciated, but occasionally, it has appreciated.

Currency depreciation is the fall in the value of one currency in terms of another currency. For example if the dollar falls from 100 yen to 80 yen, the dollar depreciates by 20 percent. The U.S. dollar depreciated against the Japanese yen from 1986 through 1988, from 1991 through 1995, and from 1998 through 2000.

Currency appreciation is the rise in the value of one currency in terms of another currency. For example if the dollar rises from 100 yen to 120 yen, the dollar appreciates by 20 percent. The U.S. dollar appreciated against the yen in 1989 and 1990, from 1996 to mid-1998, and in 2001 and 2002.

We've just expressed the value of the U.S. dollar in terms of the yen. But we can express the value of

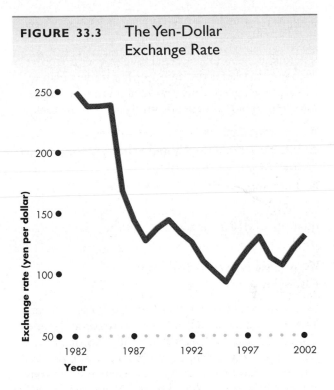

FIGURE 33.3   The Yen-Dollar Exchange Rate

The exchange rate is the price at which two currencies can be traded. The yen-dollar exchange rate, expressed as yen per dollar, shows that the dollar has generally fallen in value — depreciated — against the yen. But since 1995, it has generally risen.

Source: Economic Report of the President, 2002.

the dollar in terms of any currency. We can also express the exchange rate of the yen in terms of the dollar as a number of dollars per yen. When the U.S. dollar appreciates against the yen, the yen depreciates against the dollar.

Why does the U.S. dollar fluctuate in value? Why does it sometimes depreciate and sometimes appreciate? What happened during 2001 to make the dollar appreciate against the yen and in 2000 to make it depreciate? To answer these questions, we need to understand what determines the exchange rate.

The exchange rate is a price — the price of one country's money in terms of another country's money. And like all prices, demand and supply determine the exchange rate. So to understand what determines the exchange rate, we need to study demand and supply in the foreign exchange market. We'll begin by looking at the demand side of the market.

Demand in the Foreign Exchange Market

The quantity of dollars demanded in the foreign exchange market is the amount that traders plan to buy during a given time period at a given exchange rate. This quantity depends on three main factors:

- The exchange rate
- Interest rates in the United States and other countries
- The expected future exchange rate

We first look at the relationship between the quantity of dollars demanded and the exchange rate.

The Law of Demand for Foreign Exchange

People do not buy dollars because they enjoy them. The demand for dollars is a *derived demand*. People demand dollars so that they can buy U.S.-made goods and services (U.S. exports). They also demand dollars so that they can buy U.S. assets such as bonds, stocks, businesses, and real estate. Nevertheless, the law of demand applies to dollars just as it does to anything else that people value.

Other things remaining the same, the higher the exchange rate, the smaller is the quantity of dollars demanded in the foreign exchange market. For example, if the price of the U.S. dollar rises from 100 yen to 120 yen but nothing else changes, the quantity of U.S. dollars that people plan to buy in the foreign exchange market decreases. Why does the exchange rate influence the quantity of dollars demanded?

There are two separate reasons, and they are related to the two sources of the derived demand for dollars:

- Exports effect
- Expected profit effect

Exports Effect The larger the value of U.S. exports, the larger is the quantity of dollars demanded on the foreign exchange market. But the value of U.S. exports depends on the exchange rate. The lower the exchange rate, with everything else the same, the cheaper are U.S.-produced goods and services, so the more the United States exports and the greater is the quantity of U.S. dollars demanded on the foreign exchange market to pay for these exports.

Expected Profit Effect The larger the expected profit from holding dollars, the greater is the quantity of dollars demanded in the foreign exchange market. But expected profit depends on the exchange rate. The lower the exchange rate, other things remaining the same, the larger is the expected profit from buying dollars and the greater is the quantity of dollars demanded on the foreign exchange market.

To understand this effect, suppose you think the dollar will be worth 120 yen by the end of the month. If today, a dollar costs 115 yen, you buy dollars today. But a person who thinks that the dollar will be worth 115 yen at the end of the month does not buy dollars today. Now suppose the exchange rate falls to 110 yen per dollar. More people think they can profit from buying dollars, so the quantity of dollars demanded today increases.

For the two reasons we've just reviewed, other things remaining the same, when the foreign exchange rate rises, the quantity of dollars demanded decreases, and when foreign exchange rate falls, the quantity of dollars demanded increases. Figure 33.4 shows the demand curve for U.S. dollars in the foreign exchange market. In this figure, when the foreign exchange rate rises, other things remaining the same, there is a decrease in the quantity of dollars demanded and a movement up along the demand curve as shown by the arrow. When the exchange rate falls, other things remaining the same, there is an increase in the quantity of dollars demanded and a movement down along the demand curve as shown by the arrow.

Changes in the Demand for Dollars

A change in any influence on the dollars that people plan to buy in the foreign exchange market other than the exchange rate brings a change in the demand for dollars and a shift in the demand curve for dollars. Demand either increases or decreases. These other influences are

- Interest rates in the United States and other countries
- The expected future exchange rate

Interest Rates in the United States and Other Countries People and businesses buy financial assets to make a return. The higher the interest rate that people can make on U.S. assets compared with foreign assets, the more U.S. assets they buy. What

FIGURE 33.4   The Demand for Dollars

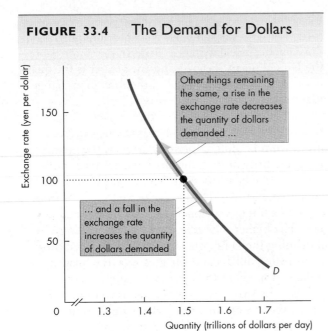

Other things remaining the same, a rise in the exchange rate decreases the quantity of dollars demanded ...

... and a fall in the exchange rate increases the quantity of dollars demanded

The quantity of dollars that people plan to buy depends on the exchange rate. Other things remaining the same, if the exchange rate rises, the quantity of dollars demanded decreases and there is a movement up along the demand curve for dollars. If the exchange rate falls, the quantity of dollars demanded increases and there is a movement down along the demand curve for dollars.

matters is not the level of U.S. interest rates, but the U.S. interest rate minus the foreign interest rate, a gap that is called the **U.S. interest rate differential**. If the U.S. interest rate rises and the foreign interest rate remains constant, the U.S. interest rate differential increases. The larger the U.S. interest rate differential, the greater is the demand for U.S. assets and the greater is the demand for dollars on the foreign exchange market.

The Expected Future Exchange Rate Other things remaining the same, the higher the expected future exchange rate, the greater is the demand for dollars. To see why, suppose you are Toyota's finance manager. The exchange rate is 100 yen per dollar, and you think that by the end of the month, it will be 120 yen per dollar. You spend 100,000 yen today and buy $1,000. At the end of the month, the dollar is 120 yen, as you predicted it would be, and you sell the $1,000. You get 120,000 yen. You've made a

profit of 20,000 yen, or almost $167. The higher the expected future exchange rate, other things remaining the same, the greater is the expected profit and the greater is the demand for dollars.

Figure 33.5 summarizes the above discussion of the influences on the demand for dollars. A rise in the U.S. interest rate differential or a rise in the expected future exchange rate increases the demand for dollars and shifts the demand curve rightward from D_0 to D_1. A fall in the U.S. interest rate differential or a fall in the expected future exchange rate decreases the demand for dollars and shifts the demand curve leftward from D_0 to D_2.

FIGURE 33.5   Changes in the Demand for Dollars

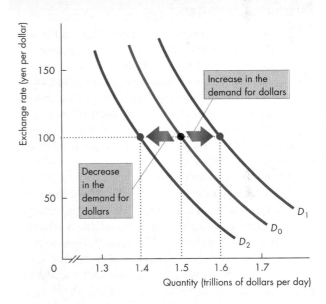

Increase in the demand for dollars

Decrease in the demand for dollars

A change in any influence on the quantity of dollars that people plan to buy, other than the exchange rate, brings a change in the demand for dollars.

The demand for dollars

Increases if:	*Decreases if:*
■ The U.S. interest rate differential increases	■ The U.S. interest rate differential decreases
■ The expected future exchange rate rises	■ The expected future exchange rate falls

Supply in the Foreign Exchange Market

The quantity of U.S. dollars supplied in the foreign exchange market is the amount that traders plan to sell during a given time period at a given exchange rate. This quantity depends on three main factors:

- The exchange rate
- Interest rates in the United States and other countries
- The expected future exchange rate

Let's look first at the relationship between the quantity of dollars supplied in the foreign exchange market and the exchange rate.

The Law of Supply of Foreign Exchange

People in the United States supply dollars in the foreign exchange market when they buy other currencies. And they buy other currencies so that they can buy foreign-made goods and services (U.S. imports). They also supply dollars and buy foreign currencies so that they can buy foreign assets such as bonds, stocks, businesses, and real estate. The law of supply applies to dollars just as it does to anything else that people plan to sell.

Other things remaining the same, the higher the exchange rate, the greater is the quantity of dollars supplied in the foreign exchange market. For example, if the price of the U.S. dollar rises from 100 yen to 120 yen but nothing else changes, the quantity of U.S. dollars that people plan to buy in the foreign exchange market increases. Why does the exchange rate influence the quantity of dollars supplied?

There are two reasons, and they parallel the two reasons on the demand side of the market:

- Imports effect
- Expected profit effect

Imports Effect The larger the value of U.S. imports, the larger is the quantity of foreign currency demanded to pay for these imports. And when people buy foreign currency, they supply dollars. So the larger the value of U.S. imports, the greater is the quantity of dollars supplied in the foreign exchange market. But the value of U.S. imports depends on

the exchange rate. The higher the exchange rate, with everything else the same, the cheaper are foreign-produced goods and services to Americans, so the more the United States imports and the greater is the quantity of U.S. dollars supplied in the foreign exchange market to pay for these imports.

Expected Profit Effect The larger the expected profit from holding a foreign currency, the greater is the quantity of that currency demanded and the greater is the quantity of dollars supplied in the foreign exchange market. But the expected profit from holding a foreign currency depends on the exchange rate. The higher the exchange rate, other things remaining the same, the larger is the expected profit from selling dollars and the greater is the quantity of dollars supplied in the foreign exchange market.

For the two reasons we've just reviewed, other things remaining the same, when the foreign

FIGURE 33.6   The Supply of Dollars

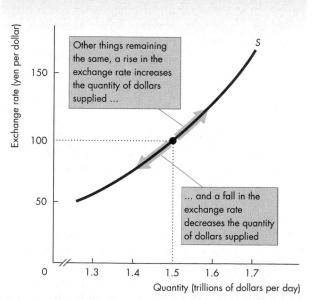

The quantity of dollars that people plan to sell depends on the exchange rate. Other things remaining the same, if the exchange rate rises, the quantity of dollars supplied increases and there is a movement up along the supply curve for dollars. If the exchange rate falls, the quantity of dollars supplied decreases and there is a movement down along the supply curve for dollars.

exchange rate rises, the quantity of dollars supplied increases and when the foreign exchange rate falls, the quantity of dollars supplied decreases. Figure 33.6 shows the supply curve for U.S. dollars in the foreign exchange market. In this figure, when the foreign exchange rate rises, other things remaining the same, there is an increase in the quantity of dollars supplied and a movement up along the supply curve as shown by the arrow. When the foreign exchange rate falls, other things remaining the same, there is a decrease in the quantity of dollars supplied and a movement down along the supply curve as shown by the arrow.

Changes in the Supply of Dollars

A change in any influence on the amount of dollars that people plan to sell in the foreign exchange market other than the exchange rate brings a change in the supply of dollars and a shift in the supply curve for dollars. Supply either increases or decreases. These other influences parallel the other influences on demand but have exactly the opposite effects. These influences are:

- Interest rates in the United States and other countries
- The expected future exchange rate

Interest Rates in the United States and Other Countries The larger the U.S. interest rate differential, the smaller is the demand for foreign assets and the smaller is the supply of dollars on the foreign exchange market.

The Expected Future Exchange Rate Other things remaining the same, the higher the expected future exchange rate, the smaller is the supply of dollars. To see why, suppose the dollar is trading at 100 yen per dollar today and you think that by the end of the month, the dollar will be 120 yen per dollar. You were planning on selling dollars today, but you decide to hold off and wait until the end of the month. If you supply dollars today, you get only 100 yen per dollar. But at the end of the month, if the rate is 120 yen per dollar as you predict, you'll get 120 yen for each dollar you supply. You'll make a profit of 20 percent. So the higher the expected future exchange rate, other things remaining the same, the smaller is the

expected profit from selling U.S. dollars today and the smaller is the supply of dollars today.

Figure 33.7 summarizes the above discussion of the influences on the supply of dollars. A rise in the U.S. interest rate differential or a rise in the expected future exchange rate decreases the supply of dollars and shifts the demand curve leftward from S_0 to S_1. A fall in the U.S. interest rate differential or a fall in the expected future exchange rate increases the supply of dollars and shifts the supply curve rightward from S_0 to S_2.

FIGURE 33.7 Changes in the Supply of Dollars

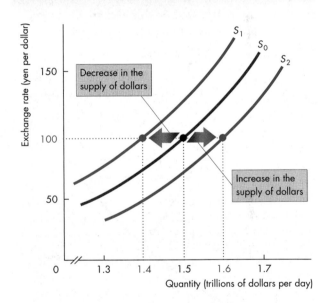

A change in any influence on the quantity of dollars that people plan to sell, other than the exchange rate, brings a change in the supply for dollars.

The supply of dollars

Increases if:	*Decreases if:*
■ The U.S. interest rate differential decreases	■ The U.S. interest rate differential increases
■ The expected future exchange rate falls	■ The expected future exchange rate rises

Market Equilibrium

Figure 33.8 shows how demand and supply in the foreign exchange market determine the exchange rate. The demand curve is D, and the supply curve is S. As in all the other markets you've studied, the price (the exchange rate) acts as a regulator.

If the exchange rate is too high, there is a surplus — the quantity supplied exceeds the quantity demanded. In Fig. 33.8, if the exchange rate is 150 yen, there is a surplus of dollars. If the exchange rate is too low, there is a shortage — the quantity supplied is less than the quantity demanded. In Fig. 33.8, if the exchange rate is 50 yen, there is a shortage of dollars.

At the equilibrium exchange rate, there is neither a shortage nor a surplus. The quantity supplied equals the quantity demanded. In Fig. 33.8, the equilibrium exchange rate is 100 yen. At this exchange rate, the quantity demanded and the quantity supplied are both $1.5 trillion a day.

The foreign exchange market is constantly pulled to its equilibrium by the forces of supply and demand. Foreign exchange dealers are constantly looking for the best price they can get. If they are selling, they want the highest price available. If they are buying, they want the lowest price available. Information flows from dealer to dealer through the worldwide computer network, and the price adjusts second by second to keep buying plans and selling plans in balance. That is, price adjusts minute by minute to keep the market at its equilibrium.

Changes in the Exchange Rate

If the demand for dollars increases and the supply of dollars does not change, the exchange rate rises. If the demand for dollars decreases and the supply of dollars does not change, the exchange rate falls. Similarly, if the supply of dollars decreases and the demand for dollars does not change, the exchange rate rises. If the supply of dollars increases and the demand for dollars does not change, the exchange rate falls.

These predictions about the effects of changes in demand and supply are exactly the same as those for any other market.

Why the Exchange Rate Is Volatile   Sometimes the dollar depreciates, and at other times, it appreciates but the quantity of dollars traded each day barely changes. Why? The main reason is that supply and demand are not independent of each other in the foreign exchange market.

When we studied the demand for dollars and the supply of dollars, we saw that unlike the situation in other markets, the demand side and the supply side of the market have some common influences. A change in the expected future exchange rate or a change in the U.S. interest rate differential changes both demand and supply and in opposite directions. These common influences on both demand and supply explain why the exchange rate can be volatile at times even though the quantity of dollars traded does not change.

Everyone in the market is potentially either a demander or a supplier. Each has a price above which he or she will sell and below which he or she will buy. Let's see how these common supply and demand effects work by looking at two episodes: one in which the dollar appreciated and one in which it depreciated.

FIGURE 33.8   Equilibrium Exchange Rate

The demand curve for dollars is D, and the supply curve is S. If the exchange rate is 150 yen per dollar, there is a surplus of dollars and the exchange rate falls. If the exchange rate is 50 yen per dollar, there is a shortage of dollars and the exchange rate rises. If the exchange rate is 100 yen per dollar, there is neither a shortage nor a surplus of dollars and the exchange rate remains constant. The market is in equilibrium.

A Depreciating Dollar: 1998–2000 Between 1998 and 2000, the dollar fell from 131 yen to 108 yen per dollar. Figure 33.9(a) explains this fall. In 1998, the demand and supply curves were those labeled D_{98} and S_{98}. The exchange rate was 131 yen per dollar. During 1999, traders expected the U.S. dollar to depreciate against the yen. They expected a lower exchange rate. As a result, the demand for dollars decreased and the supply of dollars increased. The demand curve shifted leftward to D_{00}, and the supply curve shifted rightward to S_{00}. The exchange rate fell to 108 yen per dollar.

An Appreciating Dollar: 2000–2002 Between 2000 and 2002, the dollar appreciated against the yen. It rose from 108 yen to 131 yen per dollar. Figure 33.9(b) explains why this happened. In 2000, the demand and supply curves were those labeled D_{00} and S_{00}. The exchange rate was 108 yen — where the supply and demand curves intersect. During the next two years, currency traders expected the yen to depreciate against the dollar. The demand for yen decreased. As a result, the demand for dollars increased, and the supply of dollars decreased. The demand curve shifted from D_{00} to D_{02}, and the supply curve shifted from S_{00} to S_{02}. These two shifts reinforced each other, and the exchange rate rose to 131 yen per dollar.

Exchange Rate Expectations

The changes in the exchange rate that we've just examined occurred in part because the exchange rate was *expected to change*. This explanation sounds a bit like a self-fulfilling prophecy. But what makes expectations change? The answer is new information about the deeper forces that influence the value of money. There are two such forces:

- Purchasing power parity
- Interest rate parity

FIGURE 33.9   Exchange Rate Fluctuations

(a) 1998 to 2000

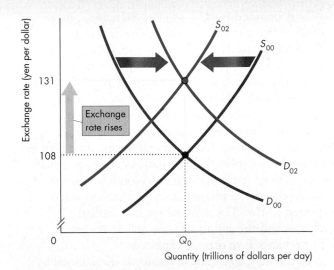

(b) 2000 to 2002

The exchange rate fluctuates because in the foreign exchange market changes in demand and supply are not independent of each other. Everyone is a potential buyer and seller in the foreign exchange market. Between 1998 and 2000 (in part a), currency traders expected the dollar to depreciate. The demand for dollars decreased, the supply of dollars increased, and the dollar depreciated. Between 2000 and 2002 (in part b), currency traders expected the dollar to appreciate. The demand for dollars increased, the supply of dollars decreased, and the dollar appreciated.

Purchasing Power Parity Money is worth what it will buy. But two kinds of money — U.S. dollars and Canadian dollars, for example — might buy different amounts of goods and services. Suppose a Big Mac costs $4 (Canadian) in Toronto and $3 (U.S.) in New York. If the Canadian dollar exchange rate is $1.33 Canadian per U.S. dollar, the two monies have the same value. You can buy a Big Mac in either Toronto or New York for either $4 Canadian or $3 U.S.

The situation we've just described is called **purchasing power parity**, which means *equal value of money*. If purchasing power parity does not prevail, some powerful forces go to work. To understand these forces, let's suppose that the price of a Big Mac in New York rises to $4 U.S., but in Toronto it remains at $4 Canadian. Suppose the exchange rate remains at $1.33 Canadian per U.S. dollar. In this case, a Big Mac in Toronto still costs $4 Canadian or $3 U.S. But in New York, it costs $4 U.S. or $5.33 Canadian. Money buys more in Canada than in the United States. Money is not of equal value in both countries.

If all (or most) prices have increased in the United States and not increased in Canada, then people will generally expect that the value of the U.S. dollar on the foreign exchange market must fall. In this situation, the exchange rate is expected to fall. The demand for U.S. dollars decreases, and the supply of U.S. dollars increases. The exchange rate falls, as expected. If the exchange rate falls to $1.00 Canadian and there are no further price changes, purchasing power parity is restored. A Big Mac now costs $4 in either U.S. or Canadian dollars in both New York and Toronto.

If prices increase in Canada and other countries but remain constant in the United States, then people will generally expect that the value of the U.S. dollar on the foreign exchange market is too low and that it is going to rise. In this situation, the exchange rate is expected to rise. The demand for U.S. dollars increases and the supply of U.S. dollars decreases. The exchange rate rises, as expected.

Ultimately, the value of money is determined by the price level, which in turn is determined by aggregate supply and aggregate demand (see Chapter 21, pp. 484–489). So the deeper forces that influence the exchange rate have tentacles that spread throughout the economy. If prices in the United States rise faster than those in other countries, the exchange rate falls. And if prices rise more slowly in the United States than in other countries, the exchange rate rises.

Interest Rate Parity Money is worth what it can earn. Again, two kinds of money — Canadian dollars and U.S. dollars, for example — might earn different amounts. For example, suppose a Canadian dollar bank deposit in Toronto earns 5 percent a year and a U.S. dollar bank deposit in New York earns 3 percent a year. In this situation, why does anyone deposit money in New York? Why doesn't all the money flow to Toronto? The answer is because of exchange rate expectations. Suppose people expect the Canadian dollar to depreciate by 2 percent a year. This 2 percent depreciation must be subtracted from the 5 percent interest to obtain the net return of 3 percent a year that an American can earn by depositing funds in a Toronto bank. The two returns are equal. This situation is one of **interest rate parity**, which means *equal rates of return*.

Adjusted for risk, interest rate parity always prevails. Funds move to get the highest return available. If for a few seconds a higher return is available in New York than in Toronto, the demand for U.S. dollars rises and the exchange rate rises until expected rates of return are equal.

The Fed in the Foreign Exchange Market

Interest rates in the United States are determined by the demand for and supply of money (see Chapter 28, pp. 665–666). But the supply of money is influenced by the Fed, so ultimately, the exchange rate is influenced by monetary policy. When interest rates in the United States rise relative to those in other countries, the demand for U.S. dollars increases, the supply of U.S. dollars decreases, and the exchange rate rises. (Similarly, when interest rates in the United States fall relative to those in other countries, the demand for U.S. dollars decreases, the supply of U.S. dollars increases, and the exchange rate falls.)

But the Fed can intervene directly in the foreign exchange market. It can buy or sell dollars and try to smooth out fluctuations in the exchange rate. Let's look at the foreign exchange interventions the Fed can make.

Suppose the Fed wants the exchange rate to be steady at 120 yen per dollar. If the exchange rate rises above 120 yen, the Fed sells dollars. If the exchange rate falls below 120 yen, the Fed buys dollars. By these actions, the Fed changes the supply of dollars and keeps the exchange rate close to its target rate of 120 yen.

FIGURE 33.10   Foreign Exchange
Market Intervention

Initially, the demand for dollars is D_0, the supply of dollars is S, and the exchange rate is 120 yen per dollar. The Fed can intervene in the foreign exchange market to keep the exchange rate close to its target rate (120 yen in this example). If demand increases from D_0 to D_1, the Fed sells dollars to increase supply. If demand decreases from D_0 to D_2, the Fed buys dollars to decrease supply. Persistent intervention on one side of the market cannot be sustained.

Figure 33.10 shows this Fed intervention in the foreign exchange market. The supply of dollars is S, and initially, the demand for dollars is D_0. The equilibrium exchange rate is 120 yen per dollar. This exchange rate is the Fed's target rate, shown by the horizontal red line in the figure.

When the demand for dollars increases and the demand curve shifts rightward to D_1, the Fed sells $0.1 trillion. This action increases the supply of dollars by $0.1 trillion and prevents the exchange rate from rising. When the demand for dollars decreases and the demand curve shifts leftward to D_2, the Fed buys $0.1 trillion. This action decreases the supply of dollars by $0.1 trillion and prevents the exchange rate from falling.

If the demand for dollars fluctuates between D_1 and D_2 and on the average is D_0, the Fed can repeatedly intervene in the way we've just seen. Sometimes

the Fed buys and sometimes it sells, but on the average, it neither buys nor sells.

But suppose the demand for dollars increases permanently from D_0 to D_1. The Fed cannot now maintain the exchange rate at 120 yen per dollar indefinitely. To do so, the Fed would have to sell dollars every day. When the Fed sells dollars in the foreign exchange market, it buys foreign currency. So the Fed would be piling up foreign currency.

Now suppose the demand for dollars decreases permanently from D_0 to D_2. Again the Fed cannot maintain the exchange rate at 120 yen per dollar indefinitely. To do so, the Fed would have to buy dollars every day. When the Fed buys dollars in the foreign exchange market, it uses its holdings of foreign currency. So the Fed would be losing foreign currency. Eventually, it would run out of foreign currency and would then have to abandon its attempt to fix the exchange rate.

REVIEW QUIZ

1 What is the exchange rate and how is it determined?
2 What are the influences of interest rates and the expected future exchange rate on the demand for and supply of dollars in the foreign exchange market?
3 How do changes in the expected future exchange rate influence the actual exchange rate?
4 How do purchasing power parity and interest rate parity affect exchange rate expectations?
5 How can the Fed influence the foreign exchange market?

◆ *Reading Between the Lines* on pp. 798–799 looks at the collapse of the Argentine peso in 2002.

In the final chapter, we expand our view of the global economy and study global stock markets. These are the markets in which firms borrow the funds that finance their investment in new capital. Those funds often cross national borders, and when they do so, they move through the foreign exchange markets and show up in the capital account of the balance of payments. Keep what you've learned about the balance of payments and the foreign exchange market in mind as you work through the stock markets chapter.

The Collapse of the Argentine Peso

THE NEW YORK TIMES, January 4, 2002

Argentina's New Leader Will Present Economic Plan Today

BUENOS AIRES With a substantial devaluation of their currency now certain, Argentines braced for the worst today as President Eduardo Duhalde and his newly appointed cabinet discussed ways to cushion the blow and avoid a repetition of the riots and protests that toppled his predecessor last month.

Economists and political leaders predict that the government will lower the exchange rate of the peso, which by law has been valued at one to one with the dollar for the last decade, by 30 to 40 percent. Mr. Duhalde, who on Tuesday became Argentina's fifth president in two weeks, is scheduled to present an emergency economic package to Congress on Friday that would immediately overturn that policy....

With the shift away from the old exchange policy not yet official and banks refusing to handle foreign exchange transactions, a black market for dollars quickly sprang up, with 1.4 pesos required to obtain a dollar. In neighboring countries, where thousands of Argentines are on summer vacation, the peso's value dropped by up to 50 percent and many merchants began refusing to accept Argentine credit cards.

An abandonment of the one-to-one peg has long been expected, and many Argentines, along with domestic and foreign-owned companies, began moving their assets from pesos into dollars months ago. "This is the end of a story that has already been announced," Mr. Ruckauf [the newly appointed foreign minister] said.

As a result of such actions, the Central Bank's reserves fell by $18 billion last year and 24 percent of all deposits left the financial system, as Mr. Duhalde acknowledged in a somber inaugural speech Tuesday night....

Essence of the Story

- Argentina pegged the value of its peso at one U.S. dollar in 1992.

- At the beginning of 2002, economists and political leaders predicted that the value of the peso would fall by 30 to 40 percent.

- Banks refused to handle foreign exchange transactions, and in black markets, the peso's value fell by up to 50 percent.

- People and businesses had begun to move their assets from pesos into dollars months ago.

- The Argentine Central Bank's reserves fell by $18 billion in 2001.

Economic Analysis

■ Argentina has had a long history of high inflation (see *Reading Between the Lines*, pp. 648–649.).

■ To avoid inflation, the Argentine government pegged the value of the peso to the U.S. dollar.

■ Figure 1 shows the last part of the period in which this fixed exchange rate system was in place. The peso had a constant value at 1 U.S. dollar through 2001. Then the peso crashed, first to 40 cents and then to 30 cents.

■ Figure 2 shows how the exchange rate was held constant.

■ The Argentine central bank's target exchange rate of $1.00 per peso was achieved by offsetting fluctuations in the demand for pesos with changes in the supply of pesos.

■ So long as demand fluctuated around the target level, the exchange rate target could be achieved.

■ During 2001, as people became more and more sure that the peso would fall in value, the demand for pesos decreased. The supply of pesos increased as more people offered pesos for sale.

■ Figure 3 shows the effects of these changes at the beginning of 2002.

■ The demand for pesos decreased from D_{Jan} to D_{Feb} and supply increased from S_{Jan} to S_{Feb}.

■ The peso crashed.

You're The Voter

■ Why does the foreign-exchange value of the peso matter for Argentina?

■ Could the Argentine central bank have done anything to maintain the value of the peso?

■ Could the Argentine government have done anything to maintain the value of the peso?

■ Thinking only about the economic well-being of the people of Argentina, would they have been better off if the government had implemented policies during the 1990s that prevented the 2002 devaluation of the peso?

Figure 1 The peso exchange rate

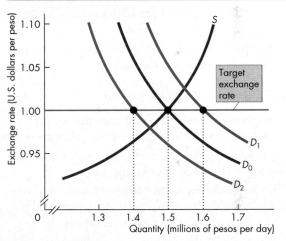

Figure 2 Pegging the peso

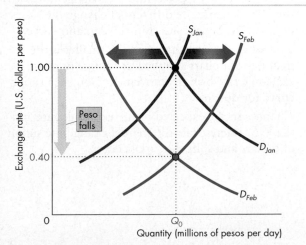

Figure 3 The peso crashes

SUMMARY

KEY POINTS

Financing International Trade (pp. 784–788)

- International trade, borrowing, and lending are financed by using foreign currency.
- A country's international transactions are recorded in its balance of payments accounts.
- The balance of payments has three accounts: current account, capital account, and official settlement account.
- Historically, the United States has been a net lender to the rest of the world, but in 1989, that situation changed and the United States became a net borrower and a net debtor.
- Net exports equal the government sector balance plus the private sector balance.

The Exchange Rate (pp. 789–797)

- Foreign currency is obtained in exchange for domestic currency in the foreign exchange market.
- The exchange rate is determined by demand and supply in the foreign exchange market.
- The lower the exchange rate, the greater is the quantity of dollars demanded. A change in the exchange rate brings a movement along the demand curve for dollars.
- Changes in the expected future exchange rate and the U.S. interest rate differential change the demand for dollars and shift the demand curve.
- The lower the exchange rate, the smaller is the quantity of dollars supplied. A change in the exchange rate brings a movement along the supply curve for dollars.
- Changes in the expected future exchange rate and the U.S. interest rate differential change the supply of dollars and shift the supply curve.

- Fluctuations in the exchange rate occur because the fluctuations in the demand for and supply of dollars are not independent.
- The Fed can intervene in the foreign exchange market to smooth fluctuations in the dollar.

KEY FIGURES AND TABLE

KEY TERMS

PROBLEMS

*1. The citizens of Silecon, whose currency is the grain, conduct the following transactions in 2002:

Item	Billions of grains
Imports of goods and services	350
Exports of goods and services	500
Borrowing from the rest of the world	60
Lending to the rest of the world	200
Increase in official holdings of foreign currency	10

a. Set out the three balance of payments accounts for Silecon.
b. Does the central bank intervene in the foreign exchange market?

2. The citizens of Spin, whose currency is the wheel, conduct the following transactions in 2002:

Item	Wheels
Imports of goods and services	100
Exports of goods and services	120
Borrowing from the rest of the world	4
Lending to the rest of the world	24
Increase in official holdings of foreign currency	0

a. Set out the three balance of payments accounts for Spin.
b. Does the central bank intervene in the foreign exchange market?

*3. The figure at the bottom of the page shows the flows of income and expenditure in Dream Land in 2000. The amounts are in millions of dollars. GDP in Dream Land is $120 million.
a. Calculate Dream Land's net exports.
b. Calculate saving in Dream Land.
c. How is Dream Land's investment financed?

4. The figure shows the flows of income and expenditure in Dream Land in 2001. The amounts are in millions of dollars. Dream Land's GDP has increased to $130 million, but all the other items whose values are provided in the figure remain the same as they were in 2000.
a. Calculate Dream Land's net exports in 2001.
b. Calculate saving in Dream Land in 2001.
c. How is Dream Land's investment financed?

*5. The table on the next page tells you about Ecflex, a country whose currency is the band. The official settlements balance is zero. Net interest income and net transfers from abroad are zero.
Calculate the following for Ecflex:
a. Imports of goods and services
b. Current account balance
c. Capital account balance
d. Net taxes
e. Private sector balance

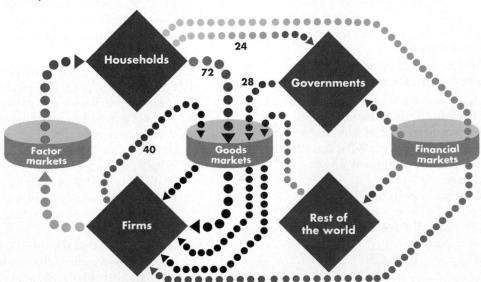

Item	Billion bands
GDP	100
Consumption expenditure	60
Government purchases of goods and services	24
Investment	22
Exports of goods and services	20
Government budget deficit	4

6. You are told the following about Ecfix, a country whose currency is the rock. The central bank intervenes to keep the exchange rate fixed.

Item	Billion rocks
GDP	400
Consumption expenditure	240
Government purchases of goods and services	100
Investment	100
Exports of goods and services	80
Saving	90

Calculate the following for Ecfix:
a. Imports of goods and services
b. Current account balance
c. Government sector balance
d. Net taxes
e. Private sector balance

*7. A country's currency appreciates, and its official holdings of foreign currency increase. What can you say about:
a. The central bank's intervention in the foreign exchange market?
b. The country's current account balance?
c. The country's official settlements account?

8. A country has a lower inflation rate than all other countries. It has more rapid economic growth. The central bank does not intervene in the foreign exchange market. What can you say about each of the following (and why):
a. The exchange rate?
b. The current account balance?
c. The expected exchange rate?
d. The interest rate differential?
e. Interest rate parity?
f. Purchasing power parity?

CRITICAL THINKING

1. Study *Reading Between the Lines* on pp. 798–799 and then answer the following questions.
   a. What happened to the Argentine peso in 2002?
   b. Why is it difficult for a central bank to peg the value of its currency when people firmly believe it is going to depreciate?
   c. If the central bank and commercial banks refuse to deal in a currency, how do people buy and sell the currency and what determines its price?
   d. If you were running Argentina, what would you try to do about the peso? Would you try to restore the old dollar standard? Why or why not?

WEB EXERCISES

1. Use the link on your Parkin Web site to visit the Bureau of Economic Analysis and find data on the United States balance of payments accounts.
   a. When did the United States last have a current account surplus?
   b. Does the United States have a surplus or a deficit in trade in goods?
   c. Does the United States have a surplus or a deficit in trade in services?
   d. What has happened to foreign investment in the United States during the past 10 years?
   e. Do you think the U.S. balance of payments record is a matter for concern? Why or why not?

2. Use the link on your Parkin Web site to visit PACIFIC (an exchange rate service) and read the page on purchasing power parity.
   a. What is purchasing power parity?
   b. Which currencies are the most overvalued relative to the U.S. dollar today?
   c. Which currencies are the most undervalued relative to the U.S. dollar today?
   d. Can you offer some suggestions as to why some currencies are overvalued and some are undervalued?
   e. Do you think that the information on overvaluation and undervaluation is useful to currency speculators? Why or why not?

CHAPTER 34

Irrational Exuberance?

On December 5, 1996, Alan Greenspan, chairman of the Federal Reserve, said that stock market investors were suffering from *irrational exuberance*. It appeared that some people agreed with Mr. Greenspan, for when the New York Stock Exchange opened the next morning, the Dow Jones Industrial Average immediately dropped by 2.3 percent. During the American night, stock prices in Japan, Hong Kong, Germany, and Britain had dropped an average of almost 4 percent. ◆ Alan Greenspan's remark was prompted by an extraordinary rise in stock prices in the United States and around the world that began in 1994 and was to continue through 1999. During these years, the Dow (as the Dow Jones Industrial Average is known) tripled! It then stopped climbing and eventually nose-dived following September 11, 2001, but only temporarily. By January 2002, prices were back at the pre–September 11 levels. ◆ How are stock prices determined? Do investors suffer from "irrational exuberance" or are their buying and selling decisions rational? How does the economy influence the stock market? And how does the stock market influence the economy?

◻ You are going to probe some interesting questions in this chapter. But first, a warning: You will not learn in this chapter which stocks to buy and how to get rich. You will, though, learn some important lessons about traps to avoid that could easily make you poor.

After studying this chapter, you will be able to

■ Explain what a firm's stock is and how its rate of return and price are related

■ Describe the global stock markets and the stock price indexes

■ Describe the long-term performance of stock prices and earnings

■ Explain what determines the price of stock and why stock prices are volatile

■ Explain why it is rational to diversify a stock portfolio rather than to hold the one stock that has the highest expected return

■ Explain how the stock market influences the economy and how the economy influences the stock market

Stock Market Basics

ALL FIRMS GET SOME OF THEIR FINANCIAL CAPITAL from the people who own the firm. A large firm has possibly millions of owners from whom it raises billions of dollars in financial capital. These owners are the firm's stockholders — the holders of stock issued by the firm.

What Is Stock?

Stock is a tradable security that a firm issues to certify that the stock holder owns a share of the firm. Figure 34.1 shows a famous stock certificate that has become a collector's item — a Walt Disney Company stock certificate. The value of a firm's stock is called the firm's **equity capital** (or just equity). The terms "stock" and "equity" are often used interchangeably.

A stockholder has *limited liability*, which means that if the firm can't pay all its debts, a stockholder's liability for the firm's debts is limited to the amount invested in the firm by that stockholder. For example, when Enron collapsed, its stockholders lost everything they had invested in the firm's stock, but they weren't forced to contribute anything to make up for Enron's remaining debts.

FIGURE 34.1   A Stock Certificate

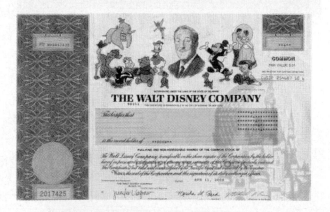

The Walt Disney Company issues a colorful stock certificate to record the ownership of its common stock. Attractive share certificates, like postage stamps and coins, become collectors' items.

Source: © Disney Enterprises, Inc.

Stockholders receive a **dividend**, which is a share of the firm's profit, in proportion to their stock holdings. For example, holders of stock in PepsiCo received a dividend of 58 cents per share during 2002.

Firms issue two types of stock:

- Preferred stock
- Common stock

Preferred stock entitles its owner to a pre-agreed dividend before common stock dividends are paid and to first claim on the firm's assets in the event that it is liquidated.

Common stock holders are entitled to a share of the firm's assets and earnings and to a vote (one vote per share held) in the selection of the firm's directors.

When a firm issues stock, the buyer of the stock invests directly in the firm. In March 1986, Microsoft Corporation issued 161 million shares of common stock for $21 a share and raised a total of $3.4 billion. The buyers of those shares paid Microsoft Corporation.

Most stockholders buy stock not from the firm that issues it but from other holders who bought the stock from yet other holders. On an average day during the past ten years, 14 million Microsoft shares have changed hands. Microsoft didn't receive anything from these transactions and doesn't even keep track of who owns its stock. It hires another firm, Mellon Investor Services, to do that job and to issue share certificates.

What Is a Stock Exchange?

People buy and sell stock on a stock exchange. A **stock exchange** is an organized market on which people can buy and sell stock. In the United States, the shares of the stock of the major corporations are traded on the New York Stock Exchange (NYSE). High-tech stocks are traded on the National Association of Securities Dealers Automated Quotation (NASDAQ) system. Other stocks are traded on the American Stock Exchange and on regional stock exchanges such as the Pacific Stock Exchange in Los Angeles and San Francisco.

Some stock exchanges — the New York Stock Exchange is one of them — are physical trading arenas. Traders shout and signal their buy and sell orders on the trading floor of the exchange. In the case of the New York Stock Exchange, trades take place on the trading floor on Wall Street in New York City.

Other stock exchanges — NASDAQ is one of them — do not have a trading floor. These more recently created or upgraded stock exchanges trade through a computer and telecommunications network that links together buyers and sellers from all parts of the world. The NASDAQ computer system enables more than 1.3 million traders in 83 countries to trade more than 4,000 (mainly high-tech) stocks.

NASDAQ is a global stock exchange with large operations in Canada, Japan, and Europe as well as the United States. The other major stock exchanges in the global economy are those in London, Frankfurt, Tokyo, and Hong Kong.

Stock Prices and Returns

You can find the price and other information about the stocks of most of the large firms in the daily newspaper. You can also find the same information (and much more) on a newspaper's Web site. The Web sites of the stock exchanges and of major stock dealers also provide a wealth of data on stocks. You can also install software such as MarketBrowser that provides an easy way of viewing stock prices and making graphs of the recent price history. (Your Parkin Web site provides the links that will get you to these Web resources.)

To read the stock market reports, you need to know the meaning of a few technical terms that we'll now review.

The point of buying stock is to earn an income from it. A **stock price** is the price at which one share of a firm's stock trades on a stock exchange. The price is expressed like any other price: in dollars and cents. For example, on March 2, 2002, the price of a share of Procter & Gamble stock was $89.94. The price can change from minute to minute and almost certainly will change over the trading day, and it can be tracked on the Internet (with a short time delay). Because the price keeps changing, in addition to tracking the current price, people also pay attention to the high and low prices during the previous year and the change from day to day.

The annual **return** on a stock consists of the stock's dividend plus its capital gain (or minus its capital loss) during the year. A stock's **capital gain** is the increase in its price, and a stock's **capital loss** is the decrease in its price. For example, between March 2001 and March 2002, the price of Procter & Gamble stock increased from $79.10 to $89.94, a capital gain of $10.84.

The absolute return — the number of dollars earned from the stock — is not very informative because the stock might be cheap or costly. More informative is the return per dollar invested. So we express the return, or its components, as a percentage of the stock price. The dividend expressed as a percentage of the stock price is called the stock's **dividend yield**. For example, during the year from March 2001 to March 2002, Procter & Gamble paid dividends of $1.56. Expressed as a percentage of the price of the stock in March 2001, the dividend yield was 1.7 percent.

The return on a stock expressed as a percentage of the stock price is called the stock's **rate of return**. For example, the return of a Procter & Gamble share in the year from March 2001 to March 2002 was a dividend of $1.56 plus a capital gain of $10.84, or $12.40. The rate of return was $12.40 as a percentage of $79.10, the price of a share in March 2001, which is 15.3 percent.

Earnings and the Price-Earnings Ratio

A firm's accounting profit is called the firm's **earnings**. A firm's directors decide how much of the earnings to pay out as dividends and how much to retain — called *retained earnings* — to invest in new capital and expand the firm.

Because earnings are the ultimate source of income for stockholders, a lot of attention is paid to a firm's earnings. And those earnings must be calculated and reported to meet standards of accuracy determined by federal authorities that include the Securities and Exchange Commission and the Financial Accounting Standards Board. Following the Enron debacle during 2001, these standards have been reviewed and will be the object of an ongoing review for some time.

Earnings are the source of stockholder returns, but it is the relationship between a stock price and earnings that matters most to the stockholder. So another number that is routinely calculated for each stock is its **price-earnings ratio** — the stock price divided by the most recent year's earnings. For example during 2001, Procter & Gamble's reported earnings were $2.14 per share, so its price-earnings ratio was $89.94 divided by $2.14, which is 42.

The price-earnings ratio is the inverse of earnings per dollar invested. For example, because in March 2002 the price of share of Procter & Gamble stock was $89.94 and the earnings per share during 2001 were $2.14, earnings per dollar invested were $2.14 ÷ $89.84 = 0.0238, or 2.38 percent. Check that 0.0238, earnings per dollar invested, equals the inverse of the price-earnings ratio and equals 1/42.

Now that you've reviewed some of the key vocabulary of the stock market, let's look at the stock market report.

Reading the Stock Market Report

Figure 34.2 shows part of a *Wall Street Journal* stock market page. (The format varies from one newspaper to another, but the content is similar in all of them.) You can see some numbers for Procter & Gamble that might seem familiar. They are some of the numbers that we've just used to illustrate the technical terms used in the report. Figure 34.2 also provides the Microsoft line from the stock market report.

The first column shows the year-to-date percentage change. The next two columns show the range of prices for the stock (expressed in dollars) over the preceding year. This information is useful because it tells you about the volatility of the stock. Some stocks fluctuate a lot more than others. By glancing at the numbers in these two columns, you can get a quick sense of how volatile the price is. In this example, the price of Microsoft stock ranged from a low of $47.50 to a high of $76.15, a range of $28.65 and more than

50 percent of the lowest price. Following the firm's name is the ticker symbol, MSFT for Microsoft and PG for Procter & Gamble. This symbol appears on real-time reports of the stock price. You need to know the symbol for any stocks that you own so that you can easily check their prices during the trading day.

The dividend paid, expressed in dollars, comes next. In this example, Microsoft didn't pay a dividend and Procter & Gamble paid $1.56 per share. The dividend yield — the dividend as a percentage of the stock's closing price — comes next, followed by the price-earnings ratio. The next column records the volume of trades in hundreds during the day. This number is the actual number of shares bought and sold. In this example, 1,770,000 Microsoft shares and 6,267,000 Procter & Gamble shares changed hands during the day.

The next column shows the closing price, and the final column shows the change in price over the day.

Stock Price Indexes

Because thousands of different stocks are traded on the world's stock markets every business day, we need a handy way of summarizing the thousands of different stock prices. Investors want to know not only how their own stocks have performed, but also how they have performed relative to other stocks on the average.

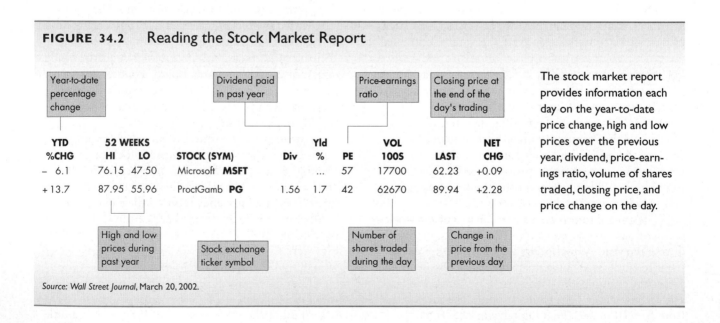

FIGURE 34.2   Reading the Stock Market Report

YTD %CHG	52 WEEKS HI	52 WEEKS LO	STOCK (SYM)	Div	Yld %	PE	VOL 100S	LAST	NET CHG
– 6.1	76.15	47.50	Microsoft **MSFT**		...	57	17700	62.23	+0.09
+ 13.7	87.95	55.96	ProctGamb **PG**	1.56	1.7	42	62670	89.94	+2.28

Year-to-date percentage change

Dividend paid in past year

Price-earnings ratio

Closing price at the end of the day's trading

High and low prices during past year

Stock exchange ticker symbol

Number of shares traded during the day

Change in price from the previous day

The stock market report provides information each day on the year-to-date price change, high and low prices over the previous year, dividend, price-earnings ratio, volume of shares traded, closing price, and price change on the day.

Source: Wall Street Journal, March 20, 2002.

To make these comparisons and to indicate the general movements in the market, index numbers of the average stock prices are calculated and published. You will encounter hundreds of different stock price indexes, but three main U.S. stock price indexes to watch for are the

- S&P Composite Index
- Dow Jones Industrial Average (DJIA)
- NASDAQ Index

S&P Composite Index The S&P Composite Index (also known as the S&P 500) is an average of the prices of 500 stocks traded on the New York Stock Exchange, the NASDAQ, and the American Stock Exchange. The index is calculated and published by Standard & Poor's (S&P), a New York financial information and services company. Figure 34.3 shows the breadth of coverage of this index, which provides one of the most comprehensive guides to the state of the stock market. Notice in Fig. 34.3 the importance of consumer products in the index.

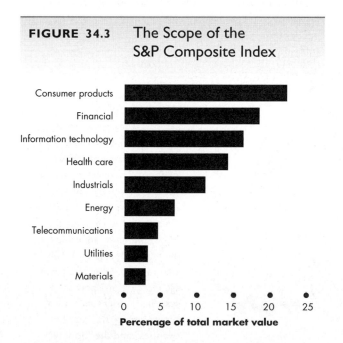

FIGURE 34.3 The Scope of the S&P Composite Index

Percentage of total market value

The 500 stocks in the S&P Composite Index cover all parts of the economy. Consumer products are the largest component of the index.

Source: www.spglobal.com.

DJIA The DJIA, or "the Dow," as it is often called, is perhaps the best-known stock price index. The Dow Jones Company is the owner of the *Wall Street Journal*, and because of this link, the Dow is the most widely and rapidly reported barometer of the state of the New York stock market.

Although the DJIA is widely quoted, it is not as broadly representative as the S&P Composite index. It is an average of the prices of just 30 stocks of major U.S. corporations traded on the New York Stock Exchange. In 2002, these corporations are Philip Morris Companies, Inc.; Eastman Kodak Co.; J.P. Morgan Chase & Co.; General Motors Corp.; E.I. DuPont de Nemours & Co.; SBC Communications, Inc.; Caterpillar, Inc.; Merck & Co., Inc.; International Paper Co.; Minnesota Mining & Manufacturing Co.; Exxon Mobil Corp.; Honeywell International, Inc.; General Electric Co.; Hewlett-Packard Co.; Procter & Gamble Co.; Alcoa, Inc.; Coca-Cola Co.; Boeing Co.; Citigroup, Inc.; United Technologies Corp.; Johnson & Johnson; AT&T Corp.; Walt Disney Co.; McDonald's Corp.; American Express Co.; International Business Machines Corp.; Wal-Mart Stores, Inc.; Home Depot, Inc.; Intel Corp.; and Microsoft Corp.

NASDAQ Index The NASDAQ index is the average price of the stocks traded on this global electronic stock exchange. Like the Dow, this index looks at only part of the market — in this case, the high-tech part.

Four indexes track the state of the world's other major stock markets. The are the

- FTSE 100
- DAX
- Nikkei
- Hang Seng

FTSE 100 The FTSE 100 (pronounced "footsie") is an index calculated by FTSE, a financial information services firm owned by the *Financial Times* (FT) and the London Stock Exchange (SE). (The *Financial Times* is Europe's leading business and financial daily newspaper and rivals the *Wall Street Journal* outside the United States.)

DAX The DAX index is an average of prices on the Frankfurt stock exchange in Germany.

Nikkei The Nikkei index is the average of prices on the Tokyo stock exchange.

Hang Seng The Hang Seng index is average of prices on the Hong Kong stock exchange.

Stock Price Performance

How has the stock market performed in recent years and over the longer term? Do stock prices generally rise? How much do they fluctuate? To answer these questions, we'll look at some actual stock price data, using the broadest index, the S&P Composite. But first, we need to make two technical points.

Inflation Adjustments Stock prices, like all prices, need to be corrected for inflation. So rather than looking at the actual S&P index numbers, we deflate them to remove the effects of inflation and examine *real* stock price indexes.

Ratio Scale Graphs Stock prices rise and fall, but over the long term, they rise. The interesting question about stock price changes is not the absolute change but the percentage change. For example, a

10 point change in the S&P Composite Index was a 1 percent change in stock prices in 2002 but a 10 percent change in stock prices in 1982. To reveal percentage changes, we graph stock prices using a ratio scale (or logarithmic scale). On a ratio scale, the distance between 1 and 10 equals that between 10 and 100 and between 100 and 1,000. Each distance represents a tenfold increase.

Stock Prices

Figure 34.4 shows the real S&P Composite index over 130 years measured on a ratio scale. The figure also shows earnings per share over the same period.

Focus first on stock prices (shown by the red line in the figure). Notice the general upward trend of the real stock price index. The index in 2001 was 926, 33 times its 1871 value of 29. This increase translates to a 2.7 percent per year increase on the average.

This average rate of increase masks some subperiods of spectacular increases and spectacular decreases in stock prices. The largest increases occurred during the "roaring twenties" and the "booming nineties." Between 1920 and 1929, on the eve of the Great Depression, stock prices increased by almost 19

FIGURE 34.4 Stock Prices and Earnings

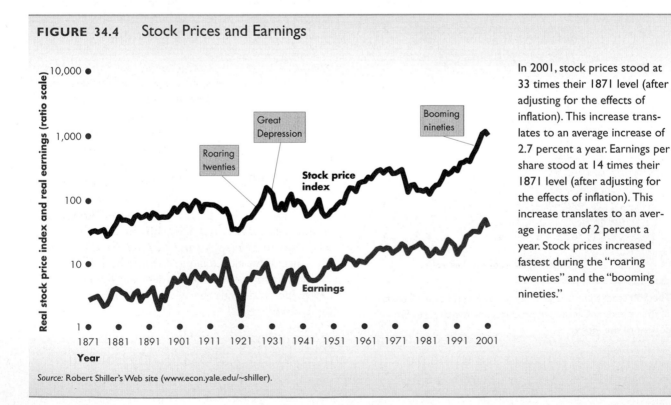

In 2001, stock prices stood at 33 times their 1871 level (after adjusting for the effects of inflation). This increase translates to an average increase of 2.7 percent a year. Earnings per share stood at 14 times their 1871 level (after adjusting for the effects of inflation). This increase translates to an average increase of 2 percent a year. Stock prices increased fastest during the "roaring twenties" and the "booming nineties."

Source: Robert Shiller's Web site (www.econ.yale.edu/~shiller).

percent a year. Between 1991 and 2000, they increased by 15 percent a year, and between 1995 and 2000, the rate of increase hit 24 percent a year.

The most spectacular period of falling stock prices occurred during World War I (1914–1918), the opening years of the Great Depression (the early 1930s), and the mid-1970s.

Earnings Per Share

Stocks are worth owning because of what they earn. Like stock prices, earnings per share have increased over the long term. But the rate of increase in earnings per share is less than the rate of increase in stock prices. Earnings per share in 2001 were 14 times their 1871 level, which translates to a growth rate of 2 percent per year on the average.

Figure 34.5 repackages the information contained in Fig. 34.4 and looks at the price-earnings ratio over the 130 years from 1871 to 2001. The average price-earnings ratio has been 13.9. But there is a lot of variation around this average value. The low values of around 6 occurred in 1916, 1950, and 1979. The high values of around 27 occurred in 1894, 1921, 1931, and the period from 1998 into 2001.

Figure 34.5 is important for the perspective in which it places the stock market's recent performance. Stock prices were high and increased rapidly during the late 1990s and into 2001. And the price-earnings ratio increased to a level not seen since the opening years of the Great Depression.

Figure 34.5 also provides a reminder that in all previous periods when the price-earnings ratio was above average, it eventually fell below the average.

Being a ratio of stock prices and earnings, the price-earnings ratio can change either because stock prices change or because earnings change. The price-earnings ratio can fall sharply because either stock prices fall sharply or earnings rise sharply. But all the cases in which the price-earnings ratio has fallen sharply are ones in which stock prices have fallen sharply. For this reason, some people are concerned that the stock market of the 1990s and 2000 increased by too much and that a sharp fall is coming some time in the future.

What does it mean to say that stock prices have increased by too much? To answer this question, we need to understand the forces that determine stock prices and the relationship between prices and earnings. That is the task of the next section.

FIGURE 34.5   The Price-Earnings Ratio

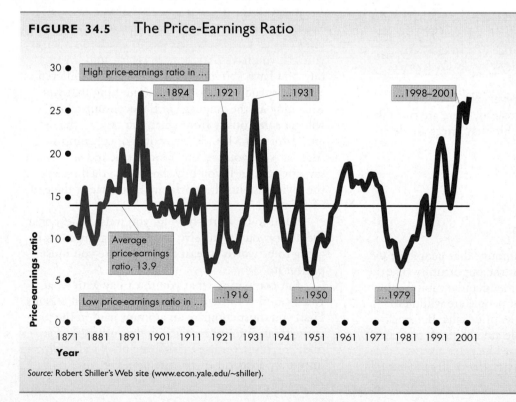

The price-earnings ratio has swung between a low of around 6 in 1916, 1950, and 1979 and a high of around 27 in 1894, 1921, 1931, and 1998–2001. The average price-earnings ratio is 13.9. When the price-earnings ratio exceeds the average, it eventually falls below the average.

Source: Robert Shiller's Web site (www.econ.yale.edu/~shiller).

REVIEW QUIZ

1 What is a stock and what is the distinction between a preferred stock and a common stock?

2 What are the two sources of return from a stock?

3 What is a stock exchange and what are the leading stock exchanges in the United States and around the world?

4 What is a price-earnings ratio and how is it calculated?

5 What is the most comprehensive stock price index for the United States? How does it differ from some other major indexes?

6 Describe the major trends and fluctuations in U.S. stock prices, earnings per share, and the price-earnings ratio since 1871.

How Are Stock Prices Determined?

YOU'VE SEEN THAT STOCK PRICES GENERALLY RISE over long periods but fluctuate a lot over shorter periods. What determines the price of a stock? Why is the long-term trend upward? Why do stock prices fluctuate so much?

There is no firm and universally agreed-upon answer to these questions. Instead, there are two possible types of answers. They are that prices are determined by

■ Market fundamentals
■ Speculative bubbles

Market Fundamentals

The price of a stock is the amount that people *on the average* are willing to pay for the opportunity that the stock provides to earn a dividend and a capital gain. If a stock price exceeds what people are willing to pay, they sell the stock and its price falls. If a stock price is less than what people are willing to pay, they buy and the stock price rises. The price always settles down at the amount that people are willing to pay.

The *market fundamentals* price that people are willing to pay is a price that is based on the deep sources of value that make a stock worth holding. These sources of value are

1. The activities of the firm that issued the stock
2. The stream of profits that these activities generate
3. The stream of dividend payments to stockholders
4. The degree and uncertainty surrounding profits and dividends
5. The attitudes of stockholders toward the timing and uncertainty of the stream of dividends

We're now going to discover how these deep sources of value of a firm's stock combine to determine the market fundamentals price of the stock. To do so, we're going to figure out how much you would be willing to pay for a stock or be willing to accept to sell it.

Price, Value, and Willingness to Pay The market fundamentals value of a stock is the price that people *on the average* are willing to pay for the opportunity that the stock provides to earn a dividend and a capital gain. To figure out how this price is determined, let's look at your decision to buy or sell a stock.

Suppose the price of a stock that you own is $1. You're trying to figure out whether to buy 50 more units of this stock or to sell the 50 units you own. If you sell, you have $50 more to spend, and if you buy, you have $50 less to spend — a $100 difference. You can spend $100 today on something that you will enjoy. In the language of the economist, you will get some utility from what you buy — the marginal utility of $100 dollars worth of consumption. Alternatively, you can buy more stock and sell it later, say, after a year. If you buy the stock, you'll receive the dividend plus the stock's market price at the end of the year.

For it to be worth buying, you must believe that the utility you will receive from owning the stock is going to be worth at least the $1 a share you must pay for it.

But comparing what you must pay with what you'll gain is a difficult exercise for two main reasons. First, you must compare an amount paid in the present with an amount received in the future. And second, you must compare a definite price today with an uncertain dividend and future price.

Present Versus Future People are impatient. We prefer good things to happen sooner rather than later, other things remaining the same. Suppose that you're offered the chance to take an exotic trip that really excites you and are told that you can go right away or after a year. Which would you choose (other things remaining the same)? Most of us would take the trip right away. Because we prefer good things now more than later, we must be compensated for delaying consumption.

Certainty Versus Uncertainty People prefer certainty to uncertainty, other things remaining the same. Suppose you're offered the opportunity to pay $50 for a chance to win $100 on the flip of a coin. Would you accept the offer? Most people would not. Accepting the offer would give you a 50 percent chance of gaining $50 and a 50 percent chance of losing $50. On the average, you get nothing from this offer. Your *expected return* is zero. Most people need to be compensated for taking risks, and the bigger the risk, the bigger is the compensation that must be offered to make bearing the risk worthwhile.

In figuring out what you're willing to pay for a stock, you can see that, for two reasons, you will not be willing to pay as much as the amount that you expect to receive in dividend and from selling the stock. You're going to get the returns later and you're going to face uncertainty, so you must be compensated for both of these consequences of buying a stock.

Discounting Future Uncertain Returns Another way of expressing the relationship between the price you're willing to pay and what you expect to get back is to *discount* the uncertain future amount. You get a discount when a shop lowers the price of an item. And you will insist on a discount if you buy a stock.

To determine the discounted price, we multiply the original price by a **discount factor**. If you get a 20 percent discount on something, you pay 80 percent, or 0.8, of the original price. The discount factor is 0.8.

We can use the idea of a discount factor to link the highest price you're willing to pay for a stock to the amount you'll get back from the stock a year later. Let's call this price P. Suppose that your discount factor is 0.8, that you believe that the stock will pay a dividend of 5¢, and that its price next year will be $1.20. Then the highest price you're willing to pay is

$$P = 0.8 \times (\$0.05 + \$1.20) = \$1.$$

In this example, you would be on the fence. If the price were a bit less than $1, you'd buy, and if the price were a bit more than $1, you'd sell the stock that you already own.

Because people buy if the price is less than the highest price they are willing to pay and sell if the price is greater than the highest price they are willing to pay, the market price moves toward the average of what people are willing to pay. If the price exceeded the average of what people are willing to pay, there would be more sellers than buyers and the price would fall. If the price was less than the average of what people are willing to pay, there would be more buyers than sellers and the price would rise. Only if the price equals the average of what people are willing to pay is there no tendency for it to rise or fall.

The Stock Price Equation Call the price of a stock P_1, the dividend D_1, the price at the end of a year P_2, and the discount factor b_1. Then the stock price is the expected value of the discounted uncertain future dividend and stock price. That is,

$$P_1 = \text{Expected value of } [b_1(D_1 + P_2)].$$

Expected Future Stock Price You've seen that the stock price depends on expectations about the future stock price. So to work out what you're willing to pay for a stock today, you must forecast next period's price.

The market fundamentals method assumes that an investor's forecast of a future stock price is a rational expectation. A **rational expectation** is a forecast that uses all the available information, including knowledge of the relevant economic forces that influence the variable being forecasted.

But the stock price equation tells us how the price at one time depends on the expected price a year later. This same stock price equation relationship applies to the current period and all future periods. So if we call next period's price P_2, next period's discount factor b_2, next period's dividend D_2, and the price at the end of next period P_3, you can see that the stock price equation next year will be

$$P_2 = \text{Expected value of } [b_2(D_2 + P_3)].$$

That is, the price next period depends on the expected dividend next period and the price at the end of the next period.

This relationship repeats period after period into the future. And each period's expected future price depends on the dividend expected in that period along with the price at the end of the period.

Table 34.1 illustrates the link between the current price and the expected future price, dividend, and discount factor. In period 1, the price depends on expectations about the period-2 price. In period 2, the price depends on expectations about the period-3 price. And in period 3, the price depends on expectations about the period-4 price. This relationship repeats indefinitely to period N.

Because each period's price depends on the expected price in the following period, the dividend stream, D_1, D_2, D_3, ... D_N, is the only fundamental that determines the price of a stock.

Market Fundamentals Price   The market fundamental stock price depends only on the stream of expected future dividend payments. If the dividend is expected to rise, the stock price rises. And starting from a given dividend, if the dividend is expected to grow at a faster rate, the stock price rises.

But dividends depend on profit, or earnings, so if earnings are expected to increase, dividends will also be expected to increase — if not right away, then at some point in the future. So if earnings increase, the stock price increases. And starting from a given level of earnings, if earnings are expected to grow more quickly, the stock price rises.

TABLE 34.1   Rational Expectations

$P_1 =$ Expected value of $[b_1(D_1 + P_2)]$

$P_2 =$ Expected value of $[b_2(D_2 + P_3)]$

$P_3 =$ Expected value of $[b_3(D_3 + P_4)]$

$P_N =$ Expected value of $[b_N(D_N + P_{N+1})]$

The core market fundamental is the expected dividend that will be earned each period out into the indefinite future. Rational expectations of future prices and future discount factors are driven by this core fundamental.

Notice that it is changes in expected future earnings and dividends that drive changes in stock price, not changes in *the actual* earnings or dividends. But expectations about the future don't change without reason. And when actual earnings change, investors project some of that actual change into the future. So fluctuations in actual earnings bring fluctuations in stock prices.

In reality, the link between earnings and stock prices is a loose one. You can see just how loose by glancing back at Fig. 34.5 and noting the large swings that range between 6 and 27 in the price-earnings ratio. The booming stock prices of the late 1990s, for example, outpaced the growth of earnings during that same period by a huge margin.

For this reason, some economists believe that stock prices can be understood only as speculative bubbles. Let's now look at this approach.

Speculative Bubbles

A **speculative bubble** is a price increase followed by a price plunge, both of which occur because people expect them to occur and act on that expectation.

Suppose that most people believe that stock prices are going to rise by 30 percent next year. With such a huge price rise, stocks provide the best available rate of return. The demand for stocks increases, and stock prices rise by the expected amount immediately.

Conversely, suppose that most people believe that stock prices are going to *fall* by 30 percent next year. With such a huge price fall, stockholders will earn less than people who simply sit on cash. In this situation, the demand for stocks collapses and a selling spree brings stock prices tumbling by the expected amount.

Why might either of these events occur? And why would a bubble burst? Why would a price collapse follow a price rise?

Guessing Other People's Guesses   Part of the answer to the questions just posed arises from the fact that forecasting future stock prices means forecasting other people's forecasts — or, more accurately, guessing other people's guesses.

The most famous English economist of the twentieth century, John Maynard Keynes, described the challenge of the stock market investor as being like that of trying to win the prize in a "select the most beautiful person" contest. Each entrant must pick the most beautiful person from a group of ten photographs. The winner is selected at random from all those who chose the photograph that most other entrants chose. So the challenge is not to pick the most beautiful person, but to pick the one that most people will pick. Or is it to pick the one that most people think that most people will pick? Or is it to pick the one that most people think that most people think that most people will pick? And so on!

Because no one knows the correct choice and because everyone faces the same challenge and shares the same sources of information, people are likely to use similar rules of thumb and theories to guide them. So people might behave in a herdlike way and form and act upon similar expectations.

The booming stock market of the 1990s provides an example of the possibility of a speculative bubble.

The Booming Nineties: A Bubble?

Some economists believe that the booming stock market of the 1990s occurred because the market fundamentals changed. They see the stock price rise as the consequence of a "new economy" in which the rational expectation is that earnings will grow in the future at a more rapid rate than in the past.

Other economists believe that the market of the booming nineties was a speculative bubble. Prominent among those who take this view is Robert Shiller, a professor at Yale University, who explains his view in a popular and readable book, *Irrational Exuberance*.

According to Robert Shiller, the late 1990s stock price rise was a bubble encouraged by 12 "precipitating factors":

1. The arrival of the Internet at a time of solid earnings growth
2. A sense that the United States had triumphed over its former rivals
3. A cultural change that favors business and profit
4. A Republican Congress and cuts in capital gains taxes
5. The baby boom and its perceived effects on the stock market
6. An expansion of media reporting of business news
7. Increasingly optimistic forecasts by "experts"
8. The expansion of pension plans with fixed contributions
9. The growth of mutual funds
10. The fall in inflation
11. The expansion of stock trading opportunities
12. A rise of gambling opportunities

Many of these factors directly influence stockholder expectations, and all of them encouraged an optimistic outlook for stock prices during the late 1990s. Probably no one investor thought that all of these factors would bring rising stock prices, but almost every investor believed that more than one of the factors would bring rising prices.

According to the speculative bubble view, eventually the factors that encourage rising stock prices weaken to the point at which prices stop rising and then begin to fall and possibly crash.

In 2002, the Internet and the information age remained a strong force for rising prices. So did the expansion of trading opportunities, especially on-line opportunities. The major new factor was the long-term campaign against terrorism. But the effects of this campaign on average stock prices were not clear at the beginning of 2002. The reason is that the economy must adjust to the new situation by reallocating resources away from travel and tourism and toward security and defense goods and services. Some sectors will expand, and some will shrink. The impact on average stock prices might be positive or negative.

REVIEW QUIZ

1 What is the market fundamentals view of the forces that determine stock prices?
2 What is the speculative bubble view of the forces that determine stock prices?
3 List five factors that you think might have encouraged the booming stock market of the 1990s.

You've seen that there are two views about the forces that determine stock prices. No one knows which view is correct. And no one can predict stock prices. For these reasons, rational stockholders diversify their holdings across a number of stocks. Let's see how diversification spreads risks.

Risk and Return

STOCK PRICES FLUCTUATE IN UNPREDICTABLE ways, and stockholders might receive a large capital gain or incur a large capital loss. But stocks differ in both their expected return and risk, and generally, the greater the risk, the higher is the expected return from a stock. We call the additional return that is earned for bearing an additional risk a **risk premium**. Let's see why a risk premium arises.

Risk Premium

Recall the stock price equation:

$$P_1 = \text{Expected value of } [b_1(D_1 + P_2)],$$

Suppose that two stocks have the same expected dividend, D_1, and the same expected future price, P_2, but one is riskier than the other. Because people dislike risk and must be compensated for bearing it, a riskier return is discounted more than a safe return — the discount factor, b_1, is smaller for the riskier return. Because b_1 is smaller, the price of a stock P_1 is lower for the riskier stock. But if the price of the riskier stock is lower, the expected return from holding it is greater than the expected return from the safer stock.

Because expected return increases with risk, a person earns the highest expected return by holding only the one stock — the one with the highest expected return. But this investment strategy is not usually the best one. The reason is that by diversifying stock holdings across a number of different stocks, an investor can lower the risk. To do so, the investor must accept a lower expected return. There is a tradeoff between risk and expected return.

Let's see how and why diversification lowers risk. To do so, we'll look at some actual stock purchases that you could have made in January 2001 and see what your investments would have been worth in 2002 with different degrees of diversification.

Portfolio Diversification

Table 34.2 shows the prices of five stocks in January 2001 and January 2002. Suppose that in January 2001, you had $1,000 to invest and put it all into just one of these five stocks. You might have been lucky and chosen Procter & Gamble (P&G), in which case your $1,000 grew to $1,139 over the year. But you might have been very unlucky and chosen Enron, in which case you lost your entire investment.

TABLE 34.2   Five Stock Prices

	Price in January 2001	Price in January 2002	Value in 2002 of $1,000 in 2001
Enron	60	0	0
McDonald's	29	27	931
Microsoft	61	64	1,049
P&G	72	82	1,139
Wal-Mart	57	60	1,053

Now suppose that instead of investing in only one of these stocks, you had put $500 into each of Enron and Procter & Gamble. In this case, your investment would have been worth $569.50 at the end of the year — a loss, but not as big as if you'd gone for only Enron.

Now imagine that you diversified even more, putting $200 each into Enron, Microsoft, Procter & Gamble, McDonald's, and Wal-Mart. In this case, your investment would have been worth $834 at the beginning of 2002.

You could spread your risks even more by investing in a mutual fund — a fund that is managed by investment specialists and that is diversified across a large number of stocks.

You can see that lowering risk means accepting a lower return. The highest return across the five stocks in Table 34.2 comes from buying only Procter & Gamble. But at the beginning of 2001, you might equally have thought that buying Enron would provide the highest return. Because you can't predict which individual stock is going to perform best, it pays to diversify and trade off a lower expected return for a lower risk.

REVIEW QUIZ

1 Why does a stock's return include a risk premium?
2 How does diversification across a number of stocks lower the risk that a stockholder faces?

We next look at the links between the stock market and the rest of the economy.

The Stock Market and the Economy

THE LINKS BETWEEN THE STOCK MARKET AND the rest of the economy that we're now going to look at run in two directions: effects from the rest of the economy *on* the stock market and effects on the rest of the economy *from* the stock market. We'll look first at influences *on* the stock market, which fall into three broad groups:

- Trends and cycles in earnings growth
- The Federal Reserve's monetary policy
- Taxes

Trends and Cycles in Earnings Growth

You've seen that expected future earnings are the fundamental influence on stock prices. Current earnings are known, but future earnings can only be forecasted. And the central question on which investors must take a position is the *expected growth rate* of earnings.

If earnings are expected to grow more rapidly, the market fundamentals value of a stock rises relative to its current earnings — the price-earnings ratio rises. Conversely, if earnings are expected to grow more slowly, the market fundamentals value of a stock falls relative to its current earnings — the price-earnings ratio falls.

The nature and pace of technological change and the state of the business cycle are the main influences on earnings growth. And expectations about future earnings growth are based on the best information that people can obtain about future technological change and business cycle developments.

The long-term trend in earnings growth has been remarkably constant at about 2 percent a year (after the effects of inflation are removed). But earnings growth has fluctuated a great deal around its trend. Figure 34.6 shows these fluctuations. The figure highlights the interesting fact that there have been only three main periods during which earnings have grown rapidly to reach a new higher level: the 1890s, 1950s and 1960s, and 1990s. There was only one other period of rapid earnings growth, from 1921 to 1931, but this episode was a temporary burst of growth from an extremely low level that did not take earnings back to their previous peak of 1918.

Each period during which earnings grew rapidly to a new level was one in which far-reaching new

---

FIGURE 34.6   Three Bursts of Earnings Growth

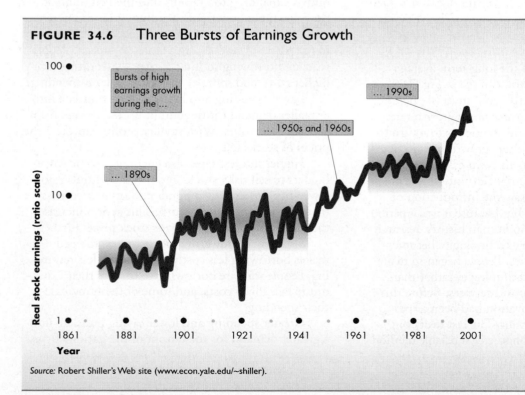

Earnings grew rapidly during three periods of rapid technological change: the 1890s (railroad, telegraph, electricity); 1950s and 1960s (interstate highway system, plastics, transistor, and television); and 1990s (Internet and information technologies).

Source: Robert Shiller's Web site (www.econ.yale.edu/~shiller).

technologies spread. During the 1890s, it was the railroad, telegraph, and electricity. During the 1950s and 1960s, it was the interstate highway system, plastics, the transistor, and television. And during the 1990s, it was the Internet and associated information technologies.

Although earnings are the fundamental source of value for stocks, the connection between earnings growth and stock prices cannot be used to make reliable predictions of stock prices. Stock prices did increase more rapidly than usual during the periods of rapid earnings growth. But they outpaced earnings growth — increased by more than was justified by the growth of earnings. And during the 1920s, stock prices grew beyond the levels that were supported by the underlying earnings fundamentals.

Some people have argued that the 1990s were special — unique — and marked a new era for permanently faster earnings growth, arising from the information technologies that brought the exploding Internet. Does the earnings growth rate change permanently when a major new technology spreads? And are we living today in a "new economy"?

A New Economy? It is a well-documented fact that the spread of the Internet was unusually rapid. Not since the spread of television during the 1950s has there been such a rapid penetration of a new technology.

It is also a solid fact that the pace of earnings growth was unusually rapid during the 1990s — 13 percent a year compared to the long-term average of 2 percent a year. But as you can see in Fig. 34.6, earnings growth was similarly rapid in earlier periods, only to return to its long-term average growth rate.

The only exception to this tendency to return to the preceding long-term average growth rate occurred more than 200 years ago, in an event called the Industrial Revolution. The Industrial Revolution was possibly unique, not because it saw the introduction of powerful new technologies but because it was a period in which for the first time in human history, research and the development of new technologies became commercially viable activities. People began to make a living by inventing new technologies rather than merely by producing goods and services. Before this period, invention and innovation had been a spasmodic and relatively rare event. The last really big invention had been the chronometer, a reliable method of keeping time on ships that improved the reliability of navigation.

It is still too soon to be sure, but more and more people are coming to the view that the "new economy" is just another stage in the evolution of the old economy. If this view is correct, the stock market of the early 2000s remains overvalued relative to its market fundamentals. If the "new economy" view is correct, the stock market has correctly incorporated the future earnings growth that the new economy will bring.

The Federal Reserve's Monetary Policy

The Federal Reserve (Fed) influences the nominal interest rates. Whether you've studied the Fed's monetary policy or not, you can understand how the Fed influences the stock market by seeing how interest rates affect stock prices.

If the Fed takes actions that raise interest rates, stock prices usually fall. Conversely, if the Fed takes actions that lower interest rates, stock prices usually rise. But the Fed's influence on stock prices is short lived, and the timing of the influences depends on whether the Fed's actions are anticipated or surprise the market.

Interest Rates and Stock Prices When the economy is expanding too rapidly and the Fed wants to slow down the growth of spending, it raises interest rates. By raising interest rates, the Fed makes borrowing more costly and lending more rewarding. People who are borrowing to finance their expenditure face higher costs, and some of them cut back on spending.

Lower spending and higher saving translate into a smaller demand for the output of the nation's firms and smaller profits. With smaller profits expected, the prices of stocks fall.

Higher interest rates also encourage some stockholders to sell risky stocks and put their funds into lower-risk, lower-return bonds and other securities that now yield a higher return. This action increases the supply of stocks and lowers stock prices further.

Similarly, by lowering interest rates, the Fed makes borrowing less costly and lending less rewarding. People who are borrowing to finance their expenditure face lower costs, and some of them increase their spending.

Greater spending and lower saving translate into a greater demand for the output of the nation's firms, and larger profits. With larger profits expected, the prices of stocks rise.

Lower interest rates on bonds and other securities also encourage some bond holders to sell bonds and put their funds into higher-risk, higher-return stocks. This action increases the demand for stocks and raises stock prices still further.

Anticipating the Fed Because the Fed's interest rate actions influence stock prices in the way we've just seen, it is profitable to anticipate the Fed's future actions. If the Fed is expected to raise interest rates in the near future, then stock prices are expected to fall in the near future. Selling stocks before the price falls and buying them back after the price has fallen is profitable. So if a large number of people expect the Fed to raise interest rates, they sell stock. The selling action increases supply and lowers the stock price before the Fed acts. The Fed has caused the stock price to fall, but the stock price falls *before* the Fed acts. (This timing relationship is an example of the *post hoc* fallacy — see pp. 13–14.)

Taxes

Taxes can influence stock prices in a number of ways, some direct and some indirect. Three types of tax can affect stock markets:

- Capital gains tax
- Corporate profits tax
- Transactions (Tobin) tax

Capital Gains Tax The capital gains tax is a tax on the income that people earn when they *realize* a capital gain. A **realized capital gain** is a capital gain that is obtained when a stock is sold for a higher price than the price paid for it. People who hold onto stocks that have increased in value also enjoy a capital gain, but they do not pay a tax on that gain until they sell the stock and realize the gain.

When a capital gains tax is introduced or when the rate of capital gains tax is increased, stock prices fall, other things remaining the same. The reason is that the capital gains tax lowers the after-tax return on stocks and so lowers the price that people are willing to pay for stocks.

The lowering of the capital gains tax rate during the 1980s and 1990s probably contributed to the booming stock prices of the 1990s.

Corporate Profits Tax The corporate profits tax is an income tax on the profits of corporations. If this

tax is increased, corporate after-tax profits fall. The firm has smaller earnings from which to pay dividends and invest in new capital. So the market fundamentals values of firms fall, and so do stock prices.

Transactions (Tobin) Tax Transactions on the stock market are not taxed. But their value is enormous, and a tax set at a tiny rate would raise a huge amount of tax revenue for the government.

James Tobin, an economist at Yale University (who died in 2002), proposed that stock market transactions be taxed — hence the name "the Tobin tax." Tobin believes that such a tax would discourage speculative buying and selling of stocks and make the stock market more efficient. The evidence on transactions taxes in other markets, notably real estate markets, does not support the view that a transactions tax lowers speculation.

Let's now change directions and look at influences *from* the stock market to the rest of the economy. We'll look at the influences of stock prices on

- Wealth, consumption expenditure, and saving
- The distribution of wealth

Wealth, Consumption Expenditure, and Saving

Wealth is the market value of assets. The influence of wealth on consumption expenditure and saving is called the **wealth effect**. *Disposable income* equals income minus taxes. A household can do only two things with its disposable income: spend it on consumption goods and services or save it. The **saving rate** is saving as a percentage of disposable income. The greater is wealth, the smaller is the saving rate.

How do stock prices influence the saving rate? The answer depends on how we measure saving (and, related, how we measure disposable income).

There are two definitions of saving that are equivalent, provided that we measure everything in a consistent way. The first definition is

$$\text{Saving} = \frac{\text{Disposable}}{\text{income}} - \frac{\text{Consumption}}{\text{expenditure}}.$$

The second definition arises from the fact that saving adds to wealth. That is,

$$\frac{\text{Wealth at}}{\text{end of year}} = \frac{\text{Wealth at}}{\text{start of year}} + \frac{\text{Saving during}}{\text{the year}}$$

or

$$\text{Saving} = \text{Change in wealth.}$$

The first definition of saving focuses on the fact that saving is what is left over after buying consumer goods and services. The second definition focuses on the fact that saving adds to wealth.

Because the two definitions of saving are equivalent, it must be the case that

$$\frac{\text{Disposable}}{\text{income}} = \frac{\text{Consumption}}{\text{expenditure}} + \frac{\text{Change}}{\text{in wealth.}}$$

In the data on income and wealth, disposable income does not include capital gains and losses. In the data on wealth, capital gains and losses *are* included. So there is a measurement discrepancy between saving measured using the first definition, which excludes capital gains, and saving measured using the second definition, which includes capital gains.

Figure 34.7 shows you what has happened to the saving rate based on the first measure and excludes capital gains. The saving rate averaged 9 percent and was on a slightly upward trend during the 1960s, 1970s, and 1980s. But during the 1990s, the saving rate collapsed, and by 2000, it was less than 1 percent.

This collapse of the personal saving rate coincided with the explosion of stock prices through the 1990s.

You might expect that if people are enjoying capital gains on the stock market, they will think of these gains as being part of their saving. So they will not be concerned if their saving rate *excluding* capital gains falls.

So what happened to the saving rate defined to include capital gains? Figure 34.8 answers this question for the period 1995–2000. While the saving rate excluding capital gains was collapsing, the saving rate including capital gains increased from about 15 percent in 1995 to almost 40 percent in 1998 and 2000.

Which measure of saving is the correct one? Neither! The rate that excludes capital gains is

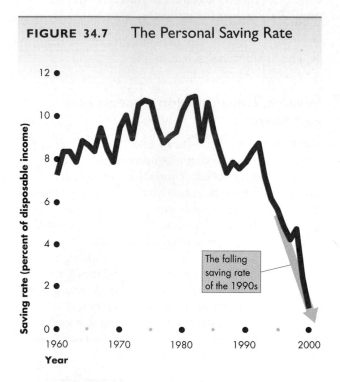

FIGURE 34.7   The Personal Saving Rate

The personal saving rate averaged 9 percent of disposable income during the 1960s, 1970s, and 1980s. It then collapsed to less than 1 percent by 2000.

Source: Bureau of Economic Analysis.

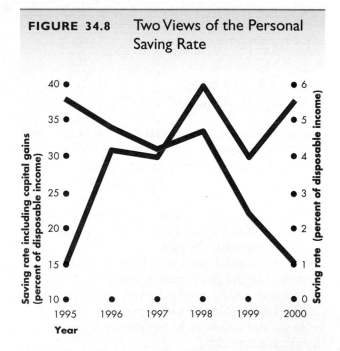

FIGURE 34.8   Two Views of the Personal Saving Rate

The personal saving rate including capital gains increased, while the saving rate excluding capital gains collapsed.

Source: Bureau of Economic Analysis.

incorrect because it omits an important source of changes in wealth. But the rate that includes capital gains is incorrect because those gains are not realized. And if everyone attempted to realize their gains, the stock market would almost surely crash, thereby wiping out some unknown proportion of the gains. So the truth lies at some unknown place between the two available measures.

The Distribution of Wealth

When stock prices are rising as rapidly as they did from 1995 to 2000, stockholders enjoy spectacular increases in their wealth. Do all income groups share in these increases in wealth? Or are the increases concentrated among the already wealthy?

The answer to this question depends on the distribution of stockholdings. It turns out that the wealthier households are those that tend to hold stocks. So the wealthiest have gained the most.

The data on wealth distributions end in 1998. But even these data tell an amazing story. You can see the data in Fig. 34.9. Here, we plot the mean wealth in 1992, 1995, and 1998 of households in five income groups ranging from those who earn less than $10,000 a year to those who earn more than $100,000 a year. The wealth data are in 1998 dollars, which means that they are adjusted to remove the effects of inflation.

Notice that the wealth of the four lowest-income groups barely changes. In contrast, the wealth of the highest-income group increases. In fact, the increase in wealth of the highest-income group exceeds the level of wealth of the next highest group. Between 1995 and 1998, households that have an income of $100,000 or more a year enjoyed an increase in average wealth of more than $300,000. The average wealth of households that earn between $50,000 and $99,999 was only $275,000 in 1998.

While we cannot be sure that all the wealth changes shown in Fig. 34.9 resulted from the rising stock prices, much of the change must have come from that source. Whether the changes in the distribution of wealth will be permanent depends on the future of stock prices. If stock prices collapse, much of the gain in wealth by the highest-income group will be reversed. And many families will wish that they had not lowered their saving rate.

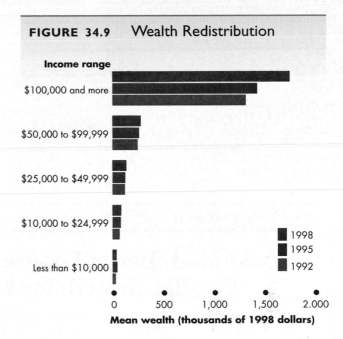

FIGURE 34.9   Wealth Redistribution

Income range

$100,000 and more

$50,000 to $99,999

$25,000 to $49,999

$10,000 to $24,999

Less than $10,000

■ 1998
■ 1995
■ 1992

Mean wealth (thousands of 1998 dollars)
0   500   1,000   1,500   2,000

The wealth of the highest-income households increased between 1995 and 1998 by more than the level of wealth of other households.

Source: Board of Governors of the Federal Reserve System.

REVIEW QUIZ

1 What are the main trends in earnings growth?
2 What events are associated with the three periods of rapid earnings growth?
3 How does the Federal Reserve's monetary policy influence the stock market?
4 How do taxes influence the stock market?
5 How does the stock market influence saving?
6 How does the stock market influence the distribution of wealth?

◆ You've learned the two main approaches to understanding stock prices, seen why portfolio diversification is a good idea, and seen how the stock market and the economy interact. In *Reading Between the Lines* on pp. 820–821, we apply some of what you've learned to the stock market in 2002.

The Stock Market in Action

THE WASHINGTON TIMES, JANUARY 1, 2002

Stocks End Year of Losses; Analysts Predict Growth for 2002

The stock market made a strong comeback after the September 11 terrorist attacks but failed to recoup a long string of earlier losses, leaving the major indexes down for a second straight year in the poorest showing in a generation.

"New economy" technology stocks took the biggest hit, with the NASDAQ Composite Index dropping an additional 21 percent last year after plummeting 39 percent in 2000. Tech stocks were the darlings of investors during the economic boom of the 1990s, when they enjoyed spectacular yearly gains that topped out with the NASDAQ's 89 percent rise in 1999, a record for any stock index.

The "old economy" stocks that inhabited the Dow Jones Industrial Average never boasted such extraordinary returns but suffered milder losses last year by comparison, declining by 7 percent after a 6.4 percent drop in 2000.

The blue-chip Standard and Poor's 500 index, reflecting the woes of large multinational corporations in a world recession, fell 13 percent last year after a 10 percent loss in 2000.

In keeping with the tone for the year, selling by investors seeking to post losses for tax purposes drove down the indexes in the final day of trading yesterday. The Dow fell 116 points to 10,021, and the NASDAQ shed 36 points to close at 1,951.

With the 2000-01 bear market now in many ways surpassing the deep bear market of 1974-75, most stock analysts believe the worst is behind and that the market can look forward to a year of growth, bolstered by a recovering U.S economy.

"We think the S&P 500 and NASDAQ will see double-digit gains over the course of 2002," said David M. Blitzer, chief investment strategist with Standard & Poor's. But "stocks face some formidable hurdles" from the lingering recession and traumas of last year.

...

Essence of the Story

■ Stock prices fell in 2001 for the second straight year.

■ The prices of technology stocks, which had increased spectacularly during the 1990s, fell most.

■ The NASDAQ Composite Index fell by 21 percent in 2001 after falling by 39 percent in 2000.

■ The Dow Jones Industrial Average fell by 7 percent in 2001 and by 6.4 percent in 2000.

■ The Standard & Poor's 500 index fell by 13 percent in 2001 and by 10 percent in 2000.

■ With the 2000–2001 price fall surpassing that of 1974–1975, stock analysts believe that prices will rise by more than 10 percent — "double-digit gains" — during 2002 as the U.S. economy expands.

Economic Analysis

■ This news article is typical of stock market reporting in its drama creation and optimism.

■ The three figures show the data to which the article refers and place 2000 and 2001 in a longer term perspective.

■ You can see in Fig. 1 that the price fall on the NASDAQ was about as deep in 2000–2001 as in 1973–1974, but from a much larger increase in the previous year.

■ In Fig. 2 and Fig. 3, you can see that the Dow Jones Industrial Average and the S&P Composite fell by much more in 1973– 1974 than in 2000–2001.

■ The three figures also show the huge volatility of the stock market.

■ Pay attention to the numbers on the *y*-axes of the graphs. Prices on the NASDAQ swing between 80 percent rises and 40 percent falls. Prices on the Dow and the S&P swing between 40 percent rises and 30 percent falls.

■ The news article talks about a "bear market." A bear market is one in which prices are falling. The opposite is a "bull market," in which prices are rising.

■ The optimism for 2002 is based on historical observation that you can see in the figures: Stock prices usually rebound after a big decline.

■ The market was expecting such a rebound at the beginning of 2002.

Figure 1 NASDAQ Composite

Figure 2 Dow Jones Industrial Average

Figure 3 S&P Composite

SUMMARY

KEY POINTS

Stock Market Basics (pp. 804–810)

- A stock is a tradable security issued by a firm to certify that its holder owns a share of the firm, is entitled to receive a share of the firm's profit (a dividend), and can vote at stockholder meetings.
- The return on a stock consists of a dividend plus a capital gain (or minus a capital loss).
- A firm's accounting profit (called earnings) is used to calculate the price-earnings ratio.
- S&P Composite, DJIA, and NASDAQ index provide information about average stock prices.
- The price-earnings ratio between 1871 and 2001 has ranged from 6 to 27 and averaged 13.9.

How Are Stock Prices Determined? (pp. 810–813)

- The market fundamentals price is the discounted present value of the stream of expected future dividend payments, which in turn depend on expected future earnings.
- Some economists believe that stock prices can be understood only as speculative bubbles — periods of rising prices followed by price plunges, both of which occur because people expect them to occur and act on that expectation.

Risk and Return (p. 814)

- Stocks differ in their expected return and risk, and the greater the risk, the higher is the stock's risk premium.
- An investor can lower risk by diversifying across a number of stocks.

The Stock Market and the Economy (pp. 815–819)

- Technological change and the state of the business cycle influence earnings growth and stock prices.
- Earnings growth has come in three main bursts: the 1890s, 1950s and 1960s, and 1990s.
- Each period of rapid earnings growth was also a time in which major new technologies spread.

- When the Fed raises interest rates, stock prices fall, and when the Fed cuts interest rates, stock prices rise. The change in stock prices precedes the Fed's anticipated actions.
- The capital gains tax and corporate profits tax affect stock prices. A transactions (Tobin) tax would probably not deter speculation.
- As stock prices increased during the 1990s, the saving rate excluding capital gains collapsed but the saving rate including capital gains increased.
- As stock prices increased during the 1990s, the distribution of wealth became more unequal.

KEY FIGURES AND TABLE

KEY TERMS

PROBLEMS

*1. On January 2, 2001, the price of a share of Coca-Cola stock was $60.81. On December 31, 2001, the price was $47.15. During 2001, Coca-Cola paid dividends that totaled 54¢ a share. Coca-Cola's reported accounting profit during 2001 was $1.58 per share.
   a. What was the dividend yield on Coca-Cola stock during 2001?
   b. What was the return on Coca-Cola stock during 2001?
   c. What was the capital gain or loss on Coca-Cola stock during 2001?
   d. What was the rate of return on Coca-Cola stock during 2001?
   e. What were Coca-Cola's earnings during 2001?
   f. What was Coca-Cola's price-earnings ratio on December 31, 2001?

2. On January 2, 2001, the price of a share of General Motors (GM) stock was $52.19. On December 31, 2001, the price was $48.60. During 2001, GM paid a dividend of $2 a share. GM's reported accounting profit during 2001 was $1.40 per share.
   a. What was the dividend yield on GM stock during 2001?
   b. What was the return on GM stock during 2001?
   c. What was the capital gain or loss on GM stock during 2001?
   d. What was the rate of return on GM stock during 2001?
   e. What were GM's earnings during 2001?
   f. What was GM's price-earnings ratio on December 31, 2001?

*3. The financial pages report that the Dow is up by 5 percent, the S&P 500 is up by 8 percent, and the NASDAQ is up by 15 percent. Write a report that interprets these numbers. What can you infer from the data about the changes in stock prices in different sectors of the economy?

4. The financial pages report that the Dow is down by 15 percent, the S&P 500 is down by 10 percent, and the NASDAQ is down by 25 percent. Write a short report that interprets these numbers. What can you infer from the data about the changes in stock prices in different sectors of the economy?

*5. You are trying to figure out whether to buy some stock. You are confident that the stock will pay a dividend of $3 a share next year, and you think that you'll be able to sell the stock at the end of the year for $30 a share. Your discount factor is 0.9. What is the most that you'd be willing to pay for this stock?

6. You are trying to figure out whether to buy some stock. You are confident that the stock will pay a dividend of $5 a share next year, and you think that you'll be able to sell the stock at the end of the year for $30 a share. Your discount factor is 0.8. What is the most that you'd be willing to pay for this stock?

*7. The price of a stock that you're thinking of buying is $20 a share. Your discount factor is 0.75. The firm has announced its dividend for next year of $1 share. What is the lowest expected price next year that would make it rational for you to go ahead and buy the stock?

8. The price of a stock that you're thinking of buying is $100 a share. Your discount factor is 0.7. The firm has announced that it will pay no dividend next year. What is the lowest expected price next year that would make it rational for you to go ahead and buy the stock?

*9. Suppose there are two pharmaceutical stocks that you might buy: Merck and Pfizer. Merck will provide a return of 50 percent if the firm makes a major breakthrough on its new drug and a 10 percent return otherwise. There is only a 10 percent chance that the firm will make the breakthrough. Pfizer will provide a return of 20 percent if the firm achieves a cost saving and a 15 percent return otherwise. There is a 50 percent chance that the firm will achieve the cost saving.
   a. What is the expected return from investing in Merck?
   b. What is the expected return from investing in Pfizer?
   c. What is the chance of making a return of 50 percent by investing only in Merck?
   d. What is the chance of making a return of 10 percent by investing only in Merck?
   e. What is the chance of making a return of 20 percent by investing only in Pfizer?
   f. What is the chance of making a return of 15 percent by investing only in Pfizer?

g. If you invest in both Merck and Pfizer in equal amounts, what is your expected return?

h. If you invest in both Merck and Pfizer in equal amounts, what is your chance of making a return of 50 percent?

i. If you invest in both Merck and Pfizer in equal amounts, what is your chance of making a return of 10 percent?

j. Explain why it might be rational to diversify across Merck and Pfizer.

10. Suppose there are two soft drink stocks that you might buy: Coke and Pepsi. Coke will provide a return of 20 percent if the firm's Harry Potter advertising campaign is successful and a 10 percent return otherwise. There is a 60 percent chance that the advertising campaign will be successful. Pepsi will provide a return of 16 percent if the firm achieves a cost saving and a 14 percent return otherwise. There is a 50 percent chance that the firm will achieve the cost saving.

a. What is the expected return from investing in Coke?

b. What is the expected return from investing in Pepsi?

c. What is the chance of making a return of 20 percent by investing only in Coke?

d. What is the chance of making a return of 10 percent by investing only in Coke?

e. What is the chance of making a return of 16 percent by investing only in Pepsi?

f. What is the chance of making a return of 14 percent by investing only in Pepsi?

g. If you invest in both Coke and Pepsi in equal amounts, what is your expected return?

h. If you invest in both Coke and Pepsi in equal amounts, what is your chance of making a return of 20 percent?

i. If you invest in both Coke and Pepsi in equal amounts, what is your chance of making a return of 10 percent?

j. Explain why it might be rational to diversify across Coke and Pepsi.

CRITICAL THINKING

1. Study *Reading Between the Lines* on pp. 820–821 and then answer the following questions:

a. What happened to stock prices during 2001 on the average?

b. Which stock price index fell most during 2001 and what can you infer from this price fall about the profit prospects in different parts of the economy?

c. What do you learn about the performance of "new economy" technology stocks from this news article?

d. Why do some investment strategists believe that stock prices are poised for a further rise?

e. Are the expectations of rising stock prices based on rational expectations of the fundamentals or a speculative bubble?

WEB EXERCISES

1. Use the link on your Parkin Web site to visit the New York, London, Frankfurt, Tokyo, and Hong Kong stock exchanges.

a. Get the latest index numbers from these stock exchanges and get the indexes a year ago.

b. On the basis of the data you have obtained, calculate the percentage changes in the indexes over the past year.

c. Which of the stock markets has delivered the largest percentage gain? Can you think of reasons for the differences in performance of the five stock markets?

2. Use the link on your Parkin Web site to obtain data on the prices and dividend payments over the past year for five stocks that interest you. Also obtain the value of the DJIA, S&P Composite, and NASDAQ indexes for the same period.

a. For each stock, calculate the rate of return assuming that you bought the stock one year ago.

b. For each index, calculate the percentage change over the past year and compare the performance of each stock with the indexes.

UNDERSTANDING THE GLOBAL ECONOMY

PART 11

It's a Small World

The scale of international trade, borrowing, and lending, both in absolute dollar terms and as a percentage of total world production expands every year. One country, Singapore, imports and exports goods and services in a volume that exceeds its Gross Domestic Product. The world's largest nation, China, returned to the international economic stage during the 1980s and is now a major producer of manufactured goods. ◆ International economic activity is large because today's economic world is small and because communication is so incredibly fast. But today's world is not a new world. From the beginning of recorded history, people have traded over large and steadily increasing distances. The great Western civilizations of Greece and Rome traded not only around the Mediterranean but also into the Gulf of Arabia. The great Eastern civilizations traded around the Indian Ocean. By the Middle Ages, the East and the West were trading routinely overland on routes pioneered by Venetian traders and explorers such as Marco Polo. When, in 1497, Vasco da Gama opened a sea route between the Atlantic and Indian Oceans around Africa, a new trade between East and West began, which brought tumbling prices of Eastern goods in Western markets. ◆ The European discovery of America and the subsequent opening up of Atlantic trade continued the process of steady globalization. So, the developments of the 1990s, amazing though many of them are, represent a continuation of an ongoing expansion of human horizons. ◆ These three chapters studied the interaction of nations in today's global economy. ◆ Chapter 32 described and explained international trade in goods and services. In this chapter, you came face to face with one of the biggest policy issues of all ages, free trade versus protection and the globalization debate. The chapter explained how all nations can benefit from free international trade. ◆ Chapter 33 explained some of the fundamentals of international borrowing and lending and the exchange rate. It explained the poorly understood fact that the size of a nation's international deficit depends not on how efficient it is, but on how much its citizens save relative to how much they invest. Nations with low saving rates, everything else being the same, have international deficits. ◆ This chapter also explained why foreign exchange rates fluctuate so much. ◆ Finally, Chapter 34 studied stock markets. It described these markets and it explained how stock prices are determined and why they are volatile and impossible to predict. ◆ The global economy is big news these days. And it has always attracted attention. On the next page, you can meet the economist who first understood comparative advantage, David Ricardo. And you can meet one of today's leading international economists, Jagdish Bhagwati of Columbia University.

PROBING THE IDEAS
Gains from International Trade

DAVID RICARDO *(1772–1832) was a highly successful 27-year-old stockbroker when he stumbled on a copy of Adam Smith's* Wealth of Nations *(see p. 52) on a weekend visit to the country. He was immediately hooked and went on to become the most celebrated economist of his age and one of the all-time great economists. One of his many contributions was to develop the principle of comparative advantage, the foundation on which the modern theory of international trade is built. The example he used to illustrate this principle was the trade between England and Portugal in cloth and wine.*

The General Agreement on Tariffs and Trade was established as a reaction against the devastation wrought by beggar-my-neighbor tariffs imposed during the 1930s. But it is also a triumph for the logic first worked out by Smith and Ricardo.

Gains from International Trade "Under a system of perfectly free commerce, each country naturally devotes its capital and labor to such employments as are most beneficial to each."

DAVID RICARDO
The Principles of Political Economy and Taxation, 1817

Until the mid-eighteenth century, it was generally believed that the purpose of international trade was to keep exports greater than imports and pile up gold. If gold was accumulated, it was believed, the nation would prosper; if gold was lost through an international deficit, the nation would be drained of money and impoverished. These beliefs are called *mercantilism,* and the *mercantilists* were pamphleteers who advocated with missionary fervor the pursuit of an international surplus. If exports did not exceed imports, the mercantilists wanted imports restricted.

In the 1740s, David Hume explained that as the quantity of money (gold) changes, so also does the price level, and the nation's *real* wealth is unaffected. In the 1770s, Adam Smith argued that import restrictions would lower the gains from specialization and make a nation poorer. Thirty years later, David Ricardo proved the law of comparative advantage and demonstrated the superiority of free trade. Mercantilism was intellectually bankrupt but remained politically powerful.

Gradually, through the nineteenth century, the mercantilist influence waned and North America and Western Europe prospered in an environment of increasingly free international trade. But despite remarkable advances in economic understanding, mercantilism never quite died. It had a brief and devastating revival in the 1920s and 1930s when tariff hikes brought about the collapse of international trade and accentuated the Great Depression. It subsided again after World War II with the establishment of the General Agreement on Tariffs and Trade (GATT).

But mercantilism lingers on. The often expressed view that the United States should restrict Japanese imports and reduce its deficit with Japan and fears that NAFTA will bring economic ruin to the United States are modern manifestations of mercantilism. It would be interesting to have David Hume, Adam Smith, and David Ricardo commenting on these views. But we know what they would say—the same things that they said to the eighteenth-century mercantilists. And they would still be right today.

THEN

In the eighteenth century, when mercantilists and economists were debating the pros and cons of free international exchange, the transportation technology that was available limited the gains from international trade. Sailing ships with tiny cargo holds took close to a month to cross the Atlantic Ocean. But the potential gains were large, and so was the incentive to cut shipping costs. By the 1850s, the clipper ship had been developed, cutting the journey from Boston to Liverpool to only 12 1/4 days. Half a century later, 10,000-ton steamships were sailing between America and England in just 4 days. As sailing times and costs declined, the gains from international trade increased and the volume of trade expanded.

Now

The container ship has revolutionized international trade and contributed to its continued expansion. Today, most goods cross the oceans in containers—metal boxes—packed into and piled on top of ships like this one. Container technology has cut the cost of ocean shipping by economizing on handling and by making cargoes harder to steal, lowering insurance costs. It is unlikely that there would be much international trade in goods such as television sets and VCRs without this technology. High-value and perishable cargoes such as flowers and fresh foods, as well as urgent courier packages, travel by air. Every day, dozens of cargo-laden 747s fly between every major U.S. city and to destinations across the Atlantic and Pacific oceans.

Jagdish Bhagwati, whom you can meet on the following pages, is one of the most distinguished international economists. He has contributed to our understanding of the effects of international trade and trade policy on economic growth and development and has played a significant role in helping to shape today's global trading arrangements.

TALKING WITH

JAGDISH BHAGWATI *is University Professor at Columbia University. Born in India in 1934, he studied at Cambridge University in England, MIT, and Oxford University before returning to India. He returned to teach at MIT in 1968 and moved to Columbia in 1980. A prolific scholar, Professor Bhagwati also writes in leading newspapers and magazines throughout the world. He has been much honored for both his scientific work and his impact on public policy. His greatest contributions are in international trade but extend also to developmental problems and the study of political economy.*

Jagdish Bhagwati

Michael Parkin talked with Jagdish Bhagwati about his work and the progress that economists have made in understanding the benefits of international economic integration since the pioneering work of Ricardo.

Professor Bhagwati, what attracted you to economics?

When you come from India where poverty hits the eye, it is easyto be attracted to economics which can be used to bring prosperity and create jobs to pull up the poor into gainful employment.

I learned later that there are two broad types of economist: those who treat the subject as an arid mathematical toy, and those who see it as a serious social science.

If Cambridge, where I went as an undergraduate, had been interested in esoteric mathematical economics, I would have opted for something else. But the Cambridge economists from whom I learned — many among the greatest figures in the discipline — saw economics as a social science. I therefore saw the power of economics as a tool to address India's poverty and was immediately hooked.

Who had the greatest impact on you at Cambridge?

Most of all, it was Harry Johnson, a young Canadian of immense energy and profound analytical gifts. Quite unlike the shy and reserved British dons, Johnson was friendly, effusive, and supportive of students who flocked around him. He would later move to Chicago where he became one of the most influential members of the market-oriented Chicago school. Another was Joan Robinson, arguably the world's most impressive female economist.

When I left Cambridge for MIT, going from one Cambridge to the other, I was lucky to transition from one phenomenal set of economists to another. At MIT, I learned much from future Nobel laureates Paul Samuelson and Robert Solow: Both would later become great friends and colleagues when I joined the MIT faculty in 1968.

After Cambridge and MIT, you went to Oxford and then back to India. What did you do in India?

I joined the Planning Commission in New Delhi, where my first big job was to find ways of raising the bottom thirty percent of India's population out of poverty to a "minimum income" level.

And what did you prescribe?

My main prescription was to "grow the pie".

My research suggested that the share of the bottom 30 percent of the pie did not seem to vary dramatically with differences in economic and political systems. So, growth in the pie seemed to be the principal (but not the only) component of an anti-poverty strategy. To supplement growth's good effects on the poor, the Indian planners were also dedicated to education, health, social reforms, and land reforms. Also, the access of the lowest-income and

> *My main prescription was to "grow the pie"… Today, this strategy has no rivals. Much empirical work shows that where growth has occurred, poverty has lessened.*

socially disadvantaged groups to the growth process and its benefits was to be improved in many ways, such as extension of credit without collateral.

Today, this strategy has no rivals. Much empirical work shows that where growth has occurred, poverty has lessened. It is nice to know that one's basic take on an issue of such central importance to humanity's well-being has been borne out by experience!

You left India in 1968 to come to America and an academic job at MIT. Why?

While the decision to emigrate often reflects personal factors — and they were present in my case — the offer of a Professorship from MIT certainly helped me make up my mind. At the time, it was easily the world's most celebrated Department: Serendipitously, the highest-ranked Departments at MIT were not in engineering and the sciences but in linguistics (which had Noam Chomsky) and economics (which had Paul Samuelson). Joining the MIT faculty was a dramatic breakthrough: I felt stimulated each year by several fantastic students and by several of the world's most creative economists.

We hear a lot in the popular press about fair trade and level playing fields. What's the distinction between free trade and fair trade? How can the playing field be unlevel?

Free trade simply means allowing no trade barriers such as tariffs, subsidies, and quotas. Trade barriers make domestic prices different from world prices for traded goods. When this happens, resources are not being used efficiently. Basic economics from the time of Ricardo tells us why free trade is good for us and why barriers to trade harm us, though our understanding of this doctrine today is far more nuanced and profound than it was at its creation.

Fair trade, on the other hand, is almost always a sneaky way of objecting to free trade. If your rivals are hard to compete with, you are not likely to get protection simply by saying that you cannot hack it. But if you say that your rival is an "unfair" trader, that is an easier sell! As international competition has grown fiercer, cries of "unfair trade" have therefore

> *Fair trade … is almost always a sneaky way of objecting to free trade.*

multiplied. The lesser rogues among the protectionists ask for "free and fair trade," whereas the worst ones ask for "fair, not free, trade."

At the end of World War II, the General Agreement of Tariffs and Trade (GATT) was established and there followed several rounds of multilateral trade negotiations and reductions in barriers to trade. How do you assess the contribution of GATT and its successor, the World Trade Organization (WTO)?

The GATT has made a huge contribution by overseeing massive trade liberalization in industrial goods among the developed countries. GATT rules, which "bind" tariffs to negotiated ceilings, prevent the raising of tariffs and have prevented tariff wars like those of the 1930s in which mutual and retaliatory tariff barriers were raised to the detriment of everyone.

The GATT was folded into the WTO at the end of the Uruguay Round of trade negotiations and is institutionally stronger. For instance, it has a binding Dispute Settlement Mechanism, whereas the GATT had no such teeth. It is also more ambitious in its scope, extending to new areas such as environment, intellectual property protection, and investment rules.

Running alongside the pursuit of multilateral free trade has been the emergence of bilateral trade agreements such as NAFTA and the EU. How do you view the bilateral free trade areas in today's world?

Unfortunately, there has been an explosion of bilateral free trade areas today. By some estimates, the ones in place and others being plotted approach 400! Each bilateral agreement gives preferential treatment to its trading partner over others. Because there are now so many bilateral agreements, such as between United States and Israel and between United States and Jordan, the result is a chaotic pattern of different tariffs depending on where a product comes from. Also, "rules of origin" must be agreed upon to determine whether a product is, say, Jordanian or Taiwanese if Jordan qualifies for a preferential tariff but Taiwan does not, and Taiwanese inputs enter the Jordanian manufacture of the product.

I have called the resulting criss-crossing of preferences and rules of origin the "spaghetti bowl" problem. The world trading system is choking under these proliferating bilateral deals. Contrast this complexity against the simplicity of a multilateral system with common tariffs for all WTO members.

We now have a world of uncoordinated and inefficient trade policies. The EU makes bilateral free trade agreements with different non-EU countries, so the United States follows with its own bilateral agreements; and with Europe and the United States doing it, the Asian countries, long wedded to multilateralism, have now succumbed to the mania.

> *We now have a world of uncoordinated and inefficient trade policies.*

Instead, if the United States had provided leadership by rewriting rules to make the signing of such bilateral agreements extremely difficult, this plague on the trading system today might well have been averted.

Despite the benefits that economics points to from multilateral free trade, the main organization that pursues this goal, the WTO, is having a very hard time with the anti-globalization movement. What can we say about globalization that puts the WTO and its work in proper perspective?

The anti-globalization movement contains a diverse set of activists. Essentially, they all claim to be stakeholders in the globalization phenomenon. But there are those who want to drive a stake through the system, as in Dracula films, and there are those who want to exercise their stake in the system. The former want to be heard; the latter, to be listened to. For a while, the two disparate sets of critics were milling around together, seeking targets of opportunity at international conferences such as WTO's November 2000 meeting in Seattle where the riots broke out. Now things have settled down; and the groups that want to work systematically and seriously at improving the global economy's functioning are much more in play.

But the WTO is also seen, inaccurately for the most part, as imposing trade sanctions that override concerns such as environmental protection. For example, U.S. legislation bans the importing of shrimp that is harvested without the use of turtle-excluding devices. India and others complained, but the WTO upheld the U.S. legislation. Ignorant of the facts, demonstrators took to the streets dressed as turtles protesting the WTO decision!

What advice do you have for a student who is just starting to study economics? Is economics a good subject in which to major?

I would say: enormously so. In particular, we economists bring three unique insights to good policymaking.

First, economists look for second and subsequent-round effects of actions.

Second, we correctly emphasize that a policy cannot be judged without using a counterfactual. It is a witticism that an economist, when asked how her husband was, said: compared to what?

Third, we uniquely and systematically bring the principle of social cost and benefit to our policy analysis.

SOLUTIONS TO ODD-NUMBERED PROBLEMS

CHAPTER 1

1. The opportunity cost of the extra 10 points is the movie forgone when you stayed home to study.

3. The opportunity cost of going to school is $9,600 of goods and services.

   The opportunity cost of going to school this summer is the highest-valued activity that you will give up so that you can go to summer school. In going to summer school, you will forgo all the goods and services that you could have bought with the income from your summer job ($6,000) plus the expenditure on tuition ($2,000), textbooks ($200), and living expenses ($1,400).

5. No, parking at this mall is not free. Yes, you did impose a cost on Harry.

   Finding a parking space takes about 30 minutes, so you incur an opportunity cost when you park your car. The opportunity cost is the highest-valued activity that you forgo by spending 30 minutes parking your car. If you would have spent those 30 minutes studying, then the opportunity cost of parking at this mall is 30 minutes of studying.

   The cost that you imposed on Harry is the additional 30 minutes that Harry will have to spend searching for a parking space.

APPENDIX TO CHAPTER 1

1a. To make a time-series graph, plot the year on the x-axis and the inflation rate on the y-axis. The graph will be a line joining all the points.

1b. (i) 1991 (ii) 1998 (iii) 1995, 1996, 1999, 2000 (iv) 1992, 1994, 1997, 1998, 2001 (v) 2000 (vi) 1992

1c. Inflation has had a fairly flat trend through these years. The line is close to horizontal.

3. To make a scatter diagram, plot the inflation rate on the x-axis and the interest rate on the y-axis. The graph will be a set of dots. The pattern made by the dots tells us that as the inflation rate increases, the interest rate usually increases.

5a. To make a graph that shows the relationship between x and y, plot x on the x-axis and y on the y-axis. The rela-

tionship is positive because x and y move in the same direction: As x increases, y increases.

5b. The slope increases as x increases. Slope is equal to the change in y divided by the change in x as we move along the curve. When x increases from 1 to 2 (a change of 1), y increases from 1 to 4 (a change of 3), so the slope is 3. But when x increases from 4 to 5 (a change of 1), y increases from 16 to 25 (a change of 9), so the slope is 9.

5c. The taller the building, the bigger is the cost of building it. The higher the unemployment rate, the higher is the crime rate. The longer the flight, the larger is the amount of fuel used.

7. The slope equals 8.

   The slope of the curve at the point where x is 4 is equal to the slope of the tangent to the curve at that point. Plot the points of the relationship and then draw a nice smooth curve through those points. Now draw the tangent line at the point where x is 4 and y is 16. Now calculate the slope of this tangent line. To do this, you must find another point on the tangent. The tangent line will cut the x-axis at 2, so another point is x equals 2 and y equals 0. Slope equals rise/run. The rise is 16 and the run is 2, so the slope is 8.

9. The slope is 7.

   The slope of the relationship across the arc when x increases from 3 to 4 is equal to the slope of the straight line joining the points on the curve at x equals 3 and x equals 4. In the graph, draw this straight line. When x increases from 3 to 4, y increases from 9 to 16. Slope equals rise/run. The rise is 7 (16 minus 9) and the run is 1 (4 minus 3), so the slope across the arc is 7.

11. The slope is –5/4.

    The curve is a straight line, so its slope is the same at all points on the curve. Slope equals the change in the variable on the y-axis divided by the change in the variable on the x-axis. To calculate the slope, you must select two points on the line. One point is at 10 on the y-axis and 0 on the x-axis, and another is at 8 on the x-axis and 0 on the y-axis. The change in y from 10 to 0 is associated with the change in x from 0 to 8. Therefore the slope of the curve equals –10/8, which equals –5/4.

13a. The slope at point a is –2, and the slope at point b is –0.75.

    To calculate the slope at a point on a curved line, draw the tangent to the line at the point. Then find a second point on the tangent and calculate the slope of the tangent.

    The tangent at point a cuts the y-axis at 10. The slope of the tangent equals the change in y divided by the change in x. The change in y equals 4 (10 minus 6) and the change in x equals –2 (0 minus 2). The slope at point a is 4/–2, which equals –2.

    Similarly, the slope at point b is –0.75. The tangent at point b cuts the x-axis at 8. The change in y equals 1.5, and the change in x equals –2. The slope at point b is –0.75.

13b. The slope across the arc AB is –1.125.

    The slope across an arc AB equals the change in y, which is 4.5 (6.0 minus 1.5) divided by the change in *x*, which equals –4 (2 minus 6). The slope across the arc *AB* equals 4.5/–4, which is –1.125.

15a. The relationship is a set of curves, one for each different temperature.

To draw a graph of the relationship between the price and the number of rides, keep the temperature at 50°F and plot the data in that column against the price. The curve that you draw is the relationship between price and number of rides when the temperature is 50°F. Now repeat the exercise but keep the temperature at 70°F. Then repeat the exercise but keep the temperature at 90°F.

15b. The relationship is a set of curves, one for each different price.

To draw a graph of the relationship between the temperature and the number of rides, keep the price at $5.00 a ride and plot the data in that row against the temperature. The curve shows the relationship between temperature and the number of rides when the price is $5.00 a ride. Now repeat the exercise but keep the price at $10.00 a ride. Repeat the exercise again and keep the price at $15.00 a ride and then at $20.00 a ride.

15c. The relationship is a set of curves, one for each different number of rides.

To draw a graph of the relationship between the temperature and price, keep the number of rides at 32 and plot the data along the diagonal in the table. The curve is the relationship between temperature and price at which 32 rides are taken. Now repeat the exercise and keep the number of rides at 27. Repeat the exercise again and keep the number of rides at 18 and then at 40.

CHAPTER 2

1a. Wendell's opportunity cost of an hour of tennis is 2.5 percentage points.

When Wendell increases the time he plays tennis from 4 hours to 6 hours, his grade in economics falls from 75 percent to 70 percent. His opportunity cost of 2 hours of tennis is 5 percentage points. So his opportunity cost of 1 hour of tennis is 2.5 percentage points.

1b. Wendell's opportunity cost of an hour of tennis is 5 percentage points.

When Wendell increases the time he plays tennis from 6 hours to 8 hours, his grade in economics falls from 70 percent to 60 percent. His opportunity cost of 2 hours of tennis is 10 percentage points. So his opportunity cost of 1 hour of tennis is 5 percentage points.

3. Wendell's opportunity cost of playing tennis increases as he spends more time on tennis

When Wendell increases the time he plays tennis from 4 hours to 6 hours, his opportunity cost is 5 percentage points. But when he increases the time he plays tennis from 6 hours to 8 hours, his opportunity cost is 10 percentage points. Wendell's opportunity cost of playing tennis increases as he spends more time on tennis.

5a. Wendell's grade in economics is 66 percent.

When Wendell increases the time he plays tennis from 4 hours to 6 hours, his opportunity cost of the additional 2 hours of tennis is 5 percentage points. So his opportunity cost of an additional 1 hour is 2.5 percentage points. So plot this opportunity cost at 5 hours on the graph (the midpoint between 4 and 6 hours). When he increases the time he plays tennis from 6 hours to 8 hours, his opportunity cost of the additional 2 hours of tennis is 10 percentage points. So his opportunity cost of the additional 1 hour of tennis is 5 percentage points. So plot this opportunity cost at 7 hours on the graph (the midpoint between 6 and 8 hours). When he increases the time he plays tennis from 8 hours to 10 hours, his opportunity cost of the additional 2 hours of tennis is 20 percentage points. So his opportunity cost of the additional 1 hour of tennis is 10 percentage points. So plot this opportunity cost at 9 hours on the graph (the midpoint between 8 and 10 hours). Wendell's opportunity cost of playing tennis increases as he spends more time on tennis. Join up the points plotted. This curve is Wendell's marginal cost of a additional hour of tennis.

Wendell uses his time efficiently if he plays tennis for 7 hours a week—marginal benefit from tennis equals its marginal cost. Wendell's marginal benefit is 5 percentage points and his marginal cost is 5 percentage points. When Wendell plays 7 hours of tennis, his grade in economics (from his *PPF*) is 66 percent.

5b. If Wendell studied for enough hours to get a higher grade, he would have fewer hours to play tennis. Wendell's marginal benefit from tennis would be greater than his marginal cost, so he would be more efficient (better off) if he played more hours of tennis and took a lower grade.

7a. Sunland's *PPF* is a straight line.

To make a graph of Sunland's *PPF* measure the quantity of one good on the *x*-axis and the quantity of the other good on the *y*-axis. Then plot the quantities in each row of the table and join up the points.

7b. The opportunity cost of 1 pound of food is 1/2 gallon of sunscreen.

The opportunity cost of the first 100 pounds of food is 50 gallons of sunscreen. To find the opportunity cost of the first 100 pounds of food, increase the quantity of food from 0 pounds to 100 pounds. In doing so, Sunland's production of sunscreen decreases from 150 gallons to 100 gallons. The opportunity cost of the first 100 pounds of food is 50 gallons of sunscreen. Similarly, the opportunity costs of producing the second 100 pounds and the third 100 pounds of food are 50 gallons of sunscreen.

The opportunity cost of 1 gallon of sunscreen is 2 pounds of food. The opportunity cost of producing the first 50 gallons of sunscreen is 100 pounds of food. To calculate this opportunity cost, increase the quantity of sunscreen from 0 gallons to 50 gallons. Sunland's production of food decreases from 300 pounds to 200 pounds. Similarly, the opportunity cost of producing the second 50 gallons and the third 50 gallons of sunscreen are 100 pounds of food.

9a. The marginal benefit curve slopes downward.

To draw the marginal benefit from sunscreen, plot the quantity of sunscreen on the *x*-axis and the willingness to pay for sunscreen (that is, the number of pounds of food that they are willing to give up to get a gallon of sunscreen) on the *y*-axis.

9b. The efficient quantity is 75 gallons a month.

The efficient quantity to produce is such that the marginal benefit from the last gallon equals the opportunity cost of producing it. The opportunity cost of a gallon of sunscreen is 2 pounds of food. The marginal benefit of the 75th gallon of sunscreen is 2 pounds of food. And the marginal cost of the 75th gallon of sunscreen is 2 pounds of food.

Busyland's opportunity cost of a pound of food is 2 gallons of sunscreen, and its opportunity cost of a gallon of sunscreen is 1/2 pound of food.

When Busyland increases the food it produces by 50 pounds a month, it produces 100 gallons of sunscreen less. The opportunity cost of 1 pound of food is 2 gallons of sunscreen. Similarly, when Busyland increases the sunscreen it produces by 100 gallons a month, it produces 50 pounds of food less. The opportunity cost of 1 gallon of sunscreen is 1/2 pound of food.

13a. Sunland sells food and buys sunscreen.

Sunland sells the good in which it has a comparative advantage and buys the other good from Busyland. Sunland's opportunity cost of 1 pound of food is 1/2 gallon of sunscreen, while Busyland's opportunity cost of 1 pound of food is 2 gallons of sunscreen. Sunland's opportunity cost of food is less than Busyland's, so Sunland has a comparative advantage in producing food.

Sunland's opportunity cost of 1 gallon of sunscreen is 2 pounds of food, while Busyland's opportunity cost of 1 gallon of sunscreen is 1/2 pound of food. Busyland's opportunity cost of sunscreen is less than Sunland's, so Busyland has a comparative advantage in producing sunscreen.

13b. The gains from trade for each country are 50 pounds of food and 50 gallons of sunscreen.

With specialization and trade, together they can produce 300 pounds of food and 300 gallons of sunscreen. So each will get 150 pounds of food and 150 gallons of sunscreen—an additional 50 pounds of food and 50 gallons of sunscreen.

CHAPTER 3

1a. The price of a tape will rise, and the quantity of tapes sold will increase.

CDs and tapes are substitutes. If the price of a CD rises, people will buy more tapes and fewer CDs. The demand for tapes will increase. The price of a tape will rise, and more tapes will be sold.

1b. The price of a tape will fall, and fewer tapes will be sold.

Walkmans and tapes are complements. If the price of a Walkman rises, fewer Walkmans will be bought. The demand for tapes will decrease. The price of a tape will fall, and people will buy fewer tapes.

1c. The price of a tape will fall and fewer tapes will be sold.

The increase in the supply of CD players will lower the price of a CD player. With CD players cheaper than they were, some people will buy CD players. The demand for CDs will increase, and the demand for tapes will decrease. The price of a tape will fall, and people will buy fewer tapes.

1d. The price of a tape will rise, and the quantity sold will increase.

An increase in consumers' income will increase the demand for tapes. As a result, the price of a tape will rise and the quantity bought will increase.

1e. The price of a tape will rise, and the quantity sold will decrease.

If the workers who make tapes get a pay raise, the cost of making a tape increases and the supply of tapes decreases. The price will rise, and people will buy fewer tapes.

1f. The quantity sold will decrease, but the price might rise, fall, or stay the same.

Walkmans and tapes are complements. If the price of a Walkman rises, fewer Walkmans will be bought and so the demand for tapes will decrease. The price of a tape will fall, and people will buy fewer tapes. If the wages paid to workers who make tapes rise, the supply of tapes decreases. The quantity of tapes sold will decrease, and the price of a tape will rise. Taking the two events together, the quantity sold will decrease, but the price might rise, fall, or stay the same.

3a. (ii) and (iii) and (iv)

The demand for gasoline will change if the price of a car changes, all speed limits on highways are abolished, or robot production cuts the cost of producing a car. If the price of a car rises, the quantity of cars bought decrease. So the demand for gasoline decreases. If all speed limits on highways are abolished, people will drive faster and use more gasoline. The demand for gasoline increases. If robot production plants lower the cost of producing a car, the supply of cars will increase. With no change in the demand for cars, the price of a car will fall and more cars will be bought. The demand for gasoline increases.

3b. (i)

The supply of gasoline will change if the price of crude oil changes. If the price of crude oil rises, the cost of producing gasoline will rise. So the supply of gasoline decreases.

3c. (i)

If the price of crude oil (a resource used to make gasoline) rises, the cost of producing gasoline will rise. So the supply of gasoline decreases. The demand for gasoline does not change, so the price of gasoline will rise and there is a movement up the demand curve for gasoline. The quantity demanded of gasoline decreases.

3d. (ii) and (iii) and (iv)

If the price of a car rises, the quantity of cars bought decrease. So the demand for gasoline decreases. The supply of gasoline does not change, so the price of gasoline falls and there is a movement down the supply curve of gasoline. The quantity supplied of gasoline decreases.

If all speed limits on highways are abolished, people will drive faster and use more gasoline. The demand for gasoline increases. The supply of gasoline does not change, so the price of gasoline rises and there is a movement up along the supply curve. The quantity supplied of gasoline increases.

If robot production plants lower the cost of producing a car, the supply of cars will increase. With no change in the demand for cars, the price of a car will fall and more cars will be bought. The demand for gasoline increases. The supply of gasoline does not change, so the price of gasoline rises and the quantity of gasoline supplied increases.

5a. The demand curve is the curve that slopes down toward to the right. The supply curve is the curve that slopes up toward to the right.

5b. The equilibrium price is $14 a pizza, and the equilibrium quantity is 200 pizzas a day.

Market equilibrium is determined at the intersection of the demand curve and supply curve.

7a. The equilibrium price is 50 cents a pack, and the equilibrium quantity is 120 million packs a week.

The price of a pack adjusts until the quantity demanded equals the quantity supplied. At 50 cents a pack, the quantity demanded is 120 million packs a week and the quantity supplied is 120 million packs a week.

7b. At 70 cents a pack, there will be a surplus of gum and the price will fall.

At 70 cents a pack, the quantity demanded is 80 million packs a week and the quantity supplied is 160 million packs a week. There is a surplus of 80 million packs a week. The price will fall until market equilibrium is restored—50 cents a pack.

9a. The supply curve has shifted leftward.

As the number of gum-producing factories decreases, the supply of gum decreases. There is a new supply schedule, and the supply curve shifts leftward.

9b. There has been a movement along the demand curve.

The supply of gum decreases, and the supply curve shifts leftward. Demand does not change, so the price rises along the demand curve.

9c. The equilibrium price is 60 cents, and the equilibrium quantity is 100 million packs a week.

Supply decreases by 40 millions packs a week. That is, the quantity supplied at each price decreases by 40 million packs. The quantity supplied at 50 cents is now 80 million packs, and there is a shortage of gum. The price rises to 60 cents a pack, at which the quantity supplied equals the quantity demanded (100 million packs a week).

11. The new price is 70 cents a pack, and the quantity is 120 million packs a week.

The demand for gum increases, and the demand curve shifts rightward. The quantity demanded at each price increases by 40 million packs. The result of the fire is a price of 60 cents a pack. At this price, there is now a shortage of gum. The price of gum will rise until the shortage is eliminated.

CHAPTER 4

1a. The price elasticity of demand is 1.25.

The price elasticity of demand equals the percentage change in the quantity demanded divided by the percentage change in the price. The price rises from $4 to $6 a box, a rise of $2 a box. The average price is $5 a box. So the percentage change in the price equals $2 divided by $5, which equals 40 percent.

The quantity decreases from 1,000 to 600 boxes, a decrease of 400 boxes. The average quantity is 800 boxes. So the percentage change in quantity equals 400 divided by 800, which equals 50 percent.

The price elasticity of demand for strawberries equals 50 divided by 40, which is 1.25.

1b. The price elasticity of demand exceeds 1, so the demand for strawberries is elastic.

3a. The price elasticity of demand is 2.

When the price of a videotape rental rises from $3 to $5, the quantity demanded of videotapes decreases from 75 to 25 a day. The price elasticity of demand equals the percentage change in the quantity demanded divided by the percentage change in the price.

The price increases from $3 to $5, an increase of $2 a videotape. The average price is $4 a videotape. So the percentage change in the price equals $2 divided by $4, which equals 50 percent.

The quantity decreases from 75 to 25 videotapes, a decrease of 50 videotapes. The average quantity is 50 videotapes. So the percentage change in quantity equals 50 divided by 50, which equals 100 percent.

The price elasticity of demand for videotape rentals equals 100 divided by 50, which is 2.

3b. The price elasticity of demand equals 1 at $3 a videotape.

The price elasticity of demand equals 1 at the price halfway between the origin and the price at which the demand curve hits the y-axis. That price is $3 a videotape.

5. The demand for dental services is unit elastic.

The price elasticity of demand for dental services equals the percentage change in the quantity of dental services demanded divided by the percentage change in the price of dental services.

The price elasticity of demand equals 10 divided by 10, which is 1. The demand is unit elastic.

7a. Total revenue increases.

When the price of a chip is $400, 30 million chips are sold and total revenue equals $12,000 million. When the price of a chip falls to $350, 35 million chips are sold and total revenue is $12,250 million. Total revenue increases when the price falls.

7b. Total revenue decreases.

When the price is $350 a chip, 35 million chips are sold and total revenue is $12,250 million. When the price of a chip is $300, 40 million chips are sold and total revenue decreases to $12,000 million. Total revenue decreases as the price falls.

7c. Total revenue is maximized at $350 a chip.

When the price of a chip is $300, 40 million chips are sold and total revenue equals $12,000 million. When the price is $350 a chip, 35 million chips are sold and total revenue equals $12,250 million. Total revenue increases as the price rises from $300 to $350 a chip. When the price is $400 a chip, 30 million chips are sold and total revenue equals $12,000 million. Total revenue decreases as the price rises from $350 to $400 a chip. Total revenue is maximized when the price is $350 a chip.

7d.   The demand for chips is unit elastic.

The total revenue test says that if the price changes and total revenue remains the same, the demand is unit elastic at the average price. For an average price of $350 a chip, cut the price from $400 to $300 a chip. When the price of a chip falls from $400 to $300, total revenue remains at $12,000 million. So at the average price of $350 a chip, demand is unit elastic.

9.   The demand for chips is inelastic.

The total revenue test says that if the price falls and total revenue falls, the demand is inelastic. When the price falls from $300 to $200 a chip, total revenue decreases from $12,000 million to $10,000 million. So at an average price of $250 a chip, demand is inelastic.

11.   The cross elasticity of demand between orange juice and apple juice is 1.17.

The cross elasticity of demand is the percentage change in the quantity demanded of one good divided by the percentage change in the price of another good. The rise in the price of orange juice resulted in an increase in the quantity demanded of apple juice. So the cross elasticity of demand is the percentage change in the quantity demanded of apple juice divided by the percentage change in the price of orange juice. The cross elasticity equals 14 divided by 12, which is 1.17.

13.   Income elasticity of demand for (i) bagels is 1.33 and (ii) donuts is –1.33.

Income elasticity of demand equals the percentage change in the quantity demanded divided by the percentage change in income. The change in income is $2,000 and the average income is $4,000, so the percentage change in income equals 50 percent.

(i) The change in the quantity demanded is 4 bagels and the average quantity demanded is 6 bagels, so the percentage change in the quantity demanded equals 66.67 percent. The income elasticity of demand for bagels equals 66.67/50, which is 1.33.

(ii) The change in the quantity demanded is –6 donuts and the average quantity demanded is 9 donuts, so the percentage change in the quantity demanded is –66.67. The income elasticity of demand for donuts equals –66.67/50, which is –1.33.

15a.   The elasticity of supply is 1.

The elasticity of supply is the percentage change in the quantity supplied divided by the percentage change in the price. When the price falls from 40 cents to 30 cents, the change in the price is 10 cents and the average price is 35 cents. The percentage change in the price is 28.57.

When the price falls from 40 cents to 30 cents, the quan-

tity supplied decreases from 800 to 600 calls. The change in the quantity supplied is 200 calls, and the average quantity is 700 calls, so the percentage change in the quantity supplied is 28.57.

The elasticity of supply equals 28.57/28.57, which equals 1.

15b.   The elasticity of supply is 1.

The formula for the elasticity of supply calculates the elasticity at the average price. So to find the elasticity at 20 cents, change the price such that 20 cents is the average price—for example, a fall in the price from 30 cents to 10 cents.

When the price falls from 30 cents to 10 cents, the change in the price is 20 cents and the average price is 20 cents. The percentage change in the price is 100. When the price falls from 30 cents to 10 cents, the quantity supplied decreases from 600 to 200 calls. The change in the quantity supplied is 400 calls and the average quantity is 400 calls. The percentage change in the quantity supplied is 100.

The elasticity of supply is the percentage change in the quantity supplied divided by the percentage change in the price. The elasticity of supply is 1.

CHAPTER 5

1a.   Equilibrium price is $1.00 a floppy disc, and the equilibrium quantity is 3 floppy discs a month.

b.   Consumers paid $3.

The amount paid equals quantity bought multiplied by the price paid. That is, the amount paid equals 3 floppy discs multiplied by $1.00 a disc.

1c.   The consumer surplus is $2.25.

The consumer surplus is the area of the triangle under the demand curve above the market price. The market price is $1.00 a disc. The area of the triangle equals (2.50 – 1.00)/2 multiplied by 3, which is $2.25.

1d.   Producer surplus is $0.75.

The producer surplus is the area of the triangle above the supply curve below the price. The price is $1.00 a disc. The area of the triangle equals (1.00 – 0.50)/2 multiplied by 3, which is $0.75.

1e.   The cost of producing the discs sold is $2.25.

The cost of producing the discs is the amount received minus the producer surplus. The amount received is $1.00 a disc for 3 discs, which is $3.00. Producer surplus is $0.75, so the cost of producing the discs sold is $2.25.

1f.   The efficient quantity is 3 floppy discs a month.

The efficient quantity is the quantity that makes the marginal benefit from the last disc equal to the marginal cost of producing the last disc. The demand curve shows the marginal benefit and the supply curve shows the marginal cost. Only if 3 floppy discs are produced is the quantity produced efficient.

3a.   The maximum price that consumers will pay is $3.

The demand schedule shows the maximum price that consumers will pay for each sandwich. The maximum price that consumers will pay for the 250th sandwich is $3.

3b. The minimum price that producers will accept is $5.

The supply schedule shows the minimum price that producers will accept for each sandwich. The minimum price
that produces will accept for the 250th sandwich is $5.

3c. 250 sandwiches exceed the efficient quantity.

The efficient quantity is such that marginal benefit from
the last sandwich equals the marginal cost of producing it.
The efficient quantity is the equilibrium quantity—200
sandwiches an hour.

3d. Consumer surplus is $400.

The equilibrium price is $4. The consumer surplus is the
area of the triangle under the demand curve above the
price. The area of the triangle is (8 − 4)/2 multiplied by
200, which is $400.

3e. Producer surplus is $400.

The producer surplus is the area of the triangle above the
supply curve below the price. The price is $4. The area of
the triangle is (4 − 0)/2 multiplied by 200, which is $400.

3f. The deadweight loss is $50.

Deadweight loss is the sum of the consumer surplus and
producer surplus that is lost because the quantity produced is not the efficient quantity. The deadweight loss
equals the quantity (250 − 200) multiplied by (5 − 3)/2,
which is $50.

5a. Ben's consumer surplus is $122.50. Beth's consumer sur-
plus is $22.50, and Bo's consumer surplus is $4.50.

Consumer surplus is the area under the demand curve
above the price. At 40 cents, Ben will travel 350 miles,
Beth will travel 150 miles, and Bo will travel 30 miles. To
find Ben's consumer surplus extend his demand schedule
until you find the price at which the quantity demanded
by Ben is zero—the price at which Ben's demand curve
cuts the y-axis. This price is 110 cents. So Ben's consumer
surplus equals (110 − 40)/2 multiplied by 350, which
equals $122.50. Similarly, Beth's consumer surplus equals
(70 − 40)/2 multiplied by 150, which equals $22.50. And
Bo's consumer surplus equals (70 − 40)/2 multiplied by
30, which equals $4.50.

5b. Ben's consumer surplus is the largest because he places a
higher value on each unit of the good than the other two
do.

5c. Ben's consumer surplus falls by $32.50. Beth's consumer
surplus falls by $12.50, and Bo's consumer surplus falls by
$2.50.

At 50 cents a mile, Ben travels 300 miles and his consumer surplus is $90. Ben's consumer surplus equals
(110 − 50)/2 multiplied by 300, which equals $90. Ben's
consumer surplus decreases from $122.50 to $90, a
decrease of $32.50. Beth travels 100 miles and her con-
sumer surplus is $10, a decrease of $12.50. Bo travels 20
miles and her consumer surplus is $2.00, a decrease of
$2.50.

CHAPTER 6

1a. Equilibrium price is $200 a month and the equilibrium
quantity is 10,000 housing units.

1b. The quantity rented is 5,000 housing units.

The quantity of housing rented is equal to the quantity
supplied at the rent ceiling.

1c. The shortage is 10,000 housing units.

At the rent ceiling, the quantity of housing demanded is
15,000 but the quantity supplied is 5,000, so there is a
shortage of 10,000 housing units.

1d. The maximum price that someone is willing to pay for
the 5,000th unit available is $300 a month.

The demand curve tells us the maximum price willingly
paid for the 5,000th unit.

3a. The equilibrium wage rate is $4 an hour, and employ-
ment is 2,000 hours a month.

3b. Unemployment is zero. Everyone who wants to work for
$4 an hour is employed.

3c. They work 2,000 hours a month.

A minimum wage rate is the lowest wage rate that a person can be paid for an hour of work. Because the equilibrium wage rate exceeds the minimum wage rate, the
minimum wage is ineffective. The wage rate will be $4 an
hour and employment is 2,000 hours.

3d. There is no unemployment

The wage rate rises to the equilibrium wage—the quantity of labor demanded equals the quantity of labor supplied. So there is no unemployment.

3e. At $5 an hour, 1,500 hours a month are employed and
1,000 hours a month are unemployed.

The quantity of labor employed equals the quantity
demanded at $5 an hour. Unemployment is equal to the
quantity of labor supplied at $5 an hour minus the quan-
tity of labor demanded at $5 an hour. The quantity sup-
plied is 2,500 hours a month, and the quantity demanded
is 1,500 hours a month. So 1,000 hours a month are
unemployed.

3f. The wage rate is $5 an hour, and unemployment is 500
hours a month.

At the minimum wage of $5 an hour, the quantity
demanded is 2,000 hours a month and the quantity supplied is 2,500 hours a month. So 500 hours a month are
unemployed.

5a. With no tax on brownies, the price is 60 cents a brownie
and 4 million a day are consumed.

5b. The price is 70 cents a brownie, and 3 million brownies a
day are consumed. Consumers and producers each pay 10
cents of the tax on a brownie.

The tax decreases the supply of brownies and raises the
price of a brownie. With no tax, producers are willing to
sell 3 million brownies a day at 50 cents a brownie. But
with a 20 cent tax, they are willing to sell 3 million
brownies a day only if the price is 20 cents higher at 70
cents a brownie.

7a. Inventory holders sell 500 boxes of rice.

Inventory holders expect the decrease in supply as a result
of the storm will raise the price to above $1.40 a box. So
inventory holders sell rice from storage.

7b. The price is $1.40 a box, and farm revenue is $2,800 per
week.

The storm cuts the quantity grown by 500 boxes to 2,000 boxes a week. The action of inventory holders maintains the price at $1.40 a box, so farm revenue equals $1.40 multiplied by 2,000 boxes.

CHAPTER 7

1a. To draw a graph of Jason's total utility from rock CDs, plot the number of CDs on the *x*-axis and Jason's utility from CDs on the *y*-axis. The curve will look similar to Fig. 7.2(a). To draw a graph of Jason's total utility from spy novels, repeat the above procedure but use the spy novel data.

1b. Jason gets more utility from any number of rock CDs than he does from the same number of spy novels.

1c. To draw a graph of Jason's marginal utility from rock CDs plot the number of CDs on the *x*-axis and Jason's marginal utility from CDs on the *y*-axis. The curve will look similar to Fig. 7.2(b). To draw a graph of Jason's marginal utility from spy novels, repeat the above procedure but use the spy novel data.

Jason's marginal utility from rock CDs is the increase in total utility he gets from one additional rock CD. Similarly, Jason's marginal utility from spy novels is the increase in total utility he gets from one additional spy novel.

1d. Jason gets more marginal utility from an additional rock CD than he gets from an additional spy novel when he has the same number of each.

1e. Jason buys 5 rock CDs and 1 spy novel.

When Jason buys 5 rock CDs and 1 spy novel he spends $60. Jason maximizes his utility when he spends all of his money and the marginal utility per dollar spent on rock CDs and spy novels is the same. When Jason buys 5 rock CDs his marginal utility per dollar spent is 2 units per dollar and when Jason buys 1 spy novel his marginal utility per dollar spent is 2 units per dollar.

3. To maximize his utility, Max windsurfs for 3 hours and snorkels for 1 hour.

Max will spend his $35 such that all of the $35 is spent and that the marginal utility per dollar spent on each activity is the same. When Max windsurfs for 3 hours and snorkels for 1 hour, he spends $30 renting the windsurfing equipment and $5 renting the snorkeling equipment—a total of $35.

The marginal utility from the third hour of windsurfing is 80 and the rent of the windsurfing equipment is $10 an hour, so the marginal utility per dollar spent on windsurfing is 8. The marginal utility from the first hour of snorkeling is 40 and the rent of the snorkeling equipment is $5 an hour, so the marginal utility per dollar spent on snorkeling is 8. The marginal utility per dollar spent on windsurfing equals the marginal utility per dollar spent on snorkeling.

5. To maximize his utility, Max windsurfs for 4 hours and snorkels for 3 hour.

Max will spend his $55 such that all of the $55 is spent and that the marginal utility per dollar spent on each

activity is the same. When Max windsurfs for 4 hours and snorkels for 3 hours, he spends $40 renting the windsurfing equipment and $15 renting the snorkeling equipment—a total of $55.

The marginal utility from the fourth hour of windsurfing is 60 and the rent of the windsurfing equipment is $10 an hour, so the marginal utility per dollar spent on windsurfing is 6. The marginal utility from the third hour of snorkeling is 30 and the rent of the snorkeling equipment is $5 an hour, so the marginal utility per dollar spent on snorkeling is 6. The marginal utility per dollar spent on windsurfing equals the marginal utility per dollar spent on snorkeling.

7. To maximize his utility, Max windsurfs for 6 hours and snorkels for 5 hours.

Max will spend his $55 such that all of the $55 is spent and that the marginal utility per dollar spent on each activity is the same. When Max windsurfs for 6 hours and snorkels for 5 hours, he spends $30 renting the windsurfing equipment and $25 renting the snorkeling equipment—a total of $55.

The marginal utility from the sixth hour of windsurfing is 12 and the rent of the windsurfing equipment is $5 an hour, so the marginal utility per dollar spent on windsurfing is 2.4. The marginal utility from the fifth hour of snorkeling is 12 and the rent of the snorkeling equipment is $5 an hour, so the marginal utility per dollar spent on snorkeling is 2.4. The marginal utility per dollar spent on windsurfing equals the marginal utility per dollar spent on snorkeling.

9. To maximize his utility, Max windsurfs for 5 hours and snorkels for 1 hour.

Because the equipment is free, Max does not have to allocate his *income* between the two activities; instead, he allocates his *time* between the two activities. Max spends 6 hours on these activities. Max allocates the 6 hours such that the marginal utility from each activity is the same. When Max windsurfs for 5 hours and snorkels for 1 hour, he spends 6 hours. His marginal utility from the fifth hour of windsurfing is 40 and his marginal utility from the first hour of snorkeling is 40—so the marginal utilities are equal.

11. The market demand curve passes through the following points: 90 cents and 3 cartons; 70 cents and 6 cartons; 50 cents and 10 cartons; 30 cents and 14 cartons; and 10 cents and 18 cartons.

At each price, the quantity demand by the market is equal to the sum of the cartons of popcorn that Shirley demands and the cartons of popcorn that Dan demands. For example, at 50 cents a carton, the quantity demanded by Shirley and Dan is 10, the sum of Shirley's 6 and Dan's 4.

CHAPTER 8

1a. Sara's real income is 4 cans of cola.

Sara's real income in terms of cans of cola is equal to her money income divided by the price of a can of cola. Sara's money income is $12, and the price of cola is $3 a can.

Sara's real income is $12 divided by $3 a can of cola, which is 4 cans of cola.

1b. Sara's real income is 4 bags of popcorn.

Sara's real income in terms of popcorn is equal to her money income divided by the price of a bag of popcorn, which is $12 divided by $3 a bag or 4 bags of popcorn.

1c. The relative price of cola is 1 bag per can.

The relative price of cola is the price of cola divided by the price of popcorn. The price of cola is $3 a can and the price of popcorn is $3 a bag, so the relative price of cola is $3 a can divided by $3 a bag, which equals 1 bag per can.

1d. The opportunity cost of a can of cola is 1 bag of popcorn.

The opportunity cost of a can of cola is the quantity of popcorn that must be forgone to get a can of cola. The price of cola is $3 a can and the price of popcorn is $3 a bag, so to buy one can of cola Sara must forgo 1 bag of popcorn.

1e. The equation that describes Sara's budget line is

$$Q_P = 4 - Q_C$$

Call the price of popcorn P_P and the quantity of popcorn Q_P, the price of cola P_C and the quantity of cola Q_C, and income y. Sara's budget equation is

If we substitute $3 for the price of popcorn, $3 for the price of cola, and $12 for the income, the budget equation becomes

$$P_P Q_P + P_C Q_C = y.$$

Dividing both sides by $3 and subtracting

$$\$3 \times Q_P + \$3 \times Q_C = \$12.$$

Q_C from both sides gives

$$Q_P = 4 - Q_C.$$

1f. To draw a graph of the budget line, plot the quantity of cola on the x-axis and the quantity of popcorn on the y-axis. The budget line is a straight line running from 4 bags on the y-axis to 4 cans on the x-axis.

1g. The slope of the budget line, when cola is plotted on the x-axis is minus 1. The magnitude of the slope is equal to the relative price of cola.

The slope of the budget line is "rise over run." If the quantity of cola decreases from 4 to 0, the quantity of popcorn increases from 0 to 4. The rise is 4 and the run is −4. Therefore the slope equals 4/−4, which is −1.

3a. Sara buys 2 cans of cola and 2 bags of popcorn.

Sara buys the quantities of cola and popcorn that gets her onto the highest indifference curve, given her income and the prices of cola and popcorn. The graph shows Sara's indifference curves. So draw Sara's budget line on the graph. The budget line is tangential to indifference curve I_0 at 2 cans of cola and 2 bags of popcorn. The indifference curve I_0 is the highest indifference curve that Sara can get onto.

3b. Sara's marginal rate of substitution is 1.

The marginal rate of substitution is the magnitude of the slope of the indifference curve at Sara's consumption point, which equals the magnitude of the slope of the budget line. The slope of Sara's budget line is −1, so the marginal rate of substitution is 1.

5a. Sara buys 6 cans of cola and 1 bag of popcorn.

Draw the new budget line on the graph with Sara's indifference curves. The budget line now runs from 8 cans of cola on the x-axis to 4 bags of popcorn on the y-axis. The new budget line is tangential to indifference curve I_1 at 6 cans of cola and 1 bag of popcorn. The indifference curve I_1 is the highest indifference curve that Sara can now get onto.

5b. Two points on Sara's demand for cola are the following: At $3 a can of cola, Sara buys 2 cans of cola. At $1.50 a can of cola, Sara buys 6 cans.

5c. The substitution effect is 2 cans of cola.

To divide the price effect into a substitution effect and an income effect, take enough income away from Sara and gradually move her new budget line back toward the origin until it just touches Sara's indifference curve I_0. The point at which this budget line just touches indifference curve I_0 is 4 cans of cola and 0.5 bag of popcorn. The substitution effect is the increase in the quantity of cola from 2 cans to 4 cans along the indifference curve I_0. The substitution effect is 2 cans of cola.

5d. The income effect is 2 cans of cola.

The income effect is the change in the quantity of cola from the price effect minus the change from the substitution effect. The price effect is 4 cans of cola (6 cans minus the initial 2 cans). The substitution effect is an increase in the quantity of cola from 2 cans to 4 cans. So the income effect is 2 cans of cola.

5e. Cola is a normal good for Sara because the income effect is positive. An increase in income increases the quantity of cola she buys from 4 to 6 cans.

7a. Pam can still buy 30 cookies and 5 comic books.

When Pam buys 30 cookies at $1 each and 5 comic books at $2 each, she spends $40 a month. Now that the price of a cookie is 50 cents and the price of a comic book is $5, 30 cookies and 5 comic books will cost $40. So Pam can still buy 30 cookies and 5 comic books.

7b. Pam will not want to buy 30 cookies and 5 comic books because the marginal rate of substitution does not equal the relative price of the goods. Pam will move to a point on the highest indifference curve possible where the marginal rate of substitution equals the relative price.

7c. Pam prefers cookies at 50 cents each and comic books at $5 each because she can get onto a higher indifference curve than when cookies are $1 each and comic books are $2 each.

7d. Pam will buy more cookies and fewer comic books.

The new budget line and the old budget line pass through the point at 30 cookies and 5 comic books. If comic books are plotted on the x-axis, the marginal rate of substitution at this point on Pam's indifference curve is equal to the relative price of a comic book at the original prices, which is 2. The new relative price of a comic book is $5/50 cents, which is 10. That is, the budget line is steeper than the indifference curve at 30 cookies and 5 comic books. Pam will buy more cookies and fewer comic books.

7e. There will be a substitution effect and an income effect.

A substitution effect arises when the relative price changes and the consumer moves along the *same* indifference curve to a new point where the marginal rate of substitution equals the new relative price. An income effect arises when the consumer moves from one indifference curve to another, keeping the relative price constant.

CHAPTER 9

1. Explicit costs are $30,000. Explicit costs are all the costs for which there is a payment. Explicit costs are the sum the wages paid ($20,000) and the goods and services bought from other firms ($10,000).

   Implicit costs are the sum of the costs that do not involve a payment. Implicit costs are the sum of the interest forgone on the $50,000 put into the firm; the $30,000 income forgone by Jack not working at his previous job; $15,000, which is the value of 500 hours of Jill's leisure (10 hours a week for 50 weeks); and the economic depreciation of $2,000 ($30,000 minus $28,000).

3a. All methods other than "pocket calculator with paper and pencil" are technologically efficient.

   To use a pocket calculator with paper and pencil to complete the tax return is not a technologically efficient method because it takes the same number of hours as it would with a pocket calculator but it uses more capital.

3b. The economically efficient method is to use (i) a pocket calculator, (ii) a pocket calculator, (iii) a PC.

   The economically efficient method is the technologically efficient method that allows the task to be done at least cost.

   When the wage rate is $5 an hour: Total cost with a PC is $1,005, total cost with a pocket calculator is $70, and total cost with paper and pencil is $81. Total cost is least with a pocket calculator.

   When the wage rate is $50 an hour: Total cost with a PC is $1,050, total cost with a pocket calculator is $610, and the total cost with paper and pencil is $801. Total cost is least with a pocket calculator.

   When the wage rate is $500 an hour: Total cost with a PC is $1,500, total cost with a pocket calculator is $6,010, and total cost with pencil and paper is $8,001. Total cost is least with a PC.

5a. Methods *A*, *B*, *C*, and *D* are technologically efficient. Compare the amount of labor and capital used by the four methods. Start with method *A*. Moving from *A* to *B* to *C* to *D*, the amount of labor increases and the amount of capital decreases in each case.

5b. The economically efficient method in (i) is method *D*, in (ii) is methods *C* and *D*, and in (iii) is method *A*.

   The economically efficient method is the technologically efficient method that allows the 100 shirts to be washed at least cost.

   (i) Total cost with method *A* is $1,001, total cost with method *B* is $805, total cost with method *C* is $420, and total cost with method *D* is $150. Method *D* has the lowest total cost.

   (ii) Total cost with method *A* is $505, total cost with

method *B* is $425, total cost with method *C* is $300, and total cost with method *D* is $300. Methods *C* and *D* have the lowest total cost.

   (iii) Total cost with method *A* is $100, total cost with method *B* is $290, total cost with method *C* is $1,020, and total cost with method *D* is $2,505. Method *A* has the lowest total cost.

7a. The four-firm concentration ratio is 60.49.

   The four-firm concentration ratio equals the ratio of the total sales of the largest four firms to the total industry sales expressed as a percentage. The total sales of the largest four firms is $450 + $325 + $250 + $200, which equals $1,225. Total industry sales equal $1,225 + $800, which equals $2,025. The four-firm concentration ratio equals ($1,225/$2,025) × 100, which is 60.49 percent.

7b. This industry is highly concentrated because the four-firm concentration ratio exceeds 60 percent.

9a. The Herfindahl-Hirschman Index is 1,800.

   The Herfindahl-Hirschman Index equals the sum of the squares of the market shares of the 50 largest firms or of all firms if there are less than 50 firms. The Herfindahl-Hirschman Index equals $15^2 + 10^2 + 20^2 + 15^2 + 25^2 + 15^2$, which equals 1,800.

9b. This industry is moderately competitive because the Herfindahl-Hirschman Index lies in the range 1,000 to 1,800.

CHAPTER 10

1a. To draw the total product curve measure *labor* on the *x*-axis and output on the *y*-axis. The total product curve is upward sloping.

1b. The average product of *labor* is equal to total product divided by the quantity of *labor* employed. For example, when 3 workers are employed, they produce 6 boats a week, so the average product is 2 boats per worker.

   The average product curve is upward sloping when the number of workers is between 1 and 8, but it becomes downward sloping when 9 and 10 workers are employed.

1c. The marginal product of *labor* is equal to the increase in total product when an additional worker is employed. For example, when 3 workers are employed, total product is 6 boats a week. When a fourth worker is employed, total product increases to 10 boats a week. The marginal product of going from 3 to 4 workers is 4 boats.

   The marginal product curve is upward sloping when up to 5.5 workers a week are employed and downward sloping when more than 5.5 workers a week are employed.

1d. (i) When Rubber Duckies produces fewer than 30 boats a week, it employs fewer than 8 workers a week. With fewer than 8 workers a week, marginal product exceeds average product and average product is increasing. Up to an output of 30 boats a week, each additional worker adds more to output than the average. Average product increases.

   (ii) When Rubber Duckies produces more than 30 boats a week, it employs more than 8 workers a week. With more than 8 workers a week, average product exceeds marginal product and average product is decreasing. For outputs greater than 30 boats a week, each additional worker adds less to output than average. Average product decreases.

3a. Total cost is the sum of the costs of all the inputs that Rubber Duckies uses in production. Total variable cost is the total cost of the variable inputs. Total fixed cost is the total cost of the fixed inputs.

For example, the total variable cost of producing 10 boats a week is the total cost of the workers employed, which is 4 workers at $400 a week, which equals $1,600. Total fixed cost is $1,000, so the total cost of producing 10 boats a week is $2,600.

To draw the short-run total cost curves, plot output on the x-axis and the total cost on the y-axis. The total fixed cost curve is a horizontal line at $1,000. The total variable cost curve and the total cost curve have shapes similar to those in Fig. 10.4, but the vertical distance between the total variable cost curve and the total cost curve is $1,000.

3b. Average fixed cost is total fixed cost per unit of output. Average variable cost is total variable cost per unit of output. Average total cost is the total cost per unit of output.

For example, when the firm makes 10 boats a week: Total fixed cost is $1,000, so average fixed cost is $100 per boat; total variable cost is $1,600, so average variable cost is $160 per boat; and total cost is $2,600, so average total cost is $260 per boat.

Marginal cost is the increase in total cost divided by the increase in output. For example, when output increases from 3 to 6 boats a week, total cost increases from $1,800 to $2,200, an increase of $400. That is, the increase in output of 3 boats increases total cost by $400. Marginal cost is equal to $400 divided by 3 boats, which is $133.33 a boat.

The short-run average and marginal cost curves are similar to those in Fig. 10.5.

5. The increase in total fixed cost increases total cost but does not change total variable cost. Average fixed cost is total fixed cost per unit of output. The average fixed cost curve shifts upward. Average total cost is total cost per unit of output. The average total cost curve shifts upward. Marginal cost and average variable cost do not change.

7a. Total cost is the cost of all the inputs. For example, when 3 workers are employed they now produce 12 boats a week. With 3 workers, the total variable cost is $1,200 a week and the total fixed cost is $2,000 a week. The total cost is $3,200 a week. The average total cost of producing 12 boats is $266.67.

7b. The long-run average cost curve is made up the lowest parts of the firm's short-run average total cost curves when the firm operates 1 plant and 2 plants. The long-run average cost curve is similar to Fig. 10.8.

7c. It is efficient to operate the number of plants that has the lower average total cost of a boat. It is efficient to operate one plant when output is less than 27 boats a week, and it is efficient to operate two plants when the output is more than 27 boats a week.

Over the output range 1 to 27 boats a week, average total cost is less with one plant than with two, but if output

exceeds 27 boats a week, average total cost is less with two plants than with one.

9a. For example, the average total cost of producing a balloon ride when Bonnie rents 2 balloons and employs 4 workers equals the total cost ($1,000 rent for the balloons plus $1,000 for the workers) divided by the 20 balloon rides produced. The average total cost equals $2,000/20, which is $100 a ride.

The average total cost curve is U-shaped, as in Fig. 10.5.

9b. The long-run average cost curve is similar to that in Fig. 10.8.

9c. Bonnie's minimum efficient scale is 13 balloon rides when Bonnie rents 1 balloon.

The minimum efficient scale is the smallest output at which the long-run average cost is a minimum. To find the minimum efficient scale, plot the average total cost curve for each plant and then check which plant has the lowest minimum average total cost.

9d. Bonnie will choose the plant (number of balloons to rent) that gives her minimum average total cost for the normal or average number of balloon rides that people buy.

CHAPTER 11

1a. Quick Copy's profit-maximizing quantity is 80 pages an hour.

Quick Copy maximizes its profit by producing the quantity at which marginal revenue equals marginal cost. In perfect competition, marginal revenue equals price, which is 10 cents a page. Marginal cost is 10 cents when Quick Copy produces 80 pages an hour.

1b. Quick Copy's profit is $2.40 an hour.

Profit equals total revenue minus total cost. Total revenue equals $8.00 an hour (10 cents a page multiplied by 80 pages). The average total cost of producing 80 pages is 7 cents a page, so total cost equals $5.60 an hour (7 cents multiplied by 80 pages). Profit equals $8.00 minus $5.60, which is $2.40 an hour.

1c. The price will fall in the long run to 6 cents a page.

At a price of 10 cents a page, firms make economic profit. In the long run, the economic profit will encourage new firms to enter the copying industry. As they do, the price will fall and economic profit will decrease. Firms will enter until economic profit is zero, which occurs when the price is 6 cents a copy (price equals minimum average total cost).

3a. (i) At $14 a pizza, Pat's profit-maximizing output is 4 pizzas an hour and economic profit is $10 an hour.

Pat's maximizes its profit by producing the quantity at which marginal revenue equals marginal cost. In perfect competition, marginal revenue equals price, which is $14 a pizza. Marginal cost is the change in total cost when output is increased by 1 pizza an hour. The marginal cost of increasing output from 3 to 4 pizzas an hour is $13 ($54 minus $41). The marginal cost of increasing output from 4 to 5 pizzas an hour is $15 ($69 minus $54). So the marginal cost of the fourth pizza is half-way between $13 and $15, which is $14. Marginal cost equals marginal revenue when Pat produces 4 pizzas an hour.

Economic profit equals total revenue minus total cost. Total revenue equals $64 ($14 multiplied by 4). Total cost is $54, so economic profit is $10.

(ii) At $12 a pizza, Pat's profit-maximizing output is 3 pizzas an hour and economic profit is –$5.

Pat's maximizes its profit by producing the quantity at which marginal revenue equals marginal cost. Marginal revenue equals price, which is $12 a pizza. Marginal cost of increasing output from 2 to 3 pizzas an hour is $11 ($41 minus $30). The marginal cost of increasing output from 3 to 4 pizzas an hour is $13. So the marginal cost of the third pizza is half-way between $11 and $13, which is $12. Marginal cost equals marginal revenue when Pat produces 3 pizzas an hour.

Economic profit equals total revenue minus total cost. Total revenue equals $36 ($12 multiplied by 3). Total cost is $41, so economic profit is –$5.

(iii) At $10 a pizza, Pat's profit-maximizing output is 2 pizzas an hour and economic profit is –$10.

Pat's maximizes its profit by producing the quantity at which marginal revenue equals marginal cost. Marginal revenue equals price, which is $10 a pizza. Marginal cost of increasing output from 1 to 2 pizzas an hour is $9 ($30 minus $21). The marginal cost of increasing output from 2 to 3 pizzas an hour is $11. So the marginal cost of the second pizza is half-way between $9 and $11, which is $10. Marginal cost equals marginal revenue when Pat produces 2 pizzas an hour.

Economic profit equals total revenue minus total cost. Total revenue equals $20 ($10 multiplied by 2). Total cost is $30, so economic profit is –$10.

3b. Pat's shutdown point is at a price of $10 a pizza.

The shutdown point is the price that equals minimum average variable cost. To calculate total variable cost, subtract total fixed cost ($10, which is total cost at zero output) from total cost. Average variable cost equals total variable cost divided by the quantity produced. For example, the average variable cost of producing 2 pizzas is $10 a pizza. Average variable cost is a minimum when marginal cost equals average variable cost. The marginal cost of producing 2 pizzas is $10. So the shutdown point is a price of $10 a pizza.

3c. Pat's supply curve is the same as the marginal cost curve at prices equal to or above $10 a pizza and the *y*-axis at prices below $10 a pizza.

3d. Pat will exit the pizza industry if in the long run the price is less than $13 a pizza.

Pat's Pizza Kitchen will leave the industry if it incurs an economic loss in the long run. To incur an economic loss, the price will have to be below minimum average total cost. Average total cost equals total cost divided by the quantity produced. For example, the average total cost of producing 2 pizzas is $15 a pizza. Average total cost is a minimum when it equals marginal cost. The average total cost of 3 pizzas is $13.67, and the average total cost of 4 pizzas is $13.50. Marginal cost when Pat's produces 3 pizzas is $12 and marginal cost when Pat's produces 4 pizzas is $14. At 3 pizzas, marginal cost is less than average total cost; at 4 pizzas, marginal cost exceeds average total cost.

So minimum average total cost occurs between 3 and 4 pizzas—$13 at 3.5 pizzas an hour.

5a. The market price is $8.40 a cassette.

The market price is the price at which the quantity demanded equals the quantity supplied. The firm's supply curve is the same as its marginal cost curve at prices above minimum average variable cost. Average variable cost is a minimum when marginal cost equals average variable cost. Marginal cost equals average variable cost at the quantity 250 cassettes a week. So the firm's supply curve is the same as the marginal cost curve for the outputs equal to 250 cassettes or more. When the price is $8.40 a cassette, each firm produces 350 cassettes and the quantity supplied by the 1,000 firms is 350,000 cassettes a week. The quantity demanded at $8.40 is 350,000 a week.

5b. The industry output is 350,000 cassettes a week.

5c. Each firm produces 350 cassettes a week.

5d. Each firm incurs an economic loss of $581 a week.

Each firm produces 350 cassettes at an average total cost of $10.06 a cassette. The firm can sell the 350 cassettes for $8.40 a cassette. The firm incurs a loss on each cassette of $1.66 and incurs an economic loss of $581a week.

5e. In the long run, some firms exit the industry because they are incurring economic losses.

5f. The number of firms in the long run is 750.

In the long run, as firms exit the industr~~~
In lon~
mu.
week, marginal cost equals average total cost and a ~~~ ~e total cost is a minimum at $10 a cassette. In the long run, the price is $10 a cassette. Each firm remaining in the industry produces 400 cassettes a week. The quantity demanded at $10 a cassette is 300,000 a week. So the number of firms is 300,000 cassettes divided by 400 cassettes per firm, which is 750 firms.

7a. The market price is $7.65 a cassette.

When the price is $7.65 a cassette, each firm produces 300 cassettes and the quantity supplied by the 1,000 firms is 300,000 cassettes a week. The quantity demanded at $7.65 is 300,000 a week.

7b. The industry output is 300,000 cassettes a week.

7c. Each firm produces 300 cassettes a week.

7d. Each firm makes an economic loss of $834 a week.

Each firm produces 300 cassettes at an average total cost of $10.43 a cassette. The firm can sell the 300 cassettes for $7.65 a cassette. The firm incurs a loss on each cassette of $2.78 and incurs an economic loss of $834 a week.

7e. In the long run, some firms exit the industry because they are incurring economic losses.

7f. The number of firms in the long run is 500.

In the long run, as firms exit the industry, the price rises. Each firm remaining in the industry produces 400 cassettes a week. The quantity demanded at $10 a cassette is 200,000 a week. So the number of firms is 200,000 cassettes divide by 400 cassettes per firm, which is 500 firms.

CHAPTER 12

1a. Minnie's total revenue schedule lists the total revenue at each quantity sold. For example, Minnie's can sell 1 bottle for $8 a bottle, which is $8 of total revenue at the quantity 1 bottle.

1b. Minnie's marginal revenue schedule lists the marginal revenue that results from increasing the quantity sold by 1 bottle. For example, Minnie's can sell 1 bottle for a total revenue of $8. Minnie's can sell 2 bottles for $6 each, which is $12 of total revenue at the quantity 2 bottles. So by increasing the quantity sold from 1 bottle to 2 bottles, marginal revenue is $4 a bottle ($12 minus $8).

3a. Marginal cost is the increase in total cost that results from increasing output by 1 unit. When Minnie's increases output from 1 bottle to 2 bottles, total cost increases by $4, so the marginal cost is $4 a bottle.

3b. Minnie's profit-maximizing output is 1.5 bottles.

The marginal cost of increasing the quantity from 1 bottle to 2 bottles is $4 a bottle ($7 minus $3). That is, the marginal cost of the 1.5 bottles is $4 a bottle. The marginal revenue of increasing the quantity sold from 1 bottle to 2 bottles is $4 ($12 minus $8). So the marginal revenue from 1.5 bottles is $4 a bottle. Profit is maximized when the quantity produced makes the marginal cost equal to marginal revenue. The profit-maximizing output is 1.5 bottles.

3c. Minnie's profit-maximizing price is $7 a bottle.

The profit-maximizing price is the highest price that Minnie's can sell the profit-maximizing output of 1.5 bottles. Minnie's can sell 1 bottle for $8 and 2 bottles for $6, so it can sell 1.5 bottles for $7 a bottle.

3d. Minnie's economic profit is $5.50.

Economic profit equals total revenue minus total cost. Total revenue equals price ($7 a bottle) multiplied by quantity (1.5 bottles), which is $10.50. Total cost of producing 1 bottle is $3 and the total cost of producing 2 bottles is $7, so the total cost of producing 1.5 bottles is $5. Profit equals $10.50 minus $5, which is $5.50.

3e. Minnie's is inefficient. Minnie's charges a price of $7 a bottle, so consumers get a marginal benefit of $7 a bottle. Minnie's marginal cost is $4 a bottle. That is, the marginal benefit of $7 a bottle exceeds Minnie's marginal cost.

5a. The profit-maximizing quantity is 150 newspapers a day and price is 70 cents a paper.

Profit is maximized when the firm produces the output at which marginal cost equals marginal revenue. Draw in the marginal revenue curve. It runs from 100 on the y-axis to 250 on the x-axis. The marginal revenue curve cuts the marginal cost curve at the quantity 150 newspapers a day.

The highest price that the publisher can sell 150 newspapers a day is read from the demand curve.

5b. The daily total revenue is $105 (150 papers at 70 cents each).

5c. Demand is elastic.

Along a straight-line demand curve, demand is elastic at all prices above the midpoint of the demand curve. The price at the midpoint is 50 cents. So at 70 cents a paper, demand is elastic.

5d. The consumer surplus is $22.50 a day and the deadweight loss is $15 a day.

Consumer surplus is the area under the demand curve above the price. The price is 70 cents, so consumer surplus equals (100 cents minus 70 cents) multiplied by 150/2 papers a day, which is $22.50 a day.

Deadweight loss arises because the publisher does not produce the efficient quantity. Output is restricted to 150, and the price is increased to 70 cents. The deadweight loss equals (70 cents minus 40 cents) multiplied by 100/2.

5e. The newspaper will not want to price discriminate unless it can find a way to prevent sharing and resale of the newspaper from those who are charged a lower price to those who are charged a higher price.

7a. The firm will produce 2 cubic feet a day and sell it for 6 cents a cubic foot. Deadweight loss will be 4 cents a day.

Draw in the marginal revenue curve. It runs from 10 on the y-axis to 2.5 on the x-axis. The profit-maximizing output is 2 cubic feet at which marginal revenue equals marginal cost. The price charged is the highest that people will pay for 2 cubic feet a day, which is 6 cents a cubic foot. The efficient output is 4 cubic feet, at which marginal cost equals price (marginal benefit). So the deadweight loss is (4 minus 2 cubic feet) multiplied by (6 minus 2 cents)/2.

7b. The firm will produce 3 cubic feet a day and charge 4 cents a cubic foot. Deadweight loss is 1 cent a day.

If the firm is regulated to earn only normal profit, it produces the output at which price equals average total cost—at the intersection of the demand curve and the *ATC* curve.

7c. The firm will produce 4 cubic feet a day and charge 2 cents a cubic foot. There is no deadweight loss.

If the firm is regulated to be efficient, it will produce the quantity at which price (marginal benefit) equals marginal cost—at the intersection of the demand curve and the marginal cost curve.

CHAPTER 13

1a. Lite and Kool produces 100 pairs a week.

To maximize profit, Lite and Kool produces the quantity at which marginal revenue equals marginal cost.

1b. Lite and Kool charges $20 a pair.

To maximize profit, Lite and Kool charges the highest price for the 100 pairs of shoes, as read from the demand curve.

1c. Lite and Kool makes a profit of $500 a week.

Economic profit equals total revenue minus total cost. The price is $20 a pair and the quantity sold is 100 pairs, so total revenue is $2,000. Average total cost is $15 a pair, so total cost equals $1,500. Economic profit equals $2,000 minus $1,500, which is $500 a week.

3a. (i) The firm produces 100 pairs.

To maximize profit, the firm produces the quantity at which marginal cost equals marginal revenue. Marginal cost is $20 a pair. The firm can sell 200 pairs at $20 a pair, so the marginal revenue is $20 at 100 pairs. (Marginal revenue curve lies halfway between the y-axis and the demand curve.)

(ii) The firm sells them for $60 a pair.

The firm sells the 100 pairs at the highest price that consumers will pay, which is read from the demand curve. This price is $60 a pair.

(iii) The firm's economic profit is zero.

The firm produces 100 pairs and sells them for $60 a pair, so total revenue is $6,000. Total cost is the sum of total fixed cost plus total variable cost of 100 pairs. Total cost equals $4,000 plus ($20 multiplied by 100), which is $6,000. The firm's profit is zero.

3b. (i) The firm produces 200 pairs.

To maximize profit, the firm produces the quantity at which marginal cost equals marginal revenue. Marginal cost is $20 a pair. At $20 a pair, the firm can sell 400 pairs (twice the number with no advertising), so the marginal revenue is $20 at 200 pairs. (The marginal revenue curve lies halfway between the y-axis and the demand curve.)

(ii) The firm sells them for $60 a pair.

The firm sells the 200 pairs at the highest price that consumers will pay—read from the demand curve. This price is $60 a pair.

(iii) The firm makes an economic profit of $1,000.

The firm produces 200 pairs and sells them for $60 a pair, so total revenue is $12,000. Total cost is the sum of total fixed cost plus the advertising cost plus total variable cost of 200 pairs. Total cost equals $4,000 plus $3,000 plus ($20 multiplied by 200), which is $11,000. The firm makes an economic profit of $1,000.

3c. The firm will spend $3,000 advertising because it makes more economic profit than when it does not advertise.

5. The firm will not change the quantity it produces or the price it charges. The firm makes less economic profit.

The firm maximizes profit by producing the output at which marginal cost equals marginal revenue. An increase in fixed cost increases total cost, but it does not change marginal cost. So the firm does not change its output or the price it charges. The firm's total costs have increased and its total revenue has not changed, so the firm makes less economic profit.

7a. The price rises, output increases, and economic profit increases.

The dominant firm produces the quantity and sets the price such that it maximizes its profit. When demand increases, marginal revenue increases, so the firm produces a larger output. The highest price at which the dominant firm can sell its output increases. Because price exceeds marginal cost, economic profit increases.

7b. The price rises, output increases, and economic profit increases.

The small firms are price takers, so the price they charge rises. Because these firms are price takers, the price is also marginal revenue. Because marginal revenue increases, the small firms move up along their marginal cost curves (supply curves) and increase the quantity they produce. Because price exceeds marginal cost, economic profit increases.

9a. The game has 2 players (A and B), and each player has 2 strategies: to answer honestly or to lie. There are 4 payoffs: Both answer honestly; both lie; A lies, and B answers honestly; and B lies, and A answers honestly.

9b. The payoff matrix has the following cells: Both answer honestly: A gets $100, and B gets $100; both lie: A gets $50, and B gets $50; A lies and B answers honestly: A gets $500, and B gets $0; B lies and A answers honestly: A gets $0, and B gets $500.

9c. Equilibrium is that each player lies and gets $50.

If B answers honestly, the best strategy for A is to lie because he would get $500 rather than $100. If B lies, the best strategy for A is to lie because he would get $50 rather than $0. So A's best strategy is to lie, no matter what B does. Repeat the exercise for B. B's best strategy is to lie, no matter what A does.

11a. The best strategy for each firm is to cheat.

If Sudsies abides by the agreement, the best strategy for Soapy is to cheat because it would make a profit of $1.5 million rather than $1 million. If Sudsies cheats, the best strategy for Soapy is to cheat because it would make a profit of $0 (the competitive outcome) rather than incur a loss of $0.5 million. So Soapy's best strategy is to cheat, no matter what Sudsies does. Repeat the exercise for Sudsies. Sudsies's best strategy is to cheat, no matter what Soapy does.

11b. Each firm makes a zero economic profit or normal profit.

If both firms cheat, each firm will lower the price in an attempt to gain market share from the other firm. In the process, the price will be driven down until each firm is making normal profit.

11c. The payoff matrix has the following cells: Both abide by the agreement: Soapy makes $1 million profit, and Sudsies makes $1 million profit; both cheat: Soapy makes $0 profit, and Sudsies makes $0 profit; Soapy cheats and Sudsies abides by the agreement: Soapy makes $1.5 million profit, and Sudsies incurs a $0.5 million loss; Sudsies cheats and Soapy abides by the agreement: Sudsies makes $1.5 million profit, and Soapy incurs $0.5 million loss.

11d. The equilibrium is that both firms cheat and each makes normal profit.

11e. Each firm can adopt a tit-for-tat strategy or a trigger strategy. Page 297 give descriptions of these strategies.

CHAPTER 14

1a. The wage rate is $6 an hour. The wage rate adjusts to make the quantity of labor demanded equal to the quantity supplied.

1b. The number of pickers hired is 400 a day. At a wage rate of $6 an hour, 400 pickers a day are hired.

1c. The income received by blue berry pickers is $2,400 an hour. Income equals the wage rate ($6 an hour) multiplied by the number of pickers (400).

3a. Marginal product of labor is the increase in total product that results from hiring one additional student. For example, if Wanda increases the number of students hired from 4 to 5, total product (the quantity of fish packed) increases from 120 to 145 pounds. The marginal product of increasing the number of students from 4 to 5 is 25 pounds of fish.

To plot the marginal product curve, the marginal product is plotted at the mid-point. For example, when the number of students increases from 4 to 5 a day, marginal product is 25 pounds of fish. The 25 pounds of fish is plotted at 4.5 students a day.

3b. Marginal revenue product of labor is the increase in total revenue that results from hiring one additional student. For example, if Wanda hires 4 students, they produce 120 pounds of fish. Wanda sells the fish for 50 cents a pound, so total revenue is $60. If Wanda increases the number of students hired from 4 to 5, total product increases to 145 pounds. Total revenue from the sale of this fish is $72.50. Marginal revenue product resulting from hiring the fifth student is $12.50 ($72.50 minus $60). Alternatively, marginal revenue product equals marginal product multiplied by marginal revenue (price). Marginal revenue product of hiring the fifth student is $12.50, which is 25 pounds of fish she sells at 50 cents a pound.

3c. One point on Wanda's demand for labor curve: At a wage rate of $12.50 an hour, Wanda will hire 4.5 students. The demand for labor curve is the same as the marginal revenue product curve.

3d. Wanda hires 6.5 students a day.

Wanda hires the number of students that makes the marginal revenue product equals to the wage rate of $7.50 an hour. When Wanda increases the number of students from 6 to 7, marginal product is 15 pounds of fish an hour, which Wanda sells for 50 cents a pound. Marginal revenue product is $7.50—the same as the wage rate. Remember the marginal revenue product is plotted at the mid-point between 6 and 7 students a day—6.5 students a day.

5a. Marginal product does not change. If Wanda hires 5.5 students a day, marginal product is still 25 pounds of fish.

5b. Marginal revenue product decreases.

If Wanda hires 5.5 students a day, marginal product is 25 pounds of fish. Now Wanda sells the fish for 33.33 cents, so marginal revenue product is now $8.33, down from $12.50.

5c. Wanda's demand for labor decreases, and her demand for labor curve shifts leftward. Wanda is willing to pay the students their marginal revenue product, and the fall in the price of fish has lowered their marginal revenue product.

5d. Wanda will hire fewer students. At the wage rate of $7.50, the number of students Wanda hires decreases as the demand for labor curve shifts leftward.

7a. Marginal revenue product does not change. If Wand hires 5.5 students an hour, marginal revenue product is 25 pounds of fish, which she sells at 50 cents a pound. So marginal revenue product remains at $12.50.

7b. Wanda's demand for labor remains the same because marginal revenue product has not changed.

7c. Wanda will hire fewer students. At the wage rate of $10 an hour, Wanda hires the number of students that makes marginal revenue product equal to $10 an hour. Wanda now hires 5.5 students an hour—down from 6.5 students an hour. The marginal product of 5.5 students is 20 pounds of fish an hour, and Wanda sells this fish for 50 cents a pound. Marginal revenue product is $10 an hour.

9. Wanda maximizes her profit when marginal revenue product equals the wage rate and when marginal revenue equals marginal cost.

When the wage rate is $7.50 an hour, Wanda hires 6.5 students an hour. Marginal revenue product is marginal product (15 pounds of fish an hour) multiplied by the price of fish (50 cents a pound), which equals $7.50 an hour.

Marginal revenue resulting from selling an additional pound of fish is 50 cents. The cost a student is $7.50 an hour and the marginal product of 15 pounds of fish, so the marginal cost of an additional pound of fish is $7.50 an hour divided by 15 pounds of fish, which is 50 cents. So when Wanda hires 6.5 students an hour, marginal revenue equals marginal cost and profit is maximized.

11. To answer this problem, we need to know the interest rate and the price that Greg expects next year. If he expects the price to rise by a percentage that exceeds the interest rate, he pumps none and waits for the higher price. If he expects the price to rise by a percentage less than the interest rate, he pumps it all now. If he expects the price to rise by a percentage equal to the interest rate, he doesn't mind how much he pumps.

13. Income of $2,400 a day is divided between opportunity cost and economic rent. Economic rent is the area above the supply curve below the wage rate. To show the economic rent on the graph, extend the supply curve until it touches the y-axis. Shade in the area above the supply curve up to the wage rate $6 an hour.

Opportunity cost is the area under the supply curve. To show the opportunity cost on the graph, shade in the area under the supply curve up to 400 pickers on the x-axis.

APPENDIX TO CHAPTER 14

1a. The wage rate is $10 a day.

The monopsony firm maximizes its profit by hiring the quantity of labor that makes the marginal cost of labor equal to the marginal revenue product of labor (see Fig. A14.2). The marginal product of the fifth worker is 10 grains per day. Gold sells for $1.40 per grain, so the marginal revenue product of the fifth worker is $14 a day. The marginal cost of the fifth worker a day equals the total labor cost of 5 workers a day minus the total labor cost of 4 workers a day. The supply of labor tells us that to hire 5 workers a day, the gold company must pay $10 a day, so the total labor cost is $50 a day. The supply of labor also tells us that to hire 4 workers a day, the gold company must pay $9 a day, so the total labor cost is $36 a day. So the marginal cost of the fifth worker is $14 a day ($50 minus $36).

The profit-maximizing quantity of labor is 5 workers because the marginal cost of the fifth worker equals the marginal revenue product of the fifth worker. The monopsony pays the 5 workers the lowest wage possible: the wage rate at which the 5 workers are willing to supply their labor. The supply of labor schedule tells us that 5 workers are willing to supply their labor for $10 a day.

1b. The gold company hires 5 workers a day.

1c. The marginal revenue product of the fifth worker is $14 a day.

CHAPTER 15

1a. Money income equals market income (wages, interest, and rent) plus cash payments from the government.

1b. To draw the Lorenz curve, plot the cumulative percentage of households on the x-axis and the cumulative percentage of income on the y-axis. Make the scale on the two axes the same. The Lorenz curve will pass through the following points: 20 percent on the x-axis and 4 percent on the y-axis; 40 percent on the x-axis and 14.8 percent on the y-axis; 60 percent on the x-axis and 32.1 percent on the y-axis; 80 percent on the x-axis and 56.3 percent on the y-axis; and 100 percent on the x-axis and 100 percent on the y-axis.

1c. U.S. money income is distributed more equally in 1967 than in 2000.

The line of equality shows an equal distribution of income. The closer the Lorenz curve is to the line of equality, the more equal is the income distribution. The Lorenz curve for the U.S. economy in 1967 lies closer to the Line of equality than does the Lorenz curve in 2000.

1d. The biggest difference in the distribution of income in the United States in 1967 and 2000 is the share of income received by the highest 20 percent. This share increased from 43.7 percent to 49.6 percent. Smaller differences are the shares received by the three middle groups, each of which decreased. The most likely explanation for these differences (and the one provided in the chapter) is that the information technologies of the 1990s are substitutes for low-skilled labor and complements of high-skilled labor. The demand for low-skilled labor has decreased relative to the supply of low-skilled labor and the wage rate of low-skilled labor has increased more slowly than the average. The demand for high-skilled labor has increased relative to the supply of high-skilled labor and the wage rate of high-skilled labor has increased faster than the average.

3a. The wage rate of low-skilled workers is $5 an hour.

The wage rate adjusts to make the quantity of labor demanded equal to the quantity supplied.

3b. Firms employ 5,000 hours of low-skilled workers a day. At a wage rate of $5 an hour, 5,000 hours are employed each day.

3c. The wage rate of high-skilled workers is $8 an hour.

Because the marginal product of high-skilled workers is twice the marginal product of low-skilled workers, firms are willing to pay high-skilled workers twice the wage rate that they are willing to pay low-skilled workers. For example, the demand curve for low-skilled workers tells us that firms are willing to hire 6,000 hours of low-skilled workers at a wage rate of $4 an hour. So with high-skilled workers twice as productive as low-skilled workers, firms are willing to hire 6,000 hours of high-skilled workers at $8 an hour. That is, the demand curve for high-skilled labor lies above the demand curve for low-skilled workers such that at each quantity of workers the wage rate for high-skilled workers is double that for low-skilled workers.

The supply of high-skilled workers lies above the supply of low-skilled workers such that the vertical distance between the two supply curves equals the cost of acquiring the high skill—$2 an hour. That is, high-skilled workers will supply 6,000 hours a day if the wage rate is $8 an hour.

Equilibrium in the labor market for high-skilled workers occurs at a wage rate of $8 an hour.

3d. Firms employ 6,000 hours of high-skilled workers a day.

5a. Market income is the income earned by factors of production in the marketplace. Labor earns wages, capital earns interest, land earns rent and entrepreneurship earns profit.

5b. To draw the Lorenz curve, plot the cumulative percentage of households on the x-axis and the cumulative percentage of market income on the y-axis. Make the scale on the two axes the same. The Lorenz curve will pass through the following points: 20 percent on the x-axis and 1.1 percent on the y-axis; 40 percent on the x-axis and 8.2 percent on the y-axis; 60 percent on the x-axis and 22.1 percent on the y-axis; 80 percent on the x-axis and 44.9 percent on the y-axis; and 100 percent on the x-axis and 100 percent on the y-axis.

5c. U.S. money income is distributed more equally in than market income in 2000.

The Lorenz curve for the U.S. money income in 2000 lies closer to the Line of equality than does the Lorenz curve for U.S. market income in 2000. Money income is distributed more equally than market income because money income includes cash payments to poor household, which increases their income.

CHAPTER 16

1a. The capacity that achieves maximum net benefit is 2.5 million gallons a day.

Net benefit is maximized at the capacity where marginal benefit equals marginal cost, which is 2.5 million gallons a day.

1b. $62.50 per person.

The efficient capacity is the one that maximizes net benefit. Total cost of the sewerage system is the sum of the marginal cost of each additional gallon of capacity. That is, total cost is the area under the marginal cost curve up to 2.5 million gallons, which equals $62.5 million. The population is 1 million, so each person will have to pay $62.50.

1c.   The political equilibrium will be a sewerage system that has a capacity of 2.5 million gallons.

If voters are well informed, the political equilibrium will be the efficient capacity.

1d.   Bureaucrats will provide a capacity of 5 million gallons.

With voters rationally ignorant, bureaucrats will maximize the budget. That is, they will increase the capacity until net benefit is zero. The total benefit from a capacity of 5 million gallons is $250 million. The total cost of a capacity of 5 million gallons is $250 million. So the net benefit from a capacity of 5 million gallons is zero.

3a.   Taxes will be progressive: B-type people will pay a higher tax rate than A-type people.

The median voter theorem tells us the tax arrangement will be that which minimizes the taxes of the median voter. The median voter is an A-type person.

3b.   The before-tax wage rate of A-type people will rise by the amount of the tax, and fewer A-type people will be employed. The after-tax wage rate will remain at $10 an hour. The before-tax wage rate of B-type people will remain at $100, and employment of B-type people will not change. The after-tax wage rate will fall by the amount of the tax.

5a.   The equilibrium wage rate is $12 an hour, and 30 hours of work are done each week.

Equilibrium wage rate is such that the quantity of labor demanded equals the quantity of labor supplied. Hours of work done equal the equilibrium quantity of labor hired.

5b.   (i) The new wage rate is $13.60 an hour. (ii) The new number of hours worked is 24 a week. (iii) The after-tax wage rate is $9.60 an hour. (iv) The tax revenue is $96.00 a week (v) Deadweight loss is $12 a week.

To work this problem, use the data provided to draw a graph like Figure 16.8b. Make sure that your graph is accurate because the solutions are not directly visible in the data table. The after-tax wage rate ($9.60) and new equilibrium quantity (24 hours) occur at the intersection of the LS curve and the LD – tax curve that you draw. The new wage rate ($13.60) is read from the LD curve at the new equilibrium quantity. The tax revenue is $4 an hour multiplied by the 24 hours employed. The deadweight loss equals the tax $4 multiplied by half the decrease in employment, which is, $4 × (30 - 24)/2 = $12.

7a.   The equilibrium price is $3 a pound, and the equilibrium quantity is 4 pounds a month.

To work this problem, use the data provided to draw a graph like Figure 18.9. Be sure to make your graph accurate so that you can read the solutions from it. The equilibrium is at the intersection of the demand curve and supply curve for cookies.

7b.   (i) The new price is $4 a pound. (ii) The new quantity is 3 pounds a month. (iii) Tax revenue is $6 a month. (iv) Deadweight loss is $1 a month.

The new price ($4 a pound) and new equilibrium quantity (3 pounds a month) occur at the intersection of the demand curve and the supply plus tax curve that you draw. The tax revenue is $2 a pound multiplied by the 3 pounds a month sold. The deadweight loss equals the tax multiplied by half the decrease in the quantity boughtæthat is, $2 × (4 – 3)/2 = $1.

CHAPTER 17

1a.   The price is 30 cents a bottle.

Elixir Springs is a natural monopoly. It produces the quantity that makes marginal revenue equal to marginal cost, and it charges the highest price it can for the quantity produced. The marginal revenue curve is twice as steep as the demand curve, so it runs from 50 on the y-axis to 1.25 on the x-axis. Marginal revenue equals marginal cost at 1 million bottles a year. The highest price at which Elixir can sell 1 million bottles a year is 30 cents a bottle, read from the demand curve.

1b.   Elixir Springs sells 1 million bottles a year.

1c.   Elixir maximizes producer surplus.

If Elixir maximizes total surplus, it would produce the quantity that makes price equal to marginal cost. That is, it would produce 2 million bottles a year and sell them for 10 cents a bottles. Elixir is a natural monopoly, and it maximizes its producer surplus.

3a.   The price is 10 cents a bottle.

Marginal cost pricing regulation sets the price equal to marginal cost, 10 cents a bottle.

3b.   Elixir sells 2 million bottles.

With the price set at 10 cents, Elixir maximizes profit by producing 2 million bottles—at the intersection of the demand curve (which shows price) and the marginal cost curve.

3c.   Elixir incurs an economic loss of $150,000 a year.

Economic profit equals total revenue minus total cost. Total revenue is $200,000 (2 million bottles at 10 cents a bottle). Total cost is $350,000 (total variable cost of $200,000 plus total fixed cost of $150,000). So Elixir incurs an economic loss of $150,000 (a revenue of $200,000 minus $350,000).

3d.   Consumer surplus is $400,000 a year.

Consumer surplus is the area under the demand curve above the price. Consumer surplus equals 40 cents a bottle (50 cents minus 10 cents) multiplied by 2 million bottles divided by 2, which is $400,000.

3e.   The regulation is in the public interest because total surplus is maximized. The outcome is efficient.

The outcome is efficient because marginal benefit (or price) equals marginal cost. When the outcome is efficient, total surplus is maximized.

5a.   The price is 20 cents a bottle.

Average cost pricing regulation sets the price equal to average total cost. Average total cost equals average fixed cost plus average variable cost. Because marginal cost is constant at 10 cents, average variable cost equals marginal cost. Average fixed cost is total fixed cost ($150,000) divided by the quantity produced. For example, when

Elixir produces 1.5 million bottles, average fixed cost is 10 cents, so average total cost is 20 cents. The price at which Elixir can sell 1.5 million bottles a year is 20 cents a bottle.

5b. Elixir sells 1.5 million bottles.

5c. Elixir makes zero economic profit.

Economic profit equals total revenue minus total cost. Total revenue is $300,000 (1.5 million bottles at 20 cents a bottle). Total cost is $300,000 (1.5 million bottles at an average total cost of 20 cents). So Elixir makes zero economic profit.

5d. Consumer surplus is $225,000 a year.

Consumer surplus is the area under the demand curve above the price. Consumer surplus equals 30 cents a bottle (50 cents minus 20 cents) multiplied by 1.5 million bottles divided by 2, which is $225,000.

5e. The regulation creates a deadweight loss, so the outcome is inefficient. The regulation is not in the public interest.

7a. The price is $500 a trip, and the quantity is 2 trips a day.

Regulation in the public interest is marginal cost pricing. Each airline charges $500 a trip and produces the quantity at which price equals marginal cost. Each airline makes 1 trip a day.

7b. The price is $750 a trip, and the number of trips is 1 trip a day (one by each airline on alternate days).

If the airlines capture the regulator, the price will be the same as the price that an unregulated monopoly would charge. An unregulated monopoly produces the quantity and charges the price that maximizes profit—that is, the quantity that makes marginal revenue equal to marginal cost. This quantity is 1 trip a day, and the highest price that the airlines can charge for that trip (read from the demand curve) is $750.

7c. Deadweight loss is $125 a day.

Deadweight loss arises because the number of trips is cut from 2 to 1 a day and the price is increased from $500 to $750. Deadweight loss equals (2 minus 1) trip multiplied by ($750 minus $500) divided by 2. Deadweight loss is $125 a day.

9. Regulation consists of rules administered by government agency to influence economic activity by determining prices, product standards and types, and the conditions under which new firms may enter an industry. Antitrust law regulates or prohibits price fixing and the attempt to monopolize. Regulation applies mainly to natural monopoly and antitrust law to oligopoly. Regulation of electric utilities is an example of regulation. The ruling against Microsoft is an example of the application of the antitrust law.

CHAPTER 18

1a. 5 tons per week are produced and the marginal cost falling on trout farmer is $167 a ton

When 5 tons a week are produced, the pesticide producers marginal cost is $75 a ton and the marginal benefit of pesticide is $75 a ton. At this quantity, the trout farmer's MC from pesticide production is $167 a ton.

1b. 3 tons per week are produced and the pesticide producer pays the farmer $100 a ton = $300 a week

The efficient quantity is 3 tons at which marginal social cost equals marginal benefit. If the trout farmer owns the lake, the cost of pollution can be forced back onto the pesticide producer, who when has the incentive to produce the efficient quantity.

1c. 3 tons per week; the rent is $1,000 minus $300 = $700 a week.

The efficient quantity is 3 tons at which marginal social cost equals marginal benefit. If the pesticide producer owns the lake, the cost of pollution is born by the pesticide producer in the form of a decreased rent from the trout farmer.

1d. Quantities in b and c are equal because the Coase theorem applies.

3a. $100 a ton.

3b. The pollution tax equals the marginal external cost—it is a Pigovian tax.

5a. 3 tons a week.

5b. $300 a permit. Pesticide producer buys permit from trout farmer for $300.

5c. The same as amount paid by producer to farmer with property rights—Pigovian tax.

7a. If schools are competitive, 30,000 students enroll and tuition is $4,000 a year.

In a competitive market, schools maximize profit. They produce the quantity at which the marginal benefit of the last student enrolled equals the marginal cost of educating the last student enrolled. Tuition is $4,000 a student.

7b. Efficient number of places is 50,000, and tuition is $4,000 a student.

The efficient number of places is such that the marginal social benefit of education equals the marginal cost of education. The marginal social benefit equals the marginal private benefit plus the external benefit. For example, the marginal social benefit of 50,000 places equals the marginal private benefit of $2,000 plus the external benefit of $2,000, which is $4,000.

CHAPTER 19

1a. Aggregate expenditure is $120 million. Aggregate expenditure is the sum of consumption expenditure, investment, government purchases, and net exports. In the figure, B is consumption expenditure, D is investment, C is government purchases, and E is net exports. Therefore aggregate expenditure equals $60 million plus $30 million plus $24 million plus $6 million, which is $120 million.

1b. Aggregate income is $120 million. Aggregate income equals aggregate expenditure, which from 1(a) is $120 million.

1c. GDP is $120 million. GDP equals aggregate expenditure, which from 1(a) is $120 million.

1d. Government budget deficit is $4 million. Government budget deficit equals government purchases minus taxes. C is government purchases, and A is taxes. So the government budget deficit equals $24 million minus $20 million, which is $4 million.

1e. Household saving is $40 million. Household saving equals aggregate income minus consumption expenditure minus taxes. From 1(b), income is $120 million. In the figure, B is consumption expenditure and A is taxes. Therefore household saving equals $120 million minus $60 million minus $20 million, which is $40 million.

1f. Government saving is minus $4 million. Government saving equals taxes minus government purchases. In the figure, A is taxes and C is government expenditure. Therefore government saving equals $20 million minus $24 million, which is minus $4 million.

1g. National saving is $36 million. National saving equals the sum of household saving and government saving. Household saving is $40 million (see answer 1e). Government saving is minus $2 million (see answer 1f). Therefore national saving equals $40 million minus $4 million, which is $36 million.

1h. Borrowing from the rest of the world is minus $6 million. Borrowing from the rest of the world equals minus net exports. E is net exports, and net exports equals $6 million. We are in surplus, so foreigners are in deficit and they must borrow from us to pay for their deficit.

3.   Martha's initial capital stock is 10 copiers, depreciation is 1 copier per year, gross investment is 5 copiers, net investment is 4 copiers, and the final capital stock is 14 copiers. Final capital stock equals initial capital stock plus net investment. Net investment equals gross investment minus depreciation.

5a. Ecoland's GDP is $1,100,000.

GDP equals the sum of consumption expenditure plus investment plus government purchases plus exports minus imports. That is, GDP equals $600,000 plus $250,000 plus $200,000 plus $300,000 minus $250,000. GDP equals $1,100,000.

5b. Expenditure approach. Income approach cannot be used because there are no data on interest, rent, depreciation, and indirect taxes and subsidies.

5c. Investment is financed by private saving plus government saving plus borrowing from the rest of the world.

Private saving equals GDP minus consumption expenditure minus net taxes, which is $300,000. Government saving the budget surplus, which equals net taxes minus government purchases. Net taxes equal taxes ($250,000) minus transfer payments ($50,000), which is $200,000. Government saving equals net taxes ($200,000) minus government purchases ($200,000), which is zero. Private saving exceeds investment by $50,000 and this amount is lent to the rest of the world.

7a. In 2002, nominal GDP is $7,000. In 2003, nominal GDP is $7,500.

Nominal GDP in 2002 is equal to total expenditure on the goods and services produced by Bananaland in 2002. Expenditure on bananas is 1,000 bunches at $2 a bunch, which is $2,000. Expenditure on sunscreen is 500 bottles at $10 a bottle, which is $5,000. Total expenditure is $7,000. So nominal GDP in 2002 is $7,000.

Nominal GDP in 2003 is equal to total expenditure on the goods and services produced by Bananaland in 2003. Expenditure on bananas is 1,100 bunches at $3 a bunch, which is $3,300. Expenditure on sunscreen is 525 bottles at $8 a bottle, which is $4,200. Total expenditure is $7,500. So nominal GDP in 2002 is $7,500.

7b. Real GDP in 2003 using base-year prices method is $7,450.

The base-year prices method is to calculate the market value of the 2003 quantities at the base-year prices of 2002. To value the 2003 output at 2002 prices, expenditure on bananas is 1,100 bunches at $2 a bunch (which is $2,200), and expenditure on sunscreen is 525 bottles at $10 a bottle (which is $5,250). So real GDP in 2003 using the base-year prices method is $7,450.

9a. The growth rate of real GDP in 2003 is 6.79 percent.

The chain-weighted output index method uses the prices of 2002 and 2003 to calculate the growth rate in 2003.

The value of the 2002 quantities at 2002 prices is $7,000. The value of the 2003 quantities at 2002 prices is $7,450. We now compare these values. The increase in the value is $450. The percentage increase is ($450/$7,000) × 100, which is 6.43 percent

The value of the 2002 quantities at 2003 prices is $7,000. The value of the 2003 quantities at 2003 prices is $7,500. We now compare these values. The increase in the value is $500. The percentage increase is ($500/$7,000) × 100, which is 7.14 percent.

The chain-weighted output index calculates the growth rate as the average of these two percentage growth rates. That is, the growth rate in 2003 is 6.79 percent

9b. The GDP deflator in 2003 is 100.33.

GDP deflator equals nominal GDP in 2003 divided by real GDP in 2003, multiplied by 100.

Real GDP in 2003 is 6.79 percent higher than real GDP in 2002. Real GDP in 2002 is $7,000, so real GDP in 2003 is $7,475.3.

GDP deflator equals ($7,500/$7,475.3) × 100 = 100.33.

9c. Real GDP in 2003 using the base-year prices method is $7,450. Real GDP in 2003 using the chain-weighted output index method is $7,475.3. The base-year prices method measure real GDP growth as being slower than the chain-weighted index measure.

CHAPTER 20

1a. Unemployment rate is 4.0 percent. The unemployment rate is the percentage of the labor force that is unemployed. The labor force is the sum of the people unemployed and the people employed. So the number of people who are unemployed is 141,544,000 minus 135,888,000, which is 5,656,000. The unemployment rate equals (the number of people unemployed divided by the labor force) multiplied by 100. That is, (5,656,000/141,544,000) × 100, which is 4.0 percent.

1b. The labor force participation rate is 67.2 percent. The labor force participation rate is the percentage of the working-age population that is in the labor force. The working-age population is 210,743,000 and the labor force is 141,544,000, so the labor force participation rate equals (141,544,000/210,743,000) ×100, which equals 67.2 percent.

1c. The employment-to-population ratio is 64.5 percent. The employment-to-population ratio is the percentage of the people of working age who have jobs. The employment-to-population ratio is equal to the number of people employed divided by the working-age population all multiplied by 100. The employment-to-population ratio is (135,888,000/210,743,000) × 100, which is 64.5 percent.

3. Unemployment decreased by 64,000. The number of people not in the labor force increased by 600,000. During 2000, employment in the United States increased by 1,375,000 and the labor force increased by 1,311,000. The number of unemployed is calculated as the labor force minus the number employed. When the labor force increased by 1,311,000 and employment increased by 1,375,000, unemployment decreased by 64,000.

5a. The number of job losers probably increased. The number of job leavers probably did not change much. The increase in the unemployment rate is an indication that the economy was slowing and possibly going into recession. Normally, in a recession, the number of job losers increases but the number of job leavers does not change much.

5b. Labor force entrants and re-entrants probably decreased. In a recession, discouraged workers remain outside the labor force. So it is likely that entrants and re-entrants decreased.

7a. The labor force in July is 11,000. It is the number employed plus the number unemployed.

7b. The unemployment rate in July is 9.1 percent. It is the number unemployed as a percentage of the labor force.

7c. The working-age population is 16,000. It is the sum of the labor force and the number of people who are not in the labor force.

7d. The employment-to-population ratio is 62.5. It is the number employed as a percentage of the working-age population.

7e. The number of people who are unemployed at the end of August is 940. It equals the number unemployed in July plus job losers, job leavers, entrants, and reentrants minus hires, recalls, and withdrawals.

7f. The number of people who are employed at the end of August is 10,050. It equals the number employed in July minus job losers and job leavers plus hires and recalls.

7g. The labor force at the end of August is 10,990. It equals the number employed plus the number unemployed.

7h. The unemployment rate at the end of August is 8.6 percent. It equals the number unemployed as a percentage of the labor force.

9a. The CPI basket is 10 bottles of juice and 5 lengths of cloth.

9b. The CPI in the current year is 107.7. It is calculated at the value of the CPI basket in current year prices multiplied by 100 and divided by the base year value of the CPI basket. The value of the CPI basket in current year

prices is: ($4 × 10) + ($6 × 5) = $70. The value in base year prices is $40 + $25 (provided in the question) which equals $65. So the CPI is ($70/$65) × 100 = 107.7.

9c. The inflation rate in the current year is 7.7 percent. It is calculated as the CPI in the current year minus the CPI in the base year expressed as a percentage of the base year CPI. Because the base year CPI is 100, the inflation rate is (107.7 − 100)×100/100 = 7.7 percent.

CHAPTER 21

1a. A deep recession in the world economy decreases aggregate demand, which decreases real GDP and lowers the price level. A sharp rise in oil prices decreases short-run aggregate supply, which decreases real GDP and raises the price level. The expectation of huge losses in the future decreases investment and decreases aggregate demand, which decreases real GDP and lowers the price level.

1b. The combined effect of a deep recession in the world economy, a sharp rise in oil prices, and the expectation of huge losses in the future decreases both aggregate demand and short-run aggregate supply, which decreases real GDP and might raise of lower the price level.

1c. The Toughtimes government might try to increase aggregate demand by increasing its purchases or by cutting taxes and the Toughtimes Fed might increase the quantity of money and lower interest rates. These policies could increase real GDP, but they would also raise the price level.

a. Make a graph with the price level on the *y*-axis and real GDP on the *x*-axis. Make the price level values run from 80 to 150 in intervals of 10, and make the real GDP values run from 150 to 650 in intervals of 50. Plot the data in the table in the graph. The *AD* curve plots the price level against the quantity of real GDP demanded. The *SAS* curve plots the price level against the quantity of real GDP supplied in the short-run.

3b. Equilibrium real GDP is $400 trillion and the price level is 100. Short-run macroeconomic equilibrium occurs at the intersection of the aggregate demand curve and the short-run aggregate supply curve.

3c. The long-run aggregate supply curve is a vertical line in your graph at real GDP of $500 billion.

5. Make a new table based on that in problem 3. Add a column headed "New real GDP demanded." Enter values in this column that equal the value in the column headed "Real GDP demanded" plus $100 billion. (For example, on the first row of your new column, you have $550 billion.) Now, using the graph that you made to answer problem 3, add a new *AD* curve by plotting the price level against "New quantity of real GDP demanded." The new equilibrium level of real GDP is $450 billion, and the price level is 110.

7. Make a new table based on that in problem 3. Add a column headed "New real GDP supplied in the short run." Enter values in this column that equal the value in the column headed "Real GDP supplied in the short run" minus $100 billion. (For example, on the first row of your new column, you have $250 billion.) Now, using the

graph that you made to answer problem 3, add a new *SAS* curve by plotting the price level against "New quantity of real GDP supplied in the short run." The new equilibrium level of real GDP is $350 billion, and the price level is 110.

9a. Point *C*. The aggregate demand curve is the red curve AD_1. The short-run aggregate supply curve is the blue curve SAS_0. These curves intersect at point *C*.

9b. Point *D*. The short-run aggregate supply curve is the red curve SAS_1. The aggregate demand curve is now the red curve AD_1. These curves intersect at point *D*.

9c. Aggregate demand increases if (1) expected future incomes, inflation, or profits increase; (2) the government increases its purchases or reduces taxes; (3) the Fed increases the quantity of money and decreases interest rates; or (4) the exchange rate decreases or foreign income increases.

9d. Short-run aggregate supply decreases if resource prices increase.

CHAPTER 22

1a. The graph is similar to Figure 7.1(a) on page 159. It plots leisure on the *x*-axis and real GDP on the *y*-axis. As leisure increases from zero to 12 hours a day, real GDP decreases from $30 to $0 a day.

1b. The table shows Crusoe's production function. It replaces leisure with labor and labor equals 12 hours a day minus leisure hours. The graph is similar to Figure 7.1(b) on page 159. It plots labor on the *x*-axis and real GDP on the *y*-axis. As labor increases from zero to 12 hours a day, real GDP increases from $0 to $30 a day.

Crusoe's Production Function

Labor	Real GDP ($ per day)
0	0
2	10
4	18
6	24
8	28
10	30
12	30

1c. When labor increases from 0 to 2 hours a day, the marginal product of labor is $5. When labor increases from 2 to 4 hours a day, the marginal product of labor is $4. When labor increases from 4 to 6 hours a day, the marginal product of labor is $3. When labor increases from 6 to 8 hours a day, the marginal product of labor is $2. When labor increases from 8 to 10 hours a day, the marginal product of labor is $1. When labor increases from 10 to 12 hours a day, the marginal product of labor is $0. Marginal product is the change in real GDP divided by the change in labor hours.

3a. The demand for labor schedule is the same as the marginal product of labor schedule. The marginal product of labor schedule is described in solution 1(c). The marginal product must be aligned with the midpoint of the change in labor. So, for example, the marginal product of $5 an hour is aligned with 1 hour of work, the midpoint between 0 and 2 hours. The graph plots a marginal product of $5 at 1 hour and a marginal product of $1 at 9 hours of labor and is a straight line between these points. At 2 hours of labor, the marginal product is $4.50.

Crusoe's Demand Schedule

Real wage rate	Quantity of Labor Demanded
$5.00	1
4.00	3
3.00	5
2.00	7
1.00	9
0.00	11

3b. The table below lists hours of labor from zero to 12 a day. Against each hour, the wage rate at which Crusoe is willing to supply labor is $4.50 an hour. Crusoe's supply curve is horizontal at $4.50 an hour.

Crusoe's Supply Schedule

Real wage rate	Quantity of Labor Supplied
$4.50	0
4.50	2
4.50	4
4.50	6
4.50	8
4.50	10
4.50	12

3c. The full-employment equilibrium real wage rate is $4.50 an hour, and the quantity of labor employed is 2 hours a day. The full-employment equilibrium real wage rate is $4.50 an hour because Crusoe is willing to work any number of hours at this wage rate. The equilibrium level of employment is 2 hours a day because this is the number of hours at which Crusoe's marginal product of labor is $4.50 an hour.

3d. Potential GDP is $10 a day. Potential GDP is $10 a day because this quantity of real GDP is produced when labor is 2 hours a day.

5a. The new production function table lists real GDP against labor hours. Real GDP is $15 at 2 hours of labor, $27 at 4 hours, $36 at 6 hours, $42 at 8 hours, $45 at 10 hours, and $45 at 12 hours. The new demand for labor schedule has labor of 2 hours at $6.75 and 9 hours at $1.50. To calculate the new demand for labor schedule, calculate the new marginal product (old marginal product multiplied by 1.5) at each level of employment.

Crusoe's New Production Function

Labor	Real GDP ($ per day)
0	0
2	15
4	27
6	36
8	42
10	45
12	45

Crusoe's New Demand Schedule

Real wage rate	Quantity of labor
$7.50	1
6.00	3
4.50	5
3.00	7
1.50	9
0	11

5b. The full-employment equilibrium real wage rate is $4.50 an hour and the quantity of labor employed is 5 hours a day. The equilibrium level of employment is 5 hours a day because this is the number of hours at which Crusoe's marginal product of labor is $4.50 an hour.

5c. Potential GDP is $31.50 a day. Potential GDP is $21 a day because this quantity of real GDP is produced when labor is 5 hours a day. (When labor is 4 hours a day, real GDP is $27 a day. When labor is 6 hours a day, real GDP is $36 a day. Therefore, when labor is 5 hours day, real GDP must be $31.50.)

5d. The increase in productivity shifts the production function upward by 50 percent. The marginal product of labor increases by 50 percent. Employment increases and so does potential GDP.

7a. Real wage rate is $3 an hour and employment is 3,000 hours a day. This wage rate and quantity of labor are at the intersection of the demand curve and the supply curve in the figure.

7b. Potential GDP is $13,500 a day. To calculate potential GDP, use the fact that the real wage rate on the demand for labor curve is the marginal product of labor. Remember that it is plotted midway between the initial and final level of real GDP from which it is calculated. Do the marginal product calculation in reverse and obtain the level of real GDP at 3,000 hours, which is $13,500 a day. Alternatively, you can calculate the potential GDP as the area under the labor demand curve, since this is the same as the marginal product curve.

7c. The natural unemployment rate is 25 percent. The natural unemployment rate occurs at full employment when job search is 1,000 hours. Employment is 3,000 hours,

and job search, which is unemployment, is 1,000 hours. The labor force (employment plus unemployment) is 4,000 hours. The natural unemployment rate is 25 percent (1,000/4,000 multiplied by 100).

CHAPTER 23

1a. Yes.

1b. Yes.

1c. No.

The firm receives a total revenue of $17 million. It spends $16 million ($10 million on the plant, $3 million on labor and $3 million on fuel). Before paying interest, the firm has a surplus of $1 million. If the interest rate is 5 percent a year, the interest cost is $0.5 million. If the interest rate is 10 percent a year, the interest cost is $1 million. If the interest rate is 15 percent a year, the interest cost is $1.5 million. So the firm earns a profit at 5 percent, breaks even at 10 percent, and incurs a loss at 15 percent. The firm will not invest to incur a loss.

3a. The graph has saving on the x-axis and the interest rate on the y-axis. Three points are plotted at $10,000 and 4 percent; $12,500 and 6 percent; and $15,000 and 8 percent. The saving supply (SS) curve passes through these points.

3b. Saving decreases, and the saving supply curve shifts leftward.

3c. Saving increases, and the saving supply curve shifts rightward.

An increase in expected future income increases consumption expenditure and decreases saving. An increase in disposable income increases both consumption expenditure and saving.

5a. 5 percent a year.

5b. $6 trillion (3050 dollars).

5c. $6 trillion (3050 dollars).

Given the saving supply schedule and the investment demand schedule, the real interest rate at which saving equals investment is 5 percent a year. At this real interest rate, saving and investment equal $6 trillion.

7a. 5 percent a year.

7b. $6 trillion (3050 dollars).

Private saving increases by an amount equal to the decrease in government saving. Total saving remains constant. So the equilibrium real interest rate and saving and investment do not change.

9a. 6 percent a year.

9b. $15 trillion (3050 dollars).

9c. $15 trillion (3050 dollars).

9d. Saving decreases, and investment increases.

To find the galactic equilibrium, find the sum of saving on Earth and Alpha Centura at each real interest rate and find the sum of investment on the two planets at each real interest rate. At a real interest rate of 6 percent a year,

galactic saving equals galactic investment at $15 trillion.
In isolation, the real interest rate on Alpha Centura is 7
percent a year. So the real interest rate on Alpha Centura
falls. Saving decreases, and investment increases.

CHAPTER 24

1. No. The economy conforms to a one-half rule.

   In this economy, an x percent increase in the capital stock
   per hour of work leads to a $0.5x$ percent increase in real
   GDP per hour of work. You can confirm this fact by calculating the percentage change in capital and real GDP at
   each of the levels provided in the table and then dividing
   the percentage change in real GDP by the percentage
   change in capital. For example, when capital increases by
   100 percent from $10 to $20, real GDP increases by 50
   percent from $3.80 to $5.70.

3a. Yes.

   Diminishing returns are present if the marginal product
   of capital diminishes as capital increases, holding technology constant. You can calculate the marginal product of
   capital from the schedule provided and see that it does
   diminish.

   The increase in real GDP per hour of work that occurred
   in the question resulted from an increase in capital and an
   advance in technology. We know this because to produce
   $10.29 in 1999 would have required a capital stock of
   $60 per hour of work, and in 2001, this output can be
   produced by a capital stock of $50. The change in real
   GDP divided by the change in capital is not the marginal
   product of labor because technology is not constant.

3b. $1.04.

   This number is calculated as the percentage increase in
   real GDP that is equal to one half the percentage increase
   in capital.

3c. $0.94.

   This number is calculated as the change in real GDP
   minus $1.04.

5a. Capital per hour of labor is $40 and real GDP per hour
   of labor is $15.

   This level of real GDP per hour of labor is the subsistence
   level at which the population is constant.

5b. Real GDP per hour of labor increases to $22.

   This level of real GDP per hour of labor is the quantity
   produced with the new technology at the original quantity of capital per hour of labor.

5c. The population begins to grow.

   The reason for the population growth is that real GDP
   per hour of labor exceeds the subsistence level.

5d. Capital per hour of labor decreases to $20.

   This is the quantity of capital per hour of labor produces
   a real GDP per hour of labor equal to $15, which is the
   subsistence level at which the population stops growing.

7. When the demand for capital raises the real interest rate
   above the target rate, the capital stock and real GDP
   begin to grow and keep on growing. In contrast, in the
   neoclassical Martha's Island, as the capital stock grows, the

real interest rate falls (because of diminishing returns) and
growth eventually ends.

CHAPTER 25

1a. The marginal propensity to consume is 0.5.

   The marginal propensity to consume is the fraction of a
   change in disposable income that is consumed. On Heron
   Island, when disposable income increases by $10 million
   per year, consumption expenditure increases by $5 mil-
   lion per year. The marginal propensity to consume is 0.5.

1b. The table that shows Heron Island's saving lists disposable
   income from zero to 40 in increments of 10. Against each
   level of disposable income are the amounts of saving,
   which equal disposable income minus consumption
   expenditure. These amounts run from −5 at zero disposable income to 15 at a disposable income of 40. For each
   increase in disposable income of $1, saving increases by
   50 cents.

1c. The marginal propensity to save is 0.5

Disposable income (millions of dollars)	Saving (millions of dollars)
0	−5
10	0
20	5
30	10
40	15

   The marginal propensity to consume plus the marginal
   propensity to save equals 1. Because consumption expenditure and saving exhaust disposable income, 0.5 of each
   dollar increase in disposable income is consumed and the
   remaining part (0.5) is saved.

3a. Autonomous expenditure is $2 billion

   Autonomous expenditure is expenditure that does not
   depend on real GDP. Autonomous expenditure equals the
   value of aggregate planned expenditure when real GDP is
   zero.

3b. The marginal propensity to consume is 0.6.

   When the country has no imports or exports and no
   income taxes, the slope of the AE curve equals the marginal propensity to consume. When income increases
   from 0 to $6 billion, aggregate planned expenditure
   increases from $2 billion to $5.6 billion. That is, when
   real GDP increases by $6 billion, aggregate planned
   expenditure increases by $3.6 billion. The marginal
   propensity to consume is $3.6 billion/$6 billion, which is
   0.6.

3c. From the graph, aggregate planned expenditure is $5.6
   billion when real GDP is $6 billion. Equilibrium expen-
   diture is $4 billion.

   Equilibrium expenditure is the level of aggregate expenditure at which aggregate planned expenditure equals real
   GDP. In terms of the graph, equilibrium expenditure
   occurs at the intersection of the AE curve and the 45∞
   line. Draw in the 45∞ line, and you'll see that the intersection occurs at $4 billion.

3d. There is no change in inventories.

When the economy is at equilibrium expenditure, inventories equal the planned level and there is no unplanned change in inventories.

3e. Firms are accumulating inventories. That is, unplanned inventory investment is positive.

When real GDP is $6 billion, aggregate planned expenditure is less than real GDP, so firms cannot sell all that they produce. Inventories pile up.

3f. The multiplier is 2.5.

The multiplier equals $1/(1 - MPC)$. The marginal propensity to consume is 0.6, so the multiplier equals $1/(1 - 0.6)$, which equals 2.5.

5a. The consumption function is $C = 100 + 0.9(Y - T)$.

The consumption function is the relationship between consumption expenditure and disposable income, other things remaining the same.

5b. The equation to the AE curve is $AE = 600 + 0.9Y$, where Y is real GDP.

Aggregate planned expenditure is the sum of consumption expenditure, investment, government purchases, and net exports. Using the symbol AE for aggregate planned expenditure, aggregate planned expenditure is:

$AE = 100 + 0.9(Y - 400) + 460 + 400$

$AE = 100 + 0.9Y - 360 + 460 + 400$

$AE = 600 + 0.9Y$

5c. Equilibrium expenditure is $6,000 billion.

Equilibrium expenditure is the level of aggregate expenditure that occurs when aggregate planned expenditure equals real GDP. That is,

$AE = 600 + 0.9Y$ and $AE = Y$

Solving these two equations for Y gives equilibrium expenditure of $6,000 billion.

5d. Equilibrium real expenditure decreases by $1,000 billion, and the multiplier is 10.

The multiplier equals $1/(1 -$ the slope of the AE curve). The equation of the AE curve tells us that the slope of the AE curve is 0.9. So the multiplier is $1/(1 - 0.9)$, which is 10. Then, the change in equilibrium expenditure equals the change in investment multiplied by 10.

7a. The quantity demanded increases by $1,000 billion.

The increase in investment shifts the aggregate demand curve rightward by the change in investment times the multiplier. The multiplier is 10 and the change in investment is $100 billion, so the aggregate demand curve shifts rightward by $1,000 billion.

7b. In the short-run, real GDP increases by less than $1,000 billion

Real GDP is determined by the intersection of the AD curve and the SAS curve. In the short run, the price level will rise and real GDP will increase but by an amount less than the shift of the AD curve.

7c. In the long-run, real GDP will equal potential GDP, so real GDP does not increase.

Real GDP is determined by the intersection of the AD curve and the SAS curve. After the initial increase in investment, money wages increase, the SAS curve shifts leftward, and in the long run, real GDP moves back to potential GDP.

7d. In the short run, the price level rises. In the long run, the price level rises.

CHAPTER 26

1a. Equilibrium expenditure decreases by $100 billion.

The government purchases multiplier is the amount by which a change in government purchases on goods and services is multiplied to determine the change in equilibrium expenditure that results. Zap has no induced taxes or imports, so the government purchases multiplier is $1/(1 - MPC)$, which equals 10. The multiplier tells us that when government purchases decrease by $10 billion, equilibrium expenditure decreases by 10 times as much or $100 billion.

1b. The government purchases multiplier is 10.

1c. Equilibrium expenditure increases by $90 billion.

The lump-sum tax multiplier equals $-MPC/(1 - MPC)$, which is -9. That is, when lump-sum taxes are changed by $10 billion, equilibrium expenditure changes by -9 times the change in lump-sum taxes. A cut in lump-sum taxes of $10 billion will increase equilibrium expenditure by $90 billion.

1d. The lump-sum tax multiplier is -9.

1e. Equilibrium expenditure decreases by $10 billion.

The decrease in government purchases decreases equilibrium expenditure by $100 billion and the cut in taxes increases equilibrium expenditure by $90 billion. So together, equilibrium expenditure decreases by $10 billion.

3a. The quantity of real GDP demanded increases by $100 billion.

The government purchases multiplier tells us that when government purchases increase by $10 billion, equilibrium expenditure increases by 10 times as much, or $100 billion. At the price level 100, the quantity of real GDP demanded increases by an amount equal to the change in equilibrium expenditure. That is, the quantity of real GDP demanded increases by $100 billion.

3b. The aggregate demand curve shifts rightward by $100 billion at each price level.

The AE curve shifts upward by $10 billion, equilibrium expenditure increases by $100 billion, and the AD curve shifts rightward by $100 billion.

3c. In the short run, real GDP increases by less than the $100 billion increase in the quantity of real GDP demanded.

In the short run, real GDP is determined by the short-run aggregate supply and aggregate demand. Because the short-run aggregate supply curve slopes upward, the price level rises and real GDP increases but by less than $100 billion.

3d. In the long run, the increase in real GDP will be zero. Real GDP will return to potential GDP.

In the short run, real GDP exceeds potential GDP and wage rates will start to rise. The short-run aggregate supply will begin to decrease and the price level will rise. The short-run aggregate supply will continue to decrease and the price level will continue to rise until real GDP equals potential GDP.

3e. The price level rises.

In the short run, aggregate demand and short-run aggregate supply determine the price level. Because the short-run aggregate supply curve slopes upward and because aggregate demand increases, the price level rises.

3f. The price level rises.

In the long run, aggregate demand and long-run aggregate supply determine the price level. The short-run aggregate supply curve shifts leftward because the money wage rate rises. Because the long-run aggregate supply curve is vertical and because aggregate demand increases, the price level rises. And it rises by more in the long run than it does in the short run.

5a. The government budget balance is zero.

The government's tax revenues equal its expenditures, so its budget is balanced.

5b. Dreamland does not have a structural or a cyclical deficit.

Because at potential GDP, the budget is balanced, Dreamland does not have a structural surplus or deficit. Because real GDP equals potential GDP, Dreamland does not have a cyclical surplus or deficit.

5c. The budget balance is a deficit of $40 million.

At a real GDP of $30 million, tax revenues equal $80 million and expenditures equal $120 million, so the budget is in deficit. The size of the deficit is $40 million.

5d. Dreamland does not have a structural deficit, but it does have a cyclical deficit of $40 million.

Because at potential GDP, the budget is balanced, Dreamland does not have a structural surplus or deficit. Because real GDP is less than potential GDP and it has a deficit, Dreamland's deficit is a cyclical deficit. The cyclical deficit is $40 million.

5e. Dreamland does not have a structural deficit but it does have a cyclical surplus of $40 million.

Because at potential GDP, the budget is balanced, Dreamland does not have a structural surplus or deficit. Because real GDP exceeds potential GDP and it has a surplus, Dreamland's surplus is a cyclical surplus. The cyclical surplus is $40 million.

CHAPTER 27

1. Of the list, money in the United States includes the quarters inside public telephones and the U.S. dollar bills in your wallet.

Money is composed of currency outside the banks and deposits at financial institutions. Currency inside the cash machines, Visa cards, checks, and loans are not money.

3. M1 increases by $1,000; M2 does not change.

M1 is the sum of currency outside the banks, traveler's checks, and checking deposits. M2 is the sum of M1 plus savings deposits, time deposits, and money market mutual funds and other deposits. The withdrawal of $1,000 from a savings account leaves M2 unchanged because the $1,000 goes into M1 types of money, which is part of M2. The $50 held as cash and the $950 held in a checking account increase M1 by $1,000.

5a. The balance sheet has the following assets: Reserves, $250 million; Loans, $1,000 million; Other assets, $1,250 million. It has the following liabilities: Deposits, $2,000 million; Other liabilities, $500 million.

Assets

Reserves	$250 million
Loans	1,000 million
Other assets	1,250 million
Total assets	2,500 million

Liabilities

Deposits	$2,000 million
Other liabilities	500 million
Total liabilities	2,500 million

5b. The reserve ratio is 12.5 peercent.

The reserve ratio is the percentage of deposits that are held as reserves. Reserves are $250 million and deposits are $2,000, so the reserve ratio is 12.5 percent.

5c. The deposit multiplier is 8.

The deposit multiplier equals 1/(required reserve ratio). The required reserve ratio is 12.5 percent, so the deposit multiplier is 8.

7a. The initial increase in the quantity of money is $1,200.

Money is equal to bank deposits and currency outside the banks. Deposits increase by $1,200, so the initial increase in the quantity of money is $1,200.

7b. The initial increase in the quantity of bank deposits is $1,200.

Deposits increase by $1,200 because the immigrant places all the new money on deposit.

7c. The bank initially lends out $1,080.

The bank has a new deposit of $1,200, and it must keep 10 percent of it ($120) as reserves and lends the rest ($1,200 minus $120), which equals $1,080.

7d. The immigrant's bank has loaned $1,080. This amount returns to the banks as new deposits. The banks keep $108 in reserves and lend a further $972.

The banks have now created deposits of $1,200 plus $1,080, which equals $2,280.

7e. The quantity of money has increased by $9,341.05.

The first loan is $1,080, and the quantity of money increases by $1,080. When this money is spent and returned to the bank as a deposit, the banks keep 10 percent of it ($108) as reserves and lend out the rest ($972). The banks create $972 of new money. So, after 2 loans, the quantity of money has increased by $1,200 + $1,080 + $972, which equals $3,252. Similar calculations reveal that after 20 loans the quantity of money increases by $9,341.05.

7f. The quantity of money increases by $12,000. Deposits increase by $12,000. Loans increase by $10,800.

The deposit multiplier is 1/0.1, which equals 10. The deposit multiplier tells us that when reserves increase by $1,200 and the required reserve ratio is 10 percent, deposits will increase by 10 times $1,200, which is $12,000.

The quantity of money increases by the amount of the increase in deposits.

Deposits increase by $12,000 and the reserve ratio is 10 percent, so reserves increase $1,200. Therefore bank loans increase by $12,000 minus $1,200, which is $10,800.

9a. Aggregate demand increases.

9b. The price level rises and real GDP increases in the short run.

9c. In the long run, real GDP returns to potential GDP and the price level is higher than it otherwise would have been by the same percentage as the percentage increase in the quantity of money.

11a. $40 million.

Because the equation of exchange tells us that $MV = PY$, we know that $M = PY/V$. Then, with $P = 200$, $Y = \$400$ million, and $V = 20$, $M = \$40$ million.

11b. $48 million.

Money grows by 20 percent, which is $8 million.

11c. 240.

Because the quantity theory holds and because the factors that influence real GDP have not changed, the price level rises by the same percentage as the increase in money, which is 20 percent.

11d. $400 billion.

Because the factors that influence real GDP have not changed, real GDP is unchanged.

11e. 20.

Because the factors that influence velocity have not changed, velocity is unchanged.

CHAPTER 28

1a. The monetary base is $45 billion.

The monetary base is the sum of the central bank's notes outside the central bank, banks' deposits at the central bank, and coins held by households, firms, and banks. There are $30 billion in notes held by households and firms, banks' deposits at the central bank are $10 billion (2/3 of $15 billion), the banks hold other reserves of $5 billion (which are notes), and there are no coins. The monetary base is $45 billion.

1b. The quantity of money is $330 billion.

In Nocoin, deposits are $300 billion and currency is $30 billion, so the quantity of money is $330 billion.

1c. The banks' reserve ratio is 5 percent.

The banks' reserve ratio is the percent of deposits that is held as reserves. In Nocoin, deposits are $300 billion and reserves are $15 billion, so the reserve ratio equals ($15 billion/$300 billion) × 100, which is 5 percent.

1d. The currency drain is 9.09 percent.

The currency drain is the percent of the quantity of money that is held as currency by households and firms. In Nocoin, deposits are $300 billion and currency is $30 billion, so the quantity of money is $330 billion. The currency drain equals ($30 billion/$330 billion) × 100, which is 9.09 percent.

3. The quantity of money increases to $333.67 billion.

The quantity of money increases by the change in the monetary base multiplied by the money multiplier. The money multiplier is the ratio of the quantity of money to the monetary base, which equals $330 billion divided by $45 billion, which equals 7.33.

That is, when the monetary base increases by $0.5 billion, the quantity of money increases by $3.67 billion. Initially, the quantity of money was $330 billion, so the new quantity of money is $333.67 billion

The change in the quantity of money is not equal to the change in the monetary base because of the multiplier effect. The open market operation increases bank reserves and creates excess reserves, which banks use to make new loans. New loans are used to make payments and some of these loans are placed on deposit in banks. The increase in bank deposits increases banks' reserves and increases desired reserves. But the banks now have excess reserves which they loan out and the process repeats until excess reserves have been eliminated.

5a. People buy bonds, and the interest rate falls.

5b. People sell bonds, and the interest rate rises.

5c. People neither buy nor sell bonds, and the interest rate remains constant at 4 percent a year.

With real GDP of $20 billion ($Y_1$ in the spreadsheet), column C shows the demand for money schedule. The quantity of money supplied is $3 billion, so the equilibrium interest rate is 4 percent a year.

If the interest rate exceeds 4 percent a year, people are holding more money than they demand. So they try to decrease the amount of money held by buying bonds. The prices of bonds rise, and the interest rate falls.

If the interest rate is less than 4 percent a year, people are holding less money than they demand. So they try to increase the amount of money held by selling bonds. The prices of bonds fall, and the interest rate rises.

If the interest rate equals 4 percent a year, people are holding exactly the quantity of money that they demand. So they take no actions to try to change the amount of money held. The interest rate remains constant.

7a. The interest rate rises to 5 percent a year.

7b. The interest rate falls to 3 percent a year.

When real GDP increases in an expansion to $30 billion ($Y_2$ in the spreadsheet), column D shows the demand for money schedule. The quantity of money supplied is $3 billion, so the equilibrium interest rate is 5 percent a year.

When real GDP decreases in a recession to $10 billion ($Y_0$ in the spreadsheet), column B shows the demand for money schedule. The quantity of money supplied is $3 billion, so the equilibrium interest rate is 3 percent a year.

9a. The money supply curve is vertical at 1 trillion 1990 yaks.

When the real money supply is 1 trillion 1990 yaks, the equilibrium interest rate is 3 percent a year at the intersection of the demand for money and supply of money curves.

9b. Must increase the quantity of real money by 0.5 trillion 1990 yaks.

When the quantity of real money increases to 1.5 trillion 1990 yaks, the equilibrium interest rate falls to 2 percent a year.

11. The AD and SAS curves intersect at a real GDP that exceeds potential GDP and there is an inflationary gap. An open market sale decreases the quantity of money and decreases aggregate demand. The AD curve shifts leftward and the inflationary gap shrinks. If the size of the open market sale is appropriate, this monetary policy action can avoid inflation. Real GDP in the long run is determined by potential GDP and the decrease in the quantity of money has no effect on real GDP in the long run.

CHAPTER 29

1a. An increase in the quantity of money, an increase in government expenditures, a tax cut, an increase in exports.

Anything that increases aggregate demand can set off a demand-pull inflation. But to sustain such an inflation, the quantity of money must keep increasing.

1b. Starting out on AD_0 and SAS_0, the price level is 120 and real GDP is at potential GDP of $7 trillion. Aggregate demand increases and the AD curve shifts rightward to AD_1. The price level rises and real GDP increases to the intersection of AD_1 and SAS_0. There is now an inflationary gap.

1c. Starting out on AD_1 and SAS_0 with an inflationary gap, the money wage rate rises and short-run aggregate supply decreases. The SAS curve starts to shift leftward towards SAS_1. The price level keeps rising, but real GDP now decreases. The process now repeats. AD shifts to AD_2, an inflationary gap opens again, the money wage rate rises again, and the SAS curve shifts toward SAS_2.

3a. An *anticipated* increase in the quantity of money, an increase in government expenditures, a tax cut, an increase in exports.

Anything that increases aggregate demand can set off an anticipated inflation as long as the event is anticipated. But to sustain such an anticipated inflation, the quantity of money must keep increasing along its anticipated path.

3b. Starting out on AD_0 and SAS_0, the price level is 120 and real GDP is at potential GDP of $7 trillion. Aggregate demand increases, and the AD curve shifts rightward to AD_1. The increase in aggregate demand is anticipated so the money wage rate rises and the SAS curve shifts to SAS_1. The price level rises, and real GDP remains at potential GDP.

3c. Starting out on AD_1 and SAS_1, a further anticipated increase in aggregate demand occurs. The AD curve shifts to AD_2, and because the increase in aggregate demand is anticipated, the money wage rate rises again and the SAS curve shifts to SAS_2. Again, the price level rises and real GDP remains at potential GDP.

5a. Both the inflation rate and the unemployment rate have increased. So the expected inflation rate has increased and the natural rate of unemployment might have increased (but has not definitely increased). Any of the events that can increase the expected inflation rate might have occurred. Most likely, the expected growth rate of the money supply has increased. If the natural rate of unemployment has not increased, the economy is in a recession, despite the fact that the inflation rate has increased.

5b. If point A is a long-run equilibrium, the $LRPC$ is vertical at an unemployment rate of 4 percent. The $SRPC$ slopes downward and passes through point A. If point A is *not* a long-run equilibrium, the $SRPC$ still passes through point A but the $LRPC$ is vertical at whatever unemployment rate is the natural rate.

5c. If point D is a long-run equilibrium, the $LRPC$ is vertical at an unemployment rate of 8 percent. The $SRPC$ slopes downward and passes through point D. If point D is *not* a long-run equilibrium, the $SRPC$ still passes through point D but the $LRPC$ is vertical at whatever unemployment rate is the natural rate.

7a. The inflation rate rises, then the unemployment rate increases, then the inflation rate falls, and finally the unemployment rate decreases. Initially any of the events that can increase the expected inflation rate might have occurred. Most likely, the expected growth rate of the money supply increased. To stop the inflation, the growth rate of the money supply might be decreases, which brings recession and an increase in the unemployment rate above the natural rate of unemployment. Now the inflation rata begins to fall. Eventually, the expected inflation rate falls and so does the unemployment rate.

7b. The natural unemployment rate is between 4 percent and 8 percent, so draw a vertical $LRPC$ at an unemployment rate of 6 percent. The $SRPC$ slopes downward and passes through point A. Then the $SRPC$ shifts upward to pass through B and eventually through D. When the economy is at point D, the expected inflation rate falls and the $SRPC$ curve shifts downward to pass through C and finally through A again..

7c. This sequence of events is most likely an unanticipated demand pull inflation and deflation.

9a. If the natural unemployment rate and the expected inflation rate remain constant between 1999 and 2003, the $SRPC$ is linear and passes through the data points listed in the table provided. Note that one of these points is the natural rate of unemployment (4 percent) and the expected inflation rate (6 percent). The $LRPC$ is vertical at an unemployment rate of 4 percent.

9b. If the actual inflation rate rises from 6 percent to 8 percent a year, the unemployment rate decreases from 4 percent to 3 percent. This change would occur if aggregate demand were expected to increase.

CHAPTER 30

1a. Possible combinations are A or D, E or G, and I or K.

A Keynesian recession results from a decrease in investment caused by a decrease in expected profit. In an extreme case, no prices change, so the move is to *A*, *E*, and *I*. But a more general possibility is that the money wage rate doesn't change but the price level falls, real wage rate rises, and the interest rate falls. In this case, the move is to *D*, *G*, and *K*.

1b.   *D*, *G*, and *L*.

A monetarist recession results from a decrease in the quantity of money. The interest rate rises, and investment decreases. Aggregate demand decreases, but the money wage rate doesn't change. Real GDP and the price level decrease, the real wage rate rises, and employment decreases. The move is to *D*, *G*, and *L*.

1c.   *D*, *G*, and *I*, *K*, or *L*.

1d.   *D*, *G*, and *I*, *K*, or *L*.

Either type of rational expectations recession results from an unanticipated decrease in aggregate demand. Any of several factors could initiate the decrease in aggregate demand, and the interest rate could rise, fall, or remain constant. Aggregate demand decreases, but the money wage rate either doesn't change or doesn't change by enough to maintain full employment. So real GDP and the price level decrease, the real wage rate rises, and employment decreases.

1e.   *C*, and *E*, *G*, or *H*, and *K*.

In a real business cycle recession, a decrease in productivity decreases the demand for labor and capital. The interest rate and the real wage rate fall and investment and employment decrease. Aggregate demand and aggregate supply decrease, so real GDP decreases but the price level might fall, rise, or remain unchanged.

3.   This recession is consistent with Keynesian or rational expectations theories (see the solutions 1a, 1c, and 1d).

5.   This recession is consistent with real business cycle theory (see the solution 1e).

7.   This recession is not consistent with any of the theories and is an unlikely combination of events. The price level does not usually rise when the real wage rate rises.

9.   This recession is consistent the real business cycle theory (see the solution 1e).

not usually fall when the real wage rate falls.

11.   This recession is consistent with monetarist theory (see the solution 1b).

13.   This recession is not consistent with any of the theories and is an unlikely combination of events. The real wage rate does not usually fall when the price level falls.

CHAPTER 31

1.   Anything that slows investment in physical or human capital or slows the pace of technological change will create a productivity growth slowdown. For the factors at work during the U.S. productivity growth slowdown of the 1970s, review pp. 555–556 of Chapter 24.

Improvements in incentives to invest in physical or human capital or to innovate and speed up the pace of technological change will counteract a productivity growth slowdown. See p. 556 of Chapter 24 and pp. 736–738 of Chapter 31.

3a.   Real GDP is $7 trillion and the price level is 110. These values are determined at the intersection of and

3b.   Real GDP falls to $6 trillion and the price level falls to 105. Then, as aggregate demand returns to the price level and real GDP return to their initial levels.

3c.   Real GDP falls to $6 trillion and the price level falls to 105. The government increases aggregate demand to and the price level and real GDP return to their initial levels. Aggregate demand then increases (because the decrease is temporary), and real GDP rises above potential GDP. An inflationary gap arises. The money wage rate rises and so does the price level. Real GDP moves back toward potential GDP.

3d.   Real GDP falls to $6 trillion, and the price level falls to 105. The economy is stuck at this point until the money wage rate falls, short-run aggregate supply increases, and the economy moves back to potential GDP at an even lower price level. This move will likely take a long time.

3e.   Real GDP falls to $6 trillion, and the price level falls to 105. The government increases aggregate demand to and the price level and real GDP return to their initial levels. Because the decrease in aggregate demand is permanent, this is the end of the action.

5a.   The economy might have gotten into its described state because of a combination of rapid money supply growth (which brings inflation) and large structural changes (which bring high unemployment and slow productivity growth).

5b.   A slowdown in money growth will lower the inflation rate. Improvements in incentives to invest in physical or human capital or to innovate and speed up the pace of technological change will speed productivity growth.

5c.   Study pp. 390–392 (736–738) and pp. 399–403 (745–749) for explanations of how these policy actions work.

7a.   These policy actions were part of a feedback rule. The actions were taken because of the crises.

7b.   The required domestic policies all decrease aggregate demand. They lower real GDP and lower the price level (compared with what would have happened).

7c.   A possible criticism, and one that some economists have made, is that the countries should have adopted policies to expand real GDP even at the risk of a rise in inflation, rather than adopt policies that decrease aggregate demand.

CHAPTER 32

1a.   0.10 computer per TV set at 10 TV sets.

1b.   0.40 computer per TV set at 40 TV sets.

1c.   0.70 computer per TV set at 70 TV sets.

1d.   The graph shows an upward-sloping line that passes through the three points described in solutions 1a, 1b, and 1c.

The opportunity cost of a TV set is calculated as the decrease in the number of computers produced divided by the increase in the number of TV sets produced as we move along the *PPF*. The opportunity cost of a TV set increases as the quantity of TV sets produced increases.

3a. Virtual Reality exports TV sets to Vital Signs.

At the no-trade production levels, the opportunity cost of a TV set is 0.10 computer in Virtual Reality and 0.30 computer in Vital Signs. Because it costs less to produce a TV set in Virtual Reality, Vital Signs can import TV sets for a lower price that it can produce them. And because a computer costs less in Vital Signs than in Virtual Reality, Virtual Reality can import computers at a lower cost than it can produce them.

3b. Virtual Reality increases the production of TV sets and Vital Signs decreases the production of TV sets. Virtual Reality decreases the production of computers and Vital Signs increases the production of computers.

Virtual Reality increases production of TV sets to export some to Vital Signs and Vital Signs decreases production of TV sets because it now imports some from Virtual Reality.

3c. Each country consumes more of at least one good and possibly of both goods.

Because each country has a lower opportunity cost than the other at producing one of the goods, total production of both goods can increase.

3d. The price of a TV set is greater than 0.10 computer and less than 0.30 computer.

The price will be higher than the no-trade opportunity cost in Virtual Reality (0.10 computer) and lower than the no-trade opportunity cost in Vital Signs (0.30 computer).

5a. Free trade increases the production of at least one good (but not necessarily both goods) in both cases because each country increases the production of the good at which it has a comparative advantage.

5b. In problem 3, the price of a TV set rises in Virtual Reality. In problem 4, it falls.

The reason is that in problem 3, Virtual Reality produces a small number of TV sets with no trade and has the lower opportunity cost per TV set. But in problem 4, Virtual Reality produces a large number of TV sets with no trade and has the higher opportunity cost per TV set. So in problem 3, Virtual Reality becomes an exporter and increases production. The price of a TV set rises. In problem 4, Virtual Reality becomes an importer and decreases production. The price of a TV set falls.

5c. In problem 3, the price of a computer rises in Vital Signs. In problem 4, it falls.

The reason is that in problem 3, Vital Signs produces a small number of computers with no trade and has the lower opportunity cost per computer. But in problem 4, Vital Signs produces a large number of computers with no trade and has the higher opportunity cost per computer. So in problem 3, Vital Signs becomes an exporter of computers and increases production. The price of a computer rises. In problem 4, Vital Signs becomes an importer of computers and decreases production. The price of a computer falls.

7a. $9 per bushel in the importing country and $1 per bushel in the exporting country.

These are the prices at which each country wishes to import and export a zero quantity.

7b. $5 per bushel.

This is the price at which the quantity demanded by the importer equals the quantity supplied by the exporter.

7c. 400 million bushels.

This is the quantity demanded and supplied at the equilibrium price.

7d. Zero.

The balance of trade is zero because the value imported equals the value exported.

9a. $6 per bushel.

The quantity demanded by the importer equals the quantity available under the quota of 300 million bushels at this price.

9b. $600 million.

The price at which the exporters are willing to sell 300 million bushels is $4 a bushel. So there is a profit of $2 a bushel. The total revenue from the quota is 300 million multiplied by $2.

9c. The importing agents to whom the quota is allocated.

CHAPTER 33

1a. A table like Table 33.1 on p. 784 with the numbers provided in the problem.

The current account shows Imports of goods and services –350 billions of grains, Exports of goods and services, 500 billions of grains, Net interest payments, unknown, and Net transfers, unknown. You cannot calculate the current account balance from these numbers because of the two unknown items.

The capital account shows Foreign investment in Silecon, 60 billions of grains, Silecon investment abroad, –200 billions of grains, and a capital account balance of –140 billions of grains (a deficit).

The official settlements account shows Increase in official Silecon reserves, –10 billions of grains (minus because it is an increase).

Because the sum of the three balances is zero, you can now calculate the current account balance, 150 billions of grains, a surplus. Exports of goods and services minus imports of goods and services equal 150 billions of grains. So the sum of Net interest income and Net transfers is zero, but we don't know the values of these two items separately.

1b. The Silecon central bank intervenes in the foreign exchange market.

We know that the central bank intervenes in the foreign exchange market because its official reserves changed.

3a. Net exports are –$20 million.

Use the fact that

$$Y = C + I + G + NX$$

and solve for NX as

$$NX = Y - C - I - G,$$

which equals

$$NX = 120 - 72 - 40 - 28 = -20.$$

3b. Saving is $24 million.

Use the fact that

$$Y = C + S + NT$$

and solve for S as

$$S = Y - C - NT,$$

which equals

$$S = 120 - 72 - 24 = 24.$$

3c. National saving and foreign borrowing finance investment.

$$I = S + NT - G - NX,$$

which equals

$$I = 24 + 24 - 28 - (-20) = 40.$$

5a. Imports of goods and services are 26 billion bands.

Use the fact that

$$Y = C + I + G + X - M$$

and solve for M as

$$M = -Y + C + I + G + X,$$

which is

$$M = -100 + 60 + 22 + 24 + 20$$

$$M = 26.$$

5b. The current account balance is − 6 billion bands (assuming that net interest income plus net transfers is zero).

Use the fact that

$$CAB = X - M$$

$$CAB = 20 - 26 = -6.$$

5c. The capital account balance is unknown.

The sum of the current account, capital account, and official settlements account is zero. The capital account balance cannot be calculated unless information is given about the official settlements account.

5d. Net taxes are 20 billion bands.

Use the fact that

$$\text{Gov. budget deficit} = G - NT,$$

so

$$NT = G - \text{Gov. budget deficit},$$

which is

$$NT = 24 - 4 = 20.$$

5e. The private sector balance is −2 billion bands (a deficit).

Use the fact that

$$\text{Private sector surplus} = S - I,$$

with

$$S = Y - C - NT,$$

or

$$\text{Private sector surplus} = Y - C - NT - I,$$

which is

$$\text{Private sector surplus} = 100 - 60 - 20 - 22$$

$$\text{Private sector surplus} = -2.$$

7a. The central bank intervenes in the foreign exchange market to limit upward movement of the exchange rate but not strongly enough to prevent some appreciation.

7b. Nothing. The current account is financed by the capital account and the official settlements account and without information about the capital account balance, we can't tell whether the current account is in surplus or deficit.

7c. The official settlements account balance is negative—an increase in reserves is like investing in other country's assets.

CHAPTER 34

1a. The dividend yield was 0.89 percent.

The dividend yield is the dividend expressed as a percentage of the stock price. The price paid on January 2 was $60.81 and the dividend was 54¢ a share, so the dividend yield during 2001 was $0.54 \times 100 \div 60.81 = 0.89$.

1b. The return was minus $13.12.

The return equals the dividend plus the capital gain or minus the capital loss. The dividend was 54¢ a share and the capital loss was $47.15 - \$60.81 = -\$13.66$, so the return was $0.54 - 13.66 = -13.12$.

1c. The capital loss as $13.66.

The capital loss is the decrease in price, which is $13.66.

1d. The rate of return was minus 21.58 percent.

The rate of return equals the return (minus $13.12 in 1b) expressed as a percentage of the purchase price, which is $-13.12 \times 100 \div 60.81 = -21.58$.

1e. Earnings are $1.58 per share (data provided in the question).

1f. 29.84

The price-earnings ratio equals the price per share divided by the earnings per share, which on 31 December 2001 was $47.15 \div 1.58 = 29.84$.

3. Your report will use the fact that the Dow contains only 30 stocks of large corporations, the S&P 500 is a broad index that covers all parts of the economy, and the NASDAQ represents the hi-tech sector. You will report that the hi-tech sector is performing better than aver and the big corporations in the Dow are performing worse than average. The S&P performance indicates the economy average, which is positive.

5. $29.70.

The highest price you would be willing to pay is your expected value of $0.9 \times (\$3 + \$30) = \$29.70$.

7. $25.67.

The lowest price at the end of the year that would make it rational for you to buy is the value of P that solves $20 = 0.75 \times (1 + P)$. The solution is $P = 20 \div 0.75 - 1 = 25.67$.

9a. 14 percent.

There is only a 1 in 10 chance of earning 50 percent and a 9 in 10 chance of earning 10 percent. The expected return is $0.1 \times 50 + 0.9 \times 10 = 5 + 9 = 14$.

9b.   17.5 percent.

There is a 5 in 10 chance of earning 20 percent and a 5 in 10 chance of earning 15 percent. The expected return is $0.5 \times 20 + 0.5 \times 15 = 10 + 7.5 = 17.5$.

9c.   10 percent.

The question tells you that the chance that Merck will earn a high return is 10 percent.

9d.   90 percent.

The question tells you that the chance that Merck will earn a high return is 10 percent. So the chance that it will not earn a high return but earn a low return is 90 percent.

9e.   50 percent.

The question tells you that the chance that Pfizer will earn a high return is 50 percent.

9f.   50 percent.

The question tells you that the chance that Pfizer will earn a high return is 50 percent. So the chance that it will not earn a high return but earn a low return is also 50 percent.

9g.   15.75 percent.

The expected return from Merck is 14 percent and the expected return from Pfizer is 17.5 percent, so if you put half your wealth in each of these stocks, you will expect to earn $0.5 \times 14 + 0.5 \times 17.5 = 15.75$.

9h.   No chance.

The best you can do is that both firms achieve the high return—50 percent for Merck and 20 percent for Pfizer. With half your wealth in each of these stocks, you will then earn $0.5 \times 50 + 0.5 \times 20 = 35$. That is, the most you can earn is 35 percent, so there is no chance of earning 50 percent.

9i.   No chance.

The worst you will do is that both firms achieve the low return—10 percent for Merck and 15 percent for Pfizer. With half your wealth in each of these stocks, you will then earn $0.5 \times 10 + 0.5 \times 15 = 12.5$. That is, the worst you can earn is 12.5 percent, so there is no chance of earning 10 percent.

9j.   It is rational to diversify because you can lower the risk. If you hold only Merck, you might earn 50 percent but you might earn only 10 percent. If you hold only Pfizer, the most you will earn is 20 percent (worse than the best with Merck), but the worst you will earn is 15 percent (better than the worst with Merck). By holding some of each, you still have a shot at some of the big return from Merck but you avoid being exposed to all of the worst of Merck.

GLOSSARY

Above full-employment equilibrium
A macroeconomic equilibrium in which real GDP exceeds potential GDP. (p. 486)

Absolute advantage A person has an absolute advantage if that person can produce more of goods with a given amount of resources than another person can; a country has an absolute advantage if its output per unit of inputs of all goods is larger than that of another country. (p. 43)

Aggregate demand The relationship between the quantity of real GDP demanded and the price level. (p. 481)

Aggregate hours The total number of hours worked by all the people employed, both full time and part time, during a year. (p. 459)

Aggregate planned expenditure The expenditure that households, firms, governments, and foreigners plan to undertake in given circumstances. It is the sum of planned consumption expenditure, planned investment, planned government purchases of goods and services, and planned exports minus planned imports. (p. 576)

Aggregate production function The relationship between the quantity of real GDP supplied and the quantities of labor and capital and the state of technology. (pp. 476, 553)

Allocative efficiency A situation in which we cannot produce more of any good without giving up some of another good that we value more highly. (p. 37)

Antitrust law A law that regulates and prohibits certain kinds of market behavior, such as monopoly and monopolistic practices. (p. 390)

Automatic fiscal policy A change in fiscal policy that is triggered by the state of the economy. (p. 610)

Automatic stabilizers Mechanisms that stabilize real GDP without explicit action by the government. (p. 614)

Autonomous expenditure The sum of those components of aggregate planned expenditure that are not influenced by real GDP. Autonomous expenditure equals investment, government purchases, exports, and the autonomous parts of consumption expenditure and imports. (p. 583)

Average cost pricing rule A rule that sets price to cover cost including normal profit, which means setting the price equal to average total cost. (pp. 273, 394)

Average fixed cost Total fixed cost per unit of output—total fixed cost divided by output. (p. 220)

Average product The average product of a resource. It equals total product divided by the quantity of the resource employed. (p. 215)

Average tax rate The percentage of income that is paid in tax. (p. 378)

Average total cost Total cost per unit of output. (p. 220)

Average variable cost Total variable cost per unit of output. (p. 220)

Balanced budget A government budget in which tax revenues and expenditures are equal. (p. 606)

Balance of payments accounts A country's record of international trading, borrowing, and lending. (p. 784)

Barriers to entry Legal or natural constraints that protect a firm from potential competitors. (p. 258)

Barter The direct exchange of one good or service for other goods and services. (p. 630)

Below full-employment equilibrium A macroeconomic equilibrium in which potential GDP exceeds real GDP. (p. 486)

Big tradeoff The conflict between equity and efficiency. (pp. 10, 113, 356)

Bilateral monopoly A situation in which there is a single seller (a monopoly) faces a single buyer (a monopsony). (p. 341)

Black market An illegal trading arrangement in which the price exceeds the legally imposed price ceiling. (p. 124)

Budget deficit A government's budget balance that is negative— expenditures exceed tax revenues. (p. 606)

Budget line The limits to a household's consumption choices. (p. 168)

Budget surplus A government's budget balance that is positive—tax revenues exceed expenditures. (p. 606)

Business cycle The periodic but irregular up-and-down movement in production and jobs. (p. 8)

Business saving Retained profits of firms plus pension funds that result from payoff deductions. (p. 527)

Capacity output The output at which average total cost is a minimum—the output at the bottom of the U-shaped *ATC* curve. (p. 283)

Capital The tools, equipment, buildings, and other constructions that businesses now use to produce goods and services. (p. 4)

Capital account A record of foreign investment in a country minus its investment abroad. (p. 784)

Capital accumulation The growth of capital resources. (p. 38)

Capital consumption The decrease in the capital stock that results from wear and tear and obsolescence. (p. 437)

Capital gain The increase in the price of a stock. (p. 805)

Capital loss The decrease in the price of a stock. (p. 805)

Capital stock The total quantity of plant, equipment, buildings, and inventories. (p. 526)

Capture theory A theory of regulation that states that the regulations are supplied to satisfy the demand of producers to maximize producer surplus—to maximize economic profit. (p. 391)

Cartel A group of firms that has entered into a collusive agreement to restrict output and increase prices and profits. (p. 291)

Central bank A bank's bank and a public authority that regulates a nation's depository institutions and controls the quantity of money. (p. 654)

Ceteris paribus Other things being equal—all other relevant things remaining the same. (p. 13)

Chain-weighted output index An index that uses the prices of two adjacent years to calculate the real GDP growth rate. (p. 442)

Change in demand A change in buyers' plans that occurs when some influence on those plans other than the price of the good changes. It is illustrated by a shift of the demand curve. (p. 61)

Change in supply A change in sellers' plans that occurs when some influence on those plans other than the price of the good changes. It is illustrated by a shift of the supply curve. (p. 65)

Change in the quantity demanded A change in buyers' plans that occurs when the price of a good changes but all other influences on buyers' plans remain unchanged. It is illustrated by a movement along the demand curve. (p. 63)

Change in the quantity supplied A change in sellers' plans that occurs when the price of a good changes but all other influences on sellers' plans remain unchanged. It is illustrated by a movement along the supply curve. (p. 66)

Classical growth theory A theory of economic growth based on the view that real GDP growth is temporary and that when real GDP per person increases above subsistence level, a population explosion brings real GDP back to subsistence level. (p. 557)

Coase theorem The proposition that if property rights exist and transactions costs are low, then private transactions are efficient. (p. 415)

Collusive agreement An agreement between two (or more) producers to restrict output, raise the price, and increase profits. (p. 291)

Command system A method of organizing production that uses a managerial hierarchy. (p. 197)

Commercial bank A firm that is licensed by the Comptroller of the Currency in the U.S. Treasury) or by a state agency to receive deposits and make loans. (p. 633)

Comparative advantage A person or country has a comparative advantage in an activity if that person or country can perform the activity at a lower opportunity cost than anyone else or any other country. (pp. 40, 764)

Competitive market A market that has many buyers and many sellers, so no single buyer or seller can influence the price. (p. 58)

Complement A good that is used in conjunction with another good. (p. 61)

Constant returns to scale Features of a firm's technology that leads to constant long-run average cost as output increases. When constant returns to scale are present, the *LRAC* curve is horizontal. (p. 227)

Consumer equilibrium A situation in which a consumer has allocated his or her available income in the way that, given the prices of goods ands services, maximizes his or her total utility. (p. 153)

Consumer Price Index An index that measures the average of the prices paid by urban consumers for a fixed "basket" of the consumer goods and services. (p. 466)

Consumer surplus The value of a good minus the price paid for it, summed over the quantity bought. (p. 105)

Consumption expenditure The total payment for consumer goods and services. (p. 435)

Consumption function The relationship between consumption expenditure and disposable income, other things remaining the same. (p. 577)

Contestable market A market in which firms can enter and leave so easily that firms in the market face competition from potential entrants. (p. 298)

Contractionary fiscal policy A decrease in government purchases or an increase in taxes. (p. 617)

Cooperative equilibrium The outcome of a game in which the players make and share the monopoly profit. (p. 297)

Copyright A government-sanctioned exclusive right granted to the inventor of a good, service, or productive process to produce, use, and sell the invention for a given number of years. (p. 421)

Cost of living The amount of money it takes to buy the goods and services that a typical family consumes. (p. 7)

Cost-push inflation An inflation that results from an initial increase in costs. (p. 681)

Council of Economic Advisers The President's council whose main work is to monitor the economy and keep the President and the public well informed about the current state of the economy and the best available forecasts of where it is heading. (p. 605)

Creditor nation A country that during its entire history has invested more in the rest of the world than other countries have invested in it. (p. 786)

Credit union A depository institution owned by a social or economic group such as firm's employees that accepts savings deposits and makes mostly consumer loans. (p. 634)

Cross elasticity of demand The responsiveness of the demand for a good to the price of a substitute or complement, other things remaining the same. It is calculated as the percentage change in the quantity demanded of the good divided by the percentage change in the price of the substitute or complement. (p. 89)

Cross-section graph A graph that shows the values of an economic variable for different groups in a population at a point in time. (p. 18)

Crowding-out effect The tendency for a government budget deficit to decrease in investment. (p. 538)

Currency The bills and coins that we use today. (p. 631)

Currency appreciation The rise in the value of one currency in terms of another currency. (p. 789)

Currency depreciation The fall in the value of one currency in terms of another currency. (p. 789)

Currency drain An increase in currency held outside the banks. (p. 659)

Current account A record of the payments for imports of goods and services, receipts from exports of goods and services, the interest income, and net transfers. (p. 784)

Cyclical surplus or deficit The actual surplus or deficit minus the structural surplus or deficit. (p. 615)

Cyclical unemployment The fluctuations in unemployment over the business cycle. (p. 464)

Deadweight loss A measure of inefficiency. It is equal to the decrease in consumer surplus and producer surplus that results from an inefficient level of production. (p. 110)

Debtor nation A country that during its entire history has borrowed more from the rest of the world than it has lent to it. (p. 786)

Deflation A process of falling cost of living. (p. 7)

Demand The relationship between the quantity of a good that consumers plan to buy and the price of the good when all other influences on buyers' plans remain the same. It is described by a demand schedule and illustrated by a demand curve. (p. 60)

Demand curve A curve that shows the relationship between the quantity demanded of a good and its price when all other influences on consumers' planned purchases remain the same. (p. 60)

Demand for labor The relationship between the quantity of labor demanded and the real wage rate when all other influences on firm's hiring plans remain the same. (p. 507)

Demand-pull inflation An inflation that results from an initial increase in aggregate demand. (p. 679)

Deposit multiplier The amount by which an increase in bank reserves is multiplied to calculate the increase in bank deposits. (p. 639)

Depository institution A firm that takes deposits from households and firms and makes loans to other households and firms. (p. 633)

Depreciation The decrease in the capital stock that results from wear and tear and obsolescence. (p. 437, 526)

Derived demand Demand for a productive resource which is derived from the demand for the goods and services produced by the resource. (p. 313)

Diminishing marginal rate of substitution The general tendency for a person to be willing to give up less of good y for to get one more unit of good x, and at the same time remain indifferent, as the quantity of good x increases. (p. 172)

Diminishing marginal returns The tendency for the marginal product of an additional unit of a factor of production is less than the marginal product of the previous unit of the factor. (p. 217)

Diminishing marginal utility The decrease in marginal utility as the quantity consumed increases. (p. 151)

Direct relationship A relationship between two variables that move in the same direction. (p. 20)

Discount factor The discounted price is the original price multiplied by the discount factor. (p. 811)

Discounting The conversion of a future amount of money to its present value. (p. 322)

Discount rate The interest rate at which the Fed stands ready to lend reserves to depository institutions. (p. 655)

Discouraged workers People who are available and willing to work but have not made specific efforts to find a job within the previous four weeks. (p. 457)

Discretionary fiscal policy A policy action that is initiated by an act of Congress. (p. 610)

Discretionary policy A policy that responds to the state of the economy in a possibly unique way that uses all the information available, including perceived lessons from past "mistakes." (p. 739)

Diseconomies of scale Features of a firm's technology that leads to rising long-run average cost as output increases. (p. 226)

Disposable income Aggregate income minus taxes plus transfer payments. (pp. 483, 576)

Dividend The share of a firm's profit paid to stockholders. (p. 804)

Dividend yield The dividend paid on a stock expressed as a percentage of the stock price. (p. 805)

Dumping The sale by a foreign firm of exports at a lower price that the cost of production. (p. 773)

Duopoly A market structure in which two producers of a good or service compete. (p. 291)

Dynamic comparative advantage A comparative advantage that a person or country possesses as a result of having specialized in a particular activity and then, as a result of learning-by-doing, having become the producer with the lowest opportunity cost. (p. 43)

Earnings A firm's accounting profit. (p. 805)

Earnings share regulation A regulation that states that profits in excess of a target level to be shared with the firm's customers. (p. 396)

Economic depreciation The change in the market value of capital over a given period. (p. 192)

Economic efficiency A situation that occurs when the firm produces a given output at the least cost. (p. 195)

Economic growth The expansion of production possibilities that results from capital accumulation and technological change. (p. 38)

Economic growth rate The percentage change in the quantity of goods and services produced from one year to the next. (p. 444)

Economic model A description of some aspect of the economic world that includes only those features of the world that are needed for the purpose at hand. p. 12)

Economic profit A firm's total revenue minus its opportunity cost. (p. 193)

Economic rent The income received by the owner of a factor of production over and above the amount required to induce that owner to offer the factor for use. (p. 330)

Economics The social science that studies the choices individuals, businesses, governments, and entire societies make and how they cope with scarcity. (p. 2)

Economic theory A generalization that summarizes what we think we understand about the economic choices that people make and the performance of industries and entire economies. (p. 12)

Economic welfare A comprehensive measure of the general state of economic well-being. (p. 444)

Economies of scale Features of a firm's technology that leads to a falling long-run average cost as output increases. (pp. 207, 226)

Economies of scope Decreases in average total cost that occur when a firm uses specialized resources to produce a range of goods and services. (p. 207)

Efficiency wage A real wage rate that is set above the full-employment equilibrium wage rate and that balances the costs and benefits of this higher wage rate to maximize the firm's profit. (p. 518)

Efficient allocation Resource use is efficient when we produce the goods and services that we value most highly. (p. 102)

Elastic demand Demand with a price elasticity greater than 1; other things remaining the same, the percentage change in the quantity demanded exceeds the percentage change in price. (p. 85)

Elasticity of demand The responsiveness of the quantity demanded of a good to a change in its price, other things remaining the same. (p. 82)

Elasticity of supply The responsiveness of the quantity supplied of a

good to a change in its price, other things remaining the same. (p. 92)

Employment Act of 1946 A landmark Congressional act that recognized a role for government actions to keep unemployment, keep the economy expanding, and keep inflation in check. (p. 604)

Employment-to-population ratio The percentage of people of working age who have jobs. (p. 458)

Entitlement spending Spending on government programs that entitle suitably qualified individuals and businesses to receive benefits and that result in transfer payments that depend on the economic state of individual citizens and businesses. (p. 613)

Entrants People who enter the labor force. (p. 461)

Entrepreneurship The human resource that organizes the other three factors of production: labor, land, and capital. Entrepreneurs come up with new ideas about what, how, when, and where to produce, make business decisions, and bear the risk that arise from their decisions. (p. 4)

Equation of exchange An equation that states that the quantity of money multiplied by the velocity of circulation equals GDP. (p. 644)

Equilibrium expenditure The level of aggregate expenditure that occurs when aggregate planned expenditure equals real GDP. (p. 584)

Equilibrium price The price at which the quantity demanded equals the quantity supplied. (p. 68)

Equilibrium quantity The quantity bought and sold at the equilibrium price. (p. 68)

Equity capital The value of a firm's stock—also called the firm's equity. (p. 804)

Excess reserves A bank's actual reserves minus its required reserves. (p. 638)

Excise tax A tax on the sale of a particular commodity. (p. 382)

Expansion A business cycle phase between a trough and a peak—phase in which real GDP increases. (p. 454)

Expansionary fiscal policy An increase in government purchases or a decrease in taxes. (p. 617)

Exports The goods and services that we sell to people in other countries. (pp. 436, 762)

External benefits Benefits that accrue to people other than the buyer of the good. (p. 250)

External costs Costs that are not borne by the producer of the good but borne by someone else. (p. 250)

External diseconomies Factors outside the control of a firm that raise the firm's costs as the industry produces a larger output. (p. 247)

External economies Factors beyond the control of a firm that lower the firm's costs as the industry produces a larger output. (p. 247)

Externality A cost or a benefit that arises from production and falls on someone other than the producer of or cost or a benefit that arises from consumption and falls on someone other than the consumer. (p. 410)

Factors of production The resources that businesses use to produce goods and services. (p. 4)

Federal budget The annual statement of the expenditures and tax revenues of the government of the United States together with the laws and regulations that approve and support those expenditures and taxes. (p. 604)

Federal funds rate The interest rate that banks charge each other on overnight loans of reserves. (p. 654)

Federal Open Market Committee The main policy-making organ of the Federal Reserve System. (p. 654)

Federal Reserve System The central bank of the United States. (p. 654)

Feedback-rule policy A rule that specifies how policy actions respond to changes in the state of the economy. (p. 739)

Final good An item that is bought by its final user during the specified time period. (p. 434)

Financial innovation The development of new financial products—new ways of borrowing and lending. (p. 636)

Firm An institution that hires factors of production and organizes those factors to produce and sell goods and services. (p. 192)

Fiscal policy The government's attempt to achieve macroeconomic objectives such as full employment, sustained economic growth, and price level stability by setting and changing taxes, making transfer payments, and purchasing goods and services. (pp. 483, 604)

Fixed-rule policy A rule that specifies an action to be pursued independently of the state of the economy. (p. 739)

Flow A quantity per unit of time. (p. 437)

Foreign exchange market The market in which the currency of one country is exchanged for the currency of another. (p. 789)

Foreign exchange rate The price at which one currency exchanges for another. (p. 789)

Four-firm concentration ratio A measure of market power that is calculated as the percentage of the value of sales accounted for by the four largest firms in an industry. (p. 202)

Free rider A person who consumes a good without paying for it. (p. 372)

Frictional unemployment The unemployment that arises from normal labor turnover—from people entering and leaving the labor force and from the ongoing creation and destruction of jobs. (p. 463)

Full employment A situation in which the quantity of labor demanded equal the quantity supplied. At full employment, there is no cyclical unemployment—all unemployment is frictional and structural. (p. 464)

Game theory A tool that economists use to analyze strategic behavior—behavior that takes into account the expected behavior of others and the mutual recognition of independence. (p. 289)

GDP deflator One measure of the price level, which is the average of current-year prices as a percentage of base-year prices. (p. 442)

General Agreement on Tariffs and Trade An international agreement signed in 1947 to reduce tariffs on international trade. (p. 769)

Goods and services All the objects that people value and produce to satisfy their wants. (p. 3)

Government debt The total amount of borrowing that the government has undertaken. It equals the sum of past budget deficits minus budget surpluses. (p. 608)

Government purchases Goods and services bought by the government. (p. 436)

Government purchases multiplier The magnification effect of a change in government purchases of goods and services on equilibrium expenditure and real GDP. (p. 610)

Government saving The government's budget surplus. (p. 527)

Government sector surplus or deficit An amount equal to net taxes minus government purchases of goods and services. (p. 787)

Gross domestic product (GDP) The market value of all goods and services produced within a country during a given time period—usually a year. (p. 434)

Gross investment The total amount spent on purchases of new capital and on replacing depreciated capital. (pp. 437, 526)

Growth accounting A method of calculating how much real GDP growth results from growth of labor and capital and how much is attributable to technological change. (p. 553)

Herfindahl-Hirschman Index A measure of market power that is calculated as the square of the market share of each firm (as a percentage) summed over the largest 50 firms (or over all firms if there are fewer than 50) in a market. (p. 202)

Human capital The knowledge and skill that people obtain from education, on-the-job training, and experience. (pp. 4, 505)

Implicit rental rate The firm's opportunity cost of using its own capital. (p. 192)

Imports The goods and services that we buy from people in other countries. (pp. 436, 762)

Incentive An inducement to take a particular action. (p. 11)

Incentive system A method of organizing production that uses a market-like mechanism inside the firm. (p. 197)

Income effect The effect of a change in income on consumption, other things remaining the same. (p. 176)

Income elasticity of demand The responsiveness of demand to a change in income, other things remaining the same. It is calculated as the percentage change in the quantity demanded divided by the percentage change in income. (p. 90)

Indifference curve A line that shows combinations of goods among which a consumer is indifferent. (p. 171)

Induced expenditure The sum of the components of aggregate planned expenditure that vary with real GDP. Induced expenditure equals consumption expenditure minus imports. (p. 583)

Induced taxes Taxes that vary with real GDP. (p. 613)

Inelastic demand A demand with a price elasticity between 0 and 1; the percentage change in the quantity demanded is less than the percentage change in price. (p. 85)

Infant-industry argument The argument that it is necessary to protect a new industry to enable it to grow into a mature industry that can compete in world markets. (p. 773)

Inferior good A good for which demand decreases as income increases. (p. 62)

Inflation A rising cost of living—a process in which the price level is rising and money is losing value. (pp. 7, 678)

Inflationary gap The amount by which real GDP exceeds potential GDP. (p. 487)

Inflation rate The percentage change in the price level from one year to the next. (p. 468)

Intellectual property rights Property rights for discoveries owned by the creators of knowledge. (p. 421)

Interest The income that capital earns. (p. 5)

Interest rate parity A situation in which the rates of return on assets in different currencies are equal. (p. 796)

Intermediate good A item that is produced by one firm, bought by another firm, and used as a component of a final good or service. (p. 434)

Inverse relationship A relationship between variables that move in opposite directions. (p. 21)

Investment The purchase of new plant, equipment, and buildings and additions to inventories. (p. 436)

Investment demand The relationship between investment and real interest rate, other things remaining the same. (p. 530)

Job leavers People who voluntarily quit their jobs. (p. 461)

Job losers People who are laid off, either permanently or temporarily, from their jobs. (p. 461)

Job rationing The practice of paying a real wage rate above the equilibrium level and then rationing jobs by some method. (p. 518)

Job search The activity of looking for acceptable vacant jobs. (p. 517)

Keynesian activist An economist who believes that fluctuations in aggregate demand combined with sticky wages (and/or sticky prices) are the main source of economic fluctuations. (p. 740)

Keynesian theory of the business cycle A theory that regards volatile expectations as the main source of economic fluctuations. (p. 708)

Labor The work time and work effort that people devote to producing goods and services. (p. 4)

Labor force The sum of the people who are employed and who are unemployed. (p. 456)

Labor force participation rate The percentage of the working-age population who are members of the labor force. (p. 457)

Labor productivity Real GDP per hour of work. (pp. 505, 553)

Labor union An organized group of workers whose purpose is to increase wages and to influence other job conditions. (p. 337)

Land All the gifts of nature that we use to produce goods and services. (p. 4)

Law of demand Other things remaining the same, the higher the price of a good, the smaller is the quantity demanded of it. (p. 59)

Law of diminishing returns As a firm uses more of a variable input, with a given quantity of other inputs (fixed inputs), the marginal product of the variable input eventually diminishes. (pp. 217, 507, 554)

Law of supply Other things remaining the same, the higher the price of a good, the greater is the quantity supplied of it. (p. 64)

Learning-by-doing People become more productive in an activity (learn) just by repeatedly producing a particular good or service (doing). (pp. 43, 505)

Legal monopoly A market structure in which there is one firm and entry is restricted by the granting of a public franchise, government license, patent, or copyright. (p. 258)

Limit pricing The practice of setting the price at the highest level that inflicts a loss on an entrant. (p. 299)

Linear relationship A relationship between two variables that is illustrated by a straight line. (p. 20)

Liquidity The property of being instantly convertible into a means of payment with little loss in value. (p. 632)

Local public good A public good that is consumed by all the people who live in a particular area. (p. 381)

Long run A period of time in which the quantities of all resources can be varied. (p. 214)

Long-run aggregate supply curve The relationship between the real GDP supplied and the price level in the long run when real GDP equals potential GDP. (pp. 476, 511)

Long-run average cost curve The relationship between the lowest attainable average total cost and output when both capital and labor are varied. (p. 225)

Long-run industry supply curve A curve that shows how the quantity supplied by an industry varies as the market price varies after all the possible adjustments have been made, including changes in plant size and the number of firms in the industry. (p. 247)

Long-run macroeconomic equilibrium A situation that occurs when real GDP equals potential GDP—the economy is on its long-run aggregate supply curve. (p. 485)

Long-run Phillips curve A curve that shows the relationship between inflation and unemployment when the actual inflation rate equals the expected inflation rate. (p. 690)

Lorenz curve A curve that graphs the cumulative percentage of income or wealth against the cumulative percentage of households or population. (p. 345)

Lump-sum taxes Taxes that do not vary with real GDP. (p. 610)

Lump-sum tax multiplier The magnification effect of a change in lump-sum taxes on equilibrium expenditure and real GDP. (p. 612)

M1 A measure of money that consists of currency and traveler's checks plus checking deposits owned by individuals and businesses. (p. 631)

M2 A measure of money that consists of M1 plus time deposits, savings deposits, and money market mutual funds and other deposits. (p. 631)

Macroeconomic long run A time frame that is sufficiently long for real GDP to return to potential GDP so that full employment prevails. (p. 476)

Macroeconomics The study of the effects on the national economy and the global economy of the choices that individuals, businesses, and governments make. (p. 2)

Macroeconomic short run A period during real GDP has fallen below or risen above potential GDP. (p. 477)

Margin When a choice is changed by a small amount or by a little at a time, the choice is made at the margin. (p.11)

Marginal benefit The benefit that a person receives from consuming one more unit of a good or service. It is measured as the maximum amount that a person is willing to pay for one more unit of the good or service. (pp. 11, 36, 102)

Marginal benefit curve A curve that shows the relationship between the marginal benefit of a good and the quantity of that good consumed. (p. 36)

Marginal cost The opportunity cost of producing one more unit of a good or service. It is the best alternative forgone. It is calculated as the increase in total cost divided by the increase in output. (pp. 11, 35, 102, 220)

Marginal cost pricing rule A rule that sets the price of a good or service equal to the marginal cost of producing it. (pp. 272, 394)

Marginal external benefit The benefit from an additional unit of a good or service that people other than the consumer enjoys. (p. 417)

Marginal external cost The cost of producing an additional unit of a good or service that falls on people other than the producer. (p. 413)

Marginal private benefit The benefit from an additional unit of a good or service that the consumer of that good or service receives. (p. 417)

Marginal private cost The cost of producing an additional unit of a good or service that is borne by the producer of that good or service. (p. 413)

Marginal product The increase in total product that results from a one-unit increase in the variable input, with all other inputs remaining the same. It is calculated as the increase in total product divided by the increase in the variable input employed, when the quantities of all other inputs are constant. (p. 215)

Marginal product of labor The

additional real GDP produced by an additional hour of labor when all other influences on production remain the same. (p. 507)

Marginal propensity to consume The fraction of an change in disposable income that is consumed. It is calculated as the change in consumption expenditure divided by the change in disposable income. (p. 578)

Marginal propensity to import The fraction of an increase in real GDP that is spent on imports. (p. 581)

Marginal propensity to save The fraction of an increase in disposable income that is saved. It is calculated as the change in saving divided by the change in disposable income. (p. 578)

Marginal rate of substitution The rate at which a person will give up good y (the good measured on the y-axis) to get an additional unit of good x (the good measured on the x-axis) and at the same time remain indifferent (remain on the same indifference curve). (p. 172)

Marginal revenue The change in total revenue that results from a one-unit increase in the quantity sold. It is calculated as the change in total revenue divided by the change in quantity sold. (p. 234)

Marginal revenue product The change in total revenue that results from employing one more unit of a resource (labor) while the quantity of all other resources remains the same. It is calculated as the increase in total revenue divided by the increase in the quantity of the resource (labor). (p. 314)

Marginal social benefit The marginal benefit enjoyed by society—by the consumer of a good or service (marginal private benefit) plus the marginal benefit enjoyed by others (marginal external benefit). (p. 417)

Marginal social cost The marginal cost incurred by the entire society— by the producer and by everyone else on whom the cost falls— and is the sum of marginal private cost and the marginal external cost. (p. 413)

Marginal tax rate The percentage of an additional dollar of income that is paid in tax. (p. 378)

Marginal utility The change in total utility resulting from a one-unit increase in the quantity of a good consumed. (p. 151)

Marginal utility per dollar spent The marginal utility from a good consumed divided by its price. (p. 153)

Market Any arrangement that enables buyers and sellers to get information and to do business with each other. (p. 44)

Market demand The relationship between the total quantity demanded of a good and its price. It is illustrated by the market demand curve. (p. 159)

Market failure A state in which the market does not allocate resources efficiently. (p. 370)

Market income The wages, interest, rent and profit earned in factor markets and before paying income taxes. (p. 344)

Market power The ability to influence the market, and in particular the market price, by influencing the total quantity offered for sale. (p. 258)

Means of payment A method of settling a debt. (p. 630)

Microeconomics The study of the choices that individuals and businesses make, the way those choices interact, and the influence governments exert on them. (p. 2)

Minimum efficient scale The smallest quantity of output at which the long-run average cost curve reaches its lowest level. (p. 227)

Minimum wage A regulation that makes the hiring of labor below a specified wage rate illegal. (pp. 127, 519)

Monetarist An economist who believes that fluctuations in the quantity of money are the main source of economic fluctuations. (p. 740)

Monetarist theory of the business cycle A theory that regards fluctuations in the quantity of money as the main source of economic fluctuations. (p. 710)

Monetary base The sum of the Federal Reserve notes, coins, and banks' deposits at the Fed. (p. 657)

Monetary policy The Fed conducts the nation's monetary policy by changing in interest rates and adjusting the quantity of money. (pp. 483, 654)

Money Any commodity or token that is generally acceptable as a means of payment. (p. 630)

Money income The sum of market income and cash payments to household by the government. (p. 344)

Money market mutual fund A fund operated by a financial institution that sells shares in the fund and holds liquid assets such as U.S. Treasury bills and short-term commercial bills. (p. 634)

Money multiplier The amount by which a change in the monetary base is multiplied to determine the resulting change in the quantity of money. (p. 659)

Money wage rate The number of dollars that an hour of labor earns. (p. 507)

Monopolistic competition A market structure in which a large number of firms compete by making similar but slightly different products. (pp. 201, 280)

Monopoly A market structure in which there is one firm, which produces a good or service that has no close substitute and in which the firm is protected from competition by a barrier preventing the entry of new firms. (pp. 201, 258)

Monopsony A market in which there is a single buyer. (p. 340)

Multiplier The amount by which a change in autonomous expenditure is magnified or multiplied to determine the change in equilibrium expenditure and real GDP. (p. 586)

Nash equilibrium The outcome of a game that occurs when player A takes the best possible action given the action of player B and player B takes the best possible action given the action of player A. (p. 290)

National saving The sum of private saving (saving by households and businesses) and government saving. (pp. 437, 532)

Natural monopoly A monopoly that occurs when one firm can supply the entire market at a lower price than two or more firms can. (p. 258)

Natural rate of unemployment The unemployment rate when the economy is at full employment. There is no cyclical unemployment; all unemployment is frictional and structural. (pp. 464, 476)

Negative externality An externality that arise from either production or consumption and that imposes an external cost. (p. 410)

Negative relationship A relationship between variables that move in opposite directions. (p. 21)

Neoclassical growth theory A theory of economic growth that proposes that real GDP grows because technological change induces a level of saving and investment that makes capital per hour of labor grow. (p. 559)

Net borrower A country that is borrowing more from the rest of the world than it is lending to it. (p. 786)

Net exports The value of exports minus the value of imports. (pp. 436, 762, 787)

Net investment Net increase in the capital stock—gross investment minus depreciation. (pp. 436, 526)

Net lender A country that is lending more to the rest of the world than it is borrowing from it. (p. 786)

Net present value The present value of the future flow of marginal revenue product generated by capital minus the cost of the capital. (p. 324)

Net taxes Taxes paid to governments minus transfer payments received from governments. (p. 436)

New classical theory of the business cycle A rational expectations theory of the business cycle that regards unanticipated fluctuations in aggregate demand as the main source of economic fluctuations. (p. 712)

New growth theory A theory of economic growth based on the idea that real GDP per person grows because of the choices that people make in the pursuit of ever greater profit and that growth can persist indefinitely. (p. 561)

New Keynesian theory of the business cycle A rational expectations theory of the business cycle that regards unanticipated fluctuations in aggregate demand as the main source of economic fluctuations but leaves room for anticipated demand fluctuations to play a role. (p. 712)

Nominal GDP The value of the final goods and services produced in a given year valued at the prices that prevailed in that same year. It is a more precise name for GDP. (p. 441)

Nonrenewable natural resources Natural resources that can be used only once and that cannot be replaced once they have been used. (p. 327)

Nontariff barrier Any action other than a tariff that restricts international trade. (p. 769)

Normal good A good for which demand increases as income increases. (p. 62)

Normal profit The expected return for supplying entrepreneurial ability. (p. 193)

North American Free Trade Agreement An agreement, which became effective on January 1, 1994, to eliminate all barriers to international trade between the United States, Canada, and Mexico after a 15-year phasing in period. (p. 770)

Official settlements account A record of the change in a country's official reserves. (p. 784)

Oligopoly A market structure in which a small number of firms compete. (pp. 201, 287)

One third rule The rule that, with no change in technology, a 1 percent increase in capital per hour of labor brings, on the average, a one third of 1 percent increase in real GDP per hour of labor. (p. 554)

Open market operation The purchase or sale of government securities—U.S. Treasury bills and bonds—by the Federal Reserve System in the open market. (p. 656)

Opportunity cost The highest-valued alternative that we give up to something. (p. 11)

Output-inflation tradeoff A tradeoff that arises because a policy action that lowers inflation also lowers output and a policy action that boosts output also increases inflation. (p. 10)

Patent A government-sanctioned exclusive right granted to the inventor of a good, service, or productive process to produce, use, and sell the invention for a given number of years. (p. 421)

Payoff matrix A table that shows the payoffs for every possible action by each player for every possible action by each other player. (p. 289)

Peak The point at which a business cycle turns from expansion into recession. (p. 454)

Perfect competition A market in which there are many firms each selling an identical product; there are many buyers; there are no restrictions on entry into the industry; firms in the industry have no advantage over potential new entrants; and firms and buyers are well informed about the price of each firm's product. (pp. 201, 234)

Perfectly elastic demand Demand with an infinite price elasticity; the quantity demanded changes by an infinitely large percentage in response to a tiny price change. (p. 85)

Perfectly inelastic demand Demand with a price elasticity of zero; the quantity demanded remains constant when the price changes. (p. 84)

Perfect price discrimination Price discrimination that extracts the entire consumer surplus. (p. 269)

Personal saving Personal disposable income minus consumption expenditure. (p. 527)

Phillips curve A curve that shows a relationship between inflation and unemployment. (p. 688)

Pigovian taxes Taxes that are used as an incentive for producers to cut back on an activity that creates an external cost. (p. 416)

Political equilibrium The outcome that results from the choices of voters, politicians, and bureaucrats. (p. 371)

Positive externality An externality that arise from either production or consumption and that provides an external benefit. (p. 410)

Positive relationship A relationship between two variables that move in the same direction. (p. 20)

Potential GDP The quantity of real GDP at full employment. (p. 465)

Poverty A situation in which a household's income is too low to be able to buy the quantities of food, shelter, and clothing that are deemed necessary. (p. 349)

Preferences A description of a person's likes and dislikes. (p. 36)

Present value The amount of money that, if invested today, will grow to be as large as a given future amount when the interest that it will earn is taken into account. (p. 322)

Price cap regulation A regulation that specifies the highest price that the firm is permitted to set. (p. 395)

Price ceiling A regulation that makes it illegal to charge a price higher than a specified level. (p. 123)

Price discrimination The practice of selling different units of a good or service for different prices or of charging one customer different prices for different quantities bought. (p. 259)

Price-earnings ratio The stock price divided by the most recent year's earnings. (p. 805)

Price effect The effect of a change in the price on the quantity of a good consumed, other things remaining the same. (p. 175)

Price elasticity of demand A units-free measure of the responsiveness of the quantity demanded of a good to a change in its price, when all other influences on buyers' plans remain the same. (p. 82)

Price floor A regulation that makes it illegal to charge a price lower than a specified level. (p. 127)

Price level The average level of prices as measured by a price index. (p. 442)

Price taker A firm that cannot influence the price of the good or service it produces. (p. 234)

Principal-agent problem The problem of devising compensation rules that induce an agent to act in the best interest of a principal. (p. 198)

Principle of minimum differentiation The tendency for competitors to make themselves identical as they try to appeal to the maximum number of clients or voters. (p. 375)

Private sector surplus or deficit An amount equal to saving minus investment. (p. 787)

Producer surplus The price of a good minus the opportunity cost of producing it, summed over the quantity sold. (p. 107)

Product differentiation Making a product slightly different from the product of a competing firm. (pp. 201, 280)

Production efficiency A situation in which the economy cannot produce more of one good without producing less of some other good. (p.33)

Production function The relationship between real GDP and the quantity of labor when all other influences on production remain the same. (p. 504)

Production possibilities frontier The boundary between the combinations of goods and services that can be produced and the combinations that cannot. (p. 32)

Productivity curve A relationship that shows how real GDP per hour of labor changes as the amount of capital per hour of labor changes with a given state of technology. (p. 553)

Profit The income earned by entrepreneurship. (p. 5)

Progressive income tax A tax on income at an average rate that increases with the level of income. (p. 355)

Property rights Social arrangements that govern the ownership, use, and disposal of resources or factors of production, goods, and services that are enforceable in the courts. (pp. 44, 414)

Proportional income tax A tax on income at a constant average rate, regardless of the level of income. (p. 355)

Public good A good or service that can be consumed simultaneously by everyone and from which no one can be excluded. (p. 372)

Public interest theory A theory of

regulation that states that regulations are supplied to satisfy the demand of consumers and producers to maximize the sum of consumer surplus and producer surplus—that is, to attain efficiency. (p. 391)

Public provision The production of a good or service by a public authority that receives its revenue from the government. (p. 419)

Purchasing power parity The equal value of different monies. (p. 796)

Quantity demanded The amount of a good or service that consumers plan to buy during a given time period at a particular price. (p. 59)

Quantity of labor demanded The labor hours hired by the firms in the economy. (p. 507)

Quantity of labor supplied The number of labor hours that all households in the economy plan to work. (p. 509)

Quantity supplied The amount of a good or service that producers plan to sell during a given time period at a particular price. (p. 64)

Quantity theory of money The proposition that in the long run, an increase in the quantity of money brings an equal percentage increase in the price level. (p. 643)

Quota A quantitative restriction on the import of a particular good, which specifies the maximum amount that can be imported in a given time period. (p. 772)

Rate of return The return on a stock expressed as a percentage of the stock price. (p. 805)

Rate of return regulation A regulation that requires the firm to justify its price by showing that the price enables it to earn a specified target percent return on its capital. (p. 395)

Rational expectation The most accurate forecast possible, a forecast that uses all the available information, including knowledge of the relevant economic forces that influence the variable being forecasted. (pp. 685, 811)

Rational ignorance The decision not to acquire information because the cost of doing so exceeds the expected benefit. (p. 376)

Real business cycle theory A theory that regards random fluctuations in productivity as the main source of economic fluctuations. (p. 715)

Real Gross Domestic Product (real GDP) The value of final goods and services produced in a given year when valued at constant prices. (p. 441)

Real income A household's income expressed as a quantity of goods that the household can afford to buy. (p. 169)

Real interest rate The nominal interest rate adjusted for inflation; the nominal interest rate minus the inflation rate. (p. 527)

Realized capital gain A capital gain that is obtained when a stock is sold for a higher price than the price paid for it. (p. 817)

Real wage rate The quantity of goods ands services that an hour's work can buy. It is equal to the money wage rate divided by the price level. (pp. 459, 507)

Recession A significant decline in activity spread across the economy, lasting for more than a few months, visible in industrial production, employment, real income, and whole-sale-retail trade. (p. 454)

Recessionary gap The amount by which potential GDP exceeds real GDP. (p. 486)

Reentrants People who reenter the labor force. (p. 461)

Reference base period The period in which the CPI is defined to be 100. (p. 466)

Regressive income tax A tax on income at an average rate that decreases with the level of income. (p. 355)

Regulation Rules administered by a government agency to influence economic activity by determining prices, product standards and types, and conditions under which new firms may enter an industry. (p. 390)

Relative price The ratio of the price of one good or service to the price of another good or service. A relative price is an opportunity cost. (pp. 58, 169)

Renewable natural resources Natural resources that can be used repeatedly without depleting what is available for future use. (p. 327)

Rent The income that land earns. (p. 5)

Rent ceiling A regulation that makes it illegal to charge a rent higher than a specified level. (p. 123)

Rent seeking Any attempt to capture a consumer surplus, a producer surplus, or an economic profit. (pp. 266, 776)

Required reserve ratio The ratio of reserves to deposits that banks are required, by regulation, to hold. (p. 638)

Reserve ratio The fraction of a bank's total deposits that are held in reserves. (p. 637)

Reserves Cash in a bank's vault plus the bank's deposits at Federal Reserve banks. (p. 633)

Return The return on a stock is the sum of the stock's dividend plus its capital gain (or minus its capital loss). (p. 805)

Risk premium The additional return that is earned for bearing an additional risk. (p. 814)

Saving The amount of income that households have left after they have paid their taxes and bought their consumption goods and services. (p. 436)

Saving function The relationship between saving and disposable income, other things remaining the same. (p. 577)

Saving rate Saving as a percentage of disposable income. (p. 817)

Savings and loan association (S&L) A depository institution that receives checking deposits and savings deposits and that makes personal, commercial, and home-purchase loans (p. 634)

Savings bank A depository institution, owned by its depositors, that accepts savings deposits and makes mortgage loans. (p. 634)

Saving supply The relationship

between saving and the real interest rate, other things remaining the same. (p. 533)

Scarcity The state in which the resources available are insufficient to satisfy people's wants. (p. 2)

Scatter diagram A diagram that plots the value of one economic variable against the value of another. (p. 19)

Search activity The time spent looking for someone with whom to do business. (p. 124)

Short run The short run in microeconomics has two meanings. For the firm, it is the period of time in which the quantity of at least one input is fixed and the quantities of the other inputs can be varied. The fixed input is usually capital—that is, the firm has a given plant size. For the industry, the short run is the period of time in which each firm has a given plant size and the number of firms in the industry is fixed. (p. 214)

Short-run aggregate supply curve A curve that shows the relationship between the quantity of real GDP supplied and the price level in the short run when the money wage rate, other resource prices, and potential GDP remain constant. (pp. 477, 511)

Short-run industry supply curve A curve that shows the quantity supplied by the industry at each price varies when the plant size of each firm and the number of firms in the industry remain the same. (p. 241)

Short-run macroeconomic equilibrium A situation that occurs when the quantity of real GDP demanded equals quantity of real GDP supplied—at the point of intersection of the *AD* curve and the *SAS* curve. (p. 484)

Short-run Phillips curve A curve that shows the tradeoff between inflation and unemployment, when the expected inflation rate and the natural rate of unemployment remain the same. (p. 688)

Shutdown point The output and price at which the firm just covers its total variable cost. In the short run, the firm is indifferent between producing the profit-maximizing output and shutting down temporarily. (p. 240)

Single-price monopoly A monopoly that must sell each unit of its output for a same price to all its customers. (p. 259)

Slope The change in the value of the variable measured on the *y*-axis divided by the change in the value of the variable measured on the *x*-axis. (p. 24)

Speculative bubble A price increase followed by a price plunge, both of which occur because people expect them to occur and act on that expectation. (p. 812)

Stagflation The combination of recession and inflation. (p. 489)

Standard of living The level of consumption that people enjoy, on the average, and is measured by average income per person. (p. 6)

Stock A quantity that exists at a point in time. (p. 437)

Stock A tradable security that a firm issues to certify that the stock holder owns a share of the firm. (p. 804)

Stock exchange An organized market on which people can buy and sell stock. (p. 804)

Stock price The price at which one share of a firm's stock trades on a stock exchange. (p. 805)

Strategies All the possible actions of each player in a game. (p. 289)

Structural surplus or deficit The budget balance that would occur if the economy were at full employment and real GDP were equal to potential GDP. (p. 615)

Structural unemployment The unemployment that arises when changes in technology or international competition change the skills needed to perform jobs or change the locations of jobs. (p. 464)

Subsidy A payment that the government makes to private producers. (p. 420)

Subsistence real wage rate The minimum real wage rate needed to maintain life. (p. 558)

Substitute A good that can be used in place of another good. (p. 61)

Substitution effect The effect of a change in price of a good or service on the quantity bought when the consumer (hypothetically) remains indifferent between the original and the new consumption situations—that is, the consumer remains on the same indifference curve. (p. 177)

Sunk cost The past cost of buying a plant that has no resale value. (p. 214)

Supply The relationship between the quantity of a good that producers plan to sell and the price of the good when all other influences on sellers' plans remain the same. It is described by a supply schedule and illustrated by a supply curve. (p. 64)

Supply curve A curve that shows the relationship between the quantity supplied and the price of a good when all other influences on producers' planned sales remain the same. (p. 64)

Supply of labor The relationship between the quantity of labor supplied and the real wage rate when all other influences on work plans remain the same. (p. 509)

Symmetry principle A requirement that people in similar situations be treated similarly. (p. 114)

Tariff A tax that is imposed by the importing country when an imported good crosses its international boundary. (p. 769)

Technological change The development of new goods and better ways of producing goods and services. (p. 38)

Technological efficiency A situation that occurs when the firm produces a given output by using the least amount of inputs. (p. 195)

Technology Any method of producing a good or service. (p. 194)

Terms of trade The quantity of goods and services that a country exports to pay for its imports of goods and services. (p. 764)

Thrift institutions Thrift institutions include savings and loan associations, savings banks, and credit unions. (p. 634)

Time-series graph A graph that measures time (for example, months or years) on the *x*-axis and the variable or variables in which we are interested on the *y*-axis. (p. 18)

Total cost The cost of all the productive resources that a firm uses. (p. 219)

Total fixed cost The cost of the firm's fixed inputs. (p. 219)

Total product The total output produced by a firm in a given period of time. (p. 215)

Total revenue The value of a firm's sales. It is calculated as the price of the good multiplied by the quantity sold. (pp. 86, 234)

Total revenue test A method of estimating the price elasticity of demand by observing the change in total revenue that results from a change in the price, when all other influences on the quantity sold remain the same. (p. 86)

Total utility The total benefit that a person gets from the consumption of goods and services. (p. 150)

Total variable cost The cost of all the firm's variable inputs. (p. 219)

Tradeoff A constraint that involves giving up one thing to get something else. (p. 9)

Transactions costs The costs that arise from finding someone with whom to do business, of reaching an agreement about the price and other aspects of the exchange, and of ensuring that the terms of the agreement are fulfilled. The opportunity costs of conducting a transaction (pp. 206, 415)

Trend The general tendency for a variable to move in one direction. (p. 18)

Trough The point at which a business cycle turns from recession into expansion. (p. 454)

Unemployment rate The percentage of the people in the labor force who are unemployed. (p. 457)

Unit elastic demand Demand with a price elasticity of 1; the percentage change in the quantity demanded equals the percentage change in price. (p. 84)

Utilitarianism A principle that states that we should strive to achieve "the greatest happiness for the greatest number of people." (p. 112)

Utility The benefit or satisfaction that a person gets from the consumption of a good or service. (p. 150)

U.S. interest rate differential A gap equal to the U.S. interest rate minus the foreign interest rate. (p. 791)

U.S. Official reserves The government's holdings of foreign currency. (p. 784)

Value The maximum amount that a person is willing to pay for a good. The value of one more unit of the good or service is its marginal benefit. (p. 104)

Velocity of circulation The average number of times a dollar of money is used annually to buy the goods and services that make up GDP. (p. 643)

Voluntary export restraint An agreement between two governments in which the government of the exporting country agrees to restrain the volume of its own exports. (p. 772)

Voucher A token that the government provides to households, which they can use to buy specified goods and services. (p. 420)

Wages The income that labor earns. (p. 5)

Wealth The market value of all the things that people own—the value of their assets. (pp. 437, 817)

Wealth effect The influence of wealth on consumption expenditure and saving. (p. 817)

Working-age population The total number of people aged 16 years and over who are not in jail, hospital, or some other form of institutional care. (p. 456)

World Trade Organization An international organization that places greater obligations on its member countries to observe the GATT rules. (p. 769)

INDEX

Key terms and pages on which they are defined appear in **bold-face**.

The Addison-Wesley Series in Economics

Abel/Bernanke
Macroeconomics

Bade/Parkin
Foundations of Microeconomics

Bade/Parkin
Foundations of Macroeconomics

Bierman/Fernandez
Game Theory with Economic Applications

Binger/Hoffman
Microeconomics with Calculus

Boyer
Principles of Transportation Economics

Branson
Macroeconomic Theory and Policy

Bruce
Public Finance and the American Economy

Byrns/Stone
Economics

Carlton/Perloff
Modern Industrial Organization

Caves/Frankel/Jones
World Trade and Payments: An Introduction

Chapman
Environmental Economics: Theory, Application, and Policy

Cooter/Ulen
Law and Economics

Downs
An Economic Theory of Democracy

Eaton/Mishkin
Online Readings to Accompany The Economics of Money, Banking, and Financial Markets

Ehrenberg/Smith
Modern Labor Economics

Ekelund/Tollison
Economics: Private Markets and Public Choice

Fusfeld
The Age of the Economist

Gerber
International Economics

Ghiara
Learning Economics: A Practical Workbook

Gordon
Macroeconomics

Gregory
Essentials of Economics

Gregory/Stuart
Russian and Soviet Economic Performance and Structure

Hartwick/Olewiler
The Economics of Natural Resource Use

Hubbard
Money, the Financial System, and the Economy

Hughes/Cain
American Economic History

Husted/Melvin
International Economics

Jehle/Reny
Advanced Microeconomic Theory

Klein
Mathematical Methods for Economics

Krugman/Obstfeld
International Economics: Theory and Policy

Laidler
The Demand for Money: Theories, Evidence, and Problems

Leeds/von Allmen
The Economics of Sports

Lipsey/Courant/Ragan
Economics

McCarty
Dollars and Sense: An Introduction to Economics

Melvin
International Money and Finance

Miller
Economics Today

Miller/Benjamin/North
The Economics of Public Issues

Mills/Hamilton
Urban Economics

Mishkin
The Economics of Money, Banking, and Financial Markets

Parkin
Economics

Parkin/Bade
Economics in Action Software

Perloff
Microeconomics

Phelps
Health Economics

Riddell/Shackelford/Stamos/ Schneider
Economics: A Tool for Critically Understanding Society

Ritter/Silber/Udell
Principles of Money, Banking, and Financial Markets

Rohlf
Introduction to Economic Reasoning

Ruffin/Gregory
Principles of Economics

Sargent
Rational Expectations and Inflation

Scherer
Industry Structure, Strategy, and Public Policy

Schotter
Microeconomics: A Modern Approach

Stock/Watson
Introduction to Econometrics

Studenmund
Using Econometrics: A Practical Guide

Tietenberg
Environmental and Natural Resource Economics

Tietenberg
Environmental Economics and Policy

Todaro/Smith
Economic Development

Waldman/Jensen
Industrial Organization: Theory and Practice

Williamson
Macroeconomics